THE AMERICAN
WOMEN'S
ALMANAC

500 YEARS OF
MAKING HISTORY

ABOUT THE AUTHOR

Deborah G. Felder is a graduate of Bard College, where she studied drama and literature. She worked as an editor at Scholastic, Inc., and has been a freelance writer and editor for over thirty years. The author of more than twenty publications, including fiction and nonfiction books and articles for middle grade, young adult, and adult readers, she has published such titles as *The 100 Most Influential Women of All Time: A Ranking Past and Present; A Century of Women: The Most Influential Events in Twentieth-Century Women's History*; and *A Bookshelf of Our Own: Works That Changed Women's Lives*. She has also written book reviews for the *New York Times Book Review, Kirkus Reviews*, and *Publishers Weekly*. She resides with her husband, Daniel Burt, in South Chatham, Massachusetts.

Also from Visible Ink Press

Black Firsts: 4,000 Ground-Breaking and Pioneering Events, 3rd edition
by Jessie Carney Smith, Ph.D.
ISBN: 978-1-57859-369-9

Freedom Facts and Firsts: 400 Years of the African American Civil Rights Experience
by Jessie Carney Smith, Ph.D. and Linda T. Wynn
ISBN: 978-1-57859-192-3

The Handy African American History Answer Book
by Jessie Carney Smith, Ph.D.
ISBN: 978-1-57859-452-8

The Handy American History Answer Book
by David L. Hudson, Jr.
ISBN: 978-1-57859-471-9

The Handy History Answer Book, 4th edition
by Stephen A. Werner, Ph.D.
ISBN: 978-1-57859-680-5

The Handy Literature Answer Book: An Engaging Guide to Unraveling Symbols, Signs and Meanings in Great Works
by Daniel S. Burt, Ph.D., and Deborah G. Felder
ISBN: 978-1-57859-635-5

Native American Almanac: More Than 50,000 Years of the Cultures and Histories of Indigenous Peoples
by Yvonne Wakim Dennis, Arlene Hirschfelder and Shannon Rothenberger Flynn
ISBN: 978-1-57859-507-5

Native American Landmarks and Festivals: A Traveler's Guide to Indigenous United States and Canada
by Yvonne Wakim Dennis and Arlene Hirschfelder
ISBN: 978-1-57859-641-6

Please visit us at www.visibleinkpress.com.

THE AMERICAN WOMEN'S ALMANAC

500 YEARS OF MAKING HISTORY

DEBORAH G. FELDER

VISIBLE
INK
PRESS

Detroit

Visible Ink Press®
43311 Joy Rd., #414
Canton, MI 48187-2075

Visible Ink Press is a registered trademark of Visible Ink Press LLC.

Most Visible Ink Press books are available at special quantity discounts when purchased in bulk by corporations, organizations, or groups. Customized printings, special imprints, messages, and excerpts can be produced to meet your needs. For more information, contact Special Markets Director, Visible Ink Press, www.visibleink.com, or 734-667-3211.

Managing Editor: Kevin S. Hile
Art Director: Mary Claire Krzewinski
Typesetting: Marco Divita
Proofreaders: Larry Baker and Shoshana Hurwitz
Indexer: Larry Baker

Front cover image: Mobilus in Mobili (Wikicommons). Back cover images: Sonya Sotomayor (Collection of the Supreme Court of the United States, Steve Petteway), Sally Ride (U.S. National Archives and Records Administration), Pocahontas (Frédéric at Wikicommons), Shirley Ann Jackson (Qilai Shen).

ISBN: 978-1-57859-636-2

Cataloging-in-Publication data is on file at the Library of Congress.

Printed in the United States of America.

CONTENTS

ACKNOWLEDGMENTS

The preparation of this book owes much to the many excellent works on women's history, biography, and women's studies, which not only provided me with necessary historical information but also offered thoughtful explication concerning the experiences and perspectives of American women past and present. I urge readers to seek out the books featured in the Further Reading at the back of this book, as well as the works produced by the women profiled, all of which will greatly expand their knowledge and understanding of the history of American women throughout the centuries.

Further acknowledgment is due to my editor, Kevin Hile, publisher Roger Jänecke, my agent, Roger Williams, my husband, Daniel Burt, and John Verrilli, whose patience, support, and help were invaluable assets throughout the writing of *The American Women's Almanac*.

PHOTO CREDITS

Expert Infantry: p. 528 (Wilma Vaught).

Federal Office of Eleanor Holmes Norton: p. 371.

Brittany "B.Monét" Fennell: p. 415.

Four Star Records: p. 258.

Fernando Frazao/Agencia Brasil: p. 289 (Gabby Douglas).

Flipflopnick (Wikicommons): p. 404.

Cindy Funk: p. 94.

G. P. Putnam's Sons: p. 195 (Susan Warner).

George Eastman House: p. 544 (Osa Johnson).

George Grantham Bain Collection, Library of Congress: pp. 182, 254 (Amy Beach), 257 (Louise Brooks), 283, 330 (Alice Hamilton), 433, 470 (Mary Emma Woolley), 471, 499 (Helena Rubinstein).

Gerald R. Ford Presidential Library: p. 250.

Gerbil (Wikicommons): pp. 320 (Elizabeth H. Blackburn), 330 (Carol W. Greider).

German Federal Archives: p. 289 (Gertrude Ederle).

Germanna Community College: pp. 429 (Diane Nash), 437.

Getty Center: p. 231 (Georgia O'Keeffe).

Gibbes Museum of Art: p. 219.

Lynn Gilbert: pp. 228, 229, 257 (Julia Child).

Giovanni Giovannetti/Grazia Neri: p. 184.

Google Books: pp. 155, 214.

Gorupdebesanez (Wikicommons): p. 243.

Goyk (Wikicommons): p. 301.

Dennis Hamilton: p. 335 (Barbara Liskov).

HAP1969 (Wikicommons): p. 268 (Frances Marion).

Harlan1000 (Wikicommons): p. 295 (Julie Krone).

The Heart Truth: pp. 299 (Danica Patrick), 306 (Kristi Yamaguchi).

Heinrich-Böll-Stiftung: p. 120.

Humanities Texas: p. 532.

International Committee of the Red Cross: p. 459 (Deborah E. Lipstadt).

International Ladies' Garment Workers' Union Archives, Kheel Center Collection, Cornell University: p. 83.

International Woman's Foundation: p. 218.

Alessio Jacona: p. 161.

Jarx Media: p. 117.

Julieoe (Wikicommons): p. 181.

Steve Jurvetson: p. 421.

The Kheel Center for Labor-Management Documentation and Archives, Cornell University: p. 88 (Rose Pesotta).

King Kong Photo/www.celebrity-photos.com: pp. 148 (Maya Angelou), 152, 164 (Nikki Giovanni), 176 (Toni Morrison), 295 (Michelle Kwan), 302 (Monica Seles), 425, 483 (Helen del Gurley Brown).

Mindy Kittay: p. 135.

Mariusz Kubik: p. 185.

Labadie Photograph Collection, University of Michigan: p. 87.

LaBloga (Wikicommons): p. 148 (Julia Alvarez).

Jennifer Lapinel-Spincken: p. 162 (Maria Irene FornÈs)

Carl Lender: pp. 151, 239.

Library of Congress: pp. 35, 37 (Alva Belmont), 38 (Harriet Stanton Blatch), 39, 40, 41, 43 (Abby Kelley Foster), 45 (Sarah Grimke and Angelina Grimke), 47 (Ida Husted Harper), 48 (Inez Milholland), 52 (Anna Howard Shaw), 54 (Lucy Stone and Mary Church Terrell), 66, 70, 76, 81, 82, 89 (Rose Schneiderman), 97, 103, 114 (Bella Abzug), 164 (Charlotte Perkins Gilman), 168 (Zora Neale Hurston and Helen Hunt Jackson), 175, 216, 222 (Dorothea Lange), 242, 263, 264 (Lillian Gish), 266 (Helen Hayes), 270, 302 (Helen Stephens), 341 (Florence Sabin), 350, 353, 355, 359 (Hattie Wyatt Caraway and Shirley Chisholm), 364, 365 (Oveta Culp Hobby), 368 (Belva Lockwood), 376, 377, 383 (Nellie Taloe Ross), 385, 386 (Martha Washington and Edith Wilson), 392, 394, 407, 410 (Grace Abbott and Jane Addams), 412, 418, 420 (Emma Goldman), 422, 435, 454, 489, 521 (Helen Fairchild), 535, 540 (Martha Jane Canary).

Life magazine: p. 36.

Alan Light: p. 399.

Henk Lindeboom/Anefo: p. 300 (Wilma Rudolph).

Litchfield Historical Society: p. 463 (Sarah Pierce).

Liu Dong'ao: p. 95.

LizaKoz (Wikicommons): p. 479 (Mary Kay Ash).

Tristan Loper: p. 174.

Los Angeles Times: p. 248.

Alex Lozupone: p. 127.

The Making Cancer History® Voices Oral History Collection, Historical Resources Center, Research Medical Library. The University of Texas MD: p. 335 (Eleanor Josephine MacDonald).

Marathona (Wikicommons): p. 303 (Kathrine Switzer).

Laura Markwardt: p. 90.

Asa Mathat / Fortune Live Media: p. 498 (Ginni Rometty).

Dana Meilijson: p. 133.

Merrimack Valley Textile Museum: p. 63.

Metro-Goldwyn-Mayer: p. 143.

Metropolitan Magazine: p. 203.

Metropolitan Museum of Art, New York: pp. 187, 213 (Mary Cassatt).

Missouri History Museum: pp. 156, 518 (Pauline Cushman), 544 (Susan Shelby Magoffin).

Momovieman (Wikicommons): p. 293 (Mia Hamm).

Larry D. Moore: pp. 179 (Joyce Carol Oates), 189 (Jane Smiley).

Max Morse: p. 504.

Ms. magazine: p. 109.

Mudforce (Wikicommons): p. 302 (Annika Sörenstam).

Museum of Fine Arts, Boston: p. 177 (Sarah Wentworth Apthorp Morton).

NASA: pp. 333, 490, 516 (Eileen Collins), 540 (Bessie Coleman), 543, 546.

Nationaal Archief, Netherlands: pp. 461 (Margaret Mead), 488.

National Archives at College Park: pp. 509, 528 (Mary Edwards Walker).

National Center for Biotechnology Information: p. 340.

National Gallery of Art: p. 356.

National Institutes of Health: p. 524 (Anita Newcomb McGee).

National Institutes of Health History Office: p. 341 (Sarah Elizabeth Stewart).

National Library of Ireland on the Commons: p. 60.

National Library of Medicine: p. 324 (Gerty Theresa Cori).

National Museum of American History: p. 73.

National Photo Collection of Israel: p. 241.

National Portrait Gallery: pp. 49, 55, 231 (Sarah Miriam Peale), 235.

Lynn Neary: p. 172.

Neddy1234 (Wikicommons): p. 423 (LaDonna Harris).

Nevada National Historical Society: p. 221.

New York Historical Society: pp. 16, 173 (Emma Lazarus), 368 (Dolley Madison).

New York Public Library: pp. 43 (Charlotte Forten), 46, 298 (Annie Oakley).

New York Star: p. 272.

New York Times: p. 430.

New York World-Telegram and Sun: pp. 126, 227, 262, 291 (Althea Gibson), 317 (Virginia Apgar), 450, 478, 494.

Nheyob (Wikicommons): p. 400.

Marcia Noe: p. 163.

Marc Nozell: p. 360.

Tim O'Brien: p. 292 (Janet Guthrie).

Office of Congressman John Delaney: p. 464.

Office of Senator Kamala Harris and US Department of Agriculture: p. 429 (Sylvia Mendez).

Open Media Ltd.: pp. 122, 131.

John Phelan: p. 443.

Post of Romania: p. 324 (Josephine Cochrane).

Queens College Silhouette Yearbook: p. 325.

Rajasekharan Parameswaran: p. 305 (Serena Williams).

Peoria Journal: p. 482.

Christopher Peterson: p. 277.

Tim Pierce: p. 114 (Anita Hill).

Michael E. Ray: p. 397.

Rebekah Jacob Gallery: p. 205 (Doris Ullman).

Kjetil Ree: p. 487 (Melinda Gates).

Richard's Free Library, Newport, New Hampshire: p. 165.

Rickmouser45 (Wikicommons): p. 547 (Sacagawea).

RKO Radio Pictures: p. 246.

RMBM Photos: p. 132.

Ronald Reagan Library: p. 378.

San Diego Air and Space Museum Archives: p. 480.

Schlesinger Library, Harvard University: pp. 220 (Lois Mailou Jones), 423 (Dorothy Height), 451 (Charlotte Hawkins Brown).

Schwabel Studio: p. 183.

Science History Institute: p. 334.

Seattle Municipal Archives: p. 474.

Gillian Zoe Segal: p. 481.

Elliot Severn: p. 338 (Carolyn Porco).

David Shankbone: pp. 158 (Joan Didion), 171, 179 (Lynn Nottage), 220 (Donna Karan), 294 (Billie Jean King), 491, 501.

Shutterstock: pp. 8, 11, 80, 107, 286 (top), 296 (Cheryl Miller), 297 (Martina Navratilova), 311, 314, 445, 446, 477.

David Sifry: p. 192 (Amy Tan).

Singhaniket255 (Wikicommons): p. 492 (Abigail Johnson).

si.robi (Wikicommons): p. 305 (Venus Williams).

Gage Skidmore: pp. 157, 298 (Diana Nyad), 424, 486.

Skloewer (Wikicommons): pp. 508, 527.

John Matthew Smith/celebrityphotos.com: pp. 273 (Meryl Streep), 279, 287 (Bonnie Blair), 294 (Jackie Joyner-Kersee), 362, 419, 420 (Myrlie Evers-Williams).

Smithsonian Institution: pp. 28, 99, 202, 222 (Edmonia Lewis), 319, 321, 323, 327, 336, 338 (Bertha Parker Pallan), 344, 502 (Madame C. J. Walker).

The Socialist Woman: p. 85.

Stage magazine: p. 167.

State Library and Archives of Florida: pp. 379, 383 (Ileana Ros-Lehtinen).

Sharon Styer: p. 223.

Supreme Court of the United States: pp. 363, 373 (Sandra Day O'Connor).

Rudolph Suroch: p. 252.

TechCrunch (Wikicommons): p. 505.

Terra Foundation for American Art, Daniel J. Terra Collection: p. 177 (Judith Sargent Murray).

Texas A&M University: p. 315.

Texas A&M University-Commerce Marketing Communications Photography: p. 414.

Time magazine: p. 225 (Claire McCardell).

University of California: p. 261 (Isadora Duncan).

University of Michigan: p. 520.

University of Pennsylvania: p. 25.

University of Wisconsin-Madison Archives: p. 459 (Gerda Lerner).

U.S. Air Force: pp. 104, 343 (Gladys West), 510, 512, 516 (Jacqueline Cochran), 524 (Nancy Harkness Love), 526.

U.S. Army: pp. 84 (Sara Nelson), 374, 521 (Kristen Marie Griest), 522 (Anna Mays Hays), 529 (Cathay Williams).

U.S. Army Material Command: p. 519.

U.S. Congress: pp. 367, 375, 384, 525.

U.S. Department of Commerce: p. 493 (Juanita Morris Kreps).

U.S. Department of Energy: p. 328.

U.S. Department of Housing and Urban Development: p. 365 (Patricia Roberts Harris).

U.S. Department of Labor: p. 369.

U.S. Department of Labor—Women's Bureau: p. 84 (Frieda S. Miller).

U.S. Department of State: p. 380 (Condoleezza Rice).

U.S. Fish and Wildlife Headquarters: p. 322.

U.S. Government: pp. 357, 366, 370, 479 (Mary Barra).

U.S. Government Printing Office: pp. 483 (Ursula Burns), 518 (Tammy Duckworth).

U.S. Health and Human Services: p. 300 (Mary Lou Retton).

U.S. House of Representatives: p. 381.

U.S. Mission Canada: p. 391 (Peggy Fleming).

U.S. National Archives and Records Administration: pp. 29, 88 (Esther Peterson), 382, 431.

U.S. National Library of Medicine: pp. 345, 517.

U.S. National Park Service: pp. 48 (Mary Ann M'Clintock), 234.

U.S. Navy: p. 523.

U.S. News & World Report: p. 101.

Usbotschaftberlin (Wikicommons): p. 503.

Ted Van Pelt: p. 296 (Nancy Lopez).

Fred Viebahn: p. 160.

Romana Vysatova: 170 (Gish Jen).

Jim Wallace: p. 134.

Warfieldian (Wikicommons): p. 6.

Warner Bros.: p. 259 (Bette Davis).

Washington State Historical Society: p. 470 (Sarah Winnemucca).

Annie Watt: p. 502 (Lillian Vernon).

Wellesley College: p. 461 (Alice Freeman Palmer).

White House Press Office: p. 475.

Willa Cather Pioneer Memorial and Educational Foundation: p. 154.

William J. Clinton Presidential Library and Museum: p. 428.

William P. Gottlieb Collection, Library of Congress: p. 267.

Albert Witzel: p. 255 (Clara Bow).

Donald Woodman: p. 213 (Judy Chicago).

World Economic Forum: pp. 457, 496, 499 (Sheryl Sandberg).

Yale University Press: p. 448.

Jacqueline Zaccor: p. 484 (Barbara Corcoran).

Kenneth C. Zirkel: pp. 380 (Ann Richards), 465.

Public domain: pp. 2, 3, 4, 13, 14, 21, 23, 37 (Antoinette Brown Blackwell), 38 (Amelia Bloomer), 42, 44, 45 (Mary Grew), 47 (Jane Hunt), 50, 51, 52 (Elizabeth Cady Stanton), 56, 57, 64, 67, 78 (Rebecca Harding Davis and Mary Dreier), 79 (Harriet Farley and Elizabeth Gurley Flynn), 86 (Leonora O'Reilly), 141, 142, 146, 147, 150, 158 (Emily Dickinson),162 (Margaret Fuller), 170 (Sarah Orne Jewett), 186, 188 (Lydia Sigourney), 191, 192 (Ida Tarbell), 197, 198 (Phyllis Wheatley and Laura Ingalls Wilder), 205 (Berenice Abbott), 208 (Cecilia Beaux and Louise Blanchard Bethune), 210, 211, 224. 225 (Maria Montoya Martinez), 232, 233, 238, 244, 250 (Marian Anderson and Dorothy Arzner), 256, 259 (Joan Ganz Cooney), 261 (Maya Deren), 266 (Katharine Hepburn), 275, 278, 282, 284, 286 (Tenley Albright), 290, 293 (Florence Griffith Joyner), 307, 310, 316, 318, 326, 337, 339, 349, 351, 390, 405, 408, 409, 413, 426, 432, 434, 436, 441, 449, 452, 455 (Fanny Jackson Coppin and Prudence Crandall), 456, 458, 460, 462, 466 (Anna Garlin Spencer), 467, 468, 469, 492 (Elizabeth Keckley), 495, 498 (Lydia E. Pinkham), 515, 522 (Jennie Irene Hodgers), 534, 536, 537, 538, 539, 542, 545, 547.

TIMELINE

1539–1620 The first European women arrive in what would become the continental United States.

1638 Charismatic Puritan spiritual advisor Anne Hutchinson is banished from the Massachusetts Bay Colony for challenging the authority of the established clergy.

1648 Margaret Brent, an English immigrant to the colony of Maryland, goes before the Maryland Assembly requesting "a vote and voyce," the first attempt by a woman to gain a vote in the American colonies. Her request is denied.

1692–1693 The Salem witch trials take place in Massachusetts. Fourteen women are convicted of witchcraft and executed; thirteen die in custody or in prison.

1718 Pennsylvania becomes the first state to declare that married women are allowed to own and manage property in their own name during the incapacity of their spouses. Subsequent states would do the same through the nineteenth century.

1727 The Ursuline Academy in New Orleans is founded by the Sisters of the Order of Saint Ursula, the earliest continually operating school for girls in America, the first free school for young women, and the first to teach women of color, including female African American slaves.

1745 Pennsylvanian frontierswoman Susanna Wright serves as a legal counselor to her mostly illiterate neighbors, preparing wills, deeds, indentures, and other contracts as well as serving as an arbitrator in property disputes.

1756 Massachusetts widow Lydia Taft is the first recorded woman to vote legally in Colonial New England (at a town meeting in Uxbridge).

1767 Tax-supported schooling for girls begins in Massachusetts. It is optional, and many towns reject it or are late to adopt the innovation.

1774 Mother Ann Lee, English leader of the United Society of Believers in Christ's Second

Coming, a Quaker sect commonly known as the Shakers for their ecstatic behavior during worship services, arrives in New York City with members of her family and several followers. They go on to perform missionary work throughout New England.

1777 New York passes laws that rescind a woman's right to vote. Other states follow: Massachusetts in 1780, New Hampshire in 1784, and New Jersey in 1807.

1787 The Young Ladies Academy opens in Philadelphia, offering an extensive academic curriculum taught by male teachers. It would become the model for the many academies and seminaries that opened in the late 1700s and early 1800s.

1787 The U.S. Constitutional Convention places voting qualifications in the hands of each state.

1799 Hannah Adams publishes *A Summary History of New England,* the first history of the United States from the *Mayflower* to the ratification of the Constitution.

1811 Women nurses are first included among personnel at U.S. Navy hospitals.

1812 During the War of 1812, two women, Mary Marshall and Mary Allen, serve as nurses aboard the SS *United States* at the request of Commodore Stephen Decatur.

1821 Emma Willard founds the Troy Female Seminary in Troy, New York, offering the most advanced education available to young women at the time and becoming the first school to offer college-level courses to women.

1825 Rebecca Lukens becomes the first female industrialist in America, taking over the management of the Brandywine Iron Works & Nail Factory and making the company one of the most successful of the American Industrial Revolution.

1826 The first American public high schools for girls open in New York and Boston.

1830 The first popular women's magazine, *Godey's Lady Book,* begins publication. It would become the most widely circulated magazine in the pre-Civil War period.

1832 Prudence Crandall admits a young black girl, Sarah Harris, to her private school for girls in Canterbury, Connecticut, establishing the first integrated classroom in the United States.

1836 Georgia Female College in Macon, Georgia, becomes the first college chartered for women in the world. It would be renamed as Wesleyan Female College in 1843.

1837 Oberlin College formally admits women students for the first time. When the college opened in 1833, it only admitted women to its college preparatory program.

1837 Mount Holyoke College is founded in Massachusetts to provide women students with the same quality of education as male-only Ivy League schools.

1848 The first women's rights convention meets in Seneca Falls, New York. Its Declaration of Sentiments declares that women, like men, are citizens with an inalienable right to the elective franchise.

1849 English-born Elizabeth Blackwell becomes the first woman to graduate from an American medical school, Geneva Medical School in Geneva, New York.

1850 Lucy Sessions completes a four-year course of study at Oberlin College and becomes the first African American woman college graduate.

1853 Congregationalist Antoinette Brown Blackwell becomes the first woman to be ordained a minister in the United States

1855 The University of Iowa becomes the first coeducational public or state university in the United States.

1856 Atmospheric scientist Eunice Newton Foote presents early research on the greenhouse effect at the annual meeting of the American Association for the Advancement of Sciences.

1856 Educator Catherine Beecher publishes the first exercise manual for women

1860 Elizabeth Palmer Peabody establishes the first English-language kindergarten in the United States in Boston.

1861 *Life in the Iron Mills,* a novella by Rebecca Harding Davis, is published. It is considered a central text in the origins of American realism and feminism.

1861–1865 During the Civil War, women provide nursing care to Union and Confederate troops at field hospitals. By the end of the war, over five hundred fully paid positions were available to women as nurses in the U.S. military.

1863 Former slave and abolitionist Harriet Tubman becomes a Union spy and leader of a band of scouts. She is the first woman to lead an armed assault during the Civil War in the Raid at Combahee Ferry.

1866 Elizabeth Cady Stanton becomes the first woman to run for the U.S. House of Representatives, even though she is not eligible to vote.

1866 Congress passes the Fourteenth Amendment (ratified by the states in 1868), providing citizenship rights and equal protection to former slaves. It is the first time the Constitution defines citizens and voters as "male."

1869 Elizabeth Cady Stanton and Susan B. Anthony found the National Woman Suffrage Association. Lucy Stone forms the American Woman Suffrage Association.

1870 Ada Kepley becomes the first American woman to graduate from law school (Northwestern University College of Law). However, state law prohibits her from practicing her profession. She is finally admitted to the Illinois bar in 1881.

1870 The Fifteenth Amendment is ratified, saying, "The rights of citizens of the United States to vote shall not be denied or abridged … on account of race, color, or previous condition of servitude." Women suffragists argue that the amendment does not specifically exclude women from the vote.

1872 Victoria Woodhull becomes the first woman to run for president. Since she will not reach the constitutionally required age of thirty-five until 1873, Woodhull and her running mate, Frederick Douglass, are denied placement on the ballot.

1872 Susan B. Anthony attempts to vote in the presidential election in Rochester, New York. She is arrested, convicted, and fined. Sojourner Truth attempts to vote in Grand Rapids, Michigan, but is refused and turned away from the polling place.

1873 The first training school for nurses—at the New England Hospital for Women and Children—graduates its first class.

1874 Mary Ewing Outerbridge (1852–1856), who was exposed to lawn tennis in Bermuda, introduces tennis to the United States, shipping equipment from Bermuda to set up the first U.S. lawn tennis court at the Staten Island, New York, Cricket and Baseball Club.

1876 Anna Oliver is the first woman to receive a BD degree from an American theological seminary.

1878 Known as the Anthony Amendment, the Women's Suffrage Amendment is introduced in Congress, beginning four decades of intense campaigning until its passage.

1879 The U.S. Supreme Court holds that the Fourteenth Amendment forbids states from barring men from jury pools based on race or color, but it "may confine the selection to males, to freeholders, to citizens, to persons within certain ages, or persons having educational qualifications."

1879 Mary Baker Eddy establishes the Church of Christ, Scientist.

1881 The American Association of University Women is founded to advance equity for women and girls through advocacy, education, and research.

1881 Pioneering nurse Clara Barton founds the American Red Cross.

1882 The YWCA in Boston hosts the first athletic games for women.

1884 Julie Rosewald of San Francisco's Temple Emanu-El becomes the first female *hazzan* (cantor) in the United States.

1885 Exhibition shooter Annie Oakley joins Buffalo Bill's Wild West show and becomes the first American woman superstar performer.

1886 The Equity Club, the first professional organization for women lawyers, is founded at the University of Michigan.

1887 Susanna Salter is elected mayor of Argonia, Kansas, becoming the first female mayor in the United States.

1887 Ellen Hansell wins the first Women's Singles tennis championship at the U.S. Open.

1889 Jane Addams and Ellen Gates Starr open Hull-House in Chicago, one of the first settlement houses in the United States.

1890 Amanda Theodosia Jones establishes the first all-women's company, the Women's Canning and Preserving Company in Chicago, Illinois.

1890 Nearly thirty years after the U.S. Congress passed the Morrill Anti-Bigamy Law prohibiting multiple marriages in U.S. territories, the Mormon Church issues a manifesto officially banning the Mormon practice of polygamy.

1890 Wyoming is the first state to grant women full voting rights.

1892 Smith College initiates intercollegiate sports for women when it introduces basketball soon after the game was invented.

1893 The Supreme Court reaffirms that the legal profession in every state may discriminate on the basis of sex.

1896 Martha Hughes Cannon of Utah becomes the first woman to be elected to a state senate in the United States.

1898 The Washington College of Law in the District of Columbia (now the law school of American University) is founded to accommodate female students who are rejected from established schools due to their gender.

1900 Women compete for the first time in the Olympics in golf and tennis at the Paris Games.

1901 Congress establishes the Army Nurse Corps. The Navy Nurse Corps is established in 1908.

1904 Helen Keller graduates Phi Beta Kappa from Radcliffe College, becoming the first deaf-blind person to earn a BA degree.

1904 Educator Mary McLeod Bethune establishes the Daytona Educational and Industrial Training School for Negro Girls, later Bethune-Cookman College.

1905 Nora Stanton Blatch Barney becomes the first woman to earn an engineering degree in the United States (civil engineering from Cornell University).

1905 American geneticist Nettie Stevens discovers the X and Y sex chromosomes.

1908 The Harvard Graduate School of Business Administration establishes the first MBA program. The first women would be admitted in 1963 and become fully integrated into the program in 1970.

1911 The Triangle Shirtwaist Fire, one of the deadliest industrial disasters in U.S. history, claims the lives of 146 New York City garment workers. Most of the 123 female victims are recently arrived immigrant women and girls aged fourteen to twenty-three.

1915 The Woman's Peace Party, forerunner of the Woman's International League for Peace and Freedom (WILPF), is established. Jane Addams serves as the WPP's first president.

1916 In defiance of the Comstock Laws (1873) legally forbidding the dissemination of "any drug medicine, article, or thing designed, adapted, or intended for preventing conception," Margaret Sanger opens the first birth control clinic in the United States.

1916 Jeannette Rankin of Montana becomes the first woman to be elected to Congress.

1917 When the United States enters World War I, women work for the war effort in industry, nursing, and in some home front jobs held by men. Women also serve abroad as nurses and ambulance drivers. The navy authorizes the enlistment of women in the Naval Reserve, becoming the first branch of the armed forces to allow women in a non-nursing capacity. More than four hundred women serving as nurses and support staff are killed in action.

1918 Annette Adams becomes the first female assistant U.S. attorney general, the highest judicial position any woman had yet held.

1920 The National American Woman Suffrage Association (NAWSA) and the National Council of Women Voters merge to form the League of Women Voters, founded to encourage women to help shape public policy once they gained the vote.

1920 The Nineteenth Amendment to the Constitution is ratified, giving women the right to vote.

1922 The first public celebration of a bat mitzvah is held at the Society for the Advancement of Judaism, a New York synagogue.

1923 Suffragists Alice Paul and Crystal Eastman propose the Equal Rights Amendment, which is introduced in Congress the same year.

1923 Pentecostal evangelist and radio celebrity Aimee Semple McPherson founds the Foursquare Church and its Angelus Temple in Los Angeles, California. It is one of the nation's first evangelical megachurches.

1923 The Amateur Athletic Union (AAU) sponsors the first national championships for women in track and field.

1926 Gertrude Ederle becomes the first woman to swim the English Channel.

1929 The Great Depression begins. During the 1930s, massive unemployment among men forces many women to find jobs to help contribute financially to their households.

1931 Alma Katherine Ledig becomes the first woman to receive an MBA degree from the Wharton School at the University of Pennsylvania.

1931 Jane Addams becomes the first American woman to receive the Nobel Prize.

1932 Hattie Wyatt Caraway (D-AR) becomes the first woman to be elected to the Senate.

1932 Babe Didrikson is named Associated Press Woman Athlete of the Year after she scores enough points at the AAU national track and field meet to win the team championship by herself.

1933 Frances Perkins becomes the first woman appointed to the U.S Cabinet when President Franklin Roosevelt names her secretary of labor.

1933 Nation of Islam founder Wallace Ford Muhammad of Detroit, Michigan, founds the Muslim Girls Training & General Civilization Class, which was developed for religious instruction and to teach domestic duties and the role of women in Muslim life.

1941–1945 During World War II, an unprecedented number of women work outside the home in war-related industries. Approximately four hundred thousand women serve in officially noncombat roles as mechanics, pilots, clerks, nurses, and ambulance drivers. Eighty-eight women are captured and held as POWs.

1942 The first Native American woman engineer, Mary Golda Ross, becomes the first woman aerospace engineer employed at the Lockheed Corporation.

1942 The Women's Army Auxiliary Corps (WAAC) is founded. It is changed to the Women's Army Corps (WAC) in 1943. The Women's Airforce Service Pilots (WASPs) are organized and fly as civil service pilots. The navy recruits women into its Navy Women's Reserve, called Women Accepted for Volunteer Emergency Service (WAVES). The Coast Guard establishes their Women's Reserve, known as SPARs (after the motto *Semper Paratus*—Always Ready).

1942 The American Birth Control League, founded by Margaret Sanger in 1921, changes its name to Planned Parenthood.

1943 The All-American Girls Softball League is formed to fill the gap left when so many major league players enlist for the war. It would become the All-American Girls Professional Baseball League that is active until 1954.

1944 Cordelia E. Cook of the U.S. Army Nurse Corps is the first woman to receive both the Bronze Star and the Purple Heart.

1945 Harvard Medical School admits women for the first time.

1946 Italian-born naturalized U.S. citizen Frances Xavier Cabrini, widely known as Mother Cabrini (1850–1917), is canonized as a Roman Catholic saint.

1948 Congress passes the Women's Armed Services Integration Act, permitting women to serve as permanent members of the military. Prior to the act, women could only serve in times of war. The first women are sworn into the regular U.S. Marine Corps.

1950 During the Korean War (1950–1953), approximately fifty thousand women serve in the military, many as Army nurses in forward-deployed M.A.S.H. units and aboard ships.

1950 Kathryn Johnston, 12, becomes the first girl to play Little League Baseball, as a member of the King's Dairy team in Corning, New York.

1952 Grace Hopper completes what comes to be called COBOL, considered the first program that allows a computer to use English-like words instead of numbers.

1954 The Wharton School at the University of Pennsylvania, the first collegiate business school in the United States, established in 1881, admits the first women to its undergraduate program.

1955 The first LPGA championship is held.

1957 The Civil Rights Act of 1957 gives women the right to serve on federal juries, but it is not until 1975 that women receive the right to serve in all fifty states, after the U.S. Supreme Court holds that states cannot systematically exclude women from juries.

1959 Barbie, the doll created by Ruth Handler of Mattel, debuts. Barbie would transform the modern toy market, becoming the most popular doll of all time.

1960 The FDA approves the birth control pill.

1960 Physician and Pharmacologist Frances Oldham Kelsey begins research into the safety of Thalidomide, a tranquilizer and painkiller prescribed for pregnant women, which had resulted in the births of severely deformed babies in Europe. Kelsey's research leads to legislation to strengthen drug regulation in the United States.

1961 The Universalists join with the Unitarian denomination in 1961 to form the Unitarian Universalist Association (UUA), the first large Christian denomination to have a majority of female ministers.

1962 The first American women are deployed to Vietnam. From 1962 to 1973, an estimated 7,5000 women served in the war, 90 percent as nurses.

1962 *Romper Room* children's TV show host Sherri Finkbine sparks controversy when she obtains an abortion in Sweden after learning that thalidomide, a drug she had taken during her pregnancy, causes birth defects.

1963 The Equal Pay Act, amended to the Fair Labor Standards Act, prohibits employers and unions from paying different wages based on sex.

1963 Betty Friedan publishes *The Feminine Mystique*, which examines the discontent experienced by a great number of women in their roles as housewives and mothers. The book sparks the Women's Movement of the 1960s and 1970s.

1964 The Civil Rights Act of 1964, one of the landmark achievements of the civil rights movement, prohibits employment discrimination on the basis of race, color, religion, sex, or national origin.

1964 Margaret Chase Smith (R-ME) becomes the first woman nominated by a major political party for the presidency

1965 Sister Mary Kenneth Keller, a Roman Catholic nun, becomes the first American woman to earn a PhD in computer science (University of Wisconsin).

1965 The Equal Employment Opportunity Commission (EEOC) is established to administer and enforce civil rights laws against workplace discrimination. However, the EEOC decides that gender-segregated job advertising in publications is permissible because it serves "the convenience of readers."

1965 Birth control is legalized for married couples. However, birth control for unmarried women remains illegal in twenty-six states.

1965 Six Catholic nuns from St. Louis, Missouri, arrive in Selma, Alabama, to join other civil rights demonstrators on a voting rights march. This event marks the start of a transition among many women religious away from their traditional duties and toward social justice initiatives.

1965 Patsy Takemoto Mink (D-HI) becomes the first woman of color and the first woman of Asian Pacific Islander descent elected to the U.S. House of Representatives.

1966 Betty Friedan and other women's rights activists found the National Organization for Women (NOW).

1967 President Lyndon B. Johnson signs an executive order banning discrimination on the basis of sex in hiring and employment in the U.S. federal workforce and on the part of government contractors.

1968 Shirley Chisholm (D-NY) becomes the first black woman to serve in Congress. In 1972, she is the first African American woman major-party presidential candidate.

1970 The first women's studies program is established at San Diego State College. Nearly forty colleges and universities have instituted women's studies programs by 1974.

1970 Astronomer Vera Rubin publishes the first evidence of dark matter.

1971 A group of 320 women, including Gloria Steinem, Bella Abzug, Shirley Chisholm, and Betty Friedan, form the National Women's Political Caucus to expand the number of women in political life.

1972 Katharine Graham becomes the first female Fortune 500 CEO as the CEO of the Washington Post Company.

1972 Sally Priesand becomes the first American woman rabbi and the first ordained by a rabbinical theological seminary.

1972 Congress passes Title IX, making discrimination based on sex in any federally funded education program in the United States illegal. Title IX would have a transformative impact on school sports programs for women.

1972 Sandra Kurtzig founds the ASK Group software producer, an early Silicon Valley startup.

1972 Forty-nine years after its introduction in Congress, the Senate passes the Equal Rights Amendment. The amendment continues to await ratification.

1973 The U.S. Supreme Court's decision in *Roe v. Wade* legalizes abortion.

1973 The U.S. Supreme Court rules unconstitutional inequities in benefits for dependents of military women. Until then, military women with dependents were not authorized housing nor were their dependents eligible for the benefits and privileges afforded the dependents of male military members.

1973 In a widely viewed event that leads to greater public acceptance of women's tennis, Billie Jean King wins the "Battle of the Sexes" tennis match against Bobby Riggs.

1974 The Women's Campaign Fund is founded, the first national organization to financially support female candidates.

1974 The Women's Sports Foundation is created by Billie Jean King to support the participation of women in sports.

1975 The U.S. Department of Defense reverses policy and allows pregnant women the option of electing to be discharged or to remain on active duty. Previous policy required women to be discharged upon pregnancy or the adoption of children.

1975 Elizabeth Ann Seton (1774–1821) becomes the first American-born U.S. citizen to be canonized by the Roman Catholic Church.

1976 The U.S. service academies (U.S. Military Academy, U.S. Naval Academy, U.S. Air Force Academy, and U.S. Coast Guard Academy) admit the first women.

1976 Buddhist scholar and nun Karuna Dharma, born Joyce Pettingill, becomes the first fully ordained member of the Buddhist monastic community in the United States.

1977 Juanita M. Kreps is the first woman and the first economist to serve as secretary of commerce.

1977 Jacqueline Means is ordained to the priesthood in the Episcopal Church, a year after church laws were changed to permit ordination.

1977 Janet Guthrie becomes the first woman to compete in the Indianapolis 500 and the Daytona 500.

1978 The Pregnancy Discrimination Act makes discrimination based on pregnancy or pregnancy-related conditions illegal.

1978 Mary E. Clarke is the first woman to achieve the rank of major general in the U.S. Army.

1978 The Association for Women in Computing is founded in Washington, D.C.

1979 Carol Shaw becomes the first woman to program and design a video game: 3D Tic-Tac-Toe for the Atari 2600.

1980 Sherry Lansing becomes the first woman to head a major Hollywood studio (20th Century Fox).

1980 Women and men are enrolled in American colleges in equal numbers for the first time. The following year, for the first time, more bachelor's degrees are conferred on women than men.

1981 Sandra Day O'Connor, a former Republican state legislator from Arizona, becomes the first woman to sit on the U.S. Supreme Court.

1982 The NCAA begins sponsoring women's basketball.

1983 Astronaut Sally Ride becomes the first American woman in space.

1984 Geraldine Ferraro becomes the first woman nominated for vice president on a major-party ticket (Democrat).

1984–1986 For the first time in history, the Naval, Air Force, and Coast Guard Academies' top graduates are woman.

1984 Women are allowed to run the Olympic marathon for the first time. Joan Benoit wins the gold medal in Los Angeles.

1985 EMILY's List is founded by Ellen P. Malcolm to fund progressive Democratic female congressional and gubernatorial candidates. EMILY is an acronym for Early Money Is Like Yeast, "making the dough rise."

1985 Virologist Flossie Wong-Staal becomes the first scientist to clone and genetically map the HIV virus, enabling the development of the first HIV blood screening tests.

1987 The first National Girls and Women in Sports Day, an annual day of observance during the first week in February, is held to acknowledge the accomplishments of female athletes and to honor the progress and continuing struggle for equality for women in sports.

1991 During Operation Desert Storm (1991–1992), approximately forty-one thousand servicewomen are deployed to the Middle East.

1991 In the first FIFA soccer Women's World Cup in China, the United States beats Norway in the final. The event is largely ignored worldwide, and only a single journalist greets the victorious American team when they return home.

1991 The Civil Rights Act of 1991 adds provisions to Title VII protections, including expanding the rights of women to sue and collect compensatory and punitive damages for sexual discrimination or harassment.

1992 The media declares the "Year of the Woman," when a record-breaking number of women are elected to Congress, including Carol Moseley Braun (D-IL), the first African American woman and the first woman of color to be elected to the U.S. Senate.

1992 Mona Van Duyn becomes the first woman named U.S. poet laureate.

1993 The Family and Medical Leave Act is passed, mandating that a woman working for a company with fifty or more employees can take up to twelve weeks of unpaid leave for a newborn child or newly adopted child (the leave is also available for men).

1993 Janet Reno becomes the first woman to serve as U.S. attorney general.

1993 Congress authorizes women to fly combat missions and serve on combat ships.

1994 Judith Rodin becomes the first woman president of an Ivy League school.

1995 Ruth Simmons becomes the first African American woman to head a major college or university when she is named president of Smith College.

1995 The American Bar Association, founded in 1878, inaugurates its first female president, Roberta Cooper Ramo.

1995 Martha McSally becomes the first American woman to fly a combat mission.

1995 Theoretical physicist Shirley Anne Jackson becomes the first woman to chair the U.S. Nuclear Regulatory Commission.

1996 Planetary scientist Margaret G. Kivelson leads a team that discovers the first subsurface, saltwater ocean on the Jovian moon Europa.

1996 At the Olympic Games in Atlanta, softball and women's soccer are included for the first time. American women win team gold in basketball, soccer, softball, and gymnastics, as well as in several other individual events.

1997 Madeleine K. Albright becomes the first woman to serve as U.S. secretary of state. She had previously served as U.S. ambassador to the United Nations.

1997 A group of Republican women found the Value in Electing Women Political Action Committee (VIEWPAC) to elect qualified Republican women to Congress.

1997 The Women's National Basketball Association (WNBA) begins its first season.

1998 In the first class-action sexual harassment lawsuit in the United States (first filed in 1988 on behalf of female workers at the EVTAC mine in Eveleth, Minnesota), the fifteen women settle just before the trial is set to begin for a total of $3.5 million.

1998 Ava Muhammad becomes the first female minister in the Nation of Islam.

1999 Carly Fiorina becomes the first woman to lead a Fortune 50 company (Hewlett-Packard).

1999 The first women graduate from the Virginia Military Institute and the Citadel.

2000 Captain Kathleen A. McGrath becomes the first woman to command a U.S. Navy warship at sea during a mission in the Persian Gulf.

2001 Elaine Chao is the first Asian American woman to serve in a presidential Cabinet. Hillary Rodham Clinton (D-NY) becomes the first woman elected to the U.S. Senate from New York and the only first lady ever to be elected to public office.

2003 The invasion of Iraq sends the largest number of women into combat in U.S. history.

2003 Geophysicist Claudia Alexander oversees the final stages of Project Galileo, a space exploration mission that reached the planet Jupiter.

2004 Colonel Linda McTague becomes the first woman to command a U.S. Air Force fighter squadron.

2005 The Supreme Court rules that retaliation against a person because that person has complained of sex discrimination is a form of intentional sex discrimination covered by Title VII.

2005 Condoleezza Rice becomes the first African American woman to serve as U.S. secretary of state (2005–2009).

2005 Sergeant Leigh Ann Hester, an Army National Guard soldier, earns the Silver Star in Iraq, becoming the first female soldier since World War II to receive the medal.

2005 Amina Wadud becomes the first woman to lead a mixed-gender Muslim congregation in Friday night prayers with no curtain to divide the women and men.

2006 The "Me Too" movement is founded to help survivors of sexual assault, particularly African American women and girls and other young women of color. The movement goes viral and expands with #MeToo in 2017, following sexual abuse allegations against film producer Harvey Weinstein.

2007 Nancy Pelosi (D-CA) becomes the first woman elected speaker of the U.S. House of Representatives.

2007 For the first time, half of the eight Ivy League schools have female presidents.

2008 Evelynn Hammonds becomes the first woman and the first African American to be named dean of Harvard College.

2008 Senator Hillary Rodham Clinton (D-NY) becomes the first woman to win a major party's presidential primary (NH) and the first woman presidential candidate represented in every primary and caucus in every state. Sarah Palin becomes the Republican Party's first woman vice presidential nominee.

2009 The Lilly Ledbetter Fair Act provides that the statute of limitations for wage discrimination claims restarts every time an unequal paycheck is issued.

2009 The military's first Female Engagement Teams are deployed to build relationships with Afghan women.

2010 A group of women led by Sandra B. Mortham founds the political action committee Maggie's List to raise funds to elect more women who support fiscal conservatism, less government, more personal responsibility, and strong national security. The organization is named after Margaret Chase Smith, the first woman elected to both houses of Congress.

2011 A year after the U.S. Navy rescinds its males-only submarine policy, women officers deploy on a submarine for the first time.

2012 Tammy Baldwin (D-WI) becomes the first openly gay or lesbian person to be elected to the U.S. Senate.

2012 Mazie Hirono (D-HI) becomes the first Asian Pacific Islander woman to be elected to the U.S. Senate. Kyrsten Sinema (D-AZ) becomes the first openly bisexual person to be elected to Congress.

2012 Vashti Murphy McKenzie becomes the first woman to be elected a bishop in the African Methodist Episcopal Church. Founded in 1816 as the first independent Protestant denomination created by African Americans, the African Methodist Episcopal Church grew out of the Free African Society, which was established in Philadelphia in 1787.

2013 New Hampshire becomes the first state to have an all-female congressional delegation (Senators Jeanne Shaheen and Kelly Ayotte and Representatives Ann McLane Kuster and Carol Shea-Porter).

2013 Defense Secretary Leon Panetta lifts all gender-based restrictions on military service.

2014 Janet Yellen becomes the first woman to lead the Federal Reserve.

2014 Haitian American Mia Love (R-UT) becomes the first black Republican woman elected to Congress.

2015 The first women soldiers graduate from Ranger School. The U.S. military opens up all combat positions to women without exception.

2015 The final of the Women's World Cup between the U.S. and Japan is the most watched soccer game in American history. The U.S. team becomes the first women's sports team honored with a ticker tape parade down New York City's Canyon of Heroes.

2016 Hillary Clinton becomes the first female presidential nominee of a major political party (Democrat). Despite winning the popular vote by almost three million, Clinton loses the Electoral College.

2016 The U.S. Department of Defense opens all combat jobs to women.

2016 The USA Gymnastic scandal breaks, alleging systematic and decade-long sexual abuse of female athletes. It would lead to the conviction of longtime team physician Larry Nasser as a serial child molester and the decertification and bankruptcy of USA Gymnastics.

2017 Nikki Haley becomes the first Indian American to serve in a Cabinet-level position when she is named the U.S. ambassador to the United Nations.

2018 Stacey Cunningham becomes the first female president of the New York Stock Exchange.

2018 Sharice Davids (D-KS) and Deb Haaland (D-NM) become the first Native American women elected to Congress.

2018 Ilhan Omar (D-MN) and Rashida Tlaib (D-MI) become the first Muslim women elected to Congress. Ayanna Pressley (D-MA) is the first African American woman elected to Congress from her state, and Alexandria Ocasio-Cortez (D-NY), at twenty-nine, becomes the youngest woman elected to serve. The four freshman representatives join together to advance a progressive legislative agenda and become known as "The Squad."

2019 For the first time in history, more than two women are competing in the same major party's presidential primary process (Democratic).

2019 Major General Laura Yeager becomes the first woman to lead a U.S. Army Infantry division.

2019 The U.S. House of Representatives passes the Equality Act, which prohibits discrimination "on the basis of sex, sexual orientation, gender identity, or pregnancy, childbirth, or a related medical condition of an individual, as well as because of sex-based stereotypes." The bill goes to the Senate, where it continues to sit without any action.

INTRODUCTION

"The past," writes historian Gerda Lerner in *Why History Matters: Life and Thought*, "becomes part of our present and thereby part of our future." From the moment women arrived in what would become the United States of America, they began to make a history that was uniquely their own. This book attempts to present that history and to enhance it with the stories of American history's most remarkable women.

The story of American women begins, like all human history, with exploration and migration, settlement, and the building of communities with their own cultures and social norms. For the vast majority of non-indigenous women during America's colonial era, the observation of these norms meant physical, social, and legal submission to the authority of the religious and secular patriarchy under which they lived. For enslaved African women, it meant submission to their male and female white owners. But the era also included women who were able to challenge and transcend these strictures; for example, the adventurous Isabel de Olvera, the daughter of a black father and an Indian mother, who accompanied a Spanish expedition to Santa Fe, where she insisted on a legal document recognizing her status as a free woman of color; the courageous spiritual advisor Anne Hutchinson, who defied the estab-

lished male clergy in Puritan New England by teaching and preaching the scriptures, a practice forbidden to women; and Phillis Wheatley, a Massachusetts slave emancipated shortly after the publication of her volume of poetry, the first book published by an African American woman. While the lives of most colonial women were confined to house, farm, or plantation, there were women who worked alongside their husbands as shopkeepers and innkeepers, ran their own businesses, and were landowners. Some women pursued careers in literature and the fine arts.

When Patience Lovell Wright found herself widowed with four children to support, she turned her hobby of molding figures from wax and clay into a successful profession, becoming the first American-born sculptor. Susanna Rowson was an actor, playwright, and author of *Charlotte Temple*, the first bestselling novel in American history.

During the American Revolution (and again, during the Civil War), women served as nurses, and in combat, as spies, and as message-bearers. Much has been made of America's Founding Fathers, but the Founding Mothers, from the first women settlers in the thirteen American colonies and those who began to venture westward to the frontier, to such well-known colonial women as Martha Washington and Abigail Adams, proved equally influential in the early history that would result in the founding and formation of the Republic.

Despite the rights enshrined in the U.S. Constitution, the status of women remained largely unchanged for many years. The women of the new nation were encouraged—in fact, expected—to be the Mothers of the Republic, whose primary function was to train sons to be good citizens and nurture daughters to be good wives and mothers. The social and legal dictates of the nation meant that the vast majority of American women were prohibited from pursuing equal educational and professional opportunities. They could not own property in most cases, they were subordinate to the will of fathers and husbands, and they were denied that most basic of citizenship rights: the right to vote. Then, during the first half of the nineteenth century, a critical minority of American women joined the abolitionist cause to press for the freedom of enslaved Africans who possessed no citizenship at all. Women's lack of equal participation with men in the abolitionist movement would reveal in glaring detail their status as second-class citizens, and this set in motion what has always been, in my view, the most important aspect of American women's history: the impressive capacity of women to individually and collectively advocate on behalf of equal rights for themselves, as well as for social, economic, legal, and political justice for all.

The long and hard-fought battle for women's rights, a campaign whose earliest proponents were the abolitionist sisters Sarah and Angelina Grimké, began with women establishing their own antislavery organizations and continued with the Seneca Falls Convention of 1848: the seminal event that would usher in the women's rights movement of the nineteenth and early twentieth centuries that is also called first-wave feminism. Thanks to Elizabeth Cady Stanton, who prepared the convention's Declaration of Rights Sentiments and insisted upon including in it a demand for votes for women, woman suffrage would become a major focus of first-wave feminism. The nineteenth amendment guaranteeing a woman's right to vote would take nearly a century to achieve, and over the decades it required the indefatigable efforts of Stanton and women like Susan

B. Anthony, Lucy Stone, Carrie Chapman Catt, and the firebrand of the group, Alice Paul. Left out of the white mainstream women's suffrage movement, African American women organized on their own behalf and featured such civil rights campaigners and suffragists as journalist and anti-lynching activist Ida Wells-Barnett.

At the same time the suffragists were working to achieve the vote for women, other movements developed in which women played a central role, and there was slow but steady progress for women in education and the professions. Although secondary schools for girls date from the eighteenth century, the nineteenth century saw the first institutions of higher education for women, the first co-ed colleges, and more women working in education, nursing, medicine, business, and the law, despite the prevailing social construct that maintained that only men were entitled to the pursuit of the latter three professions. The profession of social work and the emphasis on public and workplace health initiatives began with the settlement house movement, founded by women such as Jane Addams and Lillian Wald, to address the social, educational, and health needs of the large number of immigrants who had escaped famine and persecution in the Old World and were endeavoring to adapt to life in American cities, often living with their families in overcrowded, poorly constructed tenement apartments. Living as residents of settlement houses deepened the commitment of such well-to-do and professional women as Eleanor Roosevelt, labor activist Florence Kelley, and physician Alice Hamilton who strove to improve the lives of the working poor.

Women's involvement in the nineteenth-century labor movement was represented collectively by the strike initiatives of the "Mill Girls," who labored in the textile mills of the Northeast, and individually by Irish immigrant and self-described "hell-raiser" Mary Harris "Mother" Jones in her fight to improve conditions for coal miners and to call attention to the abuses of child labor. During the first decade of the twentieth century, a relatively short but intense women's labor movement addressed the problem of women working long hours in nonunionized, low-paying, shirtwaist-making jobs in New York City sweatshops run by owners more dedicated to profit than providing a living wage and ensuring workplace safety. The solution was to strike. Led by women garment workers, some of whom have earned a place in American history as the era's greatest labor activists, the fight for the right of women garment workers to form a local union in order to better working conditions for themselves resulted in a spectacular strike during the freezing winter of 1909–1910. Often called the Uprising of the 20,000, the women on the picket line bravely stood their ground despite beatings and clubbings by police and company-hired thugs. While women garment workers were fighting for better wages and shorter hours, a visiting nurse named Margaret Sanger was attending poor women in the New York City slums who were struggling with multiple pregnancies and sometimes dying from self-inflicted abortions. In defiance of the law, Sanger and social activist Emma Goldman provided women with information on contraception, thus beginning the birth control movement. In 1915, in response to the world war raging in Europe and the possibility that the United States would join the conflict, social reformer Jane Addams and other pacifist women founded the Woman's Peace Party, which would become the Women's International League for Peace and Freedom.

Once the vote was achieved, the impetus for women to come together in large numbers in order to effect social change was lessened; instead, smaller organizations such as the League of Women Voters and the National Council of Negro Women worked to encourage the participation of women in civic, political, economic, and educational life. The United States Women's Bureau focused on women's working conditions in factories and in household employment. Suffragist Alice Paul's 1923 proposal for an equal rights amendment would not inspire collective activism until the women's movement of the 1960s and 1970s. After serving their country on the home front and abroad as nurses and ambulance drivers during World War I, many young women entered the work force during the economically booming 1920s, as office workers and salesgirls in the large new department stores: stereotypical "women's work" to be sure, but for the single "New Woman" of the era, such jobs meant autonomy, as well as a paycheck, and a certain white-collar status that fac-

tory work could never offer them. The era also saw more young women athletes competing in intercollegiate sports and Amateur Athletic Union (AAU) and Olympic games, including the versatile Babe Didrikson, who is still considered one of the greatest athletes of all time.

The 1920s featured some of the most enduring women writers and performers in American history: Harlem Renaissance author Zora Neale Hurston; modernist Gertrude Stein; the witty poet, critic, and satirist Dorothy Parker; blues great Bessie Smith; singer and comic actor Fannie Brice; and film stars Mary Pickford and Lillian Gish.

It was the rare woman teacher, office worker, or salesgirl who continued to work outside the home once she was married. But when the Great Depression of the 1930s saw massive unemployment among men, many wives went to work to help supplement their family's income. During World War II, an unprecedented number of women worked in wartime industries at home and as nurses in military hospitals in war zones. Women also served in all branches of the military in auxiliary corps, one of the most famous of which were the Women's Airforce Service Pilots (WASPs). WASPs such as Jacqueline Cochran were trained pilots who tested and ferried aircraft and trained other pilots. After the war ended, women began to seek careers in the military. Over the next several decades and into the twenty-first century, women gained entry to military colleges, worked their way up the chains of command, and were allowed to serve in combat. By 2019, Major Laura Yeager of the Army National Guard had become the first woman assigned to lead an infantry division.

Women who had helped to build bombers and other war materiel were let go to make room for returning soldiers who needed jobs. Many women willingly went back to homemaking and producing the first children of the Baby Boom generation; some resented losing their jobs, however; a sizable cohort of single women found jobs in offices, stores, and schools. During the postwar 1950s and early 1960s, more women were pursuing college degrees but frequently leaving college to marry or marrying soon after graduation. Housewives, including those with advanced college degrees, were perceived in a manner not unlike the earlier Mothers of the Republic: glorified and ostensibly satisfied by marriage and motherhood, a state of being reinforced by advertisers and on screen. But the era was both constrictive and progressive: Although marriage and motherhood were primary goals, Baby Boom girls were also expected to excel in school and in sports. Math and science were important subjects for girls as well as boys during the early Space Age, and, although women's history was not yet a subject in college, many young women grew up knowing about the achievements of such women as Jane Addams and Clara Barton; Harriet Tubman, the heroine of the Underground Railroad; Frances Perkins, the first woman cabinet member; Jeanette Rankin, the first woman elected to the U.S. Congress; and Amelia Earhart, the first woman aviator to fly solo across the Atlantic. They were exposed to news concerning desegregation in the Jim Crow South, the Civil Rights Movement, and the promise of the Peace Corps. In 1962, President John F. Kennedy initiated the President's Commission on the Status of Women, chaired by another icon in women's history, the remarkable Eleanor Roosevelt. Intended to address inequality and gender bias in the workplace through legislation, the findings of the commission would be realized in a more concrete fashion with the various Civil Rights Acts and Titles within the acts that followed.

In 1963, the mothers and older sisters of Baby Boom girls were introduced to a book that would change the lives of many of them: *The Feminine Mystique*, written by journalist Betty Friedan to explore the discontent experienced by middle-class women in their primary roles as wives, mothers, and homemakers. The book would spark a second women's movement from the late 1960s to the early 1980s, also known as second-wave feminism. Often called the Women's Liberation Movement, second-wave feminist leaders such as Betty Friedan, journalist Gloria Steinem, politician Bella Abzug, presidential advisor Catherine East, and writers Kate Millet and Robin Morgan focused on a series of gender inequities and stereotyping at home, in the workplace, and in society at large; woman's reproductive rights, most prominently the right to have safe, legal abortions; and passage and ratification of the Equal Rights Amendment. Many of the movement's aims

were achieved through campaigns, protests, and legislation, but one of the movement's most significant accomplishments was the absorption into the collective consciousness its condemnation of gender stereotyping, questions concerning the essence of feminism, and its call for equality.

By the mid 1970s and the 1980s, large numbers of women were pursuing advanced degrees and careers in higher education, law, medicine, business, politics, government, and nonprofit organizations. The era saw the first African American woman, Shirley Chisholm, elected to Congress, and Sandra Day O'Connor become the first woman appointed to the U.S. Supreme Court. Professional women continued to face challenges, however. The "glass ceiling" prevented women from reaching the top echelons of business, and women with children were viewed with suspicion that they were on the "mommy track," distracted from their jobs because of motherhood. Tasked with domestic duties after work, many women also felt torn between their jobs, their children, and their spouses, and they wondered, in the argot of the 1980s, if it was really possible to "have it all." Flexible workplace hours to facilitate motherhood might mean fewer opportunities for advancement and even the disappearance of a job when women returned from maternity leave or after spending the first years of motherhood at home. There were women who made the choice to use day care or to become stay-at-home mothers, if such choices were financially viable. For single mothers and the working poor, then as now, few options were available.

During the politically conservative 1980s, women experienced what author Susan Faludi called a "backlash" against feminist advances, with some representatives of the media suggesting that the women's liberation movement was to blame for the unrealistic expectations of women in the workplace. However, by the 1990s, women were so firmly ensconced in every aspect of public life that the media's harangues against feminism seemed irrelevant. In fact, the ever-opportunistic media dubbed 1992 the "Year of the Woman," after an unprecedented number of women were elected to Congress.

The twenty-first century has continued to see progress for women. Although there have been influential women in the sciences since the twentieth century, including mathematician Katherine Johnson, computer programmer Grace Hopper, and such Nobel Prize recipients as physicist Rosalyn Yalow and cytogeneticist Barbara McClintock, more attention has been paid to young women who want to pursue careers in the Science, Technology, Engineering, and Mathematics (STEM) disciplines. In 2016 Hillary Clinton became the first woman in American history to be named the candidate of a major political party for the highest office in the nation. Two years later, a second "Year of the Woman" was proclaimed, this time with an even greater number of women of color, as well as women of LGBTQ communities, elected to Congress. The Me Too and other resistance movements in the wake of the presidential election of 2016, and the revelations of sexual assault and harassment by men of influence in every sphere of society, have prompted women to courageously speak out and show their willingness to organize on behalf of social change once again.

Like the abolitionists, the suffragists, and the women who formed the backbone of the Civil Rights Movement and fought for equality in the Women's Liberation Movement, the women of the twenty-first century will not remain silent when faced with injustice and inequality because they know that the price paid for silence is too high.

The list of influential women in American history is long and could fill volumes. There is no question that all the women mentioned in the history covered in this book, and more besides, deserve recognition. However, for the biographies featured here, I chose to concentrate on the stories of women, who, in my view, best represent the historical trajectory of women in America. There are icons, trailblazers, and in some cases, pioneering outliers, all of whom have much to tell us about where we have been, where we are now, and what we might become.

THE ARRIVAL OF WOMEN IN AMERICA

The first women in the area of North America that would become the United States were members of the many indigenous groups and tribes that populated the continent. The arrival of European women, who lived in patriarchal societies and were largely consigned to the private rather than public sphere, generally followed the explorations of the Spanish *conquistadores* (conquerors) and the appropriation of land and resources that began in the West Indies in the late fifteenth century and continued throughout the Americas in the sixteenth century as well as the first European attempts at colonization, particularly by the Spanish, English, and Dutch in the sixteenth and seventeenth centuries. The wars and religious rivalries occurring in Europe at this time would spill over into North America as nations and religious communities strove to gain footholds there. Women, initially thought to be too frail to endure the dangers and hardships of a journey to the New World and therefore considered too much of a hindrance in colonization efforts, would prove to be necessary to the survival of the settlements that were eventually established in North America.

Some Native Americans accepted the presence of the Europeans, offered aid, and chose alliances with the European explorers and settlers; many others aggressively rejected their intrusion. The violence resulting from European attempts to acquire and colonize territory, together with diseases the explorers and first colonists brought with them from Europe, led to large declines in indigenous populations throughout the Americas. Confrontations with and displacement of Native Americans in the United States would continue well into the nineteenth century as the nation continued to expand its territory in accordance with the principle of Manifest Destiny.

WOMEN AND THE FIRST EUROPEAN SETTLEMENTS

Histories of the age of exploration have traditionally focused on the men who made those explorations and first attempted to colonize the lands they conquered. However, the presence of women in Florida, the Southeast, and the Southwest in the sixteenth and early seventeenth centuries predate the founding of the more well-known Roanoke Colony and the early seventeenth-century settlements of Jamestown, Plymouth, and New Amsterdam.

1539: Francisca Hinestrosa and Ana Mendez

It is most likely that the first European women to set foot in what would become the continental United States accompanied Spanish explorer and *conquistador* Hernando de Soto (c. 1495–1542) on his expedition to Florida and the Southeast. In 1539, de Soto and a large number of ships, men (including soldiers, priests, craftsmen, engineers, farmers, and merchants), horses, and supplies sailed from Spanish-held Cuba to present-day Florida (which he named *Espíritu Sancto*, "Holy Spirit") and the Southeast to settle the land and claim it for Charles V of the Spanish and Holy Roman empires. De Soto's wife, Doña Isabel de Bobadilla, remained in Cuba with nine Castilian women and female slaves, although some sources claim that de Soto's wife and family, as well as the families of some of his men, also made the crossing to Florida. What is more clearly documented is the presence of Ana Mendez, the servant of Doña Isabel, and Francisca Hinestrosa on the expedition. Little information exists on Francisca Hinestrosa and even less on Ana Mendez. Hinestrosa was most likely the member of an influential Cuban family, and she may have been married to Luis de Inostrosa or Hernando Bautista, both from Seville, or she was the wife of one of de Soto's unnamed soldiers. Hinestrosa made the journey disguised as a male soldier; sources differ on whether the deception was revealed early on, afterward working as a nurse and a cook for the company, or she was identified as a woman only after her death. Hinestrosa was with de Soto and his company as they traveled throughout the Southeast, including present-day Georgia, the Carolinas, Tennessee, Alabama, and Mississippi. In each area, the expedition established winter camps in deserted or commandeered Native American villages.

While traveling to the Gulf of Mexico to meet ships from Havana with fresh supplies, de Soto and his Spaniards suffered numerous casualties and the loss of most of their possessions as the result of a battle led by Chief Tuskaloosa at the Native American fortress of Mabila in southern Alabama. De Soto moved inland and, in the early spring of 1541, set up a camp near a Chickasaw village in Mississippi in the area around present-day Tupelo. De Soto demanded porters from the village leader as well as women for domestic and sexual labor. The Chickasaws refused and attacked de Soto's camp during the night, burning huts and killing somewhere between a dozen and forty Spaniards. Among the dead was Francisca Hinestrosa, who was either unable to leave her hut because she was pregnant and in labor or, according to some sources, escaped but went back to the hut to collect

This statue that was once atop the Castillo de la Real Fuerza in Havana, Cuba, is said by locals to represent Doña Isabel de Bobadilla, who was the Spanish governor of Cuba from 1539 to 1543 as well as the wife of explorer Hernando de Soto.

her pearls. Ana Mendez survived the attack and later described her experiences with the expedition to a Spanish commission.

1564: The French Huguenot Women of Fort Caroline

Women were also among the colonists at the short-lived French settlement of Fort Caroline. The persecution of the Huguenots (Reformed Protestants) in Catholic France, which culminated in the French Wars of Religion (1562–1598; also known as the Huguenot Wars), led to greater attempts to colonize territories in the Americas where French Protestants might find refuge. The Huguenots failed to establish settlements in Brazil (1555–1567; destroyed by the Portuguese) and on Parris Island in present-day Georgia (1562; abandoned the following year). In 1564, Huguenot explorers Jean Ribault and René Goulaine de Laudonnièrre founded a third settlement in Florida on the banks of the St. John's River near present-day Jacksonville. Named Fort Caroline after the French king Charles IX and intended at first as a commercial venture and expansion of the French empire, which had begun to establish a presence in Canadian America in the early sixteenth century, the settlement ultimately served as a safe haven for Huguenots. Some three hundred settlers, including Huguenot women, were brought from France to Fort Caroline, and French soldiers and artisans built a village and fort with the help of a local Indian tribe, the Timucuans. Jean Ribault was pleased with the look and demeanor of the settlers, whom he described as "very gentle, courteous, and of good nature" and the women especially "well favored and modest."

By the spring of 1565, the settlers at Fort Caroline faced starvation, mutiny, and Indian attacks

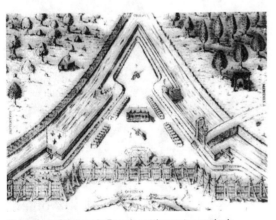

A drawing of the early French settlement near Jacksonville, Florida, Fort Caroline, which was established by French Huguenots, including some of the first women settlers from Europe.

when relations with the Timucuans deteriorated. The colony was on the verge of collapse when Jean Ribault returned from France with fresh supplies, several hundred soldiers, and more women as well as children. In August 1565, a Spanish fleet captained by Pedro Menéndez de Avilés landed up the coast from Fort Caroline and founded St. Augustine, a fort that would become the first permanent European colonial settlement in what is now the continental United States (women would arrive in St. Augustine the following year). Determined to drive out the French, considered heretics as well as a threat to Catholic Spain's claim on all of *La Florida*, Menéndez marched on Fort Caroline with about five hundred troops. The French fleet had run aground near St. Augustine during a storm, and the few soldiers who had stayed behind at the fort could not hold off Menéndez's soldiers, who massacred the majority of Fort Caroline's men and later killed Jean Ribault and his soldiers except for those who claimed to be Catholic, some impressed Breton sailors, and four artisans who were sent to St. Augustine. The site became known as *Las Matanzas* ("The Slaughters"). About twenty-six men, including René Goulaine de Laudonnièrre, managed to escape. The Spanish spared about fifty to sixty women and children, who were taken prisoner and sent to Havana. Their fate remains unknown.

1587: Virginia Dare and the Roanoke Colony

The first sixteenth-century English women colonists arrived at Roanoke Island in present-day North Carolina in July 1587. Named after the Roanoke Carolina Algonquian people who inhabited the island, Roanoke Colony is often referred to as the "Lost Colony" because of the mystery that has surrounded its disappearance. Sponsored by England's queen, Elizabeth I, and organized by soldier, explorer, and courtier Sir Walter Raleigh, the Roanoke Colony followed two voyages in 1584 and 1585. The earlier voyages were intended to first explore the area, which Raleigh named Virginia for Elizabeth, the "Virgin Queen," and then establish a permanent English presence that would challenge the commercial and religious dominance of Spain in North America. According to the charter granted to

Raleigh, the mission was to "discover, search, find out, and view such remote heathen and barbarous Lands, Countries, and territories … to have, hold, occupy, and enjoy." An attempt to fortify and colonize Roanoke during the second voyage failed, but the 1587 voyage brought some 117 men, women, and children to the site of the 1585 settlement. Among the colonists was artist John White, a veteran of the second voyage and the colony's governor, and White's daughter and son-in-law, Eleanor (also spelled Elinor and Elenora) and Ananias Dare. In August, Eleanor gave birth to a healthy baby girl, who was named Virginia in honor of England's new territory. One of two children born in the colony in 1587, Virginia Dare was the first and only female infant and the first English child born in the Americas.

The relationship between the colonists and the Croatan Indians and other local tribes John White had encountered on his previous voyage was for the most part friendly. However, by the end of the month, the Roanoke colonists' food supplies had begun to run out. Worried that they might not survive the winter since any supply ships would land at the colony's first intended site in the Chesapeake Bay area, the colonists insisted that John White return to England to inform Walter Raleigh of their situation and to ask for "supplies and other necessaries." The governor proved reluctant and demanded that the colonists put their request in writing as a decision made with "one minde." Women as well as men signed the letter, an unusual occurrence in an era when women were expected to confine themselves to domestic opinions. White, accompanied by the colony ship's pilot Simon Fernandez and his crew, sailed for England in late 1587. The inability of White to find a ship that would cross the Atlantic in winter, together with the Spanish Armada's attempted invasion of England in 1588 and the Anglo–Spanish War that followed, delayed White's return to Roanoke for three years. White was finally able to gain passage to Roanoke aboard a privateer ship. When he reached the colony on August 18, 1590—his granddaughter's third

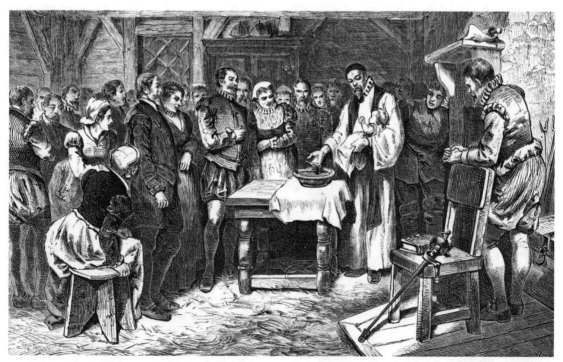

An 1876 illustration depicts the 1587 baptism of Virginia Dare, the first Englishperson born in the New World. Unfortunately, she was born in the colony of Roanoke whose settlers all mysteriously disappeared.

birthday—he found his belongings, which had been buried and hidden, and the word "CROATAN" carved into a post of the fort. The buildings had been dismantled, and no trace of the colonists or sign of a struggle was found. After a fruitless attempt to find them, John White returned to England, never to see his daughter and granddaughter again.

Despite several hypotheses, the most prevalent of which is that the Roanoke colonists had become integrated into one or more of the Native American tribes in the area, evidence concerning their fate has never been conclusive. Little Virginia Dare became an object of American myth and folklore as a symbol of innocence and purity, revered as the "first white child" in America. To punctuate that description, her name was invoked during the era of women's suffrage when an antisuffrage group in Raleigh, North Carolina, feared the extension of the right to vote to black women. In the 1980s, North Carolina feminists urged the state to pass the Equal Rights Amendment to "honor Virginia Dare." In 1999, in a perverse use of the name of a vanished little girl who was the daughter and granddaughter of immigrants, Virginia Dare became the symbol of VDARE, an anti-immigration group with ties to white supremacist, white nationalist, and alt-right movements in the United States.

1600: Isabel de Olvera

The exploration and colonization of the American Southwest included people of African ancestry. Most were enslaved Africans, of which some, mainly soldiers, were able to gain their freedom. In 1542, the Spanish enacted the *Nuevas Leyes* ("New Laws"), which forbade the formal enslavement and mistreatment of indigenous people in the occupied territories of New Spain. While only partially successful and frequently ignored, the New Laws would influence the status of mixed-race people in Spanish America.

In 1598, following the failed expedition of explorer Francisco de Coronado, Spanish *conquistador* Juan de Oñate brought 129 soldiers, two of whom were black, and their wives and children to the upper Rio Grande river to colonize Nueva México Province near Santa Fe. Two years later, Juan Guerra de Resa, a wealthy relative of Oñate, led an expedition from Querétero, Mexico, to Santa Fe in order to further bolster Spanish claims there. One woman accompanied the Guerra de Resa party: Isabel de Olvera, the daughter of a black father and an Indian mother. Concerned that her status as a mixed-race free woman of color would be challenged and her safety compromised in a pioneer outpost, Olvera insisted on filing a deposition with the *alcade* (mayor) before she left Querétero. In Olvera's deposition, she states that she has:

> … some reason to fear that I may be annoyed by some individual … and it is proper to protect my rights in such an eventuality by an affidavit showing that I am a free woman, unmarried and the legitimate daughter of Hernando, a negro [sic] and an Indian named Magdelena … I therefore request your grace to accept this affidavit, which shows that I am free and not bound by marriage or slavery. I request that a properly certified and signed copy be given to me in order to protect my rights, and that it carry fully legal authority. I demand justice.

Isabel de Olvera's deposition was signed by the mayor and three witnesses and notarized. It is perhaps the first recorded incidence of a woman receiving legal standing as a free woman of African ancestry in colonial America.

COLONIAL WOMEN IN AMERICA

After the arrival of women at St. Augustine in Spanish Florida in 1566, the history of non-indigenous American women in what would become the continental United States continues with their presence at the first permanent English and Dutch settlements in Virginia, Massachusetts, and New Netherland. The Virginia Company of London and the Dutch West India Company established two of these settlements: Jamestown in Virginia (1607) and New Amsterdam in New York (1624). The Plymouth Colony in Massachusetts (1620) was founded as a safe haven for Pilgrims—Puritan separatists who had fled England to escape the jurisdiction and perceived corruption of the Church of England and settled in Holland in 1607 before immigrating to North America—as well as a commercial enterprise for a group of investors calling themselves the Merchant Adventurers (also known as the London Company), who financed the Pilgrims' crossing on the *Mayflower*, indentured them to the company for seven years after their arrival in the New World, and recruited some fifty non-Separatist colonists to join them. The establishment of these British- and Dutch-American settlements marks the beginning of the economy, politics, culture, and society that would shape and define the Thirteen Colonies and the nation that emerged from them.

1608: The Women of Jamestown

Jamestown is notable for being the first permanent English settlement as well as the first successful British commercial colonial enterprise. Women arrived at the Jamestown settlement after it was determined that the commercial ventures that initiated colonization would be capable of generating profit for the Virginia Company and to discourage the practice of male settlers returning to England after making their fortunes. The first settlers at Jamestown in 1607 were about one hundred men and boys who, regardless of social class, were indentured to the company. In October 1608, a supply ship brought an additional 198 men as well as one woman, Margaret Forrest, and her fourteen-year-old maid, Anne Burras. Much speculation but few definitive historical facts are known about Margaret Forrest. She made the crossing with her financier husband, Thomas, and is pictured with him in an 1840 painting by John Gadsby Chapman titled *The Baptism of Pocahontas*, which hangs in the rotunda of the U.S. Capitol building. A description of the painting identifies "Mr. and Mrs. Forrest, the lady being the first gentlewoman to arrive in the colony." Anne Burras married carpenter John Laydon a few months after her arrival in what was Jamestown's first wedding, gave birth to four daughters, survived what the settlers called the "Starving Time" during the winter of 1609 to 1610, and was listed as living in Virginia as of 1625.

When colonist John Rolfe (the future husband of Pocahontas) successfully cultivated tobacco in 1611, the economic viability of Jamestown was assured but only if enough settlers were around to tend

A replica of the ship *Susan Constant,* which some say was actually called the *Sarah Constant*. It was the largest of three ships that brought the first settlers to establish the colony of Jamestown. Only two of the two hundred settlers were women: Margaret Forrest and her maid, Anne Burras.

and harvest the crop. In 1618, the Virginia Company began to offer fifty-acre tracts of land, called headrights, to men over fifteen years of age as an inducement to settle in Virginia (established settlers received two headrights), but the company feared that, without wives, the single men of Jamestown might abandon the settlement, which would threaten its stability, permanence, and, by extension, the expansion of Virginia as an English colony. In 1619, the Virginia Company acted on a scheme proposed by its treasurer, Edwin Sandys, to find "a fit hundredth … of women, maids young and uncorrupt, to make wives for the inhabitants and by that means to make the men there more settled and less movable." To make the scheme attractive to marriageable women, the company advertised incentives if they would choose husbands from among eligible suitors and immigrate to Jamestown to marry. These incentives included not only husbands but also a dowry of clothing, linens, and other furnishings; free transportation to Jamestown; free room and board while they decided on which man to choose; and a plot of land. Prior to Sandys's plan to import wives, the Virginia House of Burgesses petitioned the Virginia Company to extend to women settlers the right to own and inherit land, a right that was denied to women in England. The company claimed that in "a new plantation it is not known whether man or woman be the most necessary," and it made a similar request during the recruitment of the Jamestown wives. The men of Jamestown would be expected to reimburse the Virginia Company for its financial outlay in the form of 120 (later 150) pounds of "good leaf" tobacco. The advertised incentives proved appealing to many women, especially those of the working class, for whom the financial demands involved in setting up households meant that marriage was only attainable after years of toil in domestic service. In 1620, ninety young, English women arrived at Jamestown to become what were called "Tobacco Wives"; another fifty-seven followed in 1622.

Life was not easy for the Jamestown wives. Because the cultivation of tobacco was labor-intensive work, women were expected to bear children as soon after marriage—and as often—as possible so that eventually, all members of a family could work the fields. Since few doctors or midwives were available, childbearing in the Virginia wilderness could be a dangerous process with only neighbors on hand to assist during childbirth. The prevalence of disease, as well as other complications during childbirth, meant that infant mortality was high, and it is estimated that one-quarter of the Jamestown babies died before their first birthdays.

However, the Jamestown brides had certain benefits accompanying the incentives that had attracted them to new lives in Virginia. Married women in England were not only forbidden to own their own land because of the rule of coverture—a legal term from English Common Law meaning "covered woman"—they were also legally prohibited from selling or inheriting property, making wills, or serving as executors without their husbands' consent. The need for wives in Jamestown meant that the rules of coverture were largely ignored. If a husband should

die early, widows would be provided for and not forced to remarry out of economic necessity. However, despite the relative liberation of the Jamestown wives, the colony, as it grew, adhered to a patriarchal social contract, which held that the husband was the head of the household and made all decisions pertaining to family and property. A wife was confined to management of the house and garden unless her husband was away from home due to business, politics, or military service, an especially frequent situation for men who owned large plantations. A

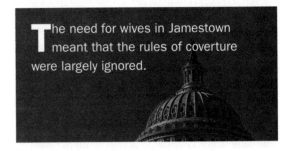

The need for wives in Jamestown meant that the rules of coverture were largely ignored.

wife would then become a "deputy husband," or the oldest son would take on his father's responsibilities regarding the family if he were old enough.

Many poor women, as well as women convicts and prostitutes eager to escape a prison sentence, were encouraged to emigrate from England to Jamestown (and other colonial settlements) as indentured servants contracted to a landowner to work without wages, usually for four to seven years, in exchange for their passage to the New World. The Virginia Company agreed to pay for the transportation of indentured servants at first, but after the headright system was established in 1618, the company convinced tobacco planters and merchants to cover the cost with the promise of land. Indentured servants labored in the tobacco fields and did other agricultural work as well as household tasks. Some women married after their term of indenture was over; others were given clothing and some money, tobacco, or other salable or tradable commodity with which to start a new life.

Pocahontas

One of the most famous women in American history, Pocahontas (c. 1596–1617) has been the subject of numerous written and oral accounts for more than four hundred years. What we know, or speculate, about the life of the woman most associated with Jamestown comes from the writings of John Smith and other leaders of the Jamestown settlement, the oral history of Virginia's Mattaponi Tribe, and through historical research. Pocahontas was the daughter of Wahunsenaca (called Chief Powhatan by the settlers), the mamanatowick (paramount chief) of the Tsenacommacah (also known as the Powhatan Chiefdom), an alliance of more than thirty Algonquin-speaking tribes that populated the Tidewater region of Virginia at the time Jamestown was founded. Named Amonoute, Pocahontas, as was the custom, was also given a private name, Matoaka (variously translated as "Flower Between Two Streams" or "Bright Stream Between the Hills"), for use on certain tribal occasions. Pocahontas (loosely translated as "Playful One") was the child's nickname. Written accounts of Pocahontas and Jamestown provide no details about her mother; historians have suggested that she may have been Wahunsenaca's first wife, who was also named Pocahontas, and that she either died in childbirth or went to live in another village (probably her native village) after her daughter's birth. If the latter is correct, then Pocahontas would have gone with her and returned to her father's village once she was weaned. Her mother would then have been free to take another husband.

As the daughter of the mamanatowick, Pocahontas would have enjoyed a more privileged and protected life than other children, but, like other Powhatan girls, she was also expected to learn the work for which women were responsible in Powhatan society. In addition to bearing and rearing children, the tasks assigned to women were many and various: building thatched houses and making household items, planting and harvesting, identifying and collecting edible plants, cooking, fetching water, gathering firewood, and tending the fires.

Pocahontas's interaction with the settlers at Jamestown began when she was a child of about eleven. According to popular history, the Jamestown leader was taken before Powhatan in his capital of Werowocomoco and forced onto the ground with

A statue of Pocahontas (born Amonute and also known as Matoaka) stands at Jamestown, Virginia. The legend of her life that was created by Captain John Smith and that survived four centuries is now being rewritten by historians seeking the truth.

his head laid upon two stones. When a warrior raised his club, ostensibly to smash in his head, Pocahontas rushed over to Smith and laid her head upon his, thus stopping the execution. Whether or not Pocahontas saved John Smith's life has long been debated as has the true meaning of the event (the intervention of Pocahontas was not mentioned in Smith's journals of 1608 and 1612, and it appeared in print for the first time in 1624 in his *Generall Historie of Virginia*). One theory suggests that the event was actually an adoption ceremony and that Smith's life was not in danger (however, he likely would not have known this). Afterward, Powhatan declared that Smith was now a member of the tribe, esteemed as "his son Nataquoud," and was given land in return for "two great guns and a grindstone." When Powhatan sent gifts of food to the hungry settlers, Pocahontas, as the chief's favorite daughter, accompanied the Indian envoys and in one case was sent to Jamestown to negotiate the release of Indian prisoners.

By the winter of 1608–1609, relations between the settlers and the Powhatan Indians deteriorated after a summer drought severely reduced the tribes' harvests. They were no longer willing to trade corn for beads and trinkets, and the English resorted to threats and burning villages to obtain food. John Smith's narrative records that Powhatan lured him and his men to Werowocomoco with the promise of corn in exchange for such commodities as swords, guns, hens, copper, and beads. When negotiations between Powhatan and Smith and his men broke down, Powhatan and his family, including Pocahontas, disappeared into the woods. That night, Pocahontas returned to warn Smith that her father intended to kill him. Smith also later recorded Pocahontas's efforts to save the life of Henry Spelman, who, with two other boys, ran away from the Powhatan village where they had been sent to learn native languages and serve as interpreters. In 1609, John Smith sailed back to England because of a gunpowder wound he sustained in an accident. Pocahontas and Powhatan were told that he had died during the voyage.

The relationship between the Powhatan Indians and the Jamestown settlers remained poor, and Pocahontas would not be mentioned again in English accounts until 1613. She had reached adulthood and marriageable age when she was about fourteen. Women in Powhatan society were free to choose their own husbands, and in 1610, after a courtship period, Pocahontas married the warrior Kocoum, who may have been a member of the Patawomeck Tribe. In 1613, when Captain Samuel Argall of Jamestown discovered that Pocahontas was living with the Patawomeck, he hatched a plan with the cooperation of Iopassus, the brother of the Patawomeck chief, to kidnap Pocahontas with the intention of holding her for ransom for the return of stolen weapons and English prisoners. Iopassus and

his wife lured Pocahontas onto Argall's ship to spend the night; the following morning, the Patawomeck couple left the ship with a copper kettle and some trinkets, but Pocahontas was not allowed to disembark. She was first brought to Jamestown, where she was put in the care of Sir Thomas Gates, who oversaw the negotiations between the English and Powhatan. Pocahontas was then sent to Henrico, an English settlement near present-day Richmond. There, she was taught the English language and English customs and given religious instruction from

> The relationship between the Powhatan Indians and the Jamestown settlers remained poor, and Pocahontas would not be mentioned again in English accounts until 1613.

Reverend Alexander Whitaker. Powhatan agreed to many of Argall and Gates's demands and, when it was clear that the English had no intention of releasing Pocahontas, did not attempt to retaliate, as his councilors advised, in order to ensure his daughter's safety.

English written history and Mattaponi oral history differ somewhat regarding what happened next. Both narratives record Pocahontas's conversion to Christianity, her baptism with the name Rebecca, and her marriage to widower John Rolfe (best known as the successful cultivator of the lucrative tobacco crop) all in 1614. According to the English written history, the marriage led to the Peace of Pocahontas, a respite from the conflicts between the settlers and the Powhatan Indians. The English narrative also records that Powhatan agreed to the proposed marriage between his daughter and Rolfe and sent Pocahontas's uncle to represent him at the wedding. Mattaponi oral history does not dispute the cessation of hostilities but maintains that Pocahontas, although cooperative for the good of her people and for her own survival, became deeply depressed when the English insisted that her father did not love her and continually repeated this fiction. When her sister, Mattachanna, arrived to care for her, Pocahontas confided to her sister that she had been raped at Jamestown. She later gave birth to a son, Thomas, whom the English narrative asserts was the son of Pocahontas and John Rolfe.

In 1616, Pocahontas, now known as Lady Rebecca Rolfe, her husband, and her son, accompanied by several Powhatan men and women, sailed for England. Their expenses were paid by the Virginia Company, which had funded the settling of Jamestown and was eager to encourage interest in Virginia. The Virginia Company decided that Pocahontas—a convert married to an Englishman—would be an excellent advertisement for the colony as well as for the company. After touring the country and attending a masque, where they sat near the king and queen, the Rolfe family settled in the rural town of Brentford. There, Pocahontas saw John Smith again and, according to English written history, reprimanded him for his treatment of Powhatan and her people and for the settlers' report that he had died during the voyage to England after his accident. She told Smith that Powhatan had suspected that Smith had not died since "your countrymen will lie much."

In March 1617, Pocahontas, her family, and the Powhatan Indians embarked upon the voyage back to Virginia. While traveling down the Thames River to the sea, Pocahontas became ill and died from an ailment historians believe may have been pneumonia or some form of dysentery (according to the Mattaponi oral history, the Powhatan Indians who traveled with them told Powhatan that she had been murdered and suspected the use of poison). On March 21, Pocahontas was buried at St. George's Church at Gravesend, a town on the south bank of the Thames Estuary. John Rolfe left the sickly Thomas with relatives in England and sailed back to Virginia. The following year, Powhatan died.

Like Sacagawea, the Shoshone woman who accompanied Meriwether Lewis and William Clark during their 1804–1806 western expedition following the Louisiana Purchase of 1803, Pocahontas has been celebrated and mythologized in American cultural history as a symbol of the relationship between Native Americans and the Europeans who came to settle in what would become the continental United States.

1619: African Women in Jamestown

By the first decades of the sixteenth century, black slavery had been established at St. Augustine in Spanish Florida. The institution of slavery in what would become the Thirteen Colonies began at Jamestown and developed gradually in Virginia and the other colonies thereafter. In the summer of 1619, John Rolfe recorded that a Dutch warship arrived at Port Comfort in present-day Hampton, Virginia. In reality, the ship was an English privateer, the *White Lion*, which was carrying Dutch letters of marque allowing it to attack and loot any Spanish or Portuguese ships it encountered en route. On board the *White Lion* were twenty African slaves, including three women, who had been forcibly removed from a Portuguese slave ship that was attempting to deliver them to Mexico. Rolfe falsified his record in order to transfer any blame of piracy from the English to the Dutch, who also operated privateers in the area. The African slaves joined the Jamestown colony as indentured servants who worked in the tobacco fields and after their terms of indenture were freed and given some land. However, as more laborers were needed to cultivate tobacco in what was a burgeoning industry, the importation of Africans became routine.

By the 1630s, it had become customary practice in some instances to hold Africans in some form of service for life. What was practice became statutory law in 1640, when John Punch, a runaway indentured servant, was captured along with two white servants. The latter servants were ordered to serve one more year of indenture; Punch was ordered to serve his master for the rest of his life. In 1670, a Virginia law defined slaves for life as all non-Chris-

> **S**he told Smith that Powhatan had suspected that Smith had not died since "your countrymen will lie much."

Black slavery became more common after the beginning of the sixteenth century, leading to more African men and women being shipped to America to become indentured servants.

tian servants who had arrived in Jamestown "by shipping." Further restrictions on the rights of Africans and the expansion of the rights of slave owners continued throughout the rest of the century, and any remaining rights for African slaves almost completely eroded by 1705 with the Virginia Slave Code, which codified the status of slaves as "property." Similar laws would be enacted throughout the Thirteen Colonies.

It is estimated that between 1700 and 1740, some forty-three thousand slaves were shipped to Virginia, the vast majority of whom were African men, women, and children. African women in Virginia—and throughout the South as colonies expanded and crops such as cotton were added to the lucrative southern agrarian economy—labored in the fields and as caretakers of white children in the households of their white mistresses, whether on large plantations or smaller, family-operated farms, but women slaves were especially valuable for the children they bore and who would, in turn, become an additional source of free labor.

Family life among the slaves could be tenuous: It was often common for children to be sold away from their mothers, mothers from their children, wives from their husbands, and husbands from their wives. The same was true in the case of African women with children born to white masters. In Solomon Northup's *Narrative of Solomon Northup, Twelve Years a Slave* (1853), Northup chronicles a slave, Eliza, who begs a planter to buy herself and her mixed-race daughter along with her son: "But it was no avail.... The bargain was agreed upon, and Randall must go alone." Soon afterward, despite further pleading, Eliza is sold away from her daughter for $700. For white landowners throughout the colonies, black Africans existed only to be bought, sold, and worked to capacity. In a record of slave narratives commissioned by the Works Project Administration titled *Born in Slavery: Slave Narratives*

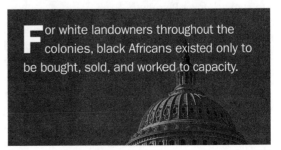

For white landowners throughout the colonies, black Africans existed only to be bought, sold, and worked to capacity.

from the Federal Writers Project 1936–1938, Abbie Lindsay, an ex-slave from Louisiana, describes the labor of slaves: "They worked, in a manner of speaking, from can to can't, from the time they could see until the time they couldn't."

THE ARRIVAL OF WOMEN IN NEW ENGLAND

They were a most unusual group of colonists. Instead of noblemen, craftsmen, and servants—the types of people who had founded Jamestown in Virginia—these were, for the most part, families—men, women, and children who were willing to endure almost anything if it meant they could worship as they pleased.

—Nathaniel Philbrick, Mayflower:
A Story of Courage, Community, and War

When the *Mayflower* Pilgrims, the earliest Europeans to permanently settle in New England, left Leiden in Holland in the summer of 1620 and landed on Cape Cod in November of the same year before establishing their colony at Plymouth, 102 passengers were on board, including eighteen women, all of whom were married. Three of the women—Susanna White, Mary Allerton, and Elizabeth Hopkins—were about six months pregnant. Only Susanna White would deliver a child—Peregrine White—who survived to reach adulthood. During the hard winter of 1620–1621, the women and children remained on board the ship while the men explored Cape Cod. The *Mayflower* then set sail again to settle in Plymouth, where the men built houses and storehouses in the new settlement. Legend has it that in March 1621, fourteen-year-old Mary Chilton became the first *Mayflower* passenger to step ashore at Plymouth.

The damp and crowded living quarters aboard the *Mayflower* most likely contributed to the spread of disease among the women and children and the high mortality rate among the women: Fourteen women died during the Pilgrims' first fall and winter in the New World. Elizabeth Hopkins's baby son, Oceanus, born while the ship was still at sea, did not survive the winter. According to the journal of

William Bradford, the first governor of Plymouth Plantation, by the fall harvest of 1621, four married women, six adolescent girls, and four little girls were the last female survivors of the voyage. They included Susanna White, Elizabeth Hopkins, and two daughters of Mary Allerton, who had died in the spring of 1621 after giving birth to a stillborn son. Thirty-nine men and boys comprised the rest of the *Mayflower* survivors.

The Legal and Social Status of Colonial Women

The Pilgrims of Plymouth Colony and the seventeenth-century English colonists who came after them to settle in much of present-day New England, established as the Massachusetts Bay Colony (1628–1686), generally adhered to the patriarchal, Puritan tradition regarding the proper status and role of women. God, it was believed, created women for the benefit of men, a belief instilled in women from girlhood and reinforced by a male-governed community in which family life dictated that men were the undisputed, lawful heads of households, and wives and children were obliged to obey them. Women were expected to dress modestly, to cover their hair and their arms, and to behave in a mild and courteous manner. They were not allowed to speak in church (where attendance was mandatory for all in the community) and, despite having been taught to read as girls in order to read the Bible, were forbidden to interpret the Scriptures, a proscription challenged in the 1630s by Puritan spiritual leader Anne Hutchinson. Women were denied a voice in the political and social decisions of the community and could not participate in town meetings or vote—a man cast his vote on behalf of his family unless he were ill, in which case his wife was generally allowed to vote in his place. Throughout the American colonies in the seventeenth and eighteenth centuries, English civil Common Law (which became the basis for federal law after the American Revolution) and its rule of coverture meant that women were forbidden to own property, conduct business, or sign contracts, although young, Puritan women engaged to be married were party to a legally binding prenuptial agreement called a precontract or contraction. Widows who had not remarried were granted an exception to these laws, and if a widow did remarry, she retained exclusive control of the property she brought to the marriage.

The status of women in the Dutch colonies was different. From 1624 until 1664, Dutch colonists in New Netherland and New Amsterdam, which included settlements in the Hudson Valley area of present-day New York State and New York City, generally lived according to the laws of Holland (known as the Kingdom of the Netherlands after its unification in 1813). This meant that Dutch women experienced more autonomy and were officially accorded more legal rights than women in British America. Women kept their birth names when they married, and children were given their fathers' first name as a surname for life. Women were legally entitled to keep any money or property they owned when they married; however, this entailed the choice of whether to marry according to *Manus*, in which a woman granted marital authority to her husband to legally represent her and become the administrator of her property, or *Usus*, in which she made a prenuptial agreement legally ensuring that she would retain sole control of her property. Women who were pregnant and unmarried could take the father to court to try to force him to marry her; if the father was already married, the woman could seek payment for childbirth costs as well as monetary support for her child.

Colonial Dutch women, who, like men, were taught a form of commercial arithmetic similar to algebra, conducted business, earned their living in various occupations, and were able to practice midwifery and medicine. Many did so while married and raising children. Examples include Sara Roeloef, a linguist who worked for several New Amsterdam businesses; Anneke Van Courtland, who oversaw the paving of the first cobbled street in the American colonies; and Margaret Philipse, who ran a shipping and import/export business.

In 1664, Charles II of England, vying with the Dutch for naval dominance, sent his brother James, the Duke of York, to claim the Dutch colonies for England. James's fleet arrived in New Amsterdam in September 1664 and easily overcame the nearly nonexistent military force of the Dutch in both New Amsterdam and New Netherland. By the following year, Richard Nicholls, the first English governor of the newly named province of New York, had introduced the Duke's Laws, which were based on English Common Law. As a result, the social and economic independence and legal rights enjoyed by Dutch women gradually eroded. Between 1664 and 1700, it became increasingly more difficult for Dutch women to continue to work, and the number of women in trade, business, and service occupations significantly declined. Fewer women were able to apply to the courts for restitution, make joint wills

Etching made around 1650 of the Dutch settlement of New Amsterdam, which we know now as New York City. Dutch women experienced more rights at this time than did British women in America.

with their husbands, or inherit property. Crimes such as theft and prostitution committed by women became more common and were punished by execution (unless they were pregnant) or by banishment from the colony.

COURTSHIP, MARRIAGE, AND MOTHERHOOD IN THE COLONIES

Marriage was the most desirable social and economic state for both women and men throughout British America, and the pressure to wed was considerable. Girls were taught from an early age the skills deemed necessary to become good wives and "helpmeets" in the home, farm, or plantation. In his 1694 wedding sermon "The Help Meet," John Cotton, the preeminent Puritan minister of the Massachusetts

Bay Colony, wrote, "Women are creatures without which there is no comfortable living for man." In order to provide a comfortable and efficiently managed home for their future husbands, girls learned such skills as spinning, sewing, knitting, cooking, cleaning, washing, and child-rearing (learned by caring for younger siblings) as well as midwifery, nursing the sick, and doctoring the wounded. They learned to make their own candles, soap, starch, brooms, and polish; order provisions; and, although formal education for the vast majority of girls was limited to learning how to read, they were taught simple arithmetic since, as wives, they would be responsible for the household bookkeeping.

Young colonial women and men spent much time together in group activities, and, even among the Puritans, courting couples were given ample privacy to get to know each other and fall in love, al-

The early male settlers in Massachusetts wanted to have women travel over from their homelands and give them the chance to share their experiences, and marry. This early etching of a Puritan wedding shows a happy couple about to take their vows.

though parents maintained strict supervision over where their children went and how long they were alone together. One New England courtship custom was the use of a "courting stick," a six- to eight-foot-long, hollow tube with an earpiece at each end so that the courting couple could whisper to each other in one room, while the rest of the family sat in another room. Another popular custom among New Englanders was borrowed from the Europeans and was known as "bundling," in which a couple spent the night together in bed with a "bundling board" between them, and sometimes, the young woman's legs were bound together in a "bundling stocking." The custom became less popular by the 1750s, during the French and Indian War (1754–1763), when it was discovered that French soldiers were bundling with women they did not plan to marry.

While young people in Puritan New England were generally free to choose their own spouses, they were bound by certain conventions: They were expected to select marriage partners from similar backgrounds and could not marry—or even court— without parental consent. Before beginning a courtship, a suitor might send small presents to the young woman he wished to marry, as well as to her mother, in the hope of gaining consent from her parents. The European tradition of arranged marriages was not observed in the American colonies: For the Puritans, a courtship leading to a covenanted marriage depended upon the free consent of the young woman and man. Young people were rarely married against their will; however, parents from well-to-do families, especially in the South, would sometimes threaten to withhold a dowry or an inheritance to ensure that a son or daughter made a lucrative financial or socially advantageous match. Many Virginians justified this aspect of sovereignty over their children by consulting a popular and influential English Anglican devotional work, *The Whole Duty of Man*, written by Royalist clergyman Richard Allestree and published anonymously in 1658 during the Cromwellian era. In it, Allestree asserts that of all the acts of disobedience "that of marrying against the consent of the parent is one of the highest ... it belongs to children to perform duty, not only to the kind and virtuous, but even to the harshest and wickedest parent."

When a Puritan couple became engaged, a betrothal ceremony followed. Commonly referred to as the "walking out" or "coming out," the event included the prenuptial contract, described by Puritan minister and author Cotton Mather (1663–1728) as a "solemnity called a Contraction ... before the consummation of marriage was allowed...." The local minister (or pastor) presided over the ceremony and delivered a sermon based on a biblical text chosen by the intended bride. After the required banns (a public announcement of betrothal) were posted at the meetinghouse for three consecutive days and the marriage date was arranged—usually for some time in November—the couple was married at home in a civil ceremony conducted by a magistrate. A modest wedding dinner followed. Couples did not exchange vows or wear rings, displays that were a feature of Anglican marriage ceremonies in the South. Virginians, for example, followed the elaborate Church of England marriage ritual: espousal, publication of the banns, a religious ceremony held in the bride's home or in a church and solemnized by a minister, a marriage feast, and sexual consummation. The Puritans, who rejected Anglican religious customs, referred to extravagant wedding displays as "vain marriage."

It was not uncommon for a Puritan bride to become pregnant once the precontract was signed, and because the couple was considered legally married, no scandal was attached to either bride or groom. The sexual transgressions of women who were not yet precontracted or who were not courting was a different matter: Unmarried women who became pregnant might be taken to court and fined, sentenced to a public whipping, or branded. If a woman refused to name the father of her child so that the court could order him to provide financial support, the child was often taken from her to be apprenticed to a tradesperson. The worst crime women could commit was adultery, especially among more prosperous families, where the possibility existed that a male child born of adultery could inherit the cuckolded husband's property. In Puritan and other strongly religious communities, both men and women who had committed adultery were forced to publicly confess their sin in church. For transgressors of high social rank and wealth, confession was the only official penance demanded; those less socially and financially connected might be "ducked" (immersed) in a pond or river, whipped, or branded.

In contrast to the southern colonies, where, especially in the seventeenth century, the mortality rate among men was high and women tended to marry before they reached their twenties, were often much younger than their husbands, experienced widowhood earlier, and remarried, New England women were generally wed in their early twenties (men in their mid-twenties), and the title "Goodwife" was conferred upon them after as a form of address. In early eighteenth-century New England, 93 percent of women married. If a woman married later or remained unmarried, it was either because she was needed at home to care for a sick or widowed parent or other family member, or she could not find a complementary mate, often one who did not conform to the high standard of spiritual, moral, and ethical behavior prized by her and the community. In seventeenth-century New

England, women who did not find a marriage partner by the time they were thirty were often unflatteringly labeled "thornbacks," a nickname for the sea skate, an ungainly looking food fish whose back and tail were covered with sharp spines. Unmarried women were considered to be potentially disruptive to the social order: A woman's failure to marry was interpreted as a sign of God's ill favor, a belief that contributed to the vulnerability of unmarried women to charges of witchcraft. By the eighteenth century, women who did not marry were seen more as objects of pity and derision rather than as necessarily threatening; they were considered ugly, bad tempered, nosy, and odd. The social and economic impetus to wed was so strong that widows and widowers were encouraged to remarry and on average did so within six months to a year. In the case of widows with few or no financial prospects, no property, and no relatives who might take them in, remarriage was an economic

Life as a Puritan woman in the seventeenth century was restrictive, to say the least. Church attendance was compulsory, of course; married women had few rights, and women who did not marry were basically ostracized (*Pilgrims Going to Church* by artist George Henry Boughton, 1867).

necessity and hopefully a more palatable option than servitude.

The social pressure against divorce was extreme and divorces difficult to obtain, but the civil covenant of the Puritan marriage meant that women were allowed to divorce their husbands in such circumstances as adultery, willful desertion, or physical cruelty with slightly greater ease than their Anglican counterparts, who were subject to a view of marriage as a dissoluble union. Sometimes, women simply ran away, often to start a new life on the newly explored frontier; in such situations, a husband might publicly announce that he was no longer responsible for his wife's debts (such announcements could be seen in newspapers well into the twentieth century). A husband might also post ads in the hope of finding his wife and retrieving whatever personal or household belongings she took with her, which, like all property, was legally his. A married couple might be granted a legal separation, but since alimony laws did not exist, this left a wife in a precarious position unless she had a generous spouse, skills with which to support herself, or access to money of her own; otherwise, she risked losing everything, including her children, who would be left in the care of their father.

Motherhood was the primary role of colonial wives between about the ages of twenty and forty-five, and a woman could expect to be pregnant or nursing for most of that time. Women generally spent about two and a half years nursing a child before becoming pregnant with the next. The bearing and rearing of numerous children was an important goal of marriage in the colonies for several reasons: To be "fruitful and multiply" and "replenish the Earth" was a scriptural mandate; to increase the colonial population was a patriotic imperative; and having children to help on the farms, in the fields, at sea, and in the home was a necessity. Parents also wanted to ensure that property would stay in the family and to ensure that they would have caregivers in their old age. A further reason was the mortality rate among infants and children: Women bore an average of nine children, only about five to seven of whom survived to reach adulthood, and it was not uncommon for a woman to bear eleven or twelve children, usually as the result of a second or third marriage. Lydia George and Elizabeth Hubbard, the first two of Puritan minister Cotton Mather's three wives, produced fifteen children between them; only six survived to adulthood, and only two outlived their father. It is estimated that some 20 percent of children died between the ages of one and five; for children born to African slaves, the mortality rate for children under ten was as high as 40 to 50 percent because of maternal malnutrition, overwork, and disease.

It was a physical and emotional hardship for women to experience continual pregnancies and childbirths. Because it was believed that hard work made for an easier labor, pregnant women continued the many chores for which they were responsible; these might include heavy lifting, carrying, slaughtering, and salting down meat. Such tasks throughout a pregnancy might result in a physically depleted condition by the time a woman was ready to give birth: Infants born to physically weakened women often died before they reached their first birthday.

Childbirth was difficult and frequently dangerous: An estimated 1 to 2 percent of all childbirths resulted in the mother's death during and after childbirth from such complications as hemorrhage, convulsions, dehydration, infection, or simply exhaustion. Women gave birth at home, and the only anesthesia or painkiller offered to them was alcohol. Midwives assisted women during childbirth with women relatives, friends, and sometimes a nurse on hand to encourage them to bear their pain with patience, prayer, and fortitude. Experienced midwives were highly valued, and midwifery was a profession (one of the few officially open to women) that could be very lucrative for practitioners: Midwives were frequently offered rent-free housing or a salary to live and practice in a community. After the birth, the new mother was kept warm to help sweat out the "poisons" accompanying childbirth and was often treated to a feast. Women from wealthy families generally convalesced for three to four weeks; women from less well-to-do families and in good health usually went back to her chores in one or two days.

By the mid-eighteenth century, wealthy women began to insist on doctors rather than midwives attending them at home during childbirth; women believed that because doctors were better educated, they would experience a safer childbirth. Rivalries between midwives and doctors developed, the former citing experience and latter claiming a better understanding, sometimes spurious, of female anatomy. In 1751, Benjamin Franklin and Dr. Thomas Moran founded Pennsylvania Hospital in Philadelphia, the earliest established public hospital in what would become the United States. However, women did not begin to give birth in a hospital until the early twentieth century, when anesthesia was more available. In 1900, midwives delivered about 50 percent of babies; by the mid-1930s, midwives delivered only 15 percent of children, mostly in rural areas.

From the time they first set foot on land, the women who came to the New World displayed much strength and courage in adapting to and coping with the realities of their lives. However, during the American Revolution, which definitively severed the relationship between the colonies and Great Britain, and after the establishment of the Republic, many women began to question the constrictive legal and social status by which they were forced to live. In the 1780s and 1790s, a new view of marriage based on mutual esteem rather than patriarchal authority in which wives were property and unmarried women were considered "unwomanly" took hold. It was a view advocated by Abigail Adams and the reformers who followed, and it was the first step toward a long, hard-fought revolution by women for the "natural and inalienable" rights enjoyed by men that would first see American women fighting for the abolition of slavery and then for a woman's right to vote.

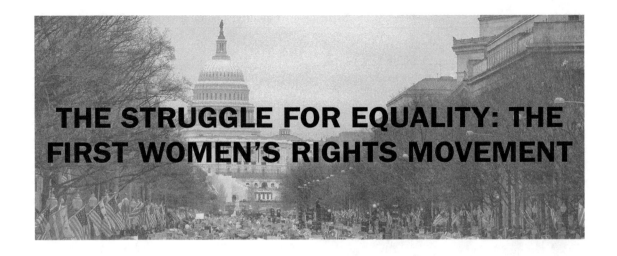

THE STRUGGLE FOR EQUALITY: THE FIRST WOMEN'S RIGHTS MOVEMENT

The struggle for women's rights that took place in the nineteenth and early twentieth centuries is sometimes referred to as first-wave feminism, a term coined by journalist Martha Weinman Lear (1932–) in 1968 to distinguish its objectives from what she called "second-wave feminism," the addressing of inequalities faced by women during the women's movement of the late 1960s to the 1980s. The foundation of the fight for equal rights for women during the first women's rights movement was the attainment of suffrage—the right to vote.

In the eighteenth century, some colonies and states did allow women with property to legally vote in local and state elections, the first recorded example of which was wealthy Massachusetts widow Lydia Chapin Taft, who legally cast her vote in town meetings in Uxbridge in 1756, 1758, and 1765. In the New Jersey State Constitution of 1776, passed two days before the Second Continental Congress declared America's independence from Great Britain, a provision was included that gave voting rights to "all inhabitants of this colony, of full age, who are worth fifty pounds … and have resided within the county … for twelve months." In 1790, the legislature added "he or she" to the law, which clarified that suffrage included unmarried women property owners (married women could not own property). African Americans were allowed to vote in New Jersey if they were free residents who owned property,

although it is considered unlikely that black residents met those requirements: Slavery was not abolished in the state until 1804; African Americans born to slave mothers after July 4 of that year were forced to serve long apprenticeships to the owners of their mothers before gaining their freedom; and after 1846, black Americans who had been born prior to abolition continued to be enslaved as lifelong indentured servants.

Many New Jersey women did vote "for Representatives in Council and Assembly; and also for all other public officers, that shall be elected by the people of the county at large." However, neither the original document nor its addendum specified an amendment procedure for this provision, and in 1807, the legislature passed a bill restricting voting rights to tax-paying, white, male residents, which was added as an amendment to the second constitution of 1844. Voting rights for women continued to erode. New York women lost the right to vote in 1777; women in Massachusetts lost the vote in 1780. New Hampshire reversed women's voting rights in 1784. By the early years of the nineteenth century, American women in every state were disenfranchised citizens, legally barred from voting in local, state, and national elections. Although several states and territories granted partial and sometimes full voting rights for women during the latter half of the 1800s and in the 1910s, it would take nearly a century and massive effort and organization before passage of the Nineteenth Amendment to the U.S. Constitution guaranteed full voting rights to every American woman in every state of the union.

By the early years of the nineteenth century, American women in every state were disenfranchised citizens, legally barred from voting in local, state, and national elections.

THE ABOLITIONIST MOVEMENT AND EQUAL RIGHTS FOR WOMEN

The organization among women that would result in the formation of women's antislavery societies and the associations that would work to gain women's suffrage had its roots in such groups as women's church sewing circles, which raised funds for charitable and missionary work, and societies dedicated to "female improvement" and literary pursuits. For free African American women in the Northeast, similar women's societies evolved into organizations like the Ohio Ladies' Education Society, which was dedicated to the founding of schools that would offer better education for their children, a goal that would continue to be of paramount importance for the empowerment and enfranchisement of black communities. One example of the growing ambition of women to come together in a purpose beyond local interests is Lucy Stone, a Massachusetts woman in her early twenties who belonged to a literary society and would go on to become one of the nineteenth century's most prominent public speakers advocating for both abolition and women's rights. In 1840, Stone wrote to one of her three brothers, "It was decided in our Literary Society the other day that ladies ought to mingle in politics, go to Congress, etc., etc. What do you think of that?" (All three brothers supported such ambitions.) Stone was responding to three developments that had oc-

curred in the 1830s: a controversy some called the "woman question," stirred up by newspapers in Massachusetts over whether or not it was appropriate for women to assume an active, public role in the political and reform initiatives of the day; the women's rights advocacy that had become a feature of William Lloyd Garrison's abolitionist newspaper *The Liberator*; and the presence of women in the abolitionist movement.

The abolition of slavery had been a particular goal of many Quakers (also known as the Society of Friends), who founded the Pennsylvania Abolition Society in 1775. The first notable American female abolitionist was Philadelphia Quaker Elizabeth Margaret Chandler (1807–1834), whose antislavery column "The Ladies Repository" appeared in the *Genius of Universal Emancipation*, a newspaper published by abolitionist and Quaker Benjamin Lundy. Quakers would remain at the forefront of abolitionist efforts when antislavery societies throughout the North were founded and the Underground Railroad gained momentum in the wake of two events that occurred in 1831. On January 1, Boston journalist William Lloyd Garrison, who had been a coeditor of Lundy's paper, and printer Isaac Knapp copublished the first issue of *The Liberator*, the influential abolitionist newspaper that would be published weekly until 1865. In the first issue of *The Liberator*, Garrison called for the immediate emancipation of slaves, writing, "On this subject I do not wish to think, or speak, or write, with moderation ... I will not equivocate, I will not excuse, I will not retreat a single inch—and I WILL BE HEARD!" The following year, Garrison included a "Ladies' Department" in *The Liberator*, which was headed by a woodcut of a Wedgwood medallion depicting a kneeling female slave in chains and inscribed with the motto "Am I Not a Woman and a Sister?".

Between 1831 and 1833, Garrison published pamphlets written by African American abolitionist, writer, lecturer, and women's rights activist Maria W. Stewart as well as the texts of four public lectures Stewart delivered, including a lecture given in Boston to the New England Anti-Slavery Society titled "Why Sit Ye Here and Die?," which demanded equal rights for African American women.

Journalist and abolitionist William Lloyd Garrison's newspaper, *The Liberator*, included a "Ladies Department" headed with the pictured art, variations of which were first published in the 1820s by British abolitionists and featured in American publications in the 1830s.

The second event that would help to galvanize abolitionist efforts in the North occurred in August 1831, when the rebellion led by Virginia slave Nat Turner resulted in the deaths of nearly two hundred slaves and some fifty whites and led to widespread repressive measures against black slaves in the South. In 1833, the American Anti-Slavery Society was founded in Philadelphia at a convention of prominent male abolitionists, many of whom were Quakers. Among the founders were William Lloyd Garrison, Quaker merchant James Mott, and Theodore Dwight Weld, an abolitionist, writer, speaker, organizer, and future husband of abolitionist and women's rights advocate Angelina Grimké. Over the objections of William Lloyd Garrison, women were permitted to attend the convention and speak from the floor but were not allowed to serve as delegates, join the society, or sign its Declaration of Sentiments and Purposes. During the convention, the only woman who exercised her right to speak was Quaker minister Lucretia Mott, the wife of James Mott. After the convention had adjourned, Mott, together with about twenty white and African American women, met to form the Philadelphia Female Anti-Slavery Society. Over the next few years, women organized similar societies in New York, Boston, and other New England towns.

In 1837, the Anti-Slavery Convention of American Women, the first of three conventions scheduled to be held from 1837–1839, met in New York City from May 9–12 with Lucretia Mott chosen as working chair. In attendance were 175 white and African American women of varying economic and social status representing twenty women's antislavery societies from ten states. The 1837 Anti-Slavery Convention of American Women marks the first gathering of American women that addressed women's rights. Delegates Angelina Grimké and her sister Sarah Grimké from the slaveholding state of South Carolina, both of whom advocated equal rights for women as well as abolition, offered resolutions for discussion. Sarah proposed calling for the "women of America … fully to discuss the subject of slavery, that they may be … qualified to act as women … on this all important subject." Angelina's resolution was more forceful:

> Resolved. That as certain rights and duties are common to all moral beings, the time has come for woman to move in that sphere which Providence has assigned her, and no longer remain satisfied in the circumscribed limits with which corrupt custom and perverted application of Scripture has encircled her; therefore that it is the duty of woman, and the province of woman, to plead her cause of the oppressed in our land and to do all that she can by her voice, and her pen, and her purse, and the influence of her example, to overthrow the horrible system of American slavery.

When Angelina Grimké wrote to Theodore Weld later in the month, a message from one of the delegates was included, which read in part, "Tell Mr. Weld that when the women got together they found they had *minds* of their own and could transact their business *without* his direction."

Subsequent meetings of the Anti-Slavery Convention of American Women were held in Philadelphia in 1838 and 1839 at a time when the city's population had grown to a sizable number of free African Americans and freed and fugitive slaves, who had joined with the city's large Quaker community in the cause of abolition. Both communities had been the victims of periodic racial, ethnic, and religious violence since the 1820s. On the morning of May 15, 1838, the second Anti-Slavery Convention of American Women was convened. The three-day convention was scheduled to take place at Pennsylvania Hall, a new building commissioned by the Pennsylvania Anti-Slavery Society as a venue for abolitionist meetings and dedicated on May 14. Angelina Grimké and Theodore Weld were married on the same day with both an African American and a white preacher presiding over the nuptials. Throughout the first day of the convention, notices calling upon "citizens who entertain a proper respect for the right of property" to interfere with the convention and to use force "if they must" against the convention attendees were distributed throughout the city. On the following day, crowds of anti-abolitionist and anti-Quaker men began to gather around the building becoming more unruly as the day went on. During the evening meeting, as abolitionist Maria Chapman spoke before the audience of three thousand, the mob threw rocks into the building, smashing windows, and shouting so loudly, Chapman could not be heard. When it was Angelina Grimké Weld's turn to speak, she refused to allow the disruptive mob to deter her and delivered a speech that went on for more than an hour. Later, in a show of solidarity and to protect the African American women attendees, white and black conventioneers left the hall together arm in arm. The women were greeted with jeers and rocks thrown at them by the crowd outside.

On the third day, the crowd outside the hall returned. The convention's organizers refused a request from the mayor to restrict the meeting to white women only and convened in the morning with a full complement of attendees. After the mayor obtained the keys to the building, locked the doors, and canceled the remaining meetings, the mob broke into the building and set fires, burning Pennsylvania Hall to the ground. An official report on the fire blamed the abolitionists for encouraging "race mixing" and inciting violence by upsetting the citizens of Philadelphia. Undaunted, the third Anti-Slavery Convention of American Women was convened as scheduled in the hall of the Pennsylvania Riding School in Philadelphia from May 1–3, 1839.

THE SENECA FALLS CONVENTION OF 1848

In July 1848, five women—abolitionist Mary Ann M'Clintock, Lucretia Mott, Martha Coffin Wright (Lucretia Mott's sister), social reformer Jane Hunt, and women's rights activist Elizabeth Cady Stanton (the only non-Quaker among them)—attended a social gathering at the home of Mrs. Hunt in Waterloo, New York. There, the five women decided to call a convention to focus exclusively on the subject of equal rights for women to take place in the nearby village of Seneca Falls. The Seneca Falls Convention would prove to be a pivotal moment in the history of American women: It was the start of the first formal women's rights movement in the United States and the beginning of the battle to achieve what became known as women's suffrage.

In the 1830s, women had been denied an equal opportunity to work alongside men for the abolitionist cause in which they believed and had called upon their capacity for organization to unite on behalf of that cause. The Grimké sisters' insistence on the inclusion of women's rights in convention resolutions to be discussed and acted upon marks the convergence of the abolitionist movement and the issue of equal rights for women. Men supported women's rights, most notably William Lloyd Garrison, who in 1838 began to address the subject in his abolitionist newspaper *The Liberator*. The paper's objective, he declared, would be to "redeem woman as well as man from a servile to an equal condition" and to support the "rights of women to their utmost extent." During the following decades, Garrison and his printers published

During the evening meeting, as abolitionist Maria Chapman spoke before the audience of three thousand, the mob threw rocks into the building, smashing windows, and shouting so loudly....

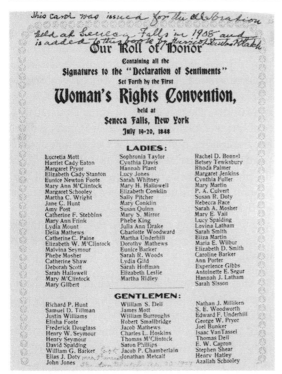

This card was issued for the celebration held at Seneca Falls in 1908 and is added to the book by Harriet Taylor Upton

Our Roll of Honor

Containing all the
Signatures to the "Declaration of Sentiments"
Set Forth by the First

Woman's Rights Convention,

held at
Seneca Falls, New York
July 19-20, 1848

LADIES:

Lucretia Mott	Sophronia Taylor	Rachel D. Bonnel
Harriet Cady Eaton	Cynthia Davis	Betsey Tewksbury
Margaret Pryor	Hannah Plant	Rhoda Palmer
Elizabeth Cady Stanton	Lucy Jones	Margaret Jenkins
Eunice Newton Foote	Sarah Whitney	Cynthia Fuller
Mary Ann M'Clintock	Mary H. Hallowell	Mary Martin
Margaret Schooley	Elizabeth Conklin	P. A. Culvert
Martha C. Wright	Sally Pitcher	Susan R. Doty
Jane C. Hunt	Mary Conklin	Rebecca Race
Amy Post	Susan Quinn	Sarah A. Mosher
Catherine F. Stebbins	Mary S. Mirror	Mary E. Vail
Mary Ann Frink	Phebe King	Lucy Spalding
Lydia Mount	Julia Ann Drake	Lovina Latham
Delia Mathews	Charlotte Woodward	Sarah Smith
Catherine C. Paine	Martha Underhill	Eliza Martin
Elizabeth W. M'Clintock	Dorothy Mathews	Maria E. Wilbur
Malvina Seymour	Eunice Barker	Elizabeth D. Smith
Phebe Mosher	Sarah R. Woods	Caroline Barker
Catherine Shaw	Lydia Gild	Ann Porter
Deborah Scott	Sarah Hoffman	Experience Gibbs
Sarah Hallowell	Elizabeth Leslie	Antoinette E. Segur
Mary M'Clintock	Martha Ridley	Hannah J. Latham
Mary Gilbert		Sarah Sisson

GENTLEMEN:

Richard P. Hunt	William S. Dell	Nathan J. Milliken
Samuel D. Tillman	James Mott	S. E. Woodworth
Justin Williams	William Burroughs	Edward F. Underhill
Elisha Foote	Robert Smallbridge	George W. Pryor
Frederick Douglass	Jacob Mathews	Joel Bunker
Henry W. Seymour	Charles L. Hoskins	Isaac VanTassel
Henry Seymour	Thomas M'Clintock	Thomas Dell
David Spalding	Saron Phillips	E. W. Capron
William G. Barker	Jacob P. Chamberlain	Stephen Shear
Elias J. Doty	Jonathan Metcalf	Henry Hatley
John Jones		Azaliah Schooley

The American concern with abolishing slavery went international when believers of the cause met in London for the World Anti-Slavery Convention. This document lists the signatories of the Declaration of Sentiments presented in the Seneca Falls women's rights convention of 1848.

editorials, petitions, tracts, and other material pertaining to women's social and legal rights, educational and professional equality, and women's suffrage.

The same year, *The Liberator* published Sarah Grimké's "Letters on the Province of Woman," a series of fifteen letters focusing on the social, religious, and legal condition of women in the United States and around the world written to Mary S. Parker, president of the Boston Female Anti-Slavery Society. At the same time, Garrison published the letters in pamphlet form under the title *Letters on the Equality of the Sexes, and the Condition of Woman.* The writings of Sarah Grimké and her assertion that God had created women equal to men and that men had usurped God's authority would have both a profound effect ten years later on the wording of the Declaration of Sentiments prepared for the Seneca Falls Convention and on the religious composition of the women who attended the convention, most of whom were Quaker and evangelist Methodist women.

By 1840, the same year Lucy Stone wrote to her brother soliciting his opinion on women's equality, Garrison's promotion of equal rights for women caused some male abolitionists, including brothers Arthur and Lewis Tappan, to leave the American Anti-Slavery Society to form the male-only American and Foreign Anti-Slavery Society. From then on, women were admitted as members of the American Anti-Slavery Society with Lucretia Mott, together with writers Lydia Maria Child and Maria Weston Chapman, serving on the society's executive committee.

In 1840, the British and Foreign Anti-Slavery Society organized the first General Anti-Slavery Convention, known variously as the World Slavery Convention and the World's Slavery Convention, to be held in London from June 12–23. At the request of Arthur Tappan, the organizers agreed to confine the convention to male delegates only: Women delegates would not be admitted. However, on the first day of the convention, a number of British and American abolitionist women, including Lucretia Mott and Elizabeth Cady Stanton, the wife of delegate Henry Brewster Stanton, took their seats on the main floor as official delegates, causing a contentious debate that lasted for hours. The majority of male delegates finally voted to set aside the upper end and one side of the hall for the women, who could watch but would not be allowed to speak or vote on convention resolutions. Several men protested the exclusion of the women from the proceedings, and four of them—William Lloyd Garrison, American writer and editor Nathaniel Peabody Rogers, British Baptist minister and abolitionist William Adam, and African American abolitionist Charles Lenox Remond—refused to take their seats on the floor as delegates. Instead, they chose to sit with the women in the makeshift spectators' gallery. When the convention adjourned, Lucretia Mott, who an Irish reporter had called "the lioness of the convention," and Elizabeth Cady Stanton met outside the hall and walked through London together. As the two women discussed the incidents of the day, they resolved to hold a convention to advocate the rights of women as soon as they returned home.

During the following eight years, Stanton and Mott met in Boston on two occasions to discuss the convention they had envisioned while in London. By their second meeting in 1847, Mott had led women's groups in Philadelphia at meetings to discuss women's rights. The same year, abolitionists friendly to the cause began to raise the possibility of such a convention. In April 1848, New York granted property rights to married women with the adoption of the Married Women's Property Act, a statute for which abolitionist and lecturer Ernestine

> In April 1848, New York granted property rights to married women with the adoption of the Married Women's Property Act....

Rose, Elizabeth Cady Stanton, and abolitionist and educator Harriet Wright Davis had been campaigning since 1836. Not long afterward, the Pennsylvania legislature adopted similar legislation. Several other states had passed such legislation earlier in the century, and more would follow New York and Pennsylvania from the 1850s to the 1870s.

On July 13, 1848, when Elizabeth Cady Stanton, Lucretia Mott, Mary Ann M'Clintock, Martha Coffin Wright, and Jane Hunt began to plan a women's rights convention, the five women chose as their first order of business the preparation of a notice that appeared in the *Seneca County Courier* on July 14. The notice announced "a convention to discuss the social, civil, and religious rights of women," which would take place on July 19 and 20 at the Wesleyan Chapel in Seneca Falls. On the first day, the meeting would be held "exclusively for women, who are earnestly invited to attend." The general public was invited to attend on the second day, when "Lucretia Mott of Philadelphia and other ladies and gentlemen will address the convention." Two days after the announcement appeared in the newspaper, Mary M'Clintock and her oldest daughters hosted a

planning meeting at her home in Waterloo to prepare a Declaration of Sentiments for the convention. After much discussion, the women turned to the Declaration of Independence for inspiration. Seated in the parlor at a round, three-legged, mahogany table (now displayed at Washington, D.C.'s Museum of American History, where it is known as the Declaration of Sentiments Table), Elizabeth Cady Stanton worked at paraphrasing portions of the Declaration of Independence to serve as a statement that would define the purpose of their convention. The three-part Declaration of Sentiments (also known as the Declaration of Rights and Sentiments) consisted of opening paragraphs comprising a declaration followed by a series of sentiments listing grievances and resolutions and closing remarks.

Between July 16 and 19, Stanton edited the list of grievances and resolutions at her home in Seneca Falls. Stanton's husband, Henry, a lawyer and politician, provided assistance by finding extracts from property laws that were unjust to women. However, when he read the final draft that would be presented at the convention, he was dismayed to see that his wife had included grievances concerning the disenfranchisement of women. Henry Stanton was planning to run for elective office and, like the majority of American men of his time, was not in favor of voting rights for women. He warned his wife that the radical addition of women's suffrage to the document would "turn the proceedings into a farce" and, rather than risk becoming associated with such an unpopular cause, left Seneca Falls for the duration of the convention. Elizabeth Cady Stanton attended the convention accompanied by her sister, Harriet Cady Eaton, and her sister's young son, Daniel.

Some causes for concern arose just before and during the convention. Lucretia Mott worried that she would not be able to come to Seneca Falls because her husband, James, who had been selected to serve as chairman of the event, was ill. Fortunately, he recovered in time to attend the convention, although Mary Ann M'Clintock's husband, Thomas, would chair the evening session on the second day. On the morning of the first day, the women gathered at the Wesleyan Chapel only to find the church doors locked. The solution was to lift Daniel up

Elizabeth Cady Stanton's husband, Henry, was a politician, journalist, abolitionist, and respected orator who also had a background as student of theology. He proved a valuable ally to the suffragists.

through an open window to unlock the doors. Mott was also concerned that because the brief notice in the *Seneca County Courier* had only appeared in one issue and it was the all-important haying season, convention turnout would be low. However, Mott's fears were not realized: By the second day, three hundred people were in attendance at the meeting with some having come to Seneca Falls in farm wagons from a radius of fifty miles. Although the notice stated that the first day of the convention would be held exclusively for women, some forty men showed up. They were allowed to attend but were asked to remain silent during the proceedings.

The convention opened with an eloquent speech delivered by Elizabeth Cady Stanton, the beginning of which was an assertion of her belief that she would not have ventured to speak out "were I not nerved

by a sense of right and duty, did I not feel that the time had come for the question of woman's wrongs to be laid before the public, did I not believe that woman herself must do this work; for woman alone can understand the height, the depth, the length and breadth of her degradation." The two-day meeting included speeches by several women, among them Lucretia Mott, who provided a social and moral context for the fight for women's rights by citing the progress of other reform movements. The Declaration of Sentiments was read on both days, and resolutions taken from the list of rights and grievances were discussed and voted upon.

The next to last resolution concerned women's suffrage and resulted in some opposition: "Resolved, that it is the duty of the women of this country to secure to themselves their sacred right to the elective franchise." It was argued that such a resolution might cause the other resolutions to lose support and that resolutions should be confined to issues regarding the social, civil, and religious, rather than political, status of women. Lucretia and James Mott were opposed to the resolution, with Lucretia cautioning Stanton, "Why, Lizzie, thou will make us ridiculous. We must go slowly." But Stanton was adamant: For her, women's suffrage was the means for women to affect legislation, which in turn would lead to greater rights. Influential support came from Frederick Douglass, the only African American at the convention. Douglass, who saw parallels between equal rights for women and black emancipation and suffrage, spoke up in favor of the resolution: "In this denial of the right to participate in government, not merely the degradation of woman and the perpetuation of a great injustice happens, but the maiming and reputation of one-half of the moral and intellectual power of the government of the world." The resolution was passed, but it was the only one that was not passed unanimously. On the evening of the second day, Lucretia Mott offered a final resolution: "Resolved. That the speedy success of our cause depends upon the zealous and untiring efforts of both men and women, for the overthrow of the monopoly of the pulpit, and for the securing to woman an equal participation with men in the various trades, professions, and commerce." Lucretia Mott was the first of sixty-eight women to sign the completed Declaration of Sentiments. Forty-two men, designated as "the gentlemen present in favor of this new movement," also signed the document. One of the signatories was a nineteen-year-old farmer's daughter and seamstress, Charlotte Woodward (later Charlotte Woodward Pierce). Charlotte was the only woman at the Seneca Falls Convention who, at ninety-one, had lived to witness both the passage of the Nineteenth Amendment and the first presidential election in which women were eligible to vote.

The Declaration of Rights and Sentiments, Seneca Falls Convention, July 19–20, 1848

Below is the full text of the declaration:

When, in the course of human events, it becomes necessary for one portion of the family of man to assume among the people of the earth a position different from that which they have hitherto occupied, but one to which the laws of nature and of nature's God entitle them, a decent respect to the opinions of mankind requires that they should declare the causes that impel them to such a course.

We hold these truths to be self-evident: that all men and women are created equal; that they are endowed by their Creator with certain inalienable rights; that among these are life, liberty, and the pursuit of happiness; that to secure these rights governments are instituted, deriving their powers from the consent of the governed. Whenever any form of government becomes destructive of these rights, it is the right of those who suffer from it to refuse allegiance to it, and to insist upon the institution of a new government, laying its foundation on such principles, and organizing its powers in such form, as to them shall seem most likely to effect their safety and happiness.

Prudence, indeed, will dictate that governments long established should not be changed for light and transient causes; and accordingly all experience hath shown that mankind are more disposed to suffer, while evils are suf-

ferable, than to right themselves by abolishing the forms to which they are accustomed, but when a long train of abuses and usurpations, pursuing invariably the same object, evinces a design to reduce them under absolute despotism, it is their duty to throw off such government, and to provide new guards for their future security. Such has been the patient sufferance of the women under this government, and such is now the necessity which constrains them to demand the equal station to which they are entitled.

The history of mankind is a history of repeated injuries and usurpation on the part of man toward woman, having in direct object the establishment of an absolute tyranny over her. To prove this, let facts be submitted to a candid world.

He has not ever permitted her to exercise her inalienable right to the elective franchise.

He has compelled her to submit to laws, in the formation of which she had no voice.

He has withheld her from rights which are given to the most ignorant and degraded men—both natives and foreigners.

Having deprived her of this first right as a citizen, the elective franchise, thereby leaving her without representation in the halls of legislation, he has oppressed her on all sides.

He has made her, if married, in the eye of the law, civilly dead.

He has taken from her all right in property, even to the wages she earns.

He has made her morally, an irresponsible being, as she can commit many crimes with impunity, provided they be done in the presence of her husband. In the covenant of marriage, she is compelled to promise obedience to her husband, he becoming, to all intents and purposes, her master—the law giving him power to deprive her of her liberty, and to administer chastisement.

He has so framed the laws of divorce, as to what shall be the proper causes of divorce, in case of separation, to whom the guardianship of the children shall be given; as to be wholly regardless of the happiness of the women— the law, in all cases, going upon a false supposition of the supremacy of a man, and giving all power into his hands.

After depriving her of all rights as a married woman, if single and the owner of property, he has taxed her to support a government which recognizes her only when her property can be made profitable to it.

He has monopolized nearly all the profitable employments, and from those she is permitted to follow, she receives but a scanty remuneration.

He closes against her all the avenues to wealth and distinction, which he considers most honorable to himself. As a teacher of theology, medicine, or law, she is not known.

He has denied her the facilities for obtaining a thorough education—all colleges being closed against her.

He allows her in church, as well as State, but a subordinate position, claiming Apostolic authority for her exclusion from the ministry, and, with some exceptions, from any public participation in the affairs of the Church.

He has created a false public sentiment by giving to the world a different code of morals for men and women, by which moral delinquencies which exclude women from society, are not only tolerated but deemed of little account in man.

He has usurped the prerogative of Jehovah himself, claiming it as his right to assign for her a sphere of action, when that belongs to her conscience and her God.

He has endeavored, in every way that he could to destroy her confidence in her own powers, to lessen her self-respect, and to make her willing to lead a dependent and abject life.

Now in view of this entire disfranchisement of one-half the people of this country, their social and religious degradation—in view of

the unjust laws above mentioned, and because women do feel themselves aggrieved, oppressed, and fraudulently deprived of their most sacred rights, we insist that they have immediate admission to all the rights and privileges which belong to them as citizens of these United States.

In entering upon the great work before us, we anticipate no small amount of misconception, misrepresentation, and ridicule; but we shall use every instrumentality within our power to effect our object. We shall employ agents, circulate tracts, petition the State and national Legislatures, and endeavor to enlist the pulpit and the press in our behalf. We hope this Convention will be followed by a series of Conventions, embracing every part of the country.

SENECA FALLS TO THE SUFFRAGE MOVEMENT

The ideas presented at the Seneca Falls Convention slowly began to gain momentum with a series of women's rights conventions held from 1850 to 1860 throughout the northeastern states, which had become the nation's center of industrial and social change. In the largely agrarian South, economically and socially tied to the institution of slavery as well as to the patriarchal social constructs that had defined southern life since the colonial period, the majority of white women during the antebellum era were isolated from the movements for equal rights and opportunity that were emerging in the North. For the enslaved African American women of the South, participation in a movement for women's rights could not be envisioned until emancipation had been achieved. However, after the end of the Civil War and the reemergence of the women's rights movement and the movement toward women's suffrage among largely middle- and upper-class, white women, African American women, especially in the South, were primarily concerned with the goal of bettering black communities overall rather than seeking individual advancement. By the last decades of the nineteenth century, black women, marginalized within and then excluded from the mainstream white women's suffrage movement as well as burdened with the racism that pervaded the South during the era of "separate but equal" Jim Crow laws, would begin to organize African American women's clubs such as the Alpha Suffrage Club (1913) as a means to accomplish social reform, among which was the goal of attaining suffrage.

Two weeks after Seneca Falls, a second convention was held in Rochester, New York, which featured many of the same speakers. Among the attendees were Lucy Anthony and her daughter, Mary, the mother and sister of twenty-eight-year-old Susan B. Anthony, who expressed an interest in meeting Elizabeth Cady Stanton and Lucretia Mott after hearing her mother and sister's account of the event. In 1851, Amelia Bloomer, a women's rights and temperance activist who had attended the Seneca Falls Convention, introduced Susan B. Anthony to Elizabeth Cady Stanton. Anthony, who abandoned the temperance movement in 1852 after she was not allowed to speak at a conference because she was a woman, attended her first National Women's Rights Convention in Syracuse, New York, the same year. There, she made her first public speech on women's rights. Anthony would establish a long working

The mahogany parlor table upon which Elizabeth Cady Stanton drafted the Declaration of Sentiments is maintained at the Smithsonian Institute's National Museum of American History in Washington, D.C.

partnership with Stanton for the cause of women's suffrage and become one of the most iconic women's rights campaigners in American history.

The first statewide women's rights convention was the Ohio Women's Convention held in Salem, Ohio, in April 1850, where the organizers included the caveat that only women would be allowed to sit on the platform, speak, and vote on resolutions. The state convention held in Akron, Ohio, the following year is especially notable for a speech delivered extemporaneously by former slave Sojourner Truth, who had escaped captivity in New York with her infant daughter in 1826, the year before slavery was abolished in the state. Truth's speech, one of the most famous in American history, came to be known under the title "Ain't I a Woman?"

The first National Women's Rights Convention was held in Worcester, Massachusetts, October 23–24, 1850. Organized by educator and women's rights activist Paulina Kellogg Wright Davis and Lucy Stone, now in her late twenties and a graduate of Oberlin College, the first American college to admit both women (1837) and African Americans (1835), the convention was attended by more than one thousand women and men with delegates from eleven states, including one delegate from California, a state that had been admitted to the Union only a few weeks earlier. Among the speakers were Sojourner Truth, Lucretia Mott, William Lloyd Garrison, Frederick Douglass, and Lucy Stone, and calls were made for a woman's right to vote, to own property, and admittance to institutions of higher education, the ministry, medicine, and other professions. Missing from the event was Elizabeth Cady Stanton, who was in the last stages of pregnancy and did not want to travel. Stanton sent her regrets along with her support and a speech to be read in her name. Lucy Stone delivered a speech asserting that women wanted to be "something more than the appendages of society; we want that Woman should be the co-equal and help-meet of Man in all the interests and perils and enjoyments of human life." Stone, at her own expense, had the proceedings of the convention and the six that followed printed as booklets called Women's Rights Tracts, which she sold at her lectures and at conventions. With the exception of 1857, a National Women's Rights Convention would be held annually until 1860, and smaller gatherings took place in northeastern cities and towns.

The press was hostile at first toward the conventions. When the *New York Herald* reported on the Worcester convention of 1850, the writer irritably asked, "What do the leaders of the women's rights convention want?" and went on to suggest that women would never want to subject themselves to the rowdiness of the political process and because of childbirth and motherhood would never be able to efficiently practice a profession (attitudes women continued to experience well beyond the nineteenth century). For the rest of the decade, news stories on the conventions were confined to factual reporting, but editorial pieces were no less derisive. One example was Horace Greeley, a politician and founder and editor of the *New York Tribune* who responded to Elizabeth Cady Stanton's resolution on marriage reform at the 1860 National Women's Rights Convention by writing that the word "Women" should be replaced in the convention title with "Wives Discontented." Other than in newspapers such as the *Liberator*, little support came from the press for the cause of women's rights. To fill the gap, some women published their own newspapers and magazines focusing on women's issues such as Amelia Bloomer's *The Lily*, Paulina Wright Davis's *The Una*, and Elizabeth Cady Stanton and Susan B. Anthony's *Revolution*, the motto of which was "Men, their rights and nothing more; women, their rights and nothing less!"

During the Civil War, women activists shifted their focus back to the cause of abolition. In 1863, Elizabeth Cady Stanton and Susan B. Anthony posted a notice in the *New York Tribune* appealing to the "Loyal Women of the Nation" to meet in New York City for the purpose of organizing support for a constitutional amendment to abolish slavery. Among the women who attended the meeting along with Stanton and Anthony were such abolitionist and women's rights stalwarts as Angelina Grimké Weld, Lucy Stone, and Martha Coffin Wright. Together, the attendees formed the Women's National Loyal League (also known as the Loyal Women's National League), which embarked on a massive petition drive that would gain nearly four hundred thousand signatures. The petition, which was pre-

sented to Congress, helped to secure passage of the Thirteenth Amendment ending slavery in the United States. Among the resolutions adopted during a second convention in May 1864 was a call for equal pay for women in the field of medicine, voting rights for African American men, and the right of black men to secure employment as soldiers, sailors, and laborers with pay equal to that of white men. By August 1864, the league was disbanded after it was clear that the Thirteenth Amendment would be achieved. Although its existence was brief, the Women's Loyal National League was significant because its formation marked the beginning of a shift toward a women's movement that was more formally organized and politically active.

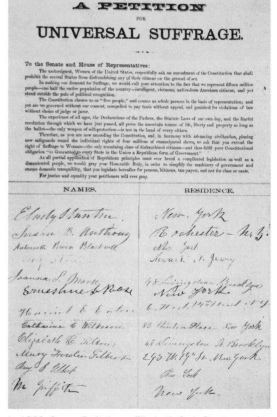

In 1863, Susan B. Anthony, Elizabeth Cady Stanton, and other prominent suffragists presented this petition to the U.S. Congress to amend the Constitution so that no state could prevent someone from voting on the basis of their sex.

Once emancipation was achieved with the implementation of the Thirteenth Amendment—the first of three Reconstruction amendments—the leaders of the women's movement once again took up the cause of women's rights. In January 1866, at a meeting of the American Anti-Slavery Society, Lucy Stone and Susan B. Anthony suggested that the society merge with the women's movement to form a new organization to advocate for the rights, including suffrage, for both African Americans and women. However, male abolitionist leaders, concerned that adding

> **W**inning the ballot for African American men would, it was argued, help pave the way for universal suffrage.

women's rights to the society's agenda would compromise the objective of gaining the vote for African American men, rejected the proposal. During the eleventh National Women's Rights Convention, held in New York on May 10, 1866, Frances Harper, an African American abolitionist and writer, spoke to the gathering to demand equal rights for all, including black women: "We are all bound up together in one great bundle of humanity, and society cannot trample on the weakest and feeblest of members without receiving the curse in its own soul.... You white women speak here of rights. I speak of wrongs.... I, as a colored woman, have had in this country an education which has made me feel as if I were in the situation of Ishmael, my hand against every man, and every man's hand against me...." The convention voted to create a new organization, the American Equal Rights Association (AERA), that would advocate for the rights of both African Americans and women. The AERA's first meeting was held in New York in 1867, where the association's president, Lucretia Mott, presented her opinion that if only African American men and not women attained suffrage, black men would oppose women's enfranchisement. Elizabeth Cady Stanton and Sojourner Truth agreed, the latter expressing herself more forcefully: "If colored men get their rights, and not colored women theirs, you see the colored men will be masters over the women, and it will be just as bad as it was before." Other members of the gathering disagreed, with the prevailing opinion that securing the ballot for one group of citizens should not be contingent on insisting upon it for another. Winning the ballot for African American men would, it was argued, help pave the way for universal suffrage. From 1866 through 1867, the AERA campaigned in Kansas, where the issues of black and women's suffrage had referenda. It was a difficult campaign during which Stanton and Anthony alienated many members of the AERA, as well as other reform activists, by unwisely forming an alliance with wealthy racist businessman George Francis Train, who advocated women's suffrage but opposed voting rights for African Americans. Despite the AERA's campaign, the ballot measure for suffrage without regard to gender or race failed.

The issue of African American suffrage caused a schism within the women's movement overall. Dissension arose over the Fourteenth Amendment, first proposed in 1865 and intended to ensure equal protection, citizenship, and voting rights for African Americans. Elizabeth Cady Stanton and Susan B. Anthony adamantly opposed the amendment on the grounds that it specified male but not female citizens (in addition, it was the first time the word "male" had been specifically introduced into the Constitution); Lucy Stone, along with other women in the movement, petitioned for the wording to be changed to include women but ultimately supported the final amendment, ratified in 1868, on its own merits as necessary to help ensure the rights of African Americans and as a first step toward universal suffrage. The same year, a proposed Fifteenth Amendment that clarified the right of African American men to vote was introduced into Congress, which read: "The right of citizens of the United States to vote shall not be denied or abridged by the United States or any State, on account of race, color, or previous condition of servitude." It did not include the word "sex," which infuriated Stanton and Anthony, who had also resented the extension of the vote to black men and not women. The Fifteenth Amendment was ratified, unchanged, in 1870.

In May 1869, Anthony and Stanton, disillusioned with the AERA's support for the Reconstruction amendments to the detriment of women's rights, as well as with its male leadership, left that organization to form the all-female National Woman Suffrage Association (NWSA). Among the prominent women's rights activists who joined Stanton (who was appointed the new organization's president) and Anthony in forming the new organization were Lucretia Mott, Martha Coffin Wright, and Ernestine Rose. The NWSA immediately set as their agenda the passage of a constitutional amendment giving women the right to vote. The same year, members of the New England Woman Suffrage Association (NEWSA), an organization that supported passage of the Fifteenth Amendment, met in Boston to discuss the formation of the American Woman Suffrage Association (AWSA). The AWSA was officially founded at a convention in Cleveland in November 1869 and counted among its leaders and members Lucy Stone, Julia Ward Howe, Sojourner Truth, and Lucy Stone's husband, Henry Blackwell. In 1870, Lucy Stone and Henry Blackwell founded the *Women's Journal*, the AWSA organ and rival newspaper to Susan B. Anthony and Elizabeth Cady Stanton's *The Revolution*, which was undergoing financial difficulties and was ultimately forced to cease publication by 1872. The *Women's Journal* would go on to become the official organ of the National American Woman Suffrage Association (NAWSA), the organization created by the merger of the NWSA and the AWSA in 1890.

Both organizations worked toward gaining suffrage, but they each had different principles and tactics. The NWSA included in its campaigns such issues as equal pay for women and easier divorce laws, criticized aspects of marriage and religion that were unjust toward women, and used litigation and confrontation to bring attention to its causes. The AWSA endorsed traditional social institutions, including marriage and religion, and relied on less militant tactics such as public speeches, petition drives, and testifying before legislatures to gain support. The organization focused on suffrage and felt that a state-by-state campaign would more easily secure success. The NWSA initially favored securing women's suffrage by working toward a constitutional amendment but in the 1880s began to lobby at the state level as well.

Women in states and territories slowly began to win the vote. The territory of Wyoming was the first, granting women's suffrage together with the right to hold public office in 1869. Among the arguments for suffrage was the prospect that it might bring more women to the territory, which then had a population of some one thousand women and six thousand men. The following year, Utah territory granted full suffrage to women. However, in 1887, the U.S. Congress passed the Edmunds–Tucker Act, which outlawed polygamy in the territory and included a clause that revoked women's suffrage. When Utah gained statehood in 1896, women won back their voting rights. From 1883 to 1896, women won the vote in four other territories and states: Washington, Montana, Colorado, and Idaho.

TERRITORIES AND STATES GRANTING WOMEN'S SUFFRAGE

States granting women the right to vote prior to the Nineteenth Amendment:

State	Year
Wyoming	1890
Colorado	1893
Utah	1896
Idaho	1896
Washington	1910
California	1911
Arizona	1912
Kansas	1912
Oregon	1912
Montana	1914
Nevada	1914
New York	1917
Michigan	1918
Oklahoma	1918
South Dakota	1918

Territories granting full voting rights before the Nineteenth Amendment and before statehood:

Territory	Year
Wyoming	1869
Utah	1870
Washington	1883
Montana	1887
Alaska	1913

States in which women could vote for president prior to the Nineteenth Amendment:

State	Year
Illinois	1913
Nebraska	1917
Ohio	1917
Indiana	1917
North Dakota	1917
Rhode Island	1917
Iowa	1919
Maine	1919
Minnesota	1919
Missouri	1919
Tennessee	1919
Wisconsin	1919

States in which women gained voting rights with the passage of the Nineteenth Amendment in 1920:

- Alabama
- Arkansas
- Connecticut
- Delaware
- Florida
- Georgia
- Kentucky
- Louisiana
- Maryland
- Massachusetts
- Mississippi
- New Hampshire
- New Mexico
- New Jersey
- North Carolina
- Pennsylvania
- South Carolina
- Texas
- Vermont
- Virginia
- West Virginia

THE FINAL BATTLE FOR SUFFRAGE

In 1890, in the hope of presenting a stronger, more united front on behalf of the women's movement, the National Woman Suffrage Association and the American Woman Suffrage Association joined together to form the National American Woman Suffrage Association (NAWSA). The new organization's first president was seventy-five-year-old Elizabeth Cady Stanton, who held the post until 1892, when she was succeeded as president by seventy-two-year-old Susan B. Anthony.

The NAWSA's internal quarrels and lack of a national headquarters weakened the organization's effectiveness. Although Anthony was an inspirational leader who shared with younger suffragists a single-minded concern with winning the vote, she was unable to unite the movement. Between 1896 and 1910, no new states granted women's suffrage, and only six states held suffrage referenda, all of which failed. The Susan B. Anthony federal women's suffrage amendment, introduced into Congress in 1878 and containing the wording that would later be used for the Nineteenth Amendment, seemed doomed. In the South, the racist Jim Crow laws were used to prevent African Americans from voting, and southern suffragists worried that a movement toward federal suffrage would call attention to the South's flagrant disregard for the citizenship, equal protection, and voting rights enshrined in the Fourteenth and Fifteenth Amendments. Some southern suffragists advocated voting rights for white women only, while others felt threatened by the inclusion of both African American women and northern immigrant "foreigners" in the political process (Elizabeth Cady Stanton had voiced similar concerns about extending the vote to male immigrants in 1869 before the Fifteenth Amendment was ratified). Susan B. Anthony and other NAWSA members felt that it would not be feasible to work on behalf of suffrage for black women until the vote was extended to all women in general, and after the conventions of 1899 and 1903, the organization separated itself from the cause of African American women's suffrage.

Susan B. Anthony stepped down as president of the NAWSA in 1900 and was replaced by Carrie

Men and women are shown lined up together to vote in Colorado. Thanks to the work of journalist and suffragist Ellis Meredith and Carrie Chapman Catt, the right to vote for Colorado women passed in 1893.

Chapman Catt, a brilliant tactician in her early forties, who devised a plan to gain support for women's suffrage at the grassroots level. After Catt left the presidency in 1904 to care for her ailing husband, she was replaced by Anna Howard Shaw, a physician and a Methodist pastor, who was a gifted speaker but a poor administrator. While the NAWSA struggled during the first decade of the twentieth century in what suffragists called "the doldrums," younger women activists founded grassroots suffrage organizations such as the College Equal Suffrage League and the Boston Equal Suffrage League for Good Government. These groups conducted door-to-door campaigns in working-class areas as well as in middle- and upper-middle-class neighborhoods in an attempt to interest women in the suffrage movement. Groups of women traveled by trolley throughout Massachusetts, making speeches at each stop and attracting crowds by holding spontaneous outdoor meetings.

In 1907, Harriot Stanton Blatch, the daughter of Elizabeth Cady Stanton, organized the Equality League of Self-Supporting Women, later renamed the Women's Political Union, in New York City. Intended to bring working-class women into the movement, among the league's members were writer Charlotte Perkins Gilman and labor activists Florence Kelley and Rose Schneiderman. By 1908, membership in the league numbered nineteen thousand women. The league lobbied unsuccessfully in Albany for a women's suffrage bill and in 1910 opened the first suffragist newsstand in New York City, which sold suffragist pamphlets, magazines, buttons, ribbons, postcards, and copies of addresses made by Susan B. Anthony. In addition, the league was responsible for initiating the suffrage parades that would become an integral part of suffragist strategy.

By 1910, the movement had encouraging victories: That year, Washington became the first state in fourteen years to pass a women's suffrage amendment; California, Oregon, Arizona, Kansas, Montana, and Illinois followed. An added spur was supplied by news of British suffragettes, who had become famous for their campaign of civil disobedience and confrontation in their determination to convince the recalcitrant, all-male Parliament to give women the right to vote. Members of the British suffragist organization, the Women's Social and Political Union (WSPU), chained themselves to public buildings, stormed the House of Commons, blew up postal boxes, and held mass marches to the Parliament. Suffragettes were sent to prison, where they organized hunger strikes and were brutally force-fed by their captors. The treatment of the suffragettes had the effect of swaying public opinion in their favor. Carrie Chapman Catt, now president of the International Woman Suffrage Alliance, took note of the suffragettes' tactics but was too consummate a politician to sanction the use of violence and militancy endorsed by the WSPU. Harriot Stanton Blatch applied British strategy in the form of parades and street-corner speeches. The most militant of the era's American women's suffrage leaders was Quaker and social worker Alice Paul, who had attended the London School of Economics. Paul had participated in WSPU demonstrations, had been repeatedly imprisoned, and had joined the hunger strikers, during which she was force-fed through her nose.

THE SUFFRAGE PARADE OF 1913

When Alice Paul returned to the United States, she and Lucy Burns, who was also a veteran of the WSPU's suffrage campaign, persuaded the NWSA leadership to endorse a massive parade and demonstration. Paul, Burns, and other NAWSA members organized a parade to be held in Washington, D.C., on March 3, 1913, the day before President Woodrow Wilson's inauguration. The parade was led by labor lawyer Inez Milholland, dressed in white and mounted on a white horse. She was followed by between five thousand and eight thousand marchers, many marching as groups, with banners proclaiming their various affiliations. The parade included five mounted brigades, twenty-

six floats, supporters from countries around the world, and such notables as Helen Keller and Montana's Jeannette Rankin, who would make history three years later when she became the first woman to be elected to the U.S. House of Representatives.

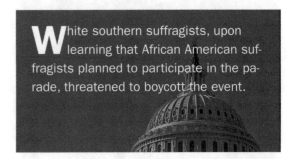

White southern suffragists, upon learning that African American suffragists planned to participate in the parade, threatened to boycott the event.

White southern suffragists, upon learning that African American suffragists planned to participate in the parade, threatened to boycott the event. In order to mollify the white southerners, the NAWSA solution was to segregate black suffragists and insist they walk at the end of the parade in a "colored delegation." When African American journalist and civil rights activist Ida B. Wells-Barnett, who had helped found the Alpha Suffrage Club in Chicago the same year, was told by the Illinois delegation that the NAWSA wanted "to keep the delegation entirely white," she refused to comply. Instead, she waited with the spectators until the suffragists in the Chicago delegation came by and then joined the parade to walk with them.

What began as a peaceful march turned violent when crowds of angry, jeering men slapped demonstrators, spit at them, and poked them with lighted cigars. A near riot broke out, which stopped the marchers before they could reach the White House. Forty people were hospitalized, and it took a cavalry troop to restore order. The behavior of the agitators only resulted in a great deal of favorable publicity for the suffrage cause and led to organized pilgrimages to Washington from all across the country with petitions collected at the grassroots level. On July 31, 1913, an automobile procession to the Capitol presented a group of senators with suffrage petitions carrying two hundred thousand signatures. Delegations began to visit President Wilson, who could no

A new strategy for making the party in power responsible for not allowing all women to have voting rights was begun with the formation of the Congressional Union of Woman Suffrage.

longer hide behind his earlier pronouncement that the issue of women's suffrage had not been brought to his attention.

AMERICAN WOMEN WIN THE RIGHT TO VOTE

In 1913, Alice Paul and Lucy Burns formed the Congressional Union for Woman Suffrage (CU), an auxiliary organization to the NAWSA. The CU's strategy for winning suffrage was to hold the party in power responsible for denying women the right to vote. Paul also proposed that the women in states that had won suffrage—some four million women— put pressure on both Democrats (the party then in power) and Republicans to change their position on women's suffrage or else they would lose votes. The NAWSA viewed Paul's strategy as harassment and politically unviable, and when Carrie Chapman Catt returned to the presidency of the NAWSA in 1915, she expelled Alice Paul from the organization. Paul responded by forming the National Women's Party (NWP) with such like-minded suffragists as Crystal Eastman (a cofounder of the Woman's Peace Party) and Maude Wood Park (later president of the League of Women Voters, founded in 1919 to encourage women to vote once the Nineteenth Amend-

ment was ratified). Both Paul and Carrie Chapman Catt planned to use their organizations to press for a federal suffrage amendment. Catt and the NAWSA would continue the suffrage campaign state by state, moving toward ratification of a federal amendment by 1920. The NWP, which numbered fifty thousand members in contrast with the NAWSA membership of two million, favored a more radical approach. During the 1916 presidential campaign, the NWP mounted a vigorous anti-Wilson campaign that ultimately failed (Wilson was reelected) nevertheless focused even more attention of the issue of women's suffrage.

After the United States entered World War I in 1917, the NWP began daily around-the-clock picketing of the White House, carrying banners that referred to "Kaiser Wilson" and proclaiming that "Democracy should begin at home," a reference to the nation's defense of democracy abroad while hypocritically denying democratic rights to women at home. Several months after the picketers, known as the Silent Sentinels, started their vigil, the police began making arrests, but since the picketers had been demonstrating legally, they were set free without sentence. When they returned to the picket lines, they were arrested on a charge of obstructing sidewalk traffic, found guilty, and imprisoned in the Occaquan workhouse in Virginia. There, Alice Paul, journalist Dorothy Day, and other picketers went on a hunger strike and were force-fed. Paul, whose hunger strike lasted for twenty-two days, was considered insane by prison officials and forced to undergo a mental examination. The courts, pressured by the public outcry over the maltreatment of the picketers, invalidated the arrests, the women were hailed as heroines, and even more favorable publicity was generated for the cause of women's suffrage. In a promising development, the House Rules Committee brought the dormant federal suffrage amendment to the floor for debate.

By 1918, the NAWSA's painstaking state-by-state initiatives and the Women's Party's dramatic demonstrations had created a public and political climate favorable to the passage of the federal suffrage amendment. On January 10, 1918, Representative Jeannette Rankin introduced the amendment onto the floor of the House. Four congressmen with determining votes voted from their sickbeds; one came from the deathbed of his suffragist wife. The final tally was 274 in favor of the amendment and 136 against. The amendment had passed with exactly one vote more than the required two-thirds.

It would take another year and a half to win over the Senate, which passed the Nineteenth Amendment on June 4, 1919. During the congressional ratification process, antisuffragist factions, known as "antis," who included southern white supremacists, northern political bosses, and the National Women's Organization to Oppose Suffrage, worked to block final passage of the amendment, but the efforts of the antis were in vain: On August 18, 1920, twenty-four-year-old Senator Harry Burn of Tennessee, whose mother had sent him a letter in which she wrote, "Hurrah and vote for Suffrage and don't keep them in doubt," cast the deciding vote in favor of ratification. The amendment carried 49–47, thus enfranchising some twenty-six million American women after seventy-two years of struggle.

By obtaining one of the most basic of individual democratic freedoms—the right to vote—women gained access to the political process that would help to shape their future. However, inclusion into the world of politics would take longer. Carrie Chapman Catt warned that obtaining the right to vote was only a first step in becoming part of that process; women would need to force their way behind the locked door that led to the rooms where political decisions on issues and on candidates were made. "If you really want women's vote to count," cautioned Catt, "make your way there."

BIOGRAPHIES

Susan B. Anthony (1820–1906)

Suffragist

Susan B. Anthony is renowned as one of the most prominent leaders of the suffragist movement in the battle to gain the vote for American women. Her efforts of more than fifty years

finally led to the passage in 1920 of the Nineteenth Amendment, also known as the Susan B. Anthony Amendment.

Born in Adams, Massachusetts, Susan Brownell Anthony was the second of the six children of Quaker abolitionist parents. Educated at a Quaker school in Philadelphia, she began her career as a teacher in rural New York State, where she campaigned for equal pay for women teachers, coeducation, and college training for girls.

In 1848, Anthony's parents and younger sister attended the first women's rights convention in Seneca Falls, New York. From them, Anthony learned of Elizabeth Cady Stanton, whose groundbreaking Declaration of Rights and Sentiments had become a rallying cry for women's rights and the suffrage movement. Anthony first met Stanton in 1851, and the two joined forces to lead the crusade for women's suffrage. In 1869, they formed the National Woman Suffrage Association to lobby for a constitutional amendment for their cause. Anthony would devote thirty years of her life to traveling around the country to gather support for women's suffrage.

Anthony and Stanton believed that women were entitled to vote under the postwar constitutional amendments that enfranchised former slaves and guaranteed equal rights to all citizens. In 1872, Anthony attempted to vote in the presidential election and was arrested, tried, found guilty, and fined $100, which she refused to pay. No action was taken to enforce the court action, however, which meant that Anthony was unable to challenge the law, as she had hoped, before the U.S. Supreme Court.

Each year beginning in 1876, advocates for women's suffrage presented Congress with a constitutional amendment extending voting rights to women, and each year, Congress ignored or rejected it. However, largely through Anthony's efforts, four states did grant women the right to vote in state and local elections. In 1890, the National Woman Suffrage Association merged with the American Woman Suffrage Association to form the National American Woman Suffrage Association (NAWSA), for which Anthony served as president from 1892 to 1900.

In 1906, the year she died, Anthony attended her last women's suffrage convention. There, she delivered the message that "failure is impossible." It would take another fourteen years and a new generation of suffragists led by Carrie Chapman Catt and Alice Paul for Anthony's conviction to become realized with the passage of the Nineteenth Amendment.

Today, Susan B. Anthony is revered as one of the most influential figures in American history for her dedication to the cause of women's rights and her leadership in the women's suffrage movement.

Alva Belmont (1853–1933)

Suffragist

Alva Belmont was a wealthy socialite who used her fortune to advance the women's rights movement as a major figure in the women's suffrage movement.

Born in Mobile, Alabama, Belmont was educated in France and married William K. Vanderbilt, the grandson of Cornelius Vanderbilt, in 1875. Although the Vanderbilts were among the richest people in the world, they were excluded from the "Four Hundred," the cream of New York society, and Alva instituted an aggressive and eventually victorious campaign to be included by commissioning a $3 million mansion on Fifth Avenue and hosting the Olympian masquerade ball, the most opulent entertainment ever seen in New York. She also had built a "cottage" in Newport that cost $9 million when completed in 1892. Alva divorced her long-unfaithful husband a year later and married Oliver Hazard Perry Belmont, an old friend of her ex-husband, who was active in yachting and horse-racing circles.

When her husband died suddenly in 1908, Alva Belmont took up the cause of women's suffrage after hearing a lecture by journalist and suffragist Ida Husted Harper. Belmont brought English suffragette Christabel Pankhurst to the United States in 1914 for a speaking tour and helped to finance Alice Paul's more militant tactics in the fight to win women the right to vote. She cowrote a suffragist operetta, *Melinda and Her Sisters*, and presented it at the Waldorf-Astoria Hotel in 1916. After American women won the right to vote in 1920, Belmont was elected

president of the National Woman's Party, a post she held for the rest of her life. She was also the founder of the Political Equality League and is credited with the line, "Pray to God. She will help you."

Dying from a stroke in 1932 in Paris, Belmont's body was returned to New York for burial. At her funeral, female pallbearers carried her coffin, and at her instructions, the suffragist slogan "Failure is Impossible" was draped across it. A crowd of 1,500 mourners turned out to pay their respect to one of the greatest patrons of the women's rights movement, who contributed so much in the fight for women's equality.

Antoinette Brown Blackwell (1825–1921)

Minister, Suffragist

The first woman to be ordained by an established Protestant denomination in the United States, Antoinette Brown Blackwell was a renowned public speaker who used her skills as a powerful advocate of abolition and women's rights.

The youngest of seven children, Blackwell grew up in Henrietta, in upstate New York. She was recognized as highly intelligent as early as age three and was accepted into the Congregational Church as a member before age nine when she began to preach during Sunday meetings. After her schooling at Monroe County Academy ended at the age of sixteen, she taught for four years, saving enough money to attend Oberlin College in 1846. She completed the literary, or ladies', course, the prescribed course of study for women students in 1847. Overcoming the objections of family, faculty, and friends, Blackwell completed the theological course in 1850, but her professors refused to license her or allow her to graduate. Instead, she became an itinerant preacher and lecturer until 1853, when she finally became an ordained Congregational minister, the first ordained female minister in the United States.

Blackwell wrote for Frederick Douglass's abolitionist paper *The North Star* and spoke in 1850 at the first National Women's Rights Convention, the beginning of a speaking tour in which she would speak out on issues of abolition, temperance, and women's rights. Despite her reputation and achievements, Blackwell was barred from addressing the World's Temperance Convention in New York in 1853 as a woman. Her changing religious convictions led her to resign to become a Unitarian minister at a church in Elizabeth, New Jersey. In 1856, she married Samuel C. Blackwell, a brother of Elizabeth Blackwell, the first woman to receive a medical degree. Although her marriage caused her to retire from public life, she continued to contribute articles to the *Woman's Journal*, a suffrage publication, and continue her studies in physical and social sciences that produced several books, including *Studies in General Science* (1869), *The Sexes Throughout Nature* (1875), *The Physical Basis of Immortality* (1876), *The Philosophy of Individuality* (1893), *The Making of the Universe* (1914), and *The Social Side of Mind and Action* (1915).

In 1920, when the Nineteenth Amendment was ratified, guaranteeing women the right to vote, Blackwell was one of only a few of the first generation of suffragists still alive to witness the realization of their hard-fought goal.

Harriot Stanton Blatch (1856–1940)
Suffragist, Writer

The daughter of Elizabeth Cady Stanton, Harriot Stanton Blatch would continue her mother's work in the women's rights movement, becoming one of its major figures.

The sixth of the eight children of Henry Brewster Stanton and Elizabeth Cady Stanton, Blatch was born in Seneca Falls, New York. She attended Vassar College, where she graduated with a degree in mathematics. She spent 1880–1881 in Germany as a tutor for young girls. She also worked with her mother and Susan B. Anthony on the *History of Woman Suffrage*, contributing a major chapter in the second volume on the history of the American Woman Suffrage Association, the rival of Stanton and Anthony's National Woman Suffrage Association. Blatch's work is said to have helped reconcile

the two organizations for their final push for a constitutional amendment for women's suffrage.

On her return voyage to the United States, she met English businessman William Henry Blatch Jr., whom she married in 1882, living for twenty years in Basinstoke, Hampshire, where her husband was brewery manager of John May & Co. Their first of two daughters, Nora Stanton Blatch Barney, would become the first U.S. woman to earn a degree in civil engineering. Blatch was active in England with famed suffragist Emmeline Pankhurst, becoming a member of the Woman's Suffrage Society. She also continued her academic work, receiving a master's degree in mathematics from Vassar for her statistical analysis of English villages.

Returning to the United States in 1902, Blatch resumed her involvement with the women's rights movement, founding the Equality League of Self-Supporting Women in 1907, which later was renamed the Women's Political Union, which eventually merged with Alice Paul's Congressional Union to form the National Woman's Party. During World War I, Blatch supported the war effort but encouraged women to get involved in peace work to prevent future wars, outlining her views in *A Woman's Point of View* (1920). Blatch entered politics, failing to win election as comptroller of the city of New York in 1921 or later as a member of the New York State Assembly, both of which she ran in as a Socialist Party candidate.

Blatch's final years were spent in a nursing home in Greenwich, Connecticut, where she completed her autobiography, *Challenging Years* (1940). The book's title is a suitable descriptor for a life spent both as a custodian of the memory of the first great generation of women's rights activists and as an activist in her own right who lived to see the goal of women's suffrage realized.

Amelia Bloomer (1818–1894)
Temperance Activist, Women's Rights Activist

Associated mainly with the fashion trend named for her, the prototrousers that challenged the constricting dresses worn by nineteenth-century women, Amelia was a women's rights and temperance activist who became the first woman to own, operate, and edit a newspaper for women.

Born Amelia Jenks in upstate Homer, New York, Bloomer received only a few years of formal education in the local district school. After working briefly as a schoolteacher at the age of seventeen, she relocated with her sister to Seneca Falls, New York, to serve as a live-in governess of her sister's three young children. In 1840, she married a Quaker newspaper editor, Dexter Bloomer, who stimulated Bloomer's interest in public affairs. She began contributing articles to newspapers on various topics and became an early member of the local women's Temperance Society. In 1848, Bloomer attended the Seneca Falls Convention organized by Elizabeth Cady Stanton and Lucretia Mott, and in 1849, Bloomer began a newspaper for women, *The Lily: A Ladies Journal Devoted to Temperance and Literature*, that included articles by women's rights advocates as well as temperance reformers.

Women's fashion in the mid-nineteenth century dictated, for modesty's sake, floor-length dresses, a full skirt beneath a tiny waist made possible with tight corsets, and from six to eight petticoats to fill out the shape of the skirts. Outfits could weigh up to fifteen pounds and caused overheating, impaired breathing, and constricted movement. In 1851, a male editor of the *Seneca County Courier*, who had opposed women's suffrage, urged women to consider switching to "Turkish pantaloons and a skirt reaching a little below the knee." Bloomer in *The Lily* chastised the writer for supporting dress reform but not women's rights. At about the same time, Bloomer's neighbor, Elizabeth Cady Stanton, had a visit from her cousin, who was wearing the very outfit being discussed, a knee-length skirt with loose pants. Stanton shortly copied the style, and Bloomer followed her lead and advocated for the fashion in *The Lily*. "I stood amazed at the furor I had unwittingly caused," Bloomer later recalled. "Some praised and some blamed, some commented, and some ridiculed and condemned." Letters began to pour into her newspapers asking for patterns, and the circulation of *The Lily* increased from five hundred per month to four thousand. The furor inextricably linked Bloomer's name with the trend, and adapters were

called Bloomerites, practitioners of Bloomerism, or, more simply, wearers of bloomers.

Although bloomers would start a revolution in women's fashion that would change core notions of femininity and practicality for women, Bloomer would play an even more important role in 1851 by introducing her neighbor Elizabeth Cady Stanton to Susan B. Anthony, which set in motion their long-standing partnership that would transform the women's rights movement in America. In 1853, Bloomer and her husband moved west and in 1854, she decided to sell her paper. Eventually, the couple settled in Council Bluffs, Iowa, where Bloomer continued to be active on the causes of temperance and women's rights until her death at the age of seventy-six in 1894.

Lucy Burns (1879–1966)

Suffragist

Lucy Burns was one of the pivotal figures in the women's suffrage movement who, allied with Alice Paul, directed the fight for the constitutional amendment, founding the Congressional Union for Woman Suffrage and the National Woman's Party.

Born in Brooklyn, New York, to an Irish Catholic family, Burns was a gifted student who attended Packer Collegiate Institute (formerly the Brooklyn Female Academy) before graduating from Vassar College in 1902. Over the next seven years, she did graduate work in linguistics, becoming the first woman to be accepted to the Yale University Graduate School. She became a high school English teacher at Erasmus Hall, a public high school in Brooklyn, and she also studied at the universities of Berlin, Bonn, and Oxford. While in England, she became interested in the struggle to secure the vote for women, became a close colleague of suffragist leaders Emmeline and Christabel Pankhurst, and endured several arrests and prison hunger strikes.

Returning to the United States in 1912, Burns joined the National American Woman Suffrage Association (NAWSA) and became, with Alice Paul, one of the leaders of its Congressional Committee. Paul and Burns endorsed a more militant program to compel Congress to act on women's suffrage, and they were able to persuade a reluctant NAWSA to authorize a suffrage parade during Woodrow Wilson's first inauguration. While the demonstration provoked violence, it also generated support for suffrage, and Burns and Paul were convinced that their radical tactic was correct, forming the Congressional Union that split with the NAWSA in 1914 to further their ends to provoke Congress to act. "Inaction," Burns stated, "establishes just as clear a record as does a policy of open hostility."

When the so-called Anthony Amendment to the Constitution made it out of the committee in 1914, Burns became the first woman to speak before congressional delegates. The Congressional Union next began organizing in the nine states where women had the right to vote ways to gain ratification. Burns traveled to California, raising the issue of suffrage in theaters, on the street, and going door-to-door. In 1915, Burns became the editor of the Congressional Union's newspaper *The Suffragist* and supported Alice Paul's radical new plan in 1916 to organize a woman's political party, which became the National Woman's Party (NWP). Burns was one of the chief organizers of the NWP's efforts to picket the White House as Silent Sentinels in 1917. Burns was arrested and sent to Occoquan Workhouse in Virginia, where she joined Alice Paul and other women in hunger strikes. Released, Burns was rearrested and imprisoned two more times before the judge gave her the maximum sentence. In prison, she endured what is remembered as the "Night of Terror," in which the women were brutalized. Burns, who remained defiant, was handcuffed with her hands above her head to her cell door for an entire night. Burns organized a hunger strike in response, and she was force-fed, as historian Eleanor Clift described it: "Five people to hold her down, and when she refused to open her mouth, they shoved the feeding tube up her nostril." It is reckoned that among the well-known suffragists, Burns spent the most time in jail.

The struggle that finally resulted in the ratification of the Nineteenth Amendment in 1920 left Burns exhausted. She retired from public life and returned to Brooklyn, where she devoted herself to the Catholic Church and her orphaned niece. Burns died in Brooklyn at the age of eighty-seven.

Carrie Chapman Catt (1859–1947)
Suffragist

While Elizabeth Cady Stanton and Susan B. Anthony are responsible for initiating the crusade for women's suffrage in the United States, the credit for completing the task and securing the passage of the Nineteenth Amendment belongs in large part to the efforts of suffragist Carrie Chapman Catt.

Born in Ripon, Wisconsin, Catt grew up on a farm and was an active, self-reliant young woman who attended Iowa State College, supporting herself by washing dishes and working in the library. After graduation in 1880, she became a high school principal in Mason City, Iowa, and then superintendent of schools before marrying newspaperman Leo Chapman in 1885.

After her husband died from typhoid fever, Catt began lecturing for women's rights and joined the Iowa Woman Suffrage Association. In 1890, she attended the first convention of the newly organized National American Woman Suffrage Association (NAWSA). When she remarried that year, she worked out with her new husband, George William Catt, an agreement that allowed her at least four months a year to do suffrage work. Catt created and headed the Organization Committee of the NAWSA to direct the group's efforts nationwide and demonstrated her characteristic strengths of careful planning, innovation, and meticulous attention to detail. When the aging president of NAWSA, Susan B. Anthony, retired in 1900, she chose Catt as her successor. Although Catt was forced to resign in 1904 because of her husband's poor health, she returned as NAWSA president in 1915 to unify a badly divided suffrage movement.

Catt realized that the way to ensure passage of the constitutional amendment rested in increasing the number of individual states that gave women the right to vote, which would in turn compel those in Congress to support the amendment granting suffrage throughout the country. Despite cofounding the Woman's Peace Party with Jane Addams in 1915, Catt encouraged women to support the war effort when the United States entered World War I in 1917, convinced that patriotism displayed by women would help secure the vote. Catt's dual strategy of increasing the number of "suffrage states" and mobilization of women behind the war effort helped to ensure eventual passage of the Nineteenth Amendment guaranteeing women the right to vote, a milestone event in American women's history.

Paulina Kellogg Wright Davis (1813–1876)

Abolitionist, Suffragist

 An abolitionist, suffragist, and lecturer, Paulina Davis was president of the National Women's Rights Committee from 1850 to 1868 and a founder of the New England Woman Suffrage Association in 1868.

Born in Bloomfield, New York, Davis moved with her family to the frontier near Niagara Falls in 1817. When both of her parents died three years later, Davis went to live with her aunt in LeRoy, New York, where she joined the Presbyterian Church. However, she became frustrated with the church's hostility toward outspoken women and its refusal to allow women to become missionaries. In 1833, Davis married Francis Wright, the son of a prosperous family from Utica, New York. The couple resigned from their church to protest its proslavery stance, served on the executive committee of the Central New York Anti-Slavery Society, and organized an antislavery convention in Utica. The Wrights were also supporters of women's rights reforms.

During this period, Davis studied women's health. After Francis Wright died in 1845, Davis moved to New York to study medicine and the following year began to lecture on anatomy and physiology to women only. After importing a medical mannequin, David used it on tours of the eastern United States, during which she lectured to women and urged them to become physicians. In 1849, she married Thomas Davis, a jewelry manufacturer, abo-

litionist, and politician from Providence, Rhode Island. The couple adopted two daughters.

In 1850, Davis stopped lecturing to focus on women's rights. The same year, she helped to organize the first National Women's Rights Convention in Worcester, Massachusetts, at which she served as chair and delivered the opening address. From 1853 to 1855, she edited the women's newspaper the *Una*. After the splintering of the New England Woman Suffrage Association, she joined the National American Woman Suffrage Association. In 1870, she published *The History of the National Women's Rights Movement*.

After her death in Providence at the age of sixty-three, Davis was eulogized by Elizabeth Cady Stanton. She was inducted into the National Women's Hall of Fame in 2002.

Grace Bustill Douglass (1782–1842)

Abolitionist, Women's Rights Activist

A member of one of the first prominent black families in the United States, Grace Bustill was a prominent abolitionist, a founding member of the Philadelphia Female Anti-Slavery Society, and vice president of the Anti-Slavery Convention of American Women.

Born in Burlington, New Jersey, Douglass was the daughter of former slave Cyrus Bustill, an outspoken opponent of slavery, and a half-Delaware Indian and half-English mother. The owner of a successful bakery business, Cyrus Bustill was the founder of Philadelphia's Free African Society, which established a school for African American children that Douglass and her siblings attended, one of the few schools for black children at the time. Douglass learned the millinery trade, and she eventually opened a successful milliner shop in Philadelphia next to her father's bakery.

In 1803 at the age of twenty-one, Douglass married Robert Douglass, a wealthy minister and barber from St. Kitts in the West Indies, and they had six children together, one of whom, Sarah Mapps Douglass, would join her mother in the abolitionist cause. Despite her comfortable life of privilege, Douglass and her daughter Sarah developed close ties with Lucretia Mott and Angelina and Sarah Grimké that led to the creation in 1833 of the

Philadelphia Female Anti-Slavery Society when they were denied membership in the male Anti-Slavery Society in Philadelphia. Douglass participated in the Anti-Slavery Convention of American Women. In 1837 and 1839, Douglass was elected vice president for the conventions.

Douglass died in 1842, a successful business-woman and philanthropist who helped to advance the abolitionist cause in America.

Sarah Mapps Douglass (1806–1882)
Abolitionist, Educator

The daughter of African American abolitionist Grace Bustill Douglass, Sarah Mapps Douglass was, like her mother, an active abolitionist as well as an educator whose paintings on her written letters are believed to be the first and earliest surviving examples of signed artwork by an African American woman.

Sarah Douglass was born in Philadelphia, the only daughter of Robert Douglass, a wealthy businessman, and Grace Bustill Douglass, who ran a successful milliner business. Her grandfather, Cyrus Bustill, was a founder of the Free African Society, which established one of the first schools for African American children. Raised in privilege, Douglass was mainly educated by private tutors before studying anatomy at the Female Medical College of Pennsylvania, becoming its first African American, female student, and the Ladies' Institute of Pennsylvania Medical University. In 1825, she began teaching in Philadelphia in a school organized by her mother, and in 1833, after teaching briefly at the Free African School for Girls, established her own school for African American girls, teaching sciences and arts. In 1838, the Philadelphia Female Anti-Slavery Society took over the school, retaining Douglass as the head. In 1854, the school merged with the Institute for Colored Youth (now Cheyney State University), and Douglass became the head of the primary school department, a position she held until her retirement in 1877. Douglass would pioneer the introduction of scientific subjects into the curriculum.

As an abolitionist and African American civil rights activist, Douglass help created the Female Literary Society, a group of African American women working to improve education and a sense of identity in the black community. It created the first social libraries specifically for African American women. With her mother, Douglass was a founding member of the biracial Philadelphia Female Anti-Slavery Society in 1833, dedicated to a total and immediate end to slavery. Describing the evolution of her activism, Douglass would write: "I had formed a little world of my own, and cared not to move beyond its precincts. But how was the scene changed when I beheld the oppressor lurking on the border of my peaceful home! I saw his iron hand stretched forth to seize me as his prey, and the cause of the slave became my own."

Crystal Eastman (1881–1928)
Attorney, Suffragist

 Lawyer, suffragist, journalist, and activist, Crystal Eastman was cofounder in 1917 of the National Civil Liberties Bureau, which would later become the ACLU, to fight government suppression of dissenters' rights during World War I.

Born in Marlborough, Massachusetts, Eastman was raised in upstate New York. Her mother, Annis Bertha Ford Eastman, was one of the first women ordained as a Protestant minister in America when she was ordained in 1889. Eastman graduated from Vassar College in 1903 and received a master's degree in sociology from Columbia University in 1904 before gaining her law degree from New York University, graduating second in her class in 1907.

The author of an influential report, "Work Accidents and the Law" (1907), Eastman was offered a position with the New York State Commission on Employer's Liability and Causes of Industrial Accidents, Unemployment and Lack of Farm Labor, working on health and safety laws in the workplace, including the first worker's compensation law. She also founded, with Alice Paul, Lucy Burns, and others, the Congressional Union in 1913, which became the National Woman's Party, that worked for the passage of the constitutional amendment giving women the right to vote. After passage of the Nineteenth Amendment in 1920, Eastman and Paul wrote the Equal Rights Amendment, which was first introduced in 1923. Eastman announced her support of the ERA and her assessment of where the women's struggle should now center in a rousing speech, "Now We Can Begin."

Lobbying against U.S. involvement in World War I, she joined the peace movement and led the New York branch of the Woman's Peace Party. Renamed the Women's International League of Peace and Freedom in 1921, it is the oldest extant women's peace organization. When the United States entered the war in 1917, Eastman organized with Roger Baldwin and Norman Thomas the National Civil Liberties Bureau to protect the rights of conscientious objectors or, in Eastman's words, "to maintain something over her that will be worth coming back to when the weary war is over." When the NCLB grew into the American Civil Liberties Union, Eastman served as its attorney-in-charge.

Eastman was once called the "most dangerous woman in America" for her outspoken nature and relentless devotion to causes that attacked the status quo. She has also been called one of the most neglected leaders in the United States, whose pioneering legislation and still active political organization she founded have impacted so many, but she has been too little credited for her sizable contributions.

Charlotte Forten (1837–1914)
Abolitionist, Educator

The first northern African American schoolteacher to go south to teach former slaves, Charlotte Forten was an abolitionist and educator whose five volumes of diaries, written before the beginning of the Civil War, is one of the only records of the life of a free black woman in the antebellum North.

Born in Philadelphia, Forten was the daughter of Robert Forten, who was a member of the Philadelphia Vigilance Committee, which provided assistance to escaped slaves. Forten went to school in Salem, Massachusetts, the only African American at the Higginson Grammar School, and entered the Salem Normal School (now Salem State University), a teacher-training school, from which she graduated in 1856. She began her teaching career in Salem,

the first African American ever hired at the Epoes Grammar School, an all-white institution.

A fervent abolitionist whose poetry was published in antislavery periodicals such as William Lloyd Garrison's *The Liberator*, Forten volunteered during the Civil War to travel to St. Helena Island in South Carolina, where the slave owners there abandoned their plantations and ten thousand slaves and the federal government set up schools for them. Forten spent two years there, chronicling her experiences in a long essay, "Life on the Sea Islands," that was published in the *Atlantic Monthly*.

Due to ill health, she returned to New England and served as secretary of the Boston branch of the Freedman's Union Commission, recruiting and training teachers of freed slaves. In 1878, at the age of forty-one, she married Francis James Grimké, the mixed-race nephew of the famous abolitionists Sarah and Angelina Grimké, a Presbyterian minister. Forten helped her husband in his ministry and in building up the African American community in Washington, D.C.

Best remembered today for her diaries that chronicle her life from 1854 to 1867, they provide an intimate look at an exceptional African American woman of her time. Notably, an entry from 1862 while teaching in South Carolina is one of the earliest references to "the blues" as a sad or depressed state of mind that was reflected in songs that were popular among the slaves that "can't be sung without a full heart and a troubled spirit." *The Journals of Charlotte Forten Grimké* were published in one volume in 1988.

Abby Kelley Foster (1811–1887)
Abolitionist, Social Reformer

A leading abolitionist and radical social reformer, Abby Kelley Foster was a central figure of the American Anti-Slavery Society, working closely with William Lloyd Garrison against slavery and, with her husband, fellow abolitionist Stephen Symonds Foster, advocated for equal rights for women. Abiding by the motto "Go where least wanted, for there you are most needed," Foster spent more than two decades traveling the country crusading for social justice and equality for all.

Born into a Quaker family in Pelham, Massachusetts, Foster was raised in Worcester, Massachusetts, and attended the New England Friends Boarding School in Providence, Rhode Island, interrupted by earning money to further her education by teaching. In 1829, she completed a final year of schooling and returned to Worcester to teach in local schools. In 1836, she moved to Lynn, Massachusetts, where fellow Quakers awakened in her the radical ideas of temperance, pacifism, and antislavery. She became a follower of William Lloyd Garrison and became secretary of the Lynn Female Anti-Slavery Society, founding with Garrison in 1838 the New England Non-Resistant Society. At the second woman's national antislavery convention, she made her first address to a mixed audience that proved so popular that she resigned her teaching job and in 1839 began a career as a reform lecturer. Denounced regularly as immoral for even daring to speak out, Foster endured harassment and sometimes mob violence. Her influence on women's activism was expressed by her successors being called Abby Kelleyites, and her version of radical abolitionism was labeled Abby Kelleyism.

In 1841, she resigned from the Quakers over their refusal to allow antislavery speakers in meetinghouses. As a woman, she faced fierce denunciation about her activism and appearing on stage with ex-slaves. "I rejoice to be identified with the despised people of color," she remarked. "If they are despised, so ought their advocates be."

Foster would influence future suffragists such as Susan B. Anthony and Lucy Stone by her example of political activism. She helped to organize and was a key speaker at the first National Women's Rights Convention in Worcester, Massachusetts, in 1850. In 1868, she was among the organizers of the founding convention of the New England Woman Suffrage Association, the first regional association advocating women's suffrage. After the Civil War, Foster supported the passage of the Fifteenth Amendment, granting voting rights to African Americans, and split with Anthony and Elizabeth Cady Stanton, who opposed the amendment because it did not include women's suffrage. After the

amendment passed, Foster worked for equal rights for both African Americans and women. In 1872, she and her husband refused to pay taxes on their jointly owned farm, arguing that since Foster could not vote, she was a victim of taxation without representation. The farm was seized and sold, repurchased for them by friends. They would continue the same protest two more times with the same result. Ill health caused Foster to suspend her public appearances, but she continued to write letters to fellow radicals and political figures on behalf of their cause until her death in 1887.

Foster was a trailblazer, not only instrumental in helping to end slavery and laying the groundwork for women's voting rights but as a highly visible, outspoken reformer at a time when women had rarely taken such an activist role.

Matilda Joslyn Gage (1826–1898)
Suffragist

Women's rights advocate Matilda Josyln Gage helped to lead and popularize the women's suffrage movement in the United States. Best known as coauthor with Elizabeth Cady Stanton and Susan B. Anthony of the first three volumes of the *History of Woman Suffrage*, Gage was one of the earliest radical feminist thinkers and historians.

As she stated, Gage was "born with a hatred for oppression" in Cicero, New York, into a committed antislavery family. Her father, Dr. Hezekiah Joslyn, was a nationally known abolitionist, and their home was a station on the Underground Railroad. In 1845, she married merchant Henry Hill Gage, with whom they had four children. Their home in Fayetteville, New York, was also a station on the Underground Railroad. Although raised in the antislavery movement, Gage would devote her life to a new cause: women's suffrage.

Gage began her public career as a lecturer at the women's rights convention in Syracuse, New York, in 1852 and was the youngest speaker present. From then on, Gage was tireless in support of the cause as a speaker and a writer who was called "one of the most logical, fearless and scientific writers of her day." From 1878 to 1881, she published and edited the *National Citizen,* a newspaper dedicated to women's causes. More radical than either Susan B. Anthony or Elizabeth Cady Stanton, Gage argued that women deserved the vote not because their feminine morality would then properly influence government, as Anthony and Stanton argued, but as a "natural right." A vocal critic of the Christian Church for its resistance to women's rights, Gage also antagonized other suffragists such as Frances Willard and members of the Woman's Christian Temperance Union. Gage became one of the founders of the National Woman Suffrage Association, serving in various offices of the organization from 1869 to 1889. In 1871, Gage joined Susan B. Anthony and other women to test the law by attempting to vote. Gage's writings include *Woman as Inventor* (1870), *Women's Rights Catechism* (1871), and *The Dangers of the Hour* (1890). With Stanton, Gage coauthored the *Declaration of Rights for Women* (1876).

In 1890, in response to the NWSA's merger with the more conservative American Woman Suffrage Association, Gage left the organization to found the Woman's National Liberal Union to advocate on behalf of the separation of church and state and to criticize the established churches as a bulwark of male supremacist teaching, positions she outlined in *Woman, Church, and State* (1893). Gage died in 1898 and was buried in Fayetteville with a tombstone that reads, "There is a word sweeter than Mother, Home or Heaven. That word is Liberty."

In 1993, a scientific historian coined the term "Matilda effect" after Gage to describe when women scientists receive less credit for their scientific work than they deserve. The term is a fitting tribute to an important, though widely overlooked and underappreciated, champion of women's rights in America.

Mary Grew (1813–1896)
Abolitionist, Suffragist

An early antislavery activist, Mary Grew was also a pioneering crusader for women's suffrage.

Grew was born in Hartford, Connecticut, but raised in Boston and Philadelphia. Her father, Henry Grew, was an esteemed abolitionist religious writer, and Mary followed his example in support of the cause in the Boston and Philadelphia Female Anti-Slavery Society. Grew's correspondence with Maria Weston Chapman concerning women's antislavery activities led to the first Anti-Slavery Convention of American Women in New York in 1837. Grew traveled with her father to the World Anti-Slavery Convention in 1840 in London, where her father sided with the British organizers in excluding women delegates and was on the opposite side of the issue as Lucretia Mott and others. Eventually, women were allowed into the convention, but they were not allowed to speak and had to sit separately from the men. Despite the humiliation for Mary, who had traveled to London to participate actively, and the other women, the event proved to be galvanizing, linking antislavery activism with women's rights and suffrage. Based on their shared experience of ostracism at the convention, Elizabeth Cady Stanton and Lucretia Mott, with Grew's assistance, began planning the Seneca Falls Convention, which eventually took place in 1848.

Grew would come to devote her focus to gaining women the right to vote. Chosen as president of the Pennsylvania Woman Suffrage Association in 1870, she served for over two decades until ill health prompted her to retire in 1892. Grew died twenty-four years before women would achieve the goal that she labored so long to make possible.

Angelina Grimké (1805–1879)
Sarah Grimké (1792–1873)
Abolitionists, Women's Rights Activists

The daughters of a wealthy, southern slave owner, the Grimké sisters were among the first American women to speak out publicly against slavery.

While growing up in Charleston, South Carolina, Sarah and Angelina Grimké became increasingly appalled by the cruelty of slavery. Sarah, who taught in a Sunday school for slaves, defied state law by teaching her pupils to read. In 1819, while visiting Philadelphia, she became impressed by the Quakers, and two years later, she shocked her family by moving there to join their sect. In 1829, Angelina went to Philadelphia as well and joined the Philadelphia Female Anti-Slavery Society, writing a letter of support to the famed abolitionist William Lloyd Garrison. The unexpected publication of the letter in Garrison's newspaper, *The Liberator*, publicly identified Angelina with the abolitionist cause. In 1836, she published an antislavery pamphlet that was destroyed by southern postmasters.

Animosity toward Angelina became so strong in the South that she was warned not to return to Charleston. At the request of the American Anti-Slavery Society, she moved to New York City to conduct meetings for women interested in the abolitionist cause. Sarah broke with the Quakers over their discriminatory treatment of African Americans at meetings and their refusal to let her speak on behalf of black members and joined her sister in New York. They toured the North, lecturing on abolitionism, and caused a sensation when they spoke to "mixed" audiences of men and women at large, public meetings. In 1837, after the Congregational churches denounced their behavior as "unwomanly" and "unnatural," the sisters turned their activism toward women's rights. They both wrote strong pamphlets asserting the right of women to speak out on moral and social issues and to have a voice in the establishment of laws.

In 1838, Angelina married antislavery activist and noted orator Theodore Weld. In 1839, the Grimkés published *American Slavery As It Is: Testimony of a Thousand Witnesses,* which would become a major source for Harriet Beecher Stowe while she was writing *Uncle Tom's Cabin.* By 1840, the Grimké sisters had largely retired from public life. Angelina was frequently ill, and Sarah helped to raise her three children. In the 1850s, the Welds and Sarah Grimké lived in New Jersey, where they ran a girls' boarding school. In 1862, they settled in the Boston area, where they taught at a girls' school. In 1868, the sisters learned that their brother had fathered two sons by a slave. They welcomed both young men into their home and gave them aid and encouragement. Their nephews, Archibald Henry Grimké and Freeman Jones Grimké, would go on to become prominent civil rights activists and spokesmen for African Americans.

Frances E. W. Harper (1825–1911)
Abolitionist, Social Reformer

 African American abolitionist and social reformer Frances Harper was a prolific author who published collections of poetry and whose novel, *Iola Leroy; or, Shadows Uplifted* (1894), was the most popular work of fiction by an African American in the nineteenth century.

Born Frances Watkins, she was the daughter of free black parents, orphaned at the age of three, and raised in Baltimore in the home of an uncle, whose school for black children she attended. At the age of thirteen, she went to work as a domestic in a Quaker household, where she had access to a wide range of literature. In 1845, she published her first collection of poems, *Forest Leaves*, when she was twenty. In 1850, she moved to Ohio to teach sewing and domestic skills at Union Seminary, a school run by abolitionist John Brown. In 1853, she joined the American Anti-Slavery Society and became a traveling lecturer for the group. Her first speech, "Education and the Elevation of Colored Race," was so popular that it led to a two-year lecture tour of Maine. She would continue to lecture throughout the East and Midwest from 1856 to 1860. Harper's story "The Two Offers" was published in 1859, making her the first black woman in America to publish a short story.

Harper became an outspoken supporter of abolitionism, Prohibition, and women's suffrage. In 1858, one hundred years before Rosa Parks, Harper refused to give up her seat or ride in the "colored" section of a Philadelphia trolley car. In 1866, she was a featured speaker at the National Women's Rights Convention, saying, "You white women speak here of rights. I speak of wrongs. I, as a colored woman, have had in this country an education which has made me feel as if I were in the situation of Ishmael, my hand against every man, and every man's hand against me.… I tell you that if there is any class of people who need to be lifted out of their airy nothings and selfishness, it is the white women of America." From 1883 to 1890, Harper was an important organizer for the National Woman's Christian Temperance Union, working with Frances Willard and others for racial and gender equality. Disappointed when Willard gave priority to white women's concerns, Harper, with Mary Church Terrell, founded the National Association of Colored Women in 1894 and served as its vice president in 1897.

The final stanza of one of Harper's best and most admired poems, "Bury Me in a Free Land," is a fitting testimony to a life of activism and accomplishment:

> I ask no monument, proud and high,
> To arrest the gaze of the passers-by;
> All that my yearning spirit craves,
> Is bury me not in a land of slaves.

Ida Husted Harper (1851–1931)

Journalist, Suffragist

Journalist and suffragist Ida Husted Harper was the authorized biographer of Susan B. Anthony, who also coedited and collaborated with Anthony on volume four of the *History of Woman Suffrage* and wrote on her own the final volumes five and six. Harper's many newspaper columns and magazine articles are indispensable for tracing the history of the women's rights struggle from the 1870s through the 1920s.

Born Ida Husted in Fairfield, Indiana, Harper finished high school at the age of seventeen and entered Indiana University as a sophomore. She left after only a year to become principal of a high school in Peru, Indiana. Soon after her marriage to lawyer Thomas Winans Harper in 1871, Harper worked for twelve years for the Terre Haute *Saturday Evening Mail* using a male pseudonym. In 1883, she launched a weekly column, "A Woman's Opinion," under her own name.

Harper met Susan B. Anthony in 1878, and they soon became friends and colleagues. In 1889, she began to work at the Terre Haute *Daily News,* becoming its managing editor, the first instance of a woman occupying that position on a daily newspaper. In 1896, she took charge of the press relations for the campaign by the National American Woman Suffrage Association for a state suffrage amendment in California. In 1897, Anthony asked Harper to write her official biography, and Harper moved into Anthony's home in Rochester, New York, to research what would eventually become the three-volume *The Life and Work of Susan B. Anthony* (1898, 1908). She also collaborated with Anthony and completed the *History of Woman Suffrage* (1902). Harper's magazine articles and columns in *Harper's Bazaar* were important in gaining support in the successful campaign of the Nineteenth Amendment.

Harper died in Washington, D.C., at the age of seventy-nine in 1931, having documented and formed popular opinion during the crucial years of the struggle for women's rights.

Jane Hunt (1812–1889)

Abolitionist, Suffragist

Quaker abolitionist, philanthropist, and suffrage supporter, Jane Hunt is best known for hosting the tea party that brought Lucretia Mott to Seneca Falls, New York, and led to the first organized meeting about women's rights, the Seneca Falls Convention, in 1848.

Born Jane Clothier Master in Philadelphia into a Quaker family, Hunt married fellow Quaker Richard Pell Hunt, a prominent local businessman and wealthy landowner. They moved to Waterloo, New York, in 1845, where their house became a station of the Underground Railroad, and the couple supported various progressive causes, including the women's rights movement. Hunt opposed the restriction of women's membership in the Quaker community and worked to end the official inequality between men's and women's meetings.

In 1848, Hunt invited the reformer Lucretia Mott to join a group of other women, including Elizabeth Cady Stanton and Mary Ann M'Clintock, to her home for tea. Mott and Stanton had met eight years before at the World Anti-Slavery Convention in London. As the women drank tea, Stanton expressed her frustration about women's subservient place in society. Women could neither vote nor own property, and few social or intellectual opportunities were open to them. The women decided to hold a women's rights convention, drafting a brief notice that read: "Woman's Rights Convention—A Convention to discuss the social, civic and religious condition and rights of Woman will be held in the Wesleyan Methodist Chapel at Seneca Falls, N.Y. on Wednesday and Thursday, the 19th and 20th of July...." The notice was posted in the *Seneca County Courier* with only eight days' notice until the convention, which was largely financed by Jane and Richard Hunt. Three hundred women and forty-two men attended, and the American women's rights movement began.

Richard Hunt died in 1856, leaving Jane a wealthy widow with six children. She would continue the family tradition of philanthropy and support for progressive causes and social reform, living in the family home in Waterloo until her death on a visit to her daughter in Chicago in 1889 at the age of seventy-seven.

Mary Ann M'Clintock (1795–1884)

Abolitionist, Suffragist

One of the five women who met for tea at the home of Jane Hunt, whose conversation on women's rights led to the first Women's Rights Convention at Seneca Falls, New York, in 1848, Mary Ann M'Clintock was involved in the abolition and temperance movements, and her organizing skills were crucial in the success of the convention and the women's movement that it ignited.

Born Mary Ann Wilson in Burlington, New Jersey, into a Quaker family, M'Clintock attended West-town School in 1814 for a year before marrying Thomas M'Clintock and moving to Philadelphia. Raising five children, M'Clintock was active in the antislavery movement in Philadelphia and was one of the founding members of its antislavery society, working closely with fellow abolitionist Lucretia Mott. In 1836, her family moved to Waterloo, New York, where the M'Clintocks were active in several social reform movements, including abolition and temperance. They offered their home to fugitive slaves as a station on the Underground Railroad, became founding members of the Western New York Anti-Slavery Society, and raised money for Irish famine relief and for the poor around Waterloo.

After the Quaker service on Sunday, July 9, 1848, M'Clintock joined neighbor Elizabeth Cady Stanton, the visiting Lucretia Mott, and Martha Wright, Mott's sister, at the Waterloo home of Jane Hunt for tea. Expressing their collective discontent with women's place in American society, they organized the first women's rights convention in the United States, which was to be held in Seneca Falls, New York. The following Sunday, M'Clintock hosted a planning session at her house, and at the meeting, M'Clintock joined Elizabeth Cady Stanton in drafting the Declaration of Sentiments at the kitchen table. Modeled after the Declaration of Independence, the document asserting that "all men and women are created equal" would become a founding statement of principles for the women's movement in America. At the convention, M'Clintock served as secretary and recruited her Quaker friends to attend. As one remarked, "I think without exception that every member [of the Waterloo Quaker meeting] was present."

M'Clintock continued to be actively involved in the women's movement she had helped to start, credited by Elizabeth Cady Stanton with supplying much-needed organizational skills. In 1856, Thomas and Mary Ann M'Clintock left Waterloo and returned to Philadelphia, where Mary Ann died in 1884.

Inez Milholland (1886–1916)

Attorney, Suffragist

A suffragist and labor lawyer, Inez Milholland was active in the National Woman's Party and led the infamous 1913 suffrage parade in Washington, D.C., riding a white horse and wearing a crown and white cape through crowds of drunken and jeering men, symbols of both defiance and inspiration.

Born in Brooklyn, New York, Milholland grew up in a wealthy family in New York and London. In England, Milholland met English suffragette Emmeline Pankhurst, and she began her involvement in social reform causes of world peace, civil rights, and women's suffrage. She attended Vassar College and was suspended for organizing a women's rights meeting. The college president, James Monroe Taylor, opposed any discussion of women's suffrage on campus and considered it "propaganda" that students needed to be protected from hearing. Milholland organized a suffrage meeting of about fifty-six people in a small cemetery adjacent to the college. In 1909, in her senior year, she persuaded President Taylor to allow a suffrage debate if no faculty were to speak. When they did so in support of women's suffrage, Taylor reaffirmed his ban on public speaking on suffrage. Milholland responded by staging a series of silent, living tableaux on behalf of the cause.

After graduation, she made her first appearance as a suffrage orator, stopping a New York campaign parade for President William Howard Taft by speaking through a megaphone from a window in a building along the parade route. It would be the beginning of her reputation as one of the most powerful and persuasive orators in the suffrage movement. Rejected because of her gender from law schools at Yale, Harvard, and Columbia, Milholland eventually earned her law degree from New York University in 1912. In the mayhem that marked the 1913 suffrage parade in Washington, D.C., that she led, violence broke out, and police were called in to restore order. After the demonstration, Milholland was described as the "most beautiful woman ever to bite a policeman's wrist."

Although she would continue speaking on behalf of suffrage, she worked for prison reform, world peace, and equality for African Americans as a member of the NAACP, the Women's Trade Union League, the National Child Labor Committee, the National American Woman Suffrage Association, and the National Woman's Party. In 1913, she married Dutch businessman Eugen Jan Boissevain, thereby losing her U.S. citizenship and the right to

take advantage of the vote for women she worked so fervently to achieve.

Milholland was the most popular and in-demand speaker in the women's movement. Suffering from pernicious anemia, her doctor warned her of the dangers of vigorous campaigning, but she refused to heed his advice. She collapsed in the middle of a speech in Los Angeles in 1916 and died. After her death, she was regarded as a martyr to the cause, and a popular poster of the day stated: "Inez Milholland Boissevain: Who Died for the Freedom of Women."

Lucretia Mott (1793–1880)
Abolitionist, Women's Rights Activist

A Quaker minister, abolitionist, and pioneer in the fight for women's rights, Lucretia Mott was born on Nantucket, an island off the coast of Massachusetts. She was the second of the seven children of a Quaker sea captain and a mother who kept a shop that sold goods her husband brought from East India.

The men of Nantucket were frequently away on sea voyages for months at a time, and the women oversaw the community's religious and business affairs in their absence. Mott would later recall that she grew up "so thoroughly imbued with women's rights that it was the most important question of my life from a very early day." Mott was educated at private and public schools in Boston, where her family had moved in 1804. At thirteen, she was sent to Nine Partners, a Quaker boarding school in Poughkeepsie, New York. Two years later, she became an unpaid assistant teacher at the school. The fact that even experienced female teachers were paid much less than male teachers impressed Mott with the need to change "the unequal condition of women."

In 1809, her family moved to Philadelphia. There, in 1811, she married James Mott, a former teacher at Nine Partners, who had taken a job in her father's hardware business. The couple had six children, one of whom, their firstborn son, died in infancy. A grieving Mott turned to her religion for comfort. By 1818, she was preaching at Quaker meetings, and in 1821, she was officially recognized as a minister.

By 1823, Mott had become involved in the abolitionist movement. In 1833, she founded and became president of the Philadelphia Female Anti-Slavery Society. She later joined the American Anti-Slavery Society when that organization began to admit women and served on its executive committee. Mott's activism turned to women's rights after she and other female representatives of the American Anti-Slavery Society, including Elizabeth Cady Stanton, were denied seats at the 1840 World Anti-Slavery Convention in London. In 1848, Mott and Stanton organized the first women's rights convention in Seneca Falls, New York. It would become the catalyst for an organized women's movement in the United States. In 1850, Mott published *Discourse on Women,* one of the pioneering American works arguing for women's equality. Mott also continued to advance the cause of black emancipation. In the 1850s, she and her husband harbored runaway slaves in their home. After slavery was abolished, Mott worked with organizations to provide economic aid for African Americans.

In 1866, she became president of the American Equal Rights Association, a group dedicated to women's suffrage, and in 1880, after more than fifty years of activism, Mott died at her country home outside Philadelphia. Like the other great founding sisters of the women's rights movement such as Elizabeth Cady Stanton and Susan B. Anthony, Mott would not live to see the result of her activism with the passage of the Nineteenth Amendment, giving women the right to vote in 1920, but the necessary preliminary work that made passage possible directly resulted from the organization and activism of Lucretia Mott.

Alice Paul (1885–1977)

Suffragist

Suffragist Alice Paul was instrumental in helping to lead the final push for a constitutional amendment guaranteeing women the right to vote. Unlike Carrie Chapman Catt, Paul took a much more militant approach to obtaining the right to vote for women, including organizing massive street demonstrations, which led to her arrest and imprisonment on several occasions.

Born in Moorestown, New Jersey, Paul was the oldest of four children in a well-to-do Quaker family. Her mother was a suffragist, and one of Paul's earliest memories was of accompanying her mother to a suffrage meeting. Paul attended Quaker schools in Moorestown before going on to Swarthmore College, graduating with a degree in biology in 1905. She studied in the New York School of Philanthropy and went on to earn a master's degree and a Ph.D. in sociology from the University of Pennsylvania.

In 1907, Paul went to England, where she became involved in the British suffrage movement, joining suffragettes in their demonstrations. She was repeatedly arrested and participated in prison hunger strikes. After returning to the United States in 1910, she continued to fight for women's suffrage, serving as chair of the Congressional Committee of the National American Woman Suffrage Association (NAWSA). However, Paul and several other committee members disagreed on strategy with NAWSA's president, Carrie Chapman Catt. In 1913, they formed their own group, the Congressional Union for Women Suffrage, and adopted more defiant tactics than NAWSA to obtain their goals.

On March 3, 1913, the eve of Woodrow Wilson's inauguration as president, Paul led more than five thousand women in a march in Washington, D.C., to press for adoption of a women's suffrage amendment. The demonstration provoked violent reactions from crowds of male onlookers; many women were hospitalized, and armed troops had to restore order. The consequence of the demonstration was an outpouring of national sympathy for the suffrage cause.

In 1916, Paul helped form the National Women's Party to work for the passage of the Nineteenth Amendment, which was finally ratified in 1920. Paul then began a crusade for an Equal Rights Amendment, which she authored in 1923 and then introduced to Congress that year. Paul also headed the Women's Research Foundation from 1927 to 1937, and in the 1930s, she helped found the World Woman's Party. In the 1940s, she was instrumental in seeing that the Charter of the United Nations included references to gender equality. Paul would campaign for the Equal Rights Amendment for nearly fifty years. In 1972, the ERA passed Congress and went to the states for ratification. By 1977, the year of Paul's death, the amendment needed only three more states for adoption. However, it ultimately failed ratification by the 1982 deadline.

Ernestine Rose (1810–1892)

Abolitionist, Suffragist

An antislavery activist, suffragist, and orator, Ernestine Rose is celebrated for her pioneering role in first-wave feminism.

Born Ernestine Potowski in the Jewish quarter of Piotkrow in Russian Poland, Rose was the only child of a rabbi. She received an unusual education for a female child of that time and place, which included the study of the scriptures in Hebrew. While growing up, she began to question her father on religious matters, which elicited the response from him that, unlike little boys, who were trained to question such matters, "Little girls should not ask questions." By the age of fourteen, Rose had rejected both the idea that women were inferior to men and the religious beliefs that supported that notion. At sixteen, after her mother died, she refused to marry the man her father had chosen for her and brought her case before the civil court rather than to the rabbinic authorities, a daring act at that time. The court ruled in her favor and allowed her to recover the inheritance her mother had left to her. Rose returned most of the money to her father and took only what she needed to leave Poland.

After traveling to Prussia, where she found that Jews were unwelcome, Rose lived in Holland, Belgium, and France. She went to England in 1832, where she met Robert Dale Owen, a utopian socialist with whom she cofounded the Association of All Classes of All Nations. Her speeches at the association's meetings began to earn her a reputation as a brilliant orator. In 1835, she married William Ella Rose, a jeweler and fellow Owenite, in a civil ceremony, and in 1836, the couple settled in New York. Called the "Queen of the Platform" for her extemporaneous and eloquent speeches on religious freedom, public education, abolition, and women's rights, Rose lectured frequently in New York and nearby states and is credited with raising the issue of women's suffrage in Michigan. She also traveled to the South, where she confronted a slaveholder who vowed he would have her tarred and feathered if she were not a woman.

Ernestine Rose attended and played a major role in nearly every New York and national antislavery and women's rights convention, working closely with such women's rights campaigners as Elizabeth Cady Stanton, Lucretia Mott, and Sojourner Truth, and toured with Susan B. Anthony, who adopted Rose's slogan, "Agitate, agitate." In 1854, she was elected president of the National Women's Rights Convention despite objections that she was an atheist. However, her candidacy was vigorously supported by Susan B. Anthony, who declared, "Every religion—or none—should have an equal right on the platform." Although Rose had abandoned Jewish religious practices, she was quick to condemn anti-Semitism, as in one case in which the editor of the *Boston Investigator*, a magazine for which Rose often wrote, attacked the Jewish people. Rose responded with a strenuous critique of anti-Semitism and a defense of Jews based on their historical contributions to secular as well as religious culture.

In 1869, after fifteen years' work, Rose, together with Stanton, was successful in securing New York legislation allowing married women to retain their own property and have equal guardianship of children. In 1883, the year after Rose's husband died while the couple was living in England, Susan B. Anthony and Elizabeth Cady Stanton traveled to London in an unsuccessful attempt to convince Rose to return to the United States.

Ernestine Rose continued to work for social justice until her death in Brighton, England, at the age of eighty-two.

Anna Howard Shaw (1847–1919)

Suffragist

A leader of the women's suffrage movement, a physician, and one of the first ordained Methodist ministers in the United States, Anna Howard Shaw was born in Newcastle-upon-Tyne in England. In 1851, she moved with her family to the United States, where her father started farming in an isolated frontier area near Big Rapids, Michigan. By the age of twelve, her father's absences, her mother's nervous breakdown, and her elder brother's illness forced Shaw to undertake the tasks of clearing the land, planting crops, finishing the building of their cabin, and caring for the family.

Shaw received a year or two of formal schooling, which she supplemented with reading on her own, and at the age of fifteen became a teacher in a frontier schoolhouse, a job that was not unusual for teenage girls at the time. During the late 1860s, she moved to Big Rapids, where she lived with her married sister and attended high school. Shaw became active in the Methodist Church, preaching her first sermon in 1870. From 1873 to 1875, she studied at Albion College in Michigan, and in 1878, she graduated from the divinity school at Boston University, the only woman in her class. While leading the Methodist congregation in East Dennis, Massachusetts, she applied to the New England Conference of the Methodist Church and the General Conference for Ordination and was denied because she was a woman and could not administer the sacraments. The General Conference revoked her license to preach. However, she was finally ordained in 1880 as the first woman minister of the Methodist Protestant Church. While ministering to her East Dennis congregation, she studied medicine at Boston University, earning her medical degree in 1886.

Shaw resigned her ministry to focus full-time on the causes of suffrage and temperance. When Susan B. Anthony became president of the newly formed National American Woman Suffrage Association in 1892, Shaw became the organization's vice president. She served as president of the NAWSA from 1904 to 1915. She was a familiar presence at suffrage demonstrations, conventions, congressional hearings, and lectures, where she spoke on suffrage in every state of the Union. Shaw also performed war work on the home front during World War I, for which she received the Distinguished Service Medal in 1919. Afterward, her intention was to return to the lecture circuit to speak on behalf of the pending suffrage amendment, but former president William Howard Taft and Harvard president A. Lawrence Lowell asked her to use her oratorical skills to speak in favor of President Woodrow Wilson's League of Nations proposal instead. In the middle of a highly successful speaking tour, the ailing Shaw fell ill with pneumonia and died not long after at her home in Moylan, Pennsylvania, at the age of seventy-two.

Elizabeth Cady Stanton (1815–1902)

Suffragist

One of the most prominent figures in the fight for women's rights in the nineteenth century, Elizabeth Cady Stanton was heading the campaign to gain equality for American women and worked to gain for women the right to vote.

Born in Johnstown, New York, where her father was a prominent attorney, Stanton learned about her father's cases when she was young and overheard stories of married women who, because of the laws of the times, could not own property, sue for divorce, or retain custody of their children after a divorce. These injustices so angered the young Stanton that she threatened to cut those specific laws from her father's law books.

After graduating from Emma Willard's Troy Female Academy, she studied law with her father and became involved with the abolitionist movement. In 1840, she met antislavery activist Henry Stanton, and they married that year. During their marriage, they had six children, one of whom, Harriot Stanton Blatch, become one of the early twentieth century's most noted women's activists. On their honeymoon, the Stantons attended the World Anti-Slavery Convention in London, where Stanton met Lucretia

Mott, one of the delegates. Stanton became determined to fight for women's rights after learning that women delegates would not be allowed to speak at the convention.

In 1848, Stanton and Mott organized the first women's rights convention in Seneca Falls, New York. A highlight of the convention was Stanton's Declaration of Rights and Sentiments, modeled on the Declaration of Independence, in which Stanton stated, "We hold these truths to be self-evident, that all men and women are created equal" and called for property rights for women, equal pay for equal work, and the first public demand for the vote for women. The convention would become the first great event in American women's history, and the Declaration of Rights and Sentiments became the founding document of the women's movement.

In 1851, Stanton met Susan B. Anthony at an antislavery lecture. The two women joined forces in the interest of women's rights, temperance, and abolition of slavery. During the Civil War, they formed the Women's Loyal National League to support the Thirteenth Amendment ending slavery. In 1869, they founded the National Woman Suffrage Association to lobby for a constitutional amendment giving women the right to vote. They also collaborated on the first volume of the *History of Woman Suffrage* and, although neither lived to see ratification in 1920 of the Nineteenth Amendment, granting women the right to vote, Stanton rightly believed that they had laid the groundwork for such an amendment.

When Elizabeth Cady Stanton died in 1902, she was recognized as the founding figure of the American women's rights movement.

Maria W. Stewart (1803–1879)

Abolitionist, Women's Rights Activist

A domestic servant who became a teacher, journalist, lecturer, abolitionist, and women's rights activist, Maria W. Stewart is believed to be the first known American woman to speak publicly to a mixed audience of men and women as well as the first African American woman to deliver public lectures speaking out against slavery and on behalf of women's rights.

Born Maria Miller, the daughter of free African American parents in Hartford, Connecticut, Stewart went to live with a minister and his family after both her parents died. She would work for the family as a servant until she was fifteen without receiving any formal education but taking advantage of the family's extensive library. Leaving the family, she supported herself as a domestic servant and completed her education at Sabbath schools. Moving to Boston, Stewart married James W. Stewart in 1826, becoming part of Boston's small free, black, middle-class community. When he died in 1829, she was left with a sizable inheritance, but she was defrauded of it by white executors of her husband's will and was forced to return to domestic service to support herself.

Stewart answered a call by abolitionist publisher William Lloyd Garrison for writings by black women, and she supplied several essays to Garrison's *The Liberator* on religion, racism, and slavery. She also began public speaking at a time when biblical injunctions against women teaching were interpreted as prohibiting women from speaking in public. Scottish-born Frances Wright created a scandal by speaking in public in 1828, and Stewart would become the first American-born public woman lecturer in 1832. Her first address, to a group of women at the African American Female Intelligence Society, advocated activism for social equality. Her second lecture, to a mixed audience, questioned whether free blacks were much more free than slaves in America given the lack of opportunity and equality they had. Garrison published her writing in the "Ladies Department" of *The Liberator* as well as in pamphlet form.

Stewart's public-speaking career lasted three years before she moved to New York in 1833, where she supported herself teaching in public schools in Manhattan and Brooklyn, becoming the principal of the Williamsburg School. She moved to Baltimore around 1853, teaching privately, then to Washington, D.C., where she taught during the Civil War in a school she established for children of families that had escaped from slavery during the war. In 1870, she was appointed head matron at the Freedman's Hospital and Asylum in Washington, a position formerly held by Sojourner Truth. She died in the hospital in which she worked in 1879. Stewart's essays and speeches are pioneering works on African American and women's rights that predate those of Frederick Douglass and Sojourner Truth.

Lucy Stone (1818–1893)
Abolitionist, Suffragist

Abolitionist and suffragist Lucy Stone was the first woman from Massachusetts to earn a college degree and helped initiate the first National Women's Rights Convention in Worcester, Massachusetts, in 1850. She influenced Susan B. Anthony to take up the cause of women's suffrage and was called by Elizabeth Cady Stanton "the first person by whom the hearty of the American public was deeply stirred on the woman question."

Born in rural Massachusetts into a farming family, Stone resisted the restrictions placed on her as a girl and by the biblical passages that suggested a divine sanction for women's subjugation. She early on resolved to "call no man my master" and went to work as a teacher to save money so she could attend college. After a semester at Mount Holyoke, she would graduate from Oberlin College in 1847. She declined an invitation to write a commencement speech that would be read by a man. With few employment options available to her, she was hired by abolitionist William Lloyd Garrison to work for his American Anti-Slavery Society, and she wrote and delivered abolitionist speeches and was often heckled and at least once physically attacked by a mob who disapproved of a woman lecturer.

In 1850, two years after the Seneca Falls Women's Rights Convention, Stone organized the first national Women's Rights Convention in Worcester, Massachusetts. For the next five years, she traveled throughout the United States on the lecture circuit. In 1855, she agreed to marry Henry Blackwell, the brother of physician Elizabeth Blackwell, and Stone daringly retained her maiden name after her marriage. In 1858, Stone and her husband refused to pay their property tax as "taxation without representation." She was prosecuted, and their household goods were seized and sold. At the end of the Civil War, Stone went to Kansas to work on the referendum for suffrage there. In 1868, Stone broke with suffragists Elizabeth Cady Stanton and Susan B. Anthony over their objection to the passage of the Fourteenth and Fifteenth Amendments to the Constitution, which granted voting rights to black men but not to women. Stone was willing to accept the measure as an abolitionist goal and continue to work for women's suffrage. When Stanton and Anthony formed the National Woman Suffrage Association, Stone, Julia Ward Howe, and others formed the American Woman Suffrage Association until the reunification of the two groups in 1890.

Stone gave her last public speech at the World's Congress of Representative Women in Chicago in 1893. Her speech, "The Progress of Fifty Years," provided both a summation of the progress of the women's movement and Stone's own contributions. "I think," she stated, "that the young women of today do not and can never know at what price their right to free speech and to speak at all in public has been earned." When she died in 1893 at the age of seventy-five, at her request, she was cremated, the first person cremated in Massachusetts. Women who continue to use their birth name after marriage are still occasionally called "Lucy Stoners" based on her pioneering example.

Mary Church Terrell (1863–1954)
Civil Rights Activist, Women's Rights Activist

The cofounder and first president of the National Association of Colored Women, Mary Church Terrell was a pioneering civil rights advocate, educator, author, and lecturer on women's suffrage and rights for African American women.

The daughter of former slaves, Terrell was born in Memphis, Tennessee. Her father was a successful businessman who became one of the South's first African American millionaires. Terrell attended Antioch College Model School in Yellow Springs, Ohio, for elementary and secondary school before entering Oberlin College, where she became one of the first African American women to graduate, earning both her bachelor's and master's degrees. She spent two years teaching at Wilberforce College, a historically black college in Ohio, before moving to Washington, D.C., where she joined the faculty teaching Latin at the M Street Colored High School (now Dunbar High School). When she married Robert Heberton Terrell, chairman of the school's language department, she was forced to resign since married women could not work as teachers.

In 1892, Terrell learned that Thomas Moss, a close friend from Memphis, had been lynched, and after Terrell and Frederick Douglass's appeal to President Benjamin Harrison failed to elicit a public condemnation, she formed the Colored Women's League in Washington to address social problems facing black communities. Four years later, Terrell helped create the National Association of Colored Women with its motto, "Lifting as We Climb." She served as president from 1896 to 1901, becoming a well-known speaker and writer. She supported the women's suffrage movement, even though some tried to exclude black women from the cause. She was the author of scholarly articles, poems, and short stories on race and gender and in 1940 produced her autobiography, *A Colored Woman in a White World,* chronicling her struggle with both gender and racial discrimination.

After World War II, Terrell fought to end legal segregation in Washington, D.C., and she lived to see the Supreme Court rule that segregation in public schools was unconstitutional. She died two months after that decision at the age of ninety.

Sojourner Truth (c. 1797–1883)
Abolitionist, Women's Rights Activist

 An illiterate ex-slave and preacher, Sojourner Truth became one of the nineteenth century's most important African Americans in both the abolitionist and women's movements and one of the most inspiring American women in U.S. history.

Born on a farm in the Hudson River Valley area of New York, Truth was the ninth child of slaves James and Betsey Bomefree. Her slave name was Is-abella, and as a child, she was sold to several owners in the area. At fourteen, she married an older slave named Thomas. The couple had five children, although Truth later claimed to have borne thirteen children. In 1826, a year before New York State law abolished slavery, she ran away from her owner and found refuge with a Quaker family, the Van Wageners, whose name she took. While working for them, she discovered that her son had been illegally sold into slavery in Alabama. She went to court in Kingston, New York, and successfully sued for his return.

In the early 1830s, Truth moved to New York City, where she worked as a domestic servant and joined the Magdelene Society, a Methodist missionary organization. In 1843, Truth experienced a calling to become a wandering preacher, changing her name to Sojourner Truth, left home with a quarter and a new dress, and began to travel throughout New York and Connecticut, preaching and singing at camp meetings and churches. She visited Northampton, Massachusetts, where she met abolitionist leader William Lloyd Garrison, who persuaded her to publish her life story. *The Narrative of Sojourner Truth* (1850) was one of the first accounts of the life of a woman slave. The book exposed the evils of slavery and became a powerful weapon in the abolitionist cause. Truth became dedicated to the movement, and she traveled widely on the anti-slavery circuit, often with Frederick Douglass, who was, like Truth, a former slave.

In 1850, Truth took up the cause of women's rights and began to lecture at women's suffrage meetings. She saw black emancipation and women's rights as issues that were inextricably linked, but her audiences often rejected the notion of mixing what they considered to be separate issues. In 1851, at the Women's Convention in Akron, Ohio, she delivered what has come to be called the "Ain't I a Woman?" speech, one of the most famous addresses in the history of the American women's movement. In it, Truth asked, "And ain't I a woman? Look at me! Look at my arm! I have ploughed and planted, and gathered into barns, and no man could head me! And ain't I a woman? I could work as much and eat as much as a man—when I could get it—and bear the lash as well! And ain't I a woman? I have borne thirteen children, and seen 'em sold off to slavery, and when I cried out with my mother's grief, none but Jesus heard me! And ain't I a woman?" As later scholars Avtar Brah and Ann Phoenix have stated, Truth's speech "deconstructs every single major truth-claim about gender in a patriarchal slave social formation" while asking her audience to compare their expectations of gender with her actual experiences.

In the 1850s, Truth settled in Battle Creek, Michigan. During the Civil War, she urged African Americans to fight for the Union, and she worked tirelessly on behalf of freed slaves. In 1864, President Lincoln received her at the White House. After the war, she worked for the Freedman's Relief Association, leading an unsuccessful campaign to obtain land grants for the settlement of African Americans in the West. She died at her home in Battle Creek after a long life in which she fought with evangelical fervor for the rights of African Americans and women, "disrupting," as scholar Nell Painter has put it, "assumptions about race, class, and gender in American society."

Victoria Woodhull (1838–1927)

Suffragist

Women's suffrage leader Victoria Woodhull is most (in)famous for being the first woman to run for president of the United States (in 1872), but other details of her extraordinary life make Woodhull one of the most exceptional women of hers or any era. She worked for a time as a traveling clairvoyant; she and her sister were the first female brokers on Wall Street; she was the first woman to start a weekly newspaper and the first woman to address a congressional committee (in 1871); she spent Election Day 1872 in jail; she was a proponent of free love who declared to her lecture audiences: "I want the love of you all, promiscuously." She broke with fellow suffragist leaders Elizabeth Cady Stanton and Susan B. Anthony, who warned British suffrage leaders that she was "lewd and indecent."

Born Victoria Claflin in the rural town of Homer, Ohio, she was one of ten children. Her mother was illiterate, and her father was a con man and snake oil salesman. Woodhull did not start elementary school until she turned eight and then attended off and on for only three years before ending her formal education by marrying at the age of fifteen. As a child with a purported gift for communicating with the dead, her father put her to work telling fortunes and contacting spirits as a traveling medical clairvoyant.

In 1868, Woodhull and her sister moved to New York City, where they met the recently widowed Cornelius Vanderbilt, who was interested in spiritualism and set them up in a stockbrokerage firm, Woodhull, Claflin, & Company, which opened in 1870 and was quite successful. With the profits, Woodhull founded *Woodhull and Claflin Weekly,* a women's rights and reform newspaper that espoused legalized prostitution and dress reform as well as the utopian social system called Pantarchy, a theory rejecting conventional marriage and advocating free love and communal management of children and property. The *Weekly* would publish the first English-language version of Karl Marx and Friedrich Engels's *Communist Manifesto.*

Woodhull attended a suffrage convention in 1869 and was converted to the cause. She convinced a Massachusetts congressman to invite her to testify before the House Judiciary Committee in 1871 to present a petition to pass "enabling legislation" of voting rights for women. Her notoriety gained her the acceptance of suffrage leaders, and she was invited by Susan B. Anthony into the National Woman Suffrage Association. Woodhull would soon, however, join with a dissident group, the National Radical Reformers, who broke from the NWSA in 1872 to form the Equal Rights Party, who nominated Woodhull for the presidency with Frederick Douglass as vice president, although he never acknowledged the nomination. A few days before the election, Woodhull was arrested for "publishing an obscene newspaper" and jailed but acquitted on a technicality six months later. In jail on Election Day, Woodhull was prevented from attempting to vote as she intended. Her name appeared in ballots in some states, but no record exists of how many votes she received because they apparently were not counted. Woodhull would try unsuccessfully to gain nominations for the presidency again in 1884 and 1892.

In 1876 after Cornelius Vanderbilt's death, his son paid Woodhull and her sister to leave the country, and they moved to England, where Woodhull met her third husband, a wealthy banker, and would reside there until her death in 1927. She devoted her later years to running a new newspaper, preserving the English home of George Washington's ancestors, running a village school, and being a champion of education reform.

Victoria Claflin Woodhull Blood Martin died at her English home at the age of eighty-eight, a woman of great contradictions and accomplishments who broke seemingly every restriction for women of her time.

Martha Coffin Wright (1806–1875)

Abolitionist, Women's Rights Activist

Called "a very dangerous woman" because of her views and actions on behalf of women's rights and abolition, Martha Coffin Wright was the younger sister of Lucretia Mott, who was one of the original five women who met to organize the historic Seneca Falls Women's Rights Convention. Wright would remain a prominent figure in the women's movement until her death at the age of sixty-eight, when she was president of the National Woman Suffrage Association. She was no stranger to drama in her life: Wright survived a shipwreck; spent time at a frontier fort; and experienced the deaths of a fiancé, her first husband, and three of her seven children while navigating the intense conflicts within the women's rights and abolitionist movements.

Born in Boston, Wright was the youngest of eight children. Her father and mother were descendants of two of the original settlers of Nantucket Island in 1662. Both of her parents were devoted Quakers who moved their family to Philadelphia when Wright was three. After her father died, her mother opened a boardinghouse. Wright attended a local school before transferring to a Quaker boarding school. When Wright was sixteen, she fell in love with a non-Quaker, and her mother only eventually consented to the marriage, but the Quaker community refused to accept the marriage and expelled her. The couple lived for a time at a frontier fort in Tampa Bay, Florida. After her husband's early death in 1826, Wright accepted the hand of another man, but his father disapproved the match, and her fiancé died before they could wed. Wright, with her year-old child in tow, taught in a Quaker girls' school in Aurora, New York, and in 1828 married David Wright, a young law student. Her home in Auburn, New York, became a station of the Underground Railroad for escaping slaves. Wright was a close friend and supporter of Harriet Tubman.

In 1848, Wright joined her sister Lucretia Mott at the home of Jane Hunt for Sunday tea with neighbors Elizabeth Cady Stanton and Mary Ann M'Clintock in Waterloo, New York, where they planned the first women's rights convention in Seneca Falls, New York. This began Wright's twenty-year dedication to women's rights and the abolition of slavery that involved extensive traveling on behalf of the American Anti-Slavery Society and the National Woman Suffrage Association, where she earned the reputation of being "one of the most judicious and clear-sighted women in the movement." Wright was an important and loyal advisor to Stanton and Anthony, who helped them organize the American Equal Rights Association in 1866 and the National Women's Suffrage Association in 1869.

In 2007, Congress passed a resolution called "Recognizing Martha Coffin Wright on the 200th anniversary of her birth and her induction into the National Women's Hall of Fame."

WOMEN AT WORK

During the colonial era into the nineteenth century, the primary accepted ideal for nonenslaved women was that of the virtuous housewife and helpmeet, and women's work was generally confined to the domestic sphere of home and assistance with the family farm or plantation. Midwives were an exception: Women gave birth at home; no hospitals or trained nurses existed; and few doctors were available, especially in rural areas, to attend to women in childbirth. Midwifery was an indispensable and respected profession as well as a potentially lucrative one for a practitioner.

As towns and cities were founded, expanded, and prospered, women in nonfarming families often worked alongside their spouses in shops, inns, and taverns and in printmaking and publishing. Widows in colonial cities were sometimes able to earn a decent living by working as craftswomen, shop owners, and administrators of their late husbands' businesses until a son became of age to take over. Women also managed inns, boardinghouses, and even prisons. However, in an era when wages were generally low, many women who lived in cities such as New York, Boston, Philadelphia, and Charleston and worked either to supplement a household income or by necessity after the death of a parent or the death or desertion of a spouse frequently faced limited employment opportunities, which left them on the edge of economic sustainability and often in poverty. Un-

trained and unskilled in the trades that were open to men, women worked as laundresses, cooks, seamstresses, wet nurses, and domestic servants for half the wages of unskilled male laborers. By the early 1800s, women were also working for wages as schoolteachers. Teaching was considered to be the most respectable profession for unmarried women, who often began work when they were in their teens.

In the 1800s, domestic work was a primary source of employment for free or newly freed African American women and unmarried, female emigrants from Ireland. Irish women began to arrive in East Coast cities during the first half of the nineteenth century and would eventually comprise 53 percent of Irish immigrants by the end of the century. More than 60 percent of Irish women worked as maids, cooks, nannies, or housekeepers. They came to the United States to leave behind their hardscrabble lives on Irish farms and to find employment opportunities and marriage prospects, which had greatly diminished during the Great Famine of 1840–1849 that devastated Ireland. Because newly arrived Irish women had few means and little knowledge of the country, they tended to stay in the cities where they landed rather than venture elsewhere for work. The advantages of working for wealthy and middle-class families included faster assimilation into American culture and wages that were higher than those of factory workers. Once Irish Americans assimilated

A circa 1914 photo shows members of the Irish Women Workers Union. Early on, Irish women made up a large number of domestic workers in American households. Such jobs are now being filled more often by black women and Latinas.

and became more economically successful, fewer women of Irish descent worked as domestics. In the twentieth century, female African American and Latinx immigrants comprised the majority of domestic workers in the United States.

THE MILL GIRLS

When an industrial economy started to emerge during the Industrial Revolution that began in Great Britain in the 1770s and spread to the United States in the 1790s and early to mid-1800s, the textile industry was the first to be affected. Eli Whitney's mechanical cotton gin, invented in 1793 and patented in 1794, revolutionized the cotton industry, greatly enhanced the South's economy, and created a ready-made clothing industry; however, the cotton gin also increased the demand for slaves, who were needed to operate the machine. Home-based clothing manufacturing became a common trade for women and, like teaching, was considered a respectable female wage-earning occupation since spinning cloth and making clothes for their families was one of women's traditional domestic tasks. One center of clothing manufacturing was Troy, New York, where hundreds of women sewed collars and cuffs at home for the city's clothing manufacturers. The home-based manufacture of "piecework" would become an integral part of the clothing industry in the mid-1800s and especially in the latter part of the nineteenth century into the twentieth, when a large influx of immigrants from Europe arrived in New York City. There, they lived and worked in their tenement apartments as well as in factory sweatshops.

In 1793, English industrialist Samuel Slater (1768–1835), who had brought his expertise in operating looms and the spinning jenny to America from Great Britain, opened the country's first factory: a water-powered textile mill on the Blackstone River in Pawtucket, Rhode Island. Slater, who would go on to open mills in Massachusetts, first employed children aged seven to twelve to operate mill machinery and then hired whole families to work in his mill, developing company-owned villages to house his workers. Hours were long and wages were low, but the factory practices Slater called the Rhode Island System, later known as the Waltham-Lowell System or simply the Lowell System, became firmly established in American industry during the Industrial Revolution and later on in the century during the development of such industries as mining.

The success of Samuel Slater's mills and the increasing demand for manufactured cloth drew the attention of Massachusetts businessman Francis Cabot Lowell (1775–1817), who formed the Boston Manufacturing Company with investors in 1813. The following year, the company built a textile mill in Waltham that featured the first power loom, based on the British model, which offered a significant technological improvement in the making of cloth. Lowell integrated the chain of tasks under a single roof, beginning what would become the American factory system in the nineteenth century. The mill became the most famous in the nation and was highly profitable for their investors. After Lowell died in 1817, his business partners opened mills on the Merrimack River in northeastern Massachusetts, which were in operation by 1823 in a planned settlement of boardinghouses and eventually ten mill complexes that would make Lowell, incorporated as a city in 1836, the center of the nation's textile manufacturing. Other mill towns in Massachusetts, New Hampshire, and Maine would be similarly developed, although not on quite as large of a scale.

Francis Cabot Lowell's further innovation, which began with the Waltham mill and continued in Lowell and other mill towns, was to recruit the unmarried daughters of New England farmers to work in the mills. These women were already skilled at making cloth and could be hired for one-third to one-half the wages men would demand. The majority of the female mill workers were in their twenties, but their ages ranged from ten years old (child labor was not completely outlawed and age regulated until 1938, when the U.S. Congress passed the Fair Labor Standards Act) to women in their thirties and included schoolteachers, widows, and young women engaged to be married. In the 1820s and 1830s,

An 1850 illustration of Lowell Mills in Massachusetts, where Francis Cabot Lowell created a new, efficient way to manufacture textiles. He also revolutionized employment by hiring young women instead of children (as was often done in manufacturing at the time) and affording them opportunities for education and advancement.

women and girls from Massachusetts, New Hampshire, Vermont, and Maine arrived at the mill towns to sign up for work, having traveled from their farmland homes aboard buckboard baggage wagons. By 1840, the Lowell mills had recruited more than eight thousand women, who comprised nearly three-quarters of the textile workforce.

> The majority of female mill workers lived in company-owned boardinghouses with twelve to thirteen "mill girls," as they became known, sharing a house....

Women and girls chose to work in the mills for a variety of reasons: curiosity; a desire for independence; to seek the educational, social, and cultural advantages offered there; to relieve their families of the financial burden of having an unmarried daughter at home; to escape from unpleasant family situations; to supplement a family income; to pay off family mortgages; to help support widowed mothers; or to help a brother pay for college. The wages women could earn at the mills were the primary attraction: They could earn more from working in a mill than as schoolteachers, domestic workers, or seamstresses, the only other jobs available to women at that time. Mill owners paid $1.25 per week for board and a flat minimum of $0.55 per week with slightly more for additional piecework. Depending upon how fast they worked, mill girls could earn anywhere from $2.00 to $4.00 per week carding, spinning, and weaving for twelve to thirteen hours in a workday that started at 5:00 A.M. and a work week that included a half day on Saturday. Mills closed on Sundays for the Sabbath, when the mill girls were expected to attend church. The typical term of employment was nine or ten months of the year with many of the young women leaving the factories to visit their homes during part of the summer. For some women, work in the mills lasted for only a few years. They left because of illness; exhaustion; a dislike of the drudgery that was the lot

of factory workers; they had earned the money they needed; they wanted to seek nonfactory work; they wanted to further their educations; they wanted to get married; or they simply wanted to go back home.

The majority of female mill workers lived in company-owned boardinghouses with twelve to thirteen "mill girls," as they became known, sharing a house managed by a woman keeper, who was often a widow, or by a husband and wife. The mill girls were strictly supervised and were reported to their supervisors for such infractions such as staying out after 10:00 P.M. or if they were overheard complaining about any aspect of their work or lives: Breaking the curfew led to a fine docked from a woman's wages; complaints would lead to immediate dismissal. Female workers were lectured on the importance of modesty, temperance, honesty, frugality, and punctuality, and in Lowell, the showcase of the textile industry, female workers were required to sign contracts agreeing to uphold these virtues. In return, the mill girls not only earned a wage but could also take advantage of the self-improvement cultural programs that were available and centered on evening get-togethers to study literature and foreign languages as well as attending lectures and meetings of religious societies. Enhancing the theme of self-improvement was the *Lowell Offering*, a company magazine published monthly from 1840 to 1845. The *Offering* featured poetry, ballads, fiction, and autobiographical sketches written by women mill workers, which were usually published anonymously or with the authors' initials. Also included were articles culled from local improvement and literary societies. Controlled by the mill owners and intended to portray the lives and work of women in the mill towns in a positive light, the *Offering* had a substantial number of subscribers and supporters throughout not only New England but also elsewhere in the United States and among foreign visitors.

THE FIRST WOMEN'S LABOR MOVEMENT

The rosy view of the comfortable, happy, and healthy lives of the mill workers publicized by the *Lowell Offering* fell short of the reality well before the magazine was first published. As early as 1828, the women and children who worked at a mill in

Paterson, New Jersey, walked off their jobs to protest the harsh working conditions, and four hundred women in the Dover, New Hampshire, mill "turned out"—that is, organized a strike—to protest the fines they were forced to pay for lateness in reporting for work. These were the first strikes by factory workers in the United States. In the 1830s, as individual mills faced competition within the booming textile industry and each nationwide financial depression (called "panics" in the nineteenth century) threatened to cut into mill owners' profits, wages would be cut, resulting in occasional strikes to protest the cuts as well as long working hours and demands from mill owners for sped-up work to produce more cloth. After a wage cut in 1834, Lowell workers went on strike, marched through the city and to several mills to encourage other women to join them, gathered at an outdoor rally, and signed

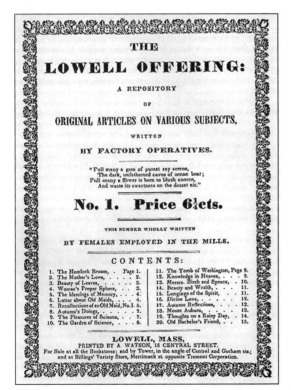

The first edition of *The Lowell Offering*, published from 1840 to 1845, intended to showcase life at the mill in a positive light. The magazine increasingly included letters and editorials on the difficult working conditions of the factory girls and labor conflicts with management.

a petition that stated, "We will not go back into the mills to work unless our wages are continued." The strike failed to sway the mill owners, who refused to comply with the women's demands, and, within a week, the mills were operating at full capacity once again. A better organized strike in 1836 saw an estimated 1,200 to 1,500 women turn out to march through Lowell to protest wage cuts and the mill owners' scheme to have the women pay the twenty cents a week for their board, which the company had previously paid. The mills' owners rejected the strikers' demands throughout the monthlong walkout, evicted women from their boardinghouses, and fired and blacklisted the leaders of the strike. The remaining women either went back to work, left the mills to pursue employment elsewhere, or returned home to their families.

Labor activism among the mill girls was not over, however. By the 1840s, the Boston merchants who owned the Massachusetts mills were using their profits to expand their business interests to such industries as insurance, shipping, and banking. The mill towns continued to grow as more mills were built, transforming rural villages and towns, such as Lawrence, Massachusetts, into hastily built, crowded cities. In the mills, owners demanded more and speedier work from the women but did not increase their wages, and new machines, such as the crank-driven loom, increased the noise, heat, and lint from the cloth and added to the unhealthy environment inside the factories. It became difficult for some of the mill girls to simply leave because the financial panic of 1837 had caused fathers to lose their farms. Many mill girls decided it was time to take action, and in 1845, twelve workers in Lowell organized the Female Labor Reform Association—the first women's labor union in the United States—which later joined with the New England Workingmen's Association to advocate for reducing the workday to ten hours. Within six months, the Female Labor Reform Association had five hundred members. The association organized large petition campaigns with two thousand signers in 1845 and more than twice that number the following year. The association organized chapters in other mill towns in Massachusetts and New Hampshire, published "Factory Tracts" to expose conditions inside the mills, testified before state legislative committees, and, even though they could not vote, campaigned against a state representative, who was one of the strongest opponents of labor reform.

The most tangible result of the Female Labor Reform Association's efforts was a change in the population of workers hired by the mill owners: Rather than keep native-born women on the loom or hire new ones, both of whom might be likely to assert themselves and seek reform, the mill owners turned to the influx of immigrants, among them Irish women who had arrived in the United States in the wake of the Irish Famine and who, they were convinced, would be happy to earn a wage and not make trouble for them. In time, however, the Irish mill workers sought reform as well with the same results as the mill girls before them.

Although the strikes and political action of the mill girls failed to achieve any reforms, they introduced the idea of trade unionism, which would come to transform the relationship between labor and management. As women continued to work in the textile mills and enter the workforce in a variety of other industries, not least of which were the garment trades, it would become necessary for them draw upon their capacity for organization in order to achieve better working conditions for themselves toward the end of the nineteenth century and well into the twentieth.

EARLY TWENTIETH-CENTURY WOMEN'S LABOR MOVEMENT

In 1912, immigrant textile workers, organized by the Industrial Workers of the World (IWW), an international labor union also known as the Wobblies, went on strike at Lawrence, Massachusetts, woolen mills over wage cuts initiated by mill owners because of a new Massachusetts law shortening the work week for women and children. The strike was ultimately successful and became known as the Bread and Roses strike. The slogan, "Bread and Roses," became the rallying cry of the labor movement after Helen Todd, a factory inspector, gave a speech before a crowd of suffragists in 1911. In her speech, Todd described a nation with "no children

in factories, no girls driven on the street to earn their bread, in the day when there shall be bread for all, and roses too." The same year, Todd wrote an article with references to "life's bread" and "the roses of life," which appeared in *The American Magazine*, and writer James Oppenheimer invoked the phrase in a poem he penned for the same magazine. The Bread and Roses strike illustrated the workers' need for the basic necessities of life and the importance of an enhanced quality of life beyond just those necessities. For the European immigrants toiling in the garment industry sweatshops and sewing piecework in the crowded tenement apartments of New York City, the promise of a better life was inextricably linked to trade unionism.

The efforts of early to mid-nineteenth-century, female textile workers to organize strikes on behalf of better working conditions had helped to lay the groundwork for the formation of unions. However, union membership and leadership in such trades as shoemaking, carpentry, mechanics, bookbinding, and, later, in the mining and garment industries were overwhelmingly male. The American Federation of Labor (AFL), founded in 1886 as an umbrella organization under which the unions were united, tended to oppose women's employment in general. Its leaders viewed working-class women as strikebreakers, too passive, and too inarticulate—a conclusion that may have shown a bias toward immigrants, for whom English was a second language.

Massachusetts militiamen confront marchers at the 1912 Bread and Roses strike in Lawrence, Massachusetts.

By 1890, 3.7 million American women had jobs; by 1900, that figure had jumped to over five million. In New York City, 350,000 women were employed, and, of this number, about sixty-five thousand women worked in the garment industry, the majority of whom were Jewish and Italian immigrants. Garment workers could spend up to 18 hours a day, night shifts included, sewing clothing in the dimly lit rooms of sweatshop factories that were stiflingly hot in the summer and drafty in the winter. Workers were forced to pay for their sewing machines out of their wages. The materials they used were flammable, sweatshops were firetraps, and machines were often cleaned and adjusted while still in use, which resulted in frequent injuries. Employers sometimes "accidentally" shortchanged female workers or agreed to salary advances in return for sexual favors. Women who did piecework at home fared little better since they lived in poorly constructed tenements that possessed many of the same hazards as the sweatshops and worked for the same employers.

Like their predecessors in the textile mills, women garment workers were paid one-half to one-third the wages of men, a discrepancy that was not corrected even when men and women did the same job. Employers justified wage inequality by claiming that women were only working for "pin" money to buy luxuries. When a 1910 government industrial commission studied the condition of female workers at the turn of the century, one of the commission members, a veteran labor leader and spokesman for the AFL, concluded that women were unqualified for wage labor and that wherever a large number of women were employed in any occupation, a point would inevitably be reached when wage equality would result in men's wages becoming as low as women's wages. Women, members of the commission argued, would be better off staying at home caring for their husbands and children. What the commission also found, but failed to mention, was that most women worked to keep themselves and their families fed, clothed, and sheltered. Some immigrant women tried to save part of their wages to help bring their families to America. Many families, both white and African American, immigrant and native born, especially counted on the extra income from wives and daughters during the times when men were laid off or became ill or injured on the job.

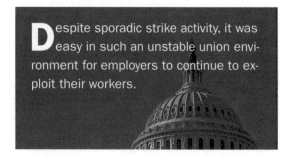

Despite sporadic strike activity, it was easy in such an unstable union environment for employers to continue to exploit their workers.

Women who belonged to local unions received higher wages and enjoyed more sanitary conditions than nonunionized women. However, in an age of monopolies and trusts, a feature of American industry that was beginning to be challenged by investigative journalists and social reformers during what has been called the Progressive Era (1890s to the 1920s) was companies producing women's garments that operated in small, isolated, competitive units, unlike large factories, which mass produced goods. Union activity was also marked by ideological disputes between socialists (who wanted state and worker control of factories) and anarchists (who advocated a radical overthrow and takeover of the existing system of employer and exploited worker). Despite sporadic strike activity, it was easy in such an unstable union environment for employers to continue to exploit their workers. By the turn of the century, it became clear that a need existed for a stable national union representing garment workers.

GARMENT WORKERS AND THE GREAT UPRISING

In June 1900, delegates from the United Brotherhood of Cloak Makers' Union No. 1 of New York and Vicinity and other interested garment workers met at New York's Labor Lyceum to form a new national union: the International Ladies' Garment Workers' Union (ILGWU). The combination of seven local unions, the ILGWU represented 2,310 garment workers in New York, New Jersey, Philadelphia, and Baltimore, Maryland. Later in June, the powerful American Federation of Labor issued a charter to the new union. By 1904, the ILGWU had 5,400 members in sixty-six locals in twenty-seven cities; by 1913, it was the AFL's third-largest affiliate union.

During its early years, the majority of ILGWU members were men, although the union's male founders and leaders could not ignore the presence of female workers, who dominated the ladies' garment industry, especially in shirtwaist (women's blouse) manufacturing. However, the men of the ILGWU agreed that women should be discouraged from union leadership in the belief that they would make poor union organizers and even worse union leaders since, in their view, women were preoccupied only with marriage. By 1903, only two delegates to the ILGWU convention were women, and five years later, it appeared that the union would be merged with the United Garment Workers union. The UGW had brought women into positions of power, but UGW locals were company unions manipulated by employers. It would take the massive efforts of women labor organizers, plus a series of strikes, to convince still nonunionized female workers that their best hope for better wages and a better life lay in unionism and to transform the ILGWU into a national union in which women were truly represented.

In November 1909, garment workers assembled at New York City's Cooper Union to hear speeches by various garment workers as well as Samuel Gompers of the AFL and Mary Dreier of the Women's Trade Union League (WTUL), an organization founded in 1903 to bring working-class women, mostly immigrants, together with well-off women to support the efforts of women to organize labor unions and eliminate sweatshop conditions. The topic of the meeting, which had been called by members of ILGWU and the United Hebrew Trades, a coalition of Jewish unions, was a proposed general strike of shirtwaist makers in response to the behavior of the Triangle Shirtwaist Company, whose workers had gone on strike two months earlier to protest the firing of workers suspected of supporting unionization. Workers from the Leiserson Company joined the striking Triangle workers; both companies used abusive and violent tactics to break the strikes. At the meeting, sixteen-year-old Clara Lemlich, a Leiserson employee recovering from a beating on the picket line, made her way onto the platform

and said in Yiddish, "I am a working girl and one of those who are on strike against intolerable conditions. I am tired of listening to speakers who talk in general terms. What we are here for is to decide whether or not we will strike. I offer a resolution that a general strike be declared—now!" Lemlich's speech galvanized her audience, and her resolution was adopted.

It was thought that no more than five thousand workers would strike; instead, between twenty and thirty thousand workers participated in the Great Uprising or the Uprising of the 20,000, as the strike variously came to be called. Supported morally and financially by the WTUL and joined for a time by well-to-do suffragists, including socialite Alva Belmont, the former granddaughter-in-law of railroad and shipping magnate Cornelius Vanderbilt, the strikers braved an unusually cold and snowy winter on the picket lines, endured beatings and clubbings by police and company-hired thugs, and risked arrest and fines until the beginning of February 1910 when the Triangle Shirtwaist Company settled the strike. The Great Uprising resulted in few concessions for the garment workers and no formal recognition for the shirtwaist makers' unions; however, it led to similar uprisings in Philadelphia, Baltimore,

Two women strikers proudly picket during the 1909-1910 Uprising of the 20,000, which was also known as the New York Shirtwaist Strike. Participants were mostly Jewish women who sewed bodices and blouses.

and Chicago, where garment workers who made men's clothing went on strike. It also focused attention on the great possibilities of unionization within the ILGWU, created solidarity among female workers, and inspired union organization among workers in the other branches of the garment industry.

THE TRIANGLE SHIRTWAIST FIRE

After the Great Uprising, garment industry employers remained intransigent concerning workers' demands for better pay, shorter working hours, and improved working conditions. The Triangle Shirtwaist Company, fearing that workers would steal shirtwaists and drop them to accomplices on the street below to resell, refused to accept demands for more fire escapes and unlocked doors. The company's callous disregard for the safety of its workers led to one of the worst industrial disasters in American women's history.

A sweatshop located on the top three floors of the Asch Building in New York's Greenwich Village (the building is now part of New York University), the Triangle Shirtwaist Company contained only two elevators and two narrow staircases with the door to one of the staircases kept locked. The building had previously experienced four recent fires and had been reported to the New York Building Department by the fire department as unsafe. Late on Saturday afternoon on March 25, 1911, some five hundred workers, the majority of them young immigrant women and most of them in their teens, were cutting fabric or sitting at sewing machines placed close together. Finished shirtwaists hung in lines above the tiers of workers, bins overflowed with scraps of material, and lint and oil-soaked rags littered the floors. Without warning, a smoldering bin of fabric burst into flames on the eighth floor. Before anyone could reach a bucket and the water barrel, the blaze spread to stacks of material piled high on the cutting tables. Soon, the entire floor was engulfed in flames. Survivors from the ninth floor, where slices of cake were being passed around to celebrate a coworker's recent engagement when the fire began, reported having seen flames shooting up through the windows and up the stairway and elevator shaft.

As the fire began to spread, the frightened workers stampeded to the elevators and found that only one, with a maximum capacity of twelve persons, was in operation. A mass of women broke down the locked doors leading to the stairwells and tumbled over one another in a desperate attempt to get to the street, where the doors opened inward. Others followed Triangle owners Max Blanck and Isaac Harris to the roof, where they escaped to another building. Other women opened windows and fell to their deaths, their bodies on fire as they fell. The one fire escape, built to support no more than a few people, collapsed under the weight of fleeing workers. A number of women remained trapped on the three floors, where they succumbed to smoke inhalation or were burned to death. When 150 firefighters arrived at the scene, they were hampered in their rescue effort by falling bodies, nets that broke under the weight of people falling from a height of eighty-five feet, ladders that only reached the sixth floor,

The 1911 Triangle Shirtwaist Factory fire in New York City was one of the worst industrial disasters in American history. Most of the 146 worker deaths were immigrant women (123) of Italian and Jewish backgrounds.

and trucks that could not pump water from the hoses beyond the seventh floor. Eighteen minutes after the fire began, 123 women between the ages of fourteen and forty-three and twenty-three men lay dead.

Over one hundred thousand mourners attended the mass funeral of the Triangle victims, and angry demonstrations occurred protesting the unsafe conditions that had led to the fire, especially on New York's Lower East Side, where most of the workers lived. When the Women's Trade Union League held a memorial meeting at the Metropolitan Opera House, among those present were many of the female philanthropists who had contributed funds for the Great Uprising. When called upon to speak, labor leader Rose Schneiderman had this to say to her audience: "I would be a traitor to these poor burned bodies, if I came here to talk good fellowship. We have tried you good people of the public and we have found you wanting.… Every year thousands of us are maimed. The life of men and women is so cheap and property so sacred.… I can't talk fellowship to those who are gathered here. Too much blood has been spilled. I know from my experience that it is up to the working people to save themselves."

An investigation into the Triangle Shirtwaist Fire exonerated company owners Blanck and Harris, the county, the state, and the insurance companies. Reforms in building safety, fire prevention, and insurance practices came too late for the twenty-three beneficiaries who, three years after the fire, received $75.00 each as payment for the loss of their loved ones. It would take the increased presence of female workers in factories during World War I and the efforts of the Women's Bureau of the U.S. Department of Labor, established in 1920—two months before women achieved the right to vote—to secure government regulations of the conditions under which women worked in order to avoid the kind of tragedy experienced by the Triangle shirtwaist makers of 1911.

THE PROTOCOL OF PEACE

The Great Uprising, the Triangle Shirtwaist Fire, the Lawrence textile strike, continued union activism, and the garment workers' strikes in Philadelphia, Baltimore, and Chicago contributed to a Pro-

tocol of Peace, which was signed by leaders of the ILGWU in 1913. A contract between labor and management and arbitrated by outside negotiators, the protocol provided for the resolution of disputes and the protection of workers' health. In the 1920s, internal disputes and a failed general strike, in which employers used gangsters from organized crime as strikebreakers and the ILGWU responded with their own thugs, nearly bankrupted and destroyed the union. However, the ILGWU rallied in the 1930s under the union presidency of David Dubinsky (1892–1982) and the prolabor policies of the administration of President Franklin D. Roosevelt. By the mid-1960s, the ILGWU was considered one the nation's most powerful and progressive labor unions with a membership of 450,000. From the late 1960s, membership declined as clothing manufacturers looked to lower their labor costs by moving their factories overseas, found new ethnic groups in the United States such as African Americans and Latinx and Asian immigrants to exploit as cheap labor, and the former industrial practice of sewing piecework at home for manufacturers returned. By 1993, ILGWU membership had declined to 150,000, and in 1995, the union merged with Amalgamated Clothing and Textile Workers to form the Union of Needletrades, Industrial, and Textile Employees (UNITE). In 2004, that union merged with the Hotel Employees and Restaurant Employees union to form UNITE HERE, a union that now primarily represents workers in the hotel, food service, commercial laundry, warehouse, and casino gambling industries.

Throughout the nearly one-hundred-year history of the ILGWU and of American labor in general, women have fought for recognition and power within the unions and made only limited gains. By the 1970s, during the height of second-wave feminism, popularly known as the Women's Liberation Movement, women with jobs in a variety of industries, most notably office workers, formed worker advocacy organizations. The same decade also saw the formation of the Coalition of Labor Union Women, a nonprofit, nonpartisan organization of trade union women affiliated with the American Federation of Labor and the Congress of Industrial Organizations (the AFL-CIO). However, a severely eroding manufacturing base in the United States in the last decades of the twentieth century, together with criticisms of the often collusive and concessionary relationship between labor and management, weakened the resolve of both women and men in the rank and file. By 2010, 11.4 percent of American workers belonged to a labor union, primarily in the public sector and in teaching, health care, and clerical work. Some corporations in the private sector such as technology were supplying workers with wages and benefits that had previously only been possible with unionization.

> **M**any workers, both women and men, are forced to work more than one job to make ends meet and have less time to spend with their families.

Conditions for American workers in the twenty-first century are certainly less difficult than they were in the nineteenth and early twentieth centuries, but problems remain. People in most industries are working longer hours for less pay and fewer benefits, and income inequality has been rising along with layoffs. Many workers, both women and men, are forced to work more than one job to make ends meet and have less time to spend with their families. Government budget cuts have made it more difficult for the Occupational Safety and Health Administration (OSHA), established in 1970, to monitor workplace conditions. In recent years, the National Labor Relations Board (NLRB), which guarantees the right of workers to form unions, bargain with their employers, and organize strikes if necessary, has appointed corporate lobbyists to its board.

Recently, women have been showing signs of renewed labor activism. On March 8, 2017, the 106th anniversary of International Women's Day, which was established to celebrate female workers and to protest their lack of representation in trade unions, the American Federation of Teachers helped rally thousands of women for Women Workers Rising, an event that coincided with a general strike called the Day without a Woman. Held at the U.S. Department of Labor in Washington, D.C., the rally called attention to the contribution of female workers as well as to the financial and workplace issues they face across a variety of industry sectors. In 2018 and 2019, teachers went on strike in states and communities across the country to advocate for higher wages and smaller classrooms and to protest budget cuts that were depriving teachers of the educational resources they needed to do their jobs.

While female workers have made some great strides toward equality in the workplace, they continue to earn seventy-nine cents for every dollar men earn. They are also disproportionally represented in nonunionized, low-income, low-esteem jobs: It is estimated that women who belong to unions earn 30.9 percent more money per week than women in nonunion jobs. Despite the often uneasy relationship between labor unions and corporate interests, unions have historically made it possible for women and minorities to close the wage gap with men and to have a voice in public policy that affects all American workers.

WOMEN AT WORK IN WARTIME

Patriotic slogans such as the one above appeared on posters during World War I to encourage women to work for the war effort once the Americans joined the fight in April 1917. For the first three years of the war, America's hard-fought struggle to remain neutral kept the nation safe from the devastating effects of the war that engulfed Europe from 1914 to 1918. The United States' late entry into what many called the Great War helped make an Allied victory possible and would cause the nation to emerge as an economic world power, ushering in the so-called American Century. For women, the war proved to be an unexpected ally: It accelerated their acceptance into the workforce in jobs formerly restricted to men and helped to ensure that the eventual outcome of the "war to make the world safe for democracy" would be the achievement of the vote for women. Many suffragists, especially those in the pacifist Woman's Peace Party (WPP), founded in 1914 by social reformer Jane Addams,

Women's Party member Crystal Eastman, writer Charlotte Perkins Gilman, and suffragist leader Carrie Chapman Catt, viewed America's entrance into the war—and war in general—as a destructive male trait that women's full representation in national life would help to correct. Some suffragists did not want to abandon the cause in favor of patriotic duty, and many, such as Alice Paul and her Women's Party, continued to vigorously advocate on behalf of winning the franchise. Although active in the WPP, Carrie Chapman Catt, president of the National American Woman Suffrage Association (NAWSA), urged NAWSA members to work for both the war effort and suffrage, fearing that the movement had too much to lose politically by opposing the war. NAWSA publicly entered the war effort, joining with other women across the country to knit socks for soldiers, can food, sell Liberty Bonds, and adjust family menus with a view toward rationing meat, bread, and butter.

When America entered the war, women were also recruited to take the place of men in the work-

Propaganda poster art such as this encouraged workers, including women, to pull together during World War I.

force who had enlisted in the military or had been drafted. Women worked in factories, oil refineries, and steel foundries and held essential positions in the manufacture of explosives, armaments, railways, automobiles, and airplanes, which were relatively new machines at the time. By the close of the war, women constituted about 20 percent of the workforce in all American manufacturing industries. Thousands of other women were hired in textile mills to produce military uniforms, and female clerical workers were recruited to work for the government, especially in the War Department. In some twenty states, women were organized into the Women's Land Army of America, which furnished fifteen thousand additional agriculture workers trained by the U.S. Farm Bureau and other organizations. One of the most important outcomes for women in the workforce during the war was the creation of the Women's Division of the Ordnance Department (WDOD), which regulated worker conditions in munitions factories and the ordnance plants where weapons were stored. By the end of the war, the U.S. Labor Department acknowledged that female workers deserved the protection of labor laws and in 1920 created the Women's Bureau, which has remained an essential lobbying resource for female workers in the fight for improved conditions and equality with men in the workplace.

Women also worked in Europe on behalf of the war effort. In June 1917, the American Women's Hospitals Service created an all-female medical force to circumvent government policy prohibiting female physicians from military service. All-female units of doctors, nurses, and ambulance drivers went to France to serve the civilian population and helped in the reconstruction of Europe after the Armistice of November 1918. The American Women's Hospitals Service would go on to provide medical care in the poor communities of Appalachia during the Great Depression of the 1930s and would eventually help female doctors to become accepted in the military, although it would take another decade before female physicians were allowed to join the military with commissions and full rank.

The presence of women in the workforce and the kinds of jobs they did during World War I challenged the conventional view that women were capable of only limited kinds of work. Their efforts on behalf of the war were greeted with national praise and public acclaim, a debt that would become an important factor in the congressional debate over the franchise for women. World War I helped to redefine the role of women in the United States, extending women's sphere of influence beyond the home, helping to provide the final impetus to achievement of the Twentieth Amendment and to pave the way for war work during World War II.

"WE CAN DO IT!": WORLD WAR II

The postwar decade of the 1920s brought postwar prosperity for many partly due to speculation in the stock market and an increasing middle class. The decade saw a rise in consumerism influenced by mass campaigns to advertise automobiles as well as new labor-saving appliances, private telephones, and the radio, which became more available because of Americans' expanded access to electricity. Young women discarded the traditional values of their elders and shortened their hemlines, cut their

> Young women discarded the traditional values of their elders and shortened their hemlines, cut their hair short, and danced to jazz music played by black musicians, all of which earned them the nickname "Flappers"....

hair short, and danced to jazz music played by black musicians, all of which earned them the nickname "Flappers," a term that originated in Great Britain to describe the open flaps of the rubber galoshes (rain boots) worn by young women there. It was the age of Prohibition, and many young women happily visited speakeasies, where alcohol was sold illegally. More white-collar jobs were available for women in American cities during the decade that reflected the burgeoning business climate of the era such as clerking in large department stores, working

in offices, and being telephone switchboard operators. Secretarial work had been a male-only profession in the nineteenth century, but the invention of the typewriter and its increased use in offices by the end of the century, as well as greater use of telephones by the start of the twentieth century, resulted in the feminization of office work since male employers considered phones and typewriters to be "women's machines."

However, large numbers of women in both cities and in rural areas still preferred the more traditional, long-term goal of marriage, motherhood, and housewifery with a husband earning a decent living for the family. For many American women, that life was altered after the Wall Street stock market crash of October 29, 1929. The Great Depression that followed in the United States and Europe was the worst economic downturn in the history of the industrialized world. By 1932, some fifteen million Americans, more than 20 percent of the U.S. population at the time, had lost their jobs, and dust storms in the Midwest led to farm foreclosures, forcing farmers and their families off their land to live in shantytowns or seek work out west. Although the New Deal policies of the administration of President Franklin D. Roosevelt helped to alleviate much of the financial suffering of Americans, the Depression was only completely relieved by the industries that produced war materiel after the United States entered World War II in 1941.

Diplomatic maneuvering, the need to solve the unemployment problem caused by the Great Depression, and a public mood of isolationism kept the United States neutral during the armed conflicts that raged in Asia and Europe between 1931 and 1941. The Depression forced many women to find wage work out of economic necessity, and they were welcomed by employers, who saw them as cheap labor, but women were generally unsupported in their efforts to make ends meet by a society that felt more comfortable with men and women in the traditional roles of breadwinner and homemaker, especially if they were white and middle class. However, after the Japanese attack on Pearl Harbor on December 7, 1941, ensured that the United States would enter the war, women were no longer told, "Don't steal a job from a man." Instead, they were urged to help the war effort by getting jobs as quickly as they could.

Although both single and married women entered the labor force in unprecedented numbers between 1941 and 1945, many initially chose to volunteer their time to help the war effort. Some three million women worked with the Red Cross, drove ambulances, served food and entertained soldiers at USO (United Service Organizations) canteens, sold war bonds, and spotted possible enemy planes for the

> The Depression forced many women to find wage work out of economic necessity, and they were welcomed by employers, who saw them as cheap labor....

Civil Defense. Women organized scrap metal drives in their communities and saved bacon grease for war materiel. However, by 1942, with the increasing number of men enlisting and drafted into the military, the labor force was becoming drained of male workers on a greater scale than World War I. Since high industrial production of such wartime weaponry as bomber planes was imperative, the U.S. government urged the industry to hire women to take the places of men. To entice women into the factories and to lessen general fears that such a gender role reversal would result in dire consequences for American society, the War Manpower Commission, with the cooperation of the media and industrial advertisers, mounted a massive recruitment campaign. The Office of War Information generated recruitment posters and pamphlets, and industry ads assured women that they could look glamorous even in coveralls. More importantly, the War Labor Board announced its intention to rule that women working in previously male jobs would be paid the same wages as men and agreed to mediate in labor disputes in order to avoid strikes.

The campaign proved so successful that some six million women took paying jobs during the war, an increase in the women's labor force from 25 percent to 36 percent. Nearly two million women went

to work in heavy industry, where they maneuvered giant overhead cranes, cleaned out blast furnaces, handled munitions, drove tanks off production lines, and worked as riveters and welders. One million women worked for the federal government in offices, handling the enormous amount of paperwork generated by the war. Still other women took over prewar jobs held by men such as bus and truck drivers, lumberjacks, train conductors, gas station operators, police officers, and lifeguards. Some 350,000 women also served in the military in clerical jobs and as nurses and commercial and military transport airplane pilots. Before the war, 72 percent of African American women worked as domestics, and 20 percent were farmhands. By the war's end, an estimated 18 percent of African American women were working in factories. Married and older women also benefited from the wartime allocation of labor: Women over thirty-five made up 75 percent of the new female labor force; 60 percent were married, and most had school-age or preschool-age children. One of the most difficult problems facing working mothers was the lack of government-sponsored daycare, an option offered to British women but unavailable to American women until 1944. Even then, daycare funding presented only a small percentage of the money needed, and federal and local programs only served 10 percent of the children of workers.

The public incarnation of female war workers was Rosie the Riveter, a character that appeared in a popular patriotic song of 1942. Rosie came to symbolize the tireless work of women in wartime industries and was depicted on posters with the slogan "We Can Do It!" as both a strong, but traditionally feminine, worker in form-fitting coveralls and as a burly, muscular woman in overalls. Magazine fiction and advertisements for products preferred to highlight the feminine qualities and traditional roles of America's Rosies along with their expertise at handling heavy equipment. One advertisement for Eureka vacuum cleaners that appeared in the popular magazine the *Saturday Evening Post* described Rosies who "leave their work benches at night to carry on with that other vitally important job of making a home for their children, and their hard-working, war-working husbands." Such advertisements reinforced society's view of Rosie the Riveter as first and

We Can Do It!

WAR PRODUCTION CO-ORDINATING COMMITTEE

The "We Can Do It!" poster is now an iconic symbol from World War II. Created by J. Howard Miller for the Westinghouse Electric & Manufacturing Company, it encouraged women to take on jobs in wartime industries and became a symbol of female patriotism in the United States. After the war, these same women were forced to leave their jobs as men returned from battle.

foremost a housewife and mother who would—and should—gladly return to her rightful place in the home when the war was over.

The work of American women during World War II helped to make victory possible, and they were irrevocably altered by their experiences. Neither they nor their daughters would forget the historical moment when millions of women began to see the promise of equality in the workplace both in the kinds of jobs they might do and the wages they could earn. However, as early as 1942, an editorial in the *Minneapolis Tribune* asked, "Where is this all going to end?… Is it hard to foresee, after the boys come marching home and they marry these emancipated young women, who is going to tend the babies in the next generation?" The more conservative values of postwar America, and the baby

boom that began in 1946, would lead most women back to the home and to idealized lives in suburban communities across the nation.

Many women continued in wage work after World War II. In the 1950s, 75 percent of women had jobs, many of them in teaching, office work, as researchers for magazines, and as airline hostesses. Office work could be particularly demeaning for women: Male employers called even middle-aged women "girls," and the standardization and eventual computerization of some tasks in the workplace made office work similar to work in factories with the result that female workers were easily replaceable and hampered in their ability to negotiate raises and advance within companies. Secretaries were expected to perform personal tasks for their male bosses such as getting coffee and shopping for wives and children, and female office workers in general were often subjected to sexual harassment on the job. Employment agencies used secret codes to rate applicants based on their appearance and their style, and an older woman's experience was frequently discounted in favor of a young woman's attractiveness. Highlighting the youth and attractiveness of women was especially common in the airline industry, where airlines advertised the sex appeal of stewardesses as a way to entice businessmen to fly with them. One example of sexually suggestive advertising was a 1971 ad campaign for National Airlines, which featured a variety of pretty, young women announcing their names with the tagline "Fly me," a slogan that was also featured in TV commercials for the airline. National also mandated that stewardesses wear "Fly me" buttons while on duty. The efforts of women during the second women's rights movement of the 1960s and 1970s to challenge the social status of women in a variety of workplaces was only partly successful: Sexist stereotyping, especially in the media, would last throughout the 1960s and into the 1970s and beyond. Even when women began to advance with the ambition of attaining upper-level and executive positions in the 1980s and 1990s, many faced a phenomenon called the "glass ceiling," the point at which they could not advance further. If a woman took maternity leave, usually without pay, or stopped working for a period of time to care for her children, she often found that her former position was unavailable.

> The efforts of women during the second women's rights movement of the 1960s and 1970s to challenge the social status of women in a variety of workplaces was only partly successful....

THE PRESIDENT'S COMMISSION ON THE STATUS OF WOMEN

In 1961, President John F. Kennedy, who had been elected largely due to the turnout of female voters, was criticized for his poor response in hiring women for high-ranking positions in his administration. When Esther Peterson, the director of the Women's Bureau of the U.S. Department of Labor and an assistant secretary of labor, approached Kennedy to urge him to establish a special commission to investigate the concerns of American women, the president, eager to repair the damage among his female constituency, agreed. Peterson's motives, like Kennedy's, were political. One concern was the Equal Rights Amendment (ERA), first drafted and submitted to Congress by Women's Party leaders Alice Paul and Crystal Eastman in 1923, which was originally named the Lucretia Mott Amendment in honor of the abolitionist and suffragist of an earlier generation and in 1943 renamed the Alice Paul Amendment. Peterson wanted to deflect any pro-ERA activity since the unions, which were strong Democratic Party supporters, opposed the amendment as harmful to protective legislation for female workers. She also wanted the proposed commission to help push through legislation mandating equal pay for equal work, an initiative favored by the unions since employers preferred to hire lower-paid female workers, which threatened male jobs.

The chair of the President's Commission on the Status of Women (PCSW) was Eleanor Roosevelt, former first lady and U.S. ambassador to the United Nations. The commission consisted of thirteen women and eleven men, who divided their work into seven investigative committees which solicited reports from women in various fields. One report that was submitted to the commission was "Images of Women in the Media," in which well-known female writers, including Betty Friedan, author of the groundbreaking work *The Feminine Mystique*, testified that the media's objectification of women rarely portrayed them as in any roles other than housewives and mothers. Dorothy Height, president of the National Council of Negro Women, chaired a committee that produced a report, "The Problem of Negro Women," which argued that too little attention had been given to the special burden of African American families and their lack of opportunities. In November 1962, Eleanor Roosevelt died, and as a tribute to her memory, the commission issued its sixty-page report, "American Women," on October 11, the anniversary of her birth. As expected, the commission's members, with the one exception of feminist lawyer and ERA supporter Marguerite Rawalt, opposed the Equal Rights Amendment, arguing that since the Supreme Court recognized gender equality as part of the Fifth and Fourteenth Amendments to the Constitution, an additional constitutional amendment was not needed "now." Rawalt fought for insertion of the word "now" in the report to allow room for a change in policy should the High Court consider altering its interpretation regarding further gender safeguards.

In its report, the commission raised the issue of women's legal inequality and called for an end to prohibitions against women jurors and restrictions on married women's rights, but the report's main achievement was its documentation of problems in employment discrimination, unequal pay, and lack of social services for working mothers. The commission recommended equal employment opportunity for women, federally and company-supported childcare, continuing education and increased vocational training for women, joint guardianship for children, and paid maternity leave. The report also urged that more women be promoted to high-level government and policy-making jobs. The government's first response to the commission's report was an executive order requiring the civil service to hire "solely on the basis of ability to meet the requirements of the position" without regard to gender. The

The Equal Pay Act of 1963 attempted to solve the inequality that existed because women were paid less than men for working similar jobs. It was expanded later by the Civil Rights Act of 1964 as well as the Education Amendments of 1972.

most important result of the report was congressional passage of the Equal Pay Act of 1963 (EPA), which was added to the Fair Labor Standards Act of 1938 as the first federal labor law prohibiting gender discrimination. Until the Equal Pay Act of 1963, only the state legislature of Wyoming had passed an equal pay law for employees of state governments.

The Equal Pay Act sought to redress the traditional concept that men, as heads of the households and principal breadwinners, were entitled to earn more than women, even when men and women did the same jobs and mandated equal pay for men and women in jobs requiring equal skill, responsibility, and effort. Subsequent legislation helped to strengthen the EPA such as the Civil Rights Act of 1964, which broadly prohibited discrimination of the basis of sex and the Bennett Amendment in Title VII of the same act, which more specifically covered discrimination by employers. The EPA's provisions originally excluded administrators, business executives, outside salespersons, and professionals, although this was amended in the Education Amendments of 1972. The EPA also left out almost two-thirds of working women, especially low-paid women in agriculture and domestic service.

The Equal Pay Act marked a significant first step toward ending wage discrimination. In 1963,

full-time, year-round female workers were earning an average of 63 percent less than male workers; by 1971, the gap had closed to 57 percent; and by the twenty-fifth anniversary of the EPA in 1998, the disparity had dropped to under 25 percent. In 2005, Senator Hillary Clinton and Representative Rosa DeLauro separately introduced the Paycheck Fairness Act to Congress to further strengthen the EPA, and in 2009, President Barack Obama signed into law the Lilly Ledbetter Fair Pay Act, an amended section of the Civil Rights Act of 1964, which addressed the 2007 Supreme Court case of *Ledbetter vs. Goodyear* regarding the statute of limitations for filing an equal-pay lawsuit.

Despite the Equal Pay Act, the legislative initiatives that followed it, and the lawsuits filed against companies in cases of wage discrimination, disagreement has occurred in determining exactly what constitutes equal skill, responsibility, and effort. A 2007 U.S. Department of Labor study concluded that the wage gap did not need correction since inequality might be due to a variety of factors, including the individual choices made by both female and male workers. This conclusion, together with a continued lack of support for working mothers regarding childcare and maternity leave, demonstrates that equality for female workers remains as much of an issue in the twenty-first century as it did in the textile mills of the nineteenth century.

BIOGRAPHIES

Mary Anderson (1872–1964)

Labor Leader

The first director of the Women's Bureau of the U.S. Department of Labor, Mary Anderson was a union leader who fought for acceptance of the principles of collective bargaining and for women in the workplace. She was the first female laborer who would head an executive department of the federal government.

Born in Lidköping, Sweden, Mary Anderson immigrated to the United States in 1888 at the age of sixteen. She went to work as a dishwasher in a lumberjacks' boardinghouse in Ludington, Michigan, and, after moving to Chicago, worked in a garment factory as a shoe stitcher. She joined the Boot and Shoe Workers' Union and was elected president of the female stitchers' Local 94 in 1900. She next became a leading member of the Women's Trade Union League in Chicago, where she worked to organize unions for women and to gain safer factory conditions for female workers. While working with the WTUL, Anderson became friends with social reformer Jane Addams, who said of Anderson, "She was not one of those feminists who are for women alone. Her heart and her brilliant mind recognized that as long as one group could be exploited society as a whole must suffer." In 1910, forty thousand garment workers in Chicago went on strike, and Anderson directed the WTUL to provide relief for distressed families. When the male-dominated United Garment Workers union called off the strike, Anderson felt that, despite their suffering, the female workers had gained little. The workers' failure to achieve the right to collective bargaining would drive Anderson's future political career.

In 1920, Anderson became the head of the Women's Bureau of the U.S. Department of Labor,

where she attempted to advance policies derived from the ideas of social justice feminism. To that end, Anderson pioneered the concept of using women's labor legislation to establish precedents to protect all workers, male and female. Under Anderson's direction, the Women's Bureau collected data on female factory workers and publishing important reports, particularly on the status of African American female workers.

After the Nineteenth Amendment was ratified guaranteeing women the right to vote, the National Women's Party, led by suffragist Alice Paul, set its next goal on the passing of an Equal Rights Amendment to end all discrimination against women. Since such an amendment would end the social justice legislation Anderson and the Women's Bureau had fought to enact, Anderson opposed the Equal Rights Amendment on the grounds that women, given the harsh conditions they faced in the workplace, needed specific protective legislation.

Anderson retired from the Women's Bureau in 1944. However, she remained active as a lobbyist for women's equality in the workplace, pressing for equal pay for factory workers. She became the legislative representative of the National Consumers League and conducted research to demonstrate wage discrimination against women in union contracts. She published her memoir, *Woman at Work*, in 1951.

Through her direct experiences as a factory worker and union member, Mary Anderson had perhaps more direct experience of women's working conditions than any other government administrator of her time. She would devote her career to raising awareness about working women while advocating and creating legislation that attacked inequality and discrimination and raised working conditions for all workers in the United States.

Sarah Bagley (1806–c. 1889)

Labor Leader

One of the Lowell, Massachusetts, "Mill Girls," Sarah Bagley would become a pioneering labor leader and social reformer. In 1846, Bagley would defy gender boundaries and expectations when she became the United States's first female telegraph operator.

Raised in rural Candia, New Hampshire, details about Bagley's early life are unknown, but she went to Lowell, Massachusetts, in 1836 to work in a cotton mill as a weaver. Despite earnings that allowed herself to save enough to make a deposit on a house for herself and her parents and siblings to live in in 1840, Bagley grew increasingly dissatisfied with working conditions and published one of the first insider's views of life for the Lowell factory girls. "Pleasures of Factory Life" was published in 1840 in the *Lowell Offering*, a literary magazine, written, edited, and published by working women. The "pleasures" Bagley recounted were, like angels' visits, "few and far between."

In 1844, Bagley and five other women met in the Anti-Slavery Hall in Lowell, where they formed the Lowell Female Reform Association to improve workers' health conditions and push for a 10-hour workday rather than the expected 12 to 14 hours per day women worked in the mills. Bagley became the president of the LFLRA, which grew to nearly five hundred members with branches in Waltham, Fall River, Manchester, Dover, and Nashua. The LFLRA published its own labor newspaper, the *Voice of Industry*, to which Bagley contributed articles and edited a women's column. She led a drive to petition the state legislature for the 10-hour day. Securing over ten thousand signatures, Begley and others testified before the Massachusetts Legislature describing the long hours and unhealthy working conditions in the mills. The legislature refused to act, claiming that working rules and conditions must be decided between the mills and the workers. However, labor and political pressure caused the Lowell textile corporations in 1847 to shorten the workday by 30 minutes. Under continuing pressure from the workers, hours were reduced to eleven in 1853 and ten in 1874.

In 1846, Bagley gave up her position as editor of the *Voice of Industry*, pushed out by those who found her writing too radical. She began to look for another job, and in 1847, only two years after Samuel Morse's first successful demonstration of the electric telegraph, Bagley was hired as a telegrapher in Springfield, Massachusetts, over strong objections. A local newspaper responded to her hiring by asking, "Can a woman keep a secret?" Bagley's efficiency as an operator si-lenced doubters and helped to open up telegraphy as an occupation for women around the country.

Mill records show that Bagley returned to work in 1848 as a weaver, lasting five months before leaving Lowell to care for her sick father. Details of her later life are sketchy. Some have suggested that she moved to Philadelphia to work as a social reformer with prostitutes and disadvantaged young women. Other records suggest that she married, moved to New York, and began working as a homeopathic physician. The date of her death is disputed.

Hattie Canty (1933–2012)
Labor Leader

Hattie Canty has been described as one of the greatest strike leaders in U.S. history. Rising from the ranks of Las Vegas hotel maids, Canty would become the president of the Las Vegas Culinary Workers' Union Local 226, which grew under her leadership to become one of the largest unions in southern Nevada.

A native of rural Alabama, Canty moved with her husband and two children to San Diego, where she worked as a cook and housekeeper. After moving to Las Vegas in 1961, she took a job as a maid at the Thunderbird Hotel. When her husband died in 1975 and she became the sole support of her eight children, Canty worked as a janitor for the Clark County School District and as a maid in private homes before taking a job at the Maxim Hotel and Casino (later the Westin Las Vegas).

Maxim workers were unionized by the Las Vegas Culinary Workers' Union Local 226, now an auxiliary of the larger union UNITE HERE, which helped secure health benefits from them as well as a pension and earnings far above the minimum wage. Canty was elected to the union's executive board in 1984, the year that Local 226 staged a successful seventy-five-day walkout against Las Vegas casinos to gain better health insurance benefits for workers. Union members elected Canty president in 1990, a position she held for over a decade. During Canty's tenure, the union was involved in the longest labor strike in American history when, in 1991, 550 culinary workers at the Frontier Hotel walked off the job over unfair labor practices by the casino's owners; the strike ended six and half years later when Frontier's new owner settled with the union.

Canty helped to found the Culinary Training Academy of Las Vegas in 1993, which helps to train thousands of workers in the hospitality industry yearly. It remains one of Canty's greatest achievements alongside her successful fight for worker's rights and improved working conditions. Hattie Canty's story of achievement from the position of maid to the presidency of one of the largest unions in the United States is a testimony to her commitment to social justice. Canty has observed, "Coming from Alabama, [labor reform] seemed like the civil rights struggle … the labor movement and the civil rights movement, you cannot separate the two of them."

Rebecca Harding Davis (1831–1910)
Author, Mill Worker

Novelist and short story writer Rebecca Harding Davis is best remembered for her story "Life in the Iron Mills," which was based on her experiences growing up in Wheeling, Virginia (later West Virginia), published in 1861. It would earn her the reputation as one of the earliest American realists in one of the first works to explore industrialization in American literature.

Born in Pennsylvania, Davis grew up in Alabama and Virginia, graduating from the Washington Female Seminary in Pennsylvania in 1848. An avid reader, Davis wrote poetry and stories from an early age, some of which were published. She achieved her greatest success when "Life in the Iron Mills" appeared in the prestigious *Atlantic Monthly* in 1861. Set in a small village that is dominated by its iron mills, the story describes its laborers as "masses of men, with dull, besotted faces bent to the ground, sharpened here and there by pain or cunning; skin and muscle and flesh begrimed with smoke and ashes." Its protagonist, Hugh Wolfe, is a laborer with artistic talent and a drive for intellectual achievement who is ground down by factory work. Davis's approach allows her readers to sympathize with her protagonist while introducing them to his grim realities in an honesty and candor that was new in Amer-

ican literature. "I want you to hide your disgust," Harding says directly to her readers, "take no heed to your clean clothes, and come right down with me—here into the thickest fog and mud and effluvia." Mixing romantic elements with its realistic setting, "Life in the Iron Mills" is a transitional literary work, a precursor to the American realism that would begin to emerge in the post-Civil War period by such writers as Mark Twain, William Dean Howells, Sarah Orne Jewett, Stephen Crane, and others.

Davis's other important works are the novels *Margaret Howth* (1863), exploring the restrictive roles of women as exemplified by a female mill worker; *Waiting for the Verdict* (1868), exploring the problems stemming from the abolition of slavery; and *John Andross* (1878), exploring political corruption.

Davis would become increasingly conservative. In *Pro Aris et Focis* (1870), she would argue that a woman's ordained role should be motherhood and that only women with "no chance of rest in a husband's house" should seek a profession. Davis's later reputation would be overshadowed by the achievements of her son, Richard Harding Davis (1864–1916), a newspaperman, magazine editor, and war correspondent.

Mary Dreier (1875–1963)
Labor Leader

A labor reformer and women's suffrage activist, Mary Elizabeth Dreier was an early leader of the Women's Trade Union League and served as chairs of the New York State Committee on Women in Industry and the New York City's Woman Suffrage Party.

Born in Brooklyn, New York, Dreier was the daughter of a well-to-do German immigrant father. After an early education from private tutors, she took classes at the New York School of Philanthropy but did not seek a college degree. Her strong religious background motivated her to undertake reform work. She met fellow reformer Frances Kellor in 1905, and the two would share a home until Kellor died in 1952. Dreier and her sister Margaret joined the New York Women's Trade Union League to organize female workers and to educate the public about urban labor conditions. Dreier would serve as the NYWTUL president from 1906 to 1914. During the 1909 strike of shirtwaist makers known as the Uprising of the 20,000, she was arrested, and the notoriety that followed her arrest led her to become a leading spokesperson for labor reform for female workers.

From 1911 to 1915, Dreier served on the New York State Factory Investigating Commission to propose factory reform legislation. In 1917, she became chair of the New York State Committee on Women in Industry of the Advisory Commission of the Council of National Defense. After the end of World War I, Dreier served on the executive committee of the New York Council for Limitation of Armaments and headed the WTUL Committee for the Outlawry of War.

The negative attitude of male trade unionists toward female workers caused Dreier to become an ardent supporter of suffrage and women's rights. She chaired the New York City's Woman Suffrage Party and served on several government and private committees on labor conditions and women's issues. Later in her career, she focused on international issues and foreign policy. She was an outspoken opponent of Nazi Germany and after World War II was a crusader against nuclear proliferation.

Dreier's position as a woman from a wealthy family could have insulated her from the struggles faced by working women. Instead, she devoted her life to the goal of improving labor conditions for women and advocating on behalf of social justice, equal rights, and peace around the world.

Harriet Farley (1813–1907)
Author, Mill Worker

Writer and editor Harriet Farley is celebrated for her direction of the *Lowell Offering,* the literary magazine written by women at the textile mills in Lowell, Massachusetts. Providing insights into the daily lives of mill workers, the *Offering* drew the admiration and interest of readers across the United States and abroad, one of which was British author Charles Dickens.

Farley grew up in Atkinson, New Hampshire, where she was educated at the local academy headed by her father. In 1837, she came to Lowell to work in a textile mill. In 1840, Farley's criticisms of working conditions in the mills was published by the *Lowell Offering*, and when it changed ownership in 1842, Farley was invited to become its editor.

Under Farley, the *Offering* offered articles that demonstrated the intelligence and refinement of the working girls and women of Lowell, spreading their notoriety as far away as England, where an anthology of selections from the *Offering* was published in 1844. Although Farley was determined to keep the *Offering* apolitical and noncontroversial, she became involved in the abolitionist movement, joining the Massachusetts Anti-Slavery Society and becoming a prominent abolitionist leader in Lowell. The *Lowell Offering* ceased publication in 1845 due to increased protests about working conditions that made the magazine's neutral stance seem too conservative and irrelevant to its current readers. From 1847 to 1850, the magazine was revived, with Farley as editor and publisher, as the *New England Offering.* Farley would move on to New York City, where she would write for the women's magazine *Godey's Lady's Book.* After her marriage, Farley gave up writing since her husband did not approve.

Farley's essays and stories have been described as "tiresomely inspirational" as well as conventional and often out of step with important issues of the women who wrote and read her magazine. However, her contribution was still significant in providing a human face and acceptable reputation of the factory girls and women who labored in the mills, who otherwise could have easily been dismissed and undervalued as mindless drudges and cogs in the factory machine. The *Offering* gave the female mill workers a claim to self-respect and dignity that would play an important role in the campaign for improved working conditions and in generating sympathy for their cause.

Elizabeth Gurley Flynn (1890–1964)
Labor Leader

Labor leader, radical reformer, and early feminist, Elizabeth Gurley Flynn played a leading role in the Industrial Workers of the World (IWW) and as a founding member of the American Civil Liberties Union.

Born in Concord, New Hampshire, the daughter of Irish immigrants, Flynn and her family moved to the Bronx, New York, in 1900. There, Flynn was educated in a local public school. "I hated poverty," she later recalled. "I was determined to do something about the bad conditions under which our family and all around us suffered." Like her parents, Flynn became a committed socialist who gave her first speech, "What Socialism Will Do for Women," at the Socialist Club in Harlem when she was just sixteen. As a result of her political activities, she was expelled from her high school.

In 1908, Flynn joined the radical labor organization the Industrial Workers of the World, called the Wobblies, and organized mine workers in Minnesota before joining the Spokane Free Speech Fight, a campaign of civil disobedience to repeal a Spokane, Washington, city ordinance prohibiting public speaking. The IWW had issued a call to members that read: "Wanted—Men to fill the Jails of Spokane," and Wobblies from across the country answered the call, including Flynn. While speaking, Flynn chained herself to a post, forcing the police to take even more time to arrest her. After Spokane, Flynn participated in 1912 in the Lawrence Textile Mill strike, known as the Bread and Roses strike. The brutal treatment of the strike workers brought national sympathy to the cause, and the strike ended with the owners granting most of the union's demands. During the strike, Joe Hill, a fellow Wobbly, wrote the ballad "The Rebel Girl" as a tribute to Flynn, who was thereafter known by that title. Flynn became one of the most important faces of the labor movement and traveled across the country, organizing in Pennsylvania, New Jersey, New York, and Massachusetts, where she was arrested more than ten times but never sentenced to prison.

During World War I, Flynn was arrested for her public opposition to American involvement and charged with violating the espionage act, though the charge was dropped. Her work defending immigrants who were being threatened with deportation due to their opposition to the war led her to help found the American Civil Liberties Union.

Elected to its board, Flynn was active in the ACLU throughout the 1920s and increasingly in International Labor Defense, a group that defended civil rights across the globe. She chaired the group for three years and was active in its campaign against the conviction of Italian immigrants and anarchists Nicola Sacco and Bartolomeo Vanzetti.

In 1936, Flynn joined the Communist Party and wrote a feminist column for the party's publication, the *Daily Worker.* During World War II, Flynn advocated for equal opportunity for women in the workplace, urging women to volunteer for the military and take war-related jobs. In the 1950s, anticommunist sentiment resulted in arrests for Flynn and other radicals on the charge of conspiracy to overthrow the government. She was convicted in 1953 and, refusing to avoid jail time by being deported, she served her prison term from 1955 to 1957. After her release, she was elected National Chairman of the Communist Party, a position she held for the rest of her life.

Flynn died in 1964 on a visit to the Soviet Union. She was given a state funeral in Red Square, but in accordance with her wishes, her remains were returned to the United States for burial in Chicago's Waldheim Cemetery near the graves of Bill Haywood and the 1886 Haymarket Market Martyrs.

Dolores Huerta (1930–)

Labor Leader

For more than thirty-five years, Dolores Huerta has fought to gain justice, dignity, and a decent standard of living for one of the country's most disadvantaged and exploited groups— the migrant farm workers.

Huerta was born Dolores Fernández in the small mining town of Dawson, New Mexico. Her father was of Native American and Mexican heritage; her mother was a second-generation New Mexican. Her parents divorced when she was a toddler, and her mother moved her daughter and two sons to Stockton, California, where Huerta grew up in a mixed neighborhood of farm workers and laborers. Unlike most Hispanic women of her generation, she continued her education after graduating from high school, receiving a degree in education from Stockton College. However, her interest soon shifted to social activism.

In 1955, Huerta began to work with the Community Service Organization, a Mexican American self-help association that sponsored voter registration drives and social reforms in the Hispanic community. Huerta was drawn to the plight of the migrant farm workers, who labored for low pay and were forced to live in cars, shacks, and tents; exposed to deadly pesticides; and deprived of health and welfare benefits. In 1962, she joined Cesar Chavez in organizing the Farm Workers Association, which later became the United Farm Workers, to fight for workers' rights, paid holidays, improved housing, unemployment insurance, and pension benefits. Huerta recruited union members and in 1965 helped to organize a nationwide grape boycott when California's grape pickers went on strike for better working conditions. Huerta was tireless in rallying support during the bitter, five-year strike. As a result of efforts of Huerta and other union leaders, the growers finally gave in and negotiated a historic contract with the union that set an hourly wage, established low-cost housing for workers, health benefits, and a total ban on toxic pesticides used in California vineyards.

During her early years in the labor movement, Huerta met her second husband, Ventura Huerta, who was also an activist. The marriage did not last partly as a result of her devotion to her work. Although she has admitted to placing her labor activities above concerns for her family, Huerta raised eleven children from her two marriages.

In 1988, during a peaceful demonstration in San Francisco, Huerta suffered broken ribs and a ruptured spleen when police officers swung their batons at protesters. The incident made headlines and caused the San Francisco police to change their crowd-control policies. Huerta recovered from her injuries and returned to work for the UFW as a negotiator and vice president. She retired from active union service in 1999.

Mary Harris "Mother" Jones (1830–1930)

Labor Leader

The most influential labor organizer in the United States in the late nineteenth and early twentieth centuries, Mary Harris "Mother" Jones was a feisty and fearless agitator who devoted her adult life to helping laborers obtain better working conditions and a decent living wage.

Mary Harris was the daughter of an Irish immigrant forced to flee arrest in Ireland for his efforts to gain Irish independence from England. Raised in Toronto, she worked as a teacher and a dressmaker, and in 1860, she accepted a teaching position in Memphis, Tennessee. The following year, she married George Jones, an ironworker and organizer for the Knights of Labor, one of the earliest American labor unions.

In 1867, a yellow fever epidemic swept through Memphis, claiming the lives of George and their four children. Jones stayed on to nurse other victims and then left for Chicago, where she opened a dressmaking shop. In 1871, her shop and home were destroyed during Chicago's Great Fire. She eventually reestablished her business and began to attend Knights of Labor meetings, where she impressed union leaders with her debating skills and knowledge of labor issues. Jones recruited more workers to the union cause and, beginning in 1891, she participated in strikes in Virginia, West Virginia, Colorado, Kansas, and Pennsylvania fighting for shorter working hours, better pay, and the right for workers to unionize. She lived wherever she found shelter, most often in workers' shanties or strikers' tent cities. Having no personal funds, she sometimes obtained income from union activities, but more often, she relied upon friends to supply her with whatever necessities she lacked. In 1897, after Jones addressed a railway union convention, union members began to refer to her as "Mother" by the union members, a name that stuck.

After taking a job as a textile mill worker to investigate working conditions for children, Mother Jones saw young children who had lost fingers or hands working with dangerous machinery. In 1903, she organized the Crusade of the Mill Children, marching with them from Pennsylvania to President Theodore Roosevelt's summer home on Long Island, New York. The march of the children—many of whom were undernourished and had suffered workplace accidents—brought public attention to their dangerous working conditions, and they helped to facilitate reforms. For her relentless agitation and success in organizing workers, Jones was called "the most dangerous woman in America."

Mother Jones herself was frequently jailed. In 1913, she was accused of inciting violence during a West Virginia strike and was convicted of conspiracy to commit murder. The governor commuted the sentence after a public outcry. The following year, her graphic account of the massacre of twenty people during a Ludlow, Colorado, miner's strike convinced President Woodrow Wilson to try to mediate the dispute.

A founding member of the Industrial Workers of the World (IWW), Mother Jones continued to agitate well into her nineties, rallying on behalf of garment, steel, and streetcar workers. She spent her last years in the home of a retired miner and his wife near Washington, D.C. On her one hundredth birthday, Jones received greetings from prominent Americans across the country, among them John D. Rockefeller Jr., whose father had owned some of the copper mines where she had led strikes.

Mary Morton Kehew (1859–1918)

Labor Leader

A labor union activist, suffragist, and social reformer, Mary Morton Kehew served as president of the Women's Educational and Industrial Union and as the first president of the National Women's Trade Union League, the first national association dedicated to organizing female workers.

Kehew was born Mary Morton Kimball in Boston, the daughter of a banker and granddaughter of a former Massachusetts governor. Privately educated in Boston and Europe, Kehew married William Brown Kehew, a wealthy businessman, in 1880. As a Boston Brahmin (a term used to describe the oldest families in Boston) and prominent society woman, Kehew was devoted to charity work and

used her social position and political connections to benefit working-class women. In 1886, she joined the Women's Educational and Industrial Union, serving as its president from 1892 to 1913. Kehew transformed this charity group into an organization focused on educating and organizing female workers, providing them with legal advice, counseling, and vocational training as well as conducting research on the lives of working women.

In 1892, Kehew formed the Union for Industrial Progress to organize women bookbinders, laundry workers, tobacco workers, and those in the needle trades. In 1903, Kehew was elected the first president of the National Women's Trade Union League with Jane Addams as vice president. Uncomfortable with public speaking, Kehew used her considerable organization skills behind the scenes, lobbying legislators and raising money among her wealthy friends. She served as president of the National Women's Trade Union League until 1913 and as board chair until her death in 1918 in Boston. Her friend and sister social reformer, Emily Greene Balch, would eulogize her as "the never-ending fairy godmother" of Boston social and labor reform.

Florence Kelley (1859–1932)

Labor Reformer

A crusading social and labor reformer, Florence Kelley was instrumental in the development of state and federal labor and social welfare legislation, including the elimination of sweatshops, minimum wage, 8-hour workdays, and the end of child labor, serving as the first general secretary of the National Consumers League and helping to create the National Association for the Advancement of Colored People (NAACP).

Kelley was born in Philadelphia. Her father was a prominent abolitionist and a founder of the Republican Party as well as a judge and longtime member of the U.S. House of Representatives. Kelley graduated from Cornell University in 1882, and after teaching evening classes for working women in Philadelphia for a year, she attended the University of Zurich, where she met her husband, Lazare Wischnewetzky, whom she married in 1884.

In 1891, she and her husband separated, and after their divorce, Kelley moved to Chicago, where she became a resident at Jane Addams's Hull-House settlement. In 1892, she began investigating slum conditions and sweatshops in the tenements, and her reports contributed to legislation that limited working hours for women, regulated tenement sweatshops, and prohibited child labor. To aid her in her advocacy, Kelley enrolled in law school at Northwestern University, graduating in 1884.

In 1899, Kelley moved to New York City and became general secretary of the newly established National Consumers League, a post she would hold until her death. She worked for federal legislation on working hours, wages, and child labor reforms. She organized some sixty local and state Consumers' Leagues, traveling the country and speaking out on social and labor reform. She helped initiate the "white label" given to stores that treated employees fairly, urging customers to only shop at businesses that displayed the "white label." Investigating labor conditions made Kelley aware of how African Americans were treated differently in the workplace, and in 1909, she helped organize the NAACP, a biracial organization founded to advance the cause of justice for African Americans. In 1912, Kelley helped to form the United States Children's Bureau, a federal agency overseeing children's welfare.

Kelley, who was active in the women's suffrage movement, served as vice president of the National American Woman Suffrage Association. She was also a founding member of the Women's International League for Peace and Freedom. During a lifetime devoted to social welfare, Kelley saw the enactment of many of the reforms for which she advocated.

Clara Lemlich (1888–1982)

Labor Activist

 A labor activist, Clara Lemlich's impassioned words in Yiddish to the garment workers gathered at New York's Cooper Union, "I am one of those who suffers from the abuses described here,

and I move that we go on a general strike," initiated the 1909–1910 Uprising of the 20,000, the massive strike of shirtwaist workers in New York's garment industry that became a critical turning point in American labor activism.

Born in the Ukrainian city of Gorodok to a Jewish family, Lemlich was raised in a predominantly Yiddish-speaking village. Following a pogrom, she immigrated to the United States in 1903 and found work in New York City's garment industry. Faced with long hours, low pay, appalling work conditions, and mistreatment from male supervisors, Lemlich joined the International Ladies' Garment Workers' Union and was elected to the executive board of Local 25 of the ILGWU.

Lemlich led several strikes of shirtwaist makers and challenged the mostly male leadership of the union. At a mass meeting at Cooper Union in support of a strike among shirtwaist workers at the Triangle Shirtwaist Company and the Leiserson Company, Lemlich listened patiently to leading figures of the American labor movement, who spoke about the need for solidarity and preparedness. Impatient with the slow pace of decision making among those present, Lemlich took the platform and demanded action, saying, "I have listened to all the speakers, and I have no further patience for talk." A vote for a general strike was carried, and approximately twenty thousand of the thirty-two thousand workers in the shirtwaist trade walked off their jobs. Lemlich would take a leading role in the strike that lasted almost three months, producing union contracts at almost every shop except the Triangle Shirtwaist Company. In 1911, the refusal of the Triangle owners to implement safety improvements cost the lives of nearly 150 garment workers during the infamous Triangle Shirtwaist Fire.

After the strike, Lemlich was blacklisted from New York garment shops. She turned her attention to the suffrage movement, helping to found the Wage Earners' League for Woman Suffrage; however, she was fired from her paid position as an organizer for refusing to moderate her radical politics to suit most middle-class suffragists. In 1913, Lemlich married Joe Shavelson, a printer, with whom she had three children and worked to organize wives and mothers around such issues as housing, food, and public education. She joined the Communist Party in 1926 and helped found the United Council of Working Class Housewives, an organization that aided wives of striking workers by setting up community kitchens and cooperative childcare. After the Communist Party created a Women's Commission in 1929, Lemlich helped form the United Council of Working Class Women that led strikes, anti-eviction demonstrations, boycotts, sit-ins, and marches. In 1935, the UCWW changed its name to the Progressive Women's Councils and began building a coalition with women's organizations not affiliated with the Communist Party. Lemlich served as the organization's first president.

After her husband became ill, Lemlich returned to the garment trade and the union movement. After a visit to the Soviet Union as a member of the American Committee to Survey Trade Union Conditions in Europe, Lemlich and other members of the committee had their passports revoked. In 1951, she was summoned to Washington to testify before the House Committee on Un-American Activities and remained under HUAC surveillance for the next two decades. After she retired from garment work in 1954, Lemlich fought a long battle with the International Ladies' Garment Workers' Union to obtain a pension. When her second husband died in 1967, Lemlich moved to California to be near her children. She entered the Jewish Home for the Aged in Los Angeles, where she persuaded the management of the home to join the United Farm Workers' boycott of grapes and lettuce and urged the workers there to organize a union.

Frieda S. Miller (1890–1973)

Labor Leader, Women's Rights Activist

A labor and women's rights activist, Frieda S. Miller is known for her efforts to address the problems of women in industry during the postwar economy. Miller pioneered several reforms that would subsequently be accepted as standard practice in the workplace.

Born in La Crosse, Wisconsin, Miller was raised by her grandparents after the death of her mother

and father. She graduated from Milwaukee's Downer College in 1911 before doing graduate work in economics, law, political science, and sociology as a fellow at the University of Chicago. In 1916, she taught social economy as a research assistant at Bryn Mawr and, in 1917, became secretary of the Philadelphia Women's Trade Union League, a post she held until 1923.

In 1928, Frances Perkins, the industrial commissioner for the State of New York, hired Miller as the director of the Bureau of Women in Industry. Miller spent several years working on legislation to create a minimum wage law for women and children, which passed in 1933. In 1938, she followed Frances Perkins, the nation's first woman secretary of labor, as the second female commissioner of labor in New York, a post she held until 1943. She then served as director of the Women's Bureau of the U.S. Department of Labor from 1944 to 1953. In 1957, Miller became a delegate to the United Nations for the International Alliance of Women and worked on various UNICEF programs until 1967, when she retired.

Sara Nelson (1974–)

Labor Leader

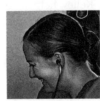

A United Airlines flight attendant since 1996, Sara Nelson is the international president of the Association of Flight Attendants-CWA, AFL-CIO, representing nearly fifty thousand flight attendants from twenty airlines. She has been described as "America's Most Powerful Flight Attendant" and a rising star of the labor movement.

Nelson grew up in Corvallis, Oregon, and earned her bachelor's degree from Principia College with majors in English and education. After graduation, faced with $45,000 in student debt, she worked for a year holding down four jobs—waiting tables, selling linens, substitute teaching, and temping at an insurance company. She has been a union activist since the beginning of her flying career. At the age of twenty-nine, Nelson was tapped by the AFA as its chief of communications. After United Airlines filed the largest corporate bankruptcy in U.S. history in 2002 and used bankruptcy to terminate the flight attendants' pension plan, Nelson announced the AFA's intent to strike and won United's concession to pay more for a pension replacement plan.

In 2011, she was elected International Vice President of the AFA, and in 2014, she was elected its president. She successfully led the AFA's No Knives Ever Again Campaign in 2013 to convince the Transportation Security Administration to reverse its decision to allow knives on passenger flights. It is widely believed that her call for a strike by airline workers helped to end the 2018–2019 government shutdown. Jonathan Ornstein, the chief executive of Mesa Airlines, has said that "I think [Nelson] is truly one of the most effective labor leaders I have ever met." Nelson's achievements have come despite the prejudice and condescension she has felt as a female flight attendant and union leader. "Even today," she has stated at a congressional hearing, "we are called pet names, patted on the rear when a passenger wants our attention, cornered in the back galley and asked about our 'hottest' layover."

A committed supporter of unions, Miller is an important advocate for labor in the twenty-first century.

Pauline Newman (1887–1986)
Labor Leader

Labor activist Pauline Newman was the first female general organizer of the International Ladies' Garment Workers' Union (ILGWU) and for six decades served as the education director of the ILGWU Health Center.

Newman was born in Kaunas, Lithuania, where her father was a teacher. As a Jew, she was not only barred from the local public school but was refused entry into Jewish schools because she was a girl. However, she convinced her father to let her sit in on his classes, and she learned to read and write in Hebrew and Yiddish. Following the death of her father in 1901, her family immigrated to New York City, where Newman, at the age of eight, began

working at the Triangle Shirtwaist Company, earning $1.50 a week and working twelve-hour days. "All we knew," Newman would recall, "was the bitter fact that after working seventy to eighty hours in a seven-day week, we did not earn enough to keep body and soul together."

As a teenager, she joined the local Socialist Literary Club to improve her English and discuss progressive political and social theories. In 1907, she helped organize one of the largest rent strikes in New York history and was hailed as a working-class hero. In 1908, having quit her job at the Triangle Shirtwaist Company, Newman won the New York State Socialist Party nomination for secretary of state, and she used her campaign to argue for women's suffrage. She was a leader of the Uprising of the 20,000, the largest general strike created and organized by American women up to that time. In recognition of her central role in organizing and sustaining the strike, Newman was appointed as the first female general organizer for the International Ladies' Garment Workers' Union, and from 1909 to 1913, she organized garment strikes around the country while continuing to campaign for women's suffrage for the Women's Trade Union League.

Newman grieved deeply for the 146 workers who had lost their lives as a result of the tragic 1911 Triangle Shirtwaist Fire; many of the victims had been her friends. Soon after, New York State established the Factory Investigation Commission (FTC), an investigative commission invested with the power to ensure worker safety. Newman was offered a job as one of the commission's first inspectors, a position she gladly accepted on New York's Factory Investigation Commission to ensure worker safety. During her work with the FTC, Newman met Frances Perkins, who would later become President Franklin D. Roosevelt's secretary of labor. Perkins helped Newman become a liaison between the labor movement and government as a lobbyist. In 1917, the Women's Trade Union League sent Miller to Philadelphia to open a new branch. While there, Newman met labor activist Frieda S. Miller, who was then an economics instructor at Bryn Mawr College. The couple moved to Greenwich Village, where they raised Miller's daughter and lived together until Miller's death in 1974.

In 1923, Newman became the educational director for the ILGWU's Health Center, the first comprehensive medical program created by a union for its members. For the next sixty years, Newman would work to promote health care for workers, adult education, and increased participation by women in the union. Following World War II, Newman was asked by the U.S. Departments of State and Labor to review postwar factory conditions across Germany. She also served as a consultant to the U.S. Public Health Service during the Truman administration.

Pauline Newman died in 1986 in the New York City home of her adopted daughter at the age of ninety-eight, having risen from a child factory worker to an influential women's trade unionist and crusader for women in the workplace.

Leonora O'Reilly (1870–1927)

Union Organizer

 A trade union organizer and suffragist, Leonora O'Reilly helped form the Women's Trade Union League, an organization dedicated to raising awareness about the exploitation of female workers and to educate them on the advantages of trade union membership.

The daughter of Irish immigrants who had escaped the Irish Potato Famine, O'Reilly was born into a working-class family and raised on the Lower East Side of New York City. When O'Reilly was one, her father died, leaving her mother, a garment worker, as the sole support of Leonora and her younger brother. At the age of eleven in 1881, O'Reilly left school to begin working as a seamstress at a color factory and, in 1886, joined the Knights of Labor, one of the earliest trade unions. In 1898, O'Reilly took art courses at New York's Pratt Institute, graduating in 1900. She was supported in her studies with the help of a wealthy Boston philanthropist who provided her with an annual salary that allowed her to leave wage work for full-time labor activism. She organized the Working Women's Society in 1886, a women's local for the United Gar-

ment Workers union in 1897, and was a founder of the Women's Trade Union League in 1903, serving as a member of its executive committee from 1903 to 1915. O'Reilly helped to organize the 1909–1910 New York City strike of female garment workers known as the Uprising of 20,000. She also led protests following the tragic Triangle Shirtwaist Fire of 1911.

O'Reilly, whose nickname was "The Agitator," was a rousing public speaker and masterful organizer. She was a founder of the group that became the National Association for the Advancement of Colored People (NAACP), an active member of the Socialist Party, the chair of the industrial committee of the New York City Woman Suffrage Party (1912), and a trade union delegate to the International Congress of Women (1915) and the International Congress of Working Women (1919).

Between 1916 and 1923, O'Reilly worked with several American organizations that supported the Irish rebellion against Great Britain. In the 1920s, O'Reilly taught courses on "the theory of the labor movement" at New York's New School for Social Research. One of the most persevering and persuasive activists of her day, Leonora O'Reilly is celebrated for her dedication to the cause of bettering the lives of female workers.

Mary Kenney O'Sullivan (1864–1943)

Union Organizer

A suffragist and union organizer during the early labor movement, Mary Kenney O'Sullivan fought against the exploitation of children and nonunionized women who labored in American factories in unsafe conditions.

Born in Hannibal, Missouri, the only child of working-class Irish immigrants, O'Sullivan began work at the age of fourteen as a bookbinder and, by the age of nineteen, had mastered every skill in the printing trade and was promoted to forewoman. However, she never earned as much as her male counterparts in the same positions, and the harsh working conditions she experienced played an important role in her growing social activism.

In 1888, O'Sullivan moved to Chicago, where she lived at Jane Addams's Hull-House settlement house, began organizing women into trade unions, and assisted social reformer Florence Kelley in Kelley's inspection of tenements and sweatshops. In 1892, Samuel Gompers, president of the American Federation of Labor, appointed O'Sullivan its first female, full-salaried general organizer, a position she held for nearly a year. During her work with the AFL, O'Sullivan organized garment workers in New York City and Troy, New York, and printers, binders, shoe workers, and carpet weavers in Massachusetts. While in Chicago, O'Sullivan was appointed one of twelve inspectors in the new city Factory Inspection Department headed by Florence Kelley.

In the mid-1890s, O'Sullivan moved to Boston, where she married journalist John O'Sullivan and worked for the Women's Educational and Industrial Union organizing rubber makers and shoe, garment, and laundry workers. After her husband died in 1902, leaving her to raise three children, O'Sullivan worked as the manager of a model tenement in South Boston as well as for the American Federation of Labor. In 1903, she cofounded the Women's Trade Union League. O'Sullivan worked to increase female participation in unions as well as voting rights, publishing a pamphlet called "Why the Working Woman Needs the Vote."

During the Lawrence Bread and Roses textile strike of 1912, O'Sullivan's relationship with the WTUL became strained as the result of clashes between the AFL, which opposed the strike and now controlled the WTUL, and the Industrial Workers of the World (IWW), which, like O'Sullivan, was a strong supporter of the walkout. The WTUL, which had been providing aid to striking workers under O'Sullivan's direction, withdrew its support and caused her to end her association with the organization.

Following the Lawrence strike, O'Sullivan worked to secure legislation for improved working conditions in Massachusetts factories. She was hired in 1914 by the state as the inspector for the Massachusetts Board of Labor and Industries to oversee the enforcement of the labor laws she helped to pass. She would hold that position until her retirement in 1934.

O'Sullivan died at the age of seventy-nine in 1943. Her bust was added in 1999 to other celebrated Massachusetts women, such as Dorothea Dix and Lucy Stone, at the Massachusetts State House.

Lucy Parsons (c. 1853–1942)
Labor Leader

An early African American labor organizer and radical reformer, Lucy Parsons was one of the nation's first minority labor and social activists. An anarchist, socialist, journalist, and union leader, Parsons was an outspoken defender of free speech and free assembly despite the relentless persecution she experienced by government agents opposed to her militancy. Parsons was described by the Chicago Police Department as "more dangerous than a thousand rioters."

Details about Parsons's upbringing and heritage are disputed. Born Lucy (or Lucia) Eldine Gonzalez in Texas, Parsons would list her birthplace as Virginia. She may have been born a slave to parents of Native American, African American, and Mexican ancestry. She has been alternately called the first "Chicana socialist labor organizer" and "the first Black woman to play a prominent role in the American left." Parsons worked as a cook and a seamstress in the home of white families and married a freed slave when she was still a teenager. The couple had one child, who died in infancy. Around 1869, Parsons met Albert Parsons, a printer and a former Confederate soldier, who she married in 1872 a few weeks before interracial unions were outlawed in Texas. The Parsonses moved to Chicago, where they frequented socialist and trade union circles, and Albert joined the Knights of Labor, the Workers Party, and the Socialist Labor Party. Lucy Parsons joined the Working Women's Union.

In 1877, the Parsonses participated in the nationwide rail workers' strike, the greatest mass strike in U.S. history. Because of his involvement, Albert was fired from his job and blacklisted in the printing trade. Lucy Parsons opened a dress shop, hosted meetings for the International Ladies' Garment

Workers' Union, and wrote for many radical publications, including *The Socialist* and *The Alarm,* an anarchist weekly, published by the Working People's Association, which she and her husband had founded in 1883. By 1886, demand for an 8-hour workday resulted in strikes across the country. In Chicago, the strikes became violent. Police disrupted a peaceful demonstration in Haymarket Square, and an unknown person threw a bomb, killing one officer, sparking a riot during which both workers and police were killed and injured. Police responded by rounding up any suspected anarchists, including Albert Parsons, who was not even at Haymarket Square at the time. He was arrested, tried, convicted, and executed in 1887. Lucy Parsons was under continual police surveillance as she petitioned for leniency for the convicted men as well as censure from the Knights of Labor, who took a strong stance against the Haymarket activists.

After her husband's execution, Parsons lived in poverty, receiving a small weekly allowance from a support group formed to help families of the Haymarket martyrs. She was still a widely known and in-demand public speaker and was often arrested for her activism. In 1905, she helped found the Industrial Workers of the World (IWW) and, in 1915, organized the Chicago Hunger Demonstration. In 1925, she began working with the National Committee of the International Labor Defense, a communist-led organization that defended labor activists. Parsons continued to give fiery speeches into her eighties. She died in a house fire in Chicago in 1942. Despite censure for her violation of virtually every restriction imposed upon the women of her time, Parsons, who has been described as "a revolutionary cadre of one," remained steadfastly opposed to economic inequality and committed to social justice.

union leaders and was branded a troublemaker. Between 1934 and 1944, Pesotta was one of the most successful labor organizers in the United States.

Born Rakhel Peisoty in Ukraine, Pesotta was exposed to anarchist views early from the books in her father's library and in a local anarchist group. She refused her parents' arranged marriage for her and immigrated to New York City in 1913, where she found work as a seamstress in shirtwaist factories. She joined the International Ladies' Garment Workers' Union (ILGWU). She would create the union's first education department in 1915 and, in 1920, was elected to an executive board position. Pesotta's charismatic personality, boundless energy, and empathy with the workers made her a sought-after and highly successful labor organizer, and she traveled the country broadcasting the union message and aiding workers' strikes and demonstrations. In 1934, she was elected as vice president of the ILGWU, a position she held for a decade.

On loan from the ILGWU, she participated with the Congress of Industrial Organizations (CIO) in several of the key labor disputes of the 1930s in Akron, Ohio, and Flint, Michigan. She protested the lack of leadership positions for women in the union and refused a fourth term on the CIO executive board, stating that "one woman vice president could not adequately represent the woman who now make up 85 percent of the International's membership of 305,000." Instead, she went back to the factory from which she began, supporting herself as a seamstress.

Following her resignation from ILGWU, she published two memoirs, *Bread upon the Waters* (1945) and *Days of Our Lives* (1958), while supporting herself largely through factory work. She resigned from her job after a cancer diagnosis and moved to Florida, where she died alone in a Miami hospital.

Rose Pesotta (1896–1965)

Labor Leader

A labor activist and anarchist, Rose Pesotta was one of the first female vice presidents of the International Garment Workers' Union (ILGWU). In that capacity, she challenged the authority of the male

Esther Peterson (1906–1997)

Workers' Rights Activist

For more than fifty years, Esther Peterson was a determined advocate for workers' rights who was honored by the National Women's Hall of Fame as "one of the nation's most effective and

beloved catalysts of change." She was a driving force in the fight for legislation to secure equal pay for equal work, creating the Presidential Commission on the Status of Women to document workplace discrimination toward women.

Born Esther Eggertsen, Peterson was the daughter of Danish immigrants. She grew up in a Mormon family in Provo, Utah, graduated from Brigham Young University in 1927, and earned a master's degree from Teachers College, Columbia University, in 1930. She held several teaching positions, including one at the innovative Bryn Mawr Summer School for Women Workers in Industry. After her marriage to Oliver Peterson in 1932, the couple moved to Boston, where she taught at the Winsor School.

In 1938, Peterson became a paid organizer for the American Federation of Teachers and then served as assistant director of education and lobbyist for the Amalgamated Clothing Workers of America (1939–1944, 1945–1948). From 1958 to 1961, she worked in Washington, D.C., as legislative representative of the industrial union department of the AFL-CIO. She would move on to various positions in the Women's Bureau of the U.S. Department of Labor, where she worked from 1961 to 1969. As assistant secretary of labor and director of the Women's Bureau in the administration of President John F. Kennedy, Peterson was the highest-ranking woman in the administration. The Presidential Commission on the Status of Women, the first such commission, focused federal attention for the first time on the status and condition of women in the workplace. Peterson was a driving force behind the passage of the Equal Pay Act of 1963 and would subsequently serve both Presidents Lyndon Johnson and Jimmy Carter as an adviser in consumer affairs. Peterson's consumer advocacy included truth in advertising, uniform packaging, unit pricing, and nutritional labeling laws.

Peterson received the Presidential Medal of Freedom in 1981 for her career as a significant voice for working women and for all consumers. Asked to provide advice to young people, she said that "your life can be satisfying and happy if you work to make a difference. Maybe the difference will be just a little tiny piece and not a big difference. But the point is to make a difference by the way you live your life."

Rose Schneiderman (1882–1972)

Labor Leader, Union Organizer

For more than fifty years, Rose Schneiderman was an influential leader in what she called "the most exciting movement in the United States—the fight of workers for the right to organize." During her long and extraordinary career, much of which was spent as president of the New York Women's Trade Union League (NYWTUL) and the national Women's Trade Union League (WTUL), Schneiderman worked tirelessly to improve conditions for American women in the workplace and to provide trade union women with schools, recreational facilities, and professional networks. Schneiderman's commitment to bettering the quality of working women's lives is typified in a famous declaration often attributed to her: "The worker must have bread, but she must have roses, too."

Born in Saven, a small village in Russian Poland, Schneiderman was the oldest of four children. Her father worked as a tailor, and her mother made custom uniforms for Russian soldiers. The family lived in one room in the back of a house where the landlady kept a saloon. Despite the resistance of education for girls, Schneiderman began attending Hebrew school at the age of four, and, at six, she also started going to public school in Russia. She would continue her schooling on and off after the family immigrated to New York City in 1890, where they lived in a two-room tenement apartment on the Lower East Side. After her father's death, Schneiderman was placed in a Jewish orphanage for a time and, at the age of thirteen, went to work as a cashier and sales clerk in a department store, working a seventy-hour week for $2.75. In 1898, she took a better paying position as a lining maker in a cap factory. Introduced to socialism and trade unionism by friends, Schneiderman recalled, "I became interested in politics. I knew nothing about trade unions or strikes and, like other young people, I was likely to look upon strikebreakers as heroic figures because they wanted to work and were willing to risk everything for it. My entire point of view was changed by the conversations I heard...."

In 1903, Scheiderman organized her shop into the first female local of the United Cloth Hat and Cap Makers' Union, and, under her leadership, membership grew to several hundred. The following year, she became the first woman to hold national office in an American labor union when she was elected to the general executive board of the United Cloth Hat and Cap Makers' Union. In 1905, she began her association with the Women's Trade Union League. Formed in 1903, the WTUL was a coalition of reformers dedicated to unionizing working women. Schneiderman would call the WTUL "the most important influence in my life," and she rose in the ranks as a masterful organizer. She would play a key role in the 1909 general strike of New York's garment workers, called the Uprising of the 20,000, one of the pivotal events of the American women's labor movement. Schneiderman helped organize picket lines, raised money for strikers, and made numerous speeches in defense of the cause.

After the strike was concluded, Schneiderman intended to complete high school and go on to college to become a teacher. Instead, she took a full-time position as an organizer with the NYWTUL, stating "my heart was in the trade-union movement." In 1918, she was elected president of the NYWTUL, a position she held until 1949. In addition to her WTUL activities, Schneiderman was an ardent suffragist and helped form the Wage Earner's League for Woman Suffrage. In 1926, now a nationally known figure, Schneiderman was elected president of the WTUL, and she turned her attention to promoting workers' education and lobbying for minimum wage and 8-hour workdays. By the 1940s, the influence of the WTUL had waned with its function of union organization and negotiation taken over by the AFL and CIO. Schneiderman, then seventy-three, observed, "They don't need us anymore. Let's step out gracefully." She retired from public life, lived quietly in Manhattan, and in 1972 died in the Jewish Home and Hospital for the Aged.

Schneiderman would write in her autobiography that "to me the labor movement was never just

a way of getting higher wages. What appealed to me was the spiritual side of a great cause that created fellowship. You wanted the girl or man who worked beside you to be treated just as you were." Schneiderman dedicated her career toward realizing this ideal, and workers today take for granted the protections won for them by Rose Schneiderman's long struggle.

Randi Weingarten (1957–)
Educator, Labor Leader

A labor leader and educator, Randi Weingarten is the current president of the American Federation of Teachers and the former president of the United Federation of Teachers. Weingarten became the first openly gay individual to be elected president of a national American labor union.

Born in New York City, Weingarten grew up in Rockland County, New York, and developed an early interest in labor unions and politics when her mother—a teacher—went on strike. Weingarten attended Cornell University and then the Cardozo School of Law. In 1986, she became counsel to the then president of the United Federation of Teachers, representing the union in several important cases and, by the early 1990s, was the union's chief contract negotiator. From 1991 to 1997, Weingarten also taught history at Clara Barton High School in Crown Heights, Brooklyn. She was elected the union's assistant secretary in 1995, treasurer in 1997, and finally president in 1998, a position she held for twelve years before becoming president of the American Federation of Teachers in 2008.

As president of the UFT, Weingarten fought for higher salaries and better training for teachers as well as merit pay. As president of the AFT, she has worked to put educational reform on the national agenda, to change how teachers are evaluated, and to improve access for all students. Weingarten has long advocated a "bottom up" approach to education reform that takes into account the views and needs of teachers and their students. Worried about the consequence of certain market-based proposals that she fears will result in the "eventual elimination of public education altogether," Weingarten sees the role of private, charter schools as complementing, rather than competing with, public schools. "Charter schools should be laboratories for innovation and creative ideas," she has asserted, "that can be scaled up so they can enrich communities."

Often a lightning rod for the contentious issues surrounding education in America, Weingarten has been a tireless advocate for teachers' rights and responsibilities as well as one of the nation's most effective contemporary labor leaders.

THE SECOND
WOMEN'S RIGHTS MOVEMENT

When American servicemen returned to the United States after the end of World War II in 1945, they either resumed the jobs at which they worked before the war, found new jobs in business and industry, went back to college, or entered college or vocational-technical schools with the help of the G.I. Bill. Women who had worked in industrial and other jobs related to the war industry and were reluctant to leave their newfound independence unwillingly quit or were let go. Other women in the wartime workforce gladly went back to caring for their husbands, children, and homes. Women were also marrying younger, starting families, and bearing more children, with only 6.8 percent of women remaining childless compared to 14 percent in 1900. Between 1946 and 1964, the years that are associated with the generation of Americans known as the baby boomers, also called the boomers, the birthrate soared. Some 3,411,000 babies were born in 1946 as compared with 2,858,000 births the previous year, and in 1957, a record 4.3 million babies were born. By the mid-1960s, over seventy million boomers had been born out of a total U.S. population of approximately 197,000,000, and about forty million of them were girls. Like the boys, baby boomer girls were the children of parents who had experienced the Great Depression, World War II, and the Korean War, events that helped to solidify a sense of patriotism and domestic values. Exhausted by the war, most Americans desired a return to normalcy, which meant that fathers went to work and mothers who did not need to work stayed home, even college-educated women with advanced degrees. Despite an increase of women in the labor pool, the mothers of the baby boomers experienced a postwar cultural backlash against women, especially married women, working outside the home and a society that encouraged both women and men to embrace traditional domestic roles. In 1945, only 18 percent of Americans approved of a married woman working if she had a husband to support her.

The 1947 best-selling book *Modern Woman: The Lost Sex* by Maryania Farnham, a psychiatrist, and Ferdinand Lundberg, a sociologist and social historian, set the tone for the time by making the case that a woman's true vocation should be a mother and homemaker and insisted that women who strayed from their natural reproductive functions and roles as nurturers were psychologically disturbed. In 1949, the Pillsbury flour company inaugurated the Grand National Recipe and Baking Contest, which became known as the Pillsbury Bake-Off, where homemakers could win up to $25,000 by displaying their cooking and baking skills. One print ad of the 1950s encouraged women to buy Heinz soups to keep husbands from "yawning at the table"; another featured a wife in a fetching bathrobe serving her husband breakfast in bed with the caption,

"Show her it's a man's world." The new medium of television also reinforced gender stereotyping with several domestic comedies in the 1950s and 1960s in which fathers generally knew best and mothers were either highly competent and calm nurturers or scatterbrained wives with husbands who needed to control them in order to diminish the damage caused by their antics. Unmarried, female TV characters in the 1950s and early to mid-1960s such as Eve Arden's caustic high school English teacher in *Our Miss Brooks* and Rose Marie's very funny television variety show writer in *The Dick Van Dyke Show* generally did not have "careers"; they had jobs, which would end once they captured and married the men of their dreams. An exception in the 1950s was *Private Secretary* with Ann Sothern as the smart and competent title secretary, who was often called upon to save her publicist boss from the various romantic and business complications in which he became entangled.

Baby boomer women born in the late 1940s and the early 1950s, as well as the generation of women born in the mid-1930s to the mid-1940s, grew up and came of age in an era that was both

Advertising in the post-war era was designed to reinforce gender stereotypes. Women were portrayed as nurturers whose role was to cook, clean, and raise children, and ads for products like this food mixer reflected that standard.

constrictive and progressive. One popular cultural notion was that the educational system was not adequately preparing young women, especially the older sisters of the baby boomers, for their proper domestic roles. To that end, some colleges featured a required course called "Marriage and Family Life Education." Women were marrying soon after high school or college, dropping out of college to marry, and giving up their jobs once wed. It was widely accepted that women went to college to obtain a "MRS" degree and that the only reason for them to become well educated was to serve as more stimulating mates for their husbands. In 1949, a progressive note was sounded when Harvard Law School announced its intention to admit female students for the first time. However, in 1950, *Educating Our Daughters: A Challenge to the Colleges* by college professor and historian Lynn White Jr. called for the rejection of male-oriented coeducational colleges and the development of programs to address the special needs of women. On the surface, that was not an unreasonable concept given the educational effectiveness of such women-only colleges as Smith, Vassar, Mount Holyoke, and Wellesley, but White went further, making his thesis both sexist and classist with the argument that college-educated women had a special duty to ensure a stable population by counteracting the "sterility" overtaking better educated and more affluent women and threatening democracy. He made the claim that colleges and universities needed to instill the idea in their female students that it was their duty to bear at least three children so that the United States might avoid a "drift toward totalitarianism." His book coincided with the infamous nude "posture" photos of male and female first-year students, a practice begun at Harvard in the 1880s, reinitiated by Harvard researcher William Sheldon in the 1940s, and overseen by physical education departments at the all-male Ivy League colleges, the elite women's "sister" colleges associated with them, and other schools from the 1940s to the 1970s. The black-and-white photos featured some forty-six thousand students over the years posing with four-inch, metal pins sticking out of their spines to determine whether a student had curvature of the spine and were intended to predict a student's personality by identifying individual body shape. The studies were carried out in the name of science, but in reality, they were an exercise in eugenics, meant to pick out the more attractive students in order to enforce better future breeding among the intellectual elite. The practice was slowly phased out over the next three decades after parents and students began to complain, and college officials took a closer look at William Sheldon's demeaning and dubious matchmaking theory. The majority of the photos were burned, but several thousand of them remain housed at the Smithsonian Institution.

The emphasis on women's traditional domestic roles that was prevalent in the 1950s and 1960s often clashed with an American secondary and college educational system that stressed academic focus and physical fitness along with home economics and

Simone de Beauvoir's groundbreaking book *The Second Sex* (1949) is credited as a major influence in the development of second-wave feminism that began in the 1960s.

male-only shop courses and a culture that was becoming defined by such liberalizing influences as rock and roll; the miniskirt and the bikini; birth control, which was finally legalized in 1965 when the Supreme Court struck down the last state law prohibiting private use of contraceptives; and the birth control pill, first made available in 1960. The social dissonance and upheavals that marked the 1960s such as the potential threat of nuclear annihilation; the assassinations of President John F. Kennedy, Robert Kennedy, and Martin Luther King Jr.; and the war in Vietnam also brought an idealism and awareness of the possibilities of social change that evolved from the Peace Corps, the civil rights movement, and the peace movement. The civil rights movement would prove to be especially inspiring to women as they began to work toward organizing a rights movement of their own in the 1960s.

Unlike the first women's rights movement of the nineteenth and early twentieth centuries, which primarily centered around women's suffrage, the second-wave feminism that resulted in the women's liberation movement of the late 1960s to the 1980s did not coalesce around a primary issue; instead, it responded to the various legal, social, sexual, and economic challenges women continued to face in the pursuit of equality. The revitalized women's movement stemmed from a variety of sources. In 1949, French existentialist Simone de Beauvoir published *The Second Sex*, a two-volume book in which she explored the question "What is a woman?" in the hierarchical, metaphysical, physiological, social, and economic context of humanity, where men are considered the default gender, while women are objectified as the "Other" and subordinate to men. *The Second Sex* is regarded as a major work of feminist philosophy and an influential text in the development of second-wave feminism. Ten years later, twenty-six-year-old writer and Smith graduate Nora Johnson wrote a prescient article for *The Atlantic Monthly* magazine called "Sex and the College Girl," the thesis of which was that young, college-educated women would be disappointed in their quest for fulfillment characterized by "a husband, a career, community work, children, and the rest." According to Johnson, the majority of women navigating this convoluted path, which women in the 1980s and beyond described as "having it all," would end up sacrificing either their professional or personal lives. In 1962, forty-year-old advertising agency executive and later *Cosmopolitan* editor-in-chief Helen Gurley Brown anticipated the "sexual revolution" with *Sex and the Single Girl*, a lively, flirtatious little book extolling the sexual and social pleasures of the unmarried state. In it, Gurley Brown observes that women "may marry or not. In today's world that is no longer the big question. Those who glom on to men so that they can collapse with relief, spend the rest of their lives shining up their status symbol, and figure they never have to reach, stretch, grow, face dragons, or make a living again are the ones to be pitied. They, in my opinion, are the unfulfilled ones." Its career-oriented message notwithstanding, *Sex and the Single Girl* anticipated what was termed the "sexual revolution," a cultural event that saw the liberalization of sexual attitudes among a large number of young women beginning in the 1960s and reaching its peak during the disco decade of the 1970s, when baby boomers were also often referred to as the "me generation" for their self-involved qualities and their emphasis on self-fulfillment rather than social responsibility.

LITERATURE AND LIBERATION

The Feminine Mystique

No other work in the history of feminist thought sounded the clarion call for a change in the status of post–World War II American women with as much reverberating success as journalist Betty Friedan's groundbreaking 1963 book *The Feminine Mystique*. The title came from the psychic distress experienced by Friedan and the women she featured in her book, whose vague feelings of aimlessness and discontent with their expected role of happy housewife she would diagnose as the "problem that has no name" and identify as the "feminine mystique." "If I am right," Freidan observes, "the problem that has no name stirring in the minds of so many American women today is not a matter of loss of femininity or too much education, or the demands of domesticity. It is far more important that anyone recognizes. It is the key to these other new and old problems which have been torturing women

and their husbands and children, and puzzling their doctors and educators for years. It may well be the key to our future as a nation and a culture. We can no longer ignore that voice within women that says 'I want something more than my husband and my children and my home.'"

The seeds of Friedan's analysis of the cultural forces that subordinated and repressed women's opportunities and desire for accomplishment beyond the role of wife, mother, and homemaker began in the 1950s, when she lost her job as a newspaper reporter after requesting her second maternity leave. She continued to write, however, submitting articles to women's magazines, whose messages extolling the joys and virtues of domesticity she would later use as sources for her assessment of the "feminine mystique." Dissatisfied with her primary role as wife and mother, Friedan began to explore the causes of her discontent. Her research revealed that women's magazines such as *Good Housekeeping* and the *Ladies' Home Journal* reinforced a traditional image of women that glorified domesticity and urged concealment of intellectual ability and deference to men with articles like "I'd Hate to Be a Man" and the suggestion that women become, as one *Ladies' Home Journal* article preached, "the fragile, feminine, dependent but priceless creature every man wants his wife to be."

Friedan found disturbing the overriding message that women's contentment lay solely in domestic accomplishments. At the same time, she wondered if other women shared her dissatisfaction with domesticity. In 1957, she sent out questionnaires to two hundred of her Smith College classmates. The answers she received convinced her that she was not alone in suffering from "the problem that has no name." When Friedan and her classmates met to discuss the results of the questionnaire during their 1957 college reunion, they canvassed Smith seniors about their aspirations. As Friedan later observed, "Try as we might, we couldn't get these fifties seniors to admit they had become interested in *anything*, at that great college, except their future husbands and children, and suburban homes.... It was as if something was making these girls defensive, inoculating them against the larger interests, dreams, and passions really good higher education can lead to."

Gender roles changed during the war years as women like this turret lathe operator joined their male counterparts in contributing to the war effort. Once the war was over, not all women returned to their former lifestyles; some preferred to pursue a career in the workforce.

Friedan next submitted an article to the *Ladies' Home Journal* and the women's magazines *McCall's* and *Redbook* titled "Are Women Wasting Their Time in College?," in which she suggested that "maybe it wasn't higher education making American women frustrated in their role as women, but the current definition of the role of women." The *Ladies' Home Journal* accepted the article, but Friedan refused to allow it to be printed after she saw that it had been rewritten to support the opposite viewpoint of her findings. She continued to research her subject, interviewing professional women and housewives on what she described as "the strange discrepancy between the reality of our lives as women and the image to which we were trying to conform." She then

decided to expand the article into a book, which was published by W. W. Norton five years after Friedan signed her contract with them.

In *The Feminine Mystique*, Friedan aimed to heighten awareness of a woman's powerlessness within the family and in society, her limited opportunities for self-expression, and the negative stereotyping and discrimination that career-minded women faced as well as the unequal salaries earned by women who did work outside the home. Drawing her conclusions from her own experiences and observations as well as from the letters, interviews, and questionnaires she compiled from educated, middle-class housewives who were struggling to find some meaning in their domestically ordered lives, Friedan concluded that the anxiety and aimlessness experienced by American women were products of a postwar fantasy of happy, suburban, female domesticity created and reinforced by educators, sociologists, psychologists, and the media.

> **F**riedan concluded that the anxiety and aimlessness experienced by American women were products of a postwar fantasy of happy, suburban, female domesticity created and reinforced by educators, sociologists, psychologists, and the media.

In the booming, if inflationary, postwar economic climate, advertisers in particular required a large class of consumers, and women, considered America's hyperconsumers, were encouraged in their roles as sex objects and domestic guardians whose longings could be satisfied by purchasing the home and beauty products companies sold. According to Friedan, women accepted their social and sexual subordination in exchange for the material and psychological advantages their passive femininity and maternal roles as wives and mothers brought them—but at the cost of feeling isolated and dehumanized in gilded, suburban castles.

After articulating the dilemma of women trapped in the feminine mystique, Friedan called for a reassertion of female identity beyond that of domestic icon, consumer, helpmate, and caregiver. It was a call to activism that rejected the characterization of women as helpless victims and asserted the need for increased education and opportunities that would allow women to grow to their full potential. In her famous conclusion to the book, Friedan writes, "Who knows what women can be when they are finally free to become themselves? Who knows what women's intelligence will contribute when it can be nourished without denying love? Who knows of the possibilities of love when men and women share not only their children, home, and garden, not only the fulfillment of their biological roles, but the responsibilities and passions

of the work that creates the human future and the full human knowledge of what they are? It has barely begun, the search of women for themselves. But the time is at hand when the voices of the feminine mystique can no longer drown out the inner voice that is driving women on to become complete."

The Feminine Mystique was brought out in a modest printing of two thousand copies. Over the next ten years, the book sold three million hardcover copies and many more in paperback, and it has never gone out of print. Friedan received numerous letters from women who wrote that they had no idea other women shared their feelings. Women were not the only buyers of *The Feminine Mystique*. As Friedan recalled in her 2000 autobiography *Life So Far*, "Many men whose wives had made those feminine mystique renunciations had bought the book for their wives, and encouraged them to go back to school or work." The book was rightly seen as a new, unifying force in a second wave of feminism, but it also drew criticism for its focus on middle-class and upper-middle-class white women, especially in the 1970s, as the women's movement was reaching its midpoint and the voices of women of color, working-class women, and lesbian women began to be heard. However, the call for reform that Friedan articulated and the movement that followed the book provided a flashpoint for debate on the status of all American women, not just Friedan's target audience.

Influential chroniclers of the movement Betty Friedan inspired with *The Feminine Mystique* include Caroline Bird Mahoney, claimed to be the first writer to use the term "sexism" in print and the author of *Born Female: The High Cost of Keeping Women Down* (1968), published under her birth name of Caroline Bird, and Kate Millett, whose *Sexual Politics*, published in 1970, characterized American society, "like all other historical societies," as patriarchal and articulated a philosophy for what was by then called the women's liberation movement or, more popularly, women's lib. The same year, Australian writer Germaine Greer published *The Female Eunuch*, in which she wrote, "I'm sick of pretending that some fatuous male's self-important pronouncements are the objects of my undivided attention." One of the most influential books of the era was *Sisterhood Is*

Powerful: An Anthology of Writings from the Women's Liberation Movement, a 1970 anthology of essays from feminist writers as well as current and historical documents addressing the need for a radical feminism to challenge the discrimination women faced from politically left-wing men and the sexism they experienced in the workplace. The theme of feminism was carried on in such important 1970s books as *The Young Woman's Guide to Liberation* (1971) by Karen DeCrow, president of the National Organization for Women (NOW) from 1974 to 1977 and the first edition of *Our Bodies, Ourselves* (1973), published by the Boston Women's Health Book Collective. A guide covering many aspects of women's health and sexuality, the best-selling book has been translated into twenty-nine languages and its most recent—and last—edition was published in 2011, in which the topic of transsexualism and transgenderism was discussed. In 1975, journalist Susan Brownmiller published *Against Our Will: Men, Women, and Rape*, a groundbreaking examination of rape as a violent display of male power and intimidation that is widely credited with changing public attitudes about rape. The 1970s also saw the emergence of fiction written by women that explored aspects of feminism and issues concerning women's sexuality and sexual freedom such as Alix Kates Shulman's *Memoirs of an Ex-Prom Queen* (1972); Erica Jong's *Fear of Flying* (1973); Judith Rossner's *Looking for Mr. Goodbar* (1975); Marilyn French's

Author of *The Feminine Mystique* and founder of the National Organization for Women (NOW), Betty Friedan (second from the left) helped launch the Second Women's Movement. Also pictured here are NOW co-chair Barbara Ireton (third from left) and attorney Marguerite Rawalt (far right).

The Women's Room (1977); and Marge Piercy's *The Moon Is Always Female* (1980).

One of the most influential explicators of the women's movement and a variety of women's concerns since its first appearance as a stand-alone supplement in *New York Magazine* in December 1971 has been *Ms.*, the first and only feminist mass-market magazine in history. Named for the honorific that was once an abbreviation for the more formal "Mistress" and periodically revived during the first five decades of the twentieth century, Ms. gradually became the default form of address for women regardless of their married state after feminist and civil rights activist Sheila Michaels used it during an appearance on the New York City radio station WBAI. A friend of feminist activist Gloria Steinem heard the interview and suggested it to her as a title for the magazine Steinem was in the process of cofounding with Dorothy Pitman Hughes.

In 1971, feminism, despite inroads in raising the consciousness of women and attracting media attention to women's issues, was dubbed by the *New York Times* as "a passing fad." According to the *Times*, "in small-town USA, women's liberation is either a joke or a bore." The subject of feminism was viewed as having limited appeal, and a magazine devoted to a feminist perspective was expected to fail. *60 Minutes* newsman Harry Reasoner weighed in with the challenge by saying "I'll give it six months before they run out of things to say," only to apologize later after the magazine proved successful with all three hundred thousand of its test copies sold out nationwide in eight days. In 1987, *Ms.* was sold to an Australian publisher, and in 1998, Gloria Steinem and other investors created Liberty Media for Women and bought *Ms.* under independent ownership. In 2001, the nonprofit organization the Feminist Majority Foundation, cofounded by former NOW president Eleanor Smeal, purchased the magazine. Gloria Steinem remains on the masthead as one of the six founding editors and serves on the advisory board.

Since its first issue, which was available on newsstands on 1972, *Ms.* has featured articles by a variety of prominent women as well as groundbreaking investigative journalism on such topics as overseas sweatshops, sex trafficking, the wage gap, the glass ceiling, date rape, and domestic violence. Although some concessions to popular culture have occurred in recent years, leading to editorial disagreements and a perceived generation gap toward third-wave feminists, *Ms.* continues to provide a forum for articles on women's concerns that, prior to its inception, other magazines had ignored or deemed too controversial or feminist to publish. *Ms.* helped raise the level and nature of the national conversation on women's experiences and firmly established itself as an essential chronicler of women's lives in the nearly fifty years since it was first published.

THE NATIONAL ORGANIZATION FOR WOMEN

The history of women in America has been greatly defined by women's capacity for organization, and the second women's movement was no exception. The most visible national women's organization of the era was the National Organization for Women (NOW), founded in 1966 by Betty Friedan, civil rights and women's activist Pauli Murray, equal rights leader and Title VII commissioner Richard Alton Graham, and forty-six other women and men. The organization was founded out of frustration over the refusal of the Equal Employment Opportunity Commission (EEOC) to address the issue of complaints made by women over job discrimination, a right mandated by the Title VII statutes of the Civil Rights Act of 1964. Newspapers continued to advertise male and female jobs in separate columns, airlines fired stewardesses who married, and some states prohibited women from waiting tables at restaurants at night. The word "sex" had been added to the list of prohibited discriminatory categories as a ploy by opponents of civil rights in an attempt to discourage passage of the bill, and after the attempt failed and the bill was passed and enacted into law, the EEOC was slow to enforce compliance and even labeled the gender provision a "fluke." The commission would be thrust into the public spotlight in 1970 when forty-six women, who worked at *Newsweek* magazine and were relegated to such low-level positions as mail clerks and researchers since company policy forbade the promotion of women

A U.S. congresswoman from Michigan who later became her state's lieutenant governor, Martha Griffiths was a supporter of Title VII and criticized the U.S. Congress for its inaction in passing laws to provide gender equality.

to the status of writers (only one woman on the magazine staff had attained the position of junior writer), hired ACLU lawyer Eleanor Holmes Norton, who filed a discrimination claim with the EEOC and a lawsuit against the magazine, both of which led to a settlement and limited gains for the *Newsweek* women. A second lawsuit in 1972 resulted in more concrete commitments from *Newsweek* regarding the promotion of women to senior editors, writers, and reporters.

Four years before the women of *Newsweek* brought their claim before the EEOC, Michigan representative Martha Griffiths, a staunch supporter of the Title VII sex provision, offered a stinging attack from the House floor on the commission's lack of effort in cases of gender discrimination. "Since when is it permissible," she asked, "for an agency charged with the duty of enforcing the law, to allude to the

assumed motive of the author of legislation as an excuse for not enforcing the law?" A few days after Griffith's attack, the Third National Conference of State Commissions on the Status of Women, the successor to the President's Commission on the Status of Women, met in Washington, D.C. Several attendees, including Betty Friedan, hoped a strong resolution would be issued condemning the EEOC's actions. Richard Graham had previously sought help from the heads of such independent women's organizations as the League of Women Voters and the American Association of University Women (AAUW) with headquarters in Washington, D.C., to lobby the EEOC for compliance with the law as other civil rights groups had done. They all declined with the assertion that they were not feminists.

Activists such as Friedan hoped that the leaders of the conference would agree to spearhead a public protest movement among women on the issue of employment equality. However, the conference's conservative leadership refused to act on the resolution since its sponsors were not official delegates to the convention. Disgruntled delegates, including women from the United Auto Workers and leaders of several state commissions, held an informal meeting in Friedan's hotel room and determined that a new organization was needed to move their agenda forward. They all chipped in five dollars and began to discuss names for the new organization. As Friedan recalled in her 2006 memoir *It Changed My Life*, "I dreamed up N.O.W. on the spur of the moment." She scribbled on a cocktail napkin that she had "to take the actions needed to bring women into the mainstream of American society, now, full equality for women, in fully equal partnership with men. NOW. The National Organization for Women." NOW was launched on June 29, 1966, with an initial membership of twenty-eight and treasury of $135.

NOW was conceived as a civil rights-type organization to lobby the government for changes that would secure equal rights for women. At the organization's second annual convention in 1967, Betty Friedan, NOW's first president, presented a bill of rights that demanded paid maternity leave, tax deductions for childcare, educational and job training, the right to legal abortions, and passage of the Equal Rights Amendment (ERA). The organization announced its opposition to any policy or practice that denied equal opportunities and by doing so created contempt for women and fostered in them "self-denigration, dependence, and evasion of responsibility." NOW also challenged traditional notions of women's roles as defined solely by marriage and motherhood with a difficult choice between home and career. "Above all," NOW asserted, "we reject the assumption that these problems are the unique responsibility of each individual woman, rather than a basic social dilemma which society must solve."

NOW's early years were contentious ones with the organization coping with a conspicuous lack of organizational skills as its leadership tried to hold together a diverse membership that grew to fifteen thousand in its first five years.

NOW's early years were contentious ones with the organization coping with a conspicuous lack of organizational skills as its leadership tried to hold together a diverse membership that grew to fifteen thousand in its first five years. Advocates for such controversial causes as legalized abortion and the ERA alienated many supporters and forced some members to withdraw. Lawyers who wanted to focus on legal and economic issues rather than social concerns left to found the Women's Equity Action League (WEAL) in 1968, and still others became frustrated with Betty Friedan's impatient and imperious leadership. Friedan would step down from the presidency in 1970 to organize the Women's Strike for Equality, which held a march in New York City on August 26 (the fiftieth anniversary of the adoption of the Nineteenth Amendment) at which more than fifty thousand people participated. The following year, Freidan, together with politicians such as Bella Abzug and Shirley Chisholm and activists Fannie Lou Hamer and Gloria Steinem, among others, formed the National Women's Political Caucus (NWPC) with the goal of increasing the number of women in all aspects of political life.

Despite its internal tensions, NOW succeeded in becoming the nation's largest and most powerful women's organization. However, conflicts over its agenda persisted. Activists pushed the organization to shift its emphasis from political to identity and cultural concerns as the women's movement in the 1970s began to be reinterpreted as personal women's liberation, and gender equality clashed with notions of gender difference. In the 1980s, which experienced a conservative backlash against the feminist advances of the 1970s, NOW increasingly came under attack for its perceived pushing of an agenda that was "antifamily" and labeled as too extreme for the majority of women. Antifeminists, such as the outspoken conservative Phyllis Schlafly, attacked the organization as having "nothing to say to the average American woman." NOW's leadership has also tried to balance calls for greater militancy, particularly concerning issues of sexual preference and gender identity, while resisting the alienation of members for whom equal opportunity in politics and the workplace, rather than social and cultural concerns, remain the principal focus. Now a mainstream organization with 550 chapters in all fifty states and Washington, D.C., the National Organization for Women has remained relevant for its willingness to debate and act upon the various and diverse concerns that continue to face American women.

THE MISS AMERICA PROTESTS

One of the ways in which the women's movement responded to gender inequality was to begin to challenge the objectification of women based on perceived notions of physical beauty. The most visible expression of women as objects to be admired and rated according to what they looked like was the Miss America pageant. On September 7, 1968, between two hundred and four hundred women, organized by the feminist group the New York Radical Women, gathered on the boardwalk in Atlantic City, New Jersey, to protest the 1969 Miss America pageant, which was being held the same day at the Boardwalk Hall. The purpose of the demonstration was to protest the pageant's focus on women's bodies rather than their minds, and, according to the letter requesting a permit for the demonstration sent by Robin Morgan, a leader of the New York Radical Women and a key organizer of the protest, to Atlantic City mayor Richard S. Jackson, "on youth rather than maturity, and on commercialism rather than humanity." She named the sponsor of the protest "Women's Liberation," which she described as a "loose coalition of small groups and individuals." The advisory sponsor was the Media Workshop, a group founded by lawyer, civil rights activist, and feminist Florynce Kennedy in 1966 to protest the media's representation of African Americans. Participants also included members of the National Organization for Women and the feminist Jeannette Rankin Brigade as well as representatives of the American Civil Liberties Union. Men were barred from taking part in the protest.

The protestors were objecting to the twentieth-century iteration of a practice that had become firmly established in American culture in the nineteenth century, when cities and states began to hold festivals

Famous for his touring circus show that he founded with James Bailey, P. T. Barnum knew how to make money by putting people and animals on display. It was Barnum who created the first beauty contest in 1854.

and carnivals at which queens were chosen. While the selection of a carnival or festival queen included such attributes as outstanding civic leadership, family connections, or popularity in the community, the physical attractiveness of candidates counted as well. These public contests helped to regularize selection procedures based on standards of physical beauty, which also affected public attitudes about the way women were supposed to look and reinforced physical beauty as central to women's lives.

The first modern beauty contest featuring a display of women's faces and bodies before judges was the 1854 creation of huckster showman Phineas T. Barnum, who had already held successful dog, bird, flower, and baby contests at his New York City American Museum. Prizes for the contest included a diamond tiara if the winner were married and a dowry if she were single. Because the first contestants were women of dubious reputation rather than the respectable beauties Barnum had hoped to attract, he turned the competition into a daguerreotype (the precursor of the photograph) contest. He offered to pay the postage of the photos that were sent to him, suggested that the women's names need not be included, and stated that he would not accept photographs from "disreputable persons." All the candidates would receive prizes and have their portraits painted from the photographs, which in turn would be exhibited in a gallery at the museum called the Congress of Beauty. Barnum's photographic beauty contest proved popular, and by the beginning of the twentieth century, the development of the halftone plate, which made photographic reproduction possible, had been adopted as a promotional device by newspapers across the country. In 1911, the *Ladies' Home Journal*, which had earlier condemned beauty contests as unwomanly, began sponsoring a competition to find the five most beautiful young women in the United States. The winners would receive a trip to New York City, where their portraits would be painted by artist Charles Dana Gibson, the creator of the Gibson Girl, the epitome of female beauty from 1895 through the first two decades of the twentieth century.

The early beauty contests often offered as prizes opportunities for careers in modeling, movies, or the theater. For many contestants, winning a beauty contest could mean the difference between living in poverty or a chance to raise one's social status. One example was silent film star Clara Bow, who was born into extreme poverty and catapulted to film fame as America's "It" girl after winning a screen test through a photographic beauty test sponsored by the fan magazine *Photoplay*. Other beauty contest winners might secure a place in one of the Broadway shows of producer–manager Lee Shubert or in the chorus of the *Ziegfeld Follies*, a stage show produced by impresario Florenz Ziegfeld that was advertised as "glorifying the American girl." Both Ziegfeld and Shubert had very specific criteria regarding how their showgirls should look and were publicly well-known men who had made careers out of choosing women who would be physically attractive to audiences. Their showgirls and female stars, together with the models and beauty contest winners women saw in person and in newspapers and magazines, represented standards of beauty and fashion and supported the notion that these were standards American women should strive for.

Beauty contests had become a regular feature at American seaside resorts by the first decade of the twentieth century. By the first Miss America beauty contest, held in Atlantic City on September 8, 1921, swimsuits for women had begun to shift from voluminous swim dresses to one-piece suits, and the bathing beauty was a recognized symbol of female beauty. Swimmer and film actress Annette Kellermann had pioneered the one-piece suit, and filmmaker and producer Mack Sennett, known for his slapstick silent comedies featuring the incompetent Keystone Kops, had become equally famous for his bevy of relatively scantily clad bathing beauties. The more revealing one-piece suits were considered scandalous by well-to-do vacationers at seaside resorts, and the Atlantic Business Men's League, promoters of the first Miss America pageant, worried that a protest would mar the event and have a negative effect on tourism. To deflect criticism, pageant managers stressed the athletic and wholesome, unsophisticated qualities of the candidates, insisted they wear knee-length swim dresses, banned makeup and bobbed hair, and chose a distinguished panel of newspaper editors and illustrators of attractive young women to serve as judges. The first Miss America, chosen from among 1,500 contestants, was fifteen-year-old Margaret Gorman from Washington, D.C. Blonde, blue-eyed, and petite, Gorman bore a striking resemblance to Mary Pickford, the most popular star of the silent film era. Her prizes included a tiara replication of the Statue of Liberty's headpiece, a large American flag fashioned into a coronation robe, and an oversize trophy worth $5,000, which featured a mermaid reclining on a base of teak wood.

The Miss America pageant continued to be held annually until the years 1928–1932, when fi-

Miss America contestants, 2004. In 1968 feminists and civil rights activists protested the Miss America Pageant, a contest they felt stressed female stereotypes of beauty rather than intelligence and diversity.

nancial problems associated with the Great Depression, as well as suggestions that the pageant promoted "loose morals," forced a temporary shutdown. When it was revived in 1933, the winner was another fifteen-year-old, who held the title for two years since no pageant occurred in 1934 and was refused the prize of a screen test because she was too young. Thereafter, the youngest age at which contestants could compete was changed to eighteen. In 1936, the talent competition was added to the pageant, and each contestant was required to have a chaperone. In the 1940s, the pageant began to offer college scholarships to winners. In 1945, when Miss New York, Bess Myerson, was crowned, she became the first and, so far, the only Jewish Miss America as well as the first winner to wear a two-piece swimsuit, a feature of the pageant introduced that year. Myerson, who resisted pressure to use a pseudonym that sounded "less Jewish," was forced to cut back on her duties as Miss America because of the considerable anti-Semitism she experienced, not least of which was the refusal of three of the pageant's sponsors to allow her to represent their companies. In 1954, the pageant was televised for the first time, thus giving viewers at home the chance to pick the beauty of their choice from the lineup of attractive young women. In 1952, the first Miss USA and Miss Universe pageants appeared, to be followed by Miss Teenage America (1961) and Little Miss America, a beauty pageant for little girls (1961). The Mrs. America pageant, established to honor married women in the United States, made its debut in 1976.

By the 1960s, the Miss America pageant had become firmly established in American culture as the ultimate display of female physical perfection. For the women who protested in Atlantic City in 1968, the pageant, which the protestors termed "The Degrading Mindless Boob-Girlie Symbol," represented not only the promotion and publicizing of women as mere objects to be emulated and desired but also a symbol of all the trappings of a standardized femininity that oppressed women. The protestors exhibited a "freedom trash can" into which they threw what they called "instruments of female torture," such as mops, pots and pans, corsets, girdles, bras, high-heeled shoes, curlers, makeup, and hair-

spray along with copies of the *Ladies' Home Journal*, *Cosmopolitan*, and *Playboy* magazines. The trashing of *Playboy* is interesting given the debut of *Playgirl* in 1973. A magazine founded in response to the popular erotic men's magazine and its rival British publication *Penthouse*, which first appeared in the United States in 1969, *Playgirl* featured similarly titillating photos but of attractive, nude men as well as articles on women's sexuality.

In addition to its trash can, the Miss America protestors picketed the pageant with signs such as "Let's Judge Ourselves as People" and "I Am a Woman—Not a Toy, Pet, or Mascot"; passed out pamphlets, one of which was written by Robin Morgan and titled "No More Miss America"; crowned a live sheep as Miss America; displayed an illustration of a woman's figure marked up as a side of beef accompanied by a sign that read "Welcome to the Miss America Cattle Auction"; and auctioned off an effigy of a woman with the pitch, "Gentlemen, I offer you the 1969 model. She's better every year. She walks. She talks. *And* she does housework." Two of the protestors, Kathie Sarachild and Carol Hanisch (also known for popularizing the phrase "the personal is political"), bought tickets for the event and entered the hall, where the outgoing 1968 Miss America, Debra Barnes Snodgrass, was giving her farewell address. Stationing themselves in the balcony, Sarachild and Hanisch unfurled a bedsheet with the words "Women's Liberation!" on it and managed several repeated shouts of "women's liber-

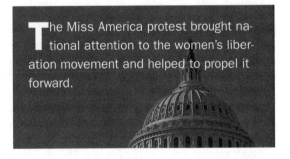

The Miss America protest brought national attention to the women's liberation movement and helped to propel it forward.

ation!" and "no more Miss America" before they were removed by the police. Snodgrass responded to the protest by saying that it diminished the thousands of contestants who were attending school and had worked hard to develop their talents.

The Miss America protest brought national attention to the women's liberation movement and helped to propel it forward. It also had one unintended result. When journalist Lindsy Van Gelder, who covered the demonstration for the *New York Post*, wrote her story on the event, she compared the tossing of bras into the garbage can with the burning of draft cards during Vietnam War protest. In the same paper on September 12, 1968, humorist Art Buchwald tailored the analogy to fit his marginally tongue-in-cheek column headlined "The Bra Burners," in which he described the protestors as "well-meaning but misled females" who "were trying to destroy everything this country holds dear." The media had a field day with the concept of bra burning, and the term "bra burners" became a permanent trope during the women's liberation movement along with the derisive descriptive "women's libbers." The protestors had, in fact, planned to burn bras but were denied a permit to do so.

The Miss America pageant was not the only beauty contest held in Atlantic City that day. Since 1940, when pageant rules requiring all contestants to be "of good health and of the white race" were dropped, no African American woman had ever competed for the title. In 1968, leaders of the Atlantic City chapter of the NAACP met with Miss America pageant officials to advocate for integration. Pageant officials responded by adding black judges to their own event and setting up a scholarship fund to encourage African American contestants. Still, without any African American state finalists already competing, it was too late for participation that year. To redress the omission of black, female contestants, regional NAACP director Philip Savage and Philadelphia entrepreneur J. Morris Anderson organized the Miss Black America Pageant, which was held at the Ritz-Carlton Hotel in Atlantic City on the same day as the Miss America pageant. The following year, the pageant was moved from Atlantic City to New York's Madison Square Garden and celebrated its fortieth anniversary in 2018. The first African American contestants began to compete in the Miss America pageant in the 1970s, and the first to win the competition was talented vocalist and actor Vanessa Williams in 1983. However, after *Penthouse* magazine published nude photographs of Williams, she

was forced to relinquish her crown to Suzette Charles, who is also African American. In 2016, Sam Haskell, a former Miss America CEO, apologized to Williams, who was serving as head judge that year, for the way in which pageant officials had handled the scandal.

By the 1990s, the Miss America pageant had introduced further changes, among them the "Focus on Achievement," during which contestants were expected to discuss a social issue. Contestants were further required to do their own hair; the evening gown competition became the evening wear competition; the winners' "reign" was changed to "year of service"; and the first hearing-impaired Miss America, Heather Whitestone, was crowned. In 1995, television viewers were invited to call in to vote on whether or not the swimsuit competition should be discontinued. The National Organization for Women called the initiative a marketing gimmick; voters nevertheless overwhelmingly elected to keep the competition. In 1998, pageant officials announced that they had lifted the ban of contestants who were divorced or who had had an abortion; the new ruling was later rescinded, and the pageant CEO who suggested it was fired. The twenty-first century has seen the first diabetic, autistic, Asian American, openly lesbian, and Indian American Miss America, Nina Davuluri. Shortly after her win in 2013, Davuluri became the target of xenophobic and racist slurs on social media. She was labeled a Muslim and an Arab and was associated with the terrorist organization Al-Qaeda. Davuluri cited the pageant's proximity to the second anniversary of 9/11, as well as anti-Indian sentiment, as causes of the harassment.

The Miss America pageant has clearly undergone many refinements since its debut in 1921. Like the contests of the 1930s, the pageant and its prizes offer young women a way to realize their ambitions and their goals, especially through the organization's scholarship programs. The fact that physical beauty remains an overriding feature of the Miss American pageant seems somewhat irrelevant now, as women's concerns have begun to shift from emulating a standard of beauty to asserting that no standards should exist at all.

THE EQUAL RIGHTS AMENDMENT

The struggle to secure passage of the Equal Rights Amendment for addition to the U.S. Constitution began when suffragist Alice Paul, leader of the National Women's Party (NWP), drafted the ERA in 1923 as the logical next step in the cause of women's rights after the suffrage victory. The text of the proposed amendment was in two sections and read: "No political, civil, or legal disabilities or inequalities on account of sex or of marriage, unless applying equally to both sexes, shall exist within the United States or any territory subject to the jurisdiction thereof" and "Congress shall have power to enforce this article by appropriate legislation."

A woman holds a protest sign in support of the ERA during the 2018 Women's March in New York City. Even though women were finally given voting rights in 1920, there is still a long way to go for them to obtain true equality in the United States.

Despite having won the vote, women continued to face discriminatory legislation throughout the country. Women in some states were denied the right to serve on juries; husbands could control the earnings of their wives; and a woman's inheritance from a husband without a will was limited to one-third of his property, while state laws granted widowers complete control over their deceased wives' estates. Husbands could determine their wives' legal residence, and the burden of responsibility for illegitimate children rested with the mother. Women were barred from certain kinds of employment, and unequal pay for working at the same job as men continued to be standard practice.

However, by asserting women's equality through the ERA, the NWP was forced to repudiate much of the protective legislation that progressive reformers had struggled to enact on behalf of women. NWP members were forced to denounce such reform measures as the recently enacted Sheppard-Towner Maternity and Infancy Protection Act, the first federally funded health care program, as well as the first welfare program, in the United States. For the NWP, the Sheppard-Towner Act singled out women as a class for special protection, as mothers, not as persons. The issue split the suffrage coalition and was opposed by nearly every other women's group out of fear that the amendment would nullify the important protections for women that had taken years of lobbying to win. For other women opposed to the ERA, suffrage was not a single victory in the long struggle for equality but the appropriate final victory that would allow women a political voice to express their concerns.

Without support among the majority of women's groups during the next five decades, the ERA languished in Congress and the Senate Judiciary Committee until the late 1960s and early 1970s, when support for the amendment gathered momentum as a result of the women's movement's impact. In 1966, the newly formed National Organization for Women, which would become the most powerful feminist organization over the next few years, called for an end to sexual discrimination in the workplace and spearheaded a campaign to work for passage of the ERA. By 1971, when the 92nd Congress began to consider passage of the ERA, supporters included not only NOW but also the League of Women Voters, the YWCA, the American Association of University Women, the watchdog group Common Cause, and the United Auto Workers, all of which mounted a mail campaign that generated thousands of letters sent to Capitol Hill. Many women in the African American community supported the amendment as well. One prominent supporter was New York congressional representative Shirley Chisholm, who gave a speech in 1970 to advocate for the passage of the ERA. In her speech, Chisholm asserted

> **B**y 1976, during the ratification process, 60 percent of African American women and 63 percent of African American men favored passage of the ERA....

that the ERA would remedy widespread sex discrimination and help men, as well as women, since it would help to protect both men and women from unsafe conditions in the workplace. By 1976, during the ratification process, 60 percent of African American women and 63 percent of African American men favored passage of the ERA, and the legislation had gained support from such prominent organizations as the NAACP, the National Council of Negro Women, the Coalition of Black Trade Unionists, the National Association of Negro Business, and the National Black Feminist Organization.

Congress, suddenly recognizing the political power of women, rushed to appease a constituency that represented more than half of the voting public. Both the House and the Senate passed the ERA by wide margins, and it was finally approved in March 1972. However, the road to ratification would be rocky because the bill included a time limit of seven years for approval by the much-needed three-fourths of the states for the essentially intact language of Alice Paul's original amendment. Since Congress had imposed no time limit for ratification of the Nineteenth Amendment, opposition to it disappeared almost immediately, whereas opposition to

the ERA would have time to strengthen as the states considered whether or not to ratify the amendment. By 1977, thirty-five states had voted to ratify the ERA—three states short of what was needed—as time began to run out for ratification in 1982 after Congress voted for a two-year extension. The amendment lost by only a few votes in Illinois, Florida, and Oklahoma. By one calculation, the ERA would have achieved ratification if seven votes had been changed.

The ERA's defeat was the result of several factors, which included a vigorous opposition campaign that managed to exploit the conflict between feminists and non- and antifeminists and the underlying tension within the women's movement over the issue of gender equality and the protection of gender differences. Groups opposed to the women's liberation movement such as Women Who Want to Be Women, Happiness of Womanhood, and Females Opposed to Equality declared their satisfaction with the status quo, which they perceived was under attack by the ERA. The amendment's most visible and formidable opponent was Phyllis Schlafly, the 1972 founder of STOP ERA. Schlafly mounted an unrelenting attack to demonize feminists and arouse deep-seated fears that the amendment would destroy the family and women's protected place in society. She linked the ERA with *Ms.* magazine and women's lib, which she charged with being "anti-family, anti-children, and pro-abortion." She characterized supporters of the ERA and women's liberation as "a series of sharp-tongued, high-pitched, whining complaints by unmarried women.... Women's lib is a total assault on the role of the American woman as wife and mother and on the family as the basic unit of society." The fearmongering of Schlafly and other ERA opponents included claims that the amendment would decriminalize rape, legalize homosexual ("gay" was not yet a common term) marriages, integrate public restrooms, end gender segregation in prisons, mandate women's combat service in the military, and make every American wife legally responsible for 50 percent of the financial support of her family, thus forcing into the workforce women who otherwise might wish to stay home with their children.

Ms. magazine cover

The anti-feminist movement reached a peak during the attempt to pass the Equal Rights Amendment. *Ms.* magazine was one of the many targets of the anti-feminists.

Opponents of the ERA successfully turned the debate over women's equality into a referendum on the traditional sanctities of motherhood and family, an issue that could not be silenced by a divided women's movement that had never fully made peace or accommodation with women who willingly defined themselves as homemakers. The women's movement of the 1970s proved insufficiently broad to include both feminists who identified their activism in terms of their careers and those for whom the ERA would ensure equality in the workplace and women who demanded different protection for their roles as mothers and family caregivers. The failure of the amendment stemmed from the inability of its proponents to satisfy the latter group that the ERA was in their best interests as well.

Since 1982, the Equal Rights Amendment has been reintroduced in every session of Congress. In 2011, the one hundredth anniversary of International Women's Day, Wisconsin representative Tammy Baldwin introduced legislation to remove the congressionally imposed time limit for ratification of the amendment. The House Judiciary Committee referred the legislation to the Subcommittee on the Constitution, which failed to vote on it before the 112th Congress ended in January 2013, thus allowing it to die in committee. In February, the New Mexico House of Representatives House Memorial No. 7 asked for removal of the deadline. The measure was received by the Senate in 2014 and published in the *Congressional Record*. In 2013, New York representative Carolyn Maloney introduced and sponsored the "New ERA," which included an additional sentence to the original text: "Women shall have equal rights in the United States and every place subject to its jurisdiction." In 2018, it appeared that the ERA had secured the thirty-eight states needed for ratification until the Virginia legislature changed course and voted against the amendment in January 2019. The year 2023 will mark the one hundredth anniversary of the amendment Alice Paul crafted with the worthy goal of constitutionally ensuring equal rights for all women in the United States.

THE LEGALIZATION OF ABORTION

Before the 1860s, when abortion in the United States was first criminalized, the performing of an abortion prior to what was known as "quickening"—the stage at which the fetus first moved in the uterus—was not considered a crime, and abortion even after quickening was not treated as much more than a minor offense. Around 1860, however, physicians became increasingly concerned regarding the upsurge in the number of abortions as well as the health consequences of the procedure. The first state laws restricting abortion were passed to protect women from septicemia, which was often a side effect of the procedure at the time. In addition, the American Medical Association was endeavoring to professionalize the practice of medicine and wanted to rid the medical community of so-called "irregular" doctors, who in their view were not "scientifically trained." These were doctors who were primarily providing abortions, and the AMA counted on legal restrictions to drive them out of business. Physicians led the campaign to prohibit abortion and tried to gain support from the clergy. However, most non-Catholic clergymen did not view abortion as a religious matter and refused to become involved in the crusade to enact restrictive legislation because of the prevailing religious belief that the soul did not come to life until after quickening. Female social reformers, who considered abortion as well as contraception a gross violation of proper womanhood and an invitation to practice sexual immorality, supported legislation but preferred to let physicians campaign for it. The medical community found its most receptive audience among legislators, who were also concerned with loosening morals and were moreover worried that the increasing use of abortion by white, middle-class, Protestant women would change the population balance. State after state began to enact laws prohibiting abortion unless a continuation of the pregnancy endangered the life of the mother.

> **P**hysicians led the campaign to prohibit abortion and tried to gain support from the clergy. However, most non-Catholic clergymen did not view abortion as a religious matter....

During the second decade of the twentieth century, when birth control advocates Margaret Sanger and Emma Goldman disseminated information on contraception and contraceptives in defiance of the federal Comstock Laws enacted in 1873 to prohibit the "Trade in, and Circulation of, Obscene Literature and Articles of Immoral Use," illegal abortion was the most widely practiced form of birth control. Even after the Comstock Laws were liberalized in 1929 and repealed in 1936, women continued to seek illegal abortions for reasons ranging from the unwillingness of a spouse or lover to use contraception to becoming pregnant as the result of rape or incest. Before the advent of the vacuum aspirator, a sharp instrument called a curette was inserted into the uterus to scrape the fetus from the uterine wall. A woman could bleed to death if the curette pierced the uterus or suffer a fatal infection if the instrument was not properly sterilized. Women with money could afford to consult a skilled abortionist. Poor women attempted to abort their fetuses using folk remedies, charms, or patent medicines, which were ineffective but harmless. Other methods that involved the insertion of coat hangers, shoe hooks, knitting needles, and douches were not only ineffective, they often led to sterility and death. In the 1930s, many women wanting to terminate pregnancies continued to rely on vaginal douching, often with deadly solutions of lye, carbolic soap, iodine, and turpentine.

In the 1950s, an estimated one million illegal abortions were performed in the United States, and over a thousand women died as a result of abdominal infections from unsanitary procedures performed by unskilled practitioners. Still others were left sterile or chronically ill and emotionally scarred. In the frightening, secret world of illegal abortion in the 1950s and 1960s, most American abortionists were only interested in collecting their fees—usually $1,000 or more in cash—and turned women away if they could not pay the asking price. Women were sometimes forced to trade sex with a male abortionist for the procedure. Concerned with speed and their own protection, abortionists often refused to use anesthesia because it would take too long for a woman to recover, thus raising the risk of discovery. Women did not receive explanations of what would happen during the procedure; birth control techniques were not discussed; and few, if any, adequate precautions were taken to prevent hemorrhages or infections. Poor women and women of color were particularly at risk from abortions: It is estimated that 75 percent of women who died as a result of illegal abortions in 1969 were women of color.

In the 1960s, members of the liberal clergy and women's groups set up their own referral services to help women obtain safer illegal abortions. One support group, the Chicago-based Jane Collective, helped over eleven thousand women get safe first- and second-trimester abortions for as little as $50, with the result that many of Chicago's expensive and unsafe abortionists were put out of business. By the end of the decade, as the women's movement

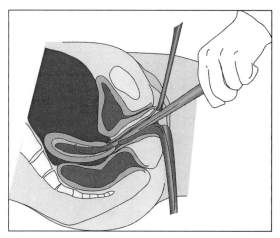

Before the invention of a vacuum aspirator for abortions, an instrument called a curette was used to scrape the uterine wall in a procedure that could often lead to a woman bleeding to death.

was gaining momentum, women's groups held demonstrations and speak-outs at which many women spoke about their experiences undergoing illegal abortions. Members of the women's movement, supported by civil liberties groups, marched, rallied, and lobbied for abortion on demand. In 1969, Betty Friedan and others in the women's movement founded the National Association for the Repeal of Abortion Laws, later renamed the National Abortion Rights Action League and, finally, NARAL Pro-Choice America. By the early 1970s, some states had liberalized their abortion laws, allowing the procedure in certain cases—for example, when pregnancy was the result of rape or incest or when a woman was under fifteen years of age. Other states allowed abortion on demand through the twenty-fourth week from the last menstrual period. Physicians, who had witnessed the cost of illegal abortions in terms of maternal injuries and deaths, argued for the overturning of restrictions. In 1972, the fledgling feminist magazine *Ms.* featured an advertisement headlined "We Have Had Abortions" that was signed by Gloria Steinem as well as such prominent women as Lillian Hellman, Susan Sontag, Barbara Tuchman, and Billie Jean King.

A number of abortion cases were brought before the U.S. Supreme Court, including one in which Norma McCorvey, a pregnant Texas woman, sued Dallas County district attorney Henry Wade for blocking her attempts to obtain an abortion. The case was adjudicated in the Supreme Court, where McCorvey was known by the alias "Jane Roe." On January 22, 1973, the court ruled 7–2 in the case of *Roe v. Wade* that abortion should be a decision between a woman and her physician. The court stated that the "right of privacy ... founded in the Fourteenth Amendment's concept of personal liberty ... is broad enough to encompass a woman's decision whether or not to terminate her pregnancy." In his majority opinion, Justice Harry A. Blackmun held that through the end of the first trimester of pregnancy, only a woman and her doctor have the legal right to decide on an abortion and that the state's interest in a woman's welfare is not "compelling" enough to warrant any interference. For the next trimester, a state could "regulate the abortion procedure in ways that are reasonably related to maternal health," including the licensing and regulation of facilities. As a result of the court's ruling, the number of illegal abortions and the rates of maternal mortality were greatly decreased.

The landmark Supreme Court decision of 1973 sparked a firestorm of controversy, which over the next five decades would grow into a contentious debate concerning women's reproductive freedom that centered on moral, religious, emotional, and political considerations and sharply divided pro-choice and prolife activists and adherents. The women's movement of the 1970s greeted the court's decision as a victory in the struggle for women's reproductive rights. Terence Cardinal Cooke of the Catholic Diocese of New York called the court's action "horrifying." Antiabortion forces led by the Catholic Church hierarchy, fundamentalist Christians, and right-to-life organizations such as Operation Rescue, founded in 1988 by New York used-car salesman Randall Terry, lobbied to eliminate abortion and used such strategies as the picketing and padlocking of abortion clinics in a policy of harassment and intimidation.

Antiabortion advocates were handed the first of several victories in 1976, when the Hyde Amendment to the health, education, and welfare appropriations bill cleared Congress by a vote of 256–114. Named for its sponsor, Illinois Republican

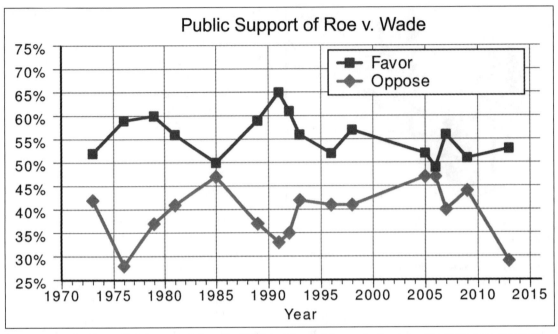

Public support for *Roe v. Wade* has varied since the 1973 decision, but those who favor abortion rights have always out-numbered those opposing them.

congressman Henry Hyde, the amendment barred the use of Medicaid funds for abortion "except where the life of the mother would be endangered if the fetus was brought to term." Critics labeled the new legislation discriminatory and unconstitutional, while supporters, apparently unaffected by the negative impact the amendment would have on the health and well-being of poor families, contended that tax revenues should not be used to fund a surgical procedure that a substantial number of Americans considered immoral.

In 1980, the Supreme Court upheld the Hyde Amendment in the case of *Harris v. McRae*. In 1989, Congress voted to authorize Medicaid payment for abortions for victims of rape and incest, but President George H. W. Bush vetoed the measure, and Congress failed to override. The same year, the Supreme Court ruled in *Webster v. Reproductive Health Services* that states could limit access to abortion. Supreme Court cases in the early 1990s upheld one of the strictest parental notification laws in the nation as well as a gag rule prohibiting counselors and doctors in federally funded clinics from pro-

viding information about abortion and referrals to doctors, a Pennsylvania law limiting access to the procedure, and a Mississippi law requiring a 24-hour waiting period. In 1993, President Bill Clinton marked the twentieth anniversary of *Roe v. Wade* by signing memoranda reversing abortion restrictions imposed during the Reagan and Bush administrations. As a result, federally funded clinics became free to provide abortion counseling; military hospitals were allowed to perform abortions; fetal tissue could be used in federally financed research; and federal aid was allowed for international family-planning programs that included abortion-related practices. The memoranda also called for a review of the policy against the importation of the abortifacient drug RU486, which became available in the United States in 2000. In 1996, Clinton vetoed a bill that would have banned late-term, sometimes known as partial-birth, abortion, a highly controversial procedure that was banned in 2003, with the ban upheld by the Supreme Court in 2007.

Since the ratification of *Roe v. Wade*, some of its opponents shifted from debate to violence. Between

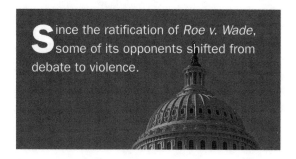

ince the ratification of *Roe v. Wade*, some of its opponents shifted from debate to violence.

1993 and 2015, numerous incidences of vandalism, arson, kidnapping, stalking, assault, attempted murder, and murder directed at individuals and organizations that provide abortions occurred, even when physicians and clinical workers did not entirely approve of the procedure but nevertheless recognized its legality and necessity. By 1998, acts of violence toward abortion providers resulted in fewer physicians willing to perform the procedure, almost no courses on abortion taught in medical schools, and little if any research on the subject. Caught between medical and political interests have been prochoice women, many of whom have witnessed the erosion of abortion rights since 1976 as well as a political and cultural assault on the nearly eighty-year-old women's health organization Planned Parenthood, an invaluable resource for women, especially those who cannot afford expensive health care. American women continue to face legal and constitutional uncertainty regarding all aspects of reproductive freedom, including birth control and abortion. As Supreme Court Justice Ruth Bader Ginsburg stated during her 1993 confirmation hearings, "The state controlling a woman would deny her full autonomy and full equality."

POSTFEMINISM

The second women's movement coincided with the coming of age of women baby boomers who, by 1976, had begun to surge into graduate school and enter the work force in great numbers. By the 1980s, many women were either giving all of their effort to advancing in their careers and delaying marriage and motherhood because of it or starting families and coping with the challenge of juggling the demands of a career, marriage, and

child-rearing. This was fueled by a new political and social conservatism during the decade, which included dissension over abortion rights and a growing print and broadcast media that fostered a new romanticizing of motherhood; public concern over children ostensibly raised by babysitters or in less than adequate daycare facilities; reactionary notions of deep-seated, hormonally driven gender differences; and the exploitation of women's anxieties over the ticking biological clock that would render them incapable of conceiving children. The term "postfeminism" was used in the 1980s to describe what many women saw as a political and cultural backlash against the second-wave feminism of the women's movement.

At the same time, the media began to label teenage women and women in their twenties, who were either born during the women's movement or too young to participate in it, the "postfeminist generation." By the millennium, postfeminists would come to describe young women who had benefited from the access to employment, education, and the more fluid family arrangements that resulted from second-wave feminism; were not inclined to push for more political changes in the equality of women; or might largely agree with the goals of feminism but did identify themselves as feminists. Along with a postfeminist consciousness came a reevaluation of what it meant to be a feminist and whether the concept of feminism was relevant at all together with a media that interpreted postfeminism as a form of feminism in which women accepted popular culture rather than rejecting it, unlike second-wave feminists. In the 1990s and 2000s, TV shows and films such as *Xena: Warrior Princess*, *Sex and the City*, *The Devil Wears Prada*, and *Bridget Jones's Diary* as well as novels dubbed "chick lit" variously portrayed women as powerful, independent, confident, sexually liberated, feminine, emotionally vulnerable, and partner- and marriage-minded.

Postfeminism, which evolved from the feminism of the second women's rights' movement, has sometimes been described as an ideology in which society is no longer defined by gender roles or as gender binary, that is, either feminine or masculine. Third-wave feminism began in the early 1990s and

An attorney and professor at Brandeis University, Anita Hill accused Supreme Court Clarence Thomas of sexual harassment during Thomas's 1991 confirmation hearing. Her allegations were dismissed and Thomas now sits on the nation's highest court.

fourth-wave feminism; it has been characterized by the examination of how systems of power contribute to the social stratification of traditionally marginalized groups as well as the use of social media to empower women, most prominently on Twitter and Facebook. In addition, terms such as toxic masculinity, gender normative, gender conforming and nonconforming, and female presenting began to enter the national vocabulary.

The use of social media has been particularly useful as a tool to connect women in common purpose, not least of which has been the #MeToo movement calling out cases of sexual abuse and sexual assault and encouraging and providing platforms for women to share their stories. Social media also rose to the occasion after the election of Donald Trump as president in 2016. Women's marches protesting Trump's presidency were scheduled to take place on January 20, 2017, and advertised on Facebook. Women heeded the call, and between three million and five million women and men participated in at least 408 marches in cities and towns across the United States, with similar marches taking place in other countries. Women's marches have taken place every January since then. It can be argued that the #MeToo movement and the resistance movement that resulted from the women's marches, together with the activism of women in TV and film to support and promote women of color, older women, and women directors and producers, comprise a third women's movement that promises to be as influential in the struggle for women's equality as the women's movements of the past.

in many ways aligned with postfeminism. Third-wave feminism has regarded race, social class, transgender rights, and the status of women and mothers in the workplace and at home as central issues; has embraced individualism and diversity; and has endeavored to redefine what it means to be a feminist in the wake of such cultural and political events as the emergence of the Riot Grrrl feminist punk subculture and the 1991 televised congressional testimony of Anita Hill, who had accused Supreme Court nominee Clarence Thomas of sexual harassment. Also emerging from third-wave feminism and carrying over into what has been called fourth-wave feminism in the 2000s and 2010s were new cultural concepts such as intersectionality, sex positivity, transfeminism, and postmodern feminism. Intersectionality in particular has been a focus of

BIOGRAPHIES

Bella Abzug (1920–1998)
Politician, Women's Rights Activist

Sometimes known as "Battling Bella" for her outspokenness and untiring efforts on behalf of women's rights and social justice as well as for her trademark wide-brimmed hats, Bella Abzug

was an attorney, a U.S. representative, a human rights activist, and a leader of the women's movement of the 1960s and 1970s.

Born Bella Savitsky in New York City and raised in the Bronx, Abzug was the daughter of Russian Jewish immigrants. Her mother was a homemaker, and her father ran a butcher shop. When her father died, Abzug, then thirteen, was told that her Orthodox synagogue only permitted the sons of deceased fathers to say the Kaddish (the mourners' prayer). Since Abzug had no brothers, she defied tradition and went to the synagogue every day for a year to recite the prayer.

Abzug attended Walton High School in New York City, where she was class president, and went on to Hunter College, a women's college in New York City. While attending Hunter, Abzug served as president of the student council and also studied at the Jewish Theological Seminary of America. She applied to the Harvard Law School but was rejected because she was a woman; instead, she earned her law degree at Columbia University. In 1944, she married Martin Abzug, a novelist and stockbroker; the couple remained married until Martin Abzug's death in 1986.

At a time when few women worked as lawyers, Abzug was admitted to the New York Bar in 1945 and began practicing at Pressman, Witt & Cammer, a law firm in New York City, where she specialized in labor law and civil rights cases. Early in her career, while working with the American Civil Liberties Union (ACLU), Abzug appealed the case of Willie McGee, an African American man accused of raping a white woman in Mississippi, convicted by an all-white jury in less than 3 minutes, and sentenced to death. Despite numerous threats from white supremacist groups, Abzug continued to challenge McGee's conviction and managed to secure a delay for his execution. Abzug ultimately lost the appeal, and McGee was executed in 1951.

Abzug was an early participant in Women Strike for Peace, an activist group founded in 1961 during America's Cold War with the Soviet Union to protest against the U.S. testing of nuclear weapons. She was also an outspoken advocate of the Equal Rights Amendment and opponent of the

Vietnam War, a stance that placed her on President Richard Nixon's "Enemies List." In 1970, Abzug ran for Congress, using as her campaign slogan, "This woman's place is in the House—the House of Representatives." She soundly defeated both the fourteen-year incumbent and a talk show host in the primary only to lose to candidate William Fitts Ryan. However, Ryan died before the general election, and Abzug defeated his widow in a Democratic Party convention to choose the replacement nominee. Abzug won the general election and served in the U.S. House of Representatives from 1971 to 1973 and again from 1973 to 1977.

While serving in Congress, Abzug was voted one of the three most influential members of the House of Representatives. She became one of the first members of Congress to support gay rights, introducing the Equality Act, the first federal gay rights bill, with cosponsor Ed Koch, who would go on to become mayor of New York City. She served as chair of the Subcommittee on Government Information and Individual Rights, which held hearings on government secrecy, and in 1975, near the end of the Vietnam War, she was part of a bipartisan delegation sent by President Gerald Ford to Saigon to assess the situation in South Vietnam. Abzug was also an author, penning *Bella: Mrs. Abzug Goes to Washington* (1972) and *The Gender Gap: Bella Abzug's Guide to Political Power for American Women* (1984), cowritten with friend and colleague Mim Kelber.

In 1976, Abzug mounted an unsuccessful bid for the U.S. Senate, losing in the primary to the popular and more moderate Daniel Patrick Moynihan, who had served in both the Nixon and Ford administrations in several capacities. Although Abzug lost the primary by less than 1 percent, news coverage did not report this fact, preferring instead to focus on the male candidates. After her failed run for the Senate, President Jimmy Carter appointed her cochair of the National Commission on the Observance of International Women's Year and cochair of the National Advisory Commission for Women. Abzug also unsuccessfully ran for mayor of New York City in 1977 and mounted two failed attempts to return to the U.S. House of Representatives from two different New York districts in 1978 and 1986.

Abzug continued to work for women's equality in the United States and abroad, founding several women's advocacy organizations, including Women U.S.A. in 1979, and leading women's rights events such as the Women's Equality Day New York March in 1980, at which she served as grand marshal. In the early 1990s, Abzug cofounded the Women's Environment and Development Organization (WEDO) and served as the organization's president. In that capacity, she became an influential leader at United Nations world conferences, held to advocate for the empowerment of women around the world. During her last years, Abzug continued her busy schedule of travel and work. In 1997, the year before her death, she received the Blue Beret Peacekeepers Award, the highest honor bestowed by the United Nations on a civilian. It was a fitting tribute to one of the most influential Americans in women's history. It also speaks to her response to those who mentioned the eye-catching hats she wore: "It's what's under the hat that counts!"

Ti-Grace Atkinson (1938–)
Author, Philosopher

An influential feminist author and philosopher, Ti-Grace Atkinson was an early proponent and explicator of radical feminism during the women's movement of the 1960s and 1970s.

Atkinson was born in Baton Rouge, Louisiana, the youngest of the seven children of a Standard Oil chemical engineer and a homemaker. She was named for her grandmother, Grace, and the "Ti" attached to her name is Cajun French for "little." Because of her father's career, the family moved a great deal, an experience Atkinson has credited with forming her awareness of the different ways in which people view the world. After an early marriage at seventeen ended in divorce several years later, she enrolled at the University of Pennsylvania, earning a BFA degree in 1964. Atkinson remained in Philadelphia for a time, where she helped found and was the first director of the Institute of Art. She then moved to New York City, where she reviewed

sculpture for *ARTnews* magazine and in 1967 entered the Ph.D. program in philosophy at Columbia University. Atkinson went on to teach at several colleges and universities over a period of twenty-six years.

Atkinson's commitment to feminism began when, as an undergraduate, she read Simone de Beauvoir's *The Second Sex* and was inspired to write to de Beauvoir, who suggested she contact Betty Friedan. Friedan encouraged Atkinson to join the newly formed National Organization for Women, which she did in 1967, serving on NOW's national board and becoming the New York chapter's president. She led NOW's efforts to end the *New York Times's* gender-segregated Help Wanted ads, but when she met with the editor, her request to change the ads was immediately rejected. Atkinson and NOW embarked on a series of demonstrations and lawsuits until the *Times* eventually agreed to publish gender-neutral ads.

In 1968, Atkinson left NOW because of the organization's unwillingness to confront such issues as abortion and marriage inequalities. She founded the October 17th Movement, which later became The Feminists, a radical feminist group active until 1973. In 1969, Atkinson and other members marched into the Manhattan Marriage Bureau to denounce marriage contracts as fraudulent. Coverage in *Life* magazine described the group as "active—and angry—female militants." In 1974, she published a radical feminist manifesto titled *Amazon Odyssey*, in which she suggested lesbianism as an alternative to marriage and motherhood.

In 1997, Atkinson moved to Cambridge, Massachusetts, to complete her doctoral dissertation and taught at Harvard and Tufts University. She retired in 2004. In 2013, Atkinson joined with other feminists to prepare an open statement titled "Forbidden Discourse: The Silencing of Feminist Criticism of 'Gender,'" a denunciation of the threats and attacks directed toward those who have challenged "the right of women to organize for their liberation separately from men, including … (male to female) transgendered people." In recent years, Atkinson's social justice advocacy has included supporting the 2014 worker's strike at Market Basket, an area grocery chain, and advocating for affordable housing, especially for elderly women and female victims of domestic violence.

Caroline Bird (1915–2011)

Author

A feminist author whose 1968 book *Born Female: The High Cost of Keeping Women Down* is considered one of the most influential works of the women's rights movement of the 1960s and 1970s, Bird was born in New York City and grew up in White Plains, New York. She attended school in Lausanne, Switzerland, and at sixteen enrolled at Vassar College, the youngest member of the class of 1935. After her junior year, Bird left college to marry Edward Menuez, a civil engineer, and later earned a BA degree at the University of Toledo and an MA degree in comparative literature at the University of Wisconsin. The couple divorced in 1945. In 1957, Bird married Thomas Mahoney, an author and journalist to whom she remained married until his death in 1981.

Born Female: The High Cost of Keeping Women Down resulted from an article on discrimination against women in business that was rejected by *The Saturday Evening Post*. The same year the book was published, Bird delivered a speech, "On Being Born Female," before the Episcopal Church Executive Council in Greenwich, Connecticut, which was subsequently published in November 1968 in the magazine *Vital Speeches of the Day*. In the speech, Bird asserts, "There is recognition abroad that we are in many ways a sexist country. Sexism is judging people by their sex when sex doesn't matter. Sexism is intended to rhyme with racism. Women are sexists as often as men." According to the *Oxford English Dictionary*, Bird's speech marks the first use of the word "sexism" in print.

Bird's other published works include *The Invisible Scar* (1966), *Everything a Woman Needs to Know to Get Paid What She's Worth* (1973), *Case Against College* (1975), *The Crowding Syndrome: Learning to Live With Too Much and Too Many* (1976), *Enterprising Women* (1976), *What Women Want* (1979), *The Two-Paycheck Marriage* (1979), *Second Careers* (1992), and *Lives of Our Own* (1995). The American Library Association named *The Invisible Scar*, a history of the Great Depression, one of the one hundred most significant books of 1966.

In 1977, Bird became an associate of the Women's Institute for Freedom of the Press (WIFP), a nonprofit publishing organization and national and international feminist network dedicated to increasing communication between women and connecting the public with different forms of female-based media. The same year, she was a consultant on the National Commission on the Observance of International Women's Year in Houston and, in 1978, cowrote the commission's report, *The Spirit of Houston*. In 1979, Bird's name and picture were included in *Supersisters*, a set of seventy-two feminist trading cards featuring women from various areas of achievement. After Bird's death in Nashville, "The Caroline Bird Papers, 1915–1995" were added to the Archives and Special Collections Library at Vassar College.

Heather Booth (1945–)

Women's Rights Activist

 A leading women's rights activist, civil rights activist, political strategist, and community organizer, Heather Booth was instrumental in the formation of the Jane Collective, an underground counseling service for women seeking safe abortions.

Born Heather Tobis in a military hospital in Brookhaven, Mississippi, where her father was serving as a physician specializing in physical therapy and cardiac rehabilitation, Booth and her two brothers were raised in Bensonhurst, Brooklyn, and on the North Shore of Long Island, where Booth attended high school. She grew up in an observant Jewish family that attended a liberal synagogue. Booth's Jewish upbringing, as well as the example of her loving, supportive parents, impressed upon her the importance of treating others with decency and respect together with the need to identify social injustice and take responsibility to correct it. An early influence on Booth's feminism was Betty Friedan's

The Feminine Mystique, the central thesis of which her mother discussed with her. While in high school, Booth joined the cheerleading team and a sorority but resigned from both when she came to believe they discriminated against students from less privileged backgrounds. She campaigned against the death penalty and joined the Congress of Racial Equality (CORE) to protest the segregationist policies of the Woolworth department store chain.

After graduating from high school, Booth attended the University of Chicago, where she graduated in 1967, with a BA degree in social sciences. Shortly after her graduation, she married Paul Booth, an antiwar activist and founder of the Students for a Democratic Society (SDS), who would later have a long career as a labor organizer. The couple, who had two sons within a few years of their marriage, met at a sit-in protesting the university's cooperation with the U.S. Selective Service, the local boards of which were drafting men to serve in the Vietnam War. Paul Booth died in 2018.

While in college, Booth joined the Student Non-Violent Coordinating Committee (SNCC) and, as the head of the campus Friends of SNCC, helped coordinate freedom schools, alternative and free schools for African Americans, on Chicago's South Side. She participated in Freedom Summer as one of many college volunteers working to register black voters in Mississippi, an experience that included frightening confrontations with white Mississippians who, in the Jim Crow South, resisted initiatives that would empower the African American community.

Booth's feminist activism began in college, where she set up women's consciousness-raising groups to address the university's bias toward male students. As the women shared their experiences of biases directed toward them, they began to gain a sense of the influence collective action might have on changing the unfair practices and dismissive attitudes they had previously accepted as the norm. Booth also helped to organize a women's studies course, began to coach women who were uncomfortable about speaking up in class, and founded the Women's Radical Action Program to document and reverse the subordinate position of women in such purportedly progressive groups as the SDS and SNCC.

In 1965, a fellow student approached Booth to help his sister, who had become suicidal after learning she was pregnant. Booth contacted the medical branch of the civil rights movement and was able to refer the woman to a reputable doctor willing to perform an illegal abortion. Booth was then asked for more referrals, and out of that came the formation of the Jane Collective, also simply known as Jane. The students who worked with the Jane Collective evaluated doctors, made referrals, counseled women, and made follow-up phone calls to women after their abortions. The group renamed itself the Abortion Counseling Service of Women's Liberation in 1969 and began to advertise in student and underground newspapers, where women seeking abortions were advised to "call Jane." The group disbanded after abortion was legalized throughout the United States in 1973.

In 1969, Booth cofounded the Chicago Women's Liberation Union (CWLU), a group formed to organize women into a collective force that would advocate for reforms to improve women's lives. Frustrated by the lack of local daycare centers in her Hyde Park, Chicago, community, Booth organized the Action Committee for Decent Childcare (ACDC), which worked to overcome legal barriers to the expansion of childcare facilities throughout Chicago and resulted in the city investing $1 million for childcare centers. In 1972, Booth and others in the CWLU published "Socialist Feminism: A Strategy for the Women's Movement," a position paper believed to mark the first appearance of the term "socialist feminism," an ideology that rose in the 1960s and 1970s as an offshoot of the feminist movement focusing on the connection between patriarchy and capitalism.

In addition to her work on behalf of women's rights, Booth has been a highly effective community organizer and has played an influential role in progressive politics on the local and national level. She has also endured considerable criticism from leading conservatives, who have labeled her a communist. In 2011, Matthew Vadum, senior vice president of the conservative think tank Capital Research Center, described Booth as one of Washington's "labor thugs" seeking to "achieve a socialist transformation of America."

The recipient of numerous awards and honors for her advocacy, Booth has appeared in several films documenting the history of feminism and the women's liberation movement. In 2016, she was the subject of the documentary *Heather Booth: Changing the World*, written, produced, and directed by filmmaker Lily Rivlin. The following year, she was interviewed in an episode of the *That's What She Said* podcast series. She continues to be a tireless advocate for social change.

Susan Brownmiller (1935–)
Journalist, Women's Rights Activist

A feminist journalist and activist, Susan Brownmiller is the author of *Against Our Will: Men, Women, and Rape*, a groundbreaking book on the titular subject, which the New York Public Library selected as one of the one hundred most important books of the twentieth century.

Brownmiller was born Susan Warhaftig in Brooklyn, New York. Her father was a salesman in New York's Garment District and later worked as a vendor for Macy's department store. Her mother was a secretary for a business in the Empire State Building. As a child, Brownmiller attended Hebrew school at the East Midwood Jewish Center in Brooklyn two afternoons a week. In "Jewish Women and the Feminist Revolution," recorded by the Jewish Women's Archive in 2010, Brownmiller credits her study of Hebrew and Jewish history as responsible for her determination "to fight against physical harm, specifically the terror of violence against women."

Brownmiller attended Cornell University from 1952 to 1954, then moved back to New York City, where she took acting classes and appeared in two off-Broadway productions. She began her career in journalism with an editorial position at one of the "true confessions" magazines popular at the time and, from 1959 to 1960, worked as assistant to the managing editor of *Coronet* magazine. By this time, she had taken the pen name of Susan Brownmiller, which she legally adopted in 1961.

From 1961 to 1968, Brownmiller was an editor of the *Albany Report*, a weekly review of the New York State Legislature, and worked as a national af-fairs researcher at *Newsweek* magazine, a reporter for the NBC-TV affiliate in Philadelphia, a staff writer for the *Village Voice* newspaper, and as a network news writer for ABC-TV in New York. After becoming a freelance writer in 1968, Brownmiller wrote book reviews, essays, and articles for several newspapers and magazines, including *The New York Times*, *The New York Daily News*, *Vogue* magazine, and *The Nation* magazine.

Brownmiller's social activism began in 1964, when she joined the Congress of Racial Equality (CORE) and the Student Non-Violent Coordinating Committee (SNCC) and participated in the sit-in movement and registered African American voters in Mississippi during Freedom Summer. In 1968, she became involved with the women's liberation movement, joining a consciousness-raising group within the New York Radical Women organization. In 1970, Brownmiller participated in an 11-hour sit-in of female workers at the *Ladies' Home Journal* to protest the lack of editorial positions for women and to demand an editorial staff solely comprised of women, who would dictate the magazine's content.

Brownmiller's idea for *Against Our Will* grew out of a 1971 New York Radical Feminists Speakout on Rape, which she helped to organize, as well as her participation in the New York Radical Feminists Conference the same year. She began to study rape throughout history, evaluated statistics, collected newspaper clippings to locate patterns in which rape has been reported in the press, researched laws that continued to legalize rape within marriage, and analyzed rape as it has been portrayed in literature, films, and music. In *Against Our Will*, Brownmiller argues that rape has been a persistent factor in our social order, a fundamental aspect of male–female relations, supported by a "rape culture" that blames the victim and exonerates (and even glamorizes) the perpetrator. Rape, as Brownmiller has observed, is "nothing more or less than a conscious process of intimidation by which men keep all women in a state of fear." Brownmiller also asserts that prostitution and pornography contribute to "the false perception of sexual access as an adjunct of male power and privilege," which objectifies and dehumanizes women. "My purpose in this book,"

Brownmiller writes, "has been to give rape its history. Now we must deny it a future."

Against Our Will received much praise and provoked a great deal of controversy ranging from criticism of Brownmiller's assertion that all men benefit from the culture of rape to its white, middle-class assumptions that deny the presence of emotional states or acts that might drive such behavior. African American educator and activist Angela Davis took issue with Brownmiller's discussion of rape and race, calling it an "unthinking partnership, which borders on racism." Nevertheless, *Against Our Will* is credited with changing public attitudes about rape and sparking discussion on how rape affects women.

Brownmiller's other works include *Shirley Chisholm*, a biography for children (1970), *Femininity* (1984), the novel *Waverly Place* (1989), and *In Our Time: Memoir of a Revolution* (1999), a chronicle of the women's movement of the 1960s and 1970s. In 2014, Brownmiller appeared in *She's Beautiful When She's Angry*, a documentary on many of the women involved in the women's movement.

Jacqueline Ceballos (1925–)
Women's Rights Activist

A feminist activist and public relations executive, Jacqueline Cebellos was born Jacqueline Michot in Mamou, Louisiana, the middle child in a family that included seven children. She attended public school in Lafayette, Louisiana, and studied music at the Southwestern Louisiana Institute, where she majored in voice. After her studies, she moved to New York City to pursue a career in opera. In 1951, Cebellos married Alavaro Cebellos, a Colombian businessman, with whom she had four children. The family moved to Bogotá, Colombia, where Jacqueline Cebellos founded the city's first opera company, and, with her husband's help, she opened an import–export clothing business in New York.

Cebellos was inspired to become active in the feminist movement after she read Betty Friedan's *The Feminine Mystique* during the breakup of her marriage. In 1967, Cebellos and her children moved to New York City, where Cebellos attended her first National Organization for Women (NOW) confer-

ence. She served on NOW's local and national boards from 1967 to 1973, was president of the New York chapter in 1971, became NOW's eastern regional director, and formed a public relations committee and speakers' bureau within the organization. She helped Betty Friedan organize the Women's Strike for Equality in 1970 and assisted Friedan in organizing demonstrations protesting the all-male staff at *The New York Times*. In 1971, she helped found the National Women's Political Caucus.

In April 1971, Cebellos participated in a debate billed as "A Dialogue on Women's Liberation," held at New York's Town Hall, and documented it in a film of the event titled *Town Bloody Hall*. The other panelists were Australian feminist Germaine Greer, author of *The Female Eunuch* (1970), columnist Jill Johnston, literary critic Diana Trilling, and author and sometime politician Norman Mailer. The debate became notorious for its heated discussion, particularly between Greer and Mailer, an avowed antifeminist regarded by most in the women's liberation movement as sexist, homophobic, and reactionary. During the debate, Cebellos made the case that women had the right and the duty "to have a voice in changing the world that is changing them."

Cebellos served as NOW's representative at the 1972 Democratic National Convention in Miami Beach and was the organization's representative to the International Women's Year Conference in Mexico in 1975. In 1974, she cofounded the Women's Forum and served as the organization's first president. She retired from public activism in 1975 to start a public relations firm dedicated to promoting women's studies courses. The firm also began the New Feminist Talent Speaker's Bureau. In 1977, she became an associate of the Women's Institute for Freedom of the Press. In the 1980s, a decade of backlash against feminism, Cebellos cofounded Veteran Feminists of America, an organization whose purpose is to "honor, record, and preserve the history of the accomplishments of women active in the feminist movement, to educate the public on the importance of the changes brought about by the women's movement, to preserve the movement's history and to inspire future generations." In 2014, Cebellos was featured in a film about the women's movement, *She's Beautiful When She's Angry*.

Kimberlé Williams Crenshaw (1959–)

Attorney, Educator

 A lawyer and educator specializing in issues pertaining to race and gender, Kimberlé Williams Crenshaw is known for the introduction and development of intersectional theory and intersectional feminism, the study of how overlapping and intersecting social identities relate to cultural and legal systems of oppression, domination, or discrimination for women and especially for women of color. Crenshaw introduced the theory of intersectionality in a 1989 paper she wrote for the University of Chicago Legal Forum entitled "Demarginalizing the Intersection of Race and Sex: A Black Feminist Critique of Antidiscrimination Doctrine, Feminist Theory, and Antiracist Politics."

Crenshaw was born in Canton, Ohio, and received a bachelor's degree in government and Africana studies from Cornell University in 1981. She earned her JD degree from Harvard Law School in 1984 and, in 1985, received a LLM degree from the University of Wisconsin Law School, where she clerked for Wisconsin Supreme Court Judge Shirley Abrahamson. She joined the faculty of the UCLA School of Law in 1986. A founder of the field of critical race theory, which examines society and culture as they relate to race, law, and power, Crenshaw is a lecturer on civil rights, critical race studies, and constitutional law. In 1995, she was appointed as a full professor at the Columbia Law School, where she is the founder and director of the Center for Intersectionality and Social Policy Studies, established in 2011. Crenshaw is also executive director of the African American Policy Forum (AAPF), a nonprofit think tank and information clearinghouse that she cofounded in 1996 and which sponsored the My Brother's Keeper Challenge, a public–private partnership with the U.S. government to foster intervention by civic leaders in the lives of young, African American men to address their unique challenges. In addition, Crenshaw wrote the background paper on race and gender discrimination for the United Nations World Conference on Racism in 2011, served as a member of the National Science Foundation's Committee to Research Violence Against Women, has been the Fulbright chair for Latin America in Brazil, and, in 2008, was awarded an in-residence fellowship at the Center of Advanced Behavioral Studies at Stanford University.

Crenshaw was on the legal team representing Anita Hill, who testified at the 1991 confirmation hearings for U.S. Supreme Court candidate Clarence Thomas that she had been sexually harassed by Thomas while working as his assistant. The case provided an example of intersectionality, with two groups expressing contrasting views: white feminists, who supported Anita Hill; and members of the African American community, who were willing to overlook Hill's experience as a woman who had been violated in order to ensure Thomas's confirmation as the second African American to sit on the Supreme Court. Crenshaw's contention was that Hill, caught between these two opposing camps, had lost her ability to bring to the conversation her voice as a black woman. Crenshaw argued that although Anita Hill helped many women to begin to recognize cases of sexual harassment, "what's not doing so well is the recognition of black women's unique experiences with discrimination."

The recipient of many honors and awards, Crenshaw has also published several works on civil rights, black feminist legal theory, racism, and the law. In 2015, *Ms.* magazine named her the Number One Most Inspiring Feminist. In 2019, Crenshaw participated in the PBS series *Reconstruction: America After the Civil War*.

Karen DeCrow (1937–2014)

Attorney, Women's Rights Activist

An attorney, author, activist, and one of the most celebrated leaders of the women's rights movement, Karen DeCrow also supported equal rights for men in child custody cases as well as the rights of both men and women to decide whether or not to become a parent.

Born Karen Lipschultz in Chicago, Illinois, De-Crow attended public schools, earned her bachelor's degree from Northwestern University's Medill School of Journalism in 1959 and, following graduation, worked as a writer and editor. After a brief first marriage, DeCrow married computer scientist Roger De-Crow in 1967. The same year, DeCrow became president of the Syracuse, New York, chapter of the National Organization for Women (NOW). She would go on to serve on NOW's National Board of Directors from 1968 until 1974. In 1969, DeCrow went back to college at the Syracuse University School of Law, graduating as the only woman in the class of 1972.

The same year DeCrow began her law studies, she and Faith Seidenberg, an attorney and activist, entered McSorley's Old Ale House, a male-only bar in New York City, and were refused service. They sued the establishment for discrimination in a case and won after the U.S. District Court in New York ruled that because it was a public place, McSorley's was in violation of the Equal Protection Clause of the U.S. Constitution. The case decision was featured on the front page of *The New York Times*.

DeCrow was elected national president of NOW in 1974. During her three-year tenure as president, NOW embarked on such initiatives as the achievement of nongovernmental status with the United Nations, supporting the ordination of the first Episcopal female priests, persuading the federal government to include sex discrimination in the Fair Housing Law, and instituting highly publicized and successful antidiscrimination suits against the Sears department store chain and AT&T. DeCrow also led campaigns to ensure that collegiate sports would be included in the provisions of Title IX as part of the Education Amendment to the Civil Rights Act of 1964. She was the last NOW president to serve without a salary or an office.

DeCrow devoted her legal career to cases promoting gender equality, eliminating age discrimination, and the protection of civil liberties. She was honored by the American Civil Liberties Union (ACLU) in 1985. She was a supporter of shared parenting after divorce, a position that was criticized by some NOW members. She campaigned for passage of the Equal Rights Amendment (ERA) in the 1970s and 1980s and traveled throughout the country to engage in some eighty debates on the ERA with antifeminist activist Phyllis Schlafly.

DeCrow's works include *The Young Woman's Guide to Liberation* (1971) and *Sexist Justice—How Legal Sexism Affects You* (1975). She was inducted into the National Women's Hall of Fame in 2009.

Andrea Dworkin (1946–2005)
Anti-Pornography Activist, Author

A writer, radical feminist, and antipornography campaigner, Andrea Dworkin sparked a heated debate in the 1980s on censorship and pornography.

The oldest of two children, Dworkin was born in Camden, New Jersey, and raised in Cherry Hill, New Jersey. Both parents were influential in inspiring in Dworkin a passion for social justice. Her father, a teacher and avowed socialist, was the grandson of a Russian Jew who had fled Russia at the age of fifteen to escape conscription in the Russian military. Her mother, the child of Jewish immigrants from Hungary, was a supporter of legal birth control and legal abortion. Dworkin's rebellious streak was evident as early as sixth grade, when school administrators punished her for refusing to sing Christmas carols.

After her graduation from high school, Dworkin attended Bennington College in Vermont. While a freshman at the school, Dworkin was arrested during an anti-Vietnam War protest held at the U.S. Mission to the United Nations and was sent to the Women's House of Detention in New York's Greenwich Village, where she was subjected to a violent internal examination from prison doctors. She wrote to the commissioner of corrections to describe this violation and testified before a grand jury, which declined to indict prison administrators. However, Dworkin's testimony, which made national and international news, helped to stir public outrage over the treatment of inmates. The Women's House of Detention was closed in 1974. Dworkin left college soon after her grand jury testimony and moved to the Greek island of Crete, where she wrote a series of poems, a novel titled *Notes on a Burning Boyfriend*, a tribute to Norman Morrison, a pacifist who had burned himself to death to protest the Vietnam War, and *Morning Hair*, a book of poems and dialogues she hand-printed after returning to the United States.

Dworkin returned to Bennington, where she continued to study literature and participated in campaigns against the college's conduct code, for contraception on campus, for the legalization of abortion, and against the war in Vietnam. After her graduation in 1968, she moved to Amsterdam to interview Dutch anarchists. While there, she married anarchist Cornelius Dirk Bruin, who physically abused her and continued to physically and emotionally harass her after she left him in 1971. While she tried to earn enough money to return to the United States, Dworkin sheltered with an expatriate friend, Ricki Abrams, who introduced her to the writings of early second-wave feminists Kate Millett, Shulamith Firestone, and Robin Morgan. The two women collaborated on a book titled *Women Hating*, which was published under Dworkin's name in 1974.

In 1972, Dworkin returned to New York, where she worked as an antiwar organizer, demonstrated on behalf of lesbian rights and against apartheid in South Africa, and joined the radical feminist movement, focusing on campaigns against violence toward women. She gained a reputation as a passionate speaker, urging her audiences to action during speeches given at the first Take Back the Night march against rape in 1978, during which three thousand women marched through the red-light district of San Francisco, and at the 1983 Midwest Regional Conference of the National Organization for Changing Men, where her speech was titled "I Want a Twenty-Four-Hour Truce During Which There is No Rape."

Dworkin's activism in the feminist antipornography movement began in 1976, when she co-organized a public picketing of *Snuff*, a low-budget "sexploitation" horror film, and the same year joined with several prominent feminists to form an antipornography group that would become Women Against Pornography in 1979. The following year,

Dworkin, feminist lawyer Catherine MacKinnon, and members of Women Against Pornography began to discuss using federal civil rights law to combat pornography. Despite several initiatives, neither Dworkin nor MacKinnon succeeded, either together or separately, to secure city ordinances against pornography. In 1986, Dworkin testified before the Attorney General's Commission on Pornography, during which she cited both *Playboy* and *Penthouse* magazines as promoting both rape and child sexual abuse. Although Dworkin's testimony was praised and intimidated some retailers into withdrawing copies of the magazines, the Washington, D.C., District Court quashed the commission's campaign on First Amendment grounds.

Dworkin was a prolific writer, whose works include *The New Woman's Broken Heart* (1980), *Pornography: Men Possessing Women* (1981), *Right-Wing Women: The Politics of Domesticated Females* (1983), *Ice and Fire* (1986), and a collection of her speeches and articles from the 1990s, *Life and Death: Unapologetic Writings on the Continuing War on Women* (1997). Dworkin's earlier speeches were published in *Our Blood* (1976) and *Letters from a War Zone* (1988). In 2002, she published her autobiography, *Heartbreak*.

In 1998, Dworkin married her longtime partner John Stoltenberg, a feminist activist, author, and magazine editor. During their marriage, Dworkin continued to publicly identify herself as a lesbian, and Stoltenberg identified himself as gay.

Catherine East (1916–1996)

Women's Rights Activist

A U.S. government researcher and feminist, Catherine East was a major formative influence on the women's movement of the 1960s and 1970s. East was born Catherine Shipe in Barboursville, West Virginia, the oldest of three children. When she was eleven, her mother suffered a nervous breakdown, and four years later, her father committed suicide. After graduating from high school, East enrolled in the teaching program at Marshall College in Charleston, West Virginia, but was forced to withdraw just before gaining enough academic credits to earn a bachelor's degree because of financial difficulties. In 1937, she married Charles East, with whom she had two daughters. East later divorced her husband. She would earn her college degree in history in 1943.

In 1939, East took a job with the U.S. Civil Service Commission as a junior civil service examiner and was later appointed chief of the commission's career service division. From 1963 to 1975, East worked for the U.S. Department of Labor, where she served as the technical advisor to President John F. Kennedy's President's Commission on the Status of Women and helped to research and write the commission's report, *American Women*. East was also appointed executive secretary for Kennedy's Interdepartmental Committee on the Status of Women and the Citizen's Advisory Council on the Status of Women. East would hold various senior advisory positions in government until she retired in 1977.

A valuable and willing conduit of information for early second-wave feminists because of her unique position within the federal government, East encouraged Betty Friedan to form an organization similar to the NAACP to advocate for women's equality. When the National Organization for Women (NOW) was founded in 1966, Betty Friedan credited East as "the midwife of the contemporary women's movement" for catalyzing her and other women to begin the crusade to end inequality. East was well placed to provide NOW with official data concerning women in the workplace and to disprove the claims of legislators who opposed women's equality. She also helped to reconcile differences between female labor activists and feminists.

After her retirement, East became a full-time activist. She worked to pass the Equal Rights Amendment (ERA), served as the women's issues coordinator during the presidential campaign of Independent John Anderson from 1979 to 1980, served on the board of NOW's Legal Defense and Education Fund from 1979 to 1983, and was the legislative director of the National Women's Political Caucus from 1983 to 1986.

East was an active member of many organizations, including the American Association of University Women (AAUW), the American Civil Liberties Union (ACLU), the National Women's Party (NWP), and Planned Parenthood. The recipient of numerous awards for her contribution to the advancement of women's equality, East was inducted into the National Women's Hall of Fame in 1994.

Susan Faludi (1959–)
Author, Journalist

An award-winning journalist and author, Susan Faludi is best known for her influential book on the conservative backlash toward American women in the 1980s, *Backlash: The Undeclared War on American Women*, published in 1991.

Faludi was born in the New York City borough of Queens and raised in Yorktown Heights, New York. Her father, Steven (later Stefánie) Faludi, a Hungarian immigrant and Holocaust survivor who died in 2015, came out as a transgender woman when he was seventy-six. Susan Faludi's interest in journalism began in fifth grade, when she conducted a poll showing that most of her classmates opposed the Vietnam War and supported the Equal Rights Amendment and the legalization of abortion. Faludi went on to attend Harvard University, where she was elected to the academic society Phi Beta Kappa and was the managing editor of *The Harvard Crimson*, for which she often wrote about women's issues such as sexual harassment on campus. She graduated summa cum laude from Harvard in 1981.

In the 1980s, Faludi's career in journalism included working as a copy clerk at *The New York Times* and wrote for the *Times*, the *Miami Herald*, the *Atlanta Journal Constitution*, the *San Jose Mercury News*, and *The Wall Street Journal* as well as other publications. In 1990, Faludi joined the San Francisco bureau of *The Wall Street Journal*, where she wrote an article exploring the human costs of the leveraged buyout of the Safeway supermarket chain. The article earned Faludi the 1991 Pulitzer Prize for exploratory journalism.

Throughout the 1980s, Faludi also wrote several articles on feminism and what she saw as a resistance to the outcomes of the women's movement that had begun in the 1960s. The pattern Faludi saw emerging from her findings comprised the genesis for *Backlash: The Undeclared War against Women*. In it, Faludi describes a backlash against feminism and the spread of negative media stereotypes, especially directed toward women with careers. The book won Faludi the National Book Critics Circle Award for general nonfiction in 1991. *Backlash* continues to be read as a classic feminist text that cautions women not to take the gains of the women's movement for granted. In 2015, the online women's magazine *Bustle* included the book on a list called "25 Bestsellers From the Last 25 Years You Simply Must Make Time to Reread."

Faludi's other works include *Stiffed: The Betrayal of the American Man* (1999), *The Terror Dream: Fear and Fantasy in Post-9/11 America* (2007), and *In the Darkroom* (2016), a memoir. In addition to her writing career, Faludi has been a fellow at the Radcliffe Institute for Advanced Study (2008–2009) and the Tallman Scholar in the Gender and Women's Studies Program at Bowdoin College (2013–2014). Since 2013, she has been a contributing editor at *The Baffler* magazine in Cambridge, Massachusetts, and in 2017, she was awarded an honorary doctoral degree from Stockholm University in Sweden. Since 2013, she has been married to author Russ Rymer, whom she met in San Francisco in 1992.

Shulamith Firestone (1945–2012)

Author, Feminist

A central figure in second-wave feminism and an early radical feminist, Shulamith Firestone was the author of *The Dialectic of Sex: The Case for Feminist Revolution* (1970). One of the most widely discussed and influential books of the women's movement, the book continues to be regarded as a classic feminist text, which is still used in many women's studies programs.

Born Shulamith Bath Shmuel Ben Ari Feuerstein in Ottawa, Ontario, Canada, Firestone was the second of six children in an Orthodox Jewish family. When Shulamith, known by her nickname, Shulie, was a child, her parents Anglicized their name to Firestone and moved to St. Louis, Missouri. Fire-

stone attended the Yavneh Teacher's Seminary in Cleveland and received a bachelor's degree from Washington University in St. Louis and a BFA degree in painting from the School of the Art Institute of Chicago (SAIC). She joined with other feminists who were denied a forum at the National Conference for New Politics in Chicago to found an independent women's caucus organized around women's issues.

While at SAIC, Firestone was the subject of a student documentary film that was never released but rediscovered in the 1990s by experimental filmmaker Elisabeth Subrin, who reshot the film with an actress playing Firestone. The film, titled *Shulie*, chronicles Firestone's life as a young student and influential second-wave feminist and feminist author. *Shulie* was the recipient of awards from the Los Angeles Film Critics Association (1998) and the New England Film and Video Festival (2000).

In 1967, Firestone moved to New York, where she cofounded the New York Radical Women (NYRW), the radical feminist group the Redstockings, named after the Blue Stockings Society, an eighteenth-century women's literary group, and the New York Radical Feminists (NYRF). With members of the NYRF, Firestone created and edited *Notes*, a feminist periodical.

The Dialectic of Sex was published when Firestone was only twenty-five. In it, she synthesizes the ideas of such historically influential thinkers as Sigmund Freud, Karl Marx, and Simone de Beauvoir as well as more recent works such as Paul Ehrlich's 1968 best-seller *The Population Bomb* into a radical theory of feminist politics. She argues that gender inequality stems from the patriarchal social structures imposed upon women because of their culturally determined reproductive and maternal roles. She calls for a feminist revolution to eliminate male privilege in order to end the social and economic oppression of women but to also render culturally irrelevant the differences between the sexes. As Naomi Wolf, the author of *The Beauty Myth*, has observed, "No one can understand how feminism has evolved without reading this radical, inflammatory, second-wave landmark."

By the early 1970s, Firestone had withdrawn from politics and begun to work as a painter, and, in the early 1980s, she began to suffer from schizophrenia. She chronicled her experiences during her hospital treatment for the disease in *Airless Spaces*, a collection of short stories on the struggles of characters living with mental illness and poverty. Shulamith Firestone died in her New York City apartment in August 2012, possibly as the result of self-induced starvation exacerbated by her illness. A memorial service was arranged in her memory.

Betty Friedan (1921–2006)

Author, Women's Rights Activist

If Catherine East was, in Betty Friedan's words, the "midwife of the contemporary women's movement" of the 1960s and 1970s, then Friedan can be considered the movement's first parent. Her groundbreaking 1963 book *The Feminine Mystique* was absorbed into the hearts and minds of American women and is widely regarded as the spark that would ignite the women's movement. Friedan would go on to become one of the most influential leaders of the movement she helped set in motion.

Born Bettye Naomi Goldstein, Friedan was born in Peoria, Illinois, the oldest child in a family of two daughters and a son. Her father, Harry, was a jeweler; her mother, Miriam Horowitz Goldstein, had been a journalist who gave up her career when her daughter was born. While growing up, Friedan often felt lonely and isolated as a Jewish child in the largely Christian community of Peoria and later ascribed her commitment to social justice as stemming from her awareness of the injustice of anti-Semitism. Friedan's sense of exclusion did not prevent her from excelling in school. A voracious reader in childhood, she was an academically gifted student who was involved in her high school newspaper. When her application to write a column for the paper was turned down, she founded a literary magazine called *Tide*, won a dramatic award (for a time she aspired to become an actor), and graduated as valedictorian of her class.

In 1938, Friedan entered Smith College, where she studied psychology. After graduating cum laude in 1943, she won a fellowship to study at the University of California–Berkeley. There, she dropped the "e" from her first name. Unwilling to commit to a doctorate and a career as a psychologist, Friedan left after a year at Berkeley to move to New York City. Due to the shortage of men in civilian jobs because of World War II, Friedan was able to find work as a journalist first for the Federated Press, a news agency for labor unions with left-wing newspapers, and later for the *UE News*, the official publication of the United Electric, Radio, and Machine Workers of America. One of her assignments was to report on the House Un-American Activities Committee (HUAC), which began investigating supposed communists in the United States not long after the war. She also authored union pamphlets arguing for workplace rights for women. In 1947, she married Carl Friedan, a theater producer, and the following year, she gave birth to the couple's first of three children. After twelve stormy years together, the Friedans divorced.

In the 1950s, Friedan was fired from her job with the *UE News* because she was pregnant with her second child and had requested her second maternity leave. She then became a freelance writer for various women's magazines. Concurrent with Friedan's growing dissatisfaction with her primary role as wife and mother was the notion, popular in American society and promoted in the magazines for which Friedan wrote, that the highest achievements to which a woman should aspire were marriage, motherhood, and homemaking. Friedan began to wonder if other women shared her discontent, and in 1957, she sent a questionnaire to two hundred of her Smith College classmates. The answers she received convinced her that her ailment, a psychic distress she came to call "the problem that has no name," was widespread. She began several years of research into the origins of, as she later wrote, "the discrepancy between the reality of our lives as women and the image to which we were trying to conform." Friedan analyzed that image and found it to be a fantasy of post-World War II, happy, suburban, female domesticity created and supported by educators, sociologists, psychologists, and the media. She called the image and the book that resulted from her research *The Feminine Mystique*. An immediate success, the book spoke to the legions of women who had sacrificed their identities and sense of self-worth by succumbing to the gilded cage of the suburban home. Although it continues to be read as a classic work in the history of twentieth-century American women, *The Feminine Mystique* has also drawn criticism over the years for its focus on the lives of white, middle- and upper-middle-class women to the exclusion of working-class women and women of color.

The Feminine Mystique was seen as a new, unifying force in second-wave feminism, and its now famous author emerged as a leading figure in the women's movement that followed. In 1966, she co-founded the National Organization for Women (NOW) and served as NOW's president until 1970. In the 1960s and 1970s, she helped found the National Association for the Repeal of Abortion Laws (1969), renamed several times and now known as NARAL Pro-Choice America, organized the Women's Strike for Equality on the fiftieth anniversary of the ratification of the Nineteenth Amendment to raise awareness of gender discrimination, and was a co-founder of the National Women's Political Caucus (1971). Through her activism within these organizations, Freidan was influential in helping to change unfair hiring practices, gender inequality, and pregnancy discrimination in the workplace.

Friedan's sometimes abrasive and imperious personality led to clashes with others in the women's movement, and as more diverse voices emerged, she was criticized for her focus on issues facing middle-class, educated, heterosexual women. Friedan's emphasis on retaining the movement's mainstream ties alienated her from younger, more radical feminists who were increasingly becoming an influential force within the women's movement. Nevertheless, Friedan remained a visible and passionate activist on behalf of women's rights, who has been described as the "mother of the modern women's movement."

In addition to her activism, Friedan taught at New York University and the University of Southern California and frequently lectured at women's conferences around the world. In 1976, she published *It Changed My Life: Writings on the Women's Movement,*

in which she assessed the progress of the movement and her relationship with it. Concerned with the splintering of the movement into smaller groups with a variety of agendas, she called for an end to polarization and a new emphasis on "human liberation." Friedan's other works include *The Second Stage* (1981), *The Fountain of Age* (1993), *Beyond Gender* (1997), and a memoir titled *Life So Far* (2000). The recipient of many awards throughout her career, Friedan's papers are held at the Schlesinger Library at Harvard University's Radcliffe Institute.

bell hooks
(pseudonym of Gloria Jean Watkins; 1952–)
Author, Educator

 Born Gloria Jean Watkins but better known by her pen name, hooks is an author, scholar, feminist, and social activist whose work has focused on intersectionality and race, capitalism, and gender in the context of oppression and class domination and has examined the varied perceptions of African American women and the development of feminist identities. She is credited with coining the terms "imperialist white-supremacist capitalist patriarchy" and "oppositional gaze," which describes the reflexive ways in which people look back at each other and which often reflects the unconscious attitudes of the "gazer."

Bell hooks was born in Hopkinsville, Kentucky, one of the six children of Veodis Watkins, a custodian, and Rosa Bell Watkins, a homemaker. Hooks began her education in racially segregated schools and has written of the difficulties she encountered when she made the transition to an integrated school with predominantly white teachers and students. After her graduation from Hopkinsville High School, she attended Stanford University, where she received her BA degree in English in 1973. She received an MA degree in English from the University of Wisconsin–Madison in 1976 and a doctorate in literature at the University of California–Santa Monica in 1983. Hooks's doctoral dissertation was on author Toni Morrison.

From 1976 to 1979, hooks was an English professor and senior lecturer in ethnic studies at the University of Southern California (UCLA), where she published her first book, a chapbook of poems titled *And There We Wept* (1978). The book was written under her pen name, which she borrowed from her outspoken maternal great-grandmother, Bell Blair Hooks, whom she greatly admired. Her decision to present her pen name in lowercase letters came from her desire for readers to focus attention on her books and her message rather than on herself.

Hooks taught English, ethnic studies, and women's studies at a variety of colleges and universities in the 1980s and 1990s. In 2004, she became a professor-in-residence at Berea College in Berea, Kentucky. In the 1980s, hooks established a support group for African American women called the Sisters of the Yam, which she later used as the title for a 1993 book celebrating black sisterhood.

When hooks was nineteen, she began writing what would become her first full-length book, *Ain't I a Woman?: Black Women and Feminism*, published in 1981. The book examines the effects of racism and sexism on African American women in the context of the civil rights and feminist movements from the women's suffrage era to the 1970s. In 1992, *Publishers Weekly* named *Ain't I a Woman?* one of the most influential books of the last twenty years. Hooks's other works include *Feminist Theory: From Margin to Center* (1984), *All About Love: New Visions* (2000), and *We Real Cool: Black Men and Masculinity* (2004). She has also published numerous scholarly articles, appeared in documentary films, participated in public lectures, and received several honors and awards. In 2014, she established the bell hooks Institute at Berea College.

Dorothy Pitman Hughes (1938–)

Child Welfare Activist, Women's Rights Activist

A feminist, child welfare advocate, and African American activist, Dorothy Pitman Hughes was the cofounder with Gloria Steinem of *Ms.* magazine. Hughes is equally celebrated for an iconic photo from 1971, in which the two women are standing side by side, each with a raised fist salute to show feminist solidarity. The photo, shot by portrait photographer Dan Wynn for *Esquire* magazine, is in the collection of the National Portrait Gallery at the Smithsonian Institution. In 2014, the two women recreated the pose for photographer Daniel Bagan, who included it in his "The Age of Beauty" series showcasing women over fifty.

Hughes was born in Lumpkin, Georgia, where her childhood was marked by an incident in which her father was beaten and left for dead on the family doorstep when she was ten years old. The family has believed that members of the Ku Klux Klan committed the crime. The incident made Hughes decide to devote her life to social justice activism.

In 1957, Hughes moved to New York City, where, throughout the 1960s, she worked as a singer and raised bail money for civil rights protestors. During the same decade, she owned and operated three childcare centers that helped to serve as a model for such centers. The same year, she cofounded *Ms.* magazine with Gloria Steinem. Hughes and Steinem formed the Women's Action Alliance, a first-of-its-kind national information center specializing in nonsexist, multiracial children's education. Throughout the 1970s, the two women toured together to speak on the issues of race, class, and gender.

In 1992, Hughes cofounded the Charles Junction Historic Preservation Society in Jacksonville, Florida. Dedicated to helping underserved women, children, and families gain access to better education, jobs, and quality of life and to foster self-reliance, the society has used the Charles Junction homestead to combat poverty through community gardening and food production. In 1994, Hughes became involved in the Upper Manhattan Empowerment Zone (UMEZ), a federal program instituted by the Clinton administration to allot federal, state, and city money for the economic development of Harlem. Hughes was part of the research team that focused on the development of small, locally owned businesses in the community and was disappointed when large businesses opened chains there, thus threatening the ability of smaller businesses to thrive. In 2012, Hughes published *I'm Just Saying ... It*

Looks Like Ethnic Cleansing: The Gentrification of Harlem, which advised African American business owners on similar government programs such as the JOBS Act initiated by President Barack Obama.

From 1997 to 2007, Hughes owned and was the CEO of an office supply and copy center business, Harlem Office Supply, the first African American woman to own such a business. In *Wake Up and Smell the Dollars!* (2011), Hughes writes about her experiences and also advocates small business ownership to African Americans as a form of empowerment. She has also been a guest lecturer at Columbia University and City College in New York City and has taught a course, "The Dynamics of Change," at the College of New Rochelle in New York. She currently owns the Gateway Bookstore in Jacksonville.

Patricia Ireland (1945–)

Attorney, Women's Rights Activist

An attorney, feminist, and social activist, Patricia Ireland served as the ninth president of the National Organization for Women (NOW) from 1991 to 2001.

Born in Oak Park, Illinois, and raised on a farm in Valparaiso, Indiana, where her family raised honeybees, Ireland was the younger of the two daughters of James Ireland, a metallurgical engineer, and Joan Filipek, a volunteer counselor with Planned Parenthood, who became the first director of the organization's local chapter. Her older sister, Kathy, was killed in a horseback riding accident when Ireland was five.

After graduating from Valparaiso High School at sixteen, Ireland entered DePauw University in Greencastle, Indiana, but after she became pregnant, she left school to travel to Japan to obtain a legal abortion. During a brief first marriage, she attended the University of Tennessee, where she studied German and earned a BA degree in 1966. She taught German for a time and married her second husband, artist James Humble. The couple moved to Miami, where Ireland took a job as a flight attendant for Pan American airlines. After Ireland discovered gender discrepancies in the airline's insurance coverage for spouses, she sought advice from the Dade County

chapter of NOW and then filed a formal complaint against the airline with the flight attendants' labor union, the Equal Opportunity Employment Commission (EEOC), and the U.S. Department of Labor, which was successful and led to a change in employee insurance coverage. Soon afterward, Ireland began to study law at Florida State University School of Law. She received her law degree from the University of Miami School of Law in 1975. While attending law school, she served on the school's law review and worked pro bono for the Dade County chapter of NOW. After her graduation, she practiced corporate law for twelve years helping corporations to implement affirmative action programs. She also continued her work with NOW. In the 1980s, Ireland served as chair of NOW's lesbian rights task force and managed Eleanor Smeal's successful campaign for the presidency of the organization.

When Ireland was named president of NOW in 1991, she was tasked with responding to the shifting concerns of women in the wake of the women's movement and the backlash of the 1980s. To that end, she worked to implement such programs as Project Stand Up for Women, an international program formed to protect abortion rights; Elect Women for a Change, designed to support women running for elective office; and the Global Feminist Program, which provided a worldwide forum for the discussion of women's issues. Ireland also organized the 1993 March on Washington for Lesbian, Gay, and Bi Equal Rights and Liberation and served as NOW's legal counsel for several landmark cases.

NOW's assertion that lesbian rights would be a top priority, together with an article in the *Advocate* newspaper revealing that Ireland, while still married to James Humble, also had a female partner with whom she lived in Washington, D.C., led to questions among its members, including Betty Friedan, concerning whether the organization's focus had become too narrow and had ceased to represent the majority of American women, whose main concern was work–life balance. Ireland responded with the contention that NOW also needed to advocate on behalf of women's rights issues that might make some people feel uncomfortable.

In 2003, Ireland was appointed CEO of the YWCA, a position she held for six months before she was asked to step down, which was possibly the result of conservative pressure on the organization. The following year, she served as national campaign manager for Senator Carol Moseley Braun's brief presidential bid. During her career, she has been a guest speaker at universities and human rights groups and has contributed articles to magazines, newspapers, and journals. Her autobiography, *What Women Want*, was published in 1996.

Florynce Kennedy (1916–2000)

Attorney, Women's Rights Activist

An attorney and an outspoken feminist activist and civil rights advocate, Florynce Kennedy was born in Kansas City, Missouri, the second of five daughters in an African American family. Her father, Wiley, was a Pullman train porter and waiter, who later owned a taxi business. In her autobiography *Color Me Flo: My Hard Life and Good Times* (1976), Kennedy describes a childhood incident that took place after the family moved to a mostly white neighborhood and her father, armed with a shotgun, successfully confronted members of the Ku Klux Klan, who had arrived at the house to drive the family out.

Kennedy graduated with honors from Lincoln High School in 1934 and afterward opened a hat shop with her sisters and worked at various jobs, including one as an elevator operator. She also organized a successful boycott against a local Coca-Cola bottler who refused to hire African American truck drivers. In 1942, after the death of her mother, Zella, Kennedy and her sister, Grayce, moved to New York City, where they shared an apartment in Harlem. She began to take prelaw classes at the Columbia University School of General Studies, graduating in 1949. When she applied to Columbia Law School, she was refused admission, ostensibly because she was a woman rather than because of her race. Neither of those reasons were acceptable to Kennedy, and she threatened to sue the school. She was admitted and graduated with her law degree in 1952 as one of eight women in her class and the second African American woman to graduate from Columbia. She worked as a clerk for a law firm and, in 1954, opened her own law office, where she handled matrimonial cases as well as some assigned criminal cases. In 1957, she married science fiction writer Charles Dye, an alcoholic, who died in 1960, not long after Kennedy had the marriage dissolved.

Kennedy's activism on behalf of women and African Americans began in 1965, when she was arrested by police who refused to believe that she lived in her home in a midtown Manhattan neighborhood because she was black. In 1966, she created the Media Workshop to advocate for more representation of African Americans in the media and stated that the group would lead boycotts of major advertisers if they did not feature African Americans in their ads. In 1968, she played a significant role in planning the Miss America Protest in Atlantic City and in recruiting other black feminists to join the protest. When several women were arrested, Kennedy represented them as their attorney. She was an early member of the National Organization for Women (NOW) but left the organization in 1970 because of her dissatisfaction with NOW's approach to change. The following year, she founded the Feminist Party, which nominated congressional representative Shirley Chisholm for president and helped to found the National Women's Political Caucus. She served on the advisory board of the Westbeth Playwrights Feminist Collective beginning in 1972.

A supporter of abortion rights, Kennedy coauthored the book *Abortion Rap* (1971) and filed tax-evasion charges with the Internal Revenue Service against the Catholic Church on the grounds that its campaign against abortion was a violation of the separation of church and state. In 1973, she was one of the lawyers in a class action suit brought before the New York District Court to repeal New York's strict abortion laws. The case was one of the first to use women who had suffered from illegal abortions as expert witnesses rather than physicians, a tactic used in the Supreme Court case *Roe v. Wade* that led to the legalization of abortion in 1973. Kennedy was also the lawyer for a similar lawsuit brought by the Women's Health Collective. In 1973, Kennedy cofounded the National Black Feminist Organization (NBFO), a group that addressed race and gender issues, including reproductive rights.

During her long career, Kennedy acted in several films and was a narrator for the 1959 film *Come Back, Africa*, which focused on African American history as well as apartheid in South Africa. Among her other writings was a piece she contributed to Robin Morgan's 1970 anthology of feminist writings *Sisterhood is Powerful*, titled "Institutionalized Oppression vs. the Female." She received a Lifetime Courageous Activist Award in 1997, was honored with the Owl Award for outstanding graduates of Columbia University in 1998, and was the recipient of the Century Award from the City University of New York (CUNY) in 1999.

Kate Millett (1934–2017)

Author, Women's Rights Activist

 A pioneering feminist author and influential figure in the women's liberation movement, Kate Millett is best known for her landmark 1970 book *Sexual Politics* and for exploring the concept of patriarchy as a social phenomenon and the primary cause of women's oppression.

Katherine Murray Millett was born in Saint Paul, Minnesota, one of three daughters in an Irish American Catholic family. Her father, an engineer, was an alcoholic who beat Millett and abandoned the family when she was fourteen. Her mother worked as a teacher and an insurance sales representative. Millett attended parochial schools in Saint Paul and graduated cum laude from the University of Minnesota in 1956 with a BA degree in English literature. She then spent two years at St. Hilda's college, Oxford, where she became the first American woman to graduate with first-class honors.

After her graduation from Oxford, Millett taught English at the University of North Carolina, leaving in the middle of the term to study art in New York City. While studying painting and sculpture, she worked as a kindergarten teacher. From 1961 to 1963, Millett studied sculpture in Japan, where she had her first one-woman show at the Minami Gallery in Tokyo and taught English at Waseda University. During her stay in Japan, she met sculptor Fumio

Yoshimura, to whom she was married from 1965 to 1985. At the time of her death, Millett was married to photojournalist Sophie Keir.

When Millett returned to New York, she taught English and exhibited her artwork at Barnard College and in Greenwich Village. In 1968, she entered the graduate program in English and comparative literature at Columbia University, earning her doctorate in 1970. Millett began her activism while teaching at Barnard and attending Columbia. She championed student rights, women's liberation, and abortion reform; became interested in the peace movement; and joined the Congress of Racial Equality (CORE), participating in CORE's civil rights protests. As a teacher at Barnard, Millett was dedicated to instilling in her students a critical awareness of their position in a patriarchal society. In 1968, the National Organization for Women (NOW), which Millett had joined in 1966, published Millett's pamphlet "Token Learning: A Study of Women's Higher Education in America," which included a stinging attack on Barnard's educational focus. This, plus Millett's radical politics and budget cuts, led to her dismissal from Barnard in December 1968. She would go on to teach at Bryn Mawr College and the University of California–Berkeley. She also founded the Women's Art Colony and Tree Farm, a community of female artists and writers and Christmas tree farm near Poughkeepsie, New York.

Sexual Politics, Millett's most celebrated work, defined the goals of second-wave feminism and was influenced in great part by *The Second Sex* (1949), French existentialist Simone de Beauvoir's classic treatise on the treatment of women throughout history. Written by Millett at the same time as her doctoral dissertation, *Sexual Politics* is considered a classic feminist text, the first book of feminist literary criticism, and one of the first feminist texts during the women's movement to produce nationwide irritation among men. The book was an immediate success and transformed Millett into a public figure. In her 1974 autobiography *Flying*, Millett discussed the difficulties she endured as the result of her notoriety, including the perception of her as arrogant and elitist, which conflicted with her status as spokeswoman for the movement and the expectation that she spoke for all women as well as the disclosure that she was a lesbian.

Millett was a member of the New York Radical Women, the Radicalesbians, and the Downtown Radical Women. She contributed the piece "Sexual Politics (in Literature)" to Robin Morgan's 1970 anthology of writing by women in the women's liberation movement, titled *Sisterhood Is Powerful*. Millett's works from the 1970s include two more autobiographical works, *Sita* (1977) and *A.D.: A Memoir* (1979). In 1982, she published *Going to Iran*, an account of political oppression in the wake of the Iranian revolution of the late 1970s. Millett, who had suffered from mental illness since 1973, chronicled her experiences as a psychiatric patient in *The Loony Bin Trip* (1990) and discussed state-sponsored torture in *The Politics of Cruelty* (1994). In *Mother Millett* (2001), Millett explored the problems of aging through the struggles of her mother. The book earned Millett the Best Books Award from the *Library Journal*.

Millett's numerous awards and honors also include the Courage Award for the Arts (2012), presented by Yoko Ono; the Lambda Pioneer Award for Literature (2011–2012); and a Foundation for Contemporary Arts award (2012). In 2011, she was honored at a Veteran Feminists of America gala, which was attended by such prominent feminists as Gloria Steinem and Susan Brownmiller. Millett was inducted into the National Women's Hall of Fame in 2013.

Robin Morgan (1941–)

Author, Editor, Women's Rights Activist

A radical feminist, writer, political theorist, social activist, journalist, and lecturer, Robin Morgan was a key figure in the women's liberation movement from its beginnings in the late 1960s and has been a leader of the international feminist movement. Morgan's 1970 anthology *Sisterhood Is Powerful*, with its feminist essays, was one of the first widely available compilations of second-wave feminist writing and has been credited with helping to start the feminist movement.

Born in Lake Worth, Florida, Robin Morgan was the daughter of Faith Morgan and Mates Morgenstern, a physician. Faith Morgan had traveled to Florida from her home in New York City to give birth in order to avoid scrutiny over her unmarried state. When Robin Morgan was a young teenager, her mother told her that her father had been killed during World War II and then changed her story to claim that he was a Holocaust survivor whose life she had saved. Both stories were untrue. In 1961, Morgan tracked down her father, who was married with a family, and met him on two occasions. In her autobiography *Saturday's Child: A Memoir* (2000), Morgan describes her two encounters with her father.

Morgan grew up in Mount Vernon, New York, and in New York City. When she was a baby, her mother and aunt entered her in baby contests and had her working as a model when she was a toddler. By the time she was four, the precocious Morgan had her own radio show, *The Little Robin Morgan Show*, and was a panelist on the radio and TV show *Juvenile Jury*. Morgan appeared in several TV shows in the 1950s, most notably in the hit television series based on the play and film *I Remember Mama*. Titled simply *Mama*, Morgan played the role of Dagmar, the youngest daughter in a family of Norwegian immigrants. She also appeared in a stage adaptation of the show as well as in summer stock theater productions. Morgan had always wanted to be a writer and at the age of fourteen, she left the cast of *Mama*, sparking a confrontation with her mother, who wanted her to continue in show business. Morgan graduated from the Wetter School in Mount Vernon in 1956 and then was privately tutored from 1956 to 1959. When her mother refused to allow her to go away to college, Morgan attended nonmatriculating undergraduate and graduate classes at Columbia University. By the time she was seventeen, she had published her poems in literary magazines, which were later collected in her first book of poems titled *Monster* (1972). In 1962, she married poet Kenneth Pitchford and, in 1969, gave birth to their son, Blake. The couple would eventually divorce.

Morgan's activism in the 1960s began when she was an editor at Grove Press and was involved in an attempt to unionize the publishing industry. She became active in the civil rights and anti-Vietnam War movements and also contributed articles and poetry to left-wing and counterculture journals. In 1967, she joined the anarchic Youth International Party, popularly known as the Yippies, but sexism within the party led to increasing tensions once Morgan and other women involved in left-wing politics became more committed to women's liberation and second-wave feminism. In 1970, she led a women's takeover of the leftist newspaper *Rat*, which represented to her a break with what she called the "toxic sexism of the left" in an article featured in the first women's edition of the paper, titled "Goodbye to All That." In 2008, she wrote "Goodbye to All That #2," concerning the misogynistic treatment of and rhetoric aimed at presidential candidate Hillary Clinton.

A founder of the New York Radical Women, Morgan was a key organizer of the Miss America pageant protest in 1968 and the same year formed the Women's International Terrorist Conspiracy from Hell (WITCH), a feminist group that used street theater (also known as guerilla theater) to call attention to sexism in society. She designed the universal symbol of the women's movement—the Venus symbol of a female but with a raised fist—and in *Sisterhood Is Powerful* coined the term "herstory." Morgan used her royalties from the book to found the first feminist foundation in the United States, the Sisterhood Is Powerful Fund, which provided grant money to women's groups in the 1970s and 1980s. She also cofounded and served on the boards of many women's groups, including the Sisterhood Is Powerful international think tank, the Women's Media Center, the Battered Women's Network Refuge, and the Feminist Women's Health Network. During her long career as an activist, she has traveled throughout the world to meet with women and to investigate the conditions under which they live. She has been an invited speaker at every major university in North America and has lectured and taught courses at a variety of academic institutions worldwide.

Morgan has been a contributing editor to *Ms.* magazine since 1979 and served as editor-in-chief from 1989 to 1994, when she stepped down to become the magazine's global consulting editor. In 1981, she received the Front Page Award for Distinguished Journalism for her *Ms.* cover story "The First Feminist Exiles for USSR." Her articles, essays, political analyses, and investigative reports have ap-

peared in many publications and have been reprinted in international publications. She has also written for online audiences, an example of which was "Letters from Ground Zero," written and posted following the September 11, 2001, attacks on New York's World Trade Center. Morgan's other published works include the nonfiction books *Going Too Far: The Personal Chronicle of a Feminist* (1977), *The Anatomy of Freedom* (1982), and *The Demon Lover* (1989). Her novels include *Dry Your Smile* (1987) and *The Burning Time* (2006). In addition to *Sisterhood Is Powerful*, Morgan published two other anthologies, *Sisterhood Is Global* (1984) and *Sisterhood Is Forever* (2003). The Robin Morgan Papers are archived at the Brigham Center for Women's History at Duke University.

Letty Cotton Pogrebin (1939–)
Women's Rights Activist

 A founding editor of *Ms.* magazine with Mary Thom, Patricia Carbine, Joanne Edgar, Nina Finkelstein, and Mary Peacock, Letty Cotton Pogrebin is an author, lecturer, and social activist. She is also celebrated for her Emmy Award-winning work as an editorial consultant on the 1972 TV special, album, and book *Free to Be ... You and Me*, a children's entertainment project emphasizing gender neutrality and identity, tolerance, and individuality, conceived, created, and produced by actor Marlo Thomas.

Born and raised in Queens, New York, Pogrebin graduated from Jamaica High School and earned a bachelor's degree in English and American literature from Brandeis University in Waltham, Massachusetts. After her graduation, she worked for the publisher Bernard Geis Associates for ten years as their director of publicity and later as vice president of the company. In 1963, she married Bert Pogrebin, a labor and employment lawyer; the couple would raise twin daughters and a son.

From 1970 to 1980, she wrote a column, "The Working Woman," for the *Ladies' Home Journal*. In the 1970s, Pogrebin was a cofounder of the Ms.

Foundation for Women and the National Women's Political Caucus. She became an associate of the Women's Institute for Freedom of the Press (WIFP) in 1977.

Pogrebin is the author of *Deborah, Golda, and Me: Being Female and Jewish in America* (1992), *Getting Over Getting Older* (1996), and *How to Be a Friend of a Friend Who's Sick* (2009), which she wrote after she was diagnosed with breast cancer. In 1982, she published *Stories for Free Children*, a collection of stories, fables, and fairy tales for young readers, which emphasizes nonsexist, multiracial, and multicultural themes.

Pogrebin has sat on the boards of several organizations, including the Director's Council of the Women in Religion Program at the Harvard Divinity School and the Women's, Gender, and Sexuality Studies Program at Brandeis University. In 2013, she was among the prominent women featured in the documentary film *Makers: Women Who Make America*.

Eleanor Smeal (1939–)

Women's Rights Activist

An activist, grassroots organizer, lobbyist, political analyst, three-term president of the National Organization for Women (NOW), and publisher of *Ms.* magazine since 2001, Eleanor Smeal is celebrated as one of the most influential leaders of second-wave feminism and the women's movement.

Born Eleanor Cutri in Ashtabula, Ohio, and raised in Erie, Pennsylvania, Smeal was the daughter of first-generation Italian Americans, who had immigrated to the United States from Italy. After graduating from Strong Vincent High School in 1957, Smeal attended Duke University in North Carolina, where women made up only 25 percent of the students enrolled there. Duke was a whites-only university for both the student body and the faculty, and Smeal advocated on behalf of integration while she was a student there. Smeal graduated Phi Beta Kappa from Duke in 1961; the university desegre-

gated two years later. At the university, Smeal met engineering student Charles Smeal, whom she married in 1963. The couple would go on to have two children. Smeal considered pursuing a law degree but abandoned that plan after discovering the discrimination female lawyers faced. She continued her studies and received a master's degree in political science and public administration from the University of Florida in 1963. Her pursuit of a Ph.D. was cut short because of a back injury, which required a year of bed rest.

Smeal's feminist activism began during the late 1960s, when she was working on her doctoral thesis concerning the attitude of female voters toward female candidates and was confronted with a lack of daycare facilities as well as an awareness that wives and mothers had no disability insurance, which she had discovered during her yearlong recuperation. In 1968, she began a four-term tenure on the board of her local League of Women Voters and, in 1970, joined the National Organization for Women (NOW).

In 1977, Smeal was elected president of NOW; she would be elected to the presidency three times, serving from 1977 to 1982 and again from 1985 to 1987. During her tenures as president, Smeal authorized a political action committee to elect feminist candidates and authorized a NOW Equal Rights Amendment (ERA) Strike Force to campaign for ratification. At the National Women's Conference in Houston, Texas, in 1977, Smeal spearheaded the effort to pass the gay rights plank in a National Plan of Action to be submitted to the U.S. government. The following year, Smeal convinced New York congressional representative Elizabeth Holtzman to bring a proposal before Congress that would extend the deadline for ratification of the ERA and was a key organizer of the March for the ERA, which featured over one hundred thousand marchers. She worked to make Social Security, which she called "institutionalized sexism at its worst," fairer to women and testified before Congress on behalf of the Family and Medical Leave Act.

When Ronald Reagan was elected U.S. president in 1980, Smeal analyzed the difference between women's and men's votes during the election and reported her findings in NOW's *National NOW*

Times, defining the difference as a "gender gap," marking the first use of a phrase that has since become commonplace. She expanded her use of the term in her 1984 book *Why Women Will Elect the Next President*. In January 1981, NOW coordinated three days of ERA actions around Reagan's inauguration and launched a national campaign to stop the president's antiabortion Human Life Amendment. NOW supported Reagan's nomination of Sandra Day O'Connor as the first female Supreme Court justice, however, with Smeal testifying at O'Connor's confirmation hearing. During Smeal's final term as president of NOW, the NOW Foundation was established, the organization brought lawsuits against antiabortion leaders, and they sought a nationwide injunction against violence directed at abortion clinics. In 1986, Smeal organized the first March for Women's Lives, an event that drew over 150,000 people to Washington, D.C., and Los Angeles in support of women's reproductive rights. In 1987, she testified against the Supreme Court nominations of conservative candidates Antonin Scalia and William Rehnquist.

After leaving NOW in 1987, Smeal cofounded the Feminist Majority Foundation, a new feminist organization dedicated to empowering both women and the men who support gender equality. Smeal is the president of the foundation, which also publishes *Ms.* magazine. She has been instrumental in several legislative initiatives, including the Freedom of Access of Clinic Entrances Act, signed into law by President Bill Clinton in 1994; the Pregnancy Discrimination Act; the Equal Credit Act; the Violence Against Women Act; and the Civil Rights Act of 1991, a labor law that guaranteed the right of employees to sue their employers for discrimination. In 2013, she contributed the piece "The Art of Building Feminist Institutions to Last" to Robin Morgan's 2003 anthology *Sisterhood Is Forever: The Women's Anthology for a New Millennium*.

Since the 1970s, Smeal has been recognized for her advocacy on behalf of women: For example, *Time* magazine featured her as one of the "50 Faces for America's Future" in 1979; the *World Almanac* chose her as one of the most influential women in the United States in 1983; *U.S. News & World Report* has named her the fourth-most influential lobbyist

in the nation. In 2015, she was inducted into the National Women's Hall of Fame.

Gloria Steinem (1934–)
Journalist, Women's Rights Activist

A feminist, journalist, and social and political activist, Gloria Steinem is perhaps the most famous—and iconic—figure in the history of second-wave feminism and the women's liberation movement that began in the late 1960s. Nationally recognized as a leader of the feminist movement as well as its spokeswoman, Steinem continues to be an influential advocate for women's rights, gender equality, and social justice.

Gloria Marie Steinem was born in Toledo, Ohio, the younger of the two daughters of Ruth and Leo Steinem. Her paternal grandmother, Pauline Perlmutter Steinem, had been a suffragist and a National American Woman Suffrage Association (NAWSA) delegate to the 1908 International Council of Women as well as the first woman to be elected to the Toledo Board of Education. Steinem's father was an itinerant antiques dealer, and the family lived and traveled around the country in a house trailer. Steinem's mother, who had suffered a severe mental breakdown before Gloria was born, spent long periods in and out of sanatoriums for the mentally ill. When the Steinems separated in 1944, Leo Steinem went to California to find work, and ten-year-old Gloria stayed with her mother in Toledo. Steinem's older sister, Susanne, was attending Smith College at the time. Steinem's parents divorced in 1946. Steinem later traced her commitment to social and political equality for women back to her experiences with her mother, attributing Ruth Steinem's inability to hold a job and the apathy of doctors regarding her mental illness to a basic hostility and bias toward women.

Steinem attended high school in Toledo and Washington, D.C., where she graduated from Western High School while living with her sister, who was working there and in New York City as a gemologist. After graduating Phi Beta Kappa from Smith College in 1956, Steinem went to India on a two-year scholarship. There, she participated in nonviolent protests against the present Indian government and briefly clerked for the chief justice of India's Supreme Court. In 1960, she began working as a writer and journalist in New York City with writing positions at the satire magazine *Help!* and at *Esquire* magazine, for which she researched and wrote an article in 1962 on the dilemmas of women forced to choose between a career and marriage. In 1963, Steinem went undercover for the arts and entertainment magazine *Show* as a Playboy Bunny waitress at New York's Playboy Club. The article Steinem wrote for the magazine revealed the sexually exploitive and underpaid conditions under which women worked at Playboy clubs and was published under the title "A Bunny's Tale." The article featured a photo of Steinem in her bunny outfit. The image caused Steinem to briefly lose assignments because, as she later observed, "I had now become a Bunny—and it didn't matter why." In 1968, after doing freelance work, which included an interview with Beatles member John Lennon and writing for the 1965 season of the satirical TV revue series *That Was the Week That Was*, she obtained a job as an editor and writer at the newly formed *New York* magazine. The following year, while working at *New York*, she covered an abortion speak-out in Greenwich Village, at which she shared of the abortion she had had in London at the age of twenty-two. Steinem credited the event as the catalyst that sparked her determination to become an active feminist.

Throughout her long career as an activist, Steinem has been involved in numerous initiatives on behalf of women. In 1969, she wrote an article for *New York* titled "After Black Power, Women's Liberation," which brought her to the forefront of the women's liberation movement. The following year, she testified before the Senate Judiciary Committee in favor of the Equal Rights Amendment (ERA) and wrote an article for *Time* magazine on a vision for gender equality titled "What Would It Be Like if Women Win." In 1971, she cofounded the National Women's Political Caucus and, as the NWPC's convener, delivered a speech called "Address to the Women of America," which defined the organization's goals and stated in part, "We are talking about a society in which there will be no roles

other than those chosen or those earned. We are really talking about humanism." The WPC continues to support gender equality as well as proequality, female candidates for public office. Another organization Steinem cofounded in 1971 was the Women's Action Alliance, which promotes nonsexist, multiracial children's education. In 1972, Steinem became the first woman to speak at the National Press Club, cofounded *Ms.* magazine, which remains a premier source of articles on issues concerning women, and helped establish the Ms. Foundation for Women. In 1977, she became an associate of the Women's Institute for Freedom of the Press (WIFP) and cofounded Voters for Choice, a prochoice political action committee.

In 1984, Steinem protested against South African apartheid at the South African embassy and was arrested along with several members of Congress and civil rights activists for disorderly conduct. In the 1990s, she helped established Take Our Daughters to Work Day, the first national effort to empower girls to learn about career opportunities. In 1992, she cofounded Choice USA, a nonprofit organization that provides support to younger women lobbying for reproductive rights. In 2005, she joined with actor Jane Fonda and writer and activist Robin Morgan to found the Women's Media Center to promote positive images of women and to encourage and support the diverse perspectives of women in the media. She has spoken out and written about female genital mutilation, feminist theory, pornography, same-sex marriage, and transgender rights.

Steinem has been the recipient of numerous honors and awards, including the Presidential Medal of Freedom, awarded to her in 2013. She has been the subject of three biographies, has produced and been featured in TV documentaries, and was the main character in *Female Force: Gloria Steinem*, a 2013 comic book created by Melissa Seymour. She is also the author of several books, including *Outrageous Acts and Everyday Rebellions* (1983); *Marilyn: Norma Jean* (with George Barris, 1986); *Revolution from Within* (1992); and *My Life on the Road* (2015). She contributed the piece "The Media and the Movement: A User's Guide" to Robin Morgan's 2003 anthology *Sisterhood Is Forever: The Women's Anthology for a New Millennium.*

In 2000, Steinem, who had eschewed marriage when she was younger because of her commitment to activism as well as marriage laws that were unfavorable to women, was married for the first time to entrepreneur and activist David Bale, the father of actor Christian Bale. The wedding was performed at the Oklahoma home of Steinem's friend, Wilma Mankiller, the first female principal chief of the Cherokee Nation. Sadly, David Bale died three years later of brain lymphoma.

Steinem has approached aging with equilibrium, asserting that it represents a new phase of life that has freed her from the "demands of gender." She is clearly not finished with the demands of activism nor is she any less a subject of interest. On January 21, 2017, the day after the inauguration of Donald Trump as president, Steinem, who had endorsed Hillary Clinton, was an honorary cochair of and speaker at the Women's March on Washington to protest Trump's presidency. In 2018, the play *Gloria: A Life*, written by Emily Mann and directed by Tony Award winner Diane Paulus, opened at the Daryl Roth Theatre in New York City. Posters for the production feature the words "History. Her Story. Our Story."

LITERATURE

The practical and social conditions of settlement in the American colonies greatly impeded the development of American literature for both women and men. From around 1582 through much of the eighteenth century, the creation of literature, which depends on sufficient leisure time to produce literary works and to sustain a readership, was antithetical to the conditions faced by the settlers, who faced a seemingly limitless, unmapped, and untamed wilderness as well as uncertain alliances and confrontations with native peoples, all of which demanded an emphasis on subsistence labor and practical survival. The circumstances of the settlers' lives were neither conducive to the production of or a market for a colonial, European American literary culture. The early American colonists had little time either to produce works of literature or to encourage their creation. What was written and published in the seventeenth century was almost exclusively religious or utilitarian in nature with little distinction between the two. For the Puritans of New England, literature itself was far more sinister than a mere luxury most could not afford. In the view of many early American churchgoers, literature was a distraction from a principal focus on salvation, and although the Puritan insistence on a direct relationship with God's words required literacy—a necessity for a literary culture—secular poetry, fiction, and drama had scant support. The first significant work printed on Boston's new printing press in 1639 was an almanac, a miscellany

of practical and moral advice that would serve as an example for the only kind of reading material in most colonial households other than the Bible. The first book published in the American colonies was the *Bay Psalm Book* in 1640, the accepted hymnal of the Massachusetts Bay Colony. This essential tool of worship was followed by sermons, devotional essays, and works on moral instruction by a distinguished group of clerics, all male.

Women in colonial America faced an almost impossible barrier to publishing. Without recourse to formal education, women largely accepted their domestic roles of wives and mothers, leaving the world of ideas, moral instruction, and self-expression to men. Female writers in colonial America would be the rare exceptions to the rule of male literary dominance. It is, therefore, both remarkable and ironic that American published poetry began with a book by a woman, Anne Bradstreet's domestic and devotional verses *The Tenth Muse Lately Sprung Up in America,* collected without her approval by her brother-in-law and published in London in 1650. It was one of the first books of poetry ever published by a woman in English. The best-selling, secular work published in the seventeenth century was also the work of a woman, the first of many Indian captivity accounts, *Narrative of the Captivity and Restauration of Mrs. Mary Rowlandson*, published in 1682. An equally famous, best-selling captivity narrative was Elizabeth Hanson's *God's Mercy Surmounting Man's Cruelty* (1728). Despite these exceptional works, little was published by colonial American female writers.

By 1700, half a million European Americans were living in all the colonies. Boston was the largest city with a population of seven thousand. The first half of the eighteenth century would begin to show a loosening of the religious grip by the Puritans in New England and the gradual emergence of Yankee secular society. The era produced some of Puritanism's greatest literary achievements, most notably Cotton Mather's epic ecclesiastical history of New England, *Magnalia Christi Americana* (1702), and the works of the last great Puritan theologian, Jonathan

A collection of both devotional and domestic poetry was the first book published by an American woman, Anne Bradstreet, when it was released in 1650.

Edwards, whose "Sinners in the Hands of an Angry God" is perhaps the most famous sermon ever written by an American, yet the Puritan spiritual interpretation of the world was challenged by secular, Enlightenment thinkers such as John Locke, Jean Jacques Rousseau, and Voltaire, whose influence is evident in America. The exemplar of the evolving, American, secular character that reflected Enlightenment ideas is unquestionably Benjamin Franklin who, as a printer and writer, played a key role in creating and cultivating an emerging American literary culture. In the years before and during the American Revolution, the first secular literature began to appear, including the first poetry celebrating American scenes as well as the first book by an African American woman, the former slave Phillis Wheatley, whose *Poems on Various Subjects, Religious and Moral* appeared in 1773. The first drama by an American to be professionally produced—Thomas Godfrey's *The Prince of Parthia*—appeared in 1767, while the first dramas by an American female playwright were the political satires *The Adulateur* (1773) and *The Group* (1775) by Mercy Otis Warren. William Hill Brown's *The Power of Sympathy* (1789) is generally considered the first American novel, but Susanna Rowson's *Charlotte Temple* (1794) was the biggest best-seller novel before Harriet Beecher Stowe's *Uncle Tom's Cabin* (1852). Hannah Webster Foster's *The Coquette* (1797) claims consideration as an important early work of American fiction as well. Both Rowson and Foster's works are sentimental romances distinguished by making a case for the rights of women and equality in the new democratic nation.

Early American literature was, therefore, late to develop in the colonies and slow to achieve distinction after independence from Great Britain. Whether written by men or women, American writing in the early decades of the eighteenth century was mainly derivative and subservient to English literary models and depreciated abroad as second-hand and second rate. In 1820, British critic Sydney Smith declared with some justification, "In the four quarters of the globe, who reads an American book? Or goes to an American play?" The need for a distinctive literature to match the originality of the American national drama became Ralph Waldo Emerson's theme in his famous 1837 address to

Harriet Beecher Stowe wrote one of the defining novels of the nineteenth century, *Uncle Tom's Cabin*, which introduced readers to a favorite literary villain, Simon Legree, who is shown here abusing the title character.

Harvard's (all-male) Phi Beta Kappa Society, "The American Scholar." Emerson declared, "Our day of dependence or long apprenticeship to the learning of other lands, draws to a close. The millions that around us are rushing into life, cannot always be fed on the sere remains of foreign harvests." Emerson urged his audience to participate in the creation of a distinctively American literary tradition.

Conditions in the nineteenth century would both benefit and hold back American writers answering Emerson's call. American publishers, printers, and booksellers began to gratify a literate market of readers with sufficient leisure time and an appetite for secular works. The Puritan resistance to the sinful pleasures of literature gradually faded, although the emerging novel would still be vulnerable to attack as unwholesome and corrupting. For women, educational opportunities increased, including admission to colleges and universities. For most of the nineteenth century, however, American female writers continued to face the long-standing prejudice that authorship risked bargaining away gentility for the suspect status of a laborer seeking crass gain in the publishing trade. Moreover, the

economic conditions of publishing would contribute to the struggles of American writers, whether male or female, as they attempted to emerge from the long shadow cast by the British. International copyright protection was not established in the United States until 1891, leaving American publishers free to pirate the latest works of popular British writers such as Walter Scott and Charles Dickens. Because American readers could enjoy the best British writers in cheap reprints with none of the expense compensating the author, scant economic incentive existed for publishers to support American writers who expected to be paid for their work. Most American writers consequently found it difficult to survive by their writing; only those who produced work of exceptional interest and distinction were awarded.

Despite these challenges, the first professional female writers, public intellectuals, and a host of best-selling female authors would emerge in the decades preceding the American Civil War. Notable trailblazing female literary figures include Ann Eliza Bleecker (1752–1783), who wrote the first fictional captivity narrative and would help to transform pastoral poetry with the realism of actuality; Sarah Wentworth Morton (1759–1846), the foremost American female poet in the years immediately following the American Revolution; Hannah Mather Crocker (1752–1783), whose *Observations on the Real Rights of Women* (1818) is the first book by an American to champion women's rights; Hannah Adams (1755–1831), the first professional American female writer who published some of the earliest scholarship by an American woman; Judith Sargent Murray (1751–1820), one of the first American proponents for women's intellectual capabilities and economic independence; Sarah Josepha Hale (1768–1879), who wrote the first American novel to take up the issue of slavery and who became the first female editor of an important national magazine; Catherine Maria Sedgwick (1789–1867), the most successful American female fiction writer in the first half of the nineteenth century; Susan Warner (1819–1885), the first American author of a book that sold one million copies; and Margaret Fuller (1810–1850), the first American female public intellectual, whose *Woman in the Nineteenth Century* (1845) is considered the first major feminist work in the United States.

WOMAN

IN THE

NINETEENTH CENTURY.

BY S. MARGARET FULLER.

" Frei durch Vernunft, stark durch Gesetze,
Durch Sanftmuth gross, und reich durch Schatze,
Die lange Zeit dein Busen dir verschling."

"I meant the day-star should not brighter rise,
Nor lend like influence from its lucent seat;
I meant she should be courteous, facile, sweet,
Free from that solemn vice of greatness, pride;
I meant each softest virtue there should meet,
Fit in that softer bosom to reside;
Only a (heavenward and instructed) soul
I purposed her, that should, with even powers,
The rock, the spindle, and the shears control
Of destiny, and spin her own free hours."

NEW-YORK:
GREELEY & McELRATH, 160 NASSAU-STREET.
W. Osborn, Printer, 88 William-street.
1845.

Margaret Fuller's 1845 work, *Woman in the Nineteenth Century,* was the first important feminist book published in the United States.

If female writers in the first half of the nineteenth century lagged significantly behind men as poets and dramatists, both of which required knowledge of the literary tradition denied to women by being excluded from higher education, the relatively new literary genre, the novel, significantly encouraged women's voices. The novel originating in Europe in the eighteenth century took up the lives and circumstances of unexceptional individuals with an emphasis on plausibility and verisimilitude. Every day, domestic life of average, middle-class characters was the raw material for this new narrative genre, and who better than the custodians of the domestic and connoisseurs of sentiment (in popular view),

women, to contribute to the growing appetite for novels. Writers such as Susan Warner, whose novel, *The Wide, Wide World* (1850), produced one of America's first fictional blockbusters, and Maria Cummins, whose novel, *The Lamplighter* (1855), the sentimental story of a Boston orphan girl, sold nearly as well. Other best-selling female novelists included E.D.E.N. Southworth, who produced more than sixty novels, and Augusta Jane Evans, who was widely known for her *St. Elmo* (1866). So many female novelists dominated the marketplace that Nathaniel Hawthorne complained to his editor in 1855: "America is now wholly given over to a damned mob of scribbling women, and I should have no chance of success while the public taste is occupied with their trash—and should be ashamed of myself if I did succeed. What is the mystery of these innumerable editions of the 'Lamplighter,' and other books neither better nor worse?—worse they could not be, and better they need not be, when they sell by the 100,000."

The greatest literary triumph of the nineteenth century (and indeed, possibly, the most influential book ever written by an American) was Harriet Beecher Stowe's *Uncle Tom's Cabin* (1852), which harnessed the power of domestic sentiment to the incendiary theme of slavery. It became the first undisputedly American international best-seller with only the Bible eclipsing it in sales. An American female writer, for the first time, achieved near-total cultural saturation. As Ralph Waldo Emerson observed, the novel found "equal interest to three audiences, namely, in the parlor, in the kitchen, and in the nursery of every home." So influential was Stowe's "moral battle cry" (in the words of Langston Hughes) that it prompted the apocryphal remark by Abraham Lincoln when he met Stowe in 1862: "So you are the little woman who wrote the book that started this great war." If Lincoln said no such thing, the remark is simply too apt to be denied.

In marked contrast to Stowe's public notoriety and influence is the alternative private and reticent case of, arguably, America's greatest and most original poet, Emily Dickinson, whose groundbreaking work found readers only posthumously. During her lifetime, fewer than a dozen of Dickinson's 1,800 poems were published. A first volume of her poetry only emerged in 1890 after Dickinson's younger sister found the trove of the poet's works four years after Dickinson's death. Her poetry, compared to the poetic conventions of nineteenth-century popular verse as written by such male poets as William Cullen Bryant, Henry Wadsworth Longfellow, and John Greenleaf Whittier or by female poets such as Lydia Maria Child, Julia Ward Howe, and Frances Harper, was simply too unconventional and eccentric to find a contemporary audience, as Dickinson no doubt realized. Dickinson instead sustained her poetic vision in private, writing instead for posterity. "I have dared to do strange things—bold things," she declared, "and have asked no advice from any." No other American female writer before or since has created such intimate and idiosyncratic verses that would, along with her contemporary, another largely ignored redefiner of poetic norms, emerge in the twentieth century as the poetic geniuses of nineteenth-century America.

Following the Civil War, the trails blazed by Stowe and others into the literary marketplace would be followed by more and more female writers who led in the twentieth century if not to parity with male writers than to increasingly equal access and recognition of women's literary contributions. Writers like Sarah Orne Jewett, Mary E. Wilkins, and Kate Chopin would make important literary contributions to the interest in local color and regionalism that would become the vanguard of the late-developing American literary realism. Edith Wharton would rival male novelists such as Henry James and William Dean Howells as a close observer of social manner and behavior. Realism began to influence

The 1937 Oscar-winning film *The Good Earth*, starring Luise Rainer and Paul Muni (pictured), was based on the 1931 novel by Pearl S. Buck, the first American woman to win the Nobel Prize in Literature.

American drama as well, and female playwrights such as Susan Glaspell and Zoe Akins made important contributions to the development of modern American drama.

One indicator of the status of American female writers is to look at the annual Pulitzer Prizes awarded to them:

Year	Author	Work
2006	Claudia Emerson	*Late Wife*
2007	Natasha Trethewey	*Native Guard*
2010	Rae Armantrout	*Versed*
2011	Kay Ryan	*The Best of It: New and Selected Poems*
2012	Tracy K. Smith	*Life on Mars*
2013	Sharon Olds	*Stag's Leap*

POETRY

Year	Author	Work
1918	Sara Teasdale	*Love Songs*
1919	Margaret Widdemer	*Old Road to Paradise*
1923	Edna St. Vincent Millay	*The Ballad of the Harp-Weaver: A Few Figs from Thistles: Eight Sonnets in American Poetry, 1922. A Miscellany.*
1926	Amy Lowell	*What's O'Clock*
1927	Leonora Speyer	*Fiddler's Farewell*
1935	Audrey Wurdemann	*Bright Ambush*
1938	Marya Zaturensk	*Cold Morning Sky*
1950	Gwendolyn Brook	*Annie Allen*
1952	Marianne Moore	*Collected Poems*
1956	Elizabeth Bishop	*Poems: North & South*
1961	Phyllis McGinley	*Times Three: Selected Verse from Three Decades*
1967	Anne Sexton	*Live or Die*
1973	Maxine Winokur Kumin	*Up Country*
1982	Sylvia Plath	*The Collected Poems*
1984	Mary Oliver	*American Primitive*
1985	Carolyn Kizer	*Yin*
1987	Rita Dove	*Thomas and Beulah*
1991	Mona Van Duyn	*Near Changes*
1993	Louise Gluck	*The Wild Irish*
1996	Jorie Graham	*The Dream of the Unified Field*
1997	Lisel Mueller	*Alive Together: New Selected Poems*

FICTION

Year	Author	Work
1921	Edith Wharton	*The Age of Innocence*
1923	Willa Cather	*One of Ours*
1924	Margaret Wilson	*The Able McLaughlins*
1925	Edna Ferber	*So Big*
1929	Julia Peterkin	*Scarlet Sister*
1931	Margaret Ayer Barnes	*Years of Grace*
1932	Pearl Buck	*The Good Earth*
1934	Caroline Miller	*Lamb in His Bosom*
1935	Josephine Winslow Johnson	*Now in November*
1937	Margaret Mitchell	*Gone with the Wind*
1939	Marjorie Kinnan Rawlings	*The Yearling*
1942	Ellen Glasgow	*In This Our Life*
1961	Harper Lee	*To Kill a Mockingbird*
1965	Shirley Ann Grau	*The Keepers of the House*
1966	Katherine Anne Porter	*The Collected Stories of Katherine Anne Porter*
1970	Jean Stafford	*Collected Stories*
1973	Eudora Welty	*The Optimist's Daughter*
1983	Alice Walker	*The Color Purple*
1985	Alison Lurie	*Foreign Affairs*
1988	Toni Morrison	*Beloved*
1989	Anne Tyler	*Breathing Lessons*
1992	Jane Smiley	*A Thousand Acres*
1994	E. Annie Proulx	*The Shipping News*
1995	Carol Shields	*The Stone Diaries*

2000	Jhumpa Lahiri	*Interpreter of Maladies*
2005	Marilynne Robinson	*Gilead*
2006	Geraldine Brooks	*March*
2009	Elizabeth Strout	*Olive Kitteridge*
2011	Jennifer Egan	*A Visit from the Goon Squad*
2014	Donna Tartt	*The Goldfinch*

DRAMA

Year	Author	Work
1921	Zona Gale	*Miss Lulu Bett*
1931	Susan Glaspell	*Alison's House*
1935	Zoe Akins	*The Old Maid*
1945	Mary Chase	*Harvey*
1956	Frances Goodrich (with Albert Hackett)	*The Diary of Anne Frank*
1958	Ketti Frings	*Look Homeward, Angel*
1981	Beth Henley	*Crimes of the Heart*
1983	Marsha Norman	*'night Mother*
1989	Wendy Wasserstein	*The Heidi Chronicles*
1998	Paula Vogel	*How I Learned to Drive*
1999	Margaret Edson	*Wit*
2002	Suzan-Lori Parks	*Topdog/Underdog*
2009	Lynn Nottage	*Ruined*
2012	Quiara Alegria Hudes	*Water by the Spoonful*
2014	Annie Baker	*The Flick*
2017	Lynn Nottage	*Sweat*
2018	Martyna Majok	*Cost of Living*

GENERAL NONFICTION

Year	Author	Work
1963	Barbara W. Tuchman	*The Guns of August*
1968	Ariel Durant (with Will Durant)	*Rousseau and Revolution*
1972	Barbara W. Tuchman	*Stilwell and the American Experience in China*
1973	Frances FitzGerald	*Fire in the Lake: The Vietnamese and the Americans in Vietnam*
1974	Annie Dillard	*Pilgrim at Tinker Creek*
1983	Susan Sheehan	*Is There No Place on Earth for Me?*
1996	Tina Rosenberg	*The Haunted Land: Facing Europe's Ghosts after Communism*
2002	Diane McWhorter	*Carry Me Home: Birmingham, Alabama, the Climactic Battle of the Civil Rights Revolution*
2003	Samantha Power	*A Problem from Hell: America and the Age of Genocide*
2004	Anne Applebaum	*Gulag: A History*
2006	Caroline Elkins	*Imperial Reckoning: The Untold Story of Britain's Gulag in Kenya*
2015	Elizabeth Kolbert	*The Sixth Extinction: An Unnatural History*

The presence of so many women on annual listings of the best literary achievements throughout the twentieth and twenty-first centuries stems from several factors: Beginning in the nineteenth century, education for women widened to include colleges and universities, while the stigma against women in the trade of literature declined. In examining the Pulitzer lists, you can see a recognition of women's literary contributions not just as an exception to the rule of male superiority but, increasingly, to an indication that American literary practice must include women's perspectives. Although some of the female writers on the list are of their time alone, today unread and unknown, others would enter the canon of unavoidable literary figures. You simply cannot adequately treat American literary history any longer without reference to such female writers as Millay, Lowell, Wharton, Cather, and Glaspell.

What is also evident in looking at the prizewinners in the post-World War II period is the increasingly widening of literary perspectives by race and gender. American literature through much of its history was the province of white, male writers. Increasingly, in the second half of the twentieth century and beyond, other voices claimed consideration. Gender perspectives joined with ethnic perspectives to help redefine American literature from a multicultural, globalist perspective. Writers would help to provoke and then record racial, gender, and sexual liberation in the second half of the twentieth century. They shifted what was formerly on the margins of American norms to its center. Writers of color, women, gays, and lesbians, along with writers of diverse ethnic backgrounds of either gender, altered accepted standards of American identity and experience.

Toni Morrison in 1993 became the second American woman and the first writer of color to be awarded the Nobel Prize in Literature, heading a distinguished list of successful and acclaimed African American writers who included women such as Alice Walker, Terry McMillan, Maya Angelou, Audre Lord, Rita Dove, and many more. Prominent Asian American female writers include Maxine Hong Kingston, Amy Tan, and Cathy Song. Leading Hispanic female writers include Lorna Dee Cisneros, Sandra Cisneros, and Julia Alvarez. Native American female writers include Leslie Marmon Silko, Louise Erdrich, and Paula Gunn Allen.

At the end of the millennium and into the twenty-first century, American writers, particularly female writers, continued to struggle with American destiny and identity, issues that have dominated the national debate since the nation's founding. What has changed markedly is the unprecedented diversity of opinion and imaginative expression that have emerged out of the social and cultural upheavals of the post-World War II period.

If American literature begins with the discovery of America, it has been sustained by its continuing discovery of Americans, particularly American women. Despite the fact that the consensus is lacking about what precisely America has become and where it is headed, American perspectives on those questions have never been as wide-ranging or as challenging by the inclusion of so many voices, particularly the voices of American women writers.

BIOGRAPHIES

Hannah Adams (1755–1831)
Historian

A historian and scholar, Hannah Adams published some of the earliest scholarship by a woman in America and is considered the first professional American female writer.

Born in Medford, Massachusetts, Adams (a distant cousin of John Adams) was encouraged in her reading by her Harvard-educated father, who worked as a farmer and bookseller and who took in boarders, preparing them for college. Impressed with Adams's passion for learning, they taught her Greek and Latin. During the Revolution, Adams assisted her family by sewing and lace making. After the war, she earned a modest income tutoring neighboring young men in Latin and Greek, helping to prepare them for the college education she was denied. Adams was given a copy of Thomas Broughton's *Historical Dictionary of All Religions from the Creation of the World to the Present Time* (1742) but objected to its lack of tolerance for some religions. She began to research the subject and, from a side job knitting and sewing, earned enough to buy paper to make a blank notebook for a new reference work in which she intended "to avoid giving the least preference of one denomination above another," presenting the arguments and beliefs of each religious sect in the believers' own words.

The result was *An Alphabetical Compendium of the Various Sects Which Have Appeared from the Beginning of the Christian Era to the Present Day* in 1784, only the fifth book by an American woman (after Anne Bradstreet, Mary Rowlandson, Elizabeth Hanson, and Mercy Otis Warren) to be published. Despite the first edition selling out, Adams's agent took all the profits, and Adams labored on a second, more profitable edition titled *A View of Religions*, which appeared in 1791. She earned enough from this edition to devote all her attention to her historical research, publishing *A Summary History of New England* in 1799, the first history of the United States from the *Mayflower* to the ratification of the Constitution. Despite failing eyesight, Adams continued to publish, including *Truth and Excellence of the Christian Religion* (1804), *History of the Jews* (1812), and *Letters on the Gospels* (1826). *A Memoir of Miss Hannah Adams* appeared a year after her death in 1831. At one time one of the most famous women in America, Hannah Adams was one of the pioneer female intellectuals in America who proved that a woman could both earn respect and a living by her scholarly pursuits.

Louisa May Alcott (1832–1888)

Novelist

A novelist and poet, Louisa May Alcott is the author of one of the most beloved novels of all time, *Little Women* (1868), based on the author's childhood experiences in Concord, Massachusetts, with her three sisters. Regarded as a children's literature classic, *Little Women* and its several sequels are written with a sophistication that defies a restriction to young readers. It can be appreciated as a women's novel, one with a strong feminist subtext. Alcott's protagonist, the March sisters, and their wise, principled mother represent five versions of nineteenth-century womanhood, as the novel dramatizes the completeness and self-sufficiency of their nearly all-female universe.

Many telling similarities exist between the March family of *Little Women* and Alcott's own family. Like the spirited, literary-inclined Jo March, Louisa May Alcott was the second oldest of four sisters. Alcott's father, Bronson Alcott, was one of the foremost intellectuals of his day and was variously a schoolmaster, educational innovator, school superintendent, transcendentalist, and lecturer. Frequently absent from home, leaving his family in genteel poverty, the family turned to one another for support with Louisa turning to writing to bring in a family

income after trying her hand at work as a seamstress, domestic servant, governess, and teacher.

In 1851, she published a poem in a magazine. Additional poems and serialized stories followed. A first book, *Flower Fables*, a collection of fairy tales, appeared in 1854. She achieved her first notoriety as a writer for *Hospital Sketches* (1863), which drew on her experiences as an army nurse in Washington, D.C. Her first novel, *Moods* (1864), a psychological study of a failed marriage, failed with critics. Henry James, who praised the book's "every-day virtues," felt she lacked the ability to "handle the great dramatic passions" and suggested that she should be "satisfied to describe only that which she has seen."

Alcott would respond with *Little Women*, which showcased her close observation of domestic life in a development story of the four March sisters and their mother as their father is serving in the Civil War. Their stories, extended in the sequels *Good Wives* (1869), *Little Men* (1871), and *Jo's Boys* (1886), became international best-sellers, selling millions of copies and spawning three movies and two miniseries.

Alcott's novel may idealize the comforting coziness of nineteenth-century domestic life with, as one of Alcott's biographers puts it, "the vividness of a Currier & Ives print," but in Meg, Jo, Beth, and Amy, Alcott created characters whose strengths and failings, struggles and triumphs are as easily recognized to contemporary readers as they were instructive for young women marching toward a new concept called "feminism" more than one hundred years ago.

Paula Gunn Allen (1939–2008)

Novelist, Poet

A poet, novelist, and literary scholar, Paula Gunn Allen was the daughter of a Lebanese American father and a Pueblo Sioux mother. Allen became one of the most important Native American writers and scholars to link feminism with Native American studies and, through her editing of several important anthologies, helped to establish the canon of Native American literature while raising appreciation for its achievement.

Born Paula Marie Francis in Albuquerque, New Mexico, Allen grew up in a small village bordering the Laguna Pueblo reservation in New Mexico. Allen attended a mission school on the reservation and a boarding school in Albuquerque before receiving a BA and an MFA in creative writing from the University of Oregon and her Ph.D. from the University of New Mexico. A teaching career followed at the University of New Mexico, Fort Lewis College in Colorado, San Diego State University, the University of California–Berkley, and UCLA. Her scholarship on Native American cultures led to the groundbreaking book *The Sacred Hoop: Recovering the Feminine in American Indian Traditions* (1986), which broke with previous patriarchal understandings of Native American cultures that downplayed or ignored the central roles women played.

Allen's creative work in poetry and fiction dramatizes the complex heritage of Native Americans and the challenges of history and assimilation on identity and values. Her poetry is collected in such volumes as *Shadow Country* (1982), *Skin and Bones* (1988), and *Life Is a Fatal Disease* (1996). Her novel, *The Woman Who Owned the Shadows* (1983), reflects her own upbringing. Her *Studies in American Indian Literature: Critical Essays and Course Designs* (1983) is considered a landmark in Native American literary criticism.

Julia Alvarez (1950–)

Essayist, Novelist, Poet

A novelist, poet, and essayist, Dominican American writer Julia Alvarez has earned a reputation as one of the most popular and critically acclaimed contemporary Latinx writers. Her novels, poetry, and essays explore cultural collision and female identity, giving voice to the marginalized and silenced.

Born in New York City, Alvarez was raised in the Dominican Republic before returning to New York in 1960 when the political situation on the island forced her family to flee. Alvarez experienced alienation, homesickness, and discrimination, often called a "spic" by her classmates. Sent to a boarding school, she attended Connecticut College before transferring to Middlebury College, where she

earned her BA degree. She earned a master's degree from Syracuse University in 1975. Alvarez began her career as a writer-in-residence for the Kentucky Arts Commission traveling the state and offering writing workshops at elementary schools, high schools, colleges, and community centers. She was a visiting professor in creative writing at the University of Vermont before becoming a tenured professor at her alma mater, Middlebury, where she continues to teach.

Alvarez continued to publish widely, despite her teaching commitments, with essays appearing in national magazines. Her first book of poetry, *Homecoming,* was published in 1984. Never intending to become a fiction writer, Alvarez was approached by an influential agent of Latinx fiction who encouraged her and found a publisher for her breakthrough book, *How the Garcia Girls Lost Their Accents* (1991), fifteen connected stories about life before and after immigration from the Dominican Republic to New York City. Treating issues of identity and assimilation in the conflict between two cultures, Alvarez's novel was both a critical and popular success. *In the Time of Butterflies,* a fictionalized account of the killing of three sisters who opposed Trujillo, followed in 1994, and *Yo!* (1997) revisits the Garcia sisters, with one now a successful novelist. *In the Name of Salomé* (2000) fictionalizes the life of Dominican nineteenth-century poet Salomé Ureña.

Alvarez has said, "Because of who I am, where I come from, what my heritage is, the stories I have to tell come out of a certain history, background and certain spot on this earth." Alvarez's strength as a writer is in her ability to transform characters and settings from the Dominican Republic into universal human experiences.

Maya Angelou (1928–2014)

Essayist, Memoirist, Poet

One of America's most popular and acclaimed American poets, storytellers, and essayists, Maya Angelou was also a memoirist whose most famous work, *I Know Why the Caged Bird Sings*

(1969), became a pioneering work on gender and race and one of the first autobiographies by an African American woman. Selected by Bill Clinton to read her poem "On the Pulse of Morning" at his 1993 inauguration, Angelou was proclaimed "the black woman's poet laureate."

Born Marguerite Anni Johnson in St. Louis, Missouri, Angelou and her brother were sent to live with her grandmother in Arkansas when her parents' marriage collapsed. Angelou recorded in *I Know Why the Caged Bird Sings* how she was raped by her mother's boyfriend when she was seven. When the man was murdered by her uncles for his crime, Angelou felt responsible and stopped talking, remaining mute for the next five years. During these silent years, Angelou developed her love for books and reading and her ability to listen and observe the world around her. Angelou credits a teacher, Mrs. Bertha Flowers, with helping her to speak again. At the age of fourteen, she and her brother moved with their mother to Oakland, California, where Angelou attended the California Labor School and, at the age of sixteen, became the first black, female cable car conductor in San Francisco. She married a white ex-sailor in 1950, and, after they separated, Angelou sang at the Purple Onion cabaret in San Francisco before becoming a cast member of a touring production of *Porgy and Bess*.

In the 1950s, inspired by Dr. Martin Luther King, Angelou became the northern coordinator of Dr. King's SCLC. In the 1960s, she moved to Cairo with her son and to Ghana. Returning to the United States in the mid-1960s, Angelou was encouraged by author James Baldwin and an editor at Random House to write an autobiography. *I Know Why the Caged Bird Sings,* which chronicles Angelou's childhood, became an immediate popular and critical success and the first of six autobiographical volumes, completing the final volume, *A Song Flung up to Heaven,* in 2002. Her memoirs helped to define the evolving genre of creative nonfiction that employs fiction-writing techniques such as dialogue and nonchronological narrative.

Angelou also became a popular poet in such collections as *Just Give Me a Cool Drink of Water 'fore I Diiie* (1971), which was nominated for a Pulitzer

Prize, *Oh Pray My Wings Are Gonna Fit Me Well* (1975), *And Still I Rise* (1978), and *Shaker, Why Don't You Sing?* (1983). Her *Complete Collected Poems* appeared in 1994. She also pursued a career in film and television, becoming the first black woman to have a screenplay (*Georgia, Georgia*) produced in 1972, and received an Emmy nomination for her performance in *Roots* in 1977. She became the first African American woman to direct a major film, *Down in the Delta*, in 1998.

Over a remarkably productive and diverse career, Maya Angelou was an unapologetic voice for racial and gender empowerment. Angelou deserves the credit for writing, in the words of critic Hilton Als, "about blackness from the inside, without apology or defense."

Elizabeth Bishop (1911–1979)

Memoirist, Poet

Poet and memoirist Elizabeth Bishop published sparingly, producing only 101 poems during her lifetime. The work of a perfectionist and a writer uncomfortable with the confessional style of postwar poets such as Robert Lowell, Sylvia Plath, and John Berryman, Bishop's work has been increasingly appreciated since her death in 1979, influencing multiple poets such as James Merrill, John Ashbery, Robert Pinsky, Amy Clampitt, and Sandra McPherson, such that more than one literary critic has claimed her as one of the most important American poets of the twentieth century.

Born in Worcester, Massachusetts, Bishop lived with her grandparents in Nova Scotia after the death of her father when she was one year old and her mother's breakdown and commitment to a mental asylum. She attended Vassar College, where she met poet Marianne Moore, who would become a lifelong friend. After graduation, she lived in New York and traveled extensively in France, Spain, Ireland, Italy, and North Africa. In 1938, she moved to Key West, Florida, and began work on the poems that were collected in her first volume, *North and South* (1946). From 1951 until 1973, she lived in Brazil, alternating for a number of years between that country and teaching at Harvard. Her second collection, *Poems: North & South/A Cold Spring* (1955), won the Pulitzer Prize. *Questions of Travel* (1965) reflected her experiences living abroad. In Brazil, Bishop lived with architect Lota de Macedo Soares until 1967, when Soares committed suicide. In 1970, she received a National Book Award for *The Complete Poems,* and in 1974, she moved permanently to Boston, teaching at Harvard full time. Her last book of poems to appear in her lifetime was *Geography III* (1977). *The Complete Poems, 1927–1979* appeared posthumously in 1983, followed by *The Collected Prose,* a compilation of essays and short stories, in 1984.

Bishop's poems are notable for their vividly observed details, a conversational tone, and a movement toward symbolic resolution. Bishop specialized in exploring the contrasts between childhood and adulthood, dreams versus waking, and a northern versus southern perspective, in which complex and nuanced awareness is presented through precisely rendered images and details. Important poems include "Sestina," "I Am in Need of Music," "The Fish," "One Art," "Insomnia," "First Death in Nova Scotia," and "A Miracle for Breakfast." Bishop has become one of the modern poets to be most reckoned with. As fellow poet Eavan Boland has stated, "Elizabeth Bishop is the most disruptive and mysterious of modern poets; disruptive because no one expected a poet of such cool and desolate intelligence to upset the apple cart of twentieth-century poetry, and mysterious because it's still not clear how this happened. How someone who, in James Merrill's words, undertook the 'lifelong impersonation of an ordinary woman' could have dazzled and subverted the modernist canon."

Ann Eliza Bleecker (1752–1783)

Epistolarian, Poet

Although she never published any of her work during her lifetime, Ann Eliza Bleecker's poems, letters, and fiction are both innovative and distinguished in their perspective on the Ameri-can Revolution. She wrote what is believed to be the first fictional captivity narrative and transformed the conventions of pastoral poetry with the realism of actuality.

Born in New York City, the youngest child in a successful merchant family and members of the American Dutch aristocracy, Ann was known for her precocious writing ability, expressed in verses she shared with her family and friends. In 1769, she married John James Bleecker, who gave up a law practice in Poughkeepsie, New York, in 1771 for farming on the frontier about eighteen miles north of Albany. There, Ann gave birth to two daughters and wrote poetry about both the loveliness and loneliness of country life. During the Revolution, when her husband was away serving in the New York militia, Ann and her two young daughters fled south to avoid the British force, under General John Burgoyne, that invaded New York from Canada. Her poem, "Written in the Retreat from Burgoyne," captures their harrowing experience, in which both her infant daughter and her mother died. After Burgoyne's surrender in 1777, Ann, her daughter, and her sister journeyed back to the family farm, but her sister died during the journey. In 1779, Ann was forced to flee back to Albany again, and in 1781, her husband was taken prisoner by Loyalists that resulted in a breakdown from which she never fully recovered. She died at the age of thirty-three, leaving behind manuscripts of poetry and prose that her daughter edited and published.

The Posthumous Works of Ann Eliza Bleecker, a collection of letters, poems, and prose, was published in 1793, detailing life on the front lines of the American Revolution and a rare firsthand account of women's lives during that period. Her pastoral poetry, which avoids the conventional idealization of rural life for its often harsh realities, would open up a new style of American poetry that treats the beauty of the countryside but does not turn away from the horrifying impact of war, suffering, death, and destruction that reflected Bleecker's direct experiences. *The History of Maria Kittle* (1797), set during the French and Indian War, is a fictionalized elaboration of the author's own experiences fleeing from the British that offers possibly the first fictional accounts of Native Americans, who become the author's projection of all the savagery and brutality of her war experience.

Judy Blume (1938–)

Novelist

 A novelist who writes for children, young adults, and adults, Judy Blume, from her debut novel *The One in the Middle Is the Green Kangaroo* (1968), would transform fiction for young readers. Blume's innovation was to introduce formerly out-of-bounds subjects and themes, which resonated with and reflected the concerns of her readers. With sales in excess of seventy million copies worldwide, Blume is the most widely read writer for young readers ever.

Born Judy Sussman in Elizabeth, New Jersey, Blume was raised by her dentist father and homemaker mother, who passed on her love of reading to her daughter. While attending New York University, Blume met John Blume, an attorney whom she married in 1959. The couple had two children, a daughter and a son. Seeking a creative outlet as a homemaker, Blume began to write children's novels while taking writing courses at NYU. Her third novel, *Are You There, God? It's Me, Margaret* (1970), became a notorious breakthrough best-seller. It is narrated by an eleven-year-old girl on the onset of puberty who deals honestly with issues of menstruation and bodily development. Several cities started movements to have the book banned from libraries. Today, the book is regarded as a trailblazing classic of young-adult literature.

Blume continued to offer challenging subjects in works, including divorce in *It's Not the End of the World* (1972) and *Just as Long as We're Together* (1987), bullying in *Blubber* (1974), masturbation in *Then Again, Maybe I Won't* (1971) and *Deenie* (1973), sexuality in *Forever...* (1975), and family issues in *Here's to You, Rachel Robinson* (1993). Asked about her subjects, particularly sexuality, Blume has observed, "I think I write about sexuality because it was uppermost in my mind when I was a kid: the need to know, and not know how to find out. My father delivered these little lectures to me, the last one when I was 10, on how babies are made. But questions about what I was feeling, and how my body could feel, I *never* asked my parents."

Blume has also written adult novels, including *Wifey* (1978), *Smart Women* (1983), *Summer Sisters* (1998), and *In the Unlikely Event* (2015).

Anne Bradstreet (1612–1672)

Poet

A colonial American poet, Anne Bradstreet has the distinction of being the first American female author of a book, the first female poet ever published in both England and America, and the first writer from the New World to be recognized as an accomplished and important poet.

Born in Northampton, England, to a wealthy, Puritan family, Bradstreet was well educated for a woman of her time, tutored in several languages, history, and literature. She came to America in 1630, arriving first in Salem, Massachusetts, before becoming one of the founding settlers in Newe Towne, which became Boston. She married in 1632, and both her father and husband would serve as governors of the Massachusetts Bay Colony. Giving birth to eight children between 1633 and 1652, Bradstreet relocated with her family to Ipswich, a then-frontier town thirty miles north of Boston, where she wrote most of the poems for her first collection, and finally to North Andover, Massachusetts, where she died at the age of sixty from tuberculosis.

In 1650, Bradstreet's brother-in-law arranged for publication of her first collection of poems, *The Tenth Muse Lately Sprung Up in America,* "by a Gentlewoman of those Parts." She had to endure several attacks by reviewers who were shocked at the impropriety of a female author. Bradstreet's modern reputation as the first noteworthy American poet is based mainly on intimate verse explorations of religious and domestic experience, written primarily after 1650 and published posthumously in a second edition of her works, *Severall Poems Compiled with Great Variety of Wit and Learning*, in 1678 that included revisions of her earlier works and a dozen new works found among her papers after her death. They include "The Flesh and the Spirit"; "On the Burning of Her Home," a short, spiritual autobiography in prose; "Religious Experience"; and "Contemplation," which many regard as her greatest poetic achievement. To Bradstreet belongs the distinction of bringing into poetry intimate observations of ordinary, domestic details joined to the most profound religious and existential themes. In a fundamental sense, the American poetic tradition begins with Anne Bradstreet.

Gwendolyn Brooks (1917–2000)

Poet

One of the most revered and distinguished poets of the twentieth century, Gwendolyn Brooks was the first African American to win a Pulitzer Prize for Poetry and, in 1976, became the first black woman to be inducted into the National Institute of Arts and Letters. Able to move effortlessly between formal conventions and eloquent language and street talk and the rhythm of black urban life, which became her distinctive subject, Brooks produced a treasury of important and influential works which were all informed by her original and humanistic vision.

Although born in Topeka, Kansas, Brooks grew up on the South Side of Chicago, her mother a teacher and her father a janitor who studied to become a doctor. Her parents taught her the value of literature and learning, and Brooks began to write at the age of seven, composing her first poem, a two-line verse. She filled notebooks with her poetry from the age of eleven. At thirteen, her poem "Eventide" was published in *American Childhood* magazine. Despite her writing success, Brooks's school years were largely unhappy. She was ridiculed for her dark skin by blacks who regarded light skin as the standard of beauty and shunned by whites for being black. Brooks would use her school experiences as the basis for her 1953 novel *Maud Martha*, one of

the first novels to explore the theme of a black girl's coming of age. After graduating from high school, Brooks attended a junior college and produced a newspaper focusing on racial and cultural issues. In 1939, she married writer Henry Lowington Blakely, whom she had met through her involvement with the NAACP. The first of the couple's two children was born in 1940.

Brooks's first poetry collection, *A Street in Bronzeville*, was published in 1945, the same year she was selected as one of ten women to receive the *Mademoiselle* magazine Merit Award for Distinguished Achievement. Her second collection, *Annie Allen* (1949), received the Pulitzer Prize for Poetry. In the 1950s, she published a novel, *Maud Martha,* about a woman who stands up to a racist store clerk. She continued through the 1950s and 1960s to publish volumes of children's poetry and adult collections, including *The Bean Eaters* (1960), *Selected Poems* (1963), and *Riot* (1969). Her subject matter dealt with the experiences of the African American community with a style that rivaled such modernist writers as Ezra Pound and T. S. Eliot.

In 1967, Brooks attended the Second Black Writers' Conference at Fisk University and was influenced by the energy and perspective of the black writers she met there. The experience would lead to the exploration of the implications of her own black identity. Before 1967, she recalled, "I wasn't writing consciously with the idea that blacks *must* address blacks, *must* write about blacks.... I'm trying to create new forms, trying to do something that would be presented in a tavern atmosphere." She set out "to clarify my language," creating poems in new forms that would be "direct without sacrificing the kinds of music, the picture making I've always been interested in." Her first collection in her new style was *In the Mecca* (1968), subtle portraits of black urban life. From the 1970s to the 1990s, Brooks continued to publish important volumes: *Aloneness* (1971), *Beckonings* (1975), *Primer for Blacks* (1980), *Blacks* (1987), *Winnie* (1988), and *Children Come Home* (1991). In all her works, an original and unique poetic voice is heard capturing the intimate experiences of daily life. As Brooks once described her method, she "scrapes life with a fine-tooth comb."

Margaret Wise Brown (1910–1952)

Children's Author

A prolific children's book writer of beloved classics such as *Goodnight Moon* and *The Runaway Bunny*, Margaret Wise Brown possessed an almost uncanny ability to convey a child's experience and perspective that through her works would help to transform children's literature.

The daughter of wealthy parents, Brown was born in Brooklyn, New York, and attended private schools in New York, Massachusetts, and Switzerland. After graduating from Hollins College in Virginia in 1932, Brown worked at the Bank Street Experimental School in New York City, where she was enlisted to participate in a new approach to children's literature that emphasized real-world experiences rather than the fairy tales and fables of previous books for children. Based on the relatively new science of psychology and observations of how children themselves told stories, Brown wrote about familiar things—animals, the sounds of the city, bedtime rituals—attempting to speak to her readers in their own language, aided by Brown's own keen observational skills. Brown's first children's book, *When the Wind Blew,* was published in 1937, to be followed by her *Here and Now* stories and the *Noisy Book* series. Brown teamed with illustrator Clement Hurd to produce the children's picture book classics *The Runaway Bunny* (1942) and, arguably, the most popular of all children's books, *Goodnight Moon* (1947). It is based on Brown's own childhood ritual of saying goodnight to the toys and other objects in the nursery where she slept. Described as less a story and more "an incantation," *Goodnight Moon* has charmed (and soothed) parents and children alike for decades.

Brown died at the age of forty-two of an embolism shortly after suffering from an attack of appendicitis. At the time of her death, she had published over one hundred books while leaving behind over seventy unpublished manuscripts. Her books remain in print and have been reissued with new illustrations, suggesting that Brown's gift of seeing the world through a child's eyes and imagination continues to resonate and that her books remain part of bedtime rituals in households around the world.

Pearl S. Buck (1892–1973)

Novelist

In 1938, writer and novelist Pearl Sydenstricker Buck became the third American and the first of two American women to receive the Nobel Prize in Literature for "her rich and truly epic descriptions of peasant life in China and for her biographical masterpieces." Buck was a tireless advocate of women's rights and of Chinese and Asian cultures.

Born in West Virginia to Presbyterian missionaries, Buck moved to China when she was five months old, remaining there until 1911, when she returned to the United States for college at Randolph-Macon Woman's College in Lynchburg, Virginia. She described her childhood as living in "several worlds": the "small, white, clean Presbyterian world of my parents" and the "big, loving merry not-too-clean Chinese world." After graduation, she returned to China, and from 1914 to 1932, she served as a missionary, marrying fellow missionary John Lossing Buck in 1917. Together, they moved to Suzhou, Anhui Province, the region she would memorialize in *The Good Earth*. From 1920 to 1933, the couple lived in Nanjing, where they taught at the University of Nanking. They were swept up in the violence known as the Nanking Incident of 1927 that pitted Chiang Kai-shek's nationalist and communist forces and local warlords against each other. They sought refuge in Japan, where Buck lived for a year before returning to China and devoting herself full time as a professional writer, publishing essays and stories in various magazines in the 1920s.

Buck published a first novel, *East Wind: West Wind*, in 1930 and, working each morning in the attic room of their bungalow in Nanking, completed her masterpiece, *The Good Earth,* published in 1931, the first book of a trilogy that includes *Sons* (1932) and *A House Divided* (1935). The trilogy, collectively called *The House of Earth*, provides an intimate saga of a family and village life in China in the early years of the twentieth century. Buck's realistic and sympathetic depiction of Chinese life and culture was groundbreaking. According to scholar Kang Liao, Buck played a "pioneering role in demythologizing China and the Chinese people in the American mind." By her death in 1973, Buck would publish over seventy books, including novels, a collection of short stories, biographies, an autobiography, poetry, drama, children's books, and translations from the Chinese.

After returning to live in the United States in 1934, living in a farmhouse in Bucks County, Pennsylvania, Buck became active in the American civil rights and women's rights movements. In 1942, she and her second husband, Richard Walsh, founded the East and West Association, which was dedicated to cultural exchange and understanding between Asia and the West. In 1949, she established Welcome House, the first international, interracial adoption agency, and in 1964, she established the Pearl S. Buck Foundation, providing scholarships for thousands of Asian children. In 1973, Buck was inducted into the National Women's Hall of Fame and in 1983 was honored with a postage stamp, part of the Great Americans series. In 2004, *The Good Earth* returned to the best-seller list when it was selected by Oprah Winfrey for her book club.

Willa Cather (1873–1947)
Novelist, Short Story Author

Novelist and short-story writer Willa Cather can be described as the last great nineteenth-century American writer in the twentieth century. Adrift and dispossessed by the modern world, which, she lamented, "broke in two in 1922 or thereabouts" (1922 was the magnum opus year of modernism with the publication of T. S. Eliot's *The Waste Land* and James Joyce's *Ulysses*), Cather left little doubt which side of the divide she was on by celebrating in her writing the departed world of the past. However, Cather contributed far more than nostalgia for the bygone; by exploring the emotional contours of the past, Cather offered a definition of the American identity based on its frontier and immigrant experience, explaining America's present by investigating its past.

Born in 1873 in Virginia, Cather moved to the Nebraska prairie village of Red Cloud as a child, leaving for schooling at the state university in Lincoln. After graduating in 1895, she went to work editing a home magazine in Pittsburgh and later as a drama and music reviewer for a Pittsburgh newspaper. After a stint as a high school English teacher, in 1906, she began work as an editor for *McClure's* magazine, a job she held until 1911 when she resigned to pursue a writing career. After her first novel, *Alexander's Bridge*, was published in 1912, Cather, encouraged by Maine regionalist writer Sarah Orne Jewett to focus on the region she knew best, published the first novel of her Prairie Trilogy, *O Pioneers*, in 1913, followed by *The Song of the Lark* (1915) and *My Antonia* (1918).

My Antonia, though her fourth novel, was the first that most completely reflected her realization that "life began for me when I ceased to admire and began to remember." The novel would celebrate both the elemental landscape of the Nebraska prairie and the intensity and idiosyncrasies of its inhabitants, particularly the immigrants who first carved lives from the unforgiving wilderness. Its vivid depiction of people and places is focused on the life of a Czech farm girl, Antonia Shimerda, and the impact she had on the narrator, Jim Burden, over her lifetime that tells the story of the settling and transformation of the Nebraskan frontier. The novel is one of the greatest pastoral elegies in American literature, celebrating all that is elemental and archetypal through its heroine, Antonia, one of a core group of essential female characters in American literature.

Cather's subsequent works continued to explore her past, the most distant past, and an increasingly disappointing present in comparison. *One of Ours* (1921), set during World War I, was inspired by the death of Cather's cousin on the Western Front; *A Lost Lady* (1923) is based on a woman Cather knew when she was growing up in Red Cloud; *My Mortal Enemy* (1926) is a bitter story of a woman who comes to regret having married for love; and *The Professor's House* (1935) deals with a man's midlife crisis and expresses many of Cather's own anxieties during the period. Cather turned to the past in *Death Comes for the Archbishop* (1926), based on the lives of nineteenth-century French clerical missionaries in New Mexico, which is widely regarded as her masterpiece; *Shadows on the Rock* (1931), set in seventeenth-century Quebec; and *Sapphira and the Slave Girl* (1940), which takes place in the village of Cather's birth in the years before the Civil War.

Over her long and productive career, Cather remained dedicated to her art, foregoing matrimony and children to pursue her writing. Since most of her close relationships were with women, Cather has been offered up as an early example of a lesbian author; little evidence contradicts the facts of her celibacy and her primary relationship with her art.

Lydia Maria Child (1802–1880)

Novelist, Poet

A novelist, poet, and rights activist, Lydia Child is primarily remembered today as the author of the Thanksgiving children's poem *Thanksgiving Day* (1857), which begins, "Over the river and through the wood, / To Grandfather's house we'll go." Child was among the most influential nineteenth-century female writers and a tireless crusader for excluded groups in American society: Native Americans, slaves, and women. She established the first American monthly for children, the *Juvenile Miscellany* (1826), published an early antislavery work, *Appeal in Favor of That Class of Americans Called Africans* (1833), and was a pioneering advocate for women's suffrage and sex education as well as being the author of *A History of the Condition of Women in Various Ages and Nations* (1835).

Born Lydia Maria Francis in Medford, Massachusetts, she was educated at a local school and later in Maine, where she trained to be a teacher. There, she experienced Native American life, which became the subject of her first novel, *Hobomok* (1824), a controversial historical romance set during Puritan times (regarded as the first historical novel

set in New England) that sympathetically portrayed the marriage between a Native American and a white girl. Other novels include *The Rebels* (1825), set in pre-Revolutionary Boston, *Philothea* (1836), set in ancient Greece, and *A Romance of the Republic* (1867), which deals with abolitionism.

After marrying lawyer and aspiring politician David Lee Child in 1828, Lydia Child became increasingly involved in political causes, exploring the Indian removal crisis in *The First Settlers of New-England: or, Conquests of the Pequods, Narragansets, and Pokanokets* (1829). Her most popular work from her early married years was the manual *The Frugal Housewife, Dedicated to Those Who Are Not Ashamed of Economy* (1829). As her husband's career faltered, she relied on her writing to support them. In the 1830s, she became an outspoken abolitionist, blaming both the North and the South for the existence of slavery and calling for its immediate eradication. Sales of her works plummeted, and she was forced to resign as the editor of the *Juvenile Miscellany*, which she had founded in 1826. Despite the financial toil, Child persisted in her antislavery view, reaching the pinnacle of her fame as an activist after the 1859 John Brown raid at Harpers Ferry prompted her to publish the pamphlet *Correspondence between Lydia Maria Child and Gov. Wise and Mrs. Mason of Virginia* (1860). She would edit the memoirs of Harriet Jacobs, *Incidents in the Life of a Slave Girl* (1861), and would publish a book written especially for emancipated slaves, *The Freedmen's Book* (1865), which promoted self-respect and self-reliance and challenging prevailing notions of racial inferiority.

Over a long and productive career that produced more than fifty books, Child used her considerable literary talent to tackle the most vexing and intractable issues of the day.

Alice Childress (1916–1994)

Novelist, Playwright

For more than four decades, African American novelist, playwright, and actor Alice Childress was an unapologetic chronicler of lives too often forgotten or deemed insignificant in America. "My writing attempts to interpret the 'ordinary' because they are not ordinary," she stated. "Each human is uniquely different. Like snowflakes, the human pattern is never cast twice. We are uncommonly and marvelously intricate in thought and action, our problems are most complex and, too often, silently borne." Childress gave voice to those burdens while celebrating how we are both similar and different from one another.

Born Alice Herndon in Charleston, South Carolina, Childress moved to Harlem when her parents separated to live with her grandmother, who would encourage her interest in reading and writing. Leaving high school after only two years after the death of her grandmother, Childress supported herself at low-paying jobs while becoming involved in the Harlem theater scene. In 1934, she married actor Alvin Childress, and the couple had a daughter. Childress studied drama at the American Negro Theatre and performed there throughout the 1940s, winning acclaim (and a Tony nomination) for her performance in Philip Yordan's *Anna Lucasta* (1944), which became the longest-running all-black play in Broadway history. In 1949, she began her writing career with the one-act play *Florence,* which she also directed and starred in. It would preview many of the themes of her work, including working-class life, racial politics, and the empowerment of black women. *Just a Little Simple*, an adaptation of a Langston Hughes novel, followed in 1950, and *Gold through the Trees* (1952) earned her the distinction of being one of the first African American women to have her work professionally produced on the New York stage. Her play *Trouble in Mind* (1955) won an Obie Award for the best off-Broadway play of the 1955–1956 season, making Childress the first African American woman to win the award. Her next dramatic work, *Wedding Band: A Love/Hate Story* (1962), set in South Carolina and dealing with an interracial love affair, was so scandalous that no New York theater would stage it, and it premiered in 1966 at the University of Michigan and in Chicago. It would not appear in New York until 1972 at the New York Shakespeare Festival. It was later filmed for television, but many stations refused to air it. Her other plays include *String* (1969), *Wine in the Wilderness* (1969), *Mojo: A Black Love Story*

(1970), *Sea Island Song* (1977), and *Moms: A Praise Play for a Black Comedienne* (1987).

Childress is also known for her young-adult novels, particularly *A Hero Ain't Nothin' but a Sandwich* (1973), recounting the rehabilitation of a thirteen-year-old heroin addict, which became a film in 1977; *A Short Walk* (1979), which was nominated for a Pulitzer Prize; *Rainbow Jordan* (1981); and *Those Other People* (1989).

All of Childress's works confront difficult social issues of racism and gender and class dynamics not as a theorist but as an advocate of the humanity she saw so clearly around her.

Kate Chopin (1850–1904)
Novelist, Short Story Author

A novelist and short-story writer widely considered the most important early feminist writer in America, Chopin's novel *The Awakening* (1899) is regarded as a groundbreaking classic. Kate Chopin was forced by the untimely death of her husband into a reassessment of her previous conventional role of wife, which led to a literary career in which she tested and challenged many of her era's assumptions about gender and race that still have the capacity to shock and question conventional beliefs.

Born in St. Louis, Missouri, as Katherine O'Flaherty to a successful businessman who had emigrated from Ireland and a well-connected member of the ethnic French community in St. Louis, Chopin graduated from the Sacred Heart Convent in St. Louis in 1868 and two years later married New Orleans businessman Oscar Chopin. Settling in New Orleans, the couple had six children between 1871 and 1879. When Oscar Chopin's cotton brokerage failed, the family moved to Cloutiersville in northwestern Louisiana to manage several small plantations and a general store. When Oscar Chopin died in 1882, he left his wife with considerable debt. When she was unable to make the plantation and general store succeed, Chopin sold the property and returned to St. Louis. Within a year, her mother died, and Chopin struggled with depression. A doctor and family friend suggested that Chopin try writing as a therapy.

Chopin was successful in publishing a number of stories and articles in newspapers and magazines based on her Louisiana experiences, drawing on the local color of Creole life. Her first novel was *At Fault* (1890), and her stories were collected in *Bayou Folk* (1894) and *A Night in Acadia* (1897). In works like "The Story of an Hour," Chopin moved beyond regionalism to dramatize gender issues and female empowerment. In "Désirée's Baby," she tackles the theme of miscegenation. It was in *The Awakening* (1899), a powerful study of confinement felt by a woman in the conventional gender roles of wife and mother, that Chopin orchestrated a full-frontal assault on gender standards of the time in scenes that proved to be far too frank and daring for contemporary readers. The novel was forgotten until rediscovered by literary scholars in the 1950s, when it claimed a preeminent place as one of the most groundbreaking novels dealing with gender and women's liberation ever produced in America.

Sandra Cisneros (1954–)

Essayist, Novelist, Poet

One of the leading figures in contemporary Chicana literature, Mexican American novelist, poet, and essayist Sandra Cisneros has explored central issues of cultural and sexual identity in experimental and diverse literary forms.

Born in Chicago, the only daughter in a family with six sons, Cisneros was raised both in Chicago and in her father's family home in Mexico City, a duality "always straddling two countries … but not belonging to either culture" that would become central to her writing. Cisneros earned a BA degree from Loyola University and an MFA from the University of Iowa. After earning her degrees, Cisneros taught former high school dropouts at the Latino Youth High School in Chicago. In 1984, her breakthrough coming-of-age novel *The House on Mango Street* was published to great popularity and critical acclaim.

Treating the life of Mexican Americans growing up in Chicago, the novel has sold more than six million copies and has become required reading in high schools and colleges across the country.

Cisneros's poetry collections include *Bad Boys* (1980), *My Wicked Ways* (1987), and *Loose Woman* (1994). Her short-story collection *Woman Hollering Creek and Other Stories* (1991) won the PEN Center West Award for Best Fiction. She returned to long fiction with *Carmelo* (2002), an autobiographical novel, and *Have You Seen Marie?* (2012). *A House of My Own* (2015) is a memoir.

Devoted to giving voice to perspectives on American life and identity often ignored, reflecting a bilingual, multicultural consciousness, Cisneros has stated, "I'm a translator. I'm an amphibian. I can travel in both worlds. What I'm saying is very important for the Latino community, but it is also important for the white community to hear. What I'm saying in my writing is that we can be Latino and still be American."

Hannah Mather Crocker (1752–1829)

Essayist

An essayist and the great-great-granddaughter of the founder of the Massachusetts Mather Dynasty, Hannah Mather Crocker is celebrated for her 1818 *Observations on the Real Rights of Women*, the first book by an American author to champion women's rights.

Born in Boston's North End, Crocker was the daughter of Samuel Mather, a Congregationalist minister, and Hannah Hutchinson, sister of Thomas Hutchinson, Boston's governor. Her father believed strongly in the importance of educating women, and she was widely educated in language, history, theology, and literature. As a teenager, Crocker served as a spy for the American forces during the lead-up to the American Revolution. In 1779, she married Joseph Crocker, a captain in the American army who shared his wife's advocacy of women's rights. During their marriage, she gave birth to ten children between 1780 and 1795 while becoming involved in Freemasonry, particularly on behalf of women, founding a women's lodge.

After the death of her husband and raising her children, Crocker began her career as a writer. In 1815, Crocker published *Series of Letters on Freemasonry* from "A Lady of Boston," a defense of Freemasonry, in which she wrote that "it will be thought by many, a bold attempt for a female to even dare enter on the subject at all." She followed it in 1818 with her most important work, *Observations on the Real Rights of Women, with Their Appropriate Duties, Agreeable to Scripture, Reason and Common Sense,* which argued for women's equality with men based on Christian justice and defended Mary Wollstonecraft's argument in *A Vindication on the Rights of Woman* (1792). Crocker powerfully contributed to the debate about the potential and possibilities for women in the early years of the American republic.

Emily Dickinson (1830–1886)

Poet

Despite having published fewer than a dozen of her nearly 1,800 poems during her lifetime, Emily Dickinson has emerged as almost certainly the greatest of all American female writers and, arguably, America's greatest poet. She managed to transform the events of an almost completely private interior life into universal and existential relevance.

The details of that life can be quickly summarized: born, lived, and died in Amherst, Massachusetts. She was one of the three children of Edward Dickinson, lawyer, legislator, and treasurer of Amherst College. Emily was educated at Amherst Academy and attended Mount Holyoke Female Seminary for a short time. After her schooling, she became increasingly reclusive, confining herself to a small circle of family and a few trusted friends while attending to her assigned household responsibilities. She rarely left home except for brief visits to Washington, Philadelphia, and Boston. Emotional relationships with at least two men are suspected, but little evidence is available. In her middle years, Dickinson acquired a reputation as an eccentric recluse who dressed perpetually in white and was rarely seen even by visitors to the Dickinson home.

Dickinson was encouraged in her writing by her girlhood friend and classmate, author Helen Hunt Jackson, and by author and abolitionist Thomas Wentworth Higginson. After her death, Dickinson's sister found the rich cache of her poetry among her papers. All are short lyrics, most untitled, compressed and penetrating, harnessed by the narrow limits of the rhymed quatrains of the Protestant hymn book but pushed to an expressiveness by rhythmic variations and unconventional rhymes. The emotional and intellectual weight she gives to her images transforms her verse from deceptively simple quatrains to wider, more cosmic speculation on God, death, and love in a lively, witty, and ironic intensity. Dickinson anticipates by several decades modern poetry's techniques of elliptical thought and ambiguity. Throughout her work, an intense, rebellious, and completely original poet is revealed. One of her poems provides a fitting testimony to her remarkable contribution to world literature:

> This is my letter to the world
> That never wrote to me,—
> The simple news that Nature told,
> With Tender magisty.
> Her message is committed
> To hands I cannot see,
> For love of her, sweet Countrymen,
> Judge tenderly of me!

Joan Didion (1934–)

Essayist, Novelist

In a long and distinguished writing career, Joan Didion has been acclaimed as one of America's greatest cultural critics, whose novels and essays document the social unrest and psychological fragmentation of modern life, whether measured in public or personal terms. Readers in the future who may want to experience what it was like to live through some of the decisive moments of the late twentieth century will have Didion to rely upon.

The daughter of an officer in the U.S. Army Air Corps, Didion was born in Sacramento, California. Because her family relocated across the country so often, Didion did not attend school on a regular basis and has written that moving so often made her feel like a perpetual outsider. She read fervently from a young age and recalls writing observations down as early as age five. Graduating from the University of California–Berkeley in 1956, Didion won an essay contest sponsored by *Vogue* that led to a research assistant position at the magazine. During her seven years at *Vogue,* she worked her way up to associate feature editor. Homesick for California, she also wrote her first novel, *Run River* (1963). Fellow writer John Gregory Dunne helped her edit the book, and the two married, returning to California in 1964.

From this point on, California would become Didion's principal subject as a metaphor to understand contemporary American life. Her first essay collection, *Slouching towards Bethlehem*, appeared in 1968. A second collection, *The White Album*, was published in 1979. Novels include *Play It As It Lays* (1970), set in Hollywood, and *A Book of Common Prayer* (1977) dramatizes lives reflecting the cultural disintegration of the times. The book-length essay *Salvador* (1983) reflects her two-week trip to El Salvador. *Democracy* (1984) tells the story of a CIA officer's love affair against the backdrop of the Cold War and Vietnam. *Miami* (1987) examines the Cuban expatriate community. *The Last Thing He Wanted* (1996) treats shady arms deals in Central America.

Didion collaborated with her husband on screenplays, including *Panic in Needle Park* (1971), *Play It As It Lays* (1972), *A Star Is Born* (1976), *True Confessions* (1981), and *Up Close and Personal* (1996). In 2003, John Gregory Dunne suffered a fatal heart attack. At the same time, their daughter fell gravely ill and subsequently died. Didion reflects on both in *The Year of Magical Thinking* (2005), winner of the National Book Award for Nonfiction, and *Blue Nights* (2011).

In 2007, Didion received the National Book Foundation's annual Medal for Distinguished Contribution to American Letters, in which she is aptly celebrated as "an incisive observer of American politics and culture for more than forty-five years" and that "her distinctive blend of spare, elegant prose and fierce intelligence has earned her books a place in the canon of American literature as well as the admiration of generations of writers and journalists."

Hilda "H. D." Doolittle (1886–1961)
Essayist, Novelist, Poet

A novelist and memoirist as well as one of the most important poets of the twentieth century, Hilda Doolittle, or H. D. as she was known, was an innovative and experimental modernist and a leader of the Imagist movement. Known for her poetry, she also wrote novels, memoirs, essays, and translations. Outspoken and unapologetic about her sexuality and questioning of gender roles in her life and works, H. D. would become an important forerunner figure of the LGBT community when her works were rediscovered and reevaluated in the 1970s and 1980s.

Doolittle was born in Bethlehem, Pennsylvania, into a close-knit Moravian community in which her mother had been a founding member. Her father was an astronomer who relocated his family when he became a professor at the University of Pennsylvania. Her father encouraged his favorite daughter to pursue science, but Doolittle preferred more artistic interests. She attended Bryn Mawr College and was a classmate of future poet Marianne Moore, who became a lifelong friend. She also befriended Ezra Pound and William Carlos Williams, both students at the University of Pennsylvania, who also would become influential forces in her life and poetic career. Affairs with both Pound and poet Frances Josepha Gregg initiated Doolittle's lifelong questioning of gender and sexuality and the conflict between her heterosexuality and lesbianism. In 1911, she set off for a short visit to Europe. It would become the locus for her activities for much of the rest of her life. Living in London, through Pound, she met fellow artists such as William Butler Yeats, T. S. Eliot, May Sinclair, and Wyndham Lewis, who would become important mentors and influences in her development as a poet. In 1912, Doolittle gave Pound three works, "Epigram," "Hermes of the Ways," and "Priapus," and Pound was impressed by their clarity and vividness, characteristics that he would advocate in the poetic methods of Imagism, which Pound popularized. Regarding "Do-little," an unfortunate surname for an ambitious poet, she began to sign her work "H. D. Imagiste." Pound would promote H. D.'s work by praising her poems as "objective—no slither; direct—no excessive use of adjectives, no metaphors that won't permit examination. It's straight talk, straight as the Greek!" One member of her circle, British writer and poet Richard Aldington, she married in 1913.

Doolittle's earliest volumes are *Sea Garden* (1916), *Hymen* (1921), *Heliodora and Other Poems* (1924), and *Collected Poems* (1925). She would pioneer the modern poetic methods of free verse and was among the earliest writers to employ stream-of-consciousness narrative that James Joyce popularized. Beginning in the 1920s, Doolittle wrote a number of experimental novels, some based on classical antiquity such as *Palimpsest* (1926) and *Hedylus* (1928) and others drawing on her biography and the struggles of a female artist such as *Asphodel* and *HERmione*, both not published until 1981. In the 1930s, Doolittle became a patient of Sigmund Freud. She would chronicle her experiences with Freud and psychoanalysis in *Tribute to Freud* (1956). In the 1940s, she produced the memoir *The Gift*, which treats her Moravian childhood and social and cultural development during her lifetime. It was published in full in 1999. Another volume, *End to Torment* (1979), treats her relationship with Ezra Pound. A book-length epic poem, *Helen in Egypt*, a revisionist depiction of the Helen story and the Trojan War, was published in 1961, the year of Doolittle's death. Her *Collected Poems, 1912–1944* was published in 1983.

Doolittle's importance and legacy as an important American modernist was reaffirmed beginning in the 1970s by feminist critics who radically challenged the conventional view of literary modernism as a primary male enterprise by such figures as Pound, Eliot, and Joyce. Doolittle's importance lies in the modernist tradition and as an early force in the challenge to gender and sexual orthodoxy. Her influence can be seen in the works of such poets and writers as Denise Levertov, Barbara Guest, Adrienne Rich, Susan Howe, Robert Duncan, and Allen Ginsberg.

Rita Dove (1952–)
Essayist, Novelist, Poet

A poet, novelist, and essayist, Rita Dove was the second black woman ever to win the Pulitzer Prize for Poetry (Gwendolyn Brooks was the first) and from 1993 to 1995 was the first African American to serve as U.S. Poet Laureate Consultant in Poetry to the Library of Congress. During her long and distinguished writing career, Dove has been an outspoken advocate on behalf of women and the power of poetry and literature to inspire and enlighten.

Born in Akron, Ohio, Rita Dove was the daughter of one of the first black chemists in the tire industry. Encouraged by her parents academically, Dove was named a presidential scholar, one of the top one hundred high-school graduates in the country, and attended Miami University in Ohio as a national merit scholar. After graduation, she received a Fulbright scholarship to study in Germany and later earned an MFA at the Iowa Writers' Workshop, where she met her husband, German writer Fred Viebahn. Her first poetry collection, *The Yellow House on the Corner*, appeared in 1980. It was followed by *Museum* (1983); *Thomas and Beulah* (1986), which received the Pulitzer Prize; *Grace Notes* (1989); *Mother Love* (1995); *On the Bus with Rosa Parks* (1999); and *Sonata Mulattica* (2009).

Dove's poetry is distinguished by its lyricism, sharply realized details drawn from her life, and the experiences of African Americans that range widely to include her grandparents' lives and marriage in early twentieth-century Ohio and the battles of the Civil Rights era. As fellow poet Brenda Shaughnessy has expressed, "Dove is a master of transforming a public or historical element—reenvisioning a spectacle and unearthing the heartfelt, wildly original private thoughts such historical moments always contain."

Dove has also published the short-story collection *Fifth Sunday* (1990), the novel *Through the Ivory Gate* (1992), and a verse drama, *The Darker Face of the Earth* (1996), that reimagines the Oedipus myth in the context of Southern slavery. A professor of creative writing at Arizona State University, since 1989, she has had the chair of commonwealth professor of English at the University of Virginia.

Louise Erdrich (1954–)

Novelist, Poet, Short Story Author

An acclaimed and popular novelist, short-story writer, and poet who explores her own mixed-race heritage as a Native American and German American, Erdrich, in the words of one critic, "is weaving a body of work that goes beyond portraying contemporary Native American life … to explore the great universal questions—questions of identity, pattern versus randomness, and the meaning of life itself."

Born in Little Falls, Minnesota, the daughter of a Chippewa Indian mother and a German American father, Erdrich grew up in North Dakota, where her parents taught at a school run by the Bureau of Indian Affairs. Erdrich was part of the first class of women to be admitted to Dartmouth College, and she met there her future husband, anthropologist Michael Dorris, who was hired to chair the newly established Native American Studies Department, whose courses led Erdrich to explore her own ancestry, which would eventually inspire her writing. After graduating, Erdrich was a visiting poet and teacher for the Dakota Arts Council before earning a master's degree in writing from Johns Hopkins in 1979 and returning to Dartmouth as a writer-in-residence.

In 1982, Erdrich received the Nelson Algren Fiction Award for her short story "The World's Greatest Fisherman," which became the first chapter of her debut novel, *Love Medicine* (1984), which coincided with the publication of her first collection of poems, *Jacklight* (1984), which centers on the conflict between Native and non-Native cultures while celebrating family bonds and the ties of kinship. *Love Medicine,* a series of linked stories of several members of an extended Chippewa family, won the National Book Critics Award. Her subsequent novels include *The Beet Queen* (1986); *Tracks* (1988); *The Bingo Palace*

(1994); *Tales of Burning Love* (1997); *The Antelope Wife* (1996); *The Last Report on the Miracles of Little No Horse* (2001); *The Master Butchers Singing Club* (2003); *The Plague of Doves* (2009), a finalist for the Pulitzer Prize for Fiction; and *The Round House* (2012), winner of the National Book Award for Fiction. They represent an ever-expanding fictional universe centered on Erdrich's own Dakota region but extends to universal questions of culture, identity, and human nature. Erdrich's poetry collections include *Baptism of Desire* (1989) and *Original Fire* (2003).

Erdrich has observed that "primarily I am just a storyteller, and I take [stories] where I find them. I love stories whether they function to reclaim old narratives or occur spontaneously. Often, to my surprise, they do both."

Edna Ferber (1885–1968)

Novelist, Playwright

After a remarkably productive writing career during which she produced novels, plays, and poems, the *New York Times* said in its obituary of Edna Ferber, "Her books were not profound, but they were vivid, and had a sound sociological basis. She was among the best-read novelists in the nation, and critics of the 1920s and 1930s did not hesitate to call her the greatest American woman novelist of her day."

Ferber summarized her background: "I am an American Jewish child, a woman born in the Middle West in the middle eighties." Born in Kalamazoo, Michigan, Ferber's Hungarian family settled in Appleton, Wisconsin, when she was twelve. Dreaming initially of becoming an actress, Ferber instead began her writing career shortly after high school. Writing a prize-winning essay led to her going to work on the local Appleton newspapers, publishing her first short stories that focused on a new phenomenon: women in the business world. Collections included *Roast Beef Medium* (1913), *Personality Plus* (1914), and *Emma McChesney & Co.* (1915). Her second published novel, *The Girls* (1921), earned critical praise, and her next, *So Big* (1925), won the Pulitzer Prize and was made into a film. Other best-selling successes followed, including *Show Boat* (1926), which became a musical and a movie; *Cimarron*

(1930), treating the 1889 Oklahoma land rush; and *Saratoga Trunk* (1941), which was about a notorious Creole woman who returns to her native New Orleans to marry a Texas gambler.

Ferber collaborated with George S. Kaufman in several successful plays, including *Minick* (1924), *The Royal Family* (1927), *Dinner at Eight* (1932), and *Stage Door* (1936). Her later novels included *Giant* (1952), set in Texas, which became a major motion picture, and *Ice Palace* (1958), set in Alaska.

Rarely did Ferber's stories, novels, and plays fail to connect with her readers and audiences, who were drawn to her American scenes and sentiment. About her writer's life, Ferber wrote, "Life can't ever really defeat a writer who is in love with writing, for life itself is a writer's lover until death—fascinating, cruel, lavish, warm, cold, treacherous, constant."

Maria Irene Fornés (1930–2018)
Playwright

A playwright and director who dominated the experimental theater world for four decades, Maria Irene Fornés specialized in daring, poetic, and emotionally forceful dramas. Despite having had only one play ever produced on Broadway, which closed in previews, Fornes influenced countless fellow playwrights and was admired by generations of theater critics and practitioners.

Born in Havana, Fornés immigrated to the United States at the age of fifteen. Her first career was as a painter and, after moving to Paris in the 1950s to study art, was greatly influenced by a French production of Samuel Beckett's *Waiting for Godot* and the possibilities and impact of the theater. However, she did not begin writing for the stage until the 1960s. Her first play, *There! You Died!*, later renamed *Tango Palace*, was first produced by the San Francisco Actor's Workshop in 1963 and by the New York City Actors Studio in 1964. It was followed by *The Successful Life of 3* and *Promenade* (1965), for which Fornés won the first of eight Obie Awards, the off-Broadway equivalent of the Tonys. Reflecting on her dramatic method, Fornés explained, "I com-

pose my plays guided not by story line but more by energies that take place within each scene, and the energies that place within one scene and the scene that follows." Her best-known play is *Fefu and Her Friends* (1977), one of the landmark works of feminist theater in which eight women in the 1930s reveal their conflicts, anxieties, and rivalries. It has been described by critic Richard Eder as "the dramatic equivalent of a collection of poems."

Other plays, most of which Fornés also directed, include *Mud* (1983), about a woman's attempt to escape her stifling life on a remote farm; *The Conduct of Life* (1985), about a young woman's self-awareness; *Abingdon Square* (1987), which was set during the AIDS epidemic; and *Letters from Cuba* (2000), which was based on the letters of her brother, who never left Havana. Fornés received an Obie Award for Lifetime Achievement in 1982 for a career that helped to define the American avant-garde theater.

Margaret Fuller (1810–1850)
Author, Editor, Journalist

The first full-time book reviewer, author, editor, and journalist, Margaret Fuller also produced what is considered to be the first major feminist work in the United States, *Woman in the Nineteenth Century* (1845). Susan B. Anthony would write that Fuller "possessed more influence on the thought of American women than any woman previous to her time."

Born in Cambridge, Massachusetts, the first child of Congressman Timothy Fuller, her father provided her with an education as rigorous as any boy's, forbidding her the standard feminine fare of the time such as etiquette books and sentimental novels. Educated at schools in Boston and Groton, Fuller would earn by the time she was thirty the reputation of being the best-read person—male or female—in New England and became the first woman to be allowed to use the library at Harvard. Fuller's reputation as an intellectual drew prominent women, including the wives of Ralph Waldo Emerson and Nathaniel

Hawthorne, Lydia Maria Child, and Mrs. Theodore Parker to a series of subscription *Conversations* that Fuller hosted from 1839 to 1844, giving women a rare forum to discuss academia and issues of the day.

With Emerson, Fuller founded *The Dial,* a literary and philosophical journal that Fuller edited and to which she contributed articles and reviews, including in 1843 her groundbreaking feminist manifesto "The Great Lawsuit," which called for women's equality. When *The Dial* ceased publication in 1844, Fuller moved to New York to join Horace Greeley's *New York Tribune* as a literary critic and reviewer. In 1845, she expanded her *Dial* essay "The Great Lawsuit" into *Woman in the Nineteenth Century*, a classic of the women's movement. In 1846, she became the first female foreign correspondent for the *Tribune*. In Italy, she fell in love with Giovanni Ossoli, a lieutenant of Giuseppe Mazzini in the cause of Italian Unification, with whom she had a son. On the front lines in the revolution for the establishment of a Roman Republic that failed, Fuller, Ossoli, and her son sailed back to America, where, within one hundred yards of Fire Island, their ship went aground and sank, and no trace of Fuller, Ossoli, or her son were ever found.

Edgar Allan Poe, who both admired Fuller's integrity as a writer and decried some of her ideas, famously declared that "humanity is divided into men, women, and Margaret Fuller," a testimony to a singular figure in American women's history.

Susan Glaspell (1876–1948)
Playwright

Called by British theater critic Michael Billington "American drama's best-kept secret," Glaspell is widely regarded as a pioneering feminist writer and America's first important modern female playwright, who cofounded the Provincetown Players, the country's first modern theater company.

Born in Iowa, Glaspell was raised on a rural homestead. Her father was a hay farmer, and her mother was a public school teacher. Educated in public schools in Davenport, Iowa, Glaspell went to

work at eighteen as a reporter for a local newspaper. At twenty-one, she defied conventional wisdom that college made women unfit for marriage, enrolling at Drake University and majoring in philosophy. Upon graduation, she became one of the few full-time female journalists, working on the *Des Moines Daily News* covering the state legislature and murder cases. While covering the conviction of a woman accused of murdering her abusive husband, she abruptly resigned to devote her attention to writing.

She began to publish the first of over fifty short stories in *Harper's* and *The Ladies' Home Journal*, which financed her move to Chicago, where she wrote her first novel, *The Glory of the Conquered* (1909). In 1913, Glaspell married fellow writer George Cram Cook, and the couple moved to New York City's Greenwich Village as members of America's first avant-garde artistic movement. Glaspell became a leading member of Heterodoxy, an early feminist debating society. Glaspell and Cook went to Provincetown, Massachusetts, in the summer of 1915, where they founded a "creative collective" that became known as the Provincetown Players, performing plays by group members in a refurbished fishing wharf. Glaspell would be instrumental in supporting the career of Eugene O'Neill, whose early work was mounted by the Players. Working with the company also stimulated Glaspell's own dramatic work, including her first play, *Trifles* (1916), a dramatic version of her short story "A Jury of Her Peers," which was based on the murder trial she had covered in Des Moines and has been called an early feminist masterpiece and one of the greatest works of American drama. Her other major plays are *Inheritors* (1921), following three generations of a pioneer family in one of the first modern historical dramas; *The Verge* (1921), an early expressionistic drama; and *Alison's House* (1930), based on the life of Emily Dickinson, which received the Pulitzer Prize for Drama.

Glaspell also wrote several novels, including *The Visioning* (1911), *Lifted Masks* (1912), *Fidelity* (1915), *Brook Evans* (1928), and *Judd Rankin's Daughter* (1945). Although at the time of her death she was regarded as "one of the nation's most widely read novelists," her novels fell out of print, and her work was neglected for many years until feminist critics in the 1970s began a reevaluation of her career. Glaspell is often cited as an overlooked writer deserving of inclusion in the literary canon and exalted as "the first lady of American drama."

Charlotte Perkins Gilman (1860–1935)
Novelist, Short Story Author

 A short-story writer, novelist, and feminist activist, Charlotte Perkins Gilman is best known today for her much-anthologized and powerful, yet still disturbing, short story "The Yellow Wallpaper," which she based on her experiences as a wife and mother. Gilman would become an early feminist and outspoken women's rights advocate.

Born in Hartford, Connecticut, Gilman's father, Frederick Beecher Perkins, was the grandson of Lyman Beecher and the nephew of Harriet Beecher Stowe, and he abandoned his family shortly after Charlotte's birth. After home tutoring and a short stay at the Rhode Island School of Design, Gilman went to work designing greeting cards before marrying Charles Stetson, an artist, in 1884.

Suffering from postnatal depression after the birth of their daughter, Gilman was placed under the care of noted neurologist S. Weir Mitchell, who prescribed complete inactivity at home, denying her any stimulation from writing or drawing. To escape from this mental imprisonment, which aggravated her nervous breakdown, Gilman escaped with her daughter to California in 1887, after which she divorced her husband and lost custody of her child. To expose Mitchell's debilitating treatment, she wrote "The Yellow Wallpaper," which was published in 1892. In it, the narrator describes her growing delusions under the strict regime of her husband, ending either in her eventual liberation or total madness. The reader must decide. The story would be rediscovered by feminist scholars in the 1970s and proclaimed a masterpiece as one of the earliest, yet still one of the most effective, psychological dramatizations of the impact of a woman's subjugation under a patriarchal system of control and repression.

Gilman supported herself by lecturing, editing, and teaching while beginning to write the works that would gain her a reputation as one of the earliest feminist theorists and the leading intellectual in the women's movement in the United States at the turn of the century. These included *Women and Economics* (1898), which argued that women's economic dependence on men is harmful to all humanity, and *Concerning Children* (1900) and *The Home* (1904), which advocated for radical changes in the family and domestic work to liberate women for a more productive life. *Man-Made World* (1911) and *His Religion and Hers* (1923) supported a greater role for women in political and religious life to decrease conflict and improve public policy. Gilman also published novels, including *What Diana Did* (1910), *The Crux* (1911), and utopian novels offering feminist solutions to social problems *Moving the Mountain* (1911), *Herland* (1915), and *With Her in Ourland* (1916).

In 1900, she married her cousin George Houghton Gilman, and the couple lived happily in New York and Connecticut until his death in 1934. Gilman went to live with her daughter in California, where, ill with cancer and fearing that her productive life was over, she committed suicide in 1935.

Nikki Giovanni (1943–)
Poet

 One of America's foremost contemporary poets, Nikki Giovanni has been creating original and compelling poetry for nearly half a century. Her first collection, *Black Feeling Black Talk* (1968), grew out of her response to the assassinations of Martin Luther King Jr., Malcolm X, Medgar Evers, and Robert Kennedy as well as her perceived urgency to raise awareness about the plight and rights of black Americans. Subsequent collections have maintained Giovanni's focus on racial and gender inequality and the conflicts inherent in the American experience.

Giovanni was born Yolande Cornelia Giovanni Jr. in Knoxville, Tennessee, but was largely raised in a predominantly black suburb of Cincinnati, Ohio. She attributed her appreciation for African American culture and heritage from her grandmother, whose vernacular speech and storytelling would become an important legacy for Giovanni's career as a poet. Giovanni graduated from Nashville's Fisk University and did graduate work at the University of Pennsylvania and Columbia.

Giovanni achieved her initial fame as one of the leading authors of the Black Arts Movement, whose strong and often militant African American perspective caused her to be dubbed the "poet of the Black Power Revolution." Her first three collections, *Black Talk* (1968), *Black Judgement* (1968), and *Re: Creation* (1970), reflect themes of black power and consciousness. Later collections reflect her experiences as a single mother, and *Spin a Soft Black Song* (1971), *Ego-Tripping* (1973), and *Vacation Time* (1980) are collections of poems for children. *Those Who Ride the Night Winds* (1983) show her returning to political concerns, celebrating black American heroes and heroines. Later collections include *Blues: For All the Changes* (1999), *Quilting the Black-Eyed Pea* (2002), *Bicycles: Love Poems* (2009), and *Chasing Utopia: A Hybrid* (2013).

Gemini: An Extended Autobiographical Statement on My First Twenty-Five Years of Being a Black Poet (1971), nominated for the National Book Award, provides Giovanni's assessment of her life and career. Other nonfiction works include *Racism 101* (1994), dealing with the civil rights movement and its aftermath.

Named by Oprah Winfrey one of her "25 Living Legends," Giovanni has written, "Writing is … what I do to justify the air I breathe. I have been considered a writer who writes from rage and it confuses me. What else do writers write from? A poem has to say something. It has to make some sort of sense; be lyrical; to the point; and still able to be read by whatever reader is kind enough to pick up the book."

Sarah Josepha Hale (1788–1879)

Poet

It is Sarah Josepha Hale who is responsible for the one poem virtually everyone knows by heart: "Mary Had a Little Lamb" (1830). It is Hale as well who is principally responsible for

Thanksgiving becoming a national holiday. Other accomplishments of this remarkable woman include one of the first novels by either gender to take up the issue of slavery, the first female editor of an important national magazine, and a tireless activist for women's education and property rights.

Born Sarah Josepha Buell in Newport, New Hampshire, and self-educated, Hale read whatever books were available but complained that "few were written by Americans, and none by women," and she was determined at an early age "to promote the reputation of my own sex, and do something for my own country." She went to work as a schoolteacher at eighteen and, in 1813, married a young lawyer, David Hale. Raising five children, Sarah was encouraged by her husband in her writing, which appeared in local newspapers. David Hale died unexpectedly of pneumonia in 1822, leaving Sarah with five children to raise on her own. Concluding the existence of "very few employments in which females can engage with any hope of profit," she decided that literature was "my best resource." She found success placing poems and stories in leading periodicals that encouraged her to attempt a novel, *Northwood: A Tale of New England* (1827), set in the early years of the nation, which contrasted life in the North and in the South, attacking slavery, which she called "a stain on our national character."

The positive reception she received led to an offer to become the editor of a new magazine aimed at women (the first of its kind) called *Ladies' Magazine*. It would become the *American Ladies Magazine*, reflecting Hale's policy of publishing only original work by American writers, particularly female writers, and, finally, *Godey's Lady Book*, which became the most circulated magazine of the period. Hale served as editor and a principal contributor from 1837 until 1877, becoming one of the most influential women of the mid-nineteenth century, using her position to advance the cause of women's education and employment opportunities. Although she did not support women's suffrage, believing that women should not be involved in politics, she had no reservations about promoting women authors, and her most famous publication was *Woman's Record: or Sketches of All Distinguished Women, from the Creation to A.D. 1854*, which included one of the first biographical dictionaries devoted exclusively to American female writers. Many of the writers listed debuted in print in the magazine that Hale edited.

Lorraine Hansberry (1930–1965)
Playwright

The first African American woman to have a play produced on Broadway, Lorraine Hansberry is justly known as the foremother of African American drama, whose play, *A Raisin in the Sun*, has entered the canon of classic American family dramas of the twentieth century.

Hansberry was born in Chicago, the youngest of the four children of Carl Hansberry, a successful real estate agent. In 1938, her father purchased a home in a white neighborhood, an event that provoked racial tension in legally segregated Chicago and provided the genesis of *A Raisin in the Sun*. After an attack in which a brick was thrown through a window, narrowly missing the young Lorraine, the Hansberrys were evicted. With the help of the NAACP, the case went to the Supreme Court, which resulted in a decision that prohibited racially restricted real estate covenants. The Hansberrys would return to their home but, in the words of the future playwright, endured "a hellishly hostile white neighborhood."

Lorraine attended a mostly white high school, excelling in English and history and becoming president of the debating society. She went on to the University of Wisconsin for two years before moving to New York City, where she wrote for the *Young Progressives of America* magazine and worked on the staff of *Freedom,* a radical, black monthly published in Harlem. Hansberry wrote articles on women's rights, civil rights, the arts, African history, and politics. After marrying Robert Nemiroff, whom she met on a picket line at New York University, she began work on three plays, including *The Crystal Stairs*, begun in 1956, changing the title to *A Raisin in the Sun* in 1957. It would take a year and a half to get the play, featuring African American central characters by an unknown, African American, female playwright, produced. Eventually, funding was raised from African American cultural leaders such as Harry

Belafonte. An African American, Lloyd Richards, was hired as director, Sidney Poitier agreed to star, and *A Raisin in the Sun* debuted on Broadway on March 11, 1959.

Coming at a time in which racial segregation laws were being overturned and the modern civil rights movement was taking shape, *A Raisin in the Sun* was both groundbreaking and revelatory. It tells the story of the Younger family in the working-class South Side area of Chicago, who attempt to leave the ghetto for a home in the white suburbs. Tracing the trajectory of the American Dream and the brutal discrepancy between ideals and reality, *A Raisin in the Sun* is an intimate portrait of African American family life and the racial divide that operates in America. A critical and popular success, *A Raisin in the Sun* ran for nearly two years and earned its author the distinction of becoming the youngest playwright and the first black dramatist to win the New York Drama Critics Circle Award. Hansberry wrote the screenplay for the 1961 film version of her play.

Hansberry died in 1965, at the age of thirty-four, after a short battle with pancreatic cancer on the day her second play, *The Sign in Sidney Brustein's Window*, closed on Broadway. Robert Nemiroff has edited two collections of her work in *To Be Young, Gifted and Black* (1969) and *Les Blancs: The Collected Last Plays of Lorraine Hansberry* (1972). In a career so tragically cut short, Lorraine Hansberry has left an enduring mark on American literature and social history.

Elizabeth Hanson (1684–1737)
Memoirist

Elizabeth Hanson is the author of one of most frequently read and reprinted captivity narratives in colonial America, *God's Mercy Surmounting Man's Cruelty* (1728), an account of Hanson's capture and life among the Abenaki in 1725. In contrast to other captivity narratives, in particular Mary Rowlandson's *The Sovereignty & the Goodness of God* (1682), Hanson's account is distinguished by its literary style and polish.

A Quaker woman from Dover, New Hampshire, Hanson was seized and taken, along with her four children, in an Abenaki attack during the Drummer's War (1722–1725), fought along the border between Canada and New England. After five months in captivity, a French family ransomed two of her children. She was then reunited with her husband, who also managed to find another of their daughters; however, the oldest daughter remained in captivity until marriage to a Frenchman secured her escape. Hanson's husband died during a final attempt to retrieve his daughter.

Hanson's account of her experiences with the Abenaki was valued for the details she provided on Abenaki customs and daily life as well as for her devotional account of her Quaker faith, in which she attributed her survival not to her own resources but to God's mercy and leniency.

Lillian Hellman (1905–1984)

Playwright

One of the most powerful dramatic voices in American literature in the twentieth century, playwright, screenwriter, and memoirist Lillian Hellman was also known for her relentless and outspoken opposition to social and political injustice.

Hellman was born in New Orleans, where her father owned a shoe store on Canal Street until his partner made off with the store's funds and bankrupted him. The Hellmans and their five-year-old daughter made a fresh start in New York City, dividing their year between New York and New Orleans. Hellman studied at New York University and Columbia and began work as a publisher's reader, book reviewer, and theater publicist. In 1925, she married press agent Arthur Kober, and the couple moved to Paris, where Kober edited an English-language magazine. They divorced in 1932. Hellman was encouraged to write plays by her longtime companion, detective novelist and screenwriter Dashiell Hammett, whom she met in Hollywood while working as a scenario reader. While working as a play reader for a New York producer, Hellman began to write her first play, *The Children's House*, which had its Broadway debut in 1934. The play

concerns two women, who run a girls' school, whose lives are destroyed when a student publicly accuses them of lesbianism. The homoerotic subject matter caused the play to be banned in Boston, but it became a Broadway hit. A second play, *Days to Come,* about a strike in a small, Ohio town, closed after a week's run.

Her confidence shaken, Hellman abandoned playwriting for a time for screenwriting as well as dispatches from the Spanish Civil War, the beginning of Hellman's antifascist activities. Determined to recapture the success of her first play, Hellman chose for the subject of her third play a turn-of-the-century, southern family whose money is obtained through deceitful business practices and opportunism and whose lives are defined and ultimately dominated by acquisition and arrogance. The result was her masterpiece *The Little Foxes*, which opened on Broadway to commercial and critical success in 1939. Acknowledged as a classic of American drama, *The Little Foxes* is a taut, precisely crafted play depicting aspects of American life that were rarely depicted onstage before. In her depiction of the Hubbard family, Hellman "meant to be neither misanthropic nor cynical, merely truthful and realistic."

Throughout the 1940s and 1950s, Hellman increasingly wrote plays that reflected her political activism, including the antifascist works *Watch on the Rhine* (1941) and *The Searching Wind* (1944). *Another Part of the Forest* (1946) returns to the Hubbard family of *Little Foxes* but is set twenty years before the action of the first play. *Autumn Garden* (1951) draws on her family experiences, exploring the disappointments of women in middle age, and *Toys in the Attic* (1961) continues the story of the same women, exploring love that grows destructive. Blacklisted in the 1950s for her leftist activism, Hellman continued to write and speak out against injustice, turning from drama to memoirs dealing with her social, political, and artistic life. They include *An Unfinished Woman* (1969), *Pentimento* (1973), and *Scoundrel Time* (1976). All through a contentious life of both achievement and setbacks, Lillian Hellman was unapologetic and tireless in her passion for exposing the flaws in human nature and the crippling effects of society and politics on the individual.

Zora Neale Hurston (1891–1960)

Novelist, Short Story Author

An anthropologist, novelist, short-story writer, and essayist, Zora Neale Hurston was one of America's most influential African American writers. A central figure in the Harlem Renaissance of the 1920s and 1930s, Hurston recorded and incorporated black folk tales and traditions into her work, invigorating American literature with the power and expressiveness of the African American vernacular. A brash and opinionated woman, she produced a series of novels and folklore collections that significantly gave voice to segments of American society, most notably women and African Americans who had previously been silent or unheard.

Hurston was born in Eatonville, Florida, the first incorporated black community in the United States. Her father was the mayor of Eatonville and a Baptist preacher. The town's vibrant folk tradition and its frequent "lying" sessions of tall tales had a great impact on Hurston, who absorbed many of the stories told by her elders and eventually began to make up tales of her own. When her mother died and her father remarried, Hurston was passed about from boarding school to friends and relatives. At sixteen, she worked as a wardrobe girl for a traveling light opera troupe. Quitting the show in Baltimore, she went to work as a maid for a white woman, who arranged for Hurston to attend high school. From 1918 to 1924, Hurston studied part-time at Howard University in Washington, D.C., while working as a manicurist. She eventually studied anthropology at Barnard College while writing poems, plays, articles, and stories. After graduation, she went on to Columbia University to study with eminent cultural anthropologist Franz Boas. Hurston did field research first in Eatonville, collecting data that she would include in her folklore collections and novels, and later in Haiti and Jamaica.

Hurston's two important folklore collections are *Mules and Men* (1935) and *Tell My Horse* (1938). Her novels include *Jonah's Gourd Vine* (1934), *Their Eyes Were Watching God* (1937), *Moses, Man of the Mountain* (1939), and *Seraph on the Sewanee* (1948).

Her autobiography, *Dust Tracks on the Road*, was published in 1942.

Hurston's biographer, Robert Hemenway, captures her complexities and contradictions, calling her "flamboyant yet vulnerable, self-centered yet kind, a Republican conservative and an early black nationalist." African American critics complained that the folk elements in her works were demeaning and one-dimensional, and few during Hurston's lifetime credited her work as a major source of vernacular strength and lyrical power. Convinced of the vitality and promise of the African American community—no doubt influenced by her experience in Eatonville—Hurston opposed legislation that forced integration, and her stand alienated her from other African Americans, who pushed for assimilation into mainstream white culture. Her advocacy of the strength and vibrancy of black culture predated the black power and cultural movements that began in the 1960s.

During Hurston's later years, her works were neglected, and she lived in extreme poverty, working for a time as a maid, librarian, and newspaper columnist. At her death in 1960, she was buried in an unmarked grave in a cemetery in Fort Pierce, Florida, until writer Alice Walker, who was instrumental in restoring Hurston's reputation, had a headstone erected. Today, Hurston is acknowledged as one of the most important African American writers of the twentieth century. Her masterpiece *Their Eyes Were Watching God* has been described by Hemenway "as one of the most poetic works of fiction by a black writer in the first half of the twentieth century, and one of the most revealing treatments in modern literature of a woman's quest for a satisfying life."

Helen Hunt Jackson (1830–1885)

Novelist, Poet

The author of five collections of poetry, Helen Hunt Jackson is mainly remembered for her activism on behalf of Native American rights in two important and influential works, the history of exposing government mistreatment titled *A Century*

of Dishonor (1881) and the popular fictional account of the plight of southern California's dispossessed Mission Indians, *Ramona* (1884).

Born Helen Maria Fiske in Amherst, Massachusetts, where she was a classmate and lifelong friend of Emily Dickinson, Jackson married Edward Hunt, a U.S. Army captain, in 1852. After both of their two sons died and her husband was killed in a nautical accident, Jackson began writing poetry reflecting her loss and sorrow in magazines beginning in 1866, then publishing collections, including *Verses* (1870) and *Easter Bells* (1884). She published novels, children's books, and travel books, usually anonymously, with the pseudonym "H. H." Frequently in ill health, she moved to Colorado on her doctor's recommendation, marrying banker and railroad executive William Sharpless Jackson there in 1875.

In 1879, Jackson attended a reception in Boston of representatives of two tribes who were touring the East to gain public support in their fight against confiscations of tribal lands by the U.S. government. Jackson, who had never previously taken any interest in reform movements, set out to write the well-researched *A Century of Dishonor* and, with Abbot Kinney, the government-commissioned *Report on the Conditions and Needs of the Mission Indians* (1883). Disappointed that her nonfiction writings failed to provoke the reforms she desired, Jackson, no doubt inspired by the example of Harriet Beecher Stowe's *Uncle Tom's Cabin*, decided to write a novel "in which will be set forth some Indian experiences in a way to move people's hearts."

Set in southern California shortly after the Mexican–American War, *Ramona* dramatizes the racial discrimination and hardships of a mixed-race Irish Native American orphan girl, who falls in love with Alessandro, a Mission Indian. When they elope, the prejudice they experience drives Alessandro mad, and he dies. Despite the novel's popular and critical success, *Ramona* fell short of what Jackson intended. Although she set out "to move people's hearts" in support of Native American rights, much of the immense popularity of the novel stemmed from the book's romance and its exotic depiction of colonial California life under Spanish and Mexican rule.

Jackson lived for just a year after *Ramona* was published. Her work and career have served as an example for later writers committed to social reform in their works.

Shirley Jackson (1916–1965)
Short Story Author

One of the pioneering and trailblazing writers of psychological suspense, the supernatural, and horror, Shirley Jackson has haunted countless readers with her most famous story, "The Lottery." Known best for this single work, Jackson, who produced six novels, two memoirs, and over two hundred short stories during her two-decade writing career, deserves more credit and critical attention, according to critic Elaine Showalter, who has described Jackson's work as the single most important mid-twentieth-century body of literary output yet to have its value reevaluated by critics.

Born in San Francisco, Jackson began writing poetry and short stories as a young teenager. She entered Syracuse University in 1937, where she published her first short story, "Janice," and became the fiction editor of the campus humor magazine. At Syracuse, Jackson met her future husband, Stanley Edgar Hyman, and, after their graduation in 1940, the couple moved to New York City's Greenwich Village and created a literary magazine, *Spectre*. While working odd jobs, Jackson wrote the initial stories that began to be published in *The New Republic* and *The New Yorker* while giving birth to the first of the couple's four children. When Hyman was offered a teaching position at Vermont's Bennington College, they moved into an old house in North Bennington, where Jackson completed her first novel, *The Road through the Wall* (1948), the same year that *The New Yorker* published her iconic story "The Lottery," her chilling tale of a rural community's sacrificial ritual, which prompted widespread public outrage and the largest volume of mail ever received by the magazine. "The Lottery" has been translated into most of the world's languages and is possibly the best-known short story of the twentieth century. Her novels, such as *The Haunting of Hill House* (1959), widely regarded as the best ghost story ever written, and *We Have Always Lived in the Castle* (1962) as well as her short fiction established her as a master of gothic horror and psychological suspense. Much of her work displays supernatural elements and horror against a backdrop of ordinary life and unexceptional characters. At the age of forty-eight, Jackson died unexpectedly of heart failure.

Although recognized for her contribution to the fictional subgenres of fantasy, horror, and the psychological thriller, wider recognition for Jackson's work has been slow, and she has been regarded mainly as a skilled practitioner of horror stories. A more recent biography and critical reappraisal, *A Rather Haunted Life* (2016) by Ruth Franklin, set out to challenge that consensus by arguing that Jackson should be read not only as a major figure in the American gothic tradition (with links to Hawthorne, Poe, and James) but also as a significant protofeminist chronicler of mid-twentieth-century women's lives. In Franklin's view, Jackson used supernatural elements not to cater to popular taste but "to plumb the depths of the human condition" and particularly to explore the "psychic damage to which women are especially prone." As Franklin shows, the motif of the isolated woman needing to escape a miserable family or a claustrophobic community recurs again and again in Jackson's work. Beneath the surface of Jackson's stories is the tension she herself felt between her role as wife and homemaker and her vocation as a writer in which her work and her life, in Franklin's view, "constitutes nothing less than the secret history of American women of her era."

Gish Jen (1955–)
Novelist, Short Story Author

In 2000, when asked to name his successor in the twenty-first century, author John Updike chose Gish Jen. In 2012, writer Junot Diaz called Jen "the great American novelist we have always been hearing about." She has, in a series of cross-cultural works exploring lives both in America and China, become one of the most dominant contemporary figures in articulating a multicultural identity.

Born Lilian Jen in New York City to Chinese immigrant parents from Shanghai, Jen grew up in Yonkers and Scarsdale, New York, adopting the name Gish in high school after the actress Lillian Gish. She graduated from Harvard in 1977, majoring in English. After studying business briefly at Stanford, Jen took a position teaching English in Shandong, China, before completing an MFA at the Writer's Workshop of the University of Iowa in 1983. Jen subsequently married David O'Connor, moving with him to Silicon Valley in California where he worked. Relocating to Cambridge, Massachusetts, in 1985, Jen failed to find a secretarial job at Harvard but was awarded a fellowship at Radcliffe's Bunting Institute that allowed her to begin her first novel.

Typical American was published in 1991, describing Chinese immigrants who pursue the American Dream while struggling with assimilation. In it, and in subsequent books, Jen explores the nature of American identity from an Asian perspective. Her second novel, *Mona in the Promised Land* (1996), describes a Chinese American adolescent who converts to Judaism. Her third novel, *The Love Wife* (2004), considers a multiethnic family, including Asians, Asian Americans, and white Americans. *World and Town* (2010) explores American life post-9/11. *Who's Irish?* (1999) collects short stories that have earned Jen acclaim as a master of the story form.

Issues of culture, race, and gender that are at the center of Jen's fiction are also explored in her nonfiction books, which include *Tiger Writing: Art, Culture, and the Interdependent Self* (2013) and *The Girl at the Baggage Claim: Explaining the East–West Culture Gap* (2017). The subtitle of the *The Girl at the Baggage Claim* can stand as a fitting descriptor of Jen's overall intention in her work: to bridge gaps in our collective identity in search of viable synthesis for our pluralistic society and increasingly globalist consciousness.

Sarah Orne Jewett (1849–1909)
Novelist, Short Story Author, Poet

A short-story writer, novelist, and poet, Jewett was one of the leading figures in the post-Civil War local color movement that would contribute to the development of American literary realism. She is commonly regarded as the most distinguished American regional writers of the nineteenth century.

Sarah Orne Jewett was born and lived most of her life in South Berwick, Maine, the daughter of a physician who encouraged her close observation of nature and people and frequently accompanied her father on his rounds of local fishermen and farmers. She graduated from Berwick Academy in 1865 and published her first stories at the age of nineteen, inspired, at least in part, by Harriet Beecher Stowe's *Pearl of Orr Island* (1862), which demonstrated for her the literary uses with which the Maine landscape and customs could be put. A short story, "Mr. Bruce," was accepted by the prestigious *Atlantic Monthly*, which earned Jewett the praise of its editor, the dean of American realism, William Dean Howell, for her "uncommon feeling for talk," in which he told her, "I hear your people."

Jewett's reputation rests on the books she published from 1885 to 1896, including the collections of stories *A White Heron* (1886), *The King of Folly Island* (1888), *Strangers and Wayfarers* (1890), *A Nature of Winby* (1893), *The Life of Nancy* (1895), and what is generally regarded as her best book, *The Country of the Pointed Firs* (1896). All show Jewett's skill in capturing natural and domestic detail with precision and insights that raise local color and regional subjects into often profound and moving universal themes. Jewett's artistry would earn praise from Henry James and Willa Cather, who would credit Jewett as a major influence in her own writing career.

A carriage accident in 1902 effectively ended Jewett's writing career, and she died in her South Berwick home from a stroke in 1909. Her contribution to American literature is considerable, showing later writers, both male and female, how much can be gained from a close and sensitive study of the people and places that are closest to hand. Jewett would demonstrate that American scenes and characters could serve for important literary purposes.

Jamaica Kincaid (1949–)

Novelist, Short Story Author

A novelist, short-story writer, and essayist, Jamaica Kincaid's rich and provocative literary work draws on her dual perspective of her native Antigua and her life in America. Both shed light on the other in poetically imagined and challenging explorations of cultural "belonging."

Born Elaine Potter Richardson in St. John's, Antigua, Kincaid moved to New York City when she was sixteen, working as an au pair. She won a photography scholarship to attend Franconia College in New Hampshire but returned to New York after two years. In 1973, she took the name Jamaica Kincaid and, the following year, began regularly submitting articles to *The New Yorker*, where she became a staff writer in 1976. In 1979, she married composer Allen Shawn, the son of longtime *New Yorker* editor William Shawn and the brother of actor Wallace Shawn.

Kincaid's first book, *At the Bottom of the River*, a collection of short stories and essays published in 1983, mixed lyrical reflections on her Caribbean background with often bitter and angry indictments of colonial oppression and racial conflict. The autobiographical novels *Annie John* (1984) and *Lucy* (1990) followed. Her long essay, *A Small Place* (1988), a full-frontal attack on the colonial despoilation of Antigua, was rejected by *The New Yorker* for its angry tone, but it later appeared in book form. Central themes of family relationships, identity, and colonialism inform *The Autobiography of My Mother* (1996), and *My Brother* (1997) is a searing account of her younger brother's death from AIDS.

Weaving together elements of autobiography, magical realism, and polemical attacks on oppression in all its aspects, Kincaid's writing has been described as "fearless" and was praised by Susan Sontag for its "emotional truthfulness." As critic Fernanda Eberstadt has observed, "Kincaid's force and originality lie in her refusal to curb her tongue, in an insistence on home truths that spare herself least of all."

Maxine Hong Kingston (1940–)

Memoirist, Novelist

A memoirist and novelist, Maxine Hong Kingston's *The Woman Warrior* (1976) is one of the singular achievements in modern American literature. It was the first work by an Asian American writer to gain widespread popularity and critical acclaim, revolutionizing accepted literary forms, creating a new genre that has been called "the creative memoir" or creative nonfiction, and pioneering an ongoing and important exploration of the American experience from personal, ethnic, cultural, and gender perspectives. It has been followed by other works of both technical daring and vivid authenticity that have elevated Kingston into the highest rank of American writers.

The oldest of the six American-born children of Chinese immigrants, Kingston was born in Stockton, California. His father, trained in China as a scholar and teacher, first worked in America as a laborer, saving enough to invest in a laundry in New York's Chinatown. Her mother, separated from her husband for fifteen years in China, worked as a physician before joining her husband in 1939 in California, where he managed an illegal gambling house. During World War II, they opened a laundry, where Maxine and her siblings were put to work as soon as they were old enough to help. Speaking only Chinese until she started school, Kingston eventually excelled as a student, publishing her first essay, "I Am an American," in *American Girl* in 1955 while still in high school. Attending the University of California–Berkeley on a scholarship, she married fellow student Earll Kingston and worked for five years teaching English and mathematics at a California high school. Disillusioned with 1960s drug culture and the ineffectiveness of the protest movement against the Vietnam War, the couple and their young son left California in 1967, bound for Japan. Stopping off in Hawaii, they would remain there for the next seventeen years with Kingston teaching at several high schools and business and technical colleges as she began work on her first book.

The Woman Warrior was originally intended to be combined with the stories that eventually made up *China Men* (1980) to form "one big book" exploring identity formation and cultural conflict faced by Chinese Americans, based on Kingston's family history and experiences. Avoiding the restrictions of standard autobiographies, which she identified as dealing with "exterior things" or "big historical events that you publicly participated in," Kingston focused instead on what she called "real stories,"

narratives mixing facts and the imagination, dramatizing "the rich, personal inner life." The result brought attention to one of the first Asian American experiences written from a radically new, poetic, and luminous method that would be widely imitated by future memoirists and writers of creative nonfiction. Kingston would continue to explore central issues of race, gender, and politics in such works as *Tripmaster Monkey: His Fake Book* (1989), *To Be a Poet* (2002), *The Fifth Book of Peace* (2003), *Veterans of War, Veterans of Peace* (2006), and *I Love a Broad Margin to My Life* (2011).

Jhumpa Lahiri (1967–)
Novelist, Short Story Author

 One of the most acclaimed and honored of contemporary writers, Lahiri specializes in the American immigrant experience, particularly among those from East India, while uncovering universal themes that have resonated with a wide and diverse readership.

Lahiri was born Nilanjana Sudheshna Lahiri in London to Bengali parents who emigrated from Calcutta. When Lahiri was a small child, her father, a university librarian, relocated the family to the United States for work, and they eventually settled in South Kingstown, Rhode Island. Her family nickname, Jhumpa, was used by her teachers, who found it easier to pronounce than her actual first name. Lahiri has observed that during her school years, she "felt intense pressure to be two things, loyal to the old world and fluent in the new." Lahiri attended Barnard College before earning three master's degrees (in literature, creative writing, and comparative literature) and her doctorate in Renaissance studies at Boston University in 1997. A two-year fellowship at Provincetown's Fine Arts Work Center followed.

Her early short stories were rejected, as she recalls, "for years" until her debut collection, *Interpreter of Maladies*, was published in 1999. Its stories about the assimilation and relationship challenges of Indians and Indian immigrants received the Pulitzer Prize for Fiction (only the seventh time a story collection had won the award). In 2003, Lahiri published her first novel, *The Namesake*, about the cultural clash between Indian parents and their Americanized son and daughter. A second story collection, *Unaccustomed Earth*, appeared in 2008, debuting at number one on *The New York Times* best-seller list. A second novel, *The Lowland*, was published in 2013, short-listed for the Man Booker Prize and a finalist for the National Book Award for Fiction.

Recognized as a master craftsperson, Lahiri is renowned for both the subtlety of her construction and the emotional power she generates from closely observed details of life.

Emma Lazarus (1849–1887)

Poet

 A poet best known for her 1883 sonnet "The New Colossus," with its famous lines "Give me your tired, your poor, / Your huddled masses yearning to be free," which is inscribed on the pedestal of the Statue of Liberty, Lazarus is an example of a writer transformed by a cause and a consciousness driven by her awakened sense of her own Jewish identity, which made her one of the first prominent and successful writers to explore the struggles of Jews in America.

Born in New York City into a wealthy family, Lazarus was educated at home by private tutors. Her first book of verse, *Poems and Translations* (1867), was published while she was still a teenager. A second volume of poetry, *Admetus and Other Poems*, followed in 1871, along with a novel, *Alide: An Episode in Goethe's Life*, in 1874; a verse drama, *The Spagnoletto*, in 1876; and a translation of Heinrich Heine's poems in 1881. As precocious and talented as these works were, attracting attention and praise from Ralph Waldo Emerson and others, Lazarus's early verse is conventionally romantic. It was only after a reawakening of her Jewish identity that Lazarus's work assumed the focus and passion that helped establish her as more than a prodigy and dilettante and allowed her to produce works that have been admired for their passionate advocacy of the dispossessed and persecuted.

The initial stimulus in exploring her own Jewish heritage came after reading George Eliot's *Daniel Deronda* (1876) with its central theme of Jewish identity and the prejudice to which Jews were exposed. After the Russian pogroms of 1881 that followed the assassination of Tsar Alexander II, who killed or displaced thousands of Jews, many of whom immigrated to New York, Lazarus took up their cause. Lazarus helped to establish the Hebrew Technical Institute in New York to provide vocational training to assist Jewish immigrants to become self-supporting. She founded the Society for the Improvement and Colonization of East European Jews, a forerunner organization of the Zionist movement in which Lazarus promoted the creation of a Jewish state thirteen years before Theodor Herzl.

In 1882, she published *Songs of a Semite*, which announced her arrival as a distinctive Jewish American writer in such important poems as "The Crowning of the Red Cock"; "The Banner of the Jew"; "Dance to Death," a verse drama, which is considered her best work; and *By the Waters of Babylon*, a poetic sequence published in 1887. Her collected poems were published in 1889.

Her most famous poem, "The New Colossus," was written in 1883 to raise money to construct the pedestal for the Statue of Liberty. Her poem was praised for giving the statue, a gift from France, a spirited purpose, but it was not mentioned in the dedication ceremony in 1886 and did not appear in her *New York Times* obituary after she died a year later from cancer at the age of thirty-eight. It was only in 1903 that her words, which embodied the American vision of liberty, were cast in bronze and affixed to the statue.

Harper Lee (1926–2016)

Novelist

 Harper Lee has the distinction among American novelists of having written, arguably, the most popular twentieth-century novel, *To Kill a Mockingbird* (1960). A 1991 survey by the Library of Congress found that the novel was rated behind only the Bible for books that are "most often cited as making a difference." As recently as 2018, *To Kill a Mockingbird* topped PBS's Great American Read survey of the United States's best-loved novel. This is a singular achievement for a first novel from an unknown Alabama novelist, which was, until a year before the author's death more than fifty years later, her only published book. As historian Joseph Crespino has observed, "In the twentieth century, *To Kill a Mockingbird* is probably the most widely read book dealing with race in America, and its protagonist, Atticus Finch, the most enduring fictional image of racial heroism."

Nelle Harper Lee was born in Monroeville, Alabama, the youngest of the four children of Frances Cunningham (Finch) and Amasa Coleman Lee, a former newspaper editor who practiced law and served in the Alabama State Legislature. After graduating from Monroe County High School, Lee attended Huntingdon College in Montgomery and the University of Alabama in Tuscaloosa, where she studied law and wrote for the university newspaper. In 1949, Lee moved to New York City, working as an airline reservation agent, while writing fiction in her spare time. A gift of a year's wages allowed her to write full time, and in 1957, Lee delivered the manuscript of *Go Set a Watchman* to her agent, who elicited a positive response from an editor at J. B. Lippincott. Lee was encouraged to revise what the editor described as "more a series of anecdotes than a fully conceived story." Multiple drafts followed for the next two years, and *To Kill a Mockingbird* emerged by 1960, becoming an immediate best-seller and being awarded the Pulitzer Prize for Fiction. "I never expected any sort of success with *Mockingbird*," Lee recalled. "I was hoping for a quick and merciful death at the hands of the reviewers, but at the same time I sort of hoped someone would like it enough to give me encouragement."

Set in a small Alabama town in the 1930s, *To Kill a Mockingbird* draws extensively on Lee's own childhood experiences with Lee the model for the six-year-old tomboy scout, the narrator, and her family, particularly her lawyer father, who becomes the moral center of the book, Atticus Finch, who unsuccessfully defends an African American who is charged with assaulting a white woman. The power of the novel comes from Lee's gripping evocation of

Depression-era southern life with its combination of graciousness and nostalgia for the past and the effects of racial prejudice and violence that corrode a community.

From the time of its publication until her death in 2016, Lee granted few interview requests and made even fewer public appearances, living quietly in Monroeville. Except for a few short essays, she published nothing until 2015, when *Go Set a Watchman*, the continuation of the Finch family story (but actually not so much a sequel as Lee's initial version of what would become *To Kill a Mockingbird*), came out. The fact that Lee, in declining health, would finally agree to publish the book after so many years and formerly adamant opposition raised questions about whether she had been manipulated to do so. Even more controversial was the portrait of Atticus Finch, who is shown, in the words of reviewer Michiko Kakutani, "affiliating with raving anti-integration, anti-black crazies." In many ways, the reaction that greeted *Go Set a Watchman* underscores the protectiveness that readers have for a beloved classic and its indelible impact on generations of readers for whom *To Kill a Mockingbird* is both a moral touchstone and near-sacred text.

Lois Lowry (1937–)

Novelist

The winner of two Newbery Medals for *Number of Stars* (1990) and *The Giver* (1994), Lois Lowry, author of more than forty-five children's books, is a pioneering writer who has explored difficult topics such as racism, suicide, murder, and the Holocaust, which have rarely been explored in works for young readers.

Lowry was born Lois Ann Hamersberg in Honolulu, Hawaii. Her father was a career military officer, an Army dentist, and she was the middle of three children. Following World War II, the family moved to Tokyo, where her father was stationed from 1949 to 1950. Lowry went through junior high school in a special school for military families and then back to the United States for high school.

She attended Pembroke College in Brown University for two years before her marriage, at the age of nineteen, to U.S. Navy officer Donald Grey Lowry, living in California, Connecticut, Florida, South Carolina, and finally Cambridge, Massachusetts, where Donald attended Harvard Law School before finally moving his family of four children to Portland, Maine.

As her children grew up, Lowry completed her bachelor's degree while developing a passion for photography, taking pictures to accompany the articles she began to submit as a freelance journalist. An editor encouraged her to write a children's book, which resulted in *A Summer to Die* (1977), her first book, published when she was forty. Best-selling and critically acclaimed works followed, including the Anastasia Krupnik, Tate family, and Gooney Bird series of novels. Her most popular and controversial books are the Giver Quartet—*The Giver* (1993), *Gathering Blue* (2000), *Messenger* (2004), and *Son* (2012), her chronicle of a futuristic society whose theme of questioning authority has led some schools in America to assign her books while others have prohibited their inclusion in classroom studies.

As Lowry has stated about her long and distinguished career, "My books have varied in content and style. Yet it seems to me that all of them deal, essentially, with the same general theme: the importance of human connections ... the vital need for humans to be aware of their interdependence, not only with each other, but with the world and its environment."

Edna St. Vincent Millay (1892–1950)

Poet

Nancy Milford, in her 2001 biography of Edna St. Vincent Millay, *Savage Beauty*, celebrated the famous poet of the Jazz Age as "the herald of the New Woman," who produced the lines that would become the "anthem of her generation":

My candle burns at both ends:
It will not last the night;
But ah, my foes, and oh, my friends—
It gives a lovely light!

Ephemeral and damaged, Millay would become one of the most famous chroniclers of the Roaring Twenties with its collapse and inevitable hangover in poems and plays with both a technical sophistication and an unsparing honesty. As critic Carl Van Doren asserted, "Not since Sappho" had a woman "written as outspokenly as Millay."

Born and raised in the coastal Maine town of Rockland, Millay (whose middle name comes from the hospital in New York where her uncle's life had been saved shortly before her birth) was encouraged in her literary interests and her independence by her family. By the age of fifteen, Millay had published her first poem in the popular children's magazine *St. Nicholas* and the anthology *Current Literature*. After graduating from Vassar College in 1917 and publishing her first collection, *Renascence: and Other Poems*, she moved to Greenwich Village, where she described her life as "very, very poor and very, very merry." She acted with the Provincetown Players, who produced some of her plays, and in 1924 founded the Cherry Lane Theater "to continue the staging of experimental drama."

Millay moved beyond the avant-garde with the publication of *A Few Figs from Thistles* (1920), which moved beyond the romantic lyricism of her first collection to embody the cynical irony perfectly matched to the post-World War I mood. In 1923, she won the Pulitzer Prize for Poetry for *The Harp-Weaver and Other Poems*, the same year she married businessman Eugen Boissevain. The couple purchased a farm in upstate Austerlitz, New York, which inspired some of Millay's finest work, including *Three Plays* (1926); *The King's Henchman* (1927); *The Buck in the Snow and Other Poems* (1928); *Fatal Interview* (1931), a sonnet sequence; *Wine from These Grapes* (1934); *Conversation at Midnight* (1937); *Huntsman, What Quarry?* (1939); and *Make Bright the Arrows* (1940). Her later work reflects a darkening of her view, reflecting the political turmoil of the time. Her *Collected Lyrics* appeared in 1941, and *Collected Poems* appeared after her death in 1956.

The great English writer Thomas Hardy once said that America had two great attractions: the skyscraper and the poetry of Edna St. Vincent Millay. Even if less read today than in the past, rediscovery justifies the effort even if only to capture with a rare intimacy and artistry a significant era in American literary history in the first half of the twentieth century.

Marianne Moore (1887–1972)

Poet

Marianne Moore is the greatest American female modernist poet of the twentieth century. Frequently included in the exclusive group of such modernist American poets as T. S. Eliot, William Carlos Williams, Wallace Stevens, and Ezra Pound, Moore's poetry was marked by a precision of language and an acute observation and celebration of nature and humanity. Her poetry often contrasts with the brilliant but ironic, cerebral stance of other modernists in being both accessible and of the highest technical caliber and innovation. Moore became one of modern literature's great exceptions: a poetical virtuoso who could also command a large, diverse readership.

Born near St. Louis, Moore spent most of her first twenty years in Carlisle, Pennsylvania. Attending Bryn Mawr, she published her first poems in campus literary magazines. The poet H. D. (Hilda Doolittle) was one of her classmates, who, after Moore graduated and taught for a time at the Carlisle Indian school, helped select and arrange her first collection, *Poems* (1921). A second collection, *Observations* (1924), began to display Moore's characteristic work in free verse; longer poems such as "Marriage" and "An Octopus"; and syllabic verse, highlighting the natural rhythm of speech and intricate pattern of rhymes.

Moore served as the editor of the influential literary magazine *Dial* from 1925 to 1929 and published *Selected Poems* in 1935, followed by *The Pangolin and Other Verse* (1936); *What Are Years* (1941); and *Nevertheless* (1944), which included the antiwar poem "In Distrust of Merits" that W. H. Auden considered one of the best poems to come out of World War II. Her *Collected Poems* (1951) won both the Pulitzer Prize and National Book Award, and in 1953, she received the prestigious Bollingen Prize. *The Complete Poems of Marianne Moore* appeared in 1967 and was reissued in 1981.

Through her long, productive career, Moore produced works that displayed both the specific and the universal, displaying the capacity of containing in language all the vitality and mystery of both the ordinary and the extraordinary all around us.

Toni Morrison (1931-2019)

Novelist

When novelist, essayist, editor, and teacher Toni Morrison was awarded the 1993 Nobel Prize in Literature, she became the first African American, and only the second American woman (after Pearl S. Buck), to be so honored. It was a remarkable achievement for a writer who did not publish her first book until she was thirty-nine. Her reputation today is secure as one of the most important American fiction writers, whose works dominate any listing of the most important achievements in the second half of the twentieth century and beyond.

Morrison was born Chloe Anthony Wolford in Lorain, Ohio, a child of the Great Depression. Her grandparents had been sharecroppers in the South, and their stories of the racial violence they faced made a strong impression on her as a young girl. In 1949, Morrison entered Howard University, where she majored in English and the classics and began to call herself Toni. After earning a master's degree from Cornell University in 1953, she began teaching, first at Texas Southern University in Houston and later at Howard. In 1958, she married Harold Morrison, a Jamaican architect, and they had two children.

After Morrison's marriage ended in divorce in 1965, she moved with her two children to New York City to become a senior editor at Random House and, to cope with the breakup of her marriage, she turned to writing. Morrison published her first novel, *The Bluest Eye*, in 1970. Her second, *Sula* (1975), was partly composed during her daily commute to work. Both works were praised for their poetic prose, emotional intensity, and original interpretation of the African American experience from the female perspective. Her third novel, *Song of Solomon* (1977), won the National Book Critics Award and allowed

Morrison to devote herself full time to her writing career. A string of powerful novels followed, including the Pulitzer Prize-winning *Beloved* (1987), widely considered her masterpiece and one of the most humanly compelling explorations of the psychic cost and legacy of slavery ever written. "In *Beloved*," Morrison stated, "I wanted to look at the ways in which slavery affected women specifically, particularly the ways in which a slave woman could be a mother." In subsequent works, such as *Jazz* (1992), *Paradise* (1997), *Love* (2003), *A Mercy* (2008), *Home* (2012), and *God Help the Child* (2015), Morrison accomplished the rare feat of producing works of dazzling and original poetic and narrative virtuosity and clear-eyed, challenging explorations of race and gender in American society that have appealed to a wide, popular audience. Devoted to the process of "re-membering," that is, restoring the physical and emotional realities of American history, Morrison's works serve as a kind of interior, heartfelt repossession of the American past and the nation's struggle for self-definition and liberation.

Sarah Wentworth Apthorp Morton (1759–1846)

Novelist

Although unread today, Sarah Wentworth Apthorp Morton was in her time the foremost American female poet in the years immediately following the American Revolution. Her work celebrated the achievement and spirit of independence of the new nation, but she also found herself at the center of a notorious scandal and family tragedy that would inspire the very first American novel.

Morton was born in Boston to a well-to-do merchant family that provided her with a classical education. In 1781, she married Boston lawyer and politician Perez Morton, who would serve as speaker of the Massachusetts House of Representatives and Massachusetts attorney general. When Sarah's sister Fanny came to live with the family in the mid-1780s, she had an affair with Sarah's husband, giving birth to his child in 1787. Once the affair became public,

Fanny committed suicide. The scandal provided the basis for the publication of the first American novel, *The Power of Sympathy Or, the Triumph of Nature* (1789) by William Hill Brown, a Boston neighbor of the Mortons. Sarah would later reconcile with her husband; they continued to live together, and Perez Morton continued his distinguished political career.

Although she never dealt with the scandal in her works, the pain it caused may have been the determining factor in her decision to become a serious poet as compensation for her distress. Her first published poem, "Invocation to Hope," was published soon after the scandal under the pseudonym Constantina, but she later changed her pen name to Philenia, the name she used for her most famous works. They include *Ouabi, or the Virtues of Nature: An Indian Tale in Four Cantos* (1790), a long, book-length poem that was one of the first to use Native American themes in American poetry; "The African Chief" (1792), which describes a slave's decision to die in order to escape his enslavement, was frequently reprinted and recited by later abolitionists; and *Beacon Hill, a Local Poem, Historic and Descriptive* (1797), which dramatizes the Battle of Bunker Hill, the siege of Boston, and the Declaration of Independence, celebrating the spirit of sacrifice and the founding principles of the new nation. A companion volume, *The Virtues of Society, a Tale Founded on Fact* (1799), dedicated to Abigail Adams, esteemed the principles of American freedom, compassion, and justice. The power of Morton's emotional and moral vision earned the praise of her contemporaries, who honored her with the title of the American Sappho.

Judith Sargent Murray (1751–1820)

Essayist, Playwright, Poet

An essayist, playwright, poet, and advocate of women's rights, Murray was one of the first American proponents of women's intellectual capabilities and need for economic independence. Her essay, "On the Equality of the Sexes," written in 1779 but not published until 1790, predated Mary Wollstonecraft's *Vindication of the Rights of Woman* (1792), generally regarded as the foundational document of women's movements in the United States and Great Britain. Over a long literary career, Murray published essays, poems, and drama, which established her reputation as one of the leading intellectuals of her day.

Murray was born in Gloucester, Massachusetts, into a wealthy, ship-owning family. Educated at home by her brother's tutor, who was preparing him for Harvard, Murray had the run of the family's library, where she read history, philosophy, geography, and literature. At eighteen, Murray married a ship captain and supported American independence during the Revolution, despite the considerable family economic ties to Britain. She began to publish her first poems and essays in the 1780s.

Her principal work, "On the Equality of the Sexes," is a description of women's involvement in history and literature, tracing women's contribution to public events throughout world history. She argues against any limitations of women's roles based on the notion that women are not mentally equal to men, asserts that women's presumed intellectual inferiority is a result of culture, not nature, and urges that women should be allowed to develop and express their considerable imaginative and intellectual capabilities. In her later writing, Murray adopted male pen names because she wanted readers to consider her ideas seriously and not dismiss them as coming from a woman. In 1798, she published a three-volume collection of essays and plays, *The Gleaner*, which helped to establish her reputation as a leading author and intellectual. Murray's extensive collection of letters, twenty volumes in all, were discovered in 1984, and they constitute one of the few surviving collections of writing by women during a crucial period of American history from the Revolution through the early history of the republic.

Marsha Norman (1947–)

Playwright, Screenwriter

A playwright, screenwriter, and novelist who was awarded the 1983 Pulitzer Prize for Drama for her play *'night, Mother*, Marsha Norman has been an important presence in American theater for more than three decades.

Born in Louisville, Kentucky, Norman received her bachelor's degree from Agnes Scott College in Georgia and a master's degree from the University of Louisville. She worked as a journalist for *The Louisville Times*, as a writer for Kentucky Educational Television, as a teacher at elementary schools in Louisville, and with young children and adolescents in mental hospitals and mental institutions.

One of her students whom she met working at Kentucky's Central State Hospital would inspire her first play, *Getting Out* (1977), about a young woman attempting to escape a life of prostitution. It was first produced at the Actors Theatre of Louisville before transferring to off-Broadway in 1979. Her first full-length play, *Circus Valentine* (1978), treats a traveling circus and its star attraction, Siamese twins. Her next play, *'night, Mother*, dealing frankly with suicide, brought Norman great acclaim. Her next play, *Traveler in the Dark* (1984), was a critical failure, and Norman shifted her focus to screen work, writing the 1986 movie adaptation of *'night, Mother*. She won a Peabody Award for her writing for the HBO television series *In Treatment*. She successfully returned to the stage, winning the 1992 Tony Award and a Drama Desk Award for her book of the Broadway musical *The Secret Garden*. She also wrote the book for the Broadway musical *The Color Purple* (2005), for which she received a Tony nomination. Additional plays include *Trudy Blue* (1999) and *The Master Butchers Singing Club* (2010). Her *Collected Plays* appeared in 1996 with instructive introductions and essays on playwriting. Norman has been, since 1994, a faculty member and cochair of the playwriting department at New York's Juilliard School.

A committed advocate on behalf of neglected women's voices and experiences, Norman has written, "We have to hear the stories of women at all ages of their lives in order to really present a picture of what it felt like to be alive in our time. That's what our job is as writers is to present that and create it. Our job as writers isn't to make as much money as we can. Our job is to create a record of this time. That's why if you leave out women and the stories of women, we failed at our mission. All of us. Men and women."

Lynn Nottage (1964–)

Playwright

 The first and, so far, only American woman to have won the Pulitzer Prize for Drama twice, Lynn Nottage has built her career on dramatizing the lives of individuals adrift and marginalized in society, whose stories have been long ignored or forgotten.

Born in Brooklyn, New York, Nottage wrote her first play by the age of eight, inspired by the women in her family—her grandmother, mother, and other women who worked as nurses and teachers in her Brooklyn neighborhood. After graduating from New York's High School of Music and Art, she earned her BA degree from Brown University in 1986 and her MFA degree in playwriting at the Yale School of Drama in 1989.

After working for four years as national press officer for Amnesty International, Nottage became a full-time playwright in the 1990s. Her early plays—*Crumbs from the Table of Joy* (1995), *Por'-Knocker*s (1995), and *Mud, River, Stone* (1997)—treat various periods of American history from unexpected and formerly ignored vantage points and characters. After a break of nearly seven years from playwriting, Nottage created *Intimate Apparel* (2003), about the lives of African American seamstresses, in 1905, which won the Drama Critics' Circle Award for Best Play. *Fabulation, or the Re-Education of Undine* (2004) follows a successful African American publicist forced to return to her former life in Brooklyn and her working-class relatives. Nottage won the first of her Pulitzer Prizes for *Ruined* (2008), which dramatizes Congolese women surviving civil war. Her second Pulitzer was for *Sweat* (2015), about a group of factory workers and friends who are divided by layoffs and a strike. Her other plays include *By the Way, Meet Vera Stark* (2011), *Mlima's Tale* (2018), and *Floyd's* (2019).

Nottage's plays dramatize complex social problems and their impact on a wide range of characters. As the MacArthur Foundation stated in their 2007 MacArthur Fellowship to Nottage: "Nottage's imaginative exploration of history, her ability to find resonance in unexpected moments in the past, and her sensitive evocation of social concerns have made her a powerful voice in theater."

Joyce Carol Oates (1938–)

Novelist, Short Story Author

 A prolific and popular novelist, short-story writer, poet, and essayist, Joyce Carol Oates published her first novel in 1964 and has followed it by at least one book annually and often two books a year in a body of work that includes more than fifty-five novels, over thirty collections of short stories, eight volumes of poetry, several plays, and many works of literary criticism and reviews. Oates's almost superhuman ability to produce literature has been harnessed to an unerring knack for reflecting and predicting the cultural moment. Future generations examining American life in the second half of the twentieth century and beyond could not do better than to read the works of Joyce Carol Oates.

Oates was born in rural upstate New York, the setting of many of her novels, which also reflect the Depression-era experience of her working-class parents. She attended the same one-room schoolhouse her mother attended and early on became captivated by reading, calling a gift of Lewis Carroll's *Alice in Wonderland* "the great treasure of my childhood, and the most profound literary influence of my life. This was love at first sight." She became the first member of her family to complete high school and attended Syracuse University on a scholarship, majoring in English. Oates produced the manuscript of a novel every semester, most of which she discarded. At the age of nineteen, she won the "college short story" contest sponsored by *Mademoiselle* before graduating as valedictorian and earning an MA from the University of Wisconsin. Pursuing a Ph.D. at Rice University, Oates made the decision to become a full-time writer after one of her short stories was selected for the volume *The Best American Short Stories*.

Her first book, a volume of short stories, *By the North Gate*, appeared in 1963, while her first published novel, *With Shuddering Fall*, appeared a year later. Oates would win the National Book Award for her novel *them* (1969); her novels *Black Water* (1992), *What I Lived For* (1994), and *Blonde* (2000) and the short-story collections *The Wheel of Love* (1970) and *Lovely, Dark, Deep: Stories* (2014) were each finalists for the Pulitzer Prize. One central theme that can be traced in the rich diversity of Oates's writing is an attempt to encapsulate American experience, tracing the historical and political impact on her characters—individuals struggling against cultural tides that they cannot control, often with violent consequences.

Oates married fellow University of Wisconsin graduate student Raymond J. Smith in 1961. After his death from complications of pneumonia in 2008, Oates wrote, "Set beside his death, the future of my writing scarcely interests me at the moment." However, Oates would characteristically translate her grief into writing, producing the acclaimed *A Widow's Memoir*, about her nearly forty-seven-year marriage. A professor of creative writing at Princeton University since 1978, Oates is currently a professor emerita in the humanities. Fellow writer John Gardner described the "alarming phenomenon of Joyce Carol Oates." She is certainly a phenomenon of nature in her apparently endless energy and inquiry as well as alarming to any who may wish to follow her example. Only one Joyce Carol Oates can really exist in this world.

Flannery O'Connor (1924–1964)

Novelist, Short Story Author

One of the most important fiction writers of post-World War II American literature, Flannery O'Connor's novels and short stories, filled with stark, brutal comedy, disturbing violence, and grotesque characters, explore the difficulty and necessity of spiritual belief and redemption in a world increasingly devoid of meaning and transcendence. A Catholic southerner, O'Connor labored with patience and determination to express her uncompromising moral vision, remaining unmoved by demands that her fiction should conform to another's standard. She

once declared that she could "wait a hundred years for readers." It has not taken her that long for her to be recognized as one of the most influential writers of the twentieth century.

Born in Savannah, Georgia, Mary Flannery O'Connor was an only child, precocious and independent, preferring the company of adults to other children, loving reading and writing. When O'Connor was twelve, her father became terminally ill with lupus erythemetosis, the same illness that would later afflict her. She and her mother moved to Milledgeville, Georgia, where O'Connor attended high school and Georgia State College for Women. Her family was devoutly Catholic in the predominantly Protestant South, which no doubt contributed to the religious themes in O'Connor's works and cultivated in her the sense of being both a member of the southern community but also somewhat apart and critically distant from it.

After college, O'Connor studied at the Writer's Workshop at the University of Iowa, where she perfected her craft and had her first short story published. She won the Rinehart-Iowa Fiction Award on the basis of the draft of what would become her first novel, *Wise Blood*, the story of a religious backwoodsman who rejects the fundamentalist faith in which he was raised and founds his own religion, the Church of Christ Without Christ, which leads to violence and disaster.

In 1950, O'Connor returned to Georgia for Christmas and was diagnosed with lupus, which, although incurable, could be controlled with medications developed since her father's death. After a year of nearly total immobility, O'Connor moved with her mother to a small dairy farm near Milledgeville, where she would spend the rest of her life. She managed to produce a steady flow of short stories. *Wise Blood* was finally published in 1953, and her first story collection, *A Good Man Is Hard to Find*, appeared in 1955. A second novel, *The Violent Bear It Away*, was published in 1959. In 1963, O'Connor's health declined, and her lupus reactivated. She died of kidney failure in 1964. The following year, her last collection of stories, *Everything That Rises Must Converge*, was published.

Despite her early death and years of illness, O'Connor had produced a significant body of work that stands as some of the most original and provocative fiction of the twentieth century.

Tillie Olsen (1912–2007)

Essayist, Short Story Author, Novelist

Although her literary output is small—a collection of short stories, a novel, and a selection of lectures and essays—Tillie Olsen's impact in exploring the connections of class, race, and gender in American life is considerable. Her essay collection, *Silences*, perfectly encapsulates Olsen's central project: to give voice to the experiences of those, particularly women and the laboring poor, who too often have been ignored.

Olsen was born Tillie Lerner to Russian Jewish parents in Nebraska, who had been involved in the 1905 Russian Revolution against the czar and fled to America when the uprising failed. Olsen's father provided for his family as a farm worker, painter, paper hanger, candy maker, and packing-house worker while maintaining his political commitment by serving as state secretary of the Nebraska Socialist Party. Educated in public schools in Omaha, Olsen left school early to support her family in a variety of menial jobs while also becoming active in socialist politics. In 1931, she was arrested for encouraging Kansas City packing-house workers to unionize. By 1934, she had moved to San Francisco, where she was jailed for participating in the infamous Bloody Thursday Longshoreman's Strike. In 1943, she married printer and union organizer Jack Olsen and raised their four daughters in a working-class neighborhood, supporting the family by working as a waitress, secretary, and laundress.

Having abandoned a novel about the Great Depression, *Yonnondio*, in 1937, Olsen did not take up writing again until the 1950s, when she enrolled in a writing class at San Francisco State University and won a Stanford University creative-writing fellowship. She published her acclaimed short story

"I Stand Here Ironing" in 1956 and the universally acclaimed collection *Tell Me a Riddle* in 1961, which established Olsen's reputation as one of the contemporary masters of the modern short story. Her stories, expressed in dialect-rich verisimilitude, focus on the perspectives of working-class characters, particularly women, whose stamina and endurance are tested under the constricting conditions and deadening routine of their unglamorous lives. As the mother of four children, forced for many years to work at low-paying jobs, Olsen would draw on her own experiences to give voice to those whose lives and experiences have gone largely unrecorded. It is both the fate of her characters to be silenced by their circumstances and the near-fate of Olsen herself that she explores in *Silences* (1978).

Written in the early days of the women's movement in the 1960s and 1970s, Olsen's essays offered a new perspective on gender and empowerment of neglected voices. Not since Virginia Woolf's *A Room of One's Own* had a female writer offered such a radical gender- and class-based conceptualization of literary history and literary possibilities. As critic Annie Gottlieb has argued, "Probably she is not the first, but to me Tillie Olsen *feels* like the first, both to extend 'universal' human experience to females and to dignify uniquely female experience as a source of human knowledge."

Cynthia Ozick (1928–)

Essayist, Novelist, Short Story Author

A novelist, short-story writer, and essayist who has dealt almost exclusively with the challenges faced by American Jews in the modern world, Cynthia Ozick has turned her subject into profound and universal explorations of the struggle for spiritual survival and belief in the face of seemingly insurmountable obstacles.

Ozick was raised in the Bronx, New York, where her Russian immigrant parents ran a pharmacy. Ozick helped out by delivering prescriptions. She attended public school and recalls stones being thrown at her, being called a Christ-killer, and being publicly humiliated for refusing to sing Christmas carols. Nevertheless, Ozick excelled academically, attending Hunter College High School in Manhattan and graduating from New York University in 1949 before receiving a master's degree from Ohio State University. She wrote her thesis on the novels of Henry James, and although she has stated that her decision to become a writer dates "from the first moment of sentience," it was the discovery of Henry James at the age of seventeen that she received the calling "to serve as a priest at the altar of literature."

In 1952, Ozick married Bernard Hallote, an attorney, and, after a year in Boston, where she worked as a department store copywriter, the couple moved into her parents' home in the Bronx. After abandoning a first novel, Ozick spent seven years, from 1957 to 1963, on her first published novel, *Trust* (1966), a nuanced exploration of identity and self-discovery. "In writing *Trust*," Ozick has stated, "I began as an American novelist and ended as a Jewish novelist." She would evolve through her first novel the repeated themes that would dominate her subsequent work: the opposing claims of two dominating impulses—the pagan and the sacred—as her characters struggle to define their relationship to idols that they worship. Subsequent novels include *The Cannibal Galaxy* (1983), *The Messiah of Stockholm* (1987), *The Puttermesser Papers* (1997), *Heir to the Glimmering World* (2004), and *Foreign Bodies* (2010). Short fiction collections include *The Pagan Rabbi and Other Stories* (1971), *Bloodshed and Three Novellas* (1976), *Levitation: Five Fictions* (1982), and *Collected Stories* (2007). Ozick's "The Shawl" and the novella *Rosa*, published in the collection *The Shawl* (1989), have been universally praised as among the most powerful depictions ever of the horror of the Holocaust in literature and as Ozick's greatest achievements. A literary critic and theorist as well as a practitioner, Ozick's essay collections include *Art and Ardor* (1983), *Metaphor & Memory* (1989), *Fame & Folly* (1996), *Quarrel & Quandary* (2000), *The Din in the Head* (2006), and *Critics, Monsters, Fanatics, and Other Literary Essays* (2016). Ozick's achievement has been ably summarized by critic Elaine M. Kauvar, who has described her as a "master of the meticulous sentence and champion of the moral sense of art."

Dorothy Parker (1893–1967)
Essayist, Poet, Screenwriter, Short Story Author

Although Dorothy Parker wrote many stories, essays, poetry collections, plays, and screenplays, she is known principally for her wit and famous *bon mots*, achieving that rarest of titles in American letters: that of public intellectual and epigrammatic satirist. Indeed, it can be argued that Dorothy Parker was the first American woman to become notorious not just for what she wrote but for what she said. A longtime contributor and critic for *Vanity Fair* and *The New Yorker* as well as a founding member of the informal gathering of literati known as the Algonquin Round Table, Parker issued pronouncements that have become classics, such as:

* "Men seldom make passes at girls who wear glasses."
* "Take me or leave me; or, as is the usual order of things, both."
* "I hate writing; I love having written."
* "I can't write five words but I change seven."
  And her famous, wickedly macabre rhyme:

Razors pain you,

Rivers are damp,

Acids stain you,

And drugs cause cramp.

Guns aren't lawful,

Nooses give,

Gas smells awful.

You might as well live.

Born Dorothy Rothschild in New Jersey, Parker's father was an affluent New York garment manufacturer and a Talmudic scholar. After her mother died when Parker was four, Parker's father remarried a Roman Catholic, and Dorothy was sent to the Blessed Sacrament Convent School in New York, where Parker quipped that she was expelled for describing the Immaculate Conception as "spontaneous combustion." She finished her education at a progressive New Jersey boarding school. Earning her living playing piano at a dancing school, Parker sold her first poem to *Vanity Fair* magazine in 1914, where she was later hired as a staff writer after working as an editorial assistant captioning photos for *Vogue*. She married a Wall Street stockbroker, Edwin Parker, in 1917; they would separate in 1922 and divorce in 1928. She achieved her initial notoriety writing as a theatre reviewer and, along with humorist Robert Benchley and playwright Robert E. Sherwood, began lunching daily at the Algonquin Hotel, becoming the founding members of the so-called Round Table, a loose collection of writers, actors, critics, and wits who included George S. Kaufman, Alexander Woollcott, Edna Ferber, Harpo Marx, and others. Fired from *Vanity Fair* because her criticism too often offended powerful producers, Parker began a long association with *The New Yorker* from its founding in 1925. She would continue to contribute to the magazine until 1957.

Parker's first poetry collection, *Enough Rope* (1926), became a surprise best-seller; a second collection, *Sunset Gun*, appeared in 1928. She won the O. Henry Prize in 1928 for her short story "Big Blonde" and published her first story collection, *Lament for the Living*, in 1930. *After Such Pleasures*, a second collection, followed in 1933. According to critic Dean Flower, Parker was "not only the best epigrammatic poet of the century but, in her laconic short stories was at least the equal of Hemingway and Lardner." From the 1920s through the 1950s, she wrote five plays, including what she regarded as her best, *The Ladies of the Corridor* (1953). She also wrote or cowrote more than twenty films, teaming with Alan Campbell, whom she married in 1935 (then divorced in 1947, remarried in 1950, and separated from in 1952). They received an Oscar nomination for *A Star Is Born* (1937). Increasingly, in the 1930s and 1940s, Parker was an outspoken social activist on behalf of the Loyalist cause in Spain. Suspected as a communist, Parker was blacklisted in Hollywood. She returned to New York and wrote book reviews for *Esquire* and participated as a guest and panelist on several radio programs. Having mastered virtually every available literary genre and gaining a reputation as one of the most formidable personalities of her age, Parker died from a heart attack at the age of seventy-three. Acerbic to the last, her last words on her headstone read: "Excuse My Dust."

Suzan-Lori Parks (1963–)

Novelist, Playwright, Screenwriter

 A playwright, novelist, and screenwriter and the first African American woman to win the Pulitzer Prize for Drama, Parks has been celebrated by her fellow playwright August Wilson as "an original" whose "fierce intelligence and fearless approach to craft subvert theatrical conventions and produce a mature and inimitable art that is as exciting as it is fresh."

A Kentucky native, Parks grew up in a military family. Her father, a career Army officer, was stationed in West Germany, where Parks attended middle school and a German high school. Parks has said that the experience showed her "what it feels like to be neither white nor black, but simply foreign." Returning to the United States, Parks lived and attended school in Kentucky, Texas, California, North Carolina, Maryland, and Vermont before going to Mount Holyoke College, earning her degree in English literature and German in 1985. She studied with writer James Baldwin, who encouraged her to become a playwright and who said that she "may become one of the most valuable artists of our time."

After Parks studied acting at London's Drama Studio, her first play to be produced, *Betting on the Dust Commander*, debuted in 1987 in a bar in Manhattan's Lower East Side, dramatizing a couple's 110-year married life. Parks won Obie Awards for her next play, *Imperceptible Mutabilities in the Third Kingdom* (1989). *Topdog/Underdog* (1999), for which she won the Pulitzer Prize, reflects African American identity and experience through the relationship between two brothers. The play drew comparisons to Ralph Ellison's landmark 1952 novel *Invisible Man*, in which Parks atomizes the consequences of being African American and male in America. Parks followed her success by setting out to write 365 plays in a year, which have been produced by performing arts groups around the world, taking turns until the entire cycle was performed. Parks's other plays include *The American Play* (1994), *Venus* (1996), *In the Blood* (1999), *Fucking A* (2000), *The Book of Grace* (2010), *Father Comes Home from the Wars (Parts 1, 2, and 3)* (2014), and *White Noise* (2019).

Parks has also written the radio play *Pickling* (1990), the screenplay *Girls 6* (1996), and the television adaptation of Zora Neale Hurston's *Their Eyes Were Watching God* (2005). Her first novel, *Getting Mother's Body*, was published in 2003. Awarded the MacArthur Foundation fellowship in 2001, the award celebrated Parks for her "compelling stories and characters that dramatize the complex influences that form both individual and collective identity" and challenge us "to reconsider our perceptions of others and ourselves."

Sylvia Plath (1932–1963)

Novelist, Poet

In a tragically foreshortened life, poet, novelist, and short-story writer Sylvia Plath became, and has remained, one of the most celebrated and controversial American postwar poets. A writer of almost unbearable intensity, Plath would open up formerly out-of-bounds poetic subjects, utilizing methods derived from her lacerating self-exposure that would help to shape much of the poetry that followed her.

Born in Boston, Plath was the oldest child of Otto and Aurelia Schoeber Plath. Her father had emigrated from Germany and had earned a doctorate in entomology from Harvard. He met Plath's mother, an Austrian immigrant, while teaching at Boston University. Plath's father died suddenly when she was eight years old, and the trauma of his death would become a central theme in her writing. Many have speculated that Plath's determined assault on academic and artistic achievement became a way of gaining symbolic approval from her missing father. Plath began publishing poetry while in high school and won a scholarship to prestigious Smith College.

During her junior year, she was selected as a guest editor for the college issue of *Mademoiselle* magazine. After a month in New York City, depressed over being rejected from a creative-writing seminar at Harvard, Plath attempted suicide. She became a patient in a mental hospital and began the therapy that allowed her to return to Smith in 1954. The circumstances leading up to and following her breakdown and suicide attempt would provide the narrative material for her novel *The Bell Jar*, which has been called "the most compelling and controlled account of a mental breakdown to have appeared in American fiction." It was published in 1963, just two weeks before Plath's suicide.

After winning a Fulbright fellowship to study at Cambridge University, she met the aspiring English poet Ted Hughes, whom she married in 1959. Plath's first volume of poetry, *Colossus*, appeared in 1960, the same year she gave birth to her daughter, Frieda. In 1961, Plath began work on *The Bell Jar* in an isolated village in rural Devon, England, while pregnant with her son, Nicholas, in 1962. Although despondent over the breakup of her marriage when she learned that Hughes was having an affair and exhausted from caring for her two infant children, Plath managed to finish her novel, begin a second, and wrote many of her greatest poems, which later appeared in the posthumous collection *Ariel* (1965). Moving to London, Plath would write a final letter to her mother stating that "I have been a bit grim—the upheaval over, I am seeing the finality of it all, and being catapulted from the cow-like happiness of maternity into loneliness and grim problems is no fun." She killed herself on February 11, 1963.

Barely known outside contemporary poetry circles, Plath's death at the age of thirty inevitably influenced the reception of her work, and she became one of the best-known American female poets of the twentieth century. In richly suggestive and painfully honest poems such as "Lady Lazarus," "Daddy," "Fever 103," "Poppies in July," and "Ariel" as well as in the confessional *The Bell Jar*, Plath found a new language and perspective on contemporary women's lives and consciousness. Her *Collected Poems* won the Pulitzer Prize for Poetry in 1982.

E. Annie Proulx (1935–)

Novelist, Short Story Author

 Few contemporary American writers have had either the impact or the accolades garnered by Annie Proulx. With an eye for regional truths and untapped fictional sources, Proulx is the author of darkly comic fiction that dramatizes strikingly original characters set against equally insistent and unusual landscapes.

Edna Annie Proulx was born in Norwich, Connecticut, the oldest of five children. Her father was an executive of a textile company who had come to the United States from Quebec. The family would move frequently throughout New England and North Carolina because of her father's job. Proulx attended Colby College in Maine briefly before leaving for a number of different jobs, including waiting tables and working at a post office. She eventually earned a bachelor's degree from the University of Vermont in 1969 and a master's degree from Sir George Williams University in Montreal and pursued but did not complete a Ph.D. Proulx moved back to Vermont, where she lived for more than thirty years through what she has described as her "wild" time, in which she was married and divorced three times, winding up as a single parent to three sons. Proulx supported herself as a freelance journalist and, in the early 1980s, wrote a series of "how-to" books on such topics as making cider, salad gardening, and making fences, walls, and walkways. She founded her own newspaper, the *Vershire Behind the Times*, that appeared from 1984 to 1986 and wrote and mostly published two short stories a year. In 1994, she moved to a ranch in Wyoming and spent part of the year in northern Newfoundland. She now resides outside of Seattle.

Her first short-story collection, *Heart Songs, and Other Stories*, was published in 1988 to be followed by her first novel, *Postcards* (1992), published when Proulx was fifty-six. Her next book, *The Shipping News* (1993), describing a family who leaves the United States to settle in Newfoundland, was awarded both the Pulitzer Prize and the National Book Award. About her new celebrity status the book caused, Proulx has written, "It's not good for one's view of human nature." More accolades would follow with her next novel, *Accordion Crimes* (1996), which treats the immigrant experience, and especially with *Close Range: Wyoming Stories* (1999), which includes two O. Henry Prize-winning stories, "The Mud Below" and "Brokeback Mountain." The latter story about two male ranch hands whose friendship becomes a sexual relationship was made into a critically acclaimed 2005 film and in 2014 into an opera with a libretto by Proulx that premiered at the Teatro Real in Madrid.

Later works include *That Old Ace in the Hole* (2002) about life in the Texas Panhandle; *Bad Dirt: Wyoming Stories 2* (2004); *Fine Just the Way It Is: Wyoming Stories 3* (2003), a memoir; *Bird Cloud* (2011), which treated the building of her home in Wyoming; and the novel *Barkskins* (2016) about a woodcutter in New France in the seventeenth century and their descendants in the timber industry into the twenty-first century.

In her meticulously researched and crafted works, Proulx demonstrates the power and possibility of seeing the world with clarity and honest reflection.

Adrienne Rich (1929–2012)

Poet

One of the most acclaimed poets of the post-World War II period, Adrienne Rich was also an important essayist and public intellectual who powerfully contributed to the debate over women's identity and empowerment.

Born in Baltimore, Rich was the daughter of a pathologist who worked as a professor at Johns Hopkins Medical School. Educated at home until the fourth grade, Rich was encouraged in her writing, and her first book, *Ariadne*, a three-act play and poems, was privately printed when she was only ten. She graduated from Radcliffe College in 1951, the same year that her first collection of poetry, *A Change of World*, was published in the prestigious Yale Series of Younger Poets. W. H. Auden, who selected Rich's collection for the series, declared that her poems "speak quietly but do not mumble, respect their elders, but are not cowed by them, and do not tell fibs."

In 1953, Rich married Alfred Conrad, a Harvard economist, and they had three sons between 1955 and 1959. Preoccupied with her responsibilities as a wife and mother, Rich saw her writing languish; she broke her silence in 1963 with the important collection *Snapshots of a Daughter-In-Law.* Moving to New York City, Rich began her own teaching career at Swarthmore, Columbia, Brandeis, and City College. In 1970, Rich's husband committed suicide, and in 1976, Rich came out as a lesbian, beginning a long-term relationship with writer Michelle Cliffe. During this period, Rich published some of her most important works, including *Leaflets* (1971), the National Book Award-winning *Diving into the Wreck* (1973), and *The Dream of Common Language* (1977).

Rich's works capture in intense and striking images the challenges that women face under a repressive social system that denies their human potential and expresses the urgency to achieve a liberating and autonomous self-identity. Her prose works include *Of Woman Born: Motherhood as Experience and Institution* (1976), *On Lies, Secrets, and Silences* (1979), *Blood, Bread, and Poetry* (1986), and *A Human Eye: Essays in Art in Society.* They are distinguished for their erudite, lucid, and imaginative treatments of politics, feminism, history, racism, and many other topics. Over a long and distinguished career, Rich reflected at a deeply personal level the evolving women's movement and the major political and social changes of postwar American society. As Rich summarizes in the essay *Credo of a Passionate Skeptic*: "I began as an American optimist, albeit a critical one, formed by our racial legacy and by the Vietnam War … I became an American Skeptic, not as to the long search for justice and dignity, which is part of all human history, but in the light of my nation's leading role in demoralizing and destabilizing that search, here at home and around the world. Perhaps just such a passionate skepticism, neither cynical nor nihilistic, is the ground for continuing."

Mary Rowlandson (c. 1637–1711)
Memoirist

Memoirist Mary Rowlandson was the author of one of the most famous and popular examples of colonial American prose chronicles. Her account of her spiritual and physical travails during her twelve-week captivity among Indians in 1676 is the first best-selling American book and a work that set the standard for subsequent captivity narratives.

Born Mary White in Somerset, England, her family settled in Salem in the Massachusetts Bay Colony sometime before 1650 before moving in 1653 to the Massachusetts frontier town of Lancaster, where she married Reverend Joseph Rowlandson and gave birth to four children between 1658 and 1669. During King Phillip's War in 1675, Lancaster was attacked by a Native American raiding party, who killed thirteen settlers and captured twenty-four, including Rowlandson and three of her children. For the next twelve weeks, they accompanied the Indians in the wilderness as they mounted more raids and avoided the English militia. Rowlandson was ransomed with money raised by public subscription of the women of Boston, where Mary eventually settled after the death of her husband. Her account of her captivity, *The Soveraignty & the Goodness of God, Together with the Faithfulness of His Promises Displayed; Being a Narrative of the Captivity and Restauration of Mrs. Mary Rowlandson*, was published in Cambridge, Massachusetts, and London in 1682. Since then, thirty editions of the book have been published.

Rowlandson's captivity narrative, one of the first to be published and the first popular literary success in America, combines often harrowing, vivid details with a spiritual autobiography of survival and faith. It would also serve as an important primary source for later accounts of the Puritans in New England, colonial histories, and eyewitness reports on Native American customs.

Susanna Rowson (1762–1824)
Novelist, Playwright, Poet

 Author of the first best-selling novel in American history, Susanna Rowson was also a poet, playwright, actress, and educator who pioneered female education in America, opening and operating the Academy for Young Ladies in Boston

in 1797, one of the first postprimary schools for girls in the country.

Rowson was born in Plymouth, England. Her father was a Royal Navy officer, who was posted to Boston. Following the death of her mother, Susanna joined him there in 1766. Her father remarried, and Susanna was largely self-educated at the family's home in Hull, Massachusetts. During the Revolution, Rowson's father remained loyal to the crown and was placed under house arrest and, in 1778, was deported with his family to England, where Susanna found work as a governess of the duchess of Devonshire. While working as a governess, Susanna began writing poetry, short stories, and novels, and the duchess helped Susanna publish her first novel, *Victoria*, in 1786, the same year that Susanna married William Rowson, a trumpeter in the Royal House Guards. He became bankrupt in 1792, and the couple turned to the theater to support themselves. Susanna continued to write, publishing a long poem, *A Trip to Parnassus*, in 1788 and five novels in rapid succession. She performed as a character actress in a traveling troupe and completed her first play, *Slaves in Algiers, or A Struggle for Freedom* (1794). It included the popular song "America, Commerce and Freedom," a tribute to her adopted country. Also in 1794, she published in America *Charlotte Temple*, a novel that had first appeared in England in 1791.

Charlotte Temple is a sentimental romance that tells the story of an English girl seduced by a dashing British officer, who elopes with him after a promise of marriage and moves to New York, where he abandons her to die in childbirth. The novel struck a powerful chord with American readers, going through two hundred editions and read by an estimated half a million people, the biggest-selling novel in America until Harriet Beecher Stowe's *Uncle Tom's Cabin* (1852). Some were so moved by the plight of the heroine that they made a pilgrimage to her supposed burial place at New York's Trinity Churchyard. One of the central themes of *Charlotte Temple* was the need for better education for young women, which Rowson put into practice after moving back to Boston and opening the Academy for Young Ladies, serving as headmistress until 1822, two years before her death. The boarding school attracted the New England elite to its innovative curriculum, which emphasized not only the traditional female accomplishments such as music, drawing, and domestic economy but also subjects like mathematics and science, usually taught only to men. Rowson's fictional heroines are often conventional, passive victims of circumstances, but Rowson's own life in predominantly male occupations describes a very different course open to women.

Catherine Maria Sedgwick (1789–1867)
Biographer, Novelist

A novelist, biographer, and children's writer, Catherine Sedgwick was the most famous and successful American female fiction writer in the first half of the nineteenth century. Along with her contemporary, James Fenimore Cooper, Sedgwick helped to pioneer indigenous American literature through her themes and settings. Sedgwick likewise drew inspiration from the American past in stories that embodied the American character and identity.

Born in Stockbridge, Massachusetts, the daughter of Judge Theodore Sedgwick, who would serve as speaker of the U.S. House of Representatives, Catherine attended a local school as well as a boarding school in Albany and a finishing school in Boston. She was encouraged by her four brothers to pursue a writing career to which she devoted herself exclusively, never marrying, though rejecting frequent proposals from admirers of her books. She took advantage of demands in periodicals for stories with American settings and themes and published her first novel, *A New England Tale*, in 1822, a critical look at New England Puritans and a sympathetic treatment of the Quakers whom they persecuted. *Redwood* (1824) explored the Shaker community and received praise and comparison to the works of Maria Edgeworth, Walter Scott, and James Fenimore Cooper.

Sedgwick's most enduring novel is *Hope Leslie or, Early Times in Early Times in the Massachusetts* (1827), a historical romance set during the Pequot War in about 1636. In a stark contrast with Cooper's *The Last of the Mohicans*, published the previous year, Sedgwick's novel accepts marriage between an Indian man and a white woman. Other novels include *Clarence; or, a Tale of Our Own Times* (1830), a novel of manners; and *The Linwoods; or, 'Sixty Years Since' in America* (1835), a historical romance set during the American Revolution, transplanting Scott's subtitle for *Waverley* and formula for the historical novel to America.

Sedgwick, whose works were rediscovered in the 1970s by feminist literary scholars, deserves appreciation for her role in evoking unique American settings and themes in the developing American literary canon while at the same time offering an alternative woman's perspective on core issues of American identity and values.

Ntozake Shange (1948–2018)

Essayist, Novelist, Playwright, Poet

 Best known for her early play *for colored girls who have considered suicide/when the rainbow is enuf* (1975), Ntozake Shange was an African American feminist activist whose powerful and daring works include fifteen plays, nineteen poetry collections, six novels, five children's books, and three essay collections.

Born Paulette Williams in Trenton, New Jersey, Shange was educated at Barnard College and the University of Southern California, where she earned a master's degree in American Studies. In 1971, she changed her name, which means in African "she who comes with her own things" and "she who walks like a lion," and began writing poetry while teaching courses in the humanities, women's studies, and African American studies at California colleges and also performing as a dancer and performance artist. *For colored girls,* which she described as a "choreopoem," a blend of poetry, music, dance, and drama, first appeared off-Broadway in 1975 before transferring to Broadway in 1976, where it electrified audiences and provoked debate. In the words of critic Mel Gussow, "Miss Shange was a pioneer in terms of her subject matter: the fury of black women at their double subjugation in white male America."

Two-time Pulitzer Prize-winning playwright Lynn Nottage has observed that the play "definitely spoke to a generation of young women who didn't feel invited into a theater space, who suddenly saw representation of themselves in a very honest way, and understood that they could occupy that space for the first time."

Subsequent productions include *A Photograph: A Study of Cruelty* (1977); *Boogie Woogie Landscape* (1978); *Spell No. 7: A Geechee Quick Magic Trance Manual* (1979), which received an Obie Award; *Black and White Two Dimensional Planes* (1979); *From Okra to Greens: A Different Kind of Love Story* (1984); and *The Love Space Demands* (1991). Her novels are *Sassafrass* (1976), *Cypress & Indigo* (1982), and *Betsey Brown* (1985). Poetry collections include *Nappy Edges* (1978), *Some Men* (1981), *A Daughter's Geography* (1983), *Three Pieces* (1992), and *Wild Beauty* (2017). Essay collections include *See No Evil* (1984) and *If I Can Cook You Know God Can* (1999). All of Shange's works—drama, poetry, fiction, and nonfiction—are informed by a poetic expressiveness, an experimental approach that violates accepted forms in search of new syntheses, and a relentless truthfulness that challenges conventional wisdom.

Lydia Sigourney (1791–1865)

Novelist, Poet

 Now largely forgotten, Lydia Sigourney, or, as most of her contemporaries would have known her, Mrs. Sigourney, was the most well-known and popular American female poet for much of the first half of the nineteenth century. Her verse and novels, based on newspaper reports, particularly death notices, had a wide commercial appeal that allowed her to become one of the first American female writers to establish a successful writing career. After her death, poet John Greenleaf Whittier wrote of the so-called "Sweet Singer of Hartford": "She sang alone, ere womanhood had known / The gift of song which fills the air to-day: / Tender and sweet, a music all her own."

The only daughter of a gardener/handyman in Norwich, Connecticut, Lydia attracted the attention of her father's wealthy employer, which led to support for her education from the influential Wadsworth family in Hartford. Through their help, Lydia established schools for young women in both Norwich and Hartford that offered more than the expected "feminine" subjects like music, art, and needlework with instruction in mathematics, history, science, and philosophy. The first of her sixty-seven books, *Moral Pieces in Prose*, was published anonymously to acclaim in 1815. She gave up teaching when she married Charles Sigourney, a prominent Hartford widower, in 1819 but continued her writing, despite her husband's disapproval, publishing conduct books *Letters to Young Ladies* (1833) and *Letters to My Pupils* (1837). As her husband's finances faltered, she turned to writing as her occupation, producing a steady stream of readers, poetry, travel books, and novels, including *A History of Marcus Aurelius* (1836); *Lucy Howard's Journal* (1858), a memoir; *The Faded Hope* (1853); and a collected edition of her poetry, *Poetical Works of Mrs. L. H. Sigourney* (1850).

Until recently, literary historians have dismissed much of Sigourney's writing as "hack work" despite her popularity: conventionally sentimental and lugubrious in its frequent consideration of death and dying. More recently, feminist literary scholars such as Annie Finch and Nina Baym have taken a renewed interest in Sigourney in the ways in which she both promulgated conventional views and challenged them and navigated the complex marketplace as a female writer in the first half of the nineteenth century.

Jane Smiley (1949–)

Novelist

Pulitzer Prize-winning novelist Jane Smiley has become an admired and popular chronicler of both the American landscape and experience. The author of more than thirty books, Smiley has produced a rich and deep fictional resource examining American life (and beyond) through various comic, satiric, and tragic lenses.

Born in Los Angeles, Smiley grew up in the suburbs of St. Louis. She earned her BA degree from Vassar College in 1971 and her MA and MFA from the University of Iowa. After spending a year abroad in Iceland on a Fulbright scholarship, Smiley returned to Iowa as a professor of English at Iowa State University from 1981 to 1996 before turning to writing full time.

Smiley's first novel, *Barn Blind* (1980), focuses on the relationship between a ranch wife and her children. A second novel, *At Paradise Gate* (1981), continues her exploration of family life in the face of the father's imminent death. After publishing *Duplicate Keys* (1984), a mystery set in Manhattan, and *The Age of Grief* (1987), a novella and story collection, Smiley produced a sweeping historical novel, *The Greenlanders* (1988), centered on a fourteenth-century family. It was followed by Smiley's best-known novel, *A Thousand Acres* (1991), a reimagining of Shakespeare's *King Lear* on an Iowa family farm. It won both the Pulitzer Prize and the National Book Critics Circle Award. Her subsequent novels include *Moo* (1995), *The All-True Travels and Adventures of Lidie Newton* (1998), *Horse Heaven* (2000), *Ten Days in the Hills* (2007); and *Private Life* (2010); *Some Luck* (2014), *Early Warning* (2015), and *Golden Age* (2015) make up her *Last Hundred Years* trilogy, tracing a century in the life of an Iowa family.

Smiley has also published young-adult novels, a biography of Charles Dickens, a book on craft-working in the Catskills, and a biography of American physicist John Vincent Atanasoff, *The Man Who Invented the Computer* (2010), as well as the critical study *Thirteen Ways of Looking at the Novel* (2005).

Smiley's production stands as an important reflection on American life and the stories that make up the American experience.

Susan Sontag (1933–2004)

Critic, Essayist, Novelist

An essayist, critic, and novelist as well as a teacher, philosopher, filmmaker, and political activist, Susan Sontag is perhaps best summarized as a public intellectual who for four of the most turbulent decades in American political and cultural history remained at the center of debate, influencing in her essays and books the intellectual conversations of her time.

Born Susan Rosenblatt to a couple engaged in the fur trade in China, Sontag was raised in New York City by a nanny. Her father, whom she rarely saw, died when she was five, and, after her mother remarried, she took her stepfather's surname. Her family settled in California, and Sontag graduated from North Hollywood High School at the age of fifteen. She would graduate from the University of Chicago at the age of eighteen. There, she married her sociology instructor, a marriage that lasted eight years. When her husband took a teaching post at Brandeis, Sontag entered graduate school at Harvard, earning master's degrees in both English and philosophy. In 1952, the couple had a son. Sontag would continue her studies at Oxford University and the University of Paris. In Paris, Sontag met Cuban American playwright María Irene Fornés, with whom she moved back to New York in 1959. In New York, Sontag lectured in philosophy at City College and Sarah Lawrence and later on in religion at Columbia.

Sontag began her literary career at the age of thirty, publishing an experimental novel, *The Benefactor* (1963). *Death Kit* followed four years later. Although she would become famous for her essays and criticism, she thought of herself principally as a writer of fiction. Her short story "The Way We Live Now," dealing with the AIDS epidemic, was published to great acclaim in 1986, and Sontag wrote two best-selling novels, *The Volcano Lover* (1992) and *In America* (2000), both works of historical fiction.

Sontag's chief impact and notoriety would come with her critical writing and essays. An early essay, "Notes on 'Camp'" (1964), challenged established artistic categories while identifying irony as a prevalent response to the cultural moment. In *Against Interpretation and Other Essays* (1968), Sontag made the case for a sensory response to art, arguing that intuitive response, not interpretation or analysis, was key to artistic understanding. Sontag had defined the 1960s zeitgeist, which she further elaborated on in *Styles of Radical Will* (1969). In *On Pho-*

tography (1967), Sontag provocatively laid down core aesthetic principles that would help define photography and raise its status as an art form while cautioning about its implications and warning that images may replace direct experience and thereby limit reality. In *Illness as Metaphor* (1978) and *AIDS and Its Metaphors* (1988), Sontag daringly treats the social and artistic perceptions of illness. Reflecting her own experience with breast cancer, Sontag asserted that the most truthful way to view illness is to resist thinking of it as a punishment.

Sontag wrote and directed four feature films: *Duet for Cannibals* (1969), *Brother Carl* (1971), *Promised Lands* (1974), and *Unguided Tour* (1983). Her plays *Alice in Bed* and *Lady from the Sea* have been produced worldwide. She also directed plays in the United States and Europe, most notably a production of Samuel Beckett's *Waiting for Godot* in the summer of 1993 in besieged Sarajevo, where Sontag lived working in a hospital, teaching theater, and doing radio commentary. Sontag died in New York City in 2004. Over a lifetime of trying to reinvent herself and evading simplistic labels, Sontag insisted that she was a modernist in the tradition of twentieth-century French intellectuals. The result was that she stretched her considerable intellectual reach far and wide, producing important and lasting work that bespeaks a core belief in her mission: "Be serious, be passionate, wake up."

Gertrude Stein (1874–1946)
Essayist, Novelist, Playwright, Poet

A novelist, essayist, playwright, and poet, Gertrude Stein is chiefly remembered today for coining the term "The Lost Generation"; for her Paris salon of the 1920s, where she encouraged and aided such literary and artistic greats as Hemingway and Picasso; for the line "Rose is a rose is a rose is a rose"; and for her relationship with Alice B. Toklas. She was perhaps the most famous woman of the age as well as one of the leading innovators in modern literature, influencing such diverse figures as James Joyce, the French New Novelists, and the writers of the Beat Generation.

Born in Allegheny, Pennsylvania, the youngest of seven children, Stein grew up in Oakland, California, where her father made a fortune investing in real estate. Raised by governesses and tutors, Stein formed her principal bond with her older brother, whom she followed to Harvard, where she enrolled in the Harvard Annex, soon to become Radcliffe College. In 1897, she entered Johns Hopkins University Medical School intending to become a physician, but after four years, she lost interest and dropped out. In 1903, she joined Leo in Paris at the address that would become one of the most famous in twentieth-century cultural history—27 Rue de Fleurus—the most celebrated salon in Paris, a magnet for artists, writers, intellectuals, and hangers-on in the world of the avant-garde.

In 1909, Stein published her first book, *Three Lives*, in which she attempted to duplicate what modern painters were achieving in their art: tone and texture through a pattern of repetition that suggests the equal importance of each element. Her revolutionary approach found few readers but many admirers, including Californian Alice B. Toklas, who became Stein's secretary, lover, and lifelong companion. Stein's next project, written from 1906 to 1909, was a massive, one-thousand-page work, *The Making of Americans*, a history based on three generations of Stein's family, with no dialogue or action. It remained unpublished until 1925. Stein published a volume of Cubist-inspired poetry, *Tender Buttons*, in 1914 that prompted one reviewer to dub her "the Mama of Dada." Her first commercial success was *The Autobiography of Alice B. Toklas* (1933), which chronicles Stein and Toklas's lives together. The book's success led to a lecture tour of America and Stein's reflections on her native country, *Everybody's Autobiography* (1937). During World War II, Stein and Toklas remained in Paris during the Occupation, and she produced two final works based on the war years, *Wars I Have Seen* (1945) and *Brewsie and Willie* (1946).

Gertrude Stein's presence in literary and gender history is central. She set out to liberate language for new and distinctive purposes while pursuing an equally liberating sense of gender identity, a pioneer both in language and sexuality.

Harriet Beecher Stowe (1811–1896)

Novelist

 The author of the most read and most controversial novel of the nineteenth century, Harriet Beecher Stowe produced in *Uncle Tom's Cabin* (1852) the first great American literary phenomenon: only the Bible sold more copies in nineteenth-century America, and the novel became the first American work of literature that achieved worldwide cultural saturation. It is the first great social purpose or political novel in America that served to coalesce (and polarize) attitudes toward race that could be considered a contributing factor in the outbreak of the American Civil War. Few writers, either male or female, have ever been as forceful or as influential as Harriet Beecher Stowe.

Stowe was born in Litchfield, Connecticut, the daughter of Lyman Beecher, one of the best-known clergymen of his day. She attended the Hartford Female Seminary, run by her older sister Catherine, where she received an education in the classics, languages, and mathematics, subjects usually reserved for male students. In 1832, she joined her father, who had become the president of Cincinnati's Lane Theological Seminary. There, she met Calvin Ellis Stowe, a widower and professor at the seminary. They married in 1836 and raised seven children together. It was across the border in Kentucky that Stowe would view the impact of slavery directly. She also listened to the stories of the fugitive slaves who sheltered at the Stowe home after escaping to the North on the Underground Railroad.

In 1850, Stowe moved with her family to Brunswick, Maine, where her husband was teaching at Bowdoin College. When the U.S. Congress passed the Fugitive Slave Law mandating the return of escaped slaves in the North, Stowe became determined to write a story about the problem of slavery, stating, "I feel now that the time is come when even a woman or a child who can speak a word for freedom and humanity is bound to speak … I hope every woman who can write will not be silent." The first installment of *Uncle Tom's Cabin* appeared in serial form in *The National Era* newspaper from June 1851 to April 1852 and in book form in March 1852. In less than a year, the novel had sold an unprecedented three hundred thousand copies. Stowe's ability to dramatize the emotional and physical effects of slavery on individuals, so much more effective than any previous abolitionist tract, electrified readers, exciting great adulation in the North and virulent attack in the South as well as praise from around the world. Thomas Macaulay in England declared her novel "the most valuable addition America has made to English literature." Tolstoy considered it the highest achievement ever of moral art. Dramatizations, without Stowe's authorization, flooded the stage, and it has been estimated that between 1853 and 1930, it never ceased to be performed.

Stowe answered critics who charged her with exaggeration and invention of the plight of her characters in *A Key to Uncle Tom's Cabin* (1853), which documented the abuses she had dramatized. Stowe would take up the cause of slavery again in *Dred: A Tale of the Great Dismal Swamp* (1856) before retreating from overtly political subjects in novels that drew on her memories of childhood in New England, including *The Minister's Wooing* (1859), *The Pearl of Orr's Island* (1862), and *Old Town Folks* (1869). She would continue to publish novels, stories, articles, and essays into the 1890s.

Amy Tan (1952–)

Essayist, Novelist, Short Story Author

A novelist, short-story writer, and essayist, Amy Tan is a critically acclaimed and widely read contemporary chronicler of the Chinese American experience, particularly the lives and conflicts of women, which she explored in her bestselling novel *The Joy Luck Club* (1989).

Born and raised in Oakland, California, Tan was expected to become a physician by her Chinese-born parents. Tan majored in English at San Jose State in California, and, after graduate work at the University of California–Berkeley, she began her career as a technical writer. She turned to fiction as a distraction from the demands of her work, inspired

from reading Louise Erdrich's novel of Native American family life, *Love Medicine.*

Tan's hobby resulted in *The Joy Luck Club,* which linked stories told by four Chinese, immigrant women and their four American-born daughters, who struggle to bridge the generational and cultural gap. The novel stayed on the *New York Times* bestseller list for nine months. One reviewer observed that the book "is that rare find, a first novel that you keep thinking about, keep telling your friends about long after you've finished reading it." In 1993, Tan coauthored the screenplay for the film version, the first major movie to treat the Chinese American experience. Tan's follow-up, *The Kitchen God's Wife* (1991), concerns a daughter who learns of her mother's Chinese past. *The Hundred Secret Senses* (1995) focuses on the relationship between two sisters. Tan's fourth novel, *The Bonesetter's Daughter* (2001), returns to the theme of the cultural clash between a Chinese mother and her American-born daughter. *Saving Fish from Drowning* (2005) examines American tourists visiting China and Burma, while *The Valley of Amazement* (2013) returns to mother–daughter relations set among the courtesans of Shanghai in the early twentieth century. In 2017, Tan published *Where the Past Begins*, a memoir that recounts her childhood, her relationship with her mother, and her evolution as a writer.

Tan's achievement over a productive career has been to demonstrate the power exerted by cultural heritage and the search for some kind of constructive synthesis between the past and the present, between generations, and between languages as well as the roles that can limit us but can adapt to suit experience.

Ida M. Tarbell (1857–1944)

Journalist

A journalist, biographer, and historian, Ida Tarbell was a pioneering figure of investigative journalism. The leading muckraking journalist during the Progressive Era of the early twentieth century, Tarbell's famous critical study *The History of the Standard Oil Company* (1902) is one of the great landmarks in journalism history. Its exposé of the shady business practices of John D. Rockefeller, America's richest figure, would help bring about the dissolution of the Standard Oil monopoly in 1911, when the Supreme Court ruled that the company was in violation of the Sherman Antitrust Act.

Born in a log cabin in Erie County, Pennsylvania, Tarbell was educated at Allegheny College and taught briefly before becoming an editor for the Chautauqua Literary and Scientific Circle from 1883 to 1891. She next traveled to Paris to research a projected biography of a leading female leader of the French Revolution, Madame Marie-Jeanne Roland. Tarbell enrolled at the Sorbonne and supported herself by writing articles about Parisian life for American magazines. She failed to complete her biography of Roland but, after her return to America in 1894, began a biographical series on Napoleon. A series of popular works on Abraham Lincoln followed. In 1899, she was hired to work as an editor for *McClure's* magazine, where she set out to expose the practices of John D. Rockefeller's Standard Oil Company. Tarbell's father had worked in the Pennsylvania oil fields, and she was compelled to undertake her investigation by the conviction that her father had been victimized by the company's practices. Originally serialized in nineteen parts beginning in 1902 in *McClure's*, Tarbell's *The History of the Standard Oil Company* was published in book form in 1904. Tarbell's exposé created a sensation and provoked a public outcry at the practices of Standard Oil that Tarbell had so meticulously documented and was praised for its monumental scope and careful documentation. One reviewer from the *Economic Journal* declared, "It is difficult to write about Miss Tarbell's remarkable achievement without using language approaching the edge of hyperbole. So careful is she in her facts, so sane in her judgments, that she seems to have reached the high-water mark of industrial history."

Tarbell's work ushered in the era of muckraking journalism, and her powerful investigative reporting would be followed by such important works as Lincoln Steffens's *The Shame of the Cities* (1904) on urban political machines; Upton Sinclair's *The Jungle* (1906) on the U.S. meat-packing industry; and Edwin Markham's *Children in Bondage* (1914) on child labor. In 1906, Tarbell helped to launch the *American Magazine*, writing a series of investigative articles on tariffs and their impact, which became the book *The Tariff in Our Times* (1911). As in her work on Standard Oil, Tarbell was able to make complex topics understandable to the general reader. She would lecture widely and serve on several presidential panels addressing industrial and social issues through the early 1920s.

A contrarian in regard to women's rights, Tarbell rose to the pinnacle of male-dominated journalism and was outspoken in asserting women's rights, but she opposed women's suffrage, alienated by the more militant aspects of movement. She instead recommended that women should embrace home and family life as a proper sphere for women and that the drive for suffrage was "a misguided war on men." She collected her essays on women in *The Business of Being a Woman* (1912). Tarbell completed her autobiography, *All in a Day's Work*, in 1939 when she was eighty-two. She was working on another book, *Life after Eighty*, when she died in 1946 at the age of eighty-six.

Barbara Tuchman (1912–1989)

Historian

Historian and writer Barbara Tuchman achieved a rare literary accomplishment by turning the past into best-selling books accessible to millions of readers. With her characteristic clarity, Tuchman observed that "the unrecorded past is none other than our old friends, the tree in the primeval forest which fell without being heard." She saw her vocation as supplying that unheard sound. The winner of two Pulitzer Prizes, Tuchman specialized in telling the story of the past with the eye and understanding of a novelist, shaping the formless past into riveting and revealing drama.

Born Barbara Wertheim, a member of a wealthy New York City banking family, Tuchman's interest in history was first stimulated by her childhood reading of Lucy Fitch Perkins's *Twins* series that described children of various nationalities during different historical periods. Works of historical fiction followed, which fired her imagination about the past. Educated at New York's Walden School and Radcliffe College, Tuchman spent summers with her family in Europe and accompanied her grandfather to the World Economic Conference of 1933 in London. After graduation, she took a job as a researcher and editorial assistant with the Institute of Pacific Relations in Tokyo, publishing magazine articles about her experiences. She covered the civil war in Spain for *The Nation* magazine, which helped prompt her first book, *The Lost British Policy: Britain and Spain Since 1700*, in 1938. In 1940, she married Manhattan physician Lester R. Tuchman, and, after a two-year stint on the Far East desk of the Office of War Information during World War II, Tuchman focused on raising the couple's three children.

In the 1950s, Tuchman struggled to resume her research and writing. "It was a struggle," she recalled. "I had three small children and no status whatsoever.... To come home, close a door and feel that it was your place to work, that was very difficult, particularly when you were—well, just a Park Avenue matron." Added to the challenge was the issue of being a woman in a field dominated by men and pursuing her interests without any graduate training. However, Tuchman did not feel her lack of academic credentials was a drawback. Rejecting the academic historian's tendency to "stuff in every item of research to be found," Tuchman undertook the difficult task of "selecting and shaping a readable story."

In 1956, Tuchman published her first major historical work, *Bible and Sword: England and Palestine from the Bronze Age to Balfour*, a study of British Palestinian policy. Her first popular success was *The Zimmermann Telegram* (1958), a gripping story of Germany's attempt to incite Mexico to enter World War I against the Allies. In 1963, Tuchman became the first woman to receive the Pulitzer Prize for General Nonfiction with *The Guns of August*, a detailed account of the first month of World War I. She followed it with *The Proud Tower* (1966), a study of the cultural and political forces that led to the conflict. In all three, Tuchman demonstrates her remarkable ability to discover the telling detail, to trace the significant thread that brings the past alive, and to create memorable and rounded historical figures. She won a second Pulitzer for *Stilwell and the American Experience in China, 1911–1945* (1971) and

gained a remarkable best-seller with *A Distant Mirror* (1978), which brought fourteenth-century Europe to vivid life. Her final histories were *The March of Folly: From Troy to Vietnam* (1984) and *The First Salute* (1988), a study of the American Revolution.

Tuchman embraced the role of historian not as a collector of dry historical artifacts or minutiae but as a compelling teacher and synthesizer who linked the lessons of the past with the world of her audience. Few have mastered the art of historical narrative as expertly as Barbara Tuchman.

Anne Tyler (1941–)
Novelist, Short Story Author

One of the most admired and popular of contemporary American writers, Anne Tyler has made a necessity and a virtue of the local, which she renders with the eye of the connoisseur of the ordinary into extraordinary literary creations.

Although she is associated with Baltimore, Maryland, where she lives and where most of her books are set, Tyler was born in Minnesota and grew up in North Carolina. She lived on a Quaker commune in the mountains from the ages of seven to eleven caring for the livestock and doing farming chores. She was schooled in art, carpentry, cooking, and other subjects in a tiny schoolhouse, supplemented by correspondence courses. When her family moved to Raleigh, North Carolina, eleven-year-old Tyler had never used a telephone. As she recalls, this unorthodox upbringing enabled her to view "the normal world with a certain amount of distance and surprise." With access now to libraries, Tyler plunged into writers such as Eudora Welty, whom Tyler credits with showing her that stories could be about everyday details of life, not just about major events.

Tyler attended Duke University, where she majored in Russian literature, which led, after graduation, to graduate study at Columbia University. She left after completing her coursework but not her thesis to return to Duke University as a Russian bibliographer in the library. It was there that she met Taghi Modarressi, a resident in child psychiatry at Duke Medical School, and they married in 1963.

Raising two daughters and relocating to Baltimore, Tyler published nothing from 1965 to 1970.

Between 1970 and 1974, Tyler completed three novels, the last of which, *Celestial Navigation*, brought her national recognition. The best known of her novels—*Dinner at the Homesick Restaurant* (1982), *The Accidental Tourist* (1985), and *Breathing Lessons* (1988)—were all finalists for the Pulitzer Prize for Fiction, with *Breathing Lessons* winning the prize. Later books include *Ladder of Years* (1995), *A Patchwork Planet* (1998), *The Amateur Marriage* (2004), *The Beginner's Goodbye* (2012), *A Spool of Blue Thread* (2015), *Vinegar Girl* (2016), and *Clock Dance* (2018). All draw on the fictional territory of family life and marriage relationships rooted in Tyler's experience of life that derives from her Baltimore home.

Susan Warner (1819–1885)

Novelist

A novelist and author of religious and children's fiction, Susan Warner earns the distinction for becoming the first American author of a book that sold one million copies. Along with her sister, Warner produced thirty novels as well as children's fiction and theological works. Her success would encourage other women to enter the literary market, prompting Nathaniel Hawthorne's famous complaint about the "damned mob of scribbling women."

Born into a well-to-do Manhattan family, Susan was educated at home by her father and expected to marry well. This plan collapsed when Susan's father lost his fortune in the financial crash of 1837 and, with it, any dowry to attract desirable husbands for his daughters. The family moved to a farmhouse on an island in the Hudson River opposite West Point, where Susan and her sister, Anna Bartlett Warner (1827–1915), were forced into hard physical labor to keep up the household, work that had previously been done by their servants. When creditors threatened to take their remaining furniture, the sisters turned to writing to earn money. Susan's first

attempt, *The Wide, Wide World* (1850), was an immediate popular success. It is a sentimental, domestic tale featuring a heroine who endures the early death of her mother, the collapse of the family fortune, and a demanding, uncaring aunt and is forced to make her own important life decisions according to her religious beliefs; the book is based on Warner's own experiences. Despite becoming perhaps the most circulated story by an American writer in multiple editions and translations, Warner, who sold the copyright, earned no royalties.

She responded with more of the same: *Queechy* (1852) also concerns the spiritual development of a young girl; *The Hills of the Shatemuc* (1856), which sold ten thousand copies on its first day of publication; *The Old Helmet* (1863); and *A Story of Small Beginnings* (1872). *Melbourne House* (1864), *Daisy* (1868), and *Daisy on the Field* (1869) take up the abolitionist cause, while relief for female factory workers is a central theme of *Wych Hazel* (1876) and *The Gold of Chickaree* (1876).

Warner's didactive sentimentalism found a wide contemporary audience. Later literary historians have been more dismissive, while some attempts by feminist literary critics have found more interest, at least in *The Wide, Wide World*, as a supreme example of the period domestic novel that reveals much about the gender assumptions and family dynamics of Warner's era.

Mercy Otis Warren (1728–1814)

Historian, Playwright, Poet

In an era in which political debate was exclusively a male preserve, poet, playwright, and historian Mercy Otis Warren entered the fray during the decisive years of the American Revolution, becoming the first American female playwright, political satirist, and leading female intellectual of the Revolution and the early republic.

Warren was born in Barnstable, Massachusetts, the third of thirteen children, only six of whom survived to adulthood. Her father, James Otis, was a farmer and an attorney who served in the Massachusetts House of Representatives, and her mother, Mary Allyne, was a *Mayflower* descendant. Warren took advantage of an uncle's extensive library in order to educate herself, pursuing an interest in history and politics. In 1754, she married James Warren, who would also become elected to the Massachusetts House of Representatives, where he served as speaker. He was also president of the Massachusetts Provincial Congress and became a correspondent and advisor to many political leaders, including Samuel Adams, John Hancock, Patrick Henry, Thomas Jefferson, George Washington, and John Adams, who became Mercy Warren's literary mentor.

Warren began writing political dramas that denounced British policies and officials in Massachusetts. Her 1772 satire *The Adulator* (published anonymously) attacked British colonial governor Thomas Hutchinson. Two additional plays, *Defeat* (1773) and *The Group* (1775), similarly lambasted British colonial policies. In 1788, she published *Observations on the New Constitution*, whose ratification she opposed as a committed Jeffersonian Republican and anti-federalist. In 1790, Warren published *Poems, Dramatic and Miscellaneous*, the first of her works that bear her name and the third book of poetry (after Anne Bradstreet and Phillis Wheatley) produced by an American woman. From the outset of the American Revolution, Warren recorded its history, published in 1805 as *History of the Rise, Progress, and Termination of the American Revolution*, which was among the first historical works published by a woman in America. Warren lived to the age of eighty-six remaining active as a correspondent with her political friends, having marked out new territory for a woman in America as a public intellectual whose considerable literary talents were devoted to the most pressing political and cultural issues of her day.

Wendy Wasserstein (1950–2006)

Playwright

Playwright Wendy Wasserstein can be regarded as the dramatist of the generation of American, college-educated women who came of age in the late 1960s as second-wave feminism and the women's movement was beginning to redefine and reshape gender assumptions. Her most famous play, *The Heidi Chronicles* (1988), is one of the defining literary and cultural documents of that era and established Wasserstein as one of the most important contemporary playwrights.

Wasserstein was born in Brooklyn, New York. Her father was a prosperous textile manufacturer; her mother was an amateur dancer. Taken to the theater regularly, Wasserstein remembers feeling like something was missing in the plays she saw. "Where are the girls?" she wondered. She did not start writing for the stage until, while attending Mount Holyoke College, she enrolled in a writing class at nearby Smith College. After graduating in 1971, she became one of the first students in a new creative-writing program at City College, where Wasserstein studied with novelist Joseph Heller and playwright Israel Horovitz before receiving her master's degree in 1973. Her first produced work was her thesis, a play called *Any Woman Can't*. She went on to the Yale School of Drama, where she earned an MFA degree in 1976.

Her first widely known play, *Uncommon Women and Others* (1972), involves a group of Mount Holyoke students who consider their relationships with men and their futures as well as the arrival of feminism on college campuses in the late 1960s with its dual legacy of liberation and guilt. *Isn't It Romantic*, with many of the same themes, followed in 1981. *Miami* (1986) is a musical comedy about a teenage boy on a Florida vacation with his parents. *The Heidi Chronicles* (1988) was the first of her plays to be performed on Broadway and won the Pulitzer Prize for Drama. The play dramatizes the costs and consequences of "having it all" as art history professor Heidi Holland assesses her life, career, and what is missing after liberation. Several plays followed, including *The Sisters Rosensweig* (1992), *An American Daughter* (1997), *Old Money* (2002), and *Third* (2005). She also published essays in *Bachelor Girls* (1990) and *Shiksa Goddess* (2001). A first novel, *Elements of Style*, was published after her death from cancer at the age of fifty-six in 2006. All share elements that made *The Heidi Chronicles* such an effective and important drama: a perceptive sense of the forces of generation, family, and the past that form a woman's identity.

Eudora Welty (1909–2001)
Novelist, Short Story Author

 Over a distinguished and productive literary career, novelist and short-story writer Eudora Welty demonstrated the possibilities of the local and regional to dramatize universal themes about human nature and human experience. One of the leading voices of the Southern Renaissance along with William Faulkner, Robert Penn Warren, Katherine Anne Porter, and Flannery O'Connor, Welty has been admired as a master stylist and quiet visionary of the world she inhabited for close to a century.

Born in Jackson, Mississippi, which would remain her lifelong home, Welty was educated in the Jackson Public School system before attending Mississippi State College for Women and then the University of Wisconsin, where she received her bachelor's degree. After graduate work at the Columbia University School of Business, Welty worked for a local Jackson radio station, wrote a society column for a Memphis newspaper, and did publicity work for the WPA during the Depression. Her first publication was a short story, "Death of a Traveling Salesman," in 1936. A collection of stories, *A Curtain of Green*, followed in 1941, containing the much-admired and anthologized stories "Why I Live at the P.O." and "A Worn Path." Her stories vary widely in tone from comic to tragic, from realism to surrealism, but all are anchored by a close and intimate observational skill derived from Welty's deep familiarity and understanding of her locale.

Longer forms followed, including her first novel *The Robber Bridegroom* (1942), the novella *Delta Wedding* (1946), and a cycle of interrelated stories called *The Golden Apples* (1949). After publishing seven distinguished works of fiction over a fourteen-year period, Welty was forced into a hiatus for nearly a decade to care for her ailing mother. She returned to writing, publishing what many believe are her masterpieces, *Losing Battles* (1970) and *The Optimist's Daughter* (1972), winner of the Pulitzer Prize for Fiction, both masterful explorations of family relations anchored by sharply realized details of Mississippi geography and customs.

Gracious and unassuming, Welty became an admired mentor to younger writers. Her reflections on her career and insights about writing are collected in *The Eye of the Story* (1979), *One Writer's Beginning* (1984), and *On Writing* (2002). In 1980, she received the Presidential Medal of Freedom, in 1985 the National Medal of Arts, and in 1992 the PEN/Malamud Award for the Short Story.

Edith Wharton (1862–1937)
Novelist

Edith Wharton is arguably the first great American female novelist. Encouraged by her mentor Henry James to write about what she knew best—the complex web of elite New York society—Wharton treated the status of women in that world at the turn of the century in several enduring, fictional classics.

Born in 1862 in a house near Washington Square in New York City, Edith Newbold Jones was the only daughter of socially prominent parents, descended from aristocratic, Old New York families. Educated by private tutors, she divided her time annually in New York, Europe, and Newport, Rhode Island. Delighting in reading and storytelling, she secretly wrote a novella at the age of fifteen, and a collection of her poetry was privately printed at sixteen. In 1885, she married Edward Wharton, a wealthy Bostonian, and assumed her expected role as a young society hostess. Married to a man with whom she had little in common, she suffered periodic bouts of depression that culminated in a nervous breakdown in 1898. During the prescribed rest cure, freed from her social obligations, Wharton resumed her creative writing, publishing a first collection of short stories, *The Greater Inclination*, in 1899, an event that she described as breaking the "chains that had held me for so long in a kind of torpor. For nearly twelve years, I had tried to adjust myself to my marriage; but now I was overmastered by the longing to meet people who shared my interests." She then embarked on the unfashionable artist and intellectual life as a writer, breaking with her social set, which viewed a professional writing career for a woman as scandalous.

Her first novel, *The Valley of Decision* (1902), was a historical novel set in eighteenth-century Italy.

The novella *Sanctuary* followed in 1903 before she produced her first masterwork, *The House of Mirth* (1905), a subtle drama of manners set in the fashionable New York City social world Wharton knew intimately that dramatizes the cost to the central female protagonist, Lily Bart, in challenging gender and social norms. After moving to France in 1907, Wharton produced the least typical, but most widely read, of her books, *Ethan Frome* (1914), a grim tragedy of farming life. *The Custom of the Country* (1913) returns to her usual New York City setting and, following *Summer* (1917), set in New England, and two novels reflecting her wartime experiences, *The Marne* (1918) and *A Son at the Front* (1923), Wharton published her masterpiece, *The Age of Innocence* (1920), which won her the Pulitzer Prize. In it, Wharton offers a nuanced and satirical view of social life in New York in the 1870s focused on the marriage of Newland Archer to May Welland and the consequences of his attraction to his unconventional cousin Ellen Olenska.

Wharton continued to publish important works throughout the 1920s and 1930s, including self-assessments of her writing method and career, *The Writing of Fiction* (1925) and *A Backward Glance* (1934). She remains an influential and powerful contributor to the American literary canon.

Phillis Wheatley (c. 1753–1784)

Poet

The first published African American female poet and, after Anne Bradstreet, the second published American female poet, Phillis Wheatley, with the 1773 publication of her book *Poems on Various Subjects*, also became the first African American to publish a book and the first to attempt to make a living from her writing.

Born in West Africa, she was sold into slavery at the age of seven or eight, transported to the American colonies, and purchased by the Wheatley family in Boston, who provided her surname; her given name comes from the slave ship she arrived in, *The Phillis*. The Wheatleys' eighteen-year-old daughter

Mary taught her to read and write and encouraged her verse writing. She was freed in 1773, shortly after her book of poems was published in England. Wheatley married a freed black grocer in 1778, enduring the deaths of two infant daughters and the imprisonment of her husband for debt. She failed to find a publisher or patron for a second poetry collection and was forced to support her infant son as a scullery maid in a boardinghouse. She died at the age of thirty-one.

Wheatley's first published poem, "An Elegiac Poem, on the Death of That Celebrated Divine, and Eminent Servant of Jesus Christ, the Reverend and Learned George Whitfield," a tribute to the leading minister of the religious revivalist movement of the 1740s and 1750s, known as the Great Awakening, at the age of fourteen, earned her the attention of Boston's literary elite and established her as a prodigy. Some doubted that a female African slave could have been the author, and Wheatley was forced in 1772 to defend her authorship in court, where a group of Boston luminaries, including Thomas Hutchinson, the governor, concluded that she had indeed written the poems attributed to her. Their attestation was included as the preface to her collection, published in England. Included is "On Being Brought from Africa to America," in which she recalls, "Twas mercy brought me from my Pagan land. / Taught my benighted soul to understand / That there's a God, that there's a Saviour too: / Once I redemption neither sought nor knew." Wheatley's classicism (she mastered Greek and Latin), expressed in her allusions, poetic forms, and subjects (mainly religious), is remarkable for a woman of her time, making her one of the earliest and most accomplished American female writers.

Laura Ingalls Wilder (1867–1957)

Novelist

Laura Ingalls Wilder is best known for her eight-volume *Little House* children's book series, published between 1932 and 1943, based on her own experiences of frontier life. Regarded

as a children's literature classic, Wilder's works are unique in that they reflect their author's progress from childhood, through adolescence, and on to married life, "growing up" in language and style as Wilder's own experiences matured.

Wilder was born in the Big Woods region of Wisconsin, the second of five children. When she was two years old, the family settled in 1869 in the Indian country of Kansas, near current-day Independence, Kansas. In 1871, they were on the move again back to Wisconsin and then on to Minnesota and South Dakota, where, at the age of fifteen, she began teaching in a one-room schoolhouse while attending high school. She married Almanzo Wilder in 1885 and gave birth to her daughter, Rose, in 1886. Almanzo's illness from diphtheria left him partially paralyzed, and a fire destroyed their South Dakota home. In 1894, the Wilders moved to Mansfield, Missouri, settling in a log cabin on an undeveloped property that eventually became a prosperous poultry, dairy, and fruit farm. Wilder's writing career began in 1911 with articles and columns in the *Missouri Ruralist*. A regular feature, "As a Farm Woman Thinks" found a receptive audience for Wilder's domestic subject, and she was encouraged by her daughter to develop her writing talents.

After the stock market crash of 1929 wiped out the family's investments, Wilder was prompted to earn additional income by recasting her memories of childhood into a book called *Pioneer Girl*. Her publisher encouraged her to develop and expand her story into a series, and the first book, *Little House in the Big Woods*, appeared in 1932, followed by *Farmer Boy* (1933), *Little House on the Prairie* (1935), *On the Banks of Plum Creek* (1937), *By the Shores of Silver Lake* (1939), *The Long Winter* (1940), *Little Town on the Prairie* (1941), and *These Happy Golden Years* (1943). A ninth volume, *The First Four Years*, which chronicles Laura and Almanzo's early married life, was published posthumously in 1971. Each of the *Little House* books chronicles portions of Wilder's experiences, somewhat altered from the particulars of Wilder's actual biographical chronology. They achieved great success due to their intimate portrayals of frontier and family life.

Despite her popularity and acclaim for her classic series, controversy has clouded Wilder's legacy. One issue has been the extent to which her daughter Rose Wilder Lane was responsible for the production of her mother's books and whether she was in fact a coauthor. More recently, the American Library Association's lifetime achievement award, the Laura Ingalls Wilder Medal, was renamed the Children's Literature Legacy Award in 2018 due to charges of racist language and bias against Native Americans and African Americans in Wilder's books.

ART AND APPLIED ARTS

What is the difference between the terms "art" and "applied arts"? The two art forms often overlap—for example, book and magazine illustration—but what mainly separates them is the categorization of art as fine art, meaning art intended to create pleasure or for its capacity to stimulate the intellect such as painting, sculpture, or photography, while applied arts refers to the application of an aesthetic approach in creating objects or pictures to be used rather than simply viewed and can include a subset called the decorative arts. Examples are pottery, religious articles, textile and fashion design, interior decoration, architecture, commercial photography, and photojournalism.

When asked to name influential artists throughout history, it generally takes a conscious effort on the part of most people to include more than a few women on the list, yet women as well as men have created art and been influential in the world of art since the beginning of human history. Studies of cave paintings during the Paleolithic era often show human handprints, 75 percent of which have been identified as belonging to women. The studies of early ethnographers and cultural anthropologists showed that women were often the principal artisans in Neolithic communities, creating pottery, textiles, baskets, painted surfaces, and jewelry and collaborating with men on larger projects. References have been found to women as artists and artisans during the Classical

Antiquity era, which comprised the Greco-Roman world between the eighth century B.C.E. and the sixth century C.E. Pliny the Elder, a Roman historian, claimed that the first drawing ever made was by a woman, Dibutades, who traced the silhouette of her lover on a wall. The majority of female artists who followed her received little attention until the late twentieth century. One writer who did pay attention very early on was Christine de Pizan, an Italian/French author, rhetorician, and critic of the Renaissance who paid tribute to several female artists such as illustrator Hildegard of Bingen in her 1405 protofeminist work *The Book of the City of Ladies.*

Several factors contributed to the exclusion of women from the records of art history. Art forms such as applied and decorative arts were considered crafts or merely utilitarian items to be manufactured and sold; women who did not come from artist families or find a patron were at a disadvantage when attempting to develop their talents, and women were denied entrance into most of the academies that in the eighteenth century began to train and exhibit the work of male artists. Those women who managed to receive training in the arts and produce artwork were considered by men to be either inferior artists or had become successful because they had simply imitated the work of their fathers, husbands, brothers, or other male artists. During the colonial period, American female artists, especially white women from well-to-do families, would fare slightly better, but for many of them, the making of fine art was a hobby rather than a vocation.

The first examples of American women's art are the baskets, pottery, quillwork, paintings on leather, and quillwork produced by Native American women long before the first European settlers arrived in America. Once reserved for display in museums of ethnography, these works of art have become included in the exhibits of fine art museums. The designs of Native American women have become major influences on modern art for their traditional use of geometric and abstract patterns, although animals, birds, and flowers were sometimes incorporated into their artwork.

The first art created by American women of European descent during the colonial period reflected the domestic arts and skills they learned while growing up. Women were taught to sew and embroider at a young age and often created needlework samplers: pieces of embroidery or cross-stitching that frequently included the alphabet, motifs that might include figures such as flowers and birds, aphorisms or biblical extracts, and decorative borders and the embroiderer's name and date of completion. Women were also tasked with the making of rugs and quilts from a young age, and because a shortage of fabric had occurred, they pieced together leftover scraps to create utilitarian items with designs that became works of art. Like the household items produced by Native American women, these examples of folk art have been included in the collections of fine art museums. The first exhibition of early American folk art in the United States took place in 1924 at a gallery owned by art collector and arts patron Gertrude Vanderbilt Whitney and managed by Whitney's personal secretary and folk art enthusiast Juliana Force (1876–1948).

Until the founding of the first women's academies and colleges and the advent of public education, American women who created fine art in the eighteenth century and for much of the nineteenth century were hampered in their training by their lack of educational opportunity and their exclusion from professional art academies. Another hindrance in the training of female artists in the nineteenth

Sculptor and art collector Gertrude Vanderbilt Whitney, who was born into the Vanderbilt family fortune, founded the Whitney Museum of American Art in New York City in 1930.

century was the inability of women to draw from nude models or to study anatomy, considered unseemly and unimportant for young women in ladies' academies and for those who took private drawing classes. Instruction was limited and constrained since the development of women's artistic abilities was regarded as just one more socially acceptable skill to be displayed by an accomplished woman, like music or needlework.

Female artists during the colonial era and well into the nineteenth century were either the daughters or wives of artists and were taught at home, received training in the countries from which they emigrated, were able to secure the interest of male painters who agreed to teach them, or were self-taught. Notable colonial examples include Henrietta Deering Johnston, an Irish immigrant, who was the first to create portraits in pastels; Patience Lovell Wright, one of nine siblings in a strictly observant Quaker family, who taught herself to mold figures in dough and clay and went on to become the first

American professional sculptor, modeling portraits in wax; and portrait miniaturist Hetty Sage Benbridge, the wife of portrait painter Charles Benbridge, who was aided in her technique by American painter Charles Willson Peale, best known for his portraits of leaders of the American Revolution and for establishing one of the first museums in the United States.

Formal training for female artists began when American art academies, such as the Pennsylvania Academy of Fine Arts (1805) and the National Gallery of Design (1863), slowly started to admit women in the mid- to late nineteenth century. However, in 1818, Sarah Miriam Peale (1800–1885), the daughter of Charles Willson Peale and a portrait painter considered to be the first American woman to succeed as a professional painter, exhibited her first full-size portrait at the Pennsylvania Academy of Fine Arts, founded in 1805. In 1824, Sarah and her sister, Anna Claypoole Peale (1791–1878), a portrait miniaturist and still-life painter, became the first women to be accepted into the academy. It wasn't until 1844 that the academy set aside its statue gallery for the exclusive use of women on certain days of the week. The same year, Sarah Worthington Peter (1800–1877), the daughter of the governor of Ohio and a patron of the arts, opened the Philadelphia School of Design for Women to provide training in such arts as engraving, textile design, illustration, and furniture carving to assist single and destitute women in finding employment in trades that required these skills. Other art schools, such as the Cooper Institute of Design for Women in New York (1854), would follow. By the 1870s, women in the first art academies were allowed to draw the male nude but only in segregated, so-called "Ladies' Life" classes. Although membership in the National Academy of Design, an honorary association of artists founded in New York in 1825, was essential to an artist's prestige, only one woman was elected to full membership before 1900: portrait miniaturist Ann Hall, who had earlier participated in exhibitions at the American Academy of Fine Arts. In 1889, a group of female artists, recognizing the need for women to achieve equality with men in the art world, founded the Women's Art Club of New York to support the ambitions of their sister artists and to exhibit their work. The organization was renamed the National Association of Women Painters and Sculptors in 1913 and, since 1941, has been known as the National Association of Women Artists, Inc. (NAWA).

The participation of American women in the art of photography began in the nineteenth century with portrait photography first as a hobby and then

Studio photographer Zaida Ben-Yusuf created portraits of the elite members of New York society with such skill and quality that years later the Smithsonian mounted an exhibition of her work. This is a self-portrait she took in 1901.

as a profession. Two of the earliest and most accomplished amateur portrait photographers are Marian Hooper Adams (1843–1885), a Washington, D.C., socialite and wife of historian Henry Adams, who photographed and developed portraits of friends, family, and politicians; and Sarah Choate Sears (1858–1935), a Massachusetts artist and art collector, who received international recognition for her portraits and flower studies. In 1890, Alice Boughton (1866–1943), who had studied both art and photography at the Pratt School of Art and Design in Brooklyn, New York, was one of the first women to open a studio in New York City, becoming one the city's most distinguished professional portrait photographers. In 1897, Zaida Ben-Yusef (1869–1933), a German Algerian woman who had immigrated to the United States from Great Britain in 1895, established a studio on New York's Fifth Avenue, where she gained a reputation for her portraits of wealthy, fashionable, and famous Americans. In 2008, the Smithsonian National Portrait Gallery mounted an exhibition dedicated to her work.

Some photographers practiced the art of pictorialism, an aesthetic movement in which a straightforward photograph is manipulated to create an artistic image that, like a painting, drawing, or engraving, is intended to evoke an emotional reaction from the viewer. Pictorialism was popular from the late nineteenth century until about 1915, but the practice continued until the late 1920s, when it was supplanted by the modernism that influenced both visual and performing arts. One notable pictorialist was Doris Ulmann (1882–1934), who documented the Appalachia and Gullah communities of the American South. In the 1930s, the documentation of Americans in rural and urban communities, as well as urban architecture and design, became hallmarks of the work of photographers Berenice Abbott, Dorothea Lange, and Margaret Bourke-White, who would also become America's first female photojournalist.

The last half of the nineteenth century was the era known as the Gilded Age for the opulance displayed by the families who had become rich as a result of the rise of American industry; the wives of the wealthy avidly collected fine art, were patrons of the arts, founded art museums, and featured women's art in exhibitions. Notable examples include Isabella Stewart Gardner (1840–1924), whose collection of European art and turn-of-the-century American art filled her Boston mansion, which she would convert to the Isabella Gardner Museum in 1903, and Louisine Havemeyer (1840–1929), a suffragist and a founder of the National Women's Party as well as an art collector, whose collection is displayed at the Metropolitan Museum of Art. Chicago businesswoman and socialite Bertha Palmer (1849–1918) built an extensive collection of French Impressionists, which occupies a significant space in the Art Institute of Chicago. Palmer served as president of the "Board of Lady Managers" during the planning for a Women's Building at the World's Columbian Exposition held in Chicago in 1893. After interviewing fourteen female architects to design the building, the board chose Sophia Hayden (1868–1953), the first female graduate of the four-year program in architecture at the Massachusetts Institute of Technology. The Women's Building featured exhibits of works by women that included works of both fine art and applied art. In 1930, sculptor, art collector, and arts patron Gertrude Vanderbilt Whitney (1875–1942) founded the Whitney Museum of American Art in New York City, whose first director was Juliana Force. Peggy Guggenheim (1898–1979), an art collector, socialite, and niece of businessman and philanthropist Solomon R. Guggenheim, who would establish the foundation that would create the Solomon R. Guggenheim Museum of Art in New York City, opened the Peggy Guggenheim Collection in Venice, Italy, in her former home in 1951.

American women's work in the applied arts of fashion and interior design would evolve in the twentieth century. Interior design was not considered an art or a profession in the United States until 1905, and from the eighteenth century until the 1940s, American female dressmakers largely copied the styles of the period in which they lived after the couture looks of male and female European designers, most notably French designer Coco Chanel, who, in the 1920s, introduced what became regarded as staples of women's sportswear, itself modeled, in part, on menswear. Until ready-to-wear designer clothing became widely available at the start of the twentieth century, wealthy women often purchased their dresses directly from Europe. By the

1950s, designers such as Claire McCardell and Bonnie Cashin had become influential shapers of American women's fashion. They, in turn, would be followed during the rest of the twentieth century and beyond by such well-known and influential American designers as Donna Karan, Anne Klein, Diane von Furstenberg, Caroline Herrera, Betsey Johnson, Norma Kamali, Tracy Reese, and Vera Wang.

Despite the greatly increased presence of women in the fine and applied arts as creators or administrators, a gender disparity in the representation of women in the art world remains. From 2007 to 2013, only 27 percent of female artists were featured in the 590 exhibitions by nearly seventy institutions in the United States, and only 30 percent of artists represented by commercial galleries were women. The Pritzker Architecture Prize has been awarded to only 7 percent of women since its establishment in 1979, and none of the winners have been American women. Although women direct 47.6 percent of museums in the United States, they lag behind men in the directorships of museums with budgets over $15

million and continue to earn only seventy cents for every dollar earned by male museum directors. Such gender inequity has been particularly challenging for female artists of color. To help call attention to the lack of parity experienced by female artists, the National Museum of Women in the Arts in Washington, D.C., initiated #5WomenArtists in 2016, asking those on social media to name five female artists. The initiative is intended to work toward promoting gender equity in the art world, but it is also an effective method of raising awareness about the remarkable work of female artists past and present in the United States and around the world.

BIOGRAPHIES

Berenice Abbott (1898–1991)
Photographer

Celebrated for her photographs of twentieth-century New York City architecture and urban design as well as her portraits of cultural figures and studies of scientific subjects, Berenice Abbott was born Bernice Abbott in Springfield, Ohio, where she was raised by her divorced mother. After attending Ohio State University for two semesters, she moved to New York City in 1918, where she spent four years studying sculpture and drawing on her own and then continued her studies in Berlin. From 1923 to 1935, she worked in Paris as a darkroom assistant to the American Dadaist and surrealist artist Man Ray. In 1925, she set up her own photography school in Paris and produced several portraits of such well-known expatriates, artists, and writers as James Joyce, Andre Gide, Marcel Duchamp, Jean Cocteau, and Edna St. Vincent Millay. It was around this time that Abbott adopted "Berenice," the French spelling of her first name. She also discovered the work of French documentary photographer Eugene Atget, little known outside Paris. After Atget's death in 1927, Abbott saved his prints and negatives from destruction and began promoting his work, which was acquired by the Museum of Modern Art in New York City in 1968.

Choosing to focus on the photographic arts, Doris Ulmann found her main subjects in the American South and chronicled the lifestyles of the local residents so their stories could be seen by Americans from all walks of life.

When Abbott returned to New York City in 1929, she opened a portrait studio, participated in modernist photography exhibitions, and published her photographs. Inspired by Atget's work and the writings of historian Lewis Mumford, who had criticized urban architectural design influenced by the post-Civil War industrial era, Abbott began to document the skyscrapers of the city's changing architecture as well as the fast tempo of city life in a project she called *Changing New York*. In 1934, the Museum of the City of New York hosted Abbott's first solo exhibition, which received critical acclaim, especially from art critic and historian Elizabeth McCausland (1899–1965), who would assist Abbott with her project and become her life partner. The couple traveled together from Florida to Maine so that Abbott could document the small towns and growing automobile-related architecture. Some 2,500 negatives resulted from the trip. In 1935, Abbott's *Changing New York* project became the Federal Art Project of the Works Progress Administration in 1935, and in 1939, a selection from her 305 photographs was featured along with text by McCausland in the book *Changing New York*, published shortly before the opening of the New York World's Fair the same year.

In the late 1930s, Abbott turned her attention to science, producing images of medical technology and inventing photography equipment such as a darkroom distorter, picture composer, thumb camera, and Hi-Shot Shoulder Pod, which would allow her to enhance the realistic quality of her photographs. In 1947, she founded the corporation House of Photography to develop, promote, and sell some of her inventions. The company was in operation until 1959. From 1934 to 1958, she taught photography at the New School for Social Research. In 1941, she published *A Guide to Better Photography*, in which she asserted her commitment to straight photography and realism.

After the death of Elizabeth McCausland, Abbott moved to Monson, Maine, where she spent the last decades of her life in the home she had purchased in 1954. She documented the state and published her photographs in a 1968 book called *A Portrait of Maine*. The year after her death, an award-winning 1992 documentary on her life, *Berenice Abbott: A View of the 20ᵗʰ Century* by filmmakers Fay Wheeler and Martha Wheelock, featured a first-person narrative by Abbott as well as two hundred of her black-and-white photographs.

Diane Arbus (1923–1971)
Photographer

Once considered a cult photographer, Diane Arbus is now considered one of photography's greatest artists, having changed culture's definition of *odd*, *unusual*, or *freak*. She paved the way for experimental photographers from Robert Mapplethorpe to Andy Warhol to Katharina Bosse and many others who have shown us different ways to view the world. Her vision and courage to go deeper than the superficial is her enduring legacy.

Arbus was born to affluent New York parents, Gertrude and David Nemerov. Encouraged to pursue the arts, Arbus's sister became an accomplished painter, and her brother, Howard Nemerov, became a Pulitzer Prize-winning poet. All three attended the Ethical Culture Fieldston School. At fourteen, Diane met Allan Arbus, a photographer and later an artist, and the two conducted a clandestine affair for four years before marrying in 1941, shortly after Arbus's eighteenth birthday. The couple had two children during their twenty-year marriage.

Creating the Allan and Diane Arbus Studio in 1946, they became successful fashion photographers. In 1957, Arbus quit the studio to pursue independent work. Excruciatingly shy, yet almost obsessively curious, she began to transform and deepen photography beyond recording pretty landscapes and portraiture of elegantly staged people. Her subjects offered a kind of cultural anthropology of outsiders from drag queens to junkies, from midgets to nudists, and many people who were considered freaks or odd by conventional standards. Looking at an Arbus photograph can be disconcerting, alarming, or exciting but never boring. Her photographs are stories with great subtexts that she may, or may not, have intended.

Acknowledgment of her work came in the form of two Guggenheim fellowships, in 1963 and 1966, and an exhibition of her work at the Museum of Modern Art in 1967. While awaiting recognition,

Arbus took on many jobs and assignments from teaching photography to researching press photography at the Museum of Modern Art and then returning to commercial photography.

She became the first American and first woman to show her photographs at the 1972 Venice Biennale. Beset by depression throughout her life, Arbus committed suicide in 1971 at the age of forty-eight. When the Museum of Modern Art presented a posthumous exhibition in 1972, it was viewed by more than seven million people, sealing her reputation as one of the most outstanding contemporary artists of the twentieth century. It was the most popular photographic exhibition since The Family of Man, developed by Edward Steichen in 1955. Arbus said of her photographs, "What I'm trying to describe is that it's impossible to get out of your skin into someone else's … that somebody else's tragedy is not the same as your own."

Ruth Asawa (1926–2013)

Sculptor

Japanese American artist Ruth Asawa received her first art training in an internment camp during World War II. She is best known for her wire sculptures, borrowing techniques from Mexican basket weavers and inspired by plants, shells, and spider webs. Her works are on display in the Guggenheim Museum and the Whitney Museum of American Art in New York City and San Francisco's de Young Museum. She was a founder of the San Francisco School of the Arts, which was renamed the Ruth Asawa San Francisco School of the Arts in 2010 in her honor.

Asawa was born in Norwalk, California, to Japanese immigrant parents, who operated a truck farm until her family was interned during World War II. Her art training began in the camp, where she learned to draw from several Japanese American animators from The Walt Disney Studios. She was able to enroll in the Milwaukee State Teachers College in 1943 but was prevented from graduating because of animosity toward her Japanese heritage, which prevented her from required student teaching. From 1946 to 1949, she attended Black Mountain

College. There, she met and married architect Albert Lanier, and the couple had six children together.

Inspired by a trip to Mexico in 1947, Asawa began to adapt the basket-weaving techniques she observed there in her wire sculptures. Her first public sculpture, titled *Andrea's Fountain*, was installed in San Francisco in 1968. Although some were dismayed by her abstract designs, her sculptures were so popular with the public that she designed several more fountains, and she was dubbed the "fountain lady." As one art critic has observed, "Ruth was ahead of her time in understanding how sculpture could function to define and interpret space. This aspect of her work anticipates much of the installation work that has come to dominate contemporary art." Azawa also designed two memorials to Japanese internment: the Internment Memorial Sculpture in San Jose, California, and San Francisco State University's Garden of Remembrance.

An ardent advocate for arts education, Azawa lobbied politicians and foundations to support programs in the arts for young children in San Francisco. Her work culminated in the establishment in 1982 of a public arts high school in San Francisco.

Judy Baca (1946–)

Muralist

An American Chicana artist, activist, and professor, Judy Baca is best known as the director of the mural project that created one of the largest murals in the world, *The Great Wall of Los Angeles*. She is the cofounder and artistic director of the Social and Public Art Resource Center based in Venice, California.

Born in Los Angeles to Mexican American parents, she was raised in the Watts neighborhood of the city in an all-female household consisting of her grandmother, mother, and aunts. Baca was not allowed to speak Spanish in elementary school and did not know English very well. She was told by her teachers to go paint in the corner while the others studied. She gradually mastered English, graduated from high school in 1964, and earned a bachelor's degree from California State University–Northridge in 1969 and a master's degree in art in 1979. She wanted to make art that was accessible beyond the constraints of galleries and museums. "I thought to myself," she recalled, "if I get my work into galleries, who will go there? People in my family hadn't ever been in a gallery in their entire lives. My neighbors never went to galleries…. And it didn't make sense to me at the time to put art behind some guarded wall." This led to Baca's concentration on mural art and the creation of several important works, including in 1970 *Las Vistas Nuevas* and *Mi Abuelita*, which brought together rival gang members as artists under Baca's supervision. She was the founder of the first City of Los Angeles Mural Program in 1974, which evolved into a community arts organization, the Social and Public Art Resource Center. Throughout Los Angeles and in national and international venues, Baca's projects have been created in impoverished neighborhoods that have been revitalized and energized by her murals. Her most monumental work, *The Great Wall of Los Angeles*, covers a mile-long stretch of a flood control channel in the San Fernando Valley and employed more than four hundred at-risk youth and their families along with other artists, oral historians, ethnologists, and community members depicting the multicultural history of California from prehistory through the 1950s. Baca's other important works include *The World Wall: A Vision of the Future without Fear*, a movable painting that shows the world with no violence in panels, which travels around the world with host countries adding to the collection. In 1996, she created *La Memoria de Nuestra Tierra* for the Denver International Airport. Also in 1996, Baca began teaching at the University of California–Los Angeles, and in 1998, she served as a master artist-in-residence at Harvard University.

Cecilia Beaux (1855–1942)

Painter

Cecilia Beaux was one of the most successful portrait painters of late nineteenth and early twentieth centuries.

Beaux's mother died just twelve days after her daughter's birth, and Beaux's widowed father left her to be raised by relatives in New York City and Philadelphia.

She was educated at home and at a Philadelphia finishing school. At sixteen, she took up the study of art under the tutelage of an artist cousin, Catharine Drinker Janvier. In 1883, she opened a studio in Philadelphia, and her first major work, a full-length portrait of her sister and nephew, *Last Days of Infancy*, was exhibited in 1885 at the Pennsylvania Academy of the Fine Arts and in 1886 at the Paris Salon.

After travel and study in Europe in 1888–1889, she returned to her Philadelphia studio and gained considerable success as a portrait painter. In 1895, she became the first female instructor at the Pennsylvania Academy of the Fine Arts, and in 1896, she exhibited six portraits at the Paris Salon. She moved to New York in 1900, where her reputation as the rival of John Singer Sargent in the art of fashionable portraiture led to a series of important commissions, including portraits of Mrs. Theodore Roosevelt and Mrs. Andrew Carnegie.

Following an injury in 1924, she stopped painting but published her autobiography, *Background with Figures*, in 1930. She was elected to the American Academy of Arts and Letters in 1933, and in 1935, the academy presented a retrospective exhibition of some sixty-five of her works, solidifying her reputation as one of America's great portrait painters.

Louise Blanchard Bethune (1856–1913)

Architect

The first professional female architect in the United States, Louise Blanchard Bethune designed some 150 buildings in Buffalo, New York, and throughout New England in the late nineteenth and early twentieth centuries and was the first woman to be elected to the American Institute of Architects.

Born Jennie Louise Blanchard in Waterloo, New York, she graduated from Buffalo High School in 1874, and in 1881, she married architect Robert Bethune. She planned to attend architecture school at Cornell University, but at the time, women were considered unsuited to the demanding profession of architecture. Determined to enter the profession,

coats (1952), industrial zippers (1955), and jump-suits (1957). She created the poncho by cutting a hole in a blanket to stay warm while driving her convertible. She became one of the first designers to create and popularize women's sportswear, which began to define the new modern woman.

Mary Cassatt (1845–1926)

Painter

The only woman in the Impressionist group of artists who helped to redirect modern art, Mary Cassatt is universally regarded as the greatest female artist of the nineteenth century. She has also been called "the most significant American artist, male or female, of her generation." As friend and influential art editor and critic Forbes Watson said, rejecting her title as America's best female painter, "Much more interesting and revealing would be a list of men who painted better than Mary. It would be a very short list."

Born in Pittsburgh, Pennsylvania, Cassatt was the daughter of a successful stockbroker and real estate speculator. She was inspired to become a painter when at the age of seven, she accompanied her family on an extended four-year European trip to France and Germany, where she was exposed to great European works of art for the first time. While there, she developed an enduring love for Paris and French culture and was determined to return to study painting.

In 1861, she began to study at the Pennsylvania Academy of Fine Arts. When she declared to her father her intention to become a professional painter, he said, "I would almost rather see you dead." However, he supported her decision to return to Europe to study, and, in 1866, she moved to Paris and began her training by copying paintings in museums. After additional time in Italy and Spain, she began exhibiting regularly in the 1870s at the Paris Salon, but she stopped when its jury disapproved of the avant-garde direction of her work. In 1877, Edgar Degas invited her to exhibit with the Independents (called Impressionists by hostile critics). As Degas told Cassatt, "Most women paint as though they are trimming

hats.... Not you." Cassatt and the other Impressionists began the greatest redefinition of art since the Renaissance. Committed to truthful depiction of ordinary life, the Impressionists sought to recreate an artist or viewer's impressions of a scene and explored the effect of light on a subject. Cassatt's works are characterized by their unusual angles of vision and natural and unposed portraits. Cassatt is most famous for her many depictions of mothers and their children.

In 1893, Cassatt bought a chateau in Oise, where she lived and worked until her death. In 1904, she was made a chevalier of the French Legion of Honor. Her artistic greatness was finally recognized in the United States when the Pennsylvania Academy and the Chicago Institute awarded her several prizes (all of which Cassatt rejected). Cassatt lost her eyesight in her later years and was forced to stop painting. She died at her chateau at the age of eighty-two, having achieved during her long life the double distinction of pioneering a new art and a new role for female artists.

Judy Chicago (1939–)

Artist, Educator

Judy Chicago is considered the founder of American feminist art, who in the 1970s founded the first feminist art program in the United States. Her most well-known work is *The Dinner Party*, permanently installed in the Elizabeth A. Sackler Center for Feminist Art at the Brooklyn Museum, which celebrates the accomplishments of women throughout history, and is widely regarded as the first epic feminist artwork.

Born in Chicago as Judith Cohen, her father was a labor organizer and a Marxist. During the McCarthy era in the 1950s, he was investigated and had difficulty supporting his family, dying in 1953. Encouraged in her love of art by her mother, Chicago knew by the age of five that she "never wanted to do anything but make art." She attended UCLA, where she became politically active. In 1965, Chicago displayed work in her first solo show in Los Angeles. Gallery owner Rolf Nelson nicknamed her "Judy Chicago" because of her strong Chicago accent. Asked why she did not participate in the California Women in the Arts exhibit, she answered, "I won't show in any group defined as Woman, Jewish, or California. Someday when we all group up there will be no labels." She took up auto bodywork to learn the spray-painting techniques that would later define her style of fusing color and surface in many media, which would become a hallmark of her work in later years. She also learned boat building to create sculpture and pyrotechnics to understand how to develop fireworks. With such knowledge, she displayed in her art a diverse range of skills that were incorporated into her metal and fiberglass sculptures and fireworks installations.

The Dinner Party took her more than five years to complete: a monumental project that resulted in a huge triangle (measuring 48x43x36') of thirty-nine place settings, each commemorating a female image: goddess, pharaoh, artist, or political figure. More than four hundred people, nearly all women, volunteered to work on the project. Her next large work, *Birth Project*, took five years (1980–1985) and celebrates a woman's role as the giver of life with images of labor. In the *Holocaust Project*, Chicago illustrated the poetry of Harvey Mudd in a three thousand-square-foot exhibition, complete with audio tour, videotape, and documentation panels.

Chicago's works are in the permanent collections of museums worldwide. She has had more than fifteen one-woman shows. In 1970, Chicago developed the Feminist Art Program at California State University–Fresno. After more than four decades, Chicago continues to be an influential feminist artist, author, and educator. With a determination to remake artistic expression and express contemporary reality, Chicago has persisted in continuing to challenge and innovate.

Minna Wright Citron (1896–1991)

Painter

Best known for her Social Realist images of New York City, Minna Citron's paintings and prints focus on the roles of women, often in a satirical manner.

Born in Newark, New Jersey, she began to study art later in life in 1924 at the Brooklyn Institute of

Arts and Sciences while married and taking care of her two children. By 1928, she was studying at the Art Students League with John Sloan and Kenneth Hayes Miller, whose satirical depictions of city life influence her own style. She had her first solo exhibition at the New School for Social Research in 1930.

Like Isabel Bishop, Minna Citron was part of the 14th Street School of urban realists, who depicted scenes from Union Square in New York City. She also worked as an art teacher and as a muralist as part of the Federal Art Project. After World War II, she traveled abroad to Paris, and her later work became more abstract, incorporating three-dimensional printmaking and assemblage. In the 1970s, she strongly identified with the women's movement and embraced feminism. She continued to work into her nineties. Her work is represented in many museums, including the Metropolitan Museum of Art, the Museum of Modern Art, and the Whitney Museum of American Art.

Caresse Crosby (1891–1970)

Fashion Designer

American patron of the arts and the "literary godmother to the Lost Generation of Expatriate Writers in Paris," Caresse Crosby was the first recipient of a patent for the modern brassiere.

Born Mary Phelps Jacobs in New Rochelle, New York, she came from a prominent New England family whose ancestors included the Plymouth Colony's first governor and Robert Fulton, famed steamboat developer. As she described her background, she was raised "in a world where only good smells existed."

Her contribution to fashion occurred when she was nineteen and dressing for a debutante's ball. Slipping the delicate evening gown over the whalebone corset that was the standard undergarment for women at the time, she disliked the way the corset protruded from her plunging neckline and the sheer fabric. She asked her maid for a pair of silk handkerchiefs, a cord, some pink ribbon, a needle, and thread. She then created the foundation for the modern bra. She dubbed her creation a "brassiere" and filed a patent application, which was approved in 1914. She then started the Fashion Form Brassiere Company in Boston to produce her wireless bras. She would close her shop and sell the patent to Warner Brothers Corset Company for $1,500—an acquisition that would earn the company $15 million over the next thirty years. "I can't say the brassiere will ever take as great a place in history as the steamboat," she declared, "but I did invent it."

After a failed first marriage, she fell in love with and married Harry Crosby and moved with him to France, where they founded the Black Sun Press, which would publish the early work of such writers as Ernest Hemingway, Henry Miller, Anaïs Nin, Kay Boyle, and Hart Crane. They embraced the bohemian life and were at the center of expatriate life in Paris in the 1920s. After Crosby's death in a murder–suicide or double suicide with his mistress, she remarried and lived on a Virginia plantation outside of Washington, D.C. She died in Rome at the age of seventy-eight. Writer Anaïs Nin described her as "a pollen carrier, who mixed, stirred, brewed, and concocted friendships."

Lilly Daché (1898–1989)
Millinery Designer

French-born milliner Lilly Daché established a thriving made-to-order hat business in the United States in the 1930s and 1940s that featured striking innovations, including the cloche hat, the turban, hats woven of kitchen twine, glass- and lucite-encrusted hats, and swagger hats, associated with the actress Marlene Dietrich.

She left school at the age of fourteen and was apprenticed to her aunt, a milliner in Bordeaux, and later to the famous milliner Caroline Reboux of Paris. In 1924, Daché moved to New York City, where she worked as a salesclerk at Macy's department store and then at a small milliner's shop. She would eventually buy out her employer, and the shop began to feature her innovative hat designs, which included draped turbans, brimmed hats molded to the head, half hats, visored caps for war workers, cone-tipped berets, colored snoods, and elaborate floral creations.

In 1937, Daché moved her operation to a building on East 56th Street, which combined her retail sales, wholesale trade, workroom, and living space. She would eventually employ the designer Halston and the hair stylist Kenneth before both went into business for themselves. By 1949, Daché was also designing accessories, costume jewelry, and perfume. Her celebrity clients included Sonja Henie, Audrey Hepburn, Carole Lombard, and Marlene Dietrich. In 1968, she retired and died in France at the age of ninety-one.

Elaine de Kooning (1918–1989)
Painter

Considered by many to be the voice of the Abstract Expressionism art movement in her numerous articles as a critic for *ARTnews*, Elaine de Kooning was herself an important artist, best known for her Expressionistic portraiture.

Born Elaine Fried in New York City, she developed her interest in art through museum trips and the encouragement of her mother. After graduating from Erasmus Hall High School in Brooklyn and briefly attending Hunter College, in 1938, she was introduced to artist Willem de Kooning. They were married in 1943. She began writing for *ARTnews* in 1949 to ease their dire poverty. In the early 1940s, she began painting self-portraits and portraits of family and friends as a way of differentiating herself from her husband, who was working in an increasingly abstract style. In numerous series—"bullfights," "basketball players," and "Bacchus"—de Kooning brought the methods of Abstract Expressionism to bear on figurative subjects.

Her first solo exhibitions were in the 1950s, and her works were included in major museum exhibitions, most notably The Fifties: Aspects of Painting in New York (1980). She is perhaps best known for her portrait of John F. Kennedy, commissioned by the Truman Library, in which she created hundreds of sketches and at least two dozen canvases in her attempt to capture his character and essence.

De Kooning taught at numerous colleges, including Yale University and the Parsons New School for Design. Her paintings are included in the collection of major American museums such as the

Guggenheim Museum and the Museum of Modern Art. In 2016, de Kooning was one of twelve female artists featured in the Women in Abstract Expressionism show created by the Denver Art Museum, designed to highlight the unique talents and perspectives of female artists who were often dismissed or overshadowed by their fellow male artists. For de Kooning, who was often overshadowed by her more famous husband, the exhibition provided an occasion for a reevaluation of her and other female artists in the evolution and development of modern art.

Elsie de Wolfe (1859–1950)

Interior Decorator

The first professional interior designer in America, Elsie de Wolfe was the preeminent interior designer and taste maker for much of the first half of the twentieth century. According to *The New Yorker*, "Interior design as a profession was invented by Elsie de Wolfe."

Born in New York City, de Wolfe was privately educated in New York and Edinburgh, Scotland, where she lived with maternal relatives. She was presented at Queen Victoria's court in 1883 and entered London and New York society. The death of de Wolfe's father in 1890 left the family in financial difficulty, and de Wolfe turned to the stage, forming her own touring company in 1901 before retiring from the stage in 1905.

De Wolfe next turned her attention to interior decoration, at the time an almost exclusively masculine field. Her reputation as a stage set designer and her society connections helped her advance in the field. Architect Stanford White helped her win a commission to design the interior of the Colony Club, New York's first social club for women. There, she displayed her signature style: simplicity, airiness (through the use of mirrors and light-hued paint and fabrics), and a visual unity that contrasted markedly with the popular Victorian cluttered style. Among de Wolfe's distinguished clients were Amy Vanderbilt, Anne Morgan, the Duke and Duchess of Windsor, and Henry Clay and Adelaide Frick as

she transformed the interiors of wealthy homes from dark wood, heavily curtained interiors into light, intimate spaces. Her book, *The House in Good Taste*, would influence several generations of designers.

By 1926, *The New York Times* described de Wolfe as "one of the most widely known women in New York social life." The same year, she married British diplomat Sir Charles Mendl and moved to Beverly Hills, California, where she shocked the world by becoming most likely the first woman to dye her hair blue, performing handstands to impress her friends, and covering eighteenth-century footstools in leopard-skin chintzes. Her autobiography, *After All*, was published in 1935.

Clare Falkenstein (1908–1997)

Artist

One of America's most experimental and productive twentieth-century artists, sculptor, painter, printmaker, and jewelry designer Clare Falkenstein was best known for her wire and fused glass sculptures, which explored the concept of infinite space.

Born in Coos Bay, Oregon, Falkenstein moved with her family to Berkeley, California, in 1920. She received a BA degree from the University of California–Berkeley in 1930, where she studied art, anthropology, and philosophy. While still a student, she had her first solo exhibition. In the early years of her career, she worked mainly with clay to create abstract ceramic sculptures. From clay, she moved to wood as a sculptural medium, producing the *Set Structures*, a series of wood sculptures made between 1941 and 1944, which led to her first solo exhibition in New York. These works, which she called "exploding volumes," were intended to be taken apart and reassembled by the viewer.

In 1947, while on the faculty of the California School of Fine Arts (now the San Francisco Art Institute), she began working with alternative materials such as sheet aluminum, wire, glass, and plastic. She moved to Paris in 1950 and began creating open wire sculptures there. She created several large-scale commissions, including the railing of the Galleria Spazio, Rome (1958) and the gates of the Palazzo Venier de Leoni, Venice (1961). In 1963, Falkenstein created a monumental sculpture for the fountain of the California Federal Savings corporate headquarters in Los Angeles, featuring over a ton of copper tubing and colored glass. It would be the first of several public art commissions she would complete in California. Later in life, she shifted away from large, physically demanding metal sculptures and turned to painting. She died in Venice, California, at the age of eighty-nine, having produced over her long career over four thousand sculptures, paintings, and drawings.

Audrey Flack (1931–)
Painter, Sculptor

Painter and sculptor Audrey Flack is a pioneer of photorealism, one of the first artists to use a projection of a photograph as an aid to painting, and is the first photorealistic painter whose work was included in the permanent collection of the Museum of Modern Art. She also is the first female artist, along with Mary Cassatt, to be included in Anthony Janson's influential textbook *History of Art*.

Flack began studying art at Cooper Union in New York from 1948 to 1951 before going to Yale University to work with Abstract Expressionist painter Josef Albers, who would influence her early style. She returned to New York to study art history at New York University's Institute of Fine Arts in 1953 and to improve her ability to paint in a realistic manner and enrolled at the Art Students League to study anatomy.

In the 1960s, Flack pioneered photorealism, becoming one of the first painters to use photographs as the foundation for her work. Her achievement is evident in *Kennedy Motorcade, November 22, 1963* (1964); her paintings of mundane objects such as perfume bottles; and *Farb Family Portrait* (1969–1970), in which a slide of a family portrait is projected onto the canvas as a guide for painting. Applying paint in layers with an airbrush, Flack created a number of iconic works such as a portrait of Michelangelo's *David* (1971). Through the 1970s, Flack composed primarily still lifes, including *Royal Flush* (1977), a close-up hyperrealistic painting of a table strewn with money, playing cards, cigars, cigarettes, beer, and whiskey. Other notable works include her *Vanitas* series, including *World War II* (1976–1977), *Marilyn* (1977), and *Wheel of Fortune* (1977–1978). Beginning in the 1980s, Flack switched from painting to sculpture in a series of pieces such as *Egyptian Rocket Goddess* (1990) and *Medusa* (1991), reinterpreting mythological figures that evoke a feminist message.

Flack is the author of *On Painting* (1986), *The Daily Muse* (1989), and *Art & Soul* (1991). She continues to produce important works that extend the boundary of modern artistic expression.

Helen Frankenthaler (1928–2011)
Painter

One of the most important figures in postwar American painting, Helen Frankenthaler, like her fellow Abstract Expressionist Jackson Pollock, significantly redefined the methods and meaning of modern visual art that had held sway since the Renaissance.

Frankenthaler was born in New York City. Her father, Alfred Frankenthaler, was a respected New York State Supreme Court judge. She grew up privileged and was encouraged to pursue a professional career. She studied art at the private Dalton School and Bennington College in Vermont, where she graduated in 1949. She returned to paint full-time and would associate with the central figures of the New York School of postwar artists, including Willem de Kooning, Lee Krasner, and Jackson Pollock. She became an exponent of Abstract Expressionism like many in the group, but her method of paint application was markedly original: thinning the oil paint to the consistency of watercolor so it would soak into and stain the canvas rather than accumulate on its surface. Her "soak-in" or "stain painting" technique, inspired by Pollock's drip style, produced a striking and diaphanous use of color, as in her well-known masterwork *Mountains and Sea* (1953). Although working in a field dominated by male artists and critics, Frankenthaler gained solo exhibitions and respect from her peers. In the 1960s, she began to use acrylics, and her later exhibits included lithographs and works on paper. Important later works include *This Morning's Weather* (1982), *Seeing the Moon on a Hot Summer Day* (1987), *Warming Trend* (2002), *Ebbing* (2002), and *Yoruba* (2002).

In 1958, Frankenthaler married American painter Robert Motherwell. They would divorce in 1971, and Frankenthaler bought a second home and studio in Connecticut, where she produced welded-steel sculptures, prints, and illustrated books. She received the National Medal of Arts in 2001. Although she achieved great success in the art world dominated by men, Frankenthaler did not consider herself a feminist. "For me, being a 'lady painter' was never an issue," she observed. "I don't resent being a female painter. I don't exploit it. I paint." She died in her Connecticut home at the age of eighty-three, having established and endowed the Helen Frankenthaler Foundation, dedicated to promoting greater public interest in and understanding of the visual arts.

Wilhelmina Weber Furlong (1878–1962)

Painter

Considered America's first female modern artist and its first female modernist painter, Wilhelmina Weber Furlong was a pioneering figure of modern Impressionism and Expressionism at the turn of the twentieth century and the outset of the American modernist movement.

Born in St. Louis, Missouri, Furlong studied art and trained in Paris from 1897 to 1906, where she associated with Pablo Picasso and Paul Cézanne, and from 1906 to 1913, she painted in Mexico City before moving to New York City, where she lived and worked until 1947.

Furlong was associated with the Art Students League as a secretary–treasurer and a member of its board along with her husband, artist Thomas Furlong. Her circle of friends and associates included Edward Hopper, Alexander Calder, Rockwell Kent, Thomas Hart Benton, and Willem de Kooning. Her works cover the gamut of modernist styles from Impressionism to Expressionism during a productive career that spanned from 1892 to 1962. As one of the only female artists at the center of the American modernist movement, she endured critical neglect and attacks in a male-dominated artistic and critical community. She excelled in Impressionistic and Expressionistic still lifes and landscapes.

Helen Hardin (1943–1984)

Painter

One of the most accomplished Native American painters in the modern age, Helen Hardin produced works with geometric patterns based on Native American symbols and motifs, creating a fusion of traditional folk art with modernist techniques.

Born in Albuquerque, New Mexico, she was the daughter of Santa Clara Pueblo artist Pablita Velarde and Herbert Hardin, a police officer. Her first language was Tewa, and she was named Tsa-Sah-Wee-Eh or "Little Standing Spruce." Describing her mixed heritage, she described herself as "Anglo socially and Indian in art." By the age of six, she won prizes for her drawing and began selling her work when she was nine. Although influenced by her mother's works, Hardin wanted to create her own style. While in high school, she was featured in *Seventeen* magazine. She attended the University of New Mexico to study architecture and art. She had her first one-person shows in 1962 and 1964.

Hardin's works consisted of meticulously drawn, colorful, abstracted images of Katsina figures and Native American scenes. *New Mexico Magazine* declared that Hardin had brought a "new look" to Native American art. She would become famous for painting complex works that combined colorful images and symbols from her Native American heritage with modern abstract art techniques. Her best-known works included *Bountiful Mother* (1980), which represented two aspects of motherhood from pueblo and Hopi culture, the Corn Mother and Mother Earth; the self-portrait *Metamorphosis* (1981); and the series that included *Changing Woman*, *Medicine Woman*, and *Listening Woman*, paintings that portrayed the "intellectual, emotional, and sensitive" aspects of womanhood. Her work demonstrated how traditional artistic conventions can be combined creatively with modern themes and techniques. Diagnosed with breast cancer in 1981, Hardin died in New Mexico at the age of forty-one.

Edith Head (1897–1981)

Costume Designer

A winner of eight Academy Awards for Costume Design, Edith Head is Hollywood's most famous costume designer, whose career spanned fifty-eight years, in which she defined the style of classic Hollywood, dressing such movie stars as Grace Kelly, Cary Grant, Paul Newman, John Wayne, Elizabeth Taylor, Marlene Dietrich, and many more.

Born Edith Claire Posener in San Bernadino, California, she was the daughter of a mining engineer and grew up in various towns and camps in Arizona, Nevada, and Mexico. She earned a BA degree from the University of California–Berkeley in 1919 and a master's degree in romance languages from Stanford University in 1920. After teaching French for a time, she studied art in evening classes at the Otis Art Institute and Chouinard Art College. She married Charles Head in 1923 (the marriage ended in divorce in 1936), and in 1924, despite lacking costume design experience, twenty-six-year-old Head was hired as a costume sketch artist at Paramount Pictures. She began designing costumes for silent films and by the 1930s had established herself as one of Hollywood's leading costume designers, working at Paramount for forty-three years.

Head became the first woman to head the design department of a major film studio, in charge of the costume department with a staff of hundreds. She became America's best-known and most successful Hollywood designer, noted for her wide range of costume designs from elegant simplicity to glitziness. She also was skilled in dealing with temperamental actors and directors. She was nominated for an unprecedented thirty-four Academy Awards, winning a record eight for *The Heiress* (1949), *Samson and Delilah* (1949), *All about Eve* (1950), *A Place in the Sun* (1951), *Roman Holiday* (1953), *Sabrina* (1954), *The Facts of Life* (1960), and *The Sting* (1973).

Head was the author of an autobiography, *The Dress Doctor* (1959), and a self-help book, *How to Dress for Success* (1967). She died just four days before her eighty-fourth birthday.

Henrietta Johnston (c. 1674–1729)

Painter

The earliest recorded female artist in America, Henrietta Deering Johnston is one of the first female portrait painters and the first known pastelist in the American colonies.

Born Henrietta de Beaulieu to a French Huguenot family in Dublin, she married Reverend Gideon Johnston in 1705, who in 1707 procured an appointment as rector to a church in Charleston (then Charles Town) in the Carolina colony. On the voyage, he missed the ship's departure from the Medieras, and Henrietta and her children sailed into Charleston without him. He finally reached them after being marooned for twelve days on an offshore island without food and water, only to find that another cleric had taken over his church. It took several months of negotiations before he regained control of his congregation.

She supplemented the family's income by drawing portraits of local citizens. As Gideon wrote in a letter in 1709, "Were it not for the assistance my wife gives me by drawing of pictures which can last but a little time in a place so ill I [should] not have been able to live." She was one of the few (if not the only) portrait artists in town, and her skills were much in demand. Her portraits were created on sheets of paper in pastel chalk that she most likely brought with her from Ireland. Her works have been described as crude but competent and "direct and uncompromising."

In 1716, Gideon Johnston drowned in a boating accident on Charleston Bay, and little is known of what happened to Henrietta afterward, though she may have traveled to New York since several pastels are attributed to her that are signed "New York" and dated 1725. In 1727, she was back in Charleston, where her burial is registered as 1728.

Some forty portraits of prominent people in Charleston are known, most created between 1707 and 1720, and about thirty of her works survive, some of the earliest professional art produced in America.

Lois Mailou Jones (1905–1998)

Painter

The longest-surviving artist of the Harlem Renaissance, Lois Mailou Jones achieved fame as an African American expatriate artist in Paris in the 1930s and 1940s. She incorporated influences from Africa and the Caribbean into her paintings and produced some of the first nonportrait paintings by an African American.

Born in Boston, she early on displayed a passion for drawing, and her parents encouraged her interest by enrolling her in the High School of Practical Arts in Boston, where she majored in art. In 1927, she graduated from the School of the Museum of Fine Arts and continued her education at the Boston Normal School of Arts and the Designers Art School in Boston. After chairing the art department at an all-black prep school in North Carolina in 1928, she accepted a faculty position at Howard University in Washington, D.C. In 1937, she took a sabbatical from Howard to study art in Paris.

Her most celebrated Parisian painting is *Les Fetiches*, a depiction of African masks in five distinct, ethnic styles reflecting her previous travels to Africa and Haiti, influences that Jones more and more incorporated into works. She painted outdoors, in the French tradition, producing landscapes and street scenes while contributing to Paris exhibitions and relishing the freedom from racial prejudice that she found in France. In 1953, she married artist Louis Vergniaud Pierre-Noël of Haiti, and she began to incorporate into her work brighter colors and a more Expressionistic style from Haitian art. In the 1960s and 1970s, African influences reemerged in her work. In the 1980s and 1990s, Jones continued to produce important new work until she was felled by a massive heart attack on her eighty-fourth birthday. A 1990 retrospective exhibition toured the country and brought her nationwide attention and critical acclaim, which had eluded her for much of her career because her work defied typical subjects deemed suitable for African American artists. In 1994, the Corcoran Gallery of Art opened The World of Lois Mailou Jones exhibition with a public apology for its past racial discrimination. She died at the age of ninety-two at her home in Washington, D.C., after a seventy-year artistic career.

Donna Karan (1948–)

Fashion Designer

Donna Karan is one of the most successful and influential contemporary fashion designers ever. She has changed the ways women dress in the modern world with an emphasis on simplicity and comfort and has extended her fashion sense into an industry-leading fashion empire.

She was born Donna Ivy Faske in Forest Hills, New York. Her father was a tailor, and her mother was a model and showroom representative in New York's Garment District. She began her career in fashion at the age of fourteen, lying about her age to secure a job selling clothes in a boutique. She attended New York's Parsons School of Design but quit school in 1968 to begin working for sportswear designer Anne Klein.

After Klein died in 1974, Karan was promoted to chief designer with the chief responsibility for the Anne Klein fall collection. With her former classmate Louis Dell'Olio as a designer, the pair won the Coty American Fashion Critics Award in 1977 and 1981, and the Anne Klein Co. flourished partly owing to Karan's marketing a less expensive designer collection, Anne Klein II, which debuted in 1983.

In 1984, Karan launched Donna Karan Co., serving as chief designer, with the bridge line DKNY debuting in 1988. The company extended its fashion line by selling blue jeans, men's wear, and a children's line in addition to accessories, hosiery, and perfume. Karan popularized mix-and-match clothing in soft fabrics and neutral colors as well as being known for her signature bodysuits, dark tights, sarong-wrap skirts, fitted jackets, and heavy pieces of jewelry.

In 1996, the company went public, and in 2001, it was acquired by the conglomerate LVMH, with Karan keeping control of her name and remaining chief designer. In 2007, she founded Urban Zen, a line of clothing, accessories, and wellness goods, and in 2015, she stepped down as chief designer of Donna Karan, serving only as an adviser. The same year, she published her memoir, *My Journey*.

The recipient of many awards and honors, she became the first American ever to receive Fashion Group International's Superstar Award in 2003. In 2004, she received the Lifetime Achievement Award from the Council of Fashion Designers of America.

Louisa Keyser (Dat-So-Lo-Lee) (c. 1829–1925)

Basket Weaver

 Celebrated Native American basket weaver Louisa Keyser or Dat-So-Lo-Lee was a member of the Washo people of northwestern Nevada, whose skills came to national prominence during the Arts and Crafts movement of the early twentieth century. She was called "Magic Fingers." Each of her baskets are unique, with some of her best designs coming from dream visions.

She was born in a Washo village near present-day Sheridan, Nevada, near Lake Tahoe. She spent many hours of her childhood alone, rejected by other children in the tribe because she was fat and not pretty. She spent her time watching her mother and grandmother weave baskets, learning how to gather reeds and willow stems and making colorful dyes out of tree bark and roots. She worked all winter weaving baskets, selling them in the spring. Each basket was unique and so complex in their symmetry and design that some would take as long as two years to complete. No other basket weaver has approached her level of skill and creativity.

She met a merchant in Carson City, Nevada, who recognized her artistry and bought whatever she created, documenting each of the 120 baskets she produced from 1895 to 1925. She died at the age of ninety-six, her vision long since gone due to the eyestrain of basket weaving. Today, her baskets are regarded as priceless works of art and are on display primarily in Nevada museums.

Lee Krasner (1908–1984)

Painter

Despite being overshadowed by her far more famous husband, Jackson Pollock, and ignored as a "peripheral talent," Lee Krasner was an important and unique contributor to the New York School of Abstract Expressionism, which defined postwar modern art. Krasner was one of two painters in New York working in completely abstract styles prior to World War II and is now regarded as a key transitional figure who connected early twentieth-century art with the new ideas of postwar America. She is one of the few female artists to have had a retrospective show at the Museum of Modern Art.

She was born Lena Krassner, the sixth of the seven children of Jewish emigrants from Odessa. She decided to become an artist at the age of thirteen and was accepted to Washington Irving High School, the only public high school in New York City that offered women professional art training. She went on to study at the Women's Art School of Cooper Union and at the National Academy of Design.

From 1934 to 1943, she was able to work full time as an artist in the New Deal's Federal Art Project. During this period, influenced by Picasso and Matisse, Krasner developed her own style of geometric abstraction and began exhibiting her work along with other American abstract artists. In 1942, she met painter Jackson Pollock, and they married in 1945, moving to a farm in East Hampton, New York. Each influenced the other. Krasner was inspired by Pollock's "drip paintings" in her *Little Images* paintings. Often working on a small scale, Krasner's work contrasted with the other Abstract Expressionists along with her commitment to maintaining some figuration—patterns from nature and calligraphic elements such as Hebrew letters—and her sense of control compared to the automatism practiced by her peers. Throughout the 1960s and 1970s, Krasner continued to explore color and rhythmic form in paintings and collages.

After Pollock's death in 1956, Krasner devoted the rest of her life to promoting Pollock's art and ensuring his legacy at the expense of her own reputation. In 1978, Krasner was finally accorded her rightful place alongside Pollock, Mark Rothko, and the others in the exhibition Abstract Expressionism: The Formative Years. Krasner died at the age of seventy-five, and six months after her death, the Museum of Modern Art held a retrospective exhibition of her work, which *The New York Times* declared "clearly defines Krasner's place in the New York School" and that she "is a major, independent artist of the pioneer Abstract Expressionist generation, whose stirring work ranks high among that produced here in the last half-century."

Dorothea Lange (1895–1965)

Photographer

Dorothea Lange's photographs chronicled the despair of Americans forced into poverty during the years of the Great Depression. Her powerful images of destitute people helped to create a national awareness of their plight and became classics of documentary photography.

She was born Dorothea Nutzhorn in Hoboken, New Jersey; her father abandoned the family when she was a young girl, and her mother resumed using her maiden name for herself and her children. After graduating from high school in 1913, Lange was determined to become a photographer, although she knew very little about the work. While attending the New York Training School for Teachers, she went to work as an apprentice for portrait photographers, and she studied with renowned artist and photographer Clarence H. White.

In 1918, Lange went to San Francisco, where she worked as a photofinisher and joined a camera club. In 1919, she started a portrait photography business, and Lange's studio became a gathering place for many artists, including painter Maynard Dixon, whom Lange married in 1920. Throughout the decade, her successful business supported the couple and their two children.

In the early 1930s, Lange abandoned her lucrative career to photograph the victims of the Depression. Her first attempt resulted in one of the most famous photographs ever, "White Angel Bread-line," which shows a sad-faced, unemployed man staring down at the cup he holds in his hands, his back to the men in line for food. Her photographs of migrant workers for the California State Emergency Relief fund led to the first state-run camps for migrants. In 1935, Lange divorced Dixon and married Paul Taylor, an economist who had worked with her on the project. From 1935 to 1942, Lange traveled around the country photographing rural Americans for the Farm Security Administration. Her work was reproduced in numerous magazines and newspapers as well as in books and exhibits and had an enormous impact on the public. Her famous photograph "The Migrant Mother," which shows a destitute woman holding a baby while two children lean over her shoulder, was published worldwide to raise funds for medical supplies.

During World War II, the government hired Lange to document the mass relocation of Japanese Americans in internment camps. However, her sympathetic view of the internees caused the government to suppress the photographs, and they were unavailable until after the war. In the 1950s, Lange produced photo essays for *Life* magazine and worked with photographer Edward Steichen on his remarkable exhibition of people around the world, The Family of Man. In 1966, a year after her death, a retrospective exhibition of Lange's work opened at New York's Museum of Modern Art. Her study of American women, *The American Country Woman*, was published that year as well.

Edmonia Lewis (1845–1907)

Sculptor

The first woman of African American and Native American ancestry to achieve distinction as a professional sculptor, Edmonia Lewis is known for incorporating themes related to her heritage in Neoclassical-style sculpture. She was the only black woman in the nineteenth century to enter the American artistic mainstream.

She was born near Albany, New York, to a Chippewa Indian mother and African American father. Both of her parents died by the time she was nine, and two maternal aunts raised her. In 1856, Lewis attended McGrawville, a New York Baptist abolitionist school. As Lewis recalled, "Until I was twelve years old I led this wandering life, fishing and swimming … and making moccasins. I was then sent for three years in [McGrawville], but was declared to be wild—they could do nothing with me." In 1859, she attended the Oberlin Academy Preparatory School before entering Oberlin College but left in 1863, having endured racial discrimination, abuse, assault, and unfounded charges of theft of artists' material.

In 1864, she moved to Boston, where she began to pursue her career as a sculptor, assisted by abolitionist William Lloyd Garrison, who introduced her to established sculptors in the area. Instructed by sculptor Edward Augustus Brackett, Lewis chose her subjects from the most famous abolitionists of the day: John Brown and Colonel Robert Gould Shaw. Sales of plaster-cast reproductions allowed her to move to Rome, where she lived and worked for most of the rest of her life. Her studio became a must-stop for those on the Grand Tour. Frederick Douglass visited her, and Ulysses S. Grant sat for her. Inspired by the Emancipation Proclamation, she carved *The Freed Woman and Her Child* (1866) and *Forever Free* (1867). She also turned to Native American themes to create *The Marriage of Hiawatha* (1868) and *The Old Arrow Maker and His Daughter*. Her other notable works include busts of Garrison (1866) and Abraham Lincoln (1871). Her career reached its peak in 1876, when her sculpture *The Death of Cleopatra* was exhibited at the Philadelphia Centennial Exposition. In the 1880s, Neoclassicism declined in popularity, as did Lewis's artwork, although she continued sculpting marble altars and other works for Roman Catholic patrons. Lewis died in London in 1907.

Maya Lin (1959–)

Architect

In 1981, a committee of architects, artists, and designers selected the winning design for a Vietnam Veterans Memorial in Washington, D.C. They chose the work of twenty-one-year-old Maya Lin, who at the time was still an undergraduate student at Yale University. Her design of a V-shaped, black, granite wall listing the names of the nearly sixty thousand men and women killed or missing in action in Vietnam was a striking and controversial conception that radically differed from heroic monuments of the past.

Maya Ying Lin was born in Athens, Ohio, the daughter of parents who had fled China just before the Communist Revolution of 1949. Her father was a ceramic artist and dean of the Ohio University art school; her mother was a poet and professor of Asian and English literature. As a student, Lin demonstrated an aptitude for both mathematics and art. She entered Yale University, where she studied architecture and sculpture, though teachers encouraged her to choose either one discipline or the other. "I would look at my professors, smile, and go about my business," she recalled. "I consider myself both an artist and an architect. I don't combine them, but each field informs the other."

During the controversy surrounding her design for the Vietnam Memorial, Lin was subjected to racial and sexist slurs from those who felt that an Asian American woman was an inappropriate designer for a monument honoring those who lost their lives in a war fought against the Vietnamese. Through the often bitter debate, Lin held firm to her conviction that her design "does not glorify war or make an antiwar statement. It is a place for private reckoning." Dismissed by some critics as a "black gash of shame," Lin's design struck a special chord with veterans and the families and friends of the fallen who came to touch the names of loved ones and leave personal mementos behind. Lin had created, in the words of one admiring critic, "a very psychological memorial … that brings out in people the realization of loss and a cathartic healing process." The Wall, as it has come to be called, has become the most visited monument in America, attracting more than one million people a year, a testimony to a great artist's simple but profound vision and the courage of her convictions.

In 1986, Lin earned a master's degree in architecture and went on to design the Civil Rights Memorial in Montgomery, Alabama, the Museum for African Art in New York City, and a monument commemorating women at Yale University. She has also designed numerous public and private buildings, landscape designs, and sculptures. In her many environmentally themed works, she has raised awareness of the environmental crisis. In 2000, she published the book *Boundaries,* and in 2009, Lin created the building for the Museum of Chinese in America near New York City's Chinatown. Since 2010, Lin has been working on what she calls her "final memorial": the What is Missing? Foundation, which commemorates the biodiversity that has been lost. Using sound, media, science, and art in temporary installations and on the Internet, What is Missing? appears in multiple sites simultaneously.

Married to New York photography dealer Daniel Wolf, Lin is the mother of two daughters. In 2005, Lin was elected to the Academy of Arts and Letters as well as the National Women's Hall of Fame. In 2009, she received the National Medal of Arts from President Barack Obama.

Evelyn Beatrice Longman (1874–1954)

Sculptor

 Evelyn Beatrice Longman was the first female sculptor to be elected as a full member of the National Academy of Design in 1919. She created many well-known monuments and memorials around the country, including *Genius of Electricity* atop AT&T's corporate headquarters in Manhattan and assisting Daniel Chester French on the Lincoln Memorial in Washington, D.C.

She was born on a farm near Winchester, Ohio, and went to work at the age of fourteen in a Chicago dry-goods store. She was inspired to become a sculptor when she visited the 1893 World's Columbian Exposition. She attended Olivet College in Michigan for a year before returning to Chicago to study anatomy, drawing, and sculpture at the School of the Art Institute of Chicago. In 1901, she moved to New York, where she studied with Hermon Atkins MacNeil and Daniel Chester French.

In 1904, she produced her first large-scale public sculpture for the Louisiana Purchase Exposition, a male figure, *Victory*, that was given a place of honor on the top of the fair's centerpiece building, Festival Hall. *Genius of Electricity* followed in 1915. In 1918, she was hired by Nathaniel Horton Batchelder, the headmaster of Loomis Chaffee School, to sculpt a memorial to honor his late wife. Two years later, she married Batchelder and moved to Connecticut. For the next thirty years, Longman completed dozens of commissions throughout the United States, including *Spirit of Victory* (1926) in Bushnell Park, Hartford, Connecticut; *Victory of Mercy* (1947), Loomis Chaffee School; and *Edison* (1952) at the Naval Research Laboratory in Washington, D.C.

Longman died on Cape Cod, where she had moved her studio after her husband's retirement. A collection of Ann Lowe's designs is held at the Costume Institute at the Metropolitan Museum of Art. Others are on display at the Smithsonian Institute.

Ann Cole Lowe (1898–1981)

Fashion Designer

The first African American to become a distinguished fashion designer, Ann Lowe designed one-of-a-kind dresses for high-society clients from the 1920s through the 1960s, including the wedding dress worn by Jacqueline Bouvier when she married Senator John F. Kennedy.

Born in Clayton, Alabama, Lowe was the great-granddaughter of a skilled seamstress slave and a white plantation owner. Her mixed-race grandmother was freed after being purchased by a freeman named General Cole. Ann learned to sew from her and her mother, who made dresses for southern society women. After marrying at the age of fourteen, she left her husband after he wanted her to give up working as a seamstress. In 1917, she moved with her son to New York City, where she enrolled at the St. Taylor Design School. After graduating in 1919, she moved to Tampa, Florida, where she opened her first dress salon. By 1928, she returned to New York City and began to work on commission for Neiman Marcus, Saks Fifth Avenue, Henri Bendel, and other prominent retailers.

In 1946, Lowe designed the dress that actress Olivia de Havilland wore to accept the Academy

Award for Best Actress. Designs for some of the nation's most prestigious families, including the Rockefellers, the Lodges, the DuPonts, and the Posts, followed. During her career, Lowe had her own label and a store on Fifth Avenue. At Saks, Lowe become the head designer of The Adam Room, a special in-house boutique that catered to the social elite. She retired in 1972.

Maria Montoya Martinez (1887–1980)

Potter

Native American artist Maria Martinez is widely credited with reviving and preserving the fading art of traditional pueblo pottery as a cultural legacy of her people.

Born at San Ildefonso Pueblo, about twenty miles northwest of Santa Fe, New Mexico, she learned pottery skills at an early age watching her aunt, grandmother, and father's cousin work on their pottery in the 1890s. At the time, tinware and enamelware had become readily available in the Southwest, making the creation of traditional cooking and serving pots less necessary. Martinez married Julian Martinez, a member of her pueblo in 1904, and together, they mastered the traditional craft of pueblo pottery. She crafted, shaped, and polished the pots while her husband painted them.

During an excavation in 1908 led by professor of archaeology Edgar Lee Hewett, examples of black-on-white biscuit ware pottery were discovered, and Hewitt sought out skilled pueblo potters who could repair and recreate the pieces he had found. This led him to Martinez and her husband, and Hewitt encouraged them to continue producing pottery in the traditional manner. Their skill in making black-on-black pots and teaching their techniques would make their pueblo a center of tourism and Native American crafts.

Martinez won many awards for her work and presented her pottery at many world fairs. In 1973, she received a grant from the National Endowment for the Arts to found a Martinez pottery workshop

to continue the artistic legacy that she had done so much to save.

Claire McCardell (1905–1958)

Fashion Designer

Credited with creating American sportswear, Claire McCardell revolutionized and modernized what women wore. Breaking with the dominance of Parisian fashion and an age of stiff crinolines, corsets, girdles, and padded shoulders, McCardell helped to introduce an "American look," emphasizing freedom and flexibility in fashion and a casual, athletic, and unstructured look that began to define modern fashion.

McCardell grew up in Frederick, Maryland. Her father was a Maryland state senator and president of the Frederick County National Bank. As a child, she was nicknamed "Kick" for her ability to stand up to the boys in the neighborhood. She was fascinated by fashion from an early age and wanted to move to New York City to study fashion design at the age of sixteen. Her father convinced her to enroll in the home economics program at Hood College instead, but after two years, she moved to New York and entered Parsons (then known as the New York School of Fine and Applied Art). In 1927, McCardell continued her studies at the Parsons branch in Paris. After graduation, she worked odd jobs sketching at a fashionable dress shop, painting flowers on paper lampshades, and modeling for the B. Altman department store.

In the late 1930s, she began work as an assistant designer for Robert Turk, and, in 1932, after his death, McCardell was asked to finish his fall line for Turk's Townley Frocks. Not interested in copying European high fashion, McCardell sought inspiration in art and street fashion and began to introduce innovations such as sashes, string ties, and menswear details. She modernized the dirndl and pioneered matching separates. In 1938, she introduced the monastic dress, a simple, bias-cut tent dress with no seamed waist but with a versatile belt that could be adapted for any woman's figure.

Sold exclusively by Best & Co., the dress sold out in a day. Townley went out of business trying to stop knockoffs, but it reopened in 1940 with the company's label, "Claire McCardell Clothes by Townley," making her one of the first American designers to have name recognition.

During World War II, as other designers had to contend with limited availability of some materials, McCardell flourished under the restrictions, introducing denim, calico, and wool jersey, which were readily available. She popularized the ballet flat in response to the shortage of leather. She introduced a line of separates that made nine outfits out of five pieces. By 1955, McCardell was on the cover of *Time* magazine surrounded by models wearing her designs, which typified the American sportswear look she had popularized.

McCardell's life and work were cut short when she was diagnosed with terminal colon cancer in 1957. She completed her final collection from her hospital bed and checked out of the hospital to introduce her final runway show. She died at the age of fifty-two, and her family decided to close her label. In 1990, *Life* named her one of the one hundred most important Americans of the twentieth century.

Joan Mitchell (1925–1992)

Painter

A prominent member of the so-called "second generation" of American Abstract Expressionists, Joan Mitchell, along with artists such as Lee Krasner, Helen Frankenthaler, and Elaine de Kooning, was one of the few female painters of her era to gain critical and public acclaim, best known for her large abstract paintings and energized, colorful brushstrokes.

Born in Chicago, Mitchell was the daughter of poet Marion Strobel and physician James Herbert Mitchell. As a teenager, she was a nationally ranked figure skater. After two years at Smith College (1942–1944), she studied at the School of the Art Institute of Chicago, earning a BFA degree in 1947. On a postgraduate fellowship to France, she got married in 1949 to fellow Chicagoan Barney Rosset, the soon-to-be owner of Grove Press (the couple divorced in 1952). They moved to New York City,

where she met painters Willem de Kooning, Franz Kline, Grace Hartigan, and Jackson Pollock and participated in the landmark Ninth Street Show of Abstract Expressionist art and became a member of the predominantly male Eighth Street Club, founded by artists of the New York School. She studied at Columbia and New York University, allowing her to complete an MFA degree from the Art Institute of Chicago in 1952. From 1953 to 1965, she exhibited regularly at the Stable Gallery in New York.

Her abstract canvases are expansive, often covering multiple panels, depicting landscapes and using paint on unprimed canvas or white ground. She has described her painting as "an organism that turns in space." Moving to Paris in 1959, she shifted from the bright colors of her earlier compositions to more somber hues and dense central masses of color. Her later work has been described as "very violent and angry." As art historian Linda Nochlin explains, the "meaning and intensity [of Mitchell's paintings] are produced structurally, as it were, by a whole series of oppositions: dense versus transparent strokes; gridded structure versus more chaotic, ad hoc construction; weight on the bottom of the canvas versus weight at the top; light versus dark; choppy versus continuous strokes; harmonious and clashing juxtapositions of hue—all are potent signs of meaning and feeling."

Mitchell died in Paris at the age of sixty-seven. In 2018, her painting *Blueberry* (1969) set an auction record when it sold at Christie's for $16.6 million. Sales of her work help to fund the Joan Mitchell Foundation, which provides grants for sculptors and painters in the United States.

Julia Morgan (1872–1957)

Architect

One of the most prolific and influential woman architects in the United States, Julia Morgan was the first woman to earn an architect's license in California, where she designed more than seven hundred buildings over her long career. She is best known for her work on the Hearst Castle in San Simeon, California, and is the first woman awarded the American Institute of Architect' highest honor, the AIA Gold Medal, which was awarded posthumously in 2014.

Julia Morgan was born in San Francisco. Her father was a mining engineer, and Morgan and her four siblings were raised in a large Victorian house in Oakland. She enrolled at the University of California, Berkeley, and after graduating in 1894 with a degree in civil engineering, she studied and worked with architect Bernard Maybeck, who encouraged her to apply to the École des Beaux-Arts in Paris, the world's most prestigious architecture school. The first woman admitted to the school and the first to graduate, Morgan was awarded four medals for outstanding work in design and drawing during her three years there. After returning to San Francisco with her degree in 1902, Morgan went to work for architect John Galen Howard. Despite her status as an important member of Howard's staff, she grew increasingly dissatisfied by the lack of recognition from her male colleagues and the low salary Howard paid her because she was a woman, so she decided to open her own architecture office.

Morgan's early commissions were obtained with the help of feminist and philanthropist Phoebe Apperson Hearst, the mother of newspaper magnate William Randolph Hearst. These included the design of two buildings on Mrs. Hearst's estate and a bell tower on the campus of Mills College. Morgan also designed several private homes. After the devastating San Francisco earthquake of 1906, she was asked to redesign and rebuild the city's once-luxurious Fairmont Hotel, which had been severely damaged. Her work on the hotel established her reputation and led to numerous other commissions. Over the next decade, Morgan designed houses, stores, churches, offices, and educational and public buildings. Although she was not active in the feminist movement of the first two decades of the twentieth century, she employed many women architects and drafters, and she provided financial support to women students.

After World War I, Morgan began working for William Randolph Hearst. For nearly twenty years, in addition to her regular work, she designed, built,

and added on to Hearst's San Simeon castle, guest houses on the Hearst family ranch, Hearst newspaper facilities, and family mansions in California and Mexico. One of her most famous non-Hearst commission during this time was the 1929 construction of the Berkeley City Club, a women's hotel and club. In 1937 Morgan stopped working for Hearst, whose publishing empire had fallen into financial difficulty. During World War II, she was forced to reduce her practice due to a shortage of labor and materials. She retired in 1946 and traveled extensively until her death from a stroke.

Anna Mary Robertson "Grandma" Moses (1860–1961)

Folk Artist

 A farmer's wife known first as Mother Moses and then Grandma Moses, Anna Mary Robertson Moses was a self-taught painter who began her career in her late seventies and became renowned for the simple realism of her paintings, many of which depict farm life.

Moses was born on a farm in Greenwich, New York, the third of ten children. Her father ran a flax mill and was a farmer. As a child, Moses attended a one-room school in Bennington, Vermont, just across the New York state border. The school is now the Bennington Museum, which houses the largest collection of Moses's works. Moses first painted as a child using lemon and grape juice as colors for landscapes. She created other works of art with such materials as ground ochre, grass, flour paste, and sawdust. At the age of twelve, Moses left home to perform chores for a wealthy family who lived on a nearby farm and for fifteen years kept house, cooked, and sewed for wealthy families, one of whom noted her interest in their Currier & Ives prints of bucolic scenes and purchased chalk and wax crayons for Moses so that she could create her own artwork.

When Moses was twenty-seven, she married hired man Thomas Salmon Moses, and the couple established themselves on a farm in Virginia. During the two decades they lived in Virginia, Moses gave birth to ten children, five of whom died in infancy. In 1905, after a fire destroyed their farmhouse, the family returned to New York and settled in Hoosick Falls, not far from Moses's childhood home. When her husband died in 1927, Moses continued to farm with the help of her youngest son until advancing age and bouts of arthritis forced her to retire. In the early 1930s, Moses made embroidered pictures of yarn for family and friends and was known for her beautiful quilted objects. When arthritis made embroidery painful, her sister Celestia suggested that painting would be an easier medium for her.

Moses's early style was simple and more primitive or realistic, with a lack of perspective, but as her career advanced, her nostalgic compositions of rural life from the past became more complicated and panoramic. A prolific painter, Moses generated over 1,500 canvases in three decades. She charged from three to five dollars for a painting at first; as her fame increased, her paintings commanded $8,000 to $10,000 each. Although she did not know the work of sixteenth-century Dutch painter Pieter Breughel the Elder, Moses's winter paintings are very reminiscent of that artist.

In 1939, three "Grandma" Moses paintings were included in a Museum of Modern Art exhibition titled Contemporary Unknown Painters, and the following year, Moses had her first solo exhibition, What a Farm Wife Painted, at New York's Galerie St. Etienne. More solo shows followed, and her paintings were exhibited throughout Europe and the United States over the next twenty years. The recipient of several awards and honors, Moses was the subject of a 1950s documentary of her life, which was nominated for an Academy Award. In 1952, she published her autobiography, *My Life's History*. In 1955, she was a guest on *See It Now*, a television program hosted by venerable broadcast journalist Edward R. Murrow. Moses's one hundredth birthday was celebrated by *Life* magazine, which featured her on its cover. After her death at the age of 101, several large exhibitions of her work traveled throughout the United States and abroad. In 2006, one of her most famous paintings, *Sugaring Time*, sold for $1.2 million.

Alice Neel (1900–1984)

Painter

Celebrated for her portraits of friends, family, lovers, poets, other artists, and strangers that blend realism with an Expressionistic use of line and color, Alice Neel's paintings are notable for a unique psychological insight and emotional intensity unusual in portraiture.

Alice Neel was born in Merion Square, Pennsylvania, the fourth of the five children of George Washington Neel, an accountant for the Pennsylvania Railroad, and Alice Concross Hartley Neel, a descendant of signatories of the Declaration of Independence. After her oldest brother died of diphtheria, the family moved to Colwyn, near Philadelphia, where Alice Neel attended school. After graduating from high school in 1918, Neel took the Civil Service exam and accepted a secretarial position with the U.S. Army to help with the family finances. Determined to pursue a life as an artist and despite opposition from her parents, Neel took evening art classes at the School of Industrial Art in Philadelphia. In 1921, with the help of scholarships and her savings, Neel enrolled in the fine arts program at the Philadelphia School of Design for Women, where she studied landscape painting, life drawing, and portraiture and won several awards for her portraits. In 1924, she attended a summer program sponsored by the Pennsylvania Academy of Fine Arts in Chester Springs, Pennsylvania. In 1925, Neel married Carlos Enriquez, a wealthy Cuban who had been a fellow student in the program.

Several months after their marriage, the couple moved to Havana, where the following year Neel gave birth to her first child, a daughter, who died from diphtheria in infancy. She and her husband divided their time between Cuba and New York City. In 1928, Neel's second child, Isabella Lillian (called Isabetta), was born. The child's birth was the inspiration for Neel's painting *Well Baby Clinic*, a bleak portrait of mothers and babies in a maternity clinic. After Isabetta's birth, the couple made plans to move to Paris; instead, in 1930, Enriquez unexpectedly left for Cuba, taking Isabetta with him. The loss of her child and her inability to salvage the marriage caused Neel to suffer a nervous breakdown and led to a hospitalization and a suicide attempt. After her release from the Philadelphia General Hospital in 1931, she returned to her parents' home for a time and then went back to New York. Neel and Enriquez never divorced, although they remained estranged from each other, and Neel only saw her daughter occasionally throughout her life. From the 1930s, Neel had several romantic relationships, two of which produced her sons, Richard and Hartley.

In 1933, Neel received funding from the Public Works of America Project, a Works Project Administration (WPA) initiative, which helped support her financially until 1943, after which she struggled to make ends meet. She had difficulty finding a market for her paintings and mounted only one exhibition. In the 1950s, Neel rejected the rise of Abstract Expressionism in New York and remained faithful to her representational artistic vision. Her portraits from the 1950s captured the character of her neighbors and friends in the Spanish Harlem section of New York. Committed to left-wing causes, her work attracted the attention of communist writer Mike Gold, who helped Neel to organize several exhibitions of her work. In 1960, she painted poet, art critic, and Museum of Modern Art curator Frank O'Hara, producing two portraits, one of which was flattering and the other unflatteringly critical. The paintings were well received by the magazine *Artnews* and the art critic of *The New York Times*.

During the women's movement of the late 1960s, Neel's work, which often focused on portraits of women, received renewed attention as feminist art, and by the 1970s, she was widely recognized as a major American artist. In 1974, the Whitney Museum of American Art mounted a major retrospective of her work, and in 1979, President Jimmy Carter presented her with an award for her contribution to American art. In 1980, Neel's self-portrait was seen for the first time in an exhibition of self-portraits at the Harold Reed Gallery in New York. The following year, she traveled to Moscow for an exhibition of her paintings. By then, Neel's health had begun to fail, but she continued to work and visit the studio in Vermont built by her son Hartley on his property. After her death, a memorial service was held at the Whitney, which included a poem composed and read by Beat poet Allen Ginsberg. Neel's works are represented in major museum collections throughout the United States.

Louise Nevelson (1899–1998)

Sculptor

A pioneer in the art of sculpture whose work reflects a unique and singular artistic vision, Louise Nevelson is recognized as one of the major sculptors of the twentieth century. She is known for her monumental box assemblages of complex, rhythmic abstract shapes. Her sculptures, constructed from "found objects" such as odd pieces of wood, moldings, scraps of crates, furniture legs, cast metal, and other materials and completely covered with black, gold, or white paint, have a uniform tone that gives them a mysterious, dynamic quality and accentuates the structural importance of the shadows within them. Largely ignored for much of her career, toward the end of her life, Nevelson received more public commissions for her work than any other American sculptor.

Nevelson was born Leah Berliawsky in Pereyaslav, a shtetl town near Kiev in the present-day Ukraine, the second child in an Orthodox Jewish family that would eventually include a son and three daughters. In 1902, Nevelson's father Isaac immigrated to the United States and settled in Rockland, Maine. In 1905, he sent for his wife Minna and their three children, who were met in Boston by a Russian-born relative, Joseph Dondis, who helped the children anglicize their names; Leah became Louise. In Rockland, Isaac Berliawsky began working as a junk dealer and grocer and eventually became a well-to-do landowner and builder. As a shy, Yiddish-speaking child in what she later described as a "WASP Yankee town," Louise struggled to learn English, and her immigrant family felt isolated from the Rockland community. Nevelson's feelings of shyness and sense of isolation were somewhat mitigated by what she later described as a happy home life with free-thinking parents who believed in equal rights for women.

While growing up, Nevelson excelled in her art classes and expressed a desire to become a sculptor. In 1920, she married wealthy businessman Charles Nevelson, a partner in the Nevelson Brothers Shipping Company in Boston, and the couple settled in New York City. Two years later, Nevelson gave birth to her son, Mike, who would also become a sculptor. In 1929, Nevelson enrolled full time at the Art Students League, where she studied painting and drawing with artist Kenneth Hayes Miller. At the same time, she began to feel increasingly stifled by her marriage and the life of a wealthy socialite. In 1931, she left her husband, entrusted her son to her family in Maine, and went to Munich, Germany, to study with legendary art teacher Hans Hoffman, whose cubist art form greatly affected her future work. However, soon after she arrived in Munich, Hoffman left for the United States to escape the rising tide of German fascism. While in Europe, Nevelson appeared in Austrian films as a bit player. Her experience with the shadowy and illusory appearance of movie sets as well as the lighting and look of the black-and-white films would add another dimension to her work. After living for a time in Paris and permanently separating from her husband, she returned to New York in 1932.

In the 1930s, Nevelson continued to study with Hoffman, studied sculpture with sculptor Chaim Gross, and began her own work. Her sculptures during this time were small human, animal, or abstract figures modeled in plaster or clay. In 1935, she showed her work for the first time in a show titled Young Sculptors at the Brooklyn Museum. Around this time, her son came to live with her, and despite their long separation, the two were able to forge a close relationship that lasted for the rest of Louise Nevelson's life. Like his mother, Mike Nevelson became a sculptor.

By 1941, Nevelson had gained a small amount of recognition for her work but no significant success, and she was in acute financial distress. With a courage born of desperation, she stormed into the esteemed Nierendorf Gallery in New York and insisted that Karl Nierendorf look at her work. He agreed, visited her studio, and, impressed, arranged her first solo exhibition. Nierendorf became a close friend as well as a major source of professional support, and when he died suddenly in 1947, Nevelson sank back into obscurity. A small inheritance allowed her to buy a house in New York, where she could live and work. In 1955, she began to exhibit again when her sculptures, constructed of orange crates painted black, were featured in the first of several one-woman shows at the Grand Central Moderns Gallery.

In 1957, Nevelson began to sculpt in her signature style. In her Moon Garden + One exhibition in 1958, she presented a matte black sculpture wall, *Sky Cathedral*, which was well received by critics. Art collectors began to show interest in her work, and she was offered a contract with the prestigious Martha Jackson Gallery. The following year, Nevelson was invited to exhibit at the Museum of Modern Art's Sixteen Americans show, for which she created a massive, all-white environment titled *Dawn's Wedding Feast*. In 1962, she created the all-gold wall assemblage *Dawn* for the museum and was asked to represent the United States in the sculpture section of the Venice Bienalle. For a retrospective of her work at the Whitney Museum of American Art in 1967, Nevelson created *Homage to Six Million I*, a massive, black wall dedicated to the memory of the Jewish Holocaust. Nevelson's other works include *Ice Palace I* (1967), a Plexiglas sculpture; *Bicentennial Dawn* (1976), a large, three-part wooden sculpture; and *Shadows and Flags* (1978), a group of huge steel sculptures created for the newly named Louise Nevelson Square in downtown Manhattan.

In 1978, Nevelson was elected a member of the elite Academy of Arts and Letters, and in 1983, she was awarded the academy's gold medal for sculpture. Two years later, she received the National Medal for the Arts. After her death, a memorial service was held at the Metropolitan Museum of Art. In 1994, she was again eulogized during a commemoration of the Nevelson-Berliawsky Gallery of Twentieth Century Art at the Farnsworth Museum in Rockland, Maine.

Georgia O'Keeffe (1887–1986)

Painter

One of America's most renowned and influential artists, Georgia O'Keeffe was famous for the unique way in which she used light, color, and space in her paintings.

O'Keeffe was born in Sun Prairie, Wisconsin, the second of seven children. Gifted in art as a child, she later said that she knew by the age of ten that she would be an artist. She attended a convent school in Madison, Wisconsin, until 1902, when her family moved to Williamsburg, Virginia. There, O'Keeffe continued her education at Chatham, a girls' boarding school, where she was awarded a special art diploma upon her graduation. She went on to study art at the Art Institute of Chicago and the Art Students League in New York, supporting herself by working as an advertising illustrator and teacher.

In 1915, a friend showed O'Keeffe's drawings to Alfred Stieglitz, the well-known photographer and an important figure in the New York art world. He exhibited the drawings at his famous 291 Gallery and in 1917 sponsored the first of twenty one-woman shows for O'Keeffe. In 1924, Stieglitz and O'Keeffe were married.

O'Keeffe became the only woman in a group of modern artists known as the Stieglitz Circle. She was also the subject of some five hundred photographs Stieglitz took of her from 1917 to 1937. In the 1920s, O'Keeffe began to paint abstract and magnified representations of flowers, such as *Black Iris* (1926), which are favorites of many admirers of her works.

Beginning in 1939, O'Keeffe began spending her summers in Taos, New Mexico, where she gained new inspiration for her art from the rich, colorful expanses of the land and sky. In 1946, she had the first showing of a female artist ever held at the Museum of Modern Art in New York City. The same year, Stieglitz died, and O'Keeffe moved to New Mexico permanently.

She divided her time between her house in Abiquiu and a ranch outside of town that she had purchased in 1940. She lived simply, growing her own vegetables and grinding wheat flour by hand for bread. Her paintings of cow skulls and bones, adobe buildings, desert scenes, and her studies of Taos Pueblo, an Indian village, are among her most famous and critically acclaimed works.

In the 1960s, O'Keeffe had several major showings of her art in cities throughout the United States. In 1970, she was awarded a gold medal from the National Institute of Arts and Letters for her work, and in 1977, she received the Presidential Medal of Freedom. Nearly blind in her later years, O'Keeffe continued to paint and sculpt until her death at the age of ninety-eight.

Sarah Miriam Peale (1800–1885)

Painter

The first American woman to succeed as a professional artist, Sarah Miriam Peale enjoyed a career of nearly sixty years, during which she lived on her own and supported herself with her art.

Peale was born in Philadelphia, the youngest of the three daughters of celebrated miniaturist and still-life painter James Peale, who was the younger brother of painter and politician Charles Willson Peale. Her father and uncle trained her and her sisters as artists, and Sarah served as her father's studio assistant, where her tasks included painting the finishing details in the decorative areas on his canvases. At the age of eighteen, she completed a self-portrait, a tradition in her family used to determine whether a family member could be considered a full-fledged artist rather than a student. James Peale did not pronounce the portrait a success, and Sarah left for Baltimore, Maryland, for further study with her cousin, portrait painter Rembrandt Peale, who influenced her early painting style and subject matter. Sarah Peale's 1818 self-portrait hangs in the National Portrait Gallery at the Smithsonian Institution.

From 1822 to 1847, Peale painted in Baltimore and in Washington, D.C., where she attended sessions of Congress and produced portraits of many public figures. In 1824, Peale and her sister Anna Claypoole Peale, a miniaturist and still-life painter, became the first women accepted as members of the prestigious Pennsylvania Academy of Fine Arts, the first and oldest art museum and art school in the United States. In 1831, she opened a studio in Baltimore, where she received over one hundred commissions for portraits of congressmen, diplomats, and wealthy Marylanders. The Marquis de Lafayette sat for her four times. Peale's portraits are stylistically distinctive for their decorative details as well as for realistic faces, hair, and skin.

In 1847, Peale relocated to St. Louis, Missouri, where she continued to earn a living with her work, painting mainly portraits of politicians and military figures as well as the occasional still life. She began to concentrate on still-life painting around 1860 but with more natural arrangements than her earlier paintings. In 1878, she returned to Philadelphia, where she spent her last years living with her sisters Anna and Henrietta. Most of her works are in private hands, but many others are exhibited in museums throughout the country. In 1987, several of Peale's paintings were included in the inaugural exhibition of the National Museum of Women in the Arts, American Women Artists, 1830–1930.

Augusta Savage (1892–1962)

Sculptor

A prominent artist of the Harlem Renaissance, Augusta Savage was a sculptor, teacher, and activist who worked on behalf of African Americans in the arts.

Savage was born Augusta Christine Wells in Green Cove Springs, Florida, the seventh child in a family of fourteen children. Her father, Edward Wells, a laborer and Methodist minister, strongly opposed his daughter's interest in art and objected to her childhood sculptures of small animals modeled from the red clay native to her hometown as a sinful practice reflecting the "graven images" of the Bible's Ten Commandments. In 1907, fifteen-year-old Savage married John T. Moore and

the following year gave birth to her daughter, Irene Connie Moore. Her husband died soon afterward. The second of Savage's three husbands was James Savage, a carpenter, whom she married in 1915 and whose name she retained after their divorce in the early 1920s. In 1923, Savage married Robert L. Poston, who died in 1924.

When Savage began school in West Palm Beach, Florida, where her family had relocated, a teacher encouraged her to join an art class to study clay modeling. By 1919, she was operating a booth at the Palm Beach County Fair, where she sold her clay animal figures and was awarded a ribbon and a $25 prize for the most original exhibit. In 1921, she moved to New York City with a letter of recommendation from fair superintendent George Graham Currie to sculptor Solon Borglum. Savage intended to study at the School of American Sculpture but could not afford the tuition, and Borglum suggested she apply for a scholarship to the art school Cooper Union. Savage was selected for a scholarship over 142 male applicants and so impressed the school's advisory council with her talent that she was awarded funds for her room and board when she lost her job as an apartment caretaker. Savage studied under sculptor George Brewster and received her four-year degree in three years. In 1922, while a student at Cooper Union, she applied for a summer program at the Fontainebleau School of Fine Arts sponsored by the French government but was turned down by the international judging committee because of her race. Savage's challenge of the committee's decision gained press coverage in the United States and abroad, and she was invited to study with sculptor Hermon Atkins MacNeil, the only member of the committee to support her application.

After her graduation from Cooper Union, Savage, who lived in Harlem with her family, obtained her first commission from the Harlem Library of a bust of African American author and civil rights activist W. E. B. Du Bois. Her work led to more commissions, which included busts of Marcus Garvey and NAACP leader William Pickens Sr. In 1928, she was awarded the Otto Kahn Prize for her submission *Head of a Negro* at the Harmon Foundation exhibition and the following year was acclaimed for her bust of a Harlem child, *Gamin*. Savage's new fame as an artist resulted in a scholarship to study at the Academie de la Grand Chaumiere in Paris. There, she associated with such expatriates and seminal figures of the Harlem Renaissance as authors Countee Cullen and Claude McKay.

After her return to Harlem, Savage exhibited in several galleries and took on numerous commissions, among them busts of Frederick Douglass, author and NAACP leader James Weldon Johnson, and songwriter W. C. Handy. In 1932, with a grant from the Carnegie Foundation, she founded the Savage School of Arts, which offered the largest program of free classes in New York. In 1934, she became the first African American woman to be elected to the National Association of Women Painters and Sculptors and during the decade served as president of the Harlem Artists Guild. As assistant supervisor in the Federal Arts Project, a division of the Works Project Administration (WPA), Savage was the first director of the Harlem Community Art Center. In 1939, she opened the Salon of Contemporary Negro Art in Harlem, the nation's first gallery to exhibit and sell works by black artists.

A popular display at the New York World's Fair of 1939 was Savage's sixteen-foot-tall 1937 sculpture *The Harp*, also known as *Lift Every Voice and Sing*, based on James Weldon Johnson's poem set to music. Savage, who suffered from a lack of financial resources throughout her career and who frequently worked in clay or plaster when she could not afford bronze, did not have the funds to remove the sculpture from the fairgrounds to be recast, and the piece was destroyed. Only nineteen pieces could be found for a 1988 retrospective of her work at the Schomberg Center. Savage's *Gamin* survives on permanent display at the Smithsonian Art Museum in Washington, D.C., and a life-sized version of the sculpture is in the collection of the Cleveland Museum of Art.

In 1945, Savage moved to Saugerties, New York, where she taught art to children and wrote children's stories. Shortly before her death from cancer, she moved back to New York City to live with her daughter. In 2001, her home and studio in Saugerties were listed on the New York State Register of Historic Places as the Augusta Savage House and Studio.

Jessie Willcox Smith (1863–1935)

Illustrator

Jessie Willcox Smith was a prominent illustrator during the American Golden Age of Illustration, a period that lasted from the post-Civil War era until the early twentieth century, when books and magazines began to feature full-color art, and the imagery of a small group of highly successful illustrators such as N. C. Wyeth, Maxwell Parrish, and Smith captured the American cultural imagination.

Smith, whose forte was the illustrating of children's books and magazines, was born in Philadelphia, Pennsylvania, the youngest girl in a well-to-do family. She attended private elementary schools and at sixteen was sent to Cincinnati, Ohio, to live with her cousins while finishing her education. When a friend persuaded her to attend some local art classes, Smith discovered that she had a talent for drawing. In 1884, she studied art at the Philadelphia School of Design (now the Moore Academy of Fine Arts) and the following year attended the Pennsylvania Academy of Fine Arts. There, she studied under painter and photographer Thomas Eakins, who taught her to use photography as a resource in her illustrations. In 1888, the *St. Nicholas Magazine*, a children's magazine, published Smith's illustration *Three Little Maidens All in a Row*.

After her graduation from the academy in 1888, Smith worked at the *Ladies' Home Journal* in an entry-level position in the advertising department finishing rough sketches, designing borders, and preparing advertising art. At the same time, she studied at Drexel University with illustrator and children's book author Howard Pyle, who encouraged his students, half of whom were women, to fight for the right to illustrate for the major publishing houses of the era. In the late nineteenth and early twentieth centuries, women made up some

88 percent of the subscribers of American magazines. One of the most sought-after illustrators of art reflecting a woman's perspective, Smith's work was featured in such prestigious magazines as *Colliers*, *Leslie's Weekly*, *Harper's Weekly*, *McClure's*, *Scribners*, and *Good Housekeeping* by the turn of the nineteenth century.

Smith's best-known work included a long-running series of *Mother Goose* illustrations for *Good Housekeeping* as well as illustrations for Louisa May Alcott's novels *Little Women* and *An Old-Fashioned Girl*, Henry Wadsworth Longfellow's *Evangeline*, George MacDonald's *The Princess and the Goblin*, and Robert Louis Stevenson's *A Child's Garden of Verses*. Inspired in her use of color by French Impressionist painters, Smith preferred to use real children as models so that her illustrations would convey a spontaneity she felt would be lacking in professional child actors.

From 1888 to 1932, Smith produced illustrations for more than 250 periodicals, two hundred magazine covers, sixty books, prints, calendars, and posters. Reissues of classic children's books featuring her illustrations have appeared over the years since her death. In 1936, the Pennsylvania Academy of Fine Arts held a memorial retrospective of her works. She was inducted into the Society of Illustrators Hall of Fame in 1991.

Pablita Velarde (1918–2006)

Painter

One of the most accomplished Native American painters of her generation, Pablita Velarde was born Tse Tsan, which means "Golden Dawn" in the Tewa Pueblo Indian language, on Santa Clara Pueblo near Española, New Mexico. When she was five years old, her mother died, and she was sent with two of her sisters to St. Catherine's Indian School, a mission school in Santa Fe. At the age of fourteen, she became one of the first female students of art instructor Dorothy Dunn at the Santa Fe Studio Art School at the Santa Fe Indian School. There, Velarde learned to paint in the Dunn style known as "flat painting," a technique that celebrates figurative forms by calling attention to the natural flatness of the canvas. For Velarde, the narrative style of flat painting was a way to preserve the memory of her childhood and older pueblo life. She worked in watercolor early on and later learned to prepare paints from natural pigments for what she referred to as "earth paintings." Leaders of Velarde's pueblo initially ostracized her for becoming a full-time painter. As she said in a 1979 interview, "Painting was not considered women's work in my time. A woman was supposed to be just a woman, like a housewife and a mother and a chief cook. Those were things that didn't interest me." Pueblo women who did create art were expected to make pottery to be sold at local trading posts.

In 1939, Velarde was commissioned by the National Park Service under the Works Project Administration (WPA) to depict scenes of traditional pueblo life for visitors to the Bandelier National Monument near Los Alamos, New Mexico, which contains the preserved homes of Ancestral Puebloans, dating between 1150 and 1600 C.E. She went on to exhibit her paintings throughout the United States and produce murals commissioned and funded by the WPA. In 1942, Velarde married Herbert Hardin, a graduate of the University of California, whom she had known for many years. The couple had three children and lived near Albuquerque, New Mexico.

In 1953, Velarde became the first woman to receive the Grand Purchase Award at Tulsa, Oklahoma's Philbrick Museum of Art during its Annual Exhibition of Contemporary Painting. The following year, the French government awarded Velarde and eleven other Native American artists with the Palmes Academiques for excellence in art, the first foreign honors paid to American Indian artists. In 1960, Velarde published a book of six Tewa tribal stories titled *Old Father the Storyteller*, which is illustrated with her earth-tone paintings. Velarde's other awards and honors include the New Mexico Governor's Award (1977), the Santa Fe Living Treasure (1988), and the Lifetime Achievement Award from the National Women's Caucus for Art (1990).

Patience Lovell Wright (1725–1786)

Sculptor

Famous during the colonial era and in England for her life-size and lifelike wax figures, Patience Lovell Wright is the first recognized American-born sculptor.

Born in Oyster Bay, Long Island, into a well-to-do Quaker family, Patience Lovell moved with her family to Bordentown, New Jersey, at the age of four. As children, Patience and her sisters shaped wet flour or clay, then painted their creations with plant extracts. At sixteen, she left home for Philadelphia, where she married Joseph Wright, an elderly Quaker farmer and landowner, in 1748. Patience Wright continued her childhood hobby, often amusing her three children by molding faces out of putty, bread, dough, and wax.

When her husband died in 1769, Wright was pregnant with her fourth child and in need of money to support herself and her children. At the suggestion of her neighbor Francis Hopkinson, later a signer of the Declaration of Independence, Wright turned her sculpting hobby into a full-time occupation. With her sister Rachel Wells, Wright set up a successful business molding portrait busts in tinted wax, a popular form of art at the time, and charged admission to see them. By 1770, the sisters had opened a waxworks museum in New York City and had begun to display Wright's works in Philadelphia and Charleston, South Carolina. Her portraits, many of which were of well-known figures of the day, were life-size sculptures or busts modeled from life.

They featured real clothing and glass eyes and were often posed in tableaux to suggest activities a model might have undertaken.

In 1772, after a fire destroyed many of her sculptures, Wright and her family moved to London, England, where, thanks to Benjamin Franklin and his sister Jane Mecom, she entered London society. In London, Wright attained celebrity not only for her popular waxworks show featuring historical tableaux as well as portraits of prominent actors, politicians, and members of British royalty and the nobility but also for her high spirits, independence, and informal American manners, all of which contrasted sharply with British notions of correct deportment for a woman of her class. Wright fell out of favor with the British because of her open support for the Americans during the Revolutionary War, and in 1780, she left London for Paris in an unsuccessful attempt to open a wax museum there. She returned to London in 1782 and lived with her daughter, Phoebe, and son-in-law, British painter John Hoppner.

In 1783, Wright, who wanted to return to her home in Bordentown, New Jersey, wrote to George Washington asking him if he would grant her the opportunity to model a sculpture of his likeness; Washington responded that he would be honored to sit for Wright. However, in 1785, as she was preparing to travel, she suffered a bad fall and broke her leg. She died in March of the following year. Because of the fragility of her artistic medium, few of Wright's works survive. A full-length figure of former British prime minister William Pitt, sculpted after his death, is displayed in Westminster Abbey.

MEDIA AND THE PERFORMING ARTS

The diverse categories that fall under the heading of this chapter—music, dance, theater, film, and television—have all included gifted women whose talent and innovative contributions to their art have greatly influenced American entertainment and culture. As in other professions, women in the media and performing arts have also historically faced challenges that are unique to them.

MUSIC, DANCE, AND THEATER

The history of American women in music, dance, and theater reflects the cultural traditions that originally characterized these arts, the distinctly American subgenres that evolved from them, and the cultural diversity that has enriched them. Women are recorded as composers of music as early as the Byzantine Empire (fifth century C.E. to 1453) and as singers and instrumentalists dating from the Renaissance. In 1607, women sang in the cast of *L'Orfeo*, an Italian work by Claudio Monteverdi often cited as the first opera as we know it today, but the main women's role was sung by a castrated male as was customary in Europe at the time regarding vocal music that required higher voices. However, since more women than castrati existed, women often performed main women's roles. One of the most celebrated singers of the seventeenth century was soprano Caterina Martinelli, who performed regu-

larly at the Florentine court of Duke Vincenzo and for whom Monteverdi composed his opera *L'Arianna*. In 1608, while preparing to sing the title role, eighteen-year-old Martinelli died from smallpox. The oldest opera attributed to a woman is *La liberazione di Ruggerio*, composed by musician and singer Francesca Caccini, first performed in Florence in 1625. In the eighteenth century, European women often performed in operas, sang arias and songs at private gatherings, and appeared as solo instrumental artists. American women began singing opera in the nineteenth century, but the most celebrated soloist of the century was Stockholm-born soprano Jenny Lind (1820–1887), nicknamed the "Swedish Nightingale," who performed in operas throughout Europe and undertook a very successful tour of the United States. The first American-born singer to appear in principal roles with the famed Metropolitan Opera was soprano Alwina Valleria (1848–1925). Singer and New England Conservatory of Music graduate Louisa Melvin Delos Mars was the first African American woman to compose an opera, *Leoni, the Gypsy Queen*, produced in 1889. Orchestra conducting has historically been considered primarily a male occupation, and American female conductors of opera and symphony orchestras have been rare. The first woman to conduct the orchestra at the Metropolitan Opera was American Sarah Caldwell in 1978; the first American woman to conduct a major American symphony orchestra was Marin

Alsop, who became the principal conductor and music director of the Colorado Symphony Orchestra in 1993.

American popular music is said to have originated in the nineteenth century with the music of the first African American composer, Francis Johnson, in 1818 and the sentimental, mid-century "parlor songs" of popular songwriter Stephen Foster, who, with songwriter Daniel Emmett, would popularize African rhythms in the blackface minstrel shows that watered down and misrepresented the African American experience for the consumption of white audiences. From the turn of the twentieth century through the 1950s and the early- to mid-1960s, ragtime music and the popular songs that came from New York's Tin Pan Alley, together with the genres of blues, jazz, and big band swing music, would transform and define popular American music in the 1920s and become incorporated into the styles of such twentieth-century iconic female vocalists as Bessie Smith, Billie Holiday, Ella Fitzgerald, Sarah Vaughn, Alberta Hunter, Helen Forrest, Martha Tilton, and Jo Stafford. American country

Known as the "Swedish Nightingale," soprano Jenny Lind was one of the most famous opera singers of the nineteenth century. Her tour of America in 1850 had an impact on the country's musical culture.

and western music, which originated in the South in the 1920s and is rooted in the genres of American folk music, Western music, and blues, was slow to recognize the contribution of female vocalists and songwriters. The first woman to gain fame in the genre was Kitty Wells, whose 1952 hit "It Wasn't God Who Made Honky Tonk Angels" topped the charts and made Wells the first woman to sell one million copies of a single record. Banned by the Grand Ole Opry and network television as too suggestive, Wells's song, featuring the point of view of a man whose fiancée leaves him after discovering his dalliance with a woman he met at a bar, would set the tone for the themes of love and loss characteristic of the female country vocalists who followed, including Patsy Cline, Loretta Lynn, and Tammy Wynette. Some women associated with country music, such as Emmylou Harris and Dolly Parton, have incorporated such genres as pop, folk, rock, and bluegrass into their music. Multi-award-winning Dolly Parton has been a powerhouse among country stars for her work as a singer–songwriter and bandleader as well as an interpreter of other composers' works and through her collaborations with numerous musical artists.

Pop music, which originated in the 1950s to describe both traditional popular music and all its diverse styles, included aspects of rock 'n' roll and reached its first pinnacle in the first half of the 1960s with the talent of songwriters like Carole King; girl groups such as the McGuire Sisters, the Chantels, the Shirelles, and the Supremes, fronted by Diana Ross; and solo artists including Connie Francis, Lesley Gore, Darlene Love, Dionne Warwick, and Barbra Streisand. Another popular music genre that emerged in the 1950s was soul music, which combined elements of African American gospel music, rhythm and blues, and jazz and is primarily associated with female artists like Sister Rosetta Tharpe, Aretha Franklin, Gladys Knight, Martha Reeves, Etta James, Tina Turner, and Patti LaBelle. After the advent of rock music in the mid- to late 1960s and the disco decade of the 1970s with disco's reigning female vocalists Donna Summer, Gloria Gaynor, and Thelma Houston, pop music began a resurgence in the 1980s and the 1990s with the popularity of Michael Jackson and female artists such as Madonna,

Cyndi Lauper, Whitney Houston, and Latinx singers Gloria Estefan and Selena; by the turn of the twenty-first century, the most popular American female vocalists were pop singers. One of the most versatile vocalists who began her career in the 1960s has been Linda Ronstadt, who organized a folk trio as a teenager, was the lead singer for a male band, The Stone Poneys, in the late 1960s, and went on to work with a variety of bands and solo musicians in such diverse genres as pop, country music, and Latin and mariachi music.

At the same time that rock 'n' roll was transforming popular music in the 1950s and then codified as simply "rock music" in the late 1960s, folk music became a popular genre; examples of female folk musicians include Joan Baez; Ronnie Gilbert

The sweet voice of Linda Ronstadt was first heard in 1965 when she sang with a folk/rock group, The Stone Poneys. Her career had her covering many styles of vocals from punk to Gilbert and Sullivan, always to great acclaim.

and Mary Travers of the folk groups The Weavers and Peter, Paul and Mary; Judy Collins; and Joni Mitchell, the latter two of whom would go on to combine elements of several genres in the songs they wrote and performed. Although some women played instruments in all-girl "garage" rock bands of the 1960s, rock music was primarily considered a male genre until Janis Joplin, the lead singer with the band Big Brother and the Holding Company, rose to fame after appearing at the Monterey Pop Festival in 1967. Joplin's raw and powerful voice, together with her charismatic stage presence, made her the most celebrated female rock vocalist of the era until her death from a heroin overdose in 1970 at the age of twenty-seven. Female rock artists who followed Joplin include Pat Benatar, Joan Jett, Debbie Harry of the rock band Blondie, Bonnie Raitt, Patti Smith, and Chrissie Hynde, who cofounded the band The Pretenders. Rock bands composed solely of women began to form in the 1960s and 1970s; the first to reach critical and commercial success was Fanny, which was formed in 1969 and disbanded in 1975. The most long-lived and successful all-female American bands have been Heart, The Go-Go's, and The Bangles.

The rich diversity that characterizes American dance forms dates back to the ceremonial and celebratory dances of antiquity; the European formal court dances that began to take shape during the Renaissance and out of which ballet was developed; European folk and contra dances dating from the Middle Ages; American jazz music and modern dance, both of which originated in the late nineteenth and early twentieth centuries; and the dances introduced to America from Latinx countries. Influential in the evolution of dance in performance was the cabaret, the ancestor of British music halls, burlesque, American vaudeville, and nightclubs and the precursor, along with operetta, of musical theater. Cabaret originated in French taverns and inns as preferred dining destinations during the Renaissance and as Parisian dining and musical and theatrical variety venues beginning in the eighteenth century. The most famous Parisian cabaret venues that still exist are the Folies Bergère (1869), which began by featuring such light entertainment as operettas, comic operas, and gymnastics; and the

Considered to be one of rock and roll's first female icons, Janis Joplin took the fans at the Monterey Pop Festival by storm, firmly placing her as one of the '60's first great female rockers.

Moulin Rouge (1889), best known as the birthplace of the can-can dance, which was originally introduced as a seductive dance performed by the courtesans who worked out of the building, later evolving into a can-can dance revue that was featured in cabarets throughout Europe. By the 1920s, the Folies Bergère had expanded its repertoire to include variety acts featuring comedians, singers, dancers, and a bevy of scantily clad women. In the early 1890s, Loie Fuller (1862–1928), an American actress, dancer, and choreographer in burlesque, vaudeville, and circus shows as well as an inventor of stage lighting techniques, regularly starred at the Folies Bergère, performing improvised, free-form dances that pioneered the genre of modern dance. Among the most celebrated performers at the theater was African American singer, jazz dancer, and expatriate

Josephine Baker, who appeared in her first Folies revue, *La Folie du Jour*, in 1926. Baker caused a sensation with her erotic dancing and her costume made up of a brief skirt of artificial bananas, a long necklace, and little else.

One of the most influential genres in the history of American dance is modern dance, introduced by women in Germany and the United States in the late nineteenth century as a rejection of the strict and limited set of movements and costuming that characterized the dominant tradition of Western classical and romantic ballet. A freer, more interpretive and expressive style of dance, modern dance has often drawn upon archaic dance forms and such ethnic sources as Asian and African dance for inspiration. In addition to Loie Miller, early influential modern dance pioneers include Isadora Duncan, who used Greek sculpture as a movement source and performed her dances barefoot and wearing a simple, short tunic; and Ruth St. Denis, who founded the Denishawn dance company with her husband, Ted Shawn, in 1915. St. Denis used ethnic and Asian dance styles in her work and trained her dancers in the same method. The second wave of modern dance emerged in New York City in the 1930s with the work of dancer–choreographers Martha Graham, known for her movement technique of contraction and release derived from natural breathing as well as the incorporation of narrative themes and the use of literary subjects in her dance; Doris Humphrey, who evolved a technique using the body to dramatically convey balance, falling, and recovery; and Katherine Dunham, an author, educator, anthropologist, and social activist as well as a dancer and choreographer who was an innovator in African American modern dance.

During the postwar era, dancer–choreographers Anna Sokolow and Hanya Holm were the first to bring modern dance techniques to Broadway. Sokolow frequently staged works for the New York City Opera as well as dances for the musical versions of *Street Scene* (1947) and *Camino Real* (1953). Holm staged dances for such timeless musicals as *Kiss Me, Kate* (1948), *My Fair Lady* (1956), and *Camelot* (1960). In the 1960s, dancer–choreographers such as Twyla Tharp, Yvonne Rainer, Trisha Brown, and Meredith Monk began to experiment with modern

American dancer and choreographer Anna Sokolow was noted for her pivotal role in modern dance, creating works that expressed her concerns for humanity.

dance, creating postmodern, avant-garde, and eclectic dance forms, including the fusion of traditional modern dance with ballet, social dancing, ethnic dance, jazz, and contemporary music; dances that feature the intermingling of movement and sound; and dances that utilize artwork and video to convey a complex visual experience of movement. These once experimental dance forms have been woven into the tradition of modern dance as well as into the multidisciplinary genre of performance art and the staging of dances for musical theater.

Until the advent of opera and cabaret, women's participation in theater was largely nonexistent. Men took on women's roles in Greek dramas and comedies and in the plays of William Shakespeare. In the seventeenth and eighteenth centuries, the Italian comedic entertainment of the *Commedia dell'arte*, together with an increased number of European playwrights, saw female actors begin to appear more frequently on the stage as well as British plays being written and staged by women. Female actors and playwrights often faced challenges to their success: playwrights were charged with plagiarism if their works seemed too clever for a female writer, were offered less money than male playwrights in business dealings with managers, were often expected to give away the rights to their works, and were sexually harassed. Actresses were also sexually harassed and paid less than men. Actresses who eventually did attain some artistic and financial success in Britain found even greater success with audiences when they arrived with acting troupes in the cities of colonial America where, although touring groups of players existed, theater was less developed since the market for audiences was too small to sustain urban theaters and theater companies. The most well-known American women who participated in American theater in the late eighteenth and early nineteenth centuries were playwrights, including Mercy Otis Warren (1728–1814), Susanna Rowson (1762–1824), and Sarah Pogson Smith (c. 1790). Warren, often considered the first American female playwright, wrote several successful political satires and commentaries, which were published but never staged. Rowson's 1794 play *Slaves in Algiers, or, A Struggle for Freedom* advocated for women's rights in the new American republic and was performed with Rowson in one of the roles and delivering the epilogue: "Women were born for universal sway; Men to adore, be silent and obey." In her 1805 play *The Female Enthusiast: A Tragedy in Five Acts*, Sarah Pogson Smith explored themes of American nationalism and women's equality through a sympathetic portrayal of Charlotte Corday, a French woman guillotined for assassinating radical revolutionary Jean-Paul Marat in 1793 during the French Revolution.

In the nineteenth century, two forms of theater started to become popular in the United States: vaudeville and burlesque variety shows. Both prominently featured female dancers, singers, and comediennes, but differences existed in the two genres and in how women were presented to audiences. In its early years, vaudeville encompassed such diverse entertainments as traveling circuses and medicine and minstrel shows, which included programs of song, comedy (often trading on ethnic and racial stereotypes), jugglers, and risqué material. In the early 1880s, impresario Tony Pastor, a former circus ringmaster turned theater manager, introduced "polite" vaudeville shows for more dignified urban, middle-class sensibilities, especially those of female theatergoers. Pastor eliminated the bawdiness that characterized traveling shows and centered his variety acts in several New York City theaters. Other theater managers in New York and various cities around the United States copied Pastor's success, creating vaudeville "circuits" in which performers would travel. Lasting from the 1880s until the early 1930s, when radio and film supplanted live performances (to be revived later in television variety shows), vaudeville was a showcase for many legendary female dancers, singers, and comediennes such as Lillian Russell, Fanny Brice, Eva Tanguay, Nora Bayes, Helen Morgan, Sophie Tucker, Mae West, Ethel Merman, and Ethel Waters. Female

A poster from 1898 promotes a burlesque show. Women were often prominently featured in such programs, usually wearing what was then considered scandalously skimpy clothing.

vaudeville stars were among the wealthiest independent women in the country, and many of them went on to further successful careers appearing in the Ziegfeld Follies, singing in nightclubs and on radio, and acting in musical theater and movies.

Some vaudeville stars such as Mae West, Sophie Tucker, and Fanny Brice worked in burlesque early in their careers. Burlesque, which competed with vaudeville for audiences, similarly featured variety acts but kept the flashy, uninhibited, and risqué component of early vaudeville. An offshoot of British burlesque and the English music hall, American burlesque shows, which became popular in the 1870s, were composed of songs and ribald comic sketches; assorted acts such as acrobats, magicians, and solo singers; and chorus dance numbers or a parody sketch of current politics or a takeoff of a play such as a Shakespearean drama or comedy. Burlesque was less reputable than vaudeville and considered more proletarian than the high society. Offered by the Ziegfeld Follies, burlesque featured young female singers and dancers who showed off their figures in costumes that might include tights, boots, a short tunic or dress, and, if they were playing men, a male suit jacket and top hat. These scantily clad singers, called soubrettes, were gradually replaced in burlesque by strip teasers, sometimes known by the more polite term "ecdysiasts," who bared all or nearly all and were considered stars in their own right. By 1932, some 150 strippers in the United States were famous, including fan dancer Sally Rand, Gypsy Rose Lee, and Ann Corio. By the late 1930s, burlesque shows would feature up to six strippers, along with one or two comics and a master of ceremonies. The decline of burlesque began around the same time, when New York City mayor Fiorello La Guardia began to close theaters, effectively putting burlesque out of business by the early 1940s, although some shows lingered elsewhere in the United States. By the 1970s, with nudity commonplace in movies and featured in the peep shows of New York's 42nd Street, the genre died. An attempt to revive burlesque—sometimes called neo-burlesque—began in the 1990s. Neo-burlesque has featured such performers as Dita Von Teese (born Heather Renee Sweet) and Julie Atlas Muz as well as male striptease, political satire, and performance art incorporated into shows.

In contrast to vaudeville and burlesque were the dramas, comedies, and musical comedies offered in American theaters. However, in some cases, theatrical genres overlapped. In the nineteenth and early twentieth centuries, one popular subgenre of drama was melodrama, which might feature a play based on a literary work such as Harriet Beecher Stowe's *Uncle Tom's Cabin* or the melodramatically rendered scenes from history or mythology featured at the Follies. Presented as *tableaux vivants* ("living pictures"), nude or seminude women posed like statues behind a mesh screen, a necessity since theatrical censorship prevented undressed women from moving onstage. In 1866, actress Ada Isaacs Menken played the title male role in the melodrama *Mazeppa*, based on a poem by Lord Byron that tells the story of a legendary Ukrainian military hero. In the final scene, Menken, dressed in a flesh-colored body stocking, made her entrance strapped to the back of a horse, which galloped down a ramp in the direction of the audience. Menken, who appeared to be naked, caused a sensation. Despite their shock, New York theatergoers continued to attend performances, making the play popular. Menken later reprised the role on tour in the United States and Europe.

By the turn of the twentieth century, the United States had three thousand theaters. Women, who made up the majority of theatergoers and included "matinee girls," young women who attended the theater unescorted, influenced what plays were staged and which actors would appear in leading roles. New York's Broadway, the center of theater activity, gained a reputation as a showcase for female theatergoers to display the latest fashions. Between 1870 and 1880, the number of women who described their profession on the United States census as "actress" was 780; by 1910, that number had jumped to 15,432. For successful actresses with star power, a life in the theater, much like the movie industry that was in its infancy in the first decades of the twentieth century, offered wealth, mobility, social power, and celebrity. The majority of actresses were not stars, however, and they faced the reality of a competitive and often unfriendly environment, where they sought the attention of numerous producers and theater managers who frequently responded with sexual advances. If hired for a production at a salary ranging from $10 to $25 a week in contrast to a star's $150 a week, an actress was not paid for rehearsal time and was expected to supply her own costumes, which could cost nearly $400.

One conduit to success in the mainstream theater was the Yiddish theater, which reached its peak after the large influx of Jewish immigrants arrived in the late nineteenth century. Women were influential in the Yiddish theater from the start as writers, actors, directors, producers, and drama teachers. Examples of actresses in the Yiddish theater include Sara Adler, the matriarch of the venerable Adler family of theater managers and actors who thrilled audiences with the depth of her emotional power onstage; Sara's daughter, Stella, a successful actress who became a celebrated acting teacher; and popular

Judith Malina (center) and Julian Beck (top) are shown here rehearsing at The Living Theater. Founded in 1947 in New York City, it is the oldest experimental theater in the United States.

comic actress Molly Picon, who worked on the stage, screen, and television.

In the 1950s, an Off-Broadway movement began as a reaction against the perceived commercialism of Broadway with smaller theaters in several locations in New York City and less financial obligation in mounting productions. Off-Broadway and the more avant-garde Off-Off-Broadway became the ideal venue for the production of new and often experimental plays, some of which might later secure production in Broadway theaters. Two examples are The Living Theatre, cofounded by actor Judith Malina and her husband, Julian Beck, in 1947, which began to grow in prominence in the 1950s; and the La MaMa Experimental Theatre Club, founded by African American director, producer, and fashion designer Ellen Stewart in 1961.

FILM

When moving pictures were developed at Thomas Edison's laboratories in New Jersey at the end of the nineteenth century, the first filmmakers drew upon vaudeville and burlesque for subject matter and performers. The first woman to appear in an Edison kinetoscope—a film viewed through a cabinet with a peephole—was a Spanish dancer in the film *Carmencita* in March 1894. Numerous short films featuring exotic dancers and scantily clad women followed, one of which was titled *Trapeze Disrobing Act* (1901). Similarly voyeuristic was *Peeping Tom in the Dressing Room* (1905), in which a man watches a buxom chorus girl through a keyhole as she dresses. When the women discover him, he is brought into the dressing room, where the chorus girls beat him with powder puffs. At the same time, however, early filmmakers realized that in order to create a financially viable industry, they needed to look beyond prurient subjects to attract audiences that included middle-class women. Films produced with women in mind included *Annie Oakley* (1894), in which the famed sharpshooter displayed her marksmanship, and the famous eighteen-second film *The Kiss* (1896), which featured the first on-screen kiss, delivered to vaudeville star May Irwin from Broadway actor John C. Rice. Filmmakers also made films of boxers, wrestlers, blacksmiths,

and barbershops, which allowed women views of traditionally masculine pursuits and venues from which they were normally excluded. Other scenes of everyday life included films like *Kansas Saloon Smashers* (1901), a reenactment of temperance leader Carry Nation's smashup of a hotel bar in Wichita, Kansas, and *Women of the Ghetto Bathing* (1902), which showed women and girls in turn-of-the-century swimming attire at a New York public swimming pool on "Ladies' Day."

During film's first decade, movie studios like Biograph and Vitagraph began to form in addition to the Edison Company, and filmmakers started to enhance plots and characters into complete stories that borrowed from such genres as comedy, melodrama, crime and social problem drama, and westerns. By the second decade, although films depicting

Although women were getting some feature roles in early films, they were typically cast as victims who needed to be rescued by heroic men.

current events such as the women's suffrage march of 1915 continued to be made, fictional narratives dominated the film market. Some genre films featured female leads, like *The Girl from Montana* (1907), a western in which the main character is a horsewoman who saves her lover from hanging, and *The Fatal Hour* (1908), a crime drama that tells the story of a female police operative who attempts to rescue a girl kidnapped by a Chinese "white slave" ring, a widespread cultural fear of the era. In 1914, *The Perils of Pauline*, a popular melodrama shown in weekly installments, featured Pearl White as the title character, a young woman menaced each week by various villains in a variety of dangerous circumstances. The most durable romantic film melodrama of the silent era was *Way Down East*, taken from the nineteenth-century play by Lottie Blair Parker. In the third silent-film version, which appeared in 1920, celebrated film star Lillian Gish plays a poor country girl who is seduced and abandoned by a wealthy playboy, gives birth to a child who dies, and is tossed out into a fierce snowstorm by the squire for whom she works before being rescued from an ice floe by the squire's son, who loves her.

Film studios in the increasingly popular new medium did not reveal the names of their actors because the Motion Picture Patents Company, which financially controlled the studios, worried that actors would demand more money if audiences knew their names. Audiences, however, liked to identify individual "players," as actors were called, and invented names for their favorites such as "the Biograph Girl," "the Vitagraph Girl," or, in the case of Mary Pickford, who would become the most celebrated actress in silent films, "the Girl With the Golden Hair" and, ironically, "Little Mary" after a character Pickford frequently played. The anonymity under which actors worked changed in 1910 when Carl Laemmle, a distributor turned independent producer, lured actor Florence Lawrence, famous as "the Biograph Girl," away from Biograph to his newly formed film studio, the Independent Motion Picture Company of America, known in the movie business as Imp. Laemmle concocted an elaborate publicity stunt involving a news story, planted by him, that reported Lawrence's death in a streetcar accident. Laemmle subsequently insisted that the story was a lie in-

vented by "enemies" of Imp. He further announced that Florence Lawrence, now "the Imp Girl," was alive and well and would be starring in Imp's next picture, *The Broken Oath*. Next, Laemmle had Lawrence make a public appearance in St. Louis, where throngs of excited fans mobbed her and tore off pieces of her clothing for souvenirs. By engineering such a clever, if unprincipled, publicity stunt, Laemmle, who would go on to found the highly successful Universal Studios, proved the vast popularity of movie actors, underlined their value as commercial properties, and set in motion what would become the corporate glorification and marketing of top-billed screen actors together with the publicity associated with the cultivation of new talent under the Hollywood star system. The publicity generated for leading film actors would in turn lead to the advent of highly popular movie magazines, which featured articles on the stars that, especially in the case of female stars because most readers of movie magazines were women, both glamorized them and through carefully constructed confessional narratives sought to reassure their avid fans that they were just like everyone else. In a 1936 letter to *Motion Picture* magazine, Agnes Specht, a film fan from Cleveland, Ohio, wrote: "Through [the magazines] we learn that all these glamorous people are just simple human beings like ourselves and that they have our ambitions, struggles, heartaches and hopes. And through this knowledge we understand them better." The screen magazines, together with the gossip columns of newspapers, began the celebrity juggernaut that continues in all forms of current media.

During the silent screen era into the early 1930s, before the film industry became a big business dominated by eight major film studios and the three

> The presence of female directors and producers diminished greatly during the studio era (1930–1949) as the industry became more specialized and structured....

lesser studios known as the "Poverty Row" studios, all headed by men such as Carl Laemmle, Louis B. Mayer, and the Warner Brothers, women were equally involved in nearly every aspect of film production as screenwriters, directors, actors, costume designers, script readers, script girls, film cutters and editors, set designers, and casting directors. Nearly one-quarter of Hollywood screenwriters were women, and women wrote half of all films produced and copyrighted between 1911 and 1925. The presence of female directors and producers diminished greatly during the studio era (1930–1949) as the industry became more specialized and structured, unions were formed, and creative decisions regarding most aspects of filmmaking were left to male heads of production. Female editors, directors, and screenwriters all existed, most notably Dorothy Arzner, Ida Lupino, Anita Loos, and Frances Marion as well as writers such as Dorothy Parker, who were hired to cowrite scripts or serve as "script doctors" for existing screenplays. Independent female filmmakers also existed such as Maya Deren, who made experimental film shorts in the 1940s.

The studio era, sometimes referred to as the classical or "golden" Hollywood period, saw a variety of feature films in various genres, one of which was the "women's film," formula movies sometimes referred to as "tearjerkers," which were constructed specifically to appeal to female audiences. Partly a result of the strengthening of the Motion Picture Production Code, also known as the Hays Code, which was the set of industry moral guidelines released by the major studios in 1930, rigidly enforced from 1934, and followed until 1968, the women's film, in keeping with the code, minimized or eliminated potentially controversial subjects relating to women and their status in society. For example, a precode crime drama such as *Three on a Match* (1932), which concerns the romantic and sexual misfortunes of three women, one of whom becomes addicted to drugs and commits suicide, was considered unwholesome. In contrast, the women's films that followed stricter implementation of the code encompassed melodrama, romance, and family concerns, concentrated on a female character in often difficult circumstances, and were characterized by self-sacrifice, self-denial, and

plot elements that might center on choices relating to career, motherhood, or romantic partners. The most famous example is *Now Voyager* (1942), in which Bette Davis is transformed from an overweight, unattractive spinster dominated by her dictatorial, unloving mother into a sleek, sophisticated, self-confident woman who enters into a (chaste) love affair with an unhappily married man and who must sacrifice a relationship with him in order to retain guardianship of his daughter, whom she also loves. Two women's films that retained elements of the genre but included feminist sensibilities were *Stage Door* (1937), written and directed by men, which starred Katharine Hepburn, Ginger Rogers, and several other well-known female actors as aspiring, mutually supportive actresses living in a women's theatrical boardinghouse; and *Dance, Girl, Dance* (1940), directed by Dorothy Arzner and starring Lucille Ball and Maureen O'Hara, in which O'Hara, a ballerina forced to take a job in burlesque, delivers a fiery speech

Ginger Rogers, shown here with her dancing partner Fred Astaire in the 1935 movie *Top Hat,* once famously said that she could do anything Fred did "backwards and in high heels."

from the stage castigating the voyeuristic behavior of the men in the audience.

By the 1920s, two industries were effective in Hollywood: the making of movies and the marketing of movie stars. One method used by the studios to ensure that fans would continue to yearn for the screen presence of their favorite actors was to cast them according to type. As a result, the images and personalities of female stars became etched in the public's mind as inseparable from the types of women they played. During the silent screen era, the diminutive Mary Pickford, publicized as "America's sweetheart," was typed as the spirited, but always virginal, child–woman (or boy, as in the 1921 film *Little Lord Fauntleroy*); and lively, flirtatious Clara Bow, the "It Girl," personified 1920s sex appeal. In the 1930s, Jean Harlow, in her slinky, form-fitting gowns, was Hollywood's "blonde bombshell"; languorous Greta Garbo and glamorous Marlene Dietrich projected sophisticated sexuality and the essence of female mystery; popular stars Jean Arthur and Barbara Stanwyck epitomized the tough and sassy, career-minded woman; Ginger Rogers, whose prolific career included both dramatic and comedy roles, was equally sassy in the musicals that featured her dancing with Fred Astaire "backwards and in high heels"; Myrna Loy portrayed the ideal wife–companion in the 1930s and 1940s. Marie Dressler and Shirley Temple, the two biggest box office stars of the Depression era, were symbols in their own right: Dressler, a large, unglamorous woman and an excellent comic actor, portrayed women who were tough yet vulnerable; Temple, who began her film career at the age of three, projected innocence and hope and was every parent's dream daughter. The films of the 1940s, reflecting World War II, turned such screen dream women as Betty Grable and Rita Hayworth into cheesecake "pinup girls" popular with soldiers. Joan Crawford, who had been starring in films since the late 1920s and played every kind of role from a flapper (*Our Dancing Daughters*, 1928) to a shop girl turned grasping paramour of a married man (*The Women*, 1939), was the personification of suffering womanhood in the women's film *Mildred Pierce* (1945) or the image of the vamp-on-the-make in *Humoresque* (1946). Top-billed female stars who consistently defied and challenged the constraints of

typecasting during the studio era included Katharine Hepburn and Bette Davis, both of whom frequently played strong-willed, independent women and, in the case of Davis, sometimes had disastrous results for her character.

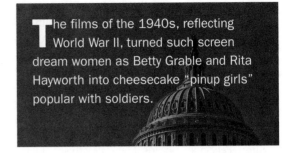

The films of the 1940s, reflecting World War II, turned such screen dream women as Betty Grable and Rita Hayworth into cheesecake "pinup girls" popular with soldiers.

In the late 1940s, the dominance of the Hollywood studios was threatened by several factors: the court-ordered breakup of the "Big Five" studios—MGM, Paramount, 20th Century Fox, Warner Brothers, and RKO—on antitrust issues; European import tariffs imposed on Hollywood films; the rise in independent film production; male and female stars who had begun to seek greater creative and economic independence from the studios that had long controlled their careers; and television, which steadily began to draw greater audiences in the newly established postwar American suburbs. By the 1960s, the studio era, with its large production costs and long-term contracts for actors and other employees in the industry, came to an end.

As studios were forced to loosen their grip on their employees and the Motion Picture Production Code gave way to the ratings system, actors became independent contractors and filmmakers became free to explore social and political themes in new ways, although the Hollywood blacklist imposed as a result of the postwar Red Scare and the House Un-American Activities Committee (HUAC) hearings that followed compromised that freedom for many in the film and television industries from the late 1940s through the 1950s. The blacklist included members of the industry who were deemed to be communists or to have communist sympathies as well as those who spoke out against HUWAC's persecution of performers, screenwriters, and directors. Blacklisted women of the era include actor and musical comedy star Judy Holliday; Oscar-nominated actor Lee Grant; actors and singers Lena Horne and Hazel Scott; writers Lillian Hellman and Dorothy Parker; celebrated acting teacher Uta Hagen; and ecdysiast Gypsy Rose Lee.

The breakdown of the studio system would gradually bring more women back into the film industry behind the camera as screenwriters, producers, directors, costume designers, and cinematographers, although the number of women in executive positions with studios lagged—and continues to lag—behind. The 1980s began to see the burgeoning of female directors and screenwriters such as Joan Micklin Silver, Penny Marshall, Claudia Weill, Nora Ephron, Penelope Spheeris, Melissa Mathison, Elaine May, and the multitalented Barbra Streisand. In the 1990s and well into the twenty-first century, female filmmakers and screenwriters such as Nancy Meyers, Tina Fey, Sofia Coppola, Greta Gerwig, Kathryn Bigelow, and Ava de Vernay as well as female actors have not only given the public outstanding films but have also been vocal advocates for greater racial

Academy Award-winning actress Judy Holliday was one of several movie stars called before the House Un-American Activities Committee.

diversity in the industry and a redefinition of the status of women on-screen and behind the camera.

Despite the overall gains made by women working in film since the 1970s and 1980s, movie stars continued to receive the most public interest, and casting women according to type remains a feature of filmmaking. Each decade since the film industry began has brought forth female movie (and, latterly, television) stars who have not only represented women of the prevailing culture in the roles they have played but who have also helped to determine, for better or for worse, how each culture has imagined its women.

TELEVISION

In 1950, only 9 percent of American households owned a television set; that figured had jumped to 90 percent by 1960. From its early years, female performers were prominently featured in television variety shows, as hosts of daytime programs, in soap operas and situation comedies, and in commercials. In the 1950s, daytime television programming was targeted especially for housewives, who might take a break from homemaking duties to watch their favorite quiz show or catch up on their favorite soap opera, each episode of which lasted for 15 minutes. After-dinner prime time viewing in the 1950s and 1960s might include such situation comedies as *I Love Lucy*, *Leave It to Beaver*, or *The Donna Reed Show*, the latter two of which featured lead female characters who typified the era's preoccupation with women as domestic and maternal goddesses.

Another popular weekly comedy show of the 1950s was *Your Show of Shows*, which featured comic actors Sid Caesar, Howard Morris, Imogene Coca, and comic actor, writer, and director Carl Reiner in a series of comedy skits and is notable for its hiring of the first female television comedy writers, Lucille Kallen (1922–1999) and Selma Diamond (1920–1985). A playwright, composer, and lyricist as well as a television writer, Kallen went on to write for the Bell Telephone Hour, a concert series imported from radio that ran on television until 1958; Diamond later became known for her acting roles in the film *It's a Mad Mad Mad Mad World* (1963) and the television sitcom *Night Court* (1984–

1992). Other pioneering women behind the television camera include Mildred Freed Allberg (1921–1984), who began her career as a typist and rose to become the executive producer of the Hallmark Hall of Fame; Lela Swift (1919–2015), a director of weekly, live, prime time anthologies and a producer on the soap operas *Dark Shadows* and *Ryan's Hope*; Lucy Jarvis (1917–), an Emmy award-winning producer of documentaries; and the hardworking film director Ida Lupino (1918–1995), who starred in her own sitcom, *Mr. Adams and Eve*, with her husband Howard Duff from 1957 to 1958 and directed television westerns, crime dramas, and situation comedies. Lupino was also the only woman to direct episodes of the original series of *The Twilight Zone* as well as the only director to star in the show. All of these women paved the way for the female producers, directors, and writers who would create and helm such memorable 1980s female-centered television shows as *Murphy Brown* (Diane English), *Roseanne* (Marcy Carsey), *Designing Women* (Linda Bloodworth-Thomason), and *Golden*

The groundbreaking television show *Julia* (1968–1971) cast Diahann Carroll in a nonstereotypical role for a black woman.

Girls (Susan Harris) as well as the western series *Lonesome Dove* (Suzanne de Passe) and the police procedural *Cagney & Lacey* (Barbara Avedon and Barbara Corday).

Television began to try to reflect the changing status of women and the experiences of African Americans in the late 1960s and 1970s. In 1968, the first weekly series to star an African American woman in a nonstereotypical role was *Julia*, an eighty-six-episode series in which singer–actor Diahann Carroll played a widowed, single mother who worked as a nurse in a doctor's office. The series is remembered now as groundbreaking, but critics at the time considered it too apolitical and an unrealistic explication of the black experience as well as criticizing it for its depiction of a fatherless black family, a cultural trope that all too often suggested a chronic instability in the African American community. By the mid-1970s and the 1980s, shows focusing on African Americans such as *Good Times*, *The Jeffersons*, and *Family Matters* featured strong female characters in relatable family units. Similarly groundbreaking shows of the late 1960s and the 1970s included *The Mary Tyler Moore Show*, starring the title actor as a single career woman working in a Minneapolis newsroom, and the multi-award-winning *The Carol Burnett Show*, a variety/sketch comedy show named for the title comedian, which lasted in prime time from 1967 to 1975 and to date is the only such television variety show starring a woman. By the mid-1990s, the first female *Star Trek* captain had appeared, and in the twenty-first century, the police procedural *Law & Order: SVU* became squarely centered in its lead female character, a police lieutenant played by Mariska Hargitay. Although strong female characters have been predominant in many series in the first decades of the twenty-first century, some have been endowed with issues that speak to stereotypes of female instability: for example, the highly competent *Nurse Jackie* is an opioid addict who sleeps with the hospital pharmacist to score pills; *Homeland*'s brilliant intelligence agent Carrie Mathison suffers from bipolar disorder, which sometimes tellingly compromises her effectiveness, and is prone to emotional outbursts, prompting some critics of the show to disparagingly call the character "cryface."

One of the most famous television journalists of her generation, Barbara Walters (left) is shown here interviewing President Gerald Ford and First Lady Betty Ford in 1976.

In the early days of television, women were markedly absent from broadcast news positions. Pioneering broadcaster Pauline Frederick (1883–1938), who began working in radio as a freelance broadcast journalist in the 1930s and was consigned to covering such women's forums as "How to Get a Husband," was told by an executive, "A woman's voice just doesn't carry authority." Undaunted, Frederick reported from the 1948 national political conventions and was finally hired at ABC, thus becoming the first female correspondent to work full time for a television network. In 1976, she became the first woman to moderate a presidential debate. Frederick was followed by Nancy Dickerson, who was hired by *CBS News's* Washington Bureau to produce a radio show called *Capital Cloakroom* and would go on to become the associate producer of the long-running news show *Face the Nation* as well as become the network's first female correspondent. The equally long-running morning news and talk show *Today* hired its first female cohost, Barbara Walters, in 1966 and its second, Jane Pauley, in 1976. The same year, Barbara Walters, who was paired with veteran broadcaster Harry Reasoner, became network television's first female national evening news coanchor on ABC. The first African American woman to anchor a major network newscast was Carole Simpson, who became a weekend anchor at ABC News. Simpson, who suffered racial slurs and sexual discrimination during her career, was also the first female moderator chosen by the Commission of Presidential Debates in 1992. In 2006, former *Today* cohost Katie Couric became the first female solo anchor when she took over the position at the *CBS Evening News* from Bob Schieffer. Questions over Couric's gravitas for such a serious job were raised, but she proved herself equal to the task during her five years in the anchor chair.

As entertainment options have widened with the advent of streaming services, women who work in film and television have seen greater opportunities. Challenges remain, but women have claimed their authority in the entertainment industry by working in increasing numbers as producers and directors and by forcefully speaking out against sexual harassment and gender discrimination and on behalf of racial inclusion and pay parity.

BIOGRAPHIES

Jay Presson Allen (1922–2006)
Playwright, Screenwriter

Best known for her screen and stage adaptations from novels, Jay Presson Allen is credited with having developed some of the best and most memorable women's stage and film roles in the 1960s and 1970s. She was one of the few women to make a living as a screenwriter when women were a rarity in the profession.

Born Jacqueline Presson in Fort Worth, Texas, the daughter of a department store manager and a buyer of women's clothing, she attended a girls' school in Dallas but skipped college, moving to California at the age of eighteen to become an actress. Instead, she turned from acting to writing. In 1948, she published a novel, *Spring Riot*, and in the 1950s, she wrote scripts for live drama television shows like the Philco Television Playhouse.

She produced the screenplay for the Alfred Hitchcock film *Marnie* (1964), but her breakthrough came with her adaptation of Muriel Spark's novel

The Prime of Miss Jean Brodie for the stage (1966) and for film (1969). Works that followed included *Forty Carats* (1968; filmed 1973), the film adaptation of *Cabaret* (1972), *Deathtrap* (1982), and the one-man stage production *Tru* (1989). "The trick in adapting," she recalled, "is not to throw out the baby with the bathwater. You can change all kinds of things, but don't muck around with the essence." Allen had the knack of creating memorable and award-winning roles, particularly for women. Maggie Smith won the Academy Award for Best Actress for *The Prime of Miss Jean Brodie;* Julie Harris won a Tony Award for *Forty Carats;* Liza Minnelli won best actress for her role as Sally Bowles in *Cabaret.*

Allen's last film work was her screenplay for the 1990 remake of *Lord of the Flies.* She disliked the finished product and had her name removed from the credits. Jay Presson Allen died at her home in Manhattan following a stroke at the age of eighty-four.

Marian Anderson (1897–1993)

Singer

Marian Anderson, who electrified and inspired audiences with her vocal power and range, is celebrated as one of the greatest singers of the twentieth century. The first African American to become a permanent member of New York City's Metropolitan Opera Company, Anderson achieved both artistic greatness and triumphed over racial discrimination with an undaunted spirit.

Anderson was born in Philadelphia, the oldest of three daughters in a poor but loving family. At the age of six, she joined the junior choir at the Union Baptist Church, where she impressed the director by learning all the vocal parts of the hymns. As a teenager, she performed at churches and local organizations, often accompanying herself on the piano. She was prevented from enrolling in a Philadelphia music school because of her race, but members of the city's black community began the "Fund for Marian's Future" to allow her to study with leading vocalists. Anderson enjoyed acting and wanted to try opera, but the exclusion, up until then, of African Americans from the field discouraged her.

In 1925, Anderson won first prize in a New York Philharmonic voice competition; however, despite her critically acclaimed performance as a soloist with the New York Philharmonic and at Carnegie Hall, she had difficulty gaining bookings for performances in the United States because of her race. Anderson received a scholarship from the Rosenwald Foundation that allowed her to study in England and Germany in the late 1920s. She then toured Europe from 1930 to 1935. When she returned to the United States for a concert, the music critic for *The New York Times* proclaimed, "Marian Anderson has returned to her native land one of the greatest singers of our time."

In 1939, in an incident that garnered national headlines, the Daughters of the American Revolution barred Anderson from performing at Constitution Hall, their national headquarters, because of her race. First Lady Eleanor Roosevelt resigned from the D.A.R. in protest, and other prominent women followed suit. Anderson subsequently performed in a concert at the Lincoln Memorial before an audience of seventy-five thousand and millions more who listened to the radio broadcast.

Anderson went on to shatter the racial barrier that had kept black singers from pursuing careers in opera by joining the Metropolitan Opera in 1955. She sang at the inaugurals of President Eisenhower and President Kennedy, and she performed again at the Lincoln Memorial during the memorable 1963 civil rights March on Washington when Martin Luther King Jr. gave his famous "I Have a Dream" speech.

For her service on behalf of racial justice and her contributions to music, Anderson received the U.S. Presidential Medal of Freedom in 1991.

Dorothy Arzner (1897–1979)

Film Director

Dorothy Arzner was the first female film director in the Hollywood studio system. From 1927 until her retirement from feature directing in 1943, she was also the only female director working in Hollywood. She made a total of twenty films and launched the careers of a number of Hollywood stars, including Katharine Hepburn, Rosalind Russell, and Lucille Ball. She was also the first woman to join the Directors Guild of America and the first woman to direct a sound film.

She was born in San Francisco but grew up in Los Angeles, where her father owned a restaurant. It was frequented by many silent film stars, including Mary Pickford, Mack Sennett, and Douglas Fairbanks and was the first place that Arzner came into contact with the movie business. After finishing high school, she enrolled at the University of Southern California studying medicine in the hopes of becoming a doctor. During World War I, she joined a local ambulance unit, but working in the office of a surgeon convinced her that a career in medicine was not for her. Instead, she tried the film industry, which was in need of workers after the war. She was given the opportunity to choose a job she preferred, and, after spending a week observing, she decided, "If one was going to be in this movie business, one should be a director because he was the one who told everyone else what to do."

She started in the script department and edited fifty-two films. Asked to edit Rudolph Valentino's film *Blood and Sand* (1922), she shot some of the bullfighting scenes for the film and intercut them with stock footage, saving the studio thousands of dollars. She caught the attention of director James Cruze and became his trusted "right arm." She used a threat to leave Paramount for Columbia to land her first directing job, *Fashions for Women* (1927).

Its success led to her directing three more silent films, and she was given the assignment to direct Clara Bow in her first talkie, *The Wild Party* (1929). Since early talkies were much harder to make, established male directors were content to stay with silent films, allowing Arzner to deal with the challenges of sound. To ease Bow's discomfort from acting beside a stationary microphone, Arzner had a technician rig a microphone on the end of a fishing rod so a technician could maneuver the mic, following Bow as she moved. Arzner had invented the "boom microphone."

In 1932, Arzner left Paramount to freelance for other studios. When MGM released *The Bride Wore Red* (1937), it advertised it as "A Woman's Love

Story Directed by Hollywood's Only Woman Director." During World War II, Arzner made training films for the Women's Army Corps. After the war, she focused on making commercials. Arzner was rediscovered in the 1970s by feminists reviewing older films to screen at film festivals. She was honored by the Director's Guild in 1975, and Katharine Hepburn sent her a congratulatory telegram reading: "Isn't it wonderful that you had such a great career, when you had no right to have a career at all?"

Josephine Baker (1906–1975)
Dancer, Singer

American-born Josephine Baker became one of the most celebrated performers ever in her adopted France, headlining the revues of the *Folies Bergère* in Paris and was dubbed "the Black Venus" and "the Creole Goddess." Baker was also the first African American to star in a major motion picture, the 1927 silent film *Siren of the Tropics*.

Born Freda Josephine McDonald in St. Louis, Missouri, Baker's parents were both entertainers, performing throughout the segregated Midwest with little success. The young Baker took odd jobs to survive, often dancing on the street, collecting money from onlookers. Eventually, she attracted the attention of an African American theater troupe, and, at the age of fifteen, Baker left home to perform with the troupe, marrying and taking her husband's last name, becoming Josephine Baker. She danced in vaudeville shows, eventually moving to New York City during the seminal era of African American history known as the Harlem Renaissance.

In 1925, Baker moved to Paris and opened *La Revue Nègre*. As Baker recalled, "I became famous first in France in the twenties. I just couldn't stand America, and I was one of the first colored Americans to move to Paris." She became a sensation for her erotic dancing and eventually headlined at the *Folies Bergère*. Her *danse sauvage* performance wearing a costume consisting of a skirt of artificial bananas became an iconic image of the Jazz Age. She became the most successful American entertainer working in France, whom Ernest Hemingway called "the most sensational woman anyone ever saw." She sang professionally for the first time in 1930 and made her screen debut four years later, making several more films before World War II curtailed her career.

During the Nazi occupation of Paris, Baker worked with the Red Cross and the French Resistance. She entertained troops in Africa and the Middle East and after the war was awarded the *Croix de Guerre* and the Legion of Honor. She retired from the stage in 1956 but was forced to come out of retirement to maintain her estate in southwestern France. Baker traveled several times to the United States to participate in civil rights demonstrations. In 1963, she spoke at the March on Washington, the only official female speaker. She introduced the "negro women for civil rights," which included Rosa Parks. In her speech, Baker declared, "I have walked into the palaces of kings and queens and into the houses of presidents. And much more. But I could not walk into a hotel in America and get a cup of coffee, and that made me mad. And when I get mad, you know that I open my big mouth. And then look out 'cause when Josephine opens her mouth, they hear it all over the world."

Baker died four days after performing in a 1975 retrospective revue celebrating her fifty years in show business, financed by Prince Rainier, Princess Grace, and Jacqueline Kennedy Onassis. The opening-night audience included Sophia Loren, Mick Jagger, Diana Ross, and Liza Minnelli. On the 110th anniversary of her birth, *Vogue* magazine included a commemoration of Baker as a performer who "radically redefined notions of race and gender through style and performance in a way that continues to echo throughout fashion and music today, from Prada to Beyoncé."

Josephine Baker was married four times and had romantic and sexual relationships with both men and women. During the course of her career, she adopted twelve children of many nationalities, whom she called her "rainbow tribe." One of them, Jean-Claude Baker (1943–2015), was adopted informally at the age of fourteen. Jean-Claude cowrote a biography of Josephine Baker, *Josephine: The Hungry Heart*, which was published in 1993.

Lucille Ball (1911–1989)
Actress, Comedian

Comic actor Lucille Ball is the most popular and influential woman in the history of early television. The star and cocreator of *I Love Lucy*, Ball continues to entertain millions of people around the world through the syndication of the show in reruns more than fifty years after its debut.

Born near Jamestown, New York, Lucille Ball left home at the age of fifteen to pursue an acting career in New York City. In acting school, she was repeatedly told that she had no talent and should return home. Determined to succeed in show business, she worked as a waitress and a model before getting her first national attention in 1933 as the Chesterfield Cigarette Girl. Ball was invited to Hollywood to try her luck in the movies, and in the late 1930s and early 1940s, she had some modest success as a featured actress in a variety of comedies and dramas.

In 1940, she married Cuban bandleader Desi Arnaz, whom she had met while the two were making a film. In 1950, the couple formed Desilu Productions to enable them to work together in movies and television. Ball and Arnaz tried to sell a husband-and-wife comedy series starring themselves to a TV network, but executives were convinced that the public would not accept the Cuban-born Arnaz as Ball's on-screen husband. To prove the networks wrong, Ball and Arnaz embarked on a nationwide tour performing their husband-and-wife sketches to live audiences. Finally, they found a sponsor for their concept, and *I Love Lucy* debuted on CBS on October 15, 1951. From 1951 to 1957, each week, nearly forty million viewers watched the zany antics of "America's Favorite Redhead." Since Ball and Arnaz controlled the production of the show, they held the residual rights to reruns, and when the show went to syndication, it made them enormously wealthy. One of the most-watched episodes concerned the birth of Lucy and Ricky Ricardo's (Ball and Arnaz's characters) baby. The birth was the culmination of a season in which Ball appeared visibly pregnant with her daughter, Lucie.

Ball and Arnaz would have a second child, Desi Arnaz Jr., in 1953.

Ball and Arnaz's collaboration ended with their divorce in 1960. In 1962, Ball bought Arnaz's share in Desilu and became sole head of the company. This made her the first woman to head a major Hollywood studio. While busy as an executive, Ball continued to perform on television as well as onstage in the musical *Wildcat* (1960) and on-screen in such films as *Critic's Choice* (1963), *Yours, Mine, and Ours* (1968), and *Mame* (1974). In the 1960s, she starred in two additional television series, *The Lucy Show* and *Here's Lucy*. In 1985, Ball played a spunky bag lady in the television movie *Stone Pillow* and in 1986 attempted a comeback, playing a grandmother in the short-lived situation comedy *Life with Lucy*.

Although all three of her 1950s and 1960s series are television rerun staples, her first series remains her funniest. With *I Love Lucy*, Ball became the first and only female actor to raise slapstick comedy to a fine art while at the same time helping to firmly establish the situation comedy as a major television entertainment form for future generations of viewers.

Ethel Barrymore (1879–1959)

Actress

In an acting career that spanned six decades, stage and screen actor Ethel Barrymore earned the title "The First Lady of the American Theater." Born Ethel Mae Blythe in Philadelphia, Barrymore was the second child of actors Maurice Barrymore (real name Herbert Blythe) and Georgiana Drew. She was the sister of actors John and Lionel Barrymore. She spent her childhood in Philadelphia attending Roman Catholic schools there. She made her professional stage debut in 1894 in a company headed by her grandmother, Louisa Lane Drew. Her first stage success was in London in *The Bells* and *Peter the Great* (1897–1898). Her first starring role on Broadway was in *Captain Jinks of the Horse Marines* (1901). Barrymore possessed a youthful stage presence with an expressive vocal and acting style that endeared her to audiences.

Barrymore's notable roles were in such plays as *Alice-Sit-by-the-Fire* (1905), *Mid-Channel* (1910), *Trelawny of the "Wells"* (1911), *Déclassé* (1919), *The Second Mrs. Tanqueray* (1924), *The Constant Wife* (1928), *Scarlet Sister Mary* (1931), *Whiteoaks* (1938), and *The Corn Is Green* (1942). She opened the Ethel Barrymore Theatre, named in her honor, with *The Kingdom of God* (1928). She also appeared in vaudeville, on radio, on television, and in several films. She made her screen debut in *The Nightingale* (1914). She won the Academy Award for Best Supporting Actress for her role in *None but the Lonely Heart* (1944). She never cared for Hollywood or working in film and centered her acting career on the Broadway stage.

Barrymore died in Hollywood two months before her eightieth birthday. She was known in the theater world as "The Duchess," a title that spoke to her status as American theater royalty.

Amy Beach (1867–1944)

Composer, Musician

One of the greatest composers of the nineteenth and early twentieth centuries, Amy Beach is best known for her *Piano Concerto* (1899) and her *Gaelic Symphony* (1896), the first symphony by an American female composer.

Born Amy Marcy Cheney in New Hampshire, she was raised in Boston. Beach possessed a precocious musical talent, composing simple melodies on the keyboard since the age of four. In 1883, at the age of sixteen, she gave her first public recital at Boston Music Hall. In 1885, she played Chopin's *Piano Concerto in F Minor* with the Boston Symphony Orchestra.

In 1885, she married Henry H. A. Beach, a surgeon and Harvard University professor, who encouraged his wife to concentrate on composition and curtail her public performing. She undertook a rigorous course of self-instruction in musical theory and composition. Her first efforts were musical settings of favorite poems. Her first major work was *Mass in E-flat* (1890), performed by the Boston Symphony and the Handel and Haydn Society, the first work by a woman to be performed by those organizations. Other important compositions include *Eilende Wolken* (1892), an aria based on a text by Friedrich von Schiller; *Festival Jubilate* (1891) for the dedication of the Woman's Building at the World's Columbian Exposition in Chicago; the *Gaelic Symphony*; *Sonata in A Minor* (1896); and *Piano Concerto in C-sharp Minor* (1899).

Beach became the most preeminent female composer in the United States with more than 150 works, nearly all of which were published, including choral works, church music, chamber works, cantatas, and songs to the words of Shakespeare, Burns, and Browning.

After an extended stay in Europe from 1910 to 1914, she returned to the United States and used her position as one of the country's best-known composers to encourage other women. She called her work "pioneer work" and said that "music is the superlative expression of life experience, and woman by the very nature of her position is denied many of the experiences that color the life of man." Beach died of chronic heart disease in her New York home at the age of seventy-seven. Beach's contribution to American music was recognized increasingly in the 1990s and subsequent years. She was inducted in 1999 into the American Classical Music Hall of Fame, and in 2000, she became the first woman to join eighty-six other composers on the granite wall of the Boston Pops' famous Hatch Shell.

Margaret Bonds (1913–1972)

Composer, Musician

Margaret Bonds is one of the first African American composers and classical performers to gain recognition in the United States. She is best known for her musical adaptations of Shakespeare and for her collaboration with Langston Hughes. She was the first African American soloist to appear with the Chicago Symphony and was an influential composer and arranger of African American spirituals, songs, instrumental works, and film music.

She was born in Chicago. Her father was a physician; her mother was an organist and music teacher who hosted many black musical luminaries. Bonds got an early start in music, finishing her first composition at the age of five. In high school, she studied with composer and pianist Florence B. Price and composer and conductor William Dawson. After graduating, not yet twenty years old, Bond won the national Wanamaker Foundation Prize for her composition "Sea Ghost," a song for voice and piano. Bond performed at the 1933 Chicago World's Fair and with the Chicago Symphony Orchestra before earning bachelor's and master's degrees in music from Northwestern University in 1933 and 1934.

Bonds went on to a successful career writing for the Glenn Miller Orchestra and regularly performing on the radio. Although she was trained as a classical musician, her work was versatile and strongly influenced by jazz and blues; musicians such as Louis Armstrong and Woody Herman performed her compositions. She is best known for her collaboration with poet Langston Hughes, writing the musical piece to accompany Hughes's poem "The Negro Speaks of Rivers" in 1941. Their partnership would continue into the 1950s and included theatrical adaptations of Hughes's works.

Over her career, Bonds mastered orchestral compositions, theatrical scores, and traditional African American spiritual arrangements. She has been widely credited with helping to create new interest in traditional African American musical forms, history, and culture.

Clara Bow (1905–1965)

Actress

With her tomboyish charm and expressive face, Clara Bow was Hollywood's first "It Girl." A box office sensation during the silent era of film in the 1920s, Bow was the embodiment of the emancipated flapper of the Roaring Twenties and the Jazz Age and its leading sex symbol.

Bow was born in Brooklyn, New York, into a poor family. She was sexually abused by her father and neglected by her mentally unbalanced mother. For Bow, the movies were the escape from the horrors of her home. At the age of sixteen, she entered a magazine's beauty contest and won a small part in the film *Beyond the Rainbow* (1922). She auditioned at New York studios and eventually received a part in *Down to the Sea in Ships* (1922). Other parts followed, and in 1923, Bow left New York for Hollywood as a contract player for Preferred Pictures and then to Paramount.

Bow's breakout film was *It* (1927), an adaptation of an Elinor Glyn novella. Its box office success led to her gaining the nickname the "It Girl." She went on to make cinematic history costarring in *Wings* (1927), which won the first Best Picture Oscar. Bow made the transition to talkies in *The Wild Party* (1929). She was named first box office draw in 1928 and 1929. At the apex of her stardom in 1929, she received more than forty-five thousand fan letters in a single month.

Her pronounced Brooklyn accent hampered her transition from silent movies to sound, however, and she retired in 1933 on a Nevada cattle ranch owned by her husband, former cowboy star Rex Bell, whom she married in 1931. In her later years, she showed symptoms of psychiatric illness. She became socially withdrawn and a recluse. She would later be diagnosed with schizophrenia. She spent her last years in a bungalow in Culver City, Nevada, where she died of a heart attack at the age of sixty.

Fanny Brice (1891–1951)

Actress, Comedian, Singer

One of America's enduring comic performers, Fanny Brice built her career on a Yiddish accent and a flair for zany parody. She is best known for creating and starring in the top-rated radio comedy series *The Baby Snooks Show*. She was also long associated with the Ziegfeld Follies and appeared in several movies, burlesque, vaudeville, and musical revues. She was called by *The New York Times* "a burlesque comic of the rarest vintage," one of the first female comedians in a field that had previously been dominated by men.

Born Fania Borach, Brice was the child of Jewish immigrants who had settled on New York's Lower East Side. When she was four, the family moved to Newark, New Jersey, where her parents bought a saloon. Brice's mother left her father and took the family to Brooklyn. Brice was a chronic truant from school and ended her formal education sometime in the eighth grade. Encouraged by success in neighborhood amateur night contests, Brice pursued a show business career. Facing roadblocks from a lack of training, she turned to burlesque, the least selective branch of the entertainment business, and spent three formative years on the eastern burlesque circuit. She settled on the name "Fanny Brice" because as she said she was tired of being called "Borax" and "Boreache."

Appearing in Max Spiegel's *The College Girls,* she had her first sizable role and specialty number with "Sadie Salome, Go Home," a "Jewish comedy song" by Irving Berlin. She sang it with a Yiddish accent, which would become her trademark. She attracted the attention of producer Florenz Ziegfeld, who hired her for his *Follies* in 1910. Brice did not conform to the prevailing notion of feminine beauty but juxtaposed to Ziegfeld's chorus of "long-stemmed American beauties" so her comic talents could shine. She eventually achieved stardom in *The Ziegfeld Follies of 1916* and *1917* and would continue to headline the *Follies* into the 1930s. In 1921, she was featured singing "My Man," which became both a big hit and her signature song. The other song most associated with her is "Second Hand Rose." In 1931, she introduced the character of Baby Snooks, the mischievous brat she had first played in vaudeville in 1912. Baby Snooks would become a *Follies* favorite, which Brice featured on radio from 1936 until her death. Brice appeared in a few motion pictures, including *My Man* (1928), *Be Yourself* (1930), *The Great Ziegfeld* (1936), and *Everybody Sing* (1938).

Six months after her appearance as Baby Snooks on the radio variety show, *The Big Show*, in 1950, she died of a cerebral hemorrhage at Hollywood's Cedars of Lebanon Hospital at the young age of fifty-nine and was eulogized on the next episode of *The Baby Snooks Show.* She has two stars on Hollywood's famous Walk of Fame.

Louise Brooks (1906–1985)

Actress

A legendary actress of the silent screen era, Louise Brooks epitomized the flapper age with her bobbed hairstyle that she helped to popularize and behavior that blatantly flaunted the accepted sexual and societal roles of women at the time.

Born in Cherryvale, Kansas, Brooks was the daughter of a lawyer who danced with the Denishawn company from 1922 to 1924 and appeared in Florenz Ziegfield's *Follies* in 1925. There, she came to the attention of Paramount Pictures producer Walter Wanger, who signed her to a five-year contract with the studio. She also attracted the attention of Charlie Chaplin, who was in town for the premiere of his film *The Gold Rush*, and the two had a two-month affair.

In Hollywood, Brooks made her screen debut in the silent film *The Street of Forgotten Men* in an uncredited role in 1925. She soon was playing the female lead in a number of silent comedies and flapper films, starring with Adolphe Menjou and W. C. Fields. She appeared in Howard Hawks's *A Girl in Every Port* (1928) and William Wellman's *Beggars of Life* (1928). Her performances attracted the attention of German film director G. W. Pabst, who cast her as the amoral, self-destructive temptress Lulu in *Pandora's Box* (1929). The film is notable for its frank treatment of modern sexual mores, including one of the first overt on-screen portrayals of a lesbian. Brooks would be nicknamed Lulu for her character, and the film would feature her naturalistic acting style without the exaggerated body language and facial expressions of customary silent-screen acting. Her acting method would become the standard, but at the time, audiences complained that she was not acting at all. Film critic Roger Ebert later noted that by employing this acting method, "Brooks became one of the most modern and effective of actors, projecting a presence that could be startling." Her next film, *Diary of a Lost Girl* (1929), also directed by Pabst, featured Brooks as a sixteen-year-old girl who is seduced and prostituted.

Brooks's innocent eroticism, along with her pale, beautiful features and bobbed brunette hair, made her both a film icon and a symbol of the flapper of the 1920s.

Brooks returned to the United States in 1930, but her independence and outspokenness, rejecting more conventional roles expected of women at the time, led her into conflict with studio executives. After appearing in smaller roles in several lesser films in the 1930s, she gave up her acting career, having made only twenty-five films. She initially returned to Kansas and then to New York City, where she worked as a salesgirl in Saks Fifth Avenue. Between 1948 and 1953, she worked as an escort, saying that "I found that the only well-paying career open to me, as an unsuccessful actress of thirty-six was that of a call girl ... and I began to flirt with the fancies related to little bottles filled with yellow sleeping pills."

She was discovered by James Card, the film curator for the George Eastman House, living as a recluse in New York. Card persuaded her to move to Rochester, New York, to be near the Eastman House film collection to study cinema and write about her past career. She began a second career as a film critic and essayist for film magazines. A collection of her writings, *Lulu in Hollywood*, was published in 1982, called by Roger Ebert "one of the few film books that can be called indispensable."

Julia Child (1912–2004)

Chef, Television Personality

A chef and cookbook author who brought the art of French cooking to kitchens across the United States, Julia Child also brought her techniques to millions with her award-winning television cooking show *The French Chef*.

Child was born Julia Carolyn McWilliams on August 15, 1912, in Pasadena, California. She was tall and athletic and grew up playing tennis, golf, and basketball. She attended a private boarding school and in 1934 graduated from Smith College, where she majored in history. After graduation, she worked as a copywriter in New York City.

During World War II, she served in the Office of Strategic Services (OSS) first as a top-secret researcher in Washington and later on assignment for the OSS in Ceylon and China. In China, she met a fellow OSS employee, Paul Child; they married after the war in 1946. In 1948, they moved to Paris, where Paul was assigned as an officer with the U.S. Information Agency (USIA). In Paris, she attended the Cordon Bleu school and through a women's cooking club met her future coauthors Simone Beck and Louisette Bertholle. Their landmark book *Mastering the Art of French Cooking*, published in 1961, became an immediate best-seller and is still in print today.

Child's NET (later PBS) television show *The French Chef* premiered in 1963 and introduced her friendly and entertaining, yet expert, style to the American public. The show won a Peabody award in 1965 and an Emmy Award in 1966 and ran nationally for ten years. She went on to publish more books, including *The French Chef Cookbook* and *Mastering the Art of French Cooking, Volume 2*. For the next thirty-five years, she continued her television and publishing career while living in Cambridge, Massachusetts. Paul Child died in 1994, and Julia moved to Montecito, California, in 2001. In her later years, she received many national and international awards, including the U.S. Presidential Medal of Freedom and France's Legion of Honor. In 1995, she established the Julia Child Foundation to support the culinary arts. The National Museum of American History at the Smithsonian Institution in Washington, D.C., includes an exhibit titled Bon Appetit! Julia Child's Kitchen.

Patsy Cline (1932–1963)

Singer

 The most popular female country singer in recording history, Patsy Cline set the standard for female vocalists, bridging the gap between country music and more mainstream audiences and inspiring scores of subsequent singers, including K. D. Lang, Loretta Lynn, Linda Ronstadt, Dolly Parton, Wynonna Judd, and Trisha Yearwood.

Cline was born Virginia Patterson Hensley in Winchester, Virginia. Her family moved nineteen times around the state before Ginny, as she was known, was fifteen, when she dropped out of school to support the family after her father deserted them. She began to sing with local country bands, sometimes accompanying herself on the guitar. By the time she was in her early twenties, now known as Patsy Cline, she was well on her way to country music stardom, having first recorded in 1955. It was the advent of television in the late 1950s that gained her a wider audience, and Cline began appearing on *Town and Country Jamboree*, a variety show broadcast every Saturday night from Washington, D.C. She also was a contestant on the CBS television show *Arthur Godfrey's Talent Scouts*, winning first prize singing "Walkin' after Midnight." She also became a regular performer on the Grand Ole Opry radio broadcast from Nashville.

Her first number-one song was "I Fall to Pieces" (1961). It was followed by the number one jukebox hit of all time, "Crazy" (written by Willie Nelson), and "She's Got You" as well as the albums *Patsy Cline Showcase* and *Sentimentally Yours*. She appeared at Carnegie Hall, the Hollywood Bowl, and Dick Clark's *American Bandstand*, demonstrating her crossover appeal beyond country and western into mainstream popular music.

Her last public performance was a benefit in Kansas City in 1963. Returning home to Nashville, she was killed in a plane crash that also took the lives of Opry stars Cowboy Copas and Hawkshaw Hawkins. Cline's singles "Leavin' on Your Mind" and "Sweet Dreams (of You)" reached the top ten after her death.

In 1973, Cline became the first solo female artist to be elected to the Country Music Hall of Fame. In the 2003 book *Remembering Patsy*, guitarist–producer Harold Bradley said of Cline, "She's taken the standards for being a country vocalist, and raised the bar. Even now, women are trying to get to that bar.... If you're going to be a country singer, and if you're not going to copy her—and must people do come to town doing just that—then you have to be aware of her technique.... It gives all the female singers coming in something to gauge their talents against. And I expect it will forever."

Joan Ganz Cooney (1929–)

Television Producer

As the creator of *Sesame Street*, perhaps the most influential educational TV program in history, Joan Ganz Cooney helped transform children's television in the United States. *Sesame Street* was created to educate preschoolers, particularly those from disadvantaged homes, in basic number, language, and reasoning skills while at the same time entertaining them with humor, music, snappy visuals, and a comical cast of muppets. The show, which premiered in 1969, would eventually reach an estimated 235 million viewers each week in more than 140 countries.

Joan Ganz Cooney was born and raised in Phoenix, Arizona. After graduating in 1951 with a degree in education from the University of Arizona, she worked as a newspaper reporter before moving to New York City in 1954 to work in television publicity. In 1962, she began producing public affairs documentaries for the New York educational television station, winning an Emmy Award for her documentary *Poverty, Anti-Poverty, and the Poor.*

In 1966, Cooney was asked to prepare a report on how television could be better used to educate the very young. She saw in the assignment a great opportunity. "I could do a thousand documentaries on poverty and poor people that would be watched by a handful of the convinced," she recalled, "but I was never really going to have an influence on my times. I wanted to make a difference." Her report, "The Potential Uses of Television in Preschool Education," demonstrated the educational value of television for preschoolers and became the genesis of *Sesame Street.*

In 1968, with the help of funding from several foundations and the federal government, Cooney cofounded the Children's Television Workshop (CTW), gathering together teams of researchers, writers, teachers, animated cartoonists, and television producers. The group designed a program that would make learning the alphabet and numbers easy and fun by using the same techniques that made cartoons and commercials so successful—animation, songs, puppets, and humorous skits.

The success of *Sesame Street* led Cooney to produce other highly regarded educational programs that focused on the building of specific skills, such as reading (*The Electric Company*), science (*3-2-1 Contact*), mathematics (*Square One*), and geography (*Where in the World Is Carmen Sandiego?*). Some critics have argued that the CTW technique of teaching children by entertaining them can lead them to expect the same kind of entertainment when they attend school. However, studies have shown that *Sesame Street* has had a positive impact on the learning skills of preschoolers. After fifty years, the program that Joan Ganz Cooney pioneered is still enormously popular and entertaining the young children of many parents who grew up watching the show.

Cooney remained the chairman and chief executive of CTW until 1990 and continued on its executive board. In 1990, she became the first female nonperformer to be inducted into the Academy of Television Arts & Sciences Hall of Fame and was awarded the U.S. Presidential Medal of Freedom in 1995.

Bette Davis (1908–1989)

Actress

Regarded as one of the greatest actors in Hollywood history, Bette Davis played an extraordinary range of characters and film genres from crime melodramas to historical and period films, romantic dramas, suspense, and comedies, always with a deftness, believability, and intensity. She won two Academy Awards for Best Actress and was nominated eight other times.

She was born Ruth Elizabeth Davis in Lowell, Massachusetts. After her parents divorced in 1916, Bette, as Davis was known, and her sister moved frequently throughout New England with their mother, who was pursuing a photography career. Davis attended Cushing Academy, a boarding school in Ashburnham, Massachusetts, where she acted in school productions and decided to pursue an acting career.

She received no encouragement because she was not conventionally pretty, but she persisted, enrolling in John Murray Anderson's Dramatic School in New York City in 1921. She made her Broadway debut in 1929 in the play *Broken Dishes*. In 1930, she was hired by Universal and made her first film, *Way Back Home*, in 1931. When she arrived in Hollywood by train, the studio representative sent to meet her train left without her because he claimed he could not identify anyone who looked like a movie star.

Dismissed for having no "sex appeal," she was given a series of minor roles before Universal dropped her option. On the verge of abandoning acting, she was given the part as the ingenue in *The Man Who Played God* (1932), and on the basis of the positive critical response, Warner Brothers signed her to a contract. With her role as the unsympathetic Mildred in *Of Human Bondage* (1934), Davis won both critical acclaim and box office popularity. She received her first best actress award for her portrayal of an alcoholic, self-destructive actress in *Dangerous* (1935) and a second for *Jezebel* (1938). A string of impressive performances followed, including *Dark Victory* (1939), *Juarez* (1939), *The Private Lives of Elizabeth and Essex* (1939), *The Letter* (1940), *The Little Foxes* (1941), *Now, Voyager* (1942), *Watch on the Rhine* (1943), *The Corn Is Green* (1945), and *All About Eve* (1950), in which she memorably played a forty-year-old stage star threatened by the machinations of a much younger and ambitious actress. In 1962, Davis made a guest appearance filling in for Raymond Burr in the television detective show *Perry Mason*. She also starred in the films *What Ever Happened to Baby Jane?* (1962), a horror film notable for the feud between Davis and her costar Joan Crawford, and a *Pocketful of Miracles* (1963).

Davis was married four times and was the mother of three children. Her first husband was Harmon "Ham" Nelson, whom she had met while a student at Cushing Academy; her last was actor Gary Merrill, her costar in *All About Eve*, to whom she was married from 1950 to 1960.

In 1977, Davis became the first woman to receive the American Film Institute Life Achievement Award, and two years later, she won an Emmy for her performance in the made-for-television movie *Strangers: The Story of a Mother and Daughter*. Health problems in her final decade slowed her, but Davis continued working until a year before her death. She died while traveling in France at the age of eighty-one after a film career during which she personified both the glamour and acting achievements of the Golden Age of Hollywood.

Agnes de Mille (1905–1993)
Choreographer, Dancer

 A choreographer, dancer, teacher, and author, Agnes de Mille was one of the most influential figures in American dance. She combined classical and modern dance with the spirited rhythms of American folk dances and helped to transform the American musical theater by bringing the beauty of ballet to a wider audience.

De Mille was a member of a distinguished American theatrical family, which included her father, playwright and director William de Mille, and her uncle, film producer–director Cecil B. de Mille. Born in New York City, she grew up in Hollywood, and, at the age of ten, after seeing the great dancer Anna Pavlova perform, was determined to become a dancer herself. Her parents discouraged her from considering a stage career and initially refused her dancing lessons; eventually they relented, and she began to study ballet. To please her parents, she deferred her dream of becoming a dancer to attend the University of California. Following graduation, de Mille went to New York City to establish a career as a dancer and choreographer. She met with little success because Broadway producers were not interested in her attempt to incorporate classical and American folk elements in her dances in place of the conventional chorus-line dancing popular at the time.

Frustrated, in the early 1930s, de Mille went to Europe, where she studied, worked, and performed for a number of years, meeting with greater success. In 1939, she returned to the United States and was asked to join the newly formed New York Ballet Theatre, which would later become the American Ballet Theatre. With this group, de Mille choreographed *Black Ritual*, the first ballet performed entirely by black dancers in a classic American ballet company. Her ballet *Rodeo*, a celebration of the American West with music by Aaron Copeland, would become a landmark in dance and theater history featuring an innovative mixture of folk dancing, modern dance, and classical ballet.

De Mille also made history with her dances for the Rodgers and Hammerstein musical *Oklahoma!* The show featured an integration of story, song, and dance for the first time in a musical comedy and ushered in a new era of sophistication and artistry in the musical theater. De Mille would also go on to choreograph such classic musicals as *Carousel* and *Brigadoon*. In the 1960s, de Mille became cofounder and president of the Society of Stage Directors and Choreographers. In 1973, she founded the Heritage Dance Theatre, which was devoted to traditional American dance. De Mille's achievement in transforming American dance was acknowledged with a Kennedy Center Award in 1980 and a National Medal for the Arts in 1986.

Maya Deren (1917–1961)
Actress, Director

Often called the "mother of American avant-garde filmmaking," Maya Deren helped transform film into an art form. Deren believed that the function of film was to create an experience, and she used her interests in dance and innovative camera techniques of multiple exposures, jump cutting, slow motion, and superimposition to achieve a visual and emotional response from her viewers.

Born Eleanora Derenkowsky in Kiev, Ukraine, she immigrated to the United States with her parents in 1922 but attended secondary school at the League of Nations School in Geneva, Switzerland, before studying journalism at Syracuse University. She graduated from New York University in 1936 and received an MA degree in literature from Smith College in 1939.

In 1940, Deren moved to Los Angeles to focus on writing poetry and doing freelance photography.

She became the assistant and publicist of dancer Katherine Dunham, touring with the Dunham dance company. In 1943, Deren purchased a used 16 mm camera, which she used to create her first and best-known film *Meshes of the Afternoon*. It is the first example of a narrative work in avant-garde American film, one of the most influential works of American experimental film, which has been credited with establishing the avant-garde film movement in the United States. It has been called an expressionistic "trance film" full of dramatic angles and innovative editing, dramatizing the ways in which the protagonist's unconscious mind works. The protagonist, played by Deren, walks to a friend's house in Los Angeles, falls asleep, and has a dream.

Deren completed five more short films before her death and left several unfinished works. In *At Land* (1944), Deren reappears as the protagonist and used imaginative editing and camera techniques to render stream of consciousness. She described *A Study in Choreography for Camera* (1945) as a pas de deux for one dancer and one camera and *Ritual in Transfigured Time* (1946) as being about the nature and process of change. In her last two films, she continued to explore the concept of creating a truly cinematic form of dance (as opposed to simply recording a performance) in *Meditations on Violence* (1948) and *The Very Eye of Night* (1954).

In addition to filmmaking, Deren lectured, taught, and wrote extensively on independent film. Her major theoretical work is *An Anagram of Ideas on Art, Form and Film* (1946). Deren died at the age of forty-four from a brain hemorrhage brought on by extreme malnutrition. Her ashes were scattered in Japan at Mount Fuji. In 1986, the American Film Institute created the Maya Deren Award to honor independent filmmakers.

Isadora Duncan (1877–1927)
Dancer

Often called the "mother of modern dance," Isadora Duncan was a trailblazing dancer and instructor whose emphasis on freer forms of movement revolutionized dance and anticipated the development of modern expressive dance. She was the first to raise interpretative dance to the status of creative art.

She was born in San Francisco, raised by her divorced mother, a piano teacher with a great appreciation for the arts. At the age of six, Duncan began to teach movement to the little children in the neighborhood. Even as a child, she rejected the rigidity of classical ballet and based her dancing on more natural rhythms and movements, which she used to interpret the works of great composers like Brahms and Beethoven. Her earliest public appearance, in Chicago and New York City, met with little success, and she left the United States at the age of twenty-one, sailing on a cattle boat for England.

There, through the patronage of the celebrated actress Mrs. Patrick Campbell, she was invited to appear at the private receptions of London's leading hostesses, where her dancing, distinguished by a complete freedom of movement, captivated those familiar only with the restrictive and conventional forms of ballet. In 1905, she toured Russia, where she came to the attention of Serge Diaghilev, who, as impresario, was soon to lead a resurgence of ballet throughout western Europe that would incorporate many of the expressive techniques Duncan featured.

Duncan's personal life was as unrestricted as her dancing. She was viewed as an early feminist, declaring she would never marry and having two children out of wedlock. She founded dance schools in the United States, Germany, and Russia with her dance students, dubbed the "Isadorables" by the press. After an accident in which her two children drowned when the car they were in fell into the Seine River, Duncan married poet Sergey Yesenin in 1922 to allow him to travel to the United States. The couple, however, were ostracized due to anti-Bolshevik paranoia, and Duncan left the United States, vowing to never return. She never did. She died in Nice, France, when her scarf got caught in the back wheels of the automobile in which she was riding. The same year of her death, her autobiography, *My Life*, was published.

Duncan left a dual legacy: as a transformative figure in the creation of modern dance as well as a woman who rejected the constraints of restrictive societal roles in search of a new freedom of activity and expression. Writer Dorothy Parker would say of Duncan: "There was never a place for her in the ranks of the terrible, slow army of the cautious. She ran ahead, where there were no paths." Dancer and choreographer Katherine Dunham, who was inspired by Duncan's example, characterized Duncan as a dancer who let dance out of the cage of the old ballet and said that Sergei Diaghilev gave structure to the new energy she unleashed.

Katherine Dunham (1909–2006)
Choreographer, Dancer

African American dancer, choreographer, anthropologist, educator, and social activist Katherine Dunham has been called the "matriarch and queen mother of black dance." She had one of the most successful dance careers of the twentieth century, directing her own dance company for many years. She introduced authentic African dance movements and exploded the possibilities of modern dance expression.

She was born Kaye Dunn in Chicago but grew up in Glen Ellyn, Illinois, about twenty-five miles west. Her father was a descendant of slaves, and her mother was of mixed French Canadian and Native American heritage. After her mother died when Dunham was three, her father remarried and moved the family to Joliet, Illinois, where Dunham graduated from high school in 1928. In high school, she studied and performed dance and opened a private dance school for young, black children. After completing Joliet Junior College, she studied anthropology and dances of the African diaspora at the University of Chicago. In 1935, on a travel fellowship, she did ethnographic study of dance in the Caribbean with fellow anthropology student Zora Neale Hurston. She would receive her bachelor's degree in social anthropology in 1936 but abandoned graduate work to relaunch her performance career.

In 1938, she joined the Federal Theatre Project in Chicago and composed a ballet, *L'Ag'Ya*, based on Caribbean dance. Two years later, she formed an all-black dance company that toured extensively, featuring works such as *Tropics* (1937) and *Le Jazz Hot* (1938), based on her research. The Dunham Company toured for two decades around the globe in fifty-seven countries, introducing to Europe for the first time to black dance as an art form. Dunham also choreographed for Broadway stage productions and opera as well as in such films as *Carnival of Rhythm* (1942), *Stormy Weather* (1943), and *Casbah* (1947).

Dunham was a social activist who fought racial discrimination and segregation, creating *Southland*, a ballet that depicted a lynching in 1951, and in 1992, at the age of eighty-three, staged a forty-seven-day hunger strike to highlight the plight of Haitian refugees. She is the author of an autobiography, *A Touch of Innocence* (1959). She received a Kennedy Center Honor in 1983 and a National Medal of Arts in 1989. She died of natural causes a month before her ninety-seventh birthday. Dance critic Wendy Perron celebrated her legacy by saying that Dunham "was the first American dancer to present indigenous forms on a concert stage, the first to sustain a black dance company.... She created and performed in works for stage, clubs, and Hollywood films; she started a school and a technique that continue to flourish; she fought unstintingly for racial justice."

Ella Fitzgerald (1917–1996)

Singer

Called "the first lady of song," "the queen of jazz," and "Lady Ella," Ella Fitzgerald was the most popular female jazz singer in the United States for more than half a century. She won fourteen Grammy Awards and sold over forty million albums. She could sing sultry ballads, sweet jazz, and imitate every instrument in an orchestra.

She was born in Newport News, Virginia, but moved to Yonkers, New York, in the early 1920s. In 1932, when Fitzgerald was fifteen, her mother died in a car accident, and Fitzgerald went to live in Harlem with her aunt. She began to skip school and worked as a lookout at a bordello and with a

numbers runner. She was eventually placed in the Colored Orphan Asylum in Riverdale in the Bronx and then to the New York Training School for Girls, a state reformatory. From 1933 through 1934, she survived by singing on the streets of Harlem. She competed at the Amateur Nights at the Apollo Theater in 1934 intending to dance but was intimidated by a local dance duo and opted to sing instead. She won first prize.

In 1935, she was introduced to drummer and bandleader Chick Webb, who was looking for a female singer. She auditioned and was a hit with audiences. She recorded several hit songs, but it was her 1938 version of the nursery rhyme "A Tisket, A-Tasket," which she cowrote, that became a major hit on the radio and one of the biggest-selling records of the decade. When Webb died in 1939, his band was renamed Ella and Her Famous Orchestra, with Fitzgerald as bandleader. She would record nearly 150 songs with the orchestra between 1935 and 1942, leaving the band at that time to begin a solo career. With the demise of the Swing era and the advent of bebop, Fitzgerald adapted by incorporating scat singing as a major part of her performance, turning her voice into an improvisational instrument. As she recalled, "I just tried to do [with my voice] what I heard the horns in the band doing." Her 1945 scat recording of "Flying Home" would be later described by *The New York Times* as "one of the most influential vocal jazz recordings of the decade ... no one before Miss Fitzgerald employed the technique with such dazzling inventiveness." From 1956 to 1964, she recorded a nineteen-volume series of "songbooks," in which she interpreted nearly 250 songs by Richard Rodgers, Cole Porter, George Gershwin, Duke Ellington, Johnny Mercer, and others. She appeared in films, on television, and in concert halls, becoming one of the best-selling jazz vocal recording artists in history.

In the 1970s, she experienced serious health problems. In 1993, complications stemming from diabetes resulted in the amputation of both of her legs below the knees. Her eyesight was affected as well. She died in her home in Beverly Hills from a stroke at the age of seventy-nine.

Aretha Franklin (1942–2018)

Singer

The first woman to be inducted into the Rock and Roll Hall of Fame, Aretha Franklin is universally acclaimed as the "queen of soul" and one of America's greatest singers in any style. Her best-known signature song, "Respect" (written by her friend Otis Redding), became an anthem for equality and freedom, setting a modern feminist archetype—sensual, strong, and long-suffering but indomitable—that Franklin echoed in other hits like "Do Right Woman—Do Right Man," "Think," "(You Make Me Feel Like) A Natural Woman," and "Chain of Fools." Franklin placed more than one hundred singles in the Billboard charts, including seventeen top-ten pop singles and twenty number-one R&B hits. She received eighteen Grammy Awards, including a lifetime achievement award in 1994. She leads the list of the 2010 "100 Greatest Singers of All Time" by *Rolling Stone*.

Franklin was born in Memphis, Tennessee. Her mother was a gospel singer and pianist; her father, C. L. Franklin, was one of the nation's most celebrated black ministers and pastor of churches in Memphis, Buffalo, and Detroit. He was known as "the man with the golden voice." Franklin taught herself to play the piano before she was ten. Around the same time, she stood on a chair and sang her first solos in church. At the age of twelve, she joined her father on tour, sharing the stage with other leading gospel performers. She became pregnant and dropped out of high school, having a child two months before her thirteenth birthday. Soon after, she had a second child by a different father.

In the late 1950s, Franklin decided to shift from gospel to secular music. She left her children with her family in Detroit and moved to New York City, where Columbia Records executive John Hammond, known for championing Billie Holiday, Bob Dylan, and Bruce Springsteen, signed her to a contract. Hammond groomed Franklin as a jazz singer, tinged with blues and gospel. In 1966, she signed with Atlantic Records, which specialized in rhythm and blues. The songs she recorded at Fame Studios in Muscle Shoals, Alabama, ignited the power of Franklin's voice, which had only been hinted at in the Columbia recordings. Hit after hit soon followed.

Despite enormous success, Franklin's personal life and family life were troubled and shadowed by tragedy. Her father was shot and killed in a home break-in in 1979. Her two marriages ended in divorce. Her brother and two sisters died of cancer in 1988, 1989, and 2002. Health issues affected her last decade. She died of pancreatic cancer at the age of seventy-seven. She was eulogized by fellow singer Mary J. Blige, who said of her, "Aretha is a gift from God. When it comes to expressing yourself through song, there is no one who can touch her. She is the reason why women want to sing."

Lillian Gish (1893–1993)

Actress

Called the "first lady of the American cinema," Lillian Gish was the film industry's first true female actor who first recognized the crucial differences between acting for the stage and for the screen, pioneering nuanced, sensitive performances with stunning emotional impact. Over an acting career spanning seventy-five years, Gish set the standard for movie acting.

Lillian Gish was born in Springfield, Ohio. Her father, an alcoholic, left the family to fend for itself, and Lillian, her sister Dorothy, who also became an actor, and their mother acted in local productions to make ends meet. Gish was six when she first appeared in front of an audience, and for the next thirteen years, she and her sister performed onstage with great success. Had Gish not made her way to films, she possibly would have been one of the great stage actresses of all time.

In 1912, she met famed director D. W. Griffith, who immediately cast her in her first films: *An Unseen Enemy*, *The One She Loved*, and *My Baby*. She would make twelve films for Griffith in 1912 alone and twenty-five in the next two years. She became the archetypal silent film heroine—the delicate damsel in distress—who captivated audiences as "America's sweetheart." In 1915, she starred in Griffith's most ambitious project, *Birth of a Nation*, as well as some of Griffith's other classics, *Intolerance* (1916), *Hearts of the World* (1918), *Way Down East* (1920), and *Orphans of the Storm* (1921). She embodied the ideal of the innocent, vulnerable heroine in performances that elicited both believability and emotional intensity.

In 1922, Gish left Griffith to work for the Tiffany Company and in 1925 for MGM. Her later films include *The White Sister* (1923), *La Bohème* (1926), *The Scarlet Letter* (1926), *The Wind* (1928), and *One Romantic Night* (1930), her first sound picture. Gish left the screen for a time and returned to the stage with great success from the 1930s through the 1970s. In 1955, she gave a memorable performance in the thriller *Night of the Hunter*, which starred Robert Mitchum and was directed by famed actor Charles Laughton.

Gish's last Broadway appearance was in *A Musical Jubilee* (1975). She continued to appear in films, and her last was with Bette Davis in *The Whales of August* (1987). Her autobiographical books include *The Movies, Mr. Griffith, and Me* (1969), *Dorothy and Lillian Gish* (1973), and *An Actor's Life for Me* (1987). She died peacefully in her sleep of heart failure at the age of ninety-nine. Through a long, productive career, Gish helped to establish the artistry of film acting and the achievement of cinema as an art form.

Martha Graham (1894–1991)

Choreographer, Dancer

 Known as the "mother of modern dance," Martha Graham revolutionized the way dancers communicate with their audiences. Born in Allegheny, Pennsylvania, Graham was the oldest of the three daughters of George Graham, a psychiatrist. Her family moved to Pittsburgh and then to Santa Barbara, California, when Graham was fourteen. She was inspired to become a dancer after attending a recital given by the popular dancer Ruth St. Denis in 1911. In 1916, Graham went to Los Angeles to enroll in the Denishawn School of Dancing run by St. Denis and her husband, dancer and choreographer Ted Shawn. Graham made her debut with the Denishawn Company in 1920, dancing the lead in an Aztec-inspired ballet, *Xochitl*, which had been created for her. She left the company in 1923 to work as a solo dancer in the Greenwich Village Follies; two years later, she accepted a teaching position at the Eastman School of Music in Rochester, New York. There, Graham worked on training her body to move in new ways to form a unique and daring style of modern dance that focused on body movement, breathing, and gravity.

Graham performed her new dance style at her first independent dance concert in 1926. Many critics disliked her choreography, but most audiences loved it. She continued to experiment, using dance to explore mood, emotion, and physical expression in ways that were completely different from classical ballet and contemporary modern dance. In 1930, Graham created one of her most famous works, *Lamentations*, a solo piece in which she wore a long tube of material that she stretched out and pulled back to show the reactions of the body to grief.

In the 1930s, Graham founded the Martha Graham School of Contemporary Dance and the Martha Graham Dance Company, both of which would become internationally renowned. In 1934, she began teaching summer workshops at Bennington College in Vermont. There, she created one of her most important works, *Letter to the World*, an interpretation of Emily Dickinson's poetry and life. Graham also created works based on other great women from literature, history, and Greek mythology such as Charlotte and Emily Brontë (*Death and Entrances*), Joan of Arc (*Seraphic Dialogue*), and Medea (*Cave of the Heart*). Her interest in American themes would result in her best-known ballet, *Appalachian Spring*, which premiered in 1944, with music by composer Aaron Copeland.

Graham was a major influence on two generations of dancers; many of her performers went on to become choreographers and directors of their own companies. She continued to dance until she was in her seventies and to create ballets and teach classes well into her nineties.

Helen Hayes (1900–1993)

Actress

In a legendary acting career that spanned eighty years, Helen Hayes earned the accolade as the "first lady of American theater." She became the first actress ever to win an Emmy, a Grammy, an Oscar, and a Tony Award.

She was born in Washington, D.C. Her mother was an actress, and her father was a salesman. Her mother enrolled her in dance classes, and from 1905 to 1909, she performed with the Columbia Players. At the age of nine, she made her Broadway debut, and a year later, she was cast in her first film, a one-reel Vitagraph film, *Jean and the Calico Cat*. She played ingenue roles during her teen years, touring in *Pollyanna* (1917). In 1920, she became the youngest actress to have her name in lights on Broadway. In 1926, she received critical and popular acclaim in James Barrie's *What Every Woman Knows*. Two years later, she married journalist and playwright Charles MacArthur, a marriage that lasted until his death in 1956.

Hayes made her talking picture debut in *The Sin of Madelon Claudet* (1931), for which she received an Academy Award. Although she made a number of films, including *A Farewell to Arms* (1932), she disliked Hollywood and soon returned to Broadway for some of her biggest stage successes in *Mary of Scotland* (1933) and *Victoria Regina* (1935), which ran for three years. She earned her first Tony Award for *Happy Birthday* (1946). Except for occasional films, she remained essentially a stage performer until 1971, when asthmatic bronchitis triggered an allergic reaction to stage dust. The year before, she won a second Academy Award for her portrayal of an elderly stowaway in the movie *Airport*. Until the mid-1980s, she divided her time between film and television work, ending her acting career as Agatha Christie's Miss Marple in three popular television movies.

Hayes published four autobiographies: *A Gift of Joy* (1965), *On Reflection* (1968), *Twice Over Lightly* (1972), and *My Life in Three Acts* (1991). Hayes died of congestive heart failure in Nyack, New York, at the age of ninety-two. Hayes intended Lillian Gish, the "first lady of American cinema," to be the beneficiary of her estate, but Gish died less than two months earlier. Hayes has the distinction of having two Broadway theaters named after her.

Katharine Hepburn (1907–2003)

Actress

Katharine Hepburn is recognized as one of the most distinguished and unique movie actresses in the history of motion pictures. In a career that spanned more than fifty years, Hepburn dazzled audiences with her portrayal of strong, spirited, independent women and won four Academy Awards, the most achieved by any actor.

Born in Hartford, Connecticut, Hepburn was the daughter of a well-to-do surgeon and a mother who scandalized conservative Hartford by working for such controversial causes as birth control and women's suffrage. The Hepburn children were encouraged to be independent, self-reliant, and inquisitive. She was educated by private tutors and at the age of sixteen entered Bryn Mawr College, where she studied drama and appeared in school productions. After graduating in 1928, Hepburn moved to New York to pursue a theatrical career. Her early stage appearances, however, were dismal failures. Her acting was artificial; her voice was high and tinny, and she suffered from stage fright. Her breakthrough came in 1932 when she was cast as the queen of the Amazons in *The Warrior's Husband*, and her beauty, athletic grace, and performance as an emancipated, spirited woman captivated audiences.

Hepburn's stage success led to movie work in Hollywood, where she received good reviews for her first film, *A Bill of Divorcement* (1932). She went on to attain stardom in a long series of memorable roles, portraying such characters as feisty Jo March in *Little Women* (1933), icy socialite Tracy Lord in *The Philadelphia Story* (1940), a world-famous political commentator in *Woman of the Year* (1942), a straitlaced missionary in *The African Queen* (1951), and Eleanor of Aquitaine in *The Lion in Winter* (1968), for which she won her third Oscar. Hepburn's other Oscar-winning performances were in the films *Morning Glory* (1933), *Guess Who's Coming to Dinner* (1967), and *On Golden Pond* (1981).

After an early brief marriage to Philadelphia socialite Ludlow Ogden Smith and her subsequent divorce, Hepburn never remarried. However, beginning in the early 1940s, she became romantically involved with her *Woman of the Year* costar Spencer Tracy. They made nine films together, and, although many inside Hollywood knew of their longtime affair, it was a well-kept secret from the public because Tracy's Roman Catholicism was an impediment to his getting a divorce. Even after his death in 1967, Hepburn would never comment publicly on their twenty-five-year relationship.

Through her long career, Hepburn led a life as far removed as possible from Hollywood stardom. Strong-minded, dignified, and outspoken, she demanded and won the respect of nearly everyone she ever worked with. A true original—on and off the screen—she has influenced generations of young women who followed her to Hollywood to make acting their career.

Billie Holiday (1915–1959)
Singer

Regarded by most jazz critics as the greatest jazz singer ever recorded, Billie Holiday revolutionized vocal performing, taking it from the accompaniment position of the big band "girl singer" to center stage and the main attraction. Her highly emotional renditions and skill in improvisation are the hallmarks of great jazz soloists. Vocal artists as far ranging in style as Sarah Vaughn, Lena Horne, Carmen McRae, and Frank Sinatra have been influenced by her. Others continue to be judged by her standard.

Born Eleanora Fagan, she grew up in Baltimore, raised by her mother and relatives. Before she was ten, she began to work for the proprietress of a local brothel performing menial chores and running errands. It was here that she first heard the recordings of Bessie Smith and Louis Armstrong, who would become major influences on her singing career. "I always wanted Bessie's sound and Pop's feeling," she recalled. In 1927, after completing fifth grade, she joined her mother in New York City, working as a maid and possibly a prostitute. She also sought work as a dancer in Harlem nightclubs; in one she was encouraged to sing, and she began to perform at various New York clubs.

Her style was unique from the start. Instead of the high-volume dramatics of Smith and Armstrong, she offered subtlety and nuance. In 1933, she was discovered by jazz enthusiast and record producer John Hammond, who arranged her first recordings within 24 hours after producing Bessie Smith's final album. Hammond recalled that Holiday "was not a blues singer, but she sang popular songs in a manner that made them completely her own. She had an uncanny ear, an excellent memory for lyrics, and she sang with an exquisite sense of phrasing." She began to tour with the Count Basie and Artie Shaw bands, becoming one of the first black performers in Shaw's otherwise all-white band.

From 1937 to 1941, Holiday performed regularly at Café Society in Greenwich Village, a club opened for the purpose of providing entertainment to integrated audiences. There, Holiday adopted as her closing number "Strange Fruit," a song about lynching and the "bitter crop" of southern racial politics. Columbia Records refused to let her record the song, but it was released on an independent label. On the Decca label, she recorded her most famous songs, "Lover Man" and her own compositions "God Bless the Child" and "Don't Explain." In 1947, Holiday entered a clinic to try to kick a drug addiction that had escalated after the collapse of her marriage to nightclub manager Jimmy Monroe. After her discharge, she was arrested for narcotics possession and served nine and a half months in a federal reformatory for women in West Virginia. Upon her release, her cabaret license was revoked, and Holiday could no longer perform in local clubs. Instead, she toured outside New York and in Europe. She continued to record and perform in the 1950s despite health issues exacerbated by drugs and alcohol. She died of liver failure at the age of forty-four. Holiday's life was a sad litany of neglect, divorce, arrests, and addiction interspersed by remarkable vocal and musical achievement. As jazz performer Anita Day observed, Billie Holiday remains "the one true genius among jazz singers.... Only somebody who'd gone through the things she did and survived, could sing from the soul the way she did."

Frances Marion (1888–1973)

Screenwriter

One of the most renowned screenwriters of the twentieth century whose twenty-five-year career spanned the silent and sound eras, Frances Marion was the first screenwriter to win two Academy Awards. She excelled at writing scripts that accentuated the strengths of specific actors and is often credited with defining the careers of Marie Dressler, Greta Garbo, Marion Davies, and Mary Pickford.

Marion was born Marion Benson Owens in San Francisco. She attended the Mark Hopkins Art Institute in San Francisco and worked as a photographer's assistant, a commercial artist, and a newspaper reporter. She moved to Los Angeles and worked as a poster artist before becoming a general assistant to pioneer female film director Lois Weber, who taught Marion screenwriting. Her friend Mary Pickford got her a job working on scenarios for film as well as original scripts for Pickford to star in, including *The Poor Little Rich Girl* (1917), *Rebecca of Sunnybrook Farm* (1917), and *The Little Princess* (1917). After serving in Europe as a combat correspondent during World War I, Marion returned to script writing and, in the 1920s, she drafted several successful scripts for Pickford, Marion Davies, Ronald Colman, and Rudolph Valentino.

Marion's first sound script was *Anna Christie* (1930), an adaptation of Eugene O'Neill's play, which was also Greta Garbo's sound debut. She also wrote *Min and Bill* (1930), which won Marie Dressler an Academy Award. Over a career that spanned the years 1915 through 1946, Marion is credited with writing three hundred scripts and over 130 produced films. Important screenplays by Marion include *The Son of the Sheik* (1926) with Rudolph Valentino, *The Champ* (1931) with Wallace Beery, *Dinner at Eight* (1933) with Marie Dressler and John Barrymore, *Camille* (1936) with Greta Garbo, *Poor Little Rich Girl* (1936) with Shirley Temple, and *Knight without Armour* (1937) with Marlene Dietrich.

She left Hollywood in 1946 to devote more time to writing stage plays and novels. In 1972, the year before her death, Marion published her memoir, *Off with Their Heads*.

Ethel Merman (1908–1984)

Singer

Known for her strong, distinctive singing voice and tough, brash performing style in Broadway musicals and on-screen, Ethel Merman has been called the "first lady of American musical comedy."

Merman was born Ethel Agnes Zimmerman in Astoria, Queens, New York. Her father was an accountant, and her mother was a teacher. Merman attended a public elementary school and William Cullen Bryant High School, which would later name its auditorium in her honor. Merman pursued a secretarial training course at school and was active in numerous extracurricular activities. A devotee of popular music, she visited local music stores to look at the weekly arrivals of sheet music. On Friday nights, the family went to vaudeville shows in Manhattan, where Merman saw such stars as Fanny Brice, Sophie Tucker, and Nora Bayes, whose singing styles she tried to emulate.

After her graduation from high school in 1924, Merman worked as a stenographer and later as a personal secretary to the president of an automobile brake manufacturing company. At night, Merman, who had no formal vocal training, sang at private parties and began appearing in nightclubs. During this time, she shortened her last name to "Merman." While appearing at Little Russia, a nightclub in Manhattan, Merman met agent Lou Irwin, who arranged an audition for Warner Brothers director Archie Mayo. She secured a six-month contract with the studio and, when no films were forthcoming, negotiated another contract, which allowed her to perform in nightclubs while waiting to be cast in films. After a series of nightclub and vaudeville engagements, which included performances at the prestigious Palace Theater as well as a few film roles, Merman won a starring role in the 1930 George and Ira Gershwin Broadway musical *Girl Crazy*. Merman's rousing rendition of "I Got Rhythm" in the musical made the song a hit and Merman a star as well as a favored performer for many of the influential songwriters of the period, including Irving Berlin and Cole Porter.

Merman followed her triumphant Broadway debut with an appearance in *George White's Scandals of 1931*. In the musical, Merman introduced the song "Life Is Just a Bowl of Cherries," which quickly became another hit. She starred in both the stage (1934) and screen (1936) versions of the popular Cole Porter musical *Anything Goes* and gave memorable performances in such musicals as *Du Barry Was a Lady* (1939), *Panama Hattie* (1940), *Something for the Boys* (1943), and *Annie Get Your Gun* (1946), in which she played sharpshooter Annie Oakley and was her biggest success. Merman's films of the 1930s and 1940s include *Kid Millions* (1934), *The Big Broadcast of 1936* (1935), *Alexander's Ragtime Band* (1938), and *Stage Door Canteen* (1943).

In the 1950s, Merman won a Tony Award for her starring role in the Broadway musical *Call Me Madam* (1950) and went on to star in the 1953 film version. In 1953, she enjoyed another huge success playing the mother of ecdysiast Gypsy Rose Lee in the musical *Gypsy*. In 1970, she stepped into the title role of matchmaker Dolly Levi in the hit musical *Hello, Dolly!* In the 1950s and 1960s, Merman appeared in the films *There's No Business Like Show Business* (1954) and *It's a Mad Mad Mad Mad World* (1963), in which she gave a memorable comic performance as the overbearing mother of comic actor Milton Berle's character. In 1977, *Mary Martin & Ethel Merman: Together on Broadway* successfully brought the two musical comedy stars together for an evening of song. Merman also cowrote two mem-

oirs: *Who Could Ask for Anything More?*, published in 1955, and *Merman*, published in 1978.

Merman was married four times and had two children with her second husband, newspaper executive Robert Levitt. Merman's fourth husband was actor Ernest Borgnine, whom she married in 1964 and divorced the same year. On the evening of her death from brain cancer, all thirty-six theaters on Broadway dimmed their lights in her honor.

Marilyn Monroe (1926–1962)

Actress

No female movie star has held the public's imagination for as long as Marilyn Monroe. A struggling, uncomfortable spirit throughout her short life, an American phenomenon during her tumultuous career, and an almost instant icon after her death from an overdose of barbiturates, Monroe possessed a face and body that, along with diligence, single-mindedness, evident talent, and the help of publicists, promoters, and photographers, transformed her into an enduring screen goddess and sex symbol.

Born Norma Jean Mortenson in Los Angeles, she was raised Norma Jean Baker, the illegitimate daughter of Gladys Monroe Baker Mortenson, a film editor who was hospitalized with paranoid schizophrenia when Monroe was seven. She would spend a sad and lonely childhood in a series of foster homes, where she was often sexually abused, as well as two years in a Los Angeles orphanage. She lived for a time with her mother's friend and coworker Grace McKee Goddard, who fostered in Monroe the idea of becoming a movie star with the movies being an escape from her daily experience.

In 1942, she dropped out of high school to marry an aircraft factory worker, James Dougherty, and she found an assembly-line job. There, she was chosen by an army photographer for *Yank* magazine to illustrate an article on female defense workers. Other modeling assignments followed. In 1946, soon after divorcing Dougherty, she was given a screen test by 20th Century Fox and a contract, then advised to change her name to "Marilyn." To go with it, she chose her mother's maiden name "Monroe." She appeared in a few bit parts in films. Her first important roles were in *Asphalt Jungle* (1950) and *All about Eve* (1950), after which the studio began to hone her image as a shapely, sexy, not-too-bright, blonde bombshell. Her movie performances reflected variations on that image. She could be comically naïve (*Gentlemen Prefer Blondes, How to Marry a Millionaire, The Seven-Year Itch, Some Like It Hot*); poignantly vulnerable and compassionate (*Bus Stop, The Misfits*); and sometimes dangerously seductive (*Niagara*). Throughout her career, her greatest desire was to be taken seriously as an actor. In 1954, she moved to New York, where she began studying at the prestigious Actors Studio.

Monroe was equally famous off-screen. Her second husband was baseball hero Joe DiMaggio, whom she wed in 1954 and divorced later that year. In 1956, she married playwright Arthur Miller and became pregnant twice, each time suffering a miscarriage. She suffered from depression and began to show signs of increasing mental and emotional instability. Her film work was marked by erratic behavior and temperamental outbursts. She divorced Miller in 1961. Filming *Something's Got to Give*, she failed to appear on the set regularly and was fired. A month later, she was found dead in her bed. Much speculation has occurred over the cause of her death, from suicide to murder. The most likely explanation remains an accidental overdose.

Like no other twentieth-century American woman, Marilyn Monroe embodied the exploitation of sexuality in the mass media and the marketing of women as sexual icons and objects, issues with which women continue to struggle.

Mary Pickford (1893–1979)

Actress

Endowed with a childlike and graceful screen presence as well as a strong knowledge of the movie business, Mary Pickford rose to become one of the most influential people in motion picture history.

Born Gladys Marie Smith in Toronto, Ontario, Canada, Pickford was the oldest child of John and Charlotte Smith. Her father, a laborer, was killed in a work-related accident when Pickford was five. Left destitute, her mother took in sewing and rented a spare room to lodgers to support herself and her three children. One boarder was the stage manager of a Toronto theater company, who hired Pickford and her sister, Lottie, for roles in a play, *The Silver King*. Other roles followed for "Baby Gladys Smith," as Pickford was billed, and she spent her childhood either in Toronto or on the road accompanied by her mother, her sister, and her brother, Jack, who was also an actor. When she could no longer find work in theater companies, fourteen-year-old Pickford went to New York alone and approached the famed producer David Belasco for a job. He changed her name to Mary Pickford and cast her in his Broadway production of *The Warrens of Virginia*.

At the age of fifteen, Pickford began her film career, working for director D. W. Griffith at his Biograph Studios. In 1912, she joined the Famous Players film company, starring in movie versions of such classic stories as *Rebecca of Sunnybrook Farm* and *A Little Princess*. In 1918, she became the first female movie star to head her own production company when she and her mother formed the Mary Pickford Film Corporation. A year later, Pickford joined Griffith and movie stars Charlie Chaplin and Douglas Fairbanks to form the film company United Artists. In 1920, Pickford and Fairbanks were married. By then, Pickford had become a multimillionaire. Nicknamed "America's sweetheart," she was the most popular actress in movies, mobbed by adoring fans wherever she went. Pickfair, Pickford and Fairbanks's mansion, was one of the most famous homes in Hollywood.

Even as an adult, the petite Pickford played youngsters' roles, starring as Pollyanna and Little Lord Fauntleroy. She shocked her fans when she had her long, golden hair cut in the 1920s. In 1929, Pickford appeared in her first "talkie," *Coquette*, for which she won an Academy Award. After starring in *Secrets* in 1933, Pickford retired from the movies to focus on producing, writing, and charity work. Pickford and Fairbanks were divorced in 1936, and soon afterward, she married actor–bandleader

Buddy Rogers, with whom she adopted two children. They remained together until her death in 1979. Pickford's last public appearance was at the 1976 Academy Awards, where she received a special Oscar for her contributions to the film industry.

Florence Price (1887–1953)

Composer

A composer whose musical style combines European classical traditions with black musical traditions, Florence Price was the first African American woman to be recognized as a symphonic composer and the first to have a composition played by a major orchestra.

Florence Beatrice Smith was born in Little Rock, Arkansas, one of three children in a mixed-race family. Her father, James, was a dentist who had been born to free black parents in Delaware, and her mother, Florence, was a music teacher who gave her children piano lessons. Price played her first recital at the age of four and had her first composition published at the age of eleven. In 1906, after graduating from Capitol High School in Little Rock as valedictorian of her class, Price was admitted to the New England Conservatory of Music in Boston. Fearing that her daughter would encounter racial prejudice in Boston, Price's mother urged her to identify as Mexican rather than black, which she did, listing her hometown as Puebla, Mexico. However, Price discovered that segregation was less severe in New England than in the South and met other African American students at the conservatory. She studied composition and counterpoint with composers Frederick Converse and George Chadwick, who suggested that Price incorporate African American musical styles such as spirituals into her compositions, which would form the basis for a distinctively American school of classical music. Price wrote several compositions as a student and earned extra money playing at church services.

After Price's graduation from the conservatory in 1906 with teaching certificates in piano and organ, she returned to Arkansas, where she taught at Shorter College in Little Rock. In 1910, she moved to Atlanta, Georgia, to take a position as head of the music department of present-day Clark Atlanta University, a historically black college. In 1912, she married Thomas J. Price, a lawyer, and the couple moved back to Little Rock, where Thomas Price had his practice. The Prices would have two daughters and a son, who was stillborn. A series of racial incidents, which included the lynching of a black man in their neighborhood in 1927, convinced the couple to leave Little Rock. Like many African American families, the Prices left the Jim Crow South to move north during the Great Migration (1916–1970). The family settled in Chicago, where Price studied composition, orchestration, and organ with various teachers and took classes in languages and liberal arts as well as music at several colleges in the city. In 1928, the G. Schirmer and McKinley musical publishing company began to issue Price's songs, piano music, and instructional pieces for piano. She also began to work on a symphony.

In 1931, after financial struggles and spousal abuse led Price to divorce her husband, she worked as an organist for silent film screenings and composed songs for radio ads under a pseudonym to help support herself and her daughters. She moved in with one of her students, Margaret Bonds, who would become a noted African American pianist and composer in her own right. In 1932, Price entered her *Symphony No. 1 in E Minor* in the annual Wanamaker music competition. The symphony won the Wanamaker Prize, a cash award of $500, and came to the notice of Chicago Symphony Orchestra conductor Frederick Stock, who included it on his program for a concert held at the Chicago Century of Progress fair in 1933. The following year, Price performed her *Piano Concerto in One Movement* with the Chicago Women's Symphony Orchestra. She performed the piece again in the late 1930s with the Detroit Symphony and composed several other orchestral works that were performed by a number of orchestras as well as the U.S. Marine Band. An admirer of Price's music was pioneering African American operatic soprano Marian Anderson, who frequently sang Price's arrangement of the spiritual *My Soul's Been Anchored in the Lord* and the composer's original arrangement of poet Langston Hughes's poem cycle *Songs to a Dark Virgin*. Leading African American singers such as opera soprano Leontyne Price and tenor Roland

Hayes also sang Price's vocal music. Besides her *Symphony in E Minor*, examples of Price's work using African American melodies and rhythms include *Concert Overture on Negro Spirituals* and *Negro Folksongs in Counterpoint*. During her career, Price composed symphonies, concertos, and other orchestral works; choral works, songs, and solo pieces for piano, chamber music, and piano and organ music; and arrangements of spirituals.

After Price's death, her work was largely forgotten, but by the twenty-first century, as more African American and female composers gained attention for their work, Price was rediscovered. The Women's Philharmonic created an album of Price's work in 2001, and in 2011, pianist Karen Walwyn and the New Black Music Repertory Ensemble performed her *Concerto in One Movement* and *Symphony in E Minor*. In 2009, a large collection of her works and papers were discovered in a house near St. Anne, Illinois, which included dozens of her scores, including two violin concertos and her fourth symphony. The Florence Price Archives at the University of Fayetteville, the Helen Walker-Hill Collection at the University of Colorado–Boulder, and the James Weldon Johnson Collection of Negro Arts and Letters at Yale University all house special collections of the works of this prolific and extraordinary composer.

Lillian Russell (1860–1922)

Actress, Singer

One of America's earliest superstar performers, Lillian Russell, known as the "American beauty," was famous for her comic opera singing. In the 1890s, she sang in the first long-distance telephone call from New York to Washington, D.C. Thomas A. Edison asked Russell to sing on one of his first voice recordings.

She was born Helen Louise Leonard in Clinton, Iowa, but raised in Chicago. Her parents separated when she was eighteen, and she moved to New York with her mother, where her mother did suffrage work for Susan B. Anthony. Russell studied singing under Leopold Damrosch and considered pursuing

an operatic career, but her very religious mother disapproved of her working in theaters. She persisted, however, and her first stage role was in the chorus of a Brooklyn company performing *H.M.S. Pinafore* in 1879. A year later, she made her New York City debut under the stage name Lillian Russell at Tony Pastor's variety theater. Pastor billed her as "Lillian Russell, the English ballad singer" to keep her mother in the dark. Her mother eventually saw her daughter perform and relented in her objections.

Russell found herself in demand, and, as she wrote in her autobiography, "I began to think it was fun to sign contracts promiscuously." She signed five contracts with five different managers for the same season, and in response to the legal tangle that ensued, she eloped to England with a musician, Edward Solomon, who would eventually be arrested for bigamy.

At the peak of her popularity, performing parts in comic operas, Russell symbolized American femininity: tall and blonde with an ample, hourglass figure. She used her popularity to support women's suffrage and women's rights, reassuring the public that having the vote would not make a woman less feminine since if Lillian Russell could advocate women's suffrage and still retain her femininity, so could others.

In 1890, Russell met "Diamond Jim" (James Buchanan) Brady, one of the richest men in America. Brady would shower Russell with so many diamonds that the press dubbed her "Diamond Lil." Russell indulged in a lavish lifestyle, supported by Brady, who broke conventions of acceptable female behavior. A woman riding a bicycle was considered shocking, but Russell's pedaling a gold-plated bicycle given by Brady helped make the bicycle acceptable for women. She also raised the level of respectability of vaudeville by teaming with comedian W. C. Fields. When her celebrated voice faded, she turned to nonsinging dramatic roles. By 1912, she mostly retired from the stage but remained active writing newspaper columns and supporting women's suffrage. In 1919, ill health forced her to leave the stage entirely after a four-decade-long career. She died at her home in Pittsburgh at the age of sixty-one. On reflection, Russell observed, "What has Life meant to me? Just a waiting game for something better. Doing as much good as possible, finding as much pleasure as possible, being as just and generous in thought and deed as possible."

Bessie Smith (1894–1937)

Singer

Bessie Smith is one of the most important figures in the history of American music. By successfully blending African and Western styles of music, she helped transform the folk tradition of the blues into an indigenous American art form with worldwide impact. Few contemporary singers of pop, jazz, or blues have not been influenced by her. An electrifying performer, she expressively and emotionally verbalized actual life. As music critic Carl van Vechten summarizes: "This was no actress, no imitator of women's woes; there was no pretense. It was the real thing."

Bessie Smith was born into a large, poor family in Chattanooga, Tennessee. Her father was a Baptist preacher who died soon after she was born; her mother died when Smith was nine, and her oldest sister became head of the family. Smith soon went to work singing on street corners for tips. She won a job as a dancer in a minstrel show, and while touring with the troupe, she met blues legend Ma Rainey, who became a lifelong friend and influence on Smith's singing style.

In 1913, Smith moved to Atlanta to become a headliner at a local club but continued to tour rural areas, performing in dance halls, cabarets, and camp meetings with F. S. Walcott's Rabbit Foot Minstrels and other traveling shows. In 1920, she formed her own troupe with herself as the star. Her rich contralto and commanding stage presence projected emotional depths never heard onstage before. Her material was drawn from vernacular African American oral tradition. As one critic observed, "More than any other singer, she set the blues tradition in terms of style and quality. She not only gave a special musical aura to this tradition but her own singing and accompaniments of the many jazz artists who

assisted her in her recordings placed her firmly in the broader jazz tradition."

Smith's recording sessions of the mid-1920s produced some of the finest work of her career. Smith used her impressive range and skill to turn her voice into another instrument in classics such as "Weeping Willow Blues," "The Bye Bye Blues," and "St. Louis Blues." Her material emphasized the daily plight of African Americans, including poverty, bootlegging, unemployment, eviction, and sexual betrayal. During the Depression, Smith's fortunes declined, as they did for many black performers, with venues closing and the record industry collapsing. A final recording session in 1933 produced the classic "Nobody Knows You When You're Down and Out." Smith continued to perform on tour until her death in an automobile accident in 1937. John Hammond incorrectly reported that Smith had died because an all-white hospital refused to admit her. She was in fact taken to an all-black hospital in Clarksdale, Mississippi, where she died from massive injuries sustained in the accident.

Smith was a great original whose life epitomized the excesses of the Roaring Twenties but whose music reflected the experience of African Americans with deep empathy and emotion. As Ralph Ellison declared, "Bessie Smith might have been a 'blues queen' to the society at large, but within the tighter Negro community where the blues were part of a total way of life, and major expression of an attitude toward life, she was a priestess, a celebrant who affirmed the values of the group and man's ability to deal with chaos."

Meryl Streep (1949–)

Actress

Known for her versatility, evident in the many characters she has portrayed on-screen, Meryl Streep is rightly considered the finest actress of her generation and one of the foremost actors in film history.

Born Mary Louise Streep but always known as "Meryl," a name her father made up, Streep was born in Summit, New Jersey, and was raised in Basking Ridge and Bernardsville, New Jersey. Her mother, Mary, was a commercial artist and art editor, and her father, William, was a pharmaceutical executive. Streep's younger brothers, Harry and Dana, are both actors.

Streep appeared in numerous school productions but was not interested in serious study of the art until she appeared in the title role of Strindberg's *Miss Julie* while she was a student at Vassar College. After graduating from Vassar in 1971, she attended the prestigious Yale School of Drama, where she played a variety of roles onstage. In 1975, she graduated from Yale with an MFA degree. After a six-week professional engagement acting in five plays at the Eugene O'Neill Theater Center's National Playwright's Conference, Streep moved to New York City. There, she won roles in producer Joseph Papp's production of *Trelawney of the Wells* and in Papp's New York Shakespeare Festival of plays performed in Central Park. At this time, she was in a serious relationship with actor John Cazale, with whom she lived until his death from cancer in 1978 at the age of forty-two.

Inspired by Robert de Niro's performance in the 1976 film *Taxi Driver*, Streep decided that she would like to act in films and began to audition for roles. She won a role in the 1977 feature film *Julia* opposite Jane Fonda, although most of her scenes were edited out. She was not happy with the way in which the scene in which she did appear was edited, and she decided to abandon film acting for a while. She continued to act in Broadway and Off-Broadway productions, receiving Tony and Drama Desk nominations for her performances. She returned to films when Robert de Niro, who had admired her onstage performance in Chekhov's *The Cherry Orchard*, suggested she play his girlfriend in the upcoming film *The Deer Hunter*. John Cazale was also cast in the film, which was released in 1978. Streep's breakthrough performance earned her an Academy Award nomination for Best Supporting Actress. Streep's portrayal of a German woman married to a Jewish artist in Nazi-era Germany in the 1978 miniseries *Holocaust* won her an Emmy Award for Outstanding Lead Actress in a Miniseries or Movie. The following year, she was cast in a supporting role as Woody Allen's ex-wife in Allen's film *Manhattan*.

Streep won a Golden Globe and her first Academy Award, that for Best Supporting Actress, for her performance as an unhappily married wife and mother in the 1979 film *Kramer vs. Kramer*, in which she starred opposite Dustin Hoffman. In the 1980s, she won acclaim for her roles in such films as *The French Lieutenant's Woman* (1981) and *Sophie's Choice* (1982), which earned her the Academy Award for Best Actress. *Premiere* magazine voted Streep's performance as a Holocaust survivor the third greatest movie performance of all time. Other notable films of the decade starring Streep include *Silkwood* (1983), *Out of Africa* (1985), and *A Cry in the Dark* (1988). In the 1990s, Streep appeared in such films as *Postcards from the Edge* (1990); the black comedy *Death Becomes Her* (1992); *The House of Spirits* (1993), based on Isabel Allende's novel; the romantic drama *The Bridges of Madison County* (1995), considered her most commercially successful film of the decade; and *Dancing at Lughnasa* (1998).

Streep continued to star in films in the first decade of the twenty-first century and also returned to the stage, where she starred as Madame Arkadina in The Public Theater's revival of Chekhov's *The Seagull*, directed by Mike Nichols. Her films of the 2000s include *Adaptation* (2002), *The Hours* (2002), and a remake of *The Manchurian Candidate* (2004). In 2003, Streep appeared in the HBO adaptation of Tony Kushner's 6-hour play *Angels in America*, also directed by Mike Nichols. Her most commercially successful film during this time was *The Devil Wears Prada* (2006), in which she plays the demanding editor of a fashion magazine. Equally successful was *Mamma Mia!* (2008), based on the stage production featuring the songs of the Swedish pop group Abba.

In 2011, Streep starred as former British prime minister Margaret Thatcher in Phyllida Lloyd's *The Iron Lady*, for which she received her second Best Actress Oscar. Other notable films of the 2010s include *Florence Foster Jenkins* (2016) and *The Post* (2017). Streep received her thirty-first Golden Globe nomination and her twenty-first Academy Award nomination for Best Actress for her portrayal of *Washington Post* publisher Katherine Graham. In 2019, she received her first main role in a television series when she joined the cast of the HBO drama series *Big Little Lies* in its second season.

Streep's other work includes the funding of a screenwriters' lab for female writers over forty years of age, called The Writers Lab. Established in 2015, The Writers Lab is administered by the nonprofit membership organization New York Women in Film & Television.

Married to sculptor Don Gummer since 1978, Streep and Gummer are the parents of a son and three daughters. Two of Streep's daughters, Mamie and Grace, are also actors.

Barbra Streisand (1942–)

Actress, Filmmaker, Singer

One of the most critically acclaimed performers and filmmakers in American history, Barbra Streisand has achieved success in multiple fields of the entertainment industry during her nearly sixty-year career and has been the recipient of numerous awards for her work.

Barbara Joan Streisand was born in Brooklyn, New York, the daughter of a high school English teacher, who died when Streisand was fifteen months old. Her mother Diana, who possessed an operatic soprano voice and sung semiprofessionally on occasion, worked as a bookkeeper to support Streisand and her older brother. Streisand began her education at the Orthodox Jewish Yeshiva of Brooklyn and then attended public school. She sang from an early age, practicing in the hallway of her apartment building and entertaining neighbors with her vocal renditions. She made her public singing debut at a PTA assembly and then sang at weddings and summer camp. In 1949, her mother remarried, and Streisand and her brother gained a half sister, the singer Rosalyn Kind.

Streisand attended Erasmus Hall High School, where she sang in choruses with future singer–songwriter and friend Neil Diamond. Determined to become an actor, she secured small roles in summer theater and took a night job working backstage at the Cherry Lane Theatre in Greenwich Village. After her graduation from high school in 1959 at the age of sixteen, Streisand moved to a small apartment in Manhattan's theater district, accepted any acting or backstage work she could get, and made the rounds of casting offices. Streisand's first singing audition was for the chorus of *The Sound of Music* in 1960. Although she did not secure a role, the director encouraged her to include her talent as a singer on her résumé. She prepared a demo tape with her boyfriend, actor–singer Barry Dennen, who was stunned at the power of her voice and suggested that she enter a talent contest at the Lion, a Greenwich Village nightclub. Streisand's performance was met with thunderous applause, and she was invited back to sing at the club for several weeks. Around this time, Streisand, who had never liked her given first name, changed its spelling to "Barbra."

After successful engagements with various nightclubs in New York, Streisand won a small but significant role in the musical comedy *I Can Get It for You Wholesale*, which opened on Broadway in 1962. Streisand's costar was Elliott Gould, whom she married in 1963 and with whom she had a son, Jason. The couple divorced in 1971. In 1998, Streisand married actor James Brolin.

Streisand's performance in *I Can Get It for You Wholesale* resulted in a Tony nomination and the New York Drama Critics' prize for Best Supporting Actress and led to numerous appearances on television shows such as *The Tonight Show*, where she appeared six times between 1962 and 1963. Her first album, *The Barbra Streisand Album*, was released in 1963, earned a place on the top ten on the Billboard chart and secured three Grammy Awards for Streisand. Since 1963, Streisand has recorded over fifty well-received studio albums and has been consistently prominent on pop music charts with such hits as "People"; "The Way We Were," from the film of the same name in which she starred; and "Evergreen," the love theme from her 1976 film remake *A Star Is Born*, which earned Streisand an Academy Award, two Grammy Awards, and three Golden Globes.

Streisand returned to Broadway in 1964 with an acclaimed performance as singer–comedian Fanny Brice in the musical comedy *Funny Girl*. She was featured on the cover of *Time* magazine and received a Tony nomination for Leading Actress in a Musical. She lost to Carol Channing, the star of

Hello, Dolly!; however, her performance in the 1968 film version of *Funny Girl* earned her an Academy Award for Best Actress, which she shared with Katharine Hepburn, who was equally honored for her performance in *A Lion in Winter*. In 1969, she was awarded a Golden Globe as Best Female Film Favorite, and, the following year, she received an honorary "Star of the Decade" Tony Award.

After *Funny Girl*, Streisand appeared as the title character in *Hello, Dolly!* (1969). Her films of the 1970s include *The Owl and the Pussycat* (1970), *The Way We Were* (1973), and *For Pete's Sake* (1974). In 1972, she set up her own production company, Barwood Films, and in 1983, she produced, directed, and starred in a film version of Isaac Bashevis Singer's story *Yentl*. She went on to produce, direct, and star in *The Prince of Tides* (1991) and *The Mirror Has Two Faces* (1996), both of which were well received. In the twenty-first century, Streisand has remained busy with philanthropic activities, intermittent film work, and live concert appearances in 2000, 2006, and 2007. Among her numerous awards and honors, Streisand received the National Medal of Arts in 2000 and an Emmy Award for her TV special *Barbra Streisand: Timeless* in 2001. Over the course of her career, she has given benefit concerts on behalf of political candidates and charities that support social causes. The Streisand Foundation, which Barbra Streisand established in 1986, continues to provide grants on behalf of such worthy social causes as preservation of the environment, voter education, the protection of civil liberties and civil rights, women's issues, and nuclear disarmament.

Maria Tallchief (1925–2013)

Ballet Dancer

Considered America's first major prima ballerina, Maria Tallchief was also the first Native American to hold that rank. In a field that featured excellent dancers, *The New York Times* called her "one of most brilliant American ballerinas of the twentieth century."

Elizabeth Marie Tallchief, known as "Betty Marie" to her family and friends, was born in Fairfax, Oklahoma, and grew up on the Osage reservation. Her father, Alexander, was a member of the Osage Nation, who had inherited oil revenues, and he was a wealthy man as a result; her mother, Ruth, was of Scottish and Irish descent. Tallchief had five siblings, three of whom were from her father's first marriage. As young children, Tallchief's Osage grandmother frequently took her and her sister, Marjorie, to ceremonial tribal dances, and Tallchief and her sister, an accomplished ballerina in her own right, studied ballet from an early age. In 1933, the family went to Los Angeles in an attempt to secure acting work for the children in Hollywood musicals. At the age of twelve, Tallchief began studying with Bronislava Nijinska, a sister of the celebrated Russian ballet dancer Vaslav Nijinsky, and David Lichine, a student of famed Russian ballerina Anna Pavlova. At the age of fifteen, she danced her first solo performance at the Hollywood Bowl in a piece staged by Madame Nijinska, *Chopin Concerto*. She danced her first pas de deaux for choreographer Ada Broadbent and attracted the interest of prima ballerina Mia Slavenska, who arranged for her to audition for Serge Denham, director of the famous Ballet Russe de Monte Carlo. Denham was impressed, but Tallchief's audition did not result in a position with the company.

Tallchief graduated from Beverly Hills High School in 1942 and won a bit part in a Judy Garland MGM movie musical called *Presenting Lily Mars*. However, she did not find the experience to be a gratifying one. Instead, at the age of seventeen, she left for New York City with a family friend, Russian American ballerina and teacher Tatiana Riabouchinska, as her chaperone. In New York, Tallchief was eventually taken on as an apprentice dancer with the Ballet Russe and while touring in Canada with the company made her first performance in the ballet *Gaite Parisienne*. After the Canadian tour, Tallchief was offered a place in the troupe when one of the dancers left due to pregnancy. When Madame Nijinska arrived at the Ballet Russe as a choreographer, she cast Tallchief as the understudy to the first ballerina in *Chopin Concerto*. During rehearsals for Agnes de Mille's ballet *Rodeo, or The Courting at Burnt Ranch*, de Mille suggested that Tallchief change her name to suggest a more European image. Proud of her heritage, a name change was a sensitive topic for Tallchief, so she compromised with the name by which she became known.

In 1944, well-known choreographer George Balanchine arrived at the Ballet Russe to stage a new ballet, *Song of Norway*. Impressed with Tallchief, he cast her as the lead ballerina's understudy. In 1946, Balanchine and Tallchief married and moved to Paris, where Tallchief became the first American ballerina to debut at the Paris Opera and was the first to appear with the Paris Opera Ballet at the Bolshoi Theatre in Moscow. She became the company's ranking soloist, and upon the couple's return to New York, she quickly became the prima ballerina of Balanchine's New York City Ballet, which opened in 1948. Balanchine created many roles especially for Tallchief, including the lead in composer Igor Stravinsky's *The Firebird* in 1949, a technically difficult role that launched Tallchief to the top of her profession. Although her marriage to Balanchine ended in 1952, Tallchief remained with the company until 1960, when she joined the American Ballet Theatre. In 1958, she created the lead role in Balanchine's *Gounod Symphony* before leaving the company to have her only child with her third husband, Chicago businessman Henry Paschen, to whom she was married from 1956 until his death in 2004.

In the 1950s and 1960s, Tallchief made guest appearances in films and on television. By the time of her retirement from dancing in 1966, she had appeared with ballet companies around the world during her career. She relocated to Chicago with her husband and from 1973 to 1979 served as the director of ballet for the Lyric Opera Company of Chicago and founded and taught at the company's ballet school. In 1981, with her sister, Marjorie, she founded the Chicago City Ballet and served as its coartistic director until its demise in 1987. In 1996, Tallchief received a Kennedy Center Honor for lifetime achievement, and in 1999, she was awarded the National Medal of the Arts by the National Endowment of the Arts. The Metropolitan Museum of Art held a special tribute to Tallchief in 2006, which was attended by the ballerina. In 2018, she was one of the first inductees into the National Native American Hall of Fame.

Barbara Walters (1929–)

Broadcast Journalist

 A pioneer for women in broadcasting, Barbara Walters was the first woman to host *The Today Show* and the first to coanchor a network evening news program. She is particularly renowned for her effective, in-depth interviews with world-renowned figures.

Walters was born in Boston, Massachusetts, one of the three children of Dena and Lou Walters. She attended schools in Boston, New York City, and Miami Beach, where her father operated a series of nightclubs. After her graduation from the Birch Wathen School in New York City in 1947, she attended Sarah Lawrence College, where she earned a bachelor's degree in English in 1951. She worked as a secretary for a small New York advertising agency for a year and then obtained a job with the local NBC station working in the publicity department and writing press releases. In 1953, she began producing a 15-minute children's show, *Ask the Camera*, and also produced a talk show hosted by gossip columnist Igor Cassini, known in the trade as "Cholly Knickerbocker." She left the show after a brief office romance with her married boss, Ted Cott, which resulted in Cott stalking her and challenging one of her dates to a fistfight on the street. She moved to WPIX, where she produced the short-lived talk show *The Eloise McElhone Show*. In 1955, she became a writer on *The Morning Show* at CBS.

In 1955, Walters married business executive Robert Henry Katz; the marriage ended in 1957. The second of Walters's three husbands was theater producer and owner Lee Guber, whom she married in 1963. The couple adopted a daughter, Jacqueline, and divorced in 1976. Walters' third husband was Merv Adelson, CEO of Lorimar Productions. The marriage lasted from 1981 to 1984; they remarried in 1986 and divorced again in 1992.

After stints as a publicist with the Tex McCrary public relations firm and as a writer for *Redbook* magazine, Walters's career began in earnest when she joined NBC's popular morning program *The Today*

Show in 1961. In an era when women were seen as decorative presences on television and not considered capable of reporting "hard news," Walters rose to become the program's regular "Today Girl," handling lighter assignments and providing the weather forecast. However, within a year, the assertive Walters had become a reporter-at-large, developing, writing, and editing her segments and interviews. In 1966, she became the show's first female host, cohosting first with Hugh Downs and then with Tom Brokaw from 1966 until 1976, when ABC hired her as the first female coanchor for a network evening news program. Walters's stint at the ABC evening news was marked by a difficult relationship with her cohost, Harry Reasoner, and ended in 1978. The following year, she began a twenty-five-year association with the ABC newsmagazine *20/20*, which she cohosted with Hugh Downs. In 1997, Walters cocreated and co-executive produced *The View*, a daytime talk-and-interview show aimed at female viewers with an audience featuring a panel of women in the entertainment industry discussing social and political issues. Walters cohosted the show until 2014, although she intermittently returned as a guest cohost afterward.

Walters became additionally famous for her in-depth series of what are sometimes known as "scoop interviews" beginning in 1977, when she jointly interviewed Egyptian president Anwar el-Sadat and Israeli prime minister Menachem Begin in the wake of the historic Camp David Accords. She would go on to interview a long list of luminaries ranging from world leaders to superstars in the entertainment, sports, and publishing industries. However, according to Walters, her most inspirational interview was with Robert Smithdas, a deaf and blind man dedicated to improving the lives of other sight- and hearing-impaired people.

In the second decade of the twenty-first century, Walters continued to host such shows as *20/20* and the documentary series *American Scandals* and to conduct interviews. Her last interview was with presidential candidate Donald Trump for ABC News in 2015.

Walters' published works include *How to Talk to Anyone About Practically Everything* (1970) and *Audition: A Memoir* (2008).

Lois Weber (1881–1939)
Director, Screenwriter

In the early years of the American motion picture industry, two directors stand out as *auteurs*—filmmakers involved in every aspect of production. One was D. W. Griffith, and the other was Lois Weber. An actor and producer as well as screenwriter and director, Lois Weber made silent films that reflected her concern with social justice and the human condition.

Born Florence Lois Weber in Allegheny, Pennsylvania, Weber was the second of the three children of George Weber, an upholsterer and decorator, and his wife Matilda. As a child, Weber was considered a musical prodigy. She left home while still in her teens and lived in poverty while working as a street-corner evangelist and social activist for the Church Army Workers. Two years later, she returned home and, after continuing her music studies for a time, began to perform as a soprano singer and pianist. She toured the United States as a concert pianist but abandoned her musical career after a piano key broke off in her hand while she was playing. She decided to pursue an acting career and left for New York City.

Weber found acting work in repertory and stock companies. She was cast as the soubrette in the farce comedy *Zig-Zag* for a Chicago-based touring company and appeared in a road company production of the popular drama *Why Girls Leave Home*. In 1904, she married Wendell Phillips Smalley, the company's leading man and manager. Around 1907, the two began working in motion pictures, often billed under the collective title "The Smalleys." During their early years at the Gaumont and Reliance studios, the couple acted together on-screen and codirected scripts written by Lois Weber. In 1912, they moved to Carl Laemmle's Universal Film Manufacturing Company, where they headed the Rex division of films. They produced one- and two-reel films each week with a stock company of actors and earned a reputation for sophisticated filmmaking. In 1914, Lois Weber became the first woman to direct a feature film when the couple completed a four-reel version of *The Merchant of Venice*. Seeking more freedom to make feature films, Weber and Smalley left Universal for Hobart Bosworth Productions, where they made such films as *Hypocrites* (1915).

When Weber and Smalley returned to Universal, Lois Weber became one of the top directors at the studio and was the sole author of scripts the couple adapted for the screen. Weber wrote, produced, and directed a series of films on the social issues of the era, including capital punishment (*The People vs. John Doe*, 1916); drug abuse (*Hop, the Devil's Brew*, 1916); and poverty and wage equality (*Shoes*, 1916). Inspired by the trial of birth control advocate Margaret Sanger, Weber made and acted in two films concerning contraception, family planning, and sex education: *Where Are My Children?* (1916) and *Hand That Rocks the Cradle* (1917).

In 1916, Weber became the first woman to be elected to the Motion Picture Directors Association. The following year, she left Universal to form her own studio. Lois Weber Productions, located on the grounds of a former estate in Los Angeles. There, she built a twelve-thousand-square-foot shooting stage and converted the home into administrative offices. She negotiated lucrative contracts with Universal and was for a time the highest paid Hollywood director. To avoid the censorship issues and controversy she had encountered with her previous social issue films, Weber began to make films focusing on women's experiences in marriage and domestic life such as *What Do Men Want?* (1921) and *Too Wise Wives* (1921). She also experimented with different working methods like split-screen techniques, sound, shooting on location whenever possible, and shooting scenes in narrative sequence.

Weber's output declined after 1922 partly due to the breakdown of her marriage (the couple would divorce in 1935) but equally likely because of the rise of the film industry as a big business and the competition that developed in the wake of the formation of the major studios, all of which were headed by men. Between 1923 and 1934, Weber wrote and directed just five feature films. By the time of her death, she was destitute and was not remembered for the nearly 350 films in which she acted or wrote and directed but rather as a "starmaker" only notable for nurturing the talents of young female actors. More than three hundred people attended her funeral, which was paid for by screenwriter and director Frances Marion. In 1960, she was awarded a star on the Hollywood Walk of Fame. Often labeled Hollywood's forgotten female director, only about twenty of Lois Weber's films have been preserved.

Oprah Winfrey (1954–)
Actress, Media Executive, Television Host

Oprah Winfrey is a show business phenomenon—an Academy Award-nominated actress, a dedicated philanthropist, and a one-woman media empire. One of the world's wealthiest entertainers, she is most famous for her long-running talk show *The Oprah Winfrey Show*, but her forays into producing and publishing have further enhanced her status as a savvy businesswoman and multitalented artist.

She was born Orpah Gail Winfrey in Kosciusko, Mississippi (she changed her birth name to Oprah because that was the way most people spelled and pronounced it). Born to an unmarried teenage mother, she grew up under difficult circumstances, primarily with her mother in Milwaukee and her father in Nashville. She graduated with honors from East Nashville High School and won a scholarship to Tennessee State University, from which she graduated in 1976.

Winfrey's media career began in high school, when she started working for a local radio station. By the age of nineteen, she was a coanchor for the evening news on Nashville's WLAC-TV. After college graduation, she was hired as a reporter and coanchor for Baltimore's WJZ-TV. Her personality and interests led her to work in the talk show format first in Baltimore and then in 1983 in Chicago. Her success in Chicago led to her own show, *The Oprah Winfrey Show*, an immediate hit, which began broadcasting nationally in 1986. For twenty-five years, her show had top ratings and had an enormous influence on U.S. culture. For example, a book selected for Oprah's Book Club would become an immediate best-seller.

Winfrey also began a screen acting career in the 1980s, and her work has included roles in *The Color Purple* (1985), for which she received an Oscar nomination, and *Beloved* (1998). In 1999, she produced the Emmy Award-winning TV movie *Tuesdays with Morrie*. Other starring or feature roles include *The Butler* (2013), *Selma* (2014), *The Immortal Life of Henrietta Lacks* (2017), and *A Wrinkle in Time* (2018). She has also served as a producer for such productions as *Their Eyes Were Watching God* (2005), *Queen Sugar* (2016), and *Love Is* (2018).

In 2011, Winfrey started her own TV network, the Oprah Winfrey Network (OWN). She has gone on to pursue many other ventures in film (her production company Harpo Films), online media (with Apple), radio (Oprah Radio), and publishing (*O* magazine). By 2003, she was the first black female billionaire and is one of the wealthiest self-made women in the United States.

Winfrey has consistently been among the top philanthropists in the United States. In 1998, she created the Oprah's Angel Network, which supported projects and provided grants to organizations around the world. She especially focused on South Africa, where she established the Oprah Winfrey Leadership Academy for Girls. She has won numerous awards for her professional and charitable work, including the U.S. Presidential Medal of Freedom in 2013.

Ellen Taaffe Zwilich (1939–)

Composer

The first woman to be awarded the Pulitzer Prize for Music, Ellen Zwilich has been called one of the most popular and frequently played living classical music composers.

Born in Miami, Florida, Zwilich is the adopted daughter of Edward Taaffe, an airline pilot, and his wife, Ruth. She began composing as a child and had studied piano, violin, and trumpet by the time she finished high school. She attended Florida State University, where she received a bachelor's degree (1960) and a master's degree (1962) in music. In 1975, she became the first woman to earn a doctorate in musical arts at the Julliard School of Music. After teaching in a small South Carolina town for a year, Zwilich moved to New York City. There, she studied violin with Ivan Galamian, worked as an usher at Carnegie Hall, and taught music at Mannes College and Hunter High School. From 1965 to 1972, Zwilich played violin with the American Symphony Orchestra under conductor Leopold Stokowski at a time when few female musicians were in major orchestras. In 1969, she married Joseph Zwilich, a Hungarian-born violinist for the Metropolitan Opera orchestra, who died in 1979.

In 1982, the American Symphony Orchestra premiered Zwilich's *Three Movements for Orchestra (Symphony No. 1)*, which won the Pulitzer Prize for the composer the following year. In addition to large-scale orchestral works, which were commissioned by the New York Philharmonic, and compositions for piano, Zwilich has composed smaller-scale works for relatively uncommon instruments such as timpani, trombone, bass trombone, bassoon, clarinet, and horn. She has also written choral works and song cycles. From 1995 to 1999, she was the first occupant of Carnegie Hall's Composer's Chair and in that capacity created the Making Music concert series focusing on live performances and lectures by composers.

Among the honors Zwilich has received during her career are the Arturo Toscanini Music Critics Award, a Guggenheim Fellowship, an award from the American Academy of Arts and Letters, and four Grammy nominations. In 1999, the magazine *Musical America* named Zwilich Composer of the Year. A member of the Academy of Arts and Letters and the Academy of Arts and Sciences, Zwilich is currently a professor of music at Florida State University.

SPORTS

It has been said that to understand a culture, look at the games it plays, and American women's organized sports provides a revealing window into changing notions of gender that have helped to define American history from colonial times.

The history of American women in sports has its roots in conventional notions accepted from the American colonial period through the nineteenth century and after of a feminine ideal antithetical to athletic participation by women. Prior to the 1870s, women's athletic activities were recreational rather than competitive, limited to a few acceptable forms of physical activities. Women, for example, could walk for exercise but rarely were encouraged to run. They could ride on horseback but not race largely because a woman's saddle made anything beyond a slow trot impossible. Women could fish but not hunt. Sports require vigor and stamina, whereas the womanly ideal through most of American history emphasized delicacy and passivity. Other elements of the ideal—modesty and propriety—were also threatened in the rough-and-tumble world of sports practiced by boys and men. For women, regarded as "fragile vessels," sporting games came with the threat of injury and the aggressive behavior contrary to the primary female attributes: the ability to attract a husband and to bear children. Physical activity was thought to be especially hazardous during menstruation, when women were "periodically weakened."

The American Indian tribes played sports and games as part of tribal ceremonies and also to teach children the skills they would need as adults. Boys and men played such games as lacrosse (a sport adopted by nonindigenous Americans) and snow snakes, a team sport; girls played a game similar to hide-and-seek called the butterfly game as well as games that would teach them about childcare. During the colonial era, men played various games, including stoolball (a game similar to cricket, imported from England), foot racing, quoits (similar to horseshoes), and skittles and ninepins (bowling). These games were designed to allow single men to show off and impress female spectators. More violent games or sports included wrestling and a form of football. In the eighteenth century, other games such as bowling, cricket, skinny (field hockey), and fives (handball) were popular, again for men to get exercise, channel pent-up energy, and escape from the daily grind. None included female participants. Acceptable athletic activities for women increased in the nineteenth century, when sports such as croquet, archery, bowling, tennis, and golf became opportunities for respectable social encounters with men. These activities were mainly for the upper classes, which had the leisure and means to belong to athletic clubs that facilitated play. Many men's clubs were opened to women as associate members to participate in separate activities and occasionally in coed competition. Croquet, for example, is consid-

In this painting from 1885 by Sir John Lavery called *A Rally*, a woman energetically plays an early version of tennis, one of the few sports considered appropriate for females at the time.

ered the first popular game played by men and women together; tennis and golf would follow.

When more women began to attend colleges in the latter half of the nineteenth century, attitudes toward women and sports began to change. A large barrier to women's participation in more strenuous physical activities, whether on campus or off, was women's restrictive clothing, which severely limited movement. Women's fashion in the nineteenth century dictated, for modesty's sake, floor-length dresses and full skirts beneath a tiny waist enhanced by tight corsets. Ladylike outfits such as these could weigh, with their six to eight petticoats to fill out the shape of the skirts, up to fifteen pounds, causing overheating, impaired breathing, and certainly constricting physical exertion, even if such unladylike exercise was approved. In the 1850s, however, Amelia Bloomer would help to popularize so-called "Turkish pantaloons," a knee-length skirt with loose pants. The style would link Bloomer's name with the trend, and adapters were called Bloomerites or, simply, wearers of bloomers.

If fashion began to allow more female activity, female educators would play significant roles in rejecting previous notions that enforced female passivity and opened the way for women to participate in sports. In 1856, Catherine Beecher would publish the first exercise manual for women. Mary Lyon, who founded Mount Holyoke College for women in 1836, was an early believer in daily exercise for women and required students to walk a mile each day after breakfast. When Wellesley College opened in 1875, its campus included a gymnasium for its female students to exercise, a lake for ice skating, the first rowing program for women, and a physical education requirement for graduation. Exercise and sports began to be regarded as essential for women to increase the physical stamina necessary to endure the stress and strain of higher education. As the first president of all-female Smith College remarked in his inaugural address in 1875: "We admit it would be an insuperable objection to the higher education of women, if it seriously endangered her health.... We understand that they need special safeguards.... With gymnastic training wisely adapted to their peculiar organization, we see no reason why young ladies cannot pursue study as safely as they do their ordinary employments."

Sports began to be implemented into the collegiate physical education curriculum in the second half of the nineteenth century to promote health and such social values as teamwork and skills and accomplishments that women could utilize in later years. In 1866, Vassar College fielded the first two women's amateur baseball teams and in 1895 organized the first athletic meeting for women at its Field Day competition, which featured running and jumping events. Archery, fencing, swimming, rowing, cycling, track and field athletics, and bowling were among the sports introduced into the college curriculum during the late nineteenth century to complement gymnasium training. Intercollegiate sports for women were initiated when basketball was introduced to Smith College in 1892, soon after the game was invented.

By the 1870s, female athletes in various traditional and new sports began to emerge beyond college campuses. In 1874, Mary Ewing Outerbridge would introduce lawn tennis to America, having encountered the sport while living in Bermuda. She would establish the first U.S. lawn tennis court on Staten Island, New York, initiating the enduring association of women in tennis. Women's singles competitions began at Wimbledon in 1884 and at the U.S. Open in 1887. In the 1870s, teams of female baseball players competed before paying customers. In the 1890s, the first women's golf tournaments and championships were held.

When the modern Olympics were initiated in 1896, women were not allowed to compete until the next Summer Games in Paris in 1900, when they were allowed to compete in tennis and golf. In 1904, women's archery was added; in 1908, figure skating; and in 1912, swimming and diving. In 1924, women competed at the Winter Olympics for the first time (in figure skating); at that year's Summer Games, fencing was added for women. In 1928, women's track and gymnastics debuted. The 800-meter race would be subsequently dropped when many competitors were reportedly so exhausted that they could not complete the race. It would not be restored to the Olympics until 1960. In 1932, the javelin throw was added; in 1936, the alpine skiing combined event was featured for the first time; in 1948, women competed in all of the same alpine skiing disciplines as men; and in 1952, women competed in cross-country skiing and equestrian for the first time at that year's Summer Games. Speed skating debuted in 1960; cross-country skiing and volleyball in 1964; shooting in 1968; basketball, rowing, and handball in 1976; women's field hockey in 1980; and synchronized swimming, cycling, and rhythmic gymnastics in 1984, the same year that the first-ever women's marathon would be held, won by American Joan Benoit. In 1991, the International Olympic Committee made it mandatory for all new sports applying for Olympic recognition to have female competitors. Subsequently, sports such as softball (1996), ice hockey (1998), triathlon (2000), water polo (2000), weight lifting (2000), wrestling (2004), boxing (2012), ski jumping (2014), and rugby (2016) have been added for female competitors at the Olympics.

It can be argued that women's participation in the Olympic Games has been the single greatest factor in supporting and sustaining modern women's sports.

As early as the late 1800s, women were actively forming baseball teams and playing to paying spectators. This photo shows the 1913 New York Female Giants team.

Since the vast majority of women's athletics is performed on the amateur level, the Olympics provided a regular showcase for the best female athletes from around the world in sports without a sufficient fan base to become professional leagues. Female athletes in the Olympics gradually competed in all the sports formerly restricted to men alone. In the process, through the twentieth century, the core concepts of what women could do and achieve in sports was transformed. In country club sports like tennis, golf, and swimming in the 1920s, women such as Babe Didrikson Zaharias, Helen Wills Moody, and Gertrude Ederle became famous for both their sporting prowess and their embodiment of a new conception of femininity. As scholar Susan Cahn summarizes, "They helped fashion a new ideal of womanhood by modeling an athletic, energetic femininity with an undertone of explicit joyful sexuality." Beginning in the late nineteenth century and continuing through the twentieth, women would make the transition from the oddity of playing men's sports such as baseball to achieving notoriety and distinction not as "almost men" but as accomplished female athletes.

The evolving women's movement and the struggle for equal rights and suffrage are reflected in the changing conception of both women's roles and capacity that sports in America would embody. "Bicycling has done more to emancipate women than anything else in the world," Susan B. Anthony declared. "I stand and rejoice every time I see a woman ride on a wheel. It gives women a feeling of freedom and self-reliance." The same was certainly true when more and more women took up sports like tennis and golf and began to play team sports like basketball. Women's achievements in the Olympics in the twentieth century and beyond are both a testimony to the increased number of women willing to participate and train as well as interest in women's performance that would rival the attention commanded by male athletes.

Despite the fact that amateur performance in the Olympics by women thrived and women gradually achieved parity with men, on the professional level, the record is considerably more mixed. Women, on occasion, have managed to invade the male preserve of professional sports but generally as exceptions to the rule. Tennis and golf have successfully sustained

Margaret Ives Abbott (1876–1955) was the first American woman to take first place in an Olympic event. She won the women's golf tournament at the 1900 Paris Games.

professional female athletes, although parity with men in terms of earnings and championship prize money have long been a contested issue. Among the big four professional men's sports—baseball, football, basketball, and hockey—only basketball has managed to sustain a professional women's team. The Women's National Basketball Association was founded in 1996 as the women's counterpart to the National Basketball Association, which originally had eight teams and is currently in a twelve-team league whose season follows that of the NBA. However, the WNBA pays the top female players sixty times less than the top male players. In 2010, the league reported its first-ever "cash flow positive" team; by 2011, three teams were profitable, and in 2013, six of the league's twelve teams reported a profit.

Previously, professional women's baseball teams, under the banner of the All-American Girls Professional Baseball League (made famous in the 1992 film *A League of Their Own*), competed from 1943 to 1954. Among other sports, the Women's Tennis Association (WTA) was founded in 1973 and is by far the most successful organization in women's professional sports with over 2,500 players worldwide, sponsoring fifty-four tournaments and four Grand Slam events in thirty-three countries. Failed women's professional sports leagues include Women's Professional Soccer (2007–2012), the first women's professional softball league (1976–1980), and the Women's Professional Volleyball Association (1986–1997). The National Women's Soccer League (NWSL) was established in 2012 and is still active with nine teams competing throughout the United States.

Despite the fact that professional women's sports have struggled to compete with men's professional sports leagues, it is undeniable that at least on the amateur level, the single most significant transformative impact on women's athletics has been the passage in 1972 of Title IX of the Educational Amendments Act. Although sports in the twentieth century increasingly became more acceptable as far as women's participation, on college campuses and in high schools, the inequality of facilities, support, and involvement between men and women was left unaddressed until the passage of Title IX. By declaring that "no person in the United States shall on the basis of sex, be excluded from participation in, be denied the benefits of, or be subjected to discrimination under any education program or activity receiving Federal financial assistance," Title IX threatened to remove federal funds from schools that discriminated based on gender in its programs. It forced schools to correct gender bias and produced a massive change in college and high school sports programs, so much so that sports in America can be usefully categorized "before Title IX" and "after Title IX."

In 1970, participation by women in intercollegiate sports programs was at about 7.5 percent; by 1978, that percentage had grown to almost 32 percent. Since 1971, the number of women who participated in collegiate varsity sports increased by nearly 250 percent. The average number of women's teams per school rose from 5.61 to 7.5. By 1996, 39 percent of college athletes were women, and women's sports scholarships grew from $100,000 in 1972 to $180 million. At the high school level, prior to Title IX, only one in twenty-seven girls played sports; the ratio is now one in three.

Just as important as the enhanced participation of women in sports that Title IX has ensured is the changed perception of the female athlete and increased respect for women's sports accomplishments. Skill levels have improved among female athletes. Between 1967 and 1987, for example, female marathoners have cut nearly an hour off the world record. Along with highly publicized stories of high school women successfully joining men's teams in baseball, football, and wrestling, female athletes have gained notoriety for invading male professional athletic turf. Former college star and 1976 Olympian Nancy Lieberman made headlines in 1986 when she became the first woman to play men's pro basketball for the U.S. Basketball League, and Lynette Woodard became the first female Harlem Globetrotter the same year. Female sports figures have emerged as celebrities and role models, attracting male as well as female fans, a fact that advertisers have seized upon by offering more product endorsements to female stars. Through the opportunities afforded by Title IX, the image of the female athlete has emerged as a challenge to previous ideals of women. Studies have shown that women who participate in sports have enhanced self-esteem, discipline, and a team orientation, qualities that are likely to translate into success in the corporate world beyond the playing field. Title IX has helped ensure that the female athlete is no longer an exception or a freak of nature but a normal aspect of achievement by women when given the opportunity to compete in areas once viewed as exclusive male sanctuaries.

Despite the benefits and improvements created by Title IX, significant challenges still exist for American women in sports. In 2016, a sex abuse scandal rocked the world of USA Gymnastics when gymnasts came forward to allege systematic sexual abuse while they were training and competing. The allegation stated that more than 368 female athletes, primarily minors, had been sexually abused over the past two decades "by gym owners, coaches, and staff working for gymnastic programs across the country." Longtime USAG national team doctor Larry Nassar was convicted as a serial child molester for sexual abuse under the pretense of providing medical treatment for at least fourteen years. The victims included

U.S. Women's Soccer Team players (left to right) Carli Lloyd, Megan Rapinoe (holding trophy), and Jill Ellis enjoy a ticker tape parade with Mayor Bill de Blasio after winning the championship in 2015 (they repeated the win in 2019). Four years later, Rapinoe and her teammates filed a gender discrimination lawsuit against the U.S. Soccer Federation over pay and working conditions.

USAG national team members such as Aly Raisman, Gabby Douglas, and Simone Biles. In 2018, the U.S. Olympic Committee began the process to decertify USAG as the national governing body for gymnastics in the United States, and USAG filed for bankruptcy.

In March 2019, twenty-eight members of the world champion U.S. women's soccer team filed a gender discrimination lawsuit against the U.S. Soccer Federation over pay equity and working conditions. The players alleged "institutionalized gender discrimination" affecting how much they are paid, where they play and how often, how they train, the medical treatment and coaching they receive, and even how they travel to matches. As star player Megan Rapinoe stated, "We very much believe it is our responsibility not only for our team and for future U.S. players but for players around the world—and frankly women all around the world—to feel like they have an ally in standing up for themselves, and fighting for what they believe in, and fighting for what they deserve and for what they feel like they have earned." Subsequent reports following the lawsuit have shown that the issue of pay inequality in sports is not limited to

soccer but extends to all sports in which women are paid less in salary and prize money.

Despite the fact that the playing field for men and women has been progressively leveled to allow greater access and participation by women and gender assumptions have been transformed to allow that female athletes are role models rather than oddities, it is clear that serious challenges remain in sports, as in the wider society for women, to succeed unrestricted by gender inequality and discrimination.

BIOGRAPHIES

Tenley Albright (1935–)
Figure Skater

Former figure skater Tenley Emma Albright was born in Newton, Massachusetts. At the age of eleven, she was stricken by polio and took up skating as a way to regain muscle strength.

She won her first important competition, the Eastern Juvenile Skating Championship, four months after her polio attack. National titles soon followed: U.S. Ladies Novice championship at the age of thirteen and the U.S. Ladies Junior championship the following year. She was chosen to skate at the 1952 Olympic Winter Games in Oslo, Norway, where she received a silver medal. Later that year, she won her first U.S. Championship.

In 1953, she became the first U.S. woman to win the World Championship and went on to win three more U.S. Championships (1954, 1955, and 1956). Albright reached the height of her success at the 1956 Winter Olympics in Cortina d'Ampezzo, Italy, where she became the first American female skater to win an Olympic gold medal.

Albright retired from competitive skating after the Olympics to attend Harvard Medical School, one of five women in a class of 135. She completed her degree in 1961 and became a surgeon and leader in blood plasma research. She practiced for twenty-three years, continuing as a faculty member and lecturer at Harvard Medical School and director of MIT's Collaborative Initiatives foundation. She has received many honorary degrees, serves on several boards of directors, and has continued her association with skating, serving as the first woman to serve as an officer of the U.S. Olympic Committee.

Simone Biles (1997–)

Gymnast

 Born in Columbus, Ohio, celebrated Olympic gymnast Simone Arianne Biles began training in gymnastics from the age of six and was working with a personal coach by the time she was eight. Her first national competitions were in 2012. The same year, at the U.S. National Championships, she finished third in the all-around competition and first on the vault. As a result, she was selected for the U.S. Junior National Team. She was soon competing at the senior level with outstanding performances in national and international events, leading up to the 2016 Summer Olympics in Rio de Janeiro, Brazil.

Biles and the rest of the U.S. team dominated women's gymnastics in the 2016 Olympics. Biles and the team won a gold medal in the team event (combined scores for vault, bars, beam, and floor). They named themselves "The Final Five" in honor of the retirement of team coordinator Marta Karolyi and the reduction of future Olympic gymnastics teams to four members. Biles went on to win gold in the all-around, the vault, and the floor exercises. Her four gold medals set an American record for most gold medals in women's gymnastics at a single game. To honor her accomplishments, she was selected as the Team USA flag bearer for the closing ceremonies.

After the Olympics, Biles took time off from training and wrote her autobiography *Courage to Soar: A Body in Motion, A Life in Balance* (cowritten with Michelle Burford). She returned to the national team in March 2018 and continued her superlative performances. At the U.S. Classic, she won the all-around title as well as gold medals for the floor exercises and the balance beam; at the 2018 National Championships, she placed first in every event; and at the 2018 World Championships, she led the U.S. team to a gold medal and went on to win her fourth all-around individual gold medal, a new record. Biles currently owns nineteen Olympic and World Championship medals.

Her accomplishments have gained her many awards such as Sportswoman of the Year by the Women's Sports Foundation and ESPY Award for Best Female Athlete as well as sponsors and endorsements. In January 2018, Biles stated that she was one of the many young women who had been molested by former USA Gymnastics team doctor Larry Nassar. Later that year, Biles and other survivors of the sexual abuse were awarded the Arthur Ashe Courage Award.

Bonnie Blair (1964–)

Speed Skater

 Speed skater Bonnie Kathleen Blair was born in Cornwall, New York, and raised in Champaign, Illinois, the youngest of six in a skating family. Blair skated from the age of two and at fifteen

earned a spot on the U.S. national speed skating team. Her first Olympic competition was at the 1984 Winter Olympics in Sarajevo. In the years that followed, she won world championships in short-track skating, raising hopes for the U.S. gold at the 1988 Winter Olympics in Calgary. Blair delivered the gold medal in the 500-meter competition, setting a new world record. She won bronze in the 1,000-meter competition.

She continued as a world leader in the short-track, leading up to the 1992 Winter Olympics in Albertville, where she won gold in both the 500 meters and the 1,000 meters, becoming the most decorated U.S. woman in the Winter Olympics. Because of a change in Olympics rules, the next Winter Olympics were held two years later, this time in Lillehammer. Once again, she won gold in both the 500 meters and the 1,000 meters. The Associated Press named her Female Athlete of the Year.

Blair's record of five gold medals and one bronze currently stands as the most Winter Olympic medals won by any U.S. athlete. She continued to compete after the Olympics, breaking her own world record twice before she retired in 1995. After retiring, she began working as a motivational speaker and founded the Bonnie Blair Charitable Fund.

Maureen Connolly (1934–1969)

Tennis Player

Born in San Diego, California, tennis champion Maureen Catherine Connolly learned and practiced her sport on the public courts in San Diego. By the age of fourteen, she had won fifty-six consecutive matches and in 1949 became the youngest girl ever to win the national junior championship. A sportswriter in San Diego gave her the nickname "Little Mo" because the power of her forehand and backhand matched the firepower of the USS *Missouri*, known as "Big Mo."

In 1951, at sixteen, she won her first singles title at the U.S. Championships (later the U.S.

Open) and became, at that time, the youngest winner of the top U.S. tournament. In 1953, she became the first woman to win a Grand Slam, winning all four major tournaments in a single year. She won the last nine Grand Slam singles tournaments she played, including fifty consecutive singles matches. She was named Female Athlete of the Year by the Associated Press for three straight years from 1951 through 1953. In 1954, two weeks after winning her third straight Wimbledon title, a horseback riding accident seriously injured her right leg and ended her competitive tennis career at the age of nineteen.

Connolly remained involved with tennis as a coach and journalist and wrote her autobiography, *Forehand Drive*. She cofounded the Maureen Connolly Brinker Tennis Foundation, which hosts tournaments and provides the opportunity for young people to play. She died of cancer in Dallas, Texas, at the age of thirty-four.

Donna de Varona (1947–)

Swimmer

Olympic swimmer Donna de Varona was born in San Diego, California, and was raised by a supportive, athletic family. She was unable to play Little League Baseball because she was a girl, which she later said motivated her to fight for gender equality in sports. De Varona began swimming instead and soon became a young star. She qualified for the U.S. Olympic swimming team in 1960 at the age of thirteen and was the youngest competitor at the Summer Olympics in Rome. Four years later, at the Summer Olympics in Tokyo, she won two gold medals, which she added to her eighteen world swimming records. In 1964 at the age of seventeen, she was voted Most Outstanding Woman Athlete in the World by both the Associated Press (AP) and the United Press International (UPI) and appeared on the covers of *Sports Illustrated*, *Look*, and *Life* magazines.

After the Olympics, she enrolled at the University of California–Los Angeles (UCLA). Since UCLA had no women's athletics department and she could not compete for a college team, de Varona retired from competitive swimming and in 1965 became one of the first female sportscasters in the United States. Her broadcasting career has been a long one filled with awards, but she also struggles as a woman in the male-dominated world of sportscasting. In 1976, de Varona left ABC after what she called "discriminatory barriers" and was soon working for NBC. She returned to ABC in 1983 and continued her successful career, but in April 1998, her contract was not renewed. She filed a lawsuit, charging age and gender discrimination under federal law. The suit was settled out of court in 2002, and de Varona rejoined ABC Sports.

De Varona has been a longtime advocate for women in sports. In the 1970s, she joined Billie Jean King in establishing the Women's Sports Foundation and served as its first president. She worked with the U.S. government to promote and safeguard Title IX of the Equal Education Amendments Act and in 2007 produced an award-winning documentary in observation of the thirty-fifth anniversary of its passage. De Varona currently serves on the executive board of Special Olympics International and is a member of the International Olympic Committee's Women in Sport Commission.

Gabby Douglas (1995–)

Gymnast

Born Gabrielle Christina Victoria Douglas in Newport News, Virginia, gymnast Gabby Douglas won her first competition, the Level 4 all-around gymnastics title at the 2004 Virginia State Championships, at the age of eight. In 2010, she moved to Iowa to train under a private coach and won medals in several senior tournaments.

At the 2012 U.S. National Championships, Douglas won the gold medal in uneven bars, silver in the all-around, and bronze in floor. At the 2012 Olympic Trials, she placed first in the all-around rankings and secured a spot on the U.S. women's gymnastics team, and at the Summer Olympics in

London, Douglas and her teammates ("The Fierce Five") won the team event gold medal. Douglas won gold for the individual all-around, becoming the first African American woman to win the event. Named Female Athlete of the Year by the Associated Press, Douglas continued to score well in the years leading up to the 2016 Summer Olympics in Rio de Janeiro. There, she and her teammates won their second consecutive gold medal in the team event. They named themselves "The Final Five" in honor of the retirement of team coordinator Marta Karolyi and the reduction of future Olympic gymnastics teams to four members.

Her accomplishments in 2012 led to a *Time* magazine cover, her picture on a Wheaties box, and various other media appearances. That year, she also released her autobiography *Grace, Gold, and Glory: My Leap of Faith*, which was adapted for a Lifetime film, *The Gabby Douglas Story*. She and her family had their own reality television series, *Douglas Family Gold*.

Gertrude "Trudy" Ederle (1905–2003)

Swimmer

Swimmer Gertrude Ederle was born in New York City, the daughter of German immigrants. After establishing herself as a championship swimmer, she made history on August 26, 1926, as the first woman to swim the English Channel. Her record of 14 hours, 31 minutes for the 35-mile (56-kilometer) distance held for thirty-five years.

Ederle was trained as a competitive swimmer at the Women's Swimming Association (WSA) in New York, a pioneering organization led by Charlotte "Eppy" Epstein, who led the effort to have women's swimming endorsed as a sport by the Amateur Athletic Union (AAU). Ederle joined the WSA at the age of twelve and soon set her first world record in the 880-yard freestyle. She went on to hold twenty-nine U.S. national and world records from 1921 until 1925. At the 1924 Paris Olympics, she gained a gold medal as a member of the U.S. 4

x 100-meter freestyle relay team but won only bronze medals in two other individual events, the biggest disappointment of her career.

She turned professional in 1925 and set a record swim of 22 miles (35 kilometers) from Manhattan to Sandy Hook, New Jersey, beating the record set by a man and preparing for the big prize of swimming the English Channel. The WSA sponsored her first attempt on August 18, 1925. She was disqualified when her trainer ordered another swimmer to retrieve her, fearing she was drowning. Ederle protested, and some speculated that her trainer did not want her to succeed.

With a new trainer, William Burgess, she planned her second attempt. The 1920s was a time when celebrity culture became big business, and successful accomplishments gained worldwide acclaim. Ederle obtained contracts from both the *New York Daily News* and the *Chicago Tribune*, which gave her money for her expenses and gave the newspapers exclusive rights to her story. She was not alone in her plans—another swimmer, Lillian Cannon, was training in France at the same time and was sponsored by the *Baltimore Post*, which played up a rivalry between the two swimmers. Other women were also training and attempting the swim, but none had succeeded when Ederle began her swim at 7:05 A.M. on August 6, 1926, off the coast of Cap Gris Nez, France.

The weather conditions grew worse as she swam with high winds, waves, and a squall. "After eight hours I knew I would either swim it or drown," she said later, according to the *Daily News*. After 12 hours, her trainer, following her in a boat, was worried for her safety and called, "Trudy, you must come out!" "What for?" she replied and kept going. At 9:40 P.M., after swimming 14 hours and 34 minutes, she walked up the beach at Kingsdown, England, to a blaze of lights and cheering crowds. She had beaten the men's record by nearly 2 hours, despite extra miles due to the currents—an amazing feat for any athlete.

She arrived back in the United States, where she was greeted with a ticker tape parade attended by two million people. She made money through personal appearances, played herself in a Hollywood movie, and toured the vaudeville circuit. Because a childhood bout with measles had caused her to lose partial hearing, she spent years teaching swimming to hearing-impaired children. She died in Wyckoff, New Jersey, at the age of ninety-eight.

Chris Evert (1954–)

Tennis Player

One of the most celebrated tennis players in history, Christine Marie Evert was born on December 21, 1954, in Fort Lauderdale, Florida. Her father, Jimmy, was a professional tennis coach, and tennis was a way of life in her family. In 1970, she won the national sixteen-and-under championship and later that year defeated the world number-one player, Margaret Court, at a tournament in North Carolina.

Evert played in her first Grand Slam tournament, the U.S. Open, in 1971, but it was not until 1974 that her extraordinary career really took off. That year, she won the French Open and Wimbledon championships as part of a then-record fifty-five consecutive wins. She ended the year with a 100–7 match record and her first number-one singles ranking, a ranking she gained in six of the next seven years (1975–1978, 1980, and 1981), the current record. She won at least one Grand Slam singles title a year for thirteen consecutive years from 1974 through 1986, which is also the current record. During Evert's career, she won eighteen Grand Slam singles, 154 singles titles, and thirty-two doubles titles. Her career winning percentage in singles matches is 89.97 percent (1309–146). She retired from the professional tour in 1989.

Evert remains active in the tennis world. She has served as a commentator for NBC Sports, the BBC, and ESPN. She and her family own the Evert Tennis Academy, and she is the publisher of *Tennis* magazine. In 2015, she launched a line of tennis and active apparel. In 1989, she founded Chris Evert Charities, which focuses primarily on drug and family problems, and she serves on the boards of other charitable foundations.

Peggy Fleming (1948–)

Figure Skater

Born in San Jose, California, figure skater Peggy Fleming began to compete on the junior circuit, winning her first gold medal in the Pacific Coast Juvenile Championship in 1960. She continued a string of successes and in 1964 won her first U.S. Championship as a senior-level skater, which qualified her to represent the United States at the 1964 Winter Olympic Games in Innsbruck. She did not receive a medal at the Olympics but later that year won a bronze medal at her first World Championship.

A stunning series of gold-medal wins followed: in the U.S. Championships in 1965 through 1968; World Championships in 1966 through 1968; and women's singles gold at the 1968 Winter Olympic Games in Grenoble. Although Fleming's performance at the Olympics was deemed not her best, her characteristic grace and skill dominated the competition. She was the only U.S. gold winner at the 1968 Olympics, which added to the attention and acclaim she received in the United States. She turned professional at the end of the 1968 season.

Fleming appeared in her first TV special in 1968 and went on to star in five NBC specials of her own. She regularly skated with the Ice Capades, the Ice Follies, and the Holiday on Ice programs. In 1980, Fleming began her career as a skating analyst on the ABC network. A breast cancer survivor, she became a spokesperson for women's health issues and devotes time to other philanthropic causes.

Althea Gibson (1927–2003)

Tennis Player

A pioneering African American tennis player, Althea Neale Gibson was born in Silver, South Carolina. In 1930, her parents moved to Harlem, where they lived on a block that was barricaded during the day so that neighborhood children could play organized sports. Gibson learned paddle tennis there, and by 1939, at the age of twelve, she was the New York City women's paddle tennis champion. Members of the Cosmopolitan Tennis Club noticed her athletic prowess and paid for a junior membership as well as lessons.

Many of the national tennis tournaments were closed to African Americans, so Gibson began to compete in tournaments sponsored by the American Tennis Association (ATA), an organization founded in 1916 to promote tennis for African Americans. Gibson's first tournament win was the 1941 ATA New York State Championship when she was fourteen. She was the national junior champion in 1944 and 1945 and national singles champion for ten straight years (1947–1956). During this time, Gibson attended Florida A&M University and graduated in 1953.

Despite Gibson's outstanding level of play, she was barred from entering the U.S. National Championships (now the U.S. Open). Although U.S. Tennis Association rules prohibited racial or ethnic discrimination, players gained points at official tournaments, most of which were held at white-only clubs. In 1950, in response to lobbying by ATA officials and prominent tennis stars, Gibson became the first black player to receive an invitation to the U.S. Nationals, where she played in her first tournament on her twenty-third birthday. Although she did not win a title, she gained attention for her talent and skill as well as for her barrier-breaking participation. She went on to win other tournaments and in 1952 was ranked seventh nationally by the USTA.

As an amateur, she made no money from competitions, and, after graduation, she began teaching physical education at Lincoln University in Jefferson City, Missouri. Her tennis career was reinvigorated when the U.S. State Department invited her on a six-week "goodwill tour" of Asia, where an integrated group of tennis stars played exhibition matches. She remained abroad after the tour, winning sixteen of the eighteen tournaments in Europe and Asia. In 1956, she became the first African American to win a Grand Slam tournament, the French Championships singles event.

Throughout 1957 and 1958, Gibson dominated women's tennis. In 1957, she won the Wimbledon and U.S. National singles titles, the Wimbledon and Australian doubles titles, and the U.S. mixed doubles title. In 1958, she successfully defended her Wimbledon and U.S. National singles titles and won her third straight Wimbledon doubles championship. She was the number-one-ranked woman in the world and in the United States in both 1957 and 1958 and was named Female Athlete of the Year by the Associated Press in both years as well. She became the first black woman to appear on the covers of *Sports Illustrated* and *Time*. Gibson ended her amateur career in 1958 with five Grand Slam singles titles, five Grand Slam doubles titles, and one mixed doubles title.

After relinquishing her amateur status, Gibson faced the need to make a living. No professional tours existed for women, which meant that her opportunities were limited to promotional events such as playing before Harlem Globetrotters games. She attempted a singing career and recorded an album but was not particularly successful. She appeared in the 1959 film *The Horse Soldiers* and worked as a sports commentator and advertising spokesperson. In 1960, she published her first memoir, *I Always Wanted to Be Somebody* (written with Ed Fitzgerald). Racial barriers, however, prevented her from obtaining the financial endorsements of other tennis stars.

In 1964, at the age of thirty-seven, Gibson broke another barrier as the first African American woman to join the Ladies Professional Golf Association (LPGA) tour. Although she achieved some success, the financial rewards were low, and she retired from the golf circuit in 1978.

In 1968, Gibson published her second memoir, *So Much to Live For* (with Richard Curtis). In the early 1970s, she began working in sports administration for both local and state governments in New Jersey. She also devoted time to clinics and coaching, particularly for the underprivileged. Her later years were marked by health problems, including a stroke and serious heart problems. She died in 2003.

Janet Guthrie (1938–)
Race Car Driver

A pioneering woman in the world of race car driving, Janet Guthrie was born in Iowa City, Iowa. Her father was a pilot, and Guthrie earned a pilot's license at the age of seventeen.

By the time she graduated from the University of Michigan in 1960 with a bachelor's degree in physics, she had worked as a commercial pilot and a flight instructor. After graduation, she worked as an aerospace engineer and began to modify cars for racing. Her first car was a modified Jaguar XK120.

The excitement of competition led her to join the professional race car circuit. In 1976, she began to make history as the first woman to compete in a NASCAR Cup Series race (then referred to as the Winston Cup Series). In 1977, she again made history as the first woman to qualify and compete in both the Daytona 500 and the Indianapolis 500, leading to a change in the traditional words that start the Indianapolis 500: "In company with the first lady ever to qualify at Indianapolis—gentlemen, start your engines." In 1979, she gained a career-high fifth-place finish in the Milwaukee 200, her last major race.

A consistent top-ten winner who gradually gained respect from the established male stars of the sport, she was unable to obtain funding through corporate sponsorship largely because of her gender and was forced into retirement. However, Guthrie continues to actively give her support to the sport and to young drivers.

Dorothy Hamill (1956–)
Figure Skater

Olympic figure skater Dorothy Stuart Hamill was born in Chicago, Illinois, and grew up in Greenwich, Connecticut. Hamill's first national ice skating competition was in 1969 at the U.S. Championships, where she won the novice women's title. She continued to compete both in the United States and internationally and won the U.S. championships in 1974, 1975, and 1976 and the world championship in 1976.

Hopes for a U.S. gold medal were high when Hamill entered the 1976 Winter Olympics in Innsbruck. She finished second in the individual figures, then first in the short program, and won the gold medal with a flawless long program. Viewers around the world became familiar with the move she invented, a combination of a camel and a sit-spin nicknamed "The Hamill Camel." Called "America's Sweetheart," Hamill's skating skills and her signature wedge hairstyle started a fashion trend and made her a media star.

After the Olympics, she turned professional and became a star in the Ice Capades, which she later owned and managed. She won a Daytime Emmy Award for her starring role in the 1983 figure-skating production of *Romeo & Juliet on Ice*. She also competed professionally, winning four consecutive professional world titles from 1984 to 1987. She published two books: *On and Off the Ice* (1983) and *A Skating Life: My Story* (2007). She also has been a passionate supporter of several breast cancer organizations after having been successfully treated for the disease.

Mia Hamm (1972–)

Soccer Player

Soccer star Mia Hamm was born Mariel Margaret Hamm in Selma, Alabama. She first played soccer in Florence, Italy, where her father was stationed with the U.S. Air Force, and she joined her first soccer team at five in Wichita Falls, Texas. A natural athlete, she excelled on the boys' football team in junior high school and starred on her high school soccer team. From 1989 to 1994, Hamm attended the University of North Carolina–Chapel Hill and led the women's team to four NCAA Division I Women's Soccer Championships. She was named the Atlantic Coast Conference (ACC) Player of the Year for three consecutive years.

Hamm's college stardom brought her to the U.S. women's national team in 1987. The youngest player ever to play on the team, Hamm continued to play with them until 2004. She and the team competed in the first four FIFA Women's World Cup tournaments in 1991, 1995, 1999, and 2003. Hamm led the U.S. team in the first three Olympic Games to

include women's soccer: 1996 in Atlanta (gold), 2000 in Sydney (silver), and 2004 in Athens (gold).

In 2001, Hamm was a founding player in the first professional women's soccer league in the United States, the Women's United Soccer Association (WUSA), and played for the Washington Freedom from 2001 to 2003. She and the Freedom won the Founders Cup in 2003. Hamm retired from competitive soccer in 2004 after the 2004 Summer Olympic Games. At the time, she had a record 158 international goals, which she held until 2013, when her record was broken by fellow American star Abby Wambach. Hamm's outstanding accomplishments at a time when women's soccer first reached the highest international level made her the sport's first superstar.

Since retirement, Hamm has been involved in both charitable and business ventures. In 1999, she founded the Mia Hamm Foundation following the death of her adopted brother Garrett in 1997 from complications of aplastic anemia, a rare blood disease. The foundation is dedicated to promoting awareness of and raising funds for families in need of a bone marrow or cord blood transplant. It also focuses on creating opportunities to empower women through sport. She described the importance of soccer in her life in her book *Go for the Goal: A Champion's Guide to Winning in Soccer and Life*. She has also been involved in many product endorsements, commercials, and television productions and is a co-owner of the Los Angeles Football Club of Major League Soccer.

Florence Griffith Joyner (1959–1998)

Track and Field Athlete

Born Florence Delorez Griffith in Los Angeles, California, Florence Griffith Joyner was a track and field star in elementary school and high school. She attended the University of California–Los Angeles (UCLA), where she qualified for the 1980 Summer Olympics in Moscow; however, the United States boycotted those games to protest the Soviet invasion of Afghanistan. In 1983, she again qualified for the Olympics, and at the 1984 Summer Olympics in Los Angeles, she won a silver medal for the 200-meter event.

Griffith Joyner raced only part time after the 1984 Olympics. In 1987, she married Al Joyner, also an Olympic track and field medal winner (and brother of track and field star Jackie Joyner-Kersee). In the same year, Griffith Joyner qualified for the Olympic Trials with strong showings in both the 100 meters and the 200 meters. At the Olympic Trials, she set a world record in the 100 meters of 10.49 seconds, a record that still stands. She also set a U.S. record for the 200 meters. "Flo-Jo," as she became known, continued her spectacular performances at the 1988 Summer Olympics in Seoul. She won gold for the 100 meters and gold for the 200 meters, setting a world-record time of 21.34 seconds, another record that still stands. She also helped the U.S. 4 x 100 relay team win a gold medal and the 4 x 200 team win silver.

Griffith Joyner's accomplishments at the 1988 Olympics resulted in many endorsement deals. She had always been interested in fashion, gaining attention for her unique, self-designed outfits when competing (as well as for her long, decorated fingernails), and she began a fashion design business. She also established a foundation to help underprivileged children. She announced her retirement from racing in 1989. She attempted a comeback in 1996, aiming to set the record for the 400 meters, but injuries prevented her from competing for that goal. She died at her home in Mission Viejo, California, at the age of thirty-eight after suffering a severe epileptic seizure.

Jackie Joyner-Kersee (1962–)
Track and Field Athlete

Track and field athlete Jackie Joyner-Kersee was born Jacqueline Joyner on March 3, 1962, in East St. Louis, Illinois. She was a high school star and qualified for the 1980 Olympic Trials while still in high school. At the University of California–Los Angeles (UCLA), she starred in both track and field and women's basketball from 1980

until her graduation in 1985. In 1986, she married her coach Bob Kersee (her brother, Al Joyner, was married to the late track star Florence Griffith Joyner).

From 1987 to 1998, Joyner-Kersee won gold medals for both the heptathlon (seven different track and field events) and the long jump in the Olympics, the World Championships, and the Goodwill Games. Her first Olympic medal was in the 1984 Summer Olympics in Los Angeles, where she won silver in the heptathlon. In the 1988 Summer Olympics in Seoul, she won a gold medal in the heptathlon, where she set the world record of 7,291 points, which still stands. She also won gold in the long jump. Four years later, at the Summer Olympics in Barcelona, she again won a gold medal in the heptathlon as well as a bronze medal in the long jump. Finally, in the 1996 Summer Olympics in Atlanta, she won her last medal, a bronze in the long jump. She had a brief career in professional basketball, won the heptathlon at the 1998 Goodwill Games, and then retired. Her accomplishments and long career caused *Sports Illustrated for Women* to name her as the greatest female athlete of the twentieth century.

In 1988, Joyner-Kersee established a foundation to provide opportunities for underprivileged youths in her hometown of East St. Louis, Illinois. In 2007, she joined other athletes to found an organization called Athletes for Hope, which helps professional athletes become involved in charitable causes.

Billie Jean King (1943–)
Tennis Player

One of the most admired and accomplished players in American tennis, Billie Jean King can be considered the single most influential figure in the successful fight for recognition and equal treatment of female athletes.

Billie Jean Moffit was born and raised in Long Beach, California. Both of her parents were athletes, and, as a child, she played football and softball. She took up tennis at the age of eleven and, six months after taking her first lesson, played in her first tournament. Even as a youngster, she was noted for her aggressive, athletic play that seemed to clash with the then-dominant image of the ladylike tennis player.

King won her first tournament at fifteen, when she captured the southern California girls fifteen-and-under championship and advanced to the quarterfinals of the national championship. In 1960, she reached the finals of the national championship but lost to seventeen-year-old Karen Hantze. A year later, she teamed up with Hantze to win the women's doubles championship at Wimbledon. They became the youngest pair ever to win the prestigious event.

In 1965, Billie Jean married Larry King, who became her agent, business manager, lawyer, and adviser. The following year, she won her first Wimbledon singles championship. Over the next ten years, King won a record twenty Wimbledon titles—six singles, ten doubles, and four mixed doubles. During that time, she also won four U.S. Open singles titles. In 1971, she joined the newly formed Virginia Slim tour and became the first female athlete to win $100,000 in a single year.

In 1973, King accepted a challenge to play a $100,000 winner-takes-all match against long-retired former champion Bobby Riggs, who had boasted that a female player could never beat a man, even with a great disparity in age. Earlier that year, the fifty-five-year-old Riggs had beaten thirty-one-year-old Margaret Smith Court in a $10,000 match. This time, in front of thirty thousand people at Houston's Astrodome and another forty million TV viewers, King crushed him in three straight sets.

King was a founder and president of the Women's Tennis Association, a union for players, a founder of tennis and softball leagues for professional female athletes, and a publisher of *women-Sports*, a magazine that reported on the progress of female athletes in a variety of sports. In 1976, she helped to create World Team Tennis, a league of male and female tennis professionals. She was also the first woman to coach male pro tennis players.

King was inducted into the Women's Sports Foundation Hall of Fame in 1980 and the International Tennis Hall of Fame in 1987.

Julie Krone (1963–)
Jockey

Thoroughbred jockey Julie Krone was born in Benton Harbor, Michigan, where she was riding at the age of two under the tutelage of her mother Judi, a former Michigan state equestrian champion. Although Krone won competitions as a show horse rider, her ambition was to become a professional thoroughbred jockey.

She made her debut as a professional jockey in 1981, winning the second race she competed in. She went on to a successful career, becoming the first woman to win many championships, including the Triple Crown Belmont Stakes in 1993. Later that same year, she suffered serious injuries in a fall, but she worked to regain her health and continued riding. She retired in 1999 and spent several years as a TV broadcaster, but in 2002, she returned to active racing. She succeeded in winning a number of races, including the 2003 Breeders' Cup Juvenile Fillies race. However, two sets of serious injuries led to her retirement again in 2004.

Krone is the recipient of many awards, including ESPN's Professional Female Athlete of the Year (1993) and the Women's Sports Foundation's Wilma Rudolph Courage Award (2004). In 2000, she became the first woman to be inducted into the National Museum of Racing's Hall of Fame. At her acceptance speech, she said: "I want this to be a lesson to all kids everywhere. If the stable gate is closed, climb the fence." Her autobiography, *Riding for My Life*, was published in 1995. She continues to maintain a close relationship with the thoroughbred racing business and shares her love of horses through motivational speeches, clinics, and private tutoring.

Michelle Kwan (1980–)
Figure Skater

Olympic figure skater Michelle Wingshan Kwan was born in Torrance, California. She followed her older brother and sister onto the ice and began to compete in junior events at the age of eleven. In 1994, she won the World Junior Championships. She continued to compete but did not reach her artistic prime until 1996, when she won both the U.S. Championships and the World Championships. In 1998, she won the U.S. Championships with particularly outstanding performances in both the short program and free skate.

Kwan's first Olympic appearance was at the 1998 Olympic Games in Nagano, where she won silver for the women's singles. She also competed in the 2002 Olympics, where she won bronze. She was more successful in the World Championships and the U.S. Championships. She was a five-time world champion (1996, 1998, 2000, 2001, and 2003) and a nine-time U.S. champion (1996 and 1998–2005). Due to injuries and a decision to continue her education in international studies, she gradually withdrew from competitive skating.

Kwan has worked as a broadcast analyst, starred in TV specials, and received major endorsement deals. In addition, she has worked with the U.S. State Department as a public diplomacy envoy both internationally and in the United States with the President's Council on Physical Fitness and Sports. She currently serves on the board of the Special Olympics.

Nancy Lopez (1957–)
Golfer

Championship golfer Nancy Lopez was born in Torrance, California, and raised in Roswell, New Mexico. With her father's coaching and her family's support, she soon became a nationally ranked amateur golfer, winning the New Mexico Women's Amateur at the age of twelve and leading her otherwise all-male high school golf team to a state championship. She attended the University of Tulsa on a golf scholarship and, as a freshman, won the Association of Intercollegiate Athletics for Women (AIAW) national intercollegiate golf championship.

She burst onto the LPGA Tour in 1978, when she won a record five consecutive tournaments and a total of nine for the season. She was named both LPGA Rookie of the Year and LPGA Player of the Year along with winning the Vare Trophy for lowest scoring average. Her sensational play that year, along with her fan-friendly personality, brought media attention to the LPGA and the world of women's golf. During her long career, she took time out to raise three daughters, but by the time she retired after the 2002 season, she had forty-eight tournament wins, three major championships, and $5 million in earnings.

Lopez currently resides in Florida, where she hosts an annual golf tournament to benefit the charity AIM (Adventures in Movement), an organization that helps mentally challenged, visually impaired, hearing impaired, physically handicapped, and other children and adults with special needs. She has hosted the tournament since 1981 and also serves as its national ambassador.

Cheryl Miller (1964–)
Basketball Player

A basketball player and coach, Cheryl Miller was born in Riverside, California. She was a high school basketball star and was named Street & Smith's National High School Player of the Year in both 1981 and 1982. She set California records for points scored in a single season (1,156) and points scored in a high school career (3,405).

Miller attended the University of Southern California (USC), where she led the Trojans to NCAA titles in 1983 and 1984 and was named NCAA Tournament MVP in both years. Miller scored 3,018 career points (tenth of all time in NCAA history) and was named Naismith College Player of the Year three times. In her senior season, *Sports Illustrated* named her the best player in college basketball, male or female.

While in college, Miller played for the USA National team and led the U.S. team to their first gold medal at the 1984 Summer Olympics in Los Angeles. After graduating from USC in 1986, she was drafted by several professional basketball leagues. However, knee injuries prevented her from continuing her playing career. She then began coaching at her alma mater, USC, as well as beginning a new career as a television sportscaster first with ABC Sports and then for seventeen years with TNT Sports.

In 1997, Miller returned to the court as head coach and general manager of the Phoenix Mercury in the newly formed Women's National Basketball Association (WNBA). She left that position in 2000 and resumed her broadcasting career. In 2014, she became coach of Langston University in Oklahoma, leaving that team in 2016 to coach the women's basketball team at California State University–Los Angeles.

Helen Wills Moody (1905–1998)

Tennis Player

The winner of thirty-one Grand Slam tennis tournaments during her career, Helen Wills Moody was born Helen Newington Wills in Centerville, California. She began playing tennis when she was eight years old and started to seriously practice the sport in 1919 after her family moved to Berkeley and she joined the Berkeley Tennis Club.

In September 1921, Wills won the singles and doubles titles at the California State Championships. She won her first women's national title at the age of seventeen in 1923, making her the youngest champion at that time. At the 1924 Summer Olympics in Paris, she won two gold medals, one each for singles and doubles. With her powerful serves and backhands, she dominated women's tennis; from 1926 until 1932, she did not lose a set in singles play. In 1927, she won her first Grand Slam event at Wimbledon and attained her first world number-one position. She held that position for a total of nine years, from 1927 to 1933, and again in 1935 and 1938. Wills's thirty-one Grand Slam tournament titles in singles, women's doubles, and mixed doubles included nineteen singles titles. In 1938, she won her last Wimbledon title and retired from competitive tennis.

Wills was known as a shy, introverted person and a very serious player on the court, which earned her the nickname "Little Miss Poker Face." A 1925 graduate of the University of California–Berkeley with a degree in fine arts, Wills enjoyed writing, drawing, and painting. She drew all the illustrations in her coaching book *Tennis*, published in 1928, and also wrote her autobiography, coauthored a mystery, and wrote poetry. She remained an avid tennis player into her eighties. Wills died at the age of ninety-two in Carmel, California. In her will, she bequeathed $10 million to the University of California–Berkeley to fund the establishment of what became the Helen Wills Neuroscience Institute.

Martina Navratilova (1956–)

Tennis Player

One of the greatest tennis champions ever, Martina Navratilova was born Martina Šubertová in Prague, Czechoslovakia, where she was given the last name of her stepfather after her parents divorced and her mother remarried. Both her mother and grandmother were accomplished tennis players, and Navratilova began playing at an early age. She won her first professional singles title in Orlando, Florida, at the age of seventeen. In 1975 at eighteen, she defected to the United States and was granted political asylum. She became a U.S. citizen in 1981.

Navratilova won her first Grand Slam singles title at Wimbledon in 1978 and captured the world number-one singles ranking for the first time, a ranking that she attained for a total of 332 weeks. She was the world number-one women's player in doubles for 237 weeks. Navratilova also holds records for the most singles titles (167) and the most doubles titles (177) in the U.S. Open era. In 2005, *Tennis* magazine selected her as the greatest female tennis player for the years 1975 through 2005. She is arguably the greatest female tennis player of all time.

Navratilova's career has consisted of two parts: her singles career and her doubles career. She completely dominated women's singles tennis in the late 1970s and 1980s, particularly in singles play. In 1982, she won ninety of ninety-three matches and the next year won eighty-six of eighty-seven matches. In 1983, she won the Wimbledon title and the following six Grand Slam women's singles titles. In the 1987 U.S. Open, she won the women's singles, women's doubles, and mixed doubles to become the first triple-crown champion since 1970, a record that still stands. She retired from singles play in 1994.

In 2000, Navratilova returned to the tour and played mostly doubles events and occasional singles. She continued her successes, winning twelve women's doubles titles—seven in 2003 alone—with a half dozen different partners. She won mixed doubles titles at both the Australian Open and Wimbledon in 2003, enabling her to share Billie Jean King's record of twenty combined Wimbledon titles. In 2006, she ended her career with a mixed doubles title at the U.S. Open, her 177th doubles title, at the age of forty-nine the oldest ever major champion.

In addition to her exceptional career on the tennis court, Navratilova has served as a sports broadcaster providing commentary on the Tennis Channel and the BBC. She has written an autobiography, coauthored mysteries, and published *Shape Your Self*, a guide to personal fitness and healthy living. Since coming out in 1981 as one of the first openly gay sports figures, Navratilova has been an inspiring advocate for LGBTQ rights. She is a strong supporter of many charities, including those that benefit the LGBTQ community.

Diana Nyad (1949–)

Swimmer

A distance swimmer, Diana Nyad was born Diana Sneed in New York City. After her parents divorced and her mother remarried, she was given her stepfather's surname. The family moved to Fort Lauderdale, Florida, where Nyad began swimming seriously in seventh grade. She won three Florida state high school championships, but a serious heart infection prevented her from competing in strenuous short-swim races. Instead, while in college, she began distance and marathon swimming.

Her first major win was in 1974 in the 22-mile (35-kilometer) Bay of Naples race, but she gained national prominence in 1975 with her record-setting swim around New York City's Manhattan island: 28 miles (45 kilometers) in 7 hours, 57 minutes. In 1979, she set a world record for distance swimming over open water by swimming 102 miles (164 kilometers) from North Bimini Island, Bahamas, to June Beach, Florida, in 27 hours, 41 minutes, a record that held until 2006.

In 1978, Nyad made the first of five attempts to swim from Cuba to Florida, a goal that she finally attained in 2013. She had failed twice in 2011, both times without a shark cage. During the first swim, she was forced to quit after some 29 hours because of an asthma attack; her second swim was cut short after 40 hours when she sustained painful jellyfish stings. A lightning storm and other obstacles foiled her fourth attempt in August 2012 after she had spent 60 hours in the water. On her fifth try, September 2, 2013, she achieved her goal, swimming 110 miles (180 kilometers) between Havana and Key West in approximately 54 hours. At the age of sixty-four, she became the first person to swim from Cuba to Florida without a shark cage or fins.

Nyad is the author of several books, including the memoirs *Other Shores* (1978) and *Find a Way* (2015), the latter of which focuses on her historic swim. She has served as a broadcast journalist, including work with *Wide World of Sports* and several NPR shows. She also appears as a motivational speaker and has publicly shared her experience as a survivor of childhood sexual abuse.

Annie Oakley (1860–1926)

Sharpshooter

Legendary sharpshooter Annie Oakley was born Phoebe Ann Mosey in Darke County, Ohio, and grew up in hardscrabble poverty. The sixth of nine children, Oakley's father died when she was six, and by the age of eight, she was shooting and hunting, selling the game to individuals, stores, and restaurants. By the age of fifteen, she had paid off the mortgage on her mother's farm.

Oakley's journey to international fame reached a milestone in 1875 when she met Irish-born sharpshooter and showman Frank Butler and bested him in a shooting match on the twenty-fifth shot. After their marriage, they began touring together while maintaining a home in the Oakley neighborhood of Cincinnati, from which Oakley likely adapted her stage name. In 1885, the couple joined Buffalo Bill's Wild West show, the premier western entertainment show of its era. Lakota chief Sitting Bull, also a member of the show, nicknamed her Watanya Cicilla, usually translated as "Little Sure Shot." This nickname was used in the title of an early Edison Kinetoscope movie, *Little Sure Shot of the Wild West*. Oakley performed with Buffalo Bill's show throughout North America and Europe until 1902, dazzling audiences with her skill at shooting playing cards, dimes, and cigarettes from her husband's lips.

In 1912, Oakley and Butler built a home in Cambridge, Maryland, where they lived until 1917, when they moved to North Carolina. Oakley continued her record-breaking sharpshooting displays even after an automobile accident forced her to wear a steel brace on her right leg. A philanthropist and advocate for women's rights, Oakley also financially supported the goals of young women she knew. She died from pernicious anemia in Greenville, Ohio, at the age of sixty-six. Frank Butler died eighteen days later in Ferndale, Michigan. Annie Oakley's fame has lived on in popular culture, most notably as a result of the Irving Berlin musical *Annie Get Your Gun*.

Danica Patrick (1982–)

Race Car Driver

A race car driver and the most successful woman in the history of American open-wheel racing, Danica Sue Patrick was born in Beloit, Wisconsin, and raised in Roscoe, Illinois. Patrick began racing go-karts when she was ten and, as a teenager, began winning races in national karting competitions. Her skill and desire to race led her to drop out of high school and intensely train in several driver-training programs both in the United States and the United Kingdom.

After several years of racing at various levels in different types of race cars, Patrick arrived on the national racing scene in 2005 in her first Indianapolis 500 when she led for nineteen laps and finished fourth, the first woman to lead laps and score a top-five finish in the historic race. In 2008, she became the first (and only) woman to win a major IndyCar race when she won the Indy Japan 300. In 2009, she finished a career-high third place at the 2009 Indianapolis 500. Soon after, she switched from the IndyCar Series to stock car racing. She holds the record for the highest finish by a woman in both the Indianapolis 500 and the Daytona 500. In 2015, Patrick broke Janet Guthrie's record for the most top-ten finishes in the NASCAR Cup Series. She retired from competitive racing in 2018.

Patrick has gone on to a successful career in media as TV host, racing commentator, model, and actress. She owns her own brand of wine, her own athletic–leisure clothing line, and is involved in various health and fitness charitable organizations.

Aly Raisman (1995–)

Gymnast

Olympic gymnast Aly Raisman was born Alexandra Rose Raisman in Needham, Michigan, and started gymnastics at the age of two, inspired by watching a video of the U.S. women's team gold medal win at the 1996 Summer Olympics. She began formal training and began to compete in 2009.

By 2012, Raisman's outstanding performances led to her selection for the U.S. Women's Olympics gymnastics team, and she was named captain. Expectations were high for the team, nicknamed "The Fierce Five," and they appeared on the cover of *Sports Illustrated*. They met those expectations, winning a gold medal. Raisman went on to win a bronze medal in the balance beam final and a gold medal in the floor final, the first American woman to win gold in that event.

Due to injury and college attendance, Raisman did not return to competition until 2015 when she was named to the U.S. national team and began climbing her path to the 2016 Summer Olympics in Rio de Janiero. She did well at the Olympic Trials in July 2016, was selected for the U.S. Women's Gymnastics team, and was again named captain. Once again, the U.S. team won the gold medal. After the event, they named themselves "The Final Five" in honor of the retirement of team coordinator Marta Karolyi and the reduction of future Olympic gymnastics teams to four members. Raisman won silver medals for the all-around and the floor competitions.

After her Olympic triumphs, she wrote her autobiography, *Fierce: How Competing for Myself Changed Everything*. In November 2017, Raisman stated that she was one of the many young women who had been molested by former USA Gymnastics team doctor Larry Nassar and was one of several victims who read impact statements at Nassar's sentencing. In 2018, Raisman and other survivors of the sexual abuse were awarded the Arthur Ashe Courage Award. Raisman is involved in several public service efforts as a business partner and brand ambassador.

Mary Lou Retton (1968–)

Gymnast

A gymnast who stunned judges and spectators with her superlative performances at the 1984 Summer Olympics in Los Angeles, Mary Lou Retton was born in Fairmont, West Virginia. When she was eight, Retton was inspired to take up gymnastics after watching television coverage of Romanian Nadia Comăneci and Russian Olga Korbut competing at the 1976 Summer Olympics in Montreal. With the support of her family, Retton moved to Houston to train under Romanians Béla and Márta Károlyi, who had coached Nadia Comăneci before their defection to the United States.

Retton soon began to win awards in competitions and in 1984 qualified for the Olympic Trials.

Five weeks before the start of the Olympics, she underwent an operation for a knee injury; however, she recovered in time to compete. The competition for the all-around gold medal, which includes all four women's events, was intense—Retton was competing head-to-head with Ecaterina Szabo of Romania and was trailing with two events to go. Retton scored perfect 10s on both events (floor exercise and vault) and beat Szabo by 0.05 points, becoming the first American and the first female gymnast from outside Eastern Europe to win the individual all-around gold. In addition, she won two silver medals and two bronze medals. Her accomplishments and her exuberant personality made her a media star. She was named *Sports Illustrated*'s Sportswoman of the Year and was the first female athlete to appear on a Wheaties box.

In 1986, after winning the American Cup all-around competition for the third time, Retton retired from competitive gymnastics. She attended the University of Texas–Austin, appeared as herself in several movies, and captured many commercial endorsements. Retton is also a motivational speaker and commentator for televised gymnastics.

Wilma Rudolph (1940–1994)

Track and Field Athlete

A world-record-holding track and field sprinter, Wilma Rudolph's story is one of the most inspiring in the history of American women's sports. Born in Saint Bethlehem, Tennessee, Wilma Glodean Rudolph was the twentieth of twenty-two children born to her father from two marriages. She was a sickly child who suffered from pneumonia, scarlet fever, and a bout with polio. Through the intense effort she displayed while undergoing physical therapy and the support of her family, Rudolph was able to regain strength in her legs and feet by the time she was twelve years old. In high school, she played basketball and ran track and was nicknamed "Skeeter" for her speed. Her outstanding athletic ability was recognized by Ed Temple, a legendary coach at Tennessee State University (TSU). She trained with the college team for the last two years of high school before attending TSU on an athletic scholarship in 1958.

Coached by Temple, the TSU Tigerbelles were among the top runners in the country. Five of them, including Rudolph, who was still in high school, qualified for the 1956 Summer Olympics in Melbourne. There, she was one of four Tigerbelles who won the bronze medal in the 4 x 100 relay. She continued to train and run at TSU with her eyes on the 1960 Summer Olympics in Rome. At the track and field trials, she set a world record in the 200-meter dash that stood for eight years. At the Olympics, she won a gold medal for the 100-meter dash (in a record time that was not credited because of wind speed) and then a gold medal for the 200-meter dash, setting the Olympic record. Finally, she and three other Tigerbelles repeated their gold medal win in the 4 x 100 relay, setting a new world record. Rudolph left the games with three gold medals, the most won by any American female athlete at that time.

In the 1960 Rome Olympics, the first to be televised worldwide, Rudolph's grace, speed, and beauty made her an international star and earned her the title of the "fastest woman in the world." After a post-Olympics European tour, Rudolph made a triumphant return to her hometown, now renamed Clarksville, with a parade and banquet which, as the result of Rudolph's insistence, was the first fully integrated municipal event in the city's history. Rudolph continued to race and win until her retirement from competitive racing in 1962. She graduated from TSU in 1963 with a degree in elementary education and returned to Clarksville to teach and coach at her old high school.

She spent the remainder of her life in various activities that promoted athletic development for American children, particularly those who would not otherwise have the opportunity to compete. She established and led the Wilma Rudolph Foundation, a nonprofit organization dedicated to promoting amateur athletics. Her autobiography, *Wilma: The Story of Wilma Rudolph*, was published in 1977. She also hosted a television show, served as a television

sports commentator, and worked as a hospital executive. She died of brain cancer at the age of fifty-four at her home in Brentwood, Tennessee.

Joan Benoit Samuelson (1957–)

Marathoner

The first-ever Olympic women's marathon champion, Joan Benoit Samuelson was born in Cape Elizabeth, Maine, where she excelled at sports as a child. She began as a skier and started long-distance running to help recover from a skiing accident. At North Carolina State University, she earned All-America honors and in 1978 helped lead the team to the Atlantic Coast Conference cross-country championship. In 1979, she won the Boston Marathon with the then-record-setting time of 2:35:15.

Samuelson continued to train and race while suffering from chronic heel pain, which was eventually corrected through surgery. In 1983, she again won the Boston Marathon, setting the world record of 2:22:43. Her time in the Boston Marathon held for eleven years. In 1984, she took first place in the Olympic Trials after recovering from knee surgery seventeen days before. At the Summer Olympics in Los Angeles, she won gold in the first Olympic women's marathon several hundred meters ahead of the other competitors. In 1985, she won the Chicago Marathon and set an American record time of 2:21:21, a record that would last for eighteen years.

Samuelson struggled with injuries in the years afterward but has continued to run marathons and has set a number of records in the 50+ Division. She now resides in Freeport, Maine. In addition to her running, she serves as a coach to women's cross-country and long-distance athletes as well as being a motivational speaker and sports commentator. Samuelson has written two books: *Running Tide* and *Joan Samuelson's Running for Women*. She and her husband, Scott Samuelson, are the parents of a son and a daughter, who ran the Boston Marathon with their mother in 2014.

Monica Seles (1973–)
Tennis Player

Tennis champion Monica Seles was born in Novi Sad, Serbia (formerly Yugoslavia), where, at the age of five, she began tennis lessons with her father. By the time she was nine—only three years after taking up the game—she competed in and won the Yugoslav twelve-and-under girls' championship. Seles continued to accumulate juniors' titles in Europe and the United States, and in 1986, she and her family moved to Florida for training and preparation for the professional circuit.

In 1990, sixteen-year-old Seles won six consecutive tournaments and the French Open, the youngest person to win the Grand Slam tournament. At seventeen, she again made history when she became the youngest player to take over the world number-one ranking. She continued to dominate the sport in 1992, again finishing as the number-one-ranked women's player. From 1991 to 1993, Seles won thirty-three of the thirty-four tournaments she entered, including six Grand Slam singles titles.

In April 1993, Seles was stabbed in the back by a crazed spectator during a tournament in Hamburg, Germany. Recovery was difficult, and she did not return to the court until 1995. During that time, she became she became a U.S. citizen (1994). She won her fourth Australian Open in 1996 and a bronze medal at the 2000 Summer Olympics in Sydney but never regained her number-one dominance. In 2002, her last full year on the tour, she finished the year ranked world number seven. She played her last professional match in 2003 and finally retired in 2008 with nine Grand Slam championships among her fifty-three singles titles.

Since retiring, Seles has spent time working on behalf of animal charities, teaching at tennis clinics, and speaking about the difficulties she faced while suffering from an eating disorder. In 2009, she wrote a memoir, *Getting a Grip: On My Body, My Mind, My Self*. She has also written young adult fiction and *The Academy*, a series set in an international sports boarding school.

Annika Sörenstam (1970–)
Golfer

Regarded as one of the best golfers in history, Annika Sörenstam was born in Bro near Stockholm, Sweden. She was a talented athlete from an early age, nationally ranked in tennis, soccer, and skiing. As a teenager, she focused on golf and soon became a star on the Swedish national team. She then played college golf at the University of Arizona in Tucson. In 1991, she became the first freshman to win the individual NCAA Division I Championship.

Sörenstam joined the LPGA Tour in 1993 and was an immediate star. In 1993, she was named the European Tour's Rookie of the Year and in 1994 was named U.S. Rookie of the Year. By the time she retired from competitive golf in 2008, she had won eighty-nine international tournaments—the most individual wins of any female golfer. She won ten LPGA majors and tops the LPGA's career money list with over $22 million in earnings. She is the winner of a record eight Player of the Year awards and holds the record for the lowest score in competition (59) as well as the lowest season scoring average (68.6969). In 2006, Sörenstam became a U.S. citizen and holds dual American and Swedish citizenship.

Since retiring, she has pursued various business and charitable projects primarily through her ANNIKA brand and foundation. The foundation's goal is to develop women's golf around the world and encourage children to lead healthy, active lifestyles. Sörenstam is especially involved with the Make-A-Wish Foundation. The businesses in which she is involved include high-end golf apparel, golf course design, and winemaking.

Helen Stephens (1918–1994)
Track and Field Athlete

An Olympic athlete who was never defeated in any running event or in weight events such as the shot put and discus throw during her career, Stephens was born in Fulton, Missouri, where she grew up on a farm. She first set records at the age of seventeen at the 1935 Amateur Athletic Union (AAU) Indoor Championship meet, defeating the current champion, Stella Walsh, in the 50-meter dash, winning two other events, and earning the nickname "The Fulton Flash."

At the 1936 Olympics, she won two gold medals. Her winning time of 11.5 seconds in the 100-meter race set a world record that stood for twenty-four years. She also won gold as a member of the U.S. women's relay team. Olympics rules at that time limited the number of events women could compete in, depriving Stephens of additional awards. She was named the Associated Press Athlete of the Year for 1936. At the Berlin Olympics, German chancellor Adolf Hitler approached Stephens, pinched her backside, hugged her, and then praised her as "a good Aryan type" who "should be running for Germany." According to Stephens, Hitler suggested she spend the weekend with him at Berchtesgarden, his Bavarian retreat, an invitation she refused.

Stephens retired from amateur sports soon after the Berlin Olympics, saying she was bored by the lack of good competition. She played professional baseball and basketball and in 1938 became the first woman to create, own, and manage a semiprofessional basketball team, the Helen Stephens Olympic Co-Eds. She served with the Marines during World War II and after the war worked for the U.S. Aeronautical Chart and Information Service. At the same time, she was active with the Senior Olympics program both as a director and a competitor.

Pat Summitt (1952–2016)

Basketball Coach

A women's basketball head coach who accrued the most career wins in college basketball history, Pat Summitt was born Patricia Sue Head in Clarksville, Tennessee. An outstanding basketball player in her youth, she won All-America honors at the University of Tennessee–Martin. She was cocaptain of the U.S. women's national basketball team at the first women's competition in the 1976 Summer Olympics in Montreal, helping the team win its silver medal. Eight years later at the 1984 Summer Olympics in Los Angeles, she coached the U.S. national team to a gold medal.

In 1974 at the age of twenty-two, Summitt became head coach of the University of Tennessee Lady Vols, a position she held until 2012. During that time, her teams won eight NCAA championships and a total of 1,098 wins out of 1,306 games coached, the most of any men or women's college teams. Known as one of the toughest coaches in college basketball history, Summitt was a fiery competitor with an icy stare who drove her teams to play to the best of their abilities.

Despite a diagnosis of early-onset Alzheimer's disease in 2011, Summitt completed the 2011–2012 season with the help of assistant coach Holly Warlick. Summitt stepped down in 2012 as head coach, naming Warlick as her successor. Summitt remained active as speaker, author, and mentor to young athletes. In addition to her coaching career, Summitt wrote two self-help books. A memoir, *Sum It Up* (with Sally Jenkins), was published two years before her death.

Kathrine Switzer (1947–)

Marathoner

A marathon runner, author, and sports commentator, Kathrine Virginia Switzer was born in Amberg, Germany, the daughter of a U.S. Army major who was stationed there. In 1949, the family returned to the United States and settled in Fairfax County, Virginia. Switzer began distance running at Syracuse University, training on her own since no running team existed for women at the time. In 1967, determined to run in the Boston Marathon, which did not officially allow women in the race, Switzer applied as K. V. Switzer and received an official number.

On April 19, 1967, Switzer and her fellow Syracuse runners started the race in good spirits until the press truck began to focus on the fact that

Switzer was a woman with an official number. A race official, Jock Semple, tried to rip the number from her sweatshirt until Switzer's boyfriend shoved him to the ground, an event that was captured in photos that made headlines around the world. Although women had unofficially been running the race since the year before, her boldness in running in the Men's Division spurred the women's running revolution at a time when popular theory held that women were not strong enough to run the 26.2-mile race. Switzer and others began advocating for women to be allowed in AAU races, a campaign that finally succeeded in 1971. The first Boston Marathon to officially include women was in 1972, and the first Olympic women's marathon took place in 1984 with Joan Benoit as the winner.

Switzer continued her running career after the Boston Marathon. She won the New York City Marathon in 1974, and *Runner's World* magazine named her Female Runner of the Decade (1967–1977). While continuing to run marathons, she has had a career as a fitness expert, author, and public speaker and is an Emmy Award-winning television commentator who has done broadcast work for ABC, CBS, NBC, and ESPN. Switzer's books include *Marathon Woman* and *Running and Walking for Women Over 40*.

was at the 2002 Winter Olympics in Salt Lake City, where her best result was sixth in the combined competition.

At the World Championship in 2007, Vonn won two silver medals, and the following year, she garnered her first World Cup win. She won the World Cup for the next two years (2009 and 2010) and her first World Championship in 2009. At the 2010 Winter Olympics in Vancouver, she attained her dream and won the gold medal in the downhill, the first gold for an American woman, and also won a bronze medal in the super-G. In 2012, she won her fourth World Cup overall championship; she is tied with Annemarie Moser-Pröll for most overall World Cup championships. Despite serious injuries, she continued to compete and win through 2018. At the 2018 Winter Olympics in Tokyo, she won a bronze medal in the downhill. In 2019, she announced her retirement, citing her injuries. Her total of eighty-two World Cup victories stands as the women's record and marks her as the greatest female skier in history.

Throughout her career, Vonn has made time to help many charitable efforts. She founded the Lindsey Vonn Foundation and is dedicated to providing scholarships and programming for education and sports.

Lindsey Vonn (1984–)
Skier

World Cup and Olympic skier Lindsey Vonn was born in St. Paul, Minnesota, and was taught to ski at the age of two by her grandfather, Don Kildow, in Milton, Wisconsin. Vonn's father, Alan Kildow, was a competitive skier who had won a national junior title before a knee injury ended his career at the age of eighteen. Vonn trained at Erich Sailer's renowned development ski program at Buck Hill, near Burnsville, Minnesota. In the late 1990s, Vonn's family moved to Vail, Colorado.

Von excelled as a junior competitor and at fourteen gained her first major win in the slalom at Trofeo Topolino in Italy. Her first Olympics appearance

Kathy Whitworth (1939–)
Golfer

A World Golf Hall of Famer, Kathy Whitworth was born Kathrynne Ann Whitworth in Monahans, Texas, and grew up in Jal, New Mexico, where she began playing golf at the age of fifteen. She briefly attended Odessa Junior College, where she won the 1957 and 1958 New Mexico State Amateur Championship before turning professional in 1958.

During her long career, Whitworth won eighty-eight LPGA tournaments, the most wins on both the LPGA Tour and the men's PGA tour. She was a strong driver and an excellent putter and dominated the LPGA Tour from 1963 to 1973. She was the LPGA's leading money winner from 1965 to 1968 and from 1970 to 1973. Named LPGA Player of the Year seven times, Whitworth is also a seven-time winner of the LPGA's Vare Trophy for best average. She won every major tournament except the U.S. Open and was the first female golfer to earn a million dollars in tournament play.

In addition to her playing career, Whitworth served as president of the LPGA in 1967, 1968, and 1971 and has worked to increase the commercial recognition of women's golf and the size of its prizes. Whitworth retired from competitive golf in 2005 after competing in the Women's Senior Golf Tour.

Serena Williams (1981–)

Tennis Player

A tennis champion and the younger, by a year, of the powerhouse Williams sisters, Serena Jameka Williams was born in Saginaw, Michigan. Williams and her sister Venus grew up playing tennis in Compton, California, and were coached by their parents. When Serena was nine, her family moved to West Palm Beach, Florida, to begin formal coaching and competing on the junior circuit. While her father, Richard, continued to take a strong role in coaching his daughters, he stopped sending the sisters to junior tournaments so that they could develop with less pressure and focus on school.

Serena turned professional in 1995 at the Bell Challenge in Quebec, Canada, where she lost in the first round. She won her first Grand Slam titles in 1998 in the mixed doubles at Wimbledon and the U.S. Open. When her sister, Venus, won the mixed doubles at the Australian Open and the French Open, the sisters completed a "Williams Family Mixed Doubles Grand Slam." At the 1999 U.S. Open, Serena was the first of the sisters to win a Grand Slam singles title. The following decades have seen the Williams sisters dominate the world of women's tennis. Over the course of her career, Serena has won a record twenty-three Grand Slam singles titles, the most in the U.S. Open era. Her most recent victory came with the 2017 Australian Open, gaining the record for the most wins in the U.S. Open era. In addition, she has won an impressive

fourteen Grand Slam doubles titles and two Grand Slam mixed doubles titles as well as four Olympic gold medals in doubles in 2000, 2008, and 2012 (shared with her sister Venus) and one in women's singles in 2008. In 2013 and 2015, she completed two career Grand Slams (winning all four Grand Slam singles events consecutively). Injuries and the birth of her child have caused her to take time off from competitions in recent years, but she has not yet retired.

As an exceptional tennis player and an accomplished African American woman, Serena is often in the public eye as a model for the aspirations of young women. In addition to numerous corporate sponsorships, she has appeared in music videos, television shows, and movies where she often plays herself but has also been featured in some dramatic roles. In the fashion world, she has developed several clothing and jewelry lines and also published a 2009 autobiography, *My Life: Queen of the Court*.

Williams has also devoted her time to activism and charity work. She formed the Serena Williams Foundation, which is dedicated to providing educational opportunities for underprivileged youth around the world, including schools in Africa and university scholarships in the United States. In 2016, Serena and Venus collaborated on the Williams Sisters Fund to work on various philanthropic projects together.

Venus Williams (1980–)

Tennis Player

A tennis champion and the older of the outstanding Williams sisters, Venus Ebony Starr Williams was born in Lynwood, California. She and her sister Serena began training for the sport in Compton, California, and were coached by their parents. When Venus was ten, her family moved to West Palm Beach, Florida, where she started formal coaching as well as competing on the junior circuit. However, her father, Richard, who continued to take a strong role in coaching his daughters, stopped sending the sisters to junior tournaments so that they could focus on school and develop their game with less pressure.

Venus made her professional debut in 1994 at the Best of the West Classic in Oakland, California, where she lost in a close match with the number-two seed Ariantxa Sanchez Vicario in the second round. Four years later, she won her first Grand Slam titles in the mixed doubles at the Australian Open and the French Open. When Serena Williams won the mixed doubles at Wimbledon and the U.S. Open, the sisters completed a "Williams Family Mixed Doubles Grand Slam." The following decades have seen the Williams sisters dominate the world of women's tennis. Over the course of her career, Venus has won seven Grand Slam singles titles, fourteen Grand Slam doubles titles (all with her sister Serena), and two Grand Slam mixed doubles titles. She has also won four Olympic gold medals: singles in 2000, doubles in 2000, 2008, and 2012 (shared with her sister Serena), and mixed doubles in 2016. She continues to compete on the professional circuit.

In 2007, Williams realized a longtime goal when the organizers of the Wimbledon and French Open tournaments agreed to award equal prize money to men and women. It was an initiative Williams had pursued since 2005 as a leader of the WTA and UNESCO campaign to promote gender equality in sports.

Off the court, Venus has attained success in the fields of fashion and interior design. She owns an active-wear clothing line, EleVen, in addition to her own fashion lines for other companies and also owns her own interior design firm, V*Starr Interiors. She cowrote *Come to Win; on How Sports Can Help You Top Your Profession*, published in 2010. In 2016, Venus and Serena collaborated on the Williams Sisters Fund to work on various philanthropic projects together.

Mickey Wright (1935–)

Golfer

Former LPGA champion golfer Mickey Wright was born Mary Kathryn Wright in San Diego, California. She learned golf early and, while in high school, won her first tournament, the 1952 U.S. Girls' Junior Championship. She attended Stanford University for one year but left to play golf full time. She was the 1954 amateur winner of the U.S. Open and turned professional later that year.

From 1955 to 1969, Wright dominated women's golf, winning at least one LPGA title during each season for a lifetime total of eighty-two tournaments. Her thirteen wins in 1963 remain the most wins in a single LPGA season. For five consecutive years (1960–1964), she won the Vare Trophy for the lowest yearlong average score. Wright won thirteen majors between 1958 and 1966, and she is the only player in LPGA Tour history to hold all four major titles at the same time.

Wright was known as a powerful hitter with a smooth, flawless swing, which championship golfer Ben Hogan described as the best he ever saw. In addition to her excellence on the course, she served as president of the LPGA, helping to build the organization into the premier sponsor of women's golf.

Kristi Yamaguchi (1971–)

Figure Skater

An Olympic champion figure skater, Kristine Tsuya Yamaguchi was born in Hayward, California, and grew up in Fremont. She began taking skating and ballet lessons as a child as physical therapy to correct her clubfeet. Yamaguchi began her competitive career as both a singles skater and a pairs skater, skating with another champion singles skater, Rudy Galindo. The pair won the junior U.S. title in 1986 and 1988 and the senior pairs title in 1989 and 1990.

In women's singles, Yamaguchi won her first major international gold medal at the 1990 Goodwill Games and went on to win the 1991 World Championship. She won the U.S. championship in 1992, assuring her a spot in the 1992 Winter Olympics in Albertville. In a close competition, she won the gold in women's singles and later that year again won the World Championship. She then turned professional and began touring with Stars on Ice, which she continued to do for years. She also competed on the professional skating circuit.

In 1996, Yamaguchi established the Always Dream Foundation to support the hopes and dreams of children with a special focus on early childhood literacy. She has created a women's active-wear clothing line, worked as a broadcast skating analyst, and written several books, including three children's books. In 1997, she published *Figure Skating for Dummies*, which includes a forward by skater Scott Hamilton.

Babe Didrikson Zaharias (1911–1956)

Golfer

 Considered the most outstanding female athlete in the first half of the twentieth century and possibly of any century, Babe Didrikson Zaharias was a phenomenon: a champion in basketball, track and field, and golf, also excelling in baseball, tennis, and swimming. "My goal," she once declared, "was to be the greatest athlete that ever lived." Her tenacious pursuit of that goal would change women's sports forever.

Born Mildred Didrikson, she was the child of Norwegian immigrants who settled in Beaumont, Texas. Didrikson showed remarkable athletic gifts at an early age, surpassing any child—girl or boy—in her town and received the nickname "Babe" after the great baseball star Babe Ruth, the era's reigning sports hero.

Didrikson's first organized sport was basketball, which she played in high school and on a semiprofessional team. She next took up track and field and in 1932 entered the Amateur Athletic Union women's national championship. Competing as an individual against several teams of athletes, she won six events, broke four women's world records, and won the championship, scoring twice as many points as the second-place team. Two weeks later, as a member of the U.S. team at the Summer Olympics in Los Angeles, Didrikson shattered world records in the javelin throw and the 8-meter hurdles, winning gold medals in both events. The following day, she won a silver medal in the high jump.

Despite her success, few opportunities existed for a female amateur athlete in the 1930s, and Didrikson turned professional, performing in exhibitions and on the vaudeville circuit more as a curiosity than as a respected athlete. In 1934, Didrikson followed a suggestion that she take up golf, a game that she had previously played infrequently. In 1938, while trying to qualify for a men's tournament in Los Angeles, she met and married George Zaharias, a professional wrestler.

In the 1940s, Didrikson starred on the golf course. She won the Western Open in 1940, 1944, and 1945 and, after reclaiming her amateur status, captured the 1946 National Amateur title; in 1947, she became the first U.S. woman to win the British Women's Amateur Tournament. In 1947, she turned professional again and went on to win thirty-four pro tournaments over the next several years, including three U.S. Open titles. She also helped to form the Ladies Professional Golf Association, which attracted more women to professional sports. Despite being diagnosed with cancer, Didrikson continued to compete in the 1950s, winning the U.S. Open and the All American Open in 1954. She died of cancer two years later.

In 1982, a poll taken of some of America's leading sports experts to name the ten most outstanding and influential American sports figures ranked Didrikson second behind only her namesake, Babe Ruth.

SCIENCE, MEDICINE, AND TECHNOLOGY

The participation of women in the sciences has been a fact since ancient times. The word science, from the Latin word *scientia*, variously meaning "knowledge," "a knowing," "expertness," and the appellation "scientist," once primarily assigned to men, also applies to women, who made significant contributions to the systematic understanding of nature and human nature that would evolve into today's scientific disciplines. In ancient Greece, the philosophy of natural science, the conceptual study of the physical universe, was open to women, and records exist of women's contributions to the science and art of healing dating from antiquity. One example is the first named female scientist, Agamede, cited by Homer as a healer in ancient Greece before the Trojan War (twelfth century B.C.E.). During the Middle Ages, convents, like monasteries, were important centers for scholarly, scientific research as well as worship. Outside convents, we have instances of female adepts sharing with men the pursuit of the mysteries of the protoscience of alchemy. With the emergence of the first universities in the eleventh century, the exclusion of women from higher education would severely restrict (though not completely exclude) women from participating in the scientific revolution of the seventeenth and eighteenth centuries when the experimental, empirical methods of modern science developed. The era's new science would not emerge in the universities, which mostly continued to teach the old Aris-

totelean scholastic ideas (Aristotle as interpreted by medieval clerics based on the presumptive authority of the past) and not the observational, experimental methods of the new scientists. The new natural philosophy, as science as we know it was called, would be discussed and debated in coffeehouses and at private gatherings called *salons* and disseminated in publications that did not exclude female readers or even female contributors to the debates. The Enlightenment of the eighteenth century valued the individual's capacity to make sense of the world, and, although the concept of women's equality was not yet a cultural force, individual women nevertheless claimed the right to pursue scientific knowledge and understanding.

In America, as in Europe, the chief catalyst for women's contribution to the modern science that emerged in the eighteenth century filtered back to the university, which replaced Aristotelian scholasticism beginning in the nineteenth century. Prior to the creation of women's colleges, the founding of new coeducational institutions, and the opening up of some all-male colleges and universities to women, science for women was an amateur avocation, not a profession, with women's scientific achievement the exception rather than the rule. Early American examples include botanists Jane Colden (1724–1766), described as the "first botanist of her sex in her country"; Martha Daniell Logan (1704–1779), who

Before the days of women's colleges in the United States, women such as botanist Jane Colden pursued science as an avocation.

was instrumental in seed exchanges between Britain and the North American colonies; agriculturalist Eliza Lucas Pinckney (1772–1793), who began cultivating and improving strains of the indigo plant that would be used in dyeing textiles; Margaretta Morris (1797–1867), the first practicing female entomologist in the United States, who did pioneering work on insects despite the lack of a formal education; and astronomer Maria Mitchell (1818–1889), the first American to discover a comet and the first faculty member hired at Vassar College in 1865. All of these early American female scientists were self- or home-educated and essentially outliers from the scientific male-dominated mainstream.

Women did not have the chance to demonstrate their capacity for scientific study and work for the same reason they were prevented from entering higher education in the first place. Throughout the eighteenth and nineteenth centuries, conventional gender distinctions held that women were intellectually incapable of the mathematical reasoning and rigorous analytical skills needed for higher academic work in general and science in particular. It was also generally believed that such intellectual challenges were harmful to a woman's mental development and would ruin their prospects as wives and mothers. Early in a girl's education, the majority of young women were taught the skills they would need in their rightful place in the home, while boys were taught the subjects, such as mathematics and logic, needed to succeed in the world. In colonial America, this was expressed most dramatically in the commonplace educational disparity between reading and writing for girls and boys. Colonial pedagogy dictated that girls needed to read (particularly to access religious material), but they did not need to write, which explains why so many colonial American women could only sign their names with an "X."

The evolution of scientific thought that began with the Enlightenment also contributed to the displacement of women who had served their communities for centuries as healers and midwives, usually without virtue of scientific training or diplomas. Long before obstetricians or trained surgeons came into existence, women had largely been responsible for the delivery of generations of newborns and the care of their mothers. Many midwives would be supplanted by the science that would only be available to men in the gender-restricted confines of medical schools and hospitals. It would be a mistake to undermine the breakthroughs in biology, anatomy, physiology, and medicine that led to significant discoveries that saved countless lives, but until women began to claim a similar place in medicine, those women who had long served a role in the health of their communities lost their place because of the barriers thrown up against their participation in the new science taught in universities and medical schools.

As public and private secondary schools were made available to young women in the nineteenth century and private, all-girl academies and seminaries were founded, scientific education was more often than not deemed unnecessary and certainly impractical since the notion of women pursuing a career in science was largely unthinkable. Well into the 1870s, the only acceptable profession for a woman outside the home was as a teacher, and rarely would science have been what she would teach. The exceptional secondary schools for girls that did offer instruction in mathematics and basic science were considered radical and daring.

The turning point that would dramatically affect the entrance of women into the sciences was the founding of women's colleges beginning with Mount Holyoke College in 1837. The first of the so-called "Seven Sisters," Mount Holyoke and its first president, Mary Lyon (1797–1849), established seven courses in the sciences and mathematics in order to graduate, a requirement unheard of at female seminaries. Lyon introduced students to a new and then-unusual method to learn science—laboratory experiments, which they performed themselves. She organized field trips on which students collected rocks, plants, and specimens for lab work and inspected geological formations and recently discovered dinosaur tracks. Lyon's innovations in science instruction would be replicated in the women's colleges that followed, all of which would become important training grounds

for the first significant generation of female scientists who emerged at the end of the nineteenth century and in the first half of the twentieth century. One example is Ellen Swallow Richards (1842–1911), who would become the first woman in America to receive a degree in chemistry (Vassar, 1870) and would go on to become the first woman to be admitted to the Massachusetts Institute of Technology in 1873. Mount Holyoke would also include a Department of Chemistry led by influential organic chemist Emma Perry Carr (1880–1972), and between 1920 and 1980, ninety-three Mount Holyoke graduates would later receive Ph.D.s in chemistry. At Vassar College, Maria Mitchell would train notable American astronomers Mary Whitney (1847–1921) and Antonia Maury (1866–1952); Mount Holyoke supported the career of astronomer Ann S. Young (1871–1961); and Smith College was the home of astronomer Mary Emma Byrd (1849–1934). In geology, Florence Bascom (1862–1945) would create the Department of Geology at Bryn Mawr College that would produce such notable American geologists as Ida Ogilvie (1874–1963), Julia Gardner (1882–1960), and Eleanora

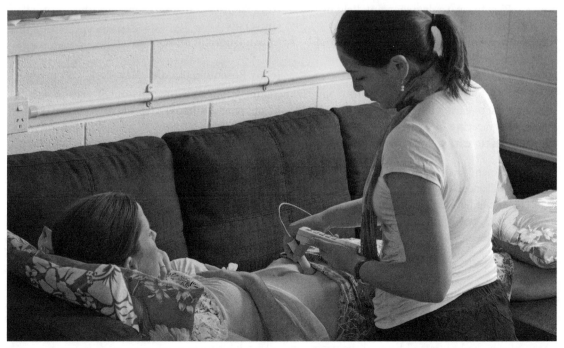

Before women were allowed to become doctors, they were long involved in the medical world as midwives. Midwifery, the precare and delivery of babies, is a career that still thrives today.

Bliss Knopf (1883–1974). Christine Ladd-Franklin (1847–1930) would receive her degree in mathematics from Vassar (1869) and would go on to do graduate work at Johns Hopkins and contribute both to mathematical and psychological research. Women trained at all-female colleges would also be responsible for opening up to women many of the graduate programs in the sciences at institutions of higher education that had slowly (and often reluctantly) agreed to implement coeducation.

Notable advanced-degree firsts for American women in the sciences include:

What is striking in looking at the biographies of many of these and other trailblazing women in the sciences profiled in this chapter is the struggle they faced in opening the door to the laboratories and science lecture halls for other women to follow. Ellen Swallow Richards provides a telling example. With both her bachelor's and master's degrees in chemistry from Vassar, Richards needed a vote by the MIT faculty to admit her as a special student in chemistry. The faculty specified that her admission "did not establish a precedent for the general admissions of females." Richards earned a BS degree from

Year	Achievement	Woman
1850	First to earn a medical degree	Lydia Folger Fowler, Central Medical College (Elizabeth Blackwell, who had earned a medical degree from Geneva College in 1849, was English born)
1866	First to earn a dental degree	Lucy Hobbs Taylor, Ohio College of Dental Surgery
1883	First to earn a pharmacy degree	Susan Hayhurst, Philadelphia College of Pharmacy
1886	First to earn a Ph.D. in mathematics	Winifred Edgerton Merrill, Columbia University
1887	First to earn a Ph.D. in chemistry	Rachel Lloyd, Swiss University of Zurich
1894	First to earn a Ph.D. in psychology	Margaret Floy Washburn, Cornell University
1903	First to earn a veterinary degree	Mignon Nicholson, McKillip Veterinary College
1905	First to earn a degree in any field of engineering	Nora Stanton Blatch (civil engineering), Cornell University
1915	First Ph.D. ever granted in industrial psychology	Lillian Gilbreth, Brown University
1929	First to earn a Ph.D. in physics	Jenny Rosenthal Bramley, New York University
1949	First to earn a Ph.D. in meterorology	Joanne Simpson, University of Chicago
1959	First to earn a Ph.D. in mechanical engineering	Lois Graham, Illinois Institute of Technology
1965	First to earn a Ph.D. in computer science	Sister Mary Kenneth Keller, University of Wisconsin

MIT in 1873 and should have been the first woman to earn an advanced degree from MIT, but the faculty refused to grant her this distinction, and MIT would not award its first Ph.D. to a woman until 1886. Hannah Marie Wormington, one of the first American women to become a professional archaeologist, became the first woman to focus on anthropology at Radcliffe College, earning her master's degree there in 1950. She became the first woman at Harvard to receive a Ph.D. in archaeology in 1954, but when she attended some classes at Harvard, she was made to sit outside the lecture hall because the professor did not allow women inside. Pioneering geologist

Florence Bascom became the first woman to receive a Ph.D. from Johns Hopkins in 1893 but was made to sit behind a screen in class in order not to distract the male students. Nobel laureate Gertrude Elion was initially unable to find a job in a research laboratory after gaining her degree in chemistry and was forced to work for the A&P supermarket chain measuring the acidity of pickle juice. The second woman to win the Nobel Prize in physics (after Marie Curie), Maria Goeppert-Mayer, would work for nine years as an unpaid researcher when her husband was hired by Johns Hopkins because university spouses could not be hired.

Examples like these both demonstrate the challenges female scientists faced just to gain access, if not full equality, with their male colleagues and puts into context the extraordinary achievements that followed when women were allowed to enter their scientific fields unfettered by gender inequality in classrooms and laboratories. The ultimate confirmation of achievement in the sciences is the Nobel Prize. The following American women have earned the award:

Despite the fact that these Nobel laureates and so many more American female scientists have effectively given the lie to the notion that science is beyond the reach or capacity of women, an argument can be made that the longtime exclusion of women from mainstream science both academically and professionally also, ironically, benefited science in significant and unexpected ways. G. Kass-Simon, in the introduction to *Women of Science: Righting the*

NOBEL PRIZE WINNERS

Year	Winner	Category	Reason for Winning
1947	Gerty Theresa Cori	Physiology or Medicine	Discovery of the course of the catalytic conversion of glycogen
1963	Maria Goeppert-Mayer	Physics	Discoveries concerning nuclear shell structure
1977	Rosalyn Sussman Yalow	Physiology or Medicine	Development of radioimmunoassays of peptide hormones
1983	Barbara McClintock	Physiology or Medicine	Discovery of mobile genetic elements
1988	Gertrude B. Elion	Physiology or Medicine	Discoveries of important principles for drug treatment
2004	Linda B. Buck	Physiology or Medicine	Discoveries of odorant receptors and the organization of the olfactory system
2009	Elizabeth Blackburn	Physiology or Medicine	Discovery of how chromosomes are protected by telomeres and the enzyme telomerase
2009	Carol W. Greider	Physiology or Medicine	Discovery of how chromosomes are protected by telomeres and the enzyme telomerase
2018	Frances Arnold	Chemistry	Discoveries of the evolution of enzymes

Record (1993), makes the case that "despite, or, more properly, because of the restrictions placed upon them, women were from time to time given a unique vantage point from which to survey their science" and thereby "were given the opportunity to so change their science or to create a new one." Excluded from the mainstream, female scientists created new streams that redefined scientific possibilities and altered history with the results of their discoveries. Some examples include Lillian Gilbreth, a pioneer in industrial and organizational psychology as an academic discipline; physician Alice Hamilton, who would do the same for public health and industrial medicine; Ellen Swallow Richards, said to have founded ecology; Rachel Carson, credited with

creating modern environmental studies; Virginia Apgar, who helped to turn the practice of anesthesiology into an important branch of medicine because her medical school advisor urged her to become an anesthesiologist rather than a surgeon because she was a woman; and Eleanor Josephine MacDonald, the world's first cancer epidemiologist at a time when epidemiologists only researched communicable diseases.

Whether by entering the mainstream or altering the mainstream, American female scientists have joined scientific fields in significant and growing numbers. Today, about 50 percent of all undergraduate science degrees go to women (women in general make up 57 percent of college graduates). This rep-

More and more women are graduating from U.S. colleges and universities with science degrees.

They still do. Finally, as of 2016, women in computer, engineering, and science occupations were paid an estimated 79.2 percent of men's annual median earnings.

PERCENTAGE OF DEGREES EARNED BY WOMEN (2014–2015)

Discipline	BA	MA	Ph.D.
Life sciences	59.0%	57.3%	53.3%
Mathematics	43.0%	40.6%	27.9%
Physical sciences	38.5%	37.5%	34.3%
Engineering	18.7%	25.2%	23.2%
Computer science	18.0%	30.4%	22.5%
All STEM fields	35.1%	32.7%	34.4%

resents a seismic shift from the days when women were excluded from lecture halls and seated behind screens; even as relatively recently as 1960, only 16 percent of undergraduate science degrees went to women. Since then, the yield of women with science degrees has tripled. On the graduate level, 41.6 percent of doctoral degrees awarded in science and engineering were, as of 2014, awarded to women, who earn 50.1 percent of doctoral degrees overall. At the faculty level (as of 2015–2016), 32.8 percent of female tenure or tenure-track faculty were full professors, compared with 52.1 percent of male tenure or tenure-track faculty. However, only 16.9 percent of tenure or tenure-track faculty in U.S. colleges of engineering are women. The life sciences have the largest percentage at 20 percent; aerospace and nuclear engineering has the lowest at 12 percent. In employment, women made up less than one-quarter (24 percent) of those employed in STEM (science, technology, engineering, and math) occupations in 2015. By the 1960s, only 1 in 100 U.S. engineers were women, while 1 in 12 chemists were women. These numbers have certainly improved but not across the board in all science fields. In 1960, men outnumbered women in computer science 3 to 1.

These numbers suggest that if women are earning science degrees in unprecedented numbers, a sizable gender gap still exists in the sciences compared to women's distribution in all academic disciplines, and women's numbers in the sciences decline sharply at the graduate and professional levels. Women have not yet reached equity with men in the sciences, and in some fields such as engineering and computer science it is still possible to describe them as predominantly (and seemingly intractably) male.

Gender disparity in STEM fields has not gone unnoticed, and scholars and researchers have been strenuously attempting to examine both its causes and solutions. A persistent stereotype that contributes to the disparity is that boys naturally do better than girls in math and science. Studies, however, have shown that girls are just as talented in math and science as boys are. Despite the evidence, the fallacy of women's lack of talent in math and science has persisted from the earliest days of women's education and became a self-fulfilling outcome, as boys are slated for success in math and science and girls are generally socialized to steer away from the sciences by the time they reach high school (confidence among girls regarding all academic pursuits has been shown to be greater in all-girls' schools, however). Studies have even shown how such deeply ingrained ideas about women and science can lead to girls performing worse on math and science tasks and tests than boys. Government surveys show that girls and boys take roughly the same number of science and math classes in high school, yet men are twice as likely to major in science, although it varies by field. Women are more likely to study biology in college; men are more likely to study engineering or computer science. Men are also more likely to obtain STEM jobs. Various societal and psychological factors have been suggested to explain why. Asked to conjure up in your mind's eye a scientist, most will imagine a male, and science as a field of study and as a career still is perceived by many as a nontraditional choice for women. While women have certainly gained acceptance and equality in certain areas of science (particularly in medicine and biology), they remain conspicuously underrepresented in other areas (such as computer science and engineering), and efforts have been made to address the disparity by organizations such as the Association for Women in Science, the Association for Women in Mathematics, Girls Who Code, and the TeachHer Initiative. Early

encouragement and enhanced opportunities in the sciences for younger students with better advising and mentoring, together with programs that engage and affirm girls' scientific skills and scholarships to support scientific study in underrepresented fields, all have been implemented to lower the barriers to women in the sciences.

Underrepresentation in certain science fields is not the only pressing issue women in the sciences face. Research has shown that harassment and other forms of sexual discrimination remain widespread. A 2018 report from the National Academy of Science, Engineering and Medicine found that up to 40 percent of female science students had been sexually harassed by faculty or staff. Female science faculty and researchers have reported entrenched and persistent bias toward female scientists in hiring, salary, start-up funds for laboratories, credit for authorship of papers, letters of recommendations, invitations to give talks at prestigious university colloquia, and at panels that are derisively described by some female

Female middle school students attend an engineering camp at Texas A&M University. A number of programs in the United States encourage young women to pursue the sciences.

scientists as "manels." "There is this belief that science is noble and unbiased, and if I'm good, I'll be recognized," said Margaret Rossiter, an emerita historian of science at Cornell. "Sometimes that's true—Marie Curie came along and got two Nobel Prizes. But often it turned out not be true, and women [are] disillusioned." In 2017, three of the four full female professors at the Salk Institute filed state gender-discrimination lawsuits claiming discrimination in access to funds for lab resources and influence. In 2018, France Córdova, director of the National Science Foundation, which funds forty thousand scientists and two thousand institutions, announced policy changes that would direct institutions that accept National Science Foundation (NSF) grants to report any findings related to harassment by a funded scientist, who then will face the possibility of losing funding. Individuals may also report harassment directly to the NSF, which may then conduct its own investigation. It remains to be seen whether calling attention to gender harassment within the science community and increased sanctions for violations can improve what many female scientists have experienced as a gender-biased and often inhospitable work environment.

Progress in science, more than any other academic discipline, is collaborative and cumulative dependent upon the open, unfettered flow of ideas to generate new knowledge. Women have played a highly significant role in that process. By completely eliminating the barriers of education, access, and social and cultural attitudes, female scientists will continue to help define and direct the scientific advances that will greatly enhance all of our lives.

BIOGRAPHIES

Hattie Elizabeth Alexander (1901–1968)

Physician

A pediatrician and microbiologist, Hattie Elizabeth Alexander won international acclaim for developing a serum to combat influenza meningitis, a common childhood disease that was previously nearly always fatal and, with the serum, re-

duced the fatality rate to 20 percent. She pioneered the study of bacterial mutation and resistance to antibiotics and became one of the first women to head a national medical association as the president of the American Pediatric Society.

Alexander was born in Baltimore, Maryland, and was more interested in athletics than academics early in her education. She attended Goucher College, graduating in 1923 with courses in bacteriology and physiology, which led to jobs as a public health bacteriologist for the U.S. Public Health Service and the Maryland Public Health Service. After three years, she enrolled at Johns Hopkins University, where she received her MD in 1930.

She continued her training in pediatrics at Johns Hopkins Hospital, Columbia-Presbyterian Medical Center in New York, and Columbia University College of Physicians and Surgeons. She was appointed adjunct assistant pediatrician at Babies Hospital and the Vanderbilt Clinic in 1933, and she remained associated with Columbia for the rest of her career. She became assistant attending pediatrician in 1938, attending pediatrician in 1951, and finally full professor in 1958.

Alexander first began researching influenza meningitis in the early 1930s. Attempts to create an anti-influenzal serum derived from horses had failed, but she noted the success of researchers using a rabbit serum to treat pneumonia. Experimenting with rabbit serums, by 1939, Alexander had developed an effective cure for influenzal meningitis and continued to refine the treatment through the early 1940s, and, within a short period, infant mortality from the disease was virtually eliminated.

Becoming one of the first medical researchers to note the development of resistance of influenza bacilli cultures to antibiotic drugs, she studied antibiotics to understand the genetic mutation of bacteria to develop resistance. Her inquiry led her into the new area of microbiological genetics. Collaborating with fellow microbiologist Grace Leidy, Alexander developed techniques that produced hereditary changes in the DNA of *Hemophilus influenzae* in 1950.

Alexander authored over 150 research papers, and her achievements were recognized by receiving the E. Mead Johnson Award for Research in Pediatrics in 1942, the Stevens Triennial Prize in 1954, and the Oscar B. Hunter Memorial Award of the American Therapeutic Society in 1961. In 1964, she was chosen as the first female president of the American Pediatric Society. After retiring in 1966, Alexander remained active as a teacher and consultant. She died of cancer in New York City at the age of sixty-seven.

Virginia Apgar (1909–1974)

Physician

 Obstetrical anesthesiologist Virginia Apgar is best known as the inventor of the Apgar score, the first standardized method for evaluating a newborn's health to determine if any immediate medical intervention is required. The test, performed in the first few minutes of a baby's life, which measures pulse and respiration and examines skin color, has saved countless newborn lives. Apgar is also responsible for groundbreaking research into the effects of anesthesia during childbirth and advocacy on the prevention of birth defects.

Born and raised in Westfield, New Jersey, Apgar was determined to become a doctor at an early age, possibly inspired by the scientific experiments of her insurance executive father, who was also an amateur inventor and astronomer, or by her older brother's early death from tuberculosis or her other brother's chronic childhood illness. She attended Mount Holyoke College, where she graduated with a major in zoology in 1929. She was admitted to Columbia University College of Physicians and Surgeons, one of the first women to be enrolled there. She graduated in 1933, and, determined to become a surgeon, she won a surgical internship at Columbia, but the chair of surgery discouraged her from continuing because other women he had trained in surgery failed to establish successful careers in surgery. Instead, Apgar was encouraged to concentrate on anesthesiology (at the time not generally recognized as a specialty and handled mostly by nurses). After completing her surgical residency, Apgar trained in the Department of Anesthesiology at the University of Wisconsin, the first in the United States, before transferring to Bellevue Hospital in New York City.

In 1938, Apgar returned to Columbia as the director of the division of anesthesiology and as an attending anesthetist. By 1946, anesthesia became an acknowledged medical specialty, and in 1949, when anesthesia research became an academic department, Apgar became the first professor of anesthesiology and the first female physician to become a full professor at the Columbia University College of Physicians and Surgeons.

Apgar's research began with the effects on the baby of anesthesia given to the mother during labor. She subsequently developed the standardized method for evaluation of the newborn's transition to life outside the womb. Despite initial resistance, the Apgar Method was subsequently accepted and is now used worldwide. In 1959, while on sabbatical leave, Apgar earned a master's degree in public health from Johns Hopkins and decided not to return to academic medicine. Instead, she devoted herself to the prevention of birth defects through public education and fundraising for research as the director of the National Foundation for Infantile Paralysis (now the March of Dimes).

Apgar maintained that "women are liberated from the time they leave the womb" and rejected the notion that being female had imposed significant limitations on her medical career. She avoided women's organizations or any public role in issues of gender equality, although she privately voiced frustration about matters of salary inequality. Apgar never married nor had any children, despite having saved the lives of so many. In 1994, she was honored with a postage stamp, and, in 1995, she was inducted into the National Women's Hall of Fame. In 2018, Google celebrated what would have been Apgar's 109th birthday with a Google Doodle.

Frances H. Arnold (1956–)

Chemist

 Chemical engineering professor Frances Arnold became only the fifth woman to win a Nobel Prize in Chemistry in 2018. She was honored for her pioneering use of directed evolution to engineer enzymes.

The daughter of a nuclear physicist, Arnold grew up in the Pittsburgh suburbs. She graduated from Pittsburgh's Taylor Allderdice High School in 1974. In 1979, she received her undergraduate degree in mechanical and aerospace engineering from Princeton University with a focus on solar energy research and her Ph.D. in chemical engineering from the University of California–Berkeley in 1985. After postdoctoral research in biophysical chemistry at Berkeley, Arnold joined the faculty at the California Institute of Technology, becoming full professor in 1996. She is currently the Linus Pauling professor of chemical engineering at Caltech.

In her research, Arnold has used the principles of evolution—the adaptation of species to different environments—to develop proteins that solve various chemical problems. In 1993, Arnold conducted the first directed evolution of enzymes, the proteins that catalyze chemical reactions. Her results have led to the development of more environmentally friendly manufacturing of chemical substances such as pharmaceuticals and the production of renewable fuels. Arnold is the coinventor of forty U.S. patents and the cofounder of Gevo, Inc., a company to make fuels and chemicals from renewable resources.

Arnold's scientific achievements were not gained without considerable personal cost. Arnold's first husband, a biochemical engineer, died of cancer in 2001. Her former partner, a prominent cosmologist, died by suicide in 2010. Arnold herself was diagnosed with breast cancer in 2005, and in 2016, her son died in an accident. "So many things in my life have gone awry," Arnold has said, yet she has persisted and succeeded in an academic field dominated by men. "If they had a special Nobel laureate for Nobel laureates," said Carolyn Bertozzi, a chemistry professor at Stanford University and friend and colleague of Arnold, "she'd be that person. Frances is an extremely strong, impressive singularity of a person."

On being only the fifth female Nobel laureate in chemistry, Arnold is confident that more women will follow her: "There are a lot of brilliant women in chemistry, a little later than some of the men, but they are amazing. We are going to see a steady stream, I predict, of Nobel prizes coming out of chemistry and given to women."

Alice Ball (1892–1916)

Chemist

African American chemist Alice Ball developed the first successful treatment for leprosy (Hansen's disease) in the early twentieth century. She was the first woman and the first African American to receive a master's degree from the University of Hawaii, and she would become the university's first female chemistry professor.

Alice Augusta Ball was born in Seattle, Washington. Her father was a newspaper editor, photographer, and lawyer. Her grandfather, James Ball Sr., was a famous photographer, one of the first African Americans in the United States to learn the process of printing photographs onto metal plates. The family moved to Honolulu during Ball's childhood in the hopes that the warmer weather would ease her grandfather's arthritis. He died shortly after, and the family returned to Seattle, where Ball attended Seattle High School, graduating in 1910. She went on to study chemistry at the University of Washington, where she earned a bachelor's degree in pharmaceutical chemistry and a second degree in pharmacy.

After graduation, Ball decided to return to Hawaii to pursue a master's degree in chemistry at the College of Hawaii (now the University of Hawaii). While there, she studied chaulmoogra oil and its chemical properties. While chaulmoogra had previously been used to treat leprosy, Ball revolutionized its use by making it injectable and able to dissolve in the bloodstream. At the time, leprosy was virtually incurable, with those diagnosed with it exiled to the Hawaiian island of Molokai. Ball's innovations would directly impact more than eight thousand people: those diagnosed with leprosy who were no longer exiled to Molokai but could be treated out of their homes. Leprosy became not a fatal disease but a curable one. Ball's solution to the problem of treating leprosy, later called the Ball Method, would be the preferred treatment until sulfonamide drugs were developed in the 1940s.

Ball did not live to see the transformation of the treatment of leprosy she had pioneered. She became ill during her research and returned to Seattle for treatment but died in 1916 at the age of twenty-four. Although the actual cause of her death is unknown, with the death certificate reading "tuberculosis," a newspaper account at the time suggested the cause may have been chlorine poisoning from a lab teaching accident.

Recognition for Ball's contribution was late in coming. In 2000, the University of Hawaii–Manoa placed a bronze plaque in front of a chaulmoogra tree on campus to honor her and her discovery. The University of Hawaii posthumously awarded her the Regents' Medal of Distinction in 2007. As scholar Paul Wermager has said about Ball, "Not only did she overcome the racial and gender barriers of her time to become one of the very few African American women to earn a master's degree in chemistry, [but she] also developed the first useful treatment for Hansen's disease. Her amazing life was cut too short at the age of 24. Who knows what other marvelous work she could have accomplished had she lived."

Florence Bascom (1862–1945)

Geologist

Pioneering American female geologist Florence Bascom is considered the "first woman geologist" in America, who founded a leading academic center of geology and would train and open the door for following generations of notable female geologists. Bascom would become the second woman to earn a Ph.D. in geology (after Mary Emilie Holmes in 1888), the first woman to earn a Ph.D. from Johns Hopkins University (1893), the first woman to work for the U.S. Geological Survey (1889), the first female geologist to present a paper before the Geological Survey in Washington (1901), and the first woman to be elected to the Council of the Geological Society of America (1924).

Bascom was born in Williamstown, Massachusetts. Her father was a professor at Williams College and later the president of the University of Wisconsin, who would provide his daughter with her first exposure to the field of geology. Her mother was a women's rights activist involved in the suffrage movement. Both parents encouraged their daughter to pursue a college education. Bascom earned her bachelor's degree in arts and letters at the University of Wisconsin in 1882. She would earn a BS degree from there in 1884 as well as a master's degree in 1887. She pursued doctoral work in geology at Johns Hopkins University, at the time a discipline for men only. She was required to sit behind a screen in class in order not to distract the male students, who were the priority. Her doctorate explored the origins and formation of the Appalachian Mountains, and she became the first woman to receive a Ph.D. from Johns Hopkins in 1893.

Bascom went to work as an assistant geologist for the U.S. Geological Survey, serving as an associate editor of the magazine *American Geologist* from 1896 to 1908. In 1906, the first edition of *American Men of Science* rated her among the top one hundred geologists in the country. After teaching at Ohio State University (1893–1895), Bascom moved to Bryn Mawr College, where, for the next thirty-three years, she created its Department of Geology and developed its library, collections, and laboratories. Her students became her colleagues: four would go on to earn doctoral degrees, and three worked for the Geological Survey. In addition to teaching, Bascom was active in field research, and her work on the geology of the Piedmont remains important today. She published more than forty scholarly articles.

Bascom would retire from teaching in 1928 but continued to work at the Geological Survey until 1936. She died of a stroke at the age of eighty-two, having laid the foundation for American female geologists. In a kind of testimony to both her career and its focus, Bascom observed in 1928, "The fascination of any search after truth lies not in the attainment … but in the pursuit, where all the powers of the mind are absorbed in the task. One feels oneself in contact with something that is infinite, and one finds a joy that is beyond expression in 'sounding the abyss of science' and the secrets of the infinite mind."

Elizabeth H. Blackburn (1948–)

Biologist

Australian American molecular biologist and biochemist Elizabeth H. Blackburn was awarded the 2009 Nobel Prize in Physiology or Medicine (along with Carol W. Greider and Jack W. Szostak) for her discoveries involving the genetic composition of telomeres (segments of DNA occurring at the ends of chromosomes) and for her contribution to the discovery of an enzyme called telomerase that replenishes the telomere.

Blackburn was born in Hobart, the capital city of Tasmania, the island that forms the southernmost state in Australia. Both of her parents were physicians, who encouraged her interest in science from an early age. When she was in her teens, her family moved to Melbourne, and she attended its university high school before earning a bachelor's and master's degree from the University of Melbourne in biochemistry. She completed her Ph.D. at Cambridge University in 1975. She pursued postdoctoral studies in molecular and cellular biology at Yale University in the laboratory of cell biologist and geneticist Joseph Gall.

Conducting research on the single-celled organism *Tetrahymena*, commonly referred to as "pond scum," Blackburn managed to uncover the molecular structure of the telomere, the section at the end of the chromosome that prevents it from disintegrating as the cell reproduces. Blackburn and her mentor, Joseph Gall, shared their findings in a landmark research study published in 1978. The same year, Blackburn joined the faculty of the University of California–Berkeley, where she began work on developing an enzyme that regulates the replication of the telomere to protect the cells of young organisms, an important breakthrough in understanding the aging process and degenerative diseases. Blackburn joined forces with a recent biology graduate, Carol W. Greider, and together, they would unlock the mystery of the telomere's regulating enzyme in 1985. News of their discovery produced worldwide attention, with some seeing in it a cure for cancer

and the means to reverse the aging process. Blackburn and Greider, however, were content to initiate a new field of inquiry into these topics with the hope that in time, new treatments for degenerative diseases and cancer would follow.

In 1990, Blackburn moved from Berkeley to the Department of Microbiology and Immunology at the University of California–San Francisco, where she chaired the department from 1993 to 1997. She continued her research on telomere biology, succeeding in more than doubling the life span of cells in the laboratory. When Blackburn and Grieder were awarded the Nobel Prize in 2009, the Swedish Academy recognized that they "have a new dimension to our understanding of the cell, shed light on disease mechanisms, and stimulated the development of potential new therapies." Other awards followed, including the 2012 American Institute of Chemists' Gold Medal as well as the Royal Medal of the Royal Society, for her contributions to the advancement of knowledge in the field.

In 2015, Blackburn became president of the Salk Institute for Biological Studies, a position she held until her retirement in 2018.

Linda Brown Buck (1947–)

Biologist

Biologist Linda Brown Buck is best known for her work on the olfactory system, for which she was awarded the 2004 Nobel Prize in Physiology or Medicine (with Richard Axel). Among Buck and Axel's discoveries was that humans have about 350 different odor receptor types found on nerve cells in the upper part of the nose and that each odor receptor is highly specialized and can detect only a small number of different odor molecules.

Buck was born in Seattle, Washington, to parents who encouraged her to believe that she could do anything she wanted to in life, to think independently, and to do something worthwhile with her life and "not settle for something mediocre." Buck received a BS degree in psychology and microbiology in 1975 from the University of Washington, taking ten years to complete her degree as she tried to determine her career path. "I wasn't sure what I wanted to do," Buck recalled. "I was filled with angst; I wanted to do something to help other people, but I didn't want to be an M.D. Then I discovered immunology and I never looked back." She completed her Ph.D. in immunology in 1980 at the University of Texas Southwestern Medical Center in Dallas.

In 1980, Buck began postdoctoral research at Columbia University, and in 1982, she joined the laboratory of Dr. Richard Axel at Columbia's Institute of Cancer Research. Inspired in 1985 by a paper written by neuroscientist Solomon Snyder about odor-detecting protein, Buck set out to unravel the puzzle of how we smell things. With Axel, Buck began looking for genes that encode receptors for odor molecules. Their research, published in 1991, was the result of three years of 12–15-hour days on the project. The paper, entitled "A Novel Multigene Family May Encode Odorant Receptors: A Molecular Basis for Odor Recognition," is considered a landmark scientific work that opened the door to the genetic and molecular analysis of the mechanism of olfaction.

After publishing their findings, Buck joined the Department of Neurobiology at Harvard Medical School, where she established her own lab to understand how the inputs from different odor receptors are organized in the nose, expanding understanding of the nervous system. In 2002, she returned to Seattle as a member of the Division of Basic Sciences at the Fred Hutchinson Cancer Research Center and was an affiliate professor of physiology and biophysics at the University of Washington.

Widely honored for her achievements, Buck has said, "Looking back over my life, I am struck by the good fortune I had to be a scientist. Very few in this world have the opportunity to do every day what they love to do, as I have. I have had wonderful mentors, colleagues, and students with whom to explore what fascinates me and have enjoyed both challenges and discoveries. I am grateful for all of these things and look forward to learning what Nature will next reveal to us."

Annie Jump Cannon (1863–1941)

Astronomer

Astronomer Annie Jump Cannon played a significant role in the development of contemporary stellar classification. Hired as an assistant at the Harvard Observatory by Edward C. Pickering, Cannon is credited with creating the Harvard Classification Scheme, the first serious attempt to organize and classify stars based on their temperatures and spectral types.

Born in Dover, Delaware, Cannon was the oldest of the three daughters of a shipbuilder and state senator. Her mother encouraged her daughter's academic pursuits and first taught her the constellations from their attic window using an old astronomy textbook. Cannon attended the Wilmington Conference Academy (now Wesley College) and in 1880 entered Wellesley College in Massachusetts, where she studied physics and astronomy. She graduated with a degree in physics, having studied under Sarah Frances Whiting, one of the few female physicists in the United States at the time, in 1884. Returning to Delaware, Cannon developed her skills in the new art of photography, traveling in 1892 through Europe taking photographs. Cannon was stricken with scarlet fever, which left her nearly deaf. In 1894 after her mother died, Cannon contacted her former instructor at Wellesley, Professor Whiting, to inquire about a job opening. Whiting hired her as a physics teacher.

The opportunity allowed Cannon to do graduate work in physics and astronomy and to learn about spectroscopy. To gain access to a better telescope, she enrolled at Radcliffe College as a special student, which led to her access to the Harvard College Observatory, where she met its director, Edward C. Pickering, who hired her as his assistant in 1896.

Cannon would become a member of Pickering's Women, a group of women Pickering hired to map and define every star in the sky. Pickering set out to obtain optical spectra of as many stars as possible and classify them by their spectra. Men in the laboratory operated the telescopes and took photographs, while the women meticulously examined the data, carried out astronomical calculations, and catalogued the photographs. Cannon simplified the classifications of stellar spectra devised by Williamina P. S. Fleming, the curator of astronomical photographs, to classes O, B, A, F, G, K, and M (using the mnemonic "Oh, Be A Fine Girl—Kiss Me!"). She also added numerical divisions, further dividing each class into steps. It was soon realized that Cannon's scheme actually was classifying stars according to their temperatures, and her spectral classifications were soon universally adopted. She would eventually obtain and classify spectra for more than 225,000 stars, publishing her work in nine volumes as the *Henry Draper Catalogue* (1918–1924).

In 1911, Cannon succeeded Fleming as curator at the observatory and, after 1924, extended her work cataloguing tens of thousands of additional stars. Cannon's work has been regarded as an invaluable contribution to astronomy, advancing the field from mere observation to theoretical and conceptual research. Cannon was honored for her achievement by receiving the first honorary doctorate awarded to a woman by Oxford University (1925) and the Henry Draper Medal of the National Academy of Sciences (1931). She was also the first woman to become an officer in the American Astronomical Society. In 1938, she was appointed to the Harvard faculty as the William Cranch Bond professor of astronomy.

Cannon never married, and it has been suggested that her deafness caused her to avoid socializing and to concentrate exclusively on her work. She officially retired from the observatory in 1940 but carried on research until her death the next year. The American Astronomical Society presents the Annie Jump Cannon Award annually to female astronomers who make important contributions to the field.

Rachel Carson (1907–1964)

Biologist

Marine biologist and nature writer Rachel Carson, perhaps more than anyone else, catalyzed the global environmental movement with her 1962 book *Silent Spring*, a controversial and groundbreaking study of the dangers of chemical pesticides. The book led to a nationwide ban on DDT and other pesticides and sparked the movement that eventually led to the creation of the U.S. Environmental Protection Agency.

Rachel Louise Carson was born in a farm in Springdale, Pennsylvania. She described herself as a "rather solitary child" who "spent a great deal of time in woods and beside streams, learning the birds and the insects and flowers. Carson became a published writer by the age of ten, writing for children's magazines. While attending the Pennsylvania College for Women (later Chatham College), she studied literature with the goal of becoming a writer. However, a required biology course ignited her passion for science, and she changed from an English major to a biology major, graduating magna cum laude in 1929. She next studied at the oceanographic institution in Woods Hole, Massachusetts, and at Johns Hopkins University, where she received a master's degree in zoology.

Carson was forced to forego the pursuit of a doctorate to support her mother and two orphaned nieces. Carson become only the second woman hired by the U.S. Bureau of Fisheries, where she worked for the next fifteen years as an aquatic biologist, writing brochures and educational materials for the public. She eventually would be promoted to editor-in-chief of all publications for the U.S. Fish and Wildlife Service.

An article she wrote for the bureau on marine life was accepted by *Atlantic Monthly,* and it grew into her first book, *Under the Sea World* (1941). In 1951, a second book, *The Sea Around Us* (1951), became a worldwide best-seller; it was translated into thirty-two languages and won the National Book Award for Nonfiction. A companion volume, *The Edge of the Sea*, was published in 1955. Both books are vivid accounts of the ocean and shorelands that combine keen scientific observation with rich, poetic descriptions.

Because of her book sales, Carson was able to move to Southport, Maine, to concentrate on her writing. She would then move to Silver Spring, Maryland, to care for her aging mother, and in

1958, she received a letter from a friend describing the devastating effects on her private bird sanctuary in Duxbury, Massachusetts, after it was sprayed with the pesticide DDT under the state's mosquito control program. Carson investigated and began to document the impact of DDT and other chemicals on plants, animals, and people. She published her findings in *Silent Spring* in 1962, detailing pesticides' effects on ecosystems and the health risk for humans. She also accused the chemical industry of spreading misinformation and public officials' inaction.

Chemical companies sought to discredit her as a communist or hysterical woman, and when a CBS special, *The Silent Spring of Rachel Carson*, aired in 1963, chemical companies pulled their ads. Fifteen million people viewed the program, and President John F. Kennedy's Science Advisory Committee validated Carson's research, launching a national debate on the use of pesticides that eventually led to the banning of DDT and increased sensitivity to environmental dangers that ignited the modern environmental movement. In addition to having won a crucial battle on behalf of the environment, Carson also touched off a much-wider debate that challenged the assumptions that industrial progress must come at the expense of the environment. *Silent Spring* had fundamentally altered the way many people saw the world and the responsibility of humans to protect it.

Carson would be honored for her work, receiving medals from the National Audubon Society and the American Geographical Society and induction into the American Academy of Arts. At the pinnacle of her notoriety and acclaim, Carson, seriously ill with breast cancer, died two years after her book's publication. In 1980, she was posthumously awarded the Presidential Medal of Freedom. According to environmental engineer and Carson scholar H. Patricia Hynes, "*Silent Spring* altered the balance of power in the world. No one since would be able to sell pollution as the necessary underside of progress so easily or uncritically." In certain fundamental ways, Carson created a new science: environmental studies.

Mary Agnes Chase (1869–1963)
Agrostologist, Botanist

Despite ending her formal education after grammar school, Mary Agnes Chase became one of the world's most outstanding agrostologists, experts on grasses, which Chase asserted "holds the Earth together." She began collecting and illustrating plants in her twenties, which became her entry to the science of agrostology.

Chase was born in Iroquois County, Illinois. After only a grammar school education, in 1893, she visited the Colombian Exposition in Chicago with her botanist nephew, and she was inspired to take up the study of the plants in northern Illinois, collecting specimens and making drawings. In 1902, she became a botanical assistant at the Field Museum of Natural History in Chicago, where her work was featured in two museum publications: *Plantae Utowanae* (1900) and *Plantae Yucatanae* (1904). In 1904, Chase joined the U.S. Department of Agriculture as a botanical illustrator and eventually became a scientific assistant in systematic agrostology in 1907 and an associate botanist in 1925. Chase collaborated closely with botanist Albert Spear Hitchcock for almost twenty years. She collaborated with Hitchcock on *The North American Species of Panicum* (1910), and she published *Tropical North American Species of Panicum* (1915) and *Grasses of the West Indies* (1917).

Chase wrote *The First Book of Grasses, the Structure of Grasses Explained for Beginners* in 1922, and in 1924, she began an eight-month field trip through eastern Brazil. She would return to Brazil in 1929–1930 and would be credited with being the first woman to scale the highest mountain in South America. Following Hitchcock's death in 1936, Chase succeeded him as senior botanist in charge of systematic agrostology and custodian of the Section of Grasses, Division of Plants at the Smithsonian's U.S. National Museum.

In addition to her research, Chase was actively involved in the women's suffrage movement and aligned with the radical Women's Party. She was jailed several times for participating in suffrage demonstrations and continued her radical activity despite threats of dismissal from the USDA. She also advocated on behalf of young, female botanists, providing training for many to enter the field.

Chase retired from the USDA in 1939 at the age of seventy but continued to work on her collections at the Smithsonian. In 1940, she surveyed Venezuela's grasses and advised the government on establishing a botanical program. In 1958, the grammar school graduate received an honorary doctorate from the University of Illinois; in 1959, she was named an honorary fellow of the Smithsonian Institution; and in 1961, she became a fellow of the Linnean Society of London.

Josephine Cochrane (1839–1913)

Inventor

Prima mașină de

Josephine Cochrane, who had no formal education in the sciences or engineering, was the inventor of the first commercially successful dishwasher. She designed the first model of her dishwasher in the shed behind her house to protect her china while it was being cleaned. Today, it is hard to imagine a home that does not have a version of Cochrane's invention.

Born Josephine Garis in Ashtabula County, Ohio, Cochrane would be raised in Valparaiso, Indiana, by her engineer father, who invented a hydraulic pump for draining marshes. Cochrane's mother died when her daughter was young. Cochrane attended private school in Indiana and later in Shelbyville, Illinois, where she completed high school. At the age of nineteen, in 1858, she married William A. Cochran. Cochrane expressed her independence by taking her husband's name but adding an "e" at the end, much to the annoyance of her in-laws. Her husband was a well-to-do dry-goods store owner, and Cochrane became a socialite and hostess. When, after a dinner party, a servant chipped the heirloom china, Cochrane refused to let the servants handle the china anymore but was averse to washing dishes by hand herself. This pro-

vided her motivation to invent a machine that could do the job for her.

Cochrane worked out a design involving water jets and a dish rack that would hold tableware and dishes in place. When her husband died suddenly in 1883, leaving behind considerable debt, what had been a speculative venture became a financial necessity, and Cochrane refined her design to market it to consumers. Cochrane's model was powered by a motor, and soapy water would squirt over the dishes to clean them. In 1886, she patented the design of the Cochrane Dishwasher. Cochrane formed the Garis–Cochran Manufacturing Company (named for Cochran's father and husband) to produce it, and the machine was showcased at the World Columbian Exposition in 1893, which helped to establish a market for it in hotels and large restaurants. Since most homes' hot-water heaters could not supply the amount of hot water the dishwasher required, the machine's large size limited home use. It would not be until the 1950s that increased availability of hot water in homes, effective dishwashing detergent, and an interest in labor-saving domestic appliances would turn the dishwasher into a consumer product. The Garis–Cochran Manufacturing Company became KitchenAid, part of the Whirlpool Corporation, and in 1949, the first KitchenAid dishwasher based on Cochrane's design was introduced to the public.

Cochrane died in Chicago at the age of seventy-four. In 2006, she was inducted into the National Inventors Hall of Fame.

Gerty Theresa Cori (1896–1957)

Medical Researcher

The first American woman (and only the third woman ever) to win a Nobel Prize in science and the first woman to be awarded the Nobel Prize in Physiology or Medicine, biochemist Gerty Theresa Cori was honored for her role in the discovery of glycogen metabolism.

Born in Prague, Czechoslovakia, Cori was encouraged by her uncle, a professor of pediatrics, to attend medical school, and she became one of only a few women to be admitted to the German University of Prague. She graduated with her MD degree in 1920 along with her classmate, Carl Cori, and the two married shortly after graduation while beginning work in clinics in Vienna. In 1922, they moved to Buffalo, New York, where Carl was hired at the State Institute for the Study of Malignant Diseases (later the Roswell Park Memorial Institute), and Cori was hired as an assistant pathologist. They began there a lifetime collaboration studying how energy is produced and transmitted in the human body, specifically how sugar (glucose) is metabolized.

Together, the Coris published some fifty papers while at Roswell with whichever researcher's name appearing first depending on who had done the bulk of the research for a given paper. In 1929, they proposed the theory that bears their name—the "Cori cycle"—to explain the movement of energy in the body from muscle to the liver and back to the muscle. They showed how glycogen in muscles is converted to glucose when energy is needed and that the muscles leave some of the sugar as lactic acid for later use. The lactic acid is recycled into glycogen by the liver, which is then stored in the muscles for later use. Their discovery of this process, the first time the cycle of carbohydrates in the human body had been fully understood and explained, would be especially useful in treating diabetes.

Although they had both developed the Cori cycle together, Carl Cori received job offers from universities, but they refused to break up their partnership and accept separate appointments. In 1931, the couple moved to St. Louis, where Carl was offered the chair of the Department of Pharmacology at Washington University School of Medicine, and Gerty was offered a position as research assistant. They remained there for the next sixteen years, with Carl made chair of the new Department of Biochemistry in 1946 and Gerty promoted to full professor. In 1947, they both were awarded the Nobel Prize for discovering the enzymes that convert glycogen to sugar and back again into glycogen. The couple would mentor six scientists, who subsequently received Nobel Prizes.

In 1957, Gerty Cori died after a decadelong struggle with myelosclerosis, although she remained active in the research laboratory until her death. In 2008, Cori was honored by the release of a U.S. postal stamp that celebrated her many important discoveries, including a new derivative of glucose, elucidating the steps of carbohydrate metabolism, and contributing to the understanding and treatment of diabetes and other metabolic diseases.

Marie Maynard Daly (1921–2003)

Biochemist

Biochemist Marie Maynard Daly was the first African American woman to earn a Ph.D. in chemistry. A researcher and teacher at the Rockefeller Institute, Columbia University, Howard University, and Yeshiva University, Daly focused on the effects of cholesterol on the mechanics of the heart, of sugar and other nutrients on the health of arteries, and of cigarette smoke on the lungs. Over her distinguished career, she made important contributions to our understanding of the causes of heart attacks and lung disease.

Daly was born in Queens, New York. Her mother was a homemaker; her father had been forced to leave his study of chemistry at Cornell University to support his family as a postal worker. He encouraged his daughter's interest in academics and science. She attended the all-girls' Hunter College High School before earning her BS degree in chemistry from Queens College in 1942 and a master's degree from New York University in 1944. Encouraged by pioneering chemist Mary Caldwell at Columbia University, Daly became in 1947 the first African American woman in the United States to earn a Ph.D. in chemistry.

Daly held teaching positions at Howard University and at Columbia. She also conducted research on the composition and metabolism of components of the cell nucleus at New York's Rockefeller Institute of Medicine. In 1955, back at Columbia and later at Albert Einstein College of Medicine at Yeshiva University from 1960 until her retirement in 1986, Daly conducted groundbreaking research discovering the link between high cholesterol and clogged arteries, which led to a better understanding of how heart attacks are caused. She also examined the effects of sugar on arteries and cigarette smoke on the lungs.

Besides her research, Daly was active in developing programs to increase the enrollment of minority students in medical school and graduate science programs. In 1988, she established a scholarship fund for African American science students at Queens College in honor of her father.

Gertrude Elion (1918–1999)

Biochemist, Pharmacologist

 Biochemist and pharmacologist Gertrude Elion received the Nobel Prize in Physiology or Medicine in 1988. Among the many drugs she developed were the first chemotherapy for childhood leukemia; the immunosuppressant that made organ transplants possible; the first antiviral medication; and treatment for lupus, hepatitis, arthritis, gout, and the first drug for effectively treating patients with AIDS. She became the fifth female Nobel laureate in Physiology or Medicine and the ninth in science—all without earning a Ph.D.

Elion was born in New York City to immigrant parents from Lithuania and Poland. An excellent student, Elion graduated from Walton High School at the age of fifteen. "I had no specific bent toward science," she recalled, "until my grandfather died of stomach cancer. I decided that nobody should suffer that much." She attended Hunter College, majoring in chemistry, and graduated in 1937. She went on to earn a master's degree from New York University in 1941. Unable to find a job in a research laboratory because she was a woman, she found work at a laboratory for A&P supermarkets performing tedious tasks such as measuring the acidity of pickle juice. "I hadn't been aware," Elion recalled, "that any doors were closed to me until I started knocking on them." She did brief stints teaching before accepting a research assistant position for George H. Hitchings (1905–1998) at Burroughs Wellcome & Company, the pharmaceutical company where she would

spend the rest of her career. While working with Hitchings, she started a Ph.D. program taking evening classes at Brooklyn Polytechnic Institute, but after several years of long commutes, she realized that she would be unable to complete her degree without becoming a full-time student. She decided instead to forego the Ph.D. and focus on her research (she would eventually receive honorary doctorates from Polytechnic and Harvard).

Working with Hitchings, Elion would revolutionize drug making using a method known as "rational drug design," replacing the conventional method of trial and error with a close study of how organic compounds operated and what could be done to interfere with harmful effects. Examining the differences between the biochemistry of normal human cells and those of cancer cells, they formulated drugs that could kill or inhibit the production of particular pathogens, leaving the normal cells undamaged. Elion would publish 225 papers on her findings, and by 1950, Hitchings and Elion successfully synthesized the compounds that for the first time interfered with the formation of leukemia cells, putting leukemia patients in remission. Elion would next discover how to make the compounds less toxic to patients with fewer side effects. This led to one of the first effective chemotherapy treatments.

Elion's innovative research method would lead to the development of multiple new drugs, including Purinethol, the first to treat leukemia; Azathioprine, the first immune-suppressive agent; Allopurinol for treating gout; Pyrimethamine for malaria; Trimethoprim for meningitis, septicemia, and bacterial infections; Acyclovir for viral herpes; and Nelarabine for cancer treatment. Elion's research has affected countless individuals.

Elion officially retired in 1983, but she continued her research, overseeing the development of azidothymidine (AZT), the first drug used in the treatment of AIDS. In 1991, she was awarded a National Medal of Science. She died at the age of eighty-one. In what can serve as a fitting testimonial and encouragement for those who will follow her, Elion observed, "Don't be afraid of hard work. Nothing worthwhile comes easily. Don't let others discourage you or tell you that you can't do it. In my day I was told women didn't go into chemistry. I saw no reason why we couldn't."

Dian Fossey (1932–1985)

Primatologist

Primatologist and conservationist Dian Fossey is considered the world's leading authority on the physiology and behavior of mountain gorillas, whom she fought to protect from game wardens, poachers, and government officials who wanted to convert gorilla habitats to farmland. Tragically, Fossey was found hacked to death in 1985 at her Rwandan forest camp. The reason for her murder and the identity of the perpetrator have never been established.

Fossey was born in San Francisco, the daughter of a fashion model and an insurance agent. Her parents divorced when Fossey was six, and her mother remarried a businessman who was a strict disciplinarian and offered Fossey little emotional support. She found solace in animals, from her goldfish to horses that Fossey trained with as an equestrienne. After high school, she followed the guidance of her stepfather and enrolled in business courses. However, a summer spent on a Montana ranch at nineteen rekindled her love of animals, and she registered for preveterinary courses at the University of California–Davis. Her parents withdrew financial support, and Fossey worked as a department store clerk, as a laboratory assistant, and as a machinist in a factory to support herself. Struggling with chemistry and physics, Fossey transferred to San Jose State College to study occupational therapy, graduating in 1954.

After working for several years at a children's hospital in Louisville, Kentucky, Fossey took her first trip to Africa in 1963, where she met anthropologist Louis Leakey and had her first glimpse of mountain gorillas. Leakey urged her to study them in their natural habitat on a long-term basis, and Fossey established the Karisoke Research Center in 1967, living in isolation in the depths of Rwanda's Virunga Mountains. With persistence and patience, Fossey was able to get the animals to become accustomed to her presence, allowing her to gather data about their behavior. Her discoveries included

how females transfer from group to group over the decades, gorilla vocalization, hierarchies, and social relationships. Fossey obtained her Ph.D. in zoology at Cambridge University by 1980 and was recognized as the world's leading authority on the physiology and behavior of mountain gorillas, which she described as "dignified, highly social, gentle giants, with individual personalities, and strong family relationships." She lectured as a professor at Cornell University from 1981 to 1983. Her account of her experiences, *Gorillas in the Mist* (1983), was an international best-seller and was made into a popular 1988 film.

Returning to Rwanda, Fossey stirred opposition and tension from her relentless campaign to protect the mountain gorillas and their natural habitat, including violent confrontations with poachers and harassment from Rwandan government officials who opposed her conservationist policies for economic development. On December 26, 1985, her slain body was discovered near her campsite. No one has been definitely charged or convicted of her murder. She is buried at the Karisoke Research Center she created in the gorilla graveyard. The foundation she created from the proceeds of her books and film continues her work of study and protection of the animals she helped make known to the world.

Lillian Moller Gilbreth (1878–1972)

Psychologist

 A pioneer in the field of industrial and organizational psychology, Lillian Moller Gilbreth is best known for applying psychology to time-and-motion studies. One of the first female engineers to receive a Ph.D., she is considered to be the first industrial/organizational psychologist, who was described in the 1940s as "a genius in the art of living" and "America's first lady of engineering," all while raising twelve children in a domestic life that would be featured in two Hollywood films.

Born Lillian Evelyn Moller in Oakland, California, she was the oldest of nine children, educated by her parents and tutors at home until she was nine, when she entered public school. She managed to convince her traditionalist father to allow her to study literature and music at the University of California–Berkeley, where she graduated in 1900 with a teaching certificate and a bachelor's degree in English. She became the university's first female commencement speaker. Intending to do graduate work in English at Columbia University with distinguished scholar Brander Matthews, she switched to psychology when she learned that Matthew did not accept female students in his classes. She would complete a master's degree in English from Berkeley in 1902. After completing one year of Ph.D. study, she met Frank Gilbreth, a wealthy construction company owner, and they married in 1904 and began their family, which would eventually include twelve children. Anxious to help her husband in his business, she changed her focus from English to psychology, and, after the family relocated to Rhode Island, Gilbreth completed her doctorate in psychology from Brown University in 1914 with an emphasis on the psychological aspects of industrial management. Gilbreth is now considered a pioneer in what is now known as organizational psychology. Working with her husband on workplace efficiency, the pair collaborated on applying principles of the social sciences to industrial management. Their method of time-and-motion study provided a systematic means of identifying and analyzing the number of movements and amount of time needed to complete a specific task. *Motion Study* (1911), *Fatigue Study* (1916), and *Applied Motion Study* (1917) published their research in groundbreaking works of organizational psychology.

Husband and wife applied their productivity methods to their own household, conducting experiments such as detailed analyses of motions to find faster and more efficient ways to wash dishes, brush teeth, and assorted domestic tasks. Two of their children, Ernestine and Frank Gilbreth Jr., collaborated on two popular accounts of the family and its organization and daily activities, *Cheaper by the Dozen* (1948) and *Belles on Their Toes* (1950), which were later made into feature films.

Frank Gilbreth suffered a fatal heart attack in 1924, leaving Gilbreth to provide for her family by herself. She became the first female professor in the engineering school at Purdue University, the first woman to be elected to the National Academy of Engineering, and the second woman to join the American Society of Mechanical Engineers. She retired from her academic position in 1948 at the age of seventy but continued to work as a consultant with General Electric to improve the design of household appliances. Before her death in 1972, she would win the Hoover Medal of the American Society of Civil Engineers and would become the first female psychologist in the United States to have a postage stamp issued in her honor in 1984.

Maria Goeppert-Mayer (1906–1972)
Physicist

Theoretical physicist Maria Goeppert-Mayer became the second woman to be awarded a Nobel Prize in Physics (after Marie Curie) and the first American woman. She is best known for proposing the nuclear shell model of the atomic nucleus: inside the nucleus, protons and neutrons are arranged in a series of layers, like the layers of an onion, with neutrons and protons rotating around each other at every level. Her discovery was foundational in the development of nuclear physics.

Goeppert-Mayer was born in Kattowitz, Germany (now Poland), the only child of a professor of pediatrics at the University of Göttingen and a former music teacher. Goeppert-Mayer was educated at a girls' grammar school operated by suffragettes. When it went bankrupt after her junior year, she passed the collegiate examination to enter the University of Göttingen without a high school diploma. She earned her Ph.D. there in 1930, the same year she married American chemical physicist Joseph Edward Mayer, and the couple moved to the United States, where he was offered a faculty position at Johns Hopkins University. Policies at the university prevented them from hiring both spouses in faculty positions, so for the next nine years, Goeppert-Mayer worked at Johns Hopkins as a volunteer associate. After becoming an American citizen in 1933, Mayer and her husband both received appointments at Columbia University, although Goeppert-Mayer's was without a salary. She gained her first paid faculty position teaching science part-time at Sarah Lawrence College.

In 1942, Goeppert-Mayer joined the Manhattan Project and worked on the separation of the uranium isotopes for the atomic bomb. Through her friend Edward Teller, Goeppert-Mayer was given a position at Columbia with the Opacity Project, a program to develop thermonuclear weapons. After the war, her husband became a professor in the Chemistry Department at the new Institute of Nuclear Studies at the University of Chicago, and Mayer became a voluntary associate professor of physics at the school. When the nearby Argonne National Laboratory was founded, Goeppert-Mayer was offered a part-time job there as a senior physicist in the Department of Theoretical Physics, although, Goeppert-Mayer admitted, "I don't know anything about nuclear physics." It was at Chicago and Argonne that Goeppert-Mayer developed the mathematical model of nuclear shells. Three other German scientists were also working on the same problem, and, although Goeppert-Mayer's discovery preceded theirs, they were able to publish first and received much of the credit. Goeppert-Mayer would collaborate with one of the scientists, Hans D. Jensen, on the book *Elementary Theory of Nuclear Shell Structure* (1950) and would share the Nobel Prize in Physics in 1963 for their work.

In 1960, Goeppert-Mayer became a full professor of physics at the University of California–San Diego. Suffering a stroke shortly after her appointment, she continued to teach and conduct research for a number of years until her death in 1972. After her death, the Maria Goeppert-Mayer Award was created by the American Physical Society to honor young, female physicists at the beginning of their careers.

Hetty Goldman (1881–1972)

Archaeologist

One of the most distinguished archaeologists of the twentieth century, Hetty Goldman was the first female faculty member at Princeton's Institute of Advanced Study and the first woman appointed to direct an archaeological excavation by the Archaeological Institute of America.

Goldman was born in New York City, the daughter of a lawyer whose father had founded the investment bank Goldman Sachs. Goldman and her three siblings attended The Sachs School, founded by their uncle Julius Sachs. Goldman graduated in 1903 from Bryn Mawr College, majoring in English and classics. She continued her classical study at Columbia University and in 1906 took a three-month tour of archaeological sites in Italy before enrolling at Radcliffe College for graduate study in classical languages and archaeology. Based on her master's thesis on Greek vase painting, Goldman became the first woman to hold the Charles Eliot Norton Fellowship to study at the American School of Classical Studies at Athens. It was her experience there that confirmed her vocation as an archaeologist. "I cannot remember the exact process," she recalled, "by which … I was transformed into a passionate excavator who was either turning up the soil of Greece or planning to return to it; but complete conversion took place on top of a hill in Boeotia." She stumbled onto a mound that did not appear natural. It was the ancient town of Eutresis, which Goldman would excavate as well as a number of other sites in Greece and Turkey, including Halae, Colophon, and Tarsus. Her first excavation was completed in 1911, and her findings would earn her a Ph.D. from Radcliffe in 1916.

In 1936, she became the first female professor in the School of Humanistic Studies at the Institute for Advanced Study in Princeton, New Jersey. In 1950, she was elected fellow of the American Academy of Arts and Science, and, following her retirement in 1956, she received, in 1960, a gold medal from the Archaeological Institute for Distinguished Archaeological Achievement, in which she was memorialized as "the dean of Classical and Near Eastern archaeology in this country."

Despite her years in the classroom and in research, Goldman would say that "excavation is my first love and fundamentally I fear I am a wandering spirit." Her adventures in pursuit of her archaeological discoveries included disruption by war, pursuit by bandits, and once traveling four thousand miles in a Model A Ford. Goldman died in 1972 at the age of ninety. Goldman would summarize her life as "like working my way through a dark tunnel with a light glimmering at the end, and gradually finding my way, by organization and comparative study, into the full light of a final arrangement that seemed to me valid."

Carol W. Greider (1961–)

Molecular Biologist

Molecular biologist Carol W. Greider was awarded (with Elizabeth H. Blackburn and Jack W. Szostak) the 2009 Nobel Prize in Physiology or Medicine for her research into telomeres (segments of DNA occurring at the ends of chromosomes) and for her discovery of an enzyme telomerase that revolutionized our understanding of the aging process and degenerative diseases and opened the door to new treatments for both.

Carol Greider was born in San Diego, the daughter of scientists: a physicist father and biologist mother. Her mother, suffering from depression, committed suicide when Greider was six, and she grew up in Davis, California, with her father and older brother. Afflicted with dyslexia, Greider managed through memorization to excel in chemistry and biology. She graduated with a bachelor's degree in biology from the University of California–Santa Barbara in 1983. Greider had difficulty getting into graduate school based on low test scores due to her dyslexia but was accepted at the University of California–Berkeley, where she began to work in Elizabeth Blackburn's laboratory on telomeres.

Blackburn and Greider searched for the telomere's mysterious regulating enzyme that protected the cell. Greider, in what the Lasker Award Committee would later describe as "a *tour de force* of biochemistry," painstakingly tried one method after another to purify and observe the proteins found in the telomeres to identify the enzyme they were searching for. After nearly eight months of failure, Greider and Blackburn altered their experiment using oligonucleotides of DNA produced in a chemical synthesizer rather than bacteria. This led to evidence of the enzymatic action they had been looking for. They named the enzyme telomerase, and the revelation of their finding caused a sensation, leading to new avenues for treatments of degenerative diseases and cancer.

In 1987, Greider received her Ph.D. from the University of California–Berkeley in molecular biology and was awarded a research fellowship at the Cold Spring Harbor Laboratory in New York, where she continued her research into telomerase. In 1990, she was named an assistant investigator at the Cold Spring Harbor Laboratory, an associate in 1992, and a full investigator in 1994. Throughout the 1990s, Greider's work with telomeres focused on cancer and the discovery that inhibiting telomerase activity in cancer cells can slow tumor growth. This research has led to telomerase as a promising subject for the development of anticancer drugs. In 1997, Greider accepted a professorship at Johns Hopkins University School of Medicine, where she serves as the director of its Department of Molecular Biology and Genetics.

In addition to the 2009 Nobel Prize, Greider has been the recipient of the Lewis S. Rosenstiel Award for Work in Basic Medical Science (1999), the Albert Lasker Basic Medical Research Award (2006), and the Wiley Prize in Biomedical Sciences (2006).

Grieder has stated, "One of the lessons I have learned in the different stages of my career is that science is not done alone. It is through talking with others and sharing that progress is made.... The ideas generated are not always the result of one person's thoughts but of the interactions between people; new ideas quickly become part of collective consciousness. This is how science moves forward and we generate new knowledge."

Alice Hamilton (1869–1970)

Physician, Researcher

A pioneer in the field of public health and industrial medicine, Dr. Alice Hamilton helped show the need for ridding U.S. factories, mines, and mills of the industrial poisons that were the cause of many illnesses and deaths of American workers. Through her research and public advocacy of better health conditions in the workplace, Hamilton saved and extended the lives of countless workers.

Hamilton grew up in Indiana and attended boarding school in Connecticut. She decided to become a doctor based on her desire for an independent and adventurous life. "I wanted to do something that would not interfere with my freedom," she recalled. "I realized that if I were a doctor, I could go anywhere I wanted—to foreign lands, to city slums—and while carrying on my profession, still be of some use." After graduating from the University of Michigan and doing research in bacteriology and pathology in Germany, in 1897, Hamilton became a professor of pathology at the Women's Medical College of Northwestern University in Chicago and went to live at Jane Addams's Hull-House. There, she founded one of the first child welfare and outpatient clinics in the United States.

Hamilton's experience working in the Chicago slums prompted her scientific interest in the environmental factors that contributed to human illnesses, and in 1911, she produced the first American study of industrial diseases. Hamilton identified the impact of lead poisoning and labeled tuberculosis as "a disease of the working classes" aggravated by poor nutrition, inadequate housing, and fatigue caused by long work shifts prevalent among mill workers.

In 1919, Hamilton became the first female professor at Harvard University. As a professor of industrial medicine at Harvard Medical School and at Harvard's School of Public Health, Hamilton lobbied for increased government programs to protect citizens against sickness, disability, unemployment, and old age. These reforms were partially realized during the New Deal of the 1930s, while other reforms she advocated, such as health programs for the elderly and indigent, were enacted as Medicare and Medicaid in the 1960s. In 1925, Hamilton published *Industrial Poisons in the United States,* the first such text on the subject, making her one of the few worldwide authorities in the field. From 1924 to 1930, she served on the Health Committee of the League of Nations.

In 1935, Hamilton retired from Harvard to serve as a special adviser on industrial medicine for the U.S. Labor Department's Bureau of Labor Standards. There, she pressed for the complete elimination of child labor, and the passage of the Fair Labor Standards Act of 1938 accomplished that goal.

Hamilton published her autobiography, *Exploring the Dangerous Trades,* in 1943, and she continued to remain active in the fields of public health and industrial medicine that she pioneered into her eighties.

Grace Hopper (1906–1992)

Computer Scientist, Navy Rear Admiral

Grace Hopper's pioneering work in computer technology helped to bring about the computer revolution. Hopper's development of the automatic programming language called COBOL (Common Business Oriented Language) helped to simplify the technology that ultimately made the computer accessible and essential.

Hopper was born in New York City and graduated from Vassar College in 1928. She went on to receive her Ph.D. in mathematics from Yale University in 1934. After teaching mathematics at Vassar for twelve years, in 1943, determined to help in the war effort, Hopper enlisted and was accepted into the WAVES (Women Accepted for Voluntary Emergency Service) branch of the Navy, even though she was considered overage and underweight. She attended the U.S. Naval Reserve Midshipman School and graduated with the rank of lieutenant junior grade. She was then assigned to the Bureau of Ordnance Computation Project at Harvard University.

At Harvard, Hopper developed the programs for the Mark I, the first automatically sequenced digital computer, a predecessor of today's electronic computer. She continued to work on the second and third series of Mark computers for the Navy before she rejoined the private sector in 1949. Working for the Eckert–Mauchly Computer Corporation, she assisted in the development of the first commercial, large-scale electronic computer, UNIVAC. Hopper and her staff would go on to create the first computer language compiler, a program that translates programming code into a machine language that a computer can understand. Her work led to the development of COBOL.

Throughout her career, Hopper maintained close contact with the naval reserve. She retired from the Navy in 1966 but was recalled to supervise the service's computer language and programs. In 1969, Hopper became the first person to receive computer science's "Man of the Year" award from the Data Processing Management Association. In 1983, President Ronald Reagan appointed her a rear admiral, and when she finally retired from the Navy in 1986 at the age of eighty, she was the oldest officer on active duty in the armed services.

Hopper later served as a senior consultant to the Digital Corporation, a position she held until her death. In 1991, Hopper became the first woman to receive, as an individual, the U.S. Medal of Technology, awarded "for her pioneering accomplishments in the development of computer programming languages."

An often combative and unorthodox computer scientist, Hopper spent her career trying to convince "the Establishment," as she called the computer science community, that computers were capable of becoming more than just highly efficient calculators. Hopper's understanding that a computer could imitate the seemingly inexhaustible process of the human intellect would set in motion one of the greatest technological revolutions in human history. Few others contributed as much to that revolution as Grace Hopper.

Harriot Kezia Hunt (1805–1875)
Physician, Women's Rights Advocate

The first American woman to practice medicine professionally, though without a medical degree, Harriot Kezia Hunt was influential for advocating the benefits of good nutrition and exercise. A women's rights activist, Hunt fought to open the medical profession to women.

Born in Boston to parents involved in the city's liberal religious community and reform culture, Hunt was, along with her sister Sarah, educated at home. When their father died in 1827, she and her sister opened a school in their parents' home

to support themselves. When Sarah became gravely ill in the early 1830s, Hunt was desperate to save her sister's life and grew frustrated with the physicians they consulted whose harsh treatments, including strong chemicals, laxatives, and bloodletting, only made Sarah weaker. Hunt began reading medical books herself and sought the advice of Elizabeth Mott and her husband Richard Dixon Mott for their unorthodox treatments. The Motts diagnosed Sarah with tuberculosis and eventually cured her. The experience would inspire Hunt to study medicine. Both sisters moved into the Motts' home to study their natural, herbalist approach to treatments. Hunt would learn from Elizabeth Mott that medicines should be natural, that doctors should consult with and listen to their patients, and that women were likely to discuss symptoms more freely with female doctors.

In 1835, Hunt opened her own consulting practice without a medical diploma. In 1843, she formed the Ladies' Physiological Society in Boston to provide a forum to promote her views on healthy living, including diet, exercise, regular bathing, good hygiene, and rest. In 1847, Hunt became the first woman to apply for admission to Harvard Medical School as a special student permitted to attend lectures, but the trustees denied her request. Three years later, after Elizabeth Blackwell had become the first woman to receive a medical degree, Hunt applied again. Although the trustees voted five to two to allow her to attend lectures, the outrage this prompted, along with Harvard's decision to accept two African American men to the medical school, prompted Hunt to withdraw her application when requested to do so. Hunt would write about this incident: "When civilization is further advanced, and the great doctrine of human rights is acknowledged, this act will be recalled and wondering eyes will stare, and wondering ears will be opened, at the semi-barbarism of the middle of the nineteenth century."

Hunt would go on to rally support for female physicians, establishing several women's groups to provide financial and moral support to female medical students as well as overcome the opposition to the medical practices she advocated, many of which would eventually enter mainstream medicine. Hunt would be granted an honorary degree from the Female Medical College of Philadelphia in 1853. Her own account of her medical career is written in *Glances and Glimpses; or, Fifty Years' Social, Including Twenty Years' Professional Life* (1856). In 1860, Hunt celebrated twenty-five years of practicing medicine. Attended by three generations of her patients, she confessed, "I have been so happy in my work; every moment occupied; how I long to whisper it in the ear of every listless woman, 'do something, if you would be happy.'" Hunt died in Boston at the age of seventy. Her grave at Mount Auburn Cemetery is marked by a statue of Hygeia, the Greek goddess of health.

Katherine Johnson (1918–)

Mathematician

 African American mathematician Katherine Johnson calculated the trajectory for America's first space missions in the 1960s that would be crucial for the success of the U.S. space program. Her achievement was celebrated in the 2016 film *Hidden Figures*, which dramatized the struggles of Johnson and other black women at NASA for equality. Dismissed as a "colored computer," Johnson and the other black women working in NASA's computing pool were separated from their white colleagues while she tracked the orbits of important missions such as Alan Shepard's Freedom 7 in 1961, John Glenn's Friendship 7 in 1962, and the various Apollo missions.

She was born Katherine Coleman in White Sulphur Springs, West Virginia. Her mother was a teacher, and her father was a blacksmith, farmer, and handyman. Johnson showed strong mathematical skills from an early age. "I counted everything: the steps, the dishes, the stars in the sky," Johnson recalls. With no secondary school to send her to, Johnson's parents enrolled her at the laboratory school on the campus of West Virginia State Institute, a black college one hundred miles away. She excelled at the school and entered West Virginia State as a freshman at the age of fifteen. She graduated at eighteen in 1937 with degrees in math education and French. She was selected as one of three black students to integrate the graduate program at

then-all-white West Virginia University, but she left after a year to get married and start a family. She would teach mathematics, French, and music in public schools in Virginia until 1952.

When she learned that job openings were available at the National Advisory Committee for Aeronautics at the Langley Aeronautical Laboratory (now the Langley Research Center), she relocated with her husband and three daughters to Newport News, Virginia, and began to work in 1953 at Langley with engineers in the Flight Research Division on issues related to airplane gust alleviation and wake turbulence. When the National Advisory Committee was transformed into the National Aeronautics and Space Administration in 1958, the engineers of the Flight Research Division became the Space Task Force, and Johnson became a member of the inner circle working on getting the United States into space. Before computers, the calculations on trajectories were done by heads, and Johnson was given some of the most crucial tasks in designing the early space missions. She also provided trajectory work for the Lunar Orbiter Program, which mapped the Moon's surface in advance of the 1969 Moon landing, and her calculations helped to synchronize the Apollo's Lunar Module with the moon-orbiting Command Module. Johnson would play a crucial role in the calculations that made possible the safe return of Apollo 13.

Johnson retired from NASA–Langley in 1986. In 2015, President Obama awarded her the Presidential Medal of Freedom, and in 2019, NASA renamed a facility in Fairmont, West Virginia, the Katherine Johnson Independent Verification and Validation Facility. Having turned one hundred in 2018, Johnson, according to her daughter, "remains in awe and honored by" all the accolades and attention she has received, but Johnson "can't imagine why people would want to honor her for just doing a good job."

Marian Koshland (1921–1997)

Immunologist

An immunologist and professor of molecular and cell biology, Marian Koshland made major contributions to the field of immunology in her work on the cholera vaccine and groundbreaking research in how antibodies fight illness.

Koshland was born in New Haven, Connecticut. Her father was a hardware salesman, and her mother was a teacher. Her interest in science was sparked when her younger brother suffered a weakened immune system from typhoid fever that made him susceptible to frequent illness, and Koshland was curious about the connection between the immune system and illness. Koshland received a bachelor's degree from Vassar College in 1942 and a master's degree from Vassar the next year, both in bacteriology. During World War II, she worked on a research team that produced a vaccine for cholera, and in 1945 and 1946, she was a research assistant on the Manhattan Project, which developed the atomic bomb. She received her doctorate in immunology from the University of Chicago in 1949.

After two years as a fellow in the Department of Bacteriology at Harvard, she joined the staff of the Brookhaven National Laboratory on Long Island, New York, first as an associate bacteriologist in the Department of Biology and then, from 1963 to 1965, as a bacteriologist. She moved to the University of California–Berkeley in 1965 initially as an associate research immunologist in the virus laboratory and then in 1966 as a lecturer in the Department of Molecular Biology. She became a professor in the Department of Microbiology and Immunology in 1970 and headed the department from 1982 to 1989.

Dr. Koshland discovered that antibodies differ in their amino acid composition, which makes them extremely efficient in fending off disease. She made the discovery by examining a molecule of phosphate and a molecule of arsenate. Although they are similar chemically, she found that they produced distinct and noticeably different antibodies when exposed to an antigen. As a colleague, Jim Allison, stated, her research "had a profound effect on theories of antibody formation and how antibody specificity was generated. Legend has it that at the annual meeting of the American Association of Immunology where she first presented her data, her talk was received by a standing ovation—quite high praise indeed."

She died of lung cancer at the age of seventy-six, survived by her husband, a biochemist at Berkeley, and five children. In her honor, the Marian Koshland Science Museum in Washington, D.C., educates the general public on the topics of her research, and the Marian E. Koshland Integrated Natural Science Center at Haverford College recognizes her considerable contribution to science.

Stephanie Kwolek (1923–2014)

Organic Chemist

Organic chemist Stephanie Kwolek invented the first of a family of synthetic fibers of exceptional strength, poly-p-phenylene terephthalamide, better known as Kevlar. For her discovery, she became the first woman to be awarded DuPont's Lavoisier Medal for technical achievement and would become in 1994 the fourth woman to be included in the National Inventors Hall of Fame.

Kwolek was born in Pittsburgh, Pennsylvania. Her father was a foundry worker but a naturalist by avocation, who died when she was ten but to whom Kwolek attributed her interest in science. From her mother, Kwolek inherited a love of fabric and sewing, and Kwolek first wanted to become a fashion designer but began studying mathematics and chemistry with the desire to teach. In 1946, she earned a BS degree with a major in chemistry from Margaret Morrison Carnegie College of Carnegie Mellon University.

Intending to become a doctor, Kwolek looked for work to earn enough money for her schooling, and she was offered a job as a chemist at Dupont Chemicals in Buffalo, New York, in 1946 to fill a vacancy left by men serving in the armed services. Kwolek found the work interesting, and she moved to DuPont's headquarters in Wilmington, Delaware, in 1950. She would remain at DuPont for four decades until her retirement in 1986. DuPont had introduced nylon just before World War II, and Kwolek conducted research in the creation of synthetic fibers. In the 1950s and 1960s, Kwolek worked with aramids or aromatic polymides, a type of polymer that can be made into strong, stiff, and flame-resistant fibers. Kwolek determined the solvents and polymerization conditions suitable for a compound that DuPont released in 1961 as a flame-resistant fiber named Nomex. Further work led her to a fiber of unprecedented stiffness and tensile strength that was released commercially in 1971 as Kevlar, which would be used in high-strength tire cord, reinforced boat hulls, and especially lightweight bulletproof vests. Speaking of her discovery, Kwolek said, "I don't think there's anything like saving someone's life to bring you satisfaction and happiness."

Kwolek's achievement was recognized with numerous awards, including in 1996 the National Medal of Technology and in 1997 the Perkins Medal presented by the Society of Chemical Industry. Kwolek is remembered in classrooms around the country for the "nylon rope trick," a classroom demonstration that she developed. Her story is celebrated in the children's book *The Woman Who Invented the Thread That Stops the Bullets: The Genius of Stephanie Kwolek* (2013) by Edwin Brit Wyckoff. She died in Delaware at the age of ninety.

Barbara Liskov (1939–)

Computer Scientist

A pioneer in the design of computer programming languages, Barbara Liskov, one of the first U.S. women to receive a doctorate in computer science, was the 2008 winner of the Turing Award, the highest honor in computer science.

Born Barbara Jane Huberman in Los Angeles, California, Liskov earned her BA degree in mathematics with a minor in physics from the University of California–Berkeley in 1961. In her classes, she had only one other female classmate; the rest were males. Intending to do graduate work in mathematics, she chose instead to move to Boston and take a position at the Mitre Corporation. There, she became interested in computers and programming. She worked at Mitre for a year before taking a programming job at Harvard, where she worked on language translation. In 1968, she become one of the first women in the United States to be awarded a Ph.D. from a computer science department, earning her degree from Stanford University. Her doctoral thesis was a computer program to play chess endgames.

After receiving her degree, she married Nathan Liskov and moved back to Boston, returning to the Mitre Corporation as a researcher from 1968 to 1972. Liskov joined the faculty at MIT in 1972, where she was the NEC professor of software science and engineering (1986–1997), the Ford professor of engineering (1997–), and an MIT institute professor (2008–). At MIT, she led the design and implementation of the CLU programming language, the basis for the object-oriented programming used in modern computer languages. She also developed the Argus language to ease implementation of programs distributed over a network such as those used in banking systems. Liskov is recognized as an authority on distrusted systems, which use several computers connected by a network. She developed a new notion of subtyping, known as the Liskov substitution principle, and her contributions have greatly influenced advanced computer system developments.

In addition to teaching and research, Liskov has served as associate provost for faculty equity. She has been recognized as one of the top fifty faculty members in the sciences in the United States, and in 2012, she was inducted into the National Inventors Hall of Fame.

Eleanor Josephine MacDonald (1906–2007)

Oncologist, Epidemiologist, Researcher

The first cancer epidemiologist ever, Eleanor Josephine MacDonald was the first to precisely determine incidence rates of cancer and one of the earliest proponents that cancer was a preventable disease.

MacDonald was born in West Somerville in Boston. Her father was an engineer at AT&T, and her mother was a concert pianist. MacDonald, also a gifted musician, graduated from Radcliffe College in 1928 with BA degrees in music and English. For four years after graduation, she performed as a concert cellist.

Her scientific career began when a friend of the family, Dr. Robert B. Greenough, chairman of the

Cancer Committee in Massachusetts, asked Mac-Donald for assistance in writing a research paper on cystic mastitis. This would lead to MacDonald becoming an epidemiologist, studying at Harvard University's School of Public Health. She took a job with the Massachusetts Department of Public Health, where she began a series of studies on cancer. Previously, epidemiologists had only researched communicable diseases. MacDonald was the first to study the incidence of cancer and other chronic diseases occurring in people older than forty. For a period of five years, she and her colleagues went door to door seeking information on the residents' health. When she presented her results, they were hailed as the first accurate calibration of cancer incidence in the country. MacDonald showed that with early detection, cancer could be treated successfully. MacDonald's approach to the problem of cancer made her the first epidemiologist in cancer research.

From 1940 to 1948, MacDonald worked for the Connecticut State Health Department, where she created the first population-based cancer record registry and follow-up program for the state. Over a six-year period, she and a volunteer checked all hospital records in the state for patients with cancer. They then traced each case to find out what had become of the patients. They found that 1,800 were still alive, and, as MacDonald recalled, "This was the beginning of follow-up for cancer patients." MacDonald's methods and procedures were widely copied nationwide.

In addition to her work in Connecticut, MacDonald worked for ten years on weekends to set up and run the statistical department at Memorial Sloane Kettering in New York as well as serving as a consultant to the National Advisory Cancer Council in Washington, D.C. In 1948, MacDonald became a full professor in epidemiology at the University of Texas MD Anderson Hospital in Houston, an association she would continue for forty-five years. Her studies included the first cancer incidence data for Hispanics and a determination that intense exposure to sunlight was linked to the rise in the occurrence of skin cancer.

MacDonald retired from her position as a professor in 1974 but continued to serve as a professor emeritus. "It has been marvelous," she recalled, "to be a pioneer. Everyone encouraged me in my work, and I did not feel they discriminated against me because I was female." She died in her home in Houston at the age of 101, having added so much to our understanding of cancer and to its treatment as a curable disease.

Barbara McClintock (1902–1992)

Botanist, Cytogeneticist

Barbara McClintock's revolutionary work in the biology of heredity helped to transform the way we understand and make use of the essential building blocks of life to eliminate disease. As a female scientist, McClintock faced numerous obstacles for nearly three decades before the scientific community understood and accepted her groundbreaking research, and she gained the recognition she deserved.

McClintock was born in Hartford, Connecticut, and when she was six years old, her father, a physician, moved the family to Flatbush, Brooklyn, New York. As a young girl, she spent time roaming about rural areas and developed a love of nature that would last a lifetime. After high school, she attended Cornell University and became interested in the study of cells and chromosomes.

While earning her master's degree and doctorate from Cornell, McClintock began her study of the chromosomes of Indian corn (maize). In the 1930s, she proved that genetic information, the coded material that determines forms of life and function, was passed on at an early stage of cell division. This discovery would be recognized as one of the cornerstones of modern genetic research. Despite such an important discovery, McClintock struggled for funding for her research and a satisfactory faculty appointment largely because she was a woman. In 1941, she was offered a one-year position at the Cold Spring Harbor Laboratory on Long Island, New York. She would spend the remainder of her life there conducting the research that would eventually earn her widespread recognition.

Continuing her research on corn, McClintock noticed different-colored spots that did not belong on the green or yellow leaves of a particular plant and tried to account for this irregularity in the passing on of the genes controlling plant color. Eventually, she concluded that genetic material could shift unpredictably from one generation to the next, that genes "jumped" from one location on the chromosomes to another, producing unexpected results. McClintock's discovery challenged the accepted view of the genetic process. Her colleagues ridiculed and dismissed her findings when she presented them at biology symposium in 1951. Nevertheless, McClintock continued her research with patience and determination.

In the 1970s, advancements in experiments by molecular biologists confirmed McClintock's conclusion from twenty years before. The scientific establishment finally understood that she had uncovered a fundamental law of genetics that helped pave the way for the breakthroughs to come in genetic engineering. In 1983, she became the first woman to be the sole recipient of a Nobel Prize in Physiology or Medicine.

McClintock died shortly after her ninetieth birthday, finally acknowledged as one the most influential geneticists and scientists of the twentieth century.

Maria Mitchell (1818–1889)

Astronomer

Considered America's first female professional astronomer, Maria Mitchell is also the first American scientist to discover a comet and the first faculty member to be hired by Vassar College when it was founded in 1861.

Mitchell, one of ten children, was born on Nantucket, an island off the coast of Massachusetts. Her Quaker parents encouraged her education, and her father, an amateur astronomer, stimulated her interest in the stars. She attended schools on Nantucket, including one run by her father. Mitchell assisted her father in his work rating chronometers for the Nantucket whaling fleet and encouraged her independent use of his telescope. From 1836 to 1856, she worked as a librarian and teacher at the Nantucket Atheneum and became a regular observer of the night skies.

In 1847, Mitchell established the orbit of a new comet, which became known as Miss Mitchell's Comet. Her discovery electrified the scientific community, gaining her a gold medal prize for her discovery from King Frederick VI of Denmark, and, in 1848, she became the first woman to be elected to the American Academy of Arts and Sciences. In 1850, she was elected to the American Association for the Advancement of Science. Leaving the Atheneum in 1856, Mitchell traveled throughout Europe meeting with other astronomers while she was also active in the antislavery and suffrage movements.

After the Civil War, Matthew Vassar recruited Mitchell to lend luster to Vassar's nine-member faculty. Mitchell and her widowed father moved into the Vassar Observatory, the first building of the college to be completed, equipped with a twelve-inch telescope, the third largest in the United States. As a teacher, Mitchell defied conventions by having her female students come out at night for classwork and celestial observations. Three of her students would later be included in the first list of Academic Men of Science in 1906.

Mitchell also was one of the founders of the American Association for the Advancement of Women (later the American Association of University Women) and served as its president in 1973. She was also elected vice president of one of the few mixed-gender professional associations at the time, the American Social Science Association. During the nation's centennial year in 1876, Mitchell delivered an important speech entitled "The Need for Women in Science."

Michell retired from Vassar in 1888 but continued her research in Lynn, Massachusetts. She died of brain disease at the age of seventy. She was one of three women elected to the Hall of Fame of Great Americans in 1905. Later astronomers honored her by naming a lunar crater on the moon the Maria Mitchell. New York's Metro North commuter railroad has a train named the *Maria Mitchell Comet*, and, in 2013, Google honored her with a doodle, showing her in cartoon form on top of a roof, gazing through a telescope at the heavens.

Bertha Parker Pallan (1907–1978)

Archaeologist

Considered the first Native American archaeologist, Bertha Parker Pallan became a distinguished and groundbreaking archaeologist who succeeded without a university education.

Bertha "Birdie" Parker Pallan was born in Chautauqua County, New York. Her mother, an Abenaki, Beulah Tahamont, was an actress, and she and her mother performed with Ringling Bros. and Barnum & Bailey Circus as as part of the Pocahontas show. Her father, Arthur C. Parker, was an archaeologist and the first president of the Society of American Archaeology, who Pallan assisted in his excavations. After her mother divorced her father in 1914, Pullan moved with her mother to Hollywood to work in films.

Pallan married Joseph Pallan in the early 1920s and had a daughter in 1925. When the marriage ended, Pallan moved to Nevada to work on an archaeological site for the Southwest Museum directed by Mark Raymond Harrington, who had married Pallan's aunt. Hired as a camp cook and expedition secretary, Pallan was instructed in archaeological methods in the field by Harrington. In 1929, she discovered and did solo excavations at the pueblo site of Scorpion Hill. In 1930, she worked at Gypsum Cave, a site believed to have the earliest evidence of human occupation in North America. Pallan cleaned, repaired, and catalogued finds as well as explored the deepest recesses of the cave. In one narrow crevice, she discovered the skull of a species of extinct giant sloth alongside ancient human tools, the most important find of the expedition, which drew the support and attention of the California Institute of Technology and the Carnegie Institute in Washington, D.C.

From 1931 to 1941, Pallan worked as an assistant in archaeology and ethnology and later as an archaeologist and ethnographer at the Southwest Museum, publishing numerous archaeological and ethnological papers in scholarly journals. Pallan has been credited with being "conscientious about recording the names of the Native people she interviewed, going so far as to give them credit as authors and co-authors," a practice that was rarely done by investigators at that time.

After leaving the Southwest Museum in 1941, Pallan returned to show business, working as a technical adviser on film projects depicting Native Americans. In the 1950s, she married Italian actor Espera Oscar de Corti, known as Iron Eyes Cody, and they hosted a television program about Native American history and folklore. She died in 1978 at the age of seventy-one. Her gravestone simply reads, "Mrs. Iron Eyes Cody."

Carolyn Porco (1953–)

Planetary Scientist

Planetary scientist Carolyn Porco was the imaging team leader on the Cassini mission in orbit around Saturn from 2004 to 2017. An expert on planetary rings and the Saturn moon Enceladus, Porco has stated that "I enjoy my career because it allows me to live my life on a plane different than most people do. My mental life is spent elsewhere—it's spent in the outer solar system." Named in 2012 as one of the twenty-five most influential people in space by *Time* magazine, Porco is renowned for translating the complexity of planetary science and its relevance to a wide popular audience.

Born in New York City, Porco was raised in an Italian American family in the Bronx, where she graduated from Cardinal Spellman High School in 1970. She earned BS degrees in physics and astronomy from the State University of New York–Stony Brook in 1974. Porco attributes her interest in outer space to an adolescent spiritual quest in which she began to wonder "what are we doing here and what's out there." By 1976, Porco was a graduate student in the Division of Geological and Planetary Sciences at the California Institute of Technology, where NASA's Jet Propulsion Laboratory is based. While there, Voyager I flew past Saturn, and Porco was assigned the imaging data on Saturn's ring system, which led her to make some significant discoveries about the rings and the planet's magnetic field.

After Porco earned her doctorate in 1983, she joined the University of Arizona's Department of Planetary Sciences and became an official member of the Voyager imaging team, which analyzed data from Voyager II's 1986 pass by Uranus and 1989 pass by Neptune. She was one of only seven women among the 178 scientists working on the Voyager mission.

In 1990, Porco become imaging team leader for the Cassini mission to Saturn, which was designed to provide new data that might reveal how the solar system was formed and how life on Earth began. "We are attempting to understand our own planet," she stated, "as one of a family of planets all born of the same parent, of the same material, at the same time." The Cassini spacecraft traveled for nearly seven years and more than two billion miles before it began orbiting Saturn in 2004. Data confirmed Porco's prediction that acoustic oscillations within the body of Saturn are responsible for the particular features in the rings of Saturn, the first demonstration that planetary rings can act like a seismograph in recording the oscillatory motions of the host planet. Porco was also the member of the imaging team for the New Horizons mission to Pluto, which made its flyby in 2015.

A recipient of numerous awards and honors for her contribution to science and public understanding, Asteroid (7231) Porco was named in her honor for her work in planetary science. In 1999, she was selected by the *London Sunday Times* as one of eighteen scientific leaders of the twenty-first century. In 2010, she was awarded the Carl Sagan Medal, awarded by the American Astronomical Society for excellence in the communication of science to the public. Since 2015, she has been a visiting distinguished scholar at the University of California–Berkeley and, since 2017, a fellow of the California Academy of Sciences.

Ellen Swallow Richards (1842–1911)

Ecologist

Called "the woman who founded ecology," one of America's first female professional chemists, and the first woman to be accepted by a scientific school (MIT), Ellen Swallow Richards is best known for pioneering the field of sanitary engineering by performing an unprecedented survey in 1890 that led to the first state water-quality standards in the United States. She was also the founder of the home economics movement that applied scientific principles to the home and to the study of nutrition.

Born in Dunstable, Massachusetts, Richards was homeschooled until her family moved in 1859 to Westford, Massachusetts, where she attended Westford Academy. In 1868, she entered Vassar College as a special student. A year later, she was admitted to the senior class and graduated in 1870 before earning an MA degree with a thesis on the chemical analysis of iron ore. It would take a vote of the faculty to allow her admission to MIT as a special student in chemistry. Richards, therefore, became the first woman to be admitted to MIT with the caveat that "her admission did not establish a precedent for the general admission of females." In 1873, Richards received a BS degree. She continued her work at MIT and would have been the first woman to have been awarded an advanced degree, but MIT refused to grant this distinction and would not award its first advanced degree to a woman until 1886.

In 1875, she married Robert H. Richards, chairman of the Department of Mine Engineering at MIT, with whom she had worked in the mineralogy laboratory. Her first postcollege work was as an unpaid chemistry lecturer at MIT from 1873 to 1878. In 1884, she was appointed as an instructor in sanitary chemistry at the newly formed MIT laboratory for the study of sanitation. Richards began her sewage treatment research analyzing water quality throughout Massachusetts in an unprecedented survey that led to the first state water-quality standards in the nation and the first modern municipal sewage treatment plant in Lowell, Massachusetts. From 1887 to 1897, Richards served as the official water analyst for the State Board of Health while continuing as an instructor at MIT, a rank she held until her death. Richards was also among the fifteen women who formed the American Association of University Women (AAUW) in 1881.

Intent on applying scientific principles to domestic issues of proper nutrition, sanitation, and physical fitness, Richards published *The Chemistry of Cooking and Cleaning: A Manual for Housekeeping* (1882), a landmark work in home economics. She set up model kitchens, opened to the public, and campaigned tirelessly for the new discipline of home economics. Her other books included *Home Sanitation: A Manual for Housekeepers* (1887), *Domestic Economy as a Factor in Public Education* (1889), *The Cost of Living* (1899), *Sanitation in Daily Life* (1907), and *Euthenics: The Science of Controllable Environment* (1912). The American Home Economics Association was formed in 1908 with Richards as its first president.

Richards died at the age of sixty-nine, having been instrumental as a foundational figure in two scientific disciplines: environmental studies and home economics. On the one-hundredth anniversary of her graduation in 1973, MIT established the Ellen Swallow Richards professorship for distinguished female faculty members.

Helen Rodríguez Trías (1929–2001)

Educator, Pediatrician, Women's Rights Activist

Pediatrician and educator Helen Rodríguez Trías was the first Latinx president of the American Public Health Association, who helped to expand the range of public health services for women and children in minority and low-income populations around the world.

Rodríguez Trías was born in New York but spent her childhood in Puerto Rico, returning to New York when she was ten. Experiencing racism and discrimination, she was placed in a class with students who were academically handicapped, even though she had good grades and knew how to speak English. She married and had three children before she decided to return to Puerto Rico to complete her education. She graduated from the University of Puerto Rico in 1957, where she was a student activist on issues of freedom of speech and Puerto Rican independence. She earned her medical degree, also from the University of Puerto Rico, in 1960. During her residency at the University Hospital–San Juan, she established the first center for the care

of newborns in Puerto Rico, and the hospital's death rate for newborns decreased by 50 percent within three years. After her residency, she established her medical practice in pediatrics on the island before returning to New York in 1970.

In New York, she began working in community medicine, heading the Department of Pediatrics at Lincoln Hospital, serving a largely Puerto Rican community in the South Bronx. She also was an associate professor of medicine at Albert Einstein College of Medicine at Yeshiva University and later taught at both Columbia and Fordham universities. Throughout the 1970s, Rodríguez Trías was an active member of the women's health movement, focusing on reproductive rights and the fight to stop sterilization abuse. She was a founding member of both the Committee to End Sterilization Abuse and the Committee for Abortion Rights and against Sterilization Abuse and testified before the U.S. Department of Health, Education, and Welfare in support of the passage of federal sterilization guidelines, which she drafted, in 1979.

In the 1980s, Rodríguez Trías served as medical director of the New York State Department of Health AIDS Institute, working on behalf of women from minority groups who were infected with HIV. In the 1990s, she served as health codirector of the Pacific Institute for Women's Health, a nonprofit research and advocacy group concerned with improving women's health worldwide. She was a founding member of both the Women's Caucus and the Hispanic Caucus of the American Public Health Association, becoming its first Latinx director. An annual APHA award, the Helen Rodríguez Trías Social Justice Award is given to a person who has worked toward social justice for underserved and disadvantaged populations.

Rodríguez Trías received the Presidential Citizen's Medal in 2001 before her death from cancer the same year. "I hope I'll see in my lifetime," she stated, "a growing realization that we are one world. And that no one is going to have quality of life unless we support everyone's quality of life…. Not on the basis of do-goodism, but because of a real commitment … it's our collective and personal health that's at stake."

Florence Sabin (1871–1953)

Medical Researcher, Physician

A physician and medical researcher, Florence Sabin was one of the most influential American female scientists of her time. Her study of the lymphatic system made it possible to understand the origin of blood cells and blood vessels, and her research on tuberculosis led to better treatment of this widespread, often fatal, disease.

Florence Rena Sabin was born in the mining town of Central City, Colorado, the youngest daughter of a mining engineer. Her mother, a teacher, died when Sabin was four, and after attending boarding schools in Denver and Illinois, she was sent at the age of twelve to live with her grandparents in Vermont. She attended Vermont Academy and Smith College, where she graduated with a BS degree in 1893. She went on to study medicine at Johns Hopkins University, and while she was a student there, she constructed accurate models of the brain that were later used as teaching aids in several medical schools.

During her medical school years, Sabin was active in the Baltimore women's suffrage movement, sometimes speaking in public on behalf of the cause. In 1900, she became the first woman to receive a medical degree from Johns Hopkins. She interned at Johns Hopkins Hospital and then turned to teaching and research on the lymphatic system. In 1917, Sabin became the first woman at Johns Hopkins to attain the position of full professor.

From 1924 to 1926, Sabin served as president of the American Association of Anatomists, and in 1925, she became the first woman to be elected to the prestigious National Academy of Science. That same year, she accepted an appointment at New York City's Rockefeller Institute (later Rockefeller University), an institution dedicated to scientific research. She became the first female member of the institute and directed a team of researchers in groundbreaking work on the biological causes of tuberculosis.

Sabin retired from the Rockefeller Institute in 1938 and returned to Colorado, where the governor appointed her chair of a state subcommittee on pub-

lic health. As a result of Sabin's work, Colorado passed the Sabin Health Bill, which led to a massive drop in the death rate from tuberculosis.

At the age of seventy-six, Sabin was appointed manager of Denver's Department of Health and Welfare. She served in that position for five years and then retired to care for her ailing sister. Sabin died of a heart attack in Denver in 1953. A bronze statue of Florence Sabin, shown sitting at her microscope, is in the Statuary Hall in the Capitol Building in Washington, D.C.

Sarah Elizabeth Stewart (1905–1976)

Oncologist, Researcher

A pioneering cancer researcher, Stewart was the first to show that cancer-causing viruses can spread from animal to animal. With her colleague Dr. Bernice Eddy, Stewart codiscovered the cancer-causing virus that now bears their names, the SE (Stewart–Eddy) polyomavirus. As a result of their work, Stewart and Eddy were twice nominated for the Nobel Prize.

Stewart was born in Tecalitlán, Jalisco, Mexico, to a Mexican mother and American engineer father. She moved to the United States at the age of five. She did her undergraduate work at New Mexico State University, graduating in 1927 and completing a master's degree from the University of Massachusetts in 1930. Stewart worked at the National Institutes of Health (NIH) from 1935 to 1944 while completing her Ph.D. in microbiology at the University of Chicago in 1939. She went on to teach microbiology at Georgetown University's School of Medicine, and once women were allowed to enroll there, she became their first female graduate in 1949 at the age of thirty-nine.

In 1951, Stewart returned to the NIH and partnered with Dr. Bernice Eddy (1903–1989) to begin their research on the viral links to cancer based on the pioneering research of Jonas Salk, whose work led to a vaccine for the virus that caused polio. In 1953, they were the first to describe the cancer-causing polyomavirus, which can be transmitted from animal to animal. In 1958, they were successful in growing the virus, which now bears their name, the SE (Stewart–Eddy) polyomavirus. In 1965, President Lyndon B. Johnson presented Stewart with the Federal Women's Award for her contribution to cancer research.

In 1971, Stewart returned to Georgetown University to teach in the Department of Pathology. She died at her home in Florida, succumbing to cancer, the disease she had spent her professional career studying.

Karen Uhlenbeck (1942–)

Mathematician

 In 2019, Karen Uhlenbeck became the first woman ever to be awarded one of mathematics's highest awards, the Abel Prize, "for her pioneering achievements in geometric partial differential equations, gauge theory, and integrable systems, and for the fundamental impact of her work on analysis, geometry, and mathematical physics." Royal Society Fellow Jim Al-Khalili has called Uhlenbeck's achievements "the most important advances in mathematics in the last 40 years."

Uhlenbeck's father was an engineer, and her mother was an artist. As a child, Uhlenbeck loved reading, which led to an interest in science. "We lived in the country," she recalled, "so there wasn't a whole lot to do. I was particularly interested in reading about science." She entered the University of Michigan intending to study physics, but she changed to mathematics, gaining her BS degree in 1964. She continued her studies at the Courant Institute at New York University. She received a master's degree in 1966 and a Ph.D. in 1968 from Brandeis University.

After graduation, she could only find temporary jobs at MIT and at Berkeley. As she recalls, "I was told ... that people did not hire women, that women were supposed to go home and have babies." Her husband, biophysicist Olke C. Uhlenbeck, was offered positions at MIT, Stanford, and Princeton, but nepotism rules did not allow her to be hired there as well. Finally, she took a position at the University of Illinois–Urbana-Champaign, and her husband

followed her. She remained there from 1971 to 1976 before being promoted to full professor at the University of Illinois–Chicago. In 1983, she was awarded the MacArthur Prize Fellowship and moved to the University of Chicago. In 1988, she became the Sid W. Richardson Foundation regents chair in mathematics at the University of Texas, where she worked for more than twenty-five years. She left Texas to become a visiting senior research scholar at Princeton University as well as visiting associate at the Institute for Advanced Study.

Uhlenbeck has described her mathematical interests in this way: "I work on partial differential equations which were originally derived from the need to describe things like electromagnetism but have undergone a century of change in which they are used in a much more technical fashion to look at the shapes of space. Mathematicians look at imaginary spaces constructed by scientists examining other problems. I started out my mathematics career by working on Palais' modern formulation of a very useful classical theory, the calculus of variations. I decided Einstein's general relativity was too hard, but managed to learn a lot about geometry of space time. I did some very technical work in partial differential equations, made an unsuccessful pass at shock waves, worked in scale invariant variational problems, made a poor stab at three-dimensional manifold topology, learned gauge field theory and then some about applications to four dimensional manifolds, and have recently been working n equations with algebraic infinite symmetries." She would help formulate the mathematical underpinning to techniques widely used by physicists in quantum field theory to describe fundamental interactions between particles and forces. She also helped pioneer the field of geometric analysis. As fellow mathematician Sun-Yung Alice Chang has stated, "She did things nobody thought about doing, and after she did, she laid the foundations of a branch of mathematics."

Throughout her career, Uhlenbeck has been a strong advocate for gender equality in science and mathematics. She is one of the founders of the Park City Mathematics Institute at the Institute of Advanced Study at Princeton, which aims to train young researchers and promote mutual understanding of the interests and challenges of mathematics. She is also the cofounder of the institute's Women and Mathematics Program created in 1993 to recruit and empower women to lead in mathematics research. "I am aware of the fact that I am a role model for young women in mathematics," Uhlenbeck has said. "It's hard to be a role model, however, because what you really need to do is show students how imperfect people can be and still succeed.... I may be a wonderful mathematician and famous because of it, but I'm also very human."

Gladys West (1930–)

Mathematician

African American mathematician Gladys West was instrumental in the creation of the Global Positioning System (GPS). One of the so-called Hidden Figures, women who were innovators in the early Air Force space program, West programmed a computer to deliver calculations for a geodetic Earth model and participated in the astronomical study that proved in the early 1960s the regularity of Pluto's motion relative to Neptune.

West was born in Dinwiddie County, Virginia, to a farming family of sharecroppers. Resisting her fate to work in the fields, West learned that the top two students in her class would be awarded scholarships to Virginia State College, and she managed to graduate as the class valedictorian. She studied mathematics at Virginia State College and, after graduation, taught for two years before returning to school for her master's degree. She would eventually receive a doctorate in 2018 from Virginia Tech.

In 1956, she became the second black woman ever hired to work at the U.S. Naval Weapons Laboratory Dahlgren Division as a mathematician. She would remain there for forty-two years. She worked among a small group of women on computing for the U.S. military before the age of reliance on computers. West participated in research on Pluto's motion and analyzing data from satellites to calculate Earth's shape. Describing her role in the development of the Global Positioning System, Captain Godfrey Weekes, commanding officer of the Naval

Surface Warfare Center, stated, "She rose through the ranks, worked on the satellite geodesy and contributed to the accuracy of GPS and the measurement of satellite data."

After retiring in 1998, West was inducted into the U.S. Air Force Hall of Fame in 2018, one of the Air Force Space Command's highest honors. West, who married in 1957 and had three children, lives in King George County, Virginia. She has said that she prefers a paper map over use of the GPS, which she helped to create.

Leona Woods (1919–1986)

Physicist

The youngest and only female member of the team that built the world's first nuclear reactor, physicist Leona Woods was an important member of the Manhattan Project that created the first atomic bomb.

Woods was born on a farm in La Grange, Illinois, the second of five children. She graduated from public high school at fourteen and received her BS degree in chemistry from the University of Chicago in 1938 at the age of eighteen. Pursuing a Ph.D. in chemistry at the University of Chicago, Woods completed her doctorate in 1942 and was recruited to join chemist Enrico Fermi and his team at Chicago, who were associated with the nationwide atomic research program known as the Manhattan Project. Fermi's wife, Laura, would describe Woods as "a tall young girl built like an athlete, who could do a man's job and do it well." Indeed, more than one job: Woods divided her time between her work with Fermi and helping her mother on the family farm. Fermi and his team worked to determine how to create a self-sustaining nuclear chain reaction, one of the keys to understanding how to construct an atomic bomb.

When Fermi's nuclear pile went critical on December 2, 1942, under the stands of an abandoned football stadium, Woods, then just twenty-three, was the only woman of the forty-two scientists present. "When do we become scared?" she purportedly asked Fermi. In 1943, Woods married fellow physicist John Marshall soon after Fermi's team moved to the Argonne National Laboratory. She soon became pregnant but hid her condition from her colleagues by wearing baggy denim. After giving birth to her son, she returned to work within a few days. Woods participated during the powering up of the first nuclear reactor. She was on hand when the B Reactor shut down after being "poisoned" by Xenon-135 and worked with the rest of the reactor team to resolve the problem. The material obtained was used to make the second nuclear bomb that was dropped on Nagasaki, Japan, on August 9, 1945. Asked years later about her involvement in the atomic weapons program, Woods was unapologetic, focusing on the fear that Germany would discover how to build a nuclear bomb ahead of the Allies and on the probability of high loss of life among the Allies fighting in the Pacific if the bombs were not used.

Following the war, Woods continued her work in chemistry with a fellowship at the University of Chicago's Institute of Nuclear Studies, Princeton's Institute of Advanced Studies, and the Brookhaven National Laboratory. In 1962, she became a professor at New York University and later joined the Department of Physics at the University of Colorado from 1964 to 1970. Her final academic position was a visiting professor of environmental studies, reflecting Woods's increasing interest in issues of climate change and food irradiation.

Hannah Marie Wormington (1914–1994)

Archaeologist

Hannah Marie Wormington was one of the first women in the United States to become a professional archaeologist. An expert on the prehistory of the Southwest, Wormington was the first female archaeologist to be elected president of the Society for American Archaeology. As James Dixon, curator of the Denver Museum of Natural History, where Wormington worked as a curator of archaeology for nearly six decades, observed, "She was one of the first and foremost women scholars in archeology in North America."

Born in Denver, Colorado, Wormington graduated from the University of Denver in 1935 and was hired to work at the Colorado Museum of Nat-

ural History (later the Denver Museum of Nature and Science), where she became curator of the Department of Archaeology and performed archaeological excavations in Colorado and Utah. She published two standard reference works of Paleo-Indian studies, *Ancient Man in North America* (1939) and *Prehistoric Indians of the Southwest* (1947). In her early career, because women in archaeology were such a rarity, she often signed her early writings "H. M." Worthington to conceal her identity.

She eventually did graduate work as the first woman to focus on anthropology at Radcliffe College, where she earned her master's degree in 1950. She then became the first woman at Harvard to receive a Ph.D. in archaeology in 1954. When she was attending classes at Harvard, she had to sit outside the lecture hall in at least one of her classes because the professor did not allow women inside.

In her nearly six-decade career, Wormington made many important contributions to the development of North American archaeological method, theory, and knowledge, particularly to our understanding of the first humans who crossed the Bering Strait land bridge from Asia around 10,000 BCE.

In 1983, the Society of American Archaeology awarded her the Distinguished Service Award, becoming the first female archaeologist to receive the award. Wormington died at the age of seventy-nine from smoke inhalation due to a fire in her home in Denver.

Chien-Shiung Wu (1912–1997)

Physicist

Chinese American experimental physicist Chien-Shiung Wu was a pioneer in the research of radioactivity. A member of the Manhattan Project, which developed the first atomic weapons, she is best known for the Wu experiment, which contradicted the law of conservation of parity. This discovery would earn her colleagues, Tsung-Dao Lee and Chen-Ning Yang, the 1957 Nobel Prize in Physics and Wu, whose contribution was not acknowledged at the time, the inaugural Wolf Prize in Physics in 1978. Her accomplishments in experimental physics earned her the accolades the "Chinese Madame Curie," the "First Lady of Physics," and the "Queen of Nuclear Research."

Born in a small town near Shanghai, Wu attended a school started by her father, who believed in education for girls and challenged the prevailing belief at the time in China. After attending a boarding school and serving as a schoolteacher from 1930 to 1934, Wu studied at the National Central University (later Nanjing University) first in mathematics and later in physics. After graduation, she did graduate work in physics at Zhejiang University. Urged to earn a Ph.D. abroad, Wu was accepted at the University of Michigan and departed for the United States in 1936. Arriving in San Francisco, she was shown the Radiation Laboratory at the University of California–Berkeley, and she enrolled there instead. She completed her Ph.D. in 1940. She married Luke Yuan, a fellow physicist, in 1942.

Unable to find a desired research position at a university, Wu became a physics instructor at Princeton University and Smith College. In 1944, she joined the Manhattan Project at the Substitute Alloy Materials Lab at Columbia University, focusing on radiation detectors. She would be instrumental in diagnosing the problem that shut down the first nuclear reactor by helping to identify poisoning by xenon-135 as the cause. After the war, she was offered a position at Columbia and began to study beta decay, which occurs when the nucleus of one element changes into another element, and was the first to confirm Enrico Fermi's theory of beta decay. In 1956, she was asked by theoretical physicists Tsung Dao Lee and Chen Ning Yang to devise an experiment to prove their theory of the law of conservation of parity, which held that all objects and their mirror images behave the same way. Wu's experiment using radioactive cobalt at near-absolute zero temperatures proved that identical nuclear particles do not always act alike. This discovery of parity violation was a major contribution to high-energy physics. Wu's book, *Beta Decay* (1965), is still a standard reference for nuclear physicists.

Wu continued making significant scientific contributions throughout her life, including helping

to answer important biological questions about blood and sickle cell anemia. She became the first woman to serve as president of the American Physical Society. Her honors include the National Medal of Science, the Comstock Prize, and the first honorary doctorate awarded to a woman at Princeton University. Wu retired in 1981 and died in New York City at the age of eighty-four after suffering a stroke. According to her wishes, her ashes were buried in the courtyard of the school her father founded and from which Wu's academic and research career was launched.

Rosalyn Sussman Yalow (1921–2011)

Medical Physicist

Medical physicist and cowinner of the 1977 Nobel Prize in Physiology or Medicine, Rosalyn Sussman Yalow was the second woman (after Gerty Cori) and the first American-born woman to be awarded a Nobel Prize in Physiology or Medicine. Yalow was the first to apply nuclear physics to medicine, developing radioimmunoassay, a method of detecting minute quantities of biologically active substances that the Nobel Prize committee credited as "the most valuable advance in basic clinical research" up to that time. For her work, Yalow was called the "Madame Curie of the Bronx."

Yalow was born in New York's South Bronx to parents from an Eastern European immigrant background, who insisted that Yalow and her brother get the education that had been denied to them. Yalow would credit her father for instilling in her the idea that girls could do anything that boys could do. A chemistry teacher at Walton High School got her excited about chemistry, but when she attended Hunter College, she switched her emphasis to physics. As a woman in physics, Yalow faced the challenge of being accepted for graduate work. Because she could type, she obtained a position as a secretary for a leading biochemist at Columbia University's College of Physicians and Surgeons after taking stenography at a business school. As Yalow recalled, "This position was supposed to provide an entry for me into graduate course, via the backdoor." However, after only a few months in her position, she received a teaching assistantship in physics at the University of Illinois, where she earned her Ph.D. in 1945. From 1946 to 1950, she returned to Hunter to teach physics while becoming a consultant in nuclear physics at the Bronx Veterans Administration Hospital. She would work there as a research physicist and assistant chief of the radioisotope service from 1950 to 1970.

Partnering with fellow physicist Solomon A. Berson, Yalow used radioactive isotopes to analyze blood for thyroid deficiencies, for the distribution of globin and serum proteins, and to study the relationship between hormones and insulin. Their work eventually led to the development of the diagnostic process RIA that was first used to study and analyze diabetes. It is now one of the most commonly used ways to screen human blood and tissue. It made possible such practical applications as the screening of blood in blood banks for hepatitis and the determination of effective dosage levels of drugs and antibiotics.

In 1970, Yalow was appointed chief of the Nuclear Medicine Service (formerly the Radioisotope Section) at the Veterans Administration Hospital. In 1976, she became the first female recipient of the Albert Lasker Basic Medical Research Award and, in 1979, became a distinguished professor at large at the Albert Einstein College of Medicine at Yeshiva University. In 1985, she accepted the position of Solomon A. Berson distinguished professor at large (named for her former partner) at the Mount Sinai School of Medicine.

After publishing more than five hundred research papers and being honored for her achievement with the National Medal of Science in 1988, Yalow, at the age of seventy-one, retired in 1992 to become senior medical investigator emerita at the VA Hospital, still working in her lab several days a week. "I am a scientist," she remarked, "because I love investigation. Even after the Nobel Prize, the biggest thrill is to go to my laboratory and hope that one day I will know something that nobody ever knew before. There are few days when it happens, but the dream is still there. That's what it means to be a scientist."

Roger Arliner Young (1889–1964)
Biologist, Zoologist

The first African American woman to receive a doctorate in zoology, Roger Arliner Young was a marine biologist who did important work on paramecia, radiation effects on sea urchin eggs, and the hydration of living cells and the fertilization process in marine organisms. In 2005, a congressional resolution recognized her and four other African American women (Ruth Ella Moore, Euphemia Lofton Haynes, Shirley Ann Jackson, and Mae Jemison) who "have broken through many barriers to achieve greatness in science."

Young was born in Clifton Forge, Virginia, but grew up in Burgettstown, Pennsylvania. Her family was poor, and she had to care for her invalid mother. In 1916, she entered Howard University to study music. However, she took her first science course with prominent black biologist Ernest Everett Just who, despite her poor grades, saw promise and started mentoring Young and encouraging her pursuit of science. She graduated with a BS degree in zoology in 1923. After graduation, she was an instructor at Howard and entered the graduate zoology program at the University of Chicago, earning her master's degree in 1926. At Chicago, she published her first research article, became the first African American woman to research and publish in the field of animal biology, and was the first to earn a Ph.D. in zoology from the University of Pennsylvania in 1940.

In 1927, Just invited Young to join his research team at the Marine Biological Laboratory in Woods Hole, Massachusetts, and, in 1929, she temporarily replaced Just, who was on a grant in Europe as the head of the Howard zoology department. Young's eyes were permanently damaged by the ultraviolet rays used in the experiments conducted at Howard, and, in 1936, she was fired from her position at Howard amid rumors about a romance between her and Just. As Young would lament, "The situation here is so cruel and cowardly that every spark of sentiment that I have held for Howard is cold." She moved on to complete her Ph.D. and hold teaching positions at the North Carolina College for Negroes and Shaw University (1940–1947) and at Jackson

State College in Mississippi. In the late 1950s, she was hospitalized for mental health problems in the State Mental Asylum. Discharged in 1962, she held one final teaching position at Southern University in New Orleans, where she died.

Despite later recognition for her contributions to marine biological research and achievements as a scientist and African American woman, Young's life was both a struggle and a testimony to her persistence, in which she endured many years of poverty and stress that undoubtedly contributed to her mental health problems.

POLITICS, GOVERNMENT, AND THE LAW

The participation of women in the legal profession, in the creation of the nation's laws, and in the implementation of public policy faced considerable obstacles throughout much of American history. Denied legal rights and the right to vote, women had no access to the decision-making power that would allow them to make laws or to adjudicate them as jurors, attorneys, judges, or legislators. In colonial America, the right to vote was reserved for property-owning, male adults. Under the English common law doctrine of coverture, husband and wife were considered "one person at law" with most interests, including the vote, governed by the husband. Unmarried women and widows could own property, enter into contracts, and sue or be sued, but they could not vote. In the first recorded attempt by a woman in America to claim voting rights, Margaret Brent (c. 1601–c. 1671), an English immigrant to the colony of Maryland, went before the Maryland Assembly to request "a vote and voyce" as an unmarried property owner. Her request was denied. Because Brent advocated for her legal prerogatives before colonial courts on multiple occasions, she is considered to be the first female lawyer in America. Although other women are included in the colonial town polling records, women in general were denied the right to vote either from the start or because state legislatures changed their laws. At the time of the American Revolution, each colony drafted their own state constitutions, and most incorporated lan-

guage excluded women from voting rights. The U.S. Constitution did not originally define who was eligible to vote but allowed each state to make that determination. Most states allowed only white, male, adult property owners to do so (by 1856, property restrictions for white males only were eliminated).

In addition to the fact that disenfranchisement excluded women from an equal role as men in choos-

A 1934 illustration depicts Margaret Brent making her case before the Maryland Assembly for a right to vote even though she was a woman who owned no property.

ing lawmakers, the lack of formal educational opportunities for women, particularly regarding legal education, was another important factor in limiting women's access to public policy making. To become lawmakers, women needed to master law. Arabella Mansfield (1846–1911) became the first American woman accepted into the legal profession in the United States when she was admitted to the Iowa Bar in 1869. She did not study at a law school but gained her legal training in her brother's law office for two years before taking the bar examination. Later in the same year, Ada H. Kepley (1847–1925) became the first American woman to graduate from a law school (Northwestern University School of Law), although she was prohibited from legal practice by state law, which denied women licenses to the "learned professions" until 1881 when the law was overturned (similar gender-restrictive professional licensing laws were in place nationwide). In 1870, Esther Morris (1814–1902) was appointed justice of the peace in Wyoming Territory, the first woman in the United States to hold a judicial position. In Wyoming later in the same year, the first gender-integrated grand juries would hear cases in Cheyenne with the chief justice overruling a motion to prohibit women from participating. His ruling stated, "It seems eminently proper for women to sit upon Grand Juries, which will give them the best possible opportunities to aid in suppressing the dens of infamy which curse the country." In 1873, the Supreme Court ruled that states had the right to exclude women from practicing law. In 1879, however, Belva Lockwood (1830–1917) gained congressional legislation establishing that women who practice law must have access to even the highest court, and the Supreme Court was compelled to allow her to plead a case before it. The first woman to be elected to a judgeship in the United States was Florence Ellinwood Allen (1884–1966) in 1914 in Ohio. Allen was also the first woman to serve on a state supreme court and the first woman to be appointed as a judge to a federal appeals court (1932). Genevieve Cline (1879–1959) was the first woman appointed to a federal court in 1928 when President Calvin Coolidge nominated her for a seat on the U.S. Customs Court.

By 1920 and the ratification of the Nineteenth Amendment, all states had admitted women to the

In 1870 Esther Hobart Morris was the first woman appointed a justice of the peace.

bar. Several elite law schools had admitted women as well; among the first in the Northeast were New York University, Cornell, and Boston University in the late 1800s and Yale at the end of World War I. Harvard Law School first accepted women in 1920, having resisted women's petitions since 1871. The top twelve law schools attended by women had eighty-four female students in 1920 (370 in 1939). The largest numbers of women attended not prestigious, established law schools but part-time law schools for women, often at night, such as Portia School of Law in Boston and Washington College of Law in the District of Columbia. In a 1925 article, deans of national law schools commented that women were as good as or better than their male classmates with several at the top of their class. However, women were told by law firms after graduation, "We want a man." In the 1920s and 1930s, firms that did hire female lawyers at all took them on only as librarians or temporary employees; some female lawyers took jobs as stenographers or went into practice with their husbands or relatives in small, local firms.

Despite the gender lag and ongoing gender gap in legal training and access to the legal profession and the as-yet closed doors that suffragist Carrie Chapman Catt insisted women must open in order to effect political change as lawmakers, women in the nineteenth and early twentieth centuries had already shown their capacity for political organization in their work with the abolitionist, suffrage, temperance, and early civil rights movements. One of the defining characteristics of American women during these years was their emergence as social and

Sadie Tanner Mossell Alexander was the first African American woman to receive a law degree from the University of Pennsylvania Law School (1927) and the first to practice law in Pennsylvania. In 1946 she was appointed to the President's Committee on Civil Rights.

political activists as well as the evolving leadership of women in their own organizations to achieve political change. Through their activism, women had gained invaluable experience as leaders, organizers, writers, and lecturers and developed considerable political expertise, which would win them the vote and pave the way for their entrance into the legislative political process.

Since each state could determine voter eligibility, women were able to vote in some states before 1920 and were elected to state and local political positions. In 1887, Susanna Salter was elected mayor of Argonia, Kansas, becoming the first female mayor in the country. In 1892, Laura Eisenhuth was elected superintendent of public instruction in North Dakota, the first woman to be elected to a statewide executive office. In 1894, three women were elected to the state legislature in the Colorado House of Representatives. Two years later, Martha Hughes Cannon from Utah became the first female state senator. Finally, in 1916, Jeannette Rankin of Montana became the first woman ever to be elected to Congress, where she served in the House of Representatives from 1917 to 1919.

Despite these early gains, women's progress in achieving equitable representation in government and law has historically been slow and gradual. The Women's Suffrage Amendment, first introduced in Congress in 1878, took four decades to accomplish; it has taken even longer for women to approach equal representation in the legislative, executive, and judicial branches of the government. Jeannette Rankin's initial call that women should make up "half the House" (or half the Senate) remains out of reach, even though women represent 52 percent of the voting-age population.

According to the Center for American Women and Politics, in 2019, 28.8 percent of the 7,383 state legislators in the United States are women. Women currently hold 510, or 25.9 percent, of the 1,972 state Senate seats and 1,619, or 29 percent, of the 5,411 state House or Assembly seats. Since 1971, the number of women serving in state legislatures has more than quintupled. Seventeen women currently serve as presidents of their state Senate or president pro tempore (34 percent); seven women serve as state-level speakers of the House (14 percent).

At the federal level, since 1917 when Jeannette Rankin began her tenure in Congress, a total of 358 women (243 Democrats, 115 Republicans) have served as U.S. representatives, delegates, or senators. Of this total, 127 (comprising 23.7 percent of the 535 members) are currently serving in Congress—102 in the House (23.4 percent) and 25 (25 percent) in the Senate. California has sent more women to Congress than any other state (43 as of 2019) with New York next with 29 women (as of 2019). One state, Vermont, has never sent a woman to either the House or the Senate. As of 2019, 74 women of color have served in Congress (70 Democrats and 4 Republicans): 42 have been black, 11 Asian American/Pacific Islander, 17 Latinx, 2 Native American, 1 Middle Eastern/North African, and 1 multiracial.

By congressional session, the breakdown of women in the House and Senate is as follows:

WOMEN IN THE U.S. CONGRESS

Congress	House	Senate
65th (1917–1919)	1	0
67th (1921–1923)	3	1
68th (1923–1925)	1	0
69th (1925–1927)	3	0
70th (1927–1929)	5	0
71st (1929–1931)	9	0
72nd (1931–1933)	7	1
73rd (1933–1935)	7	1
74th (1935–1937)	6	2
75th (1937–1939)	6	3
76th (1939–1941)	8	1
77th (1941–1943)	9	1
78th (1943–1945)	8	1
79th (1945–1947)	11	0
80th (1947–1949)	7	1
81st (1949–1951)	9	1
82nd (1951–1953)	10	1
83rd (1953–1955)	12	3
84th (1955–1957)	17	1
85th (1957–1959)	15	1

Congress	House	Senate
86th (1959–1961)	17	2
87th (1961–1963)	18	2
88th (1963–1965)	12	2
89th (1965–1967)	11	2
90th (1967–1969)	11	1
91st (1969–1971)	10	1
92nd (1971–1973)	13	2
93rd (1973–1975)	16	0
94th (1975–1977)	19	0
95th (1977–1979)	18	3
96th (1979–1981)	16	2
97th (1981–1983)	21	2
98th (1983–1985)	22	2
99th (1985–1987)	23	2
100th (1987–1989)	24	2
101st (1989–1991)	29	2
102st (1991–1993)	30	3
103st (1993–1995)	48	7
104th (1995–1997)	50	9
105th (1997–1999)	57	9
106th (1999–2001)	58	9
107th (2001–2003)	62	14
108th (2003–2005)	63	14
109th (2005–2007)	72	14
110th (2007–2009)	80	16
111th (2009–2011)	78	15
112th (2011–2013)	79	17
113th (2013–2015)	84	20
114th (2015–2017)	89	20
115th (2017–2019)	93	23
116th (2019–2021)	106	25

It would take until 1945 for the House to reach double digits of female representatives; it would not be until 2001 that the Senate managed the same. As Richard Logan Fox, author of *Gender Dynamics in Congressional Elections*, has stated, "As recently as the late 1960s, one of the surest means by which a woman could become a member of Congress was to have a husband who was a Congressman die while in office." The first Republican woman to be elected to the U.S. Senate completely on her own merits was Nancy Kassebaum of Kansas in 1978. The first Democrat was Barbara Mikulski of Maryland in 1986. Fox further argues that "the extremely low percentage of female candidates who have been elected without help of a dead relative is testimony to the social and institutional road blocks that prevent women from entering into and succeeding in electoral politics." Not only has Congress been difficult for women to access, it has also been a lonely and often inhospitable place for female members. Margaret Chase Smith served in thirteen Congressional sessions over her twenty-four-year Senate career (1948–1973): for seven of those years, she was the only female senator; for five, she had one other female Senate colleague; and for only one session, she had two. Pat Schroeder, who spent twenty-four years in the House, described the atmosphere she encountered in 1973 as an "overaged frat house." In 1993, Carol Moseley Braun joined Barbara Mikulski to defy Senate rules by wearing pants on the Senate floor. Female support staff joined them, and the rule was eventually changed to allow women to wear pants on the floor as long as they also wore a jacket.

Historically, two election cycles stand out for the unprecedented success of female candidates running for congressional office: 1992 and 2018 (1974, 1984, and 1990 were also heralded as women's years but accomplished only minor electoral gains for female candidates). In 1992, following the Clarence Thomas confirmation hearings in which the all-male Senate judiciary committee at times ridiculed Anita Hill's testimony about Thomas's sexual harassment, women entered congressional races in record numbers with 106 women winning major-party nominations for House races. In what the media dubbed "The Year of the Woman," the number of women in the House increased from thirty to forty-eight, an 11 percent increase. In the Senate, the number of

Senatorial candidates appearing at the 1992 Democratic National Convention in New York City included (far left) Carol Moseley Braun (the first African American woman elected to the U.S. Senate), Barbara Boxer (behind Braun's left shoulder), and Senator Barbara Mikulski (gesturing at bottom right).

female senators would increase from two in 1990 to nine by 1998, a dramatic increase.

In the 2018 midterm elections, women achieved their highest totals ever in both the House and the Senate, more than doubling their gains in the House from 1992 and shifting the total percentage of female senators from nine in 1994 to twenty-five. The 2018 election not only increased that percentage but also produced the most diverse U.S. Congress in history with almost one in five voting

Although 92 percent of Americans polled in 2015 responded that they would vote for a woman, that still left 8 percent who would not (well within Trump's margin of victory in key states).

members of the House and Senate a racial or ethnic minority. Minorities accounted for twenty of fifty-nine new members (34 percent). This was a striking improvement from 1981, for example, when 6 percent of members of Congress were members of a minority community. What is even more remarkable is that these newly elected female legislators represent a wide range of diversity. The new Congress following the 2018 election includes the youngest woman ever to be elected (Alexandria Ocasio-Cortes), the first Native American women (Deb Haaland and Sharice Davids), and the first Muslim women (Ilhan Omar and Rashida Tlaib). Texas sent its first Latinx women (Veronica Escobar and Sylvia Garcia) to Congress; both Connecticut and Massachusetts elected their first African American female representatives (Jahana Hayes and Ayanna Pressley); Angie Craig is the first openly gay member, elected from Minnesota; Katie Hill is the first openly bisexual congresswoman, elected from California; Sharice Davids, one of the first two Native American women elected, is also the first gay congresswoman elected from Kansas; Arizona Democrat Kyrsten Sinema is Arizona's first-ever bisexual senator. Iowa sent women to the House for the first time in its history (Abby Finkenauer and Cindy Axne). The House of

Representatives also reelected the nation's first female speaker of the House, Nancy Pelosi.

These gains are impressive, but it remains to be seen whether 2018 is a harbinger of gender equality in legislatures nationwide or just one more year of the woman achieving short-term gains with long-term equity still far from certain. Current success in legislatures will need to be balanced by inclusion and greater representation on the executive and judicial side of government. In 2016, when Hillary Clinton became the first woman in American history to be nominated as a major political party's candidate for president of the United States, she came agonizingly close to achieving her goal of becoming the first female chief executive. She received a sweeping majority of the popular vote but ultimately lost the election to Donald J. Trump. Among the many factors cited by Clinton herself and by others for her loss—the Electoral College, FBI director James Comey's last-minute reopening of the investigation into Clinton's e-mails, Russian meddling, poor campaigning by a flawed candidate—sexism was undoubtedly a contributing factor, but how much and how decisive is unclear. Although 92 percent of Americans polled in 2015 responded that they would vote for a woman, that still left 8 percent who would not (well within Trump's margin of victory in key states). Studies have shown, however, that Clinton's gender did not deter voters from choosing her. A 2018 Pew Research Center study found that 57 percent of Americans thought women brought different strengths than men to leadership roles (43 percent saw the sexes as roughly similar), and overall, those respondents saw a slight advantage in that women are seen as better at working out compromises. Despite evidence both that gender bias hurt and helped Clinton, the fact is that in her wake, an unprecedented number of women won seats in Congress in 2018 and decided to run for president in 2020. However, a widely voiced notion continues that a female presidential candidate remains a risky choice, especially when facing off against a male incumbent, even a largely unpopular one.

Compared to the federal executive, the data on women in statewide elective executive offices is just as mixed. Historically, 44 women (26 Democrats, 18 Republicans) have served as governors of thirty states (Arizona is the first state where a woman succeeded another woman as governor and the first state to have had four female governors). In 2019, 86 women hold statewide elective executive office positions across the country, 27.6 percent of the 312 available positions. Among these women, 46 are Democrats, 38 are Republicans, and 2 are nonpartisan. Fourteen, or 16.3 percent, are women of color. Nine women (6 Democrats, 3 Republicans) serve as governors in 2019 (18 percent of the national total), matching the records set from 2004 and 2007.

The key takeaway is that women currently hold record numbers of elected offices both statewide and nationally, but representation still is not proportional to the U.S. population. Women vote in higher numbers than men and have done so in every election since 1964. In 2016, 9.9 million more women than men voted (63.3 percent of eligible women went to the polls compared to 59.3 percent of eligible males), yet despite this numerical advantage, women remain well below equal representation with men in political office. A major challenge in rectifying this election gap is the way in which voters respond to female candidates: with continuing traditional notions concerning gender traits and roles. For a large number of voters, female candidates must fulfill expectations as both mothers and caretakers of the family and as extra competent public servants, more socially successful than their male counterparts, maintaining stereotypical feminine qualities while also showing a toughness and tenacity that are contrary to the traditional concepts of femininity. Given the heightened scrutiny that candidacy for national office produces, it is easy to understand why many highly qualified female candidates have chosen not to accept this unfair burden or cope with the double messages that women must endure when they enter public life. It can only be hoped that as the number of women elected to office grows, the biases against female candidates will diminish.

Women in the legal profession, from which most politicians and members of the nation's judiciary are drawn, have seen considerable gains. In 1955, the United States had approximately five thousand female lawyers (1.3 percent of the total). In 1965, only 4 percent of applicants to law schools were women. By 1973, the total of female law students was 16 percent; by 1979, it was 32 percent. By 2014, 32.9 percent of all lawyers in the nation were women, and in 2016, for the first time, women

Women U.S. senators are pictured in a 1997 meeting (left to right: Patty Murray, Susan Collins, Olympia Snowe, Carol Moseley Braun, Kay Bailey Hutchison, Barbara Mikulski, Mary Landrieu, and Dianne Feinstein).

made up a majority of law students in the nation (just over 50 percent of the seats at accredited law schools in the United States). However, despite these impressive gains, women have faced and continue to face discrimination in the legal profession. One example is Sandra Day O'Connor, the first female Supreme Court justice. When she graduated third in her law school class from Stanford University in 1952, the only job offer she received was as a legal secretary. As in business and academia, a clear gender gap remains in the legal profession. As of 2014, women make up 20.2 percent of partners in law firms, 17 percent of equity partners, and 4 percent of managing partners in the two hundred biggest law firms. In Fortune 500 corporations, 21 percent of general counsels are women, and 79 percent are men. In 2009, 21 percent of law school deans were women, 45.7 percent of associate deans, and 66.2 percent of assistant deans. In the top fifty law schools, women make up 46 percent of leadership positions on law reviews and 38 percent of editor-in-chief positions. Female lawyers' salaries were 83 percent of male lawyers' salaries in 2014.

In the judiciary, women currently make up one third of the spots on the U.S. Supreme Court. In 2012, women held 27.1 percent of all federal and state judge positions, while men held 73.9 percent. In the circuit court of appeals, 33 percent of judges are women; women make up 24 percent of federal court judges and hold about 27 percent of all state judgeships. These statistics show that the number of women on the bench has dramatically increased over the last thirty years. When the National Association of Women Judges was formed in 1979, it had one hundred members. Today, it has more than 1,250. However, an analysis by the American Constitution Society and other associations make it clear that despite the increasing gender and racial diversity of lawyers across the country, no state has a bench that adequately reflects the populations judges serve. This so-called "gavel gap" was demonstrated in an analysis of over ten thousand sitting judges that compared the proportion of women and people of color on each state's courts to the state's total population. The result was that twenty-six states received failing scores with the proportion of women and minority judges in the judiciary as less than 60 per-

cent of their proportion in the general population. Overall, women, who make up half the U.S. population, hold less than one third of judgeships.

In surveying American women in politics and the legal profession, the inevitable conclusion to draw is that the glass is definitely half full: clear and impressive gains toward equity but still far to go and challenges to be met.

BIOGRAPHIES

Abigail Adams (1744–1818)
First Lady

The first second lady and the second first lady of the United States, Abigail Adams is one of the most remarkable women of the eighteenth and early nineteenth centuries. Ambitious for herself as well as for her husband, she was highly opinionated, and she did not hesitate to speak out on political and social issues, unlike most women of her time. She believed in the equal status of women and most importantly of a woman's right to a good education.

Born in Weymouth, Massachusetts, she was the second of the four children of Reverend William and Elizabeth Smith. A frail child, Adams would suffer from poor health all her life. She was educated by her parents and spent her girlhood reading Shakespeare and classical literature as well as teaching herself French.

In 1764, nineteen-year-old Abigail wed twenty-nine-year-old lawyer John Adams, beginning an extraordinarily happy and close partnership that would last until Abigail's death. The couple lived in Braintree, outside of Boston, on a farm that John had inherited. They had five children, four of whom survived into adulthood. Their oldest son, John Quincy Adams (1767–1848), would become the sixth U.S. president.

In 1774, John Adams went to Philadelphia as a delegate to the First Continental Congress. For the next ten years, except for very brief visits, the

Adamses lived apart. In his absence, Abigail educated the children, managed the household and farm, hired the help, and paid the bills. A capable and prudent businesswoman, she successfully carried out all of these responsibilities during the Revolutionary War, when the country was disrupted and provisions were scarce. One of the great letter writers of all time, she is perhaps best known for her famous letter to her husband, whom she addressed as "Dearest Friend," and wrote to him at least once a day. The letters, some of the best sources on life during the period, include day-to-day information on the family and farm, war news, and political insights. Her most famous letter, written in 1776, urged Adams and the other members of the Continental Congress not to forget about the nation's women. "I long to hear that you have declared an independency," she wrote. "And, by the way, in the new code of laws which I suppose it will be necessary for you to make, I desire you would remember the ladies and be more generous and favorable to them than your ancestors. Do not put such unlimited power into the hands of the husbands. Remember, all men would be tyrants if they could. If particular care and attention is not paid to the ladies, we are determined to foment a rebellion, and will not hold ourselves bound by any laws in which we have no voice or representation."

During the eight years of John Adams's service as the first vice president (1789–1796) and the four years of his presidency (1796–1800), Abigail moved back and forth between Braintree and the capitals in New York City and Philadelphia. During the last three months of Adams's presidential term, they moved to the new capital in Washington and lived in the unfinished White House. The Executive Mansion was so cold and damp that she kept fires going in the mansion's thirteen fireplaces 24 hours a day. She hung the family's laundry in what is now the East Room of the White House.

After John Adams lost the 1800 presidential election to Thomas Jefferson, the Adamses returned to Braintree. There, Abigail enjoyed seventeen quiet years as the matriarch of her large family. She died from a fever in 1818 at the age of seventy-four.

Noted historian Joseph Ellis has called Abigail Adams's correspondence with her husband "a treas-ure trove of unexpected intimacy and candor, more revealing than any other correspondence between a prominent American husband and wife in American history." Ellis argues that Abigail was the more resilient and emotionally balanced of the two and calls her one of the most extraordinary women in American history.

Madeleine Albright (1937–)
Diplomat, Secretary of State

When President Bill Clinton appointed Madeleine Albright as secretary of state in 1997, she became the first woman to hold that position and the highest-ranking woman ever to serve in the U.S. government.

Albright was born Maria Jan Korbel in Prague, Czechoslovakia. Her father was a Czech diplomat who fled to England with his wife and infant daughter when the Nazis invaded Czechoslovakia in 1938. The family briefly returned to Prague after World War II, but they fled again in 1948 when the communists assumed power. This time, they immigrated to the United States, where Albright's father became a professor of international studies at the University of Denver.

It was not until after her confirmation as secretary of state that Albright learned that her family members were Czech Jews and not Catholics as she had believed and that three of her grandparents perished in concentration camps during the war. Albright responded to the discovery of her ancestry by saying, "I have been proud of my heritage that I have known about, and I will be equally proud of the heritage that I have just been given."

Albright was interested in foreign affairs from an early age. "By the time I was eleven," she recalled, "I had lived in five countries and knew four languages. In my parents' homes, we talked about international relations all the time, the way some families talk about sports or other things around the dinner table." In 1959, Albright graduated from Wellesley College and married journalist Joseph Albright. After giving birth to twin girls and another daughter, Albright moved with her family to Washington, D.C., commuting from there to Columbia University in New York City to complete her Ph.D. in international relations. Albright later became a professor of international affairs at Georgetown University in Washington and a director of the Women in Foreign Service program at the university's School of Foreign Service.

A respected foreign policy expert on Eastern European and Russian affairs, Albright served as an adviser to Democratic presidential candidates Walter Mondale in 1984 and Michael Dukakis in 1988. In 1992, Bill Clinton named Albright as the U.S. ambassador to the United Nations, only the second woman ever to serve in that post.

The Clinton administration was divided about selecting Albright as secretary of state with one faction arguing, "anybody but Albright," but she was appointed in 1997. Not being a natural-born citizen of the United States, she was not eligible as a U.S. presidential successor and was excluded from nuclear contingency plans. However, during her tenure, Albright influenced American foreign policy, particularly in Bosnia and the Middle East. In 2000, she became one of the highest-level Western diplomats ever to meet Kim Jong-il, leader of North Korea. She won the respect of the international community for her straightforward, no-nonsense style; her in-depth knowledge of foreign affairs; and her diplomatic skills. She proved herself to be a forceful and principled architect of U.S. foreign policy who helped to promote democracy around the world.

Following Albright's term as secretary, it was rumored that she might pursue a career in Czech politics with Czech president Vaclav Havel discussing the possibility of her succeeding him. Albright was reportedly flattered but denied ever seriously considering the possibility. Instead, Albright remained active on various programs and initiatives of interest to her, including genocide prevention, and founded the Albright Group (later the Albright Stonebridge Group), an international strategy consulting firm based in Washington, D.C. Her many books include *Madam Secretary* (2003), *The Mighty and the Almighty* (2006), *Prague Winter* (20112), and *Fascism: A Warning* (2018).

Cora Reynolds Anderson (1882–1950)
Legislator, Politician

Cora Reynolds Anderson was the first woman and the first Native American to be elected to a state legislature. Born in L'Anse, Michigan, Anderson was a member of the Ojibwa tribe. She attended public schools in Michigan's Upper Peninsula before attending the Haskell Institute in Lawrence, Kansas, where she received her teacher's diploma. After graduation, she returned to Michigan to teach school for many years at the Zeba Mission in the Upper Peninsula. In 1903, she married Charles Anderson, and the couple managed a hotel in L'Anse. Interested in her community's welfare, Anderson organized the first public health service in Baraga County, Michigan, that brought the first public health nurse to the region.

In 1925, Anderson won election to the Michigan House of Representatives, a notable first for a Native American woman. She served only one term, from 1925 to 1926, before losing her seat to a redistricting. While in office, Anderson was appointed chair of the committee overseeing the Industrial Home for Girls, sat on the committees for Agriculture, Insurance, and the Northern State Normal School (now Northern Michigan University). She was also a strong advocate for public heath, campaigning against alcoholism and tuberculosis, and championed the right to recognize Native American fishing rights on Huron Bay.

After her government service, Anderson was active in the Michigan Grange, a program dedicated "to educating and elevating the American farmer," which offered free rural mail delivery and promoted pure food laws. Anderson was the Grange representative for the Upper Peninsula.

For her contribution to the state, Anderson was inducted into the Michigan Women's Hall of Fame in 2001 with a testimonial that read: "At a time when minorities, including Native Americans, were subjected to considerable economic and social discrimination, Anderson's determination to attend college and return the benefits of her education to her community was notable. Her role as educator, legislator, and public health reform leader aided the Native American community as well as the whole of society."

Hattie Wyatt Caraway (1878–1950)

Senator

Hattie Wyatt Caraway was the first woman ever to be elected to serve a full term as a U.S. senator. She also was the first woman to chair a Senate committee (in 1933) and the first woman to preside officially over the Senate (in 1943).

She was born in west-central Tennessee near rural Bakerville, the daughter of a farmer and shopkeeper. She graduated from Dickson Normal College in 1896 and taught school in rural Arkansas before marrying Thaddeus Caraway in 1902. The couple settled in Jonesboro, Arkansas, where Thaddeus had a law practice and Hattie raised their three sons. Thaddeus entered politics and served four terms in the U.S. House and two terms in the Senate.

In 1931, Thaddeus Caraway died in office, and Arkansas governor Harvey Parnell named his widow to complete Thaddeus's term, stating, "The office belonged to Senator Caraway, who went before the people and received their endorsement for it, and his widow is rightfully entitled to the honor." When Caraway first entered the Senate to take her seat, she observed, "The windows need washing!" Caraway won the special election for her husband's Senate seat, winning 92 percent of the vote. In 1932, without the support of the Arkansas political establishment, she announced her candidacy for reelection against six male contenders, stating, "The time has passed when a woman should be placed in a position and kept there only while someone else is being groomed for the job." Caraway had the support of her Senate ally, Louisiana senator and political boss Huey "Kingfish" Long, who mobilized Louisiana state employees to canvas Arkansas on Caraway's behalf. Caraway managed to win a seven-way primary and won the general election in a landslide.

In the Senate, she was nicknamed "Silent Hattie" because she spoke on the floor just fifteen times during her two terms in the Senate and was derided by some in the press who called her "the quiet grandmother who never said anything or did anything." She explained her reticence as unwillingness "to take

a minute away from the men. The poor dears love it so." While serving as a senator, Caraway had three other women join her for brief tenures of two years or less, but never did more than two women serve at a time. Caraway was a loyal supporter of President Roosevelt's New Deal policies and foreign policy, arguing for his Lend-Lease Act from the perspective of a mother with two sons in the Army. During the war, Caraway encouraged women to contribute to the war effort, but she insisted that home and family were women's primary tasks. She was, however, often reminded of women's disadvantages. When assigned the same Senate desk briefly occupied by another female senator appointed to take her husband's place, she commented, "I guess they wanted as few of them contaminated as possible." In 1943, she became the first female legislator to cosponsor the Equal Rights Amendment.

Defeated in bid for a third term in 1944, Caraway remained in Washington, serving as a member of the Federal Employees' Compensation Committee, nominated by President Roosevelt and elevated to the commission's appeals board, serving until suffering a stroke and dying at the age of seventy-six. Caraway demonstrated over a long political career that she was much more than "Silent Hattie," winning respect from her Senate colleagues, advocating a wider role for women in government, and demonstrating that political skills and abilities were not exclusively male characteristics.

Shirley Chisholm (1924–2005)

Congresswoman

The first African American woman in Congress and the first woman and African American to seek the nomination for president of the United States from one of the two major political parties, Shirley Chisholm was an inspirational trailblazer, noted for her outspoken advocacy for women and minorities.

Born Shirley Anita St. Hill in Brooklyn, New York, Chisholm was the daughter of immigrants from the West Indies island of Barbados. After graduating from Brooklyn College in 1946, Chisholm worked as a teacher in a childcare center before serving in New York City's Bureau of Child Welfare, helping to set up daycare centers for working women. In 1949, she married Conrad Chisholm. They divorced in 1977, and she subsequently married Arthur Hardwick Jr. The marriage lasted until his death in 1986. In the 1950s and early 1960s, Chisholm began to work for better minority and female participation in local politics. At that time, white males represented most neighborhoods and districts in New York, even those areas, like the one where Chisholm resided, that were made up largely by African Americans. In 1964, Chisholm ran for and won a seat in the New York Assembly, becoming one of only six African Americans in that body and the only black, female member. In 1968, Chisholm was elected as a Democrat to the U.S. House of Representatives, becoming Brooklyn's first black representative and the nation's first African American female member of Congress. At the time, only eight other African Americans were members of the House, which had only ten female members. New representatives were expected to wait their turn patiently before speaking up or offering initiatives. Chisholm did neither. She became an outspoken opponent of U.S. policy in Vietnam, a highly visible supporter of the Equal Rights Amendment, and a tireless campaigner for jobs, education, and enforcement of antidiscrimination laws. Referred to as "Fighting Shirley," she introduced more than fifty pieces of legislation and championed racial and gender equality and the plight of the poor. She was cofounder of the National Women's Political Caucus in 1971 and in 1977 became the first black woman and second woman ever to serve on the powerful House Rules Committee.

In 1972, she became the first woman to make a serious bid for the presidential nomination of a major political party. Discrimination followed her quest for the Democratic Party presidential nomination. She was blocked from participating in the televised primary debate. Still, students, women, and minorities followed her on the "Chisholm Trail," and she entered twelve primaries and garnered 152 delegates' votes (10 percent of the total). Her effort paved the way for other African American candi-

dates, including Jesse Jackson and Barack Obama, as well as the candidacy of Hillary Clinton.

Chisholm retired from Congress in 1983 to return to teaching at Mount Holyoke College, where she remained for four years. In 1985, she helped to found the National Political Congress for Black Women and served as its first president. In 1993, President Clinton named her ambassador to Jamaica, but she declined the nomination due to ill health. Chisholm authored several books, including *Unbought and Unbound* (1970) and *The Good Fight* (1973). Chisholm died in Florida at the age of eighty-one after suffering several strokes. Of her legacy, Chisholm said, "I want to be remembered as a woman ... who dared to be a catalyst of change."

Hillary Clinton (1947–)

First Lady, Secretary of State

In summarizing her résumé—First Lady of Arkansas, First Lady of the United States, first First Lady to win political office, first female senator from the State of New York, first woman to win a nominating primary of a major party, first woman nominated for president by a major party, first female presidential candidate—it is hard to argue that Hillary Clinton is the most accomplished political figure in American history. Despite her loss to Donald J. Trump in 2016, she still managed to become the third-largest popular-vote winner in American history (behind Barack Obama's two presidential elections). She is also one of the most polarizing political figures—both admired and vilified—and a projection (both good and ill) of the status of women in politics at the highest level.

Born Hillary Rodham in Chicago, she was the oldest of five children in a conservative Republican family. While attending Wellesley College in the 1960s, she shifted her political views to the left and became a committed social progressive and political activist. Attending Yale Law School, she began dating fellow law student Bill Clinton, and the couple campaigned together in Texas in 1972 for the unsuccessful Democratic presidential candidate George

McGovern. She received her law degree in 1973, having stayed on an extra year to be with Clinton. She declined his first proposal following graduation, but they eventually married in 1975.

Following her graduation from law school, she served as staff attorney for the Children's Defense Fund and was a member of the impeachment inquiry staff in Washington, D.C., to advise the House Committee on the Judiciary during the Watergate scandal. After failing the District of Columbia Bar and passing the Arkansas Bar, she made the decision to follow Clinton to Arkansas: "I chose to follow my heart instead of my head." Clinton was teaching law and running for a seat in the U.S. House of Representatives in his home state. She also began teaching criminal law courses at the University of Arkansas and became the first director of a new legal aid clinic on campus. After losing the Arkansas congressional race in 1974, Clinton was elected Arkansas attorney general in 1976, and she joined the Rose Law Firm, specializing in patent infringement and intellectual property law while also working *pro bono* in child advocacy.

In 1978, she became Arkansas's first lady when Bill Clinton was elected governor, a position she would hold from 1979 to 1981 and then again from 1983 to 1992. In 1980, she gave birth to their only child, their daughter Chelsea. Clinton drew national attention for the first time when her husband became a candidate for the 1992 Democratic presidential campaign in her defense of her husband against charges of extramarital affairs and her advocacy of careers for women instead of pursuing the traditional role as homemaker. When Bill Clinton was elected president in 1992, he named Hillary to lead a commission to draft a proposal for national health care reform. It was the most important political role ever assigned to a first lady. Although the health care initiative ultimately failed, she earned respect for her expertise and ability, though also fire from those who were uncomfortable with her prominent role in the administration as well as with allegations over supposed impropriety in real estate deals in which the Clintons had been involved with in Arkansas.

During Clinton's second term, Hillary again supported her husband despite the evidence of sexual infidelity with White House intern Monica Lewinsky that led to his impeachment. Some admired her strength and poise in private matters that were made public and sympathized with her as a victim of her husband's behavior; others criticized her as an enabler to her husband's indiscretions or accused her of cynically staying in a failed marriage to further her own political aspirations.

Before the end of the Clinton administration, Clinton was elected to the Senate from New York in 2000, making her the only woman to serve in an elected office while and after serving as first lady. In 2007, she announced her candidacy for the Democratic nomination for the U.S. presidency. No woman had ever been nominated by a major party for the presidency, and no former first lady had ever run for president. Although she lost the nomination to Barack Obama, she had received seventeen million votes during the nomination and had won 1,640 pledged delegates to Obama's 1,763. She was the first woman to run in the primary or caucus of every state, and she substantially eclipsed the totals for Shirley Chisholm's 1972 nomination run in votes and delegates won.

After a hard-fought and contentious primary, Barack Obama made the surprising decision after he was elected president of naming Clinton as U.S. secretary of state. Clinton proved to be a key team player within the administration and earned high praise for her diplomatic skills. She advocated what became known as the "Hillary Doctrine," which asserted that women's rights were critical for U.S. security interests. She visited 112 countries during her tenure as secretary of state, which ended in 2013, making her the most widely traveled secretary of state ever. *Time* magazine wrote that "Clinton's endurance is legendary."

After announcing her candidacy for the presidency in the 2016 election, Clinton endured a nomination battle with Vermont senator Bernie Sanders. She was formally nominated at the 2016 Democratic National Convention, becoming the first woman to be nominated by a major U.S. political party. Leading her opponent Donald J. Trump in all the national polls up to the election, she lost the Electoral College total needed. She had won the popular vote by almost three million and became the fifth presidential candidate in U.S. history to win the popular vote but lose the election. She won the most votes of any candidate who did not win the election. Clinton confessed to pain of her loss but called on her supporters to accept Trump as president, saying, "We owe him an open mind and a chance to lead." After losing the Democratic primary in 2008, Clinton famously said, "Although we weren't able to shatter that highest glass ceiling, thanks to you, it's got about 18 million cracks in it." After 2016, the total of cracks gained by Clinton are 65,852,514.

Geraldine Ferraro (1935–2011)

Congresswoman

 Congresswoman Geraldine Ferraro became in 1984 the first female vice presidential candidate for a major political party when asked to serve as Walter Mondale's running mate in the 1984 presidential election. The *New York Times* would write, "64 years after women won the right to vote, a woman had removed the 'men only' sign from the White House door." Although she wasn't successful, and it would be another twenty-four years before another woman would be nominated as vice president, Ferraro's nomination was a transformative event in American politics and women's history.

She was born in Newburgh, New York, the fourth child and only daughter of Dominick Ferraro, an Italian immigrant who owned a restaurant and a five-and-dime store, and her seamstress mother. She was named for her brother, Gerard, who died in an automobile accident two years before she was born. Her father would die of a heart attack when she was eight, and Ferraro would describe his passing as "a dividing line that runs through my life." Her mother sold the store and the family's house, and they moved to the South Bronx. Ferraro attended a Catholic boarding school in Tarrytown, New York. She won a scholarship to Marymount Manhattan College, graduating in 1956. She went to work as an elementary school teacher in public schools in Astoria, Queens, "because that's what women were supposed to do," she recalled. She decided, however, to attend law school and was

one of two women in her graduating class from Fordham University School of Law in 1960.

In 1960, she married John Zaccaro, whom she began dating in college. He worked as a realtor and businessman; she raised three children and worked part time as a civil lawyer in her husband's real estate business for thirteen years. Her first full-time political job came in 1974 when she was appointed assistant district attorney for Queens County. She would be assigned to the new Special Victims Bureau, prosecuting cases of rape, child abuse, spouse abuse, and domestic violence. She would head the unit from 1975 to 1977.

In 1978, Ferraro ran successfully for the House seat in New York's 9th Congressional District in Queens in 1978, emphasizing law and order, the elderly, and neighborhood preservation with the slogan "Finally, a Tough Democrat." She would be reelected in 1980 and 1982. In Congress, Ferraro focused her legislative attention on equity for women in wages, pensions, and retirement plans. She cosponsored the 1981 Economic Equity Act. In 1980, she was elected secretary of the Democratic caucus and in 1984 was appointed chair of the 1984 Democratic platform committee, the first woman to hold the post.

As Walter Mondale won the 1984 Democratic nomination, he was pushed by the National Organization for Women, the National Women's Political Caucus, and others in the party, including House Speaker Tip O'Neill, to choose a female running mate. San Francisco mayor Dianne Feinstein was considered, but Mondale selected Ferraro. She was not only the first woman to run on a major party's national ticket, she was also the first Italian American. She would face questions such as "Are you tough enough?" and "Do you think that in any way the Soviets might be tempted to try to take advantage of you simply because you are a woman?" Her selection excited Democratic activists, but polls at the time showed that only 22 percent of women were excited about her selection with 18 percent saying it was a "bad idea." Ferraro, however, proved to be an effective campaigner with a brash and confident style that at times overshadowed the more bland Mondale. Questions about her husband's finances dogged the election. It would be the first time that the press had to deal with a national candidate's husband. Ferraro dealt with the controversy in a 2-hour press conference that fellow Democrat Mario Cuomo called "one of the best performances I've ever seen by a politician under pressure."

After Mondale's defeat to Ronald Reagan, Ferraro made unsuccessful bids for the Senate in 1992 and 1998, both times losing in the Democratic primary. She was named ambassador to the UN's Human Rights Commission during the Clinton administration, cohosted CNN's *Crossfire* from 1996 to 1998, and became a regular political commentator on Fox News in 1999. In 1998, she was diagnosed with bone marrow cancer that necessitated multiple, difficult procedures. She died in a Boston hospital at the age of seventy-four. President Obama said upon her death that "Geraldine will forever be remembered as a trailblazer who broke down barriers for women, and Americans of all backgrounds and walks of life." She would say about her experience in national politics that "I am the first to admit that were I not a woman, I would not have been the vice-presidential nominee," yet she insisted that her presence on the ticket helped rather than harmed the Democrat's chances and that "throwing Ronald Reagan out of office at the height of his popularity, with inflation and interest rates down, the economy moving, and the country at peace, would have required God on the ticket, and She was not available!"

Ruth Bader Ginsburg (1933–)

Attorney, U.S. Supreme Court Justice

The second female justice on the U.S. Supreme Court (following Sandra Day O'Connor), Ruth Bader Ginsburg is a widely admired jurist for the probity of her decisions and for her indefatigable commitment to service.

Born Joan Ruth Bader in Brooklyn, New York, she grew up in a working-class neighborhood. Her father was a merchant. Her older sister died of meningitis at the age of six when Ginsburg was fourteen months old. Outside the family, Ginsburg began to go by the name "Ruth" to help teachers distinguish her from other students named Joan. The Baders

were an observant Jewish family, and she attended synagogue regularly. When she started James Madison High School, her mother was diagnosed with cancer and died just days before her daughter's graduation, which Ginsburg did not attend. As Ginsburg recalled, "My mother told me two things constantly. One was to be a lady, and the other was to be independent."

She attended Cornell University on a full scholarship, graduating with a BA degree in government in 1954. The same year, she married law student Martin D. Ginsburg. He began army service, and they had their first child in 1955. In 1956, Ginsburg enrolled in Harvard Law School, one of only nine women in a class of about five hundred men. She was asked by the law school dean, "Why are you at Harvard Law School, taking the place of a man?" When her husband took a job in New York City, Ginsburg transferred to Columbia Law School, becoming the first woman to be on two major law reviews at both Harvard and Columbia. She earned her law degree in 1959, tying for first in her class.

Despite her outstanding academic record, Ginsburg experienced gender discrimination while seeking employment after graduation. After clerking for a U.S. District Court judge (1959–1961), Ginsburg taught at Rutgers University Law School (1963–1972) and at Columbia (1972–1980), where she became the school's first female tenured law professor. In the 1970s, she also served as the director of the Woman's Rights Project of the American Civil Liberties Union, arguing six landmark cases on gender equality before the U.S. Supreme Court.

In 1980, President Jimmy Carter appointed her to the U.S. Court of Appeals for the District of Columbia where she served until she was appointed to the U.S. Supreme Court by President Bill Clinton in 1993. As a judge, Ginsburg is on the Supreme Court's moderate-liberal bloc, whose opinions are generally marked by moderation and restraint but are also a strong voice in favor of gender equality. In 1996, she wrote the court's landmark decision in *United States v. Virginia* that determined that the state-supported Virginia Military Institute could not refuse to admit women. She strongly dissented in the case of *Bush v. Gore,* which effectively decided the 2000 presidential election.

In 2010, her husband, Martin, died of cancer, ending their marriage of fifty-six years. Ginsburg would call him her biggest booster and "the only young man I dated who cared that I had a brain." The day after her husband's death, Ginsburg was back at work on the court. It is this devotion to her job and her apparently steadfast focus and energy that has turned Ginsburg into a cultural icon and the subject of two feature films, the documentary *RBG* (2018) and the biopic *On the Basis of Sex* (2018), which is about the first case she argued before the Supreme Court on gender equality. She has also become a recurring character played by Kate McKinnon on *Saturday Night Live*. In 1999, Ginsburg was diagnosed with colon cancer. She underwent surgery, chemotherapy, and radiation treatments and never missed a day on the bench. In 2018, she was hospitalized after fracturing three ribs in a fall. A day later, she returned to her regular judicial work schedule. The scan of her ribs showed cancerous nodules in her lungs, and she underwent a left lung lobectomy. On January 7, 2019, for the first time since joining the court more than twenty-five years earlier, Ginsburg missed an oral argument while she recuperated. She returned to work on February 15, 2019. Despite rumors that she may retire, Ginsburg remains determined. She has said that her work on the court has helped her cope with the death of her husband and is shooting for the record of thirty-five years on the bench, set by Justice John Paul Stevens.

When asked when enough women would be on the Supreme Court, Ruth Bader Ginsburg notoriously replied, "When there are nine."

Martha Wright Griffiths (1912–2003)

Attorney, Congresswoman, Judge, State Legislator

State legislator, judge, congresswoman, attorney, and Michigan's first female lieutenant governor, Martha Wright Griffiths was a longtime fighter for women's rights, known as "Mother of the ERA," for bringing the Equal Rights Amendment to a vote and passage in the House of Representatives. She was also instrumental in drafting the sex dis-crimination amendment to Title VII of the 1964 Civil Rights Act.

Born Martha Edna Wright in Pierce City, Missouri, she attended public schools and graduated in 1934 from the University of Missouri and from the University of Michigan Law School in 1940. In 1934, she married her college sweetheart, Hicks G. Griffiths, who would become a judge and chairman of the Michigan Democratic Party from 1949–1950. First working in the legal department of the American Automobile Insurance Association in Detroit and, during World War II, as a contract negotiator in the Detroit district for the Army Ordnance, Griffiths opened her own law practice in 1946.

Encouraged to enter politics by her husband, Griffiths won elections to the Michigan House of Representatives after her second try in 1948 and 1950. She gained the Democratic nomination for a seat in the U.S. Congress in 1952 but was defeated. In 1953, she was elected as a judge, saying, "It is at least an unusual experience to assist for four years in making laws of this state, and then sit as a judge of people charged with breaking those laws." In 1954, Griffiths unseated the incumbent to win election to the U.S. House of Representatives. She would win reelection nine more times.

In the House, Griffiths became the first female representative to gain an appointment on the powerful Ways and Means Committee. She also was assigned to the Joint Economic Committee and eventually chaired the Subcommittee on Fiscal Policy, pursuing tax reform, including tax relief for single parents, married couples, and widows. In 1964, Griffiths argued that sexual discrimination should be added to the landmark Civil Rights Act and pushed for inclusion in Title VII of the act as well as later promoting the new Equal Employment Opportunity Commission to enforce the act more vigorously. Griffiths was also pivotal in passing the Equal Rights Amendment in the House, coming to believe that a constitutional amendment was the only way to overcome the Supreme Court's history of decisions that, in Griffiths's view, denied that women were "persons" within the meaning of the Constitution. Every year since she entered the House in 1955, she introduced ERA legislation, only to see it die in the Judiciary Committee. In 1970, she managed to rally House members to support bringing the bill out of committee and onto the floor for debate and a vote. Eventually, the ERA passed by a vote of 352 to 15, but the House and Senate failed to work out their differences in conference committee before Congress adjourned, so Griffiths began the process again in 1971. This time, the legislation passed by the House was approved by the Senate without revision in 1972 (the ERA was ratified by only thirty-five of the requisite thirty-eight states and failed to become part of the Constitution).

Griffiths declined to run for an eleventh term in 1974, citing her age and a desire to spend more time with her family as her reasons for leaving. She remained active in politics, however, chairing the Rules Committee for the Democratic National Convention in 1976 and in 1982 becoming Michigan's first woman to be elected lieutenant governor. After serving as lieutenant governor from 1983 to 1991, she resumed her law practice and retired to her home in Armada, Michigan, where she died at the age of ninety-one.

Patricia Roberts Harris (1924–1985)

Attorney, Cabinet Secretary, Diplomat

Appointed by President Jimmy Carter as U.S. secretary of Housing and Urban Development and U.S. Secretary of Health, Education, and Welfare, Patricia Roberts Harris was the first African American woman to serve in a U.S. Cabinet position. She previously served as ambassador to Luxembourg under President Lyndon Johnson and was the first African American female ambassador for the United States.

Roberts was born in Mattoon, Illinois, the daughter of a railroad dining car waiter. Her parents separated when she was six years old, and she was then raised primarily by her mother and grandmother. An excellent student, Harris won a scholarship to Howard University, graduating in 1945. She married in 1955, and her husband encouraged her to enter law school. She earned her law degree from George Washington University in 1960.

Her first government job was in 1960 as an attorney in the appeals and research section of the criminal division of the U.S. Department of Justice. In 1961, she returned to Howard as an associate dean of students and lecturer at Howard's law school, becoming a full professor in 1963. After serving as delegate to the 1964 Democratic National Convention and working in Lyndon Johnson's presidential campaign, Harris was appointed ambassador to Luxembourg from 1965 to 1967, the first African American named as an American envoy. In 1969, she became the first black female dean of Howard University's School of Law.

In 1977, she joined Jimmy Carter's Cabinet. Asked during her confirmation whether Harris's background of wealth and power prevented her from becoming an effective secretary of housing and urban development with sufficient connection to the poor, she replied, "I am one of them. You do not seem to understand who I am. I am a black woman, the daughter of a dining-car waiter. I am a black woman who even eight years ago could not buy a house in some parts of the District of Columbia.... I assure you that while there may be those who forget what it meant to be excluded from the dining room of this very building, I shall not forget." When the U.S. Department of Education Organization Act was implemented in 1980, the education functions of the U.S. Department of Health, Education, and Welfare were transferred to the U.S. Department of Education. Harris remained as secretary of the renamed U.S. Department of Health and Human Services until Carter left office in 1981.

Harris mounted an unsuccessful run for mayor of Washington, D.C., in 1982, and she took a position as a full-time professor at the George Washington National Law Center, a position she held until her death from breast cancer in 1985 at the age of sixty.

Oveta Culp Hobby (1905–1995)

Cabinet Secretary

As the first secretary of the U.S. Department of Health, Education, and Welfare, Oveta Culp Hobby was the second woman (after Frances Perkins) to hold a U.S. Cabinet position. She was also the first director of the Women's Army Corps.

Born in Killeen, Texas, she was a gifted student who followed her father into law, studying at the University of Texas Law School. However, she never received a degree. At the age of twenty-one, she served as parliamentarian of the Texas House of Representatives before beginning a journalism career in 1931 when she married William Hobby, a former Texas governor and publisher of the *Houston Post*.

During World War II, Hobby went to Washington to head the newly formed women's division of the War Department's Bureau of Public Relations. There, she drafted plans for the formation of a women's auxiliary to the all-male army, which eventually resulted in the formation of the Women's Army Corps. She was given the responsibility of heading the new corps. Initially restricted to fifty-four Army jobs such as secretaries and nurses, under Hobby's leadership, the WAC eventually took on 185 more jobs such as war planning, map making, and code work, areas previously restricted to men. She also initiated a program for recruiting African American women for the officer corps. By 1943, she was overseeing the activities of more than one hundred thousand WACs in a wide variety of noncombatant positions, and her efforts made her, next to Eleanor Roosevelt, the second most important woman in the American war effort.

In 1953, President Dwight D. Eisenhower named her head of the Federal Security Agency, a non-Cabinet post, but she was invited to sit in on Cabinet meetings. The same year, she was named the first secretary, and first female secretary, of the newly established U.S. Department of Health, Education, and Welfare, which later became the U.S. Department of Health and Human Services. One of her most important decisions in her role as secretary was to approve Jonas Salk's polio vaccine. Facing opposition to her attempt to restructure Social Security payroll taxes, she resigned her post in 1955 to return to Houston to take care of her ailing husband. She resumed her association with the *Houston Post* as president and editor. She helped the newspaper develop into one of the nation's leading metropolitan dailies and to become part of a media empire of radio and television stations.

At the end of President Eisenhower's second term, he encouraged Hobby to run for the presidency, becoming the first woman considered for a U.S. presidential candidacy by an incumbent president. However, she chose not to run. She died of a stroke in Houston at the age of ninety.

Journalist, politician, and civil servant, Hobby helped pave the way for women in both military and civilian life. For a woman without a college degree, she exhibited remarkable organizational and business skills, and she proved that women could direct large organizations and serve with distinction in the most important positions in government.

Diane Joyce Humetewa (1964–)

Attorney, Judge

In 2014, Diane Joyce Humetewa made U.S. history by becoming the first Native American female federal judge and only the third Native American ever to hold such a position.

Born in Phoenix, Arizona, she is a member of the Hopi Nation. Humetewa received a BS degree from Arizona State University in 1987 and her JD degree from the Arizona State University College of Law in 1993. Her various positions before she was called to the bench include deputy counsel for the U.S. Senate Committee on Indian Affairs (1993–1996), counsel to the deputy attorney general, Office of Tribal Justice, U.S. Department of Justice (1996–1998), and senior litigation counsel (1998–2007). In 2007, she was confirmed and sworn in as the U.S. attorney for the District of Arizona, becoming the first Native American woman to serve as a U.S. attorney.

In 2013, President Barack Obama nominated Humetewa to serve as a U.S. district judge of the U.S. District Court for Arizona. She was confirmed unanimously by the Senate in 2014. Native Americans have long been pushing for increased representation on the federal bench, especially in regions of the country with high numbers of tribal- and In-dian-focused legal cases. "Let's hope Diane's confirmation is just the 'start of a slew of Native American federal judges," said Chris Stearns, former counsel to the House Natural Resources Committee and a Navajo. "There is still a massive lack of representation of Indian judges in the federal courts." The National Congress of American Indians called the appointment "historic" and that "we eagerly anticipate many more nominations of Native people to the federal bench and other offices."

Following Humetewa's judicial appointment, she has widely been suggested as a possible consensus nominee for a future vacancy on the U.S. Supreme Court.

Barbara Jordan (1936–1996)

Congresswoman

 Congresswoman, educator, and leader of the civil rights movement, Barbara Jordan was the first African American woman to be elected to Congress from a southern state. She was also the first African American and first woman to deliver a keynote address at a Democratic National Convention in 1976. She is perhaps best known for her impassioned 1974 speech during the impeachment process against President Richard Nixon in 1974, earning her widespread praise for her oratory, morals, and wisdom.

She grew up in the largest black ghetto in Houston, Texas, the youngest of three daughters in a poor family. Her father, a Baptist preacher and warehouse laborer, taught her that race and poverty had nothing to do with her intellectual potential and her ability to achieve great things if she worked hard for them. When an African American, female lawyer visited her high school on career day, Jordan decided that a career in law would be the best way she could make a difference. Educated at Texas Southern University, where she excelled at debate, Jordan received her law degree from Boston University in 1959. She began her law practice back in Houston working at home from her parents' dining room table; after three years, she finally earned enough money to open an office.

In 1962, Jordan decided to enter politics, running unsuccessfully for the state legislature. After another failed attempt two years later, she finally won in 1966, becoming the first African American since the 1870s to serve in the Texas Senate and the first African American woman ever to be elected to the Texas legislature. During her six years as a state senator, Jordan worked for social reform, cosponsoring a minimum-wage bill and a workers' compensation plan. In 1972, she became the second African American woman to be elected to Congress, following Shirley Chisholm.

Jordan rose to national prominence in 1974 as a member of the House Judiciary Committee investigating whether President Nixon was guilty of impeachable offenses in concealing presidential involvement in the Watergate burglary. In a stirring and memorable speech, Jordan justified her vote to recommend impeachment, declaring, "My faith is total. I am not going to sit here and be an idle spectator to the diminution, the subversion, the destruction of the Constitution."

In 1976, Jordan became the first African American to deliver the keynote at a national political convention. Her eloquence and principled stands on tough issues caused one writer to observe, "Few members in the long history of the House have so quickly impressed themselves upon the consciousness of the country. Jordan shocked her many supporters when she announced in 1977 that she would not seek reelection. Suffering from poor health due to leukemia and multiple sclerosis, which eventually caused her to rely on a wheelchair, Jordan left Washington to teach at the University of Texas. In 1994, she was awarded the Presidential Medal of Freedom. From 1994 until her death, Jordan chaired the U.S. Commission on Immigration Reform. President Bill Clinton said that he wanted to nominate Jordan for the U.S. Supreme Court, but her health problems prevented him from doing so. Jordan died at the age of fifty-nine from complications of pneumonia in Austin, Texas. Her 1974 speech on the articles of impeachment was listed number thirteen in American Rhetoric's Top 100 Speeches of the 20th Century, while her 1976 Democratic National Convention keynote address was listed as number five.

Belva Lockwood (1830–1917)

Activist, Attorney, Politician

In 1983, attorney, politician, educator, and activist Belva Lockwood was inducted into the National Women's Hall of Fame in Seneca Falls, New York, with this testimonial: "Using her knowledge of the law, she worked to secure women suffrage, property law reform, equal pay for equal work, and world peace. Thriving on publicity and partisanship and encouraging other women to pursue legal careers, Lockwood helped to open the legal profession to women." The second woman (after Victoria Woodhull) to run for president of the United States, Lockwood is the first woman to argue a case before the U.S. Supreme Court.

Born Belva Bennett on a farm in Niagara County, New York, Lockwood attended country schools until the age of fifteen, when she went to work as a teacher. In 1848, she married Uriah McNall, a farmer and sawmill operator. After he died in 1853, Lockwood became the sole support of her young daughter. She resumed her teaching and found time to further her education, eventually graduating from Genesee College (later Syracuse University) with honors in 1857.

In 1866, she moved to Washington, D.C., where she opened one of the earliest private coeducational schools in the capital and began to study law informally. After marrying Ezekiel Lockwood, a former Baptist minister, she applied for admission to three law schools, and all three rejected her because she was a woman. In 1871, she was finally admitted to the newly created National University Law School. Although Lockwood completed her studies in 1873, her diploma was not issued until she petitioned President Ulysses S. Grant to intercede on her behalf. Soon afterward, she was admitted to the District of Columbia Bar, which two years earlier had changed the judicial rules to allow women to practice law in the district. However, when one of Lockwood's cases came before the federal Court of Claims, the court denied her the right to argue it.

In 1876, the Supreme Court turned down her petition to gain women the right to practice their profession before the highest courts in the nation. She immediately began to lobby Congress to pass a bill to grant women equal rights as lawyers in all the courts in the country. Congress passed the bill in 1879, the same year that Lockwood argued her case before the U.S. Supreme Court, the first woman ever to do so. Lockwood went on to establish a large legal practice in Washington, concentrating on protecting the rights of workers and minorities.

Lockwood ran in the presidential elections of 1884 and 1888 as a candidate of the National Equal Rights Party. Representing a third party without a broad base of support, in 1884, she received about 4,100 votes, despite the opposition of most newspapers and the fact that women could not vote. In 1885, Lockwood claimed voter fraud, asserting that she had "received one-half the electoral votes of Oregon, and a large vote in Pennsylvania, but the votes in the latter state were not counted, simply dumped into the waste basket as false votes."

Lockwood also worked on behalf of women's rights. She cofounded the first suffrage group in Washington, D.C., and participated in drafting and presenting resolutions, petitions, and bills to Congress, including provisions for equal pay for female government workers and the extension of property rights to women. During the late 1880s, she devoted much of her attention to the cause of world peace, and in 1889, she served as a delegate to the International Peace Conference. She would attend subsequent peace conferences in Europe in 1906, 1908, and 1911. After a forty-three-year career as a lawyer, Lockwood died in Washington, D.C., at the age of eighty-six.

Dolley Madison (1768–1848)

First Lady

Dolley Madison, perhaps more than any other first lady, helped to define the role of the president's spouse, providing social occasions for members of opposing political parties so they could come together and amicably socialize, network, and negotiate. Moreover, her bravery and patriotism during a time of war later earned her a reputation as one of America's most courageous first ladies.

Born Dorothea Payne in North Carolina and raised on a plantation near Ashland, Virginia, she was the oldest daughter of nine children. Her Quaker parents doted on her and gave her the nickname "Dolley." In 1790, she married John Todd Jr., a young, Quaker lawyer, who died three years later while caring for victims of a Philadelphia yellow fever epidemic. Dolley and her sons, a two-year-old and a newborn, also became ill. She and her older son survived, but the infant died.

In 1794, after a fourteen-month courtship, she married Virginia congressman James Madison. The Quakers disowned her because she married outside her faith. This meant that she was free from their restrictions and could attend social occasions that Quakers frowned upon, such as balls and receptions.

In 1801, President Thomas Jefferson appointed Madison as his secretary of state. Since both Jefferson and his vice president, Aaron Burr, were widowers, Dolley, as the wife of the highest-ranking Cabinet official, hosted presidential dinners and receptions. She carried out her duties with warmth, wit, and charm, characteristics that would continue after her husband was elected president in 1808. During the Madison presidency, Dolley produced a social whirlwind at the White House. The Executive Mansion became a nearly endless succession of dinner parties, lawn parties, luncheons, and dances. While she was always dressed in the most glamorous fashions of the day, she was known for having the talent to inject in the most formal occasion the informal gaiety of a country dance or a small tea party that allowed her guests, often highly partisan opponents, to socialize and find common ground.

She became a heroine during the War of 1812. In August 1814, with her husband away at the front and British troops fast approaching the White House, she managed to save the famous Gilbert Stuart portrait of George Washington (though some believe it was her personal slave who saved the portrait) as well as other valuables before fleeing for safety in Virginia. The British burned the Executive Mansion, and it would not be fully restored until 1817 during James Monroe's presidency. After the British retreat, the Madisons moved to another Washington residence, the Octagon House. There, Dolley hosted several galas to celebrate the American victory over the British in 1815.

In 1817, after Madison's second term, the couple retired to his Virginia estate at Montpelier. James Madison died in 1836, and a year later, Dolley returned to Washington, where she lived for a time until Congress purchased her husband's papers in dire poverty. With funds from Congress, she was able to resume her former role as the capital's most popular hostess. She died in Washington of a stroke at the age of eighty-one.

Ellen Malcolm (1947–)

Philanthropist

Before Ellen Malcolm founded the donor network EMILY's List in 1985, no Democratic woman had ever been elected to the Senate in her own right. To give female candidates credibility and the resources to win, EMILY's List (Early Money Is Like Yeast: it "makes the dough rise") was created to encourage members to contribute to candidates that EMILY's List recommended. Over the last thirty years, EMILY's List has helped elect twenty-six Democratic women to the U.S. Senate, 150 to the House, sixteen governors, and nearly 1,100 women to state and local office, having trained nearly ten thousand women to run for office and raising more than $600 million.

She grew up in Montclair, New Jersey, the daughter of parents who met while working in the sales department at IBM. Her great-grandfather, A. Ward Ford, was an IBM founder, and Malcolm became the heir to his IBM fortune after her father died when she was eight years old. After attending Montclair Kimberley Academy, graduating in 1965, she attended Hollins College. Malcolm called herself "apolitical" until she went to work for the Eugene McCarthy presidential campaign in 1968. Malcolm would cite the Vietnam War, the assassinations of Martin Luther King Jr. and Robert Kennedy, and the counterculture of the 1960s as the factors leading to her political awakening, breaking with her mostly

Republican family and upbringing. After graduating from Hollins College in 1969, she worked for Common Cause in the 1970s, working toward ending the Vietnam War.

Following Common Cause, Malcolm became the press secretary of the National Women's Political Caucus, where Lael Stegall, the development director, expressed an interest in advising wealthy, philanthropic women on where to donate their money. When Malcolm inherited her fortune at the age of twenty-one, she began giving money to several nonprofits and, with Stegall, started the Windom Fund in 1980. In 1982, Malcolm was involved in the campaign of Missourian Harriett Woods's senate race. She lost the race due to lack of funds. Malcolm then identified her main interest to help female candidates succeed. In 1983, she hosted a breakfast with a small group of women, and they identified the goal of raising early funds or seed money to elect women to the U.S. Senate. This became EMILY's List, which Malcolm founded in 1985.

The concept of a donor network was innovative in 1985, and considerable credit to the success of female candidates for office around the country is due to Malcolm's fundraising expertise. Hillary Clinton, whose 2008 campaign for president Malcolm cochaired, called Malcolm "probably the most influential fundraiser and adviser we've seen. I don't know who can match her track record." She served as EMILY's List's president for twenty-five years, turning over leadership in 2010 to Stephanie Schriock, its current president. Malcolm is the author, with Craig Unger, of *When Women Win: EMILY's List and the Rise of Women in American Politics* (2016). She was selected in 2017 as one of *Time* magazine's 50 Women Who Made American Political History.

Carol Moseley Braun (1947–)

Senator

The first female African American senator, Carol Moseley Braun is also the first woman to defeat an incumbent U.S. senator in an election, the first female senator from Illinois, and a candidate for the Democratic nomination during the 2004 U.S. presidential election.

Born Carol Elizabeth Moseley in Chicago, Illinois, she is the daughter of a policeman father and a medical technician mother. She attended public and parochial schools in her segregated, middle-class neighborhood on the South Side of Chicago. When her parents divorced when she was in her teens, she lived with her grandmother. She earned her undergraduate degree at the University of Illinois–Chicago, graduating in 1969, and her law degree from the University of Chicago Law School in 1972. In 1973, she married Michael Braun, whom she met in law school. They had a son in 1977, and they were divorced in 1986.

She went to work as a prosecutor in the U.S. Attorney's office in Chicago from 1973 to 1977. She entered politics in 1978, winning the election to the Illinois House of Representatives. She served there for ten years with a focus on advocacy of health care, educational reform, and gun control. She became assistant leader for the Democratic majority. From 1988 to 1992, she served as the Cook County recorder of deeds but, displeased with U.S. senator Alan Dixon's support of U.S. Supreme Court nominee Clarence Thomas, she ran against him in the 1992 Democratic primary and won an upset victory on her way to capturing the Senate seat in the general election. When she entered the Senate, she was only the second African American ever in the Senate (after Republican Edward Brooke) in the twentieth century, the sole African American in the Senate for her entire term, and the first woman to serve on the Senate Finance Committee.

Moseley Braun's voting record in the Senate at times defied her reputation as a liberal Democrat. She voted in favor of the North American Free Trade Agreement, breaking with her party by voting for the Freedom to Farm Act and the Telecommunication Act of 1996. She also voted in favor of a Balanced Budget Amendment to the U.S. Constitution. She was strongly pro-choice, voting against the ban on partial-birth abortions. She also voted against the death penalty and in favor of gun-control measures. In 1993, she made headlines opposing the renewal of a patent design for the United Daughters of the Confederacy because it contained the Confederate flag, arguing that the Confederate flag "has no place in our modern times, place in this body, place in our society." Swayed by her argument, the Senate rejected the UDC's application to renew its patent. Scandal and controversy also marred her Senate term. She was subject to a Federal Election Commission investigation over unaccounted-for campaign funds. Small violations were found, but no action was taken. In 1996, Moseley Braun made a private trip to Nigeria to meet with sanctioned dictator Sani Abacha, and she subsequently defended Abacha's human rights record in Congress. In 1998, after journalist George Will wrote a column reviewing corruption allegations against her, she compared Will to a Ku Klux Klansman, later apologizing for her remarks. On a lighter note, in 1993, she and Senator Barbara Mikulski wore pants on the Senate floor to protest a ban. Female support staff soon followed, and the rule was amended allowing women to wear pants on the floor as long as they also wore a jacket.

Moseley Braun lost her Senate reelection bid in 1998. She was named American ambassador to New Zealand and Samoa in 1999, serving until the end of the Clinton administration in 2001. In 2003, she announced her candidacy for the Democratic nomination for presidency but dropped out of the race in early 2004. In 2011, she lost to Rahm Emanuel in Chicago's mayoral race and, from 2016, has been a visiting professor of political science at Northwestern University while running a private law firm, Carol Moseley Braun LLC in Chicago.

Eleanor Holmes Norton (1937–)

Congresswoman

 Eleanor Holmes Norton has, for more than three decades, served as a nonvoting member of the U.S. House of Representatives, representing the District of Columbia. Before her congressional service, President Jimmy Carter appointed her to serve as the first woman to chair the U.S. Equal Employment Opportunity Commission, having achieved distinction as a civil rights and feminist leader and a professor of law.

She was born in Washington, D.C. Her parents were both government employees who made her aware of the struggles of African Americans around her. She attended Antioch College in Yellow Springs, Ohio, where she became active in civil rights work, heading the local NAACP chapter and working to desegregate public facilities in Ohio. After graduating in 1960, she earned a master's degree in American studies at Yale University (1963) and a law degree from Yale Law School in 1964. While in law school, she traveled to Mississippi for the Mississippi Freedom Summer, where she worked with civil rights leaders such as Medgar Evers and Fannie Lou Hamer. She also expanded her social activism to women's issues. She was on the founding advisory board of the Women's Rights Law Reporter (founded in 1970), the first legal periodical in the United States to focus exclusively on the field of women's rights law, and was a signer of the Black Woman's Manifesto, a founding document of the black feminist movement.

Returning to Washington, Norton worked as a law clerk to U.S. District Court Judge A. Leon Higginbotham Jr. and became in 1965 the assistant legal director of the American Civil Liberties Union, a position she held until 1970. She famously represented the sixty female employees of *Newsweek* magazine in their successful EEOC claim against the magazine's policy of only allowing men to be reporters. Between 1970 and 1977, she headed New York City's Human Rights Commission, and in 1977, she became the first woman to chair the EEOC, a post she held until 1981.

In 1990, Norton was first elected to Congress from the District of Columbia. She has served on two major committees, the Committee on Oversight and Reform and the Committee on Transportation and Infrastructure. She has fought for full voting rights for D.C. residents and gained passage of a bill to provide tuition subsidies for D.C. residents. While serving in Congress, Norton has also been a part-time teacher in the Georgetown University Law School.

Through a busy lifetime of public service, Eleanor Holmes Norton has operated by a core principle: "You can't win what you don't fight for."

Michelle Obama (1964–)

Attorney, First Lady

 The first African American first lady of the United States, the wife of Barack Obama, the forty-fourth president of the United States from 2009 to 2017, Michelle Obama was a lawyer, a Chicago city administrator, and a community outreach worker, who has become one of the most admired contemporary American women.

Born Michelle LaVaughn Robinson in Chicago, Illinois, she was the daughter of a city water plant employee and a secretary at the Spiegel's catalog store. Her mother was a full-time homemaker until Michelle entered high school. She attended Bryn Mawr Elementary School before Whitney Young High School, Chicago's first magnet high school, established as a selective enrollment school. She followed her older brother, who graduated in 1983, to Princeton University, where she majored in sociology and minored in African American studies, graduating with a BA degree in 1985. She would say that being at Princeton was the first time she became more aware of her ethnicity and often felt "like a visitor on campus." She earned her law degree from Harvard Law School in 1988. She worked for the Harvard Legal Aid Bureau, assisting low-income tenants with housing cases, and participated in demonstrations advocating more minority teacher hiring. With her law degree, she is the third first lady (after Hillary Clinton and Laura Bush) with a postgraduate degree.

After law school, she worked as an associate in the Chicago branch of the law firm Sidley Austen. It was there, in 1989, that she met her future husband, Barack Obama, a summer intern to whom she was assigned as an adviser. After two years of dating, he proposed, and the couple married in 1992. Their two daughters were born in 1998 and 2001, respectively. In 1991, she decided to leave corporate law

for a career in public service, first working as an assistant to Mayor Richard Daley, then the assistant commissioner of planning and development for the city of Chicago. In 1993, she became executive director for the Chicago office of Public Allies, a nonprofit leadership-training program that helped young adults develop skills for future careers in the public sector. In 1996, she joined the University of Chicago as associate dean of student services, developing the school's first community service program. In 2005, she was appointed as vice president for community and external affairs at the University of Chicago Medical Center.

In 2007, she reduced her own professional work to attend to family and campaign obligations during her husband's run for the Democratic presidential nomination. She faced the dual challenge on the campaign trail and in the White House as both an African American and the wife of an African American presidential candidate, a role never before experienced, and as a woman who came of age following the feminist movement of the 1970s, which would challenge previous conceptions of a politician's wife and first lady. Adept at campaigning, her openness and honesty helped to humanize the sometimes aloof and academic Barack Obama. She became known by staffers as "the closer" for her persuasiveness on the stump. As first lady, she involved herself in various causes, including supporting military families and ending childhood obesity. To promote healthy eating, she planted a vegetable garden on the White House's South Lawn. Despite multiple interests and experience as a lawyer and public servant, when people asked her to describe herself, she did not hesitate to say that first and foremost, she was the mother of her two daughters.

After leaving the White House, she published her memoir, *Becoming* (2018), which sold ten million copies in less than six months. She has invited comparisons with Jacqueline Kennedy for her sense of style and to Hillary Clinton for her political savvy and focus. Michelle Obama succeeded in a position no other American had done before as the first African American first lady while expanding the role of what a political wife should play and could become.

Sandra Day O'Connor (1930–)

Attorney, U.S. Supreme Court Justice

In 1981, Sandra Day O'Connor became the first woman to be appointed as an associate justice to the Supreme Court in its 191-year history. Born in El Paso, Texas, Sandra Day O'Connor grew up on a very large cattle ranch on the Arizona–New Mexico border. When she wasn't in school, she learned to fix fences, ride horses, brand cattle, shoot a gun, and repair machinery. These activities endowed her with self-confidence and independence while influencing her character and future judicial temperament. After graduating from high school, she entered Stanford University at the age of sixteen and earned a degree in economics in 1950. She then remained at Stanford and received her law degree in 1952.

Despite having graduated third in a class of 102, she failed to win a position with law firms in San Francisco and Los Angeles because she was a woman; she received only one job offer—as a legal secretary. In 1952, she married her law school classmate John Jay O'Connor, and the couple worked as lawyers in Germany for three years. In 1957, they moved to Phoenix, Arizona, where O'Connor interrupted her law career for four years to raise their three sons. When O'Connor returned to work, she entered politics, serving first as an assistant state attorney general, then as a state senator, and later a county judge. In 1974, she was appointed to the Arizona Court of Appeals, where she earned a reputation for making decisions protecting the rights of women, the poor, and the mentally ill.

In 1981, President Ronald Reagan appointed O'Connor to the Supreme Court in part because of her experience in all three branches of government. Her appointment was widely condemned by conservatives, who called the nomination "a direct contradiction of the Republican platform to everything that candidate Reagan said and even President Reagan has said in regard to social issues." However, she was confirmed by the Senate with a vote of 99–0. O'Connor's service on the court since her appointment was consistent with her pledge when she

confirmed "to do equal right to the poor and to the rich." She showed her independence on the court by voting at different times with both conservative and liberal justices on important cases such as abortion rights, affirmative action, and censorship. She was often the deciding swing vote in 5–4 decisions, which caused many to call O'Connor the most influential woman in America.

In 2004, O'Connor wrote the majority opinion in one of the most closely watched court cases in decades—the ruling that ordered the federal government to allow terrorist suspects held indefinitely to meet with counsel and to contest the charges against them in court.

In 2005, O'Connor announced her retirement to spend time with her husband, who was suffering from Alzheimer's disease. He died in 2009. In 2018, O'Connor announced her retirement from public life after disclosing that she had been diagnosed with the early stages of Alzheimer's-like dementia.

O'Connor's appointment to the court helped pave the way for other women to join the nation's most powerful judicial body. In 1993, President Clinton appointed Ruth Bader Ginsburg to become the second female justice; in 2009, President Obama appointed Sonia Sotomayor as the third and first Hispanic and Latinx justice and in 2010 the fourth, Elena Kagan.

Jacqueline Kennedy Onassis (1929–1994)

First Lady

Although first lady for just the one thousand days of the presidency of John F. Kennedy, Jacqueline Kennedy remains one of the most popular of all first ladies as well as one of the most admired modern women. She helped redefine the role of first lady with her style and grace. As the first first lady born in the twentieth century, she personified the new modern woman. As the grieving widow of a martyred president, she earned the respect and gratitude of a shocked nation as it struggled to cope with the tragedy of November 22, 1963. As a former first lady, she was called "the most intriguing woman in the world," earning admiration for her charitable work and for her second career as a book editor.

She was born Jacqueline Lee Bouvier in Southampton, New York, the daughter of a stockbroker father and a mother from a prominent New York banking family. After attending college at Vassar and George Washington University, she met John F. Kennedy while working as the "Inquiring Camera Girl," interviewing people and taking their photos for a daily column in the *Washington Times-Herald.* The couple were married in 1953, a year after Kennedy's election to the Senate. She slowly adjusted to her role as a senator's wife and actively participated in JFK's successful campaign for the presidency in 1960.

As first lady, she set fashion trends with her clothes, hairstyles, and famous pillbox hat that became a trademark. She directed a major restoration of the White House and gave the first televised tour of the Executive Mansion in 1962. She and the president also hosted numerous cultural events in the White House, featuring such noted artists as cellist Pablo Casals and violinist Isaac Stern. When she traveled with the president, she was so popular with the public that, during one trip to France, JFK jokingly identified himself as "the man who accompanied Jacqueline Kennedy to Paris."

She was riding with the president in the motorcade in Dallas, Texas, on November 22, 1963, when he was shot and fatally wounded by Lee Harvey Oswald. She supervised the arrangements for her husband's funeral and inspired a stunned and grieving nation with her strength and dignity. Her popularity continued undiminished after JFK's death, and polls continually ranked her as the most admired woman in the world.

In 1968, she shocked the country when she wed Aristotle Onassis, a wealthy Greek shipping magnate, with a profligate lifestyle and a reputation for womanizing. The subsequent newspaper and magazine photos showing "Jackie O.," as the press dubbed her, living a jet-set life on Onassis's ships and in the Greek islands added to the furor. After Onassis's death in 1974, she returned permanently to the United States, dividing her time between Manhattan, Martha's Vineyard, and the Kennedy Compound in Hyannis Port, Massachusetts. In 1975, she

became a consulting editor at Viking Press, a position she held for two years before being hired at Doubleday as an editor. In addition to her work as an editor, she participated in cultural and architectural preservation, particularly in the campaign to renovate Grand Central Terminal in New York.

Jacqueline Kennedy Onassis died of cancer at the age of sixty-four and is buried next to President Kennedy at Arlington National Cemetery. She reflected on her life by saying, "I have been through a lot and have suffered a great deal. But I have had lots of happy moments as well. Every moment one lives is different from the other. The good, the bad, hardship, the joy, the tragedy, love and happiness are all interwoven into one single, indescribable whole that is called life. You cannot separate the good from the bad. And perhaps there is no need to do so, either."

Sarah Palin (1964–)

Governor

When she was selected by Senator John McCain as his vice presidential running mate in 2008, Sarah Palin, Alaskan governor from 2006 to 2009, became the first Alaskan on a national ticket of a major political party and the first Republican and second woman to be selected as a vice presidential candidate.

Born Sarah Louise Heath in Sandpoint, Idaho, the third of four children, her mother was a school secretary, and her father was a science teacher and track and field coach, who moved the family to Skagway, Alaska, when she was less than a year old, finally settling in Wasilla in 1972. After completing Wasilla High School, where she was cocaptain and point guard on the basketball team, which won the 1982 Alaska state championship, she enrolled at the University of Hawaii–Hilo before transferring to Hawaii Pacific University in Honolulu, North Idaho College, the University of Idaho–Moscow, and Matanuska-Susitna College in Alaska before returning to the University of Idaho to earn her bachelor's degree in communications in 1987.

After graduation, she worked as a television sportscaster in Anchorage and as a sports reporter for the *Mat-Su Valley Frontiersman*. In 1988, she eloped with her high school sweetheart, Todd Palin, a commercial fisherman. They would raise five children. Palin entered politics in 1992 first with a seat on the Wasilla city council, then in 1996 becoming the city's mayor, a position she held for six years. In 2002, she campaigned for the Republican nomination for the office of lieutenant governor of Alaska, and, although unsuccessful, she raised her statewide profile, which led to her successful run for governor in 2006, becoming the youngest governor in Alaska's history and the first woman to hold the post.

When she was chosen by John McCain to be his running mate in 2008, Palin became an energizing presence, especially popular with the Republican base. She, however, became a polarizing figure, attacked as unqualified, a charge that was exacerbated by numerous gaffes in interviews and on the campaign trail as well as her tendency to go off-message (described by campaign staffers as "going rogue").

Although the McCain–Palin ticket lost to the Democratic ticket of Barack Obama and Joe Biden, Palin had established herself as a leading figure in the Republican Party. She resigned her post as Alaska's governor in 2009 and became a contributor to the Fox News Channel as well as becoming the unofficial spokesperson of the populist Tea Party movement, delivering the keynote address at the first National Tea Party Convention. Intense speculation occurred that she might seek the Republican Party presidential nomination in 2012, but in 2011, she announced that she would not run. In 2015, she left Fox News and, in 2016, was a vocal supporter of Donald Trump, who ultimately won the nomination and presidency.

Palin appeared in the reality television series *Sarah Palin's Alaska* (2010–2011) and in *Bristol Palin: Life's a Tripp* (2012). Her books include the memoir *Going Rogue: An American Life* (2009), *America by Heart: Reflections on Family, Faith, and Flag* (2010), *Good Tidings and Great Joy: Protecting the Heart of Christmas* (2013), and *Sweet Freedom: A Devotional* (2015). After John McCain died in 2018, Palin was not invited to his funeral. McCain grew to regret

his selection and the inadequacy of the vetting process before choosing her as his running mate. McCann would call her "a skilled amateur performer asked to appear on Broadway twice a day." Palin would call the snub a "gut-punch" and defended herself by saying that she had become the scapegoat of a poorly run campaign looking for someone to blame. "There's still a lot of snakes in the Republican Party and in politics in general," Palin commented. "They're not going to have your back, they're not going to be loyal to you. They use you and abuse you and then kick you to the side after they get out of you what they needed."

Nancy Pelosi (1940–)
Congresswoman, Speaker of the House of Representatives

As speaker of the U.S. House of Representatives, the first woman ever to serve as speaker, Nancy Pelosi is the highest-ranking elected woman ever in U.S. history and second in the presidential line of succession, immediately after the vice president. She has served seventeen terms as a congresswoman, representing California's 12th, 5th, and 8th congressional districts. The first woman to lead her party in Congress, Pelosi has twice served as speaker (2007–2011 and 2019–present). She was the House minority leader (2003–2007 and 2011–2019) and House minority whip (2002–2003).

She was born Nancy Patricia D'Alesandro in Baltimore, Maryland. Her father, Thomas D'Alesandro Jr., was a New Deal Democrat and a Democratic congressman from Maryland as well as the mayor of Baltimore for twelve years. Pelosi's brother, Thomas D'Alesandro III, also was the mayor of Baltimore from 1967 to 1971. Pelosi helped her father at his campaign events and learned the value of social networking from her mother, who was active in politics and in organizing Democratic women. Pelosi majored in political science at Trinity College in Washington, D.C., graduating in 1962. The following year, she married Paul Pelosi, first moving to New York and then to San Francisco in 1969. While raising her family of five children, Pelosi slowly got into politics, volunteering for the Democratic Party, hosting parties, and helping with campaigns while gradually rising up in the party ranks, serving as California representative to the Democratic National Committee from 1976 to 1996 as well as the state and northern chair of the California Democratic Party.

In 1987, Pelosi won a special election for California's 8th District, which includes San Francisco. As a House member, she served on the Appropriations Committee and the Permanent Select Committee on Intelligence, becoming a strong supporter of increased funding for health research and for other health care and housing programs and initiatives. In 2001, Pelosi was elected House minority whip, the second-in-command to the minority leader and the first woman in U.S. history to hold the post. In 2001, Dick Gephardt resigned as minority leader to seek the Democratic nomination in the 2004 presidential election, and Pelosi was elected to replace him, becoming the first woman to lead a major party in the House.

After the Democrats took control of the House in the 2006 midterm elections, Pelosi was the unanimous choice for speaker. Elected in 2007, Pelosi became the first woman, the first Californian, and the first Italian American speaker of the House. In her inaugural speech as speaker, she said: "This is a historic moment—for the Congress, and for the women of this country. It is a moment for which we have waited more than 200 years. Never losing faith, we waited though the many years of struggle to achieve our rights. But women weren't just waiting; women were working. Never losing faith, we worked to redeem the promise of America, that all men and women are created equal. For our daughters and granddaughters, today, we have broken the marble ceiling. For our daughters and our granddaughters, the sky is the limit, anything is possible for them."

During her first speakership, she blocked President George W. Bush's proposed changes to Social Security to allow workers to invest a portion of their withholding into stock and bond investments. She opposed the move to impeach President Bush for the invasion of Iraq, opposed the Iraq troop surge of 2007, and, most importantly, spearheaded the passage of President Obama's Affordable Health Care

legislation during a two-month marathon session to craft the health care bill. For her successful efforts, President Obama called Pelosi "one of the best Speakers of the House the House of Representatives has ever had."

When the Democrats lost their majority in the House after the 2010 midterms, Pelosi served as House minority leader from 2011 to 2019. While blocking legislative victories by the GOP majority, Pelosi spearheaded a historic bipartisan agreement to strengthen Medicare, while her strength as a negotiator led to significant funding increases for key Democratic priorities such as an extension on expiring wind and solar renewable energy tax credits, an increase in spending to address the opioid epidemic, spending for medical research, and the largest single-year funding increase for childcare development block grants in the initiative's history. She was reelected to the speakership in January 2019, becoming the first person in more than sixty years to serve nonconsecutive terms in the post.

In some ways, Nancy Pelosi is the consummate political leader, a brilliant tactician and consensus builder who has managed to keep a diverse and contentious Democratic Party focused on achievable goals while withstanding withering attacks from the opposing party that would prefer that she fail. After Nancy Pelosi, few can question whether a woman has the capacity to lead at the highest level in politics and policy.

Frances Perkins (1880–1965)

Cabinet Secretary

 Serving as the U.S. secretary of labor from 1933 to 1945, sociologist and workers' rights advocate Frances Perkins was the first woman to hold a Cabinet-level position as well as the second-longest-serving Cabinet member in American history. In her post, Perkins helped create jobs and training programs and helped establish child labor laws, maximum work hours, minimum wage standards, and unemployment insurance—all of which brought Americans relief from the economic devastation

caused by the Great Depression while becoming standards for subsequent government public policy.

Perkins grew up in Worcester, Massachusetts, where her father ran a stationery store. She attended the Worcester Classical High School and then went on to Mount Holyoke College. After graduating in 1902, Perkins taught school in Chicago and volunteered at Jane Addams's Hull-House, where she collected wages for workers who had been cheated by their employers. In 1910, Perkins earned a master's degree from the New York School of Philanthropy and then became executive secretary of the New York City Consumers' League, working for industrial reform and the improvement of sweatshop conditions. The following year, she witnessed the Triangle Shirtwaist Fire, in which more than 146 workers—most of them women and many of them young girls—perished because of the lack of access to fire escapes. This tragic event deeply affected Perkins, and she resolved to "spend my life fighting conditions that permit such a tragedy." While working for the New York Committee on Safety, she exposed employers who were jeopardizing the health and safety of their workers.

In 1917, Perkins became the first female member of the New York State Industrial Commission and, under Governors Al Smith and later Franklin D. Roosevelt, reorganized factory inspections, settled strikes, and established a reputation as one of the nation's leading experts on labor relations. As secretary of labor under FDR, Perkins played a major role in drafting legislation and developing programs that would become the foundation of Roosevelt's New Deal. These included the Federal Emergency Relief Administration to help states assist the unemployed; the Civilian Conservation Corps and the Public Works Administration to create jobs; and the Division of Labor Standards to improve working conditions.

During World War II, Perkins helped bring business and labor together in support of the war effort, creating the character of "Rosie the Riveter" to represent women who went to work in war industries. Rosie became a symbolic national heroine and helped pave the way for the greater acceptance of women in the workplace after the war.

After leaving the Cabinet, Perkins served in the Civil Service Commission. From 1957 until her death, she was a professor at Cornell University's School of Industrial and Labor Relations. She died in New York City at the age of eighty-five. As the first female member of a presidential Cabinet, Perkins faced considerable challenges to be taken seriously, but her accomplishments are remarkable: she is responsible for the adoption of Social Security, unemployment insurance, federal laws regulating child labor, and adoption of the federal minimum wage. Few other political figures, whether female or male, could claim such comparable accomplishments. In 1980, President Jimmy Carter renamed the headquarters of the U.S. Department of Labor in Washington, D.C., the Frances Perkins Building in her honor.

Jeannette Rankin (1880–1973)

Congresswoman

Politician and women's rights advocate Jeannette Rankin was the first woman to hold federal office in the United States, elected to the House of Representatives from Montana in 1916, four years before women won the right to vote nationwide. She remains the only woman ever to be elected to Congress from Montana.

Born near Missoula in Montana Territory, Rankin was the oldest of seven children. Her father was a successful rancher and lumber merchant, and her mother had been a schoolteacher before her marriage. Rankin was educated at public schools in Missoula and, in 1902, graduated with a BS degree in biology from the University of Montana. In 1908, Rankin went to New York to study at the New York School of Philanthropy. She briefly practiced social work in Montana and Washington and then entered the University of Washington.

Beginning in 1910, Rankin became active in the suffragist movement. She urged the Montana State Legislature to give women the right to vote, served as the field secretary for the National American Woman Suffrage Association, and lobbied for suffrage in fifteen states. In 1914, her efforts paid off when her home state granted women the right to vote.

In 1916, Rankin ran for Congress as a Republican and made history when she was elected as the first female U.S. representative. In 1917, Rankin, a lifelong pacifist and a member of the Woman's Peace Party, voted against America's entry into World War I. She was denounced for her vote by the press, the church, and fellow suffragists such as NAWSA president Carrie Chapman Catt, who believed that women should support the war effort to ensure their enfranchisement. Rankin spent the rest of her term sponsoring protective legislation for children and continued to work for passage of a federal suffrage amendment.

After making an unsuccessful attempt to become Montana's first female U.S. senator, Rankin returned to private life in 1919. She spent the next twenty years working on behalf of numerous national and international peace organizations as well as continuing to push for passage of legislation designed to benefit women and children. In 1940, she won reelection to Congress, running as a Republican pacifist. On December 8, 1941, the day after the Japanese attack on Pearl Harbor, Rankin cast the single vote against U.S. entry into World War II. Because of her vote, Rankin lost any chance for reelection.

In the late 1960s, Rankin made news as she led the Jeannette Rankin Brigade, a group of feminists, pacifists, students, and other activists opposed to the Vietnam War. Well into her eighties, she demonstrated with the group in Washington, D.C., in January 1968. Shortly afterward, Rankin decided to run for Congress again, but failing health prevented her from beginning a campaign. She died in California at the age of ninety-two.

Rankin said in 1972, "If I am remembered for no other act, I want to be remembered as the only woman who ever voted to give women the right to vote." In 1985, a statue of Rankin with the inscription "I Cannot Vote for War" was installed in the U.S. Capitol's Statuary Hall. At its dedication, historian Joan Hoff-Wilson called Rankin "one of the most controversial and unique women in Montana and American political history."

Nancy Reagan (1921–2016)

First Lady

Former actress Nancy Reagan, the wife of Ronald Reagan, the fortieth president of the United States, was first lady from 1981 to 1989 and set the tone for a return to glamour and style in the White House.

Born Anne Frances Robbins in New York City, she was the only child of a salesman and an aspiring actress. She early on acquired the nickname "Nancy." When her parents separated during her infancy (they divorced in 1928), she was raised by her aunt and uncle in Bethesda, Maryland. There, she attended the Sidwell Friends School. When her mother married Chicago neurosurgeon Loyal Davis, he adopted Nancy, and she changed her last name to Davis. After graduating from the Girls' Latin School, she studied drama at Smith College, where she earned her bachelor's degree in 1943.

After graduation, through her mother's acting contact, she obtained a job with a touring company and then a role on Broadway. By 1949, she was working in Hollywood, where she eventually made eleven movies. She married Ronald Reagan in 1952, and they had two children together. She eventually gave up her acting career to care for her children and support her husband's political career. In 1967, she became first lady of California when Reagan was elected governor. She moved her family out of the governor's mansion, calling it a "fire trap," into an exclusive suburb of Sacramento. Although she was criticized as "snobbish" by the press, she eventually earned praise for her glamour, style, and youthfulness and was described by the *Los Angeles Times* as "a model first lady."

When she took up residence in the White House in 1981, she was again the target of criticism for expensive redecorating of the White House during a time of economic recession and her stylish wardrobe, although private donations were used for the renovation, and much of her official wardrobe was donated. In 1982, she reversed criticism for living lavishly by championing drug abuse awareness and education, traveling throughout the United States and abroad visiting prevention programs and rehabilitation centers. She would become known for her "Just Say No" campaign, which was criticized as simplistic, but her efforts culminated in the Drug-Free America Act, signed in 1986. In 1987, she was diagnosed with breast cancer and underwent a mastectomy. Intensely protective of her husband, she became one of President Reagan's most trusted advisers and a decisive figure in determining his schedule and priorities. Particularly, after Reagan convalesced after major surgery in 1985, she would prompt the *New York Times* to conclude that she had "expanded the role of First Lady into a sort of Associate Presidency." In her defense, she wrote in her memoirs, "For eight years I was sleeping with the president, and if that doesn't give you special access, I don't know what does."

After the Reagans left the White House in 1989, they returned to their Bel Air estate in California. She continued her antidrug work under the auspices of the Nancy Reagan Foundation. When her husband was diagnosed with Alzheimer's disease in 1994, she devoted all her time to caring for him and made few political appearances. Following his death in 2004, she became an advocate for stem cell research because of its scientific promise in the treatment of Alzheimer's disease. She died of congestive heart failure at the age of ninety-four.

Janet Reno (1938–2016)

U.S. Attorney General

The first woman ever to serve as U.S. attorney general, Janet Reno held the office during the Clinton administration from 1993 to 2001 to become the second-longest-serving attorney general in U.S. history (two other women have been in the position since Reno: Loretta Lynch from 2015 to 2017 and Sally Yates, acting attorney general, from January 20, 2017, to January 30, 2017).

Born in Miami, Florida, Reno was the first of the four children of journalist parents. Her father, a

Danish immigrant, wrote for the *Miami Herald* for forty-three years as a police reporter. Her mother was a reporter for the *Miami News* and built the Reno family home on the edge of Florida's Everglades. Reno as a girl loved canoeing, camping, and athletics and aspired to become a baseball player, a doctor, or a marine biologist. Instead, after earning a degree in chemistry from Cornell University in 1960, she enrolled at Harvard University Law school, one of only sixteen women in a class of five hundred, graduating in 1963.

From 1963 to 1971, Reno worked as a lawyer for two Miami law firms and in 1971 joined the staff of the Judiciary Committee of the Florida House of Representatives. In 1978, she was appointed state attorney for Dade County, the first woman ever named to the position of top prosecutor for a county in Florida. She held the position for fifteen years until her nomination by President Bill Clinton as U.S. attorney general in 1993. During her tenure, she had to contend with two explosive events: the deadly federal raid on the compound of a religious cult in Waco, Texas, in 1993 and the government's seizing of Elián González, a young, Cuban refugee at the center of an international custody battle. Under pressure and fierce criticism, Reno was praised for her integrity and willingness to accept responsibility. She was accused of protecting President Clinton when she refused to allow an independent counsel to investigate allegations of fundraising improprieties in the White House, and she was attacked by Clinton supporters by deciding to allow an independent inquiry into a failed Clinton land deal, the Whitewater investigation, which expanded to encompass Clinton's sexual relationship with White House intern Monica Lewinsky and Clinton's impeachment.

After leaving office, she mounted an unsuccessful bid in Florida in 2002 to unseat Governor Jeb Bush, narrowly losing the Democratic primary. She followed the defeat by touring the country lecturing on issues related to the criminal justice system. She became a founding member of the board of directors for the Innocence Project, which assists prisoners who may be exonerated through DNA testing.

In popular culture, Janet Reno was the butt of jokes about her height (six feet one inch tall) and her perceived lack of traditional femininity. She never married and did not have children. She was diagnosed with Parkinson's disease in 1995, which caused her death in 2016. She was praised by President Barack Obama for her "intellect, integrity, and fierce commitment to justice."

Condoleezza Rice (1954–)

Educator, National Security Adviser, U.S. Secretary of State

Condoleezza Rice is the first African American woman to serve as the U.S. national security adviser as well as the first black woman to serve as U.S. secretary of state (the second female secretary of state and second African American after Colin Powell), becoming the highest ranking African American female government official in U.S. history.

Rice was born in Birmingham, Alabama, the only child of a Presbyterian minister and teacher. As a child, Rice was drawn to music and dreamed of becoming a concert pianist. However, her love for international music would be transferred to her interest in international affairs. She earned a bachelor's degree in political science from the University of Denver in 1974, a master's degree from the University of Notre Dame in 1975, and a Ph.D. from the University of Denver's Graduate School of International Studies in 1981. From 1980 to 1981, Rice was a fellow at Stanford University's Arms Control and Disarmament Program, a fellowship that led to her affiliation with Stanford, where she was hired as a professor of political science in 1981. In 1993, Rice was promoted to Stanford's provost, becoming the first African American woman to serve in that position.

Beginning in the 1980s, Rice began to spend time in Washington, D.C., working as an international affairs fellow attached to the Joint Chiefs of Staff. In 1989, she became director of Soviet and East European affairs with the National Security Council and special assistant to President George H. W. Bush during the dissolution of the Soviet Union

and German reunification. In 2001, Rice was appointed national security adviser by President George W. Bush, the first black woman (and woman) to hold the post. In 2004, she became the first black woman to serve as U.S. secretary of state, serving until 2009. Rice was associated during her tenure as secretary of state with the concept of transformational diplomacy, the mission of building and sustaining democratic, well-governed states around the world.

After her service as secretary of state, Rice returned to Stanford as a political science professor and senior fellow at the Hoover Institution in 2009. In 2012, Rice and South Carolina businesswoman Darla Moore became the first women to become members of the Augusta National Golf Club, the notoriously all-male club that had repeatedly resisted admitting women. Also in 2012, Rice addressed the Republican National Convention by stating, "I think my father thought I might be president of the United States. I think he would have been satisfied with secretary of state. I'm a foreign policy person and to have a chance to serve my country as the nation's chief diplomat at a time of peril and consequence, that was enough.... My future is with my students at Stanford and in public service on issues that I care about like education reform."

Ann Richards (1933–2006)

Governor

The fiery and irrepressibly witty Ann Richards was the second female governor of Texas, serving from 1991 to 1995 (Miriam "Ma" Ferguson served two non-consecutive terms as governor of Texas from 1925 to 1927 and from 1933 to 1935). She made the transition from homemaker to national political celebrity as both a silver-haired and silver-tongued, outspoken feminist and progressive. "I did not want my tombstone to read, 'She kept a really clean house,'" she stated. "I think I'd like them to remember me by saying, 'She opened government to everyone.'"

Born Dorothy Ann Willis in Lakeview, Texas, Richards grew up near Waco, graduating from Waco

High School in 1950. She earned her bachelor's degree from Baylor University in 1954, earning a college scholarship from her strong debating skills. She married her high school sweetheart David Richards, a civil rights lawyer, and the couple moved to Austin to raise four children. She went on to gain a teaching certificate at the University of Texas in 1955 and worked as a public school teacher at Fulmore Junior High School, which she often said was the hardest job she ever had.

Her political career began when she served on the Travis County Commissioners Court in Austin for six years before being elected in 1982 as state treasurer, the first woman to be elected to statewide office in Texas in nearly fifty years. Politics took a toll, ending her marriage and leading in 1980 to her treatment for alcoholism. "I had seen the very bottom of life," she recalled. "I was so afraid I wouldn't be funny anymore. I just knew that I would lose my zaniness and my sense of humor. But I didn't. Recovery turned out to be a wonderful thing."

Richards burst onto the national political scene when she gave the keynote address at the 1988 Democratic National Convention, memorably taking aim at the Republican George Bush, saying, "Poor George, he can't help it. He was born with a silver foot in his mouth." In 1990, Richards ran for governor, pledging to increase the role of minorities and women in state government as part of her plan for a "new Texas." When elected, she added African Americans and women to the Texas Rangers law enforcement agency while creating a state lottery and improving the prison system. She lost her bid for reelection to George W. Bush and exited public service. She claimed that she never missed being in public office, and when asked what she might have done differently if she had known she was going to be a one-term governor, Richards replied, "Oh, I would probably have raised more hell." She remained, however, a tireless campaign supporter of Democratic candidates.

After the events of 9/11, in which many New Yorkers left the city, Richards moved in and would spend most of the last five years of her life there. She died of cancer at her home in Austin, one of the great originals in American political life.

Edith Nourse Rogers (1881–1960)
Congresswoman

Edith Nourse Rogers was thrust into political office when her husband, Massachusetts congressman John Jacob Rogers, died in 1925. She succeeded him and went on to a thirty-five-year career in the House of Representatives, the second-longest tenure of any woman (Marcy Kaptur, currently serving, has been in the House for thirty-six years). "The first 30 years are the hardest," Rogers once said of her House service. "It's like taking care of the sick. You start it and you like the work, and you just keep on."

Born in Saco, Maine, she was the daughter of an affluent textile factory owner. She attended the private Rogers Hall School in Lowell, Massachusetts, and finished her education abroad in Parish. Returning to the United States in 1907, she married John Jacob Rogers, a lawyer, and the couple settled in Lowell. In 1912, John Rogers was elected as a Republican to Congress and was successfully reelected to the House for six succeeding terms.

During World War I, she became a "Gray Lady" with the American Red Cross in France and inspected field hospitals with the Women's Overseas Service League. In 1918, she joined the Red Cross volunteer group in Washington, D.C., to work with hospitalized veterans, earning the epithet the "angel of Walter Reed Hospital." She was named by Presidents Warren Harding, Calvin Coolidge, and Herbert Hoover as their personal ombudsman on disabled veterans affairs.

In 1925, when her husband died after a long battle with cancer, Rogers beat Eugene N. Foss, a former Massachusetts governor, in the House race in the 5th District, called the "fighting fifth" because of its equal proportion of registered Democrats and Republicans. Rogers won a lopsided victory and stated, "I hope that everyone will forget that I am a woman as soon as possible." She would be successful in her subsequent seventeen reelection campaigns, earning admiration and respect for her 18-hour workdays, which caused the press to dub her "the busiest woman on Capitol Hill." She was also famous for her trademark orchid or gardenia pinned to her shoulder. In 1950, on the twenty-fifth anniversary of her first election, GOP colleagues hailed her as "the First Lady of the Republican Party." She served on the Foreign Affairs Committee, the Civil Service Committee, and on the Committee on Veterans' Affairs, which she chaired from 1947 to 1948 and from 1953 to 1954. She was also the first woman to preside as speaker pro tempore over the House of Representatives.

Her crowning legislative achievement came in 1941 when she introduced the Women's Army Auxiliary Corps Act to create a voluntary enrollment program for women to join the U.S. Army in a noncombat capacity. It would be signed into law in 1942 giving, as Rogers stated, "women a chance to volunteer to serve their country in a patriotic way." In 1943, it would be supplanted by Rogers's Women's Army Corps Bill, which granted official military status to the volunteers by creating the Women's Army Corps. Rogers's success opened the way for the other uniformed women's services in the Navy and Air Force.

Believed to be the Republicans' best chance to challenge Democratic Senator John F. Kennedy's re-election in 1958, Rogers declined to run. Three days before the primary for the 87th Congress (1961–1963), she died of pneumonia in a Boston hospital at the age of seventy-seven.

Eleanor Roosevelt (1884–1962)

First Lady

Historians have called Eleanor Roosevelt "the most liberated American woman of [the twentieth century]" and "the most influential woman of our times." To her husband, Franklin Delano Roosevelt, she was the "most extraordinarily interesting woman" he had ever known. She did not claim to be a feminist, yet she was the personification of the strong, independent, liberated woman. She used her influence as first lady and revered private citizen to advance the cause of hu-

man rights and, in doing so, became the conscience of the country and the most important public woman of the twentieth century.

Born in New York City into a distinguished and wealthy family, Anna Eleanor Roosevelt was the oldest of the three children of Elliott and Anna Hall Roosevelt. She was so shy and solemn as a child that her mother called her "Granny." By the age of ten, both her parents had died, and she went to live with her strict maternal grandmother. At fifteen, she enrolled at Allenswood, an English girls' school. There, she excelled at her studies, gained self-confidence, and began to develop an interest in social causes. After graduating in 1902, she returned home, where she made her debut into society. She also began to work at settlement houses and visit factories and sweatshops as a member of the National Consumers' League.

In 1905, she married her distant cousin, Franklin Roosevelt; her uncle, President Theodore Roosevelt, gave the bride away. Between 1906 and 1916, she and Franklin had six children. After he won election to the New York Senate in 1910, she worked hard to overcome her shyness so she could assist his rising political career. At the same time, she became active in groups such as the League of Women Voters and the Women's Trade Union League. Her public life expanded after her husband was stricken with polio in 1921. Beginning in 1932 with FDR's election as president and continuing throughout his twelve years in office, she traveled extensively, making speeches and meeting Americans from all walks of life, considerably expanding the role of the first lady. She would then report back to FDR on the conditions she found and the needs and concerns of the people she met. She was also a tireless advocate for bringing more women into government, for housing for the poorest Americans, and for full civil rights for minorities.

In 1933, she became the first first lady to hold a press conference. She also wrote a syndicated newspaper column, "My Day," and for a time hosted a radio show. In 1939, she publicly resigned from the Daughters of the American Revolution because the organization refused to allow African American singer Marian Anderson to perform at its Constitution Hall.

After her husband's death in 1945, Roosevelt served as U.S. delegate to the newly formed United Nations and played a key role in drafting the Universal Declaration of Human Rights, which the UN adopted in 1948. Roosevelt also served as the first U.S. representative to the UN Commission on Human Rights, serving until 1953. Her last major official position was as chair for President John F. Kennedy's Commission on the Status of Women in 1961.

In 1960, Roosevelt was diagnosed with aplastic anemia after being struck by a car in New York City. In 1962, she was given steroids, which activated a dormant case of tuberculosis in her bone marrow. She died of cardiac failure in her Manhattan home at the age of seventy-eight. Harry S. Truman would call her the "First Lady of the World" for her human rights achievements, and at her funeral service, Adlai Stevenson asked, "What other single human being has touched and transformed the existence of so many?" He added that "she would rather light a candle than curse the darkness, and her glow has warmed the world."

Ileana Ros-Lehtinen (1952–)

Congresswoman

The first Cuban American and Latinx elected to the U.S. Congress, Ileana Ros-Lehtinen was the first Republican woman to be elected to the House of Representatives from Florida, representing Florida's 27th congressional district from 1989 to 2019. She would become the first Republican in the House to support same-sex marriage.

Born Ileana Ros y Adato in Havana, Cuba, she and her family left when Fidel Castro came to power when she was eight years old. They settled in Miami, and, after graduating from Southwest High School, she attended Miami-Dade Community College, earning her AA degree in 1972, a bachelor's degree in 1975, a master's degree in 1985, both from Florida International University, and, finally, a Ph.D. in education from the University of Miami in 2004.

She pursued a career as a teacher and later the principal of Eastern Academy in Hialeah, Florida.

She was elected to the Florida House of Representatives in 1982 and to the Florida Senate in 1986, the first Hispanic woman to serve in either body. In 1989, she became the first Hispanic woman to be elected to Congress. During her career in the House, she was an outspoken opponent of dictatorships, especially of Fidel Castro, based on her personal experience fleeing Cuba. He referred to her as the "ferocious she-wolf." She also has worked on behalf of women, particularly women in the military and women in domestic violence situations. She was the lead sponsor of the Violence Against Women Act, which provides resources to prosecute those who have committed acts of violence toward women. She broke with her party in 2012 to support marriage equality, becoming the first Republican in the House to do so, and was instrumental in passing marriage-equality legislation in 2015.

In 2017, Ros-Lehtinen announced that she would not be running for reelection in 2018. After a career lasting over thirty-five years, she stated, "It's been such a delight and a high honor to serve our community for so many years and help constituents every day of the week."

Nellie Tayloe Ross (1876–1977)

Governor

Nellie Tayloe Ross was the first woman in the United States to serve as a governor. She was elected governor of Wyoming in 1924 in a special election, succeeding her husband, incumbent Democrat William Bradford Ross, who died just prior to the election. After a narrow defeat for reelection in 1926, she was appointed vice chairman of the Democratic Committee and, in 1933, became the first female director of the U.S. Mint and one of the first women to hold such an important federal post.

She was born Nellie Davis Tayloe in St. Joseph, Missouri. Her parents owned a plantation on the Missouri River but moved to Miltonvale, Kansas, in 1884. She graduated from Miltonvale High School in 1892 before attending a teacher-training college, which qualified her to teach kindergarten for four years.

In 1902, she married lawyer William B. Ross, and the couple moved to Cheyenne, Wyoming, where he established a law practice. He would become a leader in Wyoming's Democratic Party, running for office several times unsuccessfully. In 1922, he was elected governor, uniting progressives in both parties behind his candidacy. However, after little more than a year and a half in office, he died from complications of an appendectomy, and the Democratic Party nominated his widow to run for governor in the special election that followed. Although she refused to campaign, she easily won the election, becoming the first female governor in U.S. history (Miriam Ferguson was inaugurated governor of Texas just sixteen days after Ross). She would continue her late husband's progressive policies, including government assistance for poor farmers, banking reform, and laws protecting children, female workers, and miners.

After her defeat for reelection in 1926, Ross blamed her loss on her refusal to campaign for herself and her support for Prohibition. She remained active in the Democratic Party and received thirty-one votes from ten states for vice president at the 1928 Democratic National Convention. President Franklin D. Roosevelt appointed Ross as director of the U.S. Mint in 1933. She would hold the position until 1953. During her twenty-year tenure, the Mint introduced the Franklin half dollar, the Roosevelt dime, the Jefferson nickel, and the steel penny. The Mint also started making proof coins for public sale.

After her retirement, Ross contributed articles to women's magazines and traveled extensively, making her last trip to Wyoming in 1972 at the age of ninety-six. She died in Washington, D.C., at the age of 101. At the time of her death, she was the oldest ex-governor of the United States.

Pat Schroeder (1940–)

Congresswoman

 Representing Colorado in the U.S. House of Representatives for twenty-four years from 1973 to 1997 and the first female U.S. representative to be elected in Colorado, Pat Schroeder became

a forceful and respected legislator and advocate for progressive causes ranging from arms control to women's reproductive rights.

Born Patricia Scott in Portland, Oregon, she is the daughter of an aviation insurance salesman and a public school teacher. Growing up in a military family, she was raised in Texas, Ohio, and Iowa. Interested in flying, she earned her pilot's license and operated a flying service to help pay for her college tuition. She graduated from the University of Minnesota in 1961, majoring in philosophy, history, and political science. She earned her law degree from Harvard Law School in 1964, one of just fifteen women in a class of five hundred. In 1962, she married a law school classmate, James Schroeder, and the couple moved to Denver, where they raised two children.

While in law school, a professor advised Schroeder that most private firms shun women lawyers, so she took a job with the federal government for two years as a field attorney for the National Labor Relations Board. She later entered private practice, taught law, and volunteered as counsel for Planned Parenthood. Her husband encouraged her to enter the 1972 House race in the congressional district encompassing most of Denver. Without the support of the state Democratic Party, Schroeder campaigned as an anti-Vietman War, women's rights candidate who would also restore honesty in government. She managed to win the Democratic primary and defeated the first-term incumbent Republican with 52 percent of the vote, the first woman to be elected to Congress from Colorado, a state that had granted women the right to vote in 1893. She would win eleven subsequent reelection campaigns.

When she entered the House at the age of thirty-two, she was the second-youngest woman ever to be elected to Congress (her Harvard Law School classmate Elizabeth Holtzman was the youngest at thirty-one) and one of only fourteen congresswomen. She described the atmosphere as that of "an over-aged frat house." She became the first woman to serve on the House's Armed Services Committee, and she became known for advocacy on working-family issues and would play an instrumental role in the passage of the Family and Medical Leave Act of 1993 and the 1985 Military Family Act. She considered and then declined to pursue a brief run for the 1988 Democratic presidential nomination. "I learned a lot about America and a lot about Pat Schroeder," she declared, "and that's why I will not be a candidate for President," adding, "I could not figure out how to run and not be separated from those I serve. There must be a way, but I haven't figured it out yet."

Schroeder did not seek a thirteenth House term in 1996. She would title her 1998 memoir *24 Years of House Work … and the Place Is Still a Mess.* She became the president and CEO of the Association of American Publishers in 1997, a position she held for eleven years. She and her husband relocated to Celebration, Florida, and is still active in Democratic politics, currently sitting on the board of The League of Women Voters of Florida.

Margaret Chase Smith (1897–1995)

Congresswoman, Senator

One of the most powerful women in American history, Margaret Chase Smith served over eight years in the U.S. House of Representatives and twenty-four years in the Senate, which made her the longest-serving Republican female senator. She was the first woman to have been elected to both houses of Congress, and, in 1964, she became the first woman to have her name placed in nomination for the presidency at a major political party's convention.

She was born in Skowhegan, Maine, the oldest of six children. Her father, of English ancestry, a descendant of immigrants to the United States in the seventeenth century, was the town barber, and her mother worked as waitress, store clerk, and shoe factory worker. She attended local schools, worked at a local five-and-dime store when she was twelve, and on occasion shaved her father's customers when her father was busy or away from his shop. Following high school, she taught briefly at a one-room school near Skowhegan before going to work for the Maine Telephone and Telegraph Company and joining the staff of Skowhegan's weekly newspaper, owned by Clyde Smith, whom she married in 1930.

After her husband was elected as a Republican to the U.S. House of Representatives from Maine's 2nd congressional district in 1936, Smith accompanied him to Washington and served as his secretary, managing his office, handling his correspondence, and helping to write his speeches. In 1940, Clyde Smith suffered a heart attack and asked his wife to run for his House seat in the general election, urging voters to vote for her as the most qualified person to carry on his ideas and plans. He died before his term ended, and a special election was called. Smith faced no Democratic challenger to become the first woman to be elected to Congress from Maine. She would be reelected to three more terms over the course of the next eight years, never receiving less than 60 percent of the vote. In the House, Smith took a strong interest in military and national security issues. She became the first and only civilian woman to sail on a U.S. Navy ship during World War II and became known as the "mother of the WAVES" after introducing legislation that created the special female military units and championing legislation that gave women permanent status in the military following the war.

In 1948, she was elected to the Senate. While campaigning, she responded to the question whether a woman would be a good senator, saying, "Women administer the home. They set the rules, enforce them, mete out justice for violations. Thus, like Congress, they legislate; like the Executive, they administer; like the courts, they interpret the rules. It is an ideal experience for politics." Her election made her the first woman to represent Maine in the Senate and the first woman to serve in both houses of Congress. Smith became famous in the Senate for becoming the first Republican senator to stand up to the anticommunist witch hunt of her fellow Republican Senator Joseph McCarthy in 1950 in a speech on the Senate floor that came to be known as the "Declaration of Conscience," in which she attacked McCarthy's "hate and character assassination" and every American's "right to criticize … right to hold unpopular beliefs … right to protest; the right of independent thought." She would be reelected by large majorities in 1954, 1960, and 1966, was considered as a vice presidential candidate in 1952, and received several votes for the presidential nomination in 1964. She was finally defeated for reelection in 1972 mainly due to questions about her age and health. It would be the only election she ever lost in the State of Maine.

Following her departure from the Senate, Smith taught at several colleges and universities as a visiting professor and returned home to Skowhegan, where she died at the age of ninety-seven. In 2010, the political action committee Maggie's List (the Republican answer to EMILY's List) was founded, named for Smith, to "raise awareness and funds to increase the number of conservative women elected to federal public office."

Martha Washington (1731–1802)

First Lady

As the first first lady of the United States (although the term was not coined until after her death), Martha Washington became a role model and example for all the nation's first ladies who followed her.

The oldest of the eight children of John and Frances Dandridge, she was born and raised on a Virginia plantation. Like most well-to-do girls of the time, she received an education that would prepare her to manage a household. At nineteen, she married Daniel Parke Custis, a plantation owner twenty years older than his bride. The couple had four children, two of whom died in infancy. Daniel Custis died in 1757, leaving the twenty-six-year-old Martha a very wealthy woman with an eighteen-thousand-acre estate to manage.

In 1758, George Washington, then a thirty-six-year-old colonel and commander of the Virginia militia, began courting her. In 1759, they were married at her home. The couple, together with Martha's son and daughter, went to live at Washington's plantation, Mount Vernon. There, Martha looked after the large household, oversaw the dairy and smokehouse, and supervised the estate's spinning and weaving operation.

When Washington was named commander-in-chief of the Continental Army in 1775, Martha joined him at his headquarters near Boston. From that time until the end of the Revolutionary War, she spent winters with her husband at the Army's encampments. Her calm, steady, and cheerful spirit was a great comfort to her husband, especially at Valley Forge during the harsh winter of 1778, when it seemed that the war would be lost. She nursed sick and wounded soldiers, mended their clothes, made shirts, and knitted socks for them. She also encouraged other officers' wives to join her.

In 1789, George Washington became the first president of the United States, and Martha and two of her four grandchildren accompanied him to the new nation's first capital in New York City. Debate occurred over what to call her. Most people addressed her as "Lady Washington," but she preferred plain "Mrs. Washington." She gave formal dinner parties at the presidential home, appeared with the president at ceremonial occasions, and hosted weekly Friday evening receptions with Abigail Adams, the wife of Vice President John Adams. Martha has been credited with creating an elegant atmosphere surrounding the president, and her friendly but dignified manner made her a popular public figure.

After Washington's two terms in office, he and his wife retired to Mount Vernon. After George Washington's death in 1799, Martha Washington lived quietly at Mount Vernon for the next two years, dying there at the age of seventy-one. The first U.S. postage stamp honoring an American woman depicted Martha Washington, issued in 1902. She is also the only woman (other than allegorical figures such as Justice and Liberty) depicted on the face of a U.S. banknote: on the $1 silver certificate of 1886 and 1891.

Edith Wilson (1872–1961)

First Lady

Described as "America's first female president," Edith Wilson was the second wife of Woodrow Wilson, twenty-eighth president of the United States, and first lady from 1915

to 1921, taking on the duties of the president for over a year after her husband's stroke. She essentially ran the country in her husband's absence during her "stewardship," the word she used to refer to her takeover of the West Wing.

She was born Edith Bolling in Wytheville, Virginia. Her father was a circuit court judge, and the family was descended from one of the earliest English settlers to Virginia Colony. She was also, through her father, a direct descendant of Pocahontas. The seventh of eleven children, she had little formal education, taught at home mainly by her invalid grandmother. At the age of fifteen, she enrolled in a finishing school for girls, but, ill-prepared and undisciplined, she left after only one semester. She had just one more year of schooling at a private girls' school in Richmond, Virginia. While visiting her married sister in Washington, D.C., she met Norman Galt, a prominent jeweler, and the couple married in 1896, living in the capital for the next twelve years. In 1903, she gave birth to a son, who only survived a few days, and the complications of his birth left her unable to have more children. In 1908, Galt died unexpectedly.

In 1915, she was introduced to the recently widowed U.S. President Woodrow Wilson at the White House by Helen Woodrow Bones, the president's first cousin and the official White House hostess after the death of Wilson's wife, Ellen, who died in 1914. Wilson proposed soon after meeting her. Rumors swirled that Wilson had cheated on his wife with Edith and even that they had conspired to murder Ellen. Wilson wanted Edith to back out of their engagement, but she insisted instead on postponing the wedding until the end of the official year of mourning for Ellen. They married in December 1915.

Since most of her tenure as first lady involved campaign trips when they were out of the White House, during World War I, that changed the expected social pattern, and during the president's illness, Edith Wilson delegated the role of social hostess to assistants to embrace her preferred position as Wilson's constant companion, filter, and later guardian. Since Wilson largely conducted his work from a private office in the family quarters, it permitted Edith to remain at his side. When he worked from the Oval Office, she would sit in listening silently as he conducted meetings with political leaders and foreign representatives. He eventually even shared secret war codes with her, and she began screening his mail and limiting his appointments, isolating him from most of his other trusted advisers.

She was the first first lady to travel to Europe during her term, accompanying the president to the Paris Peace Conference following the Armistice ending World War I. Returning from the conference, Wilson suffered a stroke in October 1919, which left him bedridden and partly paralyzed. Until the end of Wilson's term on March 4, 1921, Edith served as shadow president, screening all of her husband's communications and deciding what matters were pressing enough for him to see. As she later wrote about her role, "I studied every paper sent from the different Secretaries or Senators and tried to digest and present in tabloid form the things that, despite my vigilance, had to go to the President. I, myself, never made a single decision regarding the disposition of public affairs. The only decision that was mine was what was important and what was not, and the very important decision of when to present matters to my husband." As her actions became more evident, her "stewardship" was attacked by one Republican senator, who called her "the Presidentress who had fulfilled the dream of the suffragettes by changing her title from First Lady to Acting First Man."

After Wilson left office, the couple retired to a house in Washington, where he died in 1924. She would spend the remaining thirty-seven years of her life preserving and protecting her husband's reputation. She died eleven months after attending the presidential inauguration of John F. Kennedy. She is buried beside her husband in Washington National Cathedral, the only presidential couple to be interred in the nation's capital.

RELIGION

Patriarchal dominance characterized the relationship between women and their religious beliefs and observances from the moment the first explorers arrived in the New World. During the seventeenth and eighteenth centuries, one woman, Anne Hutchinson, was willing to challenge that dominance; another woman, Mother Ann Lee, founded her own religious denomination. Progress in increasing the numbers of women religious leaders was slow until the emergence of many more religious denominations, together with women's rights activism during the nineteenth and twentieth centuries, resulted in more women achieving equality within their various religious hierarchies in leadership roles previously reserved only for men.

When the Spanish and French began to settle in the New World in the sixteenth and seventeenth centuries, one of their goals, apart from exploration, conquest, settlement, and the attainment of riches, was the conversion of the indigenous peoples who populated the continent of North America to Catholicism. For the French, who primarily occupied the northeast of present-day Canada and much of Maine, the gaining of converts was the result of the increasing number of missionary priests in New France together with the necessity of forging alliances with native tribes against the English. Such alliances were considered to be stronger if native peoples were converted to Christianity. In 1523, the

first priests arrived in New Spain, which included the Caribbean islands, Mexico, Florida, and the Southwest, eventually expanding into Texas and California and up the Pacific Coast. By 1526, the Spanish government ruled that two priests were to accompany any expedition, and the following year, the pope determined that native peoples were capable of understanding the tenets of the Catholic faith. Spanish missionary priests offered Native Americans a choice between slavery or obedience to the *Requermiento*, a document promising salvation, with the result that the lives of Indian *conversos* revolved around the Roman Catholic missions in New Spain.

The matrilineal structure of some tribal cultures resulted in the missionaries' use of the Virgin Mary to gain converts, which in turn led to some Indian women becoming nuns. The most famous example is Kateri Tekakawitha (1656–1680), an Algonquin Mohawk woman born in the Mohawk village of Ossernenon in present-day New York. Also known as Lily of the Mohawk, Tekakawitha converted to Roman Catholicism when she was nineteen and was baptized as Catherine in honor of St. Catherine of Siena. Shunned by some members of her village for her religious practices and accused of sorcery, she went to live at a Jesuit mission in Kahnawake, another Mohawk village in New France near present-day Montreal, where she joined other converts. Venerated for her devotion and self-abnegation, Tekakawitha was beatified by the Catholic Church in 1980 and canonized as the first Native American saint in 2012. The Puritans in New England also took steps to convert native peoples with an emphasis on urging Indians to adopt the centrality of the Bible and live in what they called "praying towns."

Although Catholics and Jews did live in British colonial America, the predominant religious culture was Protestant and, in the seventeenth century, principally Puritan (which, by 1644, would include Presbyterianism) or Anglican (Church of England). By the eighteenth century, the most numerous Protestant denominations were Congregationalism in New England, Baptism in Rhode Island, Quakerism in Pennsylvania, and Anglicanism in the South. The most dominant sects were Congregationalism and Anglicanism. However, around the time of the First Great Awakening (1730–1755), a Christian revival movement in Great Britain and America saw the emergence of organized Anglo–

Kateri Tekakwitha was the first Native American woman to become a Catholic saint. She was canonized by Pope Benedict XVI in 2012.

American, evangelical Protestant sects such as the Methodists, who were referred to by the established Protestant sects as "nonconformists" or "dissenters." With the exception of the Quakers, most of the Protestant groups in the colonies shared common Calvinist beliefs based on a literal interpretation of both the Old and New Testaments. Adherence to the scriptures, together with an unshakable faith in the hand of God in all things, comprised the basis for the way in which the colonialists led their lives and how women were viewed.

The patriarchal society that characterized the Puritans and their somewhat less austere Anglican counterparts dominated the lives of women, who were subject to the authority of their fathers and husbands. "Woman," wrote Scottish Calvinist theologian John Knox, "in her greatest perfection was made to serve and obey man." In Puritan New England as in Calvinist Scotland, theological issues were the province of men: women could not speak in church or participate in church decisions, and, although they were expected to read the Bible, they were forbidden to interpret the scriptures. Women, although responsible for the original sin because of Eve's transgression in the Garden of Eden, leading, according to the biblical book of Genesis, to Eve and Adam's expulsion from Paradise, were recognized as spiritually equal to men: in need of soul saving and predestined to an afterlife in either heaven or hell. The belief in predestination, along with other religious convictions of the established Puritan clergy, would be challenged and modified by some Puritan theologians during the Antinomian Controversy, a religious and political conflict regarding the promise and limits of religious and civil free will that took place from 1636 to 1638 in the young Massachusetts Bay Colony. Among the challengers was charismatic and influential Puritan theologian and spiritual advisor Anne Hutchinson, whose lay preaching and defiance toward male Puritan authority led to an accusation of heresy, a trial, and expulsion from the colony.

Puritan ministers, in their writings and sermons, preached that the soul was divided into the immortal masculine half and the mortal feminine half. Both men and women were enjoined to reject the machinations of Satan, who, the Puritans believed, attacked the soul by assaulting the body. Because women were considered to be "weaker vessels" in mind and body, it was believed that Satan could more easily breach their bodies to possess their souls, thus making them prone to committing immoral acts. This belief, together with the fear of increasingly widespread practices such as astrology, alchemy, and forms of "witchcraft," which ranged from practices born out of superstition to interest in the natural sciences, led to witch hunts and accusations of witchcraft aimed at both men and women. The first recorded incidence

> **B**ecause women were considered to be "weaker vessels" in mind and body, it was believed that Satan could more easily breach their bodies to possess their souls....

of a woman accused of witchcraft and executed was Alse Young, a Hartford, Connecticut, woman who was blamed for the deaths of several children and put to death in 1647. Between 1648 and 1688, eleven more women were executed for witchcraft in New England.

The most famous incidence of prosecution for witchcraft was the Salem witch trials, held between February 1692 and May 1693, in which some two hundred people, most of them women, were accused of practicing "the Devil's magic." A study in religious mass hysteria, the witch hunt that led to the trials, began innocuously enough with stories of Caribbean magical practices, including voodoo, told to the daughter and niece of Elizabeth and Samuel Parris, a Puritan minister in Salem, by the family's enslaved servant, Tituba, who was from Barbados. It became a game for the girls to act as if they were possessed by the Devil until play acting became an obsession and they began to display increasingly bizarre behavior. Samuel Parris and his wife became convinced that the girls were possessed by a demon, but when they insisted upon knowing who had bewitched them, the two children, fearing punishment, refused to confess that it was just a game. Instead, they ac-

cused various people in Salem. What resulted were more accusations and counteraccusations of devilish behavior among the townspeople, which included reports of spectral occurrences ranging from a beggar woman seen flying on a pole to a witches' meeting to the death of a child attributed to a witch's curse and an apparently bewitched cow that ran away. Warrants, arrests, confessions, and examinations occurred before local magistrates in an attempt to determine exactly who out of those accused should be prosecuted. One infamous method of examination was the "touch test," during which an accused witch, who was blindfolded, would touch someone who was having a fit. If the fit stopped, it was evidence that the accused had caused the affliction. Other evidence of witchcraft included moles or blemishes on the bodies of the accused that were insensitive to the touch and the discoveries in some homes of books on palmistry and astrology or pots of ointment. Influential minister Cotton Mather, who supported the prosecutions, weighed in on the proceedings, cautioning one judge, "Do not lay more stress on pure spectral evidence than it will bear.... It is very certain that the Devils have sometimes represented the Shapes of persons not only innocent, but also very virtuous."

In the end, seven women and girls were judged as "afflicted" by witchcraft. Twenty people, fourteen of them women, were convicted and executed by hanging. An additional thirteen women died while in custody or in prison, including the infant daughter of Sarah Good, one of the executed women; the rest either pled guilty and were pardoned, were convicted and pardoned, or were released after Massachusetts governor Sir William Phips, who had established the court that adjudicated the witch trials, finally ordered their end. Two women escaped from prison: Mary Bradbury and Mary Hollingsworth, who escaped with her husband. Tituba, who confessed to practicing witchcraft and named other women who had joined her, was imprisoned and later released after Samuel Parris sold her for the price of her prison fees.

Theories explaining the symptoms displayed by those who claimed bewitchment and who accused others of witchcraft have included rye bread infected with an ergot fungus that can cause convulsions, an encephalitis epidemic, and sleep paralysis as well as psychological motivations such as jealousy, spite, and a desire for attention. Some of the women who confessed to practicing sorcery were most likely suffering from a mental illness; other women, emotionally sensitive and swept up in the morbid evangelical hysteria that enveloped the community, confessed out of a conviction, hardwired into the psyches of the Puritans, that they existed in a state of sinfulness and must therefore be guilty of practicing the Devil's magic.

Individual and institutional acts of repentance would follow Salem's relatively brief, disconcerting outburst of religious mania. In 1697, the General Court of Massachusetts declared a day of fasting and contemplation for the deaths and incarcerations resulting from the trials, and one of the judges publicly apologized for his guilt in the proceedings. In the early eighteenth century, the court determined that the trials were unlawful and made monetary reparations to the families of the victims. Ann Putnam, one of the seven "afflicted" girls, made a public apology for her role as an accuser. The abuses of the trials led to changes in the court system that became the procedures used today to prosecute criminal cases. It took nearly three hundred years, however, for all of those convicted to be fully exonerated of the crime of witchcraft.

The theology that influenced the status of Puritan women was not a defining feature of Quakerism. A dissenting Christian group founded in England after the English Civil War of 1642–1651, the Society of Friends or, simply, the Friends preached adherence to an "inward light" or "inner light" in an individual's spiritual and meditative relationship with God and the Bible as well as an emphasis on the primacy of individual conscience, a belief that would be called upon to great effect in the nineteenth century, when Quaker women such as Sarah and Angelina Grimké took up the cause of abolition.

Many women (and some men) were subjected to court trials resulting in several executions during the Salem witch trials (from an 1892 lithograph).

Although the Puritans passed a law requiring towns with at least one hundred families to send their children to publicly funded day schools, the Quakers established schools wherever they settled that set a high educational standard for both boys and girls beyond a rudimentary knowledge of reading, writing, and basic arithmetic. Meetings at Quaker meetinghouses were divided along gender lines, but women were encouraged to speak out on moral and spiritual issues and often conducted their own meetings. Quaker ministers were not appointed; instead, they were acknowledged, which meant that any Quaker, male or female, could be recognized as a preacher. Women also served as traveling missionary ministers to gain converts to Quakerism.

Quakers had been persecuted as heretics in England and were similarly persecuted when they first arrived in New England. In 1656, when Mary Fisher and Ann Austin, the first two Quakers to arrive in colonial America, began to preach in Boston, they were imprisoned, their books were burned, most of their property was confiscated, and they were deported. In 1657, five people attended the first monthly Quaker meeting in New England, held in a private home in the town of Sandwich, Massachusetts. In 1660, Mary Dyer, a Puritan who had converted to Quakerism, was hanged in Boston Common for repeatedly defying a Puritan law banning Quakers from the Massachusetts Bay Colony. Dyer was one of four executed Quakers who came to be known as the Boston Martyrs. The following year, Charles II of England forbade the execution of Quakers in Massachusetts, and when the thirteen colonies became firmly established under British rule in 1684 and the Massachusetts Charter was revoked, a broad Toleration Act was enforced. By then, Quaker immigrants to the colonies had either been expelled and made their way to the colony of Rhode Island, founded by Puritan theologian and minister Roger Williams and known for its religious freedom, or settled in New Jersey, Pennsylvania, or parts of the South.

The Puritan theology that characterized and dominated organized religion during the early colonial period gradually gave way to the various Protestant denominations that were established in their own right. The most influential of the Protestant sects overall were the Anglicans, who dominated the social and economic climate of British colonial America and continued to be associated with cultural and social elitism throughout the eighteenth, nineteenth, and twentieth centuries. In the nineteenth and twentieth centuries, however, the emancipation of African Americans, the arrival of great numbers of immigrants, the rise of Evengelicalism, and the introduction of Eastern and Islamic religions added to the American Judeo–Christian religious tradition to create an increasingly multicultural American population with a greater diversity of religious beliefs. By the twentieth and twenty-first centuries, American women would not be denied a place in their religious communities; instead, they would reflect the nation's diversity and contribute in meaningful ways to the history of religion in the United States.

BIOGRAPHIES

Sister Joan Chittister (1936–)
Author, Nun, Theologian

A Benedictine nun, theologian, author, and speaker who has advocated on behalf of women's rights, peace initiatives, and church renewal, Sister Joan Chittister is one of the most influential religious leaders in the United States.

Chittister was born in DuBois, Pennsylvania, the daughter of Daniel and Loretta Daugherty. Her father died when she was a young child, and her mother married Harold Chittister, who Joan Chittister has described as an abusive alcoholic. However, Chittister developed enough of an attachment to her stepfather that she chose to keep his name. She received her education at a parochial school run by the Sisters of St. Joseph and at St. Benedict Academy, both in Erie, Pennsylvania. Soon after entering Erie's Benedictine community at the age of sixteen, she was stricken with polio and endured several years of intensive therapy before she was able to walk again. She took her final vows and became a teacher while at the same time studying for her undergraduate and graduate degrees. She would go on to earn a master's degree from the University of Notre Dame and a doctoral degree in speech communication theory from Penn State University.

In the 1960s, the Second Vatican Council under Pope John XXIII introduced reforms that opened up new ways for women religious (as nuns and sisters are officially known) to respond to their calling. Chittister traveled throughout the country giving talks on the ways in which women religious might work to effect change and helped spearhead the effort of the Erie Benedictine community to change from a teaching order to a force for social justice implementing education, workforce training, and child-development programs for economically challenged families in Erie. She also served as the community's prioress for twelve years. In 1971, she was elected president of the Federation of St. Scholastica, a federation of twenty monasteries of Benedictine women that was established in 1922. She has observed that she "came to feminism through faith."

In 2001, during the more conservative papal climate that followed the Second Vatican Council, a directive from the Vatican's Congregation for Institutes of Consecrated Life and Societies of Apostolic Life forbade Chittister to speak on discipleship at the Women's Ordination Worldwide Conference in Dublin. Chittister, who has asserted that ordination for women has never been her primary focus, defied the directive and spoke at the conference.

Chittister's numerous accomplishments include the presidency of the Leadership Conference of Women Religious, which represents nearly 80 percent of Catholic sisters in the United States; serving as the executive director of Benetvision, a resource and research center for contemporary spirituality; serving as a member of the TED prize-sponsored Council of Nations, an interfaith group that has developed a charter for compassion for faith organizations worldwide; and cochair of the Global Peace Initiative, a partner organization of the United Nations that facilitates a worldwide network of women peace builders with a special emphasis on Israel and Palestine.

Chittister has been a guest on several TV programs, including *60 Minutes*, *CBS News*, and Oprah Winfrey's *Super Soul Sunday*. She is a prolific, award-winning author of books and articles and writes an online column for the *National Catholic Reporter* as well as a blog for the *Huffington Post*. A noted international lecturer, the annual Joan Chittister Lecture Series was inaugurated at Mercyhurst College in Erie.

Mary Baker Eddy (1821–1910)

Author, Founder of Christian Science

A religious reformer and founder of the religious denomination the Church of Christ, Scientist, popularly known as Christian Science, Mary Baker Eddy was born Mary Morse Baker in Bow, New Hampshire, the youngest of six children. Her father, Mark Baker, was a farmer, who had been a justice of the peace and a chaplain of the New Hampshire militia. Life in the Baker household reflected the strict Spartan and repetitive Puritan tradition of Eddy's devout Congregationalist father, who believed in hard work with the Sabbath as the only day of rest, the Last Judgment, and eternal damnation. According to her biographers, Eddy and her hot-tempered father had a volatile relationship, with Mark Baker often threatening his willful daughter with harsh punishment and Eddy's mother, Abigail, a devout, quiet, and kind woman, intervening on her behalf.

Eddy's education included tutoring from her brother, Albert, and Reverend Enoch Corser, who also served as her spiritual guide. From 1838 to 1842, she attended the Holmes Academy in Plymouth and the Sanbornton Academy in present-day Tilton, New Hampshire, where the family had moved when Eddy was fifteen.

Eddy endured several painful life events beginning in the 1840s, the first of which was the death of her brother, Albert, in 1841. In 1843, Eddy married businessman George Washington Glover, and the couple moved to Charleston, South Carolina. Six months later, Glover died of yellow fever while the two were visiting Wilmington, North Carolina. Eddy, who was six months pregnant, was forced to make the long journey back to her parents' home in New Hampshire, where she gave birth to her only child, George Washington Glover III. Eddy, who had suffered ill health as a child and continued to be frail as an adult, was bedridden for several months after the birth. She attempted to earn a living by writing articles for the New Hampshire *Patriot* and Odd Fellows and Masonic publications, worked as a substitute teacher, and briefly ran her own kindergarten, where she refused to use corporal punishment. In 1849, Eddy's mother died, followed three weeks later by the death of Eddy's fiancé, lawyer John Bartlett.

Eddy's father remarried in 1850, and Eddy, who was in a vulnerable position regarding her son because of the law of coverture, which stated that a mother could not be her child's legal guardian, sent George to live with his nurse. Thereafter, George was shunted between various relatives and eventually to a family who assumed guardianship of the child without Eddy's knowledge. Eddy went to live with her sister, Abigail, who had also declined to accept George into the household. In 1853, Eddy married Daniel Patterson, a dentist, who told his wife that he would assume legal guardianship of George but never followed through on his claim. The marriage eventually broke down and ended in 1873 after Patterson deserted Eddy and she filed for divorce on the grounds of adultery. She had lost track of her son when the family with whom he was living moved to Minnesota. According to Eddy, the child was told that his mother was dead. In 1878, George Glover, then aged thirty-four, discovered that she was alive and visited her in Massachusetts. Mother and son would meet only a few times during the years that followed. Eddy's third marriage was to Asa Gilbert Eddy, whom she wed in 1877. In 1882, the couple moved to Boston, where Asa Eddy died the same year.

Eddy's frequent disabling illnesses, loss of faith in conventional and unsuccessful medical remedies, and the conviction that the cause of disease was rooted in the mind drove her to seek relief from Phineas Quimby, a mental healer who lived in Maine. From 1862 to 1865, Eddy consulted Quimby, whose applications, based on a form of mesmerism and mental suggestion, provided Eddy with only partial relief and did not speak to the biblical tradition to which she was firmly bound. Quimby died in 1886, and Eddy, after suffering a spinal injury due to a fall on the ice the same year, turned to an account of healing in the Gospels. A moment of powerful, spiritual illumination brought about a near-immediate recovery as well as a new direction she described as "a glimpse of the great fact" of "Life and of Spirit; this

Life being the sole reality of existence." For the next nine years, Eddy studied the scriptures, embarked on a program of healing work and teaching, and, in 1875, published her major work, *Science and Health*, which eventually included the six basic tenets that would form the belief system for Christian Science. Eddy's tenet regarding illness and faith reads, "Man is saved through Christ, through Truth, Life, and Love as demonstrated by the Galilean Prophet in healing the sick and overcoming sin and death." Over the years, Eddy would continue to revise and refine *Science and Health*, which included adding a subtitle to the work, "With Key to the Scriptures," in 1883.

In 1879, Eddy founded the Church of Christ, Scientist, "to reinstate primitive Christianity and its lost element of healing" in Lynn, Massachusetts, with fifteen of her students. In the 1880s, Eddy taught classes of up to one hundred students at the Massachusetts Metaphysical College in Boston, which she founded and obtained a charter for in 1881, wrote articles for the *Christian Science Journal*, founded by Eddy in 1883, and preached infrequently at church services, which were beginning to attract parishioners disaffected with mainstream Protestant denominations. With a growing congregation came controversy, which Eddy addressed through her writings clarifying the difference between Christian Science and such alternative belief systems as Theosophy and Spiritualism, which were beginning to attract attention in the latter part of the nineteenth century. Controversy over the Christian Science emphasis on healing through faith has continued, although church teaching does not require adherents to avoid all medical interventions, while maintaining that prayer is the most effective means of healing.

Eddy moved to Concord, New Hampshire, in 1889 and during the next decade began to reorganize the church, establishing The Mother Church—The First Church of Christ, Scientist in Boston and its worldwide branches. In 1895, she published the *Manual of the Mother Church*, a book of bylaws intended to govern the church, which she revised until her death. The bylaws also established the first Christian Science Reading Room at the Mother Church in Boston in 1899. In 1893, Eddy founded the *Christian Science Sentinel*, a magazine that included articles, editorials, and accounts of healing from the Christian Science perspective. In 1908, at the age of eighty-seven, Eddy founded *The Christian Science Monitor*, a global newspaper that would go on to earn seven Pulitzer Prizes. Two years later, Eddy died in Newton, Massachusetts, at the age of eighty-nine.

Mary Baker Eddy was inducted into the National Women's Hall of Fame in 1995, and the Mary Baker Eddy Library opened in 2002. The library contains one of the largest collections available to the public on this remarkable and influential American woman.

Rachel "Ray" Frank (1861–1948)

Jewish Religious Leader

An influential Jewish religious leader, Ray Frank is considered to be the first American Jewish woman to deliver sermons for the Jewish High Holidays of Rosh Hashanah and Yom Kippur.

Born in San Francisco, Frank was the daughter of Polish immigrants Bernard and Leah Frank, whom Ray Frank would later describe as liberal Orthodox Jews. Her father, a peddler, claimed descent from the eighteenth-century Jewish Talmudic scholar the Vilna Gaon. After her graduation from Sacramento High School in 1879, Frank moved to the silver-mining town of Ruby Hill, Nevada, where she taught public school. In contrast to nearby Eureka, which had more than one hundred Jewish inhabitants, including Frank's sister, Rosa, Ruby Hill was home to few Jews. The situation sparked Frank's interest in examining the causes of prejudice in her sermons, lectures, and newspaper articles in the 1890s.

In 1885, with the mining industry in decline, Frank returned to her family in Oakland, California. There, she taught Bible studies and Jewish history at the First Hebrew Congregation of Oakland's Sabbath school. At the same time, she honed her skills as a public speaker. Frank's students included future writer Gertrude Stein and Juda Leon Magnes, who

would become a prominent Reform rabbi. Frank also worked as a correspondent for several Oakland and San Francisco newspapers and contributed articles to national Jewish publications, all of which increased her visibility in the Jewish community.

In the fall of 1890, Frank's newspaper work took her to Spokane (then Spokane Falls) in Washington, which had been admitted to the Union the previous year. It was the season of Rosh Hashanah, the Jewish New Year, and Frank was shocked to find that the town had no synagogue because the Orthodox and Reform communities were so divided that they refused to share religious services. When Frank expressed her dismay, a prominent member of the Jewish community offered to arrange Rosh Hashanah services at Spokane's Opera House if she would deliver a sermon. The sermon she gave was so impressive that she was invited to give another on the eve of Yom Kippur, the next Jewish High Holiday. In her sermon on the eve of the Day of Atonement, Frank implored her audience to "drop all dissension about whether you should take off your hats during the service and other unimportant ceremonials, and join hands in one glorious cause."

The Jewish and non-Jewish press made much of Frank's achievement as the first Jewish woman to speak from a pulpit at a time when religious leadership was strictly male and traditional Judaism allocated few public religious roles to women. The press of the day dubbed Frank the "first woman since Deborah to preach in a synagogue," "the maiden in the Temple," and the "girl rabbi of the Golden West," incorrectly printing that she would be ordained. Frank insisted that she had never been interested in ordination as her goal. Nevertheless, in the 1890s, she traveled the Pacific Coast lecturing at B'nai B'rith lodges, literary societies, and synagogue women's groups. She spoke in both Reform and Orthodox synagogues, officiated at services, and read scripture at San Francisco's Temple Emanu-El.

In 1893, she spoke at the Jewish Women's Congress, held in conjunction with the Chicago World's Fair. The same year, Frank enrolled in courses in Jewish ethics and philosophy at Hebrew Union College, a Reform seminary in Cincinnati, Ohio, where, although she was not the first female student, she was the first to be taken seriously. The college's president, Rabbi Isaac Meyer Wise (a controversial figure in American history for his support of slavery), welcomed her as a "gifted lady who takes the course, to assist the cause of emancipating women in the synagogue and the congregation."

In 1898, Frank was ready for a change from her hectic schedule, and she left the United States for an extended stay in Europe. While in Munich, Germany, she met Ukrainian economics student Simon Litman. When Litman went to Zurich, Switzerland, to continue his studies, Frank accompanied him, enrolling in classes at the Zurich Polytechnikum. The couple married in 1901. In 1902, after living briefly in Paris, they went to California, where Simon Litman began teaching marketing and merchandising at the University of California–Berkeley. In 1908, the Litmans moved to Illinois, where Simon Litman had been offered a position at the University of Illinois–Urbana-Champaign. There, Frank regained her vitality and began to become involved in the Jewish community, cofounding the Hillel Jewish student organization with her husband and students and helping to organize the Sinai Temple Sisterhood, serving as its president for fifteen years.

Despite her independent spirit and impressive catalog of achievements in a religious world dominated by men, Ray Frank was an opponent of women's suffrage, a contradictory position that was not unusual at the time. Some women (labor leader Mary Harris "Mother" Jones among them) at that time felt that adherence to the singular cause of women's rights and the vote would detract from the main cause to which they were dedicated. However, when the Nineteenth Amendment was ratified in 1920, Frank helped to form the Champaign County League of Women Voters so that women would be as well informed as possible concerning their political choices.

Ray Frank Litman: A Memoir, a tribute to Frank written by her husband, was published in 1957, nine years after Frank's death at the age of eighty-seven. She had played a pivotal role in initiating and invigorating the role of women in American Jewish life and opened the door that would eventually lead to ordination for women.

Anne Hutchinson (1591–1643)
Religious Reformer

 Born Anne Marbury in Alford, Lincolnshire, England, Hutchinson was the daughter of Francis Marbury, a Church of England deacon and schoolmaster as well as a dissident minister who had been imprisoned several times and eventually placed under house arrest for his rebelliousness, which included frequent complaints to church authorities concerning the poor training of Anglican clergy. Although by the mid-sixteenth century some girls were permitted to attend school, Hutchinson was taught by her father, who gave her a better education than most girls received at the time. As a young adult, Hutchinson lived in London, where she married cloth merchant and childhood friend William Hutchinson in 1612. The Hutchinsons would go on to have fifteen children.

When the couple moved back to Alford, they began attending the services of John Cotton, a well-known Puritan scholar and minister who had recently begun to preach at St. Botolph's Church in nearby Boston, Lincolnshire. The Hutchinsons were greatly impressed by Cotton's dynamic preaching, and Anne Hutchinson began a mentor–student relationship with Cotton and under his guidance led weekly prayer meetings in her home. Another influence on Hutchinson was her brother-in-law, John Wheelwright, a minister in the nearby town of Billsby, whose preaching was similar to Cotton's. John Cotton, unlike many Puritan ministers who were removed from their pulpits for practices that ran contrary to the established Anglican Church, had managed to thrive for many years with the help of supportive aldermen and lenient bishops. However, by 1632, church authorities increased pressure on nonconforming clergy to comply, and Cotton and his wife were forced into hiding. The following year, the Cottons set sail for Boston, where John Cotton began a successful ministry. Hutchinson, feeling lost without her mentor, convinced her husband to follow Cotton to America, and, in the summer of 1634, the couple and their eleven children arrived in Boston. There, the family soon became well established in the growing settlement. While William Hutchinson continued with his thriving mercantile business, Anne Hutchinson became a midwife who was much in demand. In addition, Hutchinson provided spiritual advice to the women to whom she attended and was forthcoming to them concerning her religious beliefs. She soon began to host a weekly gathering of women at her house to discuss John Cotton's recent sermons. When these gatherings proved popular, she opened them to men. One of her male attendees was Henry Vane, the governor of the Massachusetts Bay Colony.

By 1636, rumors had started that in her meetings, Hutchinson was echoing John Cotton's complaint concerning the training of Puritan ministers, specifically that ministers were emphasizing only the covenant of works in their teaching. Puritan leaders interpreted this as a threat to their authority and political power as well as the suggestion that they were reflecting the teaching of the "faithless" Anglicans of the Church of England. Hutchinson's claims sparked the religious and political conflict known as the Antinomian Controversy, which divided the Puritan community until 1638.

When John Winthrop succeeded Henry Vane as governor in 1637, he sought to maintain religious and political conformity in the colony and, with the colony's religious leaders, decided to separate Hutchinson from her prominent friends and allies and charge her with sedition against the Puritan ministers, a serious charge at a time when little separation existed between church and state. Hutchinson was ordered to stand trial for sedition in November 1637. Further damning evidence was uncovered after Winthrop and the Puritan leaders discovered that Hutchinson had delivered the severely malformed stillborn child of Quaker Mary Dyer and had buried the infant in unconsecrated ground to avoid controversy. Nevertheless, the authorities referred to the child as a "monster" and called it a punishment from God upon both Dyer and Hutchinson.

At her "civil" trial, Hutchinson was accused of violating the fifth commandment, "honor thy father and thy mother," implying that she had defied Puritan authority, and of teaching men, a violation of Puritan religious practice forbidding women from interpreting the scriptures and publicly commenting on them. Hutchinson was defiant, proudly admitting her violation of Puritan law and asserting her difference of opinion concerning the standard Puritan view of salvation and her belief that the spirit of God had revealed itself to her. John Winthrop described Hutchinson at her trial as "a woman of haughty and fierce carriage, of a nimble wit and active spirit, a very voluble tongue, more bold than a man." She was judged a heretic and ordered to leave the Massachusetts Bay Colony by the end of March 1638. She was placed under house arrest while she awaited her "church" trial at the beginning of March. John Cotton, fearing a loss of credibility within the Puritan community, abandoned his former pupil and described her opinions as "gangrenous and spread like leprosy, and will eat out the very bowels of religion." During her church trial, held at her home church, Puritan leaders attempted to convince her to recant and confess her error in denying inherent righteousness. She refused, was found guilty of heresy, and was excommunicated.

Hutchinson left Boston for the colony of Rhode Island in April 1638 with some of her children, Mary Dyer, and about sixty to seventy followers, many of whom had also been exiled by the court. William Hutchinson had already left for Rhode Island with most of the couple's children. In May, Hutchinson, who had been pregnant during her trials, miscarried. When John Winthrop was told about Hutchinson's miscarriage, he wrote in his journal, "as she had vented misshapen opinions, so she must bring forth deformed monsters." John Cotton preached to his congregation that the miscarriage was a punishment from God for Hutchinson's crimes.

Despite Rhode Island's founding by Puritan minister and theologian Roger Williams, who had been similarly exiled from the Massachusetts Bay Colony as a refuge for those seeking religious freedom and the separation of church and state as well as the election of William Hutchinson as governor of Aquidneck Island, one of the colony's settlements, Anne Hutchinson found herself embroiled in political controversy once more. In 1639, John Winthrop sent three Puritan ministers to the settlement to force Hutchinson to recant. When she refused, she was told that Massachusetts planned to unite the Puritan colonies of New England in 1643 and that Hutchinson would no longer be welcome in Rhode Island.

After William Hutchinson died in 1642, Anne Hutchinson moved with her children and some of her followers to present-day Pelham Bay Park in New York, then part of the Dutch colony of New Netherland. There, she founded a dissident colony of like-minded believers. In 1643, the colony was destroyed in a Siwanoy Indian attack as a reprisal for massacres initiated by the colony's governor, William Kleift, as part of a series of events known as Kleift's War. Hutchinson and six of her children were killed during the raid. Winthrop and the Puritan leaders of the Massachusetts Bay Colony responded to the death of a woman Winthrop called "an instrument of Satan" and "this American Jezebel" with satisfaction.

The harsh assessments of the Massachusetts Puritans withstanding, many prominent Americans are descended from Anne Hutchinson, including the Bush family, Franklin D. Roosevelt, former Massachusetts governor Mitt Romney, and Supreme Court justice Oliver Wendell Holmes Jr. In 1987, then-Massachusetts governor Michael Dukakis pardoned Hutchinson, revoking the order of banishment by Governor John Winthrop. A statue of Hutchinson and her daughter Susanna stands in front of the Massachusetts State House in Boston and is featured on the Boston Women's Heritage Trail. Dedicated in 1922, the statue's inscription reads in part, "In memory of Anne Marbury Hutchinson, a courageous exponent of civil liberty and religious toleration."

Madalyn Murray O'Hair (1919–1995)
Atheist Rights Activist

 Dubbed the "most hated woman in America," Madalyn Murray O'Hair campaigned for four decades to protect the separation of church and state and for the rights of atheists as the founder and president of American Atheists from 1963 to 1986.

Born in Pittsburgh, Pennsylvania, she was baptized into her father's Presbyterian faith, but, she said, she came to atheism early in her life. After graduating from high school in 1936, she married John Henry Roths, a steelworker. They separated when they both enlisted for World War II service, she with the Women's Army Corps, working as a cryptographer in Italy. She had a relationship with officer William J. Murray, who refused to divorce his wife and, after she divorced Roths, adopted the name Madalyn Murray. In 1949, she completed a bachelor's degree from Ashland University and a law degree from the South Texas College of Law but did not pass the bar exam.

She moved to Baltimore, Maryland, with her son born to Murray and had another son with a boyfriend. After she enrolled her oldest son in a Baltimore public school in 1959, she sued to end the mandatory classroom prayer and Bible reading held there. The case, *Murray v. Curlett*, reached the Supreme Court, and, in an 8–1 ruling, the court banned mandated prayers in public schools, vindicating O'Hair's contention that Americans had "an unalienable right to freedom from religion as well as freedom of religion." She used the attention gained from the court case to found the group American Atheists with the aim to "defend the civil rights of non-believers, work for the separation of church and state, and address issues of First Amendment public policy."

O'Hair's campaign included the attempt to get "In God We Trust" taken off American coins and taking the phrase "under God" out of the Pledge of Allegiance. She fought for the removal of tax-exempt status for the Catholic and Mormon churches. "I love a good fight," she admitted. "I guess fighting God and God's spokesmen is sort of the ultimate, isn't it?" Her combative style led to her being called "Mad Madalyn" and the "most hated woman in America" by *Life* magazine. Despite being a target of harassment and death threats, Murray was undeterred and remained an outspoken, visible presence, insisting on the principles of separation of church and state.

In 1995, O'Hair, her son, and her granddaughter disappeared from their Austin, Texas, home. Their burned and dismembered bodies were found on a remote ranch in South Texas in 2001. David Waters, a convicted felon and former employee of American Atheists, was convicted of the extortion, kidnapping, and murder of O'Hair and her family members.

In 2013, the first atheist monument was erected in Florida with quotations from O'Hair, Thomas Jefferson, and Benjamin Franklin.

Elizabeth Ann Seton (1774–1821)

Catholic Saint, Educator

The first native-born American to be canonized as a Roman Catholic saint, Elizabeth Seton is also notable as the founder of the first Catholic girls' school in the United States and the first American congregation of religious sisters, the Sisters of Charity.

Elizabeth Ann Seton was born into a wealthy Episcopal family in New York City. Her father, Richard Bayley, who was a physician and chief health officer for the Port of New York, attended to immigrants disembarking onto Staten Island and cared for New Yorkers during a yellow fever epidemic. He later served as the first professor of anatomy at Columbia College, later Columbia University. Seton's mother, Catherine Charlton Bayley, was the daughter of an Anglican priest who was the rector of St. Andrew's Church on Staten Island. Catherine Bayley died when Elizabeth was three years old, possibly because of complications from giving birth to a third daughter, who died the following year. Bayley taught his daughters, who received a broader education than most girls of the time. In her journals, Seton expressed a particular love for nature, poetry, and music and showed her religious aspirations and an inclination for introspection and contemplation.

Richard Bayley's second wife, who he married to provide a mother for his daughters, was Charlotte Amelia Barclay, a member of the Roosevelt family. Seton's stepmother participated in her church's social ministry and often took Elizabeth with her when she visited the poor to bring them food and other items. When the Bayleys' marriage foundered and the couple separated, Seton's father traveled to London for further medical studies, and Seton and her sister were sent to live with their paternal uncle and aunt in the village of New Rochelle.

In 1794, nineteen-year-old Elizabeth married twenty-five-year-old William Seton, a wealthy importer, with whom she would have five children. The couple was socially prominent in New York society and belonged to Trinity Episcopal Church near their home on Wall Street, where Elizabeth Seton, a devout communicant, continued her former stepmother's social ministry, caring for needy neighbors and nursing the sick and dying among relatives and family friends. In 1797, she cofounded the Society for the Relief of Poor Widows with Small Children, the first charitable society in New York. She became a charter member of the society and served for a time as its treasurer.

Between 1798 and 1803, France and Great Britain were at war, and a dispute between the United States and the newly formed French Republic led to a series of attacks on American shipping as well as a British embargo of goods from France. William Seton lost several ships and was forced to declare bankruptcy. After losing their home, Elizabeth moved to her father's house with her children. Her husband, who had suffered from tuberculosis throughout most of their married life, became worse, and his doctors prescribed a visit to Italy in the hopes that a warmer climate would help to cure him. The Setons, accompanied by their oldest daughter, Anna Maria (who would succumb to the same disease in 1812), arrived in Leghorn in November 1803. The Italian authorities, fearing that the family may have brought yellow fever with them from New York, kept them in quarantine for a month. Eight days after they were released, William Seton died from tuberculosis and was buried in the Old English Cemetery in Livorno, Italy.

While waiting to return to the United States, Elizabeth and her daughter spent several months with the families of the Filicchi brothers, who were business partners of her husband. Through them, Seton became drawn to Roman Catholicism, and when she returned to New York, she began instruction. She was received into the church in 1805 at St. Peter's Church, then the city's only Catholic church, and, a year later, she was confirmed by

Right Reverend John Carroll of Baltimore, Maryland, the nation's only Catholic archbishop at the time. She chose Mary as her confirmation name because of her admiration for the Virgin Mary. To support herself and her children, Seton opened an academy for young ladies, but after the news of her conversion spread, most of her students' parents withdrew their daughters from the school. In 1807, she operated a boardinghouse for students attending a Protestant academy near her house.

In 1808, Seton was considering a move to a teaching convent in Canada when she met a visiting priest, Abbé Louis Dubourg, a member of a Sulpician community of fathers who had fled religious persecution in France during the Reign of Terror, and settled in Emmitsburg, Maryland. Father Duborg, who was president of the newly established Mount St. Mary's University in the city, invited Seton to Emmitsburg to help found a religious school for the city's small Catholic community. Seton accepted his invitation, and, in 1809 with a small group of nuns, she established the Saint Joseph's Academy and Free School for Catholic girls, the first free parochial school in the United States. Seton wrote classroom textbooks, trained Catholic sisters to become teachers, and accepted all students, regardless of their parents' ability to pay. The academy's founding marks the start of the American Catholic parochial school system.

In 1809, Seton also established the first American congregation of religious sisters dedicated to aiding the poor, the Sisters of Charity, initially called the Sisters of Charity of St. Joseph. Seton, who administered the congregation, was given the title of Mother, and in 1813, she took her vows as a nun. In 1814 and 1817, the community accepted its first missions outside Emmitsburg when it established orphanages in Philadelphia and New York. By the time of her death, the Sisters of Charity order included twenty communities.

Elizabeth Seton spent the last years of her life directing St. Joseph's Academy and her growing religious community. She died from tuberculosis in Emmitsburg at the age of forty-six. Beatified by Pope John XXIII in 1963 and canonized by Pope Paul VI in 1975, Elizabeth Seton is the patron saint of Catholic schools, seafarers, and widows. The lasting legacy of this remarkable first saint born in the United States and founder of Catholic education in America includes the naming of several schools after her, the most well known of which is Seton Hall University in New Jersey.

Wilhelmina "Minnie" Vautrin (1886–1941)
Missionary

A missionary and educator in China for twenty-eight years, Minnie Vautrin is celebrated for her courageous attempts to protect and care for her women students, as well as many Chinese refugees, between 1937 and 1938, during the Japanese invasion of Nanjing (also called Nanking), a historical event known variously as the Nanjing Massacre and the Rape of Nanjing.

Wilhelmina "Minnie" Vautrin was born in Secor, Illinois, the second of three children of Edmond Vautrin, a French immigrant and blacksmith, and his wife, Pauline, who died when Minnie was six. After living in several court-ordered foster homes, Vautrin was allowed to return to her father. She graduated from Secor High School, after which she attended Illinois State Normal University, where her need to take on jobs to earn money resulted in frequent interruptions in her studies. Despite that difficulty, she graduated first in her class in 1907 and then taught high school mathematics before continuing her studies at the University of Illinois, where she was president of the Student Volunteer Movement for Foreign Missions. In 1912, after graduating as salutatorian of her class and receiving an A.B. in science, Vautrin, who had decided to devote her life to missionary work, accepted a position offered by the Foreign Christian Missionary Society to establish a girl's school in Hofei, China. The San Ching Girls' Middle School proved a success and led to the addition of a girls' high school.

In 1918 Vautrin returned to the United States on furlough and attended Columbia University, where she received a master's degree in education the following year and accepted a position from the Foreign Christian Missionary Society to serve as president of Ginling Collge in Nanjing, one of four women's colleges in China. Vautrin, who was engaged to a fellow missionary she had met in Hofei, postponed her wedding. She would later break off the engagement and remained unmarried for the rest of her life. During her tenure at Ginling College, Vautrin introduced courses on education administration, implemented an innovative student–teacher program, and, with her students, established a free clinic for the poor and raised funds for an elementary school catering to the poor and mostly illiterate children living in homes near the campus.

In 1937 the Japanese army invaded China and defeated the Chinese National Revolutionary Army at Marco Polo Bridge near Beijing (Peking). Vautrin took steps to prepare the college and its students from the approaching Japanese army. She sent school records to Shanghai, purchased supplies, instructed students and faculty on emergency preparedness, converted campus buildings for storage and refuge, and supervised the building of trenches. After the first Japanese air raid on the city, the American embassy arranged for the evacuation of Americans, but Vautrin refused to leave. She kept a detailed diary of the events in Nanjing, and in one entry wrote, "Men are not asked to leave their ships when they are in danger and women are not asked to leave their children."

By September, only three students remained on campus. Anticipating a Japanese assault on the city, Vautrin and the other Westerners who had decided to stay organized a safety zone with approximately twenty-five refugee camps. Vautrin turned the Ginling campus into a special camp for women and children, displaying American flags and proclamations issued by the American embassy in the hope that Japanese soldiers would see that Ginling was in effect American

territory and should be left alone. In December, the Japanese army reached Nanjing, where they took control of the city and embarked upon a rampage of torture, rape, and murder. During the height of these atrocities, Ginling College harbored up to ten thousand women and children at times.

By February 1938 the other refugee camps had closed, causing many women and children to seek refuge at Ginling. Vautrin patrolled the college grounds to repel incursions of Japanese soldiers onto the campus and to rescue and care for the refugees. She administered burials, aided women in childbirth, and helped women trace their missing husbands and sons. In the midst of the mayhem, Vautrin conducted classes in industrial arts and crafts so that widowed women might be able to financially support themselves. Vautrin was also forced to make frequent visits to the Japanese embassy in order to receive proclamations prohibiting soldiers from committing atrocities at the college.

By 1940 Vautrin was mentally exhausted and deeply depressed. After suffering a nervous breakdown, a colleague accompanied her back to the United States, where she attempted to commit suicide but was unsuccessful. Shortly before her death from a second suicide attempt, she wrote in her diary, "Had I ten perfect lives, I would give them all to China."

After the end of World War II, Minnie Vautrin was posthumously awarded the Emblem of the Blue Jade by the Chinese government for her sacrifices during the Nanjing Massacre. The Nanjing Massacre Museum includes a memorial of Vautrin and there is a statue of her at Ginling (now Jinling) College. The 2007 documentary film Nanking features actor Mariel Hemingway reading excerpts from Vautrin's diary.

ACTIVISTS FOR SOCIAL CHANGE

The activists who participated in the two central movements in women's history—the suffrage and women's liberation movements—greatly influenced the lives of American women past and present. However, remarkable women throughout American history have dedicated themselves to the cause of social change through other major individual and collective initiatives. In the nineteenth and early twentieth centuries, these initiatives often took place at the same time as the suffrage movement.

In the latter half of the nineteenth century, as the women's suffrage movement was at its approximate midpoint, two social reform movements were taking shape alongside it: the temperance movement, which sought to prohibit the sale and consumption of alcohol, and the American settlement movement, founded in many cities to improve the quality of life for the poor and the swelling ranks of new immigrants.

THE TEMPERANCE MOVEMENT

The temperance movement had begun with temperance societies in the early decades of the century, and while the majority of "drys," as antidrinking and antisaloon advocates were known, were men, many women joined the cause in their concern over drunkenness and its effects on families

and the workplace. Men who drank frequently neglected their jobs and families, wages were spent on beer and whiskey instead of rent and food, and drunken men were often violent toward their wives and children. Female reformers such as Susan B. Anthony embraced the cause of temperance, although it remained a minor issue in relation to causes like abolition and women's suffrage. A number of states passed temperance laws early in the century, but most of them were soon repealed. After Maine became the first state to legislate Prohibition in 1851, other states began to call for similar legislation, and emphasis shifted from advocacy of temperance to the demand for federal Prohibition. In 1869, the Prohibition Party was formed to seek national legislation but in its early years had little political influence.

In the early 1870s, women in hundreds of small towns in the Midwest led a series of antidrinking crusades in which they entered saloons to pray and sing hymns and exhorted liquor dealers to stop selling their "demon" wares. The "Singing Sisters," as the public called the crusaders, were viewed with both admiration and derision, but their small efforts contributed to the formation of a national organization that combined evangelism with political awareness: the Women's Christian Temperance Union (WCTU). Founded in 1873 and officially declared at its national convention in Cleveland, Ohio, in

The building in this photo was home to the Women's Christian Temperance Union, the first major national women's organization. The primary focus of the WCTU was to prohibit the sale of alcoholic beverages, but it later became involved in other movements aimed at improving society.

1874, the WCTU was the first truly national women's organization with a large membership representing all parts of the country and all ranks of life, although its greatest strength was in the Midwest. The WCTU became a formidable agent of social change under the presidency of educator Frances Willard, whose motto, "Do Everything," reflected the WCTU's social activism on behalf of such causes as suffrage, health and hygiene, and age-of-consent marriage laws as well as temperance. However, the WCTU has always been primarily associated with the temperance movement, which, along with the Anti-Saloon League (founded 1893), it helped to popularize. Next to Frances Willard, the WCTU's most visible temperance worker was Carry Nation, who lectured on temperance, founded a temperance magazine, and became notorious for sweeping into saloons with a pewter hatcher, infrequently accompanied by like-minded women, to destroy liquor bottles and other saloon property. Carry Nation garnered much attention for the Prohibition effort, although she did not live to see the passage of the Volstead Act and its ratification in 1919 as the Eighteenth Amendment to the U.S. Constitution banning the manufacture and sale of alcoholic beverages in the United States. Until its repeal in 1933, the amendment represented the culmination of a half-century crusade undertaken by the women who believed that Prohibition was the only solution to the widespread problem of male alcohol abuse.

THE SETTLEMENT MOVEMENT

The settlement movement, the precursor of the profession of social work, derived its name from the poor and immigrant workers who "settled" in the tenement slums of urban neighborhoods. The movement began in London with the founding of Toynbee Hall in 1884 by Church of England cleric Samuel Barnett and his wife, Henrietta, and was started in the United States in 1886 with the estab-

lishment of the University Settlement House on New York City's Lower East Side. Two of the most well-known settlement houses that followed were Hull-House, founded in Chicago by Jane Addams and Ellen Gates Starr (1859–1940) in 1889, and the Henry Street Settlement, founded in 1893 on New York's Lower East Side by social reformer and nurse Lillian Wald. Founded to achieve social reform by bridging the gap between middle-class and wealthy Americans and the poor, settlement houses provided a variety of programs such as childcare, education for children and adults, and health care as well as cultural and recreational activities. Sponsors of settlement houses included women's colleges, theological seminaries, Christian associations, churches, and the humanist Ethical Culture Society. Volunteer settlement workers, who offered their unique skills and abilities to settlement programs and often lived in settlement houses as residents, included such notable American women as Eleanor Roosevelt, Florence Kelley, and Frances Perkins. Settlement house workers also focused on social justice reform, pioneering the fight against racial discrimination and contributing to progressive political efforts to gain legislation on housing, health and sanitation, child labor, and improved conditions in the workplace.

Founded in 1889 by Jane Addams and Ellen Gates Starr, Chicago's Hull-House was a facility that provided support for newly arrived immigrants. Hull-House became the seed of a growing social program that included five hundred homes nationwide by 1920.

One Hull-House resident, Grace Abbott, worked to advance the cause of child welfare, especially the regulation of child labor. By the 1920s, nearly five hundred settlement houses were established in cities across the United States and served a diverse population of Americans. In the 1930s, social reformer Dorothy Day, who founded the Catholic Worker Movement, continued the settlement house concept with "hospitality houses" for workers.

THE WOMAN'S PEACE PARTY

The Woman's Peace Party (WPP) was an American pacifist and feminist organization established in response to World War I (1914–1918). The first of two officially declared twentieth-century global conflicts and one of the deadliest conflagrations in human history, the war began with the assassination of Archduke Franz Ferdinand, heir to the Austro-Hungarian throne, in Sarajevo (now in Bosnia and Herzegovina) in June 1914. By the end of July, the event had triggered military mobilizations, military actions, and declarations of war among the Balkan nations, and by August 1, with war declared between Germany and Russia, the conflict began to embroil most of Europe as well as the Ottoman Empire and parts of Africa and the Middle East. On August 29, to protest the war, some 1,500 women held the Women's Peace Parade, organized and chaired by seventy-year-old Fanny Garrison Villard, the daughter of abolitionist and publisher William Lloyd Garrison. The women marched in silence down New York's Fifth Avenue behind a white banner, on which was a white dove. The event marked a shift in tactics from other peace organizations, which preferred to work for political action on behalf of peace initiatives behind the scenes. The Woman's Peace Party, which emerged from a January 1915 conference of national women's organizations in Washington, D.C., dovetailed with the suffrage movement and called for direct action since party members, which included suffrage leaders Carrie Chapman Catt and Crystal Eastman in addition to pacifists Jane Addams, future Nobel Peace Prize recipient Emily Greene Balch, epidemiologist Alice Hamilton, future congressional representative Jeannette Rankin, labor activist Florence Kelley, and Lillian Wald of the Henry Street Settlement, insisted that the equality of women was essential to peace and that it was time "for men to stand down and for the women whom they have belittled to take the seat of judgment." In her 1922 book *Peace and Bread in Time of War*, Jane Addams, who had served as the organization's president and would go on to receive the Nobel Peace Prize in 1931, described the further reasoning behind the decision to form the Woman's Peace Party: "We revolted not only against the cruelty and barbarity of war, but even more against the reversal of human relationships which war implied … we also believed that justice between men or between nations can be achieved only through understanding and fellowship … which cannot possibly be secured in the storm and stress of war."

The WPP, riding the wave of antiwar sentiment that pervaded the United States directly after the outbreak of the war in Europe, soon had twenty-five thousand members.

The WPP, riding the wave of antiwar sentiment that pervaded the United States directly after the outbreak of the war in Europe, soon had twenty-five thousand members. In April 1915, delegates from the WPP attended a peace conference of 1,136 participants from both neutral and belligerent nations at The Hague in the Netherlands, which led to the establishment of the International Committee of Women for Permanent Peace (ICWPP) with Jane Addams as president. The WPP was designated as the American arm of the ICWPP. However, by May 1915, disputes between the United States and Germany and Great Britain over wartime incidents involving transoceanic commerce had resulted in a campaign of American preparedness for war, which intensified, along with national support, after the sinking of the British ocean liner the RMS *Lusitania*. Alarmed, the WPP embarked on a campaign to mediate on behalf of neutrality, an effort that ultimately failed when President Woodrow Wilson, formerly a champion of antipreparedness, shifted his position after seeing a letter from the WPP to the secretary of the Navy, in which party members referenced the president's former stance on U.S. involvement in the European war. Neither the militant antiwar activism of Crystal Eastman, the leader of the New York branch of the WPP, or the support of Jeannette Rankin, the only member of Congress to vote against a U.S. declaration of war against the European nations fighting Russia, Great Britain, and France in 1917, had any effect on the decision to join the conflict. Membership in the WPP dwindled as many members, including party founders, quit either to join the war effort or in the belief that any wartime interest in peace was dangerous as well as treasonous. Jane Addams, who received a military citation for her work with selective service registration, as well as most of the other members of the WPP's national board, were added to the U.S. Military Intelligence Service lists of "those who did not help us to win the war." Addams, once dubbed "America's only saint," was further singled out for vilification after she pleaded for food relief for German children and defended the rights of those arrested during the postwar communist Red Scare.

In 1919, a delegation of Woman's Peace Party leaders and members attended the ICWPP's second conference in Zurich, Switzerland. There, they denounced the final terms of the peace treaty (the Treaty of Versailles) that ended World War I, which included a controversial provision called the World Guilt clause that called for Germany and its allies to pay 132 billion marks (then $31.4 billion) in reparations for the loss and damage they had caused as the aggressors in the war. The ICWPP saw the provision as an act of revenge of the victors over the vanquished and correctly predicted that it would lead to another war. The delegates decided to make the committee permanent, renamed it the Women's International League for Peace and Freedom (WILPF), and moved the headquarters of the new organization to Geneva, Switzerland. Since its founding, the WILPF has worked on its own and with the United Nations on behalf of peace, all forms of individual and collective social justice, and, more recently, environmental sustainability. In 2015, one

The Woman's Peace Party was the first women's movement formed as a reaction to the outbreak of World War I in Europe. After the sinking of the *Lusitania* and the Wilson adminstration's decision to send American troops to join the conflict, the WPP's pacisfism was viewed as unpatriotic.

hundred years after the Woman's Peace Party first met with international peace activists at the International Congress of Women in the Netherlands to form the International Committee of Women for Permanent Peace, the WILPF held its thirty-second conference in The Hague.

THE BIRTH CONTROL MOVEMENT

In the early decades of the twentieth century, Americans did not have the legal right or sanction to sell or distribute contraceptive devices in the majority of U.S. states. The prohibition against birth control had begun in the late nineteenth century as a campaign by social reform groups such as the Women's Christian Temperance Union (WCTU) and the Young Women's Christian Association (YWCA) to bring "social purity" to the nation. Although these groups encouraged public discussion of social issues such as prostitution and venereal disease, they remained puritanical on the subject of birth control, which they saw as a means of freeing men to pursue their supposedly greater sexual urges outside marriage. In 1873, passage of the Comstock Laws, a set of federal acts named after zealous antivice crusader Henry Comstock, forbade the dissemination of pornography, abortion devices, and "any drug medicine, article, or thing designed, adapted, or intended for preventing conception" and criminalized usage of the U.S. Postal Service for sending such items.

The antivice social reformers viewed the Comstock Laws as protective legislation for women, but the reality was quite different. Although women in all economic circumstances were affected by the ban on the sale and distribution of birth control information and devices, middle- and upper-class women, who were better educated in general and received more adequate health care, had some access to contraceptives. Economically disadvantaged women, many of them immigrants, whose religious and cultural beliefs dictated that husbands should not be denied sex under any circumstances and were faced with the financial reality that large families meant more wage earners, did not enjoy even limited privilege when it came to birth control and sex education. Midwives and visiting nurses sometimes assisted during births, and a physician might be called in dire cases, but childbirth in the slums was a risky experience that all too often led to infection and death for both mothers and babies. Denied information from the medical establishment on birth control and fearing contraception as well, many poor women resorted to crude and often deadly methods to end their pregnancies. In her autobiography, public health nurse and birth control advocate Margaret Sanger describes a woman she attended in a tenement on the Lower East Side of New York City in the 1910s. The woman, who had three small children, was seriously ill with an infection caused by a self-induced abortion and, during her recovery, asked Sanger how she could prevent another pregnancy. Sanger, in turn, consulted the attending doctor, who suggested that the husband be told to "sleep on the roof." Three months later, Sanger was called to the woman's home again, only to find her in a coma following another attempted self-induced abortion. The woman died ten minutes after Sanger's arrival.

The female reformers who were committed to defying the Comstock Laws included Antoinette Konikow (1869–1946), a Russian immigrant physician, cofounder of the American Socialist Party, and author of the celebrated feminist work *Voluntary Motherhood* (1923); anarchist and feminist political and social activist Emma Goldman; and, most prominently, Margaret Sanger, who opened the first birth control clinic in Brooklyn in 1916. The clinic, staffed by Sanger, her sister, Ethel Byrne, and a friend who spoke Yiddish, dispensed diaphragms, birth control advice, and copies of an article titled

An 1847 issue of *The Police Gazette* depicts Ann Trow Lowman (aka Madame Restell), a British-born American abortionist, as an evil criminal even though nonsurgical abortions were legal at the time.

"What Every Girl Should Know." The clinic lasted for ten days before it was shut down by the New York City Police Department. Both Sanger and her sister were arrested and jailed for dispensing "obscene" materials, with Ethel Byrne mounting a week-long hunger strike in protest.

In the 1920s, Sanger solicited the support of progressive reformers such as former suffrage campaigner Carrie Chapman Catt, feminist writer Charlotte Perkins Gilman, and Jane Addams. Sanger claimed to Catt that legalization of birth control was the next logical campaign for women, who had won the vote in 1920. In a letter to Sanger, Catt expressed her opinion that a movement to legalize birth control was too narrow a subject to appeal to her, adding that the sexual freedom offered by birth control would result in the perpetuation of a society based on male superiority and standards rather than a society in which men emulated the moral virtues of women and argued that any social gains provided by birth control would be offset by "some increase in immorality through safety." Charlotte Perkins Gilman, who favored a wife-as-mother model of womanhood over what some feminists viewed as the unrealistic model of the wife-as-companion, took a similar view. Jane Addams believed, with Carrie Chapman Catt, that the mission of women, ideally virtuous and nonsexual, was to curb and refine the appetites of men and flatly refused to support a birth control movement. The responses of three of the most iconic figures in American women's history illustrates the social realities of the times in which they lived and serves to remind us that feminism has never represented a single ideology or agenda that fits all women.

In 1929, due to the efforts of Margaret Sanger and other like-minded reformers, the Comstock Laws were liberalized, and in 1936, a U.S. Circuit Court of Appeals, in a case brought before it by Dr. Hannah Stone, a birth control advocate and author of the medical journal article "Therapeutic Contraceptives," ruled that physicians could dispense contraceptives "for the purpose of saving life or promoting the well-being of their patients." The court's broadly worded ruling would eventually lead to the legalization of contraceptives in all fifty states but not until 1965. By then, the birth control pill and the IUD had joined

Margaret Sanger was focused on women's reproductive rights and tried to educate women about birth control. Her outspokenness often landed her in court or even in jail, but she was firm in her beliefs that women should have the right to choose whether or not to become pregnant.

the diaphragm as viable forms of birth control for women. Just over the horizon were questions over why the responsibility for birth control was solely left to women as well as the most intense battle for women's reproductive rights women would ever wage—the fight to legalize abortion.

The women profiled here worked to better conditions for poor and working women and the mentally ill; advanced the cause of peace; advocated for children, the elderly, and Americans with physical and learning disabilities; founded a celebrated organization just for girls; brought nursing and midwife services to underserved rural populations; began a movement for women's reproductive rights; and confronted the nuclear power industry in the cause of greater safety for workers. One courageous woman of color was the first to appear before the Senate Judiciary Committee to testify concerning the sexual misconduct of a Supreme Court nominee. Still other women worked on behalf of Native American rights and have been advocates for social justice for African Americans as well as grassroots leaders, public organizers, recruiters, teachers, and protectors of black men facing white violence within each historical phase of the civil rights movement.

BIOGRAPHIES

Grace Abbott (1878–1939)
Social Worker

A pioneer in the profession of social work, Grace Abbott was dedicated to the causes of immigrant rights and child welfare, specifically the regulation and elimination of child labor.

Born in Grand Island, Nebraska, Grace Abbott was one of the four children of Othman A. Abbott, the first lieutenant governor of Nebraska. Abbott and her elder sister, Edith, who would also go on to become a pioneering social worker, were raised in a family environment that stressed the values of education, religious independence, and equality. The girls developed a concern for the oppressed from their mother, Elizabeth, a Quaker turned Unitarian, who impressed upon her children the legacy of injustice toward Native Americans (the Ponca tribe of Nebraska had experienced its own Trail of Tears in 1877) as well as the goals of the women's suffrage movement.

After graduating from Grand Island College in 1898, Grace Abbott worked as a high school teacher in her hometown. In 1903, she began graduate studies at the University of Nebraska–Lincoln and four years later moved to Chicago, where she took up residency at Jane Addams's Hull-House. She received a Ph.D. in political science from the University of Chicago in 1909 and from 1909 to 1910 wrote a series of articles on the exploitation of immigrants for the *Chicago Evening Post* titled "Within the City's Gates." From 1908 to 1917, she served as director of the Immigrants Protective League. Between 1910 and 1917, Abbott was a professor at the University of Chicago's School of Social Administration, a graduate school cofounded by her sister, Edith. In 1917, after studying the conditions at New York's Ellis Island, the entry point for immigrants to the United States, Abbott published her findings in the book *The Immigrant and the Community*. The same year, she relocated to Washington, D.C., where she organized and administered the Keating–Owen Act, the first federal initiative introduced to regulate child labor, which, although later declared unconstitutional, was the precursor of subsequent successful legislation concerning child labor.

Abbott continued to campaign for the regulation of child labor after she was named director of the U.S. Children's Bureau in 1921. She also helped to administer the Sheppard–Towner Act (1921), which allocated federal aid to states for the implementation of health programs benefiting mothers and infants. In the 1920s, she worked to pass a constitutional amendment prohibiting child labor, which never secured ratification. Abbott was also a member of the National Women's Trade Union League (NWTUL) and served as an unofficial U.S. representative of the League of Nations' Advisory Council on Traffic on Women and Children from 1922 until her retirement from public service in 1934. She was a member of President Franklin Delano Roosevelt's Council on Economic Security and helped to draft the Social Security Act of 1935. In 1938, she published the sociological text *The Child and the State*.

From 1934 until her death in 1939, Abbott was a professor of public welfare at the University of Chicago. The University of Nebraska's School of Social Work is named in her honor.

Jane Addams (1860–1935)
Social Reformer

Called the "beloved lady" of American reform, Jane Addams was a pioneering social worker, reformer, and pacifist, most widely known as the founder and director of Chicago's Hull-House settlement house. For her efforts to promote world peace, she was awarded the Nobel Peace Prize in 1931, the first American woman to receive the award.

Born in the small farming town of Cedarville, Illinois, Addams was the eighth of the nine children of John and Sarah Addams. Growing up, she was greatly influenced by her father, a prominent businessman and state senator. Highly regarded in his community, he passed on to his daughter his strong sense of civic responsibility. Addams graduated at the top of her class from Rockford Female Seminary in 1881 and planned to study medicine. However, on a trip abroad in 1888, she became impressed with Toynbee Hall, the settlement house created by British reformer Arnold Toynbee to alleviate the extreme poverty of London's East End. Returning home, Addams began to make plans to establish a similar settlement house in the United States. With her longtime friend Ellen Gates Starr, Addams moved to Chicago and began seeking financial support from philanthropists.

In 1899, they acquired and fully renovated a run-down, two-story mansion, originally built by real estate developer Charles Hull in 1856 and located in a slum neighborhood of Chicago populated by European immigrants. The goal was for educated women to share all kinds of knowledge, from basic skills to arts and literature, with the poor in the neighborhood, with the women living in the community center among the people they served. Within a year of opening Hull-House, Addams and her staff of volunteers, many of whom would become leading progressive reformers, including Florence Kelley, Alice Hamilton, and Grace and Edith Abbott, attended to the needs of the struggling immigrant community with a daycare center; kindergarten; music school; vocational, recreational, and cultural programs; and classes in sewing, cooking, dressmaking, and millinery. Hull-House would grow to thirteen buildings, including a summer camp.

Addams wrote articles and gave speeches nationally about Hull-House but also expanded her interests in social reform, successfully lobbying for the establishment of a juvenile court system, better urban sanitation and factory laws, and protective labor legislation for women. In 1907, she was a founding member of the National Child Labor Committee, which played an important role in the passage of a Federal Child Labor Law in 1916. She also served as president of the National Conference of Charities and Corrections from 1909 to 1915, the first woman to hold that title, and became active in the women's suffrage movement as an officer of the National American Women's Suffrage Association. She was also among the founders of the National Association for the Advancement of Colored People.

An outspoken pacifist, Addams was elected chair of the Woman's Peace Party, and in 1919, she became the first president of the Women's International League for Peace and Freedom. Her opposition to America's entry into World War I brought her severe criticism, but she never wavered in her pacifist beliefs. She spent much of the 1920s in Europe and Asia working for world peace, and by 1930, with the arrival of the Great Depression and the threat of a new war in Europe, Addams's pacifism and tireless social activism gained increasing credibility and respect and was recognized in 1931 when she was awarded the Nobel Peace Prize.

After her death, Addams's body lay in state in Hull-House for two days while thousands of mourners filed past to pay their respects to one of the most remarkable women of her age.

Ella Baker (1903–1986)
Civil Rights Activist

One of the most important leaders of the civil rights movement of the 1950s and 1960s, Ella Baker help to found the Southern Christian Leadership Conference and the Student Nonviolent Coordinating Committee. She spent her lifetime battling racial injustice. An influential member of multiple civil rights organizations, she was also an organizer of many small, grassroots community groups.

Born in Norfolk, Virginia, Baker grew up in North Carolina on land her grandparents had worked as slaves. After graduating as class valedictorian from Shaw University in Raleigh, North Carolina, in 1927, Baker moved to New York City to look for work. She took jobs as a waitress and a factory worker before she began writing for black publications. In 1932, she co-organized the Young Negro Cooperative League, a consumer group dedicated to helping the disadvantaged during the Depression. In the 1940s, Baker traveled throughout the segregated South to organize branches of the National Association for the Advancement of Colored People (NAACP). She became known for her determination and fearlessness in an atmosphere of racial threat and violence, in which African Americans could be killed for simply trying to register to vote.

During the Montgomery, Alabama, bus boycott of 1955–1957, which began after Rosa Parks refused to give up her seat for a white passenger, Baker organized assistance for the boycotters and other African Americans who had suffered reprisals for their civil rights activities. In 1957, she was among the founders of Dr. Martin Luther King's Southern Christian Leadership Conference to widen the opposition to racial injustice in the South. While Reverend King was the group's inspirational leader, it was Baker who managed the SCLC, which grew into sixty-five affiliates in various states.

During a wave of sit-ins by black college students in the winter of 1960, Baker saw an opportunity to harness the students' dedication and enthusiasm for social activism. She helped launch the Student Non-violent Coordinating Committee (SNCC) and taught members how to organize protests and coordinate voter registration drives. Eventually, Baker's efforts on behalf of the SNCC and the Mississippi Freedom Democratic Party, which she formed to challenge the power of the all-white state Democratic Party, contributed to the landmark passage of the Civil Rights Act of 1965, which guaranteed the protection of voting rights for all U.S. citizens, one of the major achievements of the civil rights movement.

In 1967, Baker resided in New York City and remained active in multiple causes, including the campaign to release activist and writer Angela Davis and the Puerto Rican independence movement. She died on her eighty-third birthday. Those who knew Ella Baker affectionately called her the "Fundi," a Swahili word for a learned person who passes skills and knowledge from one generation to another. In light of Ella Baker's lifetime contribution to the cause of civil rights, it is a fitting description of this remarkable woman.

Emily Greene Balch (1897–1961)

Peace Activist

An economist, sociologist, and pacifist, Emily Greene Balch dedicated her life to humanitarian causes. She was the central leader of the Women's International League for Peace and

Freedom, for which she was awarded the Nobel Peace Prize in 1946.

Balch was born in Boston into a prosperous family. Her father was a successful lawyer and one-time secretary to U.S. senator Charles Sumner. Balch attended private schools and was a member of the first graduating class of Bryn Mawr College in 1889. After graduation, she did independent study in sociology and used a fellowship from Bryn Mawr to study economics in Paris from 1890 to 1891. She completed her formal studies with courses at Harvard, the University of Chicago, and in Berlin.

In 1896, she joined the faculty of Wellesley College, promoted to professor of economics and sociology in 1913. She participated in movements for women's suffrage, racial justice, control of child labor, and better wages and conditions for workers. Increasingly, her focus centered on the problem of peace, and she attended two peace conferences in 1899 and 1907 at The Hague. The outbreak of World War I convinced her that she should dedicate her life's work to rid the world of war. She founded the Women's International Committee for Permanent Peace (later named the Women's International League for Peace and Freedom (WILPF)) in 1915. In collaboration with Jane Addams and Alice Hamilton, she published *Women at The Hague: The International Congress of Women and Its Results* (1915). She campaigned actively against America's entry into the war, and her teaching contract from Wellesley was terminated. In 1919, she accepted a position as secretary of the WILPF, headquartered in Geneva, Switzerland. She served in that position until 1922, when ill health forced her resignation, then again briefly in 1934–1935. In 1936, she was elected honorary international president.

During World War II, the horrors of the Nazis caused Balch to change her pacifistic views and defended the concept of "fundamental human rights, sword in hand." Awarded the Nobel Peace Prize (shared with John R. Mott) at the age of seventy-nine, Balch continued to support the causes that she had long embraced. She died the day after her ninety-fourth birthday in Cambridge, Massachusetts.

Daisy Lee Gatson Bates (1914–1999)
Civil Rights Activist

Newspaper publisher and civil rights activist Daisy Lee Gatson Bates played a pivotal role in the integration of Little Rock, Arkansas's Central High School in 1957, one of the most important events in the civil rights movement. She became known as the "first lady of Little Rock," who was the first African American to lie in state in the Arkansas State Capitol Building after her death.

Born Daisy Lee Gatson in Huttig, Arkansas, she was adopted as a baby after her mother's murder and her father's subsequent flight for his own safety before the prosecution of the three white men suspected of the murder could begin. She never saw her father after that. Her adoptive father, Orlee Smith, told her that the killers were never found due to a lack of interest from the police in bringing her mother's murderers to justice. As she recalled, "My life now had a secret goal—to find the men who had done this horrible thing to my mother." Gatson attended the local Huttig segregated public schools.

In 1928, when she was fifteen, she met Lucius Christopher Bates, a traveling salesman. Together, they moved to Little Rock in 1941 and were married in 1942. They established *The Arkansas State Press*, a weekly statewide newspaper advocating civil rights. She also joined the Little Rock NAACP branch and was elected president of the Arkansas Conference of Branches in 1951. She remained an active member of the national NAACP board for the next twenty years.

The 1954 Supreme Court ruling in *Brown v. Board of Education* led to a ruling to integrate Little Rock Central High School, and Bates's home, not far from Central High, became the organizing and strategy center for the nine African American students selected to desegregate the school in 1957. Bates would walk in the newly desegregated schools daily from 1957 to 1958 receiving numerous death threats, and she and her husband were forced to close *The Arkansas State Press*.

Bates was named Woman of the Year by the National Council of Negro Women in 1957. Along with the Little Rock Nine, Bates received the Spingarn Medal, the NAACP's highest award in 1958. During the yearlong struggle in Little Rock, Bates also became the friend of Dr. Martin Luther King Jr., and she subsequently was elected to the executive committee of the Southern Christian Leadership Conference. Bates would speak at the 1963 March on Washington.

In 1964, Bates moved to Washington, D.C., to work for the Democratic National Committee. She also served briefly in the administration of President Lyndon B. Johnson working on antipoverty programs. After suffering a stroke in 1965, she returned to Little Rock until 1968, when she and her husband moved to the small, rural, African American community of Mitchellville, where she established and became the director of the Mitchellville Office of Equal Opportunity Self-Help, a community service program. In 1980, after her husband's death, Bates returned to Little Rock and revived the *Arkansas State Press*. When her 1962 memoir *The Long Shadow of Little Rock* was republished in 1986, it became the first reprinted edition to receive an American Book Award. In recognition for her civil rights achievements, Arkansas named the third Monday in February George Washington's birthday and Daisy Gatson Bates Day. She died of a heart attack in Little Rock at the age of eighty-four.

Mary Breckinridge (1881–1965)
Public Health Activist

The founder of the Frontier Nursing Service, Mary Breckinridge was a pioneering advocate for American midwifery and for the establishment of neonatal and childhood medical care that dramatically reduced mortality rates of mothers and children.

She grew up in Washington, D.C., where her father was an Arkansas congressman, and in St. Petersburg, Russia, where he served as U.S. minister to Russia. She was educated in private schools in Lausanne, Switzerland, and Stamford, Connecticut.

After marrying Henry Ruffner in 1904, who died in 1906, Breckinridge earned a nursing degree from Saint Luke's Hospital School of Nursing in New York City in 1910. She married Richard Ryan Thompson in 1912. The couple had two children, but one was born prematurely and did not survive, and two years later, their son died of appendicitis. Breckinridge's husband was unfaithful, and they were divorced in 1920.

Breckinridge devoted herself to nursing to cope with the pain of her children's deaths and her divorce. She joined the American Committee for Devastated France in the aftermath of World War I, where she met French and British nurse-midwives, and realized that similarly trained nurses could meet the health care needs of rural America. She traveled to the Hebrides in Scotland in 1924 to observe models of health services in remote, rural areas. Since no midwifery course was then offered in the United States, Breckinridge received the training she needed at the British Hospital for Mothers and Babies. She returned to the United States in 1925, moved to Leslie County, Kentucky, and founded the Kentucky Committee for Mothers and Babies, which was renamed the Frontier Nursing Service. The introduction of nurse-midwives into the region brought its maternal and neonatal death rate well below the national average. Breckinridge directed the service, which led to the founding in 1929 of the American Association of Nurse-Midwives, and edited its journal while traveling around the country fundraising and promoting the Frontier Nurse Service. In 1939, she established the Frontier Graduate School of Midwifery, a training program for nurse-midwives.

Breckinridge continued to direct the Frontier Nursing Service until her death at the age of eighty-four. Her autobiography, *Wide Neighborhoods: A Story of the Frontier Nursing Service*, was published in 1952. The clinic that she first established in Kentucky still operates, now named the Mary Breckinridge Hospital. On her deathbed, Breckinridge commented on her achievement of spreading the benefits of innovative health care to remote areas of the United States: "The glorious thing about it is that it has worked!"

Ruby Bridges (1954–)

Civil Rights Activist

 In 1960, at the age of six, Ruby Bridges became the first African American student to integrate an all-white elementary school in the South. She would become an iconic symbol of the civil rights movement and its youngest activist.

The oldest of five siblings, Bridges was born into a farming family in Tylertown, Mississippi. When she was two years old, her parents moved to New Orleans, Louisiana. Her birth coincided with the U.S. Supreme Court's landmark ruling in *Brown v. the Board of Education*, which ended racial segregation in public schools. Southern states, however, continued to resist integration, and in 1959, Bridges attended a segregated New Orleans kindergarten. In 1960, a federal court ordered New Orleans to desegregate, and the school district created an entrance examination for African American students to see whether they could compete academically at the all-white school. Bridges and five other students passed the exam.

Her parents were conflicted about whether to let her attend the all-white William Frantz Elementary School, a few blocks from their home. Her father feared for his daughter's safety, while her mother wanted her to have the educational opportunities that her parents had been denied. Four federal marshals escorted Bridges and her mother to the school every day; mother and child walked past crowds screaming vicious slurs at them. She would later say that she was only frightened when she saw a woman holding a black baby doll in a coffin. The ardent segregationists pulled their children from the school, and only one of the white teachers, Boston native Barbara Henry, was willing to teach her. For the entire year, Bridges was in a class of one. She ate lunch alone and sometimes played with her teacher at recess, but she never missed a day of school that year. At Bridges's home, her father lost his job, and the grocery stores refused to sell to the family; her sharecropping grandparents were evicted. Eventually, though, others in the community, both black and white, began to show support; families gradually started to send their children back to the school, and the protests began to subside. A neighbor provided Bridges's father with a job, and others volunteered to watch the house as protectors. In Bridges's second year, Barbara Henry's contract was not renewed, the federal marshals were gone, and Bridges walked to school every day by herself. However, she had other African American students in her second-grade class, and the school began to see full enrollment again.

In 1964, artist Norman Rockwell celebrated Bridges's courage in a famous painting entitled *The Problem We All Live With*. Bridges graduated from a desegregated high school, became a travel agent, married, and had four sons. She reunited with her first teacher in the 1990s, and the pair did speaking engagements together. In 1993, Bridges began working as a parent liaison at her old elementary school, which had by that time become an all-black school. A lifelong activist for racial equality, in 1999, Bridges established The Ruby Bridges Foundation to promote tolerance and create change through education. She also published her memoir, *Through My Eyes* (1999). In 2011, Rockwell's painting, now part of the permanent collection of the Norman Rockwell Museum, was on display, at the request of President Barack Obama, in the West Wing of the White House for four months.

Tarana Burke (1973–)

Civil Rights Activist

 In 2006, Tarana Burke began using the phrase "me too" to raise awareness about the pervasiveness of sexual abuse and assault in society, and in 2017, use of the #MeToo hashtag on social media created a broader movement and a cultural phenomenon. Burke was named by *Time* magazine, among a group of other prominent activists, as "the silence breakers," making them the *Time* Persons of the Year for 2017.

She was born in the Bronx, New York, and grew up in a low-income, working-class family in a housing project. She experienced rape and sexual assault as a child and teenager. She has stated that the violence she experienced has inspired her to work to improve the lives of other victims of sexual abuse. She attended Alabama State University before transferring to and graduating from Auburn University.

After college, she began working in Selma, Alabama, with the 21st Century Youth Leadership Movement, the National Voting Rights Museum & Institute, and the Black Belt Arts and Cultural Center. In 2003, she cofounded Jendayi Aza, which became Just Be, Inc., a nonprofit, all-girls program for young, black teenagers. She coined the phrase "me too" while working at Just Be, Inc., in 2006 after hearing stories by victims of sexual abuse and was searching for the right words to express empathy with the young women and girls who disclosed their experiences to her. "Me too" was meant to express, "You are not alone. This happened to me, too." As Burke has described the expression, "On one side, it's a bold declarative statement that 'I'm not ashamed' and 'I'm not alone.' On the other side, it's a statement from survivor to survivor that says 'I see you, I hear you, I understand you and I'm here for you and I get it.'" Burke used the term to raise awareness of the pervasiveness of sexual abuse and assault.

The Me Too movement was transformed into #MeToo in 2017 when actress Alyssa Milano used the social media platform Twitter to invite those who have experienced sexual harassment, abuse, or assault to share their stories in order that "we might give people a sense of the magnitude of the problem." In the first 24 hours, the hashtag was shared in more than twelve million posts and reactions, and the #MeToo movement, connecting abuse survivors around the globe, had become a cultural phenomenon.

In 2018, Burke received the Prize for Courage from the Ridenhour Prizes, awarded to individuals who demonstrate courageous defense of the public interest and passionate commitment to social justice. Burke works as the senior director at Girls for Gender Equity and organizes workshops to help improve gender policies at schools and in the workplace. She continues to focus on helping victims of sexual violence as one of the core public faces of the #MeToo movement.

Septima Clark (1898–1987)
Civil Rights Activist

An educator and civil rights activist who developed the literacy and citizenship workshops that were crucial in the drive for voting rights for African Americans, Septima Clark was called by Martin Luther King Jr. "the mother of the movement." A schoolteacher for most of her life, Clark believed that education was the key to political power for African Americans. Her "citizenship schools," which combined the teaching of literacy and voting rights instruction, spread throughout the southeastern United States and motivated thousands of southern blacks to register to vote.

Clark was the second of eight children, born in Charleston, South Carolina. Her father was born a slave on the plantation of Joel Poinsette, a former U.S. ambassador to Mexico. Her mother grew up in Haiti. As Clark recalled, she learned patience from her father and courage from her mother, who "wasn't afraid of anyone." Both parents valued education above all, and she graduated from a private secondary school, the Avery Normal Institute in Charleston, which trained black educators in 1916.

Because Charleston's public schools barred African Americans from teaching, Clark began her career on isolated Johns Island, where she taught impoverished fourth through eighth graders to read and write in a one-room schoolhouse. She married a Navy seaman, Nerie Clark, in 1919. The couple's first child died in infancy; a son was born in 1925, but Clark's husband died shortly after. Teaching in segregated schools in various locations, she was able to earn a bachelor's degree from Benedict College in 1941 and a master's degree from Hampton Institute in 1946.

While teaching in Columbia, South Carolina, Clark began working with the National Association for the Advancement of Colored People (NAACP) to secure equal pay for black teachers, who usually received about half the salary of white teachers. She also taught informal literacy classes to adults while advocating education and equal rights in numerous organizations such as the Young Women's Christian Association (YWCA), the Federation of Women's Clubs, the Council of Negro Women, and the NAACP.

In the 1950s, Clark lost her job when the South Carolina legislature barred teachers from belonging to the NAACP. That prompted her to move in 1956 to the Highlander Folk School, an integrated school and social activism center in Tennessee. There, in 1957, Clark began opening her citizenship schools so that African Americans could meet the literacy requirements for voter registration. Her program was absorbed into the Southern Christian Leadership Conference (SCLC), and Clark traveled throughout the South training teachers for citizenship schools and assisting in SCLC marches and protests, working closely with Martin Luther King Jr. and Andrew Young. King acknowledged Clark's importance in the movement when he insisted that she accompany him to Sweden, where he was to receive the 1964 Nobel Peace Prize.

By 1970, Clark had helped to coordinate the registration of more than one million black voters. In the election of 1972, the first two African Americans from the South since Reconstruction were elected to Congress—Barbara Jordan of Texas and Andrew Young of Georgia. They, and the many who have followed them into elected office, owe a debt of gratitude to Clark's tireless efforts to extend the political power of African Americans.

Clark produced two autobiographies, *Echo in My Soul* (1962) and *Ready from Within* (1986). She retired from active SCLC work in 1970. She fought for and won reinstatement of the teaching position and back pay that had been canceled when she was dismissed in South Carolina in 1956. She later served two terms on the Charleston County School Board. When she died in 1987, Joseph E. Lowery, president of the SCLC, compared her to Harriet Tubman. Like Tubman, Lowery declared, "Septima Clark led her people to freedom through journeys from the darkness of illiteracy to the shining light of literacy."

Angela Davis (1944–)
Civil Rights Activist, Educator

A radical African American advocate on behalf of civil rights and other social issues, Angela Davis was perhaps the most notorious counterculture activist of the 1960s. She was a member of the Black Panther Party and the Communist Party of America, was twice a vice presidential candidate on the Communist Party ticket, and at one time was the third woman listed on the FBI's Ten Most Wanted Fugitive List.

Born in Birmingham, Alabama, the daughter of a service station-owner father and a schoolteacher mother, Davis lived in the "Dynamite Hill" neighborhood, so called because of all the bombings of houses intended to drive out middle-class blacks who lived there. She attended segregated local public schools. Her mother, Sallye Bell Davis, was a national leader and organizer of the Southern Negro Youth Congress, which was aimed at building alliances among African Americans in the South. Davis finished high school in New York's Greenwich Village and was awarded a scholarship to Brandeis University, one of only three black students in her class. She was influenced by philosopher Herbert Marcuse whom, Davis would say, "taught me that it was possible to be an academic, an activist, a scholar, and revolutionary." As a graduate student at the University of California–San Diego in the late 1960s, she joined several radical groups, including the Black Panthers and the Che-Lumumba Club, the all-black branch of the Communist Party.

In 1969, Davis joined the philosophy department at the University of California–Los Angeles; however, she was fired from her position because of her membership in the Communist Party. She went to court to get her job back but still left when her contract expired in 1970. Davis became a strong supporter of three prison inmates of Soledad Prison known as the Soledad Brothers, who were accused of killing a prison guard after several African American inmates had been killed in a fight with another guard. Suspected of complicity in an abortive escape and kidnapping at the Marin County courthouse involving George Jackson, one of the Soledad Brothers, Davis was a fugitive and finally was arrested in New York City in 1970 and returned to California to face charges of kidnapping, murder, and conspiracy. She was acquitted of all charges in 1972.

After a time traveling and lecturing, Davis returned to teaching as a professor of ethnic studies at San Francisco State University from 1980 to 1984

and as a professor of the history of consciousness and feminist studies at the University of California–Santa Cruz and Rutgers University from 1991 to 2008. She is the cofounder of Critical Resistance, an organization dedicated to the abolishing of the prison-industrial complex, and is the author of several books, including *Angela Davis: An Autobiography* (1974), *Women, Race, and Class* (1980), *Women, Culture and Politics* (1989), *Are Prisons Obsolete?* (2003), *Abolition Democracy* (2005), and *The Meaning of Freedom* (2012).

Dorothy Day (1897–1980)
Journalist, Social Activist

Called by New York's archbishop Cardinal Timothy M. Dolan "the saint for our times," radical Catholic social reformer Dorothy Day was the cofounder of the *Catholic Worker* newspaper and the leader of its activist movement. She is currently going through the process of canonization by the Catholic Church and was one of only four Americans mentioned by Pope Francis in his address to a joint meeting of the U.S. Congress along with Abraham Lincoln, Martin Luther King Jr., and Thomas Merton. He said of Day that "her social activism, her passion for justice and for the cause of the oppressed, were inspired by the Gospel, her faith, and the example of the saints."

She was born in Brooklyn, New York. Her father, a sportswriter, took a position with a newspaper in San Francisco and moved her family, which included three brothers and a sister, to Oakland, California, in 1904. The San Francisco Earthquake of 1906 destroyed the newspaper's facilities, and her father lost his job. The family relocated to Chicago. Day's family was Episcopalian but rarely attended church. She, on the other hand, began to attend church regularly in Chicago, studied the catechism, and was taken with the liturgy and sacred music. She also was an avid reader, particularly socially conscious works. In 1914, she attended the University of Illinois–Urbana-Champaign on a scholarship, but she left after two years and moved to New York City.

She lived on the Lower East Side and worked on the staff of several socialist publications, including *The Liberator*, *The Masses*, and *The Call*, and became a member of the Industrial Workers of the World (IWW). Day lived a bohemian life with relationships with playwright Eugene O'Neill and writer Mike Gold. She worked briefly as a nurse and continued in journalism in Chicago and New Orleans. In 1927, after years of doubt and indecision, she joined the Roman Catholic Church, an act that estranged her from her earlier radical associates.

In 1933, influenced by French-born Catholic Peter Maurin, who had developed a program of social reconstruction and the establishment of houses of hospitality to serve the urban poor, now called the Catholic Worker Movement, Day established the *Catholic Worker*, a monthly newspaper to spread the movement's message of social and personal transformation. Within three years, the paper's circulation had grown to 150,000, and the original St. Joseph's House of Hospitality in New York City had served as the model for similar houses in a number of cities. Day contributed articles about the conditions of poor people and especially about the conditions of workers and the labor movement.

In the 1940s, Day's opposition to war and her pacifist stand during the Spanish Civil War divided supporters of the movement and intensified during World War II. Day was one of the few Catholic voices who opposed the war. Opposition to Day escalated, and in 1951, Day was ordered by the Archdiocese of New York to remove the word "Catholic" from the name of her publication. She respectfully declined. Day continued her advocacy and opposition to war, speaking out against the Vietnam War and support for the work of Cesar Chavez in organizing California farm laborers. Day's autobiography, *The Long Loneliness*, was published in 1952. Active as a speaker and at demonstrations, Day suffered a heart attack and died at the St. Joseph's House of Hospitality at the age of eighty-three. During her life, Dorothy Day refused to let people "dismiss her as a saint." She spurned the suggestion that she was a saint but took seriously the importance of becoming one: in her lifelong dedication to spirituality and social welfare.

Dorothea Dix (1802–1887)

Mental Health Reformer

 A humanitarian and tireless crusader for the mentally ill, Dorothea Dix was a pioneer in American health care reform who laid the foundation for the establishment of separate facilities for people with mental illnesses. When she began her work in 1841, only thirteen mental asylums existed in the United States. By 1880, largely because of Dix's efforts, that number had increased to 123.

Dix was born in the frontier village of Hampden, Maine, at that time still part of the state of Massachusetts. After caring for her invalid mother and helping to raise her two younger brothers, at the age of twelve, Dix was sent to the Boston area to live with relatives. Mainly self-educated, Dix was a serious student with an aptitude for teaching, and at the age of fourteen, she opened a school for young children. Despite poor health brought on by overwork, she continued as a schoolmistress in the 1820s and 1830s. She also authored an elementary school science textbook and devotional works expressing her deep religious beliefs.

A crucial episode in her life occurred in 1841 when she was asked to teach a Sunday school class for women in a jail in East Cambridge, Massachusetts. There, she was appalled to find mentally ill women kept alongside criminals in foul, unheated cells. Angered by their jailer's contention that "lunatics" did not feel the cold, Dix persuaded the local court to order changes, and the women's quarters were improved. Dix next began to investigate the treatment of the mentally ill throughout Massachusetts. She presented her findings to the state legislature, arguing that the mentally ill should be freed from physical restraints and cared for in facilities separate from criminals. Her findings provoked the legislature into appropriating the funds to create state facilities for the humane care of the mentally ill. Dix then took her cause to neighboring states and succeeded in getting additional asylums open, including the first mental hospital in New Jersey, in Trenton. Dix later called that facility "my first-born child." Between 1844 and 1847, she traveled more than thirty thousand miles around the country investigating conditions for the mentally ill and lobbying for changes. As a result of this work, she was directly involved in the establishment of thirty-two state mental hospitals throughout the United States.

During the Civil War, Dix became superintendent of nurses for the U.S. Army. She helped to recruit and train thousands of nurses, and her development of the Army Nursing Corps helped to establish women as health care providers. She remained chief of nurses until 1866, when she resumed her work to reform prisons and hospitals, until her retirement in 1881, when she moved to the New Jersey State Hospital in Trenton that she had helped to create. She was designated by the state legislature a suite for her private use as long as she lived.

Marian Wright Edelman (1939–)

Children's Rights Activist

 Founder of the Children's Defense Fund, Marian Wright Edelman has been a tireless and committed advocate for the disadvantaged and powerless over her entire long career fighting for social justice.

She was born in Bennettsville, South Carolina, the youngest of five children. She credits her minister father with instilling in her an obligation to right wrongs. When African Americans in Bennettsville were not allowed to enter city parks, her father built a park for them behind his church. She attended Marlboro Training High School in Bennettsville, graduating in 1956. She attended Spelman College, the prominent institution for black women in Atlanta, Georgia, and received a scholarship to study abroad, which took her to Paris, Switzerland, and the Soviet Union. She planned to pursue a career in foreign service, but the 1960s civil rights movement drew her in to its activities. She participated in and was arrested at sit-ins in Atlanta in 1960, the same year she entered Yale Law School. She received her law degree in 1963.

After graduation, Wright worked for the National Association for the Advancement of Colored People (NAACP) Legal Defense Fund before moving to Jackson, Mississippi, to work on voter registration drives for the NAACP. She became the first African American woman to be admitted to the Mississippi Bar. In 1964, she represented civil rights activists during the Freedom Summer voting campaign. After being hired as a lawyer for the Child Development Group in Mississippi and successfully lobbying for the restoration of federal funds for the Mississippi Head Start programs, she identified her central mission to fight for children's interests.

In 1967, she met Peter Benjamin Edelman, an assistant to New York senator Robert Kennedy, while he was touring the Mississippi Delta. They married in 1968. Edelman relocated to Washington, D.C., to begin their family, which eventually included three sons. In 1968, she created the Washington Research Project for the Southern Center for Policy Research to lobby for, and assist, children in poverty. In 1971, *Time* magazine named her one of the top two hundred young leaders of America, and in 1973, Edelman launched the Children's Defense Fund (CDF) to help children stay healthy, stay in school, and avoid teenage pregnancy as well as to prevent childhood abuse and drug abuse. It quickly became the leading advocacy group for children. As its leader and principal spokesperson, Edelman has worked to persuade the U.S. Congress to overhaul foster care, support adoption, improve childcare, and extend protections of children who are disabled, homeless, abused, or neglected.

In 2018, Edelman stepped down as president of the CDF after forty-five years at its helm. She is the author of several books, including *Families in Peril: An Agenda for Social Change* (1987), *The Measure of Success: A Letter to My Children and Yours* (1992), *I'm Your Child, God: Prayers for Children and Teenagers* (2002), and *The Sea Is So Wide and My Boat Is So Small: Charting a Course for the Next Generation* (2008). In 2000, President Bill Clinton awarded her the Medal of Freedom, the highest civilian honor given in the United States. She has also received the Albert Schweitzer Prize for Humanitarianism and a MacArthur "Genius" Award.

Myrlie Evers-Williams (1933–)

Civil Rights Activist

The first woman to head the National Association for the Advancement of Colored People (NAACP), Myrlie Evers-Williams has been a tireless civil rights activist seeking justice for the 1963 murder of her husband Medgar Evers.

She was born Myrlie Louise Beasley in Vicksburg, Mississippi. Her parents separated when she was one year old, and she was raised by her grandmother and aunt, both schoolteachers. In 1950, she enrolled at Alcorn A&M College, one of the few colleges in Mississippi that accepted African American students. On her first day at school, she met and fell in love with World War II veteran Medgar Evers. The couple married in 1951 and began a family of three children. During their marriage, Myrlie Evers worked as a secretary in a life insurance company.

In 1954, Medgar Evers became the Mississippi field secretary for the NAACP, and she became his secretary and fellow organizer of voter registration drives and civil rights demonstrations. For more than a decade, husband and wife campaigned for voting rights, equal access to public accommodations, and the desegregation of the University of Mississippi. They became high-profile targets for violence, and in 1962, their home in Jackson was firebombed. In 1963, Medgar Evers was shot to death in front of their home. A white supremacist, Byron De La Beckwith was initially tried for the murder but was released as a result of a hung jury (Beckwith would be retried a third time in 1994 and finally was convicted and sentenced to life in prison). Evers was relentless in her efforts to see her husband's killer brought to justice.

Left a widow with three children, Evers relocated to California, published the memoir *For Us, the Living* (1967), earned a degree in sociology at Pomona College (1968), and made an unsuccessful run for election to the U.S. Congress (1970). She married Walter Williams in 1976, and in 1987, she was named to the Los Angeles Board of Public Works, a position she served until 1991. She remained active on the NAACP board, becoming chairperson in 1995. She left the position in 1998 and founded the Medgar Evers Institute (later the Medgar and Myrlie Evers Institute) in Jackson, Mississippi. Her autobiography, *Watch Me Fly*, appeared in 1999. In 2013, she delivered the invocation at the second inauguration of Barack Obama, the first woman and the first layperson ever to deliver the invocation at a presidential inauguration.

Emma Goldman (1869–1940)

Political Activist

It was once said of Emma Goldman that she was born to ride a whirlwind. This is an apt description of a woman who, as an anarchist, radical feminist, and advocate of birth control, free love, and free speech, agitated more fiercely and deliberately stirred up more controversy than any other social or political activist of her day. "Red Emma," as she was popularly known, was reviled and scorned for her radicalism. A consummate rebel, she fought for freedom of the individual at a time when conformity and blind obedience was becoming paramount.

Born in the Jewish ghetto of Kovno, Russia, Goldman immigrated to Rochester, New York, in 1885 to escape an arranged marriage. She went to work in a clothing sweatshop, where she earned $2.50 a week and became appalled at the terrible treatment of the workers. The experience made her distrust the capitalist system, and she became an activist in the anarchist movement, which promoted social equality without government interference.

In 1889, Goldman moved to New York City, where she met Alexander Berkman, a Russian émigré anarchist who became her longtime lover. In 1893, she was sentenced to a one-year prison term for inciting a group of unemployed workers in New York's Union Square to riot. In prison, she studied nursing, and after her release, she studied midwifery and nursing in Vienna for a year. During the first years of the twentieth century, she renounced calls for violence, especially after she learned that Leon Czolgosz, who assassinated President McKinley in 1901, claimed to have been inspired by her activities. For the next several years, Goldman traveled around the country lecturing on anarchism, social equality and justice, and workers' and women's rights. She was also one of the first to speak out publicly about women's reproductive rights, and she greatly influenced Margaret Sanger, who is credited with founding the birth control movement in the United States.

In 1917, Goldman was sentenced to two years in federal prison for speaking out against the draft during World War I. Upon her release, the U.S. government deported her to Russia. There, despite her socialist and communist sympathies, she became an outspoken critic of the Bolsheviks' suppression of civil liberties after they transformed Russia into the Soviet Union. In 1921, Goldman went to Sweden and then to Germany, where she condemned totalitarianism in newspaper articles and in her book, *My Disillusionment with Russia* (1923). In 1931, she published her autobiography, *Living My Life.*

During the Spanish Civil War (1936–1939), Goldman worked tirelessly for the doomed Republican cause against the fascist forces led by General Francisco Franco. In 1940, after she suffered a fatal stroke, the U.S. government allowed her body to be returned home for burial in a Chicago cemetery. Regarded during her life as "the most dangerous woman in America," Goldman had a lifelong uncompromising commitment to social equality and justice. Despite her controversial activities, as one historian stated, she "had lived to the end of a life of unique integrity." Goldman would be "rediscovered" by political activists and feminists in the 1960s and 1970s and is now admired and valued for significantly influencing and broadening the scope of activism on issues of gender and freedom of expression.

Temple Grandin (1947–)

Autism Advocate, Scientist

Temple Grandin is one of the first individuals on the autism spectrum to share her personal experience of autism. She first gained national attention when she was profiled in Oliver Sacks's 1995 book *An Anthropologist on Mars* (the title refers to Grandin's description of how she feels in social settings). Grandin first spoke publicly about autism in the 1980s at the request of one of the founders of the Autism Society of America. She has since become an influential and eloquent advocate for the autistic community and on behalf of the humane treatment of animals.

Born in Boston into a wealthy family, Grandin was the oldest of the four children of her father, a real estate agent and heir to the largest corporate wheat farm business in America at that time, Grandin Farms, and an actress-singer mother. Grandin was never formally diagnosed with autism but with "brain damage" at the age of two. Grandin did not begin to speak until the age of four. When she was in her teens, her mother saw a checklist on autism created by Dr. Bernard Rimland, founder of the Autism Research Institute, and thought that Grandin's symptoms indicated autism. A formal diagnosis consistent with being on the autism spectrum was only carried out when Grandin was in her forties.

To treat her condition of "brain damage," Grandin worked with a speech therapist, and a nanny was hired to play educational games with her. She was able to attend a supportive kindergarten and elementary school; she was expelled from her private high school for throwing a book at a schoolmate who taunted her. After her expulsion, Grandin's parents divorced, and she spent a summer on an Arizona ranch that would prove formative in her subsequent career interest of animal science. She was sent to a private boarding school for children with behavioral problems, where she met science teacher William Carlock, who would become an important mentor figure. Carlock gave Grandin the idea to build herself a "hug box," a device to calm herself, which Grandin later shared with others on the autism spectrum. Encouraged by Carlock in her academic potential, Grandin went on to earn a bachelor's degree in psychology from Franklin Pierce College in 1970, a master's degree in animal science from Arizona in 1975, and a doctoral degree in animal science from the University of Illinois–Urbana-Champaign in 1989. She then worked as a consultant to livestock companies, advising them on ways to improve the quality of life of their cattle. Grandin is the author of numerous scientific papers on animal behavior and has lectured widely on animal welfare. "I think using animals for food is an ethical thing to do," she has said, "but we've got to do it right. We've got to give those animals a decent life, and we've got to give them a painless death. We owe the animals respect."

As a high-functioning autistic person, Grandin has articulated her experiences to increase understanding both for those dealing with autism and the general public. She advocates early intervention, including teacher training, to address autistic children's specific fixations. She is also a champion of "neurodiversity" and opposes the notion of a comprehensive cure for autism, arguing that her contributions to the field of animal welfare would not have been possible without the insights and sensitivities that are a consequence of her autism.

In 2010, she was selected for the Time 100, an annual list of the one hundred most influential people in the world. She was the subject of the Emmy- and Golden Globe-winning biographical film *Temple Grandin.*

Fannie Lou Hamer (1917–1977)

Civil Rights Activist

 A grassroots activist for civil rights and voting rights, Fannie Lou Hamer worked to desegregate the Democratic Party in Mississippi by cofounding the Mississippi Freedom Democratic Party (MFDP). She also organized Mississippi's Freedom Summer and was a cofounder of the National Women's Political Caucus.

Born Fannie Lou Townsend in Montgomery County, Mississippi, she was the last of the twenty children of her sharecropper parents. She grew up in poverty and, at the age of six, joined her family picking cotton. From 1924 through 1930, she attended a one-room school for sharecroppers' children, open between picking seasons. At the age of twelve, she left school to support her aging parents. By the age of thirteen, she could pick between two hundred and three hundred pounds of cotton daily, despite having a leg disfigured by polio.

In 1944, she married a tractor driver, Perry Hamer, and the couple labored on a Mississippi plantation until 1962. Because Hamer was the only worker who could read and write, she also served as the plantation timekeeper. In 1961, Hamer received a hysterectomy by a white doctor without her consent while undergoing surgery to remove a uterine tumor. Such forced sterilization of black women was so widespread at the time, it was called a "Mississippi appendectomy." Unable to have children of her own, the Hamers adopted two daughters.

In 1962, Hamer became a Student Nonviolent Coordinating Committee (SNCC) organizer and led a group to register to vote at the Indianola Mississippi Courthouse. Denied due to an unfair literacy test, the group was harassed on their way home, stopped by police, and fined $100 because the bus they were in was "too yellow." In addition, Hamer was fired by the plantation owner she worked for, and much of the Hamers' property was confiscated. In 1963, after successfully registering to vote, Hamer and several other black women were arrested for sitting in a "whites-only" bus station restaurant in Charleston, South Carolina. At the jailhouse, she was brutally beaten, leaving her with lifelong injuries from a blood clot in her eye and kidney and leg damage.

In 1964, Hamer cofounded the Mississippi Freedom Democratic Party to challenge the local Democratic Party's ban on black participation. Hamer and other MFDP members went to the Democratic National Convention, where Hamer called for mandatory integrated state delegation. By 1968, racial parity in delegations became a reality, and Hamer was a member of Mississippi's first integrated delegation. Also, in 1964, Hamer helped organize Freedom Summer, which brought hundreds of college students to help with African American voter registration. She also announced her candidacy for the Mississippi House of Representatives but was barred from the ballot. A year later, Hamer, Victoria Gray, and Annie Devine became the first black women to stand in the U.S. Congress when they protested the Mississippi House election of 1964.

In the late 1960s, Hamer turned her attention from politics to economics in pursuit of greater racial equality. In 1968, she began a "pig bank" to provide free pigs to black farmers to breed, raise, and slaughter. In 1969, she launched the Freedom Farm Cooperative, which bought land that blacks could own and farm collectively. She supervised the building of two hundred units of low-income housing. In 1971, Hamer cofounded the National Women's Political Caucus to empower women to exercise their political power as a voting majority.

Extensive travel and past health issues took a toll. In 1972, Hamer was hospitalized for nervous exhaustion, and in 1974, she suffered a nervous breakdown. She died in 1977 of complications of hypertension and breast cancer at the age of fifty-nine. Her tombstone is engraved with one of her most famous statements: "I am sick and tired of being sick and tired."

LaDonna Harris (1931–)

Native American Activist

LaDonna Harris, a member of the Comanche Nation, is the founder and president of Americans for Indian Opportunity (AIO) and has been an outspoken and influential advocate for civil rights, women's rights, and world peace. In 1980, she was a vice presidential candidate in the Citizen's Party and in 2018 was among the first inductees in the National Native American Hall of Fame.

Harris is of mixed-race heritage. Her father was a white Irish American, her mother a Comanche. Her father left her mother in part because of the constant hostility they faced as a racially mixed couple. She was raised by her grandparents on a farm near the small town of Walters, Oklahoma. Until the age of six, Harris spoke only the Comanche language. In high school, she met Fred Harris, whom she married and helped put through college and law school before he was elected first to the Oklahoma Senate and then to the U.S. Senate. The couple had three children.

After his election to the Senate in 1965, she began to extend the concerns of the civil rights movement on behalf of Native Americans, working with members from sixty tribes to set goals for both economic priorities and civil rights. In Washington, Har-

ris became involved with the National Rural Housing Conference, the National Association of Mental Health, the National Committee against Discrimination in Housing, and the National Steering Committee of the Urban Coalition, which she chaired. In 1967, President Lyndon Johnson appointed her to lead the National Women's Advisory Council for the War on Poverty and named Harris the president of the newly created National Council on Indian Opportunity.

In the 1970s, Harris became a founding member of the National Women's Political Caucus and founded the Americans for Indian Opportunity. She also lobbied on behalf of the mentally ill and traveled to Latin America, Africa, and the Soviet Union as a representative of the Inter-American Indigenous Institute on behalf of world peace. In the 1980s and 1990s, Harris remained active with the AIO as its director. As she has stated, "AIO's greatest contribution to tribes and communities has always been how we organized people around important issues to find solutions that restore ownership back to the community." Over a lifetime of public service and activism, LaDonna Harris has served that community.

Dorothy Height (1912–2010)

Civil Rights Activist, Women's Rights Activist

One of the most influential and important leaders of both the civil rights and women's rights movements, Dorothy Height was for four decades the president of the National Council of Negro Women.

She was born in Richmond, Virginia, but her family moved to the steel town of Rankin, Pennsylvania, when she was five years old. She attended integrated public schools there and graduated from Rankin High School in 1929 while becoming active in antilynching campaigns. She won a college scholarship in a national oratory competition and was admitted to Barnard College but was denied entrance because the school had an unwritten policy of only admitting two black students per year. Instead, she enrolled at New York University, earning her undergraduate degree in 1932 and a master's in educational psychology in 1933. She went to work as a social worker in New York City and served as assistant executive director of the Harlem YWCA. This led to her advocacy for improved conditions for black domestic workers, her election to the national office of the YWCA, and her fight to change its integration policy. In 1957, she became the fourth president of the National Council of Negro Women (NCNW), steering the organization through the civil rights struggles of 1960s by organizing voter registration in the South, voter education in the North, and scholarship programs for student civil rights workers.

Height is credited with being the first leader of the civil rights movement to connect the inequality of women and African Americans as a linked concern. As president of the NCNW, she helped organize the March on Washington in 1963 and worked with every civil rights leader of the period, including Dr. Martin Luther King Jr., Roy Wilkins, Whitney Young, and A. Philip Randolph. She also lobbied President Dwight Eisenhower to desegregate public schools and urged President Lyndon Johnson to appoint black women into governmental positions. In 1971, she joined Gloria Steinem, Shirley Chisholm, Betty Friedan, and others to create the National Women's Political Caucus.

She died at the age of ninety-eight, having received the Presidential Medal of Freedom in 1994 and been recognized by Barnard College as an honorary alumna in 2004. At her funeral in Washington's National Cathedral, President Barack Obama called her a godmotherlike figure and hero to countless Americans through her lifetime dedicated to fighting for civil rights and women's rights. "I want to be remembered," Height had earlier said, "as someone who used herself and anything she could touch to work for justice and freedom. I want to be remembered as one who tried."

Anita Hill (1956–)
Attorney, Educator

 In 1991, lawyer and academic Anita Hill became a national figure when she accused U.S. Supreme Court nominee Clarence Thomas, her supervisor at the U.S. Department of Education and the Equal Employment Opportunity Commission, of sexual harassment. Perhaps more than any other individual, Anita Hill became both a lightning rod and test case for dealing with (and surviving) sexual harassment.

The youngest of thirteen children, Anita Hill grew up on a farm in Lone Tree, Oklahoma. She studied psychology at Oklahoma State University, earning a bachelor's degree in 1977, and earned a law degree from Yale University in 1980. She was admitted to the District of Columbia Bar in 1980 and went to work for a prominent D.C. law firm.

In 1981, she became an attorney-adviser to Clarence Thomas, who was then the assistant secretary of the U.S. Department of Education's Office for Civil Rights. When Thomas became chairman of the U.S. Equal Employment Opportunity Commission in 1982, Hill served as his assistant before leaving the job in 1983. She joined the faculty of the law school at Oral Roberts University from 1983 to 1986 before teaching commercial law and contracts at the University of Oklahoma College of Law, where she became its first tenured African American professor in 1989.

At the confirmation hearings for Clarence Thomas to replace Thurgood Marshall on the Supreme Court in 1991, Hill testified before the Senate Judiciary Committee recounting Thomas's alleged sexual harassment. The hearings were televised, and Hill was questioned by the all-male committee with several senators accusing her of lying and being delusional or worse. Thomas denied the allegations, accusing the committee of "a high-tech lynching." Other women who could have supported Hill's testimony were never called by the committee, and, in the end, Thomas was narrowly confirmed 52–48.

Hill became a polarizing figure with some believing that she was simply a scorned woman or an attention seeker and others finding her treatment by the Senate committee demeaning and sexist. The scandal motivated a number of women to enter politics, and 1992 became known as the "Year of the Woman" when a historic number of women were elected to Congress. Hill's testimony was also credited with raising awareness of workplace sexual harassment and the ways in which it needed to be handled. Following Hill's accusations, President George H. W. Bush dropped his opposition to a bill that gave harassment victims the right to seek federal damage awards, back pay, and reinstatement, and the law was passed by Congress. A year after the hearing, harassment complaints filed with the EEOC were up 50 percent, and companies started training programs to deter sexual harassment.

Hill remained on the faculty at Oklahoma University, amid calls for her resignation in 1992, until she resigned in 1996. In 1998, she joined the faculty at Brandeis University. She published her autobiography, *Speaking Truth to Power* (1997), and *Reimagining Equality: Stories of Gender, Race, and Finding a Home* (2011). She has spoken out on issues of gender and race on numerous television programs and in articles. Hill's story was dramatized in the 2016 HBO film *Confirmation*.

Coretta Scott King (1927–2006)

Civil Rights Activist

Although she is best known as the wife of famed civil rights leader Martin Luther King Jr., Coretta Scott King deserves credit for her own contributions to the cause of racial justice and as an unflagging preserver of her husband's legacy for almost four decades. She took over the leadership of the civil rights movement after her husband's assassination and broadened the scope of her activism to include opposition to apartheid and LGBT rights.

She was born in Marion, Alabama. Her great-grandmother, a former slave, presided at her birth as a midwife. Her mother was known for her musical talent and singing voice, and her daughter shared both her mother's interest and talent in music. She attended a one-room elementary school and was bussed with the other local black teenagers to the closest black high school nine miles from home by her mother. She became the leading soprano in her school, played trumpet and piano, and sang in the chorus. She went on to receive her bachelor's degree in music at Antioch College, where she was one of only three African American female students. In 1951, she won a scholarship to further her music studies at the New England Conservatory of Music in Boston. There, she met Boston University doctoral student Martin Luther King Jr. They began dating and were married in 1953.

After graduating from the conservatory in 1954, the couple moved to Montgomery, Alabama, where King took a position as the pastor of the Dexter Avenue Baptist Church. The church and the Kings' home would become centers for the civil rights movement as well as targets for white supremacists. Throughout the civil rights struggle, she appeared side by side with her husband as well as openly criticizing the movement's exclusion of women in leadership positions.

Following her husband's assassination in Memphis in 1968, she continued to support various causes, marching in a labor strike only days after King's funeral. She was an outspoken opponent of the Vietnam War and was placed under FBI surveillance for several years. She traveled internationally lecturing about racism and economic issues and supporting several women's rights causes. In 1969, she published her memoirs, *My Life with Martin Luther King, Jr.* She established the King Center to advance and preserve her husband's legacy and campaigned for the federal holiday in his honor, which was signed into law in 1983.

King was the recipient of many honors and awards, among them a medal from the American Library Association named for her in 1970, which is awarded to outstanding African American writers and illustrators of children's literature; a Candace Award for Distinguished Service from the National Coalition of 100 Black Women; the prestigious Gandhi Peace Prize by the government of India in 2004; and the creation of the Coretta Scott King Forest in the Galilee region of northern Israel to perpetuate "her memory of equality and peace." Mourners at her funeral included four former U.S. presidents, one sitting president, and one future president (Barack Obama) as well as members of the Gay and Lesbian Task Force, the Human Rights

Campaign, the National Black Justice Coalition, and representatives from Antioch College. The first African American to lie in state in the Georgia State Capitol, Coretta Scott King was eulogized as the "first lady of the civil rights movement."

Maggie Kuhn (1905–1995)
Elder Rights Activist

Founder of the Gray Panthers movement, Maggie Kuhn dedicated her life to fighting for human rights, social and economic justice, and world peace, becoming best known in the last three decades of her life for her leadership in bringing about nursing home reform, the prohibition of forced retirement, and exposing health care fraud.

Born in Buffalo, New York, Kuhn lived in Cleveland, Ohio, from 1916 until 1930. She attended the Western Reserve University's College for Women in Cleveland and traces the origin of her activism to her college days. "I think it began with my sociology courses," she recalled. "Sociology, for me, related the community to the individual, and showed us a way to act responsibly in groups." After graduation, she went to work with Cleveland's Young Women's Christian Association, where she remained for eleven years. She said that at the time, the YWCA was "the foremost advocate for working women. The women in the Y in those days were wonderfully radical. They were all socialists. They influenced me profoundly." In 1930, she moved to Philadelphia, working with the organization there, and in 1941, she transferred to the New York City YWCA. There, she studied social work and theology at Columbia University's Teachers' College and the Union Theological Seminary. At the YWCA, she organized educational and social activities for young, working-class women. In 1950, she took an executive position with the Presbyterian Church (U.S.A.) and edited its journal, *Social Progress*, which urged Presbyterians to get involved with social issues.

In 1970, after twenty years on the job and seven months before her sixty-fifth birthday, Kuhn was asked to retire. "Truthfully, in those years I didn't think of myself as about to enter the ranks of the nation's old," she said. "I was just me—neither young, old, nor middle-aged. I had never given re-

tirement much thought." Feeling dazed and hurt, she remembered, "Instead of sinking into despair, I did what came most naturally to me: I telephoned some friends and called a meeting." Each of the six women she called was also being forced into retirement. "We had no responsibility to a corporation or organization," Kuhn stated. "We could take risks, speak out. We said, 'With this new freedom we have, let's see what we can do to change the world.'"

At first, they called their organization the Consultation of Older and Younger Adults for Social Change, but the group was dubbed the Gray Panthers by a talk show host after the radical African American organization the Black Panthers. The name caught on, and they gained their first national recognition in 1971 by organizing a "black house conference" to protest the lack of African American representatives at the first White House Conference on Aging. The organization, under Kuhn's leadership, grew to 120 local networks in thirty-eight states by 1979 with more chapters across the globe. The Gray Panthers anticipated many of the issues regarding aging in America well before they would emerge nationally such as the health care crisis and homelessness. They also fought for the abolition of forced retirement and for programs in which older workers could share their expertise with younger workers.

One of the most radical social activists of the last three decades of the twentieth century, Maggie Kuhn remained both committed to the cause and vocal in her advocacy well into her eighties. In a 1979 article for *Quest* magazine, writer Garson Kanin wrote of Kuhn: "Those who fired her, fired her into the social atmosphere in the manner of a space missile, propelling her into fame and usefulness and glory."

Juliette Gordon Low (1860–1927)
Founder of Girl Scouts of America

In 1912, Juliette Gordon Low founded what would become the United States' preeminent national organization solely for girls. Later renamed the Girl Scouts of the USA, the organization focused on preparing girls to empower themselves by encouraging such individual and collective values as compassion, confidence, character, leadership, and active citizenship through its various scouting activities.

Born Juliette Gordon into a wealthy and accomplished family in Savannah, Georgia, Low was the second oldest of the six children of William Washington Gordon II, who was a Confederate captain during the Civil War and later served as a diplomat during the Spanish–American War. Low's mother, Nellie, was an unconventional woman with artistic and musical talent and a penchant for sliding down banisters in the family home. Juliette Gordon, nicknamed "Daisy" as a child, attended a Virginia boarding school operated by the granddaughters of Thomas Jefferson and concluded her schooling at an exclusive finishing school in New York.

In 1886, Low married William Low, the son of a wealthy cotton merchant. The couple moved to England, where they enjoyed a life among the British and European aristocracy. The marriage lasted until William Low's death in 1905, but it was an unhappy one with divorce discussed but never acted upon. When Low died, his wife was shocked to learn that he had left the bulk of his estate to his mistress. Juliette Low contested the will and regained $500,000, which she would later use to finance the Girl Scouts.

Low traveled extensively after her husband's death looking for some direction in her life. In 1911, while in England, she met British military hero Robert Baden-Powell and his sister, Agnes, who had founded the Boy Scouts and Girl Guides. Inspired by the Baden-Powells' work in scouting, Low organized her own troop of Girl Guides in Scotland before bringing the movement to the United States. On March 12, 1912, in Savannah, Low registered her teenage niece Daisy Gordon as the first Girl Guide in the United States. The first troop consisted of eighteen girls, who formed two patrols named the Carnation and the White Rose. In 1913, the name of the organization was changed from Girl Guides to Girl Scouts. The same year saw the first African American members of the Girl Scouts in New Bedford, Massachusetts. The first all-African American Girl Scout troops were established in 1917. However, because Low feared that an official position on the inclusion of African American girls as scouts would make southern troops quit the organization, Girl Scout troops were slow to form in the South until the 1930s and 1940s. By the 1950s, a national effort to desegregate all Girl Scout troops began.

Originally outfitted in dark blue middy blouses, skirts, and a light blue tie, the early scouts pursued badges in such diverse areas as telegraphy, farming, and electrical work. The first Girl Scout handbook featured practical advice such as how to secure a burglar with six inches of cord as well as information on subjects like ecology, organic foods, and career opportunities for women. Low paid all the expenses of the organization until 1917, when she traveled throughout the country recruiting prominent women as sponsors and leaders of Girl Scout troops.

During World War I, the Girl Scouts helped the war effort by working in hospitals, staffing railroad station canteens for trains that transported soldiers, growing vegetables, and selling war bonds. Under Low's leadership, their record of leadership and service established the Girl Scouts as a national organization, which resulted in a significant expansion of membership. By 1927, the year of Low's death, membership in the Girl Scouts had reached nearly 168,000, and by the start of the twenty-first century, membership numbered 3.5 million, making the Girl Scouts of the USA the largest voluntary organization for girls and young women in the world.

Low began the Girl Scouts with the belief that intellectual, physical, and moral strength were as important to the development of girls as learning the skills that would make them good wives, homemakers, and mothers. In the more than one hundred years since its founding, the Girl Scouts have kept to many of Low's beliefs while evolving with the times.

Wilma Mankiller (1945–2010)

Native American Activist

In 1985, Wilma Mankiller became the first female chief of a major American Indian tribe when she was elected chief of the Cherokee Nation. Overcoming many personal hardships, Mankiller devoted her career to improving the conditions of her people and changing American society's perceptions of Native Americans, especially women.

Born Wilma Pearl Mankiller in Tahlequah, Oklahoma, the capital of the Cherokee Nation, she spent her early years on her family's farm. Her great-grandfather was one of thousands of Cherokees forcibly removed from their lands in the Southeastern United States in the 1830s, forced to walk to the new "Indian territory" in Oklahoma along what became known as the Trail of Tears because of the death of at least four thousand people, a quarter of those who departed. Many more perished after arriving in Oklahoma as they tried to build new lives, poorly supplied in a rugged terrain.

Mankiller experienced her own version of the Trail of Tears when, at the age of eleven, she and her family were forced off their land by financial hardship, and, with aid from the U.S. government, they relocated to San Francisco. "I learned through this ordeal," she recalled, "about the fear and anguish that occur when you give up your home, your community, and everything you have ever known to move far away to a strange place. I cried for days, not unlike the children who had stumbled down the Trail of Tears so many years before. I wept tears … tears from my history, from my tribe's past. They were Cherokee tears."

Adjusting to life in San Francisco, Mankiller experienced cultural shock and endured taunts from her schoolmates over her last name. She finished high school and took a job as a clerk. She married Hector Hugo Olaya de Bardi in 1963, and they had two daughters. She settled into the role of wife and mother, but the social protests of the 1960s led her to a political awakening, particularly about the mistreatment of Native Americans by the U.S.

government, when Native Americans in 1969 occupied the abandoned prison of Alcatraz to call attention to their cause. "Alcatraz articulated my own feelings about being an Indian," she wrote in her autobiography.

In 1976, she moved back to Oklahoma to help create projects to improve housing and social services for the Cherokees. Her administrative skills attracted the attention of tribal leader Ross Swimmer, who asked Mankiller to serve as his running mate in the 1983 election for principal chief and deputy chief. She overcame the objections of some male tribal members, who insisted that a woman would not be a suitable leader, and she became the Cherokee Nation's first female deputy chief in 1985. When Swimmer was nominated to become the head of the Bureau of Indian Affairs, Mankiller was sworn in to replace him as principal chief of the Cherokee Nation. She would be elected to the post in her own right in 1987, the same year *Ms.* magazine named Mankiller its Woman of the Year.

As chief, she focused on education and health care, oversaw the construction of new schools, job-training centers, and health clinics. She also fostered a new spirit of independence and self-confidence within the Cherokee Nation. She was elected to a second four-year term as chief in 1991. At the same election, six women were named to serve on the fifteen-member tribal council, an event that hearkened back to the early days of the Cherokee Nation when women were an active voice in tribal affairs.

In 1993, she completed her autobiography, *Mankiller: A Chief and Her People*, which interweaves her own experiences with Cherokee and Indian history. In 1995, Mankiller was diagnosed with lymphoma and chose not to run again. Mankiller became a visiting professor at Dartmouth College and embarked on a national lecture tour speaking on health care, tribal and women's rights, and cancer awareness. For her contributions to Native American causes, Mankiller received the Presidential Medal of Freedom in 1998. She died from pancreatic cancer at the age of sixty-four. In 2018, Mankiller became one of the honorees in the first induction ceremony held by the National Native American Hall of Fame.

Sylvia Mendez (1936–)

Civil Rights Activist

At the age of eight, Sylvia Mendez was at the center of the landmark desegregation case of 1946, *Mendez v. Westminster*, which led to the end of school segregation in California's public schools and became the forerunner of the broader national ban on segregated schools in *Brown v. Board of Education* in 1954.

She was born in Santa Ana, California. Her father was an immigrant from Mexico, who had a successful agricultural business; her mother was a native of Puerto Rico. The family moved from Santa Ana to Westminster to tend a farm that they were renting from a Japanese American family that had been sent to an internment camp during World War II. In the 1940s, Westminster only had two schools: one for white students and one for Hispanics, a two-room, wooden shack with few books and fewer educational benefits. Her father wanted her to attend the "whites-only," segregated 17th Street School, and when she was eight, she joined her brothers and cousins to enroll. They were told that children with light skin would be permitted, but neither Sylvia nor her brothers could attend because of their dark skin and Hispanic surname.

Sylvia's father, Gonzalo Mendez, began to organize the community to end the injustice of the segregated school system, filing a lawsuit in the federal court in Los Angeles in 1945 on behalf of five thousand Hispanic American schoolchildren. During the trial that followed, she didn't quite grasp the significance of her parents' efforts. "I was seeing this beautiful [white] school," she recalled, "large concrete courtyard, a beautiful playground. I thought, 'I know what they're fighting for. They're fighting so I can go to that beautiful school and have a playground.'" In 1946, the judge ruled in favor of Mendez and his coplaintiffs. More than a year later, the Ninth Circuit Court of Appeals affirmed the district court's ruling, and California governor Earl Warren ordered all public schools and public spaces in California to be desegregated. In 1948, Mendez and her siblings were finally al-

lowed to attend the 17th Street School, becoming some of the first Hispanics to attend an all-white school in California. *Mendez v. Westminster* set an important precedent for ending segregation in the United States.

Mendez became a nurse and raised a family but stayed involved in activist causes, traveling around the country and teaching students about the case. In 2010, President Barack Obama awarded Mendez the Presidential Medal of Freedom for her work in advancing the cause of civil rights.

Diane Nash (1938–)

Civil Rights Activist

Cofounder of the Student Nonviolent Coordinating Committee (SNCC), civil rights activist Diane Nash was instrumental in leading the first successful civil rights campaign to integrate lunch counters and organizing the Freedom Riders to desegregate interstate travel. She also initiated the Alabama Voting Rights Project and worked on the Selma Voting Rights Movement, which helped to gain passage of the Voting Rights Act of 1965, which ensured that African Americans and other minorities were not prevented from registering and voting.

Born in Chicago, Illinois, Nash attended parochial and public schools, and in 1956, she graduated from Hyde Park High School in Chicago and began college at Howard University before transferring to Fisk University in Nashville, Tennessee. In Nashville, she experienced for the first time the segregationist Jim Crow laws and customs. Outraged, she got involved in opposition by becoming the chair for organizing nonviolent protests at Fisk and attending civil disobedience workshops. In 1960, at the age of twenty-two, she became the leader of the Nashville sit-ins at downtown lunch counters, which lasted for four months. It was unique at the time by being made up exclusively of college students. The Nashville sit-ins spread to sixty-nine cities across the country.

In 1960, nearly two hundred students involved in the nationwide sit-in movement came to

Raleigh, North Carolina, for an organizing conference under the auspices of the Southern Christian Leadership Conference. Nash became one of the founders of the Student Nonviolent Coordinating Committee (SNCC) and quit school to lead its direct-action wing. In 1961, Nash and her fellow students were arrested in Rock Hill, South Carolina, and refused the offer of bail. This instituted the "jail, no bail" strategy to call attention to the cause. Nash spent thirty days in a South Carolina jail and would be arrested dozens of subsequent times for her activities.

Nash married civil rights activist James Bevel in 1961 and moved to Jackson, Mississippi, where she began organizing voter registration and school desegregation campaigns for SCLC. In 1961, the Freedom Rides movement, started to challenge state segregation of interstate buses and facilities, was suspended after a bus was firebombed and several riders were severely injured in attacks by a mob in Birmingham, Alabama. Nash, however, called on Fisk University and other college students to fill buses and keep the Freedom Rides going. "We will not stop," she insisted. "There is only one outcome." When violence escalated and bus drivers began to refuse service to the Riders due to the dangers, Attorney General Robert Kennedy got involved and worked to keep the Rides going. Nash was fully aware of the risk to herself and the other Riders, but she was adamant that the protest continue. In 1963, President John F. Kennedy appointed Nash to a national committee to promote civil rights legislation, which would eventually evolve as the Civil Rights Act of 1964.

Nash received SCLC's Rosa Parks award from Dr. Martin Luther King Jr. in 1965, and King cited her contributions especially to the Selma right-to-vote movement, which eventually led to the Voting Rights Act of 1965. In 1966, Nash joined the Vietnam peace movement and remained involved in political and social activism throughout the 1960s. In the 1980s, she fought for women's rights. She moved back to Chicago, where she worked in real estate and education. She was described by historian David Halberstam and her pivotal role in the civil rights movement as "bright, focused, utterly fearless, with an unerring instinct for the correct tactical move at each increment of the crisis; as a leader, her instincts had been flawless, and she was the kind of person who pushed those around her to be at their best, or be gone from the movement."

Carry Nation (1846–1911)

Temperance Activist

 Although she is regarded today as something of a cartoon figure with a face that resembles the hatchet she used to smash up saloons, temperance crusader Carry Nation conduced a fierce rampage against what she called "bastions of male arrogance." Nation and her hatchet focused national attention on the abuses of alcohol and its devastating social and personal costs. She described herself as a "bulldog running along the feet of Jesus, barking at what He doesn't like" and approached her activism with a religious zeal.

Born Carrie Amelia Moore in Garrard, Kentucky (the spelling of her first name was changed later in life), she experienced childhood poverty, her mother's mental instability, and frequent bouts of ill health. Her education was intermittent, though she gained a teaching certificate from a state normal school. In 1867, she married a young physician, Charles Gloyd, whose hard drinking soon killed him, leaving Nation on her own to support a young child. In 1877, she married David Nation, a lawyer, journalist, and minister, and they eventually settled in Kansas.

Nation entered the temperance movement in 1890 when a U.S. Supreme Court decision weakened the Prohibition laws of Kansas. She joined the Women's Christian Temperance Union (WCTU), founded in 1874 by women "concerned about the problems alcohol was causing their families and society." In an era in which women lacked the same rights as men with little recourse if their husbands drank too much, the WCTU crusaded to raise awareness of the consequences of alcohol. In 1880, Kansas became the first state to adopt a constitutional provision banning the manufacture and sale of alcohol, and when the Supreme Court became in favor of the importation and sale of liquor from other states into Kansas, Nation considered that the Kansas saloons were illegally operating and that anyone could destroy them with impunity. Alone or accompanied by hymn-singing women, Nation would march into a saloon, sing, pray, and smash the bar's fixtures and stock with a hatchet. Jailed multiple times, she paid her fines from lecture tour fees and sales of souvenir hatchets. She also survived numerous physical assaults.

Much in demand on the lecture circuit, Nation published newsletters—*The Smasher's Mail*, *The Hatchet*, and the *Home Defender*—and an autobiography, *The Use and Need of the Life of Carry A. Nation* (1904). She advocated other social reforms, including women's suffrage, and railed against tobacco, foreign food, the use of corsets, and skirts of improper length.

She divorced her husband in 1901, and Nation completed her last speaking tour in 1910, owing to failing health. She moved to a farm in Arkansas that she intended to turn into a school for Prohibition. She collapsed onstage in January 1911 during what would be her final speech. She died in a hospital in Leavenworth, Kansas, and was buried in an unmarked grave in Belton, Missouri. The WCTU would later erect a stone inscribed, "Faithful to the Cause of Prohibition, She Had Done What She Could." Nation never lived to see nationwide Prohibition in America, which was established with the Eighteenth Amendment in 1920. Although the remedy of Prohibition is considered a social policy failure (repealed in 1933), the cause that Nation crusaded to cure was real enough, and she deserves more consideration than that of a hatchet-wielding crank of popular memory for gaining national attention to a serious social problem.

Rosa Parks (1913–2005)

Civil Rights Activist

Called "the first lady of civil rights" and "the mother of the freedom movement," Rosa Parks made history in December 1955 when, returning home from her job as a seamstress at a Montgomery, Alabama, department store, she was ordered by the bus driver to relinquish her seat in the "colored section" to a white passenger when the whites-only section was filled. Parks's defiance challenged the policy of racial discrimination in the South and became the spark that ignited the modern civil rights movement in the United States. Parks became an international icon of resistance to racial segregation.

She was born Rosa Louise McCauley in Tuskegee, Alabama, the granddaughter of slaves. Her mother was a teacher in a one-room, rural schoolhouse, and her father was a carpenter. When she was ten, her family moved to Montgomery. She went to an industrial school for girls and later enrolled at Alabama State Teachers College for Negroes (now Alabama State University), but she was forced to withdraw after her grandmother became ill. In 1932, she married Raymond Parks, a barber and civil rights activist. The couple struggled during the Depression, contending with racial abuse and discriminatory "Jim Crow" laws, which enforced segregation throughout the South. She took what jobs she could get and eventually managed to get her high school diploma. Determined to work for racial equality, Parks joined the National Association for the Advancement of Colored People (NAACP) in 1943, becoming the chapter's secretary.

By the time Parks boarded the bus in 1955, she was an established organizer and leader in the civil rights movement in Alabama. Many have tried to diminish Parks's active resistance by depicting her as a seamstress who simply did not want to give up her seat because she was tired. "People always say that I didn't give up my seat because I was tired," she recalled. "But that isn't true. I was not tired physically, or no more tired than I usually was at the end of a working day. I was not old, although some people have an image of me as being old then. I was forty-two. No, the only tired I was, was tired of giving in." The bus driver called the police, and Parks was arrested for violating Montgomery's transportation laws. She was tried, found guilty, and fined. In protest, the black community, led by Reverend Martin Luther King Jr., responded with a citywide bus boycott that lasted 381 days. During that time, Parks appealed her conviction, and in December 1956, the U.S. Supreme Court upheld a federal district court ruling in her favor and declared the Montgomery segregated bus system unconstitutional. The bus boycott would become the model for a nonviolent campaign of sit-ins and protests that eventually brought segregation to an end throughout the South.

As a result of her arrest, both Parks and her husband lost their jobs. They were harassed and unable to find employment in Montgomery. They moved to Detroit, Michigan, in 1957, where Parks remained active in the civil rights movement. In 1965, she became an assistant to Congressman John Conyers and remained with him until she retired in 1988.

In 1980, widowed and without immediate family, she cofounded the Rosa L. Parks Scholarship Foundation for college-bound high school seniors, donating most of her speaking fees to the foundation. In 1992, she published *Rosa Parks: My Story* and a memoir, *Quiet Strength*, in 1995. She died of natural causes in Detroit at the age of ninety-two. Parks became the first American who had not been a U.S. government official to lie in state in the rotunda of the U.S. Capitol. An estimated fifty thousand people paid their respects, and the event was broadcast on television. *Time* magazine named Parks one of the twenty most influential and iconic figures of the twentieth century. On the fiftieth anniversary of her arrest, President George W. Bush directed that a statue of Parks be placed in the U.S. Capitol's National Statuary Hall.

Josephine St. Pierre Ruffin (1842–1924)

Civil Rights Activist, Women's Rights Activist

Journalist, publisher, civil rights leader, and suffragist Josephine St. Pierre Ruffin was the editor of the *Woman's Era*, the first national newspaper published by and for African American women. She is best known for organizing the Women's Era Club in 1894, one of the first African American women's organizations that initiated the important African American clubwomen's movement.

Born in Boston, Massachusetts, Ruffin was of mixed racial ancestry and was educated in integrated public and private schools in Salem, Boston, and New York. At sixteen, she married George Lewis Ruffin, who would later become the first African American graduate of Harvard Law School and Boston's first African American municipal judge. They had five children. They were active in the abolitionist cause and helped recruit black soldiers for the Union Army during the Civil War.

In 1869, Ruffin joined Julia Ward Howe and Lucy Stone to form the American Woman Suffrage Association (AWSA) in Boston. They also founded the New England Women's Club in 1868, and Ruffin was its first biracial member. Ruffin became the editor of the weekly *Boston Courant*, a weekly black newspaper. In 1893, Ruffin founded the Woman's Era Club to further the goals of African American women and all African Americans. Opened to women of any race, the club provided scholarships and fought for reforms and racial advancement. Ruffin also founded the *Woman's Era*, the club's magazine, which was the first periodical owned, published, and managed by black women in the United States.

In 1895, Ruffin helped create one of the first national organizations for African American women, the National Federation of Afro-American Women. It would eventually merge with the Colored Women's League of Washington in 1896. Ruffin served as the first vice president of the newly formed National Association of Colored Women.

Ruffin remained active in civic and charitable work throughout her life. She was one of the fifty-six charter members of the NAACP and remained a committed advocate for both racial justice and the empowerment of African American women. She died at her home in Boston at the age of eighty-one. In 1999, she was represented in one of the six marble panels added to the Massachusetts State House honoring women from the state: Ruffin, Florence Luscomb, Mary Kenney O'Sullivan, Dorothea Dix, Sarah Parker Remond, and Lucy Stone.

Margaret Sanger (1879–1966)

Birth Control Activist

The founder of the Planned Parenthood Federation of America, Margaret Sanger devoted her life to providing women with information on birth control and fighting for the legal right to practice contraception. Sanger popularized the term "birth control" and opened the first birth control clinic in the United States.

Born Margaret Higgins in Corning, New York, Sanger was the sixth of eleven children. She saw how difficult life was for her hardworking mother, who had endured eighteen pregnancies and died of tuberculosis at the age of fifty. In 1900, after graduating from Claverack College, a secondary school in the Catskill Mountains, Sanger entered the nursing program at White Plains Hospital in New York, where she completed two years of practical nursing training.

In 1902, she married architect William Sanger, and the couple had three children. They divorced in 1920, and Sanger married oil manufacturer J. Noah Slee, although she retained Sanger's surname for the rest of her life. In 1910, Sanger began working as a midwife and visiting nurse on the Lower East Side of New York City. In this poverty-stricken neighborhood, she confronted the sickness, misery, and helplessness that many young mothers faced trying to care for their children. Childbirth in the slums was a risky experience that all too often led to serious health problems for mother and baby. However, it was against the law for anyone, including doctors, to give out birth control information. Sanger came to believe that the ability to control family size was crucial to ending the cycle of women's poverty.

Sanger began a crusade to help women receive information on family planning. In 1914, she traveled to Europe to investigate birth control techniques there. When she returned to New York, she published her findings in a monthly magazine, The Woman Rebel, which ceased publication when Sanger was charged with sending obscene materials through the mail and fined. In 1916 in Brooklyn, New York, Sanger opened the country's first birth control clinic, dispensing contraceptives and providing birth control advice. The clinic gave out copies of Sanger's pamphlet "What Every Girl Should Know." Ten days after opening, the police closed the clinic, which had already been visited by five hundred women. Sanger was arrested and jailed for thirty days. Her arrest drew extensive media attention and several affluent supporters. She appealed her conviction, and although she lost, the courts ruled that physicians could prescribe contraceptives to women for medical reasons. This exception allowed Sanger to open another clinic in 1923, staffed by female doctors and social workers. It became the model for over three hundred clinics established by Sanger throughout the country. In 1937, largely due to her efforts, the American Medical Association recognized contraception as a subject that should be taught in medical schools. In 1942, Sanger organized her clinics into the Planned Parenthood Federation of America.

Sanger retired in 1942 and moved to Tucson, Arizona. She remained a passionate advocate for birth control and women's rights. In the 1950s, Sanger convinced philanthropist and feminist Katherine McCormick to fund research into a female-controlled contraceptive, which led to the development of the first birth control pill in 1960. Sanger lived long enough to see the Supreme Court in *Griswold v. Connecticut* rule in 1965 that birth control was legal for married couples. She died in a nursing home in Tucson at the age of eighty-six. Between 1953 and 1963, Sanger was nominated for the Nobel Peace Prize thirty-one times, but she was never awarded the prize.

Karen Silkwood (1946–1974)

Nuclear Safety Activist

America's first nuclear whistle-blower, Karen Silkwood, discovered numerous health violations at the Kerr-McGee nuclear power plant in Oklahoma and testified to the Atomic Energy Commission about her concerns. She became an activist on behalf of issues of health and safety until her death in a car accident on the way to provide documentation of safety violations to a *New York Times* reporter.

She was born in Longview, Texas, and, with her two sisters, was raised in Nederland, Texas. In high school, she developed an interest in chemistry and enrolled at Lamar College in Beaumont, Texas, on a full scholarship to study medical technology. She left school, however, after her first year, married, and had three children. In 1972, she and her husband separated, and she left custody of the children to her husband while she took a job at the Kerr-McGee nuclear power plant near Crescent, Oklahoma.

At Kerr-McGee, Silkwood helped make plutonium fuel rods for nuclear reactors and joined the Oil, Chemical, and Atomic Workers Union (OCAW). Shortly after starting her job, she participated in a nine-week union strike and served as a member of the union's bargaining committee. She began to monitor the plant's health and safety practices and found evidence of spills, falsification of records, inadequate training, and missing amounts of plutonium. She and two others, local union members, went before the Atomic Energy Commission in Washington, D.C., to reveal what they had learned. As a whistle-blower, she was deemed a troublemaker at the plant and subject to ongoing harassment.

In November 1974, Silkwood discovered during a routine self-check that her body contained almost four hundred times the legal limit for plutonium contamination. Decontaminated at the plant, Silkwood was sent home with a testing kit for further analysis. She continued to show high levels of plutonium contamination. She was convinced that she had been contaminated at the plant, while the company accused her of contaminating herself to enhance her case against the plant.

Silkwood collected evidence documenting her claims and contacted a *New York Times* reporter interested in her story. On November 13, 1974, she left a union meeting to drive to Oklahoma City to meet the reporter with her evidence. Her body was found in her car, which crashed into a concrete abutment. The car contained none of the documents that union members had seen Silkwood carrying to her car before she left. Her death was

ruled an accident as a result of Silkwood falling asleep at the wheel. Damage to the bumper of the car seemed to indicate that she may have been forced off the road.

After her death, Silkwood became a heroine for both antinuclear activists and whistle-blowers. Kerr-McGee eventually settled the suit brought by Silkwood's father and children in 1986 for $1.38 million, admitting no liability. Kerr-McGee closed its nuclear fuel plant in 1975, and the U.S. Department of Energy reported the Cimarron plant as decontaminated and decommissioned in 1994.

In 1983, the film *Silkwood* appeared, directed by Mike Nichols, with Meryl Streep in the title role. Several books on the Silkwood case and the mystery surrounding her death have been published that offer multiple theories to answer the many questions surrounding Silkwood's life and death. Her activism and death have shed light on the dangers of nuclear technology as well as the heroism of whistle-blowers who challenge the powerful to expose dangerous and illegal activity.

Harriet Tubman (1820–1913)
Abolitionist, Social Activist

Known as the "Moses of her people," Harriet Tubman escaped from slavery at the age of twenty-nine and then spent years as the first woman "conductor" on the Underground Railroad helping others achieve the same freedom she had gained. She was also a nurse, a Union spy during the Civil War, and a women's suffrage supporter. She is considered the first African American woman to serve in the military and remains one of the most inspirational figures in American history.

Born Araminta Ross, the daughter of parents who had been brought from Africa in chains, Tubman had eight siblings. By the age of five, her owners rented her out to neighbors as a domestic servant and later as a field hand. At the age of twelve, she intervened to keep her master from beating an enslaved man who tried to escape. She was hit in the head with a two-pound weight, leaving her with a lifetime of severe headaches and narcolepsy. Although not legally allowed to marry, she entered a marital union with John Tubman, a free black man, in 1844, taking his last name and dubbing herself Harriet.

In 1849, after her master died, Tubman feared that she would be sold away from her family, and she fled to Philadelphia. Later, she went even farther north to Ontario, Canada. Although now free, Tubman said that her heart was still "down in the old cabin quarters, with the old folk and my brothers and sisters." Over the next ten years, she made nineteen trips to the South to lead others, including her aged parents and her sister and brothers, to freedom. Her success made her a target, and slave owners placed a $40,000 reward for her capture or death. Proud that she never "lost a passenger," Tubman was personally responsible for leading more than three hundred slaves to freedom along the Underground Railroad—the network of safe houses where abolitionists assisted runaway slaves in their journey out of bondage.

Because of Tubman's expert knowledge of the towns and transportation routes in the South, she worked during the Civil War as a Union spy and scout. Often transforming herself into an aged woman, Tubman would travel behind enemy lines and learn from the enslaved population about Confederate troop movements and supply lines. She also became a respected guerilla operative and nurse to black and white soldiers stricken with infection and disease.

After the war, she helped to establish schools for freedmen in North Carolina as well as the Harriet Tubman Home for Indigent Aged Negroes on twenty-five acres of land she purchased adjacent to her home in Auburn, New York. She joined Elizabeth Cady Stanton and Susan B. Anthony in their campaign for women's suffrage. In 1895, thirty years after the end of the Civil War, the government granted Tubman a pension of twenty dollars a month in recognition for her unpaid war work. She remained active in the cause of black women's rights serving as a delegate to the first convention of the National Federation of Afro-American Women in 1896. She spent her final years in poverty, dying of

pneumonia at the age of ninety-three. She was buried with military honors in Auburn, New York.

In 2016, the U.S. Treasury announced that Tubman's image would replace that of former president and slave owner Andrew Jackson on the twenty-dollar bill. The new bill was expected to enter circulation sometime after 2020. However, U.S. Treasury secretary Steven Mnuchin reported that no change will take place before 2024, saying, "Right now we have a lot more important issues to focus on."

Lillian Wald (1867–1940)
Public Health Activist

A pioneer advocate for community nursing, Lillian Wald founded the Henry Street Settlement, which brought health care services to the residents of New York's Lower East Side tenements. She was a champion for the causes of public health nursing, housing reform, suffrage, world peace, and the rights of women, children, immigrants, and workers.

Wald was born into a German Jewish, middle-class family in Cincinnati, Ohio, and Rochester, New York. After a private school education, she abandoned her intention to attend Vassar College for an active social life. In 1889, she entered the New York Hospital Training School for Nurses, graduating in 1891. She worked for a year as a nurse in the New York Juvenile Asylum while taking medical courses at the Women's Medical College.

In 1893, Wald was teaching a course in hygiene and home nursing to a group of immigrant women from the Lower East Side of Manhattan. Her exposure to the unsanitary conditions of tenement life convinced her to alter her plan to become a doctor to attend to the poor. "I left the laboratory and the [medical] college," she said in her autobiography, *The House on Henry Street* (1915). "What I had seen had shown me where my path lay." She moved into the Henry Street neighborhood and began working as a visiting nurse. In 1895, with aid from banker-philanthropist Jacob H. Schiff and others, she opened the Nurse's Settlement, which grew from two nurses in 1893 to ninety-two in 1913 to 250 by 1929. Services were also expanded to include nurses' training, educational programs for the community, and youth clubs. Within a few years, it became the Henry Street Settlement, an innovative leader in the social settlement movement and in the broader field of public health and social work.

Wald extended her activism to include arguing for nursing service in the local public schools, which led to a citywide public nursing program, the first in the world. In 1912, Wald's role as the founder of the new profession of public nursing was recognized when she helped found and became the first president of the National Organization for Public Health Nursing. She was also active in other areas of reform: with the National Child Labor Committee, which she and Florence Kelley founded in 1903, and with the national Women's Trade Union League and the American Union against Militarism, which she and Jane Addams helped to organize in 1914 and for which she served as president. During World War I, she headed the committee on home nursing for the Council of National Defense, and she led the Nurses' Emergency Council during the influenza epidemic of 1918–1919. She published a second autobiography, *Windows on Henry Street* (1934). Ill heath forced her to resign as the director of Henry Street in 1933 when she moved to Westport, Connecticut, where she died at the age of sixty-seven.

In 1922, Wald was named by the *New York Times* as one of the twelve greatest living American women. Wald was a pioneer in community health care who, as a medical provider, employer, and educator, paved the way for women in social services and public health.

Ida B. Wells-Barnett (1862–1931)

Civil Rights Activist

Journalist, lecturer, and social activist Ida Wells-Barnett was an outspoken advocate for civil and economic rights for African Americans and women. She is perhaps best known for her fear-

less antilynching crusade in the 1890s and as one of the founders of the National Association for the Advancement of Colored People (NAACP).

Born into slavery in Mississippi six months before Abraham Lincoln signed the Emancipation Proclamation, Wells-Barnett was educated at a high school and industrial school for freed blacks. Her parents, who were socially active in Reconstruction Era politics, instilled in her the importance of education. She enrolled at Shaw University (now Rust College) in Mississippi, a traditionally black college that her father helped to start; however, she had to drop out at the age of sixteen when both her parents and one of her siblings died in a yellow fever outbreak, leaving her to care for her six siblings. She continued her education for a time at Fisk University in Nashville and passed her teaching examination before going to work teaching at a rural school.

In 1884, when she was traveling from Memphis to Nashville, having purchased a first-class ticket, she was ordered by the train crew to move to the car for African Americans. She refused and, when forcibly removed from the train, bit one of the men on the hand. She sued the railroad, winning a $500 settlement that was later overturned by the Tennessee Supreme Court. The injustice she felt drove her to journalism, and she began writing a weekly column for some of the small, black-owned newspapers then springing up in the South and East at the time. She would eventually become a full-time journalist and acquire a financial interest in the weekly newspaper the *Memphis Free Speech and Headlight*.

She also worked as a teacher in a segregated public school in Memphis and became a vocal critic of the conditions there. In 1891, she was fired from her job for her attacks. In 1892, a lynching in Memphis of three of her friends who were falsely accused of raping three white women drove her to denounce the lynchings as motivated not under the familiar pretext of defending Southern, white womanhood but because the victims, grocery store owners, had been successful in competing with white shopkeepers. Wells-Barnett's exhaustive research into lynchings across the country confirmed her assertion that the violence aimed at African Americans was an attempt to enforce the repression of blacks in America. As a result of her vocal antilynching campaign, a white mob destroyed her newspaper's offices, and she received death threats. She left Memphis for New York but continued to write in-depth reports on lynchings in America. She also began to travel across the country to lecture and gain support for her campaign against lynching, founding antilynching societies and black women's clubs wherever she went.

In 1893, she moved to Chicago, where she wrote for the *Chicago Conservator*, established by lawyer Ferdinand Barnett, whom she married in 1895. In the same year, she published *A Red Record,* her three-year statistical study of lynchings in America. Wells-Barnett was also active in the struggle for civil rights for African Americans and women. She participated in the 1910 meeting that led to the formation of the NAACP. She also founded the Negro Fellowship League to assist African Americans who had migrated from the South to cities in the North. In 1913, she helped to form the Alpha Suffrage Club, believed to be the first black women's suffrage organization.

During World War I, the U.S. government placed Wells-Barnett under surveillance, labeling her a dangerous "race agitator." She continued her activism undeterred. In the 1920s, she fought for African American workers' rights, and in the 1930s, she made an unsuccessful bid for a seat in the Illinois Senate. She died of kidney disease at the age of sixty-eight. Her memoir, *Crusade for Justice*, which was left unfinished, was posthumously published in 1970.

Regarded as the most famous African American woman of her era, Ida Wells-Barnett has been a much-admired precursor figure of the civil rights and women's movements of the 1960s and 1970s.

Jody Williams (1950–)

Political Activist

In 1997, Jody Williams, who helped found the International Campaign to Ban Landmines (ICBL), was awarded the Nobel Peace Prize for her work toward the banning and clearing of antipersonnel mines.

Born in Brattleboro, Vermont, Williams was the second of the five children of a county judge and a mother who oversaw public housing projects. Her brother was deaf and schizophrenic, and what he experienced taught her a fundamental lesson of empathy. "I couldn't understand why people would be mean to him because he was deaf," she recalled. "That translated into wanting to stop bullies being mean to … people, just because they are weak."

Williams graduated from the University of Vermont in 1972. Struggling to figure out what to do next, she earned a master's degree in teaching Spanish and English as a second language from Brattleboro's School for International Training in 1976 and another master's from the Johns Hopkins University School of Advanced International Studies in 1984. She took teaching jobs in Mexico, the United Kingdom, and Washington, D.C., until she became the co-coordinator of the Nicaragua–Honduras Education Program (1984–1986) and deputy director of Medical Aid for El Salvador (1986–1992). In war-torn El Salvador, land mines were a constant threat to the civilian population, and she was given responsibility for providing artificial limbs to children who had lost arms and legs.

In 1991, representatives of the Vietnam Veterans of America Foundation and Mexico International, a German humanitarian organization, approached Williams to coordinate an international campaign against antipersonnel land mines. It was estimated that at the time, over one hundred million such weapons scattered across eighty countries were killing approximately seventy people (mainly civilians and children) per day, or twenty-six thousand a year. Williams became the founding coordinator of the International Campaign to Ban Landmines, which was launched in 1992. Based out of her homes in Putney, Vermont, and Washington, D.C., Williams, with no staff, set to work contacting governments and organizations around the world to gain support on the land mine issue. Under Williams's leadership, the ICBL grew to include 1,300 organizations in eighty-five countries as well as the active support in 1996 from Diana, Princess of Wales, who brought world attention to the human cost of land mines. In 1997, Williams and the ICBL were awarded the Nobel Peace Prize, and an international treaty banning land mines was signed by over one hundred countries (the United States refused to participate).

In 1998, Williams stepped down as coordinator of the ICBL but remained an ambassador for the organization around the world. In 2003, she became a visiting professor of social work and global justice at the University of Houston's Graduate School of Social Work. In 2007, she became a professor of peace and social justice at the University of Houston.

EDUCATION

An African proverb says, "If you educate a man, you educate an individual. But if you educate a woman, you educate a nation." The wisdom of this saying was slow to be acknowledged in America until the twentieth century. Access to education for all women has been a hard-won right that lagged behind the democratic achievements of the founding principles of self-determination and equality that defined the young republic. However, women as educators long provided primary education in colonial America and the new nation, although women were excluded from secondary schools and colleges and universities for much of the two centuries following the founding of the nation.

It can be argued that women's rights and education are inextricably linked. As Supreme Court Justice Sonia Sotomayor has insisted, "Until we get equality in education, we won't have an equal society." Today, women are the majority of Americans pursuing and earning college degrees. While as late as the 1970s, the proportion of men attending college was significantly higher than women—58 percent to 42 percent—that ratio has now almost reversed. The U.S. Department of Education has projected that by 2026, 57 percent of college students will be women. Ironically, since colonial days, teaching was one of the only employment options for women outside the home, yet teaching opportunities were largely at the primary level, later in the twentieth

century including the secondary-school level, and only gradually in significant numbers at the college level in the second half of the twentieth century. Today, three-quarters of all teachers in kindergarten through high school are women. In elementary and middle school, 80 percent are women. Women now hold 49 percent of the total faculty positions at colleges and universities (though only 35 percent in tenured positions). All current trends point toward parity with males in education for women, as both students and teachers, with the largest gains occurring during the women's movement of the 1960s and following, a movement that almost certainly was made possible by increased educational opportunities for women in the decades preceding.

Such encouraging data should underscore just how far women have come in American education. To reach full equality and parity with men, a sea change in cultural and gender attitudes had to occur in which the nature of women's intellectual capabilities and the social implication of women choosing work outside the home had to be redefined.

On the frontier in the early decades of colonial America, homeschooling would have been the norm, with mothers providing basic reading and writing skills for their children. As subsistence in isolated farmsteads gave way to settlements in villages, primary education in the seventeenth through nineteenth centuries took place in "dame schools," a

When Boston's Latin School (later Boston Latin) was founded in 1635, it only admitted boys and hired an all-male staff. By the 1870s, new thinking on the right of women to an education led to the founding of Boston's Girl's Latin School in1877.

model for private elementary education imported from England in which a small class of young children, male and female, would be taught, or at least cared for, by a local woman, usually in her own home. Children were taught their numbers and the alphabet, basic reading and writing, and possibly religious instruction in a model resembling both today's home daycare and kindergarten. Teaching materials generally included a hornbook primer, a psalter, and the Bible. Girls would have been taught skills such as sewing and knitting. Most girls in colonial America received their only formal education from dame schools. Boys, however, would have spent more time in their dame schools acquiring the basic skills needed to enroll in "town schools," or primary schools.

Larger towns in New England set up grammar schools, the forerunner of modern high schools. The first grammar school based on the English model in the American colonies was Boston's Latin Grammar School in 1635 (later Boston Latin School). In 1647, the Massachusetts Bay Colony passed laws requiring any township with at least one hundred households to establish a grammar school. This was the initial establishment of compulsory, government-directed public education in America. Similar laws were enacted in the other New England colonies, followed by most mid-Atlantic colonies and much later in the eighteenth century by some southern colonies. Tax-supported laws to support town schools for girls were passed in Massachusetts in 1767, but it was optional,

and many towns resisted or greatly delayed adoption. Town schools or grammar schools mainly provided primary education for boys. All but a few towns in New England specifically barred girls from town schools until the end of the eighteenth century, and even then, girls usually attended at different times of the day than the boys or when boys did not attend such as summertime or holidays. These schools provided a preparatory curriculum, including classical languages, for eventual college study that remained until the nineteenth century strictly for men.

Colonial colleges such as Harvard College (founded in 1636) and Yale College (1701) were instituted to train young men as ministers. Doctors and lawyers were trained under an apprentice system. An exception was The College of William & Mary, founded by the Virginia government in 1693. Although closely associated with the Anglican Church, it hired the first law professors and trained the sons of leading planter families in the law as well as the ministry. Eventually, American colleges' liberal arts curricula in Greek, Latin, mathematics, history, logic, ethics, and rhetoric would be embraced by young men who would pursue secular careers while offering a valuable network of alumni contacts.

The first private schools in the American colonies were established by religious groups such as Roman Catholics or Quakers as well as by unaffiliated individuals who thought they could make a living or at least supplement their incomes by taking in boarders or by teaching children or adults during the evenings or at times convenient to the students. Schoolteachers for older children, as opposed to younger children in dame schools, were invariably men, possibly with college training or degrees but with no licensing or regulatory body overseeing their work quality, which varied widely. Such private venture schools offered reading and writing instruction; courses from the classical curricula such as languages, history, and geography; and vocational skills. More formal private schools, prep schools or academies, were also established for secondary school education and preparation for college study, many with a strong religious affiliation. The oldest of these boarding schools still operating are the Collegiate School in New York City (est. 1628), Roxbury Latin School in Massachusetts (est. 1645), the Hopkins School in Connecticut (est. 1660), and Friends Select School in Pennsylvania (est. 1689). Such prep schools would become an important model for the private girls' academies and seminaries that began to be established in the eighteenth and nineteenth centuries.

Secondary schooling for girls, whether in public or private, had to contend with strong resistance. With higher education closed off to women until the 1830s and most of the professions, such as law, medicine, and business, also barring women, most parents and many girls themselves found little justification in taking a college preparatory course of study. Additionally, a commonly held belief was that the classical curricula that included the complex reasoning skills of logic and mathematics were beyond the mental capacity of females and could in fact harm girls' development and their prospects to assume their expected roles as wives and mothers. What was more acceptable, for parents who could afford it, was the finishing school concept of enhancing basic reading and writing abilities with refining lessons in languages, singing, dancing, needlework, and the like, skills that both suited a conception of a well-bred female and enhanced one's marriage prospects. The conflict between teaching social graces over scholarship, ornamental versus academic training, would animate curricular deci-

The Roman Catholic Sisters of the Order of Saint Ursula founded what was the first free private school for young women in 1727.

sions as private secondary schools, academies, and seminaries for young women were established during the second half of the eighteenth century and throughout the nineteenth.

The earliest private school for girls in America was the Ursuline Academy in New Orleans, founded by the Roman Catholic Sisters of the Order of Saint Ursula in 1727 (it was also the first free school for young women and the first to teach free women of color, Native American women, and female African American slaves). The first private Protestant boarding school for girls was the Bethlehem Female Seminary, established in 1742 in Germantown, Pennsylvania (later the Moravian Female Seminary and in 1863 Moravian College). It was the first of the female seminaries that would transform women's education in America. Seminaries and academies replaced the smaller, familylike boarding school with a larger institution run by more professionalized teachers and instruction that mimicked men's colleges. Sarah Pierce opened the Litchfield Female Academy in Litchfield, Connecticut, in 1792. Emma Willard opened the Middlebury Female Academy in 1814 before establishing the Troy Female Seminary in 1821, which, although not a college, offered college-level course instruction and was hailed as the first institute in the United States for women's higher education. Catherine Beecher, who had been educated at the Litchfield Female Academy, founded the Hartford Female Seminary in 1823. The shift in name from academy, which echoed the Ancient Greek *Akedemia*, the Platonic center of learning, to seminary signaled these schools' seriousness to provide young women with a comparable serious academic mission as a men's college. Male seminaries prepared men for the ministry; female seminaries trained women for teaching careers, or at least offered the higher education necessary, and acknowledged that women were as capable and as deserving of intellectual challenge as men.

Standing behind developments in secondary education that led to the female seminary movement and protowomen's colleges were changing attitudes toward women and education. One example was the opening in 1787 of the Young Ladies' Academy in Philadelphia. It is one of the first all-female academies in America, which would set the example for the many academies and seminaries that followed. Sponsored and supervised by important Philadelphia male religious and political leaders, including the so-called leader of the American Enlightenment and signer of the Declaration of Independence, Benjamin Rush, the Young Ladies' Academy was a public commitment of the importance of higher education for women in the new American republic. In a lecture to visitors of the school, "Thoughts upon Female Education," Rush endorsed the concept of "republican motherhood," the idea that American women's sacred contribution to the nation was to raise sons to be virtuous citizens. Rush believed that women, as the caretakers of children, must pass on values and education to their offspring, and, to qualify them for this purpose, he wanted women to be instructed in the usual branches of female education such as sewing and housekeeping as well as the principles of liberty and government. This led to Rush to urge that a woman be educated as well in history, geography, astronomy, and philosophy and "thereby qualify her not only for a general intercourse with the world but to be an agreeable companion for a sensible man." Rush's concession on behalf of education that was more than simply ornamental would be significant, and women's educational advocates such as Catherine Beecher, Emma Willard, Mary Lyon, and many others would push Rush's prescription of women's education even further toward equal access to all branches of knowledge for women.

The next major hurdle for women was higher education itself—gaining entry to existing colleges and universities reserved only for male students or creating new comparable colleges for women. Eventually, the academy and seminary movement would lead to the first women's colleges in the United States, including Georgia Female College (1836, renamed Wesleyan Female College in 1843) and Mount Holyoke Female Seminary (1837, renamed Mount Holyoke College in 1893). The first coeducational institution of higher education in the United States was Franklin College in Lancaster, Pennsylvania (est. 1787). Its initial class of seventy-eight males and thirty-six females included Rebecca Gratz, the first Jewish female college student in the United States. It quickly ran into financial difficulty and closed, reopening as an all-male school. Oberlin

COLLEGE ENROLLMENT BY WOMEN

Year	Women's Colleges Enrollment	Coed Colleges Enrollment	% of All Students
1870	6,500	2,600	21%
1890	16,800	39,500	36%
1910	34,100	106,500	40%
1930	82,100	398,700	44%

College, in 1837, would become the oldest continually operating, coeducational college in America to be followed by Hillsdale College (1844), Franklin College (1844), Baylor College (1847), Waynesburg College (1851), and Westminster College (1852). The University of Iowa became the first public or state university to become coeducational in 1855, and public state colleges and universities would follow Iowa's lead in coeducation.

The transition from single-sex to coeducational colleges and universities was by no means smooth or invariable. Some faculty at newly coeducational institutions objected to the presence of women in their classes and revived earlier notions that the rigor of higher education was either beyond the capacity of women or harmful to them. The rejection of coeducation at the most prestigious and oldest of the private colleges and universities, the Ivy League,

prompted the creation of the so-called Seven Sisters women's colleges, which included Vassar College (1861), Wellesley College (1870), Smith College (1875), Bryn Mawr College (1885), and Barnard College (1889), all modeled on the prototype of Mount Holyoke (1837), the oldest.

Enrollment by women in single-sex and coeducational colleges and universities rose steadily through the nineteenth century, particularly after the Civil War. By 1900, 70 percent of American colleges were coeducational, and within a century of the first women matriculating at an American college or university, 44 percent of all college students were women. During the first century of women in higher education in America, Elizabeth Blackwell became the first woman to earn a medical degree from an American college (Geneva Medical College, New York, in 1849). Lucy Sessions became the first

Founded in 1837, Mount Holyoke College was created from a desire to create a private women's college that would be comparable to the all-male Ivy League schools.

African American woman to earn a college degree (Oberlin College, 1850), and Mary Jane Patterson became the first African American woman to earn a bachelor's degree (Oberlin College, 1862). Mary Fellows was the first woman west of the Mississippi to receive a bachelor's degree (Cornell College, Iowa, in mathematics, 1858). Lucy Hobbs earned the first DDS degree (Ohio College of Dental Surgery, 1866). Ada Kepley became the first female graduate of an accredited law school (Union College of Law, Chicago, 1870). Harriette J. Cooke was named the first female full professor with a salary equal to that of her male colleagues (Cornell College, Iowa, 1871). Frances Willard became the first female college president (Evanston College for Ladies, Illinois, 1871). Helen Magill White was the first American woman to earn a Ph.D. (Boston University, in Greek, 1877), sixteen years after the first Ph.D.s in America were awarded by Yale University in 1861. Subsequently, women were awarded doctorates in every discipline, including the first in mathematics in 1886, in psychology in 1894, and in physics in 1929. The first woman to gain a degree in architecture was in 1878, and the first in engineering was in 1905. The first doctorates awarded to African American women were in 1921.

Despite all of this reflected progress toward educational equality and widened opportunities for women, gains did not come easily. It was more a two-step forward, one-step back progression, particularly in regard to coeducation and opening the oldest and most distinguished academic institutions to women.

Collegiate coeducation began mainly in the West at the same time early models of separate women's colleges appeared in the East and South. However, even at the justly celebrated progressive and pioneering Oberlin College, coeducation was anything but equal. Although almost all the classes women attended at Oberlin were gender mixed, fewer than 20 percent of female graduates up to 1867 earned the BA degree. The majority instead received a diploma from the four-year "ladies' course," which omitted Greek, calculus, and most of the Latin required for a BA degree. Oberlin's two-track system was deemed natural and appropriate by Oberlin's president, James H. Fairchild,

given the separate sphere of duties to which women would "properly be called" based on economic expediency and established sex roles. Oberlin's model of two-track coeducation spread through much of American higher education in the post-Civil War decade.

Resistance to coeducation was the strongest at long-established New England colleges. Harvard, for example, from the early 1870s to the founding of Radcliffe in 1894 flatly refused demands and financial inducement for coeducation at the undergraduate level. Bowdoin, Dartmouth, Trinity, and Yale did not even give serious consideration to admitting women. At other all-male institutions, despite appeals by women's rights advocates such as Victoria Woodhull and Henry Ward Beecher, petitions were rejected at Amherst, Williams, Middlebury, and Brown. Only Colby, the University of Vermont, and Wesleyan among the established New England schools decided to become coeducational institutions in 1871. Wesleyan in particular is a good example of the rocky road to parity with men for women in higher education. The increased numbers of women admitted who began to push beyond the 20 percent quota established there led to protests by current students and alumni decrying "feminization" that threatened to turn Wesleyan into, in the words of one alum, "a namby-pamby college" and "a nonentity among our fellow institutions." Female undergraduates on campus were ignored and verbally abused, and in 1909, the Board of Trustees ended coeducation. The exiled woman would become the nucleus for the newly established all-women's Connecticut College, and Wesleyan would not return to coeducation until 1970.

The alternative to coeducation accepted by several Northeastern schools was the establishment of coordinated women's colleges such as Barnard (1889), Radcliffe (1894), the Women's College at Brown (1896, renamed Pembroke College in 1928), Middlebury (1902), Colby (1905), and Tufts (1910). Higher education in the East would be separate and unequal for most of the twentieth century until the transformation of higher education by the women's movement and other factors in the 1960s through the 1980s.

Prestigious institutions of higher education such as Harvard University long resisted admitting women as students. Founded in 1636, Harvard did not admit female undergraduates until 1977.

WHEN MEN'S COLLEGES BECAME COEDUCATIONAL

Year	College or University
1969	Kenyon College
	Princeton University
	Trinity College
	Yale University
1970	Colgate University
	Johns Hopkins University
	University of Virginia
	Wesleyan University
	Williams College
1971	Bowdoin College
	Brown University
	Lehigh University
1972	College of the Holy Cross
	Dartmouth College
	Davidson College
	Duke University
1975	Amherst College
	Wofford College
1976	Claremont McKenna College
	U.S. Military Academy
1977	Harvard University
1980	Haverford College
1983	Columbia University
1985	Washington and Lee University
1997	Virginia Military Institute

By 1980, women and men enrolled in American colleges in equal numbers for the first time. 1981 was the first year in which more bachelor's degrees would be conferred on women than men in the United States, a trend that has continued every year since. American universities awarded more than 1.3 million doctoral degrees from 1920 to 1999. Science and engineering fields accounted for 62 percent, while other fields comprised the remaining 38 percent. Men accounted for 73 percent of the recipients, but the proportion of doctoral degrees earned by women rose from 15 percent in the 1920s to 41 percent by the late 1990s.

Multiple factors account for these considerable shifts toward gender parity in higher education. Compulsory schooling laws and universal public education were crucial. By 1900, thirty-four states had compulsory schooling laws that required attendance until age fourteen or higher. As a result, by 1910, 72 percent of American children attended school. By 1918, every state required students to complete elementary school. In 1910, 18 percent of fifteen- to eighteen-year-olds were enrolled in high school, and barely 9 percent of all American eighteen-year-olds graduated. By 1940, 73 percent of American youths were enrolled in high schools, and half gained a high school diploma. By 1955, 80 percent of American youths graduated from an academic high school. Women attended and graduated from high school to a greater degree than men throughout this period. Following World War II, more men were able to at-

tend college on the GI Bill, and the number of women in college decreased in the middle part of the century, but women's enrollment rebounded after the influx of college-bound GIs.

The rise in the standard of living in the twentieth century also made persistence in secondary school and college education for more Americans, male and female, possible. From 1930 until 1980, the average American after-tax income adjusted for inflation tripled, giving Americans the highest living standard in the world. Between 1949 and 1969, real median income grew by 99.3 percent, and from 1948 to 1978, the standard of living for an average American family more than doubled. In 1960, Americans, were, on average, the richest people in the world by a massive margin. Increased discretionary income allowed for investment in higher education. In 1940, 3.8 percent of the U.S. population of women attended four years of college or more; by 1959, the number increased to 6 percent; by 1970 to 8.2 percent; by 1980 to 13.6 percent; by 1990 to

By the mid-1950s, girls were attending and graduating from high school at a greater rate than boys. Today, there is about a 50/50 ratio of girls to boys in secondary schools.

18.4 percent; by 2000 to 23.6 percent; by 2010 to 29.6 percent; and by 2018 to 35.3 percent.

Finally, changes in employment and gender roles in the twentieth century would be a major contributing factor. Prior to World War II, women were persistently and systematically discriminated against in the workforce, including bans in most states on married women working. In 1940, 28 percent of women over the age of fourteen were in the labor force, while men over the age of ten had a 96 percent workforce participation rate. During the war, women entered the workforce in unprecedented numbers to replace male workers in service. In 1945, 37 percent of women were employed. By 1950, that number declined to 32 percent. Scholars have called World War II a watershed in forcing a change in attitude about women in the workforce. With high school and college education better preparing women for work, the postwar period would begin a gradual sea change in the kinds of jobs women would be subsequently qualified to hold. More and more jobs that were formerly off-limits to women came within reach, and the education needed to compete with men in the American workforce was available to more and more female students.

Perhaps the most visible sign of changes on college campuses has been the almost total shift to coeducation of all-male colleges and universities from the 1960s through the 1980s. At the beginning of the 1960s, most of the elite, long-established private colleges, particularly in the Northeast, were all male. Two decades later, virtually no single-sex male schools remained (see sidebar). Coordinated all-female colleges had merged with the all-male colleges, and coeducation had shifted from the exception to the rule. (Currently, only three private, all-male, non-religious four-year colleges exist in the United States.) Elite, long-established all-female schools, such as Sarah Lawrence and Vassar, similarly went coed around the same time, but unlike all-male schools, single-sex women's colleges have persisted, though in significantly declining numbers. Around thirty-four women's colleges in the United States are active as of 2018, down from a peak of 281 in the 1960s.

If coeducation transformed the ratio of women to men on campus, the passage in 1972 of Title IX of the Education Amendments Act would attack implicit and long-established male privilege in education. Title IX declares that "no person in the United States shall on the basis of sex be excluded from participation in, be denied the benefits of, or be subjected to discrimination under any education program or activity receiving Federal financial assistance." If coeducation redressed the balance between men and women on college campuses, Title IX was directed to eliminating the residual effects of gender bias in athletics, in hiring, and in various forms of gender discrimination and harassment. Spearheaded by women such as Bernice Sandler and others who had experienced gender bias and discrimination at colleges, Title IX required that male and female students receive equal access to admissions, resources, and financial assistance. Its impact was perhaps most visible in the increase in opportunities for female athletes by ending the privileges and resources enjoyed by male athletes on campus. However, the impact of Title IX extends far beyond the playing fields. The U.S. Department of Education under Title IX made clear that it is the responsibility of institutions of higher education "to take immediate and effective steps to end sexual harassment and sexual violence." The result has been accountability on campus in matters of gender bias and discrimination. Neither have completely disappeared, but with Title IX, the climate on campus has clearly improved regarding equal access, opportunities, and protections for gender rights.

Higher education would face far more than just the enrollment, demographic, economic, and cultural changes in the post-World War II period, however. The civil rights movement and the women's movement would transform American campuses in fundamental and unprecedented ways. Both the faculty and student body would diversify by gender and race, and the

The civil rights movement and the women's movement would transform American campuses in fundamental and unprecedented ways.

curriculum would reflect that change with women's studies, black studies, and various ethnic studies courses and programs established. Feminist theory and criticism would leave virtually no academic discipline reassessed from gender consideration.

Despite the fact that women have achieved equal access to higher education, serious barriers remain regarding educational opportunities for both men and women because of the ever-escalating cost of higher education that has left more and more graduates with ruinous debt and threats to the return of colleges and universities, particularly the most elite schools, as the preserves of only the well-to-do who can pay full freight. Recent scandals about the so-called "side door" into highly selective schools for the wealthy further undermine the admission process and colleges' commitment to merit over privilege. Legal challenges to affirmative-action policies risk colleges' managing of diversity and redressing past underrepresentation of minorities. Other challenges from a stagnant job market threaten to undermine the traditional mission of the liberal arts for more specialized technical training. At the primary- and secondary-school level, support for a voucher system in the aid of choice threatens to undermine the sustainability of public schools for all.

In 1992, the American Association of University Women (founded in 1881) issued a sobering report, "How Schools Shortchange Girls," that offered "compelling evidence that girls are not receiving the same quality, or even the quantity, of education as their brothers are." The report offered the disturbing conclusion that despite considerable gains among women in measures of academic success, "the wealth of statistical evidence must convince even the most skeptical that gender bias in schools is shortchanging girls—and compromising our country." The study suggests that a qualitative imbalance exists in gender performance in schools. Despite the fact that girls got better grades than boys and were more likely to go on to college, girls, according to the report, had less confidence in their abilities, had higher expectations of failure, and developed more modest career aspirations. The result, the report concluded, was that girls were less likely to reach their potential than boys. Included among the forty recommendations in the report for changes to correct the gender

bias girls experience in schools were enactment and enforcement of policies against sexual harassment, stricter enforcement of Title IX, the revision of the curriculum to emphasize the experiences of girls and women, to help girls develop a positive self-image, and to encourage them to study math and science to enhance career opportunities. Other recommendations included creating gender-neutral tests and incorporating teaching methods that could lower or eliminate gender gaps in the classroom.

Perhaps the greatest significance of the AAUW report was to call attention to problems faced by girls in schools that have been previously ignored. "A lot of what is going on is unintentional," observed Keith Geiger, president of the National Education Association, "but the fact is that in our schools, we treat girls differently than we do boys.... We need to raise people's consciousness and bring about constructive change." The report offers important reasons why, for example, girls and women continue to be underrepresented in science, technology, engineering, and mathematics (STEM) disciplines that, despite increased women's enrollment in colleges and universities, have remained predominantly male.

Regardless of the challenges ahead for education in America, undoubtedly, women will participate in the debates about policy changes and course corrections. Women have progressed from their limited education at a dame school to parity with men as teachers, students, and administrators. Contemporary women owe much to the women listed here, who contributed so much to make education in the United States a right for all its people.

BIOGRAPHIES

Hannah Arendt (1906–1975)
Political Scientist, Philosopher

A German-born political scientist and philosopher, Hannah Arendt is generally regarded as one of the twentieth century's most brilliant and original political theorists and one of the most celebrated and admired intellectuals of the post-World War II world. Her best-known works, *The Origins of Totalitarianism*, *The Human Condition*, *Eichmann in Jerusalem*, and *On Revolution*, are classics of political history that have lost none of their relevance. Arendt held faculty positions at several American colleges and universities, including the University of Chicago, Cornell, Columbia, Bard College, The New School for Social Research, and the University of California–Berkeley. In 1959, she became the first woman to hold the rank of full professor at Princeton University.

Arendt was born in Hanover, Germany, the only child of comfortably middle-class Jewish parents. When her father died in 1913, Arendt was raised by her mother in Königsberg, Prussia, near the battlegrounds of the eastern front in World War I. In 1920, she married German philosopher and writer Gunther Stern, who she would divorce in 1937. In 1924, Arendt studied philosophy at the University of Marburg and the Albert Ludwig University of Freiburg, earning her doctorate in philosophy at the University of Heidelberg in 1928. Forced to flee Germany when the Nazis came to power in 1933 and anti-Semitism began to increase, Arendt first lived in Paris, where she met poet and philosopher Heinrich Blucher, who she would marry in 1940. When Germany invaded France the same year, Arendt was detained by the French as an alien despite having been stripped of her German citizenship in 1937. She escaped detention and made her way with Blucher to the United States in 1941, where the couple settled in New York City. There, Arendt became a research director of the Conference of Jewish Relations, chief editor of Schocken Books, and the executive director of Jewish Cultural Reconstruction. She became a naturalized American citizen in 1951 and began her teaching career at the University of Chicago in 1963.

The Origins of Totalitarianism (1951) established her reputation as a major historian and political theorist. Her second major work, *The Human Condition* (1958), explores humanity's historical–political shift from private and public realms to a hybrid liberal social realm. In *On Revolution* (1963), Arendt focuses on the American political model of local govern-

ment. In 1961, Arendt was sent to Jerusalem by *The New Yorker* to cover the trial of Nazi war criminal Adolf Eichmann. The result was the highly controversial *Eichmann in Jerusalem* (1963), in which Arendt argued that Eichmann's crimes were not those of a wicked or depraved individual but from the sheer "thoughtlessness" of an ambitious bureaucrat. She coined the term "banality of evil" to describe Eichmann's assistance in and acceptance of the mass extermination of the Jews. Her refusal to recognize in Eichmann a more malicious evil prompted fierce denunciations from both Jewish and non-Jewish intellectuals.

Arendt died of a heart attack in her New York City apartment at the age of sixty-nine. Her career as a writer, theorist, and educator expressed her acceptance of the hazards and instability of the human condition that allowed her to articulate a new paradigm of political philosophy that ultimately reflected her abiding concern with personal and moral integrity. Her works have become required reading for a thorough understanding of modern political history.

Catherine Beecher (1800–1878)
Educational Reformer

One of the most powerful and influential voices on behalf of equal access to education for women, Catherine Beecher promoted the expansion and development of teacher training programs, arguing that teaching was more important to society than lawyers and doctors. Beecher would also be identified with the elevation and protection of women's distinct roles in the domestic sphere of American culture that led her to oppose women's suffrage to protect women from being corrupted by politics.

Beecher was the oldest daughter in one of the most famous and distinguished families in the nineteenth century. Her father was the famous clergyman Lyman Beecher and the sister of equally famous preacher Henry Ward Beecher and Harriet Beecher Stowe, author of *Uncle Tom's Cabin*. Although she grew up in an atmosphere of learning, she received little formal education, being homeschooled until she was ten and then sent to the Litchfield Female Academy, the first major educational institution for women in America. She taught herself subjects that were not normally offered to women such as math, Latin, and philosophy. Beecher became a teacher at a school in New Haven, Connecticut, in 1821 and, along with her sister, Mary, opened the Hartford Female Seminary, where she taught until 1832. Contrary to most schools for women of the era, which emphasized languages and fine arts, Beecher's seminary offered a full range of subjects, substituting textbooks in arithmetic, theology, and mental and moral philosophy, which Beecher wrote herself. She also was an early pioneer of physical education for girls, introducing calisthenics to improve health in defiance with prevailing notions of women's fragility.

In the 1830s, Beecher accompanied her father when he became president of Cincinnati's Lane Theological Seminary. Beecher opened the Western Female Institute there and also worked on the McGuffey readers, the first nationally adopted textbooks for elementary students.

In the 1840s, Beecher lectured throughout the country on behalf of women's education and the need for improved teacher training as well as publishing *A Treatise on Domestic Economy* (1841), *The Duty of American Women to Their Country* (1845), and *The Domestic Receipt Book* (1846). Her books laid out her beliefs about women's central roles as mothers and educators. In 1852, she founded the American Women's Educational Association to send teachers west to create schools in the developing frontier.

Beecher would break with her family over women's suffrage and criticized abolitionist women for exceeding their proper domestic sphere. Beecher's conservatism as an opponent of suffrage and activities outside the home needs to be understood by her equally radical empowerment of women to accept their most important calling as teachers and moral guardians of their community. Her mission to extend and enhance teaching in America and widen its reach to women would have a lasting and profound effect on education in the United States.

Ruth Benedict (1887–1948)

Anthropologist

 In 1922, Ruth Benedict taught the first anthropology course at New York's Barnard College. One of her students was Margaret Mead, and together, Benedict and Mead would become the most famous American anthropologists of the twentieth century. Benedict, regarded as America's first female anthropologist, would transform fundamental concepts in cultural anthropology. As president of the American Anthropological Association, she would become one of the first women to be recognized as a prominent leader of a learned profession.

Born in New York City, Benedict attended St. Margaret's School for Girls, a college preparatory school, before entering Vassar College in 1905. A self-described "intellectual radical," Benedict graduated in 1909 with a major in English literature. Unsure what to do next, Benedict was offered an all-expense paid tour around Europe by a wealthy trustee. On her return, she took teaching jobs at the Westlake School for Girls in Los Angeles and the Orton School for Girls in Pasadena. Still undecided about a permanent career, Benedict took a class at the New School for Social Research in New York called "Sex and Ethnology." She followed it with another anthropology course, and, as Margaret Mead recalled, "Anthropology made the first 'sense' that any ordered approach to life had ever made to Ruth Benedict." She pursued graduate work with the eminent anthropologist Franz Boas at Columbia University and received her Ph.D. in anthropology in 1923. In 1931, Boas appointed her assistant professor in anthropology.

Benedict's first books, *Tales of the Cochiti Indians* (1931) and *Zuñi Mythology* (1935), reflect her eleven-year fieldwork and research into the religion and folklore of Native Americans. From this work, Benedict produced her most important book, *Patterns of Culture* (1934), in which Benedict argued, "A culture, like an individual, is a more or less consistent pattern of thought and action." Regarded as one of the major works of intellectual history, *Pat-*

terns of Culture presented the idea that culture is not a random collection of traits but a unique patterning or organization of these traits, a core concept that stands behind modern ideas of culture and our understanding of cultural diversity. Her other books include *Race: Science and Politics* (1940), which refuted theories of racial superiority, and *The Chrysanthemum and the Sword* (1946), an examination of Japanese cultural ideas.

Benedict became a full professor at Columbia in 1948 and has been acknowledged as the most outstanding anthropologist in the United States. As Benedict asserted, "The purpose of anthropology is to make the world safe for human difference." In both her life and her work, Benedict lived by this principle.

Mary McLeod Bethune (1875–1955)

Educator, School Founder

 One of the most influential and important African American women in American history, Mary McLeod Bethune was a stalwart advocate for the African American community as an educator and political leader.

Bethune was born in Mayesville, South Carolina, one of the seventeen children of former slaves Sam and Patsy McLeod. On a scholarship, she was able to attend the Scotia Seminary in North Carolina, a school for black girls that emphasized religious and industrial education. She later studied at the Bible Institute for Home and Foreign Missions (later the Moody Bible Institute) in Chicago, where she was the only black student. After graduating in 1895 and failing to find work as a missionary, she began teaching at the Haines Institute in Georgia and the Kendall Institute in North Carolina, where she met and married teacher and salesman Albertus Bethune.

In 1904, Bethune founded a school in Daytona Beach, Florida, for the daughters of African American laborers, raising money for the school by baking pies, selling ice cream, and going door to door seeking donations. In 1923, it merged with the Cookman Institute, a men's school, to become a coeducational college, renamed Bethune–Cookman College, in 1929. Bethune served as its president until 1942, taking a break to concentrate on fundraising, then resuming the presidency until her retirement in 1947.

Bethune's efforts as an educator and advocate for improved race relations brought her to national attention. She cofounded the National Council of Negro Women in 1935 and served as its president until 1949. Bethune became the first African American female presidential adviser when Franklin Roosevelt named her director of Negro Affairs of the National Youth Administration. During World War II, Bethune was an adviser on minority affairs to Roosevelt and assisted the secretary of war in selecting officer candidates for the U.S. Women's Air Corps.

In 1930, journalist Ida Tarbell named Bethune in the top ten of her list of America's greatest women. Multiple honors followed, including becoming the first woman to receive the National Honor of Merit, Haiti's highest award. Inducted into the National Women's Hall of Fame in 1973, Bethune became the first African American woman to have a monument in her honor erected in Washington, D.C. On the pedestal is engraved a passage from her Last Will and Testament: "I leave you love. I leave you hope. I leave you the challenge of developing confidence in one another. I leave you a thirst for education."

Charlotte Hawkins Brown (1883–1961)

Educator, School Founder

 In 1902, during one of the worst periods of the Jim Crow South in which educational opportunities for black Americans were neglected or confined to vocational training, teacher Charlotte Hawkins Brown established the Palmer Memorial Institute in Sedalia, North Carolina, as a preparatory school for African Americans to ready them for higher education and vocations well above what the white or black community considered possible. The school's success would be transformative, altering the trajectory of education for African Americans.

Born in Henderson, North Carolina, Brown was the granddaughter of former slaves, who moved with her mother to Cambridge, Massachusetts, where she was raised and educated. Coming to the attention of Alice Freeman Palmer, president of Wellesley College, for her determination to improve her education, Brown attended the Cambridge English High School and college at the Salem State Normal School at Palmer's expense.

After one year of college, Brown was hired to teach at the Bethany Institute, a rural school for African American children in Sedalia, North Carolina, run by the American Missionary Association. When it decided to close the school, Brown decided to establish her own, raising money and eventually obtaining two hundred acres and constructing two buildings for the school, which she named the Palmer Memorial Institute in honor of her mentor, Alice Freeman Palmer, which opened in 1902. Countering the prevailing notion that the best education for African Americans was vocational, Brown ran a preparatory school with a rigorous academic curriculum to equip her students for college and university work. It gained national recognition for its excellence and achievement, and Brown's work was acknowledged by such eminent figures as Mary McLeod Bethune, Nannie Burroughs, Eleanor Roosevelt, W. E. B. Du Bois, and Booker T. Washington. Brown was in demand as a lecturer and speaker on education. She was also active in the suffragist movement and became president of the North Carolina Association of Colored Women's Clubs, organizing voter registration drives for black women. A recipient of multiple honorary degrees, Brown would also become the first African American elected to Boston's Twentieth Century Club, organized to honor leaders in education, art, science, and religion.

Nannie Helen Burroughs (1879–1961)
Educator, School Founder

 The founder and longtime principal of the National Training School for Women and Girls in Washington, D.C., African American educator, feminist, and civil rights activist Nannie Helen Burroughs was a powerful force for the empowerment and advancement of women through education.

The daughter of former slaves, Burroughs was born in Orange, Virginia, and moved with her mother after her father's death to Washington, D.C., where she attended the M Street High School studying business and domestic science before attending Eckstein–Norton University in Kentucky, where she left before earning a degree. Failing to find work as a teacher in the district's public schools, she moved to Philadelphia and became an editor of *The Christian Banner*, a Baptist newspaper. She returned to Washington, D.C., but despite a high rating on the civil service exam, she was refused a position in the public school system. Instead, she took a series of temporary jobs as a janitor and bookkeeper while hoping to land a teaching position.

In 1900, at the annual meeting of the National Baptist Convention in Virginia, Burroughs delivered a speech titled "How the Sisters Are Hindered from Helping," which gained national attention and became a catalyst for the formation of the largest black women's organization at the time, the Woman's Convention, which became a forum for black women to come together on religious, political, and social issues as well as religious and educational training.

In 1909, Burroughs founded the National Training School for Women and Girls, a private elementary school in Washington, D.C., the first school in the nation to provide vocational training to African American females. The school addressed a central issue for African American women, who found themselves constrained as wage laborers in service occupations. Taking as its motto "We specialize in the wholly impossible," the National Training School linked vocational training with self-esteem and self-confidence, preparing young women for higher-level jobs and entry into the wider public sphere of business and politics. The core of the school's training was what Burroughs called the "three Bs": Bible, bath, and broom, with training in printing, bookkeeping, housekeeping, stenography, dressmaking, and cooking. The goal was to imbue black women with moral values as well as to prepare them to become self-sufficient wage earners.

Burroughs, who devoted the rest of her life to the school as its principal until her death in 1961, supplied a model for education that would be imitated nationally. She opposed the common belief that industrial and classical education were incompatible and became an early advocate of teaching African American history, requiring each student to pass a course on it before graduation. Three years after her death, the school she founded was renamed the Nannie Burroughs School.

Phyllis Chesler (1940–)
Educator, Psychologist

A professor of psychology and women's studies, Phyllis Chesler is a self-described "radical feminist" and "liberation psychologist" and one of the pioneers of second-wave feminism in the period from 1963 to 1975. In her review of Chesler's account of this period and beyond, *A Politically Incorrect Feminist* (2018), Ayaan Hirsi Ali has stated, "Phyllis Chesler stands out among women in general and feminists in particular. In this dark age of identity politics, when the rights of millions of women are sacrificed at the altar of intersectionality, Phyllis Chesler keeps us all focused on universal human rights for all women."

Born into an Orthodox Jewish family in Brooklyn, Chesler's mother was a school secretary and her father a truck driver. She attended New Utrecht High School and won a full scholarship to Bard College, where she met and married a Muslim man from Afghanistan and settled in Kabul in the household of her devout Muslim father-in-law. She has described her experience there as captivity that inspired her to become an ardent feminist. Her experiences are recounted in *An American Bride in Kabul* (2003). She returned to Bard to complete her final semester and after graduating earned her Ph.D. in psychology from the New School for Social Research and embarked on a dual career as a professor and as a psychotherapist in private practice.

She began her teaching career at Richmond College on Staten Island, part of the City University of New York, and offered one of the first women's studies courses in the United States and helped inaugurate women's studies programs throughout the CUNY system. As the first woman to be hired in an all-male psychology department, Chesler experienced sexism firsthand when she was assigned to shop for the secretaries' Christmas presents and was denied funding to conduct fieldwork after resisting the sexual advances of the man in charge of the fund. Despite her many publications and service to the college and her students, Chesler received tenure at Richmond only after twenty years, a delay that Chesler blames on the sexism and anti-activism approach of much of academe.

Her many publications include *Women and Madness* (1972), which is regarded as a feminist classic; *About Men* (1978); *With Child: A Diary of Motherhood* (1979), one of the few works of second-wave feminism to focus on motherhood; *Sacred Bond: The Legacy of Baby M* (1988); *Patriarchy: Notes of an Expert Witness* (1994); *Letters to a Young Feminist* (1998); *Woman's Inhumanity to Woman* (2002); *The New Anti-Semitism* (2003); and *The Death of Feminism* (2005).

A prolific author and pioneering educator who helped establish women's studies as a university discipline, Chesler has never backed down from controversial opinions or advocating on behalf of equity and justice. As she has stated, "Holding one's own against patriarchy, just holding one's own, is not easy. Resisting it—building a resistance movement—takes all we have. And more."

Jill Ker Conway (1934–2018)
College President, Historian

The first female president of Smith College, Jill Ker Conway was a historian who explored the role of feminism in American history, an acclaimed memoirist, and an admired administrator whom the present Smith president, Kathleen McCartney, said "demonstrated a leadership that was innovative and effective."

Growing up on a sheep ranch in the remote grasslands of Australia shaped Conway's life and her belief in women's capacity to take on any challenge. "In a labor-scarce society with a shortage of human energy," Conway recalled, "the work had to be done. It never crossed anyone's mind that you didn't work up to your competence." Conway's competence was evident in her attainment of a doctorate in history at Harvard in 1969. She began her teaching career at the University of Toronto, where she became a dean in 1971 and a vice president in 1973. In 1975, she began a decade as president of Smith College at a time when many doubted the need for women's colleges. Conway would answer by extending Smith's offerings to women, who could not previously take advantage of Smith. One of Conway's most notable accomplishments at Smith was a program she initiated to help mothers on welfare to pursue higher-education degrees. Instead of giving them scholarships, they were assisted instead with rent and access to an account at local stores, which allowed them to more effectively care for their children. Because of the attention the program brought to the issue of welfare, the State of Massachusetts changed its welfare system so that scholarship students would not lose their benefits. Conway also established a program to allow nontraditional students, many with work and family obligations, to study full or part time depending on their family and work schedules. After leaving Smith, she was a visiting professor in the Program in Science, Technology, and Society at MIT.

Conway's scholarship on feminism and history resulted in such books as *The Female Experience in 18th- and 19th-Century America* (1982) and *Women Reformers and American Culture* (1987). After editing an anthology of autobiographical writing by women, *Written by Herself* (1992), and a critical study of the memoir as a literary form, *When Memory Speaks* (1998), Conway undertook her own autobiography in a series of best-selling and critically acclaimed books: *The Road from Coorain* (1989), *True North* (1994), and *A Woman's Education* (2001).

In recognition of her various accomplishments—scholar, teacher, administrator, and author—Conway was awarded the National Humanities Medal in 2013. Conway described her memoir's focus as on "what women were not supposed to acknowledge—ambition, love of adventure, risk taking." The three are fitting descriptors of Conway's life as a historian and trailblazing educator.

Anna Julia Cooper (1858–1964)

Educator

One of the most historically significant African American teachers and scholars, Anna Julia Cooper's life spanned the Civil War through the civil rights movement, which she reflected in important contributions to sociology, history, and African American studies. As a teacher and administrator, she insisted on the importance of education, particularly for African American women. Her lessons and examples of racial and gender empowerment earned her the description "mother of black feminism."

Born a slave in Raleigh, North Carolina, Cooper's father is believed to have been her mother's white master. In 1868, when Cooper was nine, she received a scholarship to enroll in the newly opened Saint Augustine's Normal School and Collegiate Institute in Raleigh, founded by the local Episcopal diocese to train teachers to educate former slaves and their families. She excelled as a student, but her feminism started early when she discovered that her male classmates were encouraged to study a more rigorous curriculum than were the female students. The experience would motivate her for the rest of her life to advocate for the education of black women.

Cooper enrolled in Oberlin College, graduating in 1884 with a BS degree in mathematics and a master's degree in 1888. In 1887, she joined the faculty at the M Street High School in Washington, D.C., established in 1870 as the Preparatory High School for Negro Youth. There, she taught mathematics, science, and Latin. While teaching, she completed her first book, *A Voice from the South: By a Black Woman of the South* (1892), which is considered the first book about black feminism. In 1902, Cooper was named principal of the school, and, under her leadership, its academic reputation increased, with several graduates being admitted to Ivy League schools. Cooper's emphasis on college preparatory courses put her at odds with critics like Booker T. Washington, who favored vocational education for blacks. Her contract was not renewed in 1905, and Cooper next taught at Lincoln University, a historically black college in Jefferson City, Missouri, and in 1910, she was rehired at M Street (renamed Dunbar High School in 1916), where she remained until 1930.

In 1911, Cooper began studying part time for a doctoral degree and received her doctorate from the Sorbonne in 1925, at the age of sixty-seven, with her dissertation, written in French but published in English, *Slavery and the French Revolutionists, 1788–1805*. Cooper became the fourth African American woman to obtain a doctorate of philosophy.

Cooper's later years were devoted to Frelinghuysen University, an extension program for working African Americans, as its president. She died in Washington, D.C., at the age of 105. Cooper has the distinction of being the only woman who is quoted in current U.S. passports: "The cause of freedom is not the cause of a race or a sect, a party or a class—it is the cause of humankind, the very birthright of humanity."

Fanny Jackson Coppin (1837–1913)

Educator

An educator and missionary, Fanny Jackson Coppin was named principal of the Institute for Colored Youth in Philadelphia in 1869, becoming the first African American woman to receive the title of school principal, a position she held until 1906.

Born a slave in Washington, D.C., Coppin gained her freedom when her aunt was able to purchase her at the age of twelve for $125. Working as a domestic servant, Coppin was determined to get an education and studied to enter the Rhode Island State Normal School, and in 1860, she attended Oberlin College, the first college in the United States to accept both black and female students. At Oberlin, she followed the "gentleman's course of study" that included Latin, Greek, and mathematics. Chosen to teach a preparatory course at Oberlin, she

was warned that her students might rebel against her because of her race. Instead, her course became one of the most popular on campus. While still a student, Coppin established a night class in reading and writing for local freedmen. In 1865, she became only the second African American woman to earn a bachelor's degree.

Coppin took a teaching position at the Institute for Colored Youth in Philadelphia (now Cheyney University of Pennsylvania), a school designed to challenge the prevailing notions that African Americans were incapable of higher learning. There, she taught her students Latin classics and New Testament Greek. In her thirty-seven years at the institute, Coppin was responsible for numerous innovations, including the introduction of an industrial training department that offered instruction in ten trades. She was named by the board of education as superintendent of schools, becoming the first African American superintendent of a school district in the United States.

Coppin married Reverend Levi Jenkins Coppin, a minister of the African Methodist Episcopal Church, in 1881. She became active in her husband's missionary work, traveling in 1902 to South Africa, where she founded the Bethel Institute, a missionary school with self-help programs. After almost a decade of missionary work, ill health forced her to return to Philadelphia, where she died in 1913. In 1926, a Baltimore teacher training school was named the Fanny Jackson Coppin Normal School (now Coppin State University) in her honor.

Prudence Crandall (1803–1890)

Educator

A Quaker schoolteacher and abolitionist, Prudence Crandall prompted a firestorm of protest when in 1832 she admitted to her private school for young girls Sarah Harris, a seventeen-year-old African American girl, thereby creating what is considered to be the first integrated classroom in the United States. White parents withdrew their children, but Crandall persisted in educating, now exclusively, young girls of color, thereby establishing the first school for African American girls in Connecticut. Her actions would lead to her imprisonment and ouster from the state.

Born in Hopkinton, Rhode Island, into a farm family, Crandall was raised in Canterbury, Connecticut, and attended the New England Friends' Boarding School in Providence, Rhode Island, studying arithmetic, Latin, and science—subjects not typically taught to girls—but embraced by Quakers who believed in equal educational opportunities. After graduating, she taught at a school in Plainfield, Connecticut, before she bought a house in 1831 with her sister Almira that would become the Canterbury Female Boarding School. The curriculum included geography, history, grammar, arithmetic, reading, and writing and was offered to the daughters of the town's wealthiest families. It was quickly ranked as one of the state's best schools, which provided its female students with an education comparable to that of prominent schools for boys.

Sensitized to the plight of slaves and people of color from reading William Lloyd Garrison's abolitionist newspaper *The Liberator*, Crandall "contemplated for a while, the manner in which I might best serve the people of color." The opportunity came when Sarah Harris, the daughter of a free African American farmer, asked to be accepted to the school to prepare for teaching other African Americans. Although her white pupils did not object, their parents did, and with a mass exodus of white students, Crandall reopened the school for African American girls, who enrolled from multiple states. Students venturing beyond the school were threatened and pelted with eggs, stones, and manure. In 1833, the Canterbury legislature passed a "black law," making it illegal to run a school that taught African American students from a state other than Connecticut. Crandall was arrested, jailed, and eventually found guilty (her conviction would be overturned by a higher court). In 1834, an angry mob attacked the school, smashing windows and furniture, and Crandall, fearing for her students' safety, finally closed the school.

Crandall married Baptist minister and abolitionist Calvin Philleo, and the couple left Connecti-

cut for Illinois, where Crandall ran a school and participated in the women's suffrage movement. In 1886, repentant Canterbury citizens, supported by Hartford resident Mark Twain, gained a small pension for Crandall from the Connecticut legislature. In 1995, the Connecticut General Assembly designated her as the state's official heroine. Her Canterbury school now houses the Prudence Crandall Museum.

Zilpah P. Grant (1794–1874)
Educator, School Founder

 The founder of the Ipswich Female Seminary in Ipswich, Massachusetts, in 1828, Zilpah Grant was an influential, nineteenth-century American educator and proponent for educational access and opportunities for women.

Born in Norfolk, Connecticut, Grant attended local schools as much as her frail health and family finances would allow since she was needed at home to help her widowed mother keep the family farm. From the age of fifteen, she taught in a variety of schools in nearby towns, and in 1820, she attended the Female Seminary in Byfield, Massachusetts, where, a year later, she became a teacher in the school. In 1824, she accepted the assignment as preceptress of the newly established Adams Female Academy in East Derry, New Hampshire, where she designed a rigorous, three-year course of study. The school flourished, and Grant's reputation was enhanced, but disagreements with the school's trustees led Grant to depart to Ipswich, Massachusetts, to found the Ipswich Female Academy. Her friend Mary Lyon, who had accompanied Grant from Byfield and served as Grant's assistant, would found the Mount Holyoke Female Seminary (later Mount Holyoke College) in South Hadley, Massachusetts, in 1834.

Grant's curriculum at the Ipswich Academy combined rigorous academic studies with moral and teacher training, which would become a model for other schools for women in nineteenth-century America. Grant closed the school when she married in 1841. In 1852, she joined the board of the American Women's Educational Association, founded by Catherine Beecher, and was active in its efforts to recruit and train teachers for schools in the West.

Evelynn Hammonds (1953–)
College Dean

In 2008, Evelynn Hammonds, a scholar on the intersection of race, gender, science, and medicine, became only the fourth black woman to receive tenure on the faculty of arts and science at Harvard University and the first woman and the first African American to be named dean of Harvard College.

Born in Atlanta, Georgia, daughter of a schoolteacher mother and postal worker father, Hammonds attended public schools before earning two undergraduate degrees: in physics from Spelman College and in electrical engineering at Georgia Tech. In 1980, Hammonds earned her master's degree in physics from MIT. After graduation, she began a five-year career as a software engineer before gaining a Ph.D. in the history of science from Harvard. Returning to MIT to teach, she became the founding director of MIT's Center for the Study of the Diversity in Science, Technology, and Medicine and helped to organize the first national academic conference for black female scholars.

Hammonds's scholarly publications include *Childhood's Deadly Scourge: The Campaign to Control Diphtheria in New York City, 1880–1930* (1999), *The Nature of Difference: Sciences of Race in the United States from Jefferson to Genomics* (2008), *The Harvard Sampler: Liberal Education for the Twenty-first Century* (2011), and *The Dilemma of Classification: The Past in the Present* (2011).

A leading contemporary scholar on race, gender, and technology, Hammonds has been a strong advocate for opportunities for minorities and women in higher education. As she explained, "When I was growing up in Atlanta during the height of the civil rights movement, no one used the word diversity. We used words like justice and equity, and perhaps we should return to those words as we seek new ways to express a commitment to diversity and to excellence."

Shirley Ann Jackson (1946–)
College President, Physicist

 The first black woman to earn a Ph.D. from the Massachusetts Institute of Technology, which was in theoretical solid-state physics, Shirley Ann Jackson was also the first black woman to be elected president and then chairman of the board of the American Association for the Advancement of Science; the first black woman to become president of a major research university, the country's oldest, Rensselaer Polytechnic Institute in New York; the first black woman to be elected to the National Academy of Engineering; and the first African American and first woman to chair the U.S. Nuclear Regulatory Commission.

Jackson's long list of impressive accomplishments was not a surprise; she declared to her mother at four years old that she would someday be called "Shirley the Great." Born into a segregated Washington, D.C., Jackson took advantage of the Supreme Court decision *Brown v. Board of Education* of 1954, which mandated the integration of the nation's schools, to attend Roosevelt Senior High School, where she participated in the school's accelerated programs in both math and science. Graduating in 1964 as valedictorian, she entered MIT, one of fewer than twenty African American students and the only one studying theoretical physics, going on to earn her doctorate in nuclear physics in 1973 and becoming only the second African American woman in the United States to earn a Ph.D. in physics.

Jackson did postdoctoral research in subatomic particles at a number of physics laboratories in the United States and in Europe before becoming a research associate at the Fermi National Accelerator Laboratory in Illinois and joining AT&T Bell Laboratories in 1978. Jackson was part of the faculty at Rutgers University from 1991 to 1995 while still consulting with Bell Labs on semiconductor theory. In 1999, Jackson became the eighteenth president of Rensselaer Polytechnic Institute. Under Jackson, Rensselaer has been transformed into a world-class technological research university due to a campaign she spearheaded that raised more than $1.25 billion and invested in state-of-the-art research facilities.

The holder of fifty-three honorary doctoral degrees from colleges and universities worldwide, Jackson, in 2016, was awarded the National Medal of Science by President Barack Obama, the nation's highest honor for contributions in science and engineering. Few individuals who have claimed "the Great" as an honorific have earned that distinction as well as Shirley Ann Jackson.

Helen Keller (1880–1968) and Anne Sullivan (1866–1936)

Lecturer, Educator

The story of Helen Keller's triumph over disability is one of the best known and most inspiring in the history of women. Born in Tuscumbia, Alabama, left blind and deaf at nineteen months after an attack of scarlet fever by the age of six, she was, as she later wrote, "a phantom living in a 'no world' … I had neither will nor intellect." She could not speak, and her parents had no way of communicating with her. She was indulged and spoiled, undisciplined, and unrestrained. Advised to confine her to a mental asylum, her parents sought the advice of a family friend, Alexander Graham Bell, who suggested they request a teacher from Boston's Perkins Institute, a training school for the blind.

In 1887, twenty-year-old Anne Sullivan arrived. The "creator of a soul," as educator Maria Montessori later called her, Sullivan had survived a sordid childhood as a half-blind orphan in a squalid Massachusetts almshouse to come to the Perkins Institute alone at fourteen, illiterate and almost as unruly as Helen was when the two met. Sullivan was provided with an education and several operations that improved her eyesight. Perhaps seeing herself in Helen, Sullivan was determined not to break the child's spirit as she took on the formidable task of trying to tame and teach her.

As Sullivan worked to discipline Helen Keller and build a trusting relationship with her, she would spell out words with her fingers into the child's hands and then give her the object she spelled to touch. It made no impression on Helen until one day, Sullivan took Keller to the water pump and let the cold water spill over one of the child's hands while spelling "water" in the other. "Suddenly I felt a misty conscious as of something forgotten," Keller later recalled, "and somehow the mystery of language was returned to me." She spelled out "water" several times and then started touching other objects while indicating a desire to know their names. In the next five months, Keller had mastered 625 words. She went on to read braille, to write using thin rulers to keep her hand in alignment, and to use a typewriter.

Sullivan accompanied Keller to the Horace Mann School in New York, where Keller took lessons in speech and was with her when she attended the Wright-Humason School for the Deaf for advanced study in speech and lip reading. When Keller entered Radcliffe College, the result of fundraising by Mark Twain, Sullivan sat beside her and spelled her lectures into her hand. In 1904, Keller graduated *cum laude*, and at her request, Sullivan mounted the platform with her and stood beside her as she received her diploma.

After Keller's graduation, she and Sullivan settled in Wrentham, Massachusetts. A year later, Sullivan married writer John Macy, who had edited Keller's first best-selling book, *The Story of My Life* (1902). Keller continued to write and, with Sullivan, embarked on a series of lecture tours, speaking on the problems of the disabled. Keller helped organize thirteen state commissions for the blind, raised funds for the American Foundation for the Blind, and lobbied for materials for the visually impaired. In 1917, Keller and Sullivan moved to Forest Hills, New York, where they lived until Sullivan's death in 1936. Keller's other books include *The World I Live In* (1908), *The Song of the Stone Wall* (1910), *Out of the Dark* (1913), *My Religion* (1927), *Mid-Stream—My Later Life* (1930), *Helen Keller's Journal* (1938), *Let Us Have Faith* (1940), *The Open Door* (1957), and a tribute to Sullivan, *Helen Keller's Teacher: Anne Sullivan Macy* (1955).

Throughout their lives, Keller and Sullivan were frequently courted and feted by presidents, royalty, and other luminaries, yet Sullivan remained true to her mission as a teacher and educator while Keller was determined not to become a celebrated oddity, albeit a heroic one. Instead, she converted her story into moving educational lessons for her many readers and audiences on the nature of disabilities and the achievements that are possible despite severe limitations. Through all her fame as one of the most influential women of all time, Keller never forgot her first and greatest teacher, her other half who made her whole. "How much of my delight in all beautiful things is innate," she wrote, "and how much is due to her influence, I can never tell. I feel that her being is inseparable from my own, and that the footsteps of my life are in hers.... There is not a talent, or an aspiration or a joy in me that has not been awakened by her loving touch."

Gerda Lerner (1920–2013)

Educator, Historian

 Historian and writer Gerda Lerner has been described as the single most influential figure in the development of women's and gender history since the 1960s. Since Lerner's establishment of an MA program at Sarah Lawrence College in 1972, women's studies programs have become standard at the majority of U.S. colleges and universities. Lerner is also the author or editor of numerous groundbreaking gender-studies books, including *The Woman in American History* (1971), *Black Women in White America* (1972), *The Female Experience* (1976), *The Majority Finds Its Past: Placing Women in History* (1979), *Teaching Women's History* (1981), and *The Creation of Feminist Consciousness* (1994).

Born Gerda Gronstein in Vienna into an affluent, Jewish, middle-class family, Lerner and her family were deported in 1939 as the persecution of Austrian Jews escalated. Lerner and her mother were imprisoned for six weeks and were only released when Lerner's father agreed to sign over his property and pharmacy business to the Nazis. Lerner would later declare, "I am a historian because of my Jewish experience." The family was broken up and dispersed. Lerner alone managed to obtain a visa to the United States, where she lived in New York, working as a waitress, salesgirl, office clerk, and X-ray technician while she learned English and began to write fiction about Nazi brutality (*The Prisoners* was published in 1940 and *The Russian Campaign* in 1943). She married film editor Carl Lerner in 1941, and the couple lived in Hollywood for several years before returning to New York with their two children when the McCarthy hearings led to the Hollywood blacklist that affected Carl Lerner's ability to find work.

At the age of thirty-eight, Lerner enrolled in college and received a bachelor's degree from the New School for Social Research and eventually a Ph.D. in history at Columbia University in 1966. The same year, Lerner became a founding member of the National Organization for Women (NOW) and, in 1968, received her first academic appointment at Sarah Lawrence College. Lerner's scholarly books and articles, written in the 1960s and 1970s, would help to establish women's history as a recognized field of study. She also significantly expanded African American history with an emphasis on the role and significance of black women in America. Realizing that writing and teaching women's history was insufficient, Lerner created the women's studies program at Sarah Lawrence and later, at the University of Wisconsin, established the country's first Ph.D. program in women's history. She continued to work as a teacher and writer at the University of Wisconsin until her death at ninety-two. *Fireweed: A Political Autobiography* (2003) traces her life from her childhood in Vienna to 1958, when her academic career began.

Lerner contributed both scholarship and activism that fundamentally altered the ways in which women have been considered and studied. As Lerner insisted, "Women's history is the primary tool for women's emancipation."

Deborah E. Lipstadt (1947–)

Educator, Historian

 Historian Deborah E. Lipstadt is the Dorot professor of modern Jewish history and Holocaust studies at Emory University, who in 1996 successfully defended a libel charge brought by

David Irving after she called him a Holocaust denier in her book *Denying the Holocaust* (1993). In effect, she proved in a British court the historical truth of Hitler's genocide of six million European Jews during World War II, exposing the denial of that truth as both wrongheaded and pernicious.

Lipstadt was born in New York City. She studied at the Hebrew Institute of Long Island and attended the City College of New York, receiving her BA in American history in 1960. She completed her master's degree in 1972 and her Ph.D. in Jewish history in 1976 from Brandeis University. She began her teaching career in history and religion at the University of Washington, the first to teach Jewish studies there. In 1979, she became a faculty member at the University of California–Los Angeles, where she was denied tenure, and she left in 1985. In 1986, her book *Beyond Belief: The American Press and the Coming of the Holocaust 1933–1945* was published. After a research fellowship at Hebrew University to explore Holocaust denial and a visiting teaching position at Occidental College, Lipstadt became an associate professor of religion at Emory College. *Denying the Holocaust* appeared in 1993, and in 1994, Lipstadt received the National Jewish Book Award for it, and President Clinton appointed her to the U.S. Holocaust Memorial Council.

When Lipstadt learned in 1995 that English author and revisionist writer on World War II David Irving was threatening to sue her for calling him a Holocaust denier, she decided to fight the charge. "In England," she wrote, "I had to prove that what I wrote was not libel. I wanted a trial that proved [I] was right when [I] called David Irving a denier." To make her case, Lipstadt recruited a team of historians, who offered three thousand pages of testimony in the legal battle that went on for five years. Ultimately, the British Royal High Court of Justice ruled in favor of Lipstadt in a trial that exposed Irving's lies, distortions of history, and anti-Semitism and sentenced him to three years in prison. In 2005, Lipstadt published *History on Trial: My Day in Court with David Irving*, describing her experiences. It was the basis of the 2016 film *Denial*. Lipstadt's latest book is *Antisemitism: Here and Now* (2019), which explores the rise of anti-Semitism in the United States and Europe.

Mary Lyon (1797–1849)
College Founder

Mary Lyon is responsible for the establishment of two colleges for women, Wheaton Female Seminary (now Wheaton College) in 1834 and Mount Holyoke Female Seminary (now Mount Holyoke College) in 1837. Both would serve as models for women's higher education in America.

Born on a remote farm in western Massachusetts, Lyon attended several district primary schools intermittently while keeping the farm running after her father died when she was five. She eventually attended Sanderson Academy and the Byfield Seminary. There, Lyon was befriended by teacher Zilpah Grant, whom she assisted in running the Adams Female Academy in New Hampshire and the Ipswich Female Seminary in Massachusetts. In 1834, Laban Wheaton asked Lyon to assist in establishing the Wheaton Female Seminary, and Lyon was responsible for creating its first curriculum, designed to rival those of men's colleges.

Lyon next set out to realize the goal of creating a school providing a liberal education for female students with moderate means by having the students share in the domestic work of the school. She raised funds for her idea and, in 1836, gained a charter to open Mount Holyoke Female Seminary, which opened with about eighty students after some four hundred applicants were turned away due to lack of space. Lyon served as the school's principal for the next twelve years, overseeing the expansion of the curriculum and the construction of new buildings. Enrollment grew to a student body of two hundred. She imposed rigorous admission and academic standards and, an early believer in daily exercise for women, required students to walk one mile daily after breakfast. She was also innovative in anticipating the changing roles for women, requiring, in the words of Mount Holyoke's biography, "seven courses in the sciences and mathematics for graduation, a requirement unheard of at other female seminaries. She introduced women to 'a new and unusual way' to learn science—laboratory experiments that they performed themselves. She organized field trips on which students collected rocks, plants, and specimens for lab work, and inspected geological formations and recently discovered dinosaur tracks." Lyon's hands-on approach to learning was innovative and original and would be widely imitated at both women's and men's colleges.

Lyon died of an infection, possibly contracted from an ill student in her care. She is buried on the Mount Holyoke campus, where Mary Lyon Hall houses the college offices, classrooms, and a chapel. The main classroom building for Wheaton Female Seminary was renamed Mary Lyon Hall on the Wheaton College campus. As evidence of her impact on education in America, dormitories and classroom buildings at Miami University, Plymouth State University, Swarthmore College, and the University of Massachusetts–Amherst have been named in her honor.

Margaret Mead (1901–1978)

Anthropologist, Educator

In 1928, twenty-seven-year-old anthropologist Margaret Mead published *Coming of Age in Samoa*, an account of her first field trip to the Pacific Islands. This groundbreaking work launched Mead's career as a pioneering researcher and helped establish her as one of the world's most celebrated social and cultural anthropologists and the most famous educator of the twentieth century.

Born and raised in Philadelphia, Margaret Mead was the oldest of the five children of her father, a professor of economics, and her mother, a sociologist and teacher. As a child, Mead was educated chiefly at home by her grandmother, later attending Barnard College and doing graduate work at Columbia, studying with the eminent anthropologist Franz Boas. In 1925, she set out to do fieldwork among the people of Polynesia, a daring act for a young woman of her time. Up until then, anthropology had largely been a male domain, but Mead brought to the science a woman's perspective and interest in the roles women play in social groups, subjects often ignored in previous research. For nine months, Mead lived in a tiny Samoan island village, learning the language and customs while observing the lifestyles of Samoan teenagers, especially their sexual practices. What she discovered and recorded in *Coming of Age in Samoa* challenged previous notions of so-called primitive peoples while contradicting some of the most deeply rooted notions concerning child rearing, mating practices, family relations, and gender assumptions. Mead helped to establish that behavior was not determined at birth but by cultural conditions that could be altered if better understood.

A second field trip produced *Growing Up in New Guinea* (1930), another commercial and critical success. Mead's subsequent studies of gender formation among three different cultures of New Guinea yielded what she considered her most important book, *Sex and Temperament in Three Primitive Societies* (1935). Mead demonstrated that gender roles were not universal and that temperament was determined by culture, not biology. Both men and women developed, in Mead's view, the personalities their society considered acceptable for their sex. "It was exciting," Mead wrote in her autobiography, *Blackberry Winter* (1972), "to strip off the layers of culturally attributed expected behavior and to feel one knew at last who one was."

Mead would go on to write over forty books on a wide range of subjects, including education, science, religion, ecology, and feminism, while lecturing at colleges and universities worldwide and serving as a curator of ethnology at New York's American Museum of Natural History. Her influence in her field was enormous, but possibly, her greatest contribution was that she made anthropology accessible to the nonscientist. She invited millions of people to look with her at other cultures and, as she wrote, "to cherish the life of the world."

Alice Freeman Palmer (1855–1902)

College President

One of the earliest female college presidents in the United States, Alice Freeman Palmer was the youngest president of Wellesley

College and the first dean of women at the University of Chicago.

Born on a New York farm, Palmer taught herself to read before entering the local school at the age of four. When she was fifteen, she shocked her parents by declaring her intention to attend college. She broke off her engagement when her fiancé discouraged her. She entered the University of Michigan in 1872, two years after the university was first forced to admit women. During and after college, Palmer took a variety of teaching positions and became her family's primary support when her father went bankrupt.

In 1879, Palmer accepted a position as a professor of history at Wellesley College, which had opened four years earlier with an all-female faculty. When Wellesley's founder, Henry Durant, died in 1881, and its first president, Ada Howard, stepped down for health reasons, Palmer was named president, even though, at the age of twenty-seven, she was the youngest member of the faculty. She would establish many of the school's governance structures that persist to this day as well as establishing a system of preparatory schools around the country for students of the college. Her position led to her becoming the most visible female educator in America, and Palmer would use the attention to advocate on behalf of college educations for women. In 1881, Palmer cofounded the Association of Collegiate Alumnae, which later became the American Association of University Women, serving as its president from 1885 to 1887 and from 1889 to 1890.

Palmer resigned from Wellesley to marry Harvard professor of philosophy George Herbert Palmer in 1887. Despite needing a year to recover from tuberculosis, she spent four years traveling the country on behalf of women's higher education. Palmer countered the prevailing notion that higher education desexed women, and her own presence as an intellectual but passionate, devoted to others but happy in her personal life, did much to change views. In 1892, she was named first dean of women at the newly created University of Chicago, a post she held until 1895. Palmer was also active organizing the Harvard Annex, which would become Radcliffe College, the "sister" college to Harvard.

Elizabeth Palmer Peabody (1804–1894)
Educator, School Founder

Regarded as the first female book publisher in America, Peabody has the additional distinction of opening the first English-language kindergarten in the United States and becoming one of the leaders of the kindergarten movement that would lead to preschool instruction throughout the country.

The daughter of two teachers, Peabody was born in Billerica, Massachusetts, and raised in Salem, Massachusetts. She was educated at her mother's school for girls, and in 1821, Peabody set up her own school, the Lancaster Boarding School. In 1825, she moved to Boston and started a successful all-girls' school first in Brookline and then in Boston. There, she met clergyman and intellectual William Ellery Channing, who introduced Peabody to Unitarianism and Transcendentalism. In 1834, she assisted Bronson Alcott in starting the Temple School in Boston. In 1837, Peabody became a charter member of the Transcendentalist Club, whose members included Margaret Fuller, Ralph Waldo Emerson, Channing, and Alcott.

In 1839, Peabody opened the West Street bookstore, which served as an intellectual center in Boston. On her own printing press, she published works by Fuller, three of Nathaniel Hawthorne's earliest books, the critical journal and organ of the Transcendentalist movement *The Dial*, and Henry David Thoreau's essay "Civil Disobedience."

She closed her shop in 1850 to return to teaching and promoting public education, particularly the ideas about preschool education derived from German theorist Friedrich Froebel, which emphasized extending education to five-year-olds with an emphasis on play, social interaction, and motor skills to ease the transition from home to schooling. Peabody opened the first English-language kindergarten in 1860. She also promoted the concept as editor of the *Kindergarten Messenger* and in lectures and articles. Peabody would serve as a strong advocate for the kindergarten movement in America that would eventually spread nationwide and has been called one of the greatest educational reform movements in American history.

Peabody's involvement with so many central figures in Boston's history and the intellectual currents they fostered earned her the honorific "the grandmother of Boston." She lived long enough to see her experiment in preschool education become accepted as standard practice in America.

Sarah Pierce (1767–1852)

Educator

An early American educator, Sarah Pierce opened a school in her home in Litchfield, Connecticut, in 1792, which would become one of the first major educational institutions for women in America. The Litchfield Female Academy would eventually enroll an estimated three thousand students from across the United States and Canada, including Catherine Beecher and Harriet Beecher Stowe.

Pierce was the daughter of a Litchfield farmer and potter. Her mother died when she was three and her father in 1783, leaving the responsibility for a stepmother and seven younger siblings to her brother John, a distinguished veteran of the American Revolution. To help support the household, Sarah and her sister Mary were sent to New York City to train to become teachers. Returning to Litchfield, Sarah brought students back with her to board in the Pierce homestead. In 1798, in response to the popularity of the school, town leaders in Litchfield raised funds to build the Female Academy next to Sarah Pierce's house. Later, in 1827, the newly incorporated Litchfield Female Academy opened in an even larger building nearby.

Pierce provided instruction in composition, geography, history, needlework, painting, and dance. In 1814, her nephew, John P. Brace, a Williams College graduate, joined the school to teach classes in logic, philosophy, and the sciences. The school's pedagogy reflected Pierce's deep belief in the intellectual equality of the sexes and her insistence that enhanced educational opportunities would not jeopardize women's roles as wives and mothers. She did not

believe that women should enter all-male colleges or professions but insisted that women's contributions in the home were as important and that women needed sufficient education to form their own opinions and that the future of the new American republic would depend on the intellectual, moral, and spiritual contributions of women as well as men.

Sarah Pierce, who never married, died at the age of eighty-three, still residing in Litchfield. The diploma that the many young women who graduated from the school Pierce founded represented the highest level of education then available to women in the United States.

Virginia Randolph (1874–1958)

Educator

The daughter of former slaves, Virginia Randolph would begin teaching in a one-room schoolhouse in Henrico County, Virginia, in 1892 and devote nearly six decades to being an innovative educator whose improved teaching method in vocational training would be adopted worldwide.

Born in Richmond, Virginia, Randolph began working at an early age to contribute to the family's finances after her father died in her early childhood. She was schooled in sewing, knitting, and crocheting by her mother, skills Randolph would later draw upon in her own teaching that began when she was sixteen. In 1892, she began working at the Mountain Road School in Henrico County, an all-black, dilapidated, and neglected one-room school. Randolph raised money for supplies and improvements while instituting a Better Homes campaign to improve the lives of the poverty-stricken families of her students. Teaching both academic subjects and vocational training, Randolph embraced "learning by doing," an innovative philosophy that gained attention from the superintendent of schools for Henrico County, who said, "Here was a teacher who thought of her work in terms of the welfare of a whole community, and of the school as an agency to help people to live better, to do their work with more skill and intelligence, and to do it in the spirit of neighborliness."

In 1908, Randolph was named the first "Jeanes supervising industrial teacher," named by the Jeanes Foundation, founded by Quaker philanthropist Anna T. Jeanes of Philadelphia to improve the African American school system. Randolph oversaw twenty-three elementary schools in Henrico County, developing the first in-service training program for black teachers and improving the curricula of the schools. Randolph's methods of improving both education and the community would become the model for all the other Jeanes teachers who followed her. Her innovations and philosophy were recorded in the *Henrico Plan*, a reference book that was widely consulted throughout the South, and her teaching techniques and philosophy would be adopted in Great Britain's African colonies. In 1938, Randolph was appointed to the Industrial School Board of Colored Children and served for many years on the Inter-Racial and Health Board for the State of Virginia.

Randolph retired after a fifty-seven-year teaching and administrative career. The Virginia Randolph Fund was founded in 1936 to honor her. The Virginia E. Randolph Cottage, which houses Randolph's home economics classroom, was declared a National Historic Landmark in 1974.

Bernice Sandler (1928–2019)

Educator

An educator and activist who directly experienced gender discrimination in her professional career, Bernice Sandler was instrumental in attaining gender equality within educational programs. Her activism for women's rights in education and instrumental role in the development, passage, and implementation of the most important modern educational reforms caused her to be known as "the godmother of Title IX."

Born Bernice Resnick in Brooklyn, New York, she graduated from Erasmus Hall High School and graduated from Brooklyn College, New York's first public coeducational liberal arts college, in psychology in 1948. She became one of the first women to be admitted into the graduate programs at the City College of New York, receiving her master's in clinical and school psychology in 1950. Despite her degrees in psychology and education, including a Ph.D. from the University of Maryland in 1969, she faced sexual discrimination while seeking the full-time positions she was qualified for. Teaching there part time, she was told that she wasn't being offered a full-time job because "you come on too strong for a woman." Other interviewers complained that women stayed home when their children were sick and that she was "just a housewife who went back to school."

Sandler's experiences drove her to serve as the chair of the Action Committee for Federal Contract Compliance of the Women's Equity Action League, an organization that enforced, through lawsuits, compliance with a federal executive order prohibiting contractors from discriminating against employees. Her experience with the Women's Equity Action League led to her work in developing, passing, and implementing Title IX, a federal civil rights law that barred sex discrimination by educational institutions that received federal funding. Title IX was passed as part of the Education Amendments of 1972. Title IX represented a seismic change in the landscape of education, requiring that male and female students have equal access to admissions, resources, and financial assistance. "Every woman who has gone to college," said Margaret Dunkle, a research colleague and friend, said, "gotten a law degree or a medical degree, was able to take shop instead of home-ec[onomics], or went to a military academy really owes [Sandler] a huge debt."

Since the passing of Title IX, Sandler remained an active supporter of women's rights and continued to work with the government and various educational institutions to pursue equity for women. As chair of the first Federal Advisory Committee on Women's Educational Equity, she was instrumental in producing a pioneering federal report on sexual harassment in colleges and universities. In 1982, she published a report describing the differences in the way men and women are treated in academic and professional settings, coining the term "chilly classroom climate," which became the focus of her book *The Chilly Classroom Climate: A Guide to Improve the Education of Women* (1996). Sandler also published extensively on sexual harassment, coining the term "gang rape" in her 1985 report *Friends Raping Friends: Could It Happen to You?*

Named a senior scholar at the Women's Research and Education Institute in Washington, D.C., Sandler was an adjunct associate professor at the Drexel University School of Medicine until her death in 2019.

Elaine Showalter (1941–)

Educator, Feminist Theorist

A founder of feminist literary criticism in the United States, Elaine Showalter is identified with gynocritics, a feminist criticism concerned with the history, themes, genres, and structures of literature written by women.

Born in Boston, Showalter earned her bachelor's degree at Bryn Mawr College, her master's degree at Brandeis University, and in 1970 her Ph.D. at the University of California–Davis. She began her teaching career at Douglass College, the women's division of Rutgers University, before joining the Princeton University faculty in 1984. When she began her teaching career, neither Rutgers nor Princeton hired female faculty members.

Showalter converted her doctoral thesis into her first book, *A Literature of Their Own: British Women Novelists from Brontë to Lessing* (1977), a foundational study that provided an influential critical perspective for analyzing literature by women. *Toward a Feminist Poetics* (1979) is one of the core texts in feminist critical theory. *The Female Malady: Women, Madness, and English Culture, 1830–1980* (1985) examines women and the practice of psychiatry. Other books include *Sexual Anarchy: Gender and Culture at the Fin de Siècle* (1990); *Sister's Choice: Tradition and Change in American Women's Writing* (1991); *Hystories: Historical Epidemics and Modern Culture* (1997); *Inventing Herself: Claiming a Feminist Intellectual Heritage* (2001); *Teaching Literature* (2003); and *A Jury of Her Peers* (2009), a survey of women's writing in America from its origin through the 1990s.

Showalter's provocative attitudes on many subjects have turned her into a lightning rod for controversy. Often iconoclastic and challenging conventional wisdom, Showalter's criticism is never dull or complacent. It provokes and encourages her readers to think through the implications she describes without relying on the dogmatic or the current trend. "I don't pay any attention to academic fashion at all," she has said. "I have no interest in it. I don't care what the latest development is in feminist theory or gender theory. It's completely irrelevant to me. I feel like these are my books. They're going to be about what I'm interested in."

Ruth Simmons (1945–)

College President

When she was appointed president of Smith College, prominent African American scholar Henry Louis Gates hailed Ruth Simmons as "the Jackie Robinson of college presidents." Simmons would go on to become the first black president of an Ivy League school and the first female president of Brown University. An education trailblazer, Simmons has earned praise for her intellect, empathy, and practical accomplishments. As Harold T. Shapiro, president of Princeton University, declared, "Ruth Simmons represents quality, Ruth Simmons represents integrity, and Ruth Simmons has a vision of how higher education can serve the society that supports it."

The great-granddaughter of slaves, Simmons was the youngest of twelve children born to sharecroppers in Grapeland, Texas. When she was seven, the family moved to a poverty-stricken neighborhood in Houston. Inspired by the hard work and determination of her mother, Simmons has stated, "The conditioning I got when I was a child was to not do anything *unless* you tried to do it at the best possible level." Simmons attended Dillard University in New Orleans on scholarship and went on to earn a master's and doctorate in romance literature from Harvard.

Simmons began her teaching career as an assistant professor of French at the University of New Orleans from 1973 to 1976 and as its assistant dean from 1975 to 1976. She moved to California State University–Northridge in 1977 as coordinator of its Liberal Studies Project, director of its international programs, and associate professor of pan-African studies. Simmons next served as the assistant and then associate dean of graduate studies at the University of Southern California before coming to Princeton University as a dean of faculty from 1986 to 1990. Finally, Simmons served as provost at Spelman College from 1990 to 1991 and Princeton's vice provost from 1992 to 1995.

In 1995, she began her next career as college president, becoming the first African American woman to head a major college or university when she became president of Smith College, a position she held until 2001, starting the first engineering program in a U.S. women's college. In 2001, Simmons became president of Brown University. During her tenure as president that continued until 2012, Simmons oversaw the largest fundraising campaign in Brown's history, $1.4 billion, principally for scholarship assistance and enhancement of Brown's science programs.

Nobel Prize-winning author Toni Morrison attempted to capture Simmons's nature by saying, "She has an unusual combination of real politics and integrity, and this very keen sense of morals which does not interfere with her generosity and her wide spiritedness. She's extremely creative in terms of solving other people's problems. And she's a lot of fun." Somewhat reluctantly forced out of retirement after leaving Brown to return to her native Texas, Simmons took over the presidency of the historically black college, Prairie View A&M, stating, "I was from a very poor family with 12 children, at a time when colleges were just desegregating. I know how important historically black colleges and universities are for kids like I was." She has also said that her involvement in both white and black institutions "provides a kind of example of how we must move through these artificial barriers that separate higher education."

Lucy Diggs Slowe (1865–1937)
College Dean

The first African American woman to serve as dean of women at any American university, Lucy Diggs Slowe was also one of the original founders of Alpha Kappa Alpha, the first sorority founded by African American women. She was also a tennis champion, becoming the first African American woman to win a national championship in any sport.

Slowe was born in Berryville, Virginia, and, after her parents' early deaths, was raised by her aunt in Lexington, Virginia, before moving to Baltimore when she was thirteen. She attended the Baltimore Colored School and became the first person from her school to attend Howard University, the top historically black college in the United States. After graduation in 1908, she returned to Baltimore to teach high school and earned her MA degree from Columbia in 1915. Slowe next went to Washington, D.C., to teach and in 1919 created the first junior high school in the district, becoming its principal, a position she held until 1922. While teaching at one of three D.C. high schools and serving as dean of girls, in 1917, she won the first women's title at the American Tennis Association's national tournament.

In 1922, Howard University appointed Slowe its first dean of women, and Slowe would serve as a college administrator at Howard for the next fifteen years until her death in 1937. She also helped organize and served as the first president of the National Association of College Women, an organization dedicated to advancing women in higher education. As Slowe argued, "If a college accepts women students and employs women faculty, it should give them the same status as it gives male students and teachers, respectively." So respected was Slowe's work on behalf of raising the status and standards for women in higher education that in 1931, she was invited to address the predominantly white National Association of Women Deans, becoming the first African American to do so.

Anna Garlin Spencer (1851–1931)
Educator

An educator and feminist, Anna Garlin Spencer was the first woman to be ordained as a minister in the state of Rhode Island. A popular lecturer, associated with the New York Society for Ethical Culture and the New York School of Philanthropy, Spencer wrote on social problems, especially those concerning women and families.

Born in Attleboro, Massachusetts, Spencer began writing for the *Providence Journal* when she was eighteen. In 1878, the same year she was ordained, she married Unitarian minister William Spencer, and, after he became an invalid, Spencer succeeded him at the Bell Street Chapel in Providence. In 1919, Spencer moved to New York, where she taught at Teachers College, Columbia University.

Spencer's books included *Women's Share in Social Culture* (1913), which argued for the need for gender equality and for women to emerge from the home and become part of the public life that once belonged exclusively to men. She promoted the concept of "individuation of women" to counter limited gender roles. *The Family and Its Members* (1922) explored the nature of family life and its changes in modern society and the new roles women should play both in family and public life. Both books were prescient in anticipating core feminist ideas that would only emerge widely thirty or more years later in the women's movement. "Can a woman become a genius of the first class?" Spencer asked. "Nobody can know unless women in general shall have equal opportunity with men in education, in vocational choice, and in social welcome of their best intellectual work for a number of generations."

Helen Vendler (1933–)

Educator, Literary Critic

Widely regarded as one of the finest and most astute literary critics of the United States, Helen Vendler is the A. Kingsley Porter professor at Harvard, the first woman to hold this endowed chair. Vendler has written books on Shakespeare, Emily Dickinson, W. B. Yeats, Wallace Stevens, John Keats, and Seamus Heaney as well as books on literary methods that have made Vendler one of the most respected guides to poetry.

For an academic so associated with poetry, it may be surprising that Vendler earned her bachelor's degree in chemistry. Born in Boston, Vendler attended Emmanuel College, went to the University of Louvain after graduation on a Fulbright fellow-

ship, then earned her Ph.D. at Harvard in 1960 with a dissertation on Yeats. Vendler began her career teaching at Cornell University and later held regular appointments at Swarthmore, Haverford, Smith College, and Boston University before joining the Harvard faculty in 1981.

Her many books include *Yeats's Vision and the Later Plays* (1963); *On Extended Wings: Wallace Stevens's Longer Poems* (1975), which won the James Lowell Prize; *The Odes of John Keats* (1983); *Seamus Heaney* (1998); and *Last Looks, Last Books: Stevens, Plath, Lowell Bishop, Merrill* (2010). She received the National Book Critics Circle Award for Criticism in 1981 for *Part of Nature, Part of Us: Modern American Poets*. All of her books are marked by an insightful, common-sense approach that eschews jargon and obscurity for elucidating readings that make the most challenging works accessible. Asked if she writes for a particular audience, Vendler has stated, "I write to explain things to myself."

Beyond the classroom, Vendler has been the consultant poetry editor to *The New York Times*, the president of the Modern Language Association, and, since 1978, the poetry critic for *The New Yorker*. In 2004, the National Endowment for the Humanities selected Vendler for the Jefferson Lecture, the U.S. federal government's highest honor for achievement in the humanities. Her lecture "The Ocean, the Bird, and the Scholar" argued for the role of the arts in the study of humanities.

Lucy Wheelock (1857–1946)

Educator

The kindergarten movement in the United States, which extended education to children between the ages of four and six, has been called the most successful education reform in U.S. history. The movement's survival is due in large part to educator Lucy Wheelock.

Kindergartens in the United States originated in the 1850s, imported by German émigrés devoted to the ideas of Friedrich Froebel, the German creator of the kindergarten preschool concept based on playing, practical activities, and social interactions, which served as part of the transition from home to school. Educators began opening English-language kindergartens, the first of which was founded in Boston in 1860.

Lucy Wheelock was born in Cambridge, Vermont, and enrolled in Boston's Chauncy Hall School after graduating from high school with the intention of preparing for college. Her discovery of the school's kindergarten altered her plan. Instead, she enrolled in the Kindergarten Training School in Boston in 1878 and a year later became, for the next decade, a kindergarten teacher at Chauncy Hall. An exponent and advocate of Froebel's ideas, Wheelock lectured at educational institutes and conventions while teaching training classes. In 1888, she founded and became the head of the Wheelock Kindergarten Training School, which became Wheelock College in 1941.

In the first decade of the twentieth century, Froebel's ideas and the entire kindergarten movement came under attack from developmental psychologists who criticized Froebel's play methods as too didactic and developmentally inappropriate for young learners. As educators began advocating for the adoption of kindergarten in public schools across the United States, tension between proponents of Froebel and opponents threatened to derail early childhood educational reform. Wheelock became a crucial force in attempting to bridge divisions to sustain the kindergarten movement. As president and a member of the International Kindergarten Union, Wheelock coauthored a report that sought a middle ground. "Discussions are profitable," she wrote, "but dissension is not so. May we not rally for the preservation of the kindergarten as a distinctive type of education practice?" Through her persistence and what was widely recognized as her captivating personality, compromises were made, and the momentum for preschool education was maintained. Wheelock believed that a child's education could lift up an entire family from poverty, and current research supports her belief. The landmark 1960s Perry Preschool Study found that children who grew up in poverty but attended a high-quality preschool were more likely to graduate from high school and gain a high-paying job than those who did not.

Today, fifteen states and Washington, D.C., mandate that students attend kindergarten, and a 2015 study showed that 87 percent of five-year-olds in America were enrolled in schools. Kindergarten education has changed considerably from the days of Froebel and Wheelock, but its persistence owes much to the role Lucy Wheelock played in sustaining the movement.

Emma Willard (1787–1870)

Educator, School Founder

The founder of the Troy Female Seminary, the first school to offer college-level education to women, Emma Willard, a committed women's rights activist, devoted her life to education and traveled widely, advocating on behalf of women's education.

Born Emma Hart on a farm in Berlin, Connecticut, the second youngest of seventeen siblings, Willard was encouraged by her father in her reading and intellectual pursuits. Teaching herself geometry, she enrolled in 1802 at the Berlin Academy, and, two years later, she began teaching the youngest children. By 1807, she became the head of a girls' school in Vermont. Unimpressed by the curriculum being offered there, she opened a boarding school for women, the Middlebury Female Academy, in 1814, based on the principles that women could master topics like mathematics and philosophy rather than the subjects offered at finishing schools.

In 1819, Willard petitioned Governor DeWitt Clinton and the New York legislature for funds, writing the pamphlet *A Plan for Improving Female Education* to persuade them of a woman's right to receive an education. In 1821, the town of Troy, New York, raised $4,000 for Willard to establish a school there. It began with ninety students, with Willard developing the courses, the teaching methods, and the textbooks. Its curriculum was unique in featuring college-level courses previously only taught in men's schools. The Troy Female Seminary offered the most advanced education available to young women at the time, and, by 1823, it had educated two hundred female teachers, who spread Willard's teaching philosophy and method throughout the country.

In 1809, Willard married John Willard, a physician, who died in 1825. The Willards had one son, John Hart Willard, and Emma Willard was stepmother to her husband's four children from a previous marriage. In 1838, Willard turned over the management of the seminary to her son and daughter-in-law and married Christopher Yates. The couple moved to Connecticut, where Willard worked to improve the school system there. Willard and Yates were divorced in 1843. She eventually moved back to Troy to be near the school she founded, spending the rest of her life teaching and advocating on behalf of women's educational opportunities. In 1895, the Troy Female Seminary was renamed the Emma Willard School in her honor, and it remains a vital educational center to this day, an enduring legacy to one of America's greatest educators.

Frances Elizabeth Willard (1838–1898)

College President, Temperance Activist

 When Frances Willard was appointed president of the newly founded Evanston College for Ladies in 1871, she became the first female president of a college or university in America. When Evanston College became the Woman's College of Northwestern University, Willard became the first dean of women at the university, one of the first female administrators of a major coeducational university. Willard, who resigned from her deanship in 1874 after a conflict with the university president, would achieve further distinction in her next career as one of the founders and longtime president of the Women's Christian Temperance Union, an organization that led the Prohibition campaign, one of the most important social reform movements in the nineteenth and early twentieth centuries.

Frances Willard was born near Rochester, New York, where her father was a farmer and her mother a schoolteacher. In 1841, the family moved to Ober-

lin, Ohio, where, at Oberlin College, her father studied for the ministry. Moving on to Wisconsin, Frances attended the Milwaukee Normal School, founded by Catherine Beecher. In 1858, the family moved to Evanston, Illinois, where her father became a banker and Frances attended the North Western Female College.

After graduating, Willard held teaching positions in Illinois, New York, and Pennsylvania. After touring Europe and the Middle East with wealthy friends during the years 1868–1870, Willard was named president of the Evanston Ladies' College. Two years later in 1873, it was absorbed by the all-male Northwestern University to become the Women's College of Northwestern University, with Willard serving as the dean of women. The same year, Willard helped to found the Association for the Advancement of Women, with its stated mission "to receive and present practical methods for securing to women higher intellectual, moral and physical conditions, and thereby to improve all domestic and social relations."

In 1874, Willard embarked on what would become her life's work on behalf of the Women's Christian Temperance Union, serving as its first corresponding secretary and later longtime president. On behalf of the organization, she undertook a fifty-day speaking tour in 1874 and subsequently averaged four hundred lectures a year for a ten-year period, averaging thirty thousand miles of travel a year. As WCTU president, Willard also argued for suffrage based on "home protection," which she described as "the movement ... to secure for all women above the age of twenty-one years the ballot as one means for the protection of their homes from the devastation caused by the legalized traffic in strong drink." Willard rejected the notion that women were the "weaker" sex and were naturally dependent on men. "Politics is the place for women," she insisted.

Willard would help to found the National Council of Women of the United States, the oldest nonsectarian organization of women in America, and became its first president in 1888. Willard died after contracting influenza while preparing to sail for England and France on behalf of the international WCTU. After her death, Willard was the first woman included among America's greatest leaders in Statuary Hall in the U.S. Capitol.

Sarah Winnemucca (c. 1844–1891)
Educator

A Native American educator, lecturer, and tribal leader, Sarah Winnemucca is known for her book *Life among the Piutes: Their Wrongs and Claims* (1883), the first known autobiography written by a Native American woman, which has been described by anthropologist Omer Steward as "one of the most enduring ethnohistorical books written by an American Indian."

A granddaughter of Truckee and daughter of Winnemucca, both Northern Paiute chiefs, she was born with the name Thocmetony (meaning "Shell Flower") in northwestern Nevada but lived in central California, where she developed an aptitude for languages, learning English, Spanish, and several Native American dialects. She returned to Nevada in 1857, where she lived briefly with a white family, who called her Sarah. During the Paiute War of 1860, she lost several family members and decided to offer her language skills as an interpreter for the Bureau of Indian Affairs. She went with her tribe when it was relocated to the Malheur Reservation in Oregon in 1872 to help free her father when he was taken hostage by the Bannocks.

In 1879, Winnemucca lectured on plight of her tribe, and her cause attracted the attention of President Rutherford B. Hayes, whose commitment to help was never kept. Winnemucca taught at a reservation school in Washington Territory and traveled to the East Coast on lecture tours to arouse public opinion on behalf of her people. The success and sales of *Life among the Piutes* led to a petition campaign with Congress passing a relief bill in 1884, but it did not change the economic status of the tribe. Winnemucca then returned to teaching at a Paiute school near Lovelock, Nevada.

A tireless advocate on behalf of her people, Winnemucca would become one of the earliest Native American women to educate white America to the tragedy that had befallen the Paiutes and other western Indian tribes.

Mary Emma Woolley (1867–1947)
College President

The first woman to be accepted to Brown University, Mary Emma Woolley would serve as the eleventh president of Mount Holyoke College from 1901 to 1937, presiding over a series of reforms that raised the standard for women's higher education, which would become a model for other institutions.

The daughter of a Congregational minister, Woolley grew up in Connecticut and Rhode Island. She attended several smaller schools run by women before completing her secondary education at the Wheaton Seminary (now Wheaton College) in Massachusetts. She returned to teach there from 1885 to 1891. She agreed to become one of the first female students at Brown University, earning her BA and MA degrees there.

In 1895, Woolley began teaching biblical history and literature at Wellesley College, where she was eventually promoted to full professor and served as a department chair. In 1900, at the age of thirty-eight, she was named president of Mount Holyoke College, becoming one of the youngest college presidents in the United States. The same year, she became the first woman to receive an honorary degree from Amherst College. Over her thirty-six-year tenure as president, Woolley was instrumental in raising academic and admission standards, salaries, and benefits while overseeing sixteen major building constructions and increasing the endowment tenfold to nearly $5 million. She abolished the college's domestic work system that required students to cook and clean for economic reasons. She was a respected supporter of female higher education, arguing that women's education needed to be justified on intellectual grounds alone and that an educated woman could achieve anything.

When she retired in 1937 at the age of seventy-four, the board of trustees, fearing Mount

Holyoke was becoming too "feminized" with male faculty in the minority, appointed a male president to succeed Woolley. She opposed the decision and refused to return to campus for the rest of her life. Woolley was an outspoken activist for women's suffrage and pacifism. She served as vice president of the American Civil Liberties Union and was an early member of the Association of Collegiate Alumnae, which in 1881 became the American Association of University Women, serving as its president from 1927 to 1933. Woolley is the subject of the play *Bull in a China Shop*, written by Mount Holyoke alumna Bryna Turner, which premiered at Lincoln Center in 2017.

Ella Flagg Young (1845–1918)

Educator

Named Chicago's superintendent of schools in 1909, Ella Flagg Young became the first female superintendent not only in Chicago but in any major American school system. Young broke through an educational glass ceiling that remains a century later. Even though 72 percent of educators are female, women currently lead only 13 percent of U.S. school districts. Young defied the odds that still apply, and her challenge to the status quo applies to her innovative teaching ideas and practices that have been widely copied.

Born in Buffalo, New York, Young did not attend school until she was ten after teaching herself how to read and write. After only a few months, she dropped out of school because she decided that she was not being intellectually challenged. At the age of fifteen, she passed the certification examination to become a teacher but was told she was too

young to teach. Later, she graduated from the Chicago Normal School in 1862, beginning a fifty-three-year teaching career from 1862 to 1915.

Young would work in virtually every aspect of public education from teacher to principal to teacher trainer to superintendent to school board member. She also found time to earn her Ph.D. at the University of Chicago in 1900 at a time when only about 5 percent of doctorates nationwide went to women. Despite her experience and accomplishments, when she interviewed for the Chicago school's superintendent job, her gender was a liability. Two board members acknowledged she was qualified but doubted her "strength" for such a position; one said, "I only wish Mrs. Young were a man." Faced with twenty-seven candidates for the position, the Chicago School Board could not agree on anyone, but Young became their unanimous selection in the second-round vote, a decision that earned national coverage in newspapers across the country.

Young brought to her teaching and administrative work innovative ideas that have subsequently found favor, such as her advocacy for increased teachers' voices and teachers' councils to determine school policies. She also argued for higher wages for teachers and greater teacher control over their curriculum design. She was an early proponent of what has come to be called "character education" and student-driven learning, arguing that "our being's end and aim is the evolution of a character which, through thinking of the right and acting for the right, shall make for right conduct, rectitude, righteousness."

In 1910, she became the first female president of the National Education Association. Her books include *Isolation in the School* (1900), *Ethics in the School* (1902), and *Some Types of Educational Theory* (1902). Young's pioneering pedagogy and innovations have since become standard practices in education.

BUSINESS LEADERS
AND ENTREPRENEURS

From the colonial era until well into the twentieth century, the phrase "women in business" was, for the most part, a contradiction in terms. While women always worked—laboring on farms and plantations, in shops and factories, or as office workers —the designation of "businesswoman" was either nonexistent or exceptional.

The first American businesses were formed in the eighteenth century and included companies that remain in business today: the perfume and soap company Caswell-Massey (1752), *The Hartford Courant* newspaper (1764), Baker's Chocolate (1765), the Ames tool company (1774), King Arthur Flour (1790), the Cigna insurance company (1792), the Dixon Ticonderoga pencil company (1795), Jim Beam distillery (1795), and J. P. Morgan Chase (1799). All of them were created and administered exclusively by men, but exceptions occurred. Eliza Lucas Pinckney (1722–1793), a scientist and businesswoman, pioneered the development of the indigo plant in textile manufacturing in a business she created; Mary Katherine Goddard (1738–1816) was the first female newspaper publisher in America; and Rebecca Lukens (1794–1854), the owner and manager of an iron and steel mill, was the first woman in the United States in the iron industry and the first female chief executive officer of an industrial company.

The delay in the establishment of women in business dates from the colonial era and the early days of the republic. Bound by English Common Law and the rule of coverture, a woman had no legal rights after she married. Married women could not create or operate a business, sign a contract, or own property; she was, essentially, her husband's property. In the early years of the republic, state law, rather than federal law, governed the rights of women, and in every state, the legal status of women depended on their marital status. Unmarried women, including widows, were called femmes soles or "women alone." They had the legal right to live where they pleased and could support themselves in any occupation that did not require a license or a college degree, which were restricted to males. Single women could enter into contracts, buy and sell real estate, or accumulate personal property. These restrictions would be in force until states enacted various Married Women's Property Acts beginning in 1839, with New York's Married Property Law in

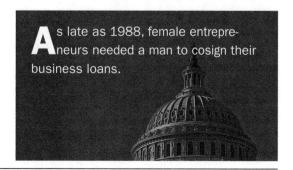

As late as 1988, female entrepreneurs needed a man to cosign their business loans.

1848 serving as the model for other states to grant women the right to own property. Restrictions on women in business would persist, however. As late as 1988, female entrepreneurs needed a man to cosign their business loans.

Cultural norms, as well as legal prohibitions, kept women from participating in the world of business. What historians have called a "cult of domesticity" designated a woman's rightful place as the home and a man's sphere as everywhere beyond. The concept of "republican motherhood" in the early days of the nation advocated that women could best serve the political and social ideals of the Republic by dedicating their energies to sustaining healthy and nurturing households. Women who stayed at home were considered more genteel than women who entered the labor force, the majority of whom did so out of necessity. Teaching—the most respectable profession open to women, especially in the nineteenth century—would usually be given up either by choice or, more often, by policy once a woman married. A woman might take over her husband's business with his death or incapacity, continue to teach in the event of widowhood, or offer dressmaking, hatmaking, and sewing services from their homes or in shops, but the notion of a career in business was not an aspiration for most women until the twentieth century. When women first ventured into the realm of business, they worked at jobs that reflected the skills they had learned at home. By the mid- to late nineteenth century, women who did not teach dominated businesses and professions dedicated to the preparation and serving of food; the manufacturing, sale, and care of clothing; and such service jobs as librarians, midwives, nurses, and household servants.

From the 1880s on, the growth in population, partly due to the arrival of new immigrants; the rise of big businesses; the transformation of the United States from a primarily rural, agrarian economy to an urban, industrial one; and the economic necessities resulting from the Great Depression and two world wars, saw an increase in women's participation as both workers and entrepreneurs. The period marked the founding and expansion of such industrial giants as Armour, International Harvester, DuPont, and Standard Oil of New Jersey (now

Exxon) as well as the introduction of national retailers like Sears Roebuck and F. W. Woolworth & Company and the birth of such technological and transportation companies as AT&T, Ford Motor Company, General Motors, and the Pennsylvania Railroad. At the same time, federal, state, and local governments also expanded. Women worked outside the home in increasing numbers, gaining jobs in such workplace venues as sweatshops and factories, as clerks in burgeoning bureaucracies, and as salesgirls and departmental supervisors in retail establishments to supplement or provide family income during the Great Depression, and on behalf of the war effort, to replace men who had been sent overseas, particularly during World War II. Women early on also ventured into management by establishing their own companies, including Madame C. J. Walker, Elizabeth Arden, Estée Lauder, and Helena Rubinstein. These early entrepreneurs avoided direct competition with male-dominated businesses by exploiting their own expertise within the female market and concentrating on selling products for the home or beauty products for female consumers. One of the ways in which female entrepreneurs have found great success is in real estate, especially in New York.

It would be the period following the end of World War II that would see the greatest transformative changes in the status of women in business.

More women entered the workplace in World War II, a phenomenon born out of necessity that continued after the war, providing work, for example, for these customer account operators shown here in 1945.

Multiple factors contributed to this transformation. Increasingly, women had access to higher education and training for higher-level jobs and were gradually competing with men on a more level playing field on campuses and, particularly in the final quarter of the twentieth century, in business as well. Historical and cultural factors contributed to an increasing number of women entering the workforce and in the expansion of the types of jobs they held.

By 1945, nearly one in four married women worked outside the home, and both married and unmarried women felt a new sense of independence and freedom doing the same work as men. However, once World War II was over and most men reclaimed their old jobs, the majority of women either left the workforce or obtained positions as office workers, teachers, or in other traditionally female jobs. The postwar prosperity of the 1950s brought the golden age of the single-income family and the stay-at-home mother, but that would change dramatically through the rest of century. In 1950, about one in three women participated in the labor force. By 1998, that number had jumped to nearly three out of every five women of working age. Among women ages sixteen or over,

the labor force participation rate was 33.9 percent in 1950 compared with 59.8 percent in 1998. Today, 47 percent of U.S. workers are women, and 70 percent of mothers with children under eighteen are in the labor force. Forty percent of mothers in the workforce are the primary earners compared to 11 percent in 1970. The proportion of women with college degrees in the labor force has quadrupled since 1970. Increasingly, women during this period have entered management positions, as this chart indicates:

PERCENTAGE OF WOMEN IN MANAGEMENT POSITIONS

Percentage	Management Field
74%	Human Resources
71%	Social and Community Services
65%	Educational Administration
46%	Food Services
45%	Marketing and Sales
27%	Chief Executives
26%	Computer and Information Services
7%	Construction

The passing of the Civil Rights Act, signed by President Lyndon Johnson in 1964, helped pave the way for increasing the numbers of women in business.

The number of new woman-owned and woman-managed businesses created has also increased dramatically. In 1970, women owned only 4.6 percent of the 8.5 million businesses in the United States. Today, woman-owned businesses account for 39 percent of all privately held companies, totaling 11.6 million companies, which employ 8 percent of the total private sector workforce, contribute 4.2 percent of total business revenue, and generate sales of $1.7 trillion. Over the past twenty years, the number of woman-owned businesses has grown 114 percent compared to the overall national growth rate of 44 percent for all businesses. By the twenty-first century, women began starting businesses at more than twice the rate of men.

Collectively, these numbers represent a substantial gender transformation of American business, in which the historical barriers to women in business have been significantly lowered, if not eliminated. Women's gains have been assisted by the passage of the Civil Rights Act of 1964, one of the landmark achievements of the civil rights movement that banned employment discrimination on the basis of race, color, religion, sex, or national origin. Title VII of the act went further by making discrimination in the workplace based on gender stereotyping illegal. For example, an employer cannot legally refuse to promote a woman due to the assumption that because she has children, she therefore needs to spend more time with them. Title VII also mandated the establishment of the Equal Employment Opportunity Commission (EEOC), the federal agency that administers and enforces civil rights laws against workplace discrimination. The EEOC, whose first complainants were female flight attendants who challenged the airline's age restrictions, ignored gender discrimination complaints at first and was largely ineffective in enforcing prohibitions against gender discrimination in employment. However, in 1980, the commission issued regulations defining sexual harassment and stated that it was a form of gender discrimination prohibited by the Civil Rights Act of 1964. In the 1986 case of *Meritor Savings Bank v. Vinson*, the Supreme Court first recognized sexual harassment as a violation of Title VII and established the standards of conduct and levels of employer liability as well as a determination that speech or conduct in itself can create a "hostile environment." Following the ruling, reported sexual harassment cases grew from ten cases registered by the EEOC per year before 1986 to 624 cases in 1987, 2,217 in 1990, and 4,626 by 1995. Currently, about 30 percent of all complaints filed annually with the EEOC are gender related (about 2,500 each year). The Civil Rights Act of 1991 added provisions to Title VII protections expanding the rights of women to sue and collect compensatory and punitive damages for sexual discrimination or harassment.

Gender discrimination is now a civil rights violation covered by Title VII of the Civil Rights Act of 1964, but gender stereotyping ... remains a prevalent obstacle for women in the workplace....

Also important in leveling the playing field for women in business was the passage in 1988 of the Women's Business Ownership Act, which addressed the needs of businesswomen by giving female entrepreneurs recognition and resources and eliminating discriminatory lending practices by banks that favored male business owners. Congress addressed four barriers to woman-owned businesses: 1) "the need for technical training to maximize growth potential of women owned business"; 2) "inequality of access to commercial credit"; 3) "virtual exclusion of women owned business from government procurement activities"; and 4) "inadequacy of information and data relative to women owned business." The act provided seed funding for women's business centers through an annual grant process by the Small Business Administration, required the U.S. Census Bureau to include C corporations when presenting data on woman-owned firms, eliminated all individual state laws that required women to have a male relative sign a business loan, and created the National Women's Business Council, a bipartisan council of female entrepreneurs and women's organizations to advise the president, Congress, and business associations on policy and program recommendations.

If employment discrimination and the challenges faced by female entrepreneurs have been addressed legislatively, other costs and consequences of women in business remain problematic. Gender discrimination is now a civil rights violation covered by Title VII of the Civil Rights Act of 1964, but gender stereotyping, much harder to regulate, remains a prevalent obstacle for women in the workplace, as women may not be thought "strong enough" to do a job that entails physical labor or "tough enough" to manage critical, high-stakes career positions. Some jobs are still seen "for men" and some "for women," even though women occupying such positions, as well as the data, challenge those assumptions. Another persistent stereotype is that women ought to be the principal caregivers for their families with work as a secondary priority. A Pew Research Center study in 2004 found that almost half of all respondents— 47 percent—felt that mothers should not work more than part time, and another 33 percent felt that they should not be working at all. In truth, women are more likely than men to put in the so-called "second shift" at night managing their homes and children. Women, therefore, face pressure and guilt from both ends: regarded as not an equal "team player" with men because of their responsibilities in the home and guilt (far more than men) over not being more present in their children's lives when away at work.

The perception that women in business have divided loyalties continues to contribute to both the wage gap between male and female workers and barriers to promotion, particularly at the highest levels of business. As women have increased their presence in more lucrative positions in American business, their wages have increased, but a wage gap continues to exist, even though, as of 2019, women were just as likely as men to be working in managerial positions. The #MeToo movement has focused discussion not just on sexual harassment in the workplace but on pay inequity. Laws prohibiting gender-based pay discrimination in the United States have been in place since the 1960s, but the pay gap has remained stuck at ten to twenty cents on the dollar over the past twenty years (with the gap even wider in higher-paying industries).

This means that the average woman at most managerial levels misses out on more than $400,000 during the course of her career. Based on a recent survey, only 16 percent of Americans think companies are doing enough to close the gender pay gap, while 60 percent attribute the gap to sexism or unconscious bias.

Statistics show that women ask for promotions and raises just as often as men, but women are still promoted more slowly. Studies have shown as well that women typically receive less feedback on their performance, get fewer high-profile assignments, and have less access to mentorship and sponsorship. Despite the fact that women have gained equity with men in professional jobs, they remain underrepresented in the upper-level business positions. In 2013, women made up 53.2 percent of professionals in the workforce, while they constitute only 38.6 percent of business officers and managers. Although women have gained a wide range of leadership positions in business in recent decades, as of 2016, they only made up about 20 percent of Fortune 500 board members and about 5 percent of Fortune 500 CEOs (as of 2017). While women

The "Me Too" movement, founded in 2006 to help survivors of sexual violence (particularly women of color), went viral as #MeToo in 2017, following sexual assault charges against film producer Harvey Weinstein.

make up 44 percent of the overall S&P 500 labor force and 36 percent of first- or mid-level officials and managers in those companies, they only comprise 25 percent of executive- and senior-level officials and managers, hold only 20 percent of board seats, and only 6 percent are CEOs. Only 6 percent of partners in venture capital firms in 2013 were women (down from 10 percent in 1999), and women made up just 20 percent of executives, senior officers, and managers in U.S. high-tech industries (in 2014). As recently as 2016, 43 percent of the 150 highest-earning public companies in Silicon Valley had no female officers at all.

In addition to the pay and promotion challenges women face in business, the #MeToo movement has raised the visibility and prevalence of sexual harassment and assault at work and the personal toll it takes on women's lives. Studies show that from almost a quarter to more than eight in ten women experience some form of workplace harassment in their lifetimes. Women who have been sexually harassed have experienced a range of negative consequences, including physical and mental health problems, career interruptions, lower earnings, and an unwillingness to attempt advancement into higher-paid careers. Sexual harassment in the workplace also results in substantial consequences for companies, including legal costs, costs related to employee turnover and lower productivity, lower motivation and commitment, and team disruption.

It remains to be seen how and when the business climate will evolve to address the concerns of the increasing presence of women in companies. All these factors and data suggest that despite the considerable progress in advancement for women in business, with the wage gap narrowed and the percentage of women climbing the management ranks steadily rising, current progress in assimilating women into business has been uneven or has stalled or stagnated. According to the World Economic Forum's 2016 Global Gender Gap index, the United States, measured globally, ranks first in women's educational attainment but only twenty-sixth in women's economic participation and opportunity. Despite their considerable progress, achievement, and success, American women continue to face con-

siderable challenges regarding both access to and equity in business.

BIOGRAPHIES

Elizabeth Arden (1878–1966)

Entrepreneur

Born Florence Nightingale Graham in Woodbridge, Ontario, Canada, Elizabeth Arden founded a cosmetic empire. By 1929, she owned 150 salons across the United States and Europe, and her company distributed one thousand products in twenty-two countries. As the sole owner of Elizabeth Arden, Inc., she became one of the wealthiest women in the world.

After dropping out of nursing school in Toronto, Arden joined her brother in New York City working as a bookkeeper for a pharmaceutical company and spending time in their labs learning about skin care. In 1908, she became an assistant to a beauty specialist, Eleanor Adair. A year later, Arden and Elizabeth Hubbard formed a brief partnership. Following their breakup, Arden established the trade name Elizabeth Arden, using "Elizabeth" to save money on her salon signage and "Arden" for a Canadian farm near her home. In 1910, she opened the first Red Door Salon on Fifth Avenue. She hired chemists to develop face creams and lotions that would become the first items in her new line of beauty products. At the time, makeup was more associated with prostitutes than respectable women, and Arden devised a marketing campaign to change the public's view of beauty products. In 1912, she traveled to France to learn beauty and makeup techniques, and she expanded her international operation in 1915, opening salons worldwide and selling her products in pharmacies and department stores. Arden was the first to introduce eye makeup to American women and pioneered the concept of the makeover. With the launch of Ardena Skin Tonic, Arden's company became the first to incorporate the founder's name into a product name. She also developed the first travel-size beauty products and was one of the first in the cosmetics business to train and send out a team of traveling demonstrators and saleswomen. By the 1930s, Red Door salons were opened in the majority of fashion capitals around the world. It would be said that only three American names were known in every corner of the globe: Singer Sewing Machines, Coca-Cola, and Elizabeth Arden.

Arden invested much of her wealth into the ownership of racehorses, and in 1945, she founded the Maine Chance Farm. In 1946, she was featured on the cover of *Time* magazine in a story about her success in the male-dominated world of horse racing. In 1947, one of Arden's thoroughbreds, Jet Pilot, won the Kentucky Derby.

Arden died in New York City at the age of eighty-seven, deliberately keeping her age a secret from the public until after her death. In 1971, the Eli Lilly corporation purchased her company for $38 million; today, its estimated value is more than $1.3 billion.

Mary Kay Ash (1918–2001)

Entrepreneur

Entrepreneur and businesswoman Mary Kay Ash was the founder of Mary Kay Inc., a cosmetic business that at the time of her death in 2001 had a sales force of over eight hundred thousand in thirty-seven countries with total sales of over $200 million.

Ash was born Mary Kathlyn Wagner in Hot Wells, Harris County, Texas. She married Ben Rogers at the age of seventeen, and they had three children. While her husband served in World War II, Ash sold books door-to-door, selling an amazing $25,000 worth in just six months. After Rogers returned home, they divorced, and Ash changed careers, going to work for Stanley Home Products. Hosting parties to encourage people to buy the company's household items, Ash was a top-earning seller and was hired away by another company, World Gifts, in 1952. Ash, however, was repeatedly passed over

for promotions and pay raises by men, and, after twenty-five years of selling, she quit in 1963.

Ash was determined to create her own business at the age of forty-five, and, with her life savings of $5,000, she purchased the formulas for skin lotions and opened a small store in Dallas. Mary Kay Cosmetics was a success from the start, turning a profit in its first year and selling close to $1 million in products by the end of the second. The marketing plan went back to her previous selling strategy through at-home parties and other events. Her innovation was in establishing incentive programs rather than establishing sales territories for her representatives, called by Ash "consultants." They bought products from Mary Kay at wholesale prices and then sold them at retail price to their customers, earning commissions from new consultants that they recruited. Encouraging women by giving them new opportunities for financial success, in 1969, Kay began to award pink Cadillacs to top sales consultants. By 1994, she had given away seven thousand cars, valued at $100 million. The company experienced record earnings and growth.

The company has been sustained by Ash's golden rule to "treat others as you want to be treated" as well as the motto "God first, family second, and career third." Ash stepped down as CEO of the company in 1987 but remained active in the business. She established the Mary Kay Charitable Foundation in 1996 to support cancer research and efforts to end domestic violence. In 2000, Lifetime Television named Ash the most outstanding woman in business in the twentieth century. As of 2014, Mary Kay Cosmetics had more than three million consultants worldwide and a wholesale volume in excess of $3 billion.

Mary Barra (1961–)

Company Executive

The chair and CEO of the General Motors Company, the largest automotive company in the United States, Barra was born Mary Teresa Makela in Royal Oak, Michigan. The family moved to Waterford, Michigan, where Barra attended public schools. Her father worked for forty years at the Pontiac car factory in Detroit, and Barra began working at the same plant at the age of eighteen as a co-op student to help pay for her college tuition. She graduated from the General Motors Institute (now Kettering University), where she obtained a BS degree in electrical engineering in 1985. In 1988, she was awarded a fellowship from GM to Stanford Business School, from which she obtained her MBA degree in 1990.

Barra continued to work for GM, working her way up to executive positions, becoming vice president of global manufacturing engineering in February 2008, vice president of human resources in July 2009, and executive vice president of global product development in February 2011. She was named CEO in January 2014, the first woman to lead an automobile manufacturer.

During Barra's first year as CEO, GM issued eighty-four safety recalls involving over thirty million cars, and she was called to testify before the U.S. Senate about the recalls and deaths attributed to a faulty ignition switch. She has directed GM's focus to the automated driverless car space, including acquisition of Strobe, a startup focused on driverless technology. She also pushed GM to develop the Chevy Bolt EV, the first electric car priced under $40,000 with a range of two hundred miles.

In 2016, *Forbes* magazine listed Barra as one of the world's most powerful women. The same year, she joined a business forum assembled by President-elect Donald Trump to provide strategic and policy advice on economic issues. She left the forum the following year after Trump's response to the white supremacist rally in Charlottesville, Virginia, in which a member of a white nationalist group killed a young woman who was protesting the rally. Currently the highest-paid CEO of the three major Detroit car companies, Barra also serves on the board of Disney, the Stanford University Board of Trustees, and several other organizations.

Barra is married to consultant Anthony Barra, who she met while she was a student at Kettering University. The Barras have two children and live in Northville, Michigan.

Olive Ann Beech (1903–1993)
Company Executive

Olive Beech was cofounder, president, and chairwoman of the Beech Aircraft Corporation, often referred to as the "First Lady of Aviation." She was born Olive Ann Mellor on September 25, 1903, in Waverly, Kansas. Her family moved first to Paola and then to Wichita. She skipped high school and began attending the American Secretarial and Business College; at eighteen, she left for a job as a bookkeeper at an electrical contracting firm.

In 1924, she began working as a secretary and bookkeeper for the Travel Air Manufacturing Company in Wichita and soon became office manager and secretary to Walter Beech, one of the company's founders. After Travel Air merged with the Curtiss-Wright Corporation, Walter Beech became president of the new corporation. Olive Ann and Walter married in 1930. In 1932, Walter quit Curtiss-Wright and, together with Olive Ann, started the Beech Aircraft Company in Wichita. Their first successful plane was the Beechcraft Staggerwing, so named because of its negatively staggered wings. To promote the plane, Olive Ann came up with the idea of sponsoring a female pilot, Louis Thaden, to compete in the Bendix transcontinental race. Thaden won the race against some of the nation's best male pilots.

Beech aircraft were recognized as some of the best in the world and were used for military as well as commercial and private uses. Olive Ann took an active role in the retooling and production needed during World War II, during which Beech Aircraft produced more than 7,400 planes. Walter died unexpectedly in 1950, and Olive Ann was elected chair of the board and president, becoming the first woman to head a major aircraft company. The company continued to be successful throughout the 1950s and 1960s, producing various components for NASA as well as aircraft. The Raytheon Corporation purchased Beech Aircraft in 1980 and in 1982 removed Beech from an active role in the business, naming her a chair emeritus. After her retirement, Beech was the recipient of numerous honors and contributed to various civic and philanthropic projects.

Carole Black (1945–)

Company Executive

As president and CEO of Lifetime Entertainment from 1999 until she retired in 2005, Carole Black led the growth of Lifetime from a cable network into a multimedia brand for women that includes Lifetime Network, which rose from sixth to first place in cable ratings in less than two years; Lifetime Movie Network; Lifetime Real Women, the reality network; Lifetime Online, an Internet site; and Lifetime Home Entertainment. Black combined her company's growth with expanding advocacy on behalf of women.

Black was born in Cincinnati, Ohio, where she attended Withrow High School, graduating in 1961 as the school's first female student body president. She graduated from Ohio State University in 1965. She began her career as a marketing executive with Proctor & Gamble in Cincinnati. After marrying and giving birth to a son, she left Proctor & Gamble in 1983 for the advertising firm DDB Needham with an emphasis on marketing specifically to women.

In 1986, Black took a position with the Walt Disney Company, where she became senior vice president of marketing and television, responsible for all branding and marketing of network and syndicated programming. During her seven years at Disney, Black worked to draw more working women, particularly working mothers, to the home-video market, a revolutionary concept that proved successful for the company. Home video grew into the company's highest profit division and helped Disney become the leading video brand worldwide. Black left Disney to head the NBC television affiliate in Los Angeles, the first woman to hold the position. She succeeded in increasing the station's female viewers and made NBC 4 the number-one news station in the area.

In 1999, Black became the first woman to head the Lifetime Television cable network. She immediately made significant changes, replacing people in top management positions, and shifted production of its daytime programming in-house as a cost savings. Lifetime became the number-one cable network for female viewers and remained so throughout Black's tenure, achieving record ratings, revenue, and profits. By 2004, Lifetime was in over eighty-five million households nationwide.

Black has been named on multiple media lists, including *BusinessWeek*'s "Top 25 Managers in Business," *Fortune*'s "50 Most Powerful Women in Business," and *Ladies' Home Journal*'s "America's 100 Most Important Women." In 2003, she was inducted into Broadcasting & Cable's Hall of Fame.

Sara Blakely (1971–)

Entrepreneur

 Billionaire businesswoman Sara Blakely is the founder of Spanx, an intimate apparel company selling pants, leggings, and shapewear that she founded with a $5,000 investment at the age of twenty-nine in 2001. Today, Spanx has an estimated $400 million in yearly sales, and Blakely has been named by *Time* magazine as one of the one hundred most influential people in the world and by *Forbes* in 2014 as the ninety-third most powerful woman in the world.

Blakely was born in Clearwater, Florida, the daughter of a trial attorney father and artist mother. After attending Clearwater High School, she graduated from Florida State University. After graduation, she worked at Walt Disney World in Orlando and as a stand-up comedian before taking a job with an office supply company selling fax machines door-to-door. She was successful and was promoted to national sales trainer at the age of twenty-five.

Forced to wear pantyhose in the hot Florida climate for her sales role, Blakely disliked the appearance of the seamed foot of the hose with open-toed shoes but liked the way control-top pantyhose eliminated panty lines and made her body appear firmer. She experimented by cutting off the feet of her pantyhose while wearing them under a pair of slacks, and the core concept for Spanx was born. She invested $5,000 and spent two years developing her concept while trying to interest established companies in her idea and design.

A prototype was completed, and Blakely completed a patent application. She used her credit card to purchase the "Spanx" trademark for $150. Blakely's innovation was to allow women to look better in certain clothes while avoiding the discomfort of slimming undergarments of the past such as girdles. Blakely initially convinced Neiman Marcus to offer her new invention, and she promoted her Spanx shapewear on the stores' sales floor. High-end stores like Bloomingdale's, Saks Fifth Avenue, and Bergdof Goodman soon followed. Initially, Blakely handled all aspects of the business, including marketing and product placement (preferring that Spanx be sold alongside shoes rather than in the hosiery section). She recruited friends and acquaintances to seek out her products at select department stores. In 2000, Oprah Winfrey, having received a product basket from Blakely, named Spanx a "favorite thing," which helped drive Spanx sales to $4 million in its first year, $10 million in its second.

Today, Spanx sells shapewear, leggings, pants, and maternity wear in sixty-five countries, and Blakely, who married in 2008 and is a mother of four, continues to run the day-to-day operation of the company, which is based in Atlanta. In 2006, she created the Sara Blakely Foundation to help women through education and entrepreneurial training, funding scholarships and donations to the Oprah Winfrey Leadership Academy for Girls. In 2013, she became the first female billionaire to the join The Giving Pledge, announced by Bill Gates and Warren Buffett, in which the world's richest people agree to donate at least half of their wealth to charity.

Gail Boudreaux (1960–)

Company Executive

Gail Boudreaux is the president and CEO of the health insurance company Anthem Inc., the second-largest American company with a woman as CEO (the largest is General Motors). Born Gail Koziara in 1960, Boudreaux grew up in Chicopee, Massachusetts, where she was a high school basketball and shot put star. She received her bachelor's degree from Dartmouth in 1982 and an MBA degree from Columbia Business School in 1989.

Boudreaux began her career at Aetna, where she worked for twenty years, and in 2002, she became president of Blue Cross/Blue Shield of Illinois. In 2008, she was named executive vice president of UnitedHealthcare, the largest division within the UnitedHealth Group, and served as the CEO from 2011 to 2014. After stepping down from United-Healthcare, she founded a health care advisory firm and, in 2017, was named president and CEO of Anthem and has completed acquisitions of several companies since then. In 2018, she was ranked number five in *Fortune*'s list of Most Powerful U.S. Women and number twelve in *Forbes*'s list of Most Powerful Women.

Boudreaux serves as a board member for several businesses and nonprofit organizations. She lives in Lake Forest, Illinois.

Lydia Moss Bradley (1816–1908)

Banker

Lydia Moss Bradley was a bank president and philanthropist and the first female member of a national bank board in the United States. Born Lydia Moss in Vevay, Indiana, Bradley grew up on the frontier and was educated at home. She began to acquire forest land and sell trees for timber as a young woman and, in 1837, married Tobias Bradley, who ran a sawmill. In 1847, the Bradleys sold their land in Indiana and moved to Peoria, Illinois, where the couple prospered in both real estate and banking. At the same time, they endured family tragedy as all six of their children died through various causes.

After Tobias Bradley died in 1867, Lydia Bradley continued to manage the family businesses. At the time of his death, Tobias Bradley was the president of the First National Bank of Peoria. Lydia inherited the stock he owned in the bank and became a member of the board of directors, making her the first woman to serve on a national bank board in the United States. Before her second marriage, Bradley had a contract drawn up to protect her assets, thus becoming one of the first American women to insist upon a prenuptial agreement.

Bradley was also noted for her philanthropic work. She founded and funded a hospital, a home for aged women, and a Universalist church in Peoria. Her most important project was the founding of Bradley Polytechnic Institute (later Bradley University) in 1896, which emphasized the value of practical skills for both men and women. She devoted the remainder of her life to the institute, which grew to become a four-year college in 1920 and a full university in 1946.

Helen del Gurley Brown (1922–2012)

Publisher

 A businesswoman, publisher, and author, Helen del Gurley Brown was editor-in-chief of *Cosmopolitan* magazine, which was both an explicator and marketer of the burgeoning sexual revolution of the 1960s and 1970s.

Brown was born Helen Marie Gurley in Green Forest, Arkansas. In 1937, Brown, her sister, and her mother moved to Los Angeles, where she attended John H. Francis Polytechnic High School and Woodbury Business College, graduating in 1941. After graduation, Brown began her career as a secretary for an advertising agency. After her writing skills were recognized, she was transferred to the copywriting department, where she became one of the highest-paid ad copywriters in the early 1960s. In 1959, she married David Brown, who would become a successful film producer.

In 1962, Brown published *Sex and the Single Girl*, a lively, provocative book extolling the professional, social, and sexual pleasures of the unmarried state, a subject that had never been explored before. The book, which predates second-wave feminism and anticipates what would be termed the "sexual revolution" in the 1960s and 1970s, was a bestseller.

In 1965, Brown became the editor-in-chief of the failing general interest magazine *Cosmopolitan*.

Brown would turn the magazine into a platform for presenting the new, sexually liberated, career-oriented single woman. Defending the magazine's covers depicting the sexy *Cosmo* girl, Brown stated, "A million times a year I defend my covers. I like skin. I like pretty. I don't want to photograph the girl next door." By 1990, *Cosmopolitan* raised its readership from eight hundred thousand copies per issue to more than 2.5 million, one of the most widely read women's magazines in the world and the sixth-best-selling newsstand magazine in any category. In 1996, after thirty-two years at the helm, Brown was replaced as editor-in-chief of *Cosmopolitan*. She remained at Hearst Publishing (the publisher of *Cosmopolitan*) as its international editor until her death in 2012. Following her death, the Helen Gurley Brown Trust was created to foster programs to help the children of New York City and advancements in education and technology, including $15 million donated to the New York Public Library and $7.5 million to the American Museum of Natural History.

Brown has been a divisive figure among feminists, who have criticized *Cosmo*'s exploitation of women's bodies and influence on women's body images while at the same time recognizing her role in advancing women's empowerment. In 1996, Brown shared with *Fortune* magazine her rules for being a good executive: pay a compliment before criticizing someone, say "no" to time wasters, do what you dread first, and work harder than anybody else.

Ursula Burns (1958–)

Company Executive

 Ursula Burns, the former CEO of Xerox and the first African American woman to head a Fortune 500 company, was born in New York, New York, the daughter of Panamanian immigrants. She received a BS degree in mechanical engineering from Brooklyn Polytechnic Institute in 1980 and an MS degree in mechanical engineering from Columbia University in 1981.

Burns began her business career at Xerox in 1980 and worked her way up the organization from technical jobs to executive jobs. Her upward trajectory was impressive: she was named president of business group operations (2002), president of Xerox (2007), CEO (2009), and chair of the Xerox board (2010). As CEO, she succeeded Anne Mulcahy and became the first woman to succeed another woman at a Fortune 500 company. She stepped down as CEO in 2016 after a corporate restructuring but remained as chair of the Xerox board until she left the board in 2017. She is now CEO of VEON, a telecom service provider.

She is a member of several business and nonprofit boards, including Uber and the New York City Ballet. She is a founding director of Change the Equation, which focuses on improving the U.S. education system in science, technology, engineering, and math (STEM). In addition to her business work, she served as leader of the White House STEM program from 2009 to 2016 and of the President's Export Council from 2015 to 2016.

Safra Ada Catz (1961–)

Company Executive

The co-CEO of the computer technology company the Oracle Corporation, Safra Catz was born in Holon, Israel, and immigrated with her family to Brookline, Massachusetts, when she was six. Catz graduated from Brookline High School, earned a BA degree from the Wharton School of Business, and then a JD degree from the University of Pennsylvania Law School in 1986.

From 1986 until 1999, Catz worked at the investment bank of Donaldson, Lufkin & Jenrette, advancing to senior vice president before moving to Oracle, where she was hired as a senior vice president in 1999 and became a director two years later. In 2004, she was named president and, the next year, drove Oracle's successful takeover of People-Soft. In 2010, Mark Hurd was named copresident, and, in 2014, Hurd and Catz were named co-CEOs after founder and CEO Larry Ellison stepped down. The highest-paid female CEO in the United States, Catz was ranked number seven in *Fortune* magazine's

list of Most Powerful Women of 2018. She also sits on the boards of the Walt Disney Co. and the Technology CEO Council.

Barbara Corcoran (1949–)

Entrepreneur

One of the ways in which women have found great success in business is in the real estate industry as brokers and as entrepreneurs, especially in New York. By 2014, women such as Bonnie Stone Sellers (Christie's International Real Estate), Dolly Lenz (Dolly Lenz Real Estate), and Diane Ramirez (Halstead Property) dominated the New York real estate market and were among the nation's most powerful business leaders. The woman who paved the way for them is Barbara Corcoran, founder of The Corcoran Group, a real estate and brokerage company. In 1973, Corcoran borrowed $1,000, quit her job as a waitress, and started a small real estate company in New York City. Over the next twenty-five years, she grew her company into a $5 billion real estate empire.

Born and raised in Edgewater, New Jersey, Corcoran attended a local Catholic elementary school and Sr. Cecilia High School in Englewood. She graduated from St. Thomas Aquinas College in New York in 1971 with a degree in education. She has admitted to having held as many as twenty jobs before she was twenty-three, including renting out apartments in New York City, although she was not yet interested in real estate as a profession. Nevertheless, in 1975, she cofounded a real estate business called The Corcoran-Simone with her boyfriend, who contributed a $1,000 loan. When the couple split up, Corcoran formed her own firm, The Corcoran Group, and began publishing *The Corcoran Report*, covering real estate trends in New York City. Having grown her company into one of the largest in the city, Corcoran sold her business for $66 million in 2001. The current president and CEO of The Corcoran Group is Pamela Liebman.

The decision to sell was prompted by her giving birth to her son, Tommy, when she was forty-five after seven years of trying to conceive a child with her husband, Bill Higgins, whom she married in 1988. However, Corcoran realized that the life of a stay-at-home mother was not enough for her. "I thought I had made a terrible mistake," she says. "I had no identity. My ego took a hit." She wrote an autobiography, *If You Don't Have Big Breasts, Put Ribbons on Your Pigtails: And Other Lessons I Learned from My Mom* (2003), and pitched herself to TV networks as a real estate expert. She landed a job on *Good Morning America*, then on the *Today* show, as a regular contributor and offered business advice on CNBC's *The Big Idea with Donny Deutsch*. In 2018, producer Mark Burnett (*Survivor*) approached Corcoran to participate in a not-yet-named reality TV show that would become *Shark Tank*. Corcoran has served on all nine seasons of *Shark Tank* as one of the investment experts who determine whether or not to financially back contestants who pitch their products and inventions on the show. Corcoran has pledged more than $5.4 million in investments in the many deals she has made. She is also the author of the best-selling book *Shark Tales: How I Turned $1,000 into a Billion Dollar Business!* (2011).

Lettie Pate Whitehead Evans (1872–1953)

Company Executive

One of the first women to direct a major corporation, Lettie Pate Whitehead Evans served on the board of directors for the Coca-Cola Company for almost two decades and was the first female board member of the company.

Born in Bedford County, Virginia, into one of Virginia's most established families, Evans was educated privately. In 1895, she married attorney Joseph Brown Whitehead, and the couple moved to Chattanooga, where they raised their two sons. Their association with the Coca-Cola Company began when Joseph Whitehead was granted the exclusive contract to bottle their beverages. The Whitehead family moved to Atlanta in 1903 to expand their thriving bottling business. When Joseph Whitehead died unexpectedly from pneumonia in 1906, Evans took over the family business and real estate assets, ac-

tively managing the bottling operation of eighty plants. In 1913, she married Colonel Arthur Kelly Evans, a retired Canadian Army officer.

In 1934, Lettie Evans sold the bottling operation, which by then had grown to over one thousand bottling plants, back to Coca-Cola in exchange for stock, and she was named to the company's board of directors. She spent her remaining years donating millions of dollars to more than thirty different organizations while serving as a trustee of Emory University, Agnes Scott College, the Virginia Museum of Fine Arts, and the American Hospital of Paris. In 1945, she created the Lettie Pate Evans Foundation, which was dedicated to charity, education, and religion, leaving her estate to the foundation when she died. That foundation, as well as the Lettie Pate Whitehead Foundation, continue to operate today and to date have donated more than $53 million to various causes.

Debbi Fields (1956–)

Entrepreneur

Known as the "Cookie Queen," Debbi Fields turned the chocolate chip cookie recipe that she perfected as a teenager into a $450 million retail business, Mrs. Fields Cookies.

Born Debra Jane Sivyer in Oakland, California, Fields was the youngest of five daughters. Her father was a welder for the U.S. Navy, and her mother was a homemaker. In 1974, she graduated from Alameda High School and attended Foothill College in Los Altos Hills, California. In 1976, she married Stanford graduate Randall Fields, the founder of the financial and economic consulting firm Fields Investment Group.

Deciding that the life of a housewife was not enough for her, Fields decided to turn her childhood hobby of baking cookies into a business. She started with the classic 1930s Toll House cookie recipe on the back of the Nestlé chocolate chips bag and began experimenting with the cookie batter. By the time she was eighteen, Fields was well known locally for her cookies, which were richer and softer than the classic recipe. In 1977, with a $50,000 loan from her skeptical husband, Fields opened a small gourmet cookie shop in a downtown Palo Alto, California, food arcade and called it Mrs. Fields' Chocolate Chippery. By noon, few customers had entered the shop, so Fields began distributing free samples outside. She earned $75 in sales that first day, exceeding her husband's prediction that she would not earn $50. Success led to expansion, first to the San Francisco Bay area, then throughout California. Between 1985 and 1988, the company opened 225 new stores. By the end of the eighties, 425 cookie stores were open across the United States and abroad with an annual retail sale of over $87 million. The product line expanded as well to include oatmeal raisin, walnut, coconut–macadamia nut, and other cookie combinations as well as brownies and a frozen cookie dessert. Fields retained personal control over all cookie-baking operations, inspecting samples of all ingredients and visiting individual stores in a rotation, closing stores that fell below her standard of perfection.

During the recession of the 1990s, Fields was forced to give up 80 percent of the company to lenders. In 1992, she began franchising existing retail store locations. She remains the company's largest shareholder and continues to be active as the company's principal spokesperson. Fields published her autobiography, *One Smart Cookie*, in 1987.

Carly Fiorina (1954–)

Company Executive

 When computer giant Hewlett-Packard named Carly Fiorina as its president and chief executive officer in 1999, it became the largest publicly held company headed by a woman. In addition, Fiorina became the first woman to lead a Fortune 50 company. By the age of forty-five, Fiorina had advanced from working as a college student in Hewlett-Packard's shipping department to becoming "the most powerful woman in American business," according to *Fortune* magazine.

Fiorina was born Cara Carleton Sneed in Austin, Texas, the daughter of a law professor and a judge who also served as a deputy attorney general in the Nixon administration; her mother was a painter. Fiorina attended Stanford University, where she majored in medieval history and philosophy and graduated in 1976. She then began studying law at UCLA but dropped out after only one semester. She next worked in a variety of jobs, including teaching English in Bologna, Italy, before going back to school to earn her MBA degree from the University of Maryland in 1980. She went on to earn an MS degree from MIT's Sloan School in 1989.

Fiorina began her business career with communications giant AT&T as an account executive in Washington, D.C., handling government accounts. In 1985, she married Frank Fiorina, an AT&T executive, and, with him, raised his two daughters from a previous marriage. Praised for her enthusiasm and drive, Fiorina transferred to AT&T's Network Systems manufacturing division, becoming its first female officer. Fiorina helped the division expand into Asia as a major provider of network systems. By 1991, she was a vice president, and by 1995, she ran the company's North American sales.

When AT&T formed Lucent Technologies, Fiorina directed the initial public offering and subsequent spin-off. She then served as president of Lucent's global service provider business. In 1999, Hewlett-Packard offered her the position as president and CEO, overseeing a $47 billion business and the world's second-largest computer manufacturer. In 2001, Fiorina staked her reputation and her position on an ambitious plan for Hewlett-Packard to acquire Compaq Computer. HP's founding families opposed the merger and used their 18 percent stock holdings to resist the $19 billion deal. In May 2002, after an eight-month proxy fight, a three-day court battle, and a bitter boardroom squabble, Fiorina's gamble paid off when Hewlett-Packard won approval for the merger with about 51 percent of shareholders agreeing to the deal. While the acquisition was a major victory for Fiorina at the time, the resulting merger produced mixed results for the company. In 2005, Fiorina resigned her position under pressure from HP's board of directors.

Fiorina followed her departure from Hewlett-Packard with political activity as an adviser to Republican senator John McCain's 2008 presidential campaign, in an unsuccessful 2012 run for the U.S. Senate from California, and as a candidate for the

Republican presidential nomination in 2016. Fiorina has also been involved in philanthropy and non-profit work as the chair of Good360, a nonprofit that helps companies donate excess merchandise to charities, and with the One Woman Initiative, an international women's empowerment program. She is also the chair and CEO of the Fiorina Foundation, a charity that has donated to numerous causes in aid of children and education.

Melinda Gates (1964–)

Company Executive, Philanthropist

Melinda Gates is an American philanthropist and a former general manager at Microsoft. She was born Melinda Ann French in Dallas, Texas, the daughter of an aerospace engineer, who encouraged Gates to follow her interest in computers. She earned a BS degree in computer science from Duke University in 1986 and an MBA degree from Duke University's Fuqua School of Business in 1987. She began work at Microsoft Corporation that year.

At Microsoft, Gates started as a product manager for multimedia and interactive products, including the multimedia encyclopedia Encarta and the trip-planning website Expedia. She worked for Microsoft for nine years, advancing to general manager of information products. She married Microsoft cofounder Bill Gates in 1994 and, with the birth of the couple's three children in 1996, decided to leave work at Microsoft to devote her time to raising her child and working on philanthropic efforts.

In 1994, Melinda and Bill Gates, along with Bill Gates's father, Bill Gates Sr., started the William H. Gates Foundation, which focused on placing computers and Microsoft products in libraries all over the United States. In 1999, the Gateses combined the Gates Foundations into the Bill & Melinda Gates Foundation. Melinda Gates expanded the foundation to include a worldwide focus on education, global poverty, and health. In 2017, the foundation had an endowment of $50.7 billion, reported to be the largest private foundation in the world.

As a result of Gates's leading role in the Gates Foundation since 2011, she has been listed among the top six on *Forbes* magazine's list of the World's 100 Most Powerful Women. In addition to working with the Gates Foundation, she has worked on increasing the role of women in technology and other businesses. She has received many U.S. and international awards for their work, including the U.S. Presidential Medal of Freedom, the U.K.'s Dame Commander of the Order of the British Empire, and France's Legion of Honor.

Mary Katherine Goddard (1738–1816)

Publisher

The most acclaimed female publisher during the American Revolution and the first female newspaper publisher in America, Mary Katherine Goddard turned enterprises begun by her undependable brother into financial successes. She is famous for printing the first copy of the Declaration of Independence, which included the names of all the signers. Named Baltimore's postmaster in 1776, she was the United States's first and only female government employee when the United States was established in 1776.

Goddard was the daughter of the postmaster of New London, Connecticut. Her brother, William, trained as a printer and set up a printing press, publishing the first newspaper in Providence, Rhode Island, the *Providence Gazette*. After William departed for Philadelphia to open a new printing business, Goddard and her widowed mother took over the management of their Providence shop and the weekly publication of the newspaper. In 1768, William was forced to sell the Providence business, and the two women joined him in Philadelphia. Goddard became the office manager and helped her brother publish the *Pennsylvania Chronicle* newspaper. William sold the business in 1774 and moved to Baltimore, where Goddard once again joined him.

In 1775, at the beginning of the Revolutionary War, Goddard became the publisher of Baltimore's first newspaper, the *Maryland Journal*. The *Journal* was one of the few newspapers that was consistently published through the war years. When she retired as its editor in 1784, the *Journal* had become the most widely read publication in the United States.

In 1777, Goddard was chosen by the Continental Congress to print the first copies of the Declaration of Independence, which included all the names of signers. The first printing, on July 4, 1776, had contained only the names of John Hancock and Charles Thomson with the other names kept secret for fear of British reprisals. By 1777, Congress ordered "an authentic copy ... with the names of the members of Congress subscribing ... be sent to each of the United States." Goddard signed the prints she produced, becoming the only woman to "sign" the Declaration of Independence.

Having made her reputation as a successful printer and publisher, a dispute with her brother caused her to leave their business. In 1775, she had been named postmaster of Baltimore, the first woman to hold such a position in the United States. She also ran a bookstore and published almanacs. Goddard kept the postmaster's job for fourteen years. In 1789, despite protests from the Baltimore community, Postmaster General Samuel Osgood removed Goddard from her position when he determined that the position required "more traveling than a woman could undertake." Goddard continued to run her bookstore until 1810. After Goddard died at the age of seventy-eight, her will freed the female slave who had been her assistant and named her as the sole beneficiary of Goddard's estate. One of Goddard's contemporaries memorialized her as "a woman of extraordinary judgment, energy, nerve, and strong good sense."

Katharine Graham (1917–2001)

Publisher

A Washington socialite who was forced to succeed her husband as president and publisher of *The Washington Post* after his death in 1963, Katherine Graham defied expectations of her competency to build the newspaper into an influential and

respected publication. In doing so, she became the most powerful woman in American journalism.

Born in New York City, Graham was the daughter of wealthy investment banker Eugene Meyer, who purchased the struggling *Washington Post* in 1933 in a bankruptcy sale. After Graham's graduation from the University of Chicago in 1933, she worked as a reporter in San Francisco before joining the editorial department of the *Post.* In 1940, she married attorney Philip Graham, who, after his service in World War II, assumed the position of publisher of the paper. He would help his father-in-law to build the business until 1948, when the Grahams bought the *Post* from Eugene Meyer. In the early 1960s, the *Post* purchased *Newsweek* magazine, expanded the radio and television operations of the company, and helped to establish an international news service. During her marriage, Katharine Graham largely retired from journalism to raise her four children and to become a prominent Washington, D.C., society hostess.

In 1963, Philip Graham, who suffered from bipolar disorder (then called manic depression), committed suicide. Suddenly, with no executive training, Katharine Graham found herself in charge of the family publishing empire. After some initial doubts as to her capacity to helm the paper, Graham gradually proved to be a bold decision maker. In an effort to improve the day-to-day leadership at the paper, Graham hired the highly regarded Ben Bradlee as the new managing editor and, in 1971, approved Bradlee's decision to publish the Pentagon Papers, the secret government documents that revealed the truth about American involvement in Vietnam, which had first appeared in *The New York Times.* The decision to publish it was a milestone event in protecting the freedom of the press, and the *Post's* action was subsequently ruled legal in a U.S. Supreme Court case. One year later, the Watergate scandal emerged, with *Post* reporters Bob Woodward and Carl Bernstein breaking the story about the connection between a burglary at Washington's Watergate complex and political corruption in the Nixon White House. The revelations ultimately led to President Nixon's resignation. Graham encouraged and financed the Watergate coverage and withstood an all-out White House attack to discredit the

Post and its investigation. In 1973, the paper was awarded the Pulitzer Prize for Public Service for its investigation of the Watergate scandal.

Graham passed the day-to-day management of the *Post* to her son, Donny, in 1979 but remained chair of the board until 1991. In 1997, she published a memoir, *Personal History*, which earned her the 1998 Pulitzer Prize for Biography or Autobiography.

Hetty Green (1834–1916)

Financier

Financier Hetty Green, nicknamed the "Witch of Wall Street," was the first woman to amass a fortune on Wall Street. Managing her own funds, investing in stocks, bonds, and real estate, she turned a $6 million family inheritance into $100 million by the time she died, making her the richest woman in America during the Gilded Age.

She was born Henrietta Howland Robinson in New Bedford, Massachusetts, into a Quaker family, who owned a large whaling fleet and a profitable China trading business. Encouraged by her grandfather in financial matters, Green once stated, "I was taught from the time I was six years old that I would have to look after my property." By the age of thirteen, she was in charge of the accounts of the family business. The sole heir of her father, who died in 1865, Green was left approximately $6 million, and, in 1867, she married millionaire businessman Edward Henry Green after he agreed to sign a prenuptial agreement stipulating that her fortune was hers alone. The couple moved to New York City, where Green began her investing career.

Green summarized her investment strategy by saying, "I buy when things are low and nobody wants them. I keep them until they go up and people are crazy to get them. This, I believe, is the secret of all successful business." Green pioneered the financial practice of what today is called "value investing," which is associated with investors like Warren Buffett. Green invested primarily in government bonds and real estate, parlaying her $6 million inheritance into a fortune worth upward of $100 million, about

$2 billion in today's money. Green's financial prowess and success invited comparisons with the age's other great financiers such as Morgan, Carnegie, and Rockefeller. However, unlike them, Green never became an industrialist. Her sole business was capital investment.

Unlike other Gilded Age tycoons, Green did nothing with her fortune except to invest it. She lived in boardinghouses, plain apartments, or hotels and became more famous for her legendary miserliness than for her financial acumen. She wore one old, black dress and undergarments that were changed only when they had been worn out, instructing her laundress to wash only the dirtiest parts of her dresses to save money on soap. It is said that she spent half a night searching for a lost two-cent stamp. Most famously, when her son broke his leg as a child, Green tried to get him admitted for treatment at a free clinic for the poor. His leg never healed properly and, after years of treatment, had to be amputated.

Green died at the age of eighty-one at her son's New York City home. She was eulogized at her death as the "Wizard of Finance" and the "Richest Woman in America." Green's two children enjoyed her fortune more than their mother ever had. Her daughter, Silvia, who died in 1951, donated a substantial portion of the family fortune to colleges, churches, hospitals, and other charities.

Ruth Handler (1916–2002)

Entrepreneur

Cofounder and president of the toy manufacturer Mattel Inc., Ruth Handler changed the face of the toy industry with her introduction of the Barbie doll in 1959. According to Mattel, every second, somewhere in the world, two Barbies are sold. More than a billion Barbies have been purchased. More Barbies exist in America than humans. According to M. G. Lord, author of the definitive study of the doll's origin, marketing, and cultural significance, "Barbie may be the most potent icon of American popular culture in the late twentieth century."

Handler was born Ruth Marianna Mosko in Denver, Colorado, to Polish Jewish immigrants. She married her high school boyfriend, Elliot Handler, and moved to Los Angeles in 1938. Starting in their garage in 1939, the Handlers began making furniture and picture frames out of two newly created plastics, Lucite and Plexiglas. Using scraps from the manufacturing process, they began to make dollhouse furniture, which proved to be more profitable than picture frames or furniture. They decided to concentrate on toy manufacturing. Elliot Handler and his business partner, Harold "Matt" Matson, had created a company named "Mattel" by combining parts of their names ("Matt" and "Elliott"). The company turned a profit in 1945, and their first big-selling toy was a toy ukulele called the "Uke-A-Doodle," released in 1947. Handler was in charge of marketing, and her husband headed up product design (Matson was bought out early in the company's history). Both were responsible for innovations that led to Mattel's success. It was the first company to make toys out of a mixture of materials and the first to realize the advantages of recycling components in a variety of toys such as placing a music box in a jack-in-the-box. Mattel's most revolutionary advancement was the use of television in its advertising. When most toys were still primarily marketed in catalogs and trade shows, the Handlers, in 1955, bought a year's exclusive sponsorship of ABC's new program *The Mickey Mouse Club*. It was a hit, and Mattel's toys flew off the shelves.

The most successful doll of all time and the apotheosis of all-American femininity originated from a racy German cartoon of a gold digger named Lilli, who became a 11.5-inch doll with a blonde ponytail, pouty lips, and sex appeal not intended for children but as a gag gift for men or as presents for girlfriends. In 1956, Handler discovered the doll while vacationing in Switzerland. Handler had wanted to create an adult doll ever since watching her daughter, Barbara, and her friends playing with adult paper dolls and observed that they "were imagining their lives as adults. They were using dolls to reflect the adult world around them.... I used to watch that over and over, and think: If only we could take this play pattern and three-dimensionalize it, we would have something special."

Handler brought the Lilli doll home and began the process of transforming it into Barbie, although her colleagues at Mattel were "all horrified by the thought of wanting to make a doll with breasts." When Barbie debuted in 1959, it was not an immediate success. Parents objected to the sexy adult doll, but television advertising drove sales, and the doll proved to be unstoppable, becoming the most popular and best-selling toy of all time.

In 1970, Handler was diagnosed with breast cancer. After a radical mastectomy, she had difficulties finding a good breast prosthesis, and she decided to make her own after concluding that "the people in this business are men who don't have to wear these." She went on to found a successful company, Ruthton Corporation, which manufactures a more realistic version of a woman's breast called "Nearly Me." In 1974, she resigned from Mattel after investigations of producing fraudulent financial reports. She blamed her illness for losing focus on her business. Handler died in California from complications of colon cancer surgery at the age of eighty-five. The doll she created has gone through several changes over the years to reflect both women's cultural and physical diversity.

Marillyn Hewson (1953–)

Company Executive

The chair, president, and CEO of Lockheed Martin Corporation, Hewson was born Marillyn Adams in Junction City, Kansas, and grew up in Alabama. Her father died when she was nine, leaving her mother to raise five children alone. She worked in high school and put herself through the University of Alabama, earning a BS degree in business administration and later an MA degree in economics.

After receiving her MA degree, she worked as an economist at the Bureau of Labor Statistics and, in 1983, joined Lockheed Martin's Marietta, Georgia, plant as an industrial engineer. She steadily worked her way up through the company, holding leadership positions in four of the company's five divisions. In 2012, she was elected to Lockheed Martin's board of directors, and, in 2013, she was named COO and soon after CEO.

As CEO of the world's largest aerospace corporation, Hewson has steered the company toward more U.S. and global defense spending (including the world's most advanced warplane, the F-35). As a result, during her tenure as CEO, Lockheed Martin's market capitalization has doubled, and total returns to shareholders have been 309 percent. Even before becoming CEO, Hewson had been listed as one of the most powerful women in business and has received many industry honors. In 2018, *Fortune* magazine identified her as number one of the 50 Most Powerful Women in Business. Hewson serves on the boards of various corporations and nonprofit organizations, including *catalyst.org*.

Barbara Holdridge (1929–)

Entrepreneur

A pioneer in the field of spoken-word recordings, Barbara Holdridge is the cofounder of Caedmon Records, a spoken-word recording company that began the audiobook business. Born Barbara Ann Cohen in New York City, Holdridge received a BA degree from Hunter College in 1950. She began graduate studies at Columbia University but in 1952 stopped her studies to collaborate with her college friend Marianne Roney (later Mantell) to create a recording business devoted to the spoken word. They named their company Caedmon Records after the earliest known English poet, Caedmon.

Caedmon's first recording was by Welsh poet Dylan Thomas and included his story "A Child's Christmas in Wales." The recording was a success, and Caedmon went on to record many other literary works as well as children's stories, speeches, and theater performances. As an entirely female-owned company, Caedmon has always been committed to gender equality and has given additional visibility to women's writings. Cademon proved to be a financial success as well, and, in 1975, the partners sold the company to D.C. Heath and Company. Holdridge remained with Caedmon for five years as president of the reorganized company, which is now a division of HarperCollins Publishers.

Holdridge moved with her husband Lawrence Holdridge to Maryland in 1959, and, in 1973, the couple purchased a historic Georgian mansion. When Holdridge began a new publishing venture in 1975, she named her new company Stemmer House after the name of the house in which she lived. Stemmer House Publishers is best known for its line of children's books and the International Design Library, a publishing imprint featuring books on folk art. In 2003, she sold the company and retired. Holdridge has received several awards for her work with Caedmon as well as for historic preservation of Stemmer House and its gardens. She currently serves on several boards of directors.

Arianna Huffington (1950–)

Company Executive, Entrepreneur

 Greek American businesswoman Arianna Huffington is the founder of *The Huffington Post* and the founder and CEO of the health and wellness startup Thrive Global. She has also been a board member of Uber since 2016.

Born Arianna Stassinopoulos, Huffington is the daughter of a Greek newspaper owner. She moved to England as a teenager and pursued an economics degree from Cambridge University, earning a master's in 1972. While at Cambridge, she served as president of its debating society, the Cambridge Union, the first foreign-born student to do so. After graduation, she lived in London for a time before relocating to the United States, settling in California with Republican politician Michael Huffington, whom she married in 1986 and divorced in 1997.

Huffington began her political and journalistic career as a Republican. She contributed to the conservative *National Review*, and, in 1994, she worked on her husband's unsuccessful campaign for U.S. Senate. In the late 1990s, however, Huffington shifted to the left politically and became active in progressive causes, particularly efforts to combat global warming. After an unsuccessful run in the 2003 California governor's race, Huffington launched *The Huffington Post* website in 2005, serving as its cofounder and editor-in-chief. It was set up as a group blog, publishing hundreds of guest contributors while providing news updates and links to other news sources and columnists. In 2011, AOL acquired *The Huffington Post* for $315 million. Huffington launched a new venture as president and editor-in-chief of the Huffington Post Media Group, which she ran until 2016, when she left to start Thrive Global, which has raised over $43 million in funding.

A prolific author, some of her books include *The Female Woman* (1973), *After Reason* (1978), *Maria Callas* (1981), *Greetings from the Lincoln Bedroom* (1998), *How to Overthrow the Government* (2000), *Pigs at the Trough* (2003), *On Becoming Fearless … In Love, Work, and Life* (2007), and *The Sleep Revolution: Transforming Your Life, One Night at a Time* (2016). Huffington was named to *Time* magazine's list of the 100 Most Influential People and to *Forbes* magazine's Most Powerful Women list.

Abigail Johnson (1961–)

Company Executive

The chair and CEO of Fidelity Investments, Inc., Abigail Pierrepont Johnson was born in Boston, Massachusetts. She received a BA degree from Hobart and William Smith College in 1984 and an MBA degree from Harvard University in 1988. After graduation, she began full-time work as an entry-level stock analyst at Fidelity Investments, an investment firm founded by her grandfather, Edward C. Johnson II, in 1946.

Johnson spent twenty-five years at Fidelity working as a portfolio manager, associate director, vice president, and, in 2001, president of Fidelity Asset Management (a division of the parent company, Fidelity Investments). She was named president of Fidelity Investments in 2012 and CEO and chair of the company in 2014.

As chief executive of one of the world's largest investment management companies with a personal net worth of approximately $16 billion, Johnson is consistently listed as one of the most powerful and wealthiest women in the world. In 2018, *Fortune* magazine ranked her number three, and *Forbes* magazine ranked her as number five. During her career,

she has been committed to ensuring that Fidelity is free of gender bias and harassment.

Elizabeth Keckley (1818–1907)

Entrepreneur

The phrase "rags to riches" is often used to describe a self-made entrepreneur from a humble or impoverished background. Elizabeth Keckley, a former slave turned entrepreneur, amply fits the description. She rose from slavery to freedom and had a successful career that led to a connection with the government elite during the Civil War period and a place as the closest confidante of First Lady Mary Todd Lincoln.

Keckley was born in Dinwiddie, Virginia, the daughter of a slave and, as she would learn before her mother's death, the white planter who owned her family. In her teens, the planter's son sent Keckley to North Carolina, where she was savagely whipped and repeatedly raped by a white store owner. She gave birth to her only child, a son, when she was twenty-three. Eventually, Keckley was transferred to owners who moved to St. Louis. To help them earn money, Keckley started a seamstress business, having been taught to sew by her mother when she was as young as three. Her talent as a seamstress kept her in high demand, allowing her to buy freedom for herself and her son for $1,200.

In 1860, she and her son moved first to Baltimore and finally to Washington, D.C., where she established her dressmaking business. Commissions for dresses among Washington's elite came in steadily, but it was a dress Keckley completed for Mrs. Robert E. Lee that helped to establish her business. She eventually became the favorite family seamstress of Jefferson Davis's wife, Varina Davis. Through a friend of Varina Davis, Keckley received an urgent commission that if completed would introduce her to the new first lady, Mary Todd Lincoln, who was looking for a "modiste" or dressmaker. Keckley made the dress for Lincoln that she wore at the inaugural festivities. Keckley, whom Lincoln addressed as "Madam Elizabeth," would become the first lady's sole designer and the creator of her wardrobe as well as Mary Todd Lincoln's most trusted confidante and constant companion. Keckley was given an intimate, insider's view of the Lincoln presidency, which she would reveal in her memoir *Behind the Scenes, or, Thirty Years a Slave, and Four Years in the White House* (1868). The book angered Mrs. Lincoln, and she and Keckley never spoke again.

Keckley continued running her dressmaking business and taught young, African American women her trade. She spent her last years in Washington's National Home for Destitute Colored Women and Children, created by the Contraband Relief Association, which Keckley had founded with the help of Mrs. Lincoln and Frederick Douglass to help former slaves who had sought refuge in the nation's capital.

Juanita Morris Kreps (1921–2010)

Company Executive, Economist

An economist, businesswoman, and public official, Juanita Morris Kreps was the first woman to serve as U.S. secretary of commerce, the first woman to sit on the board of directors of the New York Stock Exchange, and the first woman to win the Director of the Year award for the National Association of Corporate Directors.

Born Juanita Morris in Lynch, Kentucky, Kreps graduated from Berea College in 1942 before earning her master's degree (1944) and Ph.D. (1948) in economics from Duke University. She married Clifton H. Kreps Jr., also an economist, and followed him to various academic positions, teaching part time at Denison and Hofstra universities and at Queens College. In 1955, she returned to Duke as a part-time instructor, and, from 1963 to 1967, she rose through the academic ranks to become a full professor and dean of the Women's College and associate provost in 1967. In 1973, she was named Duke's first female vice president. Kreps's main field of research was the changing role of women in the labor force and its effect on society. Her published works include *Sex in the Marketplace: American Women at Work* (1971) and *Sex, Age, and Work: The Changing Composition of the Labor Force* (1975).

Kreps experienced firsthand the challenges of working women while trying to coordinate teaching positions with her husband and juggling her responsibilities of raising her three children. Kreps was an early supporter of the feminist movement, publicly supporting equal opportunity employment. One of the landmarks of the feminist movement was Kreps's appointment to U.S. secretary of commerce in 1977 by President Jimmy Carter. She was the first woman to hold the office as well as the first professional economist to do so. Kreps was only the fifth woman in U.S. history to hold any Cabinet position. She focused on U.S. trade issues, development of poor regions of the United States, and labor equity issues faced by women. Named Woman of the Year by *Ladies' Home Journal* in 1978, Kreps became the first U.S. secretary of commerce to visit China to negotiate an important trade agreement. In 1979, Kreps left her cabinet post for family reasons to return to Duke and eventually retired as vice president emerita. Kreps served on numerous corporate boards, including Eastman Kodak, AT&T, J. C. Penney, United Airlines, and R. J. Reynolds. She died in Durham, North Carolina, at the age of eighty-nine. Kreps stated to the graduates in a 1977 commencement speech at Duke, "If there is one thing I could wish for you, it would be that you sense the freedom and be sensitive to the constraints that the forces of history throw in your lap. Because you face a different world, I would further hope that you feel uninhibited by the expectations of others, remembering that their notions of success or failure are not necessarily appropriate to your time and place."

Sherry Lansing (1944–)

Company Executive

The first woman to head a major Hollywood studio, Lansing was born Sherry Lee Duhl in Chicago, Illinois. Lansing's mother, Margot, had escaped to the United States from Nazi Germany at seventeen, and her father, David, was a real estate investor who died when Lansing was nine. Her mother later remarried, and Lansing took her stepfather's last name. She graduated from the University of Chicago Laboratory Schools in 1962 and earned a BS degree at Northwestern University in 1966. She moved to Los Angeles and began working as a mathematics teacher in the Los Angeles public school system and as a model while trying to break into the movies as an actress. After appearing in two films made in 1970, *Loving* and *Rio Lobo* with John Wayne, Lansing decided to abandon acting for other work in the film industry.

Lansing began her career at MGM as a script reader and in 1972 was hired as a story editor. She advanced through the ranks to become vice president of creative affairs and in 1978 was named vice president in charge of production at Columbia Pictures. Two years later, she was chosen as president of 20th Century Fox, making her the first woman to head a major film studio. After three years, she left and teamed with producer Stanley R. Jaffe to create Jaffe/Lansing Productions. The company released a string of successful but minor films before producing the box office hit *Fatal Attraction* in 1987. In 1991, Lansing married filmmaker William Friedkin, director of the classic 1973 horror film *The Exorcist*.

Lansing returned to a studio role when she became chair of Paramount Pictures in 1992. During her tenure at Paramount, the studio produced blockbuster hits such as *Titanic*. Overall, 80 percent of the films released by Lansing were profitable, a record number for a long-term studio leader. In 2004, Lansing left the movie business to devote her time to the Sherry Lansing Foundation, which is dedicated to raising awareness and funds for cancer research. She has received numerous awards for her philanthropic work and is a board member of several corporations and nonprofits.

Estée Lauder (1906–2004)

Entrepreneur

Cofounder of Estée Lauder, Inc., a large fragrance and cosmetic company that, by 1999, accounted for nearly 50 percent of all retail beauty aids sold in America, Estée Lauder built her cosmetics empire on the motto "There are no homely women, only careless women," managing

to convince women that with the help of her products, beauty was within reach. In 1998, Lauder was the only woman on the *Time* magazine list of the Twenty Most Influential Business Geniuses of the Twentieth Century.

Born Josephine Esther Mentzer in Corona, Queens, New York City, Lauder was the daughter of Hungarian Jewish immigrants. She learned the basics of retailing, particularly the importance of the appearance of the merchandise and the value of promotions, from her father, who owned a hardware store beneath their family home. In 1914, Lauder's maternal uncle, John Schotz, a chemist, came to live with the family. He set up a laboratory in an empty stable behind their house and manufactured creams, lotions, rouge, and perfumes using natural ingredients. Lauder began selling her uncle's products to her high school classmates, calling them "jars of hope," and also started giving her classmates beauty treatments.

After Lauder married Joseph Lauter in 1930, the couple changed their surname to Lauder. Together, they founded Estée Lauder, Inc., in 1946. Instead of advertising their beauty products, they gave away samples at fashion shows and in mailings. The company employed five people and grossed $850,000 in sales in 1958. By 1973, the company employed one thousand people with $100 million in yearly sales of cosmetics and fragrances. The company sold its skin care and skin protection products only through department and specialty stores. Their product line included Youth-Dew fragrance and bath oils (added in 1953), Aramis men's products (begun in 1964), Clinique allergy-tested cosmetics (introduced in 1968), and Origins natural cosmetics (introduced in 1990). By the early twenty-first century, its products were sold in more than 140 countries with net sales approaching $8 billion annually.

Lauder would become one of the richest self-made women in the world. Stepping down from day-to-day operations of her company in 1973, Lauder devoted much of her remaining years to philanthropic efforts. For her achievements both in business and in her charitable work, she became the first woman to receive the Chevalier Commendation from the French government in 1978. She was awarded the Presidential Medal of Freedom in 2004 shortly before her death at the age of ninety-seven at her home in Manhattan. As she famously declared, "I didn't get here by dreaming or thinking about it. I got here by doing it."

Sandy Lerner (1955–)

Entrepreneur, Philanthropist

Businesswoman and philanthropist Sandy Lerner is the cofounder of Cisco Systems, Inc., the maker of the first commercially viable router that allowed computers to network to one another. The sale of her stake in the company led her to become the first female philanthropist to emerge from the booming Silicon Valley tech economy.

Born and raised in northern California, Lerner's parents divorced when she was four years old. She was raised by her two aunts and divided her time between a cattle ranch in the California Sierras and Beverly Hills. At the age of nine, Lerner bought her first steer, selling it for a profit two years later and using the money to buy two more head of cattle. By the time she entered college, she owned a registered livestock herd of thirty head of cattle, which provided the income stream that paid her college tuition. She earned an undergraduate degree in political science from California State University–Chico in 1975 and began graduate work in political studies at Claremont College. While there, she stumbled into the school's computer lab and became fascinated with the then-new machines. After learning how to operate them, she used the computers for data analysis for her political science research. She went on to earn a master's degree in econometrics from Claremont in 1977 and then entered Stanford University's graduate program for statistics and computer science, receiving her master's degree in 1981.

In 1984, Lerner cofounded Cisco Systems with her then-boyfriend and now ex-husband, Len Bosack, while working as director of computer facilities for the Stanford University Graduate School of Business. In the early days of the company, the couple built routers in their living rooms and financed the business using credit cards. The router they eventually designed had a unique multiprotocol bit of hard-ware and software that could work with many different computers. The venture capitalist they enlisted for financial support brought in John Morgridge to be the third CEO of Cisco in 1988. In 1990, after clashes with Morgridge, Lerner was fired, and, hearing the news, Bosack resigned in solidarity. The company went public the same year after $25 million in revenue the previous year. Bosack and Lerner sold off their stock, worth about $170 million.

Lerner would use her fortune to create a charitable foundation and trust to support projects of interest to her, including animal welfare and the Centre for the Study of Early Women's Writing, 1600–1830 on the site of British author Jane Austen's former home, Chawton House, which Lerner purchased. She also created a cosmetic company, Urban Decay, with its slogan, "Does Pink Make You Puke?" Lerner's punk-rock palette for nail varnish was an instant hit, taking in $9 million. It has been suggested that Urban Decay helped launch the nail polish-on-men trend.

Lerner moved to Virginia in 1995, living at Ayrshire Farm, her estate in Upperville, Virginia. Dedicated to sustainability, the farm sells its humanely raised meats and organic produce online and locally from the Home Store in Middleburg, Virginia.

Rebecca Lukens (1794–1854)

Industrialist

In 1825, when Rebecca Lukens honored her husband's deathbed request that she take over the Brandywine Iron Works and Nail Factory, she became the first woman to head an ironworks as well as America's first female industrialist. She turned the debt-ridden company into one of the Industrial Revolution's most successful enterprises.

Born Rebecca Webb Pennock, Lukens was the daughter of Quaker Isaac Penncock, who founded the Federal Slitting Mill, which processed iron into barrel hoops and nails near Coatesville, Pennsylvania, in 1793. She went to boarding school in nearby Wilmington, Delaware. She married Charles Lukens in 1813, who joined the business and leased the mill from her father. When her father died in 1824, the mill was known as the Brandywine Iron Works and Nail Factory.

When her husband died in 1825 and Lukens assumed management of the ironworks, she was pregnant with her sixth child, and the company was nearly bankrupt. Lukens supervised the completion of the largest order the mill had ever received—to make the steel plate for the first metal hulled steamboat in America, the *Codorus*, launched the same year. She saved the company from bankruptcy by making it the chief producer of boilerplates for steam engines and locomotives. The Brandywine Iron Works and Nail Factory became known for the superior quality of its products that Lukens demanded. She became a savvy businesswoman, investing in other ventures, including a warehouse, store, saddler's shop, and dwellings for her workers.

Lukens ran the company until 1847. In retirement, she wrote her autobiography for her grandchildren and had the Brandywine Mansion built as a wedding present for her daughter, where she lived until her death in 1854 at the age of sixty. After her death, the Brandywine Iron Works and Nail Factory became the publicly traded Lukens Iron and Steel and remained listed on the New York Stock Exchange until 1998, when it was purchased by Bethlehem Steel.

In 1994, *Fortune* magazine named Lukens America's first female CEO of an industrial company and inducted her into the National Business Hall of Fame. As Gene DiOrio, historical adviser to the National Iron & Steel Heritage Museum, has observed, "[Lukens] was like George Washington at Valley Forge. She faced a million instances where rather than give up and walk away, Rebecca stayed with the problem and worked her way through it. She was a shining example of courage."

Denise Morrison (1954–)

Company Executive

Denise Morrison is the former president and CEO of the Campbell Soup Company. The oldest of four sisters, Morrison was born in Elberon, New Jersey, the daughter of a business executive who encour-

aged his daughters to pursue business careers. Morrison earned a BS degree in economics and psychology from Boston College in 1975 and began her business career in sales at Procter & Gamble. She then joined Pepsi-Cola in the trade and business development area.

Morrison continued to advance her career in the food industry, working at Nestle USA and with Nabisco, Inc., where she served as senior vice president in charge of sales for the Nabisco Food Company. She then moved to Kraft Foods as an executive vice president and general manager. In 2003, she joined Campbell USA as president of global sales and, in 2010, became Campbell's chief operating officer, in charge of all the company's global businesses. She was named president and CEO of Campbell in 2011. Morrison retired in 2018.

Morrison has received numerous industry awards and awards for her leadership role as a woman in business. She is a member of several boards of directors in both the profit and nonprofit sectors. She is the former chair of Catalyst's advisory board and former president of the New Jersey Women's Forum.

Indra Nooyi (1955–)

Company Executive

The former chair and CEO of PepsiCo, Inc., Indra Nooyi was born Indra Krishnamurthy on October 28, 1955, in Madras (now Chennai), India. She received BS degrees in physics, chemistry, and mathematics from Madras Christian College in 1974 and an MBA degree from the Indian Institute of Management in Kolkata in 1976. She earned an MS degree in public and private management from the Yale School of Management in 1980.

Nooyi began her career as a product manager in India. After receiving her degree from Yale, she began working with the Boston Consulting Group as a strategy consultant. After six years as a consultant, she was hired as vice president and director of corporate strategy and planning at Motorola.

She joined PepsiCo in 1994 as a senior vice president and was named president and chief financial officer in 2001. In 2006, she was named chair and CEO, a position she held until 2018. During her twelve years running PepsiCo, she increased the company's revenues through strategic decisions that built the company rather than going for short-term gains. She also moved the company to offer healthier foods by dividing the product mix into three different areas: "fun for you," "better for you," and "good for you." She retired in 2018.

Nooyi was regularly listed as one of the most powerful women in business and the world, ranked as number one in *Fortune* magazine's annual ranking of Most Powerful Women in Business for 2006 through 2010. She has received many honorary degrees and has funded a deanship at Yale. She is a member of numerous boards, most recently Amazon. She serves as an honorary cochair for the World Justice Project, a global, multidisciplinary effort to strengthen the rule of law and create opportunity and equity.

Eliza Lucas Pinckney (1772–1793)
Agriculturalist, Entrepreneur

The first American female agriculturalist, Eliza Pinckney launched the indigo industry in pre-Revolutionary South Carolina. Planters would subsequently export thousands of pounds of it annually, making indigo a staple of the southern economy.

Pinckney was born on the island of Antigua in the Caribbean and grew up with two brothers and a sister on one of her family's sugarcane plantations. Her father, Lieutenant Colonel George Lucas, was a British Army officer and, like her siblings, Eliza was sent to London for her schooling. Her favorite subject was botany.

In 1738, when Pinckney was sixteen, the family moved to South Carolina, where her father had inherited three plantations. Pinckney, who took up the running of one of them, received various types of seeds from Antigua, where her father now served as lieutenant governor. To determine which crops could supplement the cultivation of rice, Pinckney experimented with ginger, cotton, alfalfa, and hemp

and, in 1739, began cultivating and improving strains of the indigo plant for the expanding textile market, which created a demand for its dye. After three years of experimentation and many failures, Pinckney finally proved that indigo could be successfully grown and processed in South Carolina. She used her 1744 crop to make seeds and shared them with other planters, expanding indigo production from five thousand pounds in 1745–1746 to 130,000 pounds by 1748. Indigo would become second only to rice as the South Carolina colony's commodity cash crop, and it would account for more than one-third of the total value of exports from the colony. In the so-called Indigo Bonanza, indigo planters doubled their earnings every three to four years from 1745 to 1775 when the American Revolution brought an end to trade with Britain. At the time, South Carolina was exporting over one million pounds of indigo annually with a present-day value of over $30 million.

With her success, Pinckney could afford to choose her own suitor and reject her father's recommendations. In 1744, she left the plantation to marry planter and recent widower Charles Pinckney and would eventually give birth to four children. In 1753, the family relocated to England, where Charles Pinckney served as a colonial agent for South Carolina. In 1758, after the family had returned to South Carolina, Charles died of malaria. Eliza Pinkney would spend the rest of her life overseeing the family plantations. The family supported American independence, and during the American Revolution, the British destroyed the Pinckney plantations. Two of Pinckney's sons served the cause of independence as American generals during the war, and one son, Charles Pinckney, was a signer of the Constitution as well as instrumental in introducing cotton across the South following the war. Another son, Thomas, served as the U.S. minister to Spain and Great Britain.

In 1793, Pinckney died in Philadelphia, where she had gone for medical treatment. President George Washington served as one of the pallbearers at her funeral. Valuable to posterity regarding Pinckney's role in creating the indigo market in South Carolina are her writings, published in 1850 as *The Journal and Letters of Eliza Lucas*, which provide a unique and intimate look at daily plantation life in the antebellum South.

Lydia E. Pinkham (1819–1883)

Entrepreneur

The inventor and marketer of an herbal alcoholic "women's tonic" for menstrual and menopausal problems, Lydia Pinkham has been dismissed as the "Queen of Quackery"; however, her remedy, in a modified form, remains on sale today.

Born Lydia Estes in Lynn, Massachusetts, Pinkham was the tenth of twelve children in an old Quaker family tracing its ancestry back to 1676. Pinkham was a schoolteacher and active in reform groups for abolition, temperance, women's rights, and other causes. In 1843, she married a young widower and shoe manufacturer, Isaac Pinkham, and the couple would raise four children. During the next thirty years, Pinkham brewed home remedies, collecting various recipes and sharing with her neighbors her remedy for "female complaints."

The Panic of 1873 left the family in financial straits, and one of Pinkham's sons suggested that his mother should market the herbal medicine she had been concocting for years. Shifting production from her kitchen stove to a factory, Pinkham began marketing Lydia E. Pinkham's Vegetable Compound in 1876, which became one of the best-known patent medicines of the nineteenth century. The compound was a blend of ground herbs with an alcohol content of 18 percent. She wrote the handbills with slogans such as "Only a woman can understand a woman's ills," put her image on the label, and encouraged users to write to her. Her signed responses to these letters continued even after her death, produced by the company's staff. During Pinkham's lifetime, her business grew to gross just under $300,000 a year.

In the 1920s, with increased federal regulations of drugs and advertising, the Lydia E. Pinkham Medicine Co. reduced both its claims for the compound and its alcoholic content, yet it continued to sell, and a version of it is still being marketed by Numark

Laboratories of Edison, New Jersey, called the "Lydia Pinkham Herbal Compound," which is available at Walgreens, CVS, and Rite Aid drugstore chains.

Pinkham's legacy is contested. Her tonic has been dismissed as a quack remedy, designed more as a moneymaker than for its medicinal purpose, but Pinkham has also been praised for delivering information on menstruation and menopause to women who had been poorly served by the medical establishment of the nineteenth century.

Ginni Rometty (1957–)

Company Executive

Ginni Rometty is president, chair, and CEO of IBM Corporation. She was born Virginia Marie Nicosia in Chicago, Illinois, the oldest of four children raised by a working mother. She attended Northwestern University on scholarship from General Motors, where she interned and began her career after graduation in 1979 with BS degrees in computer science and electrical engineering. The same year, she married Mark Anthony Rometty, a private equity investor.

In 1981, after two years with General Motors, Rometty joined IBM as a systems analyst in Detroit. She spent her first ten years in technical positions and, in 1991, joined IBM's consulting group. In 2002, as senior vice president of IBM Global Business Services, she helped negotiate and integrate PricewaterhouseCoopers, a multinational professional services network. In 2012, she was named president and CEO and, a year later, was named chair of the company. Under her leadership, IBM has evolved from a reliance on computers and operating system software into higher-growth areas like cloud computing and artificial intelligence.

Rometty has consistently been listed in the top ten lists of most powerful women and technology leaders, including number one in *Fortune*'s list of the 50 Most Powerful Women in Business from 2012 through 2014. She has taken a leading role in IBM organizations such as the Women's Leadership Council and has supported women in the workplace with policies such as extended parental leave. She is also a member of several for-profit and nonprofit boards.

Helena Rubinstein (1870–1965)

Entrepreneur

Polish-born cosmetician and business executive Helena Rubinstein founded Helena Rubinstein, Inc., a leading manufacturer and distributor of women's cosmetics that would make her one of the world's richest women.

Born in Krakow, Poland, the oldest of the eight daughters of a Jewish shopkeeper, Rubinstein immigrated to Australia in 1896. The diminutive Rubinstein was only four feet ten inches tall, but she was admired for her milky complexion, and people bought the jars of beauty cream she had brought with her. Realizing that a market existed for such creams, she began to make her own, adding wool grease or wax from sheep, chemically known as lanolin. Her beauty cream was a runaway best-seller, allowing Rubinstein to open salons in Australia before opening salons in London (1908) and Paris (1912).

When World War I began, Rubenstein and her husband, Polish-born American journalist Edward Titus, whom she had married in 1908, moved to New York City. There, Rubenstein opened a salon that would be the forerunner of a nationwide chain. She also began the wholesale distribution of her products, which would become the predominant activity of her business, developing hundreds of new and improved beauty aids and medicated skin care products. While competing in the lucrative American cosmetic market, Rubinstein began a lifelong rivalry with the other *grande dame* of the cosmetics industry, Elizabeth Arden. Both would become masters of marketing their products. As Rubinstein once said of her rival, "With her packaging and my product, we could have ruled the world."

In 1928, Rubinstein sold her American business to Lehman Brothers for $7.3 million, but during the Great Depression, she bought back the nearly worthless stock for less than $1 million and even-

tually created a multimillion-dollar cosmetics empire. The story of Rubinstein's early business career has been treated as a Harvard Business School case study for future MBAs.

With a personal fortune estimated at $100 million, Rubinstein maintained homes in cities around the world. A patron of the arts, she established the Helena Rubinstein Foundation in 1953 to coordinate her philanthropies, which included gifts to museums, colleges, and charities for the needy, particularly women and children. Rubinstein died of natural causes at the age of ninety-four. In 1973, Helena Rubinstein, Inc., was sold to Colgate Palmolive and is now owned by L'Oréal.

Sheryl Sandberg (1969–)

Company Executive

The chief operating officer (COO) of Facebook, Inc., Sheryl Sandberg was born in Washington, D.C., and grew up in North Miami Beach, Florida. She is the oldest of the three children of Adele Sandberg, a French teacher, and Joel Sandberg, an ophthalmologist. Her parents moved to North Miami Beach, Florida, when Sandberg was two years old. She attended North Miami Beach High School, where she was a member of the National Honor Society. She received a BA degree in economics from Harvard College in 1991 and an MBA degree from Harvard Business School in 1995. After graduation, she worked as a consultant for McKinsey & Company and then worked for Secretary of the Treasury Larry Summers, who had been her thesis advisor at Harvard.

In 2002, Sandberg joined Google, where she was responsible for advertising and sales. During her time at Google, she grew the ad and sales team from four people to four thousand. In 2008, she was hired as COO of Facebook. Her leadership, as head of business operations, changed Facebook from a money-losing business to an immensely profitable one. In 2012, she became the first woman on Facebook's board of directors. She has been a prominent spokesperson for bringing women into leadership roles in business.

Sandberg faced criticism in 2018 over her role in handling Facebook's public relations in the wake of the scandal involving Facebook and the data-mining and analysis company Cambridge Analytica regarding Russian interference in the 2016 presidential election as well as her decision to investigate financier George Soros after Soros publicly criticized tech companies, including Facebook. Although Facebook founder Mark Zuckerberg held Sandberg and her teams responsible for the public fallout resulting from the relationship between the social media site and Cambridge Analytica, Sandberg's position with Facebook remained secure.

Sandberg is the coauthor of two best-selling books. The first, *Lean In: Women, Work and the Will to Lead* (coauthored with Nell Scovell), brought the phrase "lean in" to workplace vocabulary and inspired a global community group, *LeanIn.org*, which Sandberg founded to support women striving to reach their ambitions in the business world. Her second book, *Option B: Facing Adversity, Building Resilience and Finding Joy* (coauthored with Adam Grant), grew from the challenges she faced after the 2015 death of her husband, Dave Goldberg, CEO of the online survey company SurveyMonkey.

In addition to her work at Facebook, Sandberg has served on the board of the Walt Disney Company and is a board member for the nonprofit organizations Women for Women International, the Center for Global Development, and V-Day, a global activist movement to end violence against women.

Felice Schwartz (1925–1996)

Entrepreneur

Felice Schwartz was a cofounder and longtime president of Catalyst, a national organization dedicated to advancing women in the workplace. Born Felice Toba Nierenberg in New York City, Schwartz graduated from Smith College in 1945. In 1946, she married physician Irving Schwartz, with whom she raised three children.

After her graduation from Smith, Schwartz sought to address the extremely low number of African American students at Smith and other colleges with the founding of the National Scholarship Service and Fund for Negro Students. The organization petitioned colleges and universities to admit more African American applicants and matched students with available scholarships. She left the organization in 1951 after her father's death to take over the failing family manufacturing business with her brother, which they successfully saved and sold. She later referred to her efforts as the equivalent of a master's degree in manufacturing.

Schwartz left the company to become a stay-at-home mother. During the nine years she spent raising her children, she became frustrated with the obstacles that prevented educated mothers from entering or reentering the workforce. In 1962, she started Catalyst, an organization to address the issues of working mothers, with a mission "to bring to our country's needs the unused abilities of intelligent women who want to combine work and family." She served as president of Catalyst for thirty years until her retirement in 1993. The organization remains a leading force for workforce equality with a board of directors made up of prominent business leaders, both male and female.

In 1989, Schwartz published an article in the *Harvard Business Review* titled "Management Women and the New Facts of Life," which suggested that employers create policies to help working mothers balance career and family responsibilities such as flexible work hours and high-quality daycare. Her ideas were criticized as creating a "mommy track," which Schwartz defended by saying she was writing a call to action to corporate leaders to recognize the problem and "do something about it." Her pioneering research on job sharing, dual-career couples, and parental leave has helped to bring such issues to the forefront of the conversation regarding barriers to women's progress in business.

Muriel Siebert (1928–2013)

Financier

The first woman to own a seat on the New York Stock Exchange, Muriel "Mickie" Siebert was born in Cleveland, Ohio. She attended Western Reserve

University (now Case Western Reserve University) from 1949 to 1952 but left without graduating when her father fell ill.

She began her financial career as a research trainee and worked her way up through various brokerage houses. In 1967, Siebert founded her own firm, Muriel Siebert & Co., Inc., a research and financial analysis firm. She applied for a seat on the New York Stock Exchange the same year, only to be informed that she would need to obtain a letter from a bank offering her a loan of $300,000 at the near record of the $445,000 price for a seat. However, banks refused to commit to a loan until NYSE would agree to admit her. She was finally elected to membership in December 1967, the only woman on the NYSE among 1,365 men. In 1977, she was named superintendent of banks for the State of New York with oversight of all of the banks in the state, regulating about $500 billion.

Siebert was an outspoken advocate for women in business, writing, "American business will find that women executives can be a strong competitive weapon against Japan and Germany and other countries that still limit their executive talent pool to the male 50 percent of their population." She served as president of the New York Women's Agenda, and, during her tenure, she developed a personal finance program to provide youth with financial management skills.

In 1990, she created the Siebert Entrepreneurial Philanthropic Plan, through which she shared half of her firm's profits from new securities underwriting with charities of the issuer's choice. A member of the boards of several philanthropic organizations, Siebert was the recipient of numerous honors. In 2016, Siebert Hall at the New York Stock Exchange was dedicated in her honor.

Martha Stewart (1941–)

Entrepreneur

Martha Stewart is a business executive who built her highly popular personal brand and corporation around cooking, entertaining, and decorating. She was born Martha Helen Kostryra in Jersey City, New Jersey, the second oldest in a family of six children and raised in Nutley, New Jersey, where she attended Nutley High School. Stewart's parents and grandparents taught her how to garden as well as such domestic skills as cooking, sewing, and canning and preserving. She began working as a model at thirteen and continued during and after her college years at Barnard. She graduated from Barnard in 1962 with BA degrees in history and architectural history. In 1961, while still in college, she married Andy Stewart, a law student at Yale. The couple would have a daughter, Alexis, in 1965 and divorce in 1990.

From 1967 to 1972, Stewart worked as a stockbroker for a small firm and continued to work on Wall Street until 1972, when she and her husband bought an eighteenth-century farmhouse in Westport, Connecticut. Renovation of the house brought out her talent for decorating, gardening, cooking, and hosting, and in 1976, she began a catering company, initially with a partner, which by 1986 had become a $1 million enterprise. In 1982, she published her first book, *Entertaining*, which became a best-seller and was followed by many other popular books on such subjects as cooking, gardening, wedding planning, and home decorating. In 1990, Stewart began her cooking and crafts magazine, *Martha Stewart Living*, and hosted a television show of the same name, which ran from 1993 to 2004. In 1997, Stewart, with business partner Sharon Patrick, brought together her various ventures to create a new company, Martha Stewart Living Omnimedia, which went public in 1999 with Stewart as chair, president, and CEO.

In 2003, Stewart was indicted for securities fraud and other charges related to alleged insider trading, in which she sold her stock in a company that suffered a sharp decline the next day. The securities fraud charge was dismissed, but Stewart was found guilty of conspiracy, obstruction of an agency proceeding, and making false statements to federal investigators. She was sentenced to serve a five-month term in a federal correctional facility and a two-year period of supervised release. She was also prevented from serving in any leadership role in a public company that involved preparing, auditing, or disclosing financial results. After her release in 2005, she returned to work at Martha Stewart Living Omnimedia, where she initiated such new projects as a television variety talk show titled *Martha*, also known as *The Martha Stewart Show*, which debuted in 2005, and adding to her brand of designer products for the home. She rejoined the board of directors and became chairwoman again in 2012 and, in 2015, sold her company to the Sequential Brands Group.

Lillian Vernon (1927–2015)

Entrepreneur

The founder of the Lillian Vernon Corporation, a multimillion-dollar catalog company, Lillian Vernon was born Lilli Menasche in Leipzig, Germany. When Vernon's older brother, Fred, was attacked by an anti-Jewish mob in 1933, the family left for Amsterdam and then immigrated to the United States in 1937. Vernon's father, Herman, sold lingerie and later established a manufacturing company specializing in leather goods, many of which were designed by his daughter. During World War II, Vernon worked at a women's auxiliary canteen, and Fred Menasche served as an army medic. He was killed in a grenade attack while serving in Normandy.

Vernon attended New York University from 1942 to 1949, when she married Samuel Hochberg, who worked in his parents' women's clothing store. The couple would have two sons, and Hochberg would be the first of Vernon's three husbands. In 1951, to supplement the family's income, Vernon began a mail-order service, working out of the kitchen in her home in Mount Vernon, New York. Vernon named her business the Vernon Specialties Company. She soon changed her first name to the more American-sounding "Lillian" and would formally take the last name of Vernon after her divorce from Hochberg.

Vernon used the monetary gifts she had received at her wedding to invest $2,000 in the business. She put her first advertisement in *Seventeen* magazine for personalized purses and belts and, in 1956,

created and mailed her first sixteen-page, black-and-white catalog. Her company grew steadily, finding its first niche in inexpensive, often monogrammed and personalized homemade jewelry, clothing, and gifts for young women. Vernon's catalogs attracted the attention of cosmetics companies such as Revlon, Maybelline, and Elizabeth Arden, which resulted in distribution contracts with the company. In 1965, Vernon incorporated the business as the Lillian Vernon Corporation. When Vernon and Hochberg divorced in 1969, they split the company, with Hochberg assuming control of the wholesale division and Vernon concentrating on the catalog. By 1970, the company had reached its first million-dollar sales year, and in 1987, the Lillian Vernon Corporation became the first woman-owned company to be listed on the American Stock Exchange. At the height of its popularity, the Lillian Vernon Corporation distributed nine catalogs as well as fifteen outlet stores, two websites, a business-to-business division, and a yearly revenue close to $300 million. Vernon sold the company in 2003.

Known for her leadership on behalf of women in the workplace, she was appointed by President Bill Clinton to head the National Women's Business Council in 1995, a position she held for many years. Vernon was also known for her philanthropic work, which included the founding of the Lillian Vernon Foundation to support organizations such as Citymeals-on-Wheels and the donation to New York University for the creation of the Lillian Vernon Creative Writers House. The Women's Enterprise Center created the Lillian Vernon Award to honor businesswomen who have served their community.

Madame C. J. Walker (1867–1919)

Entrepreneur

America's first black self-made millionaire, Madame C. J. Walker was the child of former slaves who attained her success by creating and marketing an innovative line of beauty products and hair-care techniques to African American women. Through her Walker System of hair care, she built a company that defined a new role for African American entrepreneurs.

Born Sarah Breedlove on a cotton plantation in Louisiana, she was orphaned at six, married at fourteen, and a mother and widow at twenty. After her husband's death in an accident, she moved to St. Louis, where she worked as a washerwoman and part-time sales agent for a manufacturer of hair products.

In 1905, she conceived her own formula for a preparation to improve the appearance of African American women's hair consisting of a shampoo, followed by the application of her Wonderful Hair Grower, a medicated pomade to combat dandruff and prevent hair loss. The final part of her hair-care system consisted of applying light oil on the hair and then straightening it with a heated metal comb. In 1906, she moved to Denver and married Charles Walker, a sales agent for a newspaper. Together, they began a successful mail-order business selling her preparations as well as demonstrating her methods door-to-door. She also began to call herself "madame" to add prestige to the company.

In 1910, Walker transferred her operations to Indianapolis and opened a manufacturing plant there that would eventually employ three thousand to five thousand workers and become the country's largest African American-owned business. Walker's agents trained at beauty colleges and schools founded by Walker and made house calls to demonstrate and sell the company's products. Dressed in the Walker uniform—white shirtwaists tucked into long, black skirts—and carrying black satchels containing hair preparations and hairdressing apparatus, the Walker agents became familiar figures in African American communities throughout the United States.

Walker and her husband divorced in 1912 over disagreements about control and the direction of the company. In 1916, she moved her headquarters to Harlem in New York City, and the business continued to thrive. By 1919, it had become the largest and most lucrative black-owned enterprise in the United States.

After having amassed a considerable fortune, Walker became a committed philanthropist, who made sizable contributions to the programs of the NAACP, the National Conference on Lynching, and homes for the aged in St. Louis and Indianapolis. She sponsored scholarships for young women at the Tuskegee Institute and led fundraising drives on behalf of noted educator Mary McLeod Bethune's Daytona Educational Training School. When Walker died in 1919, she left an estate worth $2 million, two-thirds of which went to charities, educational institutions, and African American civic organizations.

Alice Waters (1944–)

Chef, Restauranteur

Alice Waters is a chef, restaurateur, and activist who pioneered what has become known as "California cuisine" through her use of organic, locally grown food in restaurants and schools. Born and raised in Chatham Borough, New Jersey, Waters attended the University of California–Santa Barbara before transferring to UC–Berkeley. While a college student, she spent a semester abroad in Paris, where she developed her love of meals prepared from market-fresh food. After graduating from UC–Berkeley in 1967 with a degree in French cultural studies, Waters returned to Europe, where she trained as a chef in London and France.

In 1971, Waters and pastry chef Lindsey Shere opened the Chez Panisse restaurant in Berkeley. Their goal was to use organically grown ingredients from local producers and suppliers to create fresh, healthful cuisine. Chez Panisse continues to be recognized as one of the world's best restaurants. In addition to her work as a chef and restaurateur, Waters has written several cookbooks, including *Chez Panisse Cooking* (with Paul Bertolli), *The Art of Simple Food I and II*, and *40 Years of Chez Panisse*. Her memoir, *Coming to my Senses: The Making of a Counterculture Cook*, was published in 2017.

In 1996, she founded the Chez Panisse Foundation, whose mission is to "transform public education by using food to teach, nurture, and empower young people." One of her first projects was called the Edible Schoolyard Project, an organic garden and kitchen classroom in a Berkeley middle school. Waters's project has been formalized in the Berkeley school system as the School Lunch Initiative and has led to similar efforts across the country.

Meg Whitman (1956–)

Company Executive

 A business executive, political activist, and philanthropist, Meg Whitman is the former president and CEO of Hewlett-Packard Enterprises. She grew up in Cold Spring Harbor, New York, where she graduated from Cold Spring Harbor High School after three years. Whitman's early aspiration to become a doctor led her to first study math and science at Princeton University. However, after a summer spent selling advertisements for a magazine, she changed her major and received a BA degree in economics from Princeton in 1977. She earned an MBA degree from Harvard Business School in 1979. In 1980, Whitman married Griffith Harsh, a neurosurgeon at Stanford University Medical Center. The couple has two sons.

Whitman began her career in 1979 as a brand manager at Proctor & Gamble. In 1981, she and her husband moved to San Francisco, where she worked at Bain & Company and rose to the position of senior vice president. In 1989, she became vice president at the Walt Disney Corporation and then worked in executive positions at Stride Rite, FTD, and Hasbro. In 1998, she was appointed CEO of eBay, where she guided the company's explosive growth before voluntarily stepping down as CEO in 2007. However, she remained on the board of eBay to assist the company's new CEO. Whitman received several awards and honors for her work at eBay, including inclusion among *Fortune* magazine's top five Most Powerful Women list, the *Harvard Business Review*'s list of Best-Performing CEOs of the Decade, and one of the *Financial Times*' 50 Faces That Shaped the Decade.

In 2008, Whitman became involved in politics, first working for her former Bain colleague Mitt

Romney's presidential campaign and later for John McCain's 2012 presidential bid. In 2009, she won the Republican nomination for governor of California. Although she lost the election to Democratic incumbent Jerry Brown, Whitman's candidacy was particularly notable because it was largely self-funded. She spent $144 million of her own money on the race, more than any other self-funded political candidate in U.S. history.

After her campaign, Whitman returned to the business world and in 2011 was hired as president and CEO of Hewlett-Packard. She led an effort to streamline the company's management and product lines, but the results were disappointing. She resigned from Hewlett-Packard in 2018 to become the CEO and first employee of Quibi, a video-streaming platform created by media proprietor Jeffrey Katzenberg.

In 2006, Whitman and her husband created the Griffith R. Harsh IV and Margaret C. Whitman Charitable Foundation to support environmental and educational groups.

Brownie Wise (1913–1992)

Entrepreneur

Through her "party plan" system of marketing, pioneering saleswoman Brownie Wise was principally responsible for the enormous success of the home products company Tupperware. Wise, a marketing genius with an intuitive grasp of how to motivate others, teamed with inventor Earl Tupper to revolutionize the sale of home products and, in the process, became the first woman ever to appear on the cover of *Business Week*.

Born Brownie Mae Humphrey in rural Georgia, Wise was the daughter of a plumber and a hat maker. Her parents divorced when she was young, and Wise was raised by an extended family near Atlanta. More interested in fashion and dating than in studying, Wise left school after the eighth grade but dreamed of having a writing and illustrating career. In 1936, she won a contest to paint a mural at the Texas Centennial in Dallas, and, while there, she met Robert W. Wise, who was in charge of the Ford Motor Company's exhibit. They married in 1936, moved to Detroit, and had one child. After she divorced in 1942, Wise went to work as a salesperson in a clothing store and as a secretary for Bendix Aviation. To earn extra money, she started selling Stanley Home Products—cleaning aids and brushes—at home party demonstrations, and she quickly became one of the top Stanley sellers.

In 1950, Earl Tupper, who had created a company in Leominster, Massachusetts, making and selling containers for storing food, used the polyethlene manufactured by DuPont before the stiffening agent was added to the plastic to make a pliable plastic that he shaped into sealable containers. Despite the innovation of his material and design, Tupperware was not selling well in department stores. Plastic was an unfamiliar material in the home at the time, the patented seal had to be "burped" before it would work, and it was difficult for customers to grasp the concept. Wise, however, saw the potential in selling Tupperware at the kind of home parties she had run for Stanley Products. Partnering with Tupper, Wise ran the sales division, marketing his products exclusively through party plans, in which women invited friends and neighbors to a combination social event and sales presentation. She listened to the woman who worked for her and made marketing decisions based on their feedback, driven by the principle, "You build the people and they'll build the business."

In the prefeminist culture of the 1950s, when the vast majority of women did not work outside the home, Wise's social networking model motivated thousands of women to come together in their homes to sell Tupperware. Sales soared, hitting $25 million in 1954 with twenty thousand people in the network of dealers, distributors and managers, all private contractors, and the interface between the company and the consumer. Wise held pep rallies for her sales force and sponsored an annual retreat where the country's top sellers received awards and gifts. Wise also became the public face of Tupperware, appearing in women's magazines and business publications.

Wise's celebrity, together with her volatile relationship with Tupper, resulted in him firing her from the company in 1958. Tupper wanted to sell the company and decided that this would easier without such an outspoken woman in charge of sales. Without a formal contract, Wise took the company to court and was granted a one-time payment of a year's salary (around $30,000). Soon after the partners parted ways, Tupper sold his company to Dart Industries for $16 million. Wise would go on to form her own party-plan cosmetics company, Cinderella, but was unsuccessful, and she died in relative obscurity in 1992. In 2016, the Tupperware company recognized Wise's contribution by creating Brownie Wise Park in Orlando, Florida, near the company's headquarters. Her larger legacy is in creating the model for the whole field of home party businesses that has been copied by companies such as Mary Kay, LuLaRoe, Pampered Chef, and DoTerra.

Susan Wojcicki (1968–)

Company Executive

The CEO of YouTube, a subsidiary of Alphabet, Inc., the parent company of Google, Susan Wojcicki was born in Santa Clara, California, one of the three daughters of parents who are both educators. Wojcicki's sister Janet is an anthropologist and epidemiologist, while her sister Anne is the founder of the DNA testing company 23andMe. Susan Wojcicki attended Gunn High School in Palo Alto and earned a BA degree from Harvard in 1990, where she took her first computer science class and decided to pursue a career in technology. She received an MS degree in economics from the University of California–Santa Cruz in 1993 and an MBA degree from the University of California–Los Angeles in 1998.

In 1998, Wojcicki rented out garage space in her Menlo Park home to Larry Page and Sergey Brin, founders of the newly incorporated Google Inc., who briefly used it as the company's first headquarters. Wojcicki became Google employee number sixteen and the company's first marketing manager the following year. During her years at Google, she helped the company grow with the development and acquisition of a variety of products, including its acquisition of YouTube in 2006 and the video website's integration into Google. She has been the CEO of YouTube since February 2014 and has guided its growth through international marketing and new applications to approximately two billion monthly users. As a result of YouTube's financial and media success, Wojcicki consistently ranks high on the lists of Most Powerful Women in such publications as *Forbes* and *Fortune* magazines.

In addition to her position at YouTube, Wojcicki serves on the boards of several organizations and is an advocate for better working environments for women and educational opportunities in computer science for girls.

THE MILITARY

Gender equality on the battlefield has been a contentious issue ever since American colonists fought the British during the Revolutionary War. Throughout much of American history, men went to war, and women, who were to be protected and defended, mainly stayed at home. Through all of America's wars, however, women have served in essential support roles as cooks, seamstresses, and in auxiliary positions as nurses and, during World War II, pilots, but rarely in combat roles until 2014 and 2015, when the U.S. Department of Defense lifted all gender-based restrictions on military service and all combat positions were opened to women without exception. Still, in the eighteenth and nineteenth centuries, some women sought active service disguised as men or as spies and smugglers in aid of the war effort.

During the American Revolution, women who were unable to maintain their households in their husbands' absence followed the Continental Army, where they were often referred to by commanding officers as "baggage" or "necessary nuisances." Many camp followers provided services as washerwomen, cooks, nurses, seamstresses, and food scavengers. Estimates range from as many as twenty thousand women who marched with the army to a more conservative 3 percent of the camp population. In 1775, Major General Horatio Gates reported to Commander-in-Chief George Washington that "the sick

suffered much for want of good female Nurses," which led Washington to ask Congress to appoint "a matron to supervise the nurses, bedding, etc." and for nurses "to attend the sick and obey the matron's orders." This is the first instance of women being given official standing in the American military.

The Revolutionary War also marks the first instances of women in combat in the American military. Some accompanied a husband into battle; others disguised themselves as men either to collect the enlistment fee or for patriotic reasons. The most famous of the former group is the famous and possibly legendary Molly Pitcher, who attended the cannon of her fallen husband. Historians believe that she may be a generic figure representing all women in the army who may have assisted soldiers on the battlefield. Direct evidence exists for two women who did perform such duties. Mary McCauley, who may have inspired Molly Pitcher, hauled water to the cannon manned by her husband during the Battle of Monmouth (1778). After he collapsed, Mary took his place with the rest of the artillery team for the remainder of the battle. Margaret Corbin was another wife of an artillery man killed in the Battle of Fort Washington (1776). She replaced her fallen husband at his cannon and was wounded by grapeshot in the arm and chest and disabled for the rest of her life. She became the first woman to receive her husband's military pension for her courage under fire.

Legend says Molly Pitcher followed with her husband, who was an artillery man, into battle, and when he had fallen, she replaced him and continued the fight, thus becoming one of the first female combatants in the U.S. military.

The most famous of the female soldiers disguised as males was Deborah Sampson, who, based on her performance in combat, was honorably discharged and later granted a pension for her service. Other known women who disguised themselves as soldiers were Anna Maria Lane, who also was awarded a pension for her service, and Sally St. Clare (who was killed in the war). Anne Bailey (under the name of Samuel Gay) was discharged, fined, and jailed after her gender was discovered and condemned for attempting to join the army for the enlistment fee. Records exist of other women who defended their homes by shooting loyalist soldiers and women who worked as spies as well as women who delivered messages and warned troops about the movement of British and loyalist forces.

During the War of 1812, women were employed as military nurses just as they had been during the Revolution. Commodore Decatur's ship log records the names of Mary Allen and Mary Marshall as nurses on board the SS *United States*. How many women in the eighteenth and nineteenth centuries saw military service disguised as men is impossible

to estimate since only those who were ultimately discovered are recorded. One such woman is Elizabeth Newcom, who joined the Missouri Volunteer Infantry in 1847 during the Mexican–American War. She marched over six hundred miles with her unit, was discovered to be female, and was released from service but remained with the Army in some unknown capacity until she was officially mustered out in 1848. An act of Congress eventually awarded Newcom her military pay and enlistment bounty.

During the Civil War, historians conservatively estimate the number of female disguised soldiers at between 400–750. Some were compelled by patriotism, others by the promise of reliable wages, and others by a love of adventure and a chance to break free of the restrictive roles expected of them as women. As Sarah Edmonds Steele, who served in the 2nd Michigan Infantry as Franklin Flint Thompson and was the only woman to receive a veteran's pension after the war, stated, "I could only thank God that I was free and could go forward and work, and I was not obliged to stay home and weep." Many women in uniform went undetected until being wounded and sent to a field hospital. Sarah Rosetta Wakeman served two years in combat without her secret being revealed until her letters home were discovered in 1976. Those who were found to be female were usually simply sent home, though a few faced imprisonment or even institutionalization. Other women achieved distinction on both sides as spies.

Clara Barton, who ministered to the wounded on both sides during the Civil War and would go on to found the American Red Cross, would later argue that the war advanced the social position of women by fifty years. In their *History of Woman Suffrage* (1881), Susan B. Anthony, Elizabeth Cady Stanton, and Matilda Gave asserted that women's front-line service during the Civil War proved that women could perform alongside men as defenders of the republic and should therefore be accorded equal rights.

With the advent of the twentieth century, the gradual inclusion of women into official military service began in earnest, prompted both by rights women had secured and the overwhelming need for personnel in the century's conflicts. During the Spanish–American War, American military forces lost 4,600 men to diseases such as malaria, yellow fever, and typhoid while losing only four hundred to battlefield injuries. Casualties overwhelmed the Army and Navy medical departments, forcing the hiring of civilian female nurses in military hospitals. Eventually, more than 1,500 contract nurses would serve in hospitals and aboard hospital ships in the United States, the Philippines, Puerto Rico, and Hawaii. Twenty contract nurses died in service. The inability of the military medical departments to handle the number of disease-related causalities during the Spanish–American War as well as the outstanding service supplied by the contract nurses led to the creation in 1901 of the Army Nurse Corps and in 1908 the Navy Nurse Corps, in which women became official members of the American military for the first time in history.

With the creation in 1901 of the U.S. Army Nurse Corps, the number of women in the military increased considerably.

World War I, also known as The Great War (1914–1918), would be the first so-called total war in world history that effectively erased the previous distinction between combatants and noncombatants. In total war, both would be targets, and military and civilians alike would need to be mobilized, women as well as men, to participate in the war effort. With the United States officially neutral from 1914 to 1917, American female nurses served in England, France, Serbia, Russia, and even Germany under the aegis of the American Red Cross. Some American women entered foreign military services, supporting and staffing hospitals. American women's groups, such as the Children of the Frontier, collected clothing and money for refugee and repatriated children. The American Fund for French Wounded distributed hospital supplies.

When the United States entered the war in 1917, the government established a women's committee of the Council of National Defense to coordinate relief efforts. Approximately twenty-one thousand women served in the Army Nurse Corps during World War I. Two Army nurses, Edith Ayres and Helen Wood, became the first female members of the U.S. military killed in the line of duty. Over four hundred Army, Navy, and Red Cross nurses stationed overseas and in military hospitals in the United States died in the line of duty during World War I.

Female physicians were rejected by the American military but were eventually accepted as civilian contract physicians without rank. The Army Signal Corps recruited more than two hundred female telephone operators, dubbed Hello Girls, who were sworn in and issued uniforms and were subject to military discipline. Some Hello Girls served under fire. However, these "soldiers of the switchboard" were denied postwar veterans' benefits until 1977.

In 1916, Secretary of the Navy Josephus Daniels, anticipating the lack of sufficient clerical staff if the United States entered the war, determined that no regulation existed that stated a yeoman (an enlisted man in the Navy) needed to be a man, and, for the first time in history, the Navy and Marine Corps enlisted women for stateside duty so that sailors could be released for sea duty. The women served as stenographers and typists, were given the title "Yeoman

(F)," and were paid the same rate as male yeomen. Approximately 11,880 women were accepted into the Navy and 305 into the Marine Corps.

At the war's end, Congress restored restrictions on women serving in the military, and the Army and Navy Nurse Corps were reduced to their prewar sizes. However, World War I would establish several precedents regarding military service by women and women's participation in the war effort that would dramatically expand with World War II. As the United States mobilized in 1941, women would be essential in the wartime workforce to make up for departing soldiers. From the beginning of the war, women's organizations insisted that women be allowed to enlist in the services. In addition to the Army and Navy Nurse Corps, women's branches in the Army (WACs), the Navy (WAVES), the Coast Guard (SPARS), and the Marines (MCWR) were created in 1942 and 1943. Nearly 350,000 women served in the military, mostly in clerical and supply areas or as nurses. However, some one thousand women served in the Women's Air Force Service Pilots (WASP), flying commercial and military transport planes. Women also served as test pilots for the Air Force. The experiences of these daring and capable female pilots were relatively unknown until the 1980s and 1990s, when the media began to pay more attention to the exploits of unsung women in history. During wartime, the military was careful to enlist only young, unmarried women, who were not placed in positions where they would have to give orders to men. In addition, the military avoided sending them overseas as long as possible. Women with children were prohibited from enlisting. Lesbians, once discovered, were discharged. African American women, like black soldiers, were kept segregated. However, any reluctance on the part of the Army toward the inclusion of women gave way at the end of the war: In 1946, after enlistments went down, the U.S. War Department asked WAC nurses to reenlist to meet labor shortages in army

The U.S. Air Force currently has more women than any other branch of the U.S. military, including about fifty fighter pilots like these F-15 Eagle pilots from the 3rd Wing.

hospitals. In 1948, Congress passed the Women's Armed Services Integration Act, permitting women to serve as permanent members of the military. Prior to this act, women could only serve in times of war. The act placed a 2 percent ceiling on the number of women in each of the services and restricted promotions to one full colonel or Navy captain as chief of the Nurse Corps and limited the number of female officers who could serve as lieutenant colonels or Navy commanders. It also allowed the service secretaries to discharge women without specific cause and restricted women from flying aircraft engaged in combat and from assignments to ships engaged in combat.

Despite these restrictions, the makeup of the U.S. military would be transformed. With military careers now open to women, the second half of the twentieth century would demonstrate the gradual equality of women in the service with more and more women rising in the ranks and the gradual elimination of the long-held ban on women in combat. Multiple firsts followed: The first female chief petty officer (1950); the first African American woman to become an Air Force classroom instructor (1951); the first woman to deploy with the Strategic Air Command (1960); the first female marine sergeant major (1961); the first woman to hold a command in a combat zone (1962); the first woman to be promoted to brigadier general (1972); the first woman to enter ROTC (1972); the first Navy vessel to sail with a male/female crew (1972); the first female Navy pilot (1973); and the first female chaplain (1973).

In both the Korean War and the Vietnam War, women participated increasingly in front-line service. During the Korean War, 70 percent of the 540 Army nurses served in the new and experimental Mobile Army Surgical Hospital (MASH) units in Korea. These units followed the combat troops, putting women increasingly on the front lines of conflict. In the Vietnam War, approximately 7,500 American military women served in Southeast Asia, the majority as military nurses assigned to hospitals but also to air evacuation units, field units, and hospital ships. Eight of these women died in combat and are memorialized on the wall of the Vietnam Veterans Memorial. The military resisted the request of non-nursing women to be deployed to Vietnam,

but the Army eventually sent a detachment of WACs in 1966. These one hundred women worked at the U.S. Army Vietnam Headquarters in Tan Son Nhut and Long Binh as clerk-typists and administration workers. By 1968, the detachment had grown to 140 women, and communications and intelligence duties were added.

In many ways, 1973 would prove to be a significant turning point in the history of American women in the military. The draft ended, and the U.S. military became an all-volunteer force. This would result in new opportunities for women in the military, as the U.S. Armed Forces could no longer count on a steady stream of drafted male personnel and needed to attract volunteers, both men and women, to fill its ranks. In 1976, women were admitted to the service academies; eight years later in 1984, the Naval Academy's top graduate would be a woman; a year later, the Coast Guard Academy's top graduate would be female; and in 1986, a woman would be the top graduate at the Air Force Academy (the first female valedictorian at West Point was in 1995). Notable firsts in rank and ratings followed: the first female becoming a military helicopter pilot (1974); the first Coast Guard women being assigned to sea duty as crewmembers (1977); female sailors and marines being allowed to serve on noncombat ships (1978); the Coast Guard opening all assignments to women (1978); and the first woman in the U.S. Army achieving the rank of major general (1978). By 1980, over 170,000 women were on active duty, making up 8.5 percent of the U.S. Armed Forces. In some cases, the services opened positions to women, only to reconsider and close them again. In 1979, for example, the Marine Corps began assigning women to guard U.S. embassies around the world; in 1982, those assignments stopped. Army women were eligible to perform ceremonial functions such as guarding the Tomb of the Unknowns in 1978; in 1982, they were excluded again. By the end of the 1980s, however, women were barred mainly from positions that had a high probability of direct combat.

The 1990s brought the largest single deployment of women in U.S. military history, as forty-one thousand military women (7 percent of the force) participated in the first Gulf War in virtually every capacity. As Major General Jeanne M. Holm, USAF, observed, "During the operation, American military women did just about everything on land, at sea, and in the air except engage in the actual fighting, and even there the line was often blurred—it was obvious from the beginning that the front lines were not what they used to be and noncombat units regularly took casualties. In the Gulf War there were no fixed positions or clear lines in the sand." Five women were killed in action during the Gulf War, and two were captured as prisoners of war.

The final barrier for women in the military—the prohibition of serving in combat—finally fell in the 1990s when Congress authorized women to fly in combat missions (1991) and to serve on combat ships (1993). However, in 1994, the U.S. Department of Defense affirmed its rules excluding women from combat on the ground. It would not be until 2013 that Secretary of Defense Leon Panetta removed the military's ban on women serving in combat. By 2016, all combat jobs were opened to women. Considerable debate still exists over gender integration and combat, however. A 2015 Marine Corps study found that women in combat units were injured twice as often as men, were less accurate with infantry weapons, and were not as effective at removing wounded troops from the battlefield. Other studies have shown that male squads perform better on 69 percent of assigned tasks than units with women in them. Unit cohesion has been shown as lower in mixed-gender units with female soldiers reporting that they are often labeled "either standoffish or a slut." Other studies have shown advantages to having female soldiers in front-line and combat units, particularly in performing culturally

While the numbers of women in the military continued to increase, the watershed moment was when the draft ended in 1973. There were leaps forward as conditions changed for the women in the military until they were finally asked to perform in combat roles like their male counterparts.

sensitive searches at checkpoints and inside urban areas. Women were notably successful when the Army began utilizing Female Engagement Teams in Afghanistan in 2010 in intelligence gathering, relationship building, and humanitarian efforts.

Despite the contentious issue of women in combat, the gender integration of the U.S. military has drastically transformed the armed forces. When the United States ended the military draft in 1973, the U.S. Armed forces numbered 2.2 million men and women. Today, active forces are just under 1.29 million, or less than 0.5 percent of the U.S. population. When the draft ended, women represented just 2 percent of the enlisted force and 8 percent of the officer corps. Today, those numbers are 16 percent of the enlisted force (a 700 percent increase) and 18 percent of the officer corps (a 125 percent increase). Historically, the Air Force has had the highest percentage of enlisted and officer women (around 21 percent); however, by 2016, the Navy had nearly caught up. In both services, approximately one in five enlisted members and officers are women.

2016 FEMALE REPRESENTATION IN THE MILITARY BY SERVICE

Service	Army	Navy	Marines	Air Force
Officers	18%	18%	7.5%	21%
Enlisted	14%	19%	8%	19%

As the gender integration of the military has proceeded, an ongoing issue has been sexual assault and harassment in the armed forces. At least 25 percent of U.S. servicewomen report having been sexually assaulted, and up to 80 percent have been sexually harassed. A 2011 report found that women in the U.S. military were more likely to be raped by fellow soldiers than they were to be killed in combat. Other statistics have suggested that a servicewoman is more likely to be assaulted than a civilian, with a 1 in 4 likelihood of active-duty female personnel to be sexually assaulted. A 2012 Pentagon survey found that approximately twenty-six thousand women and men were assaulted that year, but of those, only 3,374 cases were reported. Highly publicized incidents of sexual assault and harassment include the 1991 Tailhook scandal, the 1996 Aberdeen scandal, the 2003 Air Force Academy sexual assault scandal,

and the 2009–2012 U.S. Air Force Basic Training scandal. In 2004, the U.S. Department of Defense created the Care for Victims of Sexual Assault Task Force that called for the creation of the Sexual Assault Prevention and Response Office (SAPRO), which is described as "the single point of authority for program accountability and oversight, in order to enable military readiness and reduce—with a goal to eliminate—sexual assault from the military." While reporting of sexual assault and its prosecution has increased, sexual abuse and harassment remain endemic in the military with women expected to become "one of the boys" and to abide by an unspoken "code of silence," fearing that reporting incidents is career suicide. Ultimately, military culture needed to evolve from a testosterone-fueled warrior culture to one in which attitude and behaviors better reflect the realities of a growing, gender-integrated armed force.

Ultimately, military culture needed to evolve from a testosterone-fueled warrior culture to one in which attitude and behaviors better reflect the realities of a growing, gender-integrated armed force.

The active-duty force of the U.S. military remains largely male dominated, but gender parity in ratings and in rank are occurring in significant numbers. Despite the fact that the military is still far from reflecting the gender distribution of the civilian population, it has been trending in that direction, and the military provides a telling microcosm of women's progress (and challenges) that it shares with other fields of American society—in education, business, and politics. Like those occupations, the military has long been a restricted, male-only preserve that has, through the persistence and accomplishment of women who have gained entrance, gradually bowed to that persistence and recognized the accomplishment of its servicewomen. Like education, business, and politics, women in the military have had to challenge long-established gender assumptions about women in positions of responsibility and leadership. The military in particular seems intractably masculine in our cultural consciousness. Imagine a warrior or a soldier, and it is likely that you will conjure up a man, not a woman—Achilles or Spartacus and not Boadicea or Joan of Arc. In crucial ways, the women profiled here challenge that stereotype with their accomplishments both in defense of their country and in blazing a trail for other women who have decided on a career in the military to follow.

BIOGRAPHIES

Marcia Anderson (1957–)

Army Officer

In 2011, Marcia Anderson, U.S. Army Reserves, became the first African American woman to achieve the rank of major general. Born in Beloit, Wisconsin, Anderson was raised in St. Louis, Missouri, and is a 1979 graduate of Creighton University, a 1986 graduate of the Rutgers School of Law, and a 2003 graduate of the U.S. Army War College, where she earned a master's degree in strategic studies. Her father served in the Army during the Korean War and wanted to work in aviation; instead, he served as a driver because of limited opportunities for African Americans in the military at the time.

Marcia Anderson's career in the military is in sharp contrast to her father's military service. Her initial intention to sign up for ROTC at Creighton because she needed a science credit would lead her to almost four decades of service in the Army, including active duty with the Army Reserve and as senior advisor to the chief of the Army Reserve on policies and programs, including budget and appropriations, personnel policies, and force structure. Anderson has helped influence military policy on diversity and inclusion, and she has given frequent talks encouraging women to seek careers with the Army.

In 2016, after thirty-seven years of service, Anderson retired from the military as deputy chief,

U.S. Army Reserve. Upon her retirement from the Army, Anderson resumed a job as clerk of the court for the U.S. Bankruptcy Court for the Western District of Wisconsin. She is married to Amos Anderson, and the couple reside near Madison, Wisconsin.

Anne Hennis Bailey (1742–1825)

Army Scout, Spy

Frontier scout Anne Bailey, better known as Mad Anne, participated as a scout and messenger during the Revolutionary War and the Northwest Indian War. Her ride in search of gunpowder to relieve the endangered Clendenin Settlement (now Charleston, West Virginia) became the basis of Charles Robb's 1861 poem "Anne Bailey's Ride."

Born Anne Hennis in Liverpool, England, Bailey came to America likely as an indentured servant in 1761, settling in Virginia's Shenandoah Valley. She married Richard Trotter, a frontiersman and veteran of General Edward Braddock's 1755 expedition to capture Fort Duquesne (modern-day downtown Pittsburgh, Pennsylvania) during the French and Indian War. Recruited to serve in the Virginia border militia, Trotter was killed by the Shawnees at the Battle of Point Pleasant in 1774 in what has been called the first battle of the American Revolution because it prevented the Shawnees from becoming British allies.

Immediately upon learning of her husband's death, Bailey adopted male attire and became a frontier scout, messenger, and spy, whose exploits, both true and legendary, earned her a reputation as the "white squaw of the Kanawha" and as "Mad Anne" for her challenge to defy conventional gender norms. It was also said that during her various scouting and messenger missions, she screamed and shrieked to convince the Shawnees in pursuit that she was possessed and could not be injured, convincing them to keep their distance. In 1788, along with her second husband, John Bailey, she moved to the Clendenin Settlement. When the settlement was besieged by Native Americans in 1791, Bailey carried out her most famous exploit: a solo ride covering one hundred miles through the forest to Fort Union (present-day Lewisburg) to obtain help for the settlers and her return to Clendenin with gunpowder.

After John Bailey died in 1802, Bailey moved deeper into the frontier in Ohio. She mostly lived in the wilderness for the next twenty years, transporting supplies for settlers and making her last ride to Charleston in 1817 at the age of seventy-five. Before her death, she was interviewed about her adventures and said, "I always carried an ax and auger, and I could chop as well as any man.... I trusted in the Almighty.... I knew I could only be killed once, and I had to die sometime."

Clara Barton (1821–1912)

Army Nurse

Called the "Angel of the Battlefield" for nursing soldiers during Civil War battles, Clara Barton went on to establish the American Red Cross, one of the most notable humanitarian organizations in the United States.

Born in North Oxford, Massachusetts, Barton was the youngest of the five children of a farmer and sawmill owner. She was educated by her older brothers and sisters and at local schools. Barton became skilled at nursing when, beginning at the age of eleven, she nursed one of her brothers through a persistent illness for two years. When she was eighteen, she began to work as a teacher in neighboring schools. In 1852, she founded one of the first free public schools in New Jersey and later moved to Washington, D.C., where she worked as a clerk in the U.S. Patent Office.

When the Civil War began, Barton witnessed the first significant battle of the war at Bull Run. Shocked to find a severe lack of first-aid facilities and provisions for the wounded, she quit her job and arranged her small residence as a storeroom, bypassing government and military red tape and inefficiency to accumulate bandages, medicine, and food for the troops. With the help of a few friends, she distributed these supplies to the Union soldiers on the battlefields. Often under fire, Barton ministered to the wounded on both the Union and the Confederate sides at every major battle in Maryland, Virginia, and South Carolina. She was officially named head nurse for one of

General Benjamin Butler's units in 1864, even though she had no formal medical training.

After the war, Barton ran the Missing Soldiers Office. While there, she helped find or identify soldiers killed or missing in action and marked thousands of graves. Barton and her assistants would eventually locate more than twenty-two thousand missing men. She spent the summer of 1865 helping to find, identify, and properly bury thirteen thousand individuals who died in the Andersonville prison camp in Georgia. From 1865 to 1868, Barton received widespread recognition for a series of lectures she delivered throughout the United States on her wartime experiences. During this time, she met Susan B. Anthony and Frederick Douglass and became active in both the women's suffrage and postwar civil rights movements.

Mentally and physically exhausted after her countrywide tours, Barton traveled to Europe in 1869 to regain her health. While in Switzerland, she learned of the International Committee of the Red Cross, which had been created in 1863 to relieve the suffering of soldiers on the battlefield. Barton managed to convince eleven European governments to respect the neutrality of ambulance and health care workers on the battlefield, who were identified by the sign of a red cross on a white background. This arrangement became part of the rules of the Geneva Convention and its international treaty regarding wartime behavior.

Back in the United States, Barton began a campaign to create an American Red Cross chapter and to push the American government into ratifying the Geneva Treaty. To help gain support, she supported Red Cross involvement in disasters such as floods, fire, railway accidents, and epidemics. In 1881, Barton organized the American Association of the Red Cross, and the following year, the U.S. Senate ratified the Geneva Treaty.

Barton would lead the American Red Cross for the next twenty-three years, providing relief in twenty-one disasters. Rejecting government subsidies, Barton appealed directly to the public for contributions, using her personal savings when funds were low.

Barton retired as president of the Red Cross in 1904 and spent her last years at her home near

Washington. Both the Glen Echo, Maryland, house in which she spent the last fifteen years of her life and the Missing Soldiers Office in Washington, D.C., are now museums.

Jacqueline Cochran (1906–1980)
Army Air Force Pilot

An important contributor to the formation of the Women's Auxiliary Army Corps (WAAC) and director of the Women's Airforce Service Pilots (WASP) during World War II, Jacqueline Cochran became the first woman to pilot a bomber across the North Atlantic. Cochran was also the first woman to break the sound barrier and, at the time of her death, held more speed, altitude, and distance-flying records than any other pilot, male or female.

Born Bessie Lee Pittman in Pensacola, Florida, Cochran was the daughter of a millwright who set up and reworked sawmills in various towns. Bessie married Robert Cochran in 1920 and had a son who died at the age of five. After the marriage ended, Cochran kept the name Cochran and began using Jacqueline as her given name. Her second husband was industrialist Floyd Odlum, whom she married in 1936. The couple remained married until Odlum's death in 1976.

Cochran, who was known to her friends as Jackie, worked as a hairdresser during the late 1920s and early 1930s first in Pensacola and then in New York City. After a friend offered Cochran a ride in her airplane, Cochran began taking flying lessons at Roosevelt Field on Long Island, learned to fly an aircraft in three weeks, soloed, and within two years had obtained her commercial pilot's license. She started a cosmetics line called Wings to Beauty and flew her own airplane around the country promoting her products. In the 1930s, she was one of a handful of barnstorming female pilots competing in air races, and by 1938, she was considered the best female pilot in the United States after setting a new transcontinental speed record as well as an altitude record.

Before the United States entered World War II, Cochran was part of Wings for Britain, an organiza-

tion that ferried aircraft to Britain, becoming the first woman to fly a bomber across the Atlantic. She volunteered for the Royal Air Force and worked for the British Air Transport Auxiliary (ATA), recruiting female pilots in the United States and taking them to England to join the ATA. In 1939, Cochran wrote to Eleanor Roosevelt proposing a women's flying division in the Army Air Force. In 1943, Cochran was named director of the Women's Airforce Service Pilots (WASP), which supplied more than a thousand auxiliary pilots for the armed forces. She was awarded the Distinguished Service Medal in 1945 and commissioned a lieutenant colonel in the Air Force Reserve. She was promoted to colonel in 1969 and retired in 1970.

In 1953, Cochran became the first woman to break the sound barrier and the first woman to pilot a jet aircraft across the Atlantic Ocean. Considered the first female pilot in the U.S. Air Force, Cochran was also the first woman to land and take off from an aircraft carrier, the first pilot to make a blind (instrument) landing, and the first pilot to fly above twenty thousand feet with an oxygen mask.

Jacqueline Cochran's biographer Maryann Bucknum Brinley called Cochran "an irresistible force.... Generous, egotistical, compassionate, sensitive, aggressive—indeed an explosive study in contradictions—Jackie was consistent only in the overflowing energy with which she attacked the challenge of being alive."

Eileen Collins (1956–)
Air Force Officer, Astronaut

The first female flight instructor in the U.S. Air Force and a NASA astronaut, retired U.S. Air Force Colonel Eileen Collins became the first woman to pilot a space shuttle (1995) and the first woman to command a space shuttle mission (1999). In all, Collins logged 38 days, 8 hours in space as a result of her NASA missions.

Collins was born in Elmira, New York, and from an early age wanted to become a pilot. Her parents would often take her to the airport to watch planes take off and land. After attending Corning Community College, Collins earned a scholarship to Syracuse University, where she graduated with majors in mathematics and economics. She would later earn an MS degree in operations research at Stanford University (1986) and an MA degree in space systems management from Webster University (1989).

Following her graduation from Syracuse, Collins was one of four women chosen for undergraduate pilot training at Vance Air Force Base, Oklahoma, where she earned her pilot wings. She taught at Vance for three years, becoming the U.S. Air Force's first female flight instructor. From 1979 to 1990, Collins taught flying at bases in Oklahoma, California, and the Air Force Academy, where she was also an assistant professor of mathematics. She eventually earned the Air Force rank of colonel.

Collins became only the second female pilot to attend the U.S. Air Force Test Pilot School, and in 1990, she was selected for the astronaut program. Along with her achievements as the first female space shuttle pilot and the first female commander of a U.S. spacecraft, Collins also commanded the important "return to flight" shuttle mission to test safety improvements in 2005 following the 2003 Columbia mission disaster that grounded the shuttle for two years. On Collins's mission, she became the first astronaut to the fly the space shuttle through a complete 360-degree pitch maneuver to check for possible damage.

In 2006, Collins retired from NASA to work part time as a shuttle mission analyst for CNN and to serve on the board of the United Services Automobile Association. Collins married pilot Pat Youngs in 1987, and they have two children.

Margaret D. Craighill (1898–1977)
Army Officer, Physician

A third-generation army officer, physician Margaret D. Craighill was the first woman to receive a commission in the U.S. Army Medical Corps. She took a leave of absence from her position as dean of the Women's Medical College in Philadelphia

to join the corps in 1943 after President Franklin D. Roosevelt signed into law the Sparkman–Johnson Bill allowing women to enter the Army and Navy Medical Corps.

Born in Southport, North Carolina, Craighill was the daughter of Colonel William Craighill and the granddaughter of Brigadier General William Price Craighill. She graduated from the University of Wisconsin in 1921 and earned a MS degree there the following year. She then enrolled in the Johns Hopkins University School of Medicine after a brief stint as a physiologist in the chemical warfare department at the Army's Edgewood (Maryland) Arsenal. From 1928 to 1937, Craighill was a private assistant in general surgery at Bellevue Hospital in New York. She also maintained a private practice in obstetrics and gynecology in Greenwich, Connecticut, and was an assistant surgeon and attending gynecologist at Greenwich Hospital. Completing her medical studies in 1924, she held a series of postgraduate positions in gynecology, surgery, and pathology at Johns Hopkins Hospital and Yale Medical School.

In 1940, Craighill was appointed acting dean of the Woman's Medical College of Pennsylvania in Philadelphia. After the United States entered World War II in 1941, Craighill volunteered for active military service and was commissioned a major and assigned to serve as a liaison with the newly established Women's Army Corps (WACS). In the course of her duties, she traveled fifty-six thousand miles visiting war zones in England, France, Italy, Africa, Iran, India, China, New Guinea, and the Philippines. Reporting on the condition of 160,000 Army nurses and WAC personnel, Craighill challenged the persistent notion that American women were unsuited for military service, noting that they were performing remarkably well in extreme climates and challenging work conditions. Craighill's reports would help to end resistance to women in the military, allowing them to serve wherever they were needed despite the conditions they faced. For her distinguished service during the war, she was promoted to lieutenant colonel and awarded the Legion of Merit.

When the war ended in 1945, Craighill became a consultant on female veterans' medical care, the first position of its kind within the Veterans Administration. After a brief return to the Woman's Medical College, she went back to school under the GI Bill to study psychiatry, entering the first class of the Menninger Foundation School of Psychiatry in Topeka, Kansas. She also studied at the New York Institute of Psychoanalysis in 1952. From 1951 to 1960, she began a private practice in medicine and psychoanalysis in New Haven, Connecticut, and served as chief psychiatrist-in-residence at the Connecticut College in New London. Craighill died at her home in Southbury, Connecticut, at the age of seventy-eight.

Pauline Cushman (1833–1893)

Spy

Actress Pauline Cushman was a spy for the Union Army during the Civil War and is regarded as the most successful of Civil War spies. Born Harriet Wood in New Orleans, Louisiana, Cushman was raised in Grand Rapids, Michigan, on a trading post for Native Americans. She moved to New York City to pursue an acting career, adopting the stage name Pauline Cushman. In 1853, she married Charles Dickinson, a musician, and they moved to Cleveland, Ohio, where the couple had two children. Dickinson enlisted in the Ohio Infantry during the Civil War, contracted dysentery, and died at home in 1862. After his death, Cushman returned to acting.

In 1863, while touring in Kentucky, a border state under Union control, Cushman was approached by Confederate sympathizers and offered money to toast Confederate president Jefferson Davis from the stage. She reported the incident to the Union provost marshal in Louisville, who suggested she accept the offer. The manager of the theater fired her on the spot, but Cushman became a Confederate celebrity. She was instructed to travel behind Confederate lines and learn all she could as a Union spy. Sometimes posing as a woman and sometimes disguised as a man, she gathered intelligence, including the battle plans of Confederate general Braxton Bragg, which she hid in her shoe. However, she was discovered and arrested. Cushman was tried, convicted, and sentenced to be hanged. While await-

ing her sentence, Cushman became sick (possibly feigning her condition), and her execution was delayed. Eventually, Union troops forced the Confederates to retreat, and she was rescued. In recognition of her service, Cushman was awarded the rank of brevet major by General James A. Garfield and made an honorary major by President Lincoln. She became known as "Miss Major Pauline Cushman," the "Spy of the Cumberland."

Too well known to be of any more service to the Union, Cushman toured the country giving lectures on her exploits as a spy and eventually settled in San Francisco, where she descended into poverty and addiction. She took a suicidal overdose of morphine in 1893 and died at the age of sixty. Her funeral was arranged by the Grand Army of the Republic, and she was buried with full military honors in the Officer's Circle at the Presidio National Cemetery.

Tammy Duckworth (1968–)

Amy Officer, Pilot

A member of the U.S. House of Representatives representing Illinois from 2013 to 2017, Tammy Duckworth was elected to the U.S. Senate in 2016. An Iraq War veteran, Duckworth served as a helicopter pilot whose combat wounds caused her to lose both of her legs. She is the first woman with a disability to be elected to Congress, the first female double amputee in the Senate, and the first senator to give birth while in office.

Ladda Tammy Duckworth was born in Thailand, the daughter of Franklin Duckworth, a U.S. Army veteran who could trace his family back to the American Revolutionary War. Duckworth's mother is Thai, of Chinese descent. Her father's work with the United Nations and with refugee organizations caused the family to move around Southeast Asia. Duckworth attended the Singapore American School and the International School Bangkok. Her family moved to Hawaii when she was sixteen, and she completed high school there in 1985 before graduating from the University of Hawaii in 1989. Duckworth later received an MA degree in international affairs from

George Washington University and a Ph.D. in human services at Capella University in 2015.

Duckworth joined the Army Reserve Officers' Training Corps while a graduate student in 1990 and became a commissioned officer in the U.S. Army in 1992, choosing to fly helicopters because it was one of the few combat jobs open to women at the time. After completing flight school, transferring to the Army National Guard and entering the Illinois Army National Guard in 1996, Duckworth was deployed to Iraq in 2004. She lost both her legs when the Black Hawk helicopter she was copiloting was hit by a rocket-propelled grenade fired by Iraqi insurgents. She was the first female double amputee in the Iraq War. Reflecting on her experience, Duckworth has stated, "I was hurt in service for my country. I was proud to go. It was my duty as a soldier to go. And I would go tomorrow."

Following her injuries, Duckworth was promoted to major and awarded the Purple Heart. During her yearlong recovery at the Walter Reed Army Hospital Medical Center, she became an activist for better medical care for wounded veterans and their families. Her activism led her to pursue a political career after her recovery. Losing her first bid for Congress in 2006, Duckworth was appointed director of the Illinois Department of Veterans' Affairs and was chosen by President Barack Obama as his assistant secretary of public and intergovernmental affairs in the U.S. Department of Veterans' Affairs.

Ever since her election to Congress in 2012 as the first disabled woman ever elected to the U.S. House of Representatives, Duckworth has been an outspoken advocate for veterans and men and women in the U.S. military.

Ann E. Dunwoody (1953–)
Army Officer

The first woman to serve as a four-star general in both the Army and the U.S. Armed Forces, Ann E. Dunwoody completed a thirty-eight-year military career in 2012. Her other notable firsts include being the first woman to com-

mand a battalion in the 82nd Airborne Division, Fort Bragg's first female general officer, and the first woman to command the Combined Arms Support Command.

Dunwoody was born at Fort Velvoir, Virginia. Her father was a career Army officer, and the family lived in Germany and Belgium while she was growing up. She graduated from Supreme Headquarters Allied Powers Europe American High School in 1971 and attended the State University of New York College–Cortland to pursue a career in physical education. During her junior year, Dunwoody attended a four-week introductory Army program followed by an eleven-week women's officer orientation course, the result of which would be a two-year commitment in the military. After graduating from Cortland in 1975, she received a commission as a second lieutenant in the Quartermaster Corps. She would later earn two master's degrees—in logistics management from the Florida Institute of Technology (1988) and in national resource strategy from the Industrial College of the Armed Forces (1995).

After her initial two-year commitment in the Army, Dunwoody decided to become a career soldier. Her major staff assignments included service as the parachute officer in the 82nd Airborne Division; strategic planner for the chief of staff of the Army; executive officer to the director, Defense Logistics Agency; and deputy chief of staff for Logistics G-4. She was deployed to Saudi Arabia for Operation Desert Shield/Operation Desert Storm in 2001 and for Operation Enduring Freedom and to Uzbekistan in support of Combined Joint Task Force-180. As commander of surface deployment and distribution command, Dunwoody supported the largest deployment and redeployment of U.S. forces since World II, and as commander of the Army Materiel Command, she was in charge of the largest commands in the Army, employing more than sixty-nine thousand personnel across all fifty states in 145 countries.

In 2008, Dunwoody was promoted to general, the first woman in the U.S. military to be promoted to that rank. Chief of Staff of the Army General Ray Odierno stated that while the promotion was significant for women, Dunwoody did not get it because of her gender: "It wasn't because you were a woman. It was because you were a brilliant, dedicated officer, and you are quite simply the best logistician the Army has ever had." Dunwoody subsequently pushed for a decrease in sexual assault in the Army as well as greater opportunities for female soldiers.

Dunwoody retired in 2012. In 2015, she published *A Higher Standard: Leadership Strategies from America's First Female Four-Star General*. It is worth noting that when Dunwoody first became a soldier, women served in the Women's Army Corps. "Over the past 38 years," Dunwoody remarked at her retirement celebration, "I have had the opportunity to witness women Soldiers jump out of airplanes, hike 10 miles, lead men and women, even under the toughest circumstance. And over the last 11 years I've had the honor to serve with many of the 250,000 women who have deployed to Iraq and Afghanistan on battlefields where there are no clear lines, battlefields where every man and woman had to be a rifleman first. And today, women are in combat, that is just a reality. Thousands of women have been decorated for valor and 146 have given their lives. Today, what was once a band of brothers has truly become a band of brothers and sisters."

Sarah Emma Edmonds (1841–1898)

Soldier, Spy

A Union soldier during the Civil War, Sarah Edmonds was known by her unsuspecting brothers-in-arms as fellow soldier "Franklin Flint Thompson." Edmonds was one of the few females known to have served in combat during the Civil War. However, Edmonds's wartime service extended beyond the battlefield. She served the war effort as a Union spy who infiltrated the Confederate Army several times and as a nurse for wounded soldiers in a Washington, D.C., hospital.

Born on a family farm in the Canadian province of New Brunswick close to the Maine border, Edmonds fled home at the age of fifteen to escape an early marriage, adopting male attire to travel more

easily. She crossed into the United States and eventually arrived in Flint, Michigan, in 1856.

Edmonds would later write in her memoir, *Unsexed, or the Female Soldier*, that when she learned about the outbreak of the war, "I was not an American—I was not obliged to stay here during this terrible strife—I could return to my native land where my parents would welcome me to the home of my childhood.... But these were not the thoughts which occupied my mind. It was not my intention, or desire, to seek my own personal ease and comfort while so much sorrow and distress filled the land. But the great question to be decided, was what can I do?" Her answer was to sign up as a male field nurse in the Second Volunteers of the U.S. Army under the alias Franklin Flint Thompson. Edmonds did hospital work for many months, participating in several campaigns, including the First and Second Battle of Bull Run, and was then reassigned as a mail carrier for her regiment, the 2nd Michigan Infantry, serving on the battlefield at Antietam, the Peninsula Campaign, Vicksburg, Fredericksburg, and other battles.

When one of General McClellan's spies was caught and executed, Edmonds volunteered for espionage work. Her first spy mission involved darkening her skin with silver nitrate to pose as a slave in a nearby Confederate military camp. She escaped to report back on Confederate troop size and weapons. A second mission had her posing as an Irish peddler behind Confederate lines. On other missions in Virginia, she again posed as a male slave and as an African American laundrywoman.

Edmonds's career as spy and soldier ended when she contracted malaria and deserted, fearing that in a military hospital, the secret of her gender would be discovered. Instead, she checked herself into a private hospital, intending to return to service once she had recuperated. She saw posters, however, listing Frank Thompson as a deserter, and rather than return to the Army under another alias or risk execution for desertion, she decided to become a female nurse at a Washington, D.C., hospital for wounded soldiers.

In 1865, Edmonds published her experiences in a best-selling book, *Nurse and Spy in the Union Army*. When her fellow soldiers learned the truth, they continued to speak highly of her military service, praising her fearlessness and acknowledging her as a good soldier. Edmonds married in 1867 and lectured on her experiences in the 1880s. She received a government pension for her military service and managed to have the charge of desertion dropped, which led to her receiving an honorable discharge. In 1897, she became the only woman to be admitted to the Grand Army of the Republic, the Civil War Army veterans' organization. She died in Texas and is buried in the Civil War cemetery in Houston. She was laid to rest a second time in 1901 with full military honors. While historians are skeptical concerning the reliability of all Edmonds's claims in her memoir, the facts that are verifiable tell the incredible story of the "beardless boy" who was one of the great soldiers of the Civil War.

Helen Fairchild (1885–1918)

Army Nurse

An Army nurse who served as a member of the American Expeditionary Force during World War I, Helen Fairchild is known for the letters she wrote home detailing the harsh realities of combat nursing during the war. She died while on duty with a British base hospital on the Western front from complications after surgery for a gastric ulcer, likely exacerbated by her exposure to poison gas.

Born in Milton, Pennsylvania, Fairchild was raised on a family farm and graduated as a nurse from Pennsylvania Hospital in 1913. After the United States joined World War I in 1917, Fairchild and sixty-three other nurses, the so-called "Pennsylvania 64," volunteered for the American Expeditionary Forces and sailed to France and Belgium for their postings in May 1917. Fairchild volunteered for front-line duty during the Third Battle of Ypres, serving as a combat nurse and being exposed to heavy shelling, including a gas attack. In letters home, Fairchild recorded the nurses' experiences at the Casualty Clearing Stations in the Ypres–Passchendaele sector, writing, "We all live in tents and wade through mud to and from the operating room where we stand in mud higher than our ankles." A doctor in

Fairchild's unit recalled, "The casualty clearing stations were frequently the scene of the most distressing sight which a human eye can witness, that is the re-wounding of already wounded men by an enemy's bomb dropped suddenly in the dead of night."

In November 1917, Fairchild developed tonsillitis and then intractable abdominal pain. An X-ray revealed a severe stomach ulcer probably connected to her poison gas exposure when, according to one account, during a gas attack, she gave up her gas mask to protect a soldier in her care. She died a few days after surgery in 1918.

Although nurses were not granted military rank at the time, Fairchild was, as Chief Nurse Margaret Dunlop wrote to Fairchild's family, "buried in her uniform of the American Army and given [a] most honored military funeral." Described by Dunlop as "the truest type of womanhood [who] stood for the very best in the nursing profession," Fairchild is today registered in the Women in Military Service for America Memorial at Arlington National Cemetery.

Kristen Marie Griest (1989–)

Army Officer

The first female Army infantry officer, Kristen Marie Griest is also one of the first women to ever graduate from the Army Ranger School, considered the toughest training in the U.S. military.

Griest was born in New Haven, Connecticut. She graduated from Amity High School in 2007 and entered the U.S. Military Academy at West Point, graduating in 2011. Griest selected the military police branch in which to serve, the only option closest to the infantry available to women at the time. She served as an MP platoon leader in the 101st Airborne Division from 2012 to 2014 and was deployed to Afghanistan in 2013, leading over one hundred missions performing convoy escorts and working with the Afghan Army. She was awarded a Bronze Star for her service.

In 2015, the Army invited Griest to join a select group of 109 women to attend the Army Ranger School, a two-month physical fitness test of grueling marches, obstacle courses, and parachute jumps with minimal food and sleep as well as twenty-seven days of mock combat patrols. After a mandatory pre-Ranger School course, only nineteen women were invited to begin Ranger School training. Griest and Shaye Haver became the first two women to earn Ranger tabs (a third, Lisa Jaster, completed the course two months later). Having shown that women are capable of handling the demands of Ranger School, the U.S. Military opened all combat positions to women without exception in December 2015.

In 2016, Griest was promoted to captain and became the first female infantry officer in the U.S. Army assigned to the 4th Ranger Training Battalion at Fort Benning as a platoon tactical trainer. She remains on active duty with the military.

Anna Mae Hays (1920–2018)
Army Officer, Nurse

Front-line nurse Anna Mae Hayes served in three wars—in the jungles of India during World War II, in Korea, and in Vietnam—and would become the first female general in the U.S. military.

Hays was born in Buffalo, New York, to parents who were officers in the Salvation Army. The family moved several times in New York and Pennsylvania, finally settling in Allentown, Pennsylvania, where Hays attended high school. In 1939, she enrolled at the Allentown General Hospital School of Nursing, graduating in 1941. She joined the Army Nurse Corps a year later and was sent to India, serving with the 20th Field Hospital on the road through the jungle into Burma. The living and working conditions were primitive with buildings constructed of bamboo, cases of dysentery, and continuous encounters with leeches and snakes. Hays served two and half years in India and in 1945 was promoted to the rank of first lieutenant.

After the war ended, Hays remained in the military serving as an operating room nurse and later as head nurse at Tilton General Hospital at Fort Dix, New Jersey, and subsequently at other hospitals in Pennsylvania and Virginia. In 1950, she was de-

ployed to Inchon during the Korean War in conditions that she later described as worse than those in India due to the cold temperatures and lack of supplies. Over a fourteen-month period, she and thirty-one other nurses treated more than twenty-five thousand patients. After her tour in Korea, Hayes was transferred to the Tokyo Army Hospital for a year and, after graduating from the Nursing Service Administration course, she was appointed head nurse at the Walter Reed Hospital in Washington, D.C. She would be one of three nurses assigned to President Dwight D. Eisenhower when he was hospitalized with ileitis. She earned her bachelor's degree in nursing education in 1958 from Columbia University and a MS degree in nursing in 1968 from the Catholic University of America.

During the Vietnam War, she traveled to the war zone three times to monitor American nurses stationed there while developing new training programs to increase the number of nurses serving overseas. In 1970, President Nixon promoted Hayes to the rank of brigadier general. Hays said at the ceremony that the stars on her uniform "reflect[ed] the dedication, selfless, and often heroic efforts of Army nurses throughout the world since 1901 in time of peace and war." After her appointment, she asked to be dropped off at the Army officers' club's front entrance, countering the expectation that female officers were expected to use the side entrance.

Following Hays's promotion, Elizabeth P. Hoisington, director of the Women's Army Corps, was also promoted to the rank of brigadier general, prompting a cartoon of two enlisted men sitting in a bar with one quipping, "Well, we've got everything, Sarge—the atomic bomb, guided missiles, the M-16 rifle, and now two lady generals."

Jennie Irene Hodgers (Albert Cashier) (1843–1915)
Soldier

One of the most famous female soldiers of the Civil War, Jennie Hodgers enlisted as Albert D. Cashier and served as part of the Army of the Tennessee participating in the Siege of Vicksburg.

After the war, Hodgers continued to live as a man, prompting many to refer to her as the first American transgender soldier.

Hodgers was born in Ireland and immigrated to America when she was still a young girl, settling in Illinois. Little is known about her early life. It is said that her uncle or stepfather dressed her in boys' clothing to find work in an all-male shoe factory and that even before the war, she adopted the identity of Albert Cashier in order to live independently.

As Cashier, she enlisted at the age of eighteen into the 95th Illinois Infantry for a three-year term. Her regiment was part of the Army of the Tennessee, and she fought in approximately forty battles, including the Siege of Vicksburg. During this campaign, Cashier was captured during a reconnaissance mission but managed to escape and return to the regiment. After the Battle of Vicksburg, Cashier entered a military hospital with chronic diarrhea but somehow managed to evade detection. Cashier participated in the Red River Campaign and the Battle of Brice's Crossroads in 1864 as well as in the Battles of Spring Hill and Franklin and the defense of Nashville. Hodgers's fellow soldiers recalled Cashier as a modest young man who kept his shirt buttoned to the chin and was teased because he was beardless. Despite her diminutive size, they recorded that she could "do as much work as anyone in the Company."

After the war, "Albert Cashier" mustered out of the service with the regiment and returned to Illinois, where she retained her male identity. Hodgers could not read or write, and the jobs available to illiterate women were extremely limited. As a man, she found work as a handyman, farm laborer, and janitor, supplementing her labor with her veteran's pension.

Hodgers's secret became known when, elderly and suffering from dementia, she entered the state hospital for the insane, where her birth gender was discovered. She was made to wear skirts for the first time in over fifty years, which she found both restrictive and humiliating. Unused to walking in long garments, she tripped and fell, breaking a hip that left her bedridden. She died in 1915, less than two years before women gained the right to serve openly—if minimally—in the Armed Forces. Given an official Grand Army of the Republic funeral, she was buried with full military honors with a tombstone inscribed "Albert D. J. Cashier, Co. G, 95 Ill. Inf."

Michelle Janine Howard (1960–)
Naval Officer

The first African American woman to command a U.S. Navy ship, Michelle Janine Howard is also the first female graduate of the U.S. Naval Academy selected for flag rank and the first woman to become a U.S. Navy four-star admiral. She was also the first African American and the first woman to serve as vice chief of naval operations and the first female four-star admiral to command operational forces when she assumed command of U.S. Naval Forces Europe and U.S. Naval Forces Africa.

The daughter of a U.S. Air Force master sergeant, Howard was born at March Air Force Base in California. After graduating from Gateway High School in Aurora, Colorado, she attended the U.S. Naval Academy, graduating in 1982, and the U.S. Army's Command and General Staff College in 1998, where she earned a master's degree in military arts and sciences.

Howard piloted her first ship, the destroyer USS *Spruance*, during her sophomore year at the Naval Academy. She served aboard the submarine tender USS *Hunley* (1982–1985) and the training aircraft carrier USS *Lexington* (1985–1987) before being named in 1990 as the chief engineer aboard the USS *Mount Hood*. She served as first lieutenant aboard the USS *Flint* (1992), the executive officer on the USS *Tortuga* (1996), and was given command of the USS *Rushmore*, becoming the first African American woman to captain a U.S. naval ship (1999). Howard became the first African American woman to lead a U.S. Navy battle group in 2009. In 2014, Howard was promoted to admiral and became the vice chief of naval operations, making her the second-highest-ranking officer in the U.S. Navy. She was named commander of naval forces in Europe and Africa in 2016, the first female four-star admiral to command operational forces, and retired from the Navy in 2017.

After her retirement, Howard became a visiting professor at George Washington University in Washington, D.C., teaching cybersecurity and international politics.

Nancy Harkness Love (1914–1976)

Army Air Force Officer

The first woman to fly aircraft for the U.S. military, Nancy Harkness Love was a World War II pilot and commander. During the war, she convinced William H. Tunner, commander of the Army Air Forces, to set up a unit of female pilots to ferry aircraft from factories to air bases. This became the Women's Auxiliary Ferrying Squadron (WAFS), which Love commanded. She would later command the newly formed Women's Airforce Service Pilots (WASP).

Born in Nancy Harkness in Houghton, Michigan, Love was the daughter of a wealthy physician. She developed a passion for aviation at an early age and obtained her pilot's license when she was sixteen. She attended Milton Academy in Massachusetts and Vassar College, where the "Flying Freshman," as she was known, earned extra money taking students for rides in an airplane she rented at a nearby airport. In 1936, Nancy Harkness married Robert M. Love, an Air Corps Reserve major, and together, they formed their own successful Boston-based aviation company, Inter City Aviation, with Nancy as a pilot. In the 1930s, she entered air races and worked as a test pilot.

In 1940, after World War II began in Europe, she assembled a group of forty-nine female pilots, called "The Originals," and submitted a proposal to Lieutenant Robert Olds of the U.S. Air Corps suggesting that the women help transport aircraft from factories to bases. Olds submitted Love's plan for integrating these civilian female pilots into the ferrying command of the U.S. Army Air Forces to General Hap Arnold, commanding general of the U.S. Army Air Forces, who turned it down after pilot Jacqueline Cochran obtained a promise from him not to act on any proposal that would not make the female pilots commissioned officers under the command of

women. By June 1942, however, both the Army and Navy were committed to using female pilots. Colonel William Tunner, who was in charge of Air Transport Command (ATC), turned to Love to recruit outstanding female pilots and was willing to defer rather than reject the idea of commissioning the women to get the program started. Love was put in charge of the Women's Auxiliary Ferry Squadron (WAFS), which began its first ferrying missions in October 1942. Love would become the first woman to fly virtually all the Army Air Force's complex, high-performance combat aircraft, including heavy bombers, and her success led the way for her original WAFS to begin ferrying combat aircraft. At its peak, the ATC Ferrying Division had three hundred female ferry pilots who, by 1944, had made 50 percent of all deliveries of fighters in the United States. When Love was awarded the Air Medal in 1945 for her wartime accomplishments, the Army Air Forces, who issued the medal, asked President Harry Truman to sign it. Robert Love, who had served in the Army Air Forces, received the Distinguished Service Medal and was decorated at the same time as his wife.

After the war, the Loves had three daughters, and Nancy Love continued working as an aviation industry leader. She also continued to champion the cause of recognition for the women who had served as WASPs. In 1948, a year after the U.S. Air Force was established as a separate branch of the U.S. military, Love was given the rank of lieutenant colonel in the U.S. Air Force Reserve. Her wish to see female pilots serving alongside men would eventually become the norm in the U.S. military.

Shortly before Love's death, the order of Fifiella, the WASP alumni organization, named her Woman of the Year. She is also enshrined in the National Aviation Hall of Fame.

Anita Newcomb McGee (1864–1940)

Army Officer, Physician

In 1898, during the Spanish–American War, physician Anita Newcomb McGee was named acting assistant surgeon general of the U.S. Army, making her the only woman up to that time permitted to wear an officer's uniform. She organized the 1,600 nurses who served during the conflict and wrote the Army Reorganization Act of 1901, which established the Army Nurse Corps as a permanent unit.

Born in Washington, D.C., McGee was born Anita Newcomb, the daughter of noted astronomer Simon Newcomb. Her mother in particular encouraged her daughter's academic pursuits. She was educated at home and elite private schools. In 1888, she married William John McGee, who supported her decision to attend medical school soon after they were married. She graduated from Columbian College (now George Washington University) in 1892, and, after an internship at the Women's Clinic in Washington and gynecology studies at Johns Hopkins University School of Medicine, she operated a private practice until 1895.

With the outbreak of the Spanish–American War, McGee learned that Army Surgeon General George M. Sternberg intended to use nurses at base hospitals for the first time since the Civil War. She petitioned Sternberg to permit only fully qualified nurses to serve, and he offered McGee the job of screening nurses. She was appointed acting assistant surgeon general of the Army for the duration of the war.

After the war, McGee drafted the legislation that established the U.S. Army Nurse Corps and helped the Navy establish a nursing corps as well. In 1899, she wrote a manual on nursing for the military. She was barred from heading the newly created Army Nurse Corps because legislation required a nurse, not a doctor, in that position. Instead, she helped to found the Society of Spanish–American War Nurses in 1900, serving as the organization's president for the next six years. She offered the society's services to the Japanese government during the Russo–Japanese War, living in Japan to work with nurses there, and was designated "superior of nurses" with the rank of an Army officer.

McGee died in 1940 and was buried with full military honors in Arlington National Cemetery. One of her contemporaries, a male Army surgeon, said of the women McGee recruited to serve in the Army Nurse Corps, "When you were coming, we did not know what we would do with you. Now we do not know what we would have done without you." His words are a testament both to contributions of men and women of the Army Nurse Corps and of McGee's work to establish the corps.

Martha McSally (1966–)

Air Force Pilot

One of the highest-ranking female pilots in the history of the Air Force, McSally was the first American woman to fly in combat following the 1991 lifting of the prohibition on female combat pilots. McSally was elected to the U.S. House of Representatives in 2014, where she served two terms. Defeated in her 2018 bid for the U.S. Senate, McSally was named to fill the Arizona Senate seat vacated by the death of John McCain.

McSally was born in Warwick, Rhode Island. After attending the all-girls' St. Mary's Academy, she earned an appointment at the U.S. Air Force Academy, graduating in 1988. After earning a master's degree from Harvard's Kennedy School of Government, McSally began pilot training and was first in her class at the Air War College.

After completing undergraduate pilot training in 1991, McSally was assigned as an instructor pilot at Laughlin Air Force Base, Texas, and when the military's combat aircraft restrictions for female pilots was lifted, McSally began fighter training in 1993. She was assigned to an operational squadron deployed to Kuwait in 1995 and flew combat patrols over Iraq, enforcing the no-fly zone over southern Iraq, becoming the first female fighter pilot to fly in combat and the first woman to command a fighter squadron. Future assignments included working as an advisor to Senator Jon Kyl of Arizona on defense and foreign affairs policy, serving with the Joint Task Force Southwest Asia in 2000 for Operation Southern Watch, and deploying to Afghanistan during Operation Enduring Freedom. In 2001, she was the plaintiff in a lawsuit against the U.S. Department of Defense challenging the military policy that required servicewomen stationed in Saudi Arabia to wear the body-covering abaya when off-base in the country. Her suit alleged that "the regulation required her to send the message that she believes women are subservient to men." In 2002, the policy was amended to state that servicewomen would no longer be required to wear the abaya but would be encouraged to do so as a show of respect to local customs. Officials claimed the decision was not made because of McSally's lawsuit.

After twenty-two years of service, McSally retired from the Air Force in 2010 to pursue a political career. She generated headlines in March 2019 when she broke a three-decade silence to announce that she had been raped by a male superior officer as a young servicewoman. She did not report the assault because it was considered a career-ending decision for women to do so. She revealed the attack during a subcommittee hearing on sexual assault in the military. "Later in my career," McSally said, "as the military grappled with scandals and their wholly inadequate responses, I felt the need to let some people know I, too, was a survivor. I was horrified at how my attempt to share generally my experiences were handled. I almost separated from the Air Force at 18 years over my despair. Like many victims, I felt the system was raping me all over again. But I didn't quit. I decided to stay and continue to serve and fight and lead."

Elsie Ott (1913–2006)

Army Officer, Nurse

In 1943, Army nurse Elsie Ott was the flight nurse on the first intercontinental air evacuation flight. She successfully oversaw the transportation of five seriously injured soldiers from India to Washington, D.C., in a six-day trip that would have taken three months by ship and ground transportation. Ott demonstrated the potential of air evacuation, and for her service, she became the first woman to receive the U.S. Air Medal.

Born in Smithtown, New York, Ott entered the Lenox Hill Hospital School of Nursing in New York City after completing high school. She worked in several different hospitals before joining the Army Nurse Corps in 1941. Given the rank of second

lieutenant, Ott took up assignments in Louisiana and Virginia before being sent to Karachi, India (now Pakistan).

In World War II, air evacuation of the wounded was untried and untested. Ott, who was assigned as the flight nurse to oversee the care of five seriously injured soldiers to be transported from India to Walter Reed Hospital in Washington, D.C., had never flown before, had not been trained regarding the effects of high altitude on injuries or illness, and was given no list of supplies needed or what to expect. She used her nursing know-how to gather basic medicine and equipment she felt might be necessary during a flight that was expected to last a week. She collected blankets, sheets, two Army cots, and two mattresses. A medical department staff sergeant accompanied Ott as her medical assistant. The flight across central Africa, with many refueling stops and overnight layovers, lasted six days, but the patients arrived safely, and Ott had proven the practicality of air evacuations. Ott confessed that when the flight arrived in Washington, she was unable to answer simple questions and couldn't even remember her name due to severe sleep deprivation. She had made detailed notes during the flight of what was needed, such as oxygen bottles, blankets, more medical supplies, and even changes of uniforms. These would become standard practices for flight nurses during future evacuations.

The Air Medal awarded to Ott for her heroic service included a citation that read in part: "The successful transportation of these patients was made possible by the efficiency and professional skill of Lieutenant Ott and her unflagging devotion to duty. It further demonstrated the practicality of long-range evacuation by air of seriously ill and wounded military personnel from theaters of operation and reflected great credit upon Lieutenant Ott and the Army Nurse Corps."

Ott returned to India and was promoted to captain before being discharged from military duty in 1946. She then married and settled in Wheaton, Illinois. A pioneering flight nurse, Elsie Ott helped to transform the methods in which casualties could be treated, which would lead to the saving of countless lives.

Emeline Piggott (1836–1919)

Spy

Confederate spy Emeline Piggott was one of the more notorious and successful of the many women who offered their services as spies during the Civil War. Raised in Harlowe Township, Carteret County, North Carolina, Piggott moved with her parents to a farm at Crab Point on the North Carolina coast during the Civil War near an encampment of soldiers of the 26th North Carolina stationed to defend the coast. Piggott began tending the sick and wounded soldiers as well as collecting mail, food, clothing, and medicine for the troops in nearby counties. The unit was set to the Battle of New Bern, and Piggott accompanied them. After New Bern fell to the Federals, she remained for several months nursing the wounded.

She offered her services to the Confederate Army as a spy and began hosting parties for Union soldiers, where she was able to gather information. She used the voluminous skirts she wore to hide contraband that she distributed to the Confederates as well as important papers she collected. In 1864, Piggott and her brother-in-law were arrested by Union soldiers on suspicion of spying while carrying supplies and messages across the lines. The brother-in-law was searched and released when no contraband was found. Piggott demanded that a white woman, not a nearby black woman, search her, and while she waited, she ate some of the incriminating messages and tore others to pieces. She was transported to New Bern for trial and endured an attempted murder with chloroform, breaking a window in her cell to breathe fresh air. Scheduled for trial on several occasions, Piggott was unexpectedly released and she returned home, where she was constantly harassed by Federal troops until the Civil War ended.

After the war, Piggott was a member of the New Bern chapter of the United Daughters of the Confederacy and organized another chapter in Morehead City that was named for her. She held the title of honorary president until her death at the age of eighty-two.

Deborah Sampson (1760–1827)

Soldier

 Called America's first female soldier, Deborah Sampson became a hero of the American Revolution when she disguised herself as a man and joined the Continental Army. She was the only woman to earn a full military pension for her participation in the Revolutionary Army.

Sampson was born in Plympton, Massachusetts. Her mother was the great-granddaughter of William Bradford, governor of Plymouth Colony. After her father abandoned the family, Sampson was raised in different households and, at the age of ten, was bound out as an indentured servant to a farmer with a large family. At eighteen, Sampson, who was self-educated, worked as a teacher and as a weaver.

In 1782, Sampson disguised herself as a man named Robert Shurtleff and joined the Fourth Massachusetts Regiment. At West Point, New York, she was given the dangerous assignment of scouting for British troop movements in Manhattan. Sampson and two sergeants led about thirty infantrymen on a raid of a Tory home that resulted in the capture of fifteen men. At the Siege of Yorktown, Sampson dug trenches and helped storm a British redoubt. For over two years, her gender escaped detection. When shot in the left thigh, she extracted the pistol ball herself to protect her identity. However, when she became ill during an epidemic, she was taken to a hospital, where she lost consciousness, and her identity was revealed when her doctor removed her clothes to treat her. Instead of revealing his discovery to Army authorities, the doctor kept her secret and took her to his house, where his wife and daughters nursed her.

After receiving an honorable discharge in 1783, Sampson returned to Massachusetts, where she married, had three children, and lived the life of a typical farmer's wife. She received a military pension from the State of Massachusetts. The story of her life, *The Female Review; or, Memoirs of an American Young Lady*, appeared in 1797, and in 1802, Sampson began a yearlong lecture tour about her experiences—

the first woman in America to do so—dressing in full military regalia.

Four years after death at the age of sixty-six, her husband petitioned Congress for pay as the spouse of a soldier. Even though they were not married at the time of her service, he was awarded payment in 1837 because, as the committee declared, the history of the American Revolution "furnished no other similar example of female heroism, fidelity, and courage."

Wilma Vaught (1930–)
Air Force Officer

One of the most highly decorated military women in U.S. history, Wilma Vaught was the first woman to deploy with an Air Force bomber unit. When she retired after twenty-eight years of service in 1985, she was one of only seven female generals in the Armed Forces and only one of three in the Air Force.

An Illinois native, Vaught earned a BS degree from the University of Illinois–Urbana-Champaign College of Business in 1952 and an MBA degree from the University of Alabama in 1968. In 1972, she became the first female U.S. Air Force officer to attend the Industrial College of the Armed Forces at Fort Lesley J. McNair in Washington, D.C.

When Vaught joined the military in the 1950s, she faced strong restrictions on the number of women who could be in the military and how they could serve. In 1957, Vaught was commissioned a second lieutenant in the Air Force and assigned as chief of the Data Services Branch at Barksdale Air Force Base in Louisiana before serving as chief of the Management Analysis Division at Zaragoza Air Base in Spain from 1959 to 1963. She became the first woman to deploy with a Strategic Air Command operational unit at Andersen Air Force Base in Guam and served in the Military Assistance Command in Saigon during the Vietnam War. Vaught was promoted to brigadier general in 1980, the first woman raised to that rank from the comptroller division. She assumed command of the U.S. Military Entrance Processing Command in 1982 and was

chairperson of the Committee of Women in the NATO Armed Forces.

When she retired from service in 1985, Vaught felt that the role of women in the military was overlooked, and she established the Women in Military Service for America Memorial, a nonprofit foundation that operates the first major national memorial honoring the nearly three million women who have served in the nation's military, dating from the American Revolution. The memorial stands at the main gateway to Arlington National Cemetery.

In 2000, Vaught was inducted into the National Women's Hall of Fame and in 2010 into the Army Women's Foundation Hall of Fame.

Mary Edwards Walker (1832–1919)
Army Officer, Surgeon

Out of nearly 3,500 Congressional Medal of Honor recipients since the award was first established in 1861, only one has been a woman, Mary Edwards Walker, a physician and the only female surgeon formally assigned field duty during the Civil War. Because she was a civilian, her medal was rescinded in 1917, two years before she died. However, Walker refused to return it, and in 1977, President Jimmy Carter restored her award, and she remains the only woman to have won the medal.

Born on a farm in Oswego, New York, Mary Edwards Walker was raised by nontraditional parents who nurtured their daughter's spirit of independence and defiance of gender roles, allowing her to wear boys' clothing during farm labor because women's clothes were too restrictive. Encouraged to gain the best possible education, her parents founded the first free schoolhouse in Oswego and sent their daughter to the progressive Falley Seminary in Fulton, New York. Walker taught to earn the money to pay her way through Syracuse Medical College, where she graduated in 1855, the only woman in her class. The same year, she married fellow medical student Albert Miller but refused to include "obey" in her vows and retained her last name. The couple set up a joint practice in Rome, New

York, but the practice failed to thrive due to public distrust of female physicians. Walker later divorced her husband because of his infidelity.

At the outbreak of the Civil War, Walker volunteered as a surgeon in the Union Army. She was rejected because she was a woman and offered the role of a nurse, which she declined, choosing instead to volunteer as a civilian surgeon. She served at the First Battle of Bull Run in 1861 and as an unpaid field surgeon near the Union front lines at the Battle of Fredericksburg and the Battle of Chickamauga. After a request to work as a spy, Walker was employed as a "contract acting assistant surgeon (civilian)" by the Army of the Cumberland, the first female surgeon employed by the U.S. Army. In 1864, she was captured by Confederate troops and arrested as a spy just after she had finished helping a Confederate doctor perform an amputation. She was sent to a POW camp in Richmond, Virginia, and after four months, she was released as part of a prisoner exchange. After her release, she was assigned to a women's prison hospital and then to an orphanage. She left government service in 1865, shortly before she was awarded the Medal of Honor.

Walker was elected president of the National Dress Reform Association in 1865 and worked with feminist organizations who widely publicized her Civil War service, but her growing eccentricity alienated women's groups. She would wear full male attire, including a wing collar, bow tie, and top hat, and was often arrested for masquerading as a man. She occasionally exhibited herself in sideshows and wrote two books, the partly autobiographical *Hit* (1871) and *Unmasked; or, the Science of Immorality* (1878).

Loretta Perfectus Walsh (1896–1925)
Naval Officer

Loretta Perfectus Walsh is the first woman to be allowed to serve in the U.S. Armed Forces as anything other than a nurse. She became the first woman to enlist in the Navy and the first woman to reach the rank of chief petty officer.

Born in Philadelphia, Walsh decided to enlist in the U.S. Navy when, in 1917, Germany an-

nounced it would resume unrestricted submarine warfare on all ships, including those from the United States. In March 1917, the Navy Department authorized the enrollment of women in the Naval Reserve, becoming the first branch of the U.S. Armed Forces to allow enlistment of women in a non-nursing capacity. Walsh, at the age of twenty, enlisted for four years, becoming the first active-duty woman in the Navy. She would subsequently become the first Navy petty officer when she was sworn in as chief yeoman twelve days before President Woodrow Wilson asked for a declaration of war on April 6, 1917.

Yeomans' duties (women were known as yeomanettes) included clerical work, recruiting for production jobs in ammunition factories, design work, drafting, translation, and radio operations. Most of the women were stationed in Washington, D.C., but some were deployed in France, Guam, and Hawaii. Notably, both male and female yeomen were paid the same, and women were given the same benefits as men, a unique feature for the time. By the end of the war, 11,275 yeomanettes were in the Navy and three hundred marinettes were in the Marine Corps. By 1919, they were all released from active duty. Walsh maintained her status until the end of her four-year commitment. Walsh became ill with influenza during the pandemic of 1918. She recovered but remained frail and eventually contracted tuberculosis, from which she died at the young age of twenty-nine.

Women who had served in the U.S. military since 1901 as nurses were civilians, despite their uniforms. Walsh would lead the vanguard of women into the ranks of the military, the first of thirteen thousand who would serve in World War I and countless others who would follow.

Cathay Williams (1844–1893)
Soldier

Cathay Williams was the first African American woman to enlist and serve in the U.S. Army. Despite the prohibition against women serving in the military, Williams enlisted in 1866 in the U.S. Regular Army under the false name of "William

Cathay." Assigned to the 38th U.S. Infantry, she was posted to New Mexico during the Indian Wars. She is also said to be the only known female Buffalo Soldier.

Williams was born in Independence, Missouri, to a freed slave and a woman still in slavery, which legally made Williams a slave. As an adolescent, Williams worked as a house slave at a household outside Jefferson City, Missouri. When Union troops occupied Jefferson City in 1861, Williams was seized as "contraband" and pressed into service with the 8th Indiana Volunteer Infantry Regiment, accompanying them in action through Arkansas, Louisiana, and Georgia.

In 1866, Williams enlisted in the U.S. Regular Army disguised as "William Cathay." She was assigned to the 38th U.S. Infantry Regiment with only her cousin and a friend, both of whom were fellow soldiers in her regiment and knew her secret. She contracted smallpox and after being hospitalized rejoined her unit in New Mexico. Frequently hospitalized thereafter, Williams was finally discovered as a woman by the surgeon at the Army post. She was discharged from the Army in 1868, but she signed up with an emerging all-black regiment that would eventually become part of the legendary Buffalo Soldiers.

Williams went to work as a cook first in New Mexico and later in Pueblo, Colorado. She married, but her husband stole her money, and she had him arrested and then moved to Trinidad, Colorado, where she worked as a seamstress. During this period, a reporter from St. Louis who had heard rumors about a female African American soldier in the Army interviewed her and published her story in 1876.

In 1889 or 1890, Williams applied for a disability pension based on her military service. Her request was denied, and it is generally believed that she died shortly afterward. Her final resting place is unknown. In 2018, the Private Cathay Williams monument bench was unveiled on the Walk of Honor at the National Infantry Museum.

EXPLORERS

The remarkable American women profiled in this chapter have been pioneers and trailblazers who, from the first women who explored and settled the American wilderness to the first woman to soar into space, have taken on daunting challenges that have called for a great deal of physical, mental, and emotional courage.

When the first European settlers arrived in Roanoke (1585), Jamestown (1607), and Plymouth (1620), the immigrant perspective was limited to the largely unknown wilderness of their immediate surroundings on the Eastern seaboard. By the eighteenth century, the earliest settlers had begun to explore the frontier farther west, defying the challenges of unknown territory and conflicts with native populations and the rival colonial powers of France and Spain. In 1763, the Treaty of Paris, which ended the Seven Years' War (called the French and Indian War in America), resulted in the loss of French holdings of lands east of the Mississippi River and what is now Canada to the British, with the lands west of the Mississippi, in addition to Florida and New Orleans, going to Spain. The end of the conflict stimulated a steady migration to frontier lands, with settlers moving over the Appalachian Mountains into western Pennsylvania and areas of Ohio, Kentucky, and Tennessee. History has celebrated the exploits of early frontiersmen such as Daniel Boone and the role they played in making the first great Western

migrations possible. Far less attention is given to the women, like Boone's wife, Rebecca, who accompanied the frontiersmen west and were expected to establish their various homes and sustain their nascent communities while giving birth to numerous children, caring for them, and educating them. Rebecca Boone's experience of hardship and struggle in an inhospitable wilderness is repeated by countless other unsung pioneer women whose contributions to building and sustaining American life are too often ignored or obscured by an emphasis on their male counterparts. Rebecca Boone's considerable accomplishments as wife, mother, midwife, doctor, leather tanner, linen maker, and sharpshooter suggest that she, like so many other early pioneer women, had to master the survival skills of her husband but with the additional responsibilities of family caretaker and community builder.

American female pioneers contradict the gender convention of the "weaker sex," who needed male protection. Pioneer women personified the self-reliance, innovation, and resourcefulness needed to meet the challenges of life on the frontier. The farm families who settled the Midwestern region between 1800 and 1840 depended on women to set up neighborhood social organizations, which often revolved around opportunities to promote community interaction and cooperation such as church membership and quilting parties. They exchanged information and tips on child-rearing, helped each other during childbirth, and organized schooling for their children. Women, like men, were required to grow the food and make the household items they needed to survive.

By 1810, the Western frontier had reached the Mississippi River. The Louisiana Purchase of 1803 doubled the size of the nation, stretching across the continent to the Pacific. The Lewis and Clark Expedition from 1804 to 1806 was the first government expedition to cross the western portion of the United States to explore and map the newly acquired territory. The Corps of Discovery, as the expedition was called, would depend on the assistance of Native American woman Sacagawea as guide, provisioner, and negotiator with the Indian tribes they encoun-

tered. Six months pregnant when she first accompanied the expedition, Sacagawea gave birth and cared for her child along the thousands of miles from the Dakota Territory to the Pacific and back to St. Louis.

Trappers, hunters, and traders were the first to travel extensively through the new Western territory. The government and private enterprises sent other explorers to the West, men like Zebulon Pike, Harriman Long, and John Charles Frémont. Missionaries would follow to bring Christianity to the Native American tribes. The first record of non-Native American women traveling in the West are two wives of traders who first traveled on the Santa Fe Trail and two wives of missionaries who traveled on the Oregon Trail. Mary Donoho traveled with her trader

Between 1804 and 1806, Meriwether Lewis and William Clark were the first to explore the West after the Louisiana Purchase. It wouldn't be long before women adventurers like Mary Donoho and Susan Shelby Magoffin followed their lead.

husband to settle in Santa Fe in 1835; in 1846, Susan Shelby Magoffin followed the trail to Santa Fe and then to Mexico City. In 1836, Marcus Whitman and Henry H. Spalding traveled west on the Oregon Trail to establish the Whitman Mission near modern-day Walla Walla, Washington. Their wives, Narcissa Whitman and Eliza Hart Spalding, became the first European American women to cross the Rocky Mountains. Both Susan Magoffin and Narcissa Whitman left valuable journal entries and letters recording their experiences, documenting for one of the first times women's perspectives on frontier life.

The greatest migration in American history followed these early pioneering women. Between 1841 and 1867, more than 350,000 settlers in family units traveled in wagon trains the 2,170 miles along the Oregon Trail to settle Oregon and California.

They left family and friends behind in farms in Illinois, Indiana, Iowa, and Missouri, lured by free land or the financial opportunities of California's gold rush. Pioneers on the journey attempted to replicate the rigid gender division of labor that characterized early nineteenth-century America. Men drove the wagons and livestock, stood guard duty, and hunted buffalo and antelope for provisions. Women got up at four o'clock each morning, collected wood or "buffalo chips" (dry animal dung used for fuel), hauled water, cooked the food, and milked cows. At the end of the day, men expected women to fix dinner, make up beds, wash clothes, and tend the children, not unlike women's domestic responsibilities at home. However, necessity along the trail often canceled strict gender role distinctions, and women often performed tasks previously reserved for men such as driving wagons, yoking cattle, and

Artist George Caleb Bingham's famous painting of Daniel Boone and his wife (on horseback), titled *Cumberland Gap*, envisions a somewhat idyllic version of what was a more arduous journey into the unknown American frontier.

loading wagons. Men on occasion were also known to assume some domestic service as cooks. In the famous 1852 painting of Daniel Boone escorting settlers through the Cumberland Gap, artist George Caleb Bingham sets the conventional image of the pioneers: Daniel Boone resolutely leading the way and his wife, Rebecca, Madonna-like with a child in her arms, the protected passenger in the wagon. However, the reality for the pioneers along the Oregon Trail was strikingly different. For one thing, wagon space was far too valuable, needed for cargo other than passengers. Men, women, and children generally walked the 2,170 miles, and despite the fact that men generally dictated the terms of travel, representing the family in group decisions, pioneer women were far from protected passengers but were essential to the success of the enterprise.

Upon reaching Oregon and California, settlers sought to reestablish the separate gender roles they had known back east, but again, pioneer life made it difficult to separate the work roles of men and women. The first few years of farming the new land required intensive labor to clear the land, fence, and plow the soil. Labor was scarce, and women and children assisted men with the field work. Men did the heaviest work such as harvesting and hauling cut wheat, but their wives assumed strenuous domestic work such as laundry and churning butter. In time, male hired hands became more available, and women gradually could withdraw from field labor to focus their attention on domestic work. Men were responsible for work outdoors in the barn and fields; women did work inside the house, including cooking, cleaning, and providing childcare. As pioneers became more settled and their homestead more established, women could conform more to the feminine ideal as the "Angel in the House," but rural families could not afford the luxury of women being merely ornamental. Pioneer homemaking, with none of the modern conveniences, was a full-time, demanding job that invalidated the gender stereotype of the passive, protected woman uncontaminated by rough labor.

Pioneer women's history, therefore, is strikingly at odds with gender conventions and assumptions. Although women's actual responsibilities and accomplishments as pioneers have been acknowl-edged in histories of the period, so much of American frontier history has until more recently been focused more on the "Great Man" model: telling the stories of the exceptional, almost always male, figures who command attention for their singular exploits and unique achievements: Kit Carson, Jim Bridger, Zebulon Pike, Wyatt Earp, Billy the Kid, Geronimo. Only two women have consistently made it into the Western frontier pantheon: Annie Oakley and Calamity Jane. In a sense, though, the essential story of the American pioneer, whether male or female, is not fully represented by either the Great Man or Great Woman. Instead, it is in the frequently obscure records of the hundreds of thousands of ordinary individuals who created a new life in the American wilderness or died trying. Their stories have increasingly been the focus of the so-called "new Western history" movement that has emerged among professional historians beginning in the 1980s. The new Western historians such as Patricia Nelson Limerick, Clyde Milner, Richard White, and others have recast the study of American frontier history by focusing on race, class, the environment, and particularly gender. The new histories of the American West will hopefully redress the balance and shed light on aspects of pioneer life that have been obscured or ignored. The female pioneers profiled here are all worthy of recognition, but it is important to note that though they may have been first or best, they were not alone. Countless other American female pioneers faced similar superhuman challenges that demand our admiration and attention.

Women pioneers were just as tough as their male counterparts. Women not only settled and farmed the land alongside men, they also bore and raised children there.

The eighteenth- and nineteenth-century pioneers who left their homes to settle the American frontier differ from explorers and adventurers largely by motivation. For the pioneers, the possible future benefit of exploration into unknown territory outweighed any present obstacles and justified their endeavors; for explorers and adventurers, meeting a challenge and testing its limits were the main motivators. They are the ultimate risk takers, compelled to go where no one has gone before or to achieve what no one has accomplished before. In the nineteenth century, at the same time that American women were challenging the restrictions that kept them from educational, professional, legal, and political equality, they were also beginning to test the notion that the adventurous life was reserved for men. In 1889, journalist Nellie Bly fascinated the world when she became the first woman to attempt to best French author Jules Verne's fictional character, Phileas Fogg, in *Around the World in Eighty Days* by traveling around the world in fewer than eighty days and, unlike Phileas Fogg, went alone, without a companion. Other examples of women's firsts include Harriet Chalmers Adams, who explored South America; Delia Akeley, the first woman to cross equatorial Africa; polar explorers Ann Bancroft, Louise Arner Boyd, and Barbara Hillary, who tested their mettle against records set by men or set new records; and world-class mountaineers like Annie Smith Peck and Sophia Danenberg.

By the twentieth century, when most of the world ceased to be unknown, the challenge for exploration came in the regions above Earth in aviation and space flight. Two American female aviators stand out: Amelia Earhart, perhaps the most famous aviation explorer of the twentieth century, whose mysterious disappearance transformed her into myth and legend; and Bessie Coleman, the first African American female pilot, who was refused admission to flying schools in the United States because of her race, learned French to obtain her pilot's license in France, and returned to the United States as a barnstorming advocate for women and African American pilots. Coleman and Earhart's achievements would lead directly to Sally Ride, the first American female astronaut in space, and Mae Jemison, the first African American woman in space.

The women profiled here speak to the qualities of strength and determination that allowed them to defy gender assumptions to claim their rightful places in American history and blaze the paths of adventure for other women to follow.

BIOGRAPHIES

Harriet Chalmers Adams (1875–1937)
Author, Explorer, Photographer

An intrepid explorer, in 1900, Harriet Chalmers Adams set out on a three-year journey through Central and South America, traveling forty thousand miles visiting every country and many of the most remote and isolated places on Earth. She would follow this with a series of daring travels and adventures. She was the only female journalist allowed in the trenches in World War I, spending three months there, and her subsequent travels in South America, Asia, and the South Pacific led the *New York Times* to declare that she "reached twenty frontiers previously unknown to white women" and was "America's greatest woman explorer."

She was born in Stockton, California. Her wandering spirit was sparked at eight years old when she and her father explored the Sierra Nevada by horseback. Homeschooled, she became fluent in Spanish and studied several other foreign languages. In 1899, she married Franklin Pierce Adams, a man who shared her fascination with travel and adventure. Financially supported by his mine engineering job, in 1900, they set out on her first major expedition, a three-year trip around South America that included crossing the Andes on horseback. At the time, many parts of South America were still unknown. To cover forty thousand miles in three years, Adams and her husband had to average thirty-seven miles a day. Adams was, according to the *New York Times*, likely the first white woman to meet twenty indigenous tribes for the first time.

When the couple returned to the United States, they settled in Washington, D.C., and Adams delivered to the National Geographic Society her massive collection of photographs and several movies of her adventures. It resulted in the first of twenty features in the magazine, and she became one of only a handful of women who contributed to *National Geographic*. She also embarked on a nationwide lecture tour, becoming one of the most popular adventure and geography lecturers of the period. In 1910, she crossed Haiti on horseback and retraced the trail of Christopher Columbus's early discoveries in America. "I've wondered why men have so absolutely monopolized the field of exploration," she told the *New York Times* in 1912. "Why did women never go to the Arctic, try for one pole or another, or invade Africa, Thibet [sic], or unknown wildernesses? I've never found my sex a hinderment; never faced a difficulty which a woman, as well as a man, could not surmount; never felt a fear of danger; never lacked courage to protect myself. I've been in tight places and have seen harrowing things."

During World War I, she served as a war correspondent for *Harper's Magazine*, the only female journalist permitted to visit the trenches. After the war, she and her husband settled in southern France, and she toured North Africa and Turkey. In Asia, she visited Siberia, the Gobi Desert, and Sumatra. Denied membership in the American Explorers Club, she helped to form the Society of Woman Geographers in 1925 and served as its president for six years. It is estimated that Adams travelled more than one hundred thousand miles.

She died in Nice, France, at the age of sixty-one. An insatiable traveler and adventurer, Adams, in her writing, photos, and lectures, brought the world to a wide audience, encouraging them in their own exploration of the world.

Delia Akeley (1869–1970)

Author, Big-Game Hunter, Explorer

The first Western woman to cross equatorial Africa, Delia Akeley traveled to areas where few non-Africans had ever journeyed, initially accompanying her husband but also going on several remarkable solo expeditions that provided important data for zoologists and anthropologists for future research.

Born Delia Denning in Beaver Dam, Wisconsin, she was the daughter of Irish immigrant parents whom she found too demanding and ran away to Milwaukee at the age of thirteen. In 1889, she married Arthur J. Reiss, a barber who helped her to find work. Sometime later, she met Carl Akeley, a hunter, naturalist, and taxidermist employed by the Milwaukee Public Museum. She assisted him in his work and relocated to Chicago when Akeley accepted a position at the Field Museum of Natural History in 1895. After divorcing Reiss, Delia married Akeley in 1902.

In 1905, the couple embarked on two major African expeditions to East Africa, collecting mammals, insects, and birds, and went to Kenya in 1906. Although she had never fired a gun before, she became an accomplished markswoman and hunter. The collection of elephants, buffaloes, birds, and gazelles they brought back in eighty-four crates to the Field Museum created a sensation with the public. In 1909, the couple was contracted to collect elephants for the American Museum of Natural History in New York, and they joined the expedition led by former president Theodore Roosevelt. In search of a bull elephant for the museum's collection, Carl Akeley was seriously injured by an attacking elephant. It was during this expedition that she began observing the behavior of monkeys, pioneering research that would be picked up by notable scientists Jane Goodall and Dian Fossey much later. The diorama that Carl Akeley created after their return can still be seen at the American Museum of Natural History.

In 1923, the couple divorced, and Carl Akeley would die in 1926 from fever in the Congo. She returned to Africa alone on two expeditions financed by the Brooklyn Museum of Arts and Sciences in 1925 and 1929, the first woman to direct a collecting expedition sponsored by a museum. She discovered several new species of animals, lived for a time with the pygmies of the Ituri Forest, became the first non-African woman to cross the continent alone, and was one of the first Westerners to explore the desert between Kenya and Ethiopia.

In 1939, she married businessman Warren D. Howe, and she remained in the public eye as a popular author and speaker on the lecture circuit. She died in Florida at the age of one hundred, succumbing not to disease or injury from her many African adventures but from old age.

Delia Akeley is one of the pioneers in the study of primates and the indigenous peoples of Africa; she opened up previously unmapped regions of the work and did much to popularize the African continent for Americans.

Susan "Doc Suzy" Anderson (1870–1960)
Frontierswoman, Physician

 Known as "Doc Suzy," Susan Anderson was one of the first women to practice medicine in Colorado and, arguably, one of the last of the great frontierswomen whose life recalls so many male and female pioneers from the nineteenth century.

She was born in Fort Wayne, Indiana, and moved with her divorced father to Cripple Creek, Colorado, during the gold rush in 1891. Her father thought that the rough mining town was no place for a young woman and encouraged her to attend medical school at the University of Michigan, where she graduated in 1897. She set up her first practice in Cripple Creek before moving to Denver and other Colorado towns as she struggled to sustain her medical career. While attending college, she was diagnosed with tuberculosis, which worsened, and she decided to move to the cold and dry climate of Fraser, Colorado, in 1907. For the next forty-nine years, Anderson, affectionately known as "Doc Suzy," served her appreciative community of lumberjacks, ranchers, railroad workers, and even animals. Most of her practice involved house calls, but she never owned a horse or a car. She was usually paid in firewood or food or bartered services and was poor for most of her life. She got by mainly on her salary as the Grand County coroner. She tended a range of patients and medical conditions, including childbirth, pneumonia during the 1918 flu pandemic, and skiing injuries. Continuing to practice in Fraser

until 1956, she died at the age of ninety in Denver and is buried in Cripple Creek.

Ann Bancroft (1955–)
Adventurer, Polar Explorer

Ann Bancroft, wilderness instructor, author, and adventurer, is one of the world's most respected polar explorers. She is the first woman to reach both the North and South Poles on foot and on sleds and is the first woman to ski across both Greenland and Antarctica.

She was born in Mendota Heights, Minnesota, and grew up in St. Paul, Minnesota. She began leading wilderness expeditions when she was eight years old. Diagnosed with dyslexia at an early age, she earned her college degree in physical education from the University of Oregon in 1981. She returned to the St. Paul area as a physical education teacher, coach, and wilderness instructor.

She joined the Steger International Polar Expedition in 1986 as the only female member. After fifty-six days, she and five other team members arrived at the North Pole by dogsled, becoming the first woman to reach the North Pole by sled and on foot. In 1992, she was the leader of the first team of women to ski across Greenland, and in 1992, she led three other women on the American Women's Expedition to Antarctica, successfully completing a sixty-seven-day, 660-mile journey in 1993, becoming the first women's team to reach the South Pole on skis. Bancroft became the first woman to have stood at both poles. She returned to Antarctica in 2001 when she and Norwegian polar explorer Liv Arnesen became the first women to complete a transcontinental crossing there, a 1,700-mile journey skiing and sailing that took ninety-four days.

In 2007, Bancroft and Arnesen trekked across the Arctic Ocean to draw attention to the threat of global warming. In 2017, Bancroft led an expedition on the Ganges River, a sixty-day, 1,500-mile journey to raise awareness of the importance of clean water. She has plans for future expeditions on every continent to raise environmental awareness.

Bancroft was named as one of most Remarkable Women of the Twentieth Century in 1998, was inducted into the National Women's Hall of Fame in 2005, and was named as one of history's greatest polar explorers in 2011.

Nellie Bly (1864–1922)

Journalist

Best known for her record-breaking trip around the world in seventy-two days in 1899 in emulation of Jules Verne's *Around the World in Eighty Days,* Nellie Bly was the most famous journalist of her day and the first female investigative reporter.

Born Elizabeth Cochran (she added an "e" to her surname later) in a small town near Pittsburgh, Pennsylvania, with only a single year of formal education, she got her start in journalism at nineteen by responding to a *Pittsburgh Dispatch* newspaper editorial, "What Girls Are Good For," that strongly opposed the idea of women's suffrage and careers for women. Her angry reply in support of women's rights so impressed the newspaper's editor that he asked her to come in for an interview—and then quickly hired her. Concerned about family disapproval of her new career, she chose as her byline "Nellie Bly" after the name of a popular Stephen Foster song. Rather than write the traditional "feminine" articles her new editor expected, Bly investigated and reported on subjects such as the hazardous and exploitative working conditions women faced in factories and the living conditions in the slums experienced by the city's poorest.

In 1887, Bly gained a job with Joseph Pulitzer's *New York World* newspaper and won national notoriety by reporting on the brutality and neglect endured by patients in mental hospitals. To get her story, Bly feigned insanity and managed to get confined for treatment at New York City's notorious asylum on Blackwell's Island. After Pulitzer secured her release, she wrote a chilling account of what she saw and experienced, prompting a public investigation that resulted in much-needed reforms. Bly subsequently went undercover as a sweatshop worker to report on the appalling working conditions faced by women in the garment industry. She also got herself

arrested for theft in order to reveal the indignities faced by female prisoners in city jails. Her firsthand accounts of the abuses of the time earned Bly the reputation as "the best reporter in America."

Her most famous adventure took place in November 1889 when she set out to break the round-the-world record "set" by Jules Verne's fictional hero, Phileas Fogg, in *Around the World in Eighty Days.* She took with her the dress she was wearing, a sturdy overcoat, several changes of underwear, and a small travel bag with essential toiletries. She carried her money in a bag tied around her neck. She was in a competition with another reporter, Elizabeth Bisland, who started the same day as Bly but was traveling the opposite way around the world. Crossing the Atlantic and the Mediterranean by ship and traveling throughout the Middle East and Asia by train, rickshaw, and sampan, she chronicled her adventures, which were followed daily in newspapers around the world. Due to rough weather on her Pacific crossing, she arrived in San Francisco two days behind schedule, but the *New York World* owner Joseph Pulitzer chartered a private train to bring her home. She returned to New York to a parade after a seventy-two-day, 6-hour, and 11-minute journey. She had circumnavigated the globe, traveling alone for almost the entire journey, a radical adventure for a woman of her day. Bisland would arrive four and a half days later.

In 1895, Bly married millionaire Robert L. Seaman and left journalism. They lived quietly together for fifteen years, and after he died in 1910, Bly tried unsuccessfully to continue his manufacturing business. After living abroad for a time, she returned to New York and spent her final years as a reporter for the *New York Journal.* She died in New York City at the age of fifty-seven.

Bly would be the inspiration for the Lois Lane character in *Superman.* She would be inducted in 1998 into the National Women's Hall of Fame.

Rebecca Boone (1739–1813)

Pioneer

History has extensively recorded the exploits of American pioneer, explorer, and frontiersman Daniel

Boone (1734–1820), one of the first folk heroes of the United States. His wife, who accompanied him into the Western wilderness, Rebecca Boone, deserves credit and acknowledgement as well.

She was born Rebecca Ann Bryan near Winchester, Virginia. When she was ten, she moved with her Quaker grandparents into the backwoods of North Carolina, where she met Daniel Boone, whose family settled near them. They began their courtship in 1753 and were married three years later when she was seventeen. Over twenty-five years, she had six sons and four daughters. Although without any formal education, she was an experienced community midwife and family doctor. She also was an accomplished leather tanner, linen maker, and sharpshooter. In the famous 1852 portrait of Daniel Boone escorting settlers through the Cumberland Gap by George Caleb Bingham, Rebecca Boone rides behind her husband as an idealized version of the pioneer frontierswoman. The reality was considerably different. Rather than being a protected passenger of her intrepid husband, she created homes for their large family in North Carolina, Virginia, Kentucky, and finally Missouri, often running the household on her own while her husband was away on long hunts and surveying trips. Husband and wife were separated for nearly four years during the Cherokee War.

In 1773, she agreed to accompanying her husband into the Western wilderness. On the way, they were attacked by Shawnees, which resulted in the death of the Boones' oldest son. They were forced to retreat back to North Carolina, where they remained for the next two years. In 1775, Daniel Boone was hired to cut a trail into Kentucky for a new settlement on land purchased from the Cherokees. Boone and thirty axemen cleared a path to the new frontier that became the Wilderness Road. In 1779, Rebecca joined the first large immigrant party to cross the Cumberland Gap and settle in Kentucky. In 1799, she accompanied her husband and other settlers across the Mississippi River into Spanish-held Missouri. Rebecca would spend the last fourteen years of her life there before her death at the age of seventy-five. Underappreciated by history, Rebecca Boone, in raising and providing for a large

family in multiple wilderness outposts, was no less courageous as her more famous husband.

Louise Arner Boyd (1887–1972)

Explorer

The first woman to fly over the North Pole, Louise Arner Boyd became an authority on the Arctic in regular expeditions there and to Greenland. She was born in San Rafael, California, into a wealthy family. Her grandfather had made a fortune in the California gold rush. Every summer, the family stayed at their ranch in the Oakland Hills, where she rode horses, hunted, fished, and camped, leading a rugged and adventurous life very different from her privileged home life. When she was a teenager, both of her brothers died of heart disease. Her mother died in 1919 and her father in 1920, leaving the family fortune to their daughter, who succeeded her father as president of the Boyd Investment Company in San Francisco.

Boyd began traveling in the 1920s, and, on a trip to Norway in 1924, she saw the Polar Ice Pack for the first time. It immediately convinced her to plan her own Arctic adventure. In 1926, she chartered a ship for a hunting and filming trip to the Arctic, gaining international notoriety for her exploits, including hunting polar bears, earning the titles of the "Arctic Diana" and "The Girl Who Tamed the Arctic." She returned to the Arctic in 1928 and participated in the search operations for explorer Roald Amundsen, who had disappeared and was never found. In 1931, she organized a scientific expedition sponsored by the American Geographical Society, the first of several trips to Greenland that mapped the coastline and collected plant specimens. Her knowledge of the east coast of Greenland became invaluable to the U.S. government after World War II broke out, and she was asked not to publish the book she was writing. She worked on a number of secret assignments for the U.S. Department of the Army, including being sent as the head of an expedition to investigate magnetic and radio phenomena in the Arctic in 1940.

After the war ended, Boyd published *The Coast of Northeast Greenland* (1948) and retired from further Arctic expeditions. She did, however, in 1955 charter a private plane to fly across the North Pole, the first woman to do so. She died in San Francisco at the age of eighty-four.

Martha Jane Canary (Calamity Jane) (1852–1903)

Pioneer, Scout

Beginning as a scout for the U.S. Army in the 1870s in the Indian Wars, Calamity Jane would become a legendary figure of the Wild West, in her own words, "the most reckless and daring rider and one of the best shots in the West."

She was born Martha Jane Canary (or Cannary) in Princeton, Missouri. Her father was a gambler, and her mother worked for a time as a prostitute. In 1865, the family moved by wagon train from Missouri to Virginia City, Montana, and her mother died along the way. In 1866, her father took the family to Salt Lake City, Utah. When he died a year later when she was fourteen, she took charge of her five younger siblings and headed to Fort Bridger, Wyoming Territory, in 1868 and on to Piedmont, Wyoming. There, she worked as a dishwasher, cook, waitress, dance-hall girl, nurse, and ox team driver. It is believed that as a teenager, she occasionally worked as a prostitute.

In 1870, she joined General George Armstrong Custer as a scout in Fort Russell, Wyoming, donning the uniform of a soldier, the beginning of her custom of dressing like a man. It was in 1872, during the Muscle Shell Indian outbreak, that she acquired her nickname. Ambushed by a large group of Indians, she managed to save the fallen Captain Egan. He, in gratitude (at least as she recounted the story), declared, "I name you Calamity Jane, the heroine of the Plains."

Leaving the Army and scouting, she traveled to Deadwood, South Dakota, in the company of "Wild Bill" Hickok. She worked as a Pony Express rider, carrying mail between Deadwood and Custer, a dis-

tance of fifty miles along one of the roughest trails in the Black Hills. By the late 1870s, Calamity Jane's exploits (actual and fabricated) captured the imagination of several magazine writers. She was dubbed in one dime novel as "The White Devil of the Yellowstone." In the 1880s, she tried ranching for a time, traveled to California and Texas, married a Texan, Clinton Burk, and gave birth to a baby girl. In 1889, they moved to Boulder, Colorado, where they ran a hotel until 1893.

Calamity Jane's reputation for riding and shooting better than most men landed her a featured role in Buffalo Bill's Wild West Show, where she performed sharpshooting astride her horse. Alcohol led to her firing. In 1900, she was found by a newspaper editor down and out and nursed her back to health. She was hired to work for the Pan American Exposition in Buffalo, New York, in 1901 but was run out of town after a drunken shooting incident. She returned to the Black Hills in 1902 for the last time, working as a cook and laundress in a brothel. Her final request when she was dying of acute alcoholism was to be buried next to "Wild Bill" Hickok in Deadwood, and her request was granted in the largest funeral to be held in Deadwood for a woman.

It is impossible to sort out fact from fiction in much of the life and adventures of Calamity Jane, but what emerges in the surviving legend is a woman who defied every gender assumption of her day while fashioning one of the most colorful (if often sad and tragic) legends for a woman in the Wild West.

Bessie Coleman (1893?–1926)

Aviator

Pioneering aviator Bessie Coleman was the first woman of African American and Native American descent to hold a pilot's license. Nicknamed "Brave Bessie," "Queen Bess," and "The Only Race Aviatrix in the World," Coleman starred in early aviation exhibitions before she was killed in a plane crash.

One of thirteen children, Coleman grew up in Waxahatchie, Texas, in a family of sharecroppers.

She worked in the cotton fields as a young girl. Her father, of Native American and African American descent, left the family in search of better opportunities in Oklahoma, leaving Bessie's mother to support the family. At the age of twelve, Coleman began attending the Missionary Baptist Church school and after graduation completed a term at the Oklahoma Colored Agricultural and Normal University (Langston University). In 1915, she moved to Chicago and worked as a manicurist. Her interest in flying developed by listening to and reading stories of World War I pilots.

As an African American, she was excluded from entering aviation schools in the United States. Undaunted, Coleman was determined to become a pilot. "The air is the only place free from prejudice," she said. "I knew we had no aviators, neither men nor women, and I knew the race needed to be represented along this most important line, so I thought it my duty to risk my life to learn aviation." She learned French, and in 1920, she was accepted at the Caudron Brothers School of Aviation in Le Crotoy, France. Black philanthropists Robert Abbott, founder of the *Chicago Defender*, and Jesse Binga, a banker, provided her tuition. In 1921, she became the first American woman to obtain an international pilot's license from the Fédération Aéronautique Internationale and the world's first black woman to earn a pilot's license. In France, she specialized in stunt flying and parachuting. Returning to the United States in 1922, she became the first African American woman to make a public flight. Coleman wanted to start a flying school for African Americans, but she earned her living barnstorming and performing aerial tricks. She toured the country giving flying lessons, performing in flight shows, and encouraging African Americans and women to learn to fly.

In 1923, she survived her first major airplane accident when her plane's engine suddenly stopped and she crashed, suffering a broken leg, cracked ribs, and facial cuts. She was back performing dangerous air tricks in 1925 before large crowds. In 1926, on a test flight with a mechanic who was piloting the plane at about three thousand feet, a loose wrench got stuck in the engine; the mechanic lost control, and the plane flipped over. Coleman was not wearing a seat belt and fell out of the open cockpit and died.

The plane crashed not far from Coleman's body, and the mechanic was killed as well.

In 2001, Coleman was inducted into the National Women's Hall of Fame, and in 2006, she became a member of the National Aviation Hall of Fame. In a tribute to her, Mae Jemison, the first African American woman in space in 1992, carried with her a photograph of Coleman on her space shuttle mission.

Sophia Danenberg (1972–)

Mountaineer

In 2006, Sophia Danenberg became the first African American and the first black woman from anywhere to reach the summit of Mount Everest. Born Sophia Marie Scott, she was raised in Chicago's suburb of Homewood by her black father and Japanese mother. After graduating from Homewood-Flossmoor High School, she entered Harvard University, studying environmental sciences and public policy, graduating in 1994. After graduation, she was a Fulbright Fellow at Keio University in Tokyo before beginning her career with United Technologies in Japan and China, managing energy and air quality projects.

Danenberg became involved in mountaineering in 1999 after a childhood friend encouraged her to try rock climbing. While doing technical climbs with her local Appalachian Mountain Club, she met her future husband David Danenberg. Her first major climb was Mount Rainier in Washington in 2002. Over the next two years, she and her husband scaled Kilimanjaro in Kenya (2002), Mount Baker in Washington (2003), and Mount Kenya (2003). In 2005, she scaled five peaks: Grand Teton (Wyoming), Mount Katahdin (Maine), Mount McKinley (Alaska), Mount Tasman (New Zealand), and Ama Dablam (Nepal).

In 2006, at the age of thirty-four, she set her sights on Everest. Along with eight others, she signed up for an "unguided" climb, which included the help of two Sherpas, weather reports, food, and oxygen. She carried her own gear and was without a guide to make decisions for her. After two months of climbing, she and her party reached the summit of Mount Everest at twenty-nine thousand feet, withstanding bad weather and, in Danenberg's case, bronchitis, frostbite, and a clogged oxygen mask.

Danenberg continues to work for United Technologies, responsible for legislative and regulatory affairs for its Global Environmental, Health, and Safety division in Hartford, Connecticut.

Amelia Earhart (1897–1937)

Aviator

 The most famous female aviator of the twentieth century, Amelia Earhart opened up the field of aviation for women as pilots and engineers. She followed her own particular path of adventure by purposely challenging and rejecting the gender roles of her time.

Born and raised in Atchison, Kansas, Earhart was a tall and lanky girl who enjoyed playing boys' sports. She graduated from Chicago's Hyde Park High School in 1916. She attended Columbia University for a year, pursuing medical studies before working as a nurse in a Toronto military hospital during World War I. She became captivated by flying when she took her first airplane ride. After taking lessons from pioneer female pilot Netta Snook, Earhart soloed for the first time in 1921. A year later, she bought her first plane, in which she set a women's altitude record of fourteen thousand feet.

In 1928, Earhart became the first woman to fly across the Atlantic Ocean as one of three crewmembers on a flight of 20 hours and 40 minutes from Newfoundland to Wales. In 1929, she became a founding member and president of the Ninety Nines, the first U.S. organization of licensed female pilots. In 1931, she married publisher George Putnam, who became her manager and the publisher of the several books she wrote about her experiences. The following year, she became the first woman—and only the second person (after Charles Lindbergh)—to make a transatlantic solo flight. On her trip across the Atlantic, she set a new speed record and earned the first Distinguished Flying Cross given to a woman.

Earhart's many flying achievements in the 1920s and 1930s made her an inspiration to women and a closely followed celebrity. She lectured extensively, encouraging women to pursue their ambitions in careers that had previously been restricted to men.

Between 1930 and 1935, Earhart set seven women's speed and distance records in a variety of aircrafts. In 1935, Earhart became the first aviator to fly solo from Honolulu, Hawaii, to Oakland, California. The same year, she flew solo from Los Angeles to Mexico City and then nonstop from Mexico City to New York. In June 1937, Earhart embarked on a daring, twenty-seven-thousand-mile trip around the equator—the longest flight in aviation history. The most dangerous part of the journey would be across the Pacific from New Guinea to the tiny island of Howland 2,500 miles away. With only primitive navigational equipment, finding such a small landmark in the middle of the Pacific was a daunting prospect.

On July 2, 21 hours after the expected 18-hour flight had begun, the Coast Guard received a final message from Earhart that she and her navigator, Fred Noonan, had approximately 30 minutes of fuel remaining but still had not sighted land. The plane's subsequent disappearance prompted the largest naval search in history but no trace of her, Noonan, or the aircraft was ever found. The fact that Earhart vanished without a trace at the height of her popularity has fueled many rumors and theories, and the mystery of her final flight contributed to the legendary status that she has gained as a great American adventurer.

Earhart has emerged as a feminist icon: independent, cool under pressure, courageous, defiant, and goal oriented. Her accomplishments in aviation inspired a generation of female aviators, including the more than one thousand female pilots of the Women Airforce Service Pilots (WASP), who ferried military aircraft and served as transport pilots in World War II.

Barbara Hillary (1931–)

Polar Explorer

After retiring from a nursing career, Barbara Hillary, in 2007 at the age of seventy-five, became the first African American woman to reach the North Pole.

She subsequently also reached the South Pole in 2011 at the age of seventy-nine, becoming the first African American woman to stand on both poles.

She was born in New York City and raised in Harlem. She never knew her father, and her mother worked as a maid. She attended the New School University in New York, earning both BA and MA degrees with a concentration in gerontology. She went to work as a nurse, focusing on staff training in concepts of patient aging and service delivery in nursing homes. She also was the founder and editor-in-chief of *The Peninsula Magazine,* a nonprofit and multiracial magazine.

Having survived breast cancer in her twenties, at the age of sixty-seven, she was diagnosed with lung cancer that was treated with surgery, which caused her to lose 25 percent of her breathing capacity. After this brush with mortality and her retirement from nursing, she began taking vacations in places that were far from tourist destinations such as dogsledding in northern Quebec and an expedition to photograph polar bears in Manitoba. When she learned that no record existed of a black woman ever reaching the North Pole, she decided to make that her next goal.

In 1986, American Ann Bancroft became the first woman ever to reach the North Pole. Hillary followed her example of reaching the North Pole on cross-country skis, although she had never skied in her life. Working with a personal trainer, she began a training regimen that included dragging a plastic sled filled with sand along a nearby beach to stimulate the weight of the supplies she would need. She solicited donations to pay for the trip. Eventually, she and two guides were dropped off by helicopter and skied sixty miles to the North Pole in 10 hours. When she reached it, she recalled, "Part of you is saying, 'I can't believe I made it this far'; another part is saying, 'Let this thing be over with'; another part, 'Damn, it's cold.'" Not only was she the first African American to reach the North Pole, but she was also one of the oldest people to do so.

Five years later, she became the first African American woman to reach the South Pole in 2011 at the age of seventy-nine. With her celebrity status from her achievements, Hillary has become an in-

spirational speaker and the subject of television profiles. In 2019, at the age of eighty-six, she set out on a two-week trek across Mongolia.

Mae Carol Jemison (1956–)
Astronaut, Physician, Scientist

In 1992, Mae Carol Jemison became the first African American woman in space when she served as a science mission specialist during an eight-day voyage on the space shuttle *Endeavour.* Jemison put into context her achievement by stating, "There have been lots of other women who had the talent and ability before me. I think this can be seen as an affirmation that we're moving ahead. And I hope it means that I'm just the first in a long line."

Jemison was born in Decatur, Alabama, the youngest of the three children of a maintenance supervisor and an elementary school teacher. Her family moved to Chicago when she was three years old for better educational and employment opportunities. As an adolescent, she was a fan of science fiction books, movies, and television programs, particularly the TV series *Star Trek.* It was, in Jemison's words, "one of the few programs that actually had women in exploration and technology roles. It also showed people from around the world working together.... It gave a real hopeful view of the universe, of groups of people, as a species." After graduating from high school in 1973, at the age of sixteen, she attended Stanford University, where she pursued a double major in chemical engineering and African American studies. She earned her medical degree in 1981 from Cornell University after having served as a medical volunteer in Cuba, Kenya, and Thailand. She completed her internship and then worked as a general practitioner in Los Angeles. In 1985, she joined the Peace Corps as a medical officer for Sierra Leone and Liberia in West Africa.

In 1987, her application for NASA's astronaut program was accepted. Jemison remembered always being fascinated with outer space and the space program, although she remembers "being irritated that there were no women astronauts." She said applying to be a shuttle astronaut was better than "waiting around in a cornfield, waiting for E.T. to pick me up or something." She was one of fifteen individuals selected out of more than two thousand applicants. After her training program, Jemison finally took off into space with six other astronauts aboard the *Endeavour* in 1992. On board, Jemison conducted experiments on motion sickness and the impact of weightlessness on bone density and the development of frog eggs. On the flight, Jemison took into orbit a photo of Bessie Coleman, the first African American woman ever to fly an airplane. She would say later that she was not driven to be the "first black woman to go into space. I wouldn't have cared less if 2,000 people had gone up before me.... I would still have had my hand up, 'I want to do this.'"

After her only space mission, Jemison resigned from NASA, explaining that her decision was based on her interest in exploring "how social sciences interact with technologies." She became a professor-at-large at Cornell University and a professor of environmental studies at Dartmouth College from 1995 to 2002. She has been a strong advocate in favor of science education and increasing minority student participation in science. She established the Jemison Group, a company that researches, develops, and markets space-age technology.

Osa Johnson (1894–1953)

Explorer, Filmmaker

Dubbed in the 1920s "The Heroine of 1,000 Thrills" and called "the greatest woman explorer and big-game hunter," Osa Johnson, with her husband, Martin Johnson, made over fourteen feature films and thirty-seven educational short films documenting their expeditions in the South Pacific, Africa, and Borneo.

Born Osa Helen Leighty in the small Kansas town of Chanute, she began her adventures when she eloped at the age of sixteen with Martin Johnson, who was passing through having recently sailed the South Seas with author Jack London. He convinced her to sing and perform Hawaiian dances for his travelogue lecture tour. In 1917, the couple embarked on their first expedition together to the Solomon Islands and the New Hebrides, where they filmed *Among the Cannibal Isles of the South Pacific* (1918). The couple would alternate between field trips and lecture tours promoting their films. In the 1920s, they made numerous trips to Africa. In the field, Martin Johnson was the principal photographer, and Osa was the hunter and pilot. Their highly successful films included *Jungle Adventures* (1921), *Head Hunters of the South Seas* (1922), *Trailing African Wild Animals* (1923), *Simba, the King of Beasts* (1928), *Across the World* (1930), *Wonders of the Congo* (1931), *Congorilla* (1932), *Baboona* (1935), and *Borneo* (1937).

In 1937, Martin was killed in a plane crash; Osa sustained serious back injuries and a broken leg. She would eventually recover and continued to lead expeditions filming location scenes for the film *Stanley and Livingstone* (1939), in which she was credited with being "the first woman ever to take the entire responsibility of an African expedition." She produced and starred in *Jungles Calling* (1938), a tribute to her late husband, and wrote the best-selling memoir *I Married Adventure* (1940), producing and starring in a film version. The lecture films *African Paradise* (1941) and *Tulagi and the Solomons* (1943) followed.

In 1953, while planning her next expedition, she suffered a heart attack in her New York hotel room, dying at the age of fifty-eight. Her obituary in the *New York Times* summarized her preference for the wild and adventure: "I can hardly wait to get back to the jungle. I prefer it out there. When I sling my rifle over my shoulder and go out into the forest, I feel as if everything belonged to me. There's no competition out there, no worry about what to wear and what other women are wearing. I am Queen of the Jungle."

Susan Shelby Magoffin (1827–1855)

Diarist, Pioneer

One of the first non-Native American women to travel on the Santa Fe Trail in the 1840s, Susan Shelby Magoffin recorded her experiences in a diary— *Down the Santa Fe Trail and into*

Mexico (1926)—one of the best sources for an account of daily experiences in the Southwest during the period.

She was born into a wealthy family on a plantation near Danville, Kentucky, the granddaughter of Isaac Shelby, a hero of the American Revolution. At eighteen, she married Samuel Magoffin, the son of an Irish immigrant who had prospered in Kentucky and was an experienced Santa Fe trader since the 1820s.

Samuel Magoffin took his bride with him on his next trading journey, leaving Independence, Missouri, on June 10, 1846. Their trip took place soon after the United States declared war against Mexico over the border of Texas, which the United States had annexed in 1845. They traveled with "fourteen big wagons with six yoke each, one baggage wagon with two yoke" along with a maid, cook, and coop for live chickens. Susan believed herself to be the first "American lady" to attempt the trip. After she suffered a miscarriage on the way, the Magoffins reached Santa Fe on August 31. From there, they headed south into Mexico, trailing behind U.S. Army troops. Her diary, therefore, also provides one of the best sources we have for U.S. Army movements in the Mexican War. While sick with yellow fever in Matamoros, she gave birth to a son, who did not survive. They returned to Kentucky in 1848.

Her diary records her excitement about making the trip, the routine of travel, and the various dangers and hardships they faced along the way on their fifteen-month trading journey. They traveled due west, across the prairies of what is now the state of Kansas, among migrating buffaloes. Mountains and deserts followed. Their southern route followed the Rio Grande to El Paso and then through the provinces of New Spain to Mexico City. Magoffin dutifully recorded all that she saw and experienced. With her health declining, the Magoffins boarded a ship from the Mexican coast to New Orleans and then north to their home in Lexington, Kentucky.

After giving birth to a daughter in Kentucky in 1851, they moved to a large estate near Kirkwood, Missouri. Magoffin's health had been damaged by the hardships of the Santa Fe expedition, and after

giving birth to a second daughter in 1855, she died and is buried in St. Louis, Missouri.

Historians long believed that Susan Shelby Magoffin was the first American white woman to travel the Santa Fe Trail. However, a claim was made by historian Marian Meyer in 1987 that a woman named Mary Donoho (1807–1880), another trader's wife, had crossed the Trail in 1835, thirteen years before Susan Magoffin. She would settle in Santa Fe, giving birth to three children there, the first American white children to claim New Mexico as their birthplace. However, unlike Donoho, Magoffin left an invaluable primary source of what a woman experienced along the Santa Fe Trail in this early period of Western settlement.

Annie Smith Peck (1850–1935)
Explorer, Mountaineer

The first person to reach the top of Peru's highest mountain, Huascaràn, Annie Smith Peck was one of the most celebrated and accomplished mountain climbers in the late nineteenth and early twentieth centuries. A dedicated suffragist, she was sixty-one when she crowned her ascent of Peru's Mount Coropuna with a "Votes for Women" pennant.

Born in Providence, Rhode Island, she was the youngest of the five children of a lawyer and state legislator. After graduating from the Rhode Island state Normal School in 1872, she graduated from the University of Michigan with degrees in Greek and classical languages in 1878, earning her master's degree in 1881. She taught Latin and speech at Purdue University from 1881 to 1883.

During a European tour in 1885, she was captivated by her first sight of the Swiss Alps and took up mountaineering. She climbed her first major mountain, California's Mount Shasta, in 1888 and the Matterhorn in 1895. In 1897, she climbed the Mexican volcanoes, Popocatépetl and Citlaltépetl; the latter, at 18,406 feet, was the highest point in the Western Hemisphere that had been attained by a woman at that point. After several ambitious climbs in Europe, she began to explore South America. In 1904, she climbed the 21,066-foot Illampu peak in Bolivia's Cordillera Real and then, in 1908, she reached the summit of the twenty-four-thousand-foot Mount Huascarán in the Peruvian Andes.

Peck supported her climbing by lecturing and writing, publishing *A Search for the Apex of South America* (1911), *The South American Tour* (1913), and *Flying over South America—20,000 Miles by Air* (1932). In 1927, the Lima Geographical Society named the north peak of Huascarán Cumbre Aña Peck in her honor. She made her last climb, of Mount Madison, New Hampshire, at the age of eighty-two. She started a world tour in 1935 but became ill while climbing the Acropolis in Athens. She died of bronchial pneumonia at the age of eighty-four.

Sally Ride (1951–2012)

Astronaut, Physicist

In June 1983, astronaut Sally Ride became the first American woman in space when she spent six days in orbit as a flight engineer aboard the space shuttle *Challenger.* She was the third woman in space overall after two Soviet cosmonauts, Valentina Tereshkova (1963) and Svetlana Savitskaya (1982). She was also the youngest American astronaut in space at the age of thirty-two in 1983.

Born in Encino, California, Ride had dreamed of being an astronaut from childhood. Growing up, she was an outstanding athlete, and for a time, she had trouble choosing a career. Initially, she seemed headed for athletics as a nationally ranked tennis player. She attended Swarthmore College, then the University of California–Los Angeles before entering Stanford University as a junior, graduating with bachelor's degrees in English and physics in 1973. She remained at Stanford to earn a master's degree and a Ph.D. in physics in 1978, specializing in astrophysics. She was working at Stanford as a teaching assistant and researcher when she joined the astronaut program at NASA.

In 1978, NASA accepted only thirty-five astronaut candidates out of eight thousand applicants.

For the first time, they selected six women, including Ride. She underwent an extensive year of training that included parachute jumping, water survival, gravity and weightlessness training, radio communications, and navigation. She also worked with the team that designed the fifty-foot remote mechanical arm that shuttle crews would use to deploy and retrieve satellites. On her 1983 flight aboard the *Challenger*, she took part in the deployment of two communications satellites and deployment and retrieval of the German-built shuttle pallet satellite. Part of Ride's job was to operate the robotic arm used to deploy and retrieve the satellite.

Ride returned to space aboard the *Challenger* in 1984 and helped to deploy the Earth Radiation Budget Satellite. Her fellow crewmember was Kathryn Sullivan, who would become the first American woman to walk in space. Ride was scheduled for a third flight aboard the *Challenger* in the summer of 1986, but that mission was canceled when the spacecraft exploded shortly after takeoff in January 1986. Ride was the only astronaut selected as a member of the special commission to investigate the disaster and to recommend changes in the space program to prevent future accidents.

Ride left NASA in 1987 to resume her teaching career at Stanford's Center for International Security and Arms Control. Two years later, she became the director of the California Space Institute, a research center at the University of California. She also became a physics professor at the University of California–San Diego. From the mid-1990s until her death, Ride led two public outreach programs for NASA involving middle-school students. She was also president and CEO of Sally Ride Science, founded in 2001, to create science programming and publications for elementary and middle school students with a particular focus on attracting girls to science.

In 1982, Ride married fellow NASA astronaut Steve Hawley. They divorced in 1987. It was revealed after Ride's death that her partner of twenty-seven years was Tam O'Shaughnessy, a school psychologist at San Diego State University, whom Ride had met when both were aspiring tennis players. Ride, therefore, is the first known LGBT astronaut. She died of pancreatic cancer at the age of sixty-one.

Sacagawea (c. 1786–c. 1812)

Frontier Guide

Sacajawea is famous for her participation in one of the most important expeditions in American history. From 1805 to 1806, she traveled with Meriwether Lewis and William Clark on their historic journey to explore the vast new territory acquired by the United States through the Louisiana Purchase, which covered thousands of miles from North Dakota to the Pacific Ocean. She played a central role in establishing contact with the Native American tribes the expedition encountered and providing invaluable assistance guiding them to the Pacific and back.

A member of the Lemhi band of the Shoshone, or Snake, Native American tribe, Sacagawea grew up in what is present-day central Idaho. When she was thirteen, a Hidastsa band of Indians captured her in a tribal battle and traded and gambled her away to Touissaint Charbonneau, a French-Canadian trapper living with the Hidatsas. She became his wife and lived with him in a village near the Missouri River in present-day North Dakota. When Lewis and Clark stopped at the village on their way west, Sacagawea and her infant son, Jean-Baptiste, went with them.

Sacagawea proved to be an invaluable member of the party as they traveled across the Great Plains and the Rocky Mountains to the Pacific Northwest and back. She led the explorers through Mandan and Shoshone villages and, acting as interpreter with her husband, helped Lewis and Clark avoid hostilities. During the journey, she reunited with her native tribe, the Lemhi Shoshones, and was overjoyed to learn that her brother had become the Lemhi chief. She convinced the Lemhi to provide the explorers with horses and to guide them across the Continental Divide. During the journey, Sacagawea gathered firewood, cooked, washed clothes, and made moccasins. She showed, Clark later reported, "equal fortitude and resolution" when, on one occasion, she saved valuable mapping instruments and records after one of the expedition's boats overturned during a storm.

When the expedition neared the Pacific Coast, Sacagawea asked to be shown the "great water," where she hoped to see a "monstrous fish." Lewis and Clark canoed with Sacagawea and Charbonneau downriver to the Pacific Ocean. There, they saw the remains of beached whales.

The members of the expedition were greeted with great acclaim when they returned to St. Louis, Missouri, on September 23, 1806. William Clark tried to help Sacagawea, Charbonneau, and their son settle there, but she became homesick for her native lands, and Charbonneau wished to return to fur trapping. In 1811, they moved to Fort Manuel on the Missouri River, on the present-day border of North and South Dakota. Sacagawea reportedly died from a fever in December 1812.

The National American Woman Suffrage Association in the early twentieth century adopted her as a symbol of women's worth and independence. In 2000, the U.S. Mint issued the Sacagawea dollar coin in her honor depicting Sacagawea and her son. In 2003, an eleven-foot-tall bronze statue of Sacagawea was unveiled in Statuary Hall in the Capitol Rotunda in Washington, D.C., becoming the first Native American woman so honored in Statuary Hall.

Narcissa Whitman (1808–1847)

Missionary, Pioneer

In 1836, Narcissa Whitman journeyed three thousand miles from her home in upstate New York to found one of the first missionary settlements in the Far West among the Cayuse Indians near modern-day Walla Walla, Washington. Traveling with her husband, Marcus Whitman, and fellow missionaries Henry Harmon Spalding and his wife, Eliza, Narcissa and Eliza became the first known non-Native American women to cross the Rocky Mountains.

Born Narcissa Prentiss in Prattsburgh, New York, she was the daughter of a carpenter and one of nine children in her family. Raised Presbyterian, at the age of eleven, she converted to the Congregationalist faith, prompted by the Second Great Awakening of evangelical fervor that swept through New England and New York in the first decades of the nineteenth century. Whitman was educated at the Franklin Academy in Prattsburgh and trained as a teacher at the Female Academy in Troy, New York. In 1834, she attended a lecture by a minister, who urged young people to become missionaries in the West. Whitman responded by applying to the American Board of Commissioners for Foreign Missions (the lands west of the Mississippi were called "foreign" because they were populated by Spanish settlers, indigenous peoples, and fur traders), the first American Christian foreign mission agency. The ABCFM would not allow single men or women to serve as missionaries, and the similarly single physician Marcus Whitman, hearing of Narcissa's application, contacted her by letter proposing marriage, and they were wed in 1836.

Shortly after their wedding, the couple set out with the first large contingent of European Americans to head west by wagon train. They traveled with another newlywed missionary couple, Henry and Eliza Spalding. They would journey by sleigh, canal barge, wagon, riverboat, horseback, and on foot for five months, averaging about fifteen miles a day on a good day. For some of the Native American communities they encountered on the way, Whitman and Eliza Spalding were the first white women they had ever seen. Whitman would write back to her sister in New York, "I never was so contented and happy before; neither have I enjoyed such health for years."

Whitman's party was the first to use the Oregon Trail, following river valleys westward from Kansas City, Missouri, to present-day Oregon. The most daunting challenge was the Continental Divide, the immense mountain range that bisected the continent and was notoriously difficult for large wagons to cross. Earlier traders, however, had discovered the Rocky Mountains's South Pass, and when the Whitman party went through this, she and Eliza Spalding became the first known white women to cross the Continental Divide.

The Whitmans and their party arrived at Walla Walla Fort, a fur-trading outpost, on September 1, 1836. The two couples built a small house and outbuildings nearby for their mission and set to work converting the nomadic Cayuse and Nez Percé tribes to both Christianity and a farming-centered lifestyle. Whitman taught Bible study classes at the mission. She gave birth to a daughter in 1837, the first white American child born in Oregon Country, but she drowned at the age of two. Whitman would slip into a depression, spending hours writing in her journals and in letters to her family in the East chronicling their difficulties. In 1847, a measles epidemic, spread by contact with the white settlers, decimated the native population and fostered resentment among the tribes that Marcus Whitman was only curing the whites while letting Indian children die. Discontent culminated in the Whitman massacre, in which the Whitmans and eleven other settlers were killed. Harsh reprisals against the Cayuse and Nez Percé tribes escalated into war.

Narcissa Whitman is the most famous as well as the most tragic of the earliest female settlers in Oregon. Her letters and journal provide an invaluable record of the challenges she faced and just how demanding was the life of the earliest settlers in the Far West.

FURTHER READING

Adam, Barry D. *The Rise of a Gay and Lesbian Movement.* New York: Twayne, 1995.

Addams, Jane. *Peace and Bread in Time of War.* New York: Macmillian, 1922.

Amott, Teresa, and Julie Matthaei. *Race, Gender, and Work: A Multi-Cultural Economic History in the United States.* Montreal: Black Rose Books, 1999.

Banner, Lois W. *American Beauty.* New York: Knopf, 1983.

Barlow, William. *"Looking Up and Down": The Emergence of Blues Culture.* Philadelphia: Temple University Press, 1989.

Basinger, Jeanine. *A Woman's View: How Hollywood Spoke to Women, 1930–1960.* New York: Knopf, 1993.

Berkin, Carol. *Revolutionary Mothers: Women and the Struggle for America's Independence.* New York: Knopf, 2005.

Bernstein, Irving. *A Caring Society. The New Deal, the Worker, and the Great Depression: A History of the American Worker, 1933–1941.* Boston: Houghton-Mifflin, 1985.

Brown, Leslie, Jacqueline Castledine, and Anne Valke, eds. *U.S. Women's History: Untangling the Threads of Sisterhood.* New Brunswick: Rutgers University Press, 2017.

Brownmiller, Susan. *In Our Time: Memoir of a Revolution.* New York: Dial Press, 1999.

Brumberg, Joan. *The Body Project: An Intimate History of American Girls.* New York: Random House, 1997.

Buhle, Mari Jo, Teresa Murphy, and Jane Gerhard. *A Concise Women's History.* New York: Pearson, 2014.

Burrell, Barbara C. *A Women's Place Is in the House: Campaigning for Congress in the Feminist Era.* Ann Arbor: University of Michigan Press, 1994.

Campbell, D'Ann. *Women at War with America: Private Lives in a Patriotic Era.* Cambridge, MA: Harvard University Press, 1984.

Clifford, Geraldine J. *Those Good Gertrudes: A Social History of Women Teachers in America.* Baltimore: Johns Hopkins University Press, 2014.

Cohen, Marcia. *The Sisterhood.* New York: Simon & Schuster, 1988.

Collins, Gail. *When Everything Changed: The Amazing Journey of American Women from 1960 to the Present.* Boston: Little Brown, 2014.

Coryell, Janet L., and Nora Faires. *A History of Women in America.* New York: McGraw-Hill, 2011.

Cott, Nancy F. *No Small Courage: A History of Women in the United States.* New York: Oxford University Press, 2004.

Degan, Marie Louise. *The History of the Woman's Peace Party.* New York: Garland, 1972.

Dicker, Rory C. *A History of U.S. Feminisms.* New York: Seal Press, 2016.

DuBois, Ellen Carol, and Lynn Dumenil. *Through Women's Eyes: An American History with Documents.* 5th ed. New York: Bedford-St. Martin's, 2018.

Eisenmann, Linda. *Higher Education for Women in Postwar America, 1945–1965.* Baltimore: Johns Hopkins University Press, 2006.

Evans, Sara M. *Born for Liberty: A History of Women in America.* New York: The Free Press, 1989.

Felder, Deborah G. *The 100 Most Influential Women of All Time: A Ranking Past and Present.* New York: Citadel Press, 2001.

———. *A Bookshelf of Our Own: Works That Changed Women's Lives.* New York: Citadel Press, 2005.

———. *A Century of Women: The Most Influential Events in Twentieth-Century Women's History.* New York: Citadel Press, 1999.

Felder, Deborah G., and Diana Rosen. *Fifty Jewish Women Who Changed the World.* New York: Citadel Press, 2003.

Flexner, Eleanor. *Century of Struggle: The Woman's Rights Movement in the United States.* 2nd ed. Cambridge: Harvard University Press, 1975.

Foner, Philip S. *Women and the American Labor Movement.* 2nd ed. Chicago: Haymarket Books, 2018.

Foster, Thomas A. *Women in Early America.* New York: NYU Press, 2015.

Fox, Richard Logan. *Gender Dynamics in Congressional Elections.* Thousand Oaks, CA: Sage Publications, 1997.

Friedan, Betty. *The Feminine Mystique.* New York: W.W. Norton, 1963.

———. *It Changed My Life: Writings on the Women's Movement.* New York: Random House., 1976.

Gordon, Linda Perlman. *Woman's Body, Woman's Right: Birth Control in America.* New York: Penguin Books, 1990.

Gordon, Lynn D. *Gender and Higher Education in the Progressive Era.* New Haven: Yale University Press, 1990.

Gwin, Minrose. *The Woman in the Red Dress: Gender, Space, and Reading.* Urbana: University of Illinois Press, 2002.

Haskell, Molly. *From Reverence to Rape: The Treatment of Women in the Movies.* 2nd ed. Chicago: University of Chicago Press, 1987.

Hine, Darlene, and Kathleen Thompson. *A Shining Thread of Hope: The History of Black Women in America.* New York: Broadway Books, 1998.

How Schools Shortchange Girls—The AAUW Report: A Study of Major Finding, on Girls and Education. New York: Marlowe & Company, 1992.

Hyman, Paula E., and Deborah Dash Moore, eds. *Jewish Women in America: An Historical Encyclopedia.* New York: Routledge, 1997.

Hymowitz, Carol, and Michaele Weissman, *A History of Women in America: From Founding Mothers to Feminists—How Women Shaped the Life and Culture of America.* New York: Bantam, 1984.

Jacobs, William Jay. *Women in American History.* Beverly Hills, CA: Benziger, Bruce & Glencoe, 1976.

Kass-Simon, G., Patricia Farnes, and Deborah Nash, eds. *Women of Science: Righting the Record.* Bloomington: Indiana University Press, 1990.

Kerber, Linda K., Jane Sherron De Hart, Cornelia Hughes Dayton, and Judy Tzu-Chun Wu. *Women's America: Refocusing the Past.* 8th ed. New York: Oxford University Press, 2015.

Kessler-Harris, Alice. *Out to Work: A History of Wage-Earning Women in the United States.* 20th ed. New York: Oxford University Press, 2003.

Kwolek-Folland, Angel. *Incorporating Women: A History of Women and Business in the United States.* Boston: Twayne, 1998.

Lepore, Jill. *These Truths: A History of the United States.* New York: Norton, 2018.

Lensky, Helen. *Out of Bounds: Women, Sports, and Sexuality.* Toronto: Women's Press, 1986.

Lerner, Gerda, ed. *Black Women in White America: A Documentary History.* New York: Vintage Books, 1992.

Ling, Huping. *Surviving on the Gold Mountain: A History of Chinese American Women and Their Lives.* Albany: SUNY Press, 1998.

Lunardini, Christine. *What Every American Should Know about Women's History: 200 Events That Shaped Our Destiny.* Holbrook, MA: Bob Adams, 1994.

Mays, Dorothy A. *Women in Early America: Struggle, Survival, and Freedom in a New World.* Santa Barbara, CA: ABC-CLIO, 2004.

Millett, Kate. *Sexual Politics.* New York: Columbia University Press, 2016.

Nadell, Pamela. *America's Jewish Women: A History from Colonial Times to Today.* New York: Norton, 2019.

Nash, Margaret A. *Women's Education in the United States, 1780–1840.* New York: Palgrave Macmillan, 2007.

Norton, Mary Beth. *Liberty's Daughters: The Revolutionary Experience of American Women, 1750–1800.* Boston: Little, Brown, 1980.

———. *Founding Mothers & Fathers: Gendered Power and the Forming of American Society.* New York: Knopf, 1996.

Riley, Glenda. *Inventing the American Woman: An Inclusive History.* 2nd ed. Arlington Heights, IL: Davidson, 1995.

Roberts, Cokie. *Founding Mothers: The Women Who Raised Our Nation.* New York: Harper, 2005.

———. *Ladies of Liberty: The Women Who Shaped Our Nation.* New York: Harper, 2008.

Rosen, Ruth. *The World Split Open: How the Modern Women's Movement Changed America.* New York: Penguin, 2006.

Rossiter, Margaret W. *Women Scientists in America: Struggles and Strategies to 1940.* Baltimore: Johns Hopkins University Press, 1982.

———. *Women Scientists in America: Before Affirmative Action, 1940–1972.* Baltimore: Johns Hopkins University Press, 1995.

Rothman, Sheila. *Woman's Proper Place: A History of Changing Ideals and Practices, 1870 to the Present.* New York: Basic Books, 1978.

Rubinstein, Charlotte Streifer. *American Women Artists: From Indian Times to the Present.* New York: Avon Books, 1982.

Rupp, Leila J., and Vera Taylor. *Survival in the Doldrums: The American Women's Rights Movement, 1945 to the 1960s.* New York: Oxford University Press, 1987.

Salter, David F. *Crashing the Old Boys' Network: The Tragedies and Triumphs of Girls and Women in Sports.* Westport, CT: Praeger, 1996.

Sawaya, Francesca. *Modern Women, Modern Work.* Philadelphia: University of Pennsylvania Press, 2004.

Schultz, Jaime. *Qualifying Times: Points of Change in U.S. Women's Sports.* Urbana: University of Illinois Press, 2014.

Sherrow, Victoria. *Encyclopedia of Women and Sports.* Santa Barbara, CA: ABC-CLIO, 1996.

———. *Women in the Military: An Encyclopedia.* Santa Barbara, CA.: ABC-CLIO, 1996.

Showalter, Elaine. *A Jury of Her Peers: American Women from Anne Bradstreet to Annie Proulx.* New York: Knopf, 2009.

Sklar, Kathryn, and Thomas Dublin. *Women and Power in American History.* 3rd ed. New York: Pearson, 2008.

Solomon, Barbara Miller. *In the Company of Educated Women: A History of Women and Higher Education in America.* New Haven: Yale University Press, 1985.

Tang, Joyce, and Earl Smith. *Women and Minorities in American Professions.* New York: SUNY Press, 1996.

Weatherford, Doris. *Milestones: A Chronology of American Women's History.* New York: Facts on File, 1997.

Weiss, Elaine. *The Woman's Hour: The Great Fight to Win the Vote.* New York: Viking Press, 2018.

Wilkerson, Isabel. *The Warmth of Other Suns: The Epic Story of America's Great Migration.* New York: Random House, 2010.

Woloch, Nancy. *Women and the American Experience.* 5th ed. New York: Knopf, 2010.

INDEX

Note:(ill.) indicates photos and illustrations.